BEST SELLER

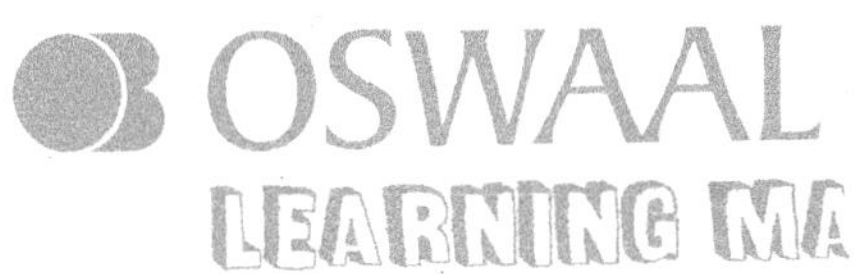

CBSE QUESTION BANK

Chapterwise & Topicwise

CLASS 11

GEOGRAPHY

(Fundamentals of Physical Geography; India: Physical Environment)

Strictly as per the latest CBSE Syllabus & Circulars released on 26th April & 6th April, 2023 (CBSE Cir No. Acad-39/2023; Acad-45/2023)

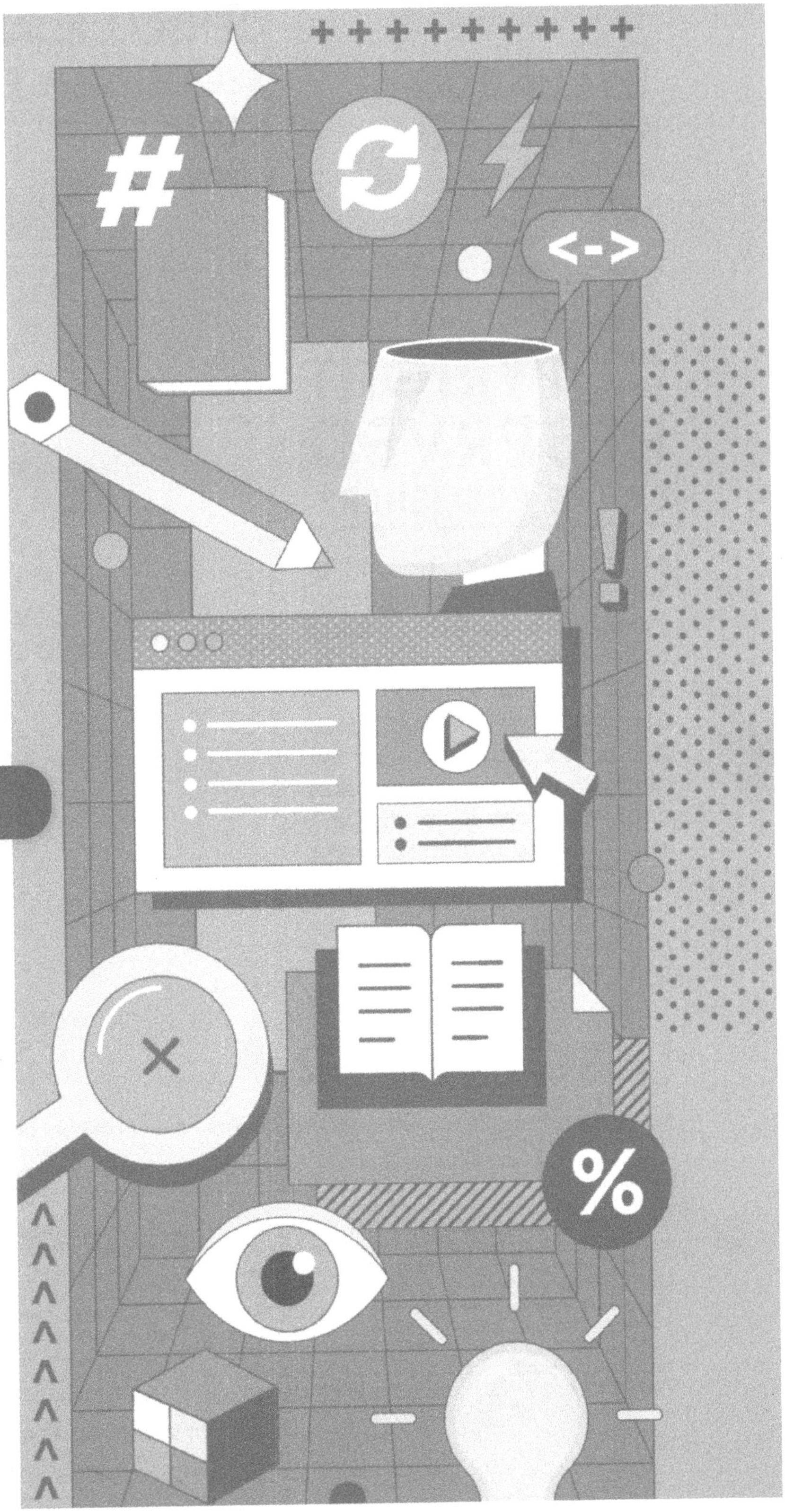

Get the #OswaalEdge

1. **100% Updated for 2023-24** with Latest Syllabus & Questions Typologies
2. **Crisp Revision** with Topic wise Revision Notes & Smart Mind Maps
3. **Extensive Practice** with 1500+ Questions and Fully Solved NCERT Textbook Questions
4. **Concept Clarity** with 1000+ Concepts & Concept Videos
5. **100% Exam Readiness** with Competency based Questions

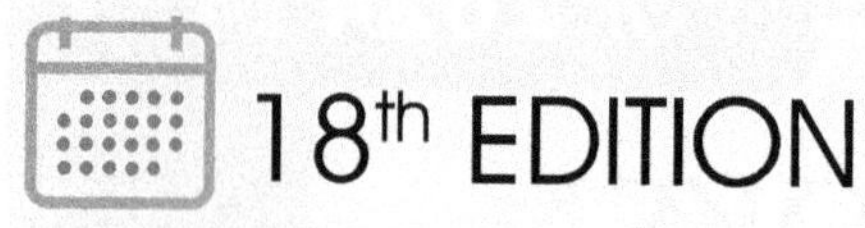
18th EDITION

YEAR 2023-24

ISBN "9789356349414"

SYLLABUS COVERED

CENTRAL BOARD OF SECONDARY EDUCATION DELHI

PUBLISHED BY

OSWAAL BOOKS & LEARNING PVT. LTD.

1/11, Sahitya Kunj, M.G. Road,
Agra - 282002, (UP) India

1/1, Cambourne Business Centre
Cambridge, Cambridgeshire
CB 236DP, United kingdom

0562-2857671

contact@oswaalbooks.com

www.OswaalBooks.com

DISCLAIMER

Printed at Repro India Ltd.

Contents

Contents

❑❑

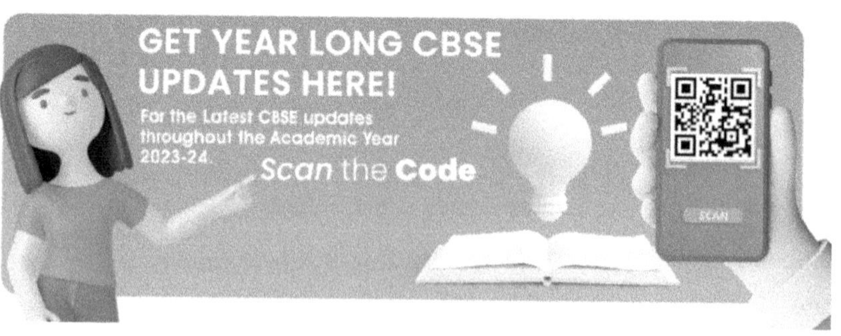

*Kindly note that this Chapter/Topic has been deleted from the Latest CBSE syllabus. Hence it is optional to study it.

What is on your wishlist for this Academic Year?

- Do better than the previous year
- Perfect every concept, every topic, and every question from the very beginning

You said it, we heard it!

Practice means to perform, repeatedly in the face of all obstacles, some act of vision, of faith, of desire. Practice is a means of inviting the perfection desired.

—Martha Graham

As we usher into a brand-new Academic Year 2023-24, Oswaal Books, with its all-new Question Banks, empowers you to perfect your learning, consistently!

These Question Banks have been updated for 2023-24 with utmost care. They are a unique blend of all the **CBSE Board Updates, Previous Years' Exam Questions,** and specially curated Questions as per the **Latest Typologies** along with best-in-class **Learning Resources.**

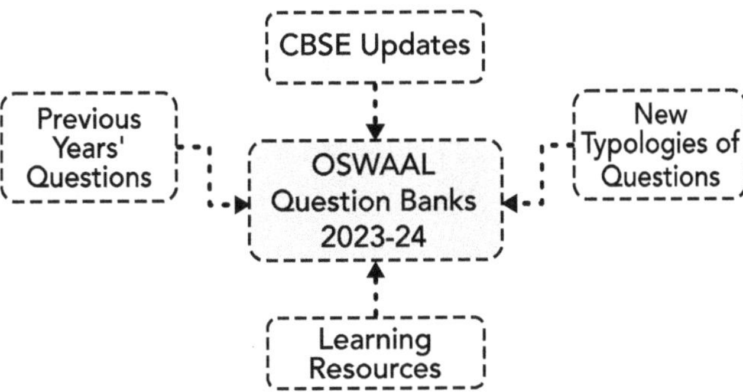

All these together will charge you with the much-needed confidence to face the boards and emerge champions. But what makes it so Unique?

1. **100% Updated** in 2023-24 with Latest Syllabus & Questions Typologies
2. **Crisp Revision** with Topic wise Revision Notes & Smart Mind Maps
3. **Extensive Practice** with 1500+ Questions & Fully Solved NCERT Textbook Questions
4. **Concept Clarity** with 1000+concepts & concept videos
5. **100% Exam Readiness** with Competency-Based Questions

For those who are looking to ramp up their preparation and to 'PERFECT' every nuance of concepts studied, these Question Banks are a must in your Boards arsenal. This is the perfect time to start your exciting journey with these Question Banks and fill in learning gaps, throughout the year with utmost ease & confidence.

This Question Bank would not have been made possible without the valuable contributions of the esteemed members of the Oswaal Editorial Board-Authors, Editors, Subject matter experts, Proofreaders & DTP operators who worked day and night to bring this incredible book to you. We are also highly grateful to our dear students for all their valuable and impeccable inputs in the making of this one-of-a-kind exam preparation tool.

All the best Students!! Be the perfectionist that you are!

Team Oswaal Books

How to use this Book

Chapter Navigation Tools

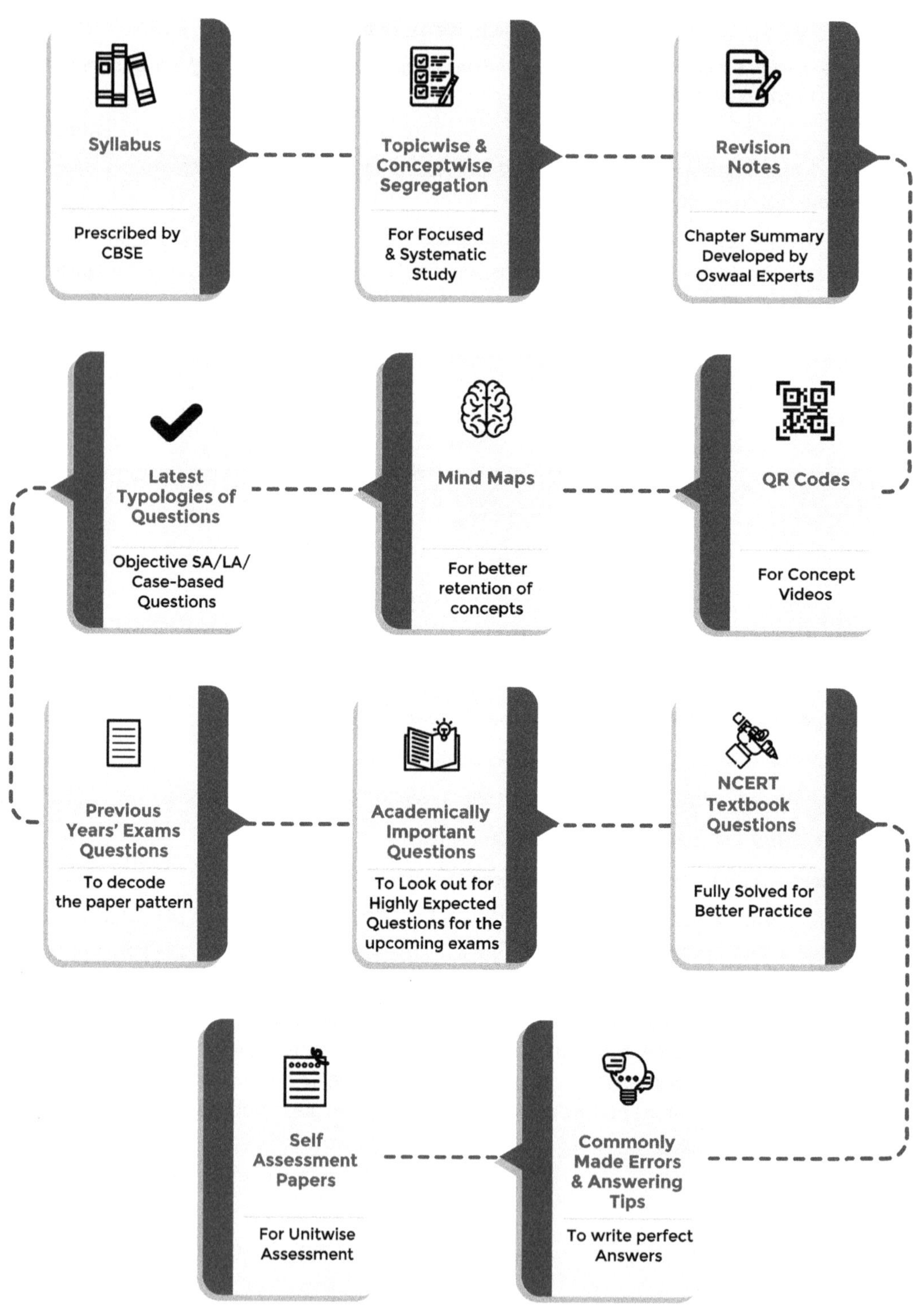
Syllabus
Prescribed by CBSE
Topicwise & Conceptwise Segregation
For Focused & Systematic Study
Revision Notes
Chapter Summary Developed by Oswaal Experts
QR Codes
For Concept Videos
Mind Maps
For better retention of concepts
Latest Typologies of Questions
Objective SA/LA/ Case-based Questions
Previous Years' Exams Questions
To decode the paper pattern
Academically Important Questions
To Look out for Highly Expected Questions for the upcoming exams
NCERT Textbook Questions
Fully Solved for Better Practice
Commonly Made Errors & Answering Tips
To write perfect Answers
Self Assessment Papers
For Unitwise Assessment

CBSE CIRCULAR 2023-24

केन्द्रीय माध्यमिक शिक्षा बोर्ड

'शिक्षा मंत्रालय भारत सरकार के अधीन एक स्वायत्त संगठन

CENTRAL BOARD OF SECONDARY EDUCATION

(An Autonomous Organisation Under the Ministry of Education, Govt. of India)

CBSE/ACADEMIC/JS(SS)/2023/

6th April, 2023
Circular No. Acad-45/2023

All Heads of Institutions affiliated to CBSE

Subject : Assessment and Evaluation Practices of the Board for the Session 2023-24

The National Education Policy, 2020 has affirmed the need to move from rote learning to learning more focused on developing the creative and critical thinking capacities of students to meet the challenges of the 21st century proactively. Accordingly, the Board has taken multiple steps towards implementation of Competency Focused Education in schools, ranging from aligning assessment to competencies, development of exemplar resources for teachers and students as well as continuous capacity building of teachers etc.

The Board has released guidelines vide Circular No. Acad- 05/2019 dated 18.01.2019; Circular No. Acad-11/2019 dated 06.03.2019; Circular No. Acad-18/2020 dated 16.03.2020; and Circular No.Acad-57/2022 dated 20.05.2022 to progressively align assessment to the vision of the NEP by including more competency-based questions in the Class X and XII Board examinations.

In continuation to these circulars, the Board is initiating further corresponding changes in the Examination and Assessment practices for the academic session 2023-24 to align assessment to Competency Focused Education. Therefore, in the forthcoming session a greater number of Competency Based Questions or questions that assess application of concepts in real-life situations will be part of the question paper.

The changes for classes IX-XII (2023-24) year-end Board Examinations are as under:

(Classes IX-X)		
Particulars	**Academic Session 2022-23**	**Academic Session 2023-24**
Composition of question paper year-end examination/ Board Examination (Theory)	• Competency Based Questions are 40% in the form of Multiple-Choice Questions, Case Based Questions, Source Based Integrated Questions or any other type. • Objective Questions are 20% • Remaining 40% Questions are Short Answer/ Long Answer Questions	• Competency Focused Questions in the form of MCQs/Case Based Questions, Source-based Integrated Questions or any other type = 50% • Select response type questions(MCQ) = 20% • Constructed response questions (Short Answer/ Long Answer type Questions, as per existing pattern) = 30%

(Classes XI-XII)		
Particulars	**Academic Session 2022-23**	**Academic Session 2023-24**
Composition of question paper year-end examination/ Board Examination (Theory)	• Competency Based Questions are 30% in the form of Multiple-Choice Questions, Case Based Questions, Source Based Integrated Questions or any other type. • Objective Question are 20% • Remaining 50% Questions are Short Answer/ Long Answer Questions	• Competency Focused Questions in the form of MCQs/Case Based Questions, Source-based Integrated Questions or any other type = 40% • Select response type questions(MCQ) = 20% • Constructed response questions (Short Answer Questions/Long Answer type Questions, as per existing pattern) = 40%

Curriculum document released by the Board for the Academic Session 2023-24 and the Sample Question Papers may also be referred to for details of the QP design of individual subjects. Learning frameworks for various subjects for classes IX-XII are now available at the https://cbseacademic.nic.in for reference.

(Dr. Joseph Emmanuel)
Director (Academics)

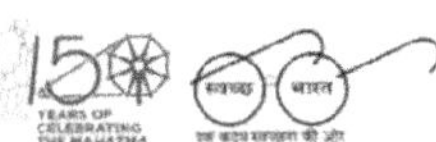

'शिक्षा सदन', 17 राऊज़ एवेन्यू, इंस्टीटूशनल एरिया, नई दिल्ली-110002
'Shiksha Sadan', 17, Rouse Avenue, Institutional Area, New Delhi – 110002

फोन/Telephone: 011-23212603 वेबसाइट/Website:http://cbseacademic.nic.in मेल/e-mail: directoracad.cbse@nic.in.

CBSE CIRCULAR 2023-24

केन्द्रीय माध्यमिक शिक्षा बोर्ड

(शिक्षा मंत्रालय भारत सरकार के अधीन एक स्वायत्त संगठन)

CENTRAL BOARD OF SECONDARY EDUCATION

(An Autonomous Organisation Under the Ministry of Education, Govt. of India)

F.1001/CBSE-Acad/Curriculum/2023 **March 31, 2023**

Cir No: Acad-39/2023

All Heads of Institutions affiliated to CBSE

Subject : Secondary and Senior School Curriculum and Sample Question Papers for the session 2023-24

1. CBSE annually provides the curriculum for classes IX to XII containing academic content, syllabus for examinations with learning outcomes, pedagogical practices, and assessment guidelines.
2. It is important that schools ensure curriculum transactions as per the directions given in the initial pages of the Curriculum document. The subjects should be taught as per the curriculum given by suitably incorporating strategies such as Art-Integrated Education, Experiential Learning, Pedagogical Plans, etc. wherever possible.
3. As CBSE has adopted National Curriculum Framework for Foundational Stage – 2022, schools offering foundational or preparatory education are advised to adhere to the recommendations regarding curriculum, pedagogy, assessment, and other areas described in detail in the NCFFS-2022 and guidelines of the Board issued from time to time.
4. Sample Question Papers with detailed designs of the Question Paper are also available on CBSE's website to reflect the impact of changes made in the curriculum. SQPs also provide students with an idea of the exam pattern and the type of questions that may be asked in the actual examination in order to ensure transparency and reduce stress. Students will also get a clear understanding of the weightage of different topics and the marking scheme to be followed by going through these Sample Question Papers.

   Schools are requested to share the Curriculum and Sample Question Papers available on **www.cbseacademic nic.in** at the given links, with all students and teachers –

   - Secondary & Senior Secondary School Curriculum –
     https://cbseacademic.nic.in/curriculum_2024.html
   - Sample Question Papers – Secondary –
     https://cbseacademic.nic.in/SQP_CLASSX_2023-24.html
   - Sample Question Papers – Senior Secondary –
     https://cbseacademic.nic.in/SQP_CLASSXII_2023-24.html

(Dr. Joseph Emmanuel)
Director (Academics)

'शिक्षा सदन', 17 राऊज़ एवेन्यू इंस्टीटूशनल एरिया, नई दिल्ली-110002

'Shiksha Sadan', 17, Rouse Avenue, Institutional Area, New Delhi – 110002

Syllabus

Latest Syllabus 2023-24
COURSE STRUCTURE : GEOGRAPHY (Code No. 029)
CLASS–XI

One Theory Paper **70 Marks**
3 Hours

Chapter No.	Chapter Name	Periods	Weightage
	Unit I: Geography as a discipline		
1.	Geography as a discipline	5	3
	Unit II: The Earth		
2.	The Origin and Evolution of the Earth	6	9
3.	Interior of the Earth	6	
4.	Distribution of oceans and continents	5	
	Unit III: Landforms		
5.	Geomorphic Processes	9	6
6.	Landform and their Evolution	9	
	Unit IV: Climate		
7.	Composition and Structure of Atmosphere	3	8
8.	Solar Radiation, Heat balance and Temperature	7	
9.	Atmospheric Circulations and Weather Systems	7	
10.	Water in the Atmosphere	4	
11.	World Climate and Climate Change (To be tested through internal assessments in the form of project and presentation)	5	
	Unit V: Water (Oceans)		
12.	Water (Oceans)	6	4
13.	Movements of Ocean Water	8	
	Unit VI: Life on the Earth		
14.	Biodiversity and Conservation (To be tested through internal assessments in the form of project and presentation)	4	–
	Map Work	5	5
	Total	89	35

Book – INDIA: Physical Environment

Chapter No.	Chapter Name	Periods	Weightage
	Unit I: Introduction		
1	India:Location	5	5
	Unit II: Physiography		
2	Structure and Physiography	18	13
3	Drainage System	14	

Syllabus

	Unit III: Climate and Natural Vegetation		
4	Climate	16	12
5	Natural Vegetation	14	
	Unit IV: Natural hazards and disasters		
6	Natural Hazards and Disasters (To be tested through internal assessment in the form of Projects and presentation)	6	–
	Map	5	5
	Total	**78**	**35**

Geography Practical Part I

Chapter No.	Chapter Name	Periods	Weightage
1	Introduction to Maps	6	3
2	Map Scale	6	4
3	Latitude Longitude and Time	8	4
4	Map Projections	10	4
5	Topographical Maps	10	4
6	Introduction to Remote Sensing	10	6
Practical file and Viva			5
Total		**50**	**30**

COURSE CONTENT

Fundamentals of Physical Geography

Chapter No. and name	Specific Learning Objective	Suggested Teaching Learning Process	Learning Outcomes
1 **Geography as a Discipline**	● To define and understand the scope and nature of Geography as a discipline. ● Branches of Geography: Physical Geography and Human Geography	Observe your surroundings and note down the variation in natural as well as cultural phenomena. Discuss with your partner: Geography is the study of "areal differentiation" **Project Work** Topic: - Forest - as a natural resource. ● Prepare a map of India showing the distribution of different types of forests. ● Write about the economic importance of forests for the country. ● Prepare a historical account of conservation of forests in India with focus on Chipko movements in Rajasthan and Uttaranchal.	**At the completion of this unit students will be able to:** ● Explain the meaning geography as an integrating discipline. ● State the fields of geography and its relation with other disciplines. ● Explain the approaches to study geography

Syllabus

2 **The Origin and Evolution of the Earth**	• To acquire knowledge about earth's origin through various theories. • To understand stages in the evolution of the earth.	Watch videos of theories (Big Bang etc.) in the class room through projector. • Presentation and interaction about the origin of the earth by students. • Students to explore more information related to the topic.	**At the completion of this unit students will be able to:** • Describe the Big Bang, Planetesimal theory, Nebular Hypothesis related to the origin of the universe.
3 **Interior of the Earth**	• To understand that the configuration of the surface of the earth is largely a product of the exogenic and endogenic processes operating in the interior of the earth	**Activity: Draw a well labelled diagram to show the interior of the earth.** • Draw a diagram of a volcano and mark the following parts: a. Magma Chamber b. Vent c. Central Pipe d. Lava flow • Draw a diagram to show the intrusive volcanic forms. • Case study of earthquakes that occurred in India in recent times and in Turkey.	**At the completion of this unit students will be able to:** • Describe direct and indirect sources of information about the interior of the earth. • Discuss Earthquakes—its causes and effects, define: Epicentre, Hypocentre, Earthquake waves and its propagation, Shadow zones, Measuring the intensity of Earthquakes. • Explain the interior structure of the earth. • Explain Volcanoes, its types and volcanic landforms.
4 **Distribution of seas and oceans**	• To describe the theory of continental drift proposed by Alfred Wegner. • To understand the present configuration of continents and oceans through plate tectonics theory.	• On the outline world map mark and label the following: a. Major plate boundaries b. Ring of fire c. Hot spot Volcanoes • Draw diagrams to show different types of plate boundaries. • Case Study: https://www.downtoearth.org.in/news/natural-disasters/out-of-the-abyss-56977	**At the completion of this unit students will be able to:** • Provide evidences in support of continental drift and force for drifting. • Explain Post drift studies, Convectional current theory, Mapping of the ocean floor, Ocean floor configuration, Concept of sea-floor spreading, • Describe theory of plate tectonics and different types of plate boundaries. • Trace the movements of Indian Plate.

Syllabus

5 **Geomorphic Processes**	• To understand various exogenic and endogenic processes responsible to bring changes in the configuration of the surface of the earth.	• Prepare a concept map to show different Exogenic and Endogenic Processes. • Students will prepare concept map on denotational processes. • Study types of weathering: Physical, Chemical, Biological and understanding their importance for human being. • Study types of mass movements and prepare a mind map.	**At the completion of this unit students will be able to:** • Differentiate between geomorphic processes and geomorphic agents. • Describe factors that affect soil formation. • Define the following terms: Exfoliation, Denudation, Weathering etc.
6 **Landforms and their Evolution**	• To understand the nature of different erosional and depositional agents and landforms made by them.	• Visit nearby landforms and draw sketches. • Draw neat and well labelled diagrams of landforms created by running water, wind and waves etc. • Watch videos of different landforms created by running water, underground water, glacier, wind, sea waves etc. • Find out the advantages and disadvantages of different landforms from the internet. • Prepare charts to show different landforms.	**At the completion of this unit students will be able to:** • Describe and draw various erosional and depositional landforms created by different agents. • Students will be able to compare and analyse various landforms • Locate different landforms (mountains, plateaus, plains) on the outline map of the world.
7 **Composition and Structure of Atmo-sphere**	• To understand the composition and structure atmosphere.	• Watch a video on the importance of different layers of the atmosphere. • Write songs based on different seasons. • Draw a neat and well labelled diagram to show different layers of the atmosphere and write the importance of each layer.	**At the completion of this unit students will be able to:** • Describe the composition and characteristics of different layers of atmosphere. • Correlate climate change with Sustainable Development Goals13: Climate Action.

Syllabus

8 **Solar Radiation, Heat Balance and Temperature**	● To understand the heating and cooling of the atmosphere and the resultant temperature distribution over the surface of the earth.	● Students to learn about the three different modes of heat transfer—convection, conduction, radiation— with the help of an activity and how they are related to the Sun and life on our planet. ● Draw a diagram to show the passage of solar radiation through the atmosphere. ● Study the figure 9.4 and 9.5 and write the distribution of surface temperature in the month of January and July.	**At the completion of this unit students will be able to:** ● Differentiate between solar radiation and terrestrial radiation. ● Give reasons for variability of insolation at the surface of the earth. ● Explain the heat budget of the planet earth. ● Describe factors controlling temperature distribution. ● Explain inversion of temperature.
9 **Atmospheric Circulation and Weather Systems**	● To understand the general atmospheric circulation and the forces that control the circulation. ● To understand the meaning of various terms related to the topic. ● To know the causes and consequences of air circulation.	● Students may read various theories and articles related to atmospheric circulation and weather system. ● Students are advised to watch live videos related to the topic winds: ● The students can be encouraged to prepare presentation on different topics in the chapter. ● Examine the weather conditions necessary for the formation of cyclones, tornadoes, hurricanes etc.	**At the completion of this unit students will be able to:** ● Describe the permanent pressure belts and the prevailing winds. ● Explain different types of winds. ● Differentiate between tropical and extra tropical cyclones. ● Realize how global warming is result of atmospheric pollution and how it can be minimised if not prevented.
10 **Water in the Atmosphere**	● To understand continuous exchange of water between the atmosphere, the oceans and the continents through the processes of evaporation, transpiration, condensation and precipitation.	● Make a list of different forms of condensation and precipitation and define them. ● Draw diagrams of different types of rainfall. ● On a world map mark and label areas of heavy, moderate, low and inadequate rainfall.	**At the completion of this unit students will be able to:** ● Explain the process of precipitation and its different forms. ● Analyse the variation in the distribution of rainfall in the world.

Syllabus

11 **Climate and Climate Change** **(To be tested through internal assessments in the form of project and presentation)**	• To define three broad approaches that have been adopted for classifying climate – Empirical Classification, Genetic Classification, and Applied Classification. • To Describe various types of climates and their groups/ subtypes. • To analyse Koeppen's Scheme of Classification of Climate. • To explain climate change and related concepts. • To evaluate the climate changes in the recent past.	• Classify climate based on various schemes by Koeppen with the help of a mind map. • Describes the causes and effects of global warming. • Evaluate the climate changes in the recent past.	**At the completion of this unit students will be able to:** • The topic can be presented in class through PPT or Project Work after conducting extensive and guided research by students.
12 **Water (Oceans)**	• To explain water cycle and summarize how an increase in demand for water leads to a water crisis. • To Illustrate major and minor ocean floor features. (mid-oceanic ridges, seamounts, submarine canyons, guyots, and atolls) • To describe horizontal and vertical distribution of oceanic temperature. • To evaluate the factors affecting the salinity of ocean waters.	• Draw a diagram to show major and minor features of ocean floor. • Study figure 13.5 and analyse the horizontal distribution of salinity in different oceans. • Locate and label the major seas on a political map of the world (As given in map list).	**At the completion of this unit students will be able to:** • Describe the basic processes involved in hydrological cycle with the help of a well labelled diagram. • Describe the relief features of the ocean floor. • Explain the process of heating and cooling of oceanic water and factors that affect temperature • distribution in the ocean • Describe the salinity of ocean waters.
13 **Movements of Ocean Water**	• To define and differentiate between tides and currents. • To describe the formation of sea waves. • To analyse the importance of tides. • To classify and describe major ocean currents and its effects.	• Mark and label the major warm and cold currents on an outline world map. (As per the given map list) • Draw a diagram of spring and neap tides.	**At the completion of this unit students will be able to:** • Explain tides, currents and waves. • Analyse the economic significance of tides. • Describe ocean currents and the forces that influence them. • Distinguish between cold and warm ocean currents.

Syllabus

14 Biodiversity and Conservation	● To explain the three major realms of the environment. ● To explain the concept of ecology. ● To analyse the features and types of aquatic ecosystems and biomes, with examples.	● Make a list of flora and fauna found in your surroundings and make a scrap book containing information and pictures of at least ten species.	**At the completion of this unit students will be able to:** ● Describe the characteristic features of the biosphere. ● Define ecology and related terms and explain the need for ecological balance. ● Recognize the abiotic and biotic factors of the ecosystem. ● To compare and contrast the features of five major biomes of the world – forest, grassland, desert, aquatic, and altitudinal.

India Physical Environment

Chapter No. and name	Specific Learning Objective	Suggested Teaching Learning Process	Learning Outcomes
1 India-Location	● To understand the geographical location of India and its significance.	● On an outline map of India mark all the neighbouring countries and compare the size of India with its neighbours. ● Make a list of all the states that share common boundary with our neighbouring countries. ● Mark and label the land boundary and coastline on an outline map of India. ● On a political map of India mark and label the states and UTs.	**At the completion of this unit students will be able to:** ● Describe the location of India mentioning the surrounding water bodies. ● Analyse the implications of living in a country with vast longitudinal and latitudinal extent and its impact on the standard time of India. ● Explain the vastness of India and the diversity that comes along with it.
2 Structure and Physiography	● To understand the evolution of different geological structures in India. ● To acquire knowledge about physiographic divisions and their subdivisions.	● Identify the physiographic and geological region you live in. Discuss the impact of physiography on the development of your region. ● On an outline map of India mark and label the physiographic divisions of India.	**At the completion of this unit students will be able to:** ● Explain the evolution of various geological structures in different parts of the country. ● Describe major physiographic divisions and the processes of their formation. ● Locate the major physical features on the map of India.

Syllabus

3 **Drainage System**	● To understand the drainage system and drainage patterns of Indian rivers. ● To understand the extent of use ability of river water and the problems associated with it.	● Have a group discussion in your class about floods-their positive and negative impact. ● Make a list of east flowing and west flowing rivers of Peninsular region.	**At the completion of this unit students will be able to:** ● Understand the major drainage systems of India. ● Analyse the causes of river water pollution. ● Differentiate between Himalayan and Peninsular rivers.
4 **Climate**	● To understand Indian monsoon: and its mechanism. ● To list the weather conditions that prevail during different seasons. ● To analyse the variation in distribution of rainfall in India.	● Students to mark and label the hottest, coldest, driest and wettest place in India. (on a political map) ● Students should be made to understand Air Quality Index. ● The Air Quality Index is a way for the government to alert people to the quality of the air and how bad the air pollution is in an area or city. They use colours to help you determine if you should go outside. ● Green - the air is good. ● Yellow - the air is moderate ● Orange - the air is unhealthy for sensitive people like the elderly, children, and those with lung diseases. ● Red – Unhealthy ● Purple - Very unhealthy ● Maroon - Hazardous	**At the completion of this unit students will be able to:** ● Discuss the factors affecting climate of the country and its effect on country's economic life. ● Understand the annual cycle of four main seasons in India. ● Able to realise the causes and problems of climate changes. ● Able to understand the concept of Global Warming.
5 **Natural Vegetation**	● To understand the relationship between vegetation belts and the climate.	● Students would be able to enhance their communication skills by debating on positive and negative impact of human activities on forest cover and wildlife. ● To mark all major types of forests on a map of India. ● Class can be divided into groups to collect information about people's (common man) participation in the conservation of forests and wildlife.	● At the completion of this topic the students will be able to: ● The students will be able to recognise the importance of forest cover in the country and its spatial distribution. ● They will learn about number of species of plants and animals in India. ● They will appreciate the efforts in conservation of forests and wild life.

Syllabus

6 **Natural Hazards and Disasters** **(To be tested through internal assessment in the form of Projects and presentation)**	• To make students aware about natural hazards and disasters happening in various parts of the country, their impact and ways to mitigate the damage caused by them.	• Divide your class into groups and allocate one disaster to each group. • Every group should think of themselves as living in a disaster prone area of their allocated topic. • All groups would give a presentation on causes ,impact and risk reduction of that disaster.	**At the completion of this unit students will be able to:** • Classifies different types of hazards and disasters. • Describes causes effects and mitigation policy for various natural disasters. • Able to identify and locate regions prone to different disasters on the map. • Understands the concept of disaster management.

Map Items for locating and labelling on outline political World Map
Fundamentals of Physical Geography

Chapter No. and name	Map Work
4 **Distribution of oceans and continents**	• Political Map of all Continents of the world. • Major Oceans of the world: Indian Ocean, Pacific Ocean, Atlantic Ocean, Arctic Ocean, Southern Ocean • Major lithospheric plates and Minor lithospheric plates, Ring of fire (Pacific Ocean), Mid-Atlantic Ridge.
9 **Atmospheric Circulations and Weather Systems**	**Major Hot Deserts of the world:** • Mojave Desert- Nevada, US • Patagonian Desert- Argentina • Sahara- Africa • Gobi Desert- Mongolia, Asia • Thar desert- India • Great Victoria desert- Australia
12 **Water(Oceans**	• Major Seas • Black sea • Baltic sea • Caspian Sea • Mediterranean Sea • North Sea • Red sea • Bay of Fundy (Canada)-Famous for the highest tides in the world
13 **Movements of Ocean Water**	**OCEAN CURRENTS-Cold currents** • Humboldt c. • California c. • Falkland c. • Canaries c. • West Australian c. • Oyashio c. • Labrador c.

	Warm currents ● Alaska c. ● Brazilian c. ● Aughlas c. ● Kuroshio c. ● Gulf stream c.
14 **Biodiversity and Conservation**	**Ecological hotspots** ● Eastern Himalaya, India ● Western ghats, India ● Indonesia, Asia ● Eastern Madagascar, Africa ● Upper Guinean forests, Africa ● Atlantic forest, Brazil ● Tropical Andes

Map Items for locating and labelling on outline political map of India
India Physical Environment

Chapter No. and name	Map Work
1 **India- Location**	● Latitudinal extent of India ● Longitudinal extent of India ● Standard Meridian of India ● Important latitude passing through India (Tropic of Cancer) ● Southern Most Point of main land of India (Kanya Kumari)
2 **Structure and Physiography**	● **Mountains:** Karakoram Range, Garo- Khasi- Jaintia hills, Aravalli Range, Vindhyan Range, Satpura Range, Western ghats & Eastern ghats ● **Peaks:** K2, Kanchenjunga, Nandadevi, Nanga Parvat, Namcha Barwa and Anaimud ● **Passes:** Shipkila, Nathula, Palghat, Bhor ghat and Thal ghat ● **Plateaus:** Malwa, Chhotnagpur, Meghalaya and Deccan Plateau. ● **Coastal Plains:** Saurashtra, Konkan, North and South Kanara, Malabar, Coromandel and Northern Circars ● **Islands:** Andaman & Nicobar Islands and Lakshadweep Islands
3 **Drainage System**	● **Rivers:** Brahmaputra, Indus, Satluj, Ganga, Yamuna, Chambal, Damodar Mahanadi, Krishna, Kaveri, Godavari, Narmada, Tapti and Luni ● **Lakes:** (Identification)Wular, Sambhar, Chilika, Kolleru, Pulicat & Vembanad ● **Straits, Bays , Gulfs:** Palk Strait, Rann of Kachch, Gulf of Kachch, Gulf of Mannar & Gulf of Khambat
4 **Climate**	● Area with highest temperature in India ● Area with lowest temperature in India ● Area with highest rainfall in India ● Area with lowest rainfall in India

Syllabus

5 **Natural Vegetation**	(Identification on an outline map of India) Tropical evergreen, Tropical deciduous, Tropical thorn, Montane and Littoral/ Swamp forests. Wildlife reserves: (locating and labeling) ● **National Parks:** Corbett, Kaziranga, Ranthambore. Shivpuri, Simlipal ● **Bird Sanctuaries:** Keoladev Ghana and Ranganathitto ● **Wild life Sanctuaries:** Periyar, Rajaji, Mudumalai, Dachigam,

Guidelines for Internal Assessment/ Geography Practical

1. A practical file must be prepared by students covering all the topics prescribed in the practical syllabus.
2. The file should be completely handwritten with a cover page, index page and acknowledgment.
3. All practical works should be drawn neatly with appropriate headings, scale, index etc. Data can be taken from the NCERT text book.
4. The practical file will be assessed at the time of term end practical examinations.
5. A written exam of 25 marks will be conducted based on prescribed practical syllabus.
6. Viva will be conducted based on practical syllabus only.
7. Written Exam– 25 Marks
8. Practical file– 03 Marks
9. Viva– 02 Marks

❑❑

Order Form

ONE FOR ALL OLYMPIADS (Multicolour)

Classes 1 to 5

Mathematics, English, Reasoning, General Knowledge, Science & Cyber

ONE FOR ALL WORKBOOKS CONCEPT-WISE (Multicolour)

Classes 1 to 5

Mathematics, English, General Knowledge, Science

NCERT WORKBOOKS (Multicolour / B W)

Classes 1 & 2

English, Hindi & Mathematics

Classes 3 to 5

English, Hindi, Mathematics & EVS

ONE FOR ALL OLYMPIADS

Classes 6 to 8

Mathematics, English, Reasoning, General Knowledge, Science & Cyber

NCERT/CBSE PULL-OUT WORKSHEETS

Classes 6 to 8

Mathematics, English, Science, Social Science, Hindi & Sanskrit

Classes 9 & 10

English Lang. & Literature, Science, Social Science & Mathematics

CBSE QUESTION BANKS (CHAPTER-WISE & TOPIC-WISE SOLVED PAPERS)

Classes 6 to 8

Mathematics, English, Science, Social Science, Hindi & Sanskrit

CBSE QUESTION BANKS (CHAPTER-WISE & TOPIC-WISE SOLVED PAPERS)

Classes 9 & 10

Hindi-A, Hindi-B, English Lang. & Lit. (With NCERT Workbook), Science, Mathematics, Social Science, Computer Applications, Sanskrit & English Communicative (With CBSE Textbook),

Classes 11 & 12

Hindi Core, English Core, Mathematics, Chemistry, Applied Mathematics, Biology, Physics, Accountancy, Economics, Business Studies, Geography, History, Political Science, Computer Science, Entrepreneurship, Informatics Practices, Physical Education, Sociology (For Class 12th Only), Psychology (For Class 12th Only)

NCERT NCERT EXEMPLAR PROBLEMS-SOLUTIONS (Hindi & English Medium)

Classes 9 & 10

Science, Mathematics, गणित, विज्ञान

NCERT NCERT EXEMPLAR PROBLEMS-SOLUTIONS (Hindi & English Medium)

Classes 11 & 12

Physics, Chemistry, Mathematics, Biology, गणित, भौतिक विज्ञान, रसायन विज्ञान, जीव विज्ञान

NCERT TEXTBOOK+EXEMPLAR

Classes 11 & 12

Physics, Chemistry, Matheamatics & Biology

CBSE 6 YEARS SOLVED PAPERS

Class 10

English Lang. & Lit, Science, Social Science, Hindi-B, Mathematics Basic, Mathematics Standard, Hindi-A, Computer Applications & Sanskrit

Class 12

Science Stream- (Chemistry, Physics, Mathematics, English Core & Biology), Commerce Stream- Economics, (Accountancy, Business Studies, Mathematics & English Core), Humanities Stream- (Geography, History, Political Science, English Core & Hindi Core)

CBSE RMT FLASH CARD

Class 10

Mathematics, English Lang. & Lit., Social Science & Science

CBSE ONE FOR ALL

Classes 9 & 10

Mathematics, English Lang. & Lit., Social Science, Science, Hindi-A, Hindi-B, Mathematics (Stand.) & Mathematics Basic

Class 12

English Core, Physics, Chemistry, Mathematics, Biology, Accoutancy, Business Studies & Economics

CBSE LMP-Last Minute Preparation System

Class 10

Combined (English Lang. & Lit., Science, Mathematics Standard & Social Science)

Class 12

Science (Physics, Chemistry, Mathematics, Biology & English Core)
Commerce (Accountancy, Business Studies, Economics, Mathematics & English Core)
Humanities (History, Geography, Political Science & English Core)

CBSE SAMPLE QUESTION PAPERS

Classes 9 & 10

Hindi-A, Hindi-B, English Lang. & Lit., Computer Appl., English Communicative, Mathematics, Science, Social Science, Sanskrit & Samajik Vigyan (For Class 10th Only)

Classes 11 & 12

Hindi Core, English Core, Mathematics, Applied Mathematics, Physics, Chemistry, Biology, Accountancy, Economics, Business Studies, Geography, History, Political Science, Computer Science, Informatics Practices, Physical Education, Entrepreneurship (For Class 12th Only), Psychology (For Class 12th Only) & Sociology (For Class 12th Only)

amazon.in Flipkart meesho JioMart snapdeal amazon kindle

Exclusive School Books Suppliers

ANDHRA PRADESH

VIJAYAWADA Sri Vikas Book Centre, 9848571114, 9440715700,

ASSAM

WEST KAMENG Dutta Book Stall, 8729948473

KARNATAKA

BANGLORE Satish Agencies, 8861630123

GUJRAT

RAJKOT Royal Stationers, 9824207514

MAHARASHTRA

PUNE Madhusheela Books & Stationery, 7875899892

JALNA Anil Paper Mart, 9422722522, (02482) 230733

TAMIL NADU

CHENNAI Bookmark-IT, 7305151653

TELANGANA

HYDERABAD Sri Balaji Book Depot , 9676996199, (040) 27613300

WEST BENGAL

KOLKATA United Book House, 9831344622

Our Distributors

ANDHRA PRADESH

VISAKHAPATHAM JBD Educational, 9246632691, 9246633693,

ANDAMAN & NICOBAR ISLAND

PORTBLAIR Krishna Book Centre, 9474205570, Kumar Book Depot, 9932082455, Kumar Book Depot, 9932082455, Sree aditya Book Centre, 8332972720, 7013300914

ASSAM

GUWAHATI Book Emporium, 9675972993, 6000763186, Ashok Publication, 7896141127, Kayaan Enterprises, (0361) 2630443, Orchid Book house, 9864624209, Newco, 9864178188

BIHAR

PATNA Nova Publisher & Distributors, (0612) 2666404, Shri Durga Pustak Mandir, 9334477386, Sharda Pustak Bhandar, 9334259293, Vikas Book Depot, 9504780402, Alka Book Agency, 9835655005, Metro Book(E&C), Ishu Pustak Bhandar, 8294576789, Gyan Ganga Limited, 6203900312

MUZAFFARPUR Pustak Bhandar, 7870834225

CHATTISGARH

AMBIKAPUR Saini Brothers, 9425582561, M.P Department Stores, 9425254264

BOKARO Bokaro Student Friends Pvt. Ltd, Bokaro, 7277931285

BHILAI Anil Book Depot, 9425234260

DURG Bhagwati Bhawani Book Depot, 0788-2327620, 9827473100

KORBA Kitab Ghar, Korba (E & C), 9425226528

RAIPUR Shri Ramdev Traders, 9981761797, Gupta Pustak Mandir, 7974220323

RAIGARH Sindhu Book Deopt, 9981935763

DELHI

DELHI Mittal Books, (011) 23288887, 9899037390, Singhania Book & Stationer, 9212028238, AoneBooks, New Delhi, 8800497047, Radhey Book Depot, 9818314141, Batheja Super Store, 9871833924, Lov Dev & Sons, Delhi (E & C), 9811182352, Zombozone, 9871274082

GUJARAT

AHMEDABAD Patel Book, 9898184248, 9824386112, 9825900335, Zaveri Agency, 9979897312, 9979890330, Hardik Book Agency, (ISC) 079-24110043 9904659821

BHAVNAGAR Samir Book Stall, Bhavnagar (ISC) 9586305305

DAHOD Collegian Book Corner, 9925501981

VAPI Goutam Book Sellers, 9081790813

VALSAD Mahavir Stationers, 9429474177

NAVSARI College Store, (ISC) NO CALL 02637-258642, 9825099121

SURAT Shopping Point, 9824108663

VADODARA Umakant Book Sellers & Stationer, 9624920709

HARYANA

ROHTAK Manish Traders, 9812556687, Swami Kitab Ghar, 9355611088, Babu Ram Pradeep Kumar, 9813214692

REWARI Sanjay book depot, 9255447231

BALLABGARH Kashi Ram Kishan lal, 9289504004, 8920567245

BHUNA Khurana Book Store, 9896572520

JAMMU

Sahitya Sangam, 9419190177

JHARKHAND

BOKARO Bokaro Student Friends, (0654) 2233094, 7360021503, Bharati Bhawan Agencies, 9431740797

RANCHI Crown Book Distributor & Publishers, (0651) 2213735, 9431173904, Pustak Mandir, 9431115138,

DUMKA Vidyarthi Pustak Bhandar, 9431310228

KARNATAKA

HUBLI Renuka Book Distributor, (0836) 2244124

BANGLORE Krishna book house, 9739847334, Hema Book Stores, 9986767000, Sapna Book House Pvt. Ltd., 9980513242, Hema Book World, (Chamrajpet) (ISC) 080-40905110 9945731121

BELLERI Chatinya book centre, 9886064731

KERALA

ERNAKULAM Academic Book House, (0484) 2376613, H & C Store, 9864196344, Surya Book House, 9847124217, 9847238314

KOTTAYAM Book Centre, (0481) 2566992

TRIVANDRUM Academic Book House, (0471) 2333349, 9447063349, Ponni Book Stall, 9037591721

CALICUT Aman Book Stall, (0495) 2721282,

MADHYA PRADESH

CHHINDWARA Pustak Bhawan, (E & C), 8982150100

GWALIOR Agarwal Book Depot, 9425116210

INDORE Bhaiya Industries, 9893326853, Sushil Prakashan,(0731) 2503333, 2535892, 9425322330, Bhaiya Store, 9425318103, Arun Prakashan, 9424890785, Bhaiya Book Centre, 9424081874, Seva Suppliers, 9826451052

JABALPUR Vinay Pustak Sadan, 8962362667, Anand Books and Stationers, 9425323508

SAGAR Princi Book Depot, Sagar, 9977277011

KATNI Shri Mahavir Agency, 9425363412

UJJAIN Shreenath Book Depot, 9827544045

BHOPAL Gupta Brother, 9644482444

MAHARASHTRA

PUNE Natraj Book Depot, (020) 24485054, 9890054092, Vikas Book House, 9921331187, Pravin Sales, 9890683475, New Saraswati Granth Bhandar, 9422323859, Akshar Books & Stationary, 7385089789, Vardhaman Educational, 9860574354, Yash Book Centre, 9890156763, Pragati Book Centre, (ISC), 9850039311, Praveen Sales, Pragati Book Centre, Pune (E & C), 9850039311

AURANGABAD Shree Sainath Agencies, 7350294089, Maya Book Centre, (ISC), 9372360150

MUMBAI Vidyarthi Sales Agencies, 9819776110, New Student Agencies, 7045065799, Shivam Books & Stationery, 8619805332

JALGAON Sharma Book Depot & Stat. (ISC), 9421393040

LATUR Yash Book House, 9637936999, Shri Ganesh Pustakalay, 9730172188

KOLHAPUR Granth the Book World, 9922295522

NAGPUR Laxmi Pustakalay and Stationers, (0712) 2727354, Vijay Book Depot, 9860122094 Renuka Book distributor, 9765406133, Novelty Book Depot, 9657690220, Karamveer Book Depot, 9923966466, Arun Book & Stationers, 9423110953

NASHIK Rahul Book Centre, 9970849681, New India Book House, 9623123458

DHULE Navjeevan Book Stall, 7020525561

YAVATMAL Shri Ganesh Pustkalaya, 9423131275

VASAI Prime Book Centre, Vasai, 9890293662

ODISHA

CUTTACK A. K. Mishra Agencies, 9437025991, 9437081319

BHUBANESHWAR M/s Pragnya, 8847888616, 9437943777, Padmalaya, 9437026922, Bidyashree, 9937017070, Books Godown, 7894281110

BARIPADA Trimurti Book World, 9437034735

KEONJHAR Students corner, 7008435418

PUNJAB

AMBALA Bharat Book Depot, 7988455354

PATIALA Goel Sons, 9463619978, Adarsh Enterprises, 9814347613

JALANDHAR Cheap Book Store, 9872223458, 9878258592, City Book Shop, 9417440753, Subhash Book Depot, 9876453625, Paramvir Enterprises, 9878626248

FEROZPUR Sita Ram book Depot, 9463039199, 7696141911

LUDHIANA Amit Book, 9815807871, Gupta Brothers, 9888200206, Bhatia Book Centre, 9815277131

CHANDIGARH Mohindra Book Depot, 9814920226

RAJASTHAN

AJMER Laxmi General Store, Ajmer, 0145- 2428942 9460652197

KOTA Vardhman Book Depot, 9571365020, 8003221190 Raj Traders, 9309232829

BHILWARA Nakoda Book Depot, (01482) 243653, 9214983594, Alankar Book Depot, 9414707462

JAIPUR Ravi Enterprises, 9829060694, Saraswati Book House, (0141) 2610823, 9829811155, Goyal Book Distt., 9460983939, 9414782130

UDAIPUR Sunil Book Store, 9828682260

JODHPUR Second Hand Book Stall, 9460004745

TRIPURA

AGARTALA Book Corner, 8794894165, 8984657146, Book Emporium, 9089230412

TAMIL NADU

COIMBATORE Majestic Book House, (0422) 2384333, CBSC Book Shop, 9585979752

CHENNAI Arraba Book Traders, (044) 25387868, 9841459105, M.R. Book Store (044) 25364596, Kalaimagal Store, (044) 5544072, 9940619404, Vijaya Stores, 9381037417, Bookmark It-Books & Stat. Store, 7305151653, M.K. Store, 9840030099, Tiger Books Pvt. Ltd., 9710447000, New Mylai Stationers, 9841313062, Prince Book House, Chennai, 0444-2053926, 9952068491, S K Publishers & Distributors, 9789865544

PUDUCHERRY Sri Lakshmi Book Seller, 7871555145

SALEM Pattu book centre, 9894816280

TRICHY P.R.Sons Book Seller, 9443370597, Rasi Publication, 9894816280

THENI Maya Book Centre, 9443929274

MADURAI Selvi Book Shoppe, 9843057435, Jayam Book Centre, 9894658036

VELLORE G.K book centre and collections, 9894517994

TELANGANA

HYDERABAD Sri Balaji Book Depot, (040) 27613300, 9866355473, Shah Book House, 9849564564 Vishal Book Distributors, 9246333166

	UTTARAKHAND		
DEHRADUN	Inder Book Agencies, 9634045280, Amar Book Depot , 8130491477, Goyal Book Store, 9897318047,	GORAKHPUR	Central Book House, 9935454590, Friends & Co., 9450277154, Dinesh book depot, 9125818274, Friends & Co., 9450277154
MUSSORIE	Ram Saran Dass Chanda kiran, 0135-2632785, 9761344588	JHANSI	Bhanu Book Depot, 9415031340
	UTTAR PRADESH	KANPUR	Radha News Agency, 8957247427, Raj Book Dist., 9235616506, H K Book Distributors, 9935146730
		LUCKNOW	Vyapar Sadan, 7607102462, Om Book Depot, 7705871398, Azad Book Depot Pvt. Ltd., 7317000250, Book Sadan, 9839487327, Rama Book Depot(Retail), 7355078254, Ashirwad Book Depot, 9235501197, Book.com, 7458922755, Universal Books, 9450302161, Sheetla Book Agency, 9235832418
AGRA	Sparsh Book Agency, 9412257817, Om Pustak Mandir, (0562) 2464014, 9319117771, Sanjay Publication, 8126699922 Arti book centre, 8630128856, Panchsheel Books, 9412257962, Bhagwati Book Store, (E & C), 9149081912	MEERUT	Ideal Book Depot, (0121) 4059252, 9837066307
ALLAHABAD	Mehrotra Book Agency, (0532) 2266865, 9415636890	NOIDA	Prozo (Global Edu4 Share Pvt. Ltd), 9318395520, Goyal Books Overseas Pvt.Ltd., 1204655555 9873387003
AZAMGARH	Sasta Sahitya Bhandar, 9450029674	PRAYAGRAJ	Kanhaiya Pustak Bhawan, 9415317109
ALIGARH	K.B.C.L. Agarwal, 9897124960, Shaligram Agencies, 9412317800, New Vimal Books, 9997398868	MAWANA	Subhash Book Depot, 9760262264
ALIGARH	T.I.C Book centre, 9808039570		WEST BENGAL
BALRAMPUR	Universal Book Center, 8933826726	KOLKATA	Oriental Publishers & Distributor (033) 40628367, Katha 'O' Kahini, (033) 22196313, 22419071, Saha Book House, (033), 22193671, 9333416484, United Book House, 9831344622, Bijay Pustak Bhandar, 8961260603, Shawan Books Distributors, 8336820363, Krishna Book House, 9123083874
BAREILLY	Siksha Prakashan, 9837829284	RENUKOOT	Om Stationers, 7007326732
DEORIA	Kanodia Book Depot, 9415277835	COOCH BEHAR	S.B. Book Distributor, Cooch behar, 9002670771
VARANASI	Gupta Books, 8707225564	KHARAGPUR	Subhani Book Store, 9046891334
MATHURA	Sapra Traders, 9410076716, Vijay Book House , 9897254292	SILIGURI	Agarwal Book House, 9832038727
FARRUKHABAD	Anurag Book Agencies, 8844007575	DINAJPUR	Krishna Book House, 7031748945
NAJIBABAD	Gupta News Agency, 8868932500, Gupta News Agency, (E & C), 8868932500	MURSHIDABAD	New Book House, 8944876176
DHAMPUR	Ramkumar Mahaveer Prasad, 9411942550		

Entrance & Competition Distributors

	BIHAR	CUTTAK	A.K.Mishra Agencies, 9437025991
PATNA	Metro Books Corner, 9431647013, Alka Book Agency, 9835655005, Vikas Book Depot, 9504780402	BHUBANESH-WAR	M/s Pragnya, 9437943777
	CHATTISGARH		PUNJAB
KORBA	Kitab Ghar, 9425226528, Shri Ramdev Traders, 9981761797	JALANDHAR	Cheap Book Store, 9872223458, 9878258592
	DELHI		RAJASTHAN
DELHI	Singhania Book & Stationer, 9212028238, Radhey Book depot, 9818314141, The Book Shop, 9310262701, Mittal Books, 9899037390, Lov Dev & Sons, 9999353491	KOTA	Vardhman Book Depot, 9571365020, Raj Traders, 9309232829
NEW DELHI	Anupam Sales, 9560504617, A ONE BOOKS, 8800497047	JAIPUR	Goyal Book Distributors, 9414782130
	HARYANA		UTTAR PRADESH
AMBALA	Bharat Book Depot, 7988455354	AGRA	BHAGWATI BOOK STORE, 9149081912, Sparsh Book Agency, 9412257817, Sanjay Publication, 8126699922
	JHARKHAND	ALIGARH	New Vimal Books, 9997398868
BOKARO	Bokaro Student Friends Pvt. Ltd, 7360021503	ALLAHABAD	Mehrotra Book Agency, (532) 2266865, 9415636890
	MADHYA PRADESH	GORAKHPUR	Central Book House, 9935454590
INDORE	Bhaiya Industries, 9109120101	KANPUR	Raj Book Dist, 9235616506
CHHINDWARA	Pustak Bhawan, 9827255997	LUCKNOW	Azad Book Depot PVT LTD, 7317000250, Rama Book Depot(Retail), 7355078254 Ashirwad Book Depot , 9235501197, Book Sadan, 8318643277, Book.com , 7458922755, Sheetla Book Agency, 9235832418
	MAHARASHTRA	PRAYAGRAJ	Format Center, 9335115561, Garg Brothers Trading & Services Pvt. Ltd., 7388100499
NAGPUR	Laxmi Pustakalay and Stationers, (0712) 2727354		UTTAR PRADESH
PUNE	Pragati Book Centre, 9850039311	DEHRADUN	Inder Book Agancies, 9634045280
MUMBAI	New Student Agencies LLP, 7045065799		WEST BENGAL
	ODISHA	KOLKATA	Bijay Pustak Bhandar Pvt. Ltd., 8961260603, Saha Book House, 9674827254 United Book House, 9831344622, Techno World, 9830168159
BARIPADA	Trimurti Book World, 9437034735		

2705

WRITING YOUR NOTES

Just in case you have forgotten today, takedown your notes!
But why is it so important?

Tools for the hands are tools for the brain writes Hetty Roessingh.
Handwritten notes are a powerful tool for encrypting embodied cognition and in turn supporting the brain's capacity for recuperation of information. If that sounds so scientiic then in simple words: Writing notes by hand help you to:

◆ Increasing your comprehension ◆ Strengthening your memory ◆ Igniting your creativity ◆ Engaging your mind ◆ Increasing your attention span

Are these reasons enough to get you started?

1. ....
2. ....
3. ....
4. ....
5. ....
6. ....
7. ....
8. ....
9. ....
10. ....
11. ....
12. ....
13. ....
14. ....
15. ....
16. ....
17. ....
18. ....
19. ....
20. ....

MIND MAP
AN INTERACTIVE MAGICAL TOOL

What?
Presenting words and concepts as pictures!!

When?
anytime, as frequency as you like till it becomes a habit!

Why?

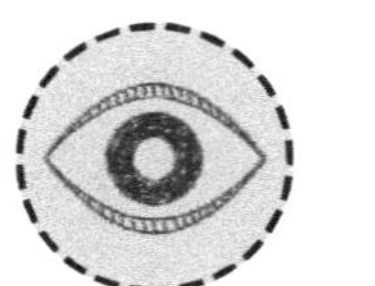

- To Unlock the imagination and come up with ideas
- To Remember facts and figures easily
- To Make clearer and better notes
- To Concentrate and save time
- To Plan with ease and ace exams

How?
With a blank sheet of paper coloured pens and your creative imagination!

Result
Learning made simple 'a winning combination'

What are Associations?

It's a technique connecting the core concept at the Centre to related concepts or ideas. Associations spreading out straight from the core concept are the First Level of Association. Then we have a Second Level of Association emitting from the first level and the chronology continues. The thickest line is the First Level of Association and the lines keep getting thinner as we move to the subsequent levels of association. This is exactly how the brain functions, therefore these Mind Maps. Associations are one powerful memory aid connecting seemingly unrelated concepts, hence strengthening memory.

New Typologies of Question introduced by CBSE for 2023-24 exam

Part A: Fundamentals of Physical Geography

Chapter 1: Geography As A Discipline

Objective Type Questions

(1 mark each)

(A) FILL IN THE BLANKS

Q. 1. Geography helps in understanding the reality in its __________ perspective. U

Ans. spatial

Q. 2. __________ geography studies the spatial pattern of natural vegetation in their habitats. R

Ans. Plant

Q. 3. Geography is a combination of both spatial as well as __________ synthesis. R

Ans. temporal

Q. 4. Population geography is closely linked with the discipline of __________. U

Ans. demography

Q. 5. The __________ geography was introduced by Alexander Von Humboldt. R

Ans. systematic

Q. 6. __________ geography studies the historical processes through which the space gets organised. U

Ans. Historical

(B) ARRANGE IN THE CORRECT ORDER

Q. 1. Arrange the following approaches in the correct order according to their development. A

1. Spatial organization
2. Regional approach
3. Areal differentiation
4. Humanistic approach

Options:

(a) 3, 2, 1, 4 (b) 4, 2, 1, 3

(c) 2, 3, 1, 4 (d) 1, 3, 2, 4

Ans. (c) 2, 3, 1, 4

Q. 2. Physical geography includes the study of: R

1. lithosphere 2. hydrosphere

3. biosphere 4. atmosphere

Options:

(a) 1, 2, 3, 4 (b) 1, 2, 4, 3

(c) 3, 4, 2, 1 (d) 1, 4, 2, 3

Ans. (d) 1, 4, 2, 3

Q. 3. Geography studies the patterns of ______ phenomena over space. U

1. location 2. concentration

3. interpretation 4. distribution

Options:

(a) 4, 1, 2, 3 (b) 2, 3, 4, 1

(c) 1, 2, 3, 4 (d) 3, 1, 4, 2

Ans. (a) 4, 1, 2, 3

Q. 4. Make correct pairs from the following two columns and mark the correct option: R

1. Meteorology	A. Population Geography
2. Demography	B. Soil Geography
3. Sociology	C. Climatography
4. Pedology	D. Social Geography

Options:

(a) 1-B, 2-C, 3-A, 4-D (b) 1-A, 2-D, 3-B, 4-C

(c) 1-D, 2-B, 3-C, 4-A (d) 1-C, 2-A, 3-D, 4-B

Ans. (d) 1-C, 2-A, 3-D, 4-B

Source-Based Questions

(3 marks each)

Q. 1. Read the passage given below and answer any three questions that follow. **(1×3=3)** A

All the branches of physical geography have interface with natural sciences. The traditional physical geography is linked with geology, meteorology, hydrology and pedology; thus, geomorphology, climatology, oceanography and soil geography, respectively, have very close link with the natural sciences as they derive their data from these sciences. Bio-geography is closely related to botany and zoology as well as ecology as human beings are located in different locational niche. A geographer should have some proficiency in mathematics and art, particularly in drawing maps. Geography is very much linked with the study of astronomical locations and deals with latitudes and longitudes. The shape of the earth is geoid, but the basic tool of a geographer is a map that is a two-dimensional representation of the earth. The problem of converting geoids into two dimensions can be tackled by projections constructed graphically or mathematically. The cartographic and quantitative techniques require sufficient proficiency in mathematics, statistics and econometrics. Maps are prepared through artistic imagination. Making sketches, mental maps and cartographic work requires proficiency in arts.

(i) All the branches of physical geography have interface with:

(a) natural sciences **(b)** physical sciences

(c) social sciences **(d)** political sciences

Ans. (a) natural sciences

(ii) Which science is closely related to botany and zoology as well as ecology?

(a) Climatology **(b)** Bio-geography

(c) Oceanography **(d)** None of the above

Ans. (b) Bio-geography

(iii) The problem of converting geoids into two dimensions can be tackled by projections constructed:

(a) graphically **(b)** mathematically

(c) Both (a) and (b) **(d)** mentally

Ans. (c) Both (a) and (b)

(iv) Making sketches, mental maps and cartographic work requires proficiency in ________.

(a) geography **(b)** english

(c) arts **(d)** subject

Ans. (c) arts

Q. 2. Read the passage given below and answer any three questions that follow. (1×3=3) U

Physical geography includes the study of lithosphere (landforms, drainage, relief and physiography), atmosphere (its composition, structure, elements and controls of weather and climate; temperature, pressure, winds, precipitation, climatic types, etc.), hydrosphere (oceans, seas, lakes and associated features with water realm) and biosphere (life forms including human beings and macro-organisms and their sustaining mechanism, viz. food chain, ecological parameters and ecological balance). Soils are formed through the process of pedogenesis and depend upon the parent rocks, climate, biological activity and time. Time provides maturity to soils and helps in the development of soil profiles. Each element is important for human beings.

Landforms provide the base on which human activities are located. The plains are utilised for agriculture. Plateaus provide forests and minerals. Mountains provide pastures, forests and tourist spots and are sources of rivers providing water to lowlands. Climate influences our house types, clothing and food habits. The climate has a profound effect on vegetation, cropping pattern, livestock farming and some industries, etc. Human beings have developed technologies that modify climatic elements in a restricted space such as air conditioners and coolers. Temperature and precipitation ensure the density of forests and quality of grasslands. In India, monsoonal rainfall sets the agriculture rhythm in motion. Precipitation recharges the ground water aquifers, which later provides water for agriculture and domestic use.

(i) Landforms provide the base on which human activities are located.

(a) True **(b)** False

(c) Somewhat true **(d)** None of the above

Ans. (a) True

(ii) What ensures the density of forests and quality of grasslands?

(a) Temperature and climate

(b) Precipitation and moisture

(c) Moisture and temperature

(d) Temperature and precipitation

Ans. (d) Temperature and precipitation

(iii) What has a profound effect on vegetation, cropping pattern, livestock farming and some industries?

(a) Politics **(b)** Climate

(c) Population **(d)** Economy

Ans. (b) Climate

(iv) What recharges the ground aquifers, which later later provides water for agriculture and domestic use?

(a) Dams **(b)** Borewells

(c) Precipitation **(d)** Humidity

Ans. (c) Precipitation

Q. 3. Read the passage given below and answer any three questions that follow. (1×3=3) U

Geography is an interdisciplinary subject of study. The study of every subject is done according to some approach. The major approaches to study geography have been (i) Systematic and (ii) Regional. The systematic geography approach is the same as that of general geography. This approach was introduced by Alexander Von Humboldt, a German geographer (1769–1859) while the regional geography approach was developed by another German geographer and a contemporary of Humboldt, Karl Ritter (1779–1859). In the systematic approach, a phenomenon is studied world over as a whole, and then the identification of typologies or spatial patterns is done. For example, if one is interested in studying about natural vegetation, the study will be done at the world level as a first step. The typologies such as equatorial rainforests or softwood conical forests or monsoon forests, etc. will be identified, discussed and delimited. In the regional approach, the world is divided into regions at different hierarchical levels, and then all the geographical phenomena in a particular region are studied. These regions may be natural, political or designated regions. The phenomena in a region are studied in a holistic manner searching for unity in diversity.

(i) What is geography?

(a) It is an interdisciplinary subject of study.
(b) It is a spatial subject of study.
(c) It is an independent subject of study.
(d) It is a hierarchical subject of study.

Ans. (a) It is an interdisciplinary subject of study.

(ii) The _________ geography approach is the same as that of general geography.

(a) regional (b) systematic
(c) human (d) historical

Ans. (b) systematic

(iii) The phenomena in a region are studied in a _______ manner searching for unity in diversity.

(a) proper (b) holistic
(c) systematic (d) None of the above

Ans. (b) holistic

(iv) In the regional approach, the world is divided into regions at different hierarchical levels.

(a) True (b) False
(c) Partially true (d) Partially false

Ans. (a) True

Chapter 2: The Origin and Evolution of the Earth

Objective Type Questions

(1 mark each)

(A) FILL IN THE BLANKS

Q. 1. _________ hypothesis considered that the planets were formed out of a cloud of material associated with a youthful sun, which was slowly rotating. R

Ans. Nebular

Q. 2. A _________ is a measure of distance and not of time. U

Ans. light year

Q. 3. _________ means Jupiter-like. R

Ans. Jovian

Q. 4. _________ suggested that initially, the earth and the moon formed a single rapidly rotating body. R

Ans. George Darwin

Q. 5. The earth was mostly in a volatile state during its ______ stage. R

Ans. primordial

Q. 6. The earth has a _________ structure. R

Ans. layered

Q. 7. The friction and collision of particles led to the formation of a disk-shaped cloud, and the planets were formed through the process of _________. R

Ans. accretion

(B) ARRANGE IN THE CORRECT ORDER

Q. 1. Arrange the stages of planet formation in the correct order. U

(i) The condensation of the gas cloud and formation of chondrules
(ii) More violent and rapid impact accretion
(iii) The accretion of gas and dust to form small bodies between 1-10 km in diameter
(iv) The gravitational collapse of a star

Options:

(a) i, ii, iv, iii (b) iv, i, iii, ii
(c) iii, iv, ii, i (d) iii, i, ii, iv

Ans. (b) iv, i, iii, ii

Q. 2. Arrange the stages of the nebular hypothesis in correct order: U

(i) Ring forms into a planet.
(ii) Central mass forms and centrifugal force balances gravitational forces and forms a ring.
(iii) Disk begins to rotate.
(iv) Self-gravity contracts a gas cloud and conservation of angular momentum pulls cloud into a disk.

Options:

(a) iv, iii, ii, i (b) iii, iv, i, ii
(c) ii, iv, iii, i (d) i, ii, iii, iv

Ans. (a) iv, iii, ii, i

Q. 3. Arrange the Big Bang Theory in the correct order: R

(i) The universe expands.

(ii) Matter created, and protons and neutrons are formed.

(iii) Atoms form; stars appear.

(iv) First galaxies appear.

Options:

(a) i, ii, iii, iv **(b)** iv, i, iii, ii

(c) ii, i, iii, iv **(d)** iii, iv, i, ii

Ans. (a) i, ii, iii, iv

Source-Based Questions

(3 marks each)

Q. 1. Read the passage given below and answer any three of the questions that follow. (1×3=3) A

The distribution of matter and energy was not even in the early universe. These initial density differences gave rise to differences in gravitational forces and it caused the matter to get drawn together. These formed the bases for development of galaxies. A galaxy contains a large number of stars. Galaxies spread over vast distances that are measured in thousands of light-years. The diameters of individual galaxies range from 80,000-150,000 light years. A galaxy starts to form by accumulation of hydrogen gas in the form of a very large cloud called nebula. Eventually, growing nebula develops localised clumps of gas. These clumps continue to grow into even denser gaseous bodies, giving rise to formation of stars. The formation of stars is believed to have taken place some 5-6 billion years ago. A light year is a measure of distance and not of time. Light travels at a speed of 300,000 km/second. Considering this, the distances the light will travel in one year is taken to be one light year. This equals to 9.461 × 1012 km. The mean distance between the sun and the earth is 149,598,000 km. In terms of light years, it is 8.311 minutes. Our Solar system consists of eight planets. The nebula from which our Solar system is supposed to have been formed, started its collapse and core formation some time 5-5.6 billion years ago and the planets were formed about 4.6 billion years ago. Our solar system consists of the sun (the star), 8 planets, 63 moons, millions of smaller bodies like asteroids and comets and huge quantity of dust grains and gases. Out of the eight planets, Mercury, Venus, Earth and Mars are called as the inner planets as they lie between the sun and the belt of asteroids. The other four planets are called the outer planets. Alternatively, the first four are called Terrestrial, meaning earth-like as they are made up of rock and metals, and have relatively high densities. The rest four are called Jovian or Gas Giant planets. Jovian means Jupiter-like. Most of them are much larger than the terrestrial planets and have thick atmosphere, mostly of helium and hydrogen. All the planets were formed in the same period sometime about 4.6 billion years ago. Till recently (August 2006), Pluto was also considered a planet. However, in a meeting of the International Astronomical Union, a decision was taken that Pluto like other celestial objects (2003 UB313) discovered in recent past may be called 'dwarf planet.

(i) A galaxy contains a large number of:

(a) Stars **(b)** Planets

(c) Moons **(d)** Hydrogen gas

Ans. (a) Stars

(ii) Why is Pluto not considered as a planet?

(a) Many other terrestrial bodies had to be accommodated

(b) It is a relatively small terrestrial body

(c) It crosses path with many planets

(d) It is a very cold terrestrial body

Ans. (b) It is a relatively small terrestrial body

(iii) Our solar system consists of the sun (the star), _______planets, __________ moons, millions of smaller bodies like asteroids and comets and huge quantity of dust grains and gases

(a) 8 planets, 62 moons **(b)** 8 planets, 63 moons

(c) 8 planets, 65 moons **(d)** 8 planets, 67 moons

Ans. (b) 8 planets, 63 moons

(iv) How is one light year measured?

(a) Distance light travels in one year

(b) Distance light travels in one minute

(c) Distance light travels in one second

(d) Distance light travels in one millisecond

Ans. (a) Distance light travels in one year

Q. 2. Read the passage given below and answer any three of the questions that follow. (1×3=3) A

The last phase in the evolution of the Earth relates to the origin and evolution of life. It is undoubtedly clear that initially the earth or even the atmosphere of the earth was not conducive for the development of life. Modern scientists refer to the origin of life as a kind of chemical reaction, which first generated complex organic molecules and assembled them. This assemblage was such that they could duplicate themselves converting inanimate matter into living substance. The record of life that existed on this planet in different periods is found in rocks in the form of fossils. The microscopic structures closely related to the present form of blue algae have been found in geological formations much older than some 3,000 million years. It can be assumed that life began to evolve sometime 3,800 million years ago.

(i) The origin and evolution of life is related to which phase of evolution of Earth?

(a) The first phase (b) The second phase
(c) The third phase (d) The last phase

Ans. (d) The last phase

(ii) Origin of life is considered as a __________ reaction.

(a) biological (b) chemical
(c) interactive (d) physical

Ans. (b) chemical

(iii) Where can the record of life that existed on this planet be found?

(a) In algae
(b) In folktales
(c) In rocks in the form of fossils
(d) All of the above

Ans. (c) In rocks in the form of fossils

(iv) It can be assumed that life began to __________ sometime 3,800 million years ago.

(a) evolve (b) dissolve
(c) sabotage (d) merge

Ans. (a) evolve

Q. 3. Read the passage given below and answer any three of the questions that follow. (1×3=3) [A]

The moon is the only natural satellite of the earth. Like the origin of the earth, there have been attempts to explain how the moon was formed. In 1838, Sir George Darwin suggested that initially, the earth and the moon formed a single rapidly rotating body. The whole mass became a dumbbell-shaped body and eventually it broke. It was also suggested that the material forming the moon was separated from what we have at present the depression occupied by the Pacific Ocean.

However, the present scientists do not accept either of the explanations. It is now generally believed that the formation of moon, as a satellite of the earth, is an outcome of "giant impact" or what is described as "the big splat". A body of the size of one to three times that of Mars collided into the earth sometime shortly after the earth was formed. It blasted a large part of the earth into space. This portion of blasted material then continued to orbit the earth and eventually formed into the present moon about 4.44 billion years ago.

(i) Early theory suggested that the Earth and the Moon were formed a double rapidly rotating body.

(a) True (b) False
(c) Partially True (d) Partially False

Ans. (b) False

(ii) The Earth has got __________ natural satellite.

(a) One (b) Two
(c) Three (d) None

Ans. (a) One

(iii) The material forming the moon was separated from what we have at present the depression occupied by the:

(a) Pacific Ocean (b) Arctic Ocean
(c) Indian Ocean (d) Arabian Ocean

Ans. (a) Pacific Ocean

(iv) During a collision between the Earth and another small planet, about the size of one to three times of Mars, the debris from this impact collected in an orbit around Earth and eventually formed the __________.

(a) Stars (b) Moon
(c) Asteroids (d) Meteoroids

Ans. (b) Moon

Chapter 3: Interior of the Earth

Objective Type Questions

(1 mark each)

(A) FILL IN THE BLANKS

Q. 1. The __________ of the surface of the Earth is largely a product of the processes operating in the interior of the earth. [U]

Ans. configuration

Q. 2. __________ give us information about the distribution of mass of the material in the crust of the earth. [U]

Ans. Gravity anomalies

Q. 3. __________ volcanoes are characterised by eruptions of cooler and more viscous lavas than basalt. [R]

Ans. Composite

Q. 4. The most easily available solid earth material is _____________. R

Ans. surface rock

Q. 5. The ______________ is greater near the Poles and less at the Equator. U

Ans. gravitational force

Q. 6. All natural earthquakes occur in the_________. R

Ans. lithosphere

Q. 7. ____________ earthquakes are generated due to sliding of rocks along a fault plane. U

Ans. Tectonic

Q. 8. The lava that is released during volcanic eruptions on cooling develops into _________rocks. R

Ans. igneous

Q. 9. The upper portion of the mantle is called _____________. R

Ans. asthenosphere

Q. 10. __________are the cooled portion of magma chambers. R

Ans. Batholiths

(B) ARRANGE IN THE CORRECT ORDER

Q. 1. Arrange the stages of earthquake occurrence in the correct order: U

(i) Influx of water and deformation in fault zone
(ii) Dilatancy and development of cracks
(iii) Build-up of elastic strain
(iv) Earthquake and aftershock

Options:

(a) i, ii, iii, iv **(b)** ii, iv, iii, i
(c) iii, ii, i, iv **(d)** iv, i, iii, ii

Ans. (c) iii, ii, i, iv

Q. 2. Arrange the occurrence of tsunami in correct order: R

(i) Rapid movement of the ocean floor displaces a column of water.
(ii) Giant waves collide with the shore causing massive damage.
(iii) Earthquake on the ocean floor.
(iv) Underwater vibrations spread creating waves that can travel up to 500 km/hr.

Options:

(a) i, ii, iv, iii **(b)** iii, i, iv, ii
(c) iv, i, ii, iii **(d)** ii, iii, i, iv

Ans. (b) iii, i, iv, ii

Q. 3. Match and arrange Descriptors and their Magnitudes in correct order: R

	Descriptor		Magnitude
i.	Great	A.	6-6.9
ii.	Major	B.	8 and higher
iii.	Strong	C.	5-5.9
iv.	Moderate	D.	7-7.9

Options:

(a) i-B, ii-D, iii-A, iv-C **(b)** i-C, ii-A, iii-D, iv-B
(c) i-A, ii-D, iii-C, iv-B **(d)** i-D, ii-C, iii-B, iv-A

Ans. (a) i-B, ii-D, iii-A, iv-C

(C) GRAPH BASED QUESTIONS

Q. 1. Study the given graph on earthquake waves carefully and answer the following questions: **(1×3=3)** U

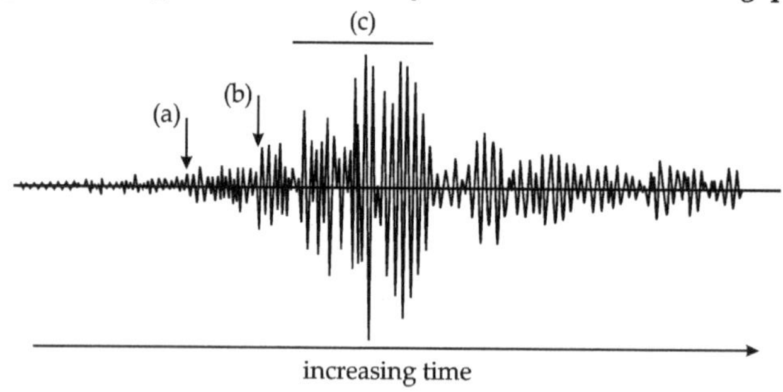

(i) What is happening at point 'a'?

(a) First arrival of P waves **(b)** First arrival of S waves
(c) Last arrival of P waves **(d)** Last arrival of S waves

Ans. (a) First arrival of P waves

(ii) What is happening at point 'b'?

(a) First arrival of S waves **(b)** Last arrival of S waves
(c) First arrival of P waves **(d)** Last arrival of P waves

Ans. (a) First arrival of S waves

(iii) What waves arrive over the interval labelled 'c'?

(a) Q waves arrivals **(b)** Surface waves arrivals
(c) Serial waves arrivals **(d)** Seismic waves arrivals

Ans. (b) Surface waves arrivals

(iv) Which waves are known as Primary Waves?

(a) S waves (b) P waves (c) C waves (d) Q waves

Ans. (b) P waves

Q. 2. Study the graph on volcanic eruption alerts issued in Barren Island from 24 Sep. 2018 to 24 Dec. 2018 and answer the questions. [1×3=3] E

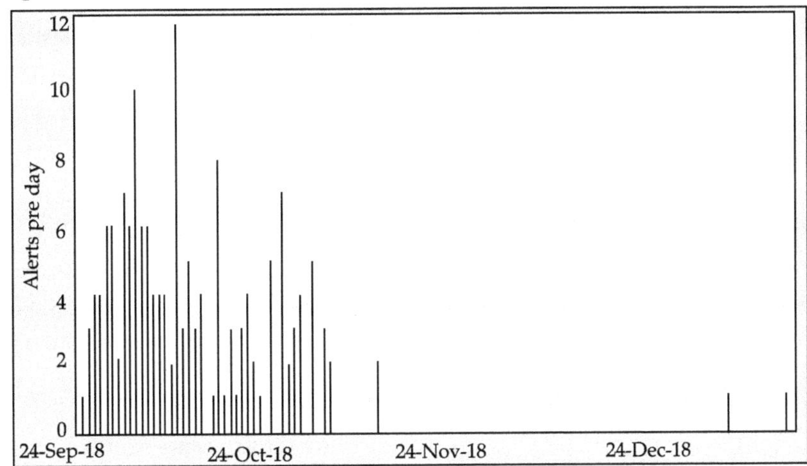

(i) In which month were the maximum alerts issued?

(a) December (b) October (c) September (d) November

Ans. (c) September

(ii) In which month were the minimum alerts issued?

(a) September (b) October (c) November (d) December

Ans. (d) December

(iii) In which month were no alerts issued?

(a) 24 Sep-24 Oct (b) 24 Oct-24 Nov (c) 24 Nov-24 Dec (d) None of the above

Ans. (c) 24 Nov-24 Dec

(iv) Where is Barren Island located?

(a) Andaman Islands (b) Indonesia (c) Japan (d) Lakshadweep

Ans. (a) Andaman Islands

Q. 3. Study the graph on number of earthquake occurrences worldwide from 2000 to 2019 and answer any three of the following questions. (1×3=3) AE

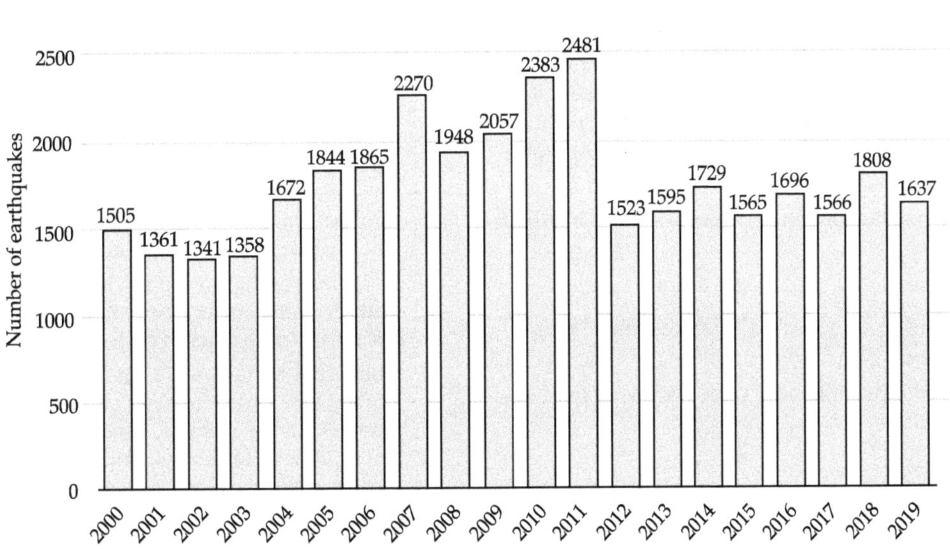

(i) Which year experienced the maximum number of earthquakes?

(a) 2010 (b) 2011

(c) 2018 (d) 2019

Ans. (b) 2011

(ii) Which year experienced the minimum number of earthquakes?

(a) 2000 (b) 2001

(c) 2002 (d) 2003

Ans. (c) 2002

(iii) How many earthquakes occurred in 2005?

(a) 1844 (b) 1845

(c) 1846 (d) 1865

Ans. (a) 1844

(iv) Which years experienced 1000 to 1500 earthquakes?

(a) 2004-2007 (b) 2001-2003

(c) 2007-2010 (d) 2016-2017

Ans. (b) 2001-2003

Source-Based Questions

(3 marks each)

Q. 1. Read the passage given below and answer any three of the questions that follow. [1×3=3] Ⓐ

Crust is the outermost solid part of the earth. It is brittle in nature. The thickness of the crust varies under the oceanic and continental areas. Oceanic crust is thinner as compared to the continental crust. The mean thickness of oceanic crust is 5 km whereas that of the continental is around 30 km. The continental crust is thicker in the areas of major mountain systems. It is as much as 70 km thick in the Himalayan region. The portion of the interior beyond the crust is called the mantle. The mantle extends from Moho's discontinuity to a depth of 2,900 km. The upper portion of the mantle is called the asthenosphere. The word 'astheno' means weak. It is considered to be extending upto 400 km. It is the main source of magma that finds its way to the surface during volcanic eruptions. The crust and the uppermost part of the mantle are called lithosphere. Its thickness ranges from 10-200 km. The lower mantle extends beyond the asthenosphere. It is in solid state. As indicated earlier, the earthquake wave velocities helped in understanding the existence of the core of the earth. The core mantle boundary is located at the depth of 2,900 km. The outer core is in liquid state while the inner core is in solid state. The core is made up of very heavy material mostly constituted by nickel and iron. It is sometimes referred to as the nife layer.

(i) Which of the following layers of earth is brittle in nature?

(a) Crust (b) Mantle

(c) Core (d) All of the above

Ans. (a) Crust

(ii) Which of the following layer is referred to as nife layer?

(a) Crust (b) Mantle

(c) Core (d) All of the above

Ans. (c) Core

(iii) What is the correct sequence of the layers of the earth from innermost to outermost?

(a) Crust – mantle – core

(b) Core – mantle – crust

(c) Crust – core – mantle

(d) Mantle – core – crust

Ans. (b) Core – mantle – crust

(iv) The core mantle boundary is located at the depth of:

(a) 2,300 km (b) 2,700 km

(c) 2,600 km (d) 2,900 km

Ans. (d) 2,900 km

Q. 2. Read the passage given below and answer any three of the questions that follow. (1×3=3) Ⓐ

The interior of the earth can be understood only by indirect evidences as no one has ever reached, or any one can reach, the interior of the earth. The configuration of the surface of the earth is largely a product of the processes operating in the interior of the earth.

Exogenic and endogenic processes are constantly shaping the landscape. A proper understanding of the physiographic character of a region remains incomplete if the effects of endogenic processes are ignored. Human life is largely influenced by the physiography of the region. Therefore, it is necessary that one gets acquainted with the forces that influence landscape development. To understand why the earth shakes or how a tsunami wave is generated, it is necessary that we know certain details of the interior of the earth.

It is interesting to know how scientists have gathered information about these layers and what are the characteristics of each of these layers.

The earth's radius is 6,370 km. No one can reach the centre of the earth and make observations or collect samples of the material. Under such conditions, you may wonder how scientists tell us about the earth's interior and the type of materials that exist at such depths. Most of our knowledge about the interior of the earth is largely based on estimates and inferences. Yet, a part of the information is obtained through direct observations and analysis of materials.

(i) The interior of the earth can be understood only by _________ evidences.

(a) indirect (b) direct

(c) integrated (d) intense

Ans. (a) indirect

(ii) Exogenic and endogenic processes are constantly shaping the ________ .

(a) Earth (b) landscape

(c) planet (d) ecosystem

Ans. (b) landscape

(iii) What has helped us gain knowledge about the interior of the Earth?

(a) Extractions (b) Experiences

(c) Inferences (d) Excavations

Ans. (c) Inferences

(iv) Human life is largely influenced by the physiography of the:

(a) Region (b) Life

(c) Mind (d) None of the above

Ans. (a) Region

Q. 3. Read the passage given below and answer any three of the questions that follow. (1×3=3) U

Different types of earthquake waves travel in different manners. As they move or propagate, they cause vibration in the body of the rocks through which they pass. P-waves vibrate parallel to the direction of the wave. This exerts pressure on the material in the direction of the propagation. As a result, it creates density differences in the material leading to stretching and squeezing of the material. Other three waves vibrate perpendicular to the direction of propagation. The direction of vibrations of S-waves is perpendicular to the wave direction in the vertical plane. Hence, they create troughs and crests in the material through which they pass. Surface waves are considered to be the most damaging waves. Earthquake waves get recorded in seismographs located at far off locations. However, there exists some specific areas where the waves are not reported. Such a zone is called the 'shadow zone'. The study of different events reveals that for each earthquake, there exists an altogether different shadow zone.

It was observed that seismographs located at any distance within 105° from the epicentre, recorded the arrival of both P and S-waves. However, the seismographs located beyond 145° from epicentre, record the arrival of P-waves, but not that of S-waves. Thus, a zone between 105° and 145° from epicentre was identified as the shadow zone for both the types of waves. The entire zone beyond 105° does not receive S-waves. The shadow zone of S-wave is much larger than that of the P-waves. The shadow zone of P-waves appears as a band around the earth between 105° and 145° away from the epicentre. The shadow zone of S-waves is not only larger in extent but it is also a little over 40 per cent of the earth surface.

(i) What do the earthquake waves do when they pass through the body of the rocks?

(a) Cause the rocks to break into small pieces.

(b) Cause vibration in the body of the rocks through which they pass.

(c) Produce body waves.

(d) Waves gather strength to cause more damage as they travel ahead.

Ans. (b) Cause vibration in the body of the rocks through which they pass.

(ii) The direction of vibrations of S-waves is perpendicular to the wave direction in the:

(a) vertical plane (b) horizontal plane

(c) perpendicular plane (d) parallel plane

Ans. (a) vertical plane

(iii) The entire zone beyond _________ does not receive S-waves.

(a) 103° (b) 145°

(c) 110° (d) 105°

Ans. (d) 105°

(iv) Which are the most damaging waves?

(a) Surface waves (b) Parallel waves

(c) Body waves (d) All of the above

Ans. (a) Surface waves

Chapter 4: Distribution of Oceans and Continents

Objective Type Questions (1 mark each)

(A) FILL IN THE BLANKS

Q. 1. The belt of ancient rocks of 2,000 million years from Brazil coast matches with those from __________ . R

Ans. western Africa

Q. 2. The age of rocks in the oceanic crust is nowhere more than _________ years old. R

Ans. 200 million

Q. 3. The age of the rocks increases as one moves away from the ________ . [U]

Ans. crest

Q. 4. ________ in 1930s discussed the possibility of convection currents operating in the mantle portion. [R]

Ans. Arthur Holmes

Q. 5. Wegener suggested that the movement responsible for the drifting of the continents was caused by ________force and ________force. [U]

Ans. pole-fleeing; tidal (½ + ½ = 1)

Q. 6. Rocks closer to the ________ ridges have normal polarity and are the youngest. [R]

Ans. mid-oceanic

Q. 7. ____________ plates are located between the South America plate and the Pacific plate. [R]

Ans. Nazca

(B) ARRANGE IN THE CORRECT ORDER

Q. 1. Arrange the Continent Drift Theory in the correct order. [U]

(i) Existence of Pangaea and Panthalassa

(ii) Laurasia and Gondwanaland form the northern and southern components.

(iii) Pangaea splits up.

(iv) Laurasia and Gondwanaland continued to break into various smaller continents that exist today.

Options:

(a) i, iii, ii, iv **(b)** i, ii, iii, iv

(c) iv, i, ii, iii **(d)** iii, iv, i, ii

Ans. (a) i, iii, ii, iv

Q. 2. Arrange the ocean floor configuration in the correct order. [R]

(i) Oceanic deeps **(ii) Deep sea plain**

(iii) Continental shelf **(iv) Continental slope**

Options:

(a) iv, ii, iii, i **(b)** iii, iv, i, ii

(c) iii, iv, ii, i **(d)** i, ii, iii, iv

Ans. (c) iii, iv, ii, i

Q. 3. Arrange the process in which tectonic plates move in the correct order. [U]

(i) Rifting

(ii) Heat convention

(iii) Continental collision

(iv) Sea floor spreading and subduction

Options:

(a) iv, ii, iii, i **(b)** i, ii, iii, iv

(c) ii, i, iv, iii **(d)** iii, iv, i, ii

Ans. (c) ii, i, iv, iii

(C) GRAPH BASED QUESTIONS

Q. 1. Study the given graph carefully and answer any three of the following questions: (1×3=3) [AE]

0 20 40 60 80 100 %
Highest mountain
Sea Level
Average height
Continental slope
Sea level
Continental Shelf
Average Depth
Ocean Basin Floor
Continent
Deepest Ocean
Height 5 0 km 5 10 Depth
100 200 300 400 500 × 10⁶km
Cumulative Area higher than Each Level

(i) According to the graph which of the following is in the correct sequence in terms of increasing height?

(a) Continental Slope–Continental Shelf–Ocean Basin Floor

(b) Continental Shelf–Continental Slope–Ocean Basin Floor

(c) Continental Shelf–Ocean Basin Floor–Continental Slope

(d) Ocean Basin Floor–Continental Slope–Continental Shelf

Ans. (d) Ocean Basin Floor–Continental Slope–Continental Shelf

(ii) According to the graph what is the average depth of the ocean?

(a) 11 km below the sea level

(b) 8 km below the sea level

(c) 4 km below the sea level

(d) 7 km below the sea level

Ans. (c) 4 km below the sea level

(iii) According to the graph what is the average height of the continent?

(a) 8 km above the sea level

(b) 1 km above the sea level

(c) 4 km above the sea level

(d) 3 km above the sea level

Ans. (b) 1 km above the sea level

(iv) According to the graph the deepest point of the ocean lies at:

(a) 11 km below the sea level

(b) 8 km below the sea level

(c) 4 km below the sea level

(d) 7 km below the sea level

Ans. (a) 11 km below the sea level

Source-Based Questions (3 marks each)

Q. 1. Read the passage given below and answer any three of the questions that follow. [1×3=3] U

The Indian Plate includes Peninsular India and the Australian continental portions. The subduction zone along the Himalayas forms the northern plate boundary in the form of continent–continent convergence. In the east, it extends through Rakinyoma Mountains of Myanmar towards the island arc along the Java Trench. The eastern margin is a spreading site lying to the east of Australia in the form of an oceanic ridge in SW Pacific. The Western margin follows Kirthar Mountain of Pakistan. It further extends along the Makrana coast and joins the spreading site from the Red Sea rift southeastward along the Chagos Archipelago. The boundary between India and the Antarctic plate is also marked by oceanic ridge (divergent boundary) running in roughly W-E direction and merging into the spreading site, a little south of New Zealand. India was a large island situated off the Australian coast, in a vast ocean. The Tethys Sea separated it from the Asian continent till about 225 million years ago. India is supposed to have started her northward journey about 200 million years ago at the time when Pangaea broke. India collided with Asia about 40-50 million years ago causing rapid uplift of the Himalayas. It also shows the position of the Indian subcontinent and the Eurasian plate. About 140 million years before the present, the subcontinent was located as south as 50°S latitude. The two major plates were separated by the Tethys Sea and the Tibetan block was closer to the Asiatic land mass. During the movement of the Indian plate towards the Eurasian plate, a major event that occurred was the outpouring of lava and formation of the Deccan Traps. This started somewhere around 60 million years ago and continued for a long period of time. Note that the subcontinent was still close to the equator. From 40 million years ago and thereafter, the event of formation of the Himalayas took place. Scientists believe that the process is still continuing and the height of the Himalayas is rising even to this date.

(i) The Indian plate includes Peninsular India and the ________ continental portions.

(a) African **(b)** Russian

(c) Australian **(d)** None of these

Ans. (c) Australian

(ii) Which of the following seas separated the Indian plate from the Asian continent till about 225 million years ago?

(a) Indian **(b)** Tethys

(c) Antarctica **(d)** Red

Ans. (b) Tethys

(iii) India collided with Asia about how many years ago causing rapid uplift of the Himalayas?

(a) 20-30 million **(b)** 30-40 million

(c) 40-50 million **(d)** 50-60 million

Ans. (c) 40-50 million

(iv) During the movement of the Indian plate towards the Eurasian plate, as a major event in how many years ago, the outpouring of lava and formation of the Deccan Traps was started?

(a) 40 million **(b)** 50 million

(c) 60 million **(d)** 70 million

Ans. (c) 60 million

Q. 2. Read the passage given below and answer any three of the questions that follow. [1×3=3] U

The shorelines of Africa and South America facing each other have a remarkable and unmistakable match. It may be noted that a map produced using a computer programme to find the best fit of the Atlantic margin was presented by Bullard in 1964. It proved to be quite perfect. The match was tried at 1,000-fathom line instead of the present shoreline.

The radiometric dating methods developed in the recent period have facilitated correlating the rock formation from different continents across the vast ocean. The belt of ancient rocks of 2,000 million years from Brazil coast matches with those from western Africa. The earliest marine deposits along the coastline of South America and Africa are of the Jurassic age. This suggests that the ocean did not exist prior to that time.

Tillite is the sedimentary rock formed out of deposits of glaciers. The Gondawana System of sediments from India is known to have its counterparts in six different landmasses of the Southern Hemisphere. At the base, the system has thick tillite indicating extensive and prolonged glaciation. Counterparts of this succession are found in Africa, Falkland Island, Madagascar, Antarctica and Australia. Overall resemblance of the Gondawana-type sediments clearly demonstrates that these land masses had remarkably similar histories. The glacial tillite provides unambiguous evidence of paleo climates and also of drifting of continents.

(i) Which shorelines have remarkable and unmistakable match?

(a) Africa and North America

(b) Africa and South America

(c) Africa and Asia

(d) Africa and Australia

Ans. (b) Africa and South America

(ii) The ____________ methods developed in the recent period have facilitated correlating the rock formation from different continents across the vast ocean.

(a) seismic dating (b) radiometric dating
(c) rock dating (d) divergent dating

Ans. (b) radiometric dating

(iii) Tillite rocks are formed out of which deposits?

(a) Glaciers (b) Clay
(c) Sand (d) Soil

Ans. (a) Glaciers

(iv) The glacial tillite provides unambiguous evidence of ________ climates.

(a) tropical (b) sub tropical
(c) paleo (d) cold

Ans. (c) paleo

Q. 3. Read the passage given below and answer any three of the questions that follow. [1×3=3] U

Since the advent of the concept of sea floor spreading, the interest in the problem of distribution of oceans and continents was revived. It was in 1967, McKenzie and Parker and also Morgan independently collected the available ideas and came out with another concept termed Plate Tectonics. A tectonic plate (also called lithospheric plate) is a massive, irregularly shaped slab of solid rock, generally composed of both continental and oceanic lithosphere. Plates move horizontally over the asthenosphere as rigid units. The lithosphere includes the crust and top mantle with its thickness range varying between 5 and 100 km in oceanic parts and about 200 km in the continental areas. A plate may be referred to as the continental plate or oceanic plate depending on which of the two occupy a larger portion of the plate. Pacific plate is largely an oceanic plate, whereas the Eurasian plate may be called a continental plate. The theory of plate tectonics proposes that the earth's lithosphere is divided into seven major and some minor plates. Young Fold Mountain ridges, trenches and/or faults surround these major plates.

(i) Plate tectonic is also known as __________ plate.

(a) atmospheric (b) lithospheric
(c) mesospheric (d) stratospheric

Ans. (b) lithospheric

(ii) Plates move horizontally over the asthenosphere as ________ units.

(a) rigid (b) individual
(c) separate (d) close

Ans. (a) rigid

(iii) According to the Theory of Plate Tectonics, Earth's lithosphere is divided into how many major plates?

(a) Four (b) Five
(c) Six (d) Seven

Ans. (d) Seven

(iv) What is the other name of Eurasian plate?

(a) Oceanic plate (b) Continental plate
(c) Ridge plate (d) European plate

Ans. (b) Continental plate

Chapter 5: Minerals and Rocks

is not in the syllabus of 2023-24

Chapter 6: Geomorphic Processes

Objective Type Questions

(1 mark each)

(A) FILL IN THE BLANKS

Q. 1. The earth's surface is being continuously subjected to __________ forces induced basically by energy. U

Ans. external

Q. 2. The _________ forces are mainly land building forces. R

Ans. endogenic

Q. 3. The __________ processes are mainly land wearing forces. R

Ans. exogenic

Q. 4. ____________ and volcanism are endogenic geomorphic processes. R

Ans. Diastrophism

Q. 5. Gravitational Force applied per unit area is called ____________. U

Ans. stress

Q. 6. Not only_________ processes differ from climate to climate, but they also differ based on the depth of the weathering mantle. U

Ans. weathering

Q. 7. __________ is an important process in the formation of soils. R

Ans. Weathering

Q. 8. Sliding of individual rock masses down the bedding, joint or fault surfaces is called ________. U

Ans. rockslide

Q. 9. _______ can occur due to expansion and contraction induced by temperature changes. R

Ans. Exfoliation

10. Weathering, mass-wasting and erosion are __________ processes. R

Ans. degradational

11. __________ processes involve uplift or warping of large parts of the earth's crust. R

Ans. Epeirogenic

(B) ARRANGE IN THE CORRECT ORDER

Q. 1. Arrange the process of soil formation in the correct order: U

(i) Translocation **(ii) Transformations**

(iii) Additions **(iv) Losses**

Options:

(a) iii, iv, ii, i (b) i, ii, iv, iii

(c) iv, iii, ii, i (d) ii, iv, i, iii

Ans. (a) iii, iv, ii, i

Q. 2. Arrange the mass movement that takes place during avalanche in the correct order : U

(i) An unstable mass of snow breaks away from a slope

(ii) Moving mass picks up even more snow as it rushes downhill

(iii) Produces a river of snow and a cloud of icy particles that rises high into the air

(iv) The snow picks up speed as it moves downhill

Options:

(a) i, iv, ii, iii (b) i, iv, iii, ii

(c) iv, ii, i, iii (d) ii, iv, i, iii

Ans. (b) i, iv, iii, ii

Q. 3. Arrange the biological weathering caused by plants in correct order: U

(i) Plant roots grow in cracks.

(ii) Roots push open the cracks.

(iii) Roots grow bigger.

(iv) Cracks grow wider and bigger.

Options:

(a) i, iii, ii, iv (b) iv, iii, i, ii

(c) ii, i, iii, iv (d) iii, i, iv, ii

Ans. (a) i, iii, ii, iv

Short Answer Type Question

(3 mark each)

Q. 1. Explain Denudation?

Ans. Denudation refers to the process by which the surface of the Earth is stripped of its outer layers, including rocks, soil, vegetation, and other geological materials. It is a natural process that occurs through various mechanisms, such as erosion, weathering, and mass wasting. Denudation can be caused by several factors, including wind, water (such as rivers, waves, and glaciers), gravity, and human activities. Over time, denudation can result in the formation of landforms like valleys, canyons, cliffs, and sediment deposition in lower-lying areas.

Long Answer Type Question

(5 mark each)

Q. 1. Differentiate between Geomorphic Process and Geomorphic agents.

Ans.

Geomorphic Process	Geomorphic agents
I. Geomorphic processes refer to the natural forces and mechanisms that actively shape the Earth's surface. These processes are responsible for creating, modifying, and destroying landforms over time. They are the dynamic forces that operate on the Earth's surface, resulting in changes to the landscape	I. Geomorphic agents, on the other hand, are the physical entities or materials that act as tools or carriers in the geomorphic processes. They are the tangible elements through which the processes operate and interact with the Earth's surface

II. Geomorphic processes can be categorized into two main types: **Endogenic Processes:** Endogenic processes are driven by internal forces originating from within the Earth's interior. These processes include tectonic activities such as volcanic eruptions, earthquakes, and mountain building. **Exogenic Processes:** Exogenic processes are driven by external forces, primarily related to weathering, erosion, transportation, and deposition of materials on the Earth's surface. These processes include the actions of water, wind, ice (glaciers), and gravity.	II. Geomorphic agents include: **Water:** Water is a prominent geomorphic agent that plays a vital role in shaping the landscape. Running water in the form of rivers, streams, and rainfall runoff erodes the land, transports sediment, and deposits it elsewhere. **Wind:** Wind is another significant geomorphic agent, especially in arid and coastal regions. Wind is also involved in weathering processes, particularly through the transport of airborne particles. **Glaciers:** Glaciers are massive bodies of ice that flow slowly over land surfaces, carving out valleys and shaping mountains through processes such as plucking and abrasion. **Gravity:** Gravity acts as a geomorphic agent by exerting force on materials, causing mass movements such as landslides, rockfalls, and soil creep.

Source-Based Questions

(3 marks each)

Q. 1. Read the passage given below and answer any three of the questions that follow. (1×3=3) AE

The endogenic and exogenic forces causing physical stresses and chemical actions on earth materials and bringing about changes in the configuration of the surface of the earth are known as geomorphic processes. Diastrophism and volcanism are endogenic geomorphic processes. Weathering, mass wasting, erosion and deposition are exogenic geomorphic processes. Any exogenic element of nature (like water, ice, wind, etc.) capable of acquiring and transporting earth materials can be called a geomorphic agent. When these elements of nature become mobile due to gradients, they remove the materials and transport them over slopes and deposit them at lower level. Geomorphic processes and geomorphic agents especially exogenic, unless stated separately, are one and the same. A process is a force applied on earth materials affecting the same. An agent is a mobile medium (like running water, moving ice masses, wind, waves and currents, etc.) which removes, transports and deposits earth materials. Do you think it is essential to distinguish geomorphic agents and geomorphic processes? Gravity besides being a directional force activating all down slope movements of matter also causes stresses on the earth's materials. Indirect gravitational stresses activate wave and tide induced currents and winds. Without gravity and gradients there would be no mobility and hence no erosion, transportation and deposition are possible. So, gravitational stresses are as important as the other geomorphic processes. Gravity is the force that is keeping us in contact with the surface and it is the force that switches on the movement of all surface material on earth. All the movements either within the earth or on the surface of the earth occur due to gradients — from higher levels to lower levels, from high pressure to low pressure areas etc.

(i) Changes in the configuration of the surface of the earth due to endogenic and exogenic forces and chemical actions on earth materials are known as:

(a) geological processes

(b) geoeconomic processes

(c) geophysical processes

(d) geomorphic processes

Ans. (d) geomorphic processes

(ii) Which of the following is an endogenic geomorphic process?

(a) Weathering (b) Erosion

(c) Deposition (d) Diastrophism

Ans. (d) Diastrophism

(iii) Which of the following is an exogenic geomorphic process?

(a) Volcanism (b) Deposition

(c) Diastrophism (d) None of these

Ans. (b) Deposition

(iv) Which of the following is a geomorphic agent?

(a) Groundwater (b) Glaciers

(c) Wind (d) All the above

Ans. (d) All the above

Q. 2. Read the passage given below and answer any three of the questions that follow. (1×3=3) U

Erosion involves acquisition and transportation of rock debris. When massive rocks break into smaller fragments through weathering and any other process, erosional geomorphic agents like running water, ground water, glaciers, wind and waves remove and transport it to other places depending upon the dynamics of each of these agents. Abrasion by rock debris carried by these geomorphic agents also aids greatly in erosion. By erosion, relief degrades, i.e., the landscape is worn down. That means, though weathering aids erosion it is not a pre-condition for erosion to take place. Weathering, mass-wasting and erosion are degradational processes. It is erosion that is largely responsible for continuous changes that the earth's surface is undergoing. Denudational processes like erosion and transportation are controlled by kinetic energy. The erosion and transportation of earth materials is brought about by wind, running water, glaciers, waves and ground water. Of these the first three agents are controlled by climatic conditions. They represent three states of matter —gaseous (wind), liquid (running water) and solid (glacier) respectively. The work of the other two agents of erosion-waves and ground water is not controlled by climate. In case of waves it is the location along the interface of litho and hydro sphere — coastal region — that will determine the work of waves, whereas the work of ground water is determined more by the lithological character of the region. If the rocks are permeable and soluble and water is available only then karst topography develops. Deposition is a consequence of erosion. The erosional agents loose their velocity and hence energy on gentler slopes and the materials carried by them start to settle themselves. In other words, deposition is not actually the work of any agent. The coarser materials get deposited first and finer ones later. By deposition depressions get filled up. The same erosional agents viz., running water, glaciers, wind, waves and ground water act as gradational or depositional agents also.

(i) What is largely responsible for continuous changes that the earth's surface is undergoing :

(a) Deposition (b) Erosion
(c) Weathering (d) Diastrophism

Ans. (b) Erosion

(ii) Denudational processes like erosion and transportation are controlled by which of the following?

(a) Kinetic energy (b) Potential energy
(c) Solar energy (d) None of these

Ans. (a) Kinetic energy

(iii) The work of two agents of erosion-waves and ground water is not controlled by:

(a) Pressure (b) Temperature
(c) Climate (d) None of the above

Ans. (c) Climate

(iv) If the rocks are permeable and soluble and water is available only then ______ topography develops.

(a) Cave (b) Speleothem
(c) Inselberg (d) Karst

Ans. (d) Karst

Q. 3. Read the passage given below and answer any three of the questions that follow: (1×3=3) U

The movements of mass may range from slow to rapid, affecting shallow to deep columns of materials and include creep, flow, slide and fall. Gravity exerts its force on all matter, both bedrock and the products of weathering. So, weathering is not a pre-requisite for mass movement though it aids mass movements. Mass movements are very active over weathered slopes rather than over unweathered materials. Mass movements are aided by gravity and no geomorphic agent like running water, glaciers, wind, waves and currents participate in the process of mass movements. That means mass movements do not come under erosion though there is a shift (aided by gravity) of materials from one place to another. Materials over the slopes have their own resistance to disturbing forces and will yield only when force is greater than the shearing resistance of the materials. Weak unconsolidated materials, thinly bedded rocks, faults, steeply dipping beds, vertical cliffs or steep slopes, abundant precipitation and torrential rains and scarcity of vegetation etc., favour mass movements.

(i) Mass movements are aided by__________.

(a) Pressure (b) Gravity
(c) Glaciers (d) Running water

Ans. (b) Gravity

(ii) Is weathering a pre-requisite for mass movement?

(a) No, it aids weathering.
(b) Yes, it's a very important pre-requisite.
(c) It is of no use.
(d) It is not related to mass movement.

Ans. (a) No, it aids weathering.

(iii) What favours mass movement?

(a) Wind (b) Cattle grazing
(c) Vertical cliffs (d) Droughts

Ans. (c) Vertical cliffs

(iv) __________ exerts its force on all matter, both bedrock and the products of weathering.

(a) Gravity (b) Pressure
(c) Earth crust (d) Steep slopes

Ans. (a) Gravity

Chapter 7: Landforms and their Evolution

Objective Type Questions

(1 mark each)

(A) FILL IN THE BLANKS

Q. 1. Several related landforms together makeup ________. R

Ans. landscapes

Q. 2. __________ meanders are very deep and wide meanders that can be found cut in hard rocks. R

Ans. Incised or entrenched (Either is correct)

Q. 3. The plain formed as a result of stream erosion is called a ________. R

Ans. peneplain

Q. 4. As meanders grow into deep loops, the same may get cut-off due to erosion at the inflection points and are left as ________. R

Ans. ox-bow lakes

Q. 5. __________ is a closed karst depression, a terrain form usually of elongated or compound structure and of larger size than a sinkhole. R

Ans. Valley sinks or Uvalas (Both are correct)

Q. 6. Bars are submerged features and when bars show up above water, they are called ________. U

Ans. barrier bars

Q. 7. The unassorted coarse and fine debris dropped by the melting glaciers is called ________. R

Ans. glacial till

Q. 8. ________ are long ridges of deposits of glacial till. U

Ans. Moraines

Q. 9. ________ is the perceptible natural movement of the air, especially in the form of a current of air blowing from a particular direction. U

Ans. Wind

Q. 10. The playa plain covered up by salts is called__________ flats. U

Ans. alkali

(B) ARRANGE IN THE CORRECT ORDER

Q. 1. Arrange the steps involved in floodplain formation in correct order. U

(i) Wide flat area is created on either side of the river due to erosion.

(ii) Interlocking spurs are removed due to erosion.

(iii) The height of the floodplain increases as material is deposited on either side of the river.

(iv) During a flood, material being carried by the river is deposited (as the river loses its speed and energy to transport material).

Options:

(a) iii, i, ii, iv **(b)** ii, i, iv, iii

(c) iv, i, iii, ii **(d)** i, ii, iii, iv

Ans. (b) ii, i, iv, iii

Q. 2. Arrange the delta development near the river in correct order:

(i) If the load is not carried away far into the sea or distributed along the coast, it spreads and accumulates as a low cone.

(ii) The load carried by the rivers is dumped and spread into the sea.

(iii) The sediment is dropped at the mouth of the river.

(iv) The coarsest materials settle out first and the finer fractions-like silts and clays are carried out into the sea. R

Options:

(a) ii, iii, i, iv **(b)** iv, iii, ii, i

(c) i, iv, ii, iii **(d)** iii, i, iv, ii

Ans. (a) ii, iii, i, iv

Q. 3. Arrange the steps involved in glacier formation in the correct order: A

(i) Enough snow accumulates to transform into ice.

(ii) Snow remains in the same area year-round.

(iii) Compression forces the snow to re-crystallize, forming grains similar in size and shape to grains of sugar.

(iv) Each year, new layers of snow bury and compress the previous layers.

Options:

(a) iv, ii, i, iii **(b)** ii, i, iii, iv

(c) iii, iv, ii, i **(d)** ii, iii, i, iv

Ans. (b) ii, i, iii, iv

Source-Based Questions

(3 marks each)

Q. 1. Read the passage given below and answer any three of the questions that follow. (1×3=3) AE

In humid regions, which receive heavy rainfall running water is considered the most important of the geomorphic agents in bringing about the degradation of the land surface. There are two components of running water. One is overland flow on general land surface as a sheet. Another is linear flow as streams and rivers in valleys. Most of the erosional landforms made by running water are associated with vigorous and youthful rivers flowing over steep gradients. With time, stream channels over steep gradients turn gentler due to continued erosion, and as a consequence, lose their velocity, facilitating active deposition. There may be depositional forms associated with streams flowing over steep slopes. But these phenomena will be on a small scale compared to those associated with rivers flowing over medium to gentle slopes. The gentler the river channels in gradient or slope, the greater is the deposition. When the stream beds turn gentler due to continued erosion, downward cutting becomes less dominant and lateral erosion of banks increases and as a consequence the hills and valleys are reduced to plains.

(i) Name the two components of running water.

(a) Overland and linear flow

(b) Vertical and horizontal flow

(c) Upward and downward flow

(d) None of the above

Ans. (a) Overland and linear flow

(ii) Why do stream channels over steep gradients turn gentler with time?

(a) Due to less flow

(b) Due to continued erosion

(c) Due to less rainwater

(d) Due to human activities

Ans. (b) Due to continued erosion

(iii) The gentler the river channels in gradient or slope, the greater is the __________.

(a) deposition (b) flow

(c) erosion (d) corrosion

Ans. (a) deposition

(iv) What happens when the stream beds turn gentler due to continued erosion?

(a) Floods occur.

(b) Hills and valleys are reduced to plains.

(c) New landforms are formed.

(d) Droughts are frequent.

Ans. (b) Hills and valleys are reduced to plains.

Q. 2. Read the passage given below and answer any three of the questions that follow. (1×3=3) U

Small- to medium-sized round to sub-rounded shallow depressions called swallow holes form on the surface of limestones through solution. Sink holes are very common in limestone/karst areas. A sinkhole is an opening more or less circular at the top and funnel-shaped towards the bottom with sizes varying in area from a few sq. m. to a hectare and with depth from a less than half a metre to thirty metres or more. Some of these forms solely through solution action (solution sinks) and others might start as solution forms first and if the bottom of a sinkhole forms the roof of a void or cave underground, it might collapse leaving a large hole opening into a cave or a void below (collapse sinks). Quite often, sinkholes are covered up with soil mantle and appear as shallow water pools. Anybody stepping over such pools would go down like it happens in quick sands in deserts. The term doline is sometimes used to refer the collapse sinks. Solution sinks are more common than collapse sinks. Quite often the surface run-off simply goes down swallow and sink hole sand flow as underground streams and re-emerge at a distance downstream through a cave opening. When sinkholes and do lines join together because of slumping of materials along their margins or due to roof collapse of caves, long, narrow to wide trenches called valley sinks or Uvalas form. Gradually, most of the surface of the limestone is eaten away by these pits and trenches, leaving it extremely irregular with a maze of points, grooves and ridges or lapies. Especially, these ridges or lapies form due to differential solution activity along parallel to sub-parallel joints. The lapie field may eventually turn into somewhat smooth limestone pavements.

(i) __________ form on the surface of limestones through solution.

(a) Deep holes (b) Swallow holes

(c) Shallow holes (d) Narrow holes

Ans. (b) Swallow holes

(ii) Which term is used to refer the collapse sinks?

(a) Soleline (b) Doline

(c) Highline (d) Fineline

Ans. (b) Doline

(iii) Quite often, sinkholes are covered up with soil mantle and appear as shallow________.

(a) water pools (b) river pools

(c) oasis (d) swimming pool

Ans. (a) water pools

(iv) Where are sinkholes commonly found?

(a) Sedimentary rocks (b) Lava

(c) Faults (d) Limestones

Ans. (d) Limestones

Q. 3. Read the passage given below and answer any three of the questions that follow. **(1×3=3)** U

Moraines are long ridges of deposits of glacial till. Terminal moraines are long ridges of debris deposited at the end (toe) of the glaciers. Lateral moraines form along the sides parallel to the glacial valleys. The lateral moraines may join a terminal moraine forming a horse-shoe shaped ridge. There can be many lateral moraines on either side in a glacial valley. These moraines partly or fully owe their origin to glacio-fluvial waters pushing up materials to the sides of glaciers. Many valley glaciers retreating rapidly leave an irregular sheet of till over their valley floors. Such deposits varying greatly in thickness and in surface topography are called ground moraines. The moraine in the centre of the glacial valley flanked by lateral moraines is called medial moraine. They are imperfectly formed as compared to lateral moraines. Sometimes medial moraines are indistinguishable from ground moraines.

(i) Where are terminal moraines found?

(a) At the end point reached by the river

(b) At the end point reached by the desert

(c) At the end point reached by the glacier

(d) At the end point of the ocean

Ans. (c) At the end point reached by the glacier

(ii) Where can the medial moraines be found?

(a) At the junction between two glaciers

(b) At the junction between two rivers

(c) At the junction between two mountains

(d) None of the above

Ans. (a) At the junction between two glaciers

(iii) Where can the lateral moraines be found?

(a) Deposited along the sides of the valleys

(b) Deposited along the sides of the glacier

(c) Deposited along the sides of the mountains

(d) Deposited along the sides of the cracks

Ans. (b) Deposited along the sides of the glacier

(iv) _________ moraines are imperfectly formed as compared to lateral moraines.

(a) Medial **(b)** Terminal

(c) Drumlin **(d)** Hummocky

Ans. (a) Medial

Chapter 8: Composition and Structure of Atmosphere

Objective Type Questions

(1 mark each)

(A) FILL IN THE BLANKS

Q. 1. _________________ is a mixture of different gases and it envelopes the earth all round. U

Ans. Atmosphere

Q. 2. The air is ________ and ________ and can be felt only when it blows as wind. R

Ans. colourless; odourless ½ + ½ = 1

Q. 3. ___________ absorbs parts of the insolation from the sun and preserves the earth's radiated heat. R

Ans. Water vapour

Q. 4. All changes in climate and weather take place in ___________. U

Ans. Troposphere

Q. 5. ____________ contains electrically charged particles known as ions. R

Ans. Ionosphere

Q. 6. The air temperature at the tropopause is about minus ________ over the Equator and about minus _________ over the Poles. R

Ans. 80°C; 45°C ½ + ½ = 1

(B) GRAPH BASED QUESTIONS

Q. 1. Study the given graph carefully and answer the following questions. **(1×3=3) U+E**

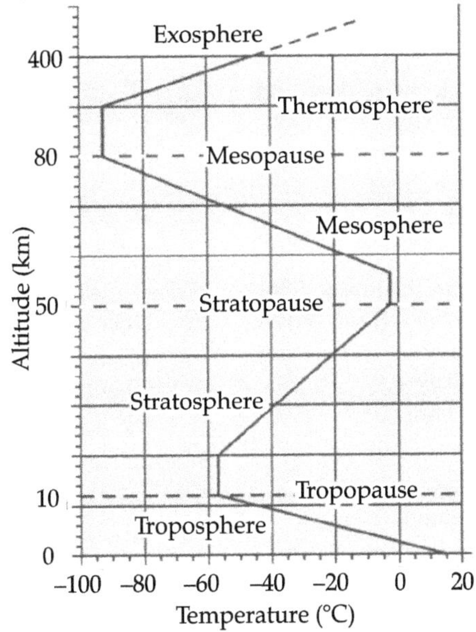

(i) According to the graph the correct sequence as per height (increasing) :

(a) Thermosphere – Stratopause – Mesosphere

(b) Stratosphere – Mesopause – Mesosphere

(c) Mesosphere – Mesopause –Thermosphere

(d) Troposphere – Mesopause – Stratosphere

Ans. (c) Mesosphere – Mesopause – Thermosphere

(ii) According to the graph the range (in km) of mesosphere is:

(a) 40 – 50 (b) 80 – 120

(c) 50 – 80 (d) 30 – 90

Ans. (c) 50 – 80

(iii) According to the graph tropopause lies between Stratosphere and :

(a) Thermosphere (b) Mesosphere

(c) Troposphere (d) Tropopause

Ans. (c) Troposphere

(iv) According to the graph the temperature range is:

(a) 0 to – 100 (b) – 5 to – 90

(c) – 10 to – 70 (d) – 20 to – 80

Ans. (b) – 5 to – 90

Source-Based Questions

(3 marks each)

Q. 1. Read the case study given below and answer any three of the questions that follow. (1×3=3) AE

Air is essential to the survival of all organisms. Some organisms like humans may survive for some time without food and water but can't survive even a few minutes without breathing air. That shows the reason why we should understand the atmosphere in greater detail. Atmosphere is a mixture of different gases and it envelopes the earth all round. It contains life-giving gases like oxygen for humans and animals and carbon dioxide for plants. The air is an integral part of the earth's mass and 99 per cent of the total mass of the atmosphere is confined to the height of 32 km from the earth's surface. The air is colourless and odourless and can be felt only when it blows as wind. The atmosphere is composed of gases, water vapour and dust particles. The proportion of gases changes in the higher layers of the atmosphere in such a way that oxygen will be almost in negligible quantity at the height of 120 km. Similarly, carbon dioxide and water vapour are found only up to 90 km from the surface of the earth.

Carbon dioxide is meteorologically a very important gas as it is transparent to the incoming solar radiation but opaque to the outgoing terrestrial radiation. It absorbs a part of terrestrial radiation and reflects back some part of it towards the Earth's surface. It is largely responsible for the greenhouse effect. The volume of other gases is constant but the volume of carbon dioxide has been rising in the past few decades mainly because of the burning of fossil fuels. This has also increased the temperature of the air. Ozone is another important component of the atmosphere found between 10 and 50 km above the Earth's surface and acts as a filter and absorbs the ultra-violet rays radiating from the sun and prevents them from reaching the surface of the Earth.

(i) Some organisms can survive without food and water for sometime but cannot survive without ________.

(a) carbon dioxide (b) air
(c) trees (d) technology

Ans. (b) air

(ii) Which gas is transparent to the incoming solar radiation but opaque to the outgoing terrestrial radiation?

(a) Oxygen (b) Nitrogen
(c) Carbon dioxide (d) Helium

Ans. (c) Carbon dioxide

(iii) Carbon dioxide is responsible for:

(a) Greenhouse effect (b) Lighting
(c) Insolation (d) Absorption

Ans. (a) Greenhouse effect

(iv) ____________ acts as a filter and absorbs the ultra-violet rays radiating from the Sun.

(a) Oxygen (b) Ozone
(c) Atmosphere (d) Ions

Ans. (b) Ozone

Q. 2. Read the case study given below and answer any three of the questions that follow. (1×3=3) U+E

Water vapour is also a variable gas in the atmosphere, which decreases with altitude. In the warm and wet tropics, it may account for four percent of the air by volume, while in the dry and cold areas of desert and polar regions, it may be less than one percent of the air. Water vapour also decreases from the Equator towards the Poles. It also absorbs parts of the insolation from the sun and preserves the earth's radiated heat. It thus, acts like a blanket allowing the earth neither to become too cold nor too hot. Water vapour also contributes to the stability and instability in the air. Atmosphere has a sufficient capacity to keep small solid particles, which may originate from different sources and include sea salts, fine soil, smoke-soot, ash, pollen, dust and disintegrated particles of meteors. Dust particles are generally concentrated in the lower layers of the atmosphere; yet, convectional air currents may transport them to great heights. The higher concentration of dust particles is found in subtropical and temperate regions due to dry winds in comparison to equatorial and polar regions. Dust and salt particles act as hygroscopic nuclei around which water vapour condenses to produce clouds.

(i) What is the percentage of water vapour found in warm and wet areas in the air by volume?

(a) 2 % (b) 4%
(c) 6% (d) 8%

Ans. (b) 4%

(ii) What is the percentage of water vapour found in the dry and cold areas of desert and polar regions?

(a) Less than 1% of air (b) Less than 2% of air
(c) Less than 3 % of air (d) Less than 4 % of air

Ans. (a) Less than 1 % of air

(iii) Dust and salt particles act as hygroscopic nuclei around which water vapour condenses to produce ________.

(a) Clouds (b) Oxygen
(c) Air (d) None of the Above

Ans. (a) Clouds

(iv) Dust particles are generally concentrated in the ________ layers of the atmosphere.

(a) upper (b) middle
(c) lower (d) no where

Ans. (c) lower

Q. 3. Read the passage given below and answer any three of the questions that follow. (1×3=3) U+E

The atmosphere consists of different layers with varying density and temperature. Density is the highest near the surface of the earth and decreases with increasing altitude. The column of atmosphere is divided into five different layers depending upon the temperature condition. They are: troposphere, stratosphere, mesosphere, thermosphere and exosphere. The troposphere is the lowermost layer of the atmosphere. Its average height is 13 km and extends roughly to a height of 8 km near the poles and about 18 km at the equator. The thickness of the troposphere is the greatest at the equator because heat is transported to great heights by strong convectional currents. This layer contains dust particles and water vapour. All changes in climate and weather take place in this layer. The temperature in this layer decreases at the rate of 1°C for every 165 m of height. This is the most important layer for all biological activity. The zone separating the troposphere from stratosphere is known as the tropopause. The air temperature at the tropopause is about minus 800°C over the Equator and about minus 45°C over the Poles. The temperature here is nearly constant, and hence, it is called the tropopause. The stratosphere is found above the tropopause and extends up to a height of 50 km. One important feature of the stratosphere is that it contains the ozone layer. This layer absorbs ultra-violet radiation and shields life on the earth from intense, harmful form of energy. The mesosphere lies above the stratosphere, which extends up to a height of 80 km. In this layer, once again, temperature starts decreasing with the increase in altitude and reaches up to minus 100°C at the height of 80 km. The upper limit of mesosphere is known as the mesopause. The ionosphere is located between 80 and 400 km above the mesopause. It contains electrically charged particles known as ions, and hence, it is known as ionosphere. Radio waves transmitted from the earth are reflected back to the earth by this layer. Temperature here starts increasing with height. The upper most layer of the atmosphere above the thermosphere is known as the exosphere. This is the highest layer but very little is known about it. Whatever contents are there, these are extremely rarefied in this layer, and it gradually merges with the outer space. Although all layers of the atmosphere must be exercising influence onus, geographers are concerned with the first two layers of the atmosphere.

(i) In which layer does the temperature remains fairly constant?

(a) Atmosphere (b) Mesophere

(c) Ionosphere (d) Tropopause

Ans. (d) Tropopause

(ii) Which is the highest layer with very little known about it?

(a) Exosphere (b) Thermosphere

(c) Atmosphere (d) Stratosphere

Ans. (a) Exosphere

(iii) Which is the most important layer for all biological activity?

(a) Troposphere (b) Stratosphere

(c) Mesosphere (d) Thermosphere

Ans. (a) Troposphere

(iv) ____________ lies above the stratosphere.

(a) Mesosphere (b) Atmosphere

(c) Thermosphere (d) None of the Above

Ans. (a) Mesophere

Chapter 9: Solar Radiation, Heat Balance and Temperature

Objective Type Questions

(1 mark each)

(A) FILL IN THE BLANKS

Q. 1. The Earth's surface receives most of its energy in short __________ . R

Ans. wavelengths

Q. 2. As the Earth is a geoid resembling a sphere, the sun's rays fall ________at the top of the atmosphere. R

Ans. obliquely

Q. 3. The transfer of heat through horizontal movement of air is called _______. R

Ans. advection

Q. 4. The convective transfer of energy is confined only to the_________. U

Ans. troposphere

Q. 5. Compared to land, the _______ gets heated slowly and loses heat slowly. R

Ans. sea

Q. 6. The Earth maintains its _____________. U

Ans. temperature

Q. 7. A reversal of the normal behaviour of temperature in the troposphere is known as _____________. R

Ans. temperature inversion

Q. 8. Temperature inversion is normal in _________ areas. U

Ans. polar

Q. 9. __________ inversion occurs most often on clear nights, when the ground cools off rapidly by radiation. R

Ans. Surface temperature

Q. 10. _________ protects plants from frost damages. R

Ans. Air drainage

(B) ARRANGE IN THE CORRECT ORDER

Q. 1. Arrange the process of terrestrial radiation in the correct order: A

(i) The earth radiates heat in the form of long waves or infrared radiation.

(ii) Solar energy reaches the Earth's surface directly or indirectly in the form of electromagnetic waves.

(iii) Whereas the earth's surface receives heat from the incoming solar radiation, it also radiates back the same amount of heat to the atmosphere as well as to the outer space.

(iv) The earth radiates heat to the layers of air which re-radiate it.

Options:

(a) i, ii, iii, iv (b) iv, i, iii, ii

(c) ii, i, iv, iii (d) iii, ii, iv, i

Ans. (c) ii, i, iv, iii

Q. 2. Arrange the convective transfer of energy in the correct order: U

(i) Transfer of energy is confined only to the troposphere.

(ii) The air in contact with the earth rises vertically on heating.

(iii) Transmits the heat of the atmosphere.

(iv) In the form of currents.

Options:

(a) ii, iv, iii, i **(b)** i, ii, iii, iv

(c) iv, iii, ii, i **(d)** iii, i, ii, iv

Ans. (a) ii, iv, iii, i

Q. 3. Arrange the Earth's heat budget in the correct order: E

(i) Incoming heat is absorbed by the Earth.

(ii) Outgoing heat escapes the Earth in the form of radiation.

(iii) Both are evenly balanced.

(iv) If the outgoing heat and incoming heat are not balanced, Earth would become either warmer or cooler with the passage of time.

Options:

(a) iv, iii, ii, i **(b)** i, ii, iii, iv

(c) ii, iii, iv, i **(d)** iv, iii, ii, i

Ans. (b) i, ii, iii, iv

(C) GRAPH BASED QUESTIONS

Q. 1. Study the given graph carefully and answer any three of the following questions : (1×3=3) E

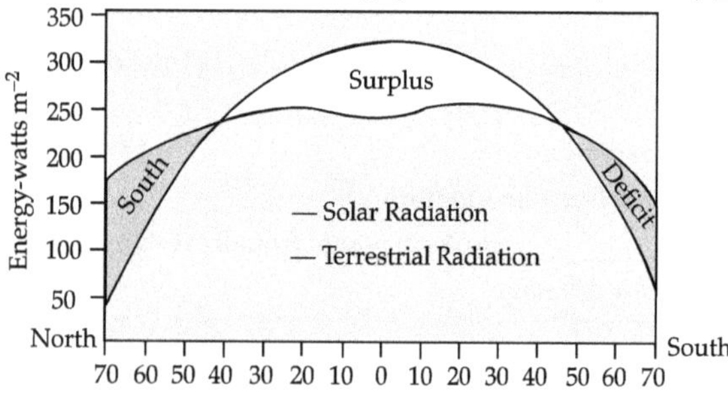

(i) According to the graph there is a surplus of net radiation balance between _______ degrees north and south.

(a) 40 **(b)** 30

(c) 35 **(d)** 45

Ans. (a) 40

(ii) According to the graph the net radiation deficit is found above the latitude of _____ in north and south.

(a) 40 **(b)** 30

(c) 50 **(d)** 45

Ans. (a) 40

(iii) According to the graph what is the measurement of the solar radiation in energy-watts m^{-2} at 0 latitude?

(a) 300 **(b)** 350

(c) 250 **(d)** 200

Ans. (a) 300

(iv) According to the graph the surplus of solar radiation is found around the:

(a) South pole **(b)** North pole

(c) Equator **(d)** Greenwich meantime

Ans. (c) Equator

Short Answer Type Question (3 mark each)

Q. 1. Describe the Prevailing winds.

Ans. Prevailing winds are the dominant wind patterns that generally blow in a consistent direction over a particular area or region. They are influenced by various factors, including the rotation of the Earth, atmospheric pressure systems, and topographical features. Prevailing winds play a crucial role in shaping climate, weather patterns, and ocean currents. Examples of prevailing winds include the trade winds, westerlies, and polar easterlies.

Long Answer Type Question (5 mark each)

Q. 1. Differentiate between Solar Radiation and Terrestrial Radiation.

Ans.

Solar Radiation	Terrestrial Radiation
I. **Source:** Solar radiation originates from the Sun as a result of nuclear fusion reactions occurring within its core.	I. **Source:** Terrestrial radiation originates from various sources on Earth, primarily as a result of natural radioactive decay processes occurring in rocks, soil, and other materials.
II. **Transmission:** Solar radiation travels through space in the form of electromagnetic waves, primarily consisting of visible light, ultraviolet (UV) radiation, and infrared (IR) radiation.	II. **Transmission:** Terrestrial radiation emanates from the Earth's surface and is composed of different types of radiation, such as alpha particles, beta particles, and gamma rays.

III. **Composition:** Solar radiation is a broad spectrum of electromagnetic radiation, including various wavelengths and energy levels.	III. **Composition:** Terrestrial radiation consists of ionizing radiation emitted by naturally occurring radioactive elements, such as uranium, thorium, and radon, present in the Earth's crust.
IV. **Intensity:** Solar radiation reaching the Earth's upper atmosphere is relatively constant, but it can vary due to factors like solar activity, Earth's orbit, and atmospheric conditions.	IV. **Intensity:** The intensity of terrestrial radiation varies depending on the geological composition of the location. Areas with high concentrations of radioactive elements will have higher levels of terrestrial radiation.
V. **Interaction with Earth:** Solar radiation interacts with the Earth's atmosphere, clouds, and surface. Some of it is absorbed by the atmosphere, while the rest reaches the Earth's surface, where it can be reflected, absorbed, or transmitted by different materials.	V. **Interaction with Environment:** Terrestrial radiation can penetrate various materials and interact with the surrounding environment. It can be absorbed by living organisms, contribute to background radiation levels, and play a role in radiometric dating and medical imaging techniques.

Q. 2. Describe the permanent pressure belts.

Ans. The permanent pressure belts are atmospheric regions characterized by relatively consistent patterns of high or low pressure that exist on Earth's surface. There are three primary permanent pressure belts: the equatorial low-pressure belt (also known as the Intertropical Convergence Zone or ITCZ), the subtropical high-pressure belts, and the subpolar low-pressure belts.

1. **Equatorial Low-Pressure Belt (ITCZ):** Located near the equator, the ITCZ is a region of low pressure where the northeast and southeast trade winds converge. This convergence leads to the upward movement of warm, moist air, resulting in frequent cloud formation and rainfall.
2. **Subtropical High-Pressure Belts:** These belts are found around 30 degrees latitude in both the Northern and Southern Hemispheres. They are characterized by stable, descending air masses that create a zone of high atmospheric pressure. The air in these belts becomes dry and warm, leading to clear skies and relatively calm weather conditions.
3. **Subpolar Low-Pressure Belts:** Positioned around 60 degrees latitude in both hemispheres, the subpolar low-pressure belts are areas of low pressure. They are formed due to the collision of cold polar air masses with relatively warmer air from the mid-latitudes. These belts are associated with stormy weather conditions and strong westerly winds.

These permanent pressure belts play a crucial role in shaping global weather patterns and influencing the distribution of precipitation and wind patterns around the Earth.

Source-Based Questions

(3 marks each)

Q. 1. Read the Passage given below and answer any three of the questions that follow. (1×3=3) E

There are different ways of heating and cooling of the atmosphere. The earth after being heated by insolation transmits the heat to the atmospheric layers near to the earth in long wave form. The air in contact with the land gets heated slowly and the upper layers in contact with the lower layers also get heated. This process is called conduction. Conduction takes place when two bodies of unequal temperature are in contact with one another, there is a flow of energy from the warmer to cooler body. The transfer of heat continues until both the bodies attain the same temperature or the contact is broken. Conduction is important in heating the lower layers of the atmosphere. The air in contact with the earth rises vertically on heating in the form of currents and further transmits the heat of the atmosphere. This process of vertical heating of the atmosphere is known as convection. The convective transfer of energy is confined only to the troposphere. The transfer of heat through horizontal movement of air is called advection. Horizontal movement of the air is relatively more important than the vertical movement. In middle latitudes, most of diurnal (day and night) variation in daily weather are caused by advection alone. In tropical regions particularly in northern India during summer season local winds called 'loo' is the outcome of advection process. The insolation received by the earth is in short waves forms and heats up its surface. The earth after being heated itself becomes a radiating body and it radiates energy to the atmosphere in long wave form. This energy heats up the atmosphere from below. This process is known as terrestrial radiation. The long wave radiation is absorbed by the atmospheric gases particularly by carbon dioxide and the other greenhouse gases. Thus, the atmosphere is indirectly heated by the earth's radiation. The atmosphere in turn radiates and transmits heat to the space. Finally, the amount of heat received from the sun is returned to space, thereby maintaining constant temperature at the earth's surface and in the atmosphere.

(i) The earth after being heated by insolation transmits the heat to the atmospheric layers near to the earth in the form of:

(a) long wave (b) short wave

(c) medium wave (d) All the above

Ans. (a) long wave

(ii) In which of the following processes, there is a flow of energy from the warmer to cooler body?

(a) Convection (b) Conduction

(c) Advection (d) Radiation

Ans. (b) Conduction

(iii) Vertical heating of the atmosphere is known as:

(a) Convection (b) Conduction

(c) Advection (d) Radiation

Ans. (a) Convection

(iv) The transfer of heat through horizontal movement of air is called:

(a) Convection (b) Conduction

(c) Advection (d) Radiation

Ans. (c) Advection

Q. 2. Read the Passage given below and answer any three of the questions that follow. (1×3=3) E

Normally, temperature decreases with increase in elevation. It is called normal lapse rate. At times, the situations are reversed and the normal lapse rate is inverted. It is called inversion of temperature. Inversion is usually of short duration but quite common none the less. A long winter night with clear skies and still air is ideal situation for inversion. The heat of the day is radiated off during the night, and by early morning hours, the earth is cooler than the air above. Over polar areas, temperature inversion is normal throughout the year. Surface inversion promotes stability in the lower layers of the atmosphere. Smoke and dust particles get collected beneath the inversion layer and spread horizontally to fill the lower strata of the atmosphere. Dense fogs in mornings are common occurrences especially during winter season. This inversion commonly lasts for few hours until the sun comes up and beings to warm the earth. The inversion takes place in hills and mountains due to air drainage. Cold air at the hills and mountains, produced during night, flows under the influence of gravity. Being heavy and dense, the cold air acts almost like water and moves down the slope to pile up deeply in pockets and valley bottoms with warm air above. This is called air drainage. It protects plants from frost damages.

(i) When does the temperature decrease?

(a) With decrease in elevation

(b) With increase in elevation

(c) With no change in elevation

(d) With recline in elevation

Ans. (b) With increase in elevation

(ii) When does inversion in temperature occur?

(a) In clear nights (b) In foggy nights

(c) In rainy nights (d) In smoggy nights

Ans. (a) In clear nights

(iii) What is a common occurrence during winter season?

(a) Dense heat (b) Dense fog

(c) Dense rain (d) None of the above

Ans. (b) Dense fog

(iv) Inversion can last for how long?

(a) Till the sun sets (b) Till the sun comes up

(c) Till the night time (d) Till the rain continues

Ans. (b) Till the sun comes up

Q. 3. Read the Passage given below and answer any three of the questions that follow. (1×3=3) U+E

The global distribution of temperature can well be understood by studying the temperature distribution in January and July. The temperature distribution is generally shown on the map with the help of isotherms. The isotherms are lines joining places having equal temperature. In general, the effect of the latitude on temperature is well pronounced, as the isotherms are generally parallel to the latitude. The deviation from this general trend is more pronounced in January than in July, especially in the Northern Hemisphere. In the Northern Hemisphere the land surface area is much larger than in the Southern Hemisphere. Hence, the effects of land mass and the ocean currents are well pronounced. In January the isotherms deviate to the north over the ocean and to the south over the continent. This can be seen on the North Atlantic Ocean. The presence of warm ocean currents, Gulf Stream and North Atlantic drift, make the Northern Atlantic Ocean warmer and the isotherms bend towards the north. Over the land the temperature decreases sharply and the isotherms bend towards south in Europe.

It is much pronounced in the Siberian plain. The mean January temperature along 60°E longitude is minus 20°C both at 80°N and 50°N latitudes. The mean monthly temperature for January is over 27°C, in equatorial oceans over 24°C in the tropics and 2°C – 0°C in the middle latitudes and –18°C to –48°C in the Eurasian continental interior.

(i) How can the global distribution of temperature be well understood?

(a) By studying the temperature distribution in June and July

(b) By studying the temperature distribution in January and July

(c) By studying the temperature distribution in July and August

(d) By studying the temperature distribution in January and February

Ans. (a) By studying the temperature distribution in June and July

(ii) How is the temperature distribution is generally shown on the map?

(a) With the help of degrees

(b) With the help of isotherms

(c) With the help of written description

(d) With the help of scale

Ans. (b) With the help of isotherms

(iii) What is the monthly temperature for January in the Eurasian continental interior?

(a) –16°C to –36°C (b) –14°C to –42°C

(c) –12°C to –40°C (d) –18°C to –48°C

Ans. (d) –18°C to –48°C

(iv) Isotherms are parallel to ______.

(a) Latitude (b) Longitude

(c) Poles (d) Equator

Ans. (a) Latitude

Chapter 10: Atmospheric Circulation and Weather Systems

Objective Type Questions (1 mark each)

(A) FILL IN THE BLANKS

Q. 1. __________ pressure also determines when the air will rise or sink. R

Ans. Atmospheric

Q. 2. ________ expands when heated and gets compressed when cooled. U

Ans. Air

Q. 3. In the lower atmosphere the pressure decreases rapidly with _________. R

Ans. height

Q. 4. A natural movement of air of any velocity is called ________. U

Ans. wind

Q. 5. The low-pressure belts are termed as the _________. R

Ans. sub-polar lows

Q. 6. __________ are lines connecting places having equal pressure. R

Ans. Isobars

Q. 7. A Ferrel Cell is a ________ pattern named after William Ferrel. R

Ans. wind circulation

Q. 8. Part of the air rising at 60° latitude diverges at high altitude towards the poles and creates the __________. U

Ans. polar cell

Q. 9. The ________of the earth about its axis affects the direction of the wind. U

Ans. rotation

Q. 10. The wind circulation around a low is called _________ circulation. U

Ans. cyclonic

Q. 11. The combined phenomenon of southern oscillation and El Nino is known as _____. R

Ans. ENSO

Q. 12. ________ are the low-latitude overturning circulations that have air rising at the Equator and air sinking at roughly 30° latitude. E

Ans. Hadley Cells

Q. 13. ________ is a type of storm system formed in middle or high latitudes. U

Ans. Extra tropical cyclone

Q. 14. The process of formation of the fronts is known as ___________. E

Ans. frontogenesis

Q. 15. The Coriolis force is absent at the _________. E

Ans. Equator

(B) ARRANGE IN THE CORRECT ORDER

Q. 1. Arrange the process of land breeze in correct order: E

(i) The air over the ocean is now warmer than the air over the land.

(ii) This causes a small temperature gradient between the ocean surface and the nearby land at night.

(iii) The land loses heat quickly after the sun goes down and the air above it cools too.

(iv) The wind will blow from the land to the ocean creating the land breeze.

Options:

(a) i, iii, ii, iv (b) iv, ii, iii, i

(c) ii, iii, iv, i (d) i, ii, iii, iv

Ans. (a) i, iii, ii, iv

Q. 2. Arrange the process of sea breeze in correct order: E

(i) During the day the land heats up faster and becomes warmer than the sea.

(ii) Over the land the air rises giving rise to a low-pressure area.

(iii) Whereas the sea is relatively cool and the pressure over sea is relatively high.

(iv) The pressure gradient from sea to land is created and the wind blows from the sea to the land.

Options:

(a) iv, ii, iii, i **(b)** iii, ii, i, iv

(c) i, ii, iii, iv **(d)** i, iv, iii, ii

Ans. (d) i, iv, iii, ii

Q. 3. Arrange the formation of cyclone in correct order: U

(i) Warm, moist air over the ocean rises upward from near the surface.

(ii) This air moves up and away from the ocean surface.

(iii) It leaves less air pressure near the surface.

(iv) As the warm air rises, it causes an area of lower air pressure below.

Options:

(a) iv, ii, iii, i **(b)** i, ii, iii, iv

(c) iv, iii, i, ii **(d)** iii, ii, i, iv

Ans. (a) i, ii, iii, iv

Short Answer Type Question (3 mark each)

Q. 1. How will you explain Air Circulation?

Ans. Air circulation refers to the movement of air on a global scale, driven by various factors such as temperature, pressure gradients, and the rotation of the Earth. It plays a crucial role in shaping weather patterns and climate around the world.

Long Answer Type Question (5 mark each)

Q. 1. Differentiate between Tropical and Extra tropical cyclones.

Ans. Tropical cyclones and extratropical cyclones are two distinct types of weather systems that have different characteristics and formation processes.

Here's a brief differentiation between the two:

Tropical cyclones	Extra tropical cyclones
1. **Location and Distribution:** These cyclones form in tropical regions over warm ocean waters near the equator, typically between 5 and 30 degrees latitude. They are commonly found in the Atlantic Ocean (hurricanes), the Pacific Ocean (typhoons), and the Indian Ocean (cyclones).	1. **Location and Distribution:** These cyclones occur in the mid-latitudes, usually between 30 and 60 degrees latitude, in both the Northern and Southern Hemispheres. They are more prevalent in areas like North America, Europe, and Asia.
2. **Formation and Energy Source:** They originate from pre-existing disturbances such as tropical waves or tropical depressions. They derive their energy primarily from warm ocean waters, where heat and moisture fuel their development and intensification.	2. **Formation and Energy Source:** These cyclones form from the interaction between contrasting air masses, such as warm and cold fronts. Their primary energy source is the horizontal temperature contrast, known as baroclinic instability, which leads to the formation of storms.
3. **Structure and Symmetry:** They possess a well-defined, compact, and symmetric structure with a warm core. They typically exhibit a central eye surrounded by an eyewall, which is a ring of intense thunderstorms.	3. **Structure and Symmetry:** These cyclones have a larger and asymmetrical structure. They lack a distinct eye and eyewall and instead have a frontal system, with a warm front ahead of the low-pressure center and a cold front trailing behind.
4. **Lifecycle and Duration:** They have a shorter lifespan, typically lasting from a few days to a couple of weeks. Their development, intensification, and dissipation are influenced by various factors such as sea surface temperatures, wind shear, and interaction with land masses.	4. **Lifecycle and Duration:** These cyclones can last for several days and sometimes even up to a week. They undergo a life cycle known as cyclogenesis, where they develop, mature, and eventually dissipate as they move along the mid-latitude storm tracks.

5. **Weather Effects:** They are known for their intense winds, heavy rainfall, storm surge, and potential for widespread damage. They often cause significant coastal flooding, destruction of infrastructure, and disruption to daily life.	5. **Weather Effects:** These cyclones can also produce strong winds and heavy precipitation, but their impacts are generally spread over a broader area. They are associated with a variety of weather conditions, including rain, snow, strong winds, and temperature changes.

Q. 2. How Global warming is result of atmospheric pollution and how it can be minimized if not prevented?

Ans. Global warming is primarily caused by the accumulation of greenhouse gases in the Earth's atmosphere, which trap heat and lead to a rise in average global temperatures. These greenhouse gases, such as carbon dioxide (CO_2), methane (CH_4), and nitrous oxide (N_2O), are released into the atmosphere through various human activities, including the burning of fossil fuels, deforestation, and industrial processes.

To minimize or mitigate global warming, several actions can be taken:

1. **Transition to renewable energy:** Shifting away from fossil fuels and promoting the use of renewable energy sources such as solar, wind, and hydroelectric power can significantly reduce greenhouse gas emissions.
2. **Energy efficiency:** Implementing energy-efficient technologies and practices can help reduce energy consumption and lower greenhouse gas emissions.
3. **Forest conservation and reforestation:** Protecting existing forests from deforestation and undertaking reforestation initiatives can enhance carbon sequestration, as trees absorb CO2 during photosynthesis.
4. **Sustainable transportation:** Promoting the use of public transportation, electric vehicles, and cycling, while reducing reliance on private vehicles powered by fossil fuels, can significantly reduce emissions from the transportation sector.
5. **Waste management:** Implementing effective waste management strategies, such as recycling and composting, can reduce methane emissions from landfills.
6. **Sustainable agriculture:** Encouraging sustainable farming practices, such as precision agriculture, agroforestry, and reduced use of synthetic fertilizers, can minimize emissions of greenhouse gases from the agricultural sector.
7. **International cooperation:** Global efforts and agreements, like the Paris Agreement, are crucial in coordinating actions among nations to address climate change collectively.

Source-Based Questions

(3 marks each)

Q. 1. Read the Passage given below and answer any three of the questions that follow. U **(1×3=3)**

When two different air masses meet, the boundary zone between them is called a front. The process of formation of the fronts is known as frontogenesis. There are four types of fronts: (a) Cold; (b) Warm; (c) Stationary; (d) Occluded. When the front remains stationary, it is called a stationary front. When the cold air moves anti clockwise cyclonic circulation. The cyclonic circulation leads to a well-developed extra tropical cyclone, with a warm front and a cold front. There are pockets of warm air or warm sector wedged between the forward and the rear cold air or cold sector. The warm air glides over the cold air and a sequence of clouds appear over the sky ahead of the warm front and cause precipitation. The cold front approaches the warm air from behind and pushes the warm air up. As a result, cumulus clouds develop along the cold front. The cold front moves faster than the warm front ultimately overtaking the warm front. The warm air is completely lifted up and the front is occluded and the cyclone dissipates. The processes of wind circulation both at the surface and aloft are closely interlinked. The extra tropical cyclone differs from the tropical cyclone in number of ways. The extra tropical cyclones have a clear frontal system towards the warm air mass, its contact zone is called the cold front, whereas if the warm air mass moves towards the cold air mass, the contact zone is a warm front. If an air mass is fully lifted above the land surface, it is called the occluded front. The fronts occur in middle latitudes and are characterised by steep gradient in temperature and pressure. They bring abrupt changes in temperature and cause the air to rise to form clouds and cause precipitation.

(i) How many types of fronts are there?

(a) One (b) Two
(c) Three (d) Four

Ans. (d) Four

(ii) A weather front formed during the process of cyclogenesis is called ________ front.

(a) Occluded (b) Contact
(c) Cold (d) Warm

Ans. (a) Occluded

(iii) When the front remains stationary, it is called a ________ front.

(a) moving (b) stationary

(c) warm (d) closed

Ans. (b) stationary

(iv) What is the contact zone of extra tropical cyclones called?

(a) Cold front (b) Warm front

(c) Zone front (d) Hot front

Ans. (a) Cold front

Q. 2. Read the Passage given below and answer any three to the questions that follow. (1×3=3) E

Other severe local storms are thunderstorms and tornadoes. They are of short duration, occurring over a small area but are violent. Thunderstorms are caused by intense convection on moist hot days. A thunderstorm is a well-grown cumulonimbus cloud producing thunder and lightening. When the clouds extend to heights where sub-zero temperature prevails, hails are formed and they come down as hailstorm. If there is insufficient moisture, a thunderstorm can generate dust-storms. A thunderstorm is characterised by intense updraft of rising warm air, which causes the clouds to grow bigger and rise to greater height. This causes precipitation. Later, downdraft brings down to earth the cool air and the rain. From severe thunderstorms sometimes spiralling wind descends like a trunk of an elephant with great force, with very low pressure at the centre, causing massive destruction on its way. Such a phenomenon is called a tornado. Tornadoes generally occur in middle latitudes. The tornado over the sea is called water spouts. These violent storms are the manifestation of the atmosphere's adjustments to varying energy distribution. The potential and heat energies are converted into kinetic energy in these storms and the restless atmosphere again returns to its stable state.

(i) __________ of short duration, occurring over a small area but are violent.

(a) Thunderstorms

(b) Tornadoes

(c) Thunderstorms and tornadoes

(d) None of the Above

Ans. (c) Thunderstorms and tornadoes

(ii) Where do tornadoes occur?

(a) Centre latitudes (b) Middle latitudes

(c) Western latitudes (d) Eastern latitudes

Ans. (b) Middle latitudes

(iii) What is the tornado over sea called?

(a) Water spouts (b) Air spouts

(c) Clear spouts (d) None of the above

Ans. (a) Water spouts

(iv) Hails are formed in which temperature?

(a) Minus one degree (b) Sub-zero degree

(c) Plus one degree (d) Zero degree

Ans. (b) Sub-zero degree

Q. 3. Read the Passage given below and answer any three of the questions that follow. (1×3=3) A+E

The rotation of the earth about its axis affects the direction of the wind. This force is called the Coriolis force after the French physicist who described it in 1844. It deflects the wind to the right direction in the northern hemisphere and to the left in the southern hemisphere. The deflection is more when the wind velocity is high. The Coriolis force is directly proportional to the angle of latitude. It is maximum at the poles and is absent at the Equator. The Coriolis force acts perpendicular to the pressure gradient force. The pressure gradient force is perpendicular to an isobar. The higher the pressure gradient force, the more is the velocity of the wind and the larger is the deflection in the direction of wind. As a result of these two forces operating perpendicular to each other, in the low-pressure areas the wind blows around it. At the Equator, the Coriolis force is zero and the wind blows perpendicular to the isobars. The low pressure gets filled instead of getting intensified. That is the reason why tropical cyclones are not formed near the Equator.

(i) The rotation of the earth about its axis affects the direction of the _______.

(a) wind (b) climate

(c) breeze (d) latitude

Ans. (a) wind

(ii) Which force acts perpendicular to the pressure gradient force?

(a) Tropical (b) Cold

(c) Warm (d) Coriolis

Ans. (d) Coriolis

(iii) The Coriolis force is zero at ________.

(a) Poles (b) Equator

(c) Oceans (d) Land

Ans. (b) Equator

(iv) Where is the Coriolis force maximum felt?

(a) At the Equator (b) At the Poles

(c) At the Latitudes (d) None of the Above

Ans. (b) At the Poles

Chapter 11: Water in the Atmosphere

Objective Type Questions (1 mark each)

(A) FILL IN THE BLANKS

Q. 1. _________ is present in the atmosphere in three forms namely – gaseous, liquid and solid. R

Ans. Water

Q. 2. A combination of smoke and fog is called_________. R

Ans. smog

Q. 3. The transformation of water vapour into water is called __________. R

Ans. condensation

Q. 4. _________ is the coating or deposit of ice that may form in humid air in cold conditions, usually overnight. R

Ans. Frost

Q. 5. A cloud of tiny water droplets suspended in the atmosphere at or near the Earth's surface limiting visibility is called _______. R

Ans. mist

Q. 6. As the _______ are formed at some height over the surface of the earth, they take various shape. R

Ans. clouds

Q. 7. In urban and industrial centres smoke provides plenty of nuclei which help the formation of _____ and ________. U

Ans. fog; mist ½ + ½ =1

(B) ARRANGE IN THE CORRECT ORDER

Q. 1. Arrange the cloud formation process in correct order: U

(i) Water travels into the sky within air as water vapour.

(ii) During day time water from different sources like pond, lake, river, sea, well, etc. get evaporated.

(iii) At a particular height the air cools.

(iv) The water vapour condenses to form minute droplets.

Options:

(a) i, ii, iii, iv (b) iv, ii, i, iii

(c) ii, i, iii, iv (d) iv, i, ii, iii

Ans. (c) ii, i, iii, iv

Q. 2. Arrange the formation of cumulous clouds in correct order: U

(i) Air on being heated, becomes light.

(ii) Air rises up in convection currents.

(iii) As air rises, it expands and loses heat.

(iv) Condensation takes place.

Options:

(a) i, ii, iii, iv (b) ii, iii, i, iv

(c) iv, ii, iii, i (d) iv, iii, ii, i

Ans. (a) i, ii, iii, iv

Q. 3. Arrange the formation of sleet in correct order: A

(i) Liquid rain forms in a warmer layer of air.

(ii) The drops form into pellets.

(iii) Rain falls down through a cooler layer just above the ground, the raindrops freeze.

(iv) The drops freeze on contact and form a glaze on objects.

Options:

(a) i, iii, ii, iv (b) iv, ii, i, iii

(c) iii, ii, i, iv (d) ii, iv, i, iii

Ans. (a) i, iii, ii, iv

Short Answer Type Question (3 mark each)

Q. 1. Explain the process of Transpiration.

Ans. Transpiration is the process by which water is transferred from land plants to the atmosphere as water vapour. It is part of the larger water cycle, which involves the exchange of water between the atmosphere, the oceans, and the continents. During transpiration, plants absorb water from the soil through their roots. This water then moves up through the plant's stem and reaches the leaves. In the leaves, water evaporates from tiny openings called stomata, which are primarily located on the underside of leaves. As water vapour is released into the air, it contributes to the moisture content of the atmosphere. This water vapour can eventually condense and form clouds, leading to precipitation in the form of rain or snow. Thus, transpiration plays a crucial role in the movement of water between the continents and the atmosphere.

Long Answer Type Question

(5 mark each)

Q. 1. Analyse the economic significance of tides.

Ans. The economic significance of tides is primarily related to their impact on various industries and activities, such as marine transportation, energy generation, fishing, and tourism. Here is a brief analysis of their economic importance:

1. **Marine Transportation:** Tides play a crucial role in determining navigational conditions for ships, particularly in coastal areas and harbors. The rise and fall of tides affect water depths, which can impact shipping routes, port access, and vessel draft limitations. By understanding tidal patterns, shipping companies can optimize their schedules, reduce risks of grounding, and ensure efficient cargo transportation.
2. **Energy Generation:** Tidal energy represents a renewable and predictable source of power. Tidal power plants harness the kinetic energy generated by tidal currents to produce electricity. These plants can contribute to a region's energy mix, reducing reliance on fossil fuels and providing a sustainable energy source. Tidal energy projects can create jobs, stimulate local economies, and promote technological advancements in the renewable energy sector.
3. **Fishing Industry:** Tides significantly influence the movement and behavior of marine organisms, including fish. They affect the availability of nutrients, water temperature, and currents, which impact fish migration patterns and breeding grounds. Understanding tidal cycles helps fishermen determine the best times and locations for fishing, increasing their chances of successful catches. This, in turn, supports the fishing industry, provides livelihoods, and supplies seafood for domestic and international markets.
4. **Tourism and Recreation:** Tidal phenomena, such as high tides, low tides, and tidal waves, attract tourists and recreational enthusiasts to coastal areas. Tidal beaches offer opportunities for swimming, surfing, and other water-based activities during certain tidal conditions. Coastal towns and cities with scenic tidal landscapes can attract visitors, boosting local tourism and related businesses, including hotels, restaurants, and souvenir shops.
5. **Environmental Impact:** Tidal movements also contribute to maintaining the health and productivity of coastal ecosystems. They support nutrient circulation, assist in flushing out pollutants, and influence sedimentation patterns. Tidal marshes and estuaries serve as critical habitats for various species, including birds and marine life. The preservation and conservation of these ecosystems have long-term economic benefits, including ecotourism, fisheries, and protection against coastal erosion.

Source-Based Questions

(3 marks each)

Q. 1. Read the Passage given below and answer any three of the questions that follow. (1×3=3) AE

The amount of water vapour in the atmosphere is added or withdrawn due to evaporation and condensation respectively. Evaporation is a process by which water is transformed from liquid to gaseous state. Heat is the main cause for evaporation. The temperature at which the water starts evaporating is referred to as the latent heat of vaporisation. Increase in temperature increases water absorption and retention capacity of the given parcel of air. Similarly, if the moisture content is low, air has a potentiality of absorbing and retaining moisture. Movement of air replaces the saturated layer with the unsaturated layer. Hence, the greater the movement of air, the greater is the evaporation. The transformation of water vapour into water is called condensation. Condensation is caused by the loss of heat. When moist air is cooled, it may reach a level when its capacity to hold water vapour ceases. Then, the excess water vapour condenses into liquid form. If it directly condenses into solid form, it is known as sublimation. In free air, condensation results from cooling around very small particles termed as hygroscopic condensation nuclei. Particles of dust, smoke and salt from the ocean are particularly good nuclei because they absorb water. Condensation also takes place when the moist air comes in contact with some colder object and it may also take place when the temperature is close to the dew point. Condensation, therefore, depends upon the amount of cooling and the relative humidity of the air. Condensation is influenced by the volume of air, temperature, pressure and humidity. Condensation takes place: (i) when the temperature of the air is reduced to dew point with its volume remaining constant; (ii) when both the volume and the temperature are reduced; (iii) when moisture is added to the air through evaporation. However, the most favourable condition for condensation is the decrease in air temperature. After condensation the water vapour or the moisture in the atmosphere takes one of the following forms — dew, frost, fog and clouds. Forms of condensation can be classified on the basis of temperature and location. Condensation takes place when the dew point is lower than the freezing point as well as higher than the freezing point.

(i) A process by which water is transformed from liquid to gaseous state is known as:

(a) Transformation (b) Evaporation

(c) Condensation (d) Vapourisation

Ans. (b) Evaporation

(ii) The temperature at which the water starts evaporating is referred to as the latent heat of:

(a) Vaporisation (b) Transformation

(c) Evaporation (d) Condensation

Ans. (a) Vaporisation

(iii) Increase in temperature _______ water absorption and retention capacity of the given parcel of air:

(a) increases

(b) decreases

(c) first increases then decreases

(d) first decreases then increases

Ans. (a) increases

(iv) The water vapour directly condensing into solid form is called:

(a) Evaporation (b) Condensation

(c) Sublimation (d) Vaporisation

Ans. (c) Sublimation

Q. 2. Read the Passage given below and answer any three of the questions that follow. (1×3=3) AE

The process of continuous condensation in free air helps the condensed particles to grow in size. When the resistance of the air fails to hold them against the force of gravity, they fall on to the earth's surface. So, after the condensation of water vapour, the release of moisture is known as precipitation. This may take place in liquid or solid form. The precipitation in the form of water is called rainfall, when the temperature is lower than the 0°C, precipitation takes place in the form of fine flakes of snow and is called snowfall. Moisture is released in the form of hexagonal crystals. These crystals form flakes of snow. Besides rain and snow, other forms of precipitation are sleet and hail, though the latter are limited in occurrence and are sporadic in both time and space. Sleet is frozen raindrops and refrozen melted snow-water. When a layer of air with the temperature above freezing point overlies a subfreezing layer near the ground, precipitation takes place in the form of sleet. Raindrops, which leave the warmer air, encounter the colder air below. As a result, they solidify and reach the ground as small pellets of ice not bigger than the raindrops from which they are formed. Sometimes, drops of rain after being released by the clouds become solidified into small rounded solid pieces of ice and which reach the surface of the earth are called hailstones. These are formed by the rain water passing through the colder layers. Hail stones have several concentric layers of ice one over the other.

(i) After the condensation of water vapour, the release of moisture is known as:

(a) Sublimation (b) Vapourisation

(c) Precipitation (d) Condensation

Ans. (c) Precipitation

(ii) The precipitation in the form of water is called:

(a) Condensation (b) Sublimation

(c) Rainfall (d) Snowfall

Ans. (c) Rainfall

(iii) Moisture is released in the form of:

(a) Pentagonal crystals (b) Tetrahedral crystals

(c) Octahedral crystals (d) Hexagonal crystals

Ans. (d) Hexagonal crystals

(iv) When a layer of air with the temperature above freezing point overlies a subfreezing layer near the ground, precipitation takes place in the form of:

(a) Hailstones (b) Rainfall

(c) Snowfall (d) Sleet

Ans. (d) Sleet

Q. 3. Read the Passage given below and answer any three of the questions that follow. (1×3=3) AE

Water vapour present in the air is known as humidity. It is expressed quantitatively in different ways. The actual amount of the water vapour present in the atmosphere is known as the absolute humidity. It is the weight of water vapour per unit volume of air and is expressed in terms of grams per cubic metre. The ability of the air to hold water vapour depends entirely on its temperature. The absolute humidity differs from place to place on the surface of the earth. The percentage of moisture present in the atmosphere as compared to its full capacity at a given temperature is known as the relative humidity. With the change of air temperature, the capacity to retain moisture increases or decreases and the relative humidity is also affected. It is greater over the oceans and least over the continents.

(i) ___________ present in the air is known as humidity.

(a) Water vapour (b) Dews

(c) Fog (d) Humidity

Ans. (a) Water vapour

(ii) The ability of the air to hold water vapour depends entirely on its________.

(a) temperature (b) humidity
(c) atmosphere (d) None of the Above

Ans. (a) temperature

(iii) The __________humidity differs from place to place on the surface of the earth.

(a) complete (b) absolute
(c) relative (d) semi

Ans. (b) absolute

(iv) ___________ humidity is greater over the oceans and least over the continents.

(a) Relative (b) Absolute
(c) Clear (d) Semi

Ans. (a) Relative

Chapter 12: World Climate and Climate Change

Objective Type Questions

(1 mark each)

(A) FILL IN THE BLANKS

Q. 1. _____________ classification attempts to organise climates according to their causes. [R]

Ans. Genetic

Q. 2. Koeppen recognised _________major climatic groups. [A]

Ans. five

Q. 3. Average temperature below 10° C for all months is experienced in ________ climates. [R]

Ans. cold

Q. 4. In __________ climates annual range of temperature is very low and annual rainfall is high. [R]

Ans. tropical humid

Q. 5. _________ climates are divided into steppe or semi-arid climate (BS) and desert climate (BW). [R]

Ans. Dry

Q. 6. In ________ climate the annual precipitation ranges between 35-90 cm. [R]

Ans. Mediterranean

Q. 7. Archaeological findings show that the _________ Desert experienced wet and cool climate around 8,000 B.C. [R]

Ans. Rajasthan

Q. 8. _________witnessed "Little Ice Age" from 1550 to about 1850. [R]

Ans. Europe

Q. 9. Dust Bowl occurred in _________. [R]

Ans. 1930s

Q. 10. The largest concentration of GHGs in the atmosphere is _________. [R]

Ans. Carbon dioxide

Q. 11. The globally averaged annual mean temperature at the end of the 20th century was about _______ above that recorded at the end of the 19th century. [R]

Ans. 0.6°C

(B) GRAPH BASED QUESTIONS

Q. 1. Read the Case Study given below and answer any three of the questions that follow: (1×3=3) [U]+[A]

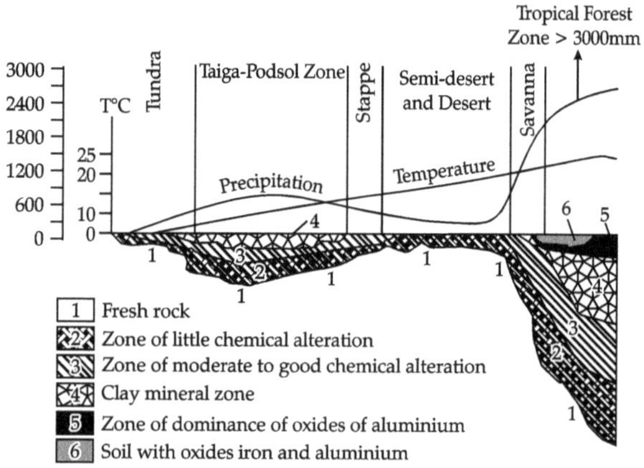

Tropical Forest Zone > 3000mm

Tundra | Taiga-Podsol Zone | Stappe | Semi-desert and Desert | Savanna

T°C; Precipitation; Temperature

1 Fresh rock
2 Zone of little chemical alteration
3 Zone of moderate to good chemical alteration
4 Clay mineral zone
5 Zone of dominance of oxides of aluminium
6 Soil with oxides iron and aluminium

(i) According to the graph the precipitation is highest in which of the following forest zone?

(a) Tundra (b) Desert
(c) Tropical (d) Steppe

Ans. (c) Tropical

(ii) According to the graph which of the following forest zone has the highest temperature?

(a) Taiga (b) Desert
(c) Tropical (d) Steppe

Ans. (c) Tropical

(iii) According to the graph which of the following zone has zone of dominance of oxides of aluminium?

(a) Taiga (b) Sawanna
(c) Tropical (d) Steppe

Ans. (c) Tropical

(iv) Clay mineral zone is found in:

(a) Taiga (b) Sawanna
(c) Tundra (d) Steppe

Ans. (a) Taiga

Q. 2. Study the given graph carefully on rise of temperature globally and answer any three of the following questions: (1×3 = 3) U+A

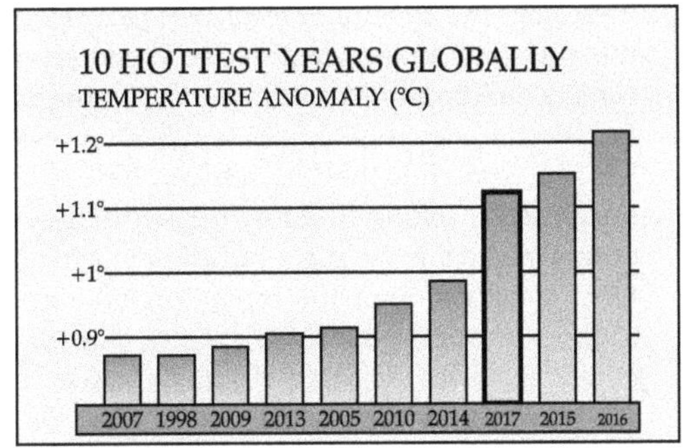

(i) In which years the temperatures increased by +0.9°C?

(a) 2007 (b) 1998

(c) 2009 (d) All of the above

Ans. (d) All of the above

(ii) Which was the last year of the 20th century to experience increase in temperature by +1°C?

(a) 1998 (b) 2007

(c) 2009 (d) 2013

Ans. (a) 1998

(iii) How much did the temperature rise by 2017?

(a) +1.1°C (b) More than +1.1°C

(c) Less than +1.1°C (d) None of the Above

Ans. (b) More than +1.1°C

(iv) The temperature rose _______ globally by 2016.

(a) More than +1.2°C (b) Less than –1.2°C

(c) More than +1.1°C (d) Less than –1.1°C

Ans. (a) More than +1.2°C

Q. 3. Study the given graph on global greenhouse gas emission and answer any three of the following questions: (1×3 = 3) U+E

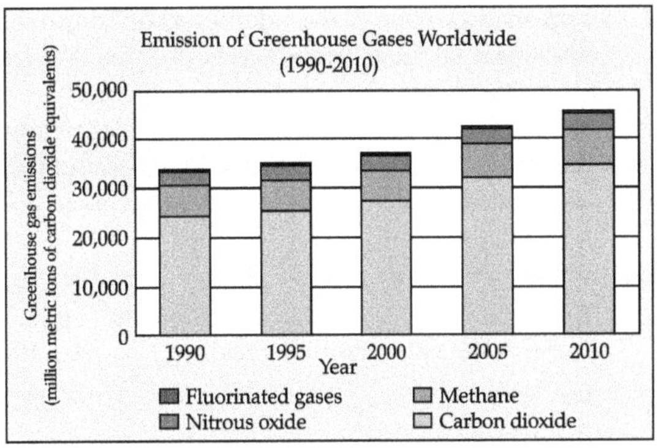

(i) Which gas had the maximum emission in 2010?

(a) Methane (b) Carbon dioxide

(c) Fluorinated gases (d) None of the above

Ans. (b) Carbon dioxide

(ii) Which gas had the minimum emission in 1990?

(a) Nitrous oxide (b) Methane

(c) Fluorinated gases (d) Carbon dioxide

Ans. (c) Fluorinated gases

(iii) How much Methane was emitted in 2005?

(a) Between 30,000-40,000 metric tons

(b) Between 40,000-50,000 metric tons

(c) Between 60,000-70,000 metric tons

(d) Between 20,000-30,000 metric tons

Ans. (a) Between 30,000-40,000 metric tons

(iv) How much Nitrous Oxide was emitted in 1990?

(a) Between 30,000 to 35,000 tons

(b) Between 35,000 to 40,000 tons

(c) Between 40,000 to 45,000 tons

(d) None of the Above

Ans. (a) Between 30,000 to 35,000 tons

Source-based Questions

(3 marks each)

Q. 1. Read the Passage given below and answer any three of the questions that follow. (1×3=3) AE

Different places on the earth's surface receive different amounts of rainfall in a year and that too in different seasons. In general, as we proceed from the Equator towards the Poles, rainfall goes on decreasing steadily. The coastal areas of the world receive greater amounts of rainfall than the interior of the continents. The rainfall is more over the oceans than on the land masses of the world because of being great sources of water. Between the latitudes 350 and 400 N and S of the Equator, the rain is heavier on the eastern coasts and goes on decreasing towards the West. But, between 450 and 650 N and S of Equator, due to the westerlies, the rainfall is first received on the western margins of the continents and it goes on decreasing towards the East. Wherever mountains run parallel to the coast, the rain is greater on the coastal plain, on the windward side and it decreases towards the leeward side. On the basis of the total amount of annual precipitation, major precipitation regimes of the world are identified as follows: The equatorial belt, the windward slopes of the mountains along the western coasts in the cool temperate zone and the coastal areas of the monsoon land receive heavy rainfall of over 200 cm per annum. Interior continental areas receive moderate rainfall varying from 100 - 200 cm per annum. The coastal areas of the continents receive moderate amount of rainfall. The central parts of the tropical land and the eastern and interior parts of the temperate lands receive rainfall varying between 50 – 100 cm per annum. Areas lying in the rain shadow zone of the interior of the continents and high latitudes receive very low rainfall-less than 50 cm per annum. Seasonal distribution of rainfall provides an important aspect to judge its effectiveness. In some regions rainfall is distributed evenly throughout the year such as in the equatorial belt and in the western parts of cool temperate regions.

(i) In general, as we proceed from the equator towards the poles, rainfall goes on ______ steadily.

(a) decreasing
(b) increasing
(c) either increasing or decreasing
(d) neither increasing nor decreasing

Ans. (a) decreasing

(ii) Between the latitudes 350 and 400 N and S of the Equator, the rain is heavier on the ________ coasts.

(a) eastern (b) western
(c) northern (d) southern

Ans. (a) eastern

(iii) In ________, the windward slopes of the mountains along the western coasts in the cool temperate zone and the coastal areas of the monsoon land receive heavy rainfall.

(a) interior continental areas
(b) temperate lands
(c) coastal areas
(d) equatorial belt

Ans. (d) equatorial belt

(iv) The central parts of the tropical land and the eastern and interior parts of the temperate lands receive rainfall varying between:

(a) 25 - 50 cm per annum
(b) 50 - 100 cm per annum
(c) 100 - 150 cm per annum
(d) 150 - 200 cm per annum

Ans. (b) 50 - 100 cm per annum

Q. 2. Read the Passage given below and answer any three of the questions that follow. (1×3=3) AE

The causes for climate change are many. They can be grouped into astronomical and terrestrial causes. The astronomical causes are the changes in solar output associated with sunspot activities. Sunspots are dark and cooler patches on the sun which increase and decrease in a cyclical manner. According to some meteorologists, when the number of sunspots increase, cooler and wetter weather and greater storminess occur. A decrease in sunspot numbers is associated with warm and drier conditions. Yet, these findings are not statistically significant. Another astronomical theory is Milankovitch oscillations, which infer cycles in the variations in the earth's orbital characteristics around the sun, the wobbling of the earth and the changes in the earth's axial tilt. All these alter the amount of insolation received from the sun, which in turn, might have a bearing on the climate. Volcanism is considered as another cause for climate change. Volcanic eruption throws up lots of aerosols into the atmosphere. These aerosols remain in the atmosphere for a considerable period of time reducing the sun's radiation reaching the Earth's surface. After the recent Pinatubo and El Cion volcanic eruptions, the average temperature of the earth fell to some extent for some years. The most important anthropogenic effect on the climate is the increasing trend in the concentration of greenhouse gases in the atmosphere which is likely to cause global warming.

(i) What are dark and cooler patches on the sun which increase and decrease in a cyclical manner called?

(a) Sunsets (b) Sunrise
(c) Sunspots (d) Sun gaps

Ans. (c) Sunspots

(ii) Volcanic eruption throws up lots of ________ into the atmosphere.

(a) aerosols (b) aerocells
(c) aeromoles (d) None of the above

Ans. (a) aerosols

(iii) What is the most important anthropogenic effect on the climates?

(a) Concentration of greenhouse gases in the atmosphere
(b) Concentration of greenhouse gases in the lithosphere
(c) Concentration of greenhouse gases in the exosphere
(d) Concentration of greenhouse gases in the ionosphere

Ans. (a) Concentration of greenhouse gases in the atmosphere

(iv) A decrease in sunspot numbers is associated with ______ and ______ conditions.

(a) warm; wet (b) warm; drier
(c) cold; humid (d) cold; drier

Ans. (b) warm; drier

Q. 3. Read the Passage given below and answer any three of the questions that follow. (1×3=3) AE

The effect of global warming may not be uniform everywhere. Nevertheless, the adverse effect due to global warming will adversely affect the life supporting system. Rise in the sea level due to melting of glaciers and ice-caps and thermal expansion of the sea may inundate large parts of the coastal area and islands, leading to social problems. This is another cause for serious concern for the world community. Efforts have already been initiated to control the emission of GHGs and to arrest the trend towards global warming. Let us hope the world community responds to this challenge and adopts a lifestyle that leaves behind a livable world for the generations to come. Temperature data are available from the middle of the 19th century mostly for western Europe. The reference period for this study is 1961-90. The temperature anomalies for the earlier and later periods are estimated from the average temperature for the period 1961-90. The annual average near-surface air temperature of the world is approximately 14°C. The time series show anomalies of annual near surface temperature over land from 1856-2000, relative to the period1961-90 as normal for the globe.

(i) The adverse effect due to global warming will adversely affect the life _______ system.

(a) supporting (b) surviving
(c) sustaining (d) suspension

Ans. (a) supporting

(ii) Efforts have already been initiated to control the emission of ________and to arrest the trend towards global warming.

(a) CHCs (b) GHGs
(c) HGHs (d) HCHs

Ans. (b) GHGs

(iii) The temperature anomalies for the earlier and later periods are estimated from the average temperature for the period:

(a) 1961-90 (b) 1972-91
(c) 1960-91 (d) 1971-90

Ans. (a) 1961-90

(iv) What is the annual average near-surface air temperature of the world?

(a) Approximately 12°C
(b) Approximately 13°C
(c) Approximately 14°C
(d) Approximately 15°C

Ans. (c) Approximately 14°C

Chapter 13: Water (Oceans)

Objective Type Questions

(1 mark each)

(A) FILL IN THE BLANKS

Q. 1. Water is a ___________ resource. U

Ans. cyclic

Q. 2. Next to air, _______ is the most important element required for the existence of life on earth. U

Ans. water

Q. 3. Nearly____ per cent of the water that falls on land returns to the atmosphere through evaporation. R

Ans. 59

Q. 4. The _______ are confined to the great depressions of the earth's outer layer. R

Ans. ocean

Q. 5. The average width of continental shelves is about _______ km. R

Ans. 80

Q. 6. Massive _________ deposits received over a long time by the continental shelves, become the source of fossil fuels. R

Ans. sedimentary

Q. 7. Canyons and trenches are observed in __________. R

Ans. continental slope

Q. 8. Seamounts are _______ in origin. U

Ans. volcanic

Q. 9. ________ is a flat-topped seamount. R

Ans. Guyots

Q. 10. The _______is a cold current in the North Atlantic Ocean. R

Ans. Labrador Current

Q. 11. The salinity of water in the surface layer of oceans depends mainly on ______and _______. U

Ans. evaporation; precipitation ½+½

(B) ARRANGE IN THE CORRECT ORDER

Q. 1. Arrange the major underwater landforms in the correct order: U+E

(i) Continental slope **(ii) Continental shelf**
(iii) Oceanic deeps **(iv) Deep sea plain**

Options:

(a) i, ii, iii, iv (b) iv, iii, ii, i
(c) ii, i, iv, iii (d) iii, iv, ii, i

Ans. (c) ii, i, iv, iii

Q. 2. Arrange the hydrologic cycle in correct order: E

(i) Collection **(ii) Evaporation**
(iii) Precipitation **(iv) Convection**

Options:

(a) i, iv, iii, ii (b) iv, ii, iii, i

(c) ii, iv, iii, i (d) iii, iv, ii, i

Ans. (c) ii, iv, iii, i

Q. 3. Arrange the salinity of ocean water in correct order: U

(i) Highly saline **(ii) Brackish**

(iii) Marginal **(iv) Saline**

Options:

(a) i, ii, iii, iv (b) ii, iv, iii, i

(c) iii, ii, iv, i (d) iv, i, ii, iii

Ans. (c) iii, ii, iv, i

Source-Based Questions

(3 marks each)

Q. 1. Read the Passage given below and answer any three of the questions that follow. (1×3=3) AE

The oceans are confined to the great depressions of the earth's outer layer. The oceans, unlike the continents, merge so naturally into one another that it is hard to demarcate them. The geographers have divided the oceanic part of the earth into five oceans, namely the Pacific, the Atlantic, the Indian Southern Ocean and the Arctic. The various seas, bays, gulfs and other inlets are parts of these four large oceans. A major portion of the ocean floor is found between 3-6 km below the sea level. The 'land' under the waters of the oceans, that is, the ocean floor exhibits complex and varied features as those observed over the land. The floors of the oceans are rugged with the world's largest mountain ranges, deepest trenches and the largest plains. These features are formed, like those of the continents, by the factors of tectonic, volcanic and depositional processes.

(i) The oceans are confined to which of the Earth's layer?

(a) Outer layer (b) Inner layer

(c) Core layer (d) None of the above

Ans. (a) Outer layer

(ii) Oceans are hard to ______.

(a) demarcate (b) adjust

(c) accommodate (d) find

Ans. (a) demarcate

(iii) Where is the major portion of the ocean floor found?

(a) 2-4 km below the sea level

(b) 3-6 km below the sea level

(c) 6-8 km below the sea level

(d) 8-10km below the sea level

Ans. (b) 3-6 km below the sea level

(iv) The __________ of the oceans are rugged with the world's largest mountain ranges, deepest trenches and the largest plains.

(a) slopes (b) floors

(c) mountains (d) All of the above

Ans. (b) floors

Q. 2. Read the Passage given below and answer any three of the questions that follow. (1×3=3) AE

The continental shelf is the extended margin of each continent occupied by relatively shallow seas and gulfs. It is the shallowest part of the ocean showing an average gradient of 1° or even less. The shelf typically ends at a very steep slope, called the shelf break. The width of the continental shelves vary from one ocean to another. The average width of continental shelves is about 80 km. The shelves are almost absent or very narrow along some of the margins like the coasts of Chile, the west coast of Sumatra, etc. On the contrary, the Siberian shelf in the Arctic Ocean, the largest in the world, stretches to 1,500 km in width. The depth of the shelves also varies. It may be as shallow as 30 m in some areas while in some areas it is as deep as 600 m. The continental shelves are covered with variable thicknesses of sediments brought down by rivers, glaciers, wind, from the land and distributed by waves and currents. Massive sedimentary deposits received over along time by the continental shelves, become the source of fossil fuels.

(i) __________ is the shallowest part of the ocean.

(a) Continental slope (b) Continental drift

(c) Continental zone (d) Continental match

Ans. (b) Continental drift

(ii) The continental shelf typically ends at a very steep slope, called the __________.

(a) shelf break (b) shelf head

(c) shelf end (d) shelf starts

Ans. (a) shelf break

(iii) Where is the Siberian Shelf located?

(a) Indian Ocean (b) Arabian Sea

(c) Arctic Ocean (d) Antarctic Ocean

Ans. (c) Arctic Ocean

(iv) The continental shelf can be as shallow as ______ metres.

(a) 10 (b) 20

(c) 30 (d) 40

Ans. (c) 30

Q. 3. Read the Passage given below and answer an three of the questions that follow. (1×3=3) U+E

The temperature-depth profile for the ocean water shows how the temperature decreases with the increasing depth. The profile shows a boundary region between the surface waters of the ocean and the deeper layers. The boundary usually begins around 100 - 400 m below the sea surface and extends several hundred of metres downward. This boundary region, from where there is a rapid decrease of temperature, is called the thermocline. About 90 per cent of the total volume of water is found below the thermocline in the deep ocean. In this zone, temperatures approach 0°C. The temperature structure of oceans over middle and low latitudes can be described as a three-layer system from surface to the bottom. The first layer represents the top layer of warm oceanic water and it is about 500 m thick with temperatures ranging between 20° and 25°C. This layer, within the tropical region, is present throughout the year but in mid latitudes it develops only during summer. The second layer called the thermocline layer lies below the first layer and is characterised by rapid decrease in temperature with increasing depth. The thermocline is 500-1,000 m thick. The third layer is very cold and extends upto the deep ocean floor. In the Arctic and Antarctic circles, the surface water temperatures are close to 0°C and so the temperature change with the depth is very slight. Here, only one layer of cold water exists, which extends from surface to deep ocean floor.

(i) The ________ profile for the ocean water shows how the temperature decreases with the increasing depth.

(a) temperature-depth
(b) area-depth
(c) altitude-depth
(d) vertical-depth

Ans. (a) temperature-depth

(ii) What is the temperature structure in the first layer of the ocean water?

(a) Ranges between 20°and 25°C
(b) Ranges between 15°and 20°C
(c) Ranges between 25°and 30°C
(d) Ranges between 35°and 40°C

Ans. (a) Ranges between 20°and 25°C

(iii) What is the water temperature in Arctic and Antarctic circles?

(a) close to 0°C (b) close to 1°C
(c) close to 1°C (d) close to 3°C

Ans. (a) close to 0°C

(iv) Which layer is characterised by rapid decrease in temperature with increasing depth?

(a) The thermocline layer
(b) The thermostat layer
(c) The thermostatic layer
(d) The thermolise layer

Ans. (a) The thermocline layer

Chapter 14: Movements of Ocean Water

Objective Type Questions (1 mark each)

FILL IN THE BLANKS

Q. 1. ________ are actually the energy which moves across the ocean surface. R

Ans. Waves

Q. 2. The highest point of a wave is called the ________. R

Ans. crest

Q. 3. The lowest point of a wave is called______. R

Ans. trough

Q. 4. ________ is the horizontal distance between two successive crests. U

Ans. Wavelength

Q. 5. An area has diurnal tide if it experiences one high and one low tide every ______ day. R

Ans. lunar

Q. 6. __________flows are of great importance in navigation. U

Ans. Tidal

Q. 7. The time between the low tide and high tide, when the tide is rising, is called the _____. R

Ans. flow/flood

Q. 8. The ___________ force acts to counter balance the gravity. R

Ans. centrifugal

Q. 9. Heating by ___________causes the water to expand. R

Ans. solar energy

Q. 10. ________ currents move very slowly, usually around 0.8-1.2 in per second. R

Ans. Deep water

Q. 11. __________ is any large system of circulating ocean currents, particularly those involved with large wind movements. [R]

Ans. A gyre

Q. 12. The movement of the water at the surface of the ocean is known as __________currents. [R]

Ans. surface

Source-Based Questions

(3 marks each)

Q. 1. Read the Passage given below and answer any three of the questions that follow. (1 × 3 = 3) [U]

The periodical rise and fall of the sea level, once or twice a day, mainly due to the attraction of the sun and the moon, is called a tide. Movement of water caused by meteorological effects (winds and atmospheric pressure changes) are called surges. Surges are not regular like tides. The study of tides is very complex, spatially and temporally, as it has great variations in frequency, magnitude and height. The moon's gravitational pull to a great extent and to a lesser extent the sun's gravitational pull, are the major causes for the occurrence of tides. Another factor is centrifugal force, which is the force that acts to counter balance the gravity. Together, the gravitational pull and the centrifugal force are responsible for creating the two major tidal bulges on the earth. On the side of the earth facing the moon, a tidal bulge occurs while on the opposite side though the gravitational attraction of the moon is less as it is farther away, the centrifugal force causes tidal bulge on the other side. The 'tide-generating' force is the difference between these two forces; i.e., the gravitational attraction of the moon and the centrifugal force. On the surface of the earth, nearest the moon, pull or the attractive force of the moon is greater than the centrifugal force, and so there is a net force causing a bulge towards the moon. On the opposite side of the earth, the attractive force is less, as it is farther away from the moon, the centrifugal force is dominant. Hence, there is a net force away from the moon. It creates the second bulge away from the moon. On the surface of the earth, the horizontal tide generating forces are more important than the vertical forces in generating the tidal bulges. The tidal bulges on wide continental shelves, have greater height. When tidal bulge shifts the mid oceanic islands, they become low. The shape of bays and estuaries along a coastline can also magnify the intensity of tides. Funnel-shaped bays greatly change tidal magnitudes. When the tide is channelled between islands or into bays and estuaries, they are called tidal currents.

(i) Movement of water caused by meteorological effects (winds and atmospheric pressure changes) are called:

(a) Surges **(b)** Tides

(c) Gravity **(d)** None of these

Ans. (a) Surges

(ii) Which of the following forces are responsible for creating the two major tidal bulges on the earth:

(a) Gravitational pull **(b)** Centrifugal force

(c) Vertical forces **(d)** Both (a) and (b)

Ans. **(d)** Both (a) and (b)

(iii) On the surface of the earth, nearest the moon, pull or the attractive force of the moon is __________ the centrifugal force.

(a) greater than **(b)** smaller than

(c) equal to **(d)** None of these

Ans. (a) greater than

(iv) When the tide is channelled between islands or into bays and estuaries, they are called tidal:

(a) Bulges **(b)** Currents

(c) Magnitudes **(d)** None of these

Ans. (b) Currents

Q. 2. Study the given graph carefully and answer any three of the following questions: (1×3=3) [E]

Waves are actually the energy, not the water as such, which moves across the ocean surface. Water particles only travel in a small circle as a wave passes. Wind provides energy to the waves. Wind causes waves to travel in the ocean and the energy is released on shorelines. The motion of the surface water seldom affects the stagnant deep bottom water of the oceans. Asa wave approaches the beach, it slows down. This is due to the friction occurring between the dynamic water and the sea floor. And, when the depth of water is less than half the wavelength of the wave, the wave breaks. The largest waves are found in the open oceans. Waves continue to grow larger as they move and absorb energy from the wind. Most of the waves are caused by the wind driving against water. When a breeze of two knots or less blows over calm water, small ripples form and grow as the wind speed increases until white caps appear in the breaking waves. Waves may travel thousands of km before rolling ashore, breaking and dissolving as surf. A wave's size and shape reveal its origin. Steep waves are fairly young ones and are probably formed by local wind. Slow and steady waves originate from far away places, possibly from another hemisphere. The maximum wave height is determined by the strength of the wind, i.e. how long it blows and the area over which it blows in a single direction. Waves travel because wind pushes the water body in its course while gravity pulls the crests of the waves downward. The falling water pushes the former troughs upward, and the wave moves to a new position. The actual motion of the water beneath the waves is circular. It indicates that things are carried up and forward as the wave approaches, and down and back as it passes.

(i) Which of the following provides energy to the waves?

(a) Wind (b) Temperature

(c) Pressure (d) Friction

Ans. (a) Wind

(ii) The largest waves are found in the:

(a) Coastal areas (b) Open Oceans

(c) Oceans Floors (d) All the above

Ans. (b) Open Oceans

(iii) As a wave approaches the beach, it slows down due to:

(a) Wind (b) Temperature

(c) Pressure (d) Friction

Ans. (d) Friction

(iv) The actual motion of the water beneath the waves is:

(a) Elliptical (b) Circular

(c) Rectangular (d) Pyramidal

Ans. (b) Circular

Q. 3. Read the Passage given below and answer any three of the questions that follow. (1×3=3) AE

Ocean currents have a number of direct and indirect influences on human activities. West coasts of the continents in tropical and subtropical latitudes (except close to the Equator) are bordered by cool waters. Their average temperatures are relatively low with an arrow diurnal and annual ranges. There is fog, but generally the areas are arid. West coasts of the continents in the middle and higher latitudes are bordered by warm waters which cause a distinct marine climate. They are characterised by cool summers and relatively mild winters with a narrow annual range of temperatures. Warm currents flow parallel to the east coasts of the continents in tropical and subtropical latitudes. This results in warm and rainy climates. These areas lie in the western margins of the subtropical anti-cyclones. The mixing of warm and cold currents helps to replenish the oxygen and favour the growth of planktons, the primary food for fish population. The best fishing grounds of the world exist mainly in these mixing zones.

(i) ________ have a number of direct and indirect influences on human activities.

(a) Ocean currents (b) Fisheries

(c) Hunting (d) Tides

Ans. (a) Ocean currents

(ii) Which coasts of the continents in tropical and subtropical latitudes (except close to the Equator) are bordered by cool waters?

(a) East (b) West

(c) North (d) South

Ans. (b) West

(iii) Where do the best fishing grounds of the world exist?

(a) Isolated zones (b) Warm zones

(c) Cold zones (d) Mixing zones

Ans. (d) Mixing zones

(iv) What happens when the warm and cold currents mix?

(a) Helps to replenish the oxygen

(b) Favours the growth of planktons

(c) Primary food for fish population

(d) All of the above

Ans. (d) All of the above

Chapter 15: Life on The Earth

is not in the syllabus of 2023-24

Chapter 16: Biodiversity and Conservation

Objective Type Questions

(1 mark each)

(A) FILL IN THE BLANKS

Q. 1. ________ is a system in constant evolution. R

Ans. Biodiversity

Q. 2. Pesticides and other pollutants such as hydrocarbons and toxic heavy metals are called ________ species. R

Ans. sensitive

Q. 3. _________ are the basic building blocks of various life forms. R

Ans. Genes

Q. 4. _________ biodiversity refers to the variation of genes within species. R

Ans. Genetic

Q. 5. Species that are not the natural inhabitants of the local habitat but are introduced into the system are called _________ species. R

Ans. exotic

Q. 6. _________ species are confined to limited areas or thinly scattered over a wider area. U

Ans. Rare

Q. 7. If species of plants and animals become endangered, they cause _________ in the environment. R

Ans. degradation

Q. 8. Tigers, elephants, rhinoceros, crocodiles, minks and birds have been categorised as _________ category. U

Ans. endangered

Source-Based Questions

(3 marks each)

Q. 1. Read the Passage given below and answer any three of the questions that follow. (1×3=3) E

Since the last few decades, growth in human population has increased the rate of consumption of natural resources. It has accelerated the loss of species and habitation in different parts of the world. Tropical regions which occupy only about one-fourth of the total area of the world, contain about three-fourth of the world human population. Over exploitation of resources and deforestation have become rampant to fulfil the needs of large population. As these tropical rain forests contain 50 per cent of the species on the earth, destruction of natural habitats has proved disastrous for the entire biosphere. Natural calamities such as earthquakes, floods, volcanic eruptions, forest fires, droughts, etc. cause damage to the flora and fauna of the earth, bringing change the biodiversity of respective affected regions. Pesticides and other pollutants such as hydrocarbons and toxic heavy metals destroy the weak and sensitive species. Species which are not the natural inhabitants of the local habitat but are introduced into the system, are called exotic species. There are many examples when a natural biotic community of the ecosystem suffered extensive damage because of the introduction of exotic species. During the last few decades, some animals like tigers, elephants, rhinoceros, crocodiles, minks and birds were hunted mercilessly by poachers for their horn, tusks, hides, etc. It has resulted in the rendering of certain types of organisms as endangered category. The International Union of Conservation of Nature and Natural Resources (IUCN) has classified the threatened species of plants and animals into three categories for the purpose of their conservation.

(i) According to the passage which of the following has increased the rate of consumption of natural resources?

(a) Pollution (b) Population
(c) Temperature (d) None of these

Ans. (b) Population

(ii) Tropical regions has occupied only about _________ of the total area of the world.

(a) 1/4 (b) 1/3
(c) 1/2 (d) 2/3

Ans. (a) 1/4

(iii) Species which are not the natural inhabitants of the local habitat but are introduced into the system are called:

(a) Sensitive species (b) Endangered species
(c) Exotic species (d) Eusocial species

Ans. (c) Exotic species

(iv) The International Union of Conservation of Nature and Natural Resources has classified the threatened species of plants and animals into how many categories?

(a) 5 (b) 7
(c) 3 (d) 6

Ans. (c) 3

Q. 2. Read the Passage given below and answer any three of the questions that follow: (1×3=3) E

The critical problem is not merely the conservation of species nor the habitat but the continuation of process of conservation. The Government of India along with 155 other nations have signed the Convention of Biodiversity at the Earth Summit held at Rio de Janeiro, Brazil in June 1992. The world conservation strategy has suggested the following steps for biodiversity conservation:

(a) Efforts should be made to preserve the species that are endangered.
(b) Prevention of extinction requires proper planning and management.
(c) Varieties of food crops, forage plants, timber trees, livestock, animals and their wild relatives should be preserved.
(d) Each country should identify habitats of wild relatives and ensure their protection.
(e) Habitats where species feed, breed, rest and nurse their young should be safeguarded and protected.

(f) International trade in wild plants and animals be regulated.

To protect, preserve and propagate the variety of species within natural boundaries, the Government of India passed the Wild Life (Protection) Act, 1972, under which national parks and sanctuaries were established and biosphere reserves declared. There are some countries which are situated in the tropical region; they possess a large number of the world's species diversity. They are called mega diversity centres. There are 12 such countries, namely Mexico, Columbia, Ecuador, Peru, Brazil, Democratic Republic of Congo, Madagascar, China, India, Malaysia, Indonesia and Australia in which these centres are located. In order to concentrate resources on those areas that are most vulnerable, the International Union for the Conservation of Nature and Natural Resources (IUCN) has identified certain areas as biodiversity hotspots. Hotspots are defined according to their vegetation. Plants are important because these determine the primary productivity of an ecosystem. Most, but not all, of the hotspots rely on species-rich ecosystems for food, firewood, cropland, and income from timber. In Madagascar, for example, about 85 percent of the plants and animals are found nowhere else in the world, Other hotspots in wealthy countries are facing different types of pressures. The islands of Hawaii have many unique plants and animals that are threatened by introduced species and land development.

(i) The Government of India along with how many other nations have signed the Convention of Biodiversity in June 1992?

(a) 165 (b) 173

(c) 158 (d) 155

Ans. (d) 155

(ii) Which of the following steps were suggested by the world conservation for biodiversity conservation:

(a) Efforts should be made to preserve the species that are endangered.

(b) Prevention of extinction requires proper planning and management.

(c) International trade in wild plants and animals be regulated.

(d) All the above

Ans. (d) All the above

(iii) To protect, preserve and propagate the variety of species within natural boundaries, the Government of India passed:

(a) Wildlife (Protection) Act, 1972

(b) Wildlife (Protection) Act, 1977

(c) Wildlife (Protection) Act, 1975

(d) Wildlife (Protection) Act, 1973

Ans. (a) Wildlife (Protection) Act, 1972

(iv) Hotspots are defined according to their:

(a) Wetlands (b) Species

(c) Vegetation (d) None of these

Ans. (c) Vegetation

(v) How many mega diversity countries are there?

(a) 10 (b) 11

(c) 12 (d) 13

Ans. (c) 12

(vi) Why are plants important?

(a) For the primary productivity of an ecosystem

(b) For the secondary productivity of an ecosystem

(c) For the survival of decomposers

(d) None of the above

Ans. (a) For the primary productivity of an ecosystem

Part B: India - Physical Environment

Chapter 1: India – Location

Objective Type Questions

(1 mark each)

(A) FILL IN THE BLANKS

Q. 1. India's territorial limit further extends towards the sea upto ______ nautical miles from the coast. R

Ans. 12

Q. 2. The USA has ________ time zones. R

Ans. seven

Q. 3. Sri Lanka and Maldives are the two island countries located in the _______ Ocean. R

Ans. Indian

Q. 4. ________ part of India extends towards the Indian Ocean. R

Ans. Peninsular

Q. 5. India accounts for _________ per cent of the world's land surface area. R

Ans. 2.4

Q. 6. India is located in the ___________ part of the continent of Asia. R

Ans. south-central

Q. 7. _________ is separated from India by the Gulf of Mannar and Palk Strait. R

Ans. Sri Lanka

Q. 8. ___________ **is located in the Arabian Sea.** R

Ans. Lakshadweep

Q. 9. **Andaman and Nicobar is located in the___________ .** R

Ans. Bay of Bengal

Q. 10. **The northern part of India lies in the _________ zone.** R

Ans. sub-tropical

Chapter 2: Structure and Physiography

Objective Type Questions

(1 mark each)

(A) FILL IN THE BLANKS

Q. 1. **Current estimation shows that the earth is approximately _____years old.** R

Ans. 460 million

Q. 2. **The ___________ mountains are tectonic in origin, dissected by fast-flowing rivers which are in their youthful stage.** E

Ans. Himalayas

Q. 3. **The Great Himalayan range is also known as the ___________range.** R

Ans. Central axial

Q. 4. **The relief and physiography of India has been greatly influenced by the______ and ___________ processes active in the Indian subcontinent.** U

Ans. geological; geomorphological **(½ + ½= 1)**

Q. 5. ___________**are the thick deposits of glacial clay and other materials embedded with moraines.** R

Ans. Karewas

Q. 6. **The ___________ river in the valley of Kashmir is still in its youth stage and yet forms meanders.** R

Ans. Jhelum

Q. 7. **The ___________ extends from the east of the Bhutan Himalayas up to the Diphu pass in the East.** R

Ans. Arunachal Himalayas

Q. 8. **Mizoram is also known as the _________ basin.** R

Ans. Molasses

Q. 9. **The _________ is the low-lying land at the foot of the Himalayas.** R

Ans. Terai

Q. 10. _________**is the only significant tributary of the river Chambal that originates from the Aravalli in the West.** R

Ans. Banas

Q. 11. **The _____________ are bound to the West by the Aravali Range.** R

Ans. Central Highlands

Q. 12. **To the Northwest of the Aravalli Hills lies the _________ Desert.** R

Ans. Great Indian

Q. 13. **The Andaman in the North and the Nicobar in the South are separated by a water body which is called the _________.** R

Ans. Ten Degree Channel

Q. 14. __________ **flows through a deep gorge after crossing Namcha Barwa.** R

Ans. Brahmaputra

Q. 15. **Lakshadweep and Minicoy are located in _____________ Sea.** R

Ans. Arabian

(B) ARRANGE IN THE CORRECT ORDER

Q. 1. **Arrange the Eastern hills as per the North -South Alignment.** E

(i) **Manipur Hills** **(ii)** **Mizo Hills**

(iii) **Patkai Hills** **(iv)** **Naga Hills**

Options:

(a) i, ii, iii, iv **(b)** iii, ii, iv, i

(c) ii, iii, iv, i **(d)** iv, ii, i, iii

Ans. (b) iii, ii, iv, i

Q. 2. **Arrange the following hills from North to South direction:** E

(i) **Zaskar Range** **(ii)** **Karakoram Range**

(iii) **Ladakh Range** **(iv)** **Shiwalik Range**

Options:

(a) iv, iii, ii, i **(b)** iii, ii, iv, i

(c) iii, iv, i, ii **(d)** ii, i, iv, iii

Ans. (c) iii, iv, i, ii

Q. 3. Arrange the following rivers from South to North direction: E

(i) **Mahanadi** (ii) **Godavari**

(iii) **Cauvery** (iv) **Krishna**

Options:

(a) i, ii, iv, iii **(b)** iii, iv, ii, i

(c) iv, iii, ii, i **(d)** ii, iii, iv, i

Ans. (b) iii, iv, ii, i

Source-Based Questions (3 marks each)

Q. 1. Read the Passage given below and answer any three of the questions that follow. (1×3=3) U

Rising from the height of 150 m above the river plains up to an elevation of 600-900 m is the irregular triangle known as the Peninsular Plateau. Delhi ridge in the northwest, (extension of Aravalis), the Rajmahal hills in the east, Gir range in the west and the Cardamom hills in the south constitute the outer extent of the Peninsular plateau. However, an extension of this is also seen in the northeast, in the form of Shillong and Karbi-Anglong plateau. The Peninsular India is made up of a series of patland plateaus such as the Hazaribagh plateau, the Palamu plateau, the Ranchi plateau, the Malwa plateau, the Coimbatore plateau and the Karnataka plateau, etc. This is one of the oldest and the most stable landmass of India. The general elevation of the plateau is from the west to the east, which is also proved by the pattern of the flow of rivers. Some of the important physiographic features of this region are tors, block mountains, rift valleys, spurs, bare rocky structures, series of hummocky hills and wall-like quartzite dykes offering natural sites for water storage. The western and north western part of the plateau has an emphatic presence of black soil. This Peninsular plateau has under gone recurrent phases of upliftment and submergence accompanied by crustal faulting and fractures. (The Bhima fault needs special mention, because of its recurrent seismic activities). These spatial variations have brought in elements of diversity in the relief of the Peninsular plateau. The north western part of the plateau has a complex relief of ravines and gorges. The ravines of Chambal, Bhind and Morena are some of the well-known examples.

(i) The __________India is made up of a series of patland plateaus such as the Hazaribagh plateau, the Palamu plateau.

(a) Peninsular **(b)** Himalayas

(c) Delta **(d)** None of the above

Ans. (a) Peninsular

(ii) The western and north western part of the plateau has an emphatic presence of ______ soil.

(a) black **(b)** red

(c) yellow **(d)** brown

Ans. (a) black

(iii) ________ is one of the oldest and the most stable landmass of India.

(a) Malwa Plateau **(b)** Punjab Plateau

(c) Aravalli Plateau **(d)** Gir Plateau

Ans. (a) Malwa Plateau

(iv) What is the general elevation of the Peninsular Plateau in India?

(a) East to West **(b)** West to East

(c) North to South **(d)** South to North

Ans. (b) West to East

Q. 2. Read the Passage given below and answer any three of the questions that follow. (1×3=3) U

Kashmir or North western Himalayas comprise a series of ranges such as the Karakoram, Ladakh, Zaskar and Pir Panjal. The north eastern part of the Kashmir Himalayas is a cold desert, which lies between the Greater Himalayas and the Karakoram ranges. Between the Great Himalayas and the Pir Panjal range lies the world-famous valley of Kashmir and the famous Dal Lake. Important glaciers of South Asia such as the Baltoro and Siachen are also found in this region. The Kashmir Himalayas are also famous for Karewa formations, which are useful for the cultivation of Zafran, a local variety of saffron. Some of the important passes of the region are Zoji La on the Great Himalayas, Banihal on the Pir Panjal, Photu La on the Zaskar and Khardung La on the Ladakh range. Some of the important fresh lakes such as Dal and Wular and salt water lakes such as Pangong Tso and Tso Moriri are also in this region. This region is drained by the river Indus, and its tributaries such as the Jhelum and the Chenab. The Kashmir and north western Himalayas are well-known for their scenic beauty and picturesque landscape. The landscape of Himalayas is a major source of attraction for adventure tourists. Srinagar, capital city of the union territory of Jammu and Kashmir is located on the banks of Jhelum river. Dal Lake in Srinagar presents an interesting physical feature. Jhelum in the valley of Kashmir is still in its youth stage and yet forms meanders – a typical feature associated with the mature stage in the evolution of fluvial land form.

(i) The north eastern part of the Kashmir Himalayas is a ________ desert.

(a) cold **(b)** hot

(c) dry **(d)** windy

Ans. (a) cold

(ii) The Kashmir Himalayas are useful for the cultivation of:

(a) Zafran **(b)** Pepper

(c) Peach **(d)** Grapes

Ans. (a) Zafran

(iii) Name the capital city of the union territory of Jammu and Kashmir.

(a) Ladakh (b) Srinagar

(c) Uri (d) Baramula

Ans. (b) Srinagar

(iv) Pangong Tso and Tso Moriri are located in:

(a) Ladakh (b) Srinagar

(c) Siachen Glacier (d) None of the above

Ans. (a) Ladakh

Q. 3. Read the Passage given below and answer any three of the questions that follow. (1×3=3) U+A

The Himachal and Uttarakhand Himalayas lies approximately between the Ravi in the west and the Kali (a tributary of Ghaghara in the east. It is drained by two major Ghaghara) systems of India, i.e., the Indus and the Ganga. Tributaries of the Indus include the river Ravi, the Beas and the Satluj, and the tributaries of Ganga flowing through this region include the Yamuna and the Ghaghara. The northernmost part of the Himachal Himalayas is an extension of the Ladakh cold desert, which lies in the Spiti subdivision of district Lahul and Spiti. All the three ranges of Himalayas are prominent in this section also. These are the Great Himalayan range, the Lesser Himalayas (which is locally known as Dhaoladhar in Himachal Pradesh and Nagtibhain Uttarakhand) and the Shiwalik range from the North to the South. In this section of Lesser Himalayas, the altitude between 1,000-2,000 m specially attracted to the British colonial administration, and subsequently, some of the important hill stations such as Dharamshala, Mussoorie, Shimla, Kaosani and the cantonment towns and health resorts such as Shimla, Mussoorie, Kasauli, Almora, Lansdowne and Ranikhet, etc. were developed in this region. The two distinguishing features of this region from the point of view of physiography are the 'Shiwalik' and 'Dun formations'. Some important duns located in this region are the Chandigarh-Kalka dun, Nalagarh dun, Dehra Dun, Harike dun and the Kota dun, etc. Dehra Dun is the largest of all the duns with an approximate length of 35-45 km and a width of 22-25 km. In the Great Himalayan range, the valleys are mostly inhabited by the Bhotias. These are nomadic groups who migrate to 'Bugyals' (the summer grasslands in the higher reaches) during summer months and return to the valleys during winters. The famous 'Valley of flowers' is also situated in this region. The places of pilgrimage such as the Gangotri, Yamunotri, Kedarnath, Badrinathand Hemkund Sahib are also situated in this part. The region is also known to have five famous Prayags.

(i) The rivers Ravi, the Beas and the Satluj are the tributaries of:

(a) Ganga (b) Indus

(c) Tista (d) None of the above

Ans. (b) Indus

(ii) What is the other name for the Lesser Himalayas?

(a) Dhaoladhar (b) Shiwalik

(c) Kasi (d) Garo

Ans. (a) Dhaoladhar

(iii) __________ is the largest of all the duns with an approximate length of 35-45 km and a width of 22-25 km.

(a) Shimla (b) Dehra Dun

(c) Kasauli (d) Solan

Ans. (b) Dehra Dun

(iv) The Great Himalayan Range is inhabited by which nomadic group?

(a) Bhotia (b) Gujjar

(c) Shepherds (d) Inuks

Ans. (a) Bhotia

Chapter 3: Drainage System

Objective Type Questions

(1 mark each)

(A) FILL IN THE BLANKS

Q. 1. The drainage pattern resembling the branches of a tree is known as __________. R

Ans. dendritic

Q. 2. When the rivers discharge their waters from all directions in a lake or depression, the pattern is known as __________. R

Ans. centripetal

Q. 3. River basins and watersheds are marked by __________. R

Ans. unity

Q. 4. The Tapi and the Periyar systems discharge their waters in the __________ Sea. R

Ans. Arabian

Q. 5. __________ lake is generally formed as a river cuts through a meander neck to shorten its course. U

Ans. Ox bow

Q. 6. The Indus River is also known as the ________. R

Ans. Sindhu

Q. 7. In Tibet, the Indus River is known as ________. R

Ans. Singi Khamban

Q. 8. The ________ is the name given to the five rivers of Punjab. R

Ans. Panjnad

Q. 9. The ________ joins the Chenab near Jhang in Pakistan. R

Ans. Jhelum

Q. 10. The ________ is formed by two streams, the Chandra and the Bhaga. R

Ans. Chenab

Q. 11. The Yamuna has its source in the ________ Glacier. R

Ans. Yamunotri

Q. 12. The ________ river rises in the Nepal Himalayas between the Dhaulagiri and Mount Everest and drains the central part of Nepal. R

Ans. Gandak

Q. 13. River ________ is known as River Jamuna in Bangladesh. R

Ans. Brahmaputra

Q. 14. The________ is the largest Peninsular river system. R

Ans. Godavari

Q. 15. The River ________ is located in Goa. R

Ans. Mandovi/ Juari **(Any One)**

(B) ARRANGE IN THE CORRECT ORDER

Q. 1. Arrange the Peninsular rivers from the longest to the shortest in the correct order: E

(i) Godavari **(ii) Krishna**

(iii) Kaveri **(iv) Narmada**

Options:

(a) iv, ii, iii, i **(b)** i, ii, iii, iv

(c) iv, iii, ii, i **(d)** ii, iii, iv, i

Ans. (b) i, ii, iii, iv

Q. 2. Arrange the course of River Ganga in the correct order: U

(i) Rises at the terminus of the Gangotri Glacier

(ii) Forms clear water of Bhagirathi River

(iii) Flows down the Himalayas

(iv) Joins the Alaknanda River

Options:

(a) iv, iii, ii, i **(b)** iii, ii, i, iv

(c) i, ii, iii, iv **(d)** ii, iii, i, iv

Ans. (c) i, ii, iii, iv

Q. 3. Arrange the course of River Jhelum in India in the correct order: E

(i) Rises from a spring at Verinag situated at the foot of the Pir Panjal

(ii) Flows through Wular Lake

(iii) Flows through Srinagar

(iv) Joins the Chenab near Jhang in Pakistan

Options:

(a) i, iii, ii, iv **(b)** i, ii, iii, iv

(c) iv, iii, ii, i **(d)** iii, ii, i, iv

Ans. (a) i, iii, ii, iv

Source-Based Questions

(3 marks each)

Q. 1. Read the Passage given below and answer any three of the questions that follow. (1×3=3) AE

The Brahmaputra, one of the largest rivers of the world, has its origin in the Chemayungdung Glacier of the Kailash range near the Mansarovar lake. From here, it traverses eastward longitudinally for a distance of nearly 1,200 km in a dry and flat region of southern Tibet, where it is known as the Tsangpo, which means 'the purifier.' The Rango Tsangpo is the major right bank tributary of this river in Tibet. It emerges as a turbulent and dynamic river after carving out a deep gorge in the Central Himalayas near Namcha Barwa (7,755 m).The river emerges from the foothills under the name of Siang or Dihang. It enters India west of Sadiya town in Arunachal Pradesh. Flowing southwest, it receives its main left bank tributaries, viz., Dibang or Sikang and Lohit; thereafter, it is known as the Brahmaputra. The Brahmaputra receives numerous tributaries in its 750 km long journey through the Assam valley. Its major left bank tributaries are the Burhi Dihing and Dhansari (South) whereas the important right bank tributaries are the Subansiri, Kameng, Manasand, Sankosh. The Subansiri which has its origin in Tibet, is an antecedent river. The Brahmaputra enters into Bangladesh near Dhubri and flows southward. In Bangladesh, the Tista joins it on its right bank from where the river is known as the Jamuna. It finally merges with the river Padma, which falls in the Bay of Bengal. The Brahmaputra is well-known for floods, channel shifting and bank erosion. This is due to the fact that most of its tributaries are large, and bring large quantity of sediments owing to heavy rainfall in its catchment area.

(i) Where does the River Brahmaputra originate?

(a) Chemayungdung Glacier

(b) Zemu Glacier

(c) Namik Glacier

(d) Siachen Glacier

Ans. (a) Chemayungdung Glacier

(ii) The ________ is the major right bank tributary of Brahmaputra river in Tibet.

(a) Rango Tsangpo (b) Tsangpo Rango

(c) Rancho Tsangpo (d) Namcha Tsangpo

Ans. (a) Rango Tsangpo

(iii) The Brahmaputra enters into Bangladesh near:

(a) Jaflong (b) Mawlynnong

(c) Dhubri (d) Langchen Khambab

Ans. (c) Dhubri

(iv) The _________ is well-known for floods, channel shifting and bank erosion.

(a) Jhelum (b) Brahmaputra

(c) Narmada (d) Tapi

Ans. (b) Brahmaputra

Q. 2. Read the Passage given below and answer any three of the questions that follow. (1×3=3) AE

The Indus River is one of the largest river basins of the world, covering an area of 11,65,000 sq. km (in India it is 321, 289 sq. km and a total length of 2,880 km (in India 1,114 km). The Indus also known as the Sindhu, is the westernmost of the Himalayan rivers in India. It originates from a glacier near Bokhar Chu (31°15'N latitude and 81°40' E longitude) in the Tibetan region at an altitude of 4,164 m in the Kailash Mountain range. In Tibet, it is known as 'Singi Khamban; or Lion's mouth. After flowing in the northwest direction between the Ladakh and Zaskar ranges, it passes through Ladakh and Baltistan. It cuts across the Ladakh range, forming a spectacular gorge near Gilgit in Jammu and Kashmir. It enters into Pakistan near Chilasin the Dardistan region. The Indus receives a number of Himalayan tributaries such as the Shyok, the Gilgit, the Zaskar, the Hunza, the Nubra, the Shigar, the Gasting and the Dras. It finally emerges out of the hills near Attock where it receives the Kabul river on its right bank. The other important tributaries joining the right bank of the Indus are the Khurram, the Tochi, the Gomal, theViboa and the Sangar. They all originate in the Sulaiman ranges. The river flows southward and receives 'Panjnad' a little above Mithankot. The Panjnad is the name given to the five rivers of Punjab, namely the Satluj, the Beas, the Ravi, the Chenab and the Jhelum. It finally discharges into the Arabian Sea, east of Karachi. The Indus flows in India only through Jammu and Kashmir. The Jhelum, an important tributary of the Indus, rises from a spring at Verinag situated at the foot of the Pir Panjal in the south-eastern part of the valley of Kashmir. It flows through Srinagar and the Wular lake before entering Pakistan through a deep narrow gorge. It joins the Chenab near Jhang in Pakistan. The Chenab is the largest tributary of the Indus. It is formed by two streams, the Chandra and the Bhaga, which join at Tandi near Keylong in Himachal Pradesh. Hence, it is also known as Chandrabhaga. The river flows for 1,180 km before entering into Pakistan. The Ravi is another important tributary of the Indus. It rises west of the Rohtang pass in the Kullu hills of Himachal Pradesh and flows through the Chamba valley of the state. Before entering Pakistan and joining the Chenab near Sarai Sidhu, it drains the area lying between the southeastern part of the Pir Panjal and the Dhauladhar ranges. The Beas is another important tributary of the Indus originating from the Beas Kund near the Rohtang Pass at an elevation of 4,000 m above the mean sea level. The river flows through the Kullu valley and forms gorges at Kati and Largi in the Dhaoladhar range. It enters the Punjab plains where it meets the Satluj near Harike. The Satluj originates in the 'Raksas tal' near Mansarovar at an altitude of 4,555 m in Tibet where it is known as Langchen Khambab. It flows almost parallel to the Indus for about 400 km before entering India, and comes out of a gorge at Rupar. It passes through the Shipkila on the Himalayan ranges and enters the Punjab plains. It is an antecedent river. It is a very important tributary as it feeds the canal system of the Bhakra Nangal project.

(i) The ________ originates from a glacier near Bokhar Chu.

(a) Satluj (b) Indus

(c) Beas (d) Ravi

Ans. (b) Indus

(ii) The Indus flows in India only through ________.

(a) Jammu and Kashmir

(b) Punjab

(c) Mizoram

(d) Nagaland

Ans. (a) Jammu and Kashmir

(iii) Which river originates near Beas Kund near the Rohtang Pass?

(a) Indus (b) Ravi

(c) Beas (d) Jhelum

Ans. (c) Beas

(iv) Which river is known as Langchen Khambab in Tibet?

(a) Satluj (b) Beas

(c) Jhelum (d) Ravi

Ans. (a) Satluj

Q. 3. Read the Passage given below and answer any three of the questions that follow. (1×3=3) AE

The Himalayan drainage system has evolved through a long geological history. It mainly includes the Ganga, the Indus and the Brahmaputra river basins. Since these are fed both by melting of snow and precipitation, rivers of this system are perennial. These rivers pass through the giant gorges carved out by the erosional activity carried on simultaneously with the uplift of the Himalayas. Besides deep gorges, these rivers also form V-shaped valleys, rapids and waterfalls in their mountainous course. While entering the plains, they form depositional features like flat valleys, ox-bow lakes, flood plains, braided channels, and deltas near the river mouth. In the Himalayan reaches, the course of these rivers is highly tortuous, but over the plains they display as strong meandering tendency and shift their courses frequently. River Kosi, also known as the 'sorrow of Bihar', has been notorious for frequently changing its course. The Kosi brings huge quantity of sediments from its upper reaches and deposits it in the plains. The course gets blocked, and consequently, the river changes its course.

(i) The _________ drainage system mainly includes the Ganga, the Indus and the Brahmaputra river basins.

(a) Peninsular (b) Himalayan

(c) Brahmaputra (d) None of the above

Ans. (b) Himalayan

(ii) The Himalayan rivers are _______ in nature.

(a) Perennial (b) Dry

(c) Destructive (d) Snow laden

Ans. (a) Perennial

(iii) The ________ brings huge quantity of sediments from its upper reaches and deposits it in the plains.

(a) Kosi (b) Krishna

(c) Mahanadi (d) Ganga

Ans. (a) Kosi

(iv) Which river is notorious for frequently changing its course?

(a) Narmada (b) Tapi

(c) Kosi (d) None of the above

Ans. (c) Kosi

Chapter 4: Climate

Objective Type Questions

(1 mark each)

(A) FILL IN THE BLANKS

Q. 1. __________ is the momentary state of the atmosphere. R

Ans. Weather

Q. 2. The monsoon regime emphasises the unity of India with the rest of ________ Asian region. U

Ans. southeast

Q. 3. While snowfall occurs in the ________, it only rains over the rest of the country. R

Ans. Himalayas

Q. 4. The _________ provides an invincible shield to protect the subcontinent from the cold northern winds. U

Ans. Himalayas

Q. 5. _________ is flanked by the Indian Ocean on three sides. R

Ans. India

Q. 6. The _________ passes through the central part of India in east-west direction. R

Ans. Tropic of Cancer

Q. 7. _________ are fast flowing, narrow, meandering air currents in the atmosphere of the Earth. U

Ans. Jet Streams

Q. 8. The _________ cyclonic disturbances originate over the Mediterranean Sea. R

Ans. western

Q. 9. The _________ jet stream steers the tropical depressions into India. R

Ans. easterly

Q. 10. The period June to September is referred to as the _________ Monsoon period. R

Ans. Southwest

Q. 11. The Inter Tropical Convergence Zone is sometimes called as the _________. U

Ans. Monsoon Trough

Q. 12. The ________ monsoons bring substantial rainfall to Tamil Nadu. R

Ans. Northeast

Q. 13. __________ is caused by the interaction between the surface layers of the tropical Pacific Ocean and the atmosphere over it. U

Ans. El Nino

Q. 14. The __________ region of India does not have any well-defined cold weather season. R

Ans. Peninsular

Q. 15. ______ monsoons do not cause rainfall as they move from land to the sea. R

Ans. Winter

(B) ARRANGE IN THE CORRECT ORDER

Q. 1. Arrange the occurrence of monsoons in India in the correct order: E

(i) Differing temperature trends over the land and ocean.

(ii) Moisture-laden winds from the Indian Ocean come to fill up the void.

(iii) They can't pass through the Himalayas region; they're forced to rise.

(iv) The gain in altitude of the clouds results in a drop in temperature.

Options:

(a) i, ii, iii, iv **(b)** iii, iv, i, ii

(c) ii, iv, iii, i **(d)** ii, iii, i, iv

Ans. (a) i, ii, iii, iv

Q. 2. Arrange the mechanism of weather in winters in the correct order: AE

(i) The weather conditions over India are generally influenced by the distribution of pressure in the Central and Western Asia.

(ii) These continental winds come in contact with trade winds over north-western India.

(iii) A high-pressure centre in the region lying to the north of the Himalayas develops.

(iv) Tropical cyclones originate over the Bay of Bengal and the Indian ocean.

Options:

(a) i, iii, ii, iv **(b)** i, ii, iii, iv

(c) ii, iii, i, iv **(d)** iv, ii, i, iii

Ans. (a) i, iii, ii, iv

Q. 3. Arrange the occurrence of El Nino in correct order: E

(i) Trade winds blow east to west across the surface of the tropical Pacific Ocean.

(ii) Brings warm moist air and warmer surface waters towards the western Pacific.

(iii) Keeping the central Pacific Ocean relatively cool.

(iv) Occurs every 3 to 5 years.

Options:

(a) i, ii, iii, iv **(b)** ii, iii, i, iv

(c) iv, i, iii, iv **(d)** iv, iii, ii, i

Ans. (a) i, ii, iii, iv

(C) GRAPH BASED QUESTIONS

Q. 1. Study the given graph of annual rain distribution in Tamil Nadu (2017) carefully and answer any three of the questions that follow : **(1×3=3)** E

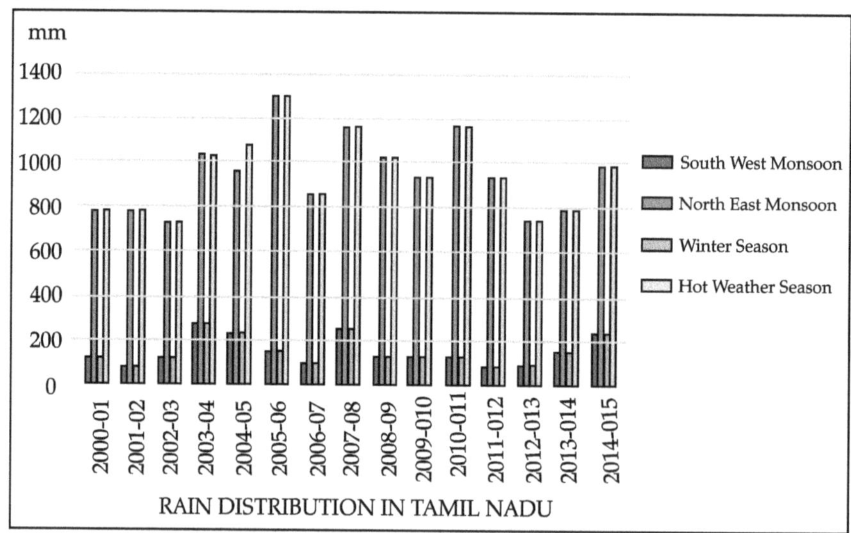

(i) The rainfall in the given graph is measured in:

(a) Centimetres **(b)** Millimetres

(c) Kilometres **(d)** None of the above

Ans. (b) Millimetres

(ii) Which year received the maximum rain from North East Monsoon?

(a) 2003-04 **(b)** 2005-06

(c) 2007-08 **(d)** 2010-11

Ans. (b) 2005-06

(iii) Which year received the maximum rain from the North East Monsoon?

(a) 2000-01 **(b)** 2003-05

(c) 2005-06 **(d)** 2007-08

Ans. (c) 2005-06

(iv) Which year received 800 mm of rainfall from both Southwest and Northeast Monsoons?

(a) 2000-01 **(b)** 2001-02

(c) 2012-13 **(d)** 2013-14

Ans. (b) 2001-02

Source-Based Questions (3 marks each)

Q. 1. Read the Passage given below and answer any three of the questions that follow. (1×3=3) U+E

The temperature of the world is significantly increasing. Carbon dioxide produced by human activities is a major source of concern. This gas, released to the atmosphere in large quantities by burning of fossil fuel, is increasing gradually. Other gases like methane, chlorofluorocarbons, and nitrous oxide which are present in much smaller concentrations in the atmosphere, together with carbon dioxide are known as greenhouse gases. These gases are better absorbers of long wave radiations than carbon dioxide, and so, are more effective at enhancing the greenhouse effect. These gases have been contributing to global warming. It is said that due to global warming the polar ice caps and mountain glaciers would melt and the amount of water in the oceans would increase. The mean annual surface temperature of the earth in the past 150 years has increased. It is projected that by the year 2,100, global temperature will increase by about 2°C. This rise in temperature will cause many other changes: one of these is arise in sea level, as a result of melting of glaciers and sea-ice due to warming. According to the current prediction, on an average, the sea level will rise 48 cm by the end of twenty first century. This would increase the incidence of annual flooding. Climatic change would promote insect-borne diseases like malaria, and lead to shift in climatic boundaries, making some regions wetter and others drier. Agricultural pattern would shift and human population as well as the ecosystem would experience change.

(i) Methane, chlorofluorocarbons and nitrous oxide along with carbon dioxide is known as:

(a) greenhouse gases **(b)** combustion gases
(c) liquid gases **(d)** solid gases

Ans. (a) greenhouse gases

(ii) Which gas is a better absorber of long wave radiations?

(a) Carbon di oxide **(b)** Methane
(c) Oxygen **(d)** Helium

Ans. (b) Methane

(iii) According to the current prediction, on an average, the sea level will rise __________ cm by the end of twenty-first century.

(a) 46 **(b)** 48
(c) 50 **(d)** 52

Ans. (b) 48

(iv) What would lead to shifts in agricultural patterns and the ecosystem?

(a) Climatic drift **(b)** Climatic change
(c) Climate variation **(d)** None of the above

Ans. (b) Climatic change

Q. 2. Read the Passage given below and answer any three of the questions that follow. (1×3=3) AE

The average annual rainfall in India is about 125 cm, but it has great spatial variations.

Areas of High Rainfall: The highest rainfall occurs along the west coast, on the Western Ghats, as well as in the sub-Himalayan areas is the northeast and the hills of Meghalaya. Here the rainfall exceeds 200 cm. In some parts of Khasi and Jaintia hills, the rainfall exceeds 1,000 cm. In the Brahmaputra valley and the adjoining hills, the rainfall is less than 200 cm.

Areas of Medium Rainfall: Rainfall between 100-200 cm is received in the southern parts of Gujarat, East Tamil Nadu, north eastern Peninsula covering Odisha, Jharkhand, Bihar, eastern Madhya Pradesh, northern Ganga plain along the sub-Himalayas and the Cachar Valley and Manipur.

Areas of Low Rainfall: Western Uttar Pradesh, Delhi, Haryana, Punjab, Jammu and Kashmir, eastern Rajasthan, Gujarat and Deccan Plateau receive rainfall between 50-100 cm.

Areas of Inadequate Rainfall: Parts of the Peninsula, especially in Andhra Pradesh, Karnataka and Maharashtra, Ladakh and most of western Rajasthan receive rainfall below 50 cm. Snowfall is restricted to the Himalayan region.

(i) What is the average rainfall received in India?

(a) 121 cm **(b)** 125 cm
(c) 130 cm **(d)** 135 cm

Ans. (b) 125 cm

(ii) How much rainfall does the Brahmaputra valley receive?

(a) More than 200 cm **(b)** Less than 200 cm
(c) More than 300 cm **(d)** Less than 300 cm

Ans. (b) Less than 200 cm

(iii) How much rainfall does Punjab, Haryana and Delhi receive?

(a) Between 40 – 80 cm **(b)** Between 80- 100 cm
(c) Between 50-100 cm **(d)** Between 100-150 cm

Ans. (c) Between 50-100 cm

(iv) In some parts of Khasi and Jaintia hills, the rainfall exceeds:

(a) 1,000 cm **(b)** 2,000 cm
(c) 3,000 cm **(d)** 4,000 cm

Ans. (a) 1,000 cm

Q. 3. Read the Passage given below and answer any three of the questions that follow. (1×3=3) AE

The months of October and November are known for retreating monsoons. By the end of September, the southwest monsoon becomes weak as the low-pressure trough of the Ganga plain starts moving southward in response to the southward march of the sun. The monsoon retreats from the western Rajasthan by the first week of September. It withdraws from Rajasthan, Gujarat, Western Ganga plain and the Central Highlands by the end of the month. By the beginning of October, the low pressure covers northern parts of the Bay of Bengal and by early November, it moves over Karnataka and Tamil Nadu. By the middle of December, the centre of low pressure is completely removed from the Peninsula. The retreating southwest monsoon season is marked by clear skies and rise in temperature. The land is still moist. Owing to the conditions of high temperature and humidity, the weather becomes rather oppressive. This is commonly known as the 'October heat'. In the second half of October, the mercury begins to fall rapidly, particularly in northern India. The weather in the retreating monsoon is dry in north India but it is associated with rain in the eastern part of the Peninsula. Here, October and November are the rainiest months of the year. The widespread rain in this season is associated with the passage of cyclonic depressions which originate over the Andaman Sea and manage to cross the eastern coast of the southern Peninsula. These tropical cyclones are very destructive. The thickly populated deltas of the Godavari, Krishna and Kaveri are their preferred targets. Every year cyclones bring disaster here. A few cyclonic storms also strike the coast of West Bengal, Bangladesh and Myanmar. A bulk of the rainfall of the Coromandel coast is derived from these depressions and cyclones. Such cyclonic storms are less frequent in the Arabian Sea.

(i) The months of October and November are known for _________ monsoons.

(a) southwest (b) retreating
(c) cyclonic (d) northwest

Ans. (b) retreating

(ii) When do the Southwest monsoon start becoming weak?

(a) End of September (b) Starting of September
(c) End of October (d) Starting of October

Ans. (a) End of September

(iii) The weather in the retreating monsoon is _______ in north India.

(a) dry (b) moist
(c) cold (d) hot

Ans. (a) dry

(iv) The retreating _________ monsoon season is marked by clear skies and rise in temperature.

(a) northeast (b) southwest
(c) western (d) None of the above

Ans. (a) northeast

Chapter 5: Natural Vegetation

Objective Type Questions

(1 mark each)

(A) FILL IN THE BLANKS

Q. 1. The Himalayan heights are marked with _________ vegetation. R

Ans. temperate

Q. 2. In the ________forests, trees reach great heights upto 60 m or above. R

Ans. tropical evergreen

Q. 3. The _________ forests have a mixture of evergreen and moist deciduous trees. R

Ans. semi-evergreen

Q. 4. _____ per cent of the world's mangrove forests is found in India. R

Ans. 7

Q. 5. To a vast number of tribal people, the ________ is a home. U

Ans. forest

Q. 6. In the _________ forests, the trees lose their leaves seasonally. R

Ans. Tropical Deciduous

Q. 7. ________ refers to the raising of trees and agriculture crops on the same land inclusive of the waste patches. U

Ans. Agro-forestry

Q. 8. _______ pertains to the raising and management of trees on public and privately owned lands in and around urban centres. R

Ans. Urban forestry

Q. 9. _______ involves the raising of trees on public or community land such as the village pasture and temple land, roadside, canal bank, strips along railway lines, and schools etc. R

Ans. Community forestry

Q. 10. The _________ Biosphere Reserve covers an area of 105,000 hectares on the southeast coast of India. R

Ans. Gulf of Mannar

(B) ARRANGE IN THE CORRECT ORDER

Q. 1. Arrange the Biosphere Reserves from the largest in area to the smallest: E

(i) Kachchh (ii) Gulf of Mannar
(iii) Sunderbans (iv) Nanda Devi

Options:

(a) i, ii, iii, iv (b) ii, iii, i, iv
(c) iv, i, iii, ii (d) ii, i, iii, iv

Ans. (a) i, ii, iii, iv

Q. 2. Arrange the tiger reserves in India from North to South: R

(i) Indravati (ii) Dudhawa
(iii) Bandhipur (iv) Simipal

Options:

(a) iv, ii, iii, i (b) i, ii, iii, iv
(c) ii, i, iv, iii (d) iii, ii, i, iv

Ans. (c) ii, i, iv, iii

Q. 3. Arrange the following tropical forest groups in the correct order of sequence based on area covered in India beginning from the largest covered area: AE

(i) **Moist Deciduous** (ii) **Dry Deciduous**
(iii) **Wet Evergreen** (iv) **Semi-Evergreen**

Options:

(a) i, ii, iii, iv **(b)** iv, i, ii, iii
(c) iii, iv, i, ii **(d)** iv, i, iii, ii

Ans. (a) i, ii, iii, iv

Source-Based Questions

(3 marks each)

Q. 1. Read the Passage given below and answer any three of the questions that follow. (1×3=3) A

In mountainous areas, the decrease in temperature with increasing altitude leads to a corresponding change in natural vegetation. Mountain forests can be classified into two types, the northern mountain forests and the southern mountain forests. The Himalayan ranges show a succession of vegetation from the tropical to the tundra, which change in with the altitude. Deciduous forests are found in the foot hills of the Himalayas. It is succeeded by the wet temperate type of forests between an altitude of 1,000-2,000 m. In the higher hill ranges of north eastern India, hilly areas of West Bengal and Uttaranchal, evergreen broad leaf trees such as oak and chestnut are predominant. Between 1,500-1,750 m, pine forests are also well-developed in this zone, with Chir Pine as a very useful commercial tree. Deodar, a highly valued endemic species grows mainly in the western part of the Himalayan range. Deodar is a durable wood mainly used in construction activity. Similarly, the chinar and the walnut, which sustain the famous Kashmir handicrafts, belong to this zone. Blue pine and spruce appear at altitudes of 2,225-3,048 m. At many places in this zone, temperate grasslands are also found. But in the higher reaches there is a transition to Alpine forests and pastures. Silver firs, junipers, pines, birchand rhododendrons, etc. occur between 3,000-4,000 m. However, these pastures are used extensively for transhumance by tribes like the Gujjars, the Bakarwals, the Bhotiyas and the Gaddis. The southern slopes of the Himalayas carry a thicker vegetation cover because of relatively higher precipitation than the drier north-facing slopes. At higher altitudes, mosses and lichens form part of the tundra vegetation. The southern mountain forests include the forests found in three distinct areas of Peninsular India viz; the Western Ghats, the Vindhyas and the Nilgiris. As they are closer to the tropics, and only 1,500 m above the sea level, vegetation is temperate in the higher regions, and subtropical on the lower regions of the Western Ghats, especially in Kerala, Tamil Nadu and Karnataka. The temperate forests are called Sholas in the Nilgiris, Anaimalai and Palani hills. Some of the other trees of this forest of economic.

Significance includes magnolia, laurel, cinchona and wattle. Such forests are also found in the Satpura and the Maikal ranges.

(i) Which of the following forests are found in the foothills of the Himalayas?

(a) Evergreen forests **(b)** Deciduous forests
(c) Alpine forests **(d)** Temperate forests

Ans. (b) Deciduous forests

(ii) Deodar, a highly valued endemic species grows mainly in which part of the Himalayan range?

(a) Eastern **(b)** Northern
(c) Western **(d)** Southern

Ans. (c) Western

(iii) Mosses and lichens are part of the:

(a) Tropical vegetation
(b) Tundra vegetation
(c) Taiga vegetation
(d) Temperate vegetation

Ans. (b) Tundra vegetation

(iv) In Nilgiris, Sholas is:

(a) Evergreen forests **(b)** Deciduous forests
(c) Alpine forests **(d)** Temperate forests

Ans. (d) Temperate forests

Q. 2. Read the Passage given below and answer any three of the questions that follow. (1×3=3) AE

The protection of wildlife has a long tradition in India. Many stories of Panchtantra and Jungle Books, etc. have stood the test of time relating to the love for wildlife. These have a profound impact on young minds. In 1972, a comprehensive Wildlife Act was enacted, which provides the main legal framework for conservation and protection of wildlife in India. The two main objectives of the Act are to provide protection to the endangered species listed in the schedule of the Act and to provide legal support to the conservation areas of the country classified as National parks, sanctuaries and closed areas. This Act has been comprehensively amended in 1991, making punishments more stringent and has also made provisions for the protection of specified plant species and conservation of endangered species of wild animals. There are 103 National parks and 535 wildlife sanctuaries in the country (Appendix V). Wildlife conservation has a very large ambit with unbounded potential for the well-being of humankind. However, this can be achieved only when every individual understands its significance and contributes his bit. For the purpose of effective conservation of flora and fauna, special steps have been initiated by the Government of India in collaboration with UNESCO's 'Man and Biosphere Programme'. Special schemes like Project Tiger (1973) and Project Elephant (1992) have been launched to conserve these species and their habitat in a sustainable manner. Project Tiger has been implemented since 1973. The main objective of the scheme is to ensure maintenance of viable population of tigers in India for scientific, aesthetic, cultural and ecological values, and to preserve areas of biological importance as natural heritage for the benefit, education and enjoyment of the people. Initially, the Project Tiger was launched in nine tiger reserves, covering an area of 16,339 sq. km, which has now increased to 44 tiger reserves, encompassing 36,988.28 sq. km of core tiger habitats distributed in 17 states. The tiger population in the country has registered an increase from 1,411 in 2006 to 1,706 in 2010. Project Elephant was launched in 1992 to assist states having free ranging population of wild elephants. It was aimed at ensuring long-term survival of identified viable population of elephants in their natural habitat. The project is being implemented in 17 states. Apart from this, some other projects such as Crocodile Breeding Project, Project Hangul and conservation of Himalayan Musk deer have also been launched by the Government of India.

(i) How many National Parks are there in the country?

(a) 101 (b) 102

(c) 103 (d) 104

Ans. (c) 103

(ii) When was the Project Tiger implemented?

(a) 1963 (b) 1973

(c) 1983 (d) 1993

Ans. (b) 1973

(iii) When was Project Elephant launched?

(a) 1992 (b) 1982

(c) 1972 (d) 1962

Ans. (a) 1992

(iv) The Comprehensive Wildlife Amendment Act was amended in ______:

(a) 1971 (b) 1981

(c) 1991 (d) 2001

Ans. (c) 1991

Q. 3. Read the Passage given below and answer any three of the questions that follow. (1×3=3) A

The Nilgiri Biosphere Reserve (NBR), the first of the fourteen biosphere reserves of India, was established in September 1986. It embraces the sanctuary complex of Wyanad, Nagarhole, Bandipur and Mudumalai, the entire forested hill slopes of Nilambur, the Upper Nilgiri plateau, Silent Valley and the Siruvani hills. The total area of the biosphere reserve is around 5,520 sq. km. The Nilgiri Biosphere Reserve possesses different habitat types, unspoilt areas of natural vegetation types with several dry scrubs, dry and moist deciduous, semi-evergreen and wet evergreen forests, evergreen sholas, grasslands and swamps. It includes the largest known population of two endangered animal species, namely the Nilgiri Tahr and the Lion-tailed macaque. The largest south Indian population of elephant, tiger, gaur, sambar and chital as well as a good number of endemic and endangered plants are also found in this reserve. The habitat of a number of tribal groups remarkable for their traditional modes of harmonious use of the environment are also found here. The topography of the NBR is extremely varied, ranging from an altitude of 250 m to 2,650 m. About 80 per cent of the flowering plants reported from the Western Ghats occur in the Nilgiri Biosphere Reserve.

(i) What does NBR stand for?

(a) Nalanda Biosphere Reserve

(b) Nilgiri Biosphere Reserve

(c) National Biosphere Reserve

(d) None of the above

Ans. (b) Nilgiri Biosphere Reserve

(ii) When was the Nilgiri Biosphere Reserve established?

(a) 1976 (b) 1986

(c) 1996 (d) 1966

Ans. (b) 1986

(iii) The total area of the biosphere reserve is around ________ sq. km.

(a) 5,520 (b) 5,000

(c) 4,500 (d) 3,500

Ans. (a) 5,520

(iv) About ________ per cent of the flowering plants reported from the Western Ghats occur in the Nilgiri Biosphere Reserve.

(a) 60 (b) 70

(c) 80 (d) 90

Ans. (c) 80

Chapter 6: Soils

is not in the syllabus of 2023-24

Chapter 7: Natural Hazards and Disasters

Objective Type Questions

(1 mark each)

(A) FILL IN THE BLANKS

Q. 1. __________ is the process present everywhere with variations in terms of magnitude, intensity and scale. R

Ans. Change

Q. 2. For a long time, geographical literature viewed _______as a consequence of natural forces. R

Ans. disaster

Q. 3. The World Conference on Disaster Management was established in May 1994 at _________. R

Ans. Yokohama

Q. 4. Every disaster is unique in terms of the local ________ factors that control it. R

Ans. socio-environmental

Q. 5. ________ are by far the most unpredictable and highly destructive of all the natural disasters. R

Ans. Earthquakes

Q. 6. The impact of ________ is less over the ocean and more near the coast where they cause large-scale devastation. R

Ans. tsunami

Q. 7. A ____________ is like a heat engine that is energised by the release of latent heat on account of the condensation of moisture that the wind gathers after moving over the oceans and seas. R

Ans. tropical cyclone or hurricane **(Any One)**

Q. 8. ___________ are relatively slow in occurrences and often occur in well-identified regions and within expected time in a year. R

Ans. Floods

Q. 9. __________ is also known as soil moisture drought. R

Ans. Agricultural drought

Q. 10. Indian agriculture has been heavily dependent on the ________ rainfall. R

Ans. monsoon

(B) ARRANGE IN THE CORRECT ORDER

Q. 1. Arrange the stages of earthquake in the correct order: E

(i) Dilatancy **(ii) Elastic build-up**
(iii) Influx of water **(iv) Earthquake**

Options:

(a) ii, i, iii, iv **(b)** i, ii, iii, iv
(c) iv, iii, i, ii **(d)** iii, iv, ii, i

Ans. (a) ii, i, iii, iv

Q. 2. Arrange the development of tropical cyclone in correct order: E

(i) Tropical disturbance **(ii) Tropical depression**
(iii) Tropical storm **(iv) Hurricane**

Options:

(a) i, ii, iii, iv **(b)** iv, iii, ii, i
(c) iii, ii, iv, i **(d)** iii, i, ii, iv

Ans. (a) i, ii, iii, iv

Q. 3. Arrange the stages of tsunami occurrence in the correct order: U

(i) Initiation **(ii) Split**
(iii) Amplification **(iv) Run-up**

Options:

(a) i, ii, iii, iv **(b)** iv, ii, i, iii
(c) ii, i, iv, iii **(d)** iii, iv, i, ii

Ans. (a) i, ii, iii, iv

Source-Based Questions

(3 marks each)

Q. 1. Read the Passage given below and answer any three of the questions that follow. (1×3=3) U+E

The speed of wave in the ocean depends upon the depth of water. It is more in the shallow water than in the ocean deep. As a result of this, the impact of tsunami is less over the ocean and more near the coast where they cause large-scale devastations. Therefore, a ship at sea is not much affected by tsunami and it is difficult to detect a tsunami in the deeper parts of sea. It is so because over deep water the tsunami has very long wave-length and limited wave-height. Thus, a tsunami wave raises the ship only a metre or two and each rise and fall takes several minutes. As opposed to this, when a tsunami enters shallow water, its wave-length gets reduced and the period remains unchanged, which increases the wave-height. Sometimes, this height can be up to 15 m or more, which causes large-scale destructions along the shores. Thus, these are also called Shallow Water Waves. Tsunamis are frequently observed along the Pacific Ring of Fire, particularly along the coast of Alaska, Japan, Philippines, and other islands of South-east Asia, Indonesia, Malaysia, Myanmar, Sri Lanka, and India etc.

After reaching the coast, the tsunami waves release enormous energy stored in them and water flows turbulently onto the land destroying port-cities and towns, structures, buildings and other settlements. Since the coastal areas are densely populated the world over, and these are also centres of intense human activity, the loss of life and property is likely to be much higher by a tsunami as compared to other natural hazards in the coastal areas.

(i) The speed of wave in the ocean depends upon the:

(a) depth of water **(b)** depth of sea bed
(c) depth of rocks **(d)** depth of waves

Ans. (a) depth of water

(ii) When tsunami enters shallow water, its wave-length gets reduced and the wave-height ______:

(a) decreases **(b)** increases
(c) remains unchanged **(d)** None of the above

Ans. (b) increases

(iii) After reaching the coast, the tsunami waves release enormous ________ stored in them.

(a) power **(b)** destruction
(c) energy **(d)** grid

Ans. (c) energy

(iv) The impact of tsunami is less over the ________:

(a) coastal areas **(b)** oceans
(c) forests **(d)** beaches

Ans. (b) oceans

Q. 2. Read the Passage given below and answer any three of the questions that follow. (1×3=3) U+E

Indian agriculture has been heavily dependent on the monsoon rainfall. Droughts and floods are the two accompanying features of Indian climate. According to some estimates, nearly 19 per cent of the total geographical area of the country and 12 per cent of its total population suffer due to drought every year. About 30 per cent of the country's total area is identified as drought prone affecting around 50 million people. It is a common experience that while some parts of the country reel under floods, there are regions that face severe drought during the same period. Moreover, it is also a common sight to witness that one region suffers due to floods in one season and experiences drought in the other. This is mainly because of the large-scale variations and unpredicability in the behaviour of the monsoon in India. Thus, droughts are widespread and common phenomena in most parts of the country, but these are most recurrent and severe in some and not so in others.

(i) ________ and floods are the two accompanying features of Indian climate.

(a) Droughts (b) Tsunami

(c) Hurricanes (d) Cyclones

Ans. (a) Droughts

(ii) How much percentage of geographical area of the country suffers from drought every year?

(a) 15 (b) 17

(c) 19 (d) 21

Ans. (c) 19

(iii) About ________ per cent of the country's total area is identified as drought prone.

(a) 15 (b) 20

(c) 25 (d) 30

Ans. (d) 30

(iv) Droughts are a ____________ occurrence.

(a) common (b) rare

(c) occasional (d) None of the above

Ans. (a) common

Q. 3. Read the Passage given below and answer any three of the questions that follow. (1×3=3) U+E

Tropical cyclones are intense low-pressure areas confined to the area lying between 30°N and 30°S latitudes, in the atmosphere around which high velocity winds blow. Horizontally, it extends up to 500-1,000 km and vertically from surface to 12-14 km. A tropical cyclone or hurricane is like a heat engine that is energised by the release of latent heat on account of the condensation of moisture that the wind gathers after moving over the oceans and seas.

Tropical cyclones are characterised by large pressure gradients. The centre of the cyclone is mostly a warm and low-pressure, cloudless core known as eye of the storm. Generally, the isobars are closely placed to each other showing high-pressure gradients. Normally, it varies between 14-17mb/100 km, but sometimes it can be as high as 60mb/100km. Expansion of the wind belt is about 10-150 km from the centre.

(i) Horizontally, the tropical cyclones extend upto:

(a) 100-500 km (b) 500-1000 km

(c) 1000-1500 km (d) 1500-2000 km

Ans. (b) 500-1000 km

(ii) What is the centre of the cyclone known as?

(a) Hand of the storm (b) Leg of the storm

(c) Eye of the storm (d) Vein of the storm

Ans. (c) Eye of the storm

(iii) Tropical cyclones are characterised by large:

(a) pressure gradients (b) heat gradients

(c) water gradients (d) moisture gradients

Ans. (b) heat gradients

(iv) Where do tropical cyclones occur?

(a) In the atmosphere around which high velocity winds blow

(b) In the atmosphere around which low velocity winds blow

(c) In the atmosphere around which zero velocity winds blow

(d) None of the above

Ans. (a) In the atmosphere around which high velocity winds blow

Part C: Fundamentals of Maps

Chapter 1: Introduction to Maps

Objective Type Questions

(1 mark each)

(A) FILL IN THE BLANKS

Q. 1. ________ pioneered land surveying and map-making as an integral part of the revenue collection procedure. R

Ans. Todarmal

Q. 2. The art and science of map-making is known as ____________. R

Ans. Cartography

Q. 3. A simplified map drawn freehand which fails to preserve the true scale or orientation is known as ____________ map. U

Ans. sketch

Q. 4. A group of maps produced at same scale, style and specifications for a country or a region is known as ________. R

Ans. map series

Q. 5. A ________ is an oblate spheroid whose shape resembles the actual shape of the Earth. R

Ans. geoid

Q. 6. ____________ is a two-dimensional form of the three-dimensional earth. R

Ans. Map

Q. 7. The first decision that a map-maker has to take is about the _____ of the map. R

Ans. scale

Q. 8. The __________ maps follow uniform colours and symbols to show details such as relief, drainage, agricultural land, forest, etc. U

Ans. topographical

Q. 9. An ________ map serves as a graphic encyclopaedia of the geographical information about the world, continents, countries or regions. U

Ans. atlas

Q. 10. The ________ maps are drawn to show the distribution, density and growth of population, age and sex composition. U

Ans. population

Source-based Questions

(3 marks each)

Q. 1. Read the Passage given below and answer any three of the questions that follow. (1×3=3) U+E

The history of map-making is as old as the history of humankind itself. The oldest map was found in Mesopotamia drawn on a clay tablet that belongs to 2,500 B.C. Greek and the Arab geographers laid the foundation of modern cartography. The measurement of the circumference of the Earth and the use of the system of geographical coordinates in map-making are some of the significant contributions of the Greeks and the Arabs. The art and science of map making was revitalised in early modern period, with extensive efforts made to minimise the effects of the transformation of the geoid onto a plane surface. The maps were drawn on different projections to obtain true directions, correct distances and to measure area accurately. The aerial photography supplemented the ground method of survey and the uses of aerial photographs stimulated map-making in the nineteenth and twentieth centuries.

(i) The history of map making is as old as the history of ________ itself.

(a) earth (b) mankind

(c) planet (d) galaxy

Ans. (b) mankind

(ii) Where was the oldest map found?

(a) India (b) Antarctica

(c) Mesopotamia (d) Egypt

Ans. (c) Mesopotamia

(iii) How old was the oldest map that was found?

(a) Belonged to 2,500 BC

(b) Belonged to 2,500 DC

(c) Belonged to 2,500 AD

(d) None of the above

Ans. (a) Belonged to 2,500 BC

(iv) What are the contributions of the Greeks and the Arabs in map-making?

(a) The measurement of the circumference of the Earth

(b) The use of the system of geographical coordinates

(c) The use of the time machine

(d) Both a and b

Ans. (d) Both a and b

Q. 2. Read the case study given below and answer any three of the questions that follow. (1×3=3) E

The foundation of map-making in India was laid during the Vedic period when the expressions of astronomical truths and cosmological revelations were made. The expressions were crystallised into 'sidhantas' or laws in classical treaties of Arya Bhatta, Varahamihira and Bhaskara, and others. Ancient Indian scholars divided the known world into seven 'dwipas'. Mahabharata conceived a round world surrounded by water.

Todarmal pioneered land surveying and map-making as an integral part of the revenue collection procedure. Besides, Sher Shah Suri's revenue maps further enriched the mapping techniques during the medieval period. The intensive topographical surveys for the preparation of up-to-date maps of the entire country, were taken up with the setting up of the Survey of India in 1767, which culminated with the map of Hindustan in 1785. Today, the Survey of India produces maps at different scales for the entire country.

(i) When was the foundation of map-making in India laid?

(a) In Mahabharata times

(b) In Vedic times

(c) In Mughal times

(d) In Modern times

Ans. (b) In Vedic times

(ii) Who produces maps at different scales for the entire country?

(a) The Survey of India (b) The Maps of Survey

(c) The Survey Maps (d) None of the above

Ans. (a) The Survey of India

(iii) Sher Shah Suri's _______ maps enriched the mapping techniques during the medieval period.

(a) physical (b) political

(c) revenue (d) social

Ans. (c) revenue

(iv) The Survey Map of India was set up in _______.

(a) 1767 (b) 1769

(c) 1771 (d) 1779

Ans. (a) 1767

Q. 3. Read the Passage given below and answer any three of the questions that follow. (1×3=3) E

We know that all maps are reductions. The first decision that a map-maker has to take is about the scale of the map. The choice of scale is of utmost importance. The scale of a map sets limits of information contents and the degree of reality with which it can be delineated on the map.

We also know that maps are a simplified representation of the three-dimensional surface of the earth on a plane sheet of paper. The transformation of all-side-curved-geoidal surface into a plane surface is another important aspect of the cartographic process. We should know that such a radical transformation introduces some unavoidable changes in directions, distances, areas and shapes from the way they appear on a geoid. A system of transformation of the spherical surface to the plane surface is called a map projection. Hence, the choice, utilisation and construction of projections is of prime importance in map-making.

(i) All maps are________.

(a) miniatures (b) reductions
(c) detailed (d) never ending

Ans. (b) reductions

(ii) The _______of a map sets limits of information contents and the degree of reality with which it can be delineated on the map.

(a) Scale (b) Distance
(c) Projection (d) Purpose

Ans. (a) Scale

(iii) The choice, utilisation and construction of projections is of prime importance in ________.

(a) map-making (b) map decision
(c) map minding (d) None of the above

Ans. (a) map-making

(iv) The transformation of all-side-curved-geoidal surface into a plane surface is another important aspect of the ________ process.

(a) map-making (b) cartographic
(c) demographic (d) All of the above

Ans. (b) cartographic

Chapter 2: Map Scale

Objective Type Questions

(1 mark each)

(A) FILL IN THE BLANKS

Q. 1. A _________ provides the relationship between the map and the whole or a part of the earth's surface shown on it. U

Ans. map scale

Q. 2. __________ of measurement is an international decimal system of weights and measures, based on the metre for length and the kilogram for mass. R

Ans. Metric system

Q. 3. __________ of measurement is prevalent in both the United States and the United Kingdom. U

Ans. English System

Q. 4. The __________defines a ratio or relationship between a unit of length on the map and the piece of Earth being referenced in the map. R

Ans. statement of scale

Q. 5. Bar scale is also known as _______ scale. R

Ans. graphical or linear **(Any One)**

Q. 6. A ___________is the ratio of distance on the map to distance on the ground. R

Ans. representative fraction

Q. 7. Representative Fraction Method is called a __________. R

Ans. universal method

Chapter 3: Latitude, Longitude and Time

Objective Type Questions

(1 mark each)

(A) FILL IN THE BLANKS

Q. 1. The rotation of the earth over its axis produces bulging at the__________. R

Ans. Equator

Q. 2. The _________ refers to the internationally recognised system of latitude and longitude used to location positions on Earth's surface. R

Ans. geographical grid

Q. 3. A network of __________ is drawn on a globe or a map to locate various places. U

Ans. imaginary lines

Q. 4. When you look at a map, the _________ is towards your right and the ________ is towards your left. U

Ans. east; west **(½ + ½ =1)**

Q. 5. The distance around the Earth is measured in _________ degrees. R

Ans. 360

Q. 6. The meridian is internationally accepted as the __________. R

Ans. Prime Meridian

Q. 7. The local time for the whole country is taken as the _________time. R

Ans. standard

Source-Based Questions (3 marks each)

Q. 1. Read the Passage given below and answer any three of the questions that follow. (1×3=3) U+E

While the world is divided into 24 time zones, there has to be a place where there is a difference in days, somewhere the day truly "starts" on the planet. The 180° line of longitude is approximately where the International Date Line passes. The time at this longitude is exactly 12 hours from the 0° longitude, irrespective of one travel westward or eastward from the Prime Meridian. We know that time increases east of the Prime Meridian and decreases to its west. Hence, for a person moving east of the Prime Meridian, the time would be 12 hours less than the time at 0° longitude. For another person moving westward, the time would be 12 hours more than the Prime Meridian. For example, a person moving eastward on Tuesday will count the day as Wednesday once the International Date Line is crossed. Similarly, another person starting his journey on the same day, but moving westward will count the day as Monday after crossing the line.

(i) The world is divided into how many time zones?

(a) 24 (b) 23
(c) 22 (d) 21

Ans. (a) 24

(ii) What is the time at 180° line of longitude?

(a) 14 hours from the 0° longitude
(b) 12 hours from the 0° longitude
(c) 16 hours from the 0° longitude
(d) 18 hours from the 0° longitude

Ans. (b) 12 hours from the 0° longitude.

(iii) The time increases __________ of the Prime Meridian.

(a) north (b) south
(c) east (d) west

Ans. (c) east

(iv) The time decreases __________ of the Prime Meridian.

(a) north (b) south
(c) west (d) east

Ans. (c) west

Q. 2. Read the case study given below and answer any three of the questions that follow. (1×3=3) AE

Unlike the parallels of latitude which are circles, the meridians of longitude are semi-circles that converge at the poles. If opposite meridians are taken together, they complete a circle, but they are valued separately as two meridians. The meridians intersect the equator at right angles. Unlike the parallels of latitude, they are all equal in length. For convenience of numbering, the meridian of longitude passing through the Greenwich observatory (near London) has been adopted as the Prime Meridian by an international agreement and has been given the value of 0°. The longitude of a place is its angular distance east or west of the Prime Meridian. It is also measured in degrees. The longitudes vary from 0° to 180° eastward and westward of the Prime Meridian. The part of the earth east of the Prime Meridian is called the eastern hemisphere and, in its west, referred to as the western hemisphere.

(i) The meridians of longitude are:

(a) Circles (b) Semi-circles
(c) Straight lines (d) None of the above

Ans. (b) Semi-circles

(ii) The meridians of longitudes converge at the __________:

(a) equator (b) poles
(c) latitudes (d) axis

Ans. (b) poles

(iii) The meridians intersect the Equator at __________ angles.

(a) intersecting (b) right
(c) acute (d) reflex

Ans. (b) right

(iv) The longitude of a place is measured in __________.

(a) angles (b) degrees
(c) kilometres (d) None of the above

Ans. (b) degrees

Q. 3. Read the Passage given below and answer any three of the questions that follow. (1×3=3) AE

We all know that the earth rotates from west to east over its axis. It makes the sun rise in the east and set in the west. The rotation of the earth over its axis takes 24 hours to complete one circle or 360° of longitudes. As 180° of longitudes fall both east and west of the Prime Meridian, the sun, thus takes 12 hours' time to traverse the eastern and western hemispheres. In other words, the sun traverses 150 of longitudes per hour or one degree of longitude in every four minutes of time. It may further be noted that the time decreases when we move from west to east and increases with our westward movement. The rate of the time at which the sun traverses over certain degrees of longitudes is used to determine the local time of an area with respect to the time at the Prime Meridian (0° Longitude).

(i) __________ of longitudes fall both east and west of the Prime Meridian.

(a) 120° (b) 140°
(c) 160° (d) 180°

Ans. (d) 180°

(ii) How much time does the Sun takes to traverse the eastern and western hemispheres?

(a) 12 hours (b) 14 hours
(c) 10 hours (d) 16 hours

Ans. (a) 12 hours

(iii) The Prime Meridian is drawn from __________.

(a) east to west (b) north to south
(c) west to east (d) south to north

Ans. (b) north to south

(iv) The rate of the time at which the sun traverses over certain degrees of longitudes is used to determine the ________ time of an area.

(a) local (b) international
(c) correct (d) day

Ans. (a) local

Chapter 4: Map Projections

Objective Type Questions (1 mark each)

(A) FILL IN THE BLANKS

Q. 1. __________ is a way to flatten a globe's surface into a plane in order to make a map. R

Ans. Map projection

Q. 2. A _________ is the best model of the earth. R

Ans. globe

Q. 3. Drawing of the _________ on a flat surface is called projection. R

Ans. graticule

Q. 4. The horizontal lines on the globe represent the parallels of _______. R

Ans. latitude

Q. 5. The __________ represents the shortest route between two points, which is often used both in air and ocean navigation. R

Ans. Great circle

Q. 6. Lexodrome or Rhumb Line is a straight line drawn on ________ projection. R

Ans. Mercator's

Q. 7. The ______ projection is a projection drawn to show Arctic and Antarctic areas. R

Ans. polar

Q. 8. ________ projections are created by setting a cone over a globe and projecting light from the centre of the globe onto the cone. R

Ans. Conical

Q. 9. _______are parallel lines that are drawn on a reference globe that will maintain a scale factor of 1.0. R

Ans. Standard parallels

Q. 10. The cylindrical equal area projection, is also known as the ________ projection. R

Ans. Lambert's

Source-Based Questions (3 marks each)

Q. 1. Read the Passage given below and answer any three of the questions that follow. (1×3=3) AE

A developable surface is one, which can be flattened, and on which, a network of latitude and longitude can be projected. A non-developable surface is one, which cannot be flattened without shrinking, breaking or creasing. A globe or spherical surface has the property of non-developable surface whereas a cylinder, a cone and a plane have the property of developable surface. On the basis of nature of developable surface, the projections are classified as cylindrical, conical and zenithal projections. Cylindrical projections are made through the use of cylindrical developable surface. A paper-made cylinder covers the globe, and the parallels and meridians are projected on it. When the cylinder is cut open, it provides a cylindrical projection on the plane sheet. A conical projection is drawn by wrapping a cone round the globe and the shadow of graticule network is projected on it. When the cone is cut open, a projection is obtained on a flat sheet. Zenithal projection is directly obtained on a plane surface when plane touches the globe at a point and the graticule is projected on it. Generally, the plane is so placed on the globe that it touches the globe at one of the poles. These projections are further subdivided into normal, oblique or polar as per the position of the plane touching the globe. If the developable surface touches the globe at the equator, it is called the equatorial or normal projection. If it is tangential to a point between the pole and the equator, it is called the oblique projection; if it is tangential to the pole, it is called the polar projection.

(i) A __________ surface is one, which can be flattened, and on which, a network of latitude and longitude can be projected.

(a) developable (b) structured
(c) non-developed (d) None of the above

Ans. (a) developable

(ii) A _________ surface is one, which cannot be flattened without shrinking, breaking or creasing.

(a) developable (b) non-developable
(c) flat (d) spherical

Ans. (b) non-developable

(iii) __________ projection is directly obtained on a plane surface when plane touches the globe at a point and the graticule is projected on it.

(a) Zenithal (b) Conical
(c) Tangible (d) Cylindrical

Ans. (a) Zenithal

(iv) If the developable surface touches the globe at the equator, it is called the _________ projection.

(a) normal (b) polar
(c) latitudinal (d) None of the above

Ans. (a) normal

Q. 2. Read the Passage given below and answer any three of the questions that follow. (1×3=3) AE

The correctness of area, shape, direction and distances are the four major global properties to be preserved in a map. But none of the projections can maintain all these properties simultaneously. Therefore, according to specific need, a projection can be drawn so that the desired quality may be retained. Thus, on the basis of global properties, projections are classified into equal area, orthomorphic, azimuthal and equi-distant projections. Equal Area Projection is also called homolographic projection. It is that projection in which areas of various parts of the earth are represented correctly. Orthomorphic or True-Shape projection is one in which shapes of various areas are portrayed correctly. The shape is generally maintained at the cost of the correctness of area. Azimuthal or True-Bearing projection is one on which the direction of all points from the centre is correctly represented. Equi-distant or True Scale projection is that where the distance or scale is correctly maintained. However, there is no such projection, which maintains the scale correctly throughout. It can be maintained correctly only along some selected parallels and meridians as per the requirement.

(i) What are the major global properties to be preserved in a map?

(a) Correctness of area
(b) Shape
(c) Direction and distance
(d) All the above

Ans. (d) All the above

(ii) What is the other name of Equal Area Projection?

(a) Homolographic projection
(b) Homoleptic projection
(c) Hoplitic projection
(d) None of the above

Ans. (a) Homolographic projection

(iii) __________ projection is one in which a globe, as of the Earth, is assumed to rest on a flat surface onto which its features are projected.

(a) Azimuthal (b) Equi-distant
(c) Stereographic (d) Orthographic

Ans. (a) Azimuthal

(iv) An __________ projection maintains scale along one or more lines, or from one or two points to all other points on the map.

(a) Equidistant (b) Gnomonic
(c) Central (d) Parallel

Ans. (a) Equidistant

Q. 3. Read the Passage given below and answer any three of the questions that follow. U (1×3=3)

On the basis of location of source of light, projections may be classified as gnomonic, stereographic and orthographic. Gnomonic projection is obtained by putting the light at the centre of the globe. Stereographic projection is drawn when the source of light is placed at the periphery of the globe at a point diametrically opposite to the point at which the plane surface touches the globe. Orthographic projection is drawn when the source of light is placed at infinity from the globe, opposite to the point at which the plane surface touches the globe.

(i) On the basis of location of the source of light, the projections can be divided into how many types?

(a) Two (b) Three
(c) Four (d) Five

Ans. (b) Three

(ii) Which projection is obtained by putting the light at the centre of the globe?

(a) Gnomonic (b) Conical
(c) Cylindrical (d) Orthogonal

Ans. (a) Gnomonic

(iii) __________ projection is drawn when the source of light is placed at the periphery of the globe at a point diametrically opposite to the point at which the plane surface touches the globe.

(a) Orthogonal (b) Stereographic
(c) Conic (d) Oblique

Ans. (b) Stereographic

(iv) __________ projection is drawn when the source of light is placed at infinity from the globe, opposite to the point at which the plane surface touches the globe.

(a) Perspective (b) Orthographic
(c) Gnomonic (d) None of the above

Ans. (b) Orthographic

Chapter 5: Topographical Maps

Objective Type Questions

(1 mark each)

(A) FILL IN THE BLANKS

Q. 1. __________ maps serve the purpose of base maps and are used to draw all the other maps. R

Ans. Topographical

Q. 2. A contour line is drawn to show places of equal __________. U

Ans. heights

Q. 3. A slope with a gentle gradient in the lower parts of a relief feature and steep in its upper parts is called the __________ slope. R

Ans. concave

Q. 4. The contour lines representing a _________ are normally close spaced at the margins with the innermost contour showing wide gap between its two sides. R

Ans. plateau

Q. 5. Small straight lines drawn on the map along the direction of maximum slope, running across the contours are known as __________. R

Ans. Hachures

Q. 6. A tongue of land, projecting from higher ground into the lower is called a _________. R

Ans. spur

Q. 7. Sometimes, a waterfall succeeds or precedes with a cascading stream forming _______ upstream or downstream of a waterfall. R

Ans. rapids

Q. 8. The contours representing a ________ merge into one another while crossing a river stream and the rapids are shown by relatively distant contour lines on a map. R

Ans. waterfall

Source-Based Questions

(3 marks each)

Q. 1. Read the Passage given below and answer any three of the questions that follow. (1×3=3) AE

Topographical maps, also known as general purpose maps, are drawn at relatively large scales. These maps show important natural and cultural features such as relief, vegetation, water bodies, cultivated land, settlements, and transportation networks, etc. These maps are prepared and published by the National Mapping Organisation of each country. For example, the Survey of India prepares the topographical maps in India for the entire country. The topographical maps are drawn in the form of series of maps at different scales. Hence, in the given series, all maps employ the same reference point, scale, projection, conventional signs, symbols and colours. The topographical maps in India are prepared in two series, i.e., India and Adjacent Countries Series and The International Map Series of the World.

(i) What is the other name of topographical maps?

(a) Simple purpose maps
(b) General purpose maps
(c) Specific purpose maps
(d) None of the above

Ans. (b) General purpose maps

(ii) What do the topographical maps depict?

(a) Relief features
(b) Water bodies
(c) Transportation networks
(d) All the above

Ans. (d) All the above

(iii) Who publishes the topographical maps?

(a) National Mapping Organisation
(b) International Mapping Organisation
(c) Survey of India
(d) National Survey Organisation

Ans. (a) National Mapping Organisation

(iv) The topographical maps in India are prepared in how many series?

(a) One (b) Two
(c) Three (d) Four

Ans. (b) Two

Q. 2. Read the Passage given below and answer any three of the questions that follow. (1×3=3) AE

Topographical maps under India and Adjacent Countries Series were prepared by the Survey of India till the coming into existence of Delhi Survey Conference in 1937. Henceforth, the preparation of maps for the adjoining countries was abandoned and the Survey of India confined itself to prepare and publish the topographical maps for India as per the specifications laid down for the International Map Series of the World. However, the Survey of India for the topographical maps under the new series retained the numbering system and the layout plan of the abandoned India and Adjacent Countries Series.

The study of topographical maps is simple. It requires the reader to get acquainted with the legend, conventional sign and the colours shown on the sheets.

The earth's surface is not uniform and it varies from mountains to hills to plateaus and plains. The elevation and depressions of the earth's surface are known as physical features or relief features of the earth. The map showing these features is called a relief map. A number of methods have been used to show the relief features of the Earth's surface on maps, over the years. These methods include hachure, hill shading, layer tints, benchmarks and spot heights and contours. However, contours and spot heights are predominantly used to depict the relief of an area on all topographical maps.

(i) Till when were the topographical maps prepared by the Survey of India?

(a) 1937 (b) 1947
(c) 1957 (d) 1967

Ans. (a) 1937

(ii) The Survey of India confined itself to prepare and publish the topographical maps for India as per the specifications laid down for the _________.

(a) International Map Series of the World
(b) International Map Series of India
(c) International Map Series of Asia
(d) None of the above

Ans. (a) International Map Series of the World

(iii) A map indicating hills, valley, mountains and other physical features of the earth is known as _________.

(a) Relief map (b) Political map
(c) Contour map (d) Outline map

Ans. (a) Relief Map

(iv) The study of topographical maps is ________.

(a) simple (b) complex
(c) difficult (d) complicated

Ans. (a) simple

Q. 3. Read the Passage given below and answer any three of the questions that follow. (1×3=3) U+E

Contours are imaginary lines joining places having the same elevation above mean sea level. A map showing the landform of an area by contours is called a contour map. The method of showing relief features through contour is very useful and versatile. The contour lines on a map provide a useful insight into the topography of an area. Earlier, ground surveys and levelling methods were used to draw contours on topographical maps. However, the invention of photography and subsequent use of aerial photography have replaced the conventional methods of surveying, levelling and mapping. Henceforth, these photographs are used in topographical mapping. Contours are drawn at different vertical intervals (VI), like 20, 50, 100 metres above the mean sea level. It is known as contour interval. It is usually constant on a given map. It is generally expressed in metres. While the vertical interval between the two successive contour lines remains constant, the horizontal distance varies from place to place depending upon the nature of slope. The horizontal distance, also known as the horizontal equivalent (HE), is large when the slope is gentler and decreases with increasing slope gradient.

(i) Contours are also called as ________ lines.

(a) straight (b) level
(c) curved (d) crossed

Ans. (b) level

(ii) A contour ________ is the vertical distance or difference in elevation between contour lines.

(a) interval (b) gap
(c) layer (d) All the above

Ans. (a) interval

(iii) Contour intervals are expressed in ________.

(a) millimetres (b) metres
(c) kilometres (d) yards

Ans. (b) meters

(iv) What is the other name of horizontal distance?

(a) Horizontal Equivalent
(b) Horizontal Equals
(c) Horizontal Heights
(d) Horizontal Heaps

Ans. (a) Horizontal Equivalent

Chapter 6: Introduction To Aerial Photographs

is not in the syllabus of 2023-24

Chapter 7: Introduction to Remote Sensing

Objective Type Questions

(1 mark each)

(A) FILL IN THE BLANKS

Q. 1. The term remote sensing was first used in the early ________. R

Ans. 1960s

Q. 2. The specific wavelength interval in the electromagnetic spectrum is called the ______. U

Ans. band

Q. 3. Any imaging or non–imaging device that receives EMR and converts it into a signal that can be recorded and displayed as photographic or digital image is called ________. R

Ans. sensors

Q. 4. _______ is the most important source of energy used in remote sensing. R

Ans. Sun

Q. 5. The ________ scanners consist of a number of detectors which are equivalent to the number obtained by dividing the swath of the sensor by the size of the spatial resolution. R

Ans. push broom

(B) ARRANGE IN THE CORRECT ORDER

Q.1. Arrange the process of interaction of energy with Earth's surface in correct order: E

(i) Reflection occurs when radiation "bounces" off the target.

(ii) Radiation redirected.

(iii) Absorption occurs when radiation is absorbed into the target.

(iv) Transmission occurs when radiation passes through a target.

Options:

(a) i, ii, iii, iv (b) ii, iii, i, iv
(c) iv, iii, i, ii (d) iii, ii, iv, i

Ans. (a) i, ii, iii, iv

Q. 2. Arrange the stages in Remote Sensing in the correct order: E

(i) Source of Energy and transmission of energy from the source to the surface of the earth

(ii) Interaction of energy with the earth's surface and propagation of reflected/emitted energy through atmosphere

(iii) Detection of the reflected energy by the sensor and conversion of energy received into photographic/ digital form of data

(iv) Extraction of the information contents from the data products; and conversion of information into Map or tabular forms

Options:

(a) i, iii, iv, ii (b) ii, i, iii, iv

(c) i, ii, iii, iv (d) iv, iii, ii, i

Ans. (c) i, ii, iii, iv

Q. 3. Arrange the steps involved in the extraction of information contents from data products: E

(i) The image is corrected.

(ii) After the image data is received at the earth station, it is processed for elimination of errors caused during image data collection.

(iii) And from analogue form of data products by applying visual interpretation methods.

(iv) Information extraction is carried out from digital images using digital image processing techniques.

Options:

(a) ii, i, iv, iii (b) iii, ii, i, iv

(c) iv, ii, i, iii (d) i, ii, iii, iv

Ans. (a) ii, i, iv, iii

Source-Based Questions

(3 marks each)

Q. 1. Read the Passage given below and answer any three of the questions that follow. (1×3=3) U+E

When energy is reflected from objects of the earth's surface, it re-enters into the atmosphere. You may be aware of the fact that atmosphere comprises gases, water molecules and dust particles. The energy reflected from the objects comes in contact with the atmospheric constituents and the properties of the original energy get modified. Whereas the Carbon dioxide (CO_2), the Hydrogen (H), and the water molecules absorb energy in the middle infrared region, the dust particles scatter the blue energy. Hence, the energy that is either absorbed or scattered by the atmospheric constituents never reaches to sensor placed on board a satellite and the properties of the objects carried by such energy waves are left unrecorded.

The sensors recording the energy that they receive are placed in a near–polar sun synchronous orbit at an altitude of 700 – 900 km. These satellites are known as remote sensing satellites (e.g. Indian Remote Sensing Series). As against these satellites, the weather monitoring and telecommunication satellites are placed in a Geostationary position (the satellite is always positioned over its orbit that synchronises with the direction of the rotation of the earth) and revolves around the earth(coinciding with the direction of the movement of the earth over its axis) at an altitude of nearly 36,000 km (e.g. INSAT series of satellites).

(i) What happens when energy is reflected from objects of the earth's surface?

(a) Its re-enters into the atmosphere

(b) It reflects into the space

(c) It re-enters the object

(d) None of the above

Ans. (a) Its re-enters into the atmosphere

(ii) What happens when energy reflected from the objects comes in contact with the atmospheric constituents?

(a) The properties of the original energy get modified.

(b) The properties of the original energy get scattered.

(c) The properties of the original energy remain the same.

(d) The properties of the original energy get disturbed.

Ans. (a) The properties of the original energy get modified.

(iii) How are the weather monitoring and telecommunication satellites placed?

(a) Remote sensing position

(b) Geostationary position

(c) Geometric position

(d) None of the above

Ans. (b) Geostationary position

Q. 2. Read the Passage given below and answer any three of the questions that follow. (1×3=3) E

The radiations received by the sensor are electronically converted into a digital image. It comprises digital numbers that are arranged in rows and columns. These numbers may also be converted into an analogue (picture) form of data product. The sensor on board, an earth-orbiting satellite electronically transmits the collected image data to an Earth Receiving Station located in different parts of the world. In India, one such station is located at Shadnagar near Hyderabad.

After the image data is received at the earth station, it is processed for elimination of errors caused during image data collection. Once the image is corrected, information extraction is carried out from digital images using digital image processing techniques and from analogue form of data products by applying visual interpretation methods.

(i) The radiations received by the sensor are electronically converted into a ________ image.

(a) magnetic (b) digital

(c) polaroid (d) All the above

Ans. (b) digital

(ii) The ________ numbers are arranged in rows and columns.

(a) digital (b) analogue

(c) pre-set (d) clocked

Ans. (a) digital

(iii) After the image data is received at the earth station, it is processed for elimination of errors caused during image ________.

(a) data collection (b) data selection

(c) data analysis (d) data numbering

Ans. (a) data collection

(iv) The Earth Receiving Station in India is located at ________.

(a) Shadnagar (b) Shahbadnagar

(c) Shahzadnagar (d) Shimla

Ans. (a) Shadnagar

Q. 3. Read the Passage given below and answer any three of the questions that follow. (1×3=3) AE

A sensor is a device that gathers electromagnetic radiations, converts it into a signal and presents it in a form suitable for obtaining information about the objects under investigation. Based upon the form of the data output, the sensors are classified into photographic (analogue) and non-photographic (digital) sensors. A photographic sensor (camera) records the images of the objects at an instance of exposure. On the other hand, a non–photographic sensor obtains the images of the objects in bit-by-bit form. These sensors are known as scanners.

In satellite remote sensing, the Multi Spectral Scanners (MSS) are used as sensors. These sensors are designed to obtain images of the objects while sweeping across the field of view. A scanner is usually made up of a reception system consisting of a mirror and detectors. A scanning sensor constructs the scene by recording a series of scan lines. While doing so, the motor device oscillates the scanning mirror through the angular field of view of the sensor, which determines the length of scan lines and is called swath. It is because of such reasons that the mode of collection of images by scanners is referred bit–by–bit. Each scene is composed of cells that determine the spatial resolution of an image. The oscillation of the scanning mirror across the scene directs the received energy to the detectors, where it is converted into electrical signals. These signals are further converted into numerical values called Digital Number (DN Values) for recording on a magnetic tape.

(i) Which device gathers electromagnetic radiations, converts it into a signal and presents it in a form suitable for obtaining information about the objects under investigation?

(a) Remote (b) Sensor

(c) Drone (d) Scanner

Ans. (b) Sensor

(ii) Which sensor obtains the images of the objects in bit-by-bit form?

(a) Photographic sensor

(b) Non-photographic sensor

(c) MSS

(d) Electric sensor

Ans. (b) Non-photographic sensor

(iii) A ________ sensor constructs the scene by recording a series of scan lines.

(a) scanning (b) motor

(c) sensory (d) photographic

Ans. (a) scanning

(iv) The oscillation of the scanning mirror across the scene directs the received energy to the detectors, where it is converted into ________signals.

(a) mechanical (b) electrical

(c) chemical (d) radioactive

Ans. (b) electrical

Chapter 8: Weather Instruments, Maps and Charts

is not in the syllabus of 2023-24

□□

KENDRIYA VIDYALAYA SANGATHAN
(AGRA REGION)
SESSION ENDING EXAMINATION 2019-20
CLASS – XI
SUBJECT - GEOGRAPHY
*(SOLVED PAPER)

**Note: This paper is solely for reference purpose only. The pattern of the question papers has been changed for 2022 Exam.*

Time : 3 Hrs. **Max. Marks : 70**

General Instructions:

(i) *There are 30 questions in all. All questions are compulsory.*

(ii) *Marks are indicated against each question.*

(iii) *Questions from serial no. 1-18 are Multiple Choice question carrying 01 mark each. Write only correct answer in your answer sheets.*

(iv) *Questions from serial no. 19-22 are Short Answer Question carrying 03 marks each. Answer to each of these questions should not exceed 80-100 words.*

(v) *Question from serial no. 23-28 are Long Answer Question carrying 05 marks each. Answer to each of these questions should not exceed 150 words.*

(vi) *Questions no. 28 & 30 are related to identification or location and labeling of geographical features on maps, carrying 5 marks each. Outline map of India and World provided to you must be attached within your answer sheet.*

Section A

Multiple Choice Questions **(1 × 18 = 18)**

1. 'Human activities are determined by nature' whose statement is this ? **1**

(a) Ratzel (b) Humboldt

(c) L.Febvre (d) E. C. Semple

2. Which one of the following scholars coined the term 'Geography' ? **1**

(a) Herodotus (b) Galileo

(c) Humboldt (d) Eratosthenes

3. Which type of volcanic eruptions have caused Deccan Trap formation ? **1**

(a) Shield (b) Flood basalt

(c) Caldera (d) Composite

OR

Nebular hypothesis was given by ....

(a) Edwin Hubble (b) Sir James Jeans

(c) Immanuel Kant (d) Chamberlin

4. Which mineral has only one element ? **1**

(a) Gold (b) Silver

(c) Graphite (d) All the above

5. Which one of the following gases constitutes the major portion of the atmosphere ? **1**

(a) Oxygen (b) Nitrogen

(c) Hydrogen (d) Carbon dioxide

6. Which one of the following is the highest cloud in the sky ? **1**

(a) Cirrus (b) Nimbus

(c) Stratus (d) Cumulus

7. Which one of the following is the most important greenhouse gas ? **1**

(a) Nitrogen (b) Oxygen

(c) Carbon dioxide (d) Helium

8. Which one of the following is the smallest ocean ? **1**

(a) Indian ocean (b) Atlantic ocean

(c) Arctic ocean (d) Pacific ocean

9. Which on of the following is included in biosphere ? **1**

(a) Only plants (b) Only animals

(c) All living and non-living things (d) All living organism

OR

Biodiversity is richer in :

(a) Tropical regions (b) Temperate regions

(c) Polar regions (d) Oceanic region

10. Which country shares the oceanic boundary with India ? **1**

(a) Srilanka (b) Pakistan

(c) Maldives (d) Both (a) & (c)

11. 1 nautical mile is equal to **1**

(a) 1.8 km (b) 1.6 km

(c) 2.1 km (d) 1.2 km

12. Which longitude has been selected as an Indian standard time ? **1**

(a) 23.5 degree North (b) 82.5 degree East

(c) 23.5 degree South (d) 82.5 degree West

13. Which one of the water bodies separates the Andaman from Nicobar Island ? **1**

(a) 9 degree channel (b) 10 degree channel

(c) 11 degree channel (d) 12 degree channel

14. .... is the largest tributary of Ganga. **1**

(a) Kali (b) Gomti

(c) Yamuna (d) Son

15. What is "Bardoli Chheerah" ? **1**

(a) Local hot weather season storms of Karnataka.

(b) Local hot weather season storms of Kerala.

(c) Local hot weather season storms of Assam.

(d) Local hot weather season storms of Maharashtra.

16. Which one of the following is the largest biosphere reserve ? **1**

(a) Nilgiri (b) Gulf of Mannar

(c) Nanda Devi (d) Cold desert

17. Which soil is ideal for the cultivation of cotton ? **1**

(a) Black (b) Alluvial

(c) Laterite (d) Peaty

18. In which of the following rivers is the Majuli Island situated ? **1**

(a) Ganga (b) Brahmaputra

(c) Godavari (d) Indus

OR

What is 'trikal' ?

(a) Scarcity of food grains (b) Shortage of water

(c) Scarcity of fodder (d) Shortage of all the three given above

Section B

Short Answer Type Questions **(3 × 4 = 12)**

19. Explain any three factors affecting the distribution of temperature of ocean water. **3**

OR

What are tides ? How are they caused ?

20. Explain any three reasons responsible for loss of biodiversity. **3**

21. Study the political map of India given below and answer the questions that follow : **3**

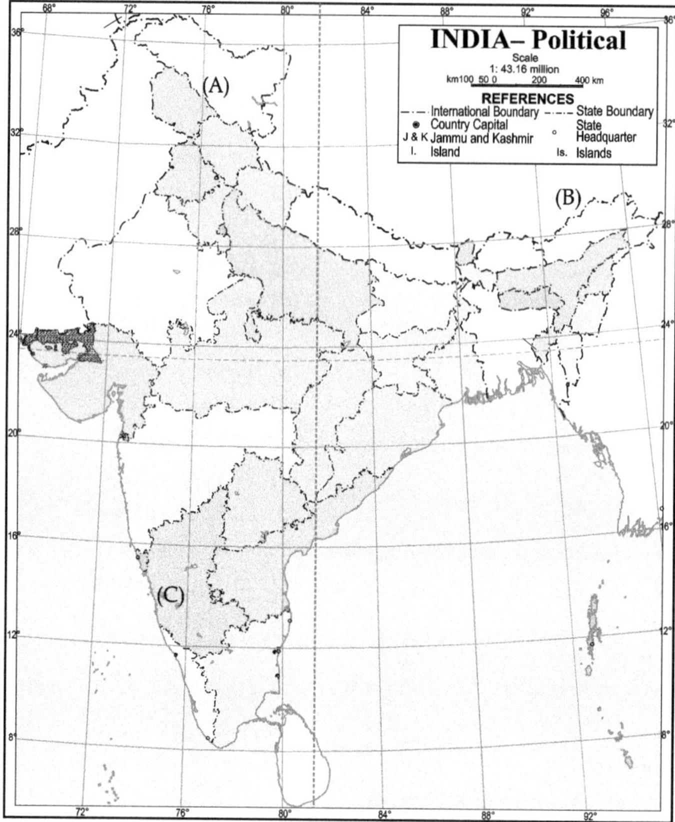

(a) Identify the newly formed union territory and write its name.

(b) Identity the mountain and write its name.

(c) Name the plateau shown in the map and write its one feature.

Note : The following question is for the **visually impaired candidates** only, in lieu of Q. No.21.

(a) Name any one neighbouring country of India.

(b) Name the highest peak of south India.

(c) Name any one peninsular river.

22. Suggest any three methods for the conservation of Soil. **3**

Section C

Long Answer Type Questions **(5 × 6 = 30)**

23. What are the evidences given in support of the continental drift theory ? **5**

24. What is Weathering ? What are the types of weathering ? **5**

OR

Explain the erosional and depositional landform made by running water.

25. Explain the heat budget of the earth with the help of diagram. **5**

OR

Differentiate between tropical and extra tropical cyclone.

26. What is Physiography ? What are the major Physiographic divisions of India ? Explain the important features of any one Physiographic river ? **(1 + 2 + 2 = 5)**

OR

What are the important characteristic features of north Indian rivers ? How are these different from Peninsular river?

27. Explain any five characteristics of Monsoon rainfall. **5**

OR

How can people's participation be effective in conserving forests and wild life.

28. What is landslide ? Explain any two consequences and two mitigation strategies of landslide. **(1 + 2 + 2 = 5)**

Section D

Map work **(2 × 5 = 10)**

29. In the given outline map of the world, the following five features (A, B, C, D & E) are shown. Identity these features and write their correct names on the lines marked near each features. **5**

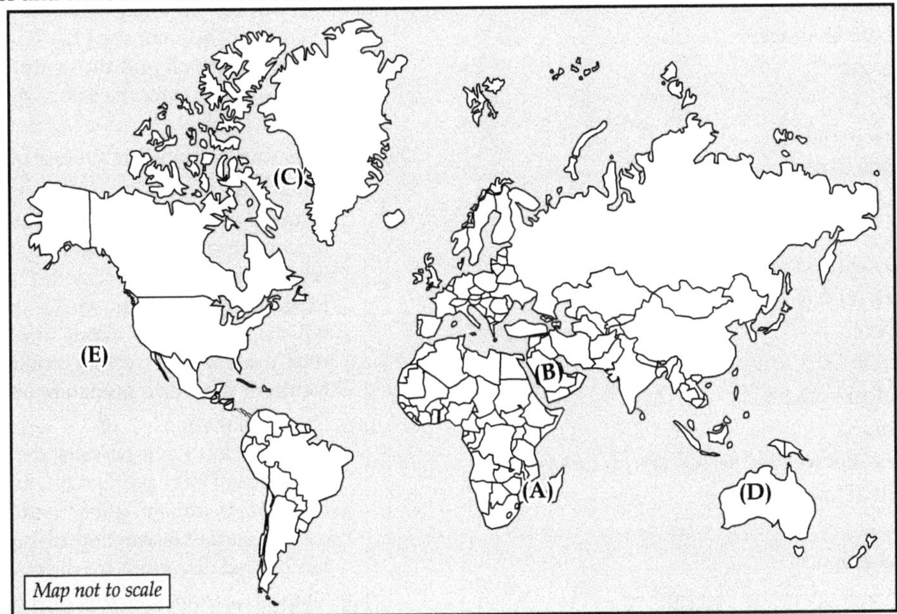

(A) Hot spot
(B) Minor Plate
(C) Cold Ocean Current
(D) Ecological hotspot
(E) Submerged mountain

Note : The following question is for the **Visually Impaired candidates** only, in lieu of Q. No. 29.

(A) Write the name of the any one cold ocean current.
(B) Write the name of any one major plate.
(C) Write the name of any one minor plate.
(D) Write the name of largest ocean of the earth.
(E) Write the name of any one ecological hotspot.

30. Located and label any five of the following in the given political map of India. **5**

(a) Lakshadweep island
(b) Malabar coast
(c) Ganga river
(d) Wettest place of the earth
(e) Nilgiri biosphere reserve
(f) Black soil region
(g) Aravali mountain

Note : The following question is for the **Visually Impaired candidates** only, in lieu of Q. No. 30.

(A) Write the name of highest peak of South India.
(B) Write the name of any one biosphere reserve of India.
(C) Write the name of rainiest place of India.
(D) Write the name of any one island of India.
(E) Write the name of largest river of south India.

ANSWERS

Section A

1. (b) Humboldt
2. (d) Eratosthenes
3. (c) Caldera

OR

(c) Immanuel Kant

4. (d) All of the Above
5. (b) Nitrogen
6. (a) Cirrus
7. (c) Carbon dioxide
8. (c) Arctic Ocean
9. (d) All living Organism

OR

(a) Tropical regions

10. (d) Both (a) & (c)
11. (a) 1.8 km
12. (b) 82°5 E
13. (b) 10 degree channel
14. (c) Yamuna
15. (c) Local hot weather season storms in Assam.
16. (b) Gulf of Mannar
17. (a) Black
18. (b) Brahmaputra

Section B

19. The factors which affect the distribution of temperature of ocean water are:

(i) Latitude : The temperature of surface water decreases from the Equator towards the Poles because the amount of insolation decreases poleward.

(ii) Unequal distribution of land and water : The oceans in the Northern Hemisphere receive more heat due to their contact with larger extent of land than the oceans in the Southern Hemisphere.

(iii) Prevailing wind : The winds blowing from the land towards the oceans drive warm surface water away from the coast resulting in the upwelling of cold water from below. It results into the longitudinal variation in the temperature. Contrary to this, the onshore winds pile up warm water near the coast and this raises the temperature.

(iv) Ocean currents : Warm ocean currents raise the temperature in cold areas while the cold currents decrease the temperature in warm ocean areas. Gulf stream (warm current) raises the temperature near the eastern coast of North America and the West Coast of Europe while the Labrador current (cold current) lowers the temperature near the North-East coast of North America.

OR

The periodical rise and fall of the sea level, once or twice a day, mainly due to the attraction of the sun and the moon, is called a tide.

The Moon's gravitational pull to a great extent and to a lesser extent the Sun's gravitational pull, are the major causes for the occurrence of tides. Another factor is centrifugal force, which is the force that acts to counter the balance of the gravity. Together, the gravitational pull and the centrifugal force are responsible for creating the two major tidal bulges on the earth.

20. Three reasons responsible for loss of biodiversity:

(i) Since the last few decades, growth in human population has increased the rate of consumption of natural resources. It has accelerated the loss of species and habitation in different parts of the world. Tropical regions which occupy only about one-fourth of the total area of the world, contain about three fourth of the world human population.

(ii) Overexploitation of resources and deforestation have become rampant to fulfil the needs of large population. As these tropical rain forests contain 50 per cent of the species on the earth, destruction of natural habitats has proved disastrous for the entire biosphere.

(iii) Natural calamities such as earthquakes, floods, volcanic eruptions, forest fires, droughts, etc., cause damage to the flora and fauna of the earth, bringing change in the biodiversity of respective affected regions.

(iv) Pesticides and other pollutants such as hydrocarbons and toxic heavy metals destroy the weak and sensitive species.

(v) There are many examples when a natural biotic community of the ecosystem suffered extensive damage because of the introduction of exotic species. During the last few decades, some animals like tigers, elephants, rhinoceros, crocodiles, minks and birds were hunted mercilessly by poachers for their horn, tusks, hides, etc. It has resulted in the rendering of certain types of organisms as endangered category.

21. (A) Ladakh

(B) Arunachal Himalayas

(C) Deccan Plateau - It receives rainfall between 50-100 cm

22. Measures taken to conserve soil are :

(i) The first step in any rational solution is to check open cultivable lands on slopes from farming.

(ii) Lands with a slope gradient of 15 - 25 per cent should not be used for cultivation. If at all the land is to be used for agriculture, terraces should carefully be made.

(iii) Over-grazing and shifting cultivation in many parts of India have affected the natural cover of land and given rise to extensive erosion. It should be regulated and controlled by educating villagers about the consequences.

(iv) Contour bunding , Contour terracing, regulated forestry, controlled grazing, cover cropping, mixed farming and crop rotation should be encouraged.

(v) In arid and semi-arid areas, efforts should be made to protect cultivable lands from encroachment by sand dunes through developing shelter belts of trees and agro-forestry. **(Any Three)**

Section C

23. Evidences in support of Continental Drift Theory are as follows :

(i) The Matching of Continents (Jig-Saw-Fit) : The shorelines of Africa and South America facing each other have a remarkable and unmistakable match. It may be noted that a map produced using a computer programme to find the best fit of the Atlantic margin was presented by Bullard in 1964. It proved to be quite perfect. The match was tried at 1,000 fathom line instead of the present shoreline.

(ii) Rocks of Same Age Across the Oceans : The radiometric dating methods developed in the recent period have facilitated correlating the rock formation from different continents across the vast ocean. The belt of ancient rocks of 2,000 million years from Brazil coast matches with those from western Africa. The earliest marine deposits along the coastline of South America and Africa are of the Jurassic Age. This suggests that the ocean did not exist prior to that time.

(iii) Tillite : It is the sedimentary rock formed out of deposits of glaciers. The Gondawana System of sediments from India is known to have its counter parts in six different landmasses of the Southern Hemisphere. At the base the system has thick tillite indicating extensive and prolonged glaciation. Counter parts of this succession are found in Africa, Falkland Island, Madagascar, Antarctica and Australia besides India. Overall resemblance of the Gondawana type sediments clearly demonstrates that these landmasses had remarkably similar histories.

(iv) Placer Deposits : The occurrence of rich placer deposits of gold in the Ghana coast and the absolute absence of source rock in the region is an amazing fact. The gold bearing veins are in Brazil and it is obvious that the gold deposits of Ghana are derived from the Brazil Plateau when the two continents lay side by side.

(v) Distribution of Fossils : When identical species of plants and animals adapted to living on land or in fresh water are found on either side of the marine barriers, a problem arises regarding accounting for such distribution. The observations that Lemurs occur in India, Madagascar and Africa led some to consider a contiguous landmass "Lemuria" linking these three landmasses.

24. Weathering is defined as mechanical disintegration and chemical decomposition of rocks through the actions of various elements of weather and climate.

Types of Weathering :

Weathering can take place in physical, chemical and biological form.

(i) The various types of physical weathering are :

(a) Unloading and Expansion : Removal of overlying rock load because of continued erosion causes vertical pressure release with the result that the upper layers of the rock expand producing disintegration of rock masses. Fractures will develop roughly parallel to the ground surface. In areas of curved ground surface, arched fractures tend to produce massive sheets or exfoliation slabs of rock. Exfoliation sheets resulting from expansion due to unloading and pressure release may measure hundreds or even thousands of metres in horizontal extent.

(b) Temperature Changes and Expansion : Various minerals in rocks possess their own limits of expansion and contraction. With rise in temperature, every mineral expands and pushes against its neighbour and as temperature falls, a corresponding contraction takes place. Because of diurnal changes in the temperatures, this internal movement among the mineral grains of the superficial layers of rocks takes place regularly. This process is most effective in dry climates and high elevations where diurnal temperature changes are drastic.

(c) Freezing, Thawing and Frost Wedging : Frost weathering occurs due to growth of ice within pores and cracks of rocks during repeated cycles of freezing and melting. This process is most effective at high elevations in mid-latitudes where freezing and melting is often repeated. Glacial areas are subject to frost wedging daily. In this process, the rate of freezing is important.

(ii) Biological weathering takes place in the following ways :

(a) Animals : Animals like rats, rabbits, etc., make burrows and holes in the rocks. They consume large quantity of soils and rocks for making their habitat and destruction of food. This loosens the rock strata and disintegration occurs.

(b) Vegetation : Long roots of plants work down into cracks of rocks. The roots of shrubs and trees reach deep into them and this lodge large blocks.

(c) Human activities : Mining, deforestation, indiscriminate cultivation of land and construction activities contribute to the biological weathering.

(iii) The various types of chemical weathering processes are :

(a) Solution : When something is dissolved in water or acids, the water or acid with dissolved contents is called solution. This process involves removal of solids in solution and depends upon solubility of a mineral in water or weak acids. On coming in contact with water many solids disintegrate and mix up as suspension in water. Soluble rock forming minerals like nitrates, sulphates, and potassium etc. are affected by this process.

(b) Carbonation : Carbonation is the reaction of carbonate and bicarbonate with minerals and is a common process helping the breaking down of feldspars and carbonate minerals. Carbon dioxide from the atmosphere and soil air is absorbed by water, to form carbonic acid that acts as a weak acid.

(c) Hydration : Hydration is the chemical addition of water. Minerals take up water and expand; this expansion causes an increase in the volume of the material itself or rock. Calcium sulphate takes in water and turns to gypsum, which is more unstable than calcium sulphate. This process is reversible and long, continued repetition of this process causes fatigue in the rocks and may lead to their disintegration.

(d) Oxidation : In weathering, oxidation means a combination of a mineral with oxygen to form oxides or hydroxides. Oxidation occurs where there is ready access to the atmosphere and oxygenated waters. The minerals most commonly involved in this process are iron, manganese, sulphur, etc. In the process of oxidation rock breakdown occurs due to the disturbance caused by addition of oxygen. Red colour of iron upon oxidation turns to brown or yellow.

(e) Reduction : When oxidised minerals are placed in an environment where oxygen is absent, reduction takes place. Such conditions exist usually below the water table, in areas of stagnant water and waterlogged ground. Red colour of iron upon reduction turns to greenish or bluish grey.

OR

The various erosional landforms made by the rivers are :

(i) Valleys : They start as small and narrow rills; the rills will gradually develop into long and wide gullies; the gullies will further deepen, widen and lengthen to give rise to valleys. Depending upon dimensions and shape, many types of valleys like V-shaped valley, gorge, canyon, etc., can be recognised. A gorge is a deep valley with very steep to straight sides and a canyon is characterised by steep step-like side slopes and may be as deep as a gorge. A gorge is almost equal in width at its top as well as its bottom.

(ii) Potholes and plunge pools : Over the rocky beds of hill-streams more or less circular depressions called potholes form because of stream erosion aided by the abrasion of rock fragments. Once a small and shallow depression forms, pebbles and boulders get collected in those depressions and get rotated by flowing water and consequently the depressions grow in dimensions. A series of such depressions eventually join and the stream valley gets deepened. At the foot of waterfalls also, large potholes, quite deep and wide, form because of the sheer impact of water and rotation of boulders. Such large and deep holes at the base of waterfalls are called plunge pools. These pools also help in the deepening of valleys.

(iii) Incised or Entrenched Meanders : In streams that flow rapidly over steep gradients, normally erosion is concentrated on the bottom of the stream channel. Also, in the case of steep gradient streams, lateral erosion on the sides of the valleys is not much when compared to the streams flowing on low and gentle slopes. Because of active lateral erosion, streams flowing over gentle slopes, develop sinuous or meandering courses. It is common to find meandering courses over floodplains and delta plains where stream gradients are very gentle. But very deep and wide meanders can also be found cut in hard rocks. Such meanders are called incised or entrenched meanders.

(iv) River terraces : River terraces are surfaces marking old valley floor or floodplain levels. They may be bedrock surfaces without any alluvial cover or alluvial terraces consisting of stream deposits. River terraces are basically products of erosion as they result due to vertical erosion by the stream into its own depositional flood plain. There can be a number of such terraces at different heights indicating former river bed levels. The river terraces may occur at the same elevation on either side of the rivers in which case they are called paired terraces. When a terrace is present only on one side of the stream and with none on the other side or one at quite a different elevation on the other side, the terraces are called non-paired terraces. Unpaired terraces are typical in areas of slow uplift of land or where the water column changes are not uniform along both the banks. **(Any Two)**

The depositional landforms made by the rivers are :

(i) **Alluvial fans :** They are formed when streams flowing from higher levels break into foot slope plains of low gradient. Normally very coarse load is carried by streams flowing over mountain slopes. This load becomes too heavy for the streams to be carried over gentler gradients and gets dumped and spread as a broad low to high cone shaped deposit called alluvial fan.

(ii) **Floodplains :** Deposition develops a floodplain just as erosion makes valleys. Floodplain is a major landform of river deposition. Large sized materials are deposited first when stream channel breaks into a gentle slope. Thus, normally, fine sized materials like sand, silt and clay are carried by relatively slow moving waters in gentler channels usually found in the plains and deposited over the bed and when the waters spill over the banks during flooding above the bed.

(iii) **Natural levees and point bars :** Natural levees and point bars are some of the important landforms found associated with floodplains. Natural levees are found along the banks of large rivers. They are low, linear and parallel ridges of coarse deposits along the banks of rivers, quite often cut into individual mounds. During flooding as the water spills over the bank, the velocity of the water comes down and large sized and high specific gravity materials get dumped in the immediate vicinity of the bank as ridges. They are high nearer the banks and slope gently away from the river.

(vi) **Meanders :** In large flood and delta plains, rivers rarely flow in straight courses. Loop-like channel patterns called meanders develop over flood and delta plains. Meander is not a landform but is only a type of channel pattern.

(Any Three)

25. The heat budget of the earth :

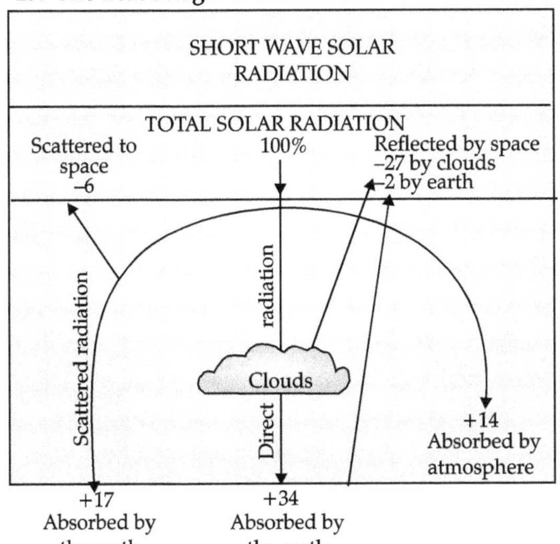

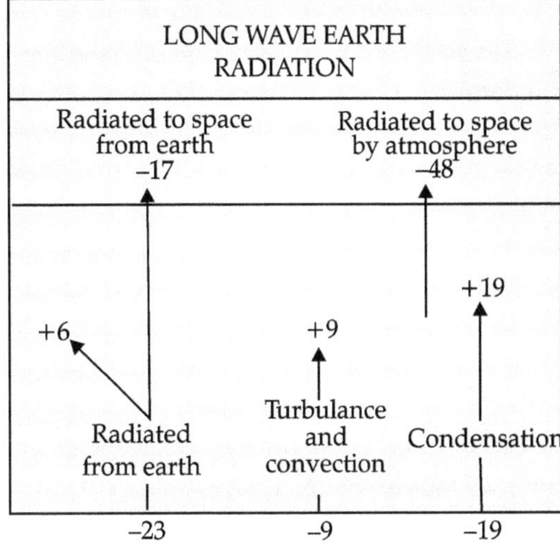

Heat budget of the earth

(i) The earth as a whole does not accumulate or loose heat. It maintains its temperature. This can happen only if the amount of heat received in the form of insolation equals the amount lost by the earth through terrestrial radiation. Consider that the insolation received at the top of the atmosphere is 100 per cent. While passing through the atmosphere some amount of energy is reflected, scattered and absorbed.

(ii) Only the remaining part reaches the earth's surface. Roughly 35 units are reflected back to space even before reaching the earth's surface. Of these, 27 units are reflected back from the top of the clouds and 2 units from the snow- and ice-covered areas of the earth. The reflected amount of radiation is called the albedo of the earth.

(iii) The remaining 65 units are absorbed, 14 units within the atmosphere and 51 units by the earth's surface. The earth radiates back 51 units in the form of terrestrial radiation. Of these, 17 units are radiated to space directly and the remaining 34 units are absorbed by the atmosphere (6 units absorbed directly by the atmosphere, 9 units through convection and turbulence and 19 units through latent heat of condensation). 48 units absorbed by the atmosphere (14 units from insolation +34 units from terrestrial radiation) are also radiated back into space.

(iv) Thus, the total radiation returning from the earth and the atmosphere respectively is 17+48=65 units which balance the total of 65 units received from the sun. This is termed the heat budget or heat balance of the earth.

OR

Basis	Tropical Cyclone	Extra-Tropical Cyclone
Characteristics	A low-pressure centre, a closed low-level atmospheric circulation, strong winds, and a spiral arrangement of thunderstorms that produce heavy rain.	A large scale low pressure weather systems that occur in the middle latitudes of the Earth.
Formation	It get intensified over warm tropical oceans and required temperature higher than 27° C, presence of the Coriolis force, small variation in the vertical wind speed, a pre existing weak low-pressure area or low-level-cyclonic circulation and upper divergent above the sea level system.	It get intensified any part of extra tropical regions of the Earth (usually between 30° and 60° latitude from the equator), either through cyclogensis or extra tropical transition.
Movement	It moves from east to west.	It moves from west to east.
Nature of Cyclone	Violent storms	Static not violent
Type	Warm Core	Cold Core

26. Physiography of an area is the outcome of structure, process and the stage of development.

The major physiological divisions of India are :

(i) The Himalayan Mountains.

(ii) The Northern Plains.

(iii) The Peninsular Plateau.

(iv) The Indian Desert.

(v) The Coastal Plains.

(vi) The Islands.

The Peninsular Plateau : The northern boundary of the Peninsular Plateau may be taken as an irregular line running from Kachchh along the western flank of the Aravalli Range near Delhi and then roughly parallel to the Yamuna and the Ganga as far as the Rajmahal Hills and the Ganga delta. Apart from these, the Karbi Anglong and the Meghalaya Plateau in the North East and Rajasthan in the West are also extensions of this block.

Characteristic features of North South Rivers and their difference from Peninsular river are as follows:

OR

S. No.	North Indian Rivers	Peninsular rivers
1. Place of origin	They originate in Himalayan mountain covered with glaciers.	They originate in the Peninsular Plateau and the Central Highland
2. Nature of flow	They are perennial because they receive water from glacier and rainfall.	They are seasonal as it is dependent on monsoon rainfall.
3. Drainage pattern	These are antecedent and consequently lead to dendritic pattern in plains.	Super imposed, rejuvenated resulting in trellis, radial and rectangular patterns.
4. Nature of river	It has long course, flowing through the rugged mountains experiencing head ward erosion and river capturing, in plains it exhibits meandering and shifting of course.	It is smaller, fixed course with well adjusted valleys.
5. Catchment area	It catchment areas include very large basins.	It catchment areas include relatively smaller basin.
6. Age of the river	These rivers are young and youthful. These are active and deepening in the valleys.	Old rivers with graded profile and have almost reached their base levels.

27. Characteristics of Monsoon Rainfall are :

(i) Rainfall received from the southwest monsoons is seasonal in character, which occurs between June and September.

(ii) Monsoonal rainfall is largely governed by relief or topography. For instance the windward side of the Western Ghats register a rainfall of over 250 cm. Again, the heavy rainfall in the north eastern states can be attributed to their hill ranges and the Eastern Himalayas .

(iii) The monsoon rainfall has a declining trend with increasing distance from the sea. Kolkata receives 119 cm during the southwest monsoon period, Patna 105 cm, Allahabad 76 cm and Delhi 56 cm.

(iv) The monsoon rains occur in wet spells of few days duration at a time. The wet spells are interspersed with rainless interval known as 'breaks'. These breaks in rainfall are related to the cyclonic depressions mainly formed at the head of the Bay of Bengal, and their crossing into the mainland. Besides the frequency and intensity of these depressions, the passage followed by them determines the spatial distribution of rainfall.

(v) The summer rainfall comes in a heavy downpour leading to considerable run off and soil erosion. Monsoons play a pivotal role in the agrarian economy of India because over three-fourths of the total rain in the country is received during the southwest monsoon season.

(vi) Its spatial distribution is also uneven which ranges from 12 cm to more than 250 cm. The beginning of the rains sometimes is considerably delayed over the whole or a part of the country.

(vii) The rains sometimes end considerably earlier than usual, causing great damage to standing crops and making the sowing of winter crops difficult. **(Any Five)**

28. Rapid sliding of large mass of bedrocks is called landslides.

Consequences of landslides :

(i) It leads to failure of transport and communication system. It can lead to road blocks, destruction of railway lines and channel-blocking due to rockfalls having far-reaching consequences.

(ii) It leads to hurdles in economic activities and destruction of natural beauty. It makes spatial interaction difficult, risky as well as a costly affair, which in turn, adversely affects the developmental activities in these areas.

Mitigation Strategies of landslides :

(i) Restriction on the construction and other developmental activities such as roads and dams, limiting agriculture to valleys and areas with moderate slopes, and control on the development of large settlements in the high vulnerability zones, should be enforced.

(ii) Some positive actions like promoting large-scale afforestation programmes and construction of bunds to reduce the flow of water should be taken.

29. (A) Madagascar

(B) Arabian Plate

(C) Labrador Ocean Current

(D) Australia

(E) Mauna Kea / Hawaii Islands

30.

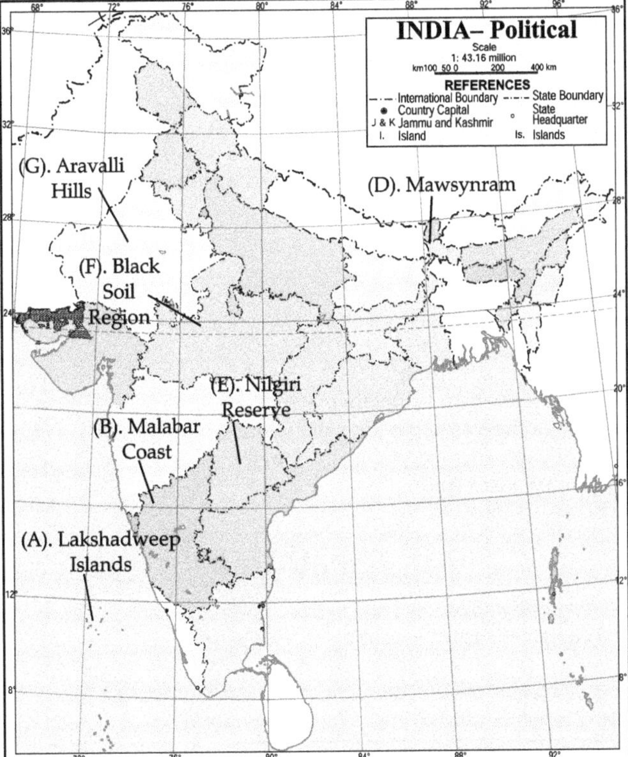

KENDRIYA VIDYALAYA SANGATHAN
(AGRA REGION)
SESSION ENDING EXAMINATION 2018-19
CLASS – XI
SUBJECT - GEOGRAPHY(THEORY)
*(SOLVED PAPER)

**Note: This paper is solely for reference purpose only. The pattern of the question papers has been changed for 2022 Exam.*

Time: 3 Hrs. **M.M.: 70**

General Instructions:

(i) *There are 22 questions in all. All questions are compulsory.*
(ii) *Marks of each question are indicated against it.*
(iii) *Question no 1 to 7 are Very Short Answer Type Questions. Answer to each of these questions should not exceed 20 words.*
(iv) *Question no 8 to 13 are Short Answer Type Questions. Answer to each of these questions should not exceed 80 words.*
(v) *Question no 14 to 20 are Long Answer Type Questions. Answer to each of these questions should not exceed 150 words.*
(vi) *Question no 21 to 22 are related to the map of the world and India for identification and location respectively.*
(vii) *The Outline maps provided to you must be attached with in your answer-book.*
(viii) *Use of templates or stencils for drawing outline map is allowed.*

Section A

1. Which gas is transparent to incoming solar radiation and opaque to outgoing terrestrial radiation? **1**

Or

Define the term "relative humidity".

2. What is thermocline? **1**

3. What are the major types of ecosystem? **1**

Or

How a food chain is differing from a food web?

4. Differentiate between a Gulf and a Strait. **1**

5. What are the elements of weather and climate? **1**

6. What is the main reason for the loss of the top soil in India? **1**

Or

What is the another name of black soil?

7. When can a hazard become a disaster? **1**

Section B

8. How does Physical Geography affect the human life? **3**

9. What are the general characteristics of Isotherms? **3**

Or

What are the factors responsible for the direction and velocity of winds?

10. Study the given data carefully and answer the following questions. **3**

Temperature data for Agra, India 2018												
Month	**Jan**	**Feb**	**Mar**	**Apr**	**May**	**Jun**	**Jul**	**Aug**	**Sep**	**Oct**	**Nov**	**Dec**
Temp. ^{0}C	10.0	12.6	34.2	37.5	48.6	48.5	48.5	40.0	32.4	30.1	23 1	00

(10.1) Which is the coldest and hottest month of the given place?
(10.2) What is the annual temperature range of the given place?
(10.3) What is the mean annual temperature of the given place?

For visually impaired candidates (in place of Q. 10)

10.1. What is the annual temperature range?
10.1. How can you calculate the mean annual temperature?
10.2. Which place received highest rainfall in the world?

11. What are the major factors that are responsible for the loss of biodiversity? 3
12. Does India need to have more than one standard time? If yes, Why do you think so? 3

Or

What are the implications of India having a long coastline?

13. What are tides? How are tides caused? 3

Section C

14. How many planets are in our solar system? What are the categories of these planets? Differentiate between them? 5

Or

What are the major types of plate boundaries? Explain.

15. "Our earth is a play field for two opposing groups of geomorphic processes. Discuss. 5

Or

How does wind perform its task in desert areas? Explain some erosional and depositional features of deserts?

16. What is a cyclone? Differentiate between tropical cyclones and extra tropical cyclones. 5

Or

Explain the classification of world climate suggested by Koeppen.

17. Name the major physical division of India. Explain any one of them. 5
18. How are Himalayan rivers different from peninsular rivers? 5
19. How can People's participation be effective in conserving forest and wild life? 5
20. What is vulnerability? Divide India into natural disaster vulnerability zone based on droughts. 5
21. On the given political map of world, five features have been marked as A, B, C, D and E, identity these features with the help of information given below and write their correct names on the lines drawn near them. 5
    - A. A trench.
    - B. A plate.
    - C. An ecological hot spot.
    - D. A warm ocean current
    - E. A cold ocean current

    For visually impaired candidates (in place of Q.21)
    - A. Name the largest tectonic plate.
    - B. How many biodiversity hotspots in the world?
    - C. Name any one biodiversity hotspots in India.
    - D. Name any one cold water current of Atlantic Ocean.
    - E. Name the lake of highest salinity in the world.

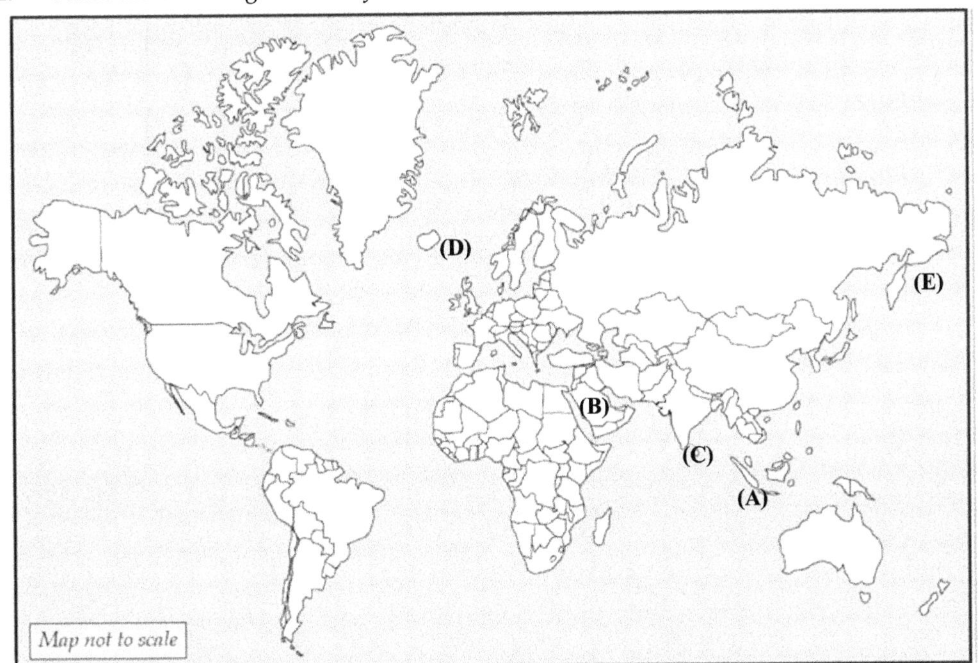

22. Locate and label any five of following on the given outline political map of India with appropriate symbols. **5**

A. Godavari river.

B. Aravalli mountain.

C. An important area of winter rainfall in south India.

D. Dachigam National Park.

E. Standard Meridian of India.

F. Tapi river

G. Mahendragiri

H. Nanda Devi

For visually impaired candidates (in place of Q.22) (Attempt any five)

A. Which river is known as Dakshin Ganga

B. Name the oldest mountain range in India.

C. Name the areas which receive rainfall in winter.

D. Name any one national park of M.P.

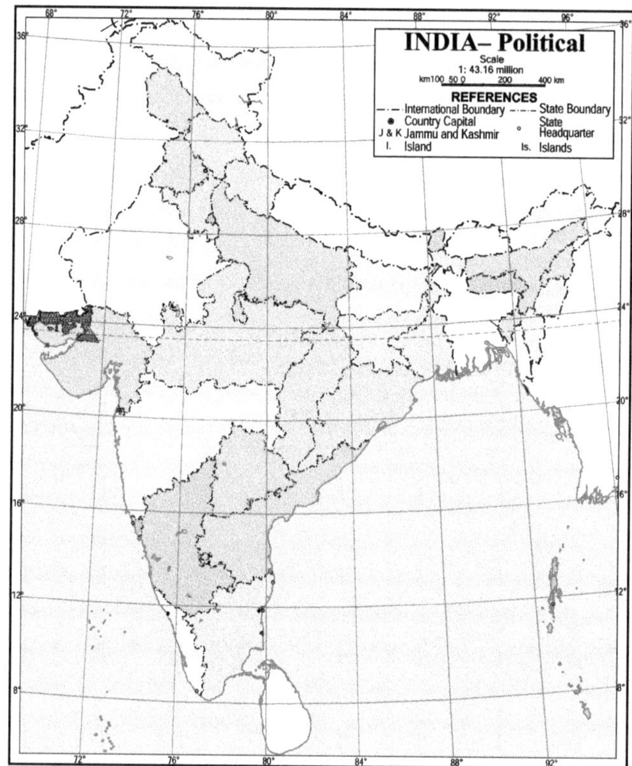

■■

ANSWERS

Section A

1. Carbon dioxide.

OR

The amount of water vapour in the air at any given time is usually less than that required to saturate the air.

2. A thermocline is the transition layer between the warmer mixed water at the surface of the ocean and the cooler deep water below.

3. The major types of ecosystems are Terrestrial (sub-divided as forests, grasslands, deserts and tundra) and Aquatic (sub-divided as fresh water and marine).

OR

Food chain is the increase in trophic level and transfer of energy through each level. And there are different types of food chains like terrestrial food chain and detritus food chain.

Food web is actually made of several food chains. One food chain gets connected to other food chain in a food web.

4. A Gulf is a deep inlet of a sea almost surrounded by land, with a narrow mouth. *Example* – Gulf of Khambat.

A Strait is a narrow passage of water connecting two large water bodies like seas and oceans. *Example* – Palk Strait.

5. The elements of climate and weather are precipitation, evaporation, pressure, solar radiation, humidity, wind speed, wind direction, etc.

6. The main reason for erosion of top soil in India is water erosion.

OR

The other name of black soil is regur soil.

7. A hazard can become a disaster when the magnitude of destruction and damage caused by it is very high.

Section B

8. Physical geography is the study of natural features and phenomena on the planet's surface and our interactions with them. These features include vegetation, climate, the local water cycle, and land formations. Geography doesn't just determine whether humans can live in a certain area or not, it also determines people's lifestyles, as they adapt to the available food and climate patterns. As humans have migrated across the planet, they have had to adapt to all the changing conditions they were exposed to.

9. The Isotherms are lines joining places having equal temperature. The temperature distribution is generally shown on the map with the help of isotherms.

OR

Factors affecting the velocity and direction of wind are:

(a) **Pressure Gradient Force -** The pressure gradient is strong where the isobars are close to each other and is weak where the isobars are apart.

(b) **Frictional Force -** It is greatest at the surface and its influence generally extends upto an elevation of 1 - 3 km. Over the sea surface the friction is minimal.

(c) **Coriolis Force -** The rotation of the earth about its axis affects the direction of the wind. This force is called the Coriolis force after the French physicist who described it in 1844. It deflects the wind to the right direction in the northern hemisphere and to the left in the southern hemisphere. The deflection is more when the wind velocity is high.

10.

10.1 The coldest month is December and the hottest month is May.

10.2 Annual temperature range = Maximum Temperature – Minimum Temperature = 48.6 – 0 = 48.6.

10.3 Mean Annual range of temperature =
10+12.6+34.2+37.5+48.6+48.5+48.5+40+
32.4+30.1+23.1+0.12=30.45°C

11. **Major factors that are responsible for the loss of biodiversity:**

(a) Overexploitation of resources and deforestation have become rampant to fulfill the needs of large population. As these tropical rain forests contain 50 per cent of the species on the earth, destruction of natural habitats have proved disastrous for the entire biosphere.

(b) Natural calamities such as earthquakes, floods, volcanic eruptions, forest fires, droughts, etc. cause damage to the flora and fauna of the earth, bringing change the biodiversity of respective affected regions.

(c) Pesticides and other pollutants such as hydrocarbons and toxic heavy metals destroy the weak and sensitive species.

12. In my point of view, I think Indian needs to have more than one standard time because India has a large longitudinal extent of about 30°.

(a) When the sun is still shining in western coast it is already night in northeast so we need two or more time zones to clearly reflect day to day changes.

(b) Time variation of 2 hours between Easternmost & the westernmost parts of our country. The sun rises two hours earlier in Arunachal Pradesh as compared to Gujarat because the earth is tilted and also it rotates in East to West direction so during rotation the Eastern part of the world experiences that sun rays earlier as compared to the western parts of the world.

(c) Other countries like USA, Canada & Russia have more than one standard time because their longitudinal extent is large. India longitudinal extent is also 30°. Therefore it is advisable to use more than one Standard Time.

OR

India's coastline is roughly 7,500 km with Arabian Sea on the West and Bay of Bengal in the East. Indian subcontinent lies in the Indian Ocean region. This geography provides India with huge advantages. Some of them are:

(a) **Maritime Trade** - This vast coastline and access to Indian Ocean allows India to trade with the most parts of the World. Arabian Sea gives it access to gulf countries which are major oil exporters. The Andaman Sea gives it access to Malacca Strait and then to South China sea. For this reason India has been a maritime nation since ancient past. It was a global trade center for spices and textile.

(b) **Tourism** - A long coastline implies good tourism potential for several states of India like Goa, Kerala and Tamil Nadu. A variety of beaches are found in India.

(c) **Cheap Transport** - Sea transport is cheaper than land transport and this implies low cost of imports and exports.

(d) **Monsoon** - The South West monsoon from Indian ocean brings good amount of rainfall to India. The agriculture thrives due to good rainfall.

(e) **Safety and Security** - The Sea borders are considered safer than land borders. There is no need for fencing like in case of land borders to check infiltration. Indian Coast Guard (ICG) protects India's maritime interests.

(f) **Climate** - The long coastline results in pleasant maritime climate near the coastal areas.

(g) **Resources** - India is heavily dependent on Indian Ocean for it's resources. India's fishing industry is one of the largest in the World. Mineral resouces extraction is also important. India has exclusive rights to explore Central Indian Ocean.

13. Tides are periodic rises and falls of large bodies of water. Tides are caused by the gravitational interaction between the Earth and the Moon. The gravitational attraction of the moon causes the oceans to bulge out in the direction of the moon. Another bulge occurs on the opposite side, since the Earth is also being pulled toward the moon (and away from the water on the far side). Since the earth is rotating while this is happening, two tides occur each day.

Section C

14. There are eight planets in our solar system – Mercury, Venus, Earth, Mars, Jupiter, Saturn, Uranus, Neptune and Pluto. Out of the eight planets, Mercury, Venus, Earth and Mars are called as the inner planets as they lie between the sun and the belt of asteroids the other four planets are called the outer planets. Alternatively, the first four are called Terrestrial, meaning earth-like as they are made up of rock and metals, and have relatively high densities. The rest four are called Jovian or Gas Giant planets. Jovian means Jupiter-like. Most of them are much larger than the terrestrial planets and have thick atmosphere, mostly of helium and hydrogen.

The difference between terrestrial and jovian planets can be attributed to the following conditions:

(a) The terrestrial planets were formed in the close vicinity of the parent star where it was too warm for gases to condense to solid particles. Jovian planets were formed at quite a distant location.

(b) The solar wind was most intense nearer the sun; so, it blew off lots of gas and dust from the terrestrial planets. The solar winds were not all that intense to cause similar removal of gases from the Jovian planets.

(c) The terrestrial planets are smaller and their lower gravity could not hold the escaping gases.

OR

There are three types of plate boundaries:

(a) **Divergent Boundaries** - Where new crust is generated as the plates pull away from each other. The sites where the plates move away from each other are called spreading sites. The best-known example of divergent boundaries is the Mid-Atlantic Ridge. At this, the American Plate(s) is/are separated from the Eurasian and African Plates.

(b) **Convergent Boundaries** - Where the crust is destroyed as one plate dived under another. The location where sinking of a plate occurs is called a subduction zone. There are three ways in which convergence can occur. These are:

(i) between an oceanic and continental plate;

(ii) between two oceanic plates; and

(iii) between two continental plates.

(c) **Transform Boundaries** - Where the crust is neither produced nor destroyed as the plates slide horizontally past each other. Transform faults are the planes of separation generally perpendicular to the mid-oceanic ridges. As the eruptions do not take all along the entire crest at the same time, there is a differential movement of a portion of the plate away from the axis of the earth. Also, the rotation of the earth has its effect on the separated blocks of the plate portions.

15. It is correct to say that our earth is a playfield for two opposing groups of geomorphic processes.

(a) We know that the earth's crust is dynamic and it moves vertically and horizontally. The internal forces of the earth operating within the earth which build up the crust have also been responsible for the variation in the outer surface of the crust.

(b) The external forces are involved to degrade the landforms built up by the internal forces. The action of the exogenic forces results in wearing down of relief of elevation and filling up of basins on the earth's surface.

(c) The endogenic forces continuously elevate or build up parts of the earth's surface and hence the exogenic processes fail to even out the relief variations of the surface of the earth.

(d) Thus variation remains as long as the opposing actions of exogenic and endogenic forces continue. So in this way our earth is a playfield for two opposing groups of processes.

OR

The wind causes the evolution of various landforms on the earth's surface. The wind is the main geomorphic agent in the hot deserts. Winds in hot deserts have greater speed which causes erosional and depositional activities in the desert. The landforms which are created by erosional and depositional activities of wind are called as Aeolian Landforms.

(a) Erosional Landforms due to Wind

(i) Pediplains - When the high relief structures in deserts are reduced to low featureless plains by the activities of wind, they are called as Pediplains.

(ii) Deflation Hollows - Deflation is the removal of loose particles from the ground by the action of wind. When deflation causes a shallow depression by persistent movements of wind, they are called as deflation hollows.

(iii) Mushroom Tables - Ventifacts are rocks that have been abraded, pitted, etched, grooved, or polished by wind-driven sand or ice crystals. These geomorphic features are most typically found in arid environments where there is little vegetation to interfere with aeolian particle transport, where there are frequently strong winds, and where there is a steady but not overwhelming supply of sand. Mushroom Tables / Mushroom rocks are Ventifacts in the shape of a mushroom. In deserts, a greater amount of sand and rock particles are transported close to the ground by the winds which cause more bottom erosion in overlying rocks than the top. This result in the formation of rock pillars shaped like a mushroom with narrow pillars with broad top surfaces.

(b) Depositional Landforms of Wind

(i) Sand dunes - Dry hot deserts are good places for sand dune formation. According to the shape of a sand dune, there are varieties of sand dune forms like Barchans, Seifs etc.

(ii) Loess - In several large areas of the world, the surface is covered by deposits of wind-transported silt that has settled out from dust storms over many thousands of years. These depositions are called as Loess.

16. Tropical cyclones are violent storms that originate over oceans in tropical areas and move over to the coastal areas bringing about large scale destruction caused by violent winds, very heavy rainfall and storm surges. This is one of the most devastating natural calamities. They are known as Cyclones in the Indian Ocean, Hurricanes in the Atlantic, Typhoons in the Western Pacific and South China Sea, and Willy-willies in the Western Australia.

The extra tropical cyclone differs from the tropical cyclone in number of ways. The extra tropical cyclones have a clear frontal system which is not present in the tropical cyclones. They cover a larger area and can originate over the land and sea. Whereas the tropical cyclones originate only over the seas and on reaching the land they dissipate. The extra tropical cyclone affects a much larger area as compared to the tropical cyclone. The wind velocity in a tropical cyclone is much higher and it is more destructive. The extra tropical cyclones move from west to east but tropical cyclones, move from east to west.

OR

The Koeppen Climate Classification System is the most widely used system for classifying the world's climates. Its categories are based on the annual and monthly averages of temperature and precipitation. The Koeppen system recognizes five major climatic types; each type is designated by a capital letter.

(a) **Tropical Moist Climate (A) :** Tropical moist climates extend northward and southward from the equator to about 15 to 25° of latitude. In these climates all months have average temperatures greater than 18° Celsius. Annual precipitation is greater than 1500 mm. Three minor Köppen climate types exist in the A group, and their designation is based on seasonal distribution of rainfall. Af or tropical wet is a tropical climate where precipitation occurs all year long. Monthly temperature variations in this climate are less than 3° Celsius. Because of intense surface heating and high humidity, cumulus and cumulonimbus clouds form early in the afternoons almost every day. Daily highs are about 32° Celsius, while night time temperatures average 22° Celsius. Am is a tropical monsoon climate. Annual rainfall is equal to or greater than Af, but most of the precipitation falls in the 7 to 9 hottest months. During the dry season very little rainfall occurs. The tropical wet and dry or savanna (Aw) has an extended dry season during winter. Precipitation during the wet season is usually less than 1000 millimeters, and only during the summer season.

(b) **Dry Climates (B) :** The most obvious climatic feature of this climate is that potential evaporation and transpiration exceed precipitation. These climates extend from 20 - 35° North and South of the equator and in large continental regions of the mid-latitudes often surrounded by mountains. Minor types of this climate include:

(i) **BW** - dry arid (desert) is a true desert climate. It covers 12% of the Earth's land surface and is dominated by xerophytic vegetation. The additional letters h and k are used generally to distinguish whether the dry arid climate is found in the subtropics or in the mid-latitudes, respectively.

(ii) **BS** - dry semiarid (steppe). Is a grassland climate that covers 14% of the Earth's land surface. It receives more precipitation than the BW either from the intertropical convergence zone or from mid-latitude cyclones. Once again, the additional letters h and k are used generally to distinguish whether the dry semiarid climate is found in the subtropics or in the mid-latitudes, respectively.

(c) **Moist Subtropical Mid-Latitude Climates (C)** - This climate generally has warm and humid summers with mild winters. Its extent is from 30 to 50° of latitude mainly on the eastern and western borders of most continents. During the winter, the main weather feature is the mid-latitude cyclone. Convective thunderstorms dominate summer months. Three minor types exist: Cfa - humid subtropical; Cs - Mediterranean; and Cfb - marine. The humid subtropical climate (Cfa) has hot muggy summers and frequent thunderstorms. Winters are mild and precipitation during this season comes from mid-latitude cyclones. A good example of a Cfa climate is the southeastern USA. Cfb marine climates are found on the western coasts of continents. They have a humid climate with short dry summer. Heavy precipitation occurs during the mild winters because of the continuous presence of mid-latitude cyclones. Mediterranean climates (Cs) receive rain primarily during winter season from the mid-latitude cyclone. Extreme summer aridity is caused by the sinking air of the subtropical highs and may exist for up to 5 months. Locations in North America are from Portland, Oregon to all of California.

(d) Moist Continental Mid-latitude Climates (D) - Moist continental mid-latitude climates have warm to cool summers and cold winters. The location of these climates is pole ward of the C climates. The average temperature of the warmest month is greater than 10° Celsius, while the coldest month is less than -3° Celsius. Winters are severe with snowstorms, strong winds, and bitter cold from Continental Polar or Arctic air masses. Like the C climates there are three minor types: Dw - dry winters; Ds - dry summers; and Df - wet all seasons.

(e) Polar Climates (E) - Polar climates have year-round cold temperatures with the warmest month less than 10° Celsius. Polar climates are found on the northern coastal areas of North America, Europe, Asia, and on the landmasses of Greenland and Antarctica. Two minor climate types exist. ET or polar tundra is a climate where the soil is permanently frozen to depths of hundreds of meters, a condition known as permafrost. Vegetation is dominated by mosses, lichens, dwarf trees and scattered woody shrubs. EF or polar ice caps has a surface that is permanently covered with snow and ice.

17. India is divided into six natural regions:

(a) The Great Himalayas

(b) The northern plains

(c) The desert region

(d) The southern plateau

(e) The coastal plains

(f) The island region

The Great Himalayas owing to the location are said to be guarding our country. The Himalayas include three main parallel ranges:

(i) **The northern-most range** is the Himadri. This range forms the backbone of the Himalayas. It contains nine of the fourteen highest peaks in the world.

(ii) **The middle range is the Himachal,** also called the Lower Himalayas.

(iii) The southern-most is the narrowest range, **the Shivalik range.**

18. Some of the key differences between the Himalayan Rivers and the Peninsular Rivers are as follows:

Himalayan Rivers	Peninsular Rivers
These rivers originate from the Himalayan mountain ranges.	These rivers originate from the peninsular plateaus in India.
They are longer and larger than the peninsular rivers.	They are comparatively smaller and shorter than the Himalayan Rivers.
They have larger basins and catchment areas.	They have smaller basins and catchment areas.
The bedrocks of these rivers are soft, sedimentary and easily erodible.	The bedrocks of these rivers are hard, and not easily erodible.
They are perennial in nature, flow throughout the year.	They are seasonal and non-perennial so may not flow throughout the year.
They are fed by the meltwater from glaciers and rains.	They are fed only by rains.
They form V-shaped valleys.	They form U-shaped valleys.
They form meanders.	They may not form meanders.
They form big deltas at their mouths where they meet the sea.	They form small rivers and estuaries.
They are antecedent rivers, i.e. they maintain their original course and pattern in spite of the changes in the rock topography.	They are consequent rivers, i.e. they flow in the direction of the slope.

19. The participation of people is crucial to the goal of effective conservation and management of forests and wildlife .This can be ensured in following ways:-

(a) **Joint Forests Management:** Through this, forests and local communities jointly manage forests and share responsibilities and user rights. Under JVM, the legal ownership remains with the government forest department and local village communities co-manages the forests and are entitled to share in forests products. This increases people' stake in protection of forests resources since they are directly dependent on forests products for their livelihood and they would like to conserve them so that they can continue reaping benefits out of the forests resources for long time. This initiative has proved to be a huge success in India in forest management and conservation efforts ever since its inception in the 1990s.

(b) **Holding regular meeting and exchange of information between the local communities and the forests officials: This is important because-**

(i) to exchange information about the progress of forest conservation initiatives, and the condition of forests resources

(ii) report of any illegal activities like poaching, smuggling and cutting of woods.

(iii) decimate information and make communities aware about new and improved techniques for forest conservation.

(iv) briefing of future plans and initiatives.

(c) **Incentives for people involved in conservation efforts :** There should be incentives for people achieving extra success in their conservation efforts by rewarding them with prize money or through permanent jobs for one or more member of their family in the forest department along with other suitable recognitions in order to boost their enthusiasm and encourage others to do the same.

(d) **Participation of NGOs and expert bodies in forestry :**

(i) to train and enhance the skills of people in conserving forests;

(ii) to inform them about the benefits and role of forests in our life;

(iii) mobilize the support of local population in conservation efforts.

20. Vulnerability is the human dimension of disasters and is the result of the range of economic, social, cultural, institutional, political and psychological factors that shape people's lives and the environment that they live in.

Drought refers to the situation of less moisture in the soil (which makes the land unproductive) and scarcity of water for drinking, irrigation, industrial uses and other purposes, usually caused by deficient/less than average rainfall over a long period of time. Some states of India feature the perennial drought such as Rajasthan, Odisha, Gujarat, Madhya Pradesh etc.Sixteen percent of the country's total area is drought-prone and approximately 50 million people are affected annually by droughts. In India about 68 percent of net sown area in the country is drought-prone. Most of the drought-prone areas identified by the Government of India lie in arid, semi-arid and sub-humid areas of the country. In the arid and semi-arid zones, very severe droughts occur once in every eight to nine years.

21.

(D) North Atlantic Drift

Oyashio Current (E)

Arabian Plate (B)

(C) Sinharaja Forest, Sri Lanka

(A) Java Trench

Map not to scale

22.

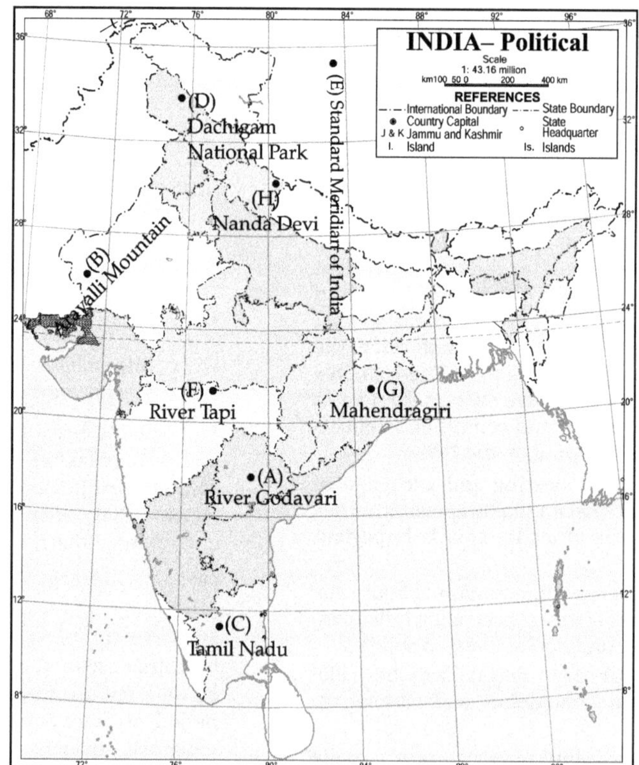

PART-A

CHAPTER 1 : GEOGRAPHY AS A DISCIPLINE

Geography as a Discipline

Geography as an Integrating Discipline

- Geography has a holistic approach.
- It helps in understanding the reality in totality in its spatial perspectives.
- It has interface with numerous natural and social sciences.

Physical Geography and Natural Sciences

All the branches of physical geography have interface with natural sciences. A geographer should have some proficiency in mathematics and arts, particularly in drawing maps.

Geography and Social Science

All the social science disciplines, viz, sociology, political science, economics and demography study different aspect of social reality.

Branches of Geography

Based on Systematic Approach

Physical

- Geomorphology
- Climatology
- Hydrology
- Soil Geography

Human

- Social / Cultural
- Population and Settlement
- Economic
- Historical
- Political

Biogeography

- Plant
- Zoo
- Ecology / Ecosystem
- Environmental

Based on Regional Approach

Regional Studies / Area Studies

- Macro regional studies
- Meso regional studies
- Micro regional studies

Regional Development

Regional Analysis

Regional Planning

- Country/Rural planning
- Town/Urban Planning

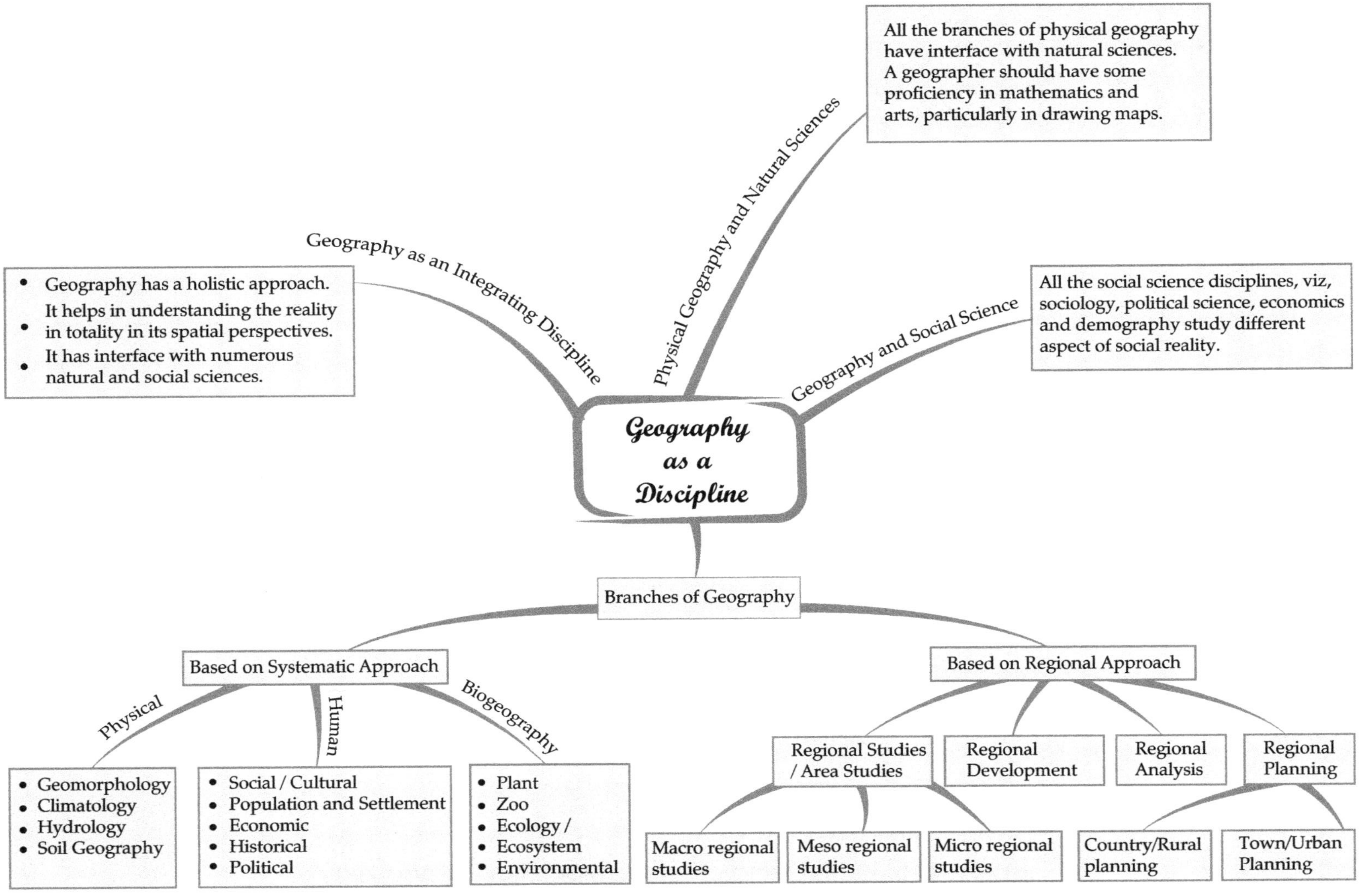

CHAPTER 2 : THE ORIGIN AND EVOLUTION OF THE EARTH

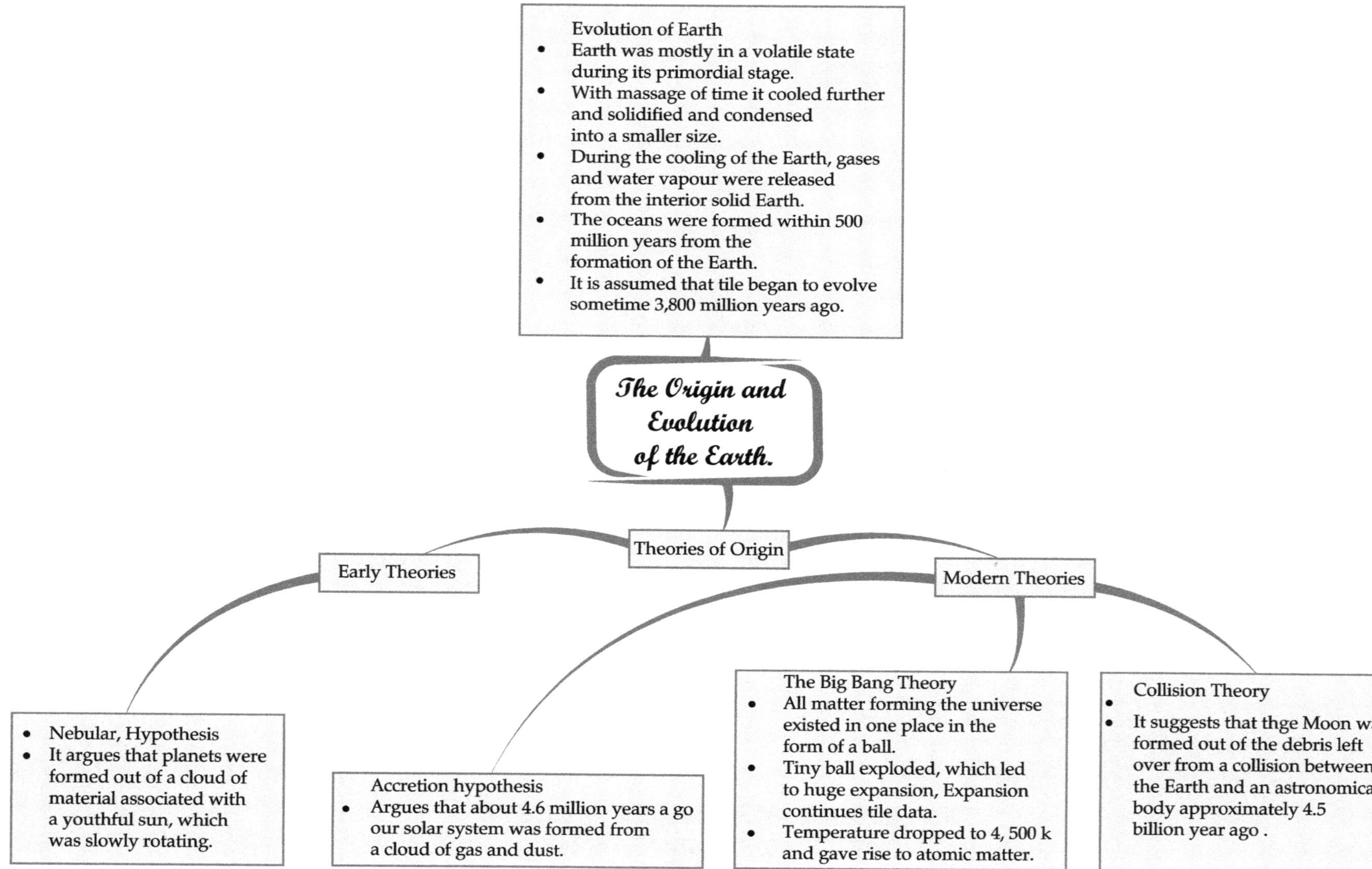

Evolution of Earth
• Earth was mostly in a volatile state during its primordial stage.
• With massage of time it cooled further and solidified and condensed into a smaller size.
• During the cooling of the Earth, gases and water vapour were released from the interior solid Earth.
• The oceans were formed within 500 million years from the formation of the Earth.
• It is assumed that tile began to evolve sometime 3,800 million years ago.
The Origin and Evolution of the Earth.
Theories of Origin
Early Theories
Modern Theories
• Nebular, Hypothesis
• It argues that planets were formed out of a cloud of material associated with a youthful sun, which was slowly rotating.
Accretion hypothesis
• Argues that about 4.6 million years a go our solar system was formed from a cloud of gas and dust.
The Big Bang Theory
• All matter forming the universe existed in one place in the form of a ball.
• Tiny ball exploded, which led to huge expansion, Expansion continues tile data.
• Temperature dropped to 4, 500 k and gave rise to atomic matter.
Collision Theory
• It suggests that thge Moon was formed out of the debris left over from a collision between the Earth and an astronomical body approximately 4.5 billion year ago .

CHAPTER 3 : INTERIOR OF THE EARTH

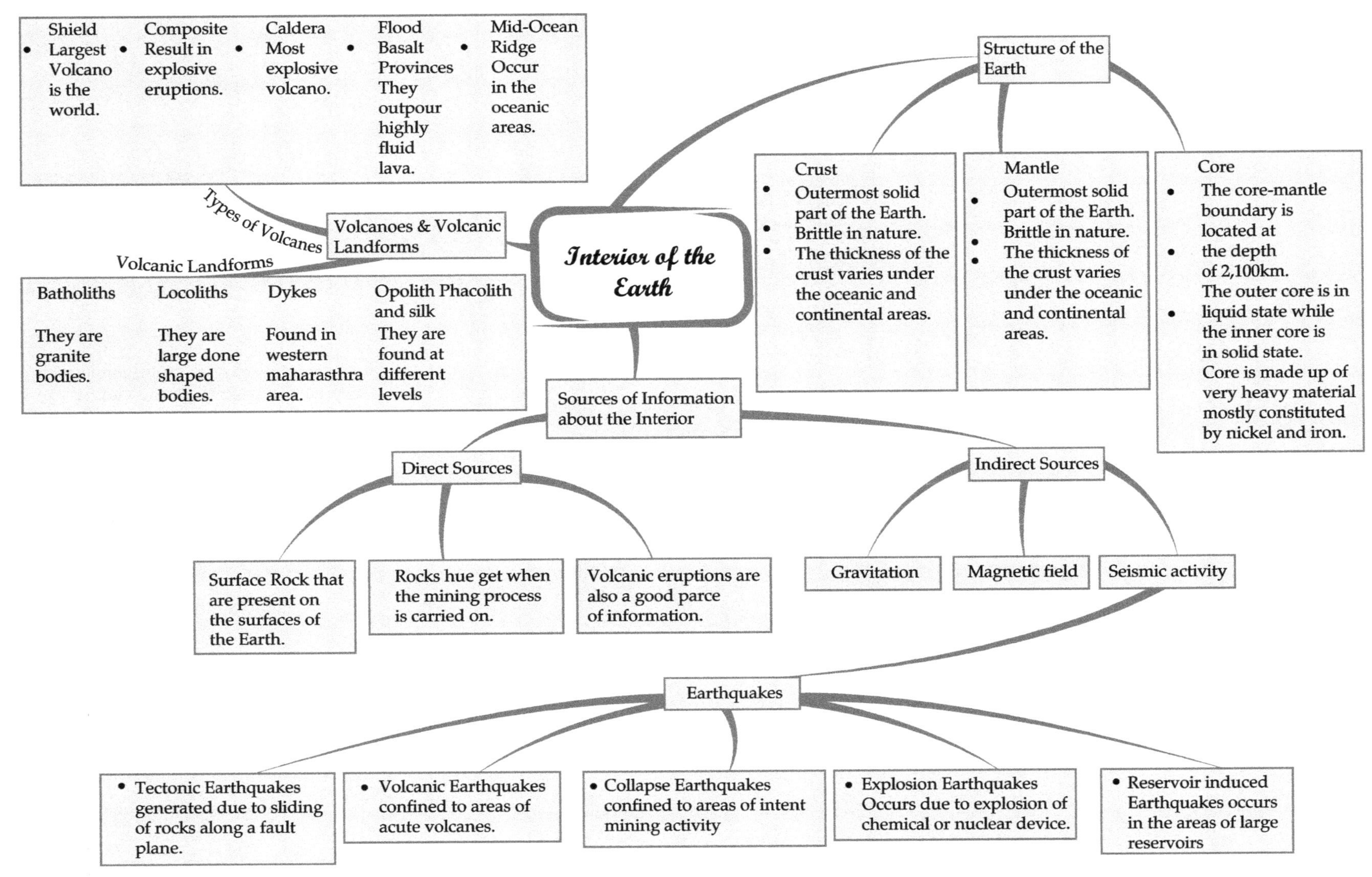
Interior of the Earth
Volcanoes & Volcanic Landforms
Types of Volcanes
• Shield Largest Volcano is the world.
• Composite Result in explosive eruptions.
• Caldera Most explosive volcano.
• Flood Basalt Provinces They outpour highly fluid lava.
• Mid-Ocean Ridge Occur in the oceanic areas.
Volcanic Landforms
Batholiths They are granite bodies.
Locoliths They are large done shaped bodies.
Dykes Found in western maharasthra area.
Opolith Phacolith and silk They are found at different levels
Structure of the Earth
Crust
• Outermost solid part of the Earth.
• Brittle in nature.
• The thickness of the crust varies under the oceanic and continental areas.
Mantle
• Outermost solid part of the Earth.
• Brittle in nature.
• The thickness of the crust varies under the oceanic and continental areas.
Core
• The core-mantle boundary is located at
• the depth of 2,100km.
The outer core is in
• liquid state while the inner core is in solid state.
Core is made up of very heavy material mostly constituted by nickel and iron.
Sources of Information about the Interior
Direct Sources
Surface Rock that are present on the surfaces of the Earth.
Rocks hue get when the mining process is carried on.
Volcanic eruptions are also a good parce of information.
Indirect Sources
Gravitation
Magnetic field
Seismic activity
Earthquakes
• Tectonic Earthquakes generated due to sliding of rocks along a fault plane.
• Volcanic Earthquakes confined to areas of acute volcanes.
• Collapse Earthquakes confined to areas of intent mining activity
• Explosion Earthquakes Occurs due to explosion of chemical or nuclear device.
• Reservoir induced Earthquakes occurs in the areas of large reservoirs

CHAPTER 4 : DISTRIBUTION OF OCEANS AND CONTINENTS

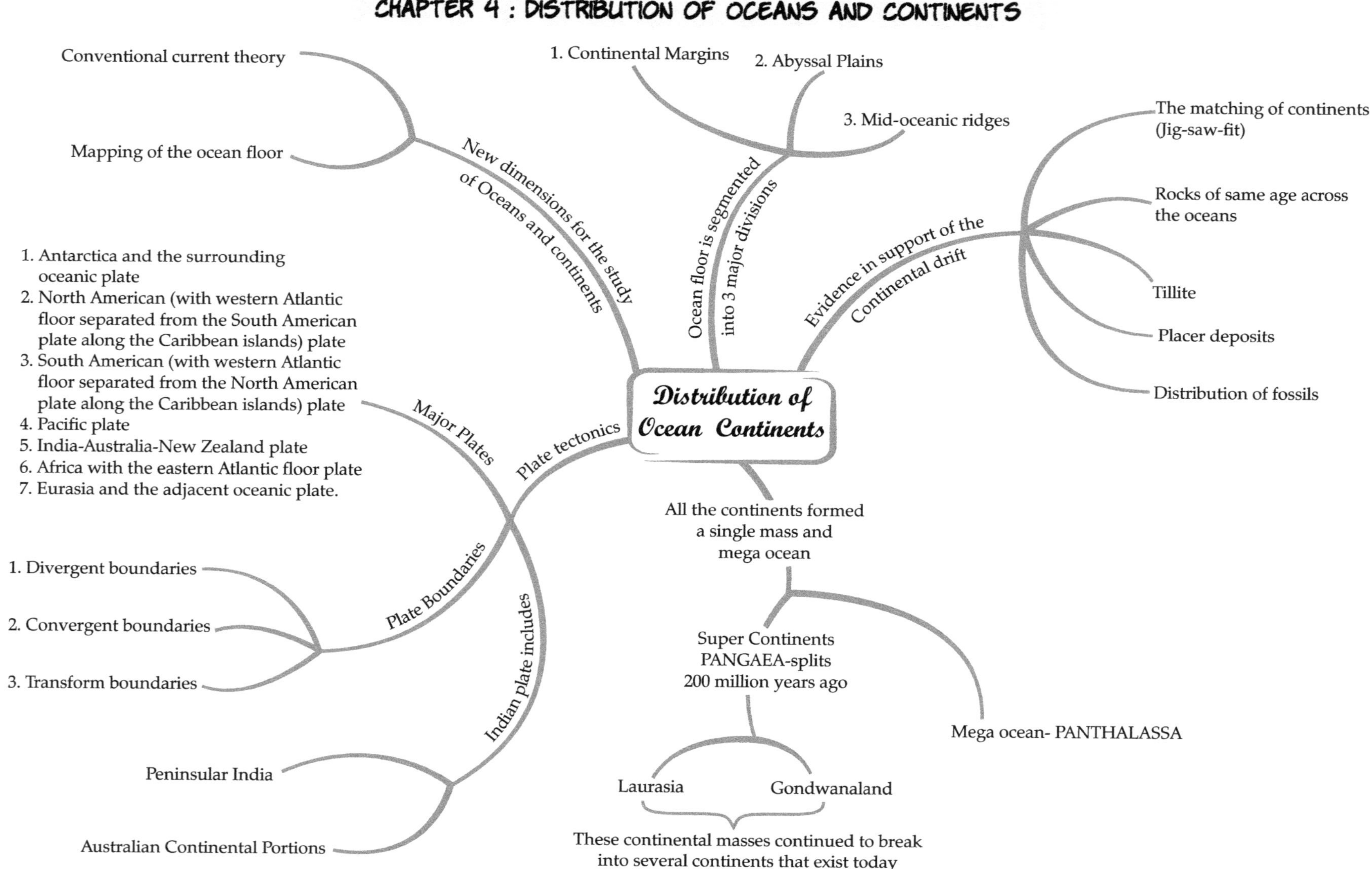

CHAPTER 5 : MINERAL & ROCKS

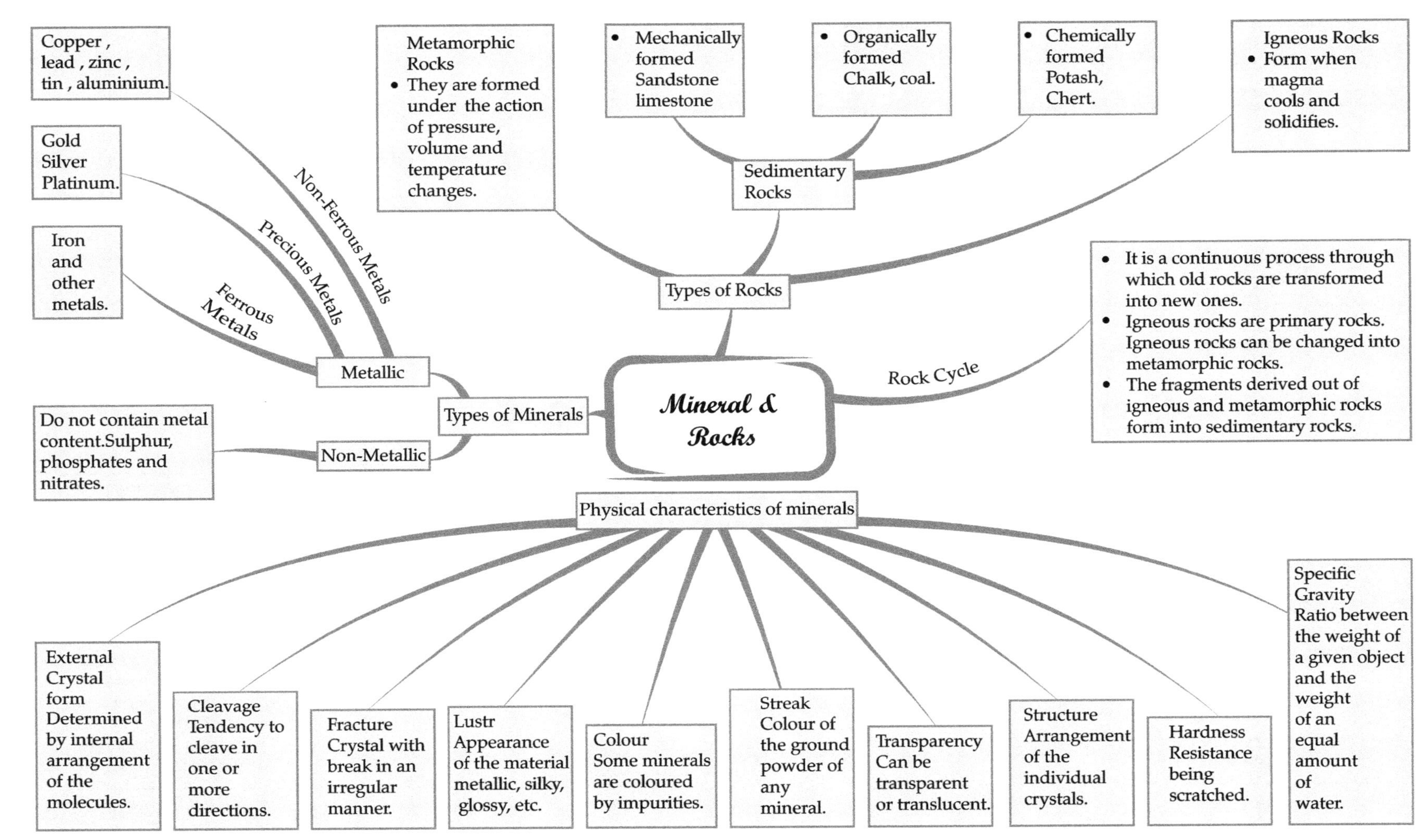
Mineral & Rocks
Types of Rocks
Metamorphic Rocks
• They are formed under the action of pressure, volume and temperature changes.
Sedimentary Rocks
• Mechanically formed Sandstone limestone
• Organically formed Chalk, coal.
• Chemically formed Potash, Chert.
Igneous Rocks
• Form when magma cools and solidifies.
Rock Cycle
• It is a continuous process through which old rocks are transformed into new ones.
• Igneous rocks are primary rocks. Igneous rocks can be changed into metamorphic rocks.
• The fragments derived out of igneous and metamorphic rocks form into sedimentary rocks.
Types of Minerals
Metallic
Non-Ferrous Metals
Copper, lead, zinc, tin, aluminium.
Precious Metals
Gold Silver Platinum.
Ferrous Metals
Iron and other metals.
Non-Metallic
Do not contain metal content.Sulphur, phosphates and nitrates.
Physical characteristics of minerals
External Crystal form Determined by internal arrangement of the molecules.
Cleavage Tendency to cleave in one or more directions.
Fracture Crystal with break in an irregular manner.
Lustr Appearance of the material metallic, silky, glossy, etc.
Colour Some minerals are coloured by impurities.
Streak Colour of the ground powder of any mineral.
Transparency Can be transparent or translucent.
Structure Arrangement of the individual crystals.
Hardness Resistance being scratched.
Specific Gravity Ratio between the weight of a given object and the weight of an equal amount of water.

CHAPTER 6 : GEOMORPHIC PROCESSES

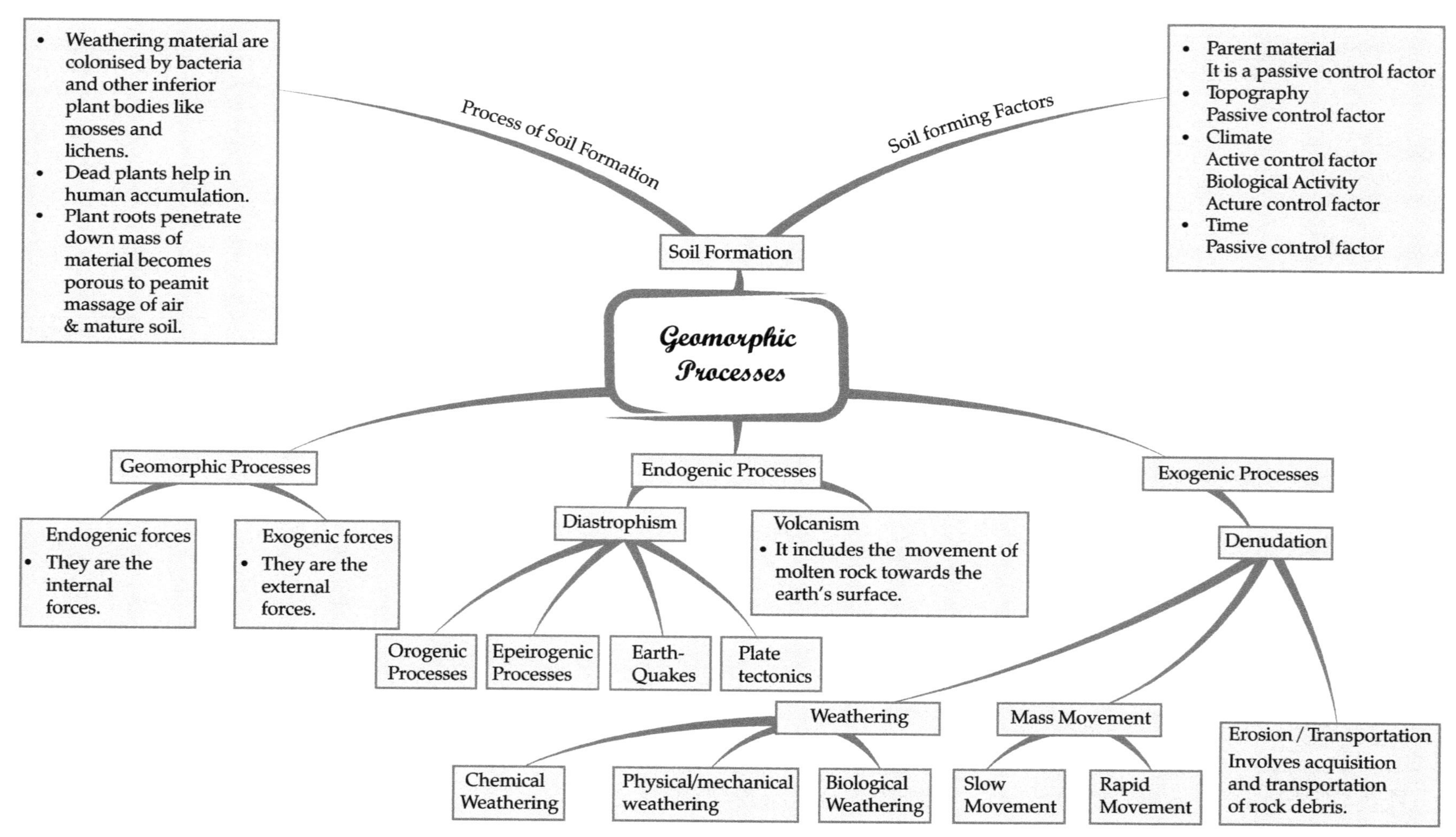

CHAPTER 7 : LANDFORMS AND THEIR EVOLUTION

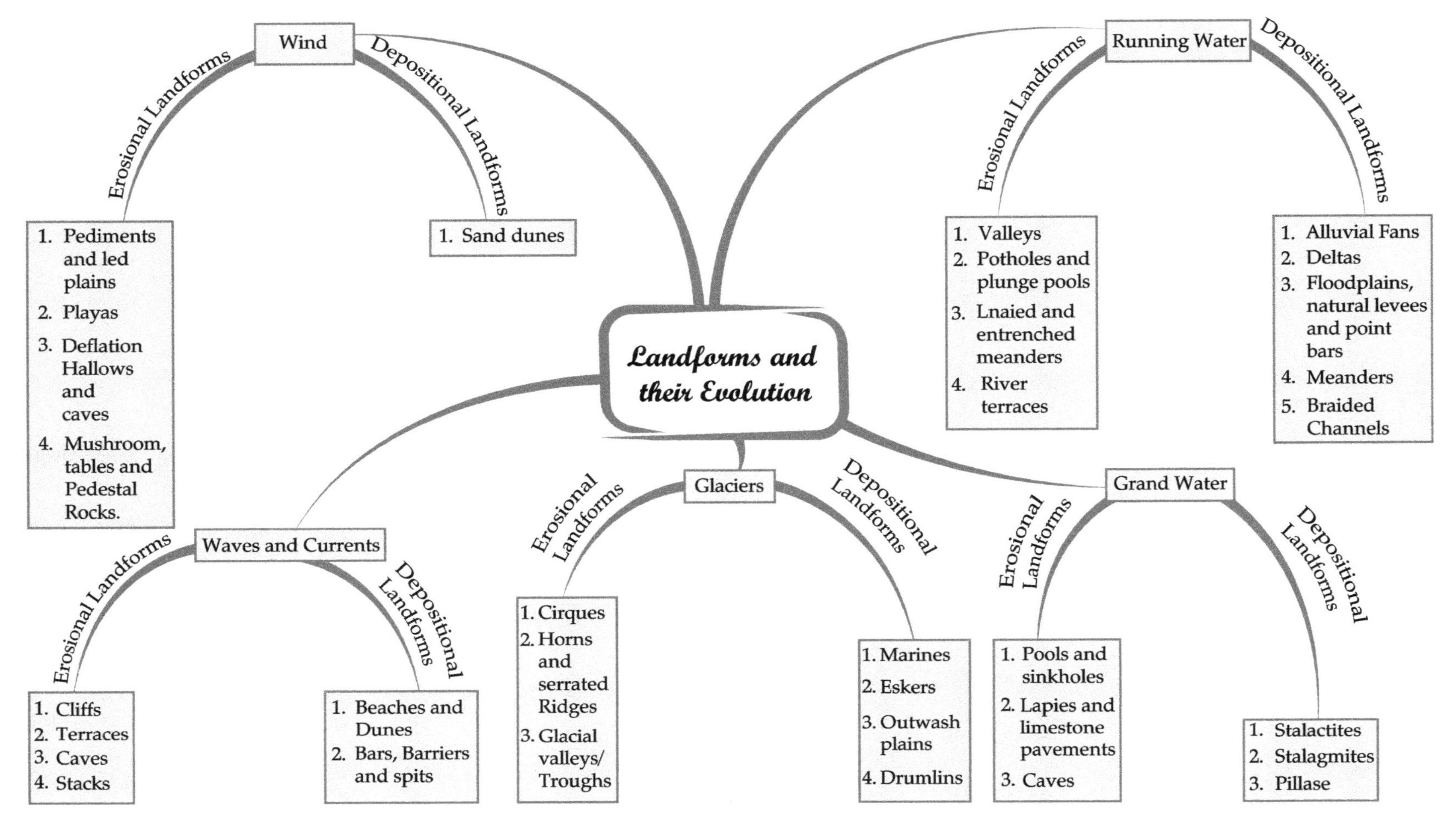
Landforms and their Evolution
Wind
Erosional Landforms
1. Pediments and led plains
2. Playas
3. Deflation Hallows and caves
4. Mushroom, tables and Pedestal Rocks.
Depositional Landforms
1. Sand dunes
Running Water
Erosional Landforms
1. Valleys
2. Potholes and plunge pools
3. Lnaied and entrenched meanders
4. River terraces
Depositional Landforms
1. Alluvial Fans
2. Deltas
3. Floodplains, natural levees and point bars
4. Meanders
5. Braided Channels
Waves and Currents
Erosional Landforms
1. Cliffs
2. Terraces
3. Caves
4. Stacks
Depositional Landforms
1. Beaches and Dunes
2. Bars, Barriers and spits
Glaciers
Erosional Landforms
1. Cirques
2. Horns and serrated Ridges
3. Glacial valleys/ Troughs
Depositional Landforms
1. Marines
2. Eskers
3. Outwash plains
4. Drumlins
Grand Water
Erosional Landforms
1. Pools and sinkholes
2. Lapies and limestone pavements
3. Caves
Depositional Landforms
1. Stalactites
2. Stalagmites
3. Pillase

CHAPTER 8 : COMPOSITION AND STRUCTURE OF ATMOSPHERE

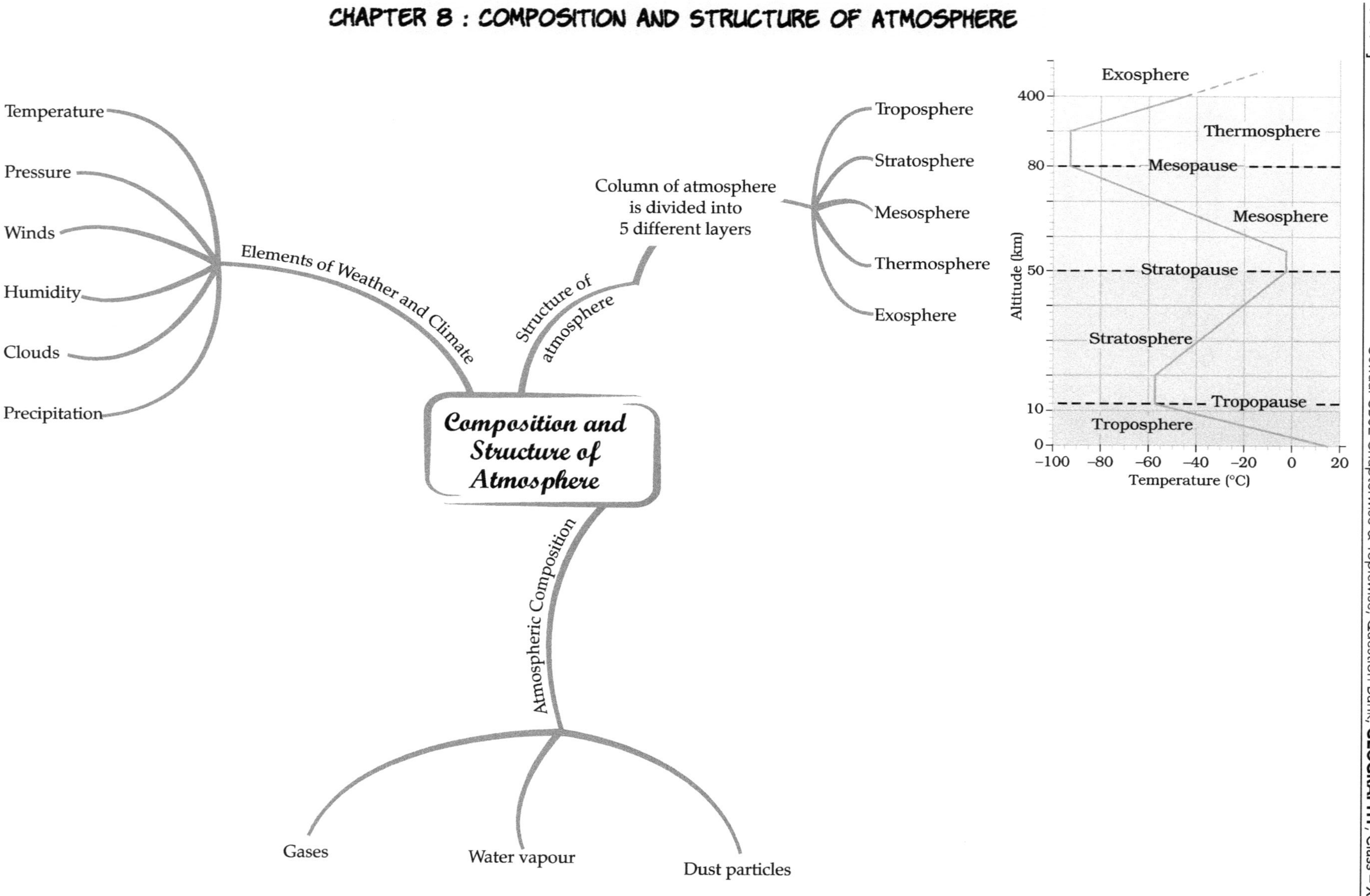

CHAPTER 9 : SOLAR RADIATIONS, HEAT BALANCE AND TEMPERATURE

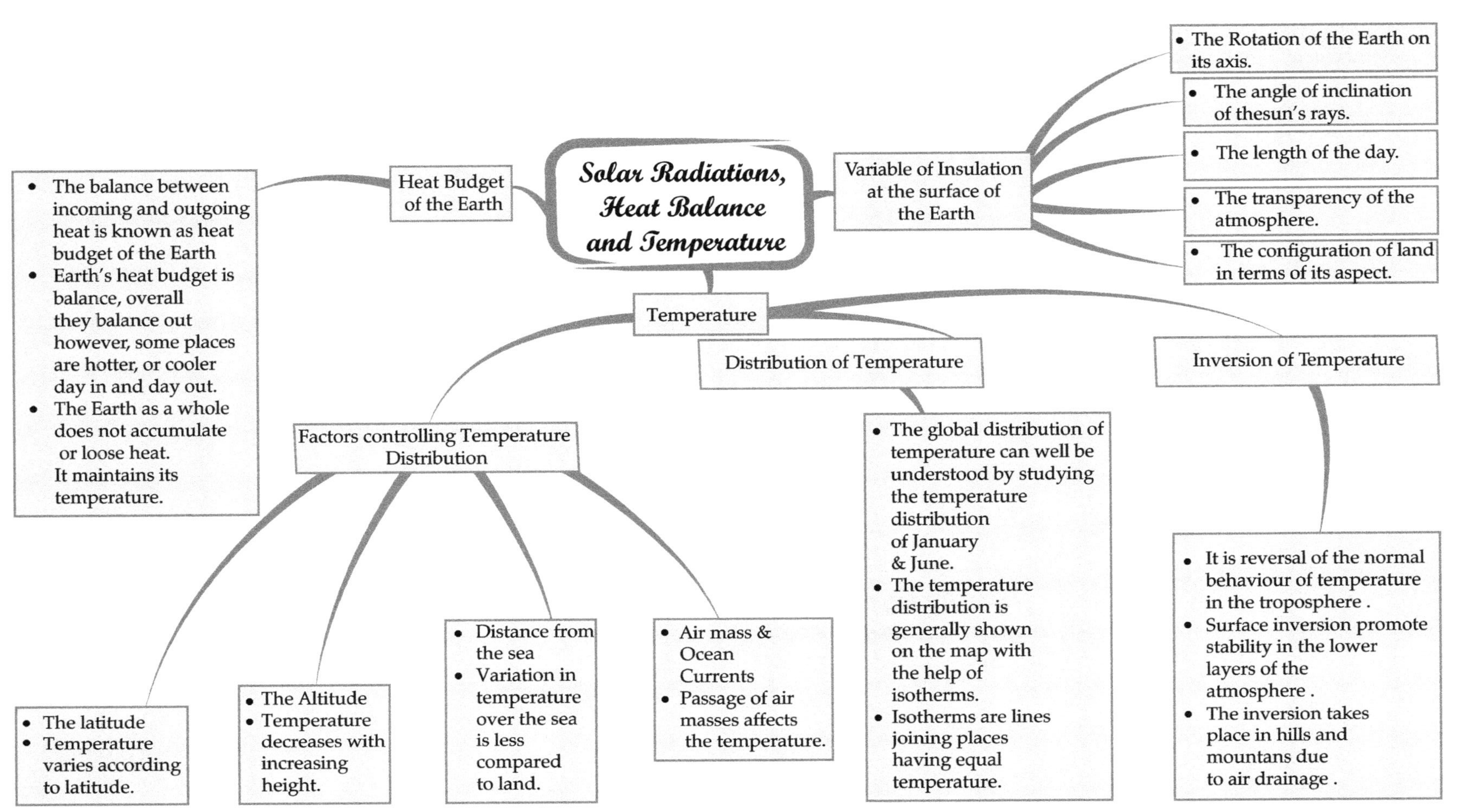

Solar Radiations, Heat Balance and Temperature
Heat Budget of the Earth
• The balance between incoming and outgoing heat is known as heat budget of the Earth
• Earth's heat budget is balance, overall they balance out however, some places are hotter, or cooler day in and day out.
• The Earth as a whole does not accumulate or loose heat. It maintains its temperature.
Variable of Insulation at the surface of the Earth
• The Rotation of the Earth on its axis.
• The angle of inclination of thesun's rays.
• The length of the day.
• The transparency of the atmosphere.
• The configuration of land in terms of its aspect.
Temperature
Factors controlling Temperature Distribution
• The latitude
• Temperature varies according to latitude.
• The Altitude
• Temperature decreases with increasing height.
• Distance from the sea
• Variation in temperature over the sea is less compared to land.
• Air mass & Ocean Currents
• Passage of air masses affects the temperature.
Distribution of Temperature
• The global distribution of temperature can well be understood by studying the temperature distribution of January & June.
• The temperature distribution is generally shown on the map with the help of isotherms.
• Isotherms are lines joining places having equal temperature.
Inversion of Temperature
• It is reversal of the normal behaviour of temperature in the troposphere .
• Surface inversion promote stability in the lower layers of the atmosphere .
• The inversion takes place in hills and mountans due to air drainage .

CHAPTER 10 : ATMOSPHERIC CIRCULATION AND WEATHER SYSTEMS

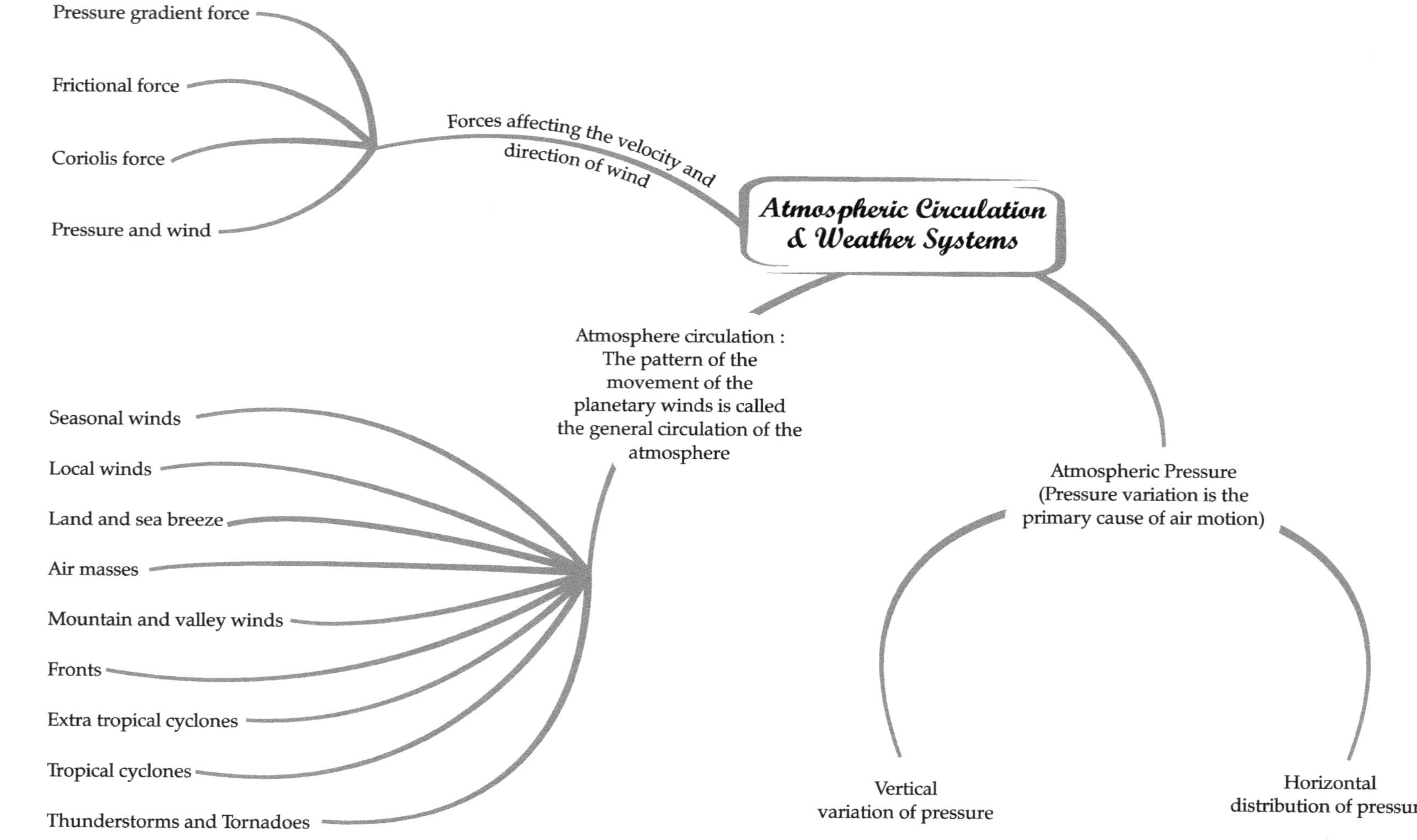
Atmospheric Circulation & Weather Systems
Forces affecting the velocity and direction of wind
Pressure gradient force
Frictional force
Coriolis force
Pressure and wind
Atmosphere circulation : The pattern of the movement of the planetary winds is called the general circulation of the atmosphere
Seasonal winds
Local winds
Land and sea breeze
Air masses
Mountain and valley winds
Fronts
Extra tropical cyclones
Tropical cyclones
Thunderstorms and Tornadoes
Atmospheric Pressure (Pressure variation is the primary cause of air motion)
Vertical variation of pressure
Horizontal distribution of pressure

CHAPTER 11 : WATER IN THE ATMOSPHERE

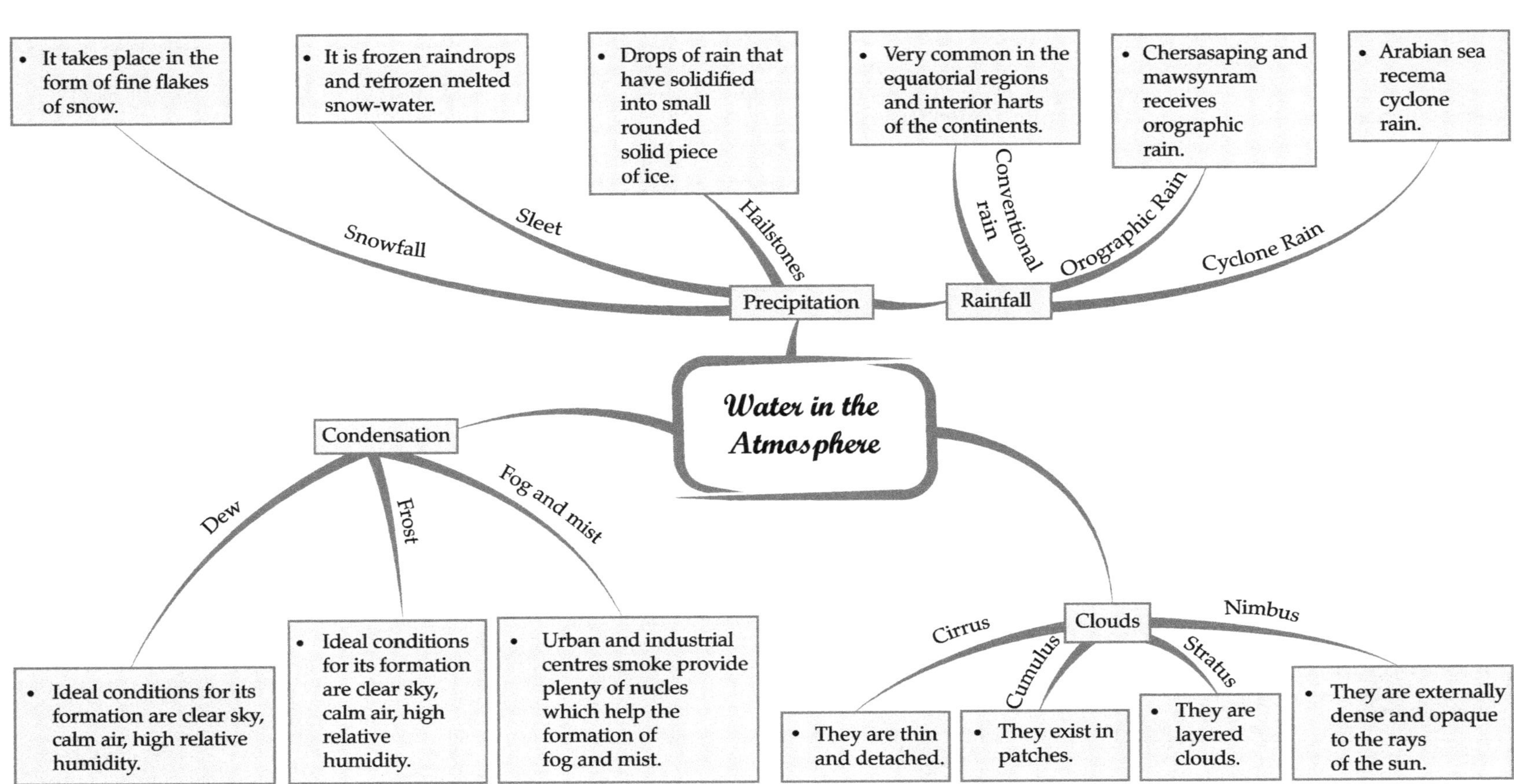

CHAPTER 12 : WORLD CLIMATE AND CLIMATE CHANGE

World climate & Climate change

Causes of Climate Change

Astronomical causes

1. Changes in solar output associated with sunspot activities
2. Miliankovitch oscillations
3. Volcanism
4. Concentration of greenhouse gases in the atmosphere causing global warming

Terrestrial causes

Greenhouses Gases (GHGs) are–
1. Chlorofluorocarbons (CFC_s)
2. Carbondioxide (CO_2)
3. Methane (CH_4)
4. Nitrous oxide (N_2O)
5. Ozone (O_3)

Koeppen's scheme of classification of climate

Group	Characteristics
A - Tropical	Average temperature of the coldest month is 18° C or higher
B - Dry Climates	Potential evaporation exceeds precipitation
C - Warm Temperate	The average temperature of the coldest month of the (Mid-latitude) climates years is higher than minus 3°C but below 18°C
D - Cold Snow Forest Climates	The average temperature of the coldest month is minus 3° C or below
E - Cold Climates	Average temperature for all months is below 10° C
H - High Land	Cold due to elevation

Climatic Types according to Koeppen

Group	Type	Letter code	Characteristics
A-Tropical Humid Climate	Tropical wet	Af	No dry season
	Tropical monsoon	am	Monsoonal, short dry season
	Tropical wet and dry	aw	Winter dry season
B-Dry Climate	Subtropical steppe	BSh	Low-latitude semi arid or dry
	Subtropical desert	BWh	Low-latitude arid or dry
	Mid-latitude steppe	BSk	Mid-latitude semi arid or dry
	Mid-latitude desert	BWk	Mid-latitude arid or dry
C-Warm temperate (Mid-latitude) Climates	Humid subtropical	Cfa	No dry season, warm summer
	Mediterranean	Cs	Dry hot summer
D-Cold Snowforest Climates	Marine west coast	Cfb	No dry season, warm and cool summer
	Humid continental	Df	No dry season, severe winter
E-Cold Climates	Subarctic	Dw	Winter dry and very severe
	Tundra	ET	No true summer
	Polar ice cap	EF	Perennial ice
H-Highland	Highland	H	Highland with snow cover

CHAPTER 13 & 14 : WATER (OCEANS) & MOVEMENTS OF OCEAN WATER

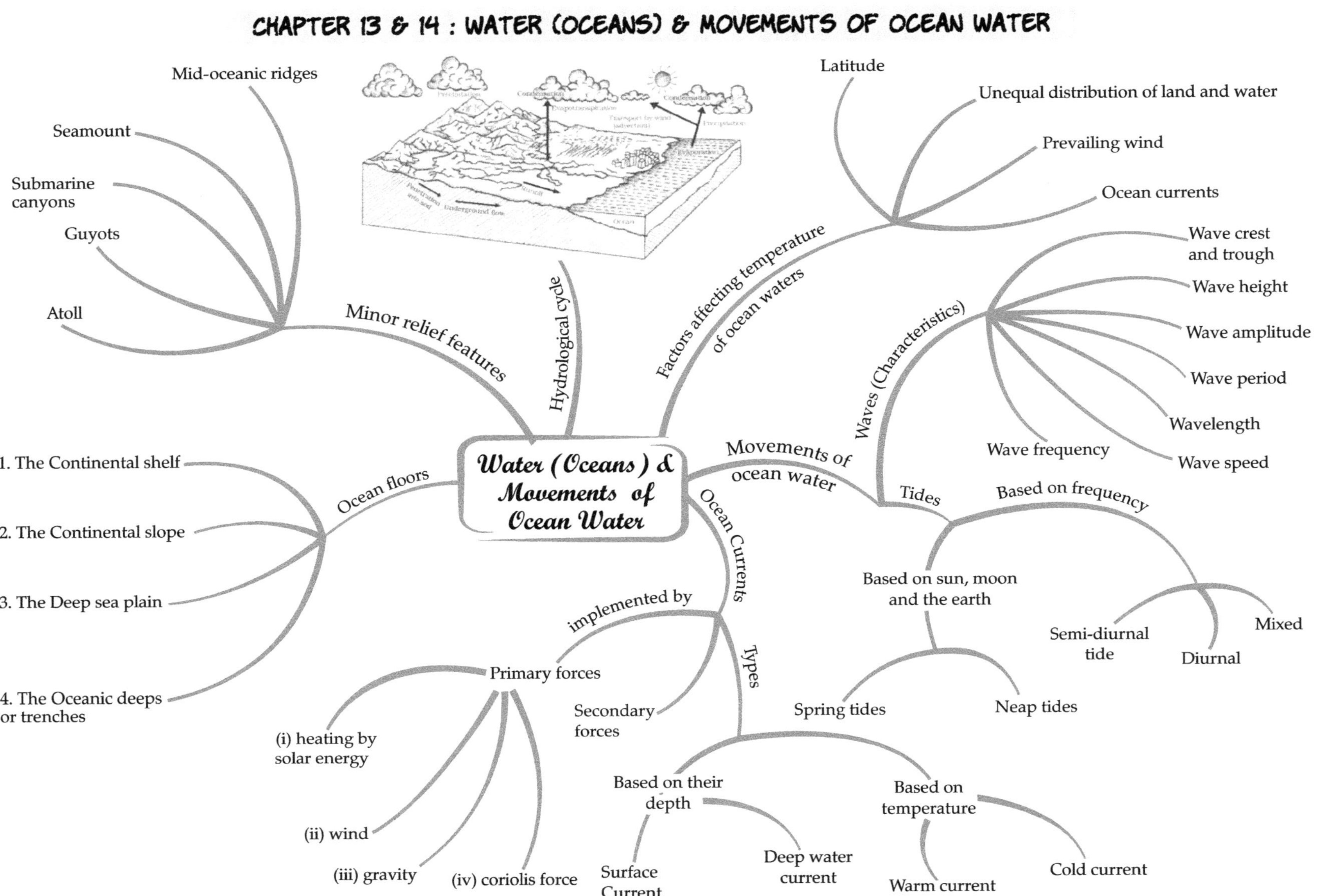
Water (Oceans) & Movements of Ocean Water
Minor relief features
Mid-oceanic ridges
Seamount
Submarine canyons
Guyots
Atoll
Hydrological cycle
Factors affecting temperature of ocean waters
Latitude
Unequal distribution of land and water
Prevailing wind
Ocean currents
Movements of ocean water
Waves (Characteristics)
Wave crest and trough
Wave height
Wave amplitude
Wave period
Wavelength
Wave speed
Wave frequency
Tides
Based on frequency
Semi-diurnal tide
Diurnal
Mixed
Based on sun, moon and the earth
Spring tides
Neap tides
Ocean Currents
implemented by
Primary forces
(i) heating by solar energy
(ii) wind
(iii) gravity
(iv) coriolis force
Secondary forces
Types
Based on their depth
Surface Current
Deep water current
Based on temperature
Warm current
Cold current
Ocean floors
1. The Continental shelf
2. The Continental slope
3. The Deep sea plain
4. The Oceanic deeps or trenches

CHAPTER 15 & 16 : LIFE ON THE EARTH & BIODIVERSITY AND CONSERVATION

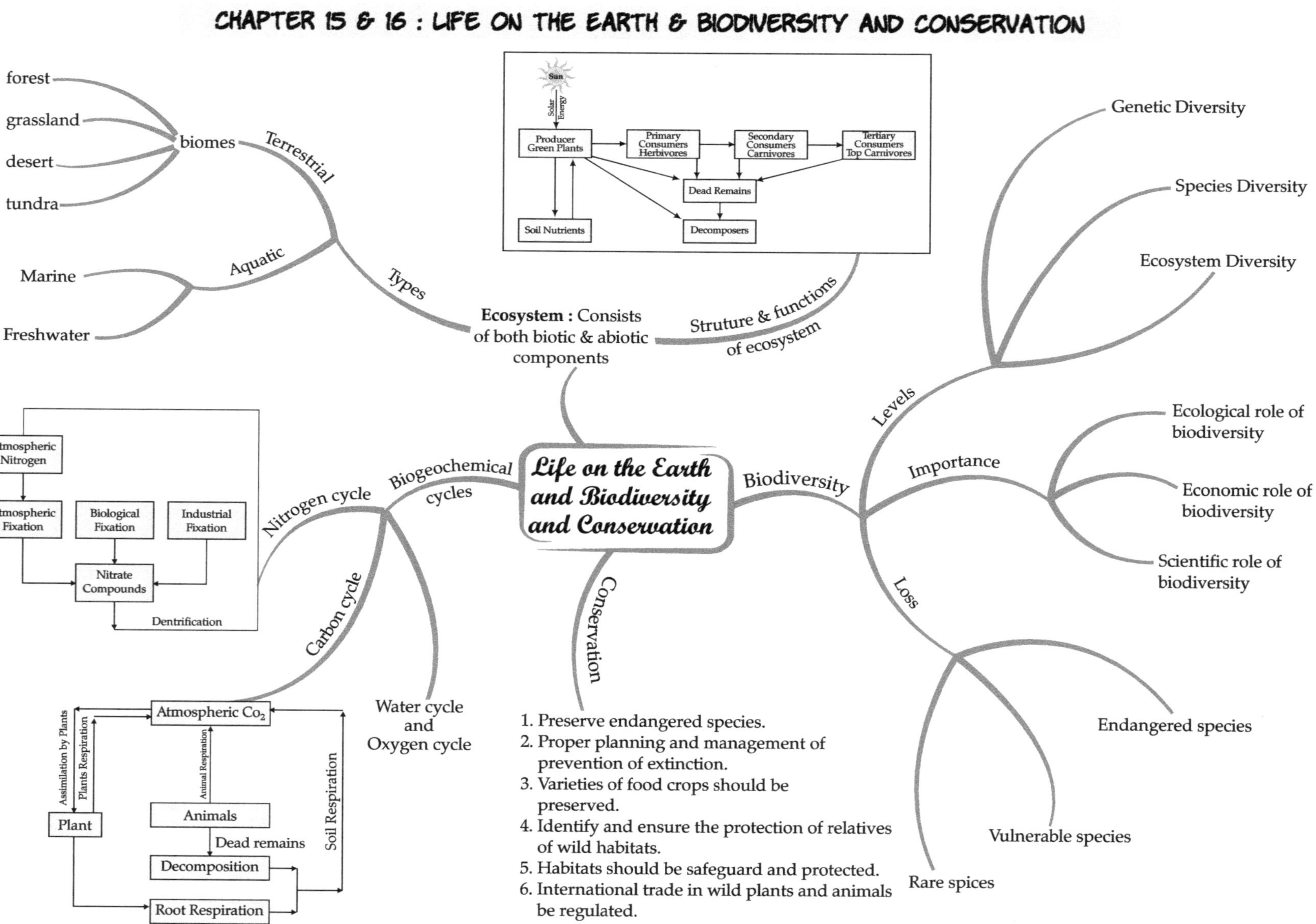

PART-B

CHAPTER 1 : INDIA-LOCATION

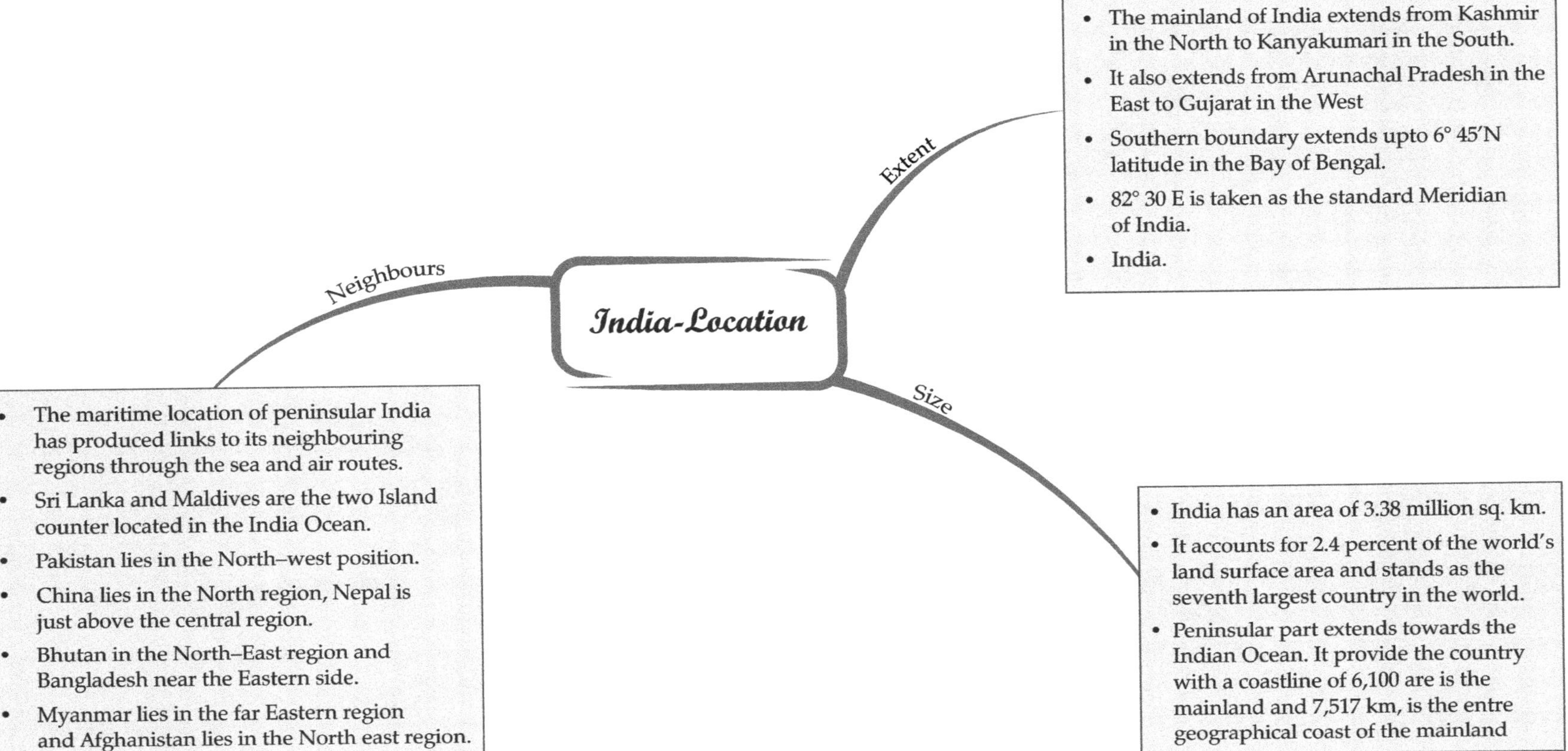

India-Location
Extent
The mainland of India extends from Kashmir in the North to Kanyakumari in the South.
It also extends from Arunachal Pradesh in the East to Gujarat in the West
Southern boundary extends upto 6° 45′N latitude in the Bay of Bengal.
82° 30 E is taken as the standard Meridian of India.
India.
Size
India has an area of 3.38 million sq. km.
It accounts for 2.4 percent of the world's land surface area and stands as the seventh largest country in the world.
Peninsular part extends towards the Indian Ocean. It provide the country with a coastline of 6,100 are is the mainland and 7,517 km, is the entre geographical coast of the mainland
Neighbours
The maritime location of peninsular India has produced links to its neighbouring regions through the sea and air routes.
Sri Lanka and Maldives are the two Island counter located in the India Ocean.
Pakistan lies in the North–west position.
China lies in the North region, Nepal is just above the central region.
Bhutan in the North–East region and Bangladesh near the Eastern side.
Myanmar lies in the far Eastern region and Afghanistan lies in the North east region.

CHAPTER 2 : STRUCTURE AND PHYSIOGRAPHY

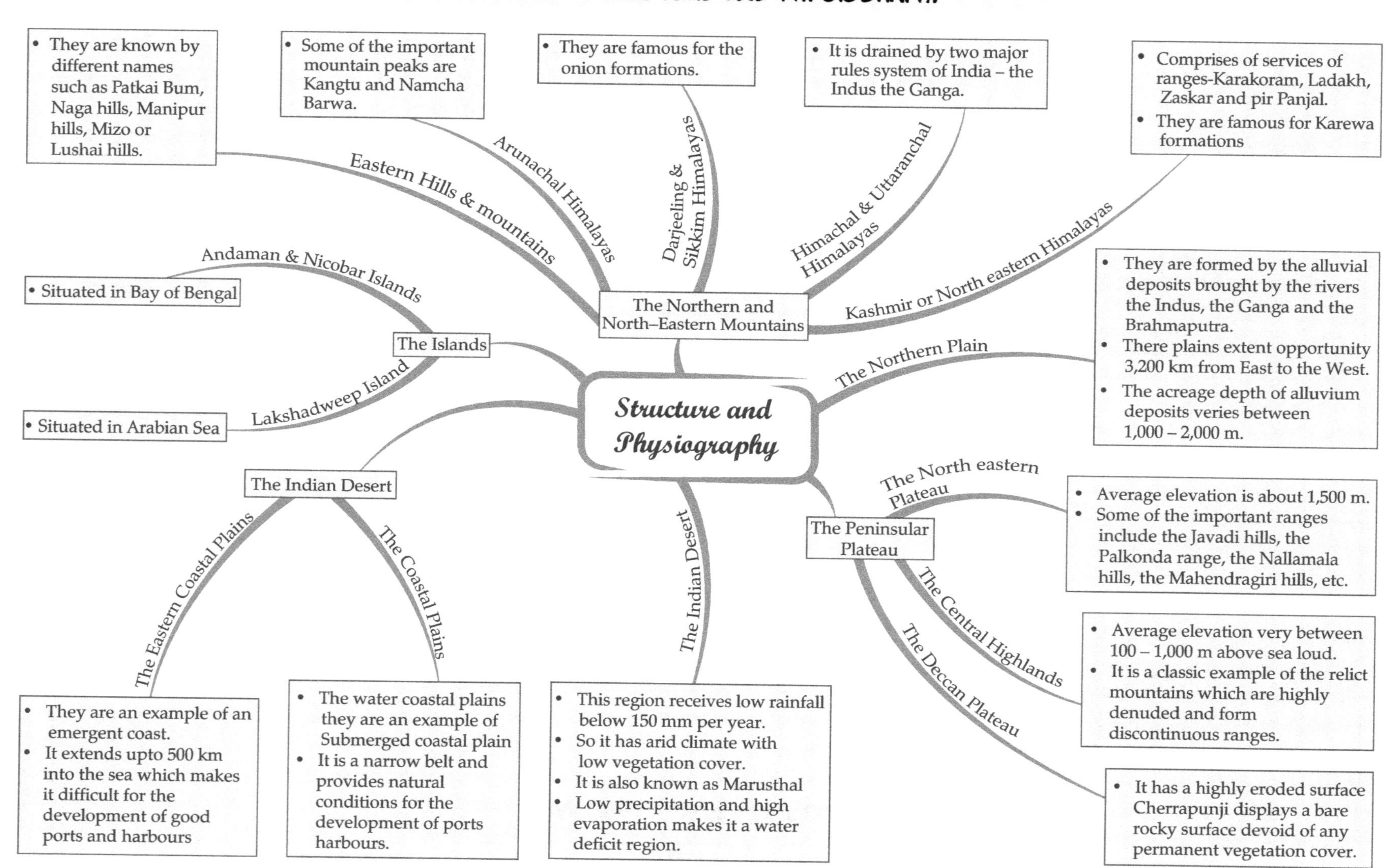

Structure and Physiography
The Northern and North–Eastern Mountains
Eastern Hills & mountains
They are known by different names such as Patkai Bum, Naga hills, Manipur hills, Mizo or Lushai hills.
Arunachal Himalayas
Some of the important mountain peaks are Kangtu and Namcha Barwa.
Darjeeling & Sikkim Himalayas
They are famous for the onion formations.
Himachal & Uttaranchal Himalayas
It is drained by two major rules system of India – the Indus the Ganga.
Kashmir or North eastern Himalayas
Comprises of services of ranges-Karakoram, Ladakh, Zaskar and pir Panjal.
They are famous for Karewa formations
The Northern Plain
They are formed by the alluvial deposits brought by the rivers the Indus, the Ganga and the Brahmaputra.
There plains extent opportunity 3,200 km from East to the West.
The acreage depth of alluvium deposits veries between 1,000 – 2,000 m.
The Peninsular Plateau
The North eastern Plateau
Average elevation is about 1,500 m.
Some of the important ranges include the Javadi hills, the Palkonda range, the Nallamala hills, the Mahendragiri hills, etc.
The Central Highlands
Average elevation very between 100 – 1,000 m above sea loud.
It is a classic example of the relict mountains which are highly denuded and form discontinuous ranges.
The Deccan Plateau
It has a highly eroded surface Cherrapunji displays a bare rocky surface devoid of any permanent vegetation cover.
The Indian Desert
This region receives low rainfall below 150 mm per year.
So it has arid climate with low vegetation cover.
It is also known as Marusthal
Low precipitation and high evaporation makes it a water deficit region.
The Indian Desert
The Coastal Plains
The water coastal plains they are an example of Submerged coastal plain
It is a narrow belt and provides natural conditions for the development of ports harbours.
The Eastern Coastal Plains
They are an example of an emergent coast.
It extends upto 500 km into the sea which makes it difficult for the development of good ports and harbours
The Islands
Andaman & Nicobar Islands
Situated in Bay of Bengal
Lakshadweep Island
Situated in Arabian Sea

CHAPTER 3 : DRAINAGE SYSTEM

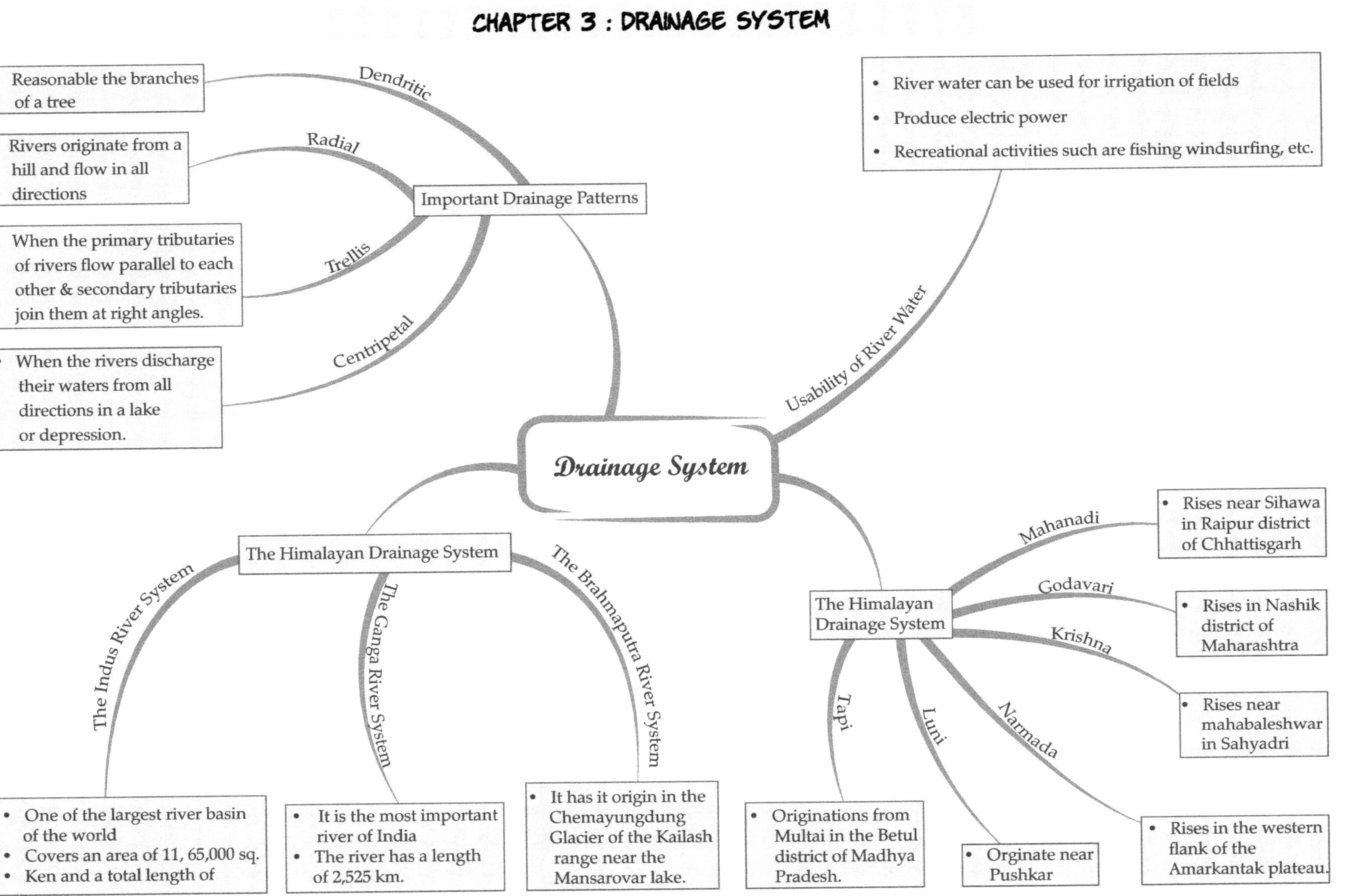
Drainage System
Important Drainage Patterns
Dendritic
• Reasonable the branches of a tree
Radial
• Rivers originate from a hill and flow in all directions
Trellis
• When the primary tributaries of rivers flow parallel to each other & secondary tributaries join them at right angles.
Centripetal
• When the rivers discharge their waters from all directions in a lake or depression.
Usability of River Water
• River water can be used for irrigation of fields
• Produce electric power
• Recreational activities such are fishing windsurfing, etc.
The Himalayan Drainage System
The Indus River System
• One of the largest river basin of the world
• Covers an area of 11, 65,000 sq.
• Ken and a total length of
The Ganga River System
• It is the most important river of India
• The river has a length of 2,525 km.
The Brahmaputra River System
• It has it origin in the Chemayungdung Glacier of the Kailash range near the Mansarovar lake.
The Himalayan Drainage System
Mahanadi
• Rises near Sihawa in Raipur district of Chhattisgarh
Godavari
• Rises in Nashik district of Maharashtra
Krishna
• Rises near mahabaleshwar in Sahyadri
Narmada
• Rises in the western flank of the Amarkantak plateau.
Luni
• Orginate near Pushkar
Tapi
• Originations from Multai in the Betul district of Madhya Pradesh.

CHAPTER 4 : CLIMATE

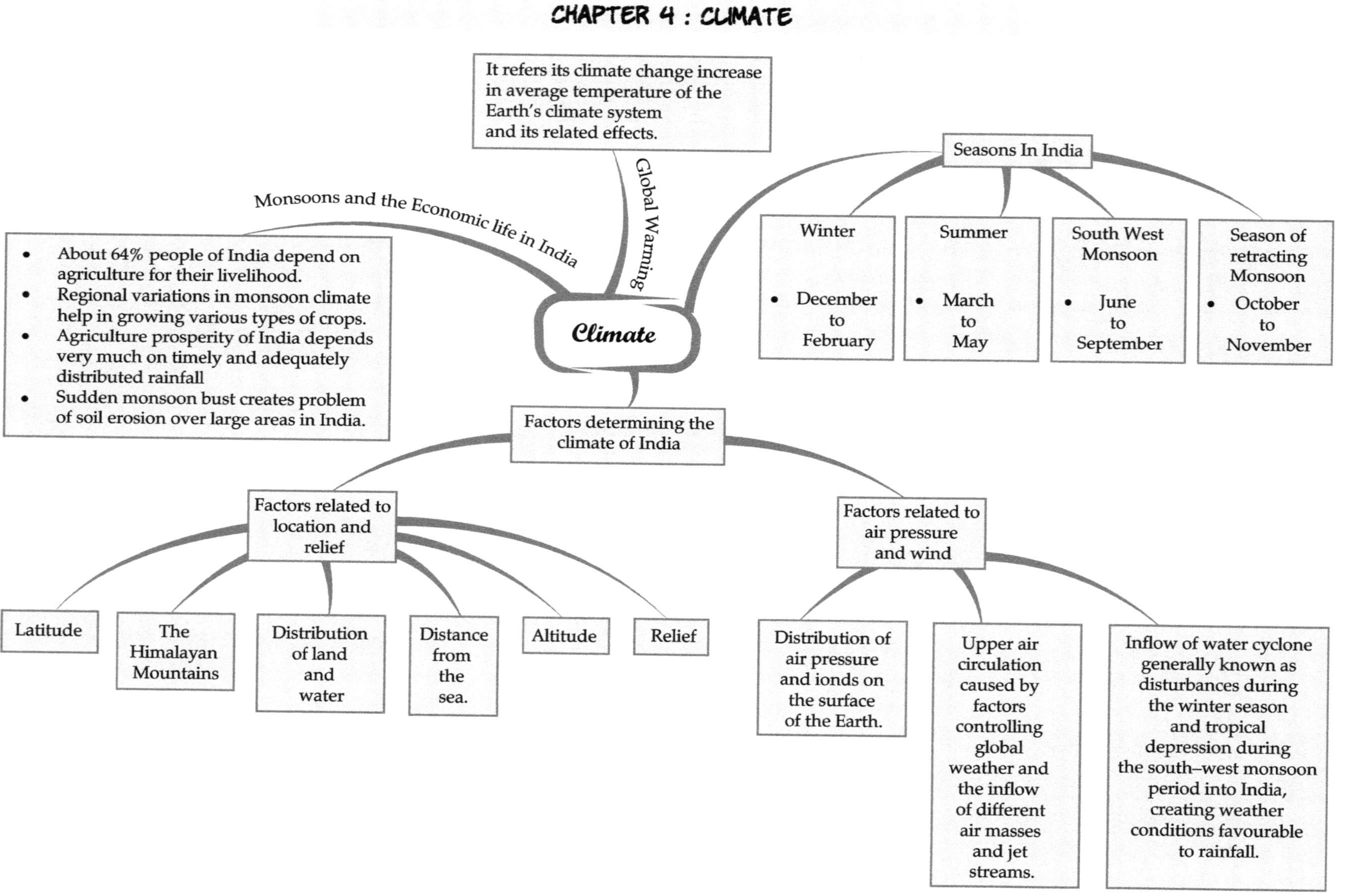
Climate
Global Warming
It refers its climate change increase in average temperature of the Earth's climate system and its related effects.
Monsoons and the Economic life in India
• About 64% people of India depend on agriculture for their livelihood.
• Regional variations in monsoon climate help in growing various types of crops.
• Agriculture prosperity of India depends very much on timely and adequately distributed rainfall
• Sudden monsoon bust creates problem of soil erosion over large areas in India.
Seasons In India
Winter • December to February
Summer • March to May
South West Monsoon • June to September
Season of retracting Monsoon • October to November
Factors determining the climate of India
Factors related to location and relief
Latitude
The Himalayan Mountains
Distribution of land and water
Distance from the sea.
Altitude
Relief
Factors related to air pressure and wind
Distribution of air pressure and iodns on the surface of the Earth.
Upper air circulation caused by factors controlling global weather and the inflow of different air masses and jet streams.
Inflow of water cyclone generally known as disturbances during the winter season and tropical depression during the south–west monsoon period into India, creating weather conditions favourable to rainfall.

CHAPTER 5 : NATURAL VEGETATION

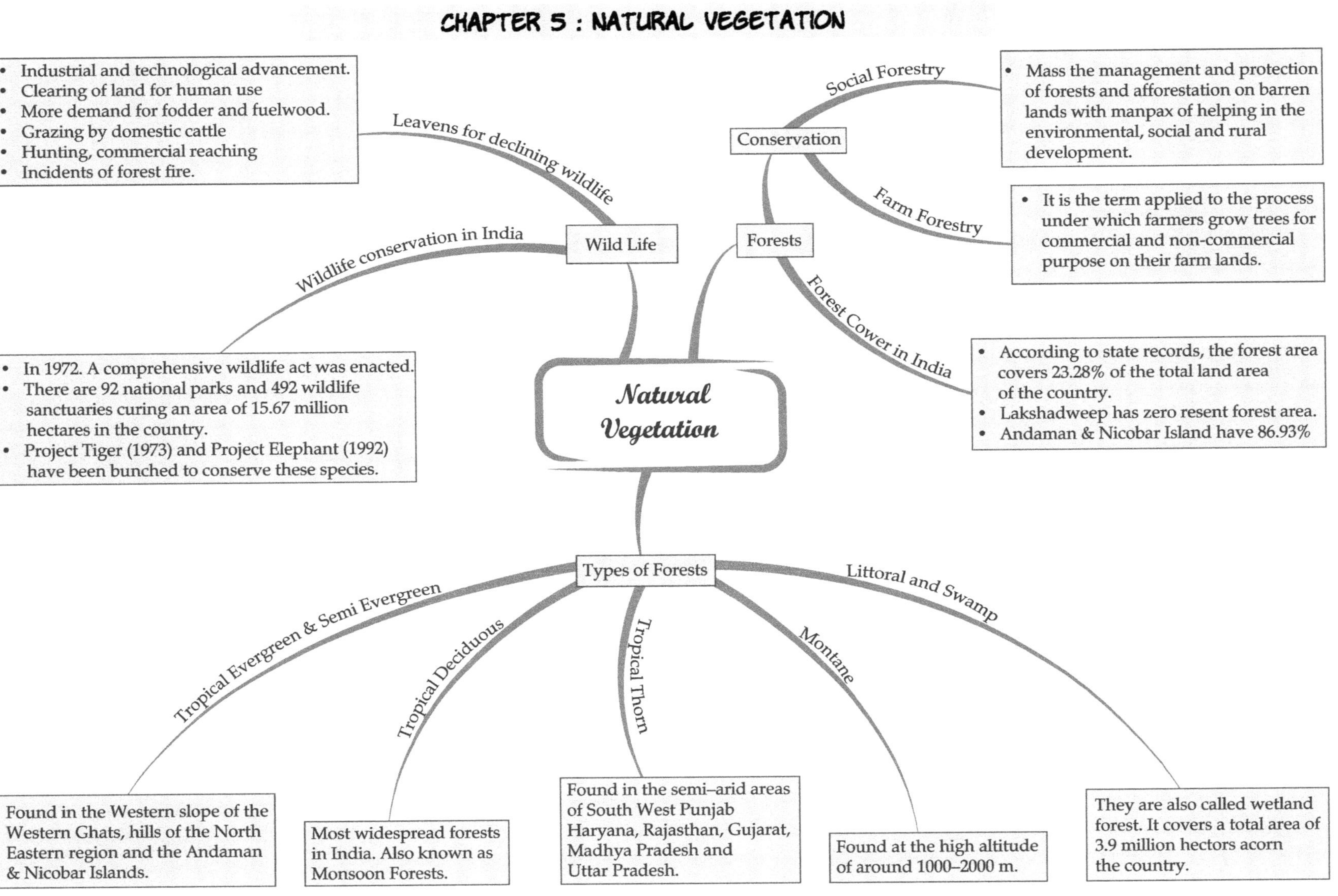

Natural Vegetation
Wild Life
Leavens for declining wildlife
• Industrial and technological advancement.
• Clearing of land for human use
• More demand for fodder and fuelwood.
• Grazing by domestic cattle
• Hunting, commercial reaching
• Incidents of forest fire.
Wildlife conservation in India
• In 1972. A comprehensive wildlife act was enacted.
• There are 92 national parks and 492 wildlife sanctuaries curing an area of 15.67 million hectares in the country.
• Project Tiger (1973) and Project Elephant (1992) have been bunched to conserve these species.
Forests
Conservation
Social Forestry
• Mass the management and protection of forests and afforestation on barren lands with manpax of helping in the environmental, social and rural development.
Farm Forestry
• It is the term applied to the process under which farmers grow trees for commercial and non-commercial purpose on their farm lands.
Forest Cower in India
• According to state records, the forest area covers 23.28% of the total land area of the country.
• Lakshadweep has zero resent forest area.
• Andaman & Nicobar Island have 86.93%
Types of Forests
Tropical Evergreen & Semi Evergreen
Found in the Western slope of the Western Ghats, hills of the North Eastern region and the Andaman & Nicobar Islands.
Tropical Deciduous
Most widespread forests in India. Also known as Monsoon Forests.
Tropical Thorn
Found in the semi–arid areas of South West Punjab Haryana, Rajasthan, Gujarat, Madhya Pradesh and Uttar Pradesh.
Montane
Found at the high altitude of around 1000–2000 m.
Littoral and Swamp
They are also called wetland forest. It covers a total area of 3.9 million hectors acorn the country.

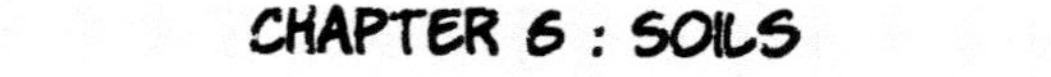

Soils

- **Soil Conservation**
  - It is a methodology to maintain soil fertility. Prevent soil erosion and exhaustion and improve the degraded condition of the soil.
  - Contour bunding contour terracing, regulated forestry, controlled growing, cover rotation are some steps taken for soil conservation.

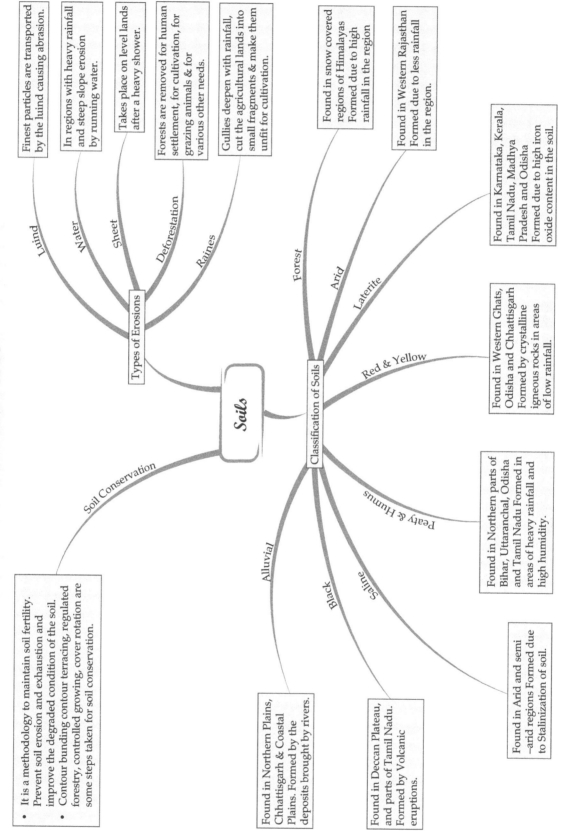

- **Types of Erosions**
  - Luind: Finest particles are transported by the luind causing abrasion.
  - Water: In regions with heavy rainfall and steep slope erosion by running water.
  - Sheet: Takes place on level lands after a heavy shower.
  - Deforestation: Forests are removed for human settlement, for cultivation, for grazing animals & for various other needs.
  - Raines: Gullies deepen with rainfall, cut the agricultural lands into small fragments & make them unfit for cultivation.

- **Classification of Soils**
  - Alluvial: Found in Northern Plains, Chhattisgarh & Coastal Plains. Formed by the deposits brought by rivers.
  - Black: Found in Deccan Plateau, and parts of Tamil Nadu. Formed by Volcanic eruptions.
  - Saline: Found in Arid and semi –arid regions Formed due to Stalinization of soil.
  - Peaty & Humus: Found in Northern parts of Bihar, Uttaranchal, Odisha and Tamil Nadu Formed in areas of heavy rainfall and high humidity.
  - Red & Yellow: Found in Western Ghats, Odisha and Chhattisgarh Formed by crystalline igneous rocks in areas of low rainfall.
  - Laterite: Found in Karnataka, Kerala, Tamil Nadu, Madhya Pradesh and Odisha Formed due to high iron oxide content in the soil.
  - Arid: Found in Western Rajasthan Formed due to less rainfall in the region.
  - Forest: Found in snow covered regions of Himalayas Formed due to high rainfall in the region

CHAPTER 7 : NATURAL HAZARDS & DISASTERS

Natural Hazards & Disasters

Disaster Management

Pre–disaster management

- Involves generating data and information about the disasters. Preparing vulnerability zoning mass & spreading answers.

During disasters

- Rescue and relief operation such as evacuation, construction of shelters.

Post disaster operations

- Involves rehabilitation and recovery of victims.

Natural Hazards Disasters in India

Earthquakes

- Frequent in Jammu & Kashmir Himachal Pradesh Uttaranchal.

Tsunami

- Frequent in Island of South east Aisa, Indonesia, Malaysia, Myanmar, Sri Lanka, India, Pacific Ring of Fire

Tropical Cyclone

- Frequent in bay of Bengal and Arabian Sea.

Floods

- Frequents in West Bengal, Bihar Punjab and Uttar Pradesh.

Droughts

- Frequent in Lass of Kutch most parts of Madhya Pradesh, Maharashtra, Andhra Pradesh, Karnataka Platea u, interior of Tamil Nadu and Southern Parts of Jharkhand and interior Odisha.

Landslides

- Frequent in Andaman and Nicobar, high rainfall slopes in the Western and the North eastern regions.

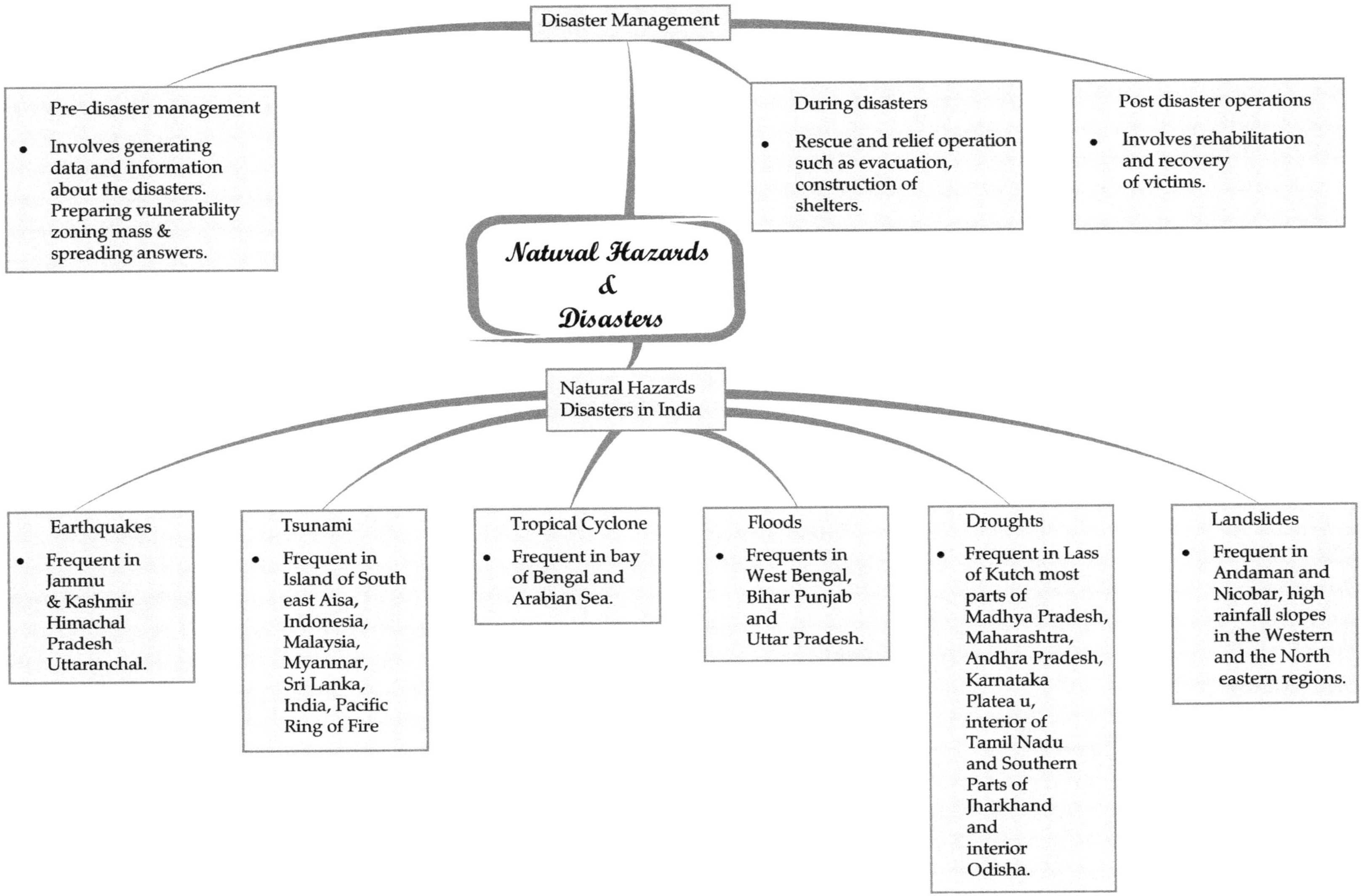

PART-C

CHAPTER 1 : INTRODUCTION TO MAPS

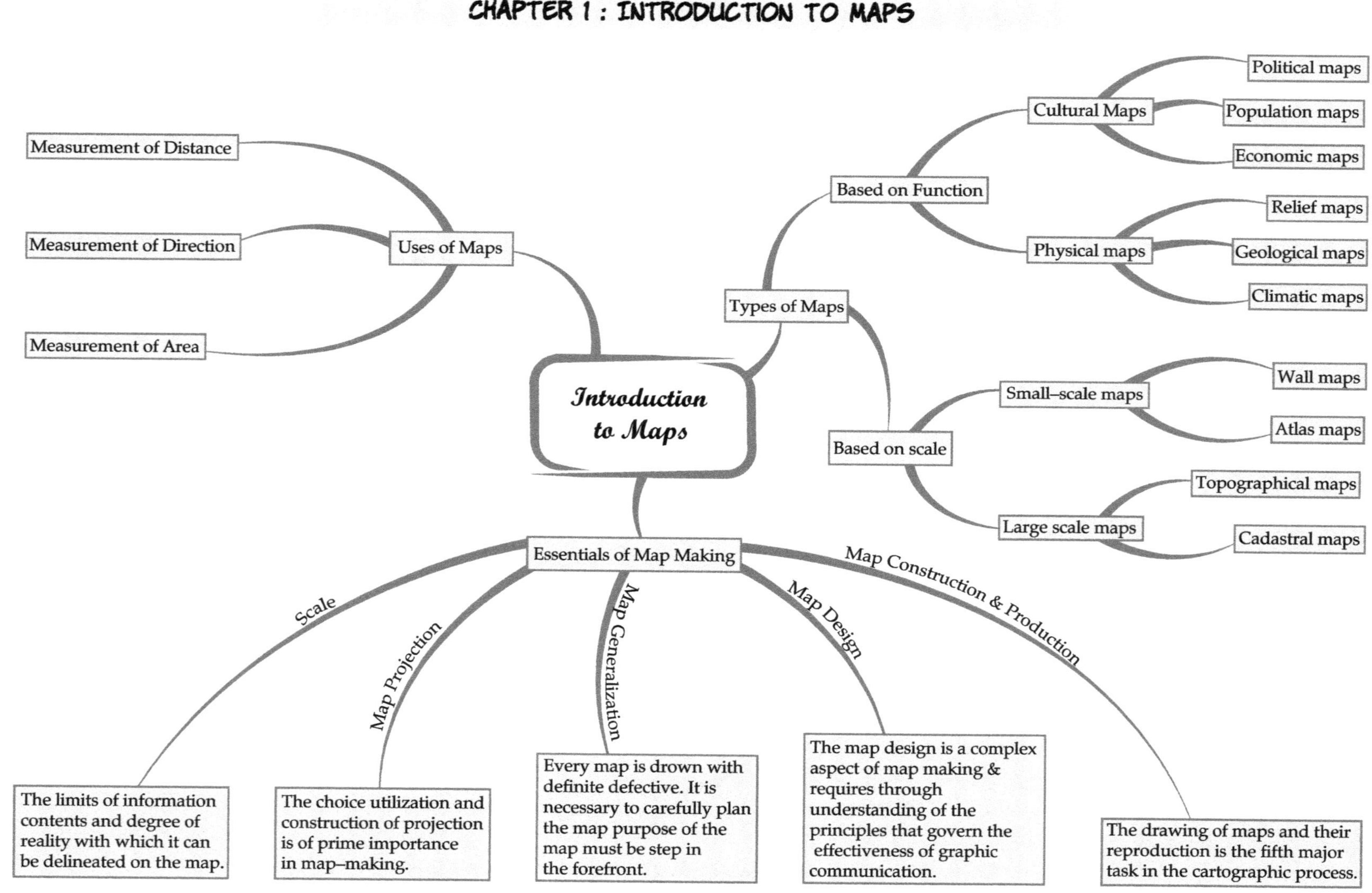

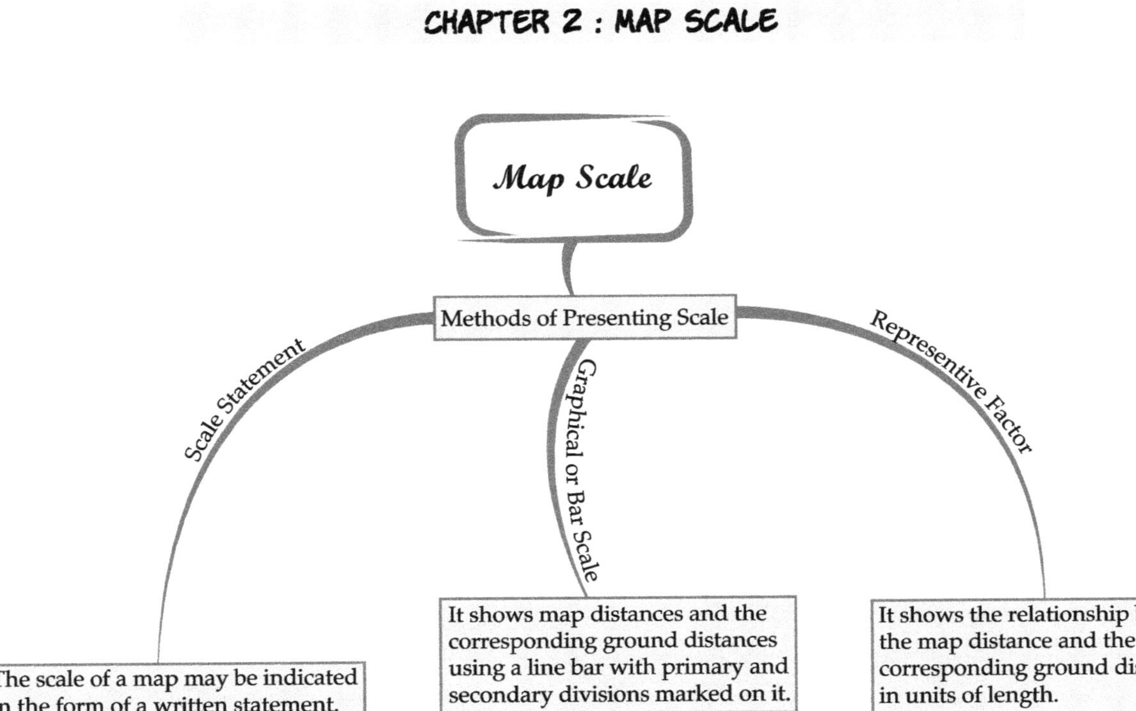
CHAPTER 2 : MAP SCALE
Map Scale
Methods of Presenting Scale
Scale Statement
Graphical or Bar Scale
Representive Factor
The scale of a map may be indicated in the form of a written statement.
It shows map distances and the corresponding ground distances using a line bar with primary and secondary divisions marked on it.
It shows the relationship between the map distance and the corresponding ground distance in units of length.

CHAPTER 3 : LATITUDE, LONGITUDE AND TIME

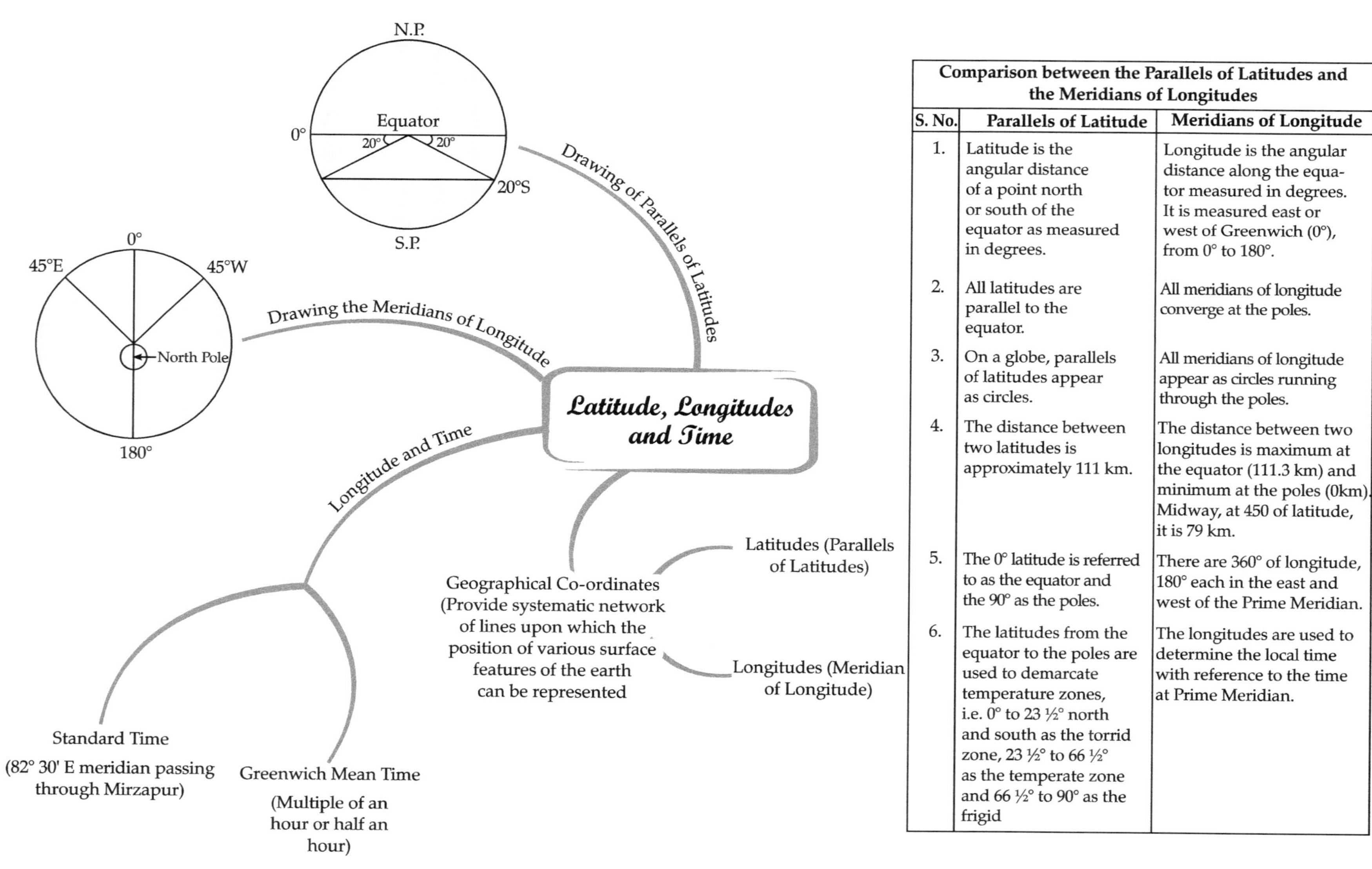

Comparison between the Parallels of Latitudes and the Meridians of Longitudes		
S. No.	**Parallels of Latitude**	**Meridians of Longitude**
1.	Latitude is the angular distance of a point north or south of the equator as measured in degrees.	Longitude is the angular distance along the equator measured in degrees. It is measured east or west of Greenwich (0°), from 0° to 180°.
2.	All latitudes are parallel to the equator.	All meridians of longitude converge at the poles.
3.	On a globe, parallels of latitudes appear as circles.	All meridians of longitude appear as circles running through the poles.
4.	The distance between two latitudes is approximately 111 km.	The distance between two longitudes is maximum at the equator (111.3 km) and minimum at the poles (0km). Midway, at 450 of latitude, it is 79 km.
5.	The 0° latitude is referred to as the equator and the 90° as the poles.	There are 360° of longitude, 180° each in the east and west of the Prime Meridian.
6.	The latitudes from the equator to the poles are used to demarcate temperature zones, i.e. 0° to 23 ½° north and south as the torrid zone, 23 ½° to 66 ½° as the temperate zone and 66 ½° to 90° as the frigid	The longitudes are used to determine the local time with reference to the time at Prime Meridian.

CHAPTER 4 : MAP PROJECTIONS

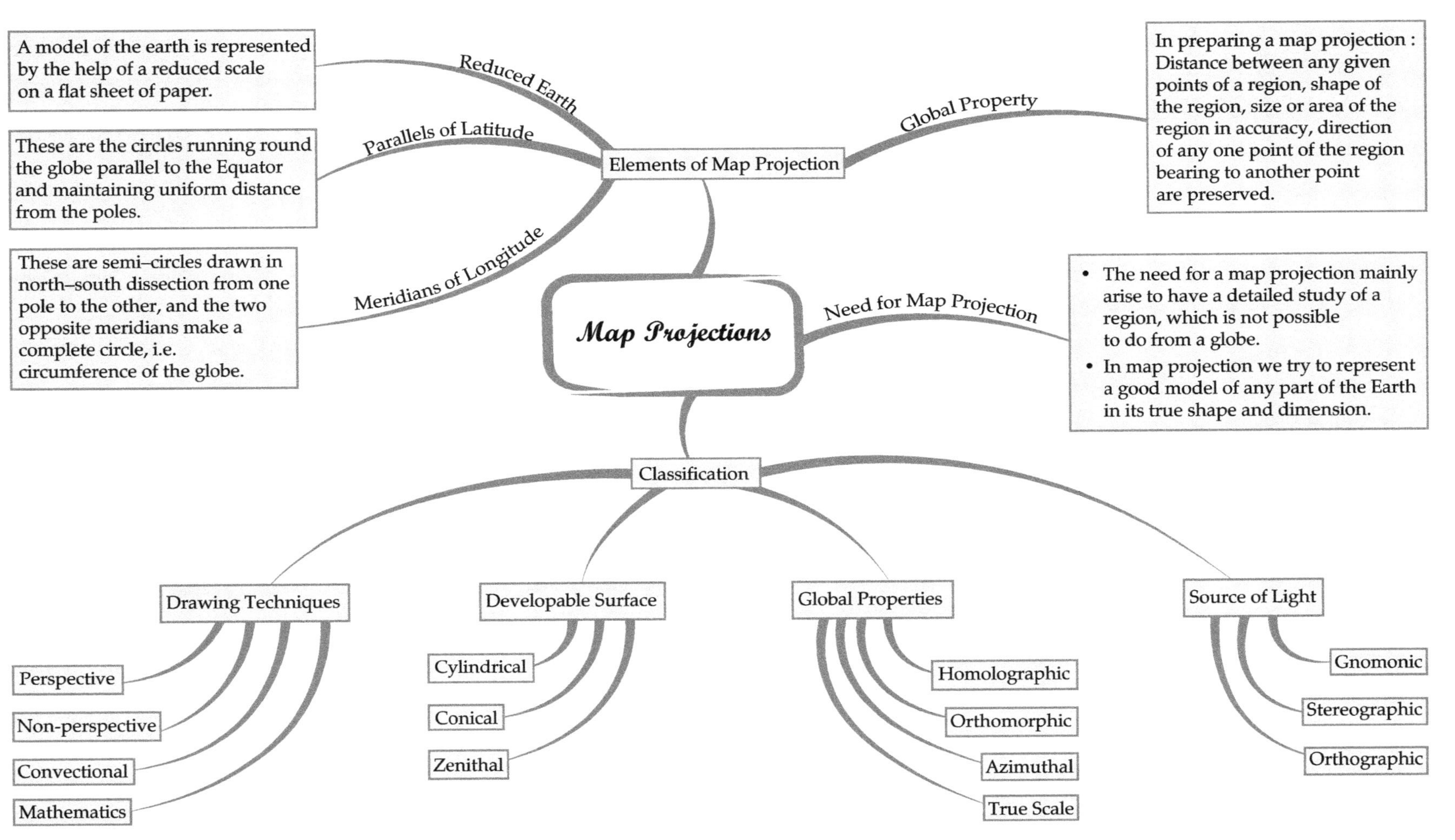

Map Projections
Elements of Map Projection
Reduced Earth
A model of the earth is represented by the help of a reduced scale on a flat sheet of paper.
Parallels of Latitude
These are the circles running round the globe parallel to the Equator and maintaining uniform distance from the poles.
Meridians of Longitude
These are semi–circles drawn in north–south dissection from one pole to the other, and the two opposite meridians make a complete circle, i.e. circumference of the globe.
Global Property
In preparing a map projection : Distance between any given points of a region, shape of the region, size or area of the region in accuracy, direction of any one point of the region bearing to another point are preserved.
Need for Map Projection
• The need for a map projection mainly arise to have a detailed study of a region, which is not possible to do from a globe.
• In map projection we try to represent a good model of any part of the Earth in its true shape and dimension.
Classification
Drawing Techniques
Perspective
Non-perspective
Convectional
Mathematics
Developable Surface
Cylindrical
Conical
Zenithal
Global Properties
Homolographic
Orthomorphic
Azimuthal
True Scale
Source of Light
Gnomonic
Stereographic
Orthographic

CHAPTER 5 : TOPOGRAPHICAL MAPS

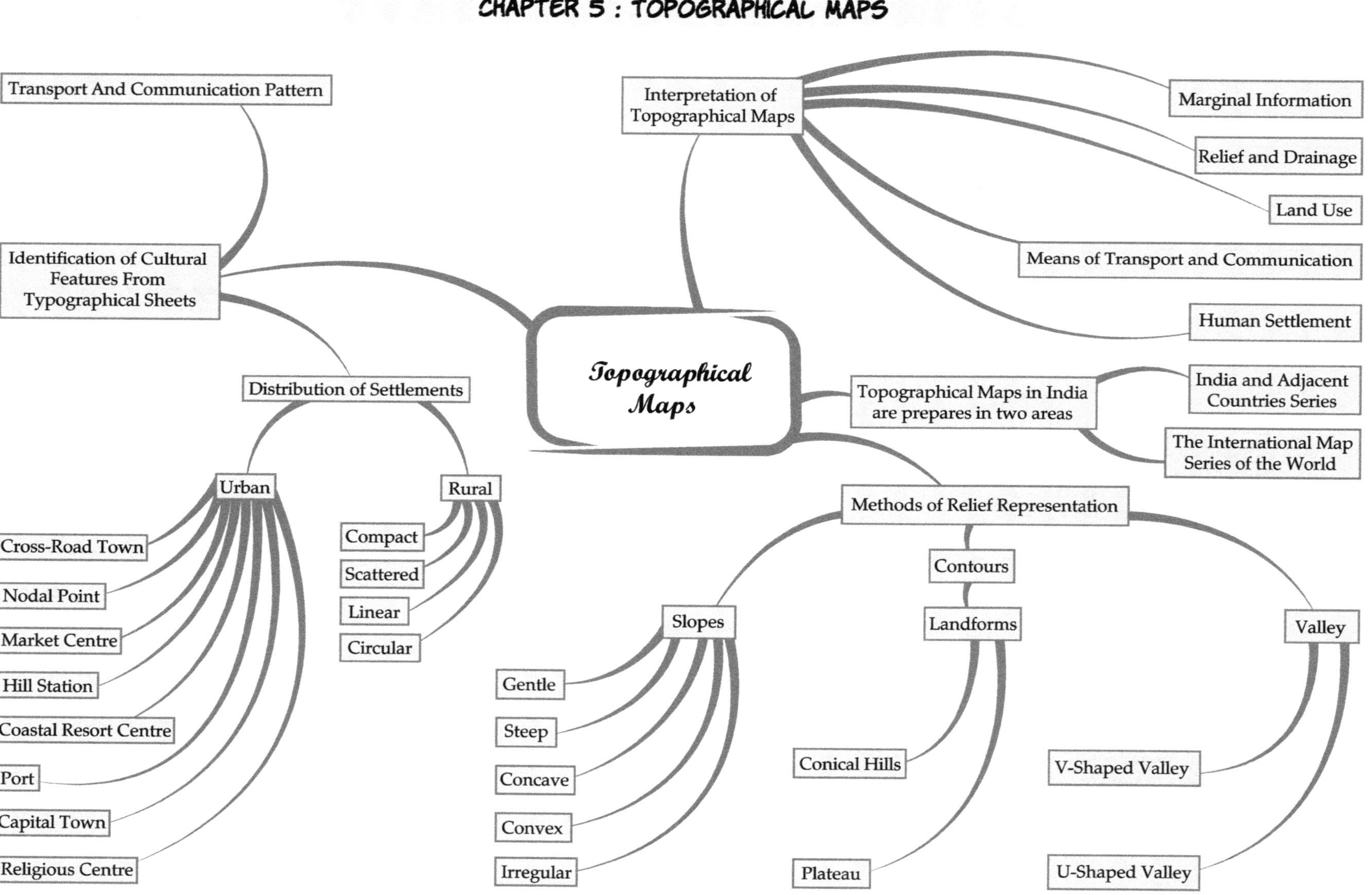

CHAPTER 6 : INTRODUCTION TO AERIAL PHOTOGRAPHS

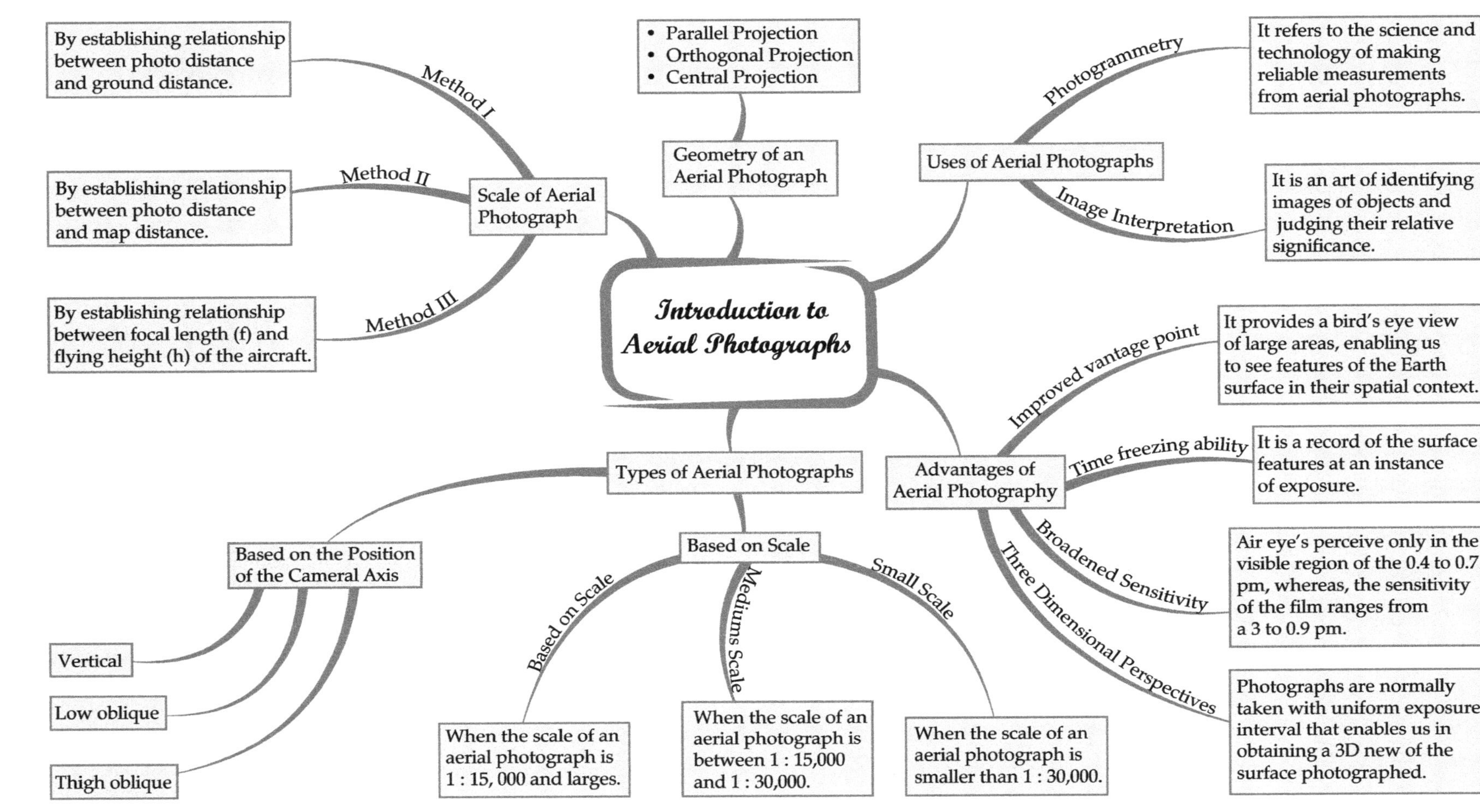
Introduction to Aerial Photographs
Scale of Aerial Photograph
Method I
By establishing relationship between photo distance and ground distance.
Method II
By establishing relationship between photo distance and map distance.
Method III
By establishing relationship between focal length (f) and flying height (h) of the aircraft.
Geometry of an Aerial Photograph
• Parallel Projection
• Orthogonal Projection
• Central Projection
Uses of Aerial Photographs
Photogrammetry
It refers to the science and technology of making reliable measurements from aerial photographs.
Image Interpretation
It is an art of identifying images of objects and judging their relative significance.
Advantages of Aerial Photography
Improved vantage point
It provides a bird's eye view of large areas, enabling us to see features of the Earth surface in their spatial context.
Time freezing ability
It is a record of the surface features at an instance of exposure.
Broadened Sensitivity
Air eye's perceive only in the visible region of the 0.4 to 0.7 pm, whereas, the sensitivity of the film ranges from a 3 to 0.9 pm.
Three Dimensional Perspectives
Photographs are normally taken with uniform exposure interval that enables us in obtaining a 3D new of the surface photographed.
Types of Aerial Photographs
Based on the Position of the Cameral Axis
Vertical
Low oblique
Thigh oblique
Based on Scale
Based on Scale
When the scale of an aerial photograph is 1 : 15, 000 and larges.
Mediums Scale
When the scale of an aerial photograph is between 1 : 15,000 and 1 : 30,000.
Small Scale
When the scale of an aerial photograph is smaller than 1 : 30,000.

CHAPTER 7 : INTRODUCTION TO REMOTE SENSING

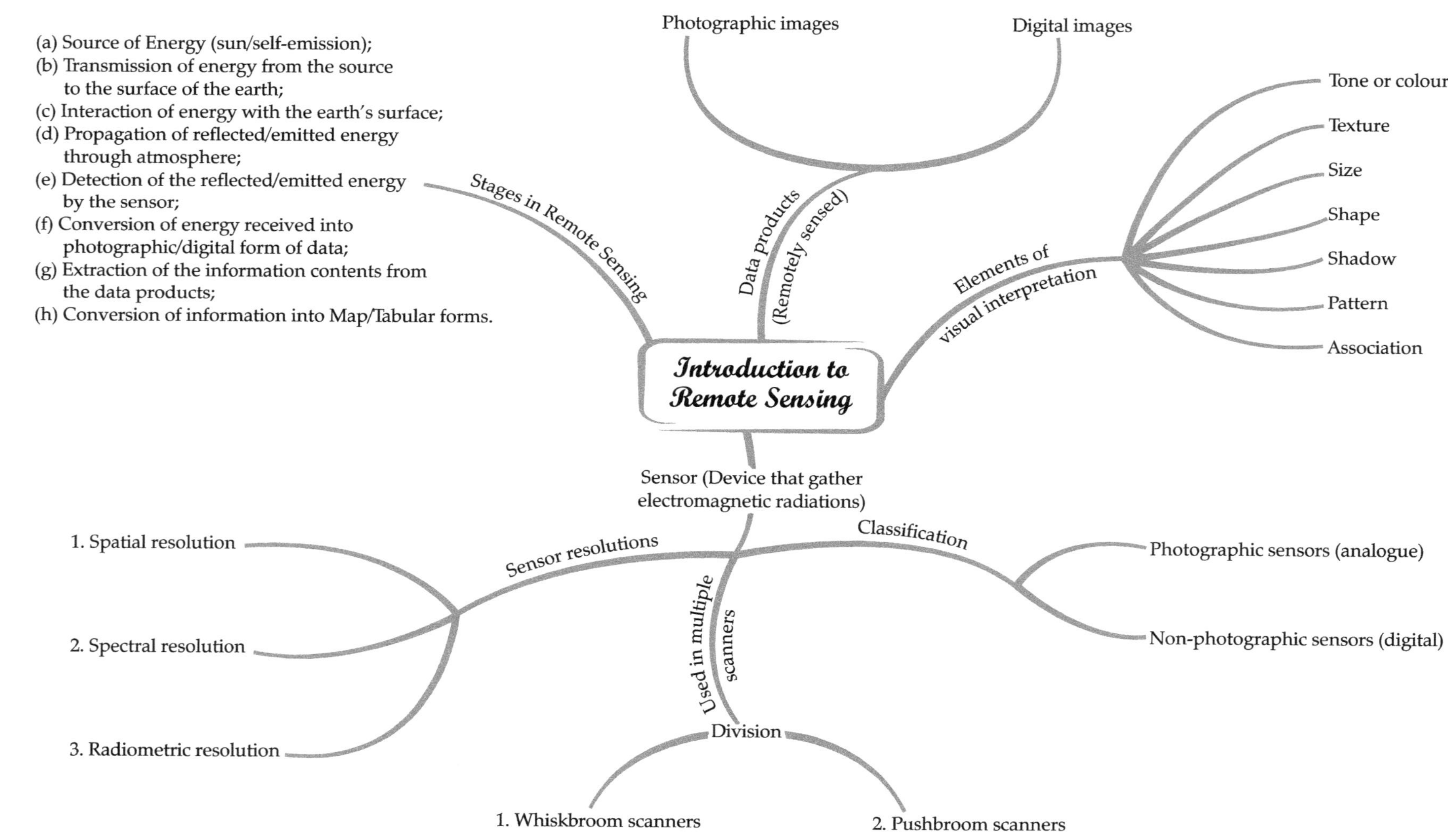

CHAPTER 8 : WEATHER INSTRUMENTS, MAPS AND CHARTS

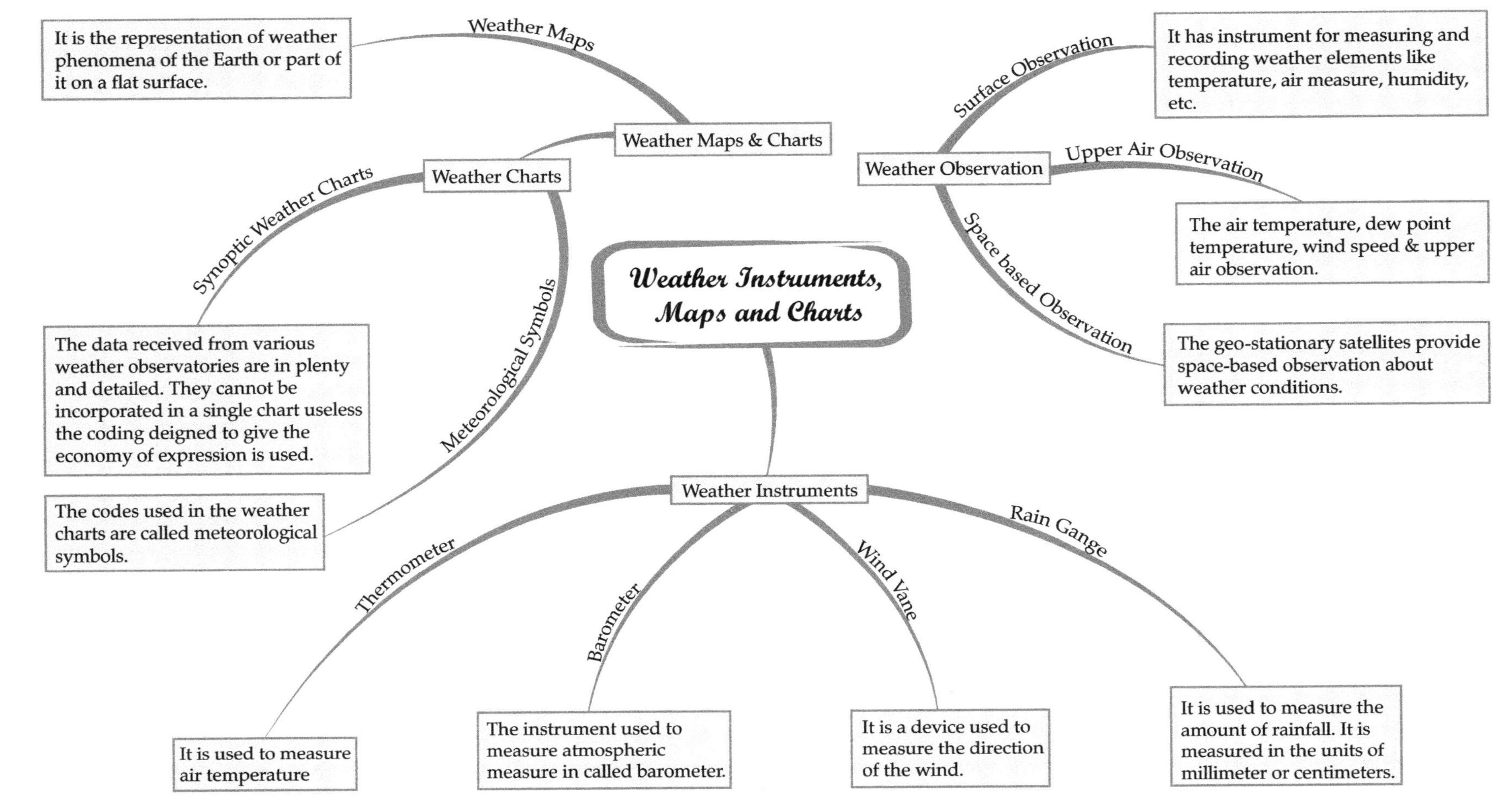
Weather Instruments, Maps and Charts
Weather Maps & Charts
Weather Maps
It is the representation of weather phenomena of the Earth or part of it on a flat surface.
Weather Charts
Synoptic Weather Charts
The data received from various weather observatories are in plenty and detailed. They cannot be incorporated in a single chart useless the coding deigned to give the economy of expression is used.
Meteorological Symbols
The codes used in the weather charts are called meteorological symbols.
Weather Observation
Surface Observation
It has instrument for measuring and recording weather elements like temperature, air measure, humidity, etc.
Upper Air Observation
The air temperature, dew point temperature, wind speed & upper air observation.
Space based Observation
The geo-stationary satellites provide space-based observation about weather conditions.
Weather Instruments
Thermometer
It is used to measure air temperature
Barometer
The instrument used to measure atmospheric measure in called barometer.
Wind Vane
It is a device used to measure the direction of the wind.
Rain Gange
It is used to measure the amount of rainfall. It is measured in the units of millimeter or centimeters.

WRITING NOTES

1. ....
2. ....
3. ....
4. ....
5. ....
6. ....
7. ....
8. ....
9. ....
10. ....
11. ....
12. ....
13. ....
14. ....
15. ....
16. ....
17. ....
18. ....
19. ....
20. ....
21. ....
22. ....
23. ....
24. ....
25. ....

PART A :

UNIT-I

Geography as a Discipline

CHAPTER

1 GEOGRAPHY AS A DISCIPLINE

Syllabus

> *Geography as an Integrated Discipline, Physical Geography and Natural Sciences, Geography and Social Sciences.*
> *Branches of Geography- Physical Geography, Human Geography, Biogeography, Branches of Geography Based on Regional Approach, Physical Geography and its Importance.*

TOPIC-1
Geography as an Integrated Discipline, Physical Geography and Natural Sciences, Geography and Social Sciences.

Revision Notes

- Geography should be studied as an independent subject as it helps us to gather knowledge about the physical environment of the Earth, human activities and their interactive relationships.
- As a student of geography, we should be curious to know about all the phenomena which vary over space. Through the study of geography, we get to know about the diverse lands and people. We also need to understand the changes that have taken place over time.
- Geography equips us to appreciate diversity and investigate into the causes responsible for creating such variations over time and space. We develop skills to understand the globe converted into maps and have a visual sense of the Earth's surface.
- We need to understand as to 'What is geography?'. In very simple words, it can be said that geography is the description of the Earth. The term 'geography' was first coined by **Eratosthenes**, a Greek scholar(276-194 BC). The word has been derived from two roots of Greek language geo (Earth) and graphos (description). Put together , they mean description of the Earth.
- Geography is different from other sciences in its subject matter and methodology but at the same time, it is closely related to other disciplines. Geography derives its data base from all the natural and social sciences and attempts their synthesis.
- Geography as a discipline is concerned with three sets of questions :
  - Some questions are concerned with the identification of the patterns of natural and cultural features over the surface of Earth. These are the questions about 'what'?
  - The second type of questions are concerned with the distribution of the natural and human/cultural features over the surface of the Earth. These are the questions about 'where'?
  - The third type of question is related to the explanation or the casual relationships between features and the processes and phenomena.
- As a social science discipline, geography studies the 'spatial organisation' and 'spatial integration.'
- Geography is a discipline of synthesis. It attempts spatial synthesis, and history attempts temporal synthesis. Its approach is holistic in nature. It recognises the fact that the world is a system of interdependencies.
- Every discipline, concerned with scientific knowledge is linked with geography as many of their elements vary over space.
- Geography helps in understanding the reality in its spatial perspective.

Know the Terms

- **Geography :** It can be defined as the description of the Earth.
- **Geographer :** An expert in the study of the Earth, the physical features of the Earth and its atmosphere and of human activities and its effects.
- **Spatial Synthesis :** It includes the formal techniques which study the entities using geographical properties.
- **Holistic Approach :** It means the overall approach that is taken up to study the subject.

Multiple Choice Questions (1 mark each)

Q. 1. Geography should be studied as an : [A]

(a) integrated subject

(b) independent subject

(c) intermingled subject

(d) interlocked subject

Ans. (b) independent subject 1

Q. 2. The term 'Holistic Approach' is related to : [R]

(a) overall approach

(b) individualistic approach

(c) seasonal approach

(d) formal approach

Ans. (a) overall approach 1

Q. 3. Geography helps in understanding the reality in its________ perspective. [A]

(a) holistic

(b) spatial

(c) overall

(d) physical

Ans. (b) spatial 1

Very Short Answer Type Questions (1 mark each)

Q. 1. Define the term 'Geography'. [U]

Ans. Geography is concerned with the description and explanation of the areal differentiation of the Earth's surface. **(Richard Hartshorne) 1**

Or

Geography studies the differences of phenomena usually related in different parts of the Earth's surface. **(Hettner)**

Q. 2. What do you mean by 'areal differentiation'? [U]

Ans. When there is similarity and dissimilarity among the physical and cultural features on the Earth's surface, it is called areal differentiation. 1

Q. 3. The term 'Geography' has been derived from where? [U]

Ans. The term 'Geography' has been derived from two roots of Greek language *geo* (Earth) and *graphos* (description). Put together, they mean description of the Earth. 1

Q. 4. How does a geographer explain a certain phenomenon? [R]

Ans. A geographer explains a certain phenomenon in a frame of cause and effect relationship, as it does not only help in interpretation but also foresees the phenomena in future. 1

Q. 5. Which discipline attempts the spatial synthesis. [U]

Ans. Geography attempts spatial synthesis. 1

Commonly Made Error

- The students tend to attempt the questions related to spatial synthesis without having proper understanding of the same.

Answering Tip

- Spatial analysis includes any of the formal techniques which study entities using their topological, geometric, or geographic properties.

Q. 6. What is a two-dimensional representation of the Earth called? [R]

Ans. The two-dimensional representation of the Earth is called a map. 1

Q. 7. Explain any two changes that have occurred in the civilization of man in course of time? [A]

Ans. Many changes have occurred in the civilization of man in course of time. They are :

(i) Man moved from stage of necessity to stage of freedom.

(ii) It created possibilities from the nature.

(iii) We find now humanised nature and naturalised man.

(iv) Space got organised with the help of transport and communication. 1

Q. 8. What do geographers study? [U]

Ans. The geographers study the variations and associations of the features on the Earth's surface. e.g., they study the different cropping patterns from place to place which is due to the difference in the climate, soil, demand, transport facility, capacity of the farmer, etc. 1

Q. 9. How can we say that Geography is an integrated discipline? [A]

Ans. Geography is an integrated discipline because it is a discipline of synthesis, it includes spatial and temporal synthesis.

Its approach is holistic in nature. It recognises the fact that the world is a system of interdependence. 1

Q. 10. What is the objective of sciences and social sciences? U

Ans. The main objective of sciences and social sciences is to understand the reality of the nature. 1

Q. 11. Describe the dialogue between nature and man? A

Ans. Dialogue between nature and man is imagined to be as follows:

(i) 'You created the soil, I created the cup.'

(ii) 'You created night, I created the lamp.'

(iii) 'You created wilderness, hilly terrains and deserts; I created flower beds and gardens.' 1

Short Answer Type Questions (3 marks each)

Q. 1. Geography being a scientific discipline , what do you think how many categories of questions is geography concerned with? Explain. U

Ans. Geography as a scientific discipline is concerned with three sets of questions:

(i) Some of the questions are related to the identification of the various patterns of natural and cultural features as found over the surface of the Earth. These are the questions about 'what'?

(ii) The second kind of questions are related to the distribution of the natural and human/cultural features over the surface of the Earth. These are the questions about 'where'?

(iii) The third kind of questions are related to the explanation or the casual relationships between features and the processes and phenomena. This aspect of geography is related to the question 'why'. (1 × 3 = 3)

AI **Q. 2. How do geographers play an important role for any country.** A

Ans. Important role of the geographers for any country :

(i) Geographers study the various similar and dissimilar features of the Earth's surface and its cause and effect relationship with the population of that particular country.

For example, a geographer will study the reasons as to why the cropping pattern differs from state to state in a country. This difference in the cropping pattern is due to the difference in climate, soil, demand, transport facilities , rainfall , etc.

(ii) A geographer helps predict the climate and the cause-effect relationship of the same. He also helps in predicting the natural calamities that might hit the country in the nearing future.

(iii) As a geographer, he studies the relationship between humans and nature which is highly dynamic. **(1 x 3 = 3)**

Q. 3. Why is geography considered as an important subject? U

Ans. Geography is considered as an important subject because :

(i) As we live on Earth, therefore, it is very important to understand the mechanism of our planet. It gives us a visual sense of the Earth's surface.

(ii) We are heavily dependent on the natural resources available on the Earth's surface. In order to know how efficiently it can be used, it is important to study geography.

(iii) Climate is a major deciding factor in the type of crops to be grown, human settlements, food to be eaten , shelter to be build , etc. To understand the interrelationship between the climate and human movements, it is important to study geography as a subject.

(iv) It also helps us connect well and understand the changes that have taken place in the evolution of the Earth . It makes our understanding of the changes that have taken place throughout the geological time better. It also helps us know the land and people in a better sense.

(Any three) (1 × 3 = 3)

Commonly Made Error

- The students do not pay much attention as to how geography as a subject can be of much importance.

Answering Tip

- Geography as a subject helps us in understanding and learning how the world's basic physical systems work and affect our everyday life.

Long Answer Type Questions (5 marks each)

Q. 1. 'Physical and human factors both are dynamic not static.' Explain. A

Ans. Physical and human factors both are dynamic not static :

(i) The factors change over a period of time as a result of the interactive processes between ever changing Earth and ever-active human beings. Primitive societies if we see were directly dependent on their immediate environment. It is only through adaptation and modifications that the humans came in terms with the nature.

(ii) The present society is an evidence of the various stages of transformation that the humans have undergone from the primitive societies who were dependent on their immediate environment to now where technology plays a major role in the utilization of various resources.

(iii) The introduction of technology made the humans less dependent on their physical environment. Technology has help reduce the amount of manpower involved, increased the efficiency, production, helped in time management, etc. The imprints of interaction between human beings and physical environment can be seen everywhere. This interaction has resulted in the creation of humanised nature and naturalised human beings and geography involves the study of this interaction between the two forces.

(iv) The development and spread of transport and communication services across the globe has helped in the space being organised in an efficient manner.

(v) It takes into consideration the associations and interrelationships between the phenomenon of space and provides apt reasoning for the patterns adapted. It also takes into consideration the relationship between the human beings and physical environment and provides explanation on their interdependence. **(1 × 5 = 5)**

TOPIC-2

Branches of Geography - Physical Geography, Human Geography, Biogeography, Branches of Geography Based on Regional Approach, Physical Geography and its Importance.

Revision Notes

➢ We all know that geography is an interdisciplinary subject of study.

➢ The major approach to the study of geography have been

- Systematic
- Regional

➢ The systematic geography was introduced by Alexander Von Humboldt, a German geographer and the regional geography was by a contemporary of Humboldt, Karl Ritter.

➢ In the systematic approach, a phenomenon is studied world-wide as a whole, and then the identification of typologies or spatial patterns is done.

➢ In the regional approach, the world is divided into regions at different hierarchical levels and then all the geographical phenomena in a particular region are studied. These regions may be natural, political or designated region.

➢ Branches of geography(based on systematic approach):

➢ **Physical Geography :**

- Geomorphology : It is devoted to the study of landforms and their evolution.
- Climatology : It is the study of the structure of atmosphere.
- Hydrology : It studies the realm of water over the surface of the earth.
- Soil Geography : It is the study of the processes of soil formation , types, etc.

➢ **Human Geography :**

- Social/cultural Geography : It is the study of society and its spatial dynamics.
- Population and Settlement Geography : It studies population growth, distribution, density , sex ratio, migration and occupational structure, etc.
- Economic Geography : It studies the activities of the people.
- Historical Geography : It studies the historical processes through which the space gets organised.
- Political Geography : It looks at the space from the angle of political events and studies boundaries, etc., to understand the political behaviour of the population.

➢ **Biogeography :**

- Plant Geography : It studies the spatial pattern of natural vegetation in their habitats.
- Zoo Geography : It studies the spatial patterns and geographical characteristics of animals and their habitats.
- Ecosystem : It deals with the scientific study of the habitats characteristics of species.
- Environmental Geography : It studies the leading environmental problems such as land gradation, pollution and concerns for conservation of environment.

➢ **Branches of geography (based on regional approach) :**

- Regional Studies/Area Studies : It comprises of Macro, Meso and Micro regional studies.
- Regional Planning : It comprises of country/rural and town/urban planning.
- Regional Development

- Regional Analysis

- Physical geography includes the study of lithosphere (landforms, drainage, relief and physiography),atmosphere, hydrosphere and biosphere.
- Each element of the physical geography is important for human beings.
- Landforms provide the base on which the human activities are located.
- The climate influences our house types, clothing , food habits, vegetation, cropping pattern, location of industries, etc.
- The study of physical geography is emerging as a discipline of evaluating and managing natural resources.
- It is important to understand the intricate relationship between physical environment and human beings.

Know the Terms

- **Systematic Approach :** It is a phenomenon which is studied world-wide as a whole, and then the identification of typologies or spatial patterns is done.
- **Regional Approach :** In this approach the world is divided into regions at different hierarchical levels and then all the geographical phenomena in a particular region are studied. These regions may be natural, political or designated region.
- **Geomorphology :** It is concerned with the study of landforms, their evolution and related processes.
- **Hydrology :** It studies the realm of water over the surface of the earth including oceans, lakes, rivers and other water bodies and its effect on different life forms including human life and their activities.
- **Population Geography :** It studies population growth, distribution, density, sex ratio, migration and occupational structure, etc.
- **Ecology :** It is concerned with the scientific study of the habitats characteristics of species.

Multiple Choice Questions (1 mark each)

Q. 1. The_______ geography was introduced by Alexander Von Humboldt. [R]

(a) systematic (b) physical
(c) economic (d) regional

Ans. (a) systematic 1

Q. 2. _________ geography studies the spatial pattern of natural vegetation in their habitats. [A]

(a) Human
(b) Plant
(c) Zoo
(d) Environmental

Ans. (b) Plant 1

Q. 3. __________comprises of country/rural and town/urban planning. [A]

(a) Regional development
(b) Regional approach
(c) Regional planning
(d) Regional segregation

Ans. (c) Regional planning 1

Q. 4. Each element of the physical geography is important for : [R]

(a) human beings (b) survival
(c) universe (d) plants

Ans. (a) human beings 1

Very Short Answer Type Questions (1 mark each)

Q. 1. What is studied under Biogeography? Name any two branches of Biogeography? [R]

Ans. Biogeography has emerged as a result of the interface between physical geography and human geography.

The branches of Biogeography are Zoo Geography, Plant Geography , Ecology and Environmental Geography. **(Any two) 1**

Q. 2. What do we study under Physical Geography? [R]

Ans. We study about the weather, soil , atmosphere, etc. 1

Q. 3. What is studied under Human Geography? [U]

Ans. Population, settlement, culture, economics and history is studied under human geography. **(Any two) 1**

Commonly Made Error

- The importance of studying physical geography is generally ignored by the students.

Answering Tip

- It is important to study physical geography as it helps to understand the geography of past times and how geography has played important roles in the evolution of people, their ideas, places and environments.

Q. 4. What does regional planning comprise of ? [A]

Ans. Regional planning comprises of country/ rural and town / urban planning. 1

Q. 5. What are the different approaches to the study of Geography? U

Ans. There are two major approaches to the study of Geography :

(i) Systematic Approach

(ii) Regional Approach. 1

Q. 6. Who introduced the concept of Systematic Approach? R

Ans. Alexander Von Humboldt introduced the concept of Systematic Approach. 1

Q. 7. Who developed the Regional Approach? R

Ans. Karl Ritter, the contemporary of Alexander Von Humboldt developed the concept of Regional Approach. 1

Q. 8. What is studied under Environmental Geography? A

Ans. Environmental Geography is concerned with the environmental problems such as land degradation, pollution and environmental conservation. 1

Q. 9. What is studied under Geomorphology? R

Ans. Geomorphology is concerned with the study of various landforms and its process of evolution. It also studies the various processes related to the landforms. 1

Q. 10. What is studied under Hydrology? U

Ans. Hydrology studies the realm of water over the surface of the earth including oceans, lakes, rivers and other water bodies and its effect on different life forms including human life and their activities. 1

Q. 11. What is studied under Economic Geography? U

Ans. Economic Geography studies the economic activities of the people including agriculture, industry, tourism, trade and transport, infrastructure and services, etc. 1

Commonly Made Error

- Economic geography is thought to have no importance in measuring the growth of the country.

Answering Tip

- Economic geography is important in developed nations such as the United States because it allows researchers to the study of human's economic activities under varying sets of conditions which is associated with production, location, distribution, consumption, exchange of resources, and spatial organization of economic activities across the world.

Q. 12. Name the sub- branches of Physical Geography. A

Ans. The sub-branches of Physical Geography are Geomorphology, Climatology, Hydrology and Soil Geography. 1

Q. 13. What are the recent techniques that help the geographer to understand the earth's surface better? R

Ans. The recent techniques that help the geographer to understand the earth's surface better are :

(i) GIS and GPS

(ii) Computer cartography 1

AI **Q.14. What makes the earth multi-dimensional?** U

Ans. The development and interrelation of various sciences such as Geology, Pedology, Oceanography, Botany, Zoology and Meteorology describe the physical features of the planet make the earth multi-dimensional. 1

Short Answer Type Questions **(3 marks each)**

Q. 1. Write any three points of difference between systematic approach and regional approach. U

Ans.

S.No.	Systematic Approach	Regional Approach
1.	The systematic approach was introduced by Alexander Von Humboldt, a German geographer.	The regional approach was developed by Karl Ritter, a contemporary of Humboldt.
2.	In this approach, the world is studied as a whole, and then identification of typologies or spatial patterns is done.	In this type of approach, the world is divided into regions at different hierarchical levels and then all the geographical phenomena in a particular region are studied. These regions may be natural, political or designated.
3.	An example of this type of approach is a geographer who is interested in studying the natural vegetation. He first will study the world at the top level . Then at the second level he will study various typologies such as tropical rainforest, equatorial rainforest, monsoon rainforest , etc.	An example of this type of approach is a geographer who is interested in studying only the natural vegetation found across the globe. He will only study the different regions such as Equator, desert region, monsoon region, etc., and not the world as a whole.

Q. 2. Differentiate between Physical Geography and Biogeography? A

Ans.

S.No.	Physical Geography	Biogeography
1.	It has developed as a subject concerned with the study of evaluation and management of natural resources.	It has emerged as a result of the interface between physical geography and human geography.

2.	Physical Geography has three branches: Geomorphology, Climatology and Hydrology.	Biogeography has three branches: Plant Geography, Ecology and Zoo Geography.
3.	This branch of geography studies abiotic elements of the earth.	Biogeography studies the biotic elements of the earth.

AI **Q.3. What are the sub-branches of Physical Geography? Explain in detail any three sub-branches ?** A

Ans. The sub-branches of Physical Geography are :

(i) **Geomorphology :** It is devoted to the study of landforms, their evolution and related processes.

(ii) **Climatology :** It encompasses the study of structure of atmosphere and elements of weather and climates and climatic types and regions.

(iii) **Hydrology :** It studies the realm of water over the surface of the earth including oceans, lakes, rivers and other water bodies and its effect on different life forms including human life and their activities.

(iv) **Soil Geography :** It is devoted to the study of the processes of soil formation, soil types, their fertility status , distribution and use.

(Any three) (1 × 3 = 3)

Q. 4. What are the sub-branches of Biogeography? Explain any three? A

Ans. Biogeography is divided into four sub-branches :

(i) **Plant Geography :** It studies the spatial pattern of natural vegetation in their habitats.

(ii) **Zoo Geography :** It studies the spatial patterns and geographic characteristics of animals and their habitats.

(iii) **Ecology/Ecosystem :** It deals with the scientific study of the habitats characteristics of species.

(iv) **Environmental Geography :** It is concerned with the world over leading to the realisation of environmental problems such as land gradation, pollution and concerns for environmental conservation. **(Any Three) (1 × 3 = 3)**

Q. 5. On the basis of regional approach, explain different branches of geography? U

Ans. On the basis of regional approach, the various branches are :

(i) **Regional Studies/Area Studies :** It comprises of Macro, Meso and Micro regional studies.

(ii) **Regional Planning :** It comprises of country /rural and town/urban planning.

(iii) **Regional Development :** It deals with the development issues of the region.

(iv) **Regional Analysis :** There are two aspects which are common to every discipline , these are:

(a) **Philosophy :**

(i) Geographical Thought

(ii) Land and Human Interaction/Human Ecology

(b) **Methods and Techniques :**

(i) Cartography including Computer Cartography

(ii) Quantitative Techniques/Statistical Techniques

(iii) Field Survey Methods

(iv) Geo-informatics comprising techniques such as Remote Sensing , GIS, GPS, etc. **(Any three)**

(1 × 3 = 3)

Q. 6. How is geography considered as an integrated discipline?

Ans. (i) Geography is considered as an integrated discipline as it is the combination of both spatial as well as temporal synthesis. As a subject, it has a holistic approach. It recognises the fact that the world as a whole is a system of interdependencies.

(ii) Today's world is considered as a global village. The well-connected transport and communication system has helped the world in becoming a unified and globalised village.

(iii) Today's technological advancement has provided better chances for monitoring the natural phenomena as well as the various social, political and economic parameters. **(1 × 3 = 3)**

Commonly Made Error

- The students fail to understand as to why geography should be studied as an integrated discipline.

Answering Tip

- Geography should be studied as an integrated discipline because it acts as a bridge between the human and the physical sciences.

Long Answer Type Questions

(5 marks each)

Q. 1. What are the sub-branches of Human Geography? Explain them in detail. A

Ans. The sub-branches of Human Geography are :

(i) **Social/Cultural Geography :** It encompasses the study of society and its spatial dynamics as well as the cultural elements contributed by the society.

(ii) **Population and Settlement Geography(Rural and Urban) :** It studies population growth, distribution, density, sex ratio, migration and occupational structure, etc. Settlement geography studies the characteristics of rural and urban settlements.

(iii) **Economic Geography :** It studies economic activities of the people including agriculture, industry, tourism, trade and transport, infrastructure and services, etc.

(iv) **Historical Geography :** It studies the historical processes through which the space gets organised. Every region has undergone some historical experiences before attaining the present-day status. The geographical features also experience temporal changes and these forms the concerns of historical geography.

(v) Political Geography : It looks at the space from the angle of political events and studies boundaries, space relations between neighbouring political units, delimitation of constituencies, election scenario and develops theoretical framework to understand the political behaviour of the population. **(1 × 5 = 5)**

Q. 2. Explain the importance of Physical Geography. U

Ans. (i) Physical Geography includes the study of lithosphere, atmosphere, hydrosphere and biosphere. Each of these elements present are termed important for the human beings.

(ii) Landforms are important as they form the base on which various human activities are located. Some of these activities are agricultural practice, human settlements, transportation facilities, establishment of industries, communication services, etc. Plains are utilized for agriculture. Plateaus provide forests and minerals. Mountains provide pastures, forests and sources of rivers. Climate influences our clothing and food habits. Climate also has a great effect on the vegetation, types of forests, cropping pattern, livestock farming, etc.

(iii) Similarly , oceans are also a great storehouse of resources. Beside fish and other sea-food, oceans are rich in mineral resources. Soils are renewable resources, which influence a number of economic activities such as agriculture. Soils provide basis for the biosphere accommodating plants, animals and micro-organisms.

(iv) Every element of physical environment is of utmost importance to the human beings. The study of physical geography is emerging as a discipline of evaluating and managing natural resources. In order to achieve this objective, it is essential to understand the intricate relationship between physical environment and human beings. Physical environment provides resources and ensures their economic and cultural development.

(v) Accelerated pace of resource utilization with the help of modern technology has created ecological imbalance in the world. Hence, a better understanding of physical environment is absolutely essential for sustainable development and also for the study of geography. **(1 × 5 = 5)**

Q. 3. Geography is an integration of social sciences and physical sciences. Explain?

Ans. (i) Geography is an integration of social sciences and physical sciences as the basic aim of both is to understand the reality of nature. All the social science disciplines, viz, sociology, political science, demography study different aspects of social reality. The branches of geography viz, social , political, economic and population and settlements are closely linked with these disciplines as each of them has spatial attributes.

(ii) The core concern of political science is territory, people and sovereignty while political geography is also interested in the study of the state as a spatial unit as well as people and their political behaviour.

(iii) History helps in knowing the man-made activities over the period of time , where as Physics helps in calculating the effect of climate on man. The change in the climate further has an influence on the occupation of the people.

(iv) Economics deal with the basic attributes of the economy such as production, distribution, exchange and consumption. Each of these attributes also has spatial aspects and here comes the role of economic geography.

(v) Mathematics and arts also have contributed to the development of geography to measure area and dimensions of the earth. Hence, it can be rightly said that all the branches of social sciences have a close relationship with the physical sciences . **(1 × 5 = 5)**

NCERT CORNER

(A) Multiple choice questions :

Q. 1. (i) Which of the following scholars coined the term 'Geography' : R

(a) Herodotus

(b) Galileo

(c) Eratosthenes

(d) Aristotle

Ans. (b) Eratosthenes.

Q. 2. (ii) Which one of the following features can be termed as 'physical feature' : R

(a) Port **(b) Plain**

(c) Road **(d) Water Park**

Ans. (c) Plain.

Q. 3. Make correct pairs from the following two columns and mark the correct option : U

Column I	Column II
1. Meteorology	A. Population Geography
2. Demography	B. Soil Geography
3. Sociology	C. Climatology
4. Pedology	D. Social Geography

(a) 1B,2C,3A,4D

(b) 1A,2D,3B,4C

(c) 1D,2B,3C,4A

(d) 1C,2A,3D,4B

Ans. (d) 1C,2A,3D,4B.

Q. 4. Which one of the following questions is related to cause-effect relationships : A

(a) Why (b) What

(c) Where (d) When

Ans. (a) Why.

Q. 5. (iv)Which one of the following disciplines attempts temporal synthesis : A

(a) Sociology (b) Geography

(c) Anthropology (d) History

Ans. (d) History.

(B) Answer the following questions in about 30 words :

Q. 1. What important cultural features do you observe while going to school? Are they similar or dissimilar? Should they be included in the study of geography or not? If yes, why? A

Ans. While going to school , we see shops, theatres, roads, temples, mosque, church, houses, government offices, etc., which represent the cultural features.

No , all these features are not similar. They are dissimilar. Yes, these features should be included in the study of geography because they play a pivotal role in understanding the human geography. They are an inseparable part of the social and cultural geography.

Q. 2. You have seen a tennis ball , a cricket ball, an orange and a pumpkin. Which one amongst these resembles the shape of the earth? Why have you chosen this particular item to describe the shape of the earth? U

Ans. We have seen tennis ball, a cricket ball, an orange and a pumpkin. Amongst them an orange resembles the shape of the earth the most because both the cricket ball as well as the tennis ball are complete circles , whereas the pumpkin is comparatively longer.

If we see the shape of the earth, it is geoid type, *i.e.*, flatter towards the poles. Hence, the shape of the orange is very similar to that of the earth.

Q. 3. Do you celebrate *Van Mahotsav* in your school? Why do we plant so many trees? How do the trees maintain ecological balance? U

Ans. Yes, we do celebrate *Van Mahotsav* in our school. We plant trees because trees give us oxygen, rubber, food, shelter, shade, paper, medicinal herbs and many other uncountable beneficial things.

Trees maintain ecological balance by taking in carbon dioxide and giving out oxygen.

Q. 4. You have seen elephants, deer, earthworms, trees and grasses. Where do they live or grow? What is the name given to this sphere? Can you describe some of the important features of this sphere? U

Ans. Yes, we have seen elephants, deer, earthworms, trees and grasses. They live and grow on the biosphere.

Some of the important features of biosphere are :

(i) The combined form of lithosphere, hydrosphere and atmosphere where life is possible is called biosphere.

(ii) Plants, animals are the biotic elements of the biosphere , whereas, the soil, water, air, etc., form the abiotic elements.

(iii) We can see the moving as well as non-moving living beings in the biosphere. Animals, human beings, insects, plants, birds, aquatic animals, etc., form the moving beings. Trees, plants, grass, etc., form the non-moving things.

Q. 5. How much time do you take to reach your school from your house? Had the school been located across the road from your house, how much time would you have taken to reach school? What is the effect of the distance between your residence and the school on the time taken in commuting? Can you convert time into space and vice-versa? U

Ans. It takes me around one hour to reach my school. Had my school been located across the road from my house, I would have taken around 2 minutes to reach my school. Due to the long distance between my residence and school lot of my time is wasted in commuting. I have left with very little time to study.

Space can be converted into time but time cannot be converted into space.

(C) Answer the following questions in about 150 words :

Q. 1. You observe every day in your surroundings that here is variation in natural as well as cultural phenomena. All the trees are not of the same variety. All the birds and animals you see, are different. All these different elements are found on the earth. Can you now argue that geography is the study of 'areal differentiation'. A

Ans. (i) We observe every day in our surroundings that there is variation in natural as well as cultural phenomena. All the trees are not of the same variety. All the birds and the trees that we get to see are different from each other.

(ii) All such varied elements are found on the earth. It is aptly said that geography is the study of 'areal differentiation' , but it cannot be said that geography is just subjected to or totally dedicated only to the study of 'areal differentiation'.

(iii) Geography as a discipline is related to space and very well takes into consideration the spatial characteristics and attributes. It takes into consideration the study of various patterns of distribution , location and concentration of phenomena over space and interprets them providing explanations for these patterns.

(iv) It takes notes of the associations and inter-relationships between the phenomenon over space and interprets them providing explanations for these patterns. It also takes the note of the associations and interrelationships between the phenomenon resulting from the dynamic interaction between human beings and their physical environment.

(v) Geography as a discipline helps us to understand the reality in totality in its spatial perspective. Thus, it can be said that geography not only takes note of the differences in the phenomena that occurs from place to place but also integrates them holistically which may be different at other places.

Q. 2. You have already studied geography, history, civics and economics as parts of social studies. Attempt an integration of these disciplines highlighting their interface. [R]

Ans. Geography as an integrated discipline :

(i) Geography and history : In different parts of the world it has been witnessed that the geographical factors have modified the course of history. Every evident region has undergone some historical experiences before attaining the present-day status. Similarly, the changes in the landforms, climate, vegetation, economic activities, occupations and cultural developments have undergone a change which been studied in the definite historical course.

(ii) Geography and civics : The major study of political science revolves around territory, people and sovereignty. Whereas, political geography is concerned with the study of the state as a spatial unit as well as the study of the people and their political behaviour.

(iii) Geography and economics : Economics is concerned with the basic features of the economy of the country such as the production, distribution, exchange, consumption, profit and loss, etc. Each of these features have certain spatial aspects and this is where the role of economic geography comes in. Economic geography studies the various aspects of production, distribution, exchange, consumption , profit and loss.

Project Work

Select forest as a natural resource :

Q. 1. Prepare a map of India showing the distribution of different types of forests. [A]

Ans.

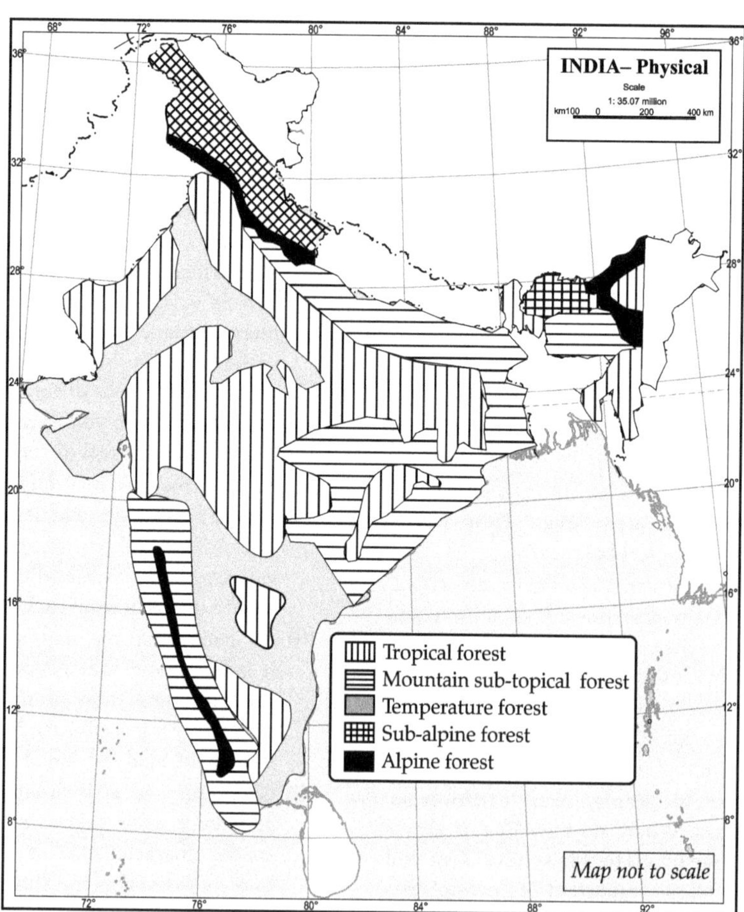

Types of forests found in India

(i) Tropical forests

(a) Tropical moist forests

(b) Tropical dry forests

(ii) Montane sub-tropical forests

(iii) Temperate forests

(iv) Sub-alpine forests

(v) Alpine forests

Detailed Answer :

Nearly 24.39 per cent of the total area in India is covered with forests.

(i) **Tropical forests :** These are also known as tropical rain forests. In India such forests are found in regions receiving more than 250 cm average annual rainfall. These forests are found in Andaman & Nicobar Islands, Western coasts and parts of Karnataka, Annamalai Hills, Assam and Bengal.

(ii) **Montane Sub-tropical forests :** These forests are found in region of fairly high rainfall but where temperature differences between winter and summer are less marked. Trees in these forests are broad leaved. These forests are found in the Himalayas where humidity and temperature are relatively low.

(iii) **Temperate forests :** These forests are found in areas of lesser rainfall. The trees are high, sometimes up to 45 metres tall. The dominant elements of vegetation are oak and conifers.

(iv) **Sub-alpine forests :** These forests are found throughout Himalayas from Ladakh in the west to Arunanchal Pradesh in the east at the altitude from 2800 m to 3800 m. Annual rainfall is less than 65 cm.

(v) **Alpine forests :** Plants growing at the altitude from 2900 m to 6000 m are called alpine forests. In India, alpine flora occurs in Himalayas between 4500 metres and 6000 metres.

Q. 2. Write about the economic importance of forests for the country. U

Ans. Forests play an important role in the economic development of a country. They provide several goods which serve as raw materials for many industries. Wood grown in the forests serves as a source of energy for rural households.

(i) Most of the world's paper is made from wood and one rather reliable index to the degree of economic development of a country is as per capita consumption of paper. As an economy develops economically, paper is used as packaging material, in communications and in scores of other uses.

(ii) While it has long been recognised that forests play many roles in the economic development of a country in addition to providing wood fiber for many uses, the non-wood outputs of forests are coming increasingly to be recognised and valued everywhere in the world. Forests have watershed values especially in areas with fragile and easily eroded soils, tree cover may be highly valuable simply as protection to the watershed.

(iii) Forests are valued as a place for outdoor decoration. The kinds of forests most valuable for outdoor recreation are not always the same as the kinds most valuable for wood production and vice-versa. National parks and biosphere reserves sanctuaries are a great attraction to the tourists. Tourists in the parks, sanctuaries and biosphere reserves brings revenue to the authorities that manage them.

(iv) Agricultural activities are allowed to the local communities and employment is provided to the people. Timber management also generates country tax relief. In our current economic environment this is more important than ever, as it provides income struggling local budgets.

(v) Forests are the home for many species of wildlife including mammals, reptiles and birds. Some of these forms of wildlife are clearly valuable to man. Some other goods provided by the forests are food, biomass, pulp and paper , rayon , fibres, lac, wooden articles and medicinal plants.

(vi) Forests sustain a lot of full-time jobs derived from truck-loading, logging, trucking, paper production, manufacturing building materials and lumber. Many other jobs are created in businesses such as the expanding printing industry , etc. **(Any five)**

Q. 3. Prepare a historical account of conservation of the forests in India with focus on Chipko Movements in Rajasthan and Uttarakhand. R

Ans. In Rajasthan, the Khejri Village of Jodhpur protecting green Khejri trees, that considered sacred by the village community. This incident was a forebear of the 20th century Chipko Movement. In this incident about 363 Bishnois were died. The whole incident was taken place in 1730 AD.

To stop the ruthless cutting of trees in the Himalayas, a unique movement, Chipko was started by illiterate tribal women in the Tehri Garhwal district of Uttarakhand in 1972.

The word 'Chipko' means 'to hug' or ' to embrace' and the movement derived its name from the dramatic circumstances in which it was born.

In 1978 when the women of Advani village hugged the trees, faced police firing and later courted arrest.

The movement continued under the leadership of Shri Sunder Lal Bahuguna. He undertook a people's march through about 3000 km in the hilly region of the Himalayas to protest against the felling of trees. Ultimately Chipko Movement got the success and a large number of trees could be saved from cutting.

The movement inspired people to work on water management, energy conservation, afforestation and recycling, issues of environmental degradation and methods of conservation in Himalayas and throughout India.

OSWAAL LEARNING TOOLS

For Suggested Online Videos

Visit : *https://qrgo.page.link/Vrnbb* **Or Scan the Code**

To learn from NCERT Prescribed Videos

Or Scan the Code **Visit :** *https://qrgo.page.link/545fS*

❑❑

UNIT-II

The Earth

CHAPTER 2

THE ORIGIN AND EVOLUTION OF THE EARTH

Syllabus

- *Early Theories: Origin of the Earth, Modern Theories: Origin of the Universe, The Star Formation, Formation of the Planets.*
- *Our Solar System, The Moon.*
- *Evolution of the Earth, Evolution of Lithosphere, Evolution of Atmosphere and Hydrosphere, Origin of Life.*

TOPIC-1

Early Theories: Origin of the Earth, Modern Theories: Origin of the Universe, The Star Formation, Formation of the Planets.

Revision Notes

- A large number of hypotheses were put forth by different philosophers and scientists regarding the origin of the earth.
- One of the earlier and popular arguments was by German philosopher Immanuel Kant. Mathematician Laplace revised it in 1796. It is known as Nebular Hypothesis.
- The hypothesis considered that the planets were formed out of a cloud of material associated with a youthful sun, which was slowly rotating.
- Later in 1900, Chamberlain and Moulton considered that a wandering star approached the sun. As a result, a cigar-shaped extension of material was separated from the solar surface.
- Sir James Jeans and later Sir Harold Jeffrey supported this argument. These arguments are called the Binary Theories. In 1950, Otto Schmidt in Russia and Carl Weizascar in Germany somewhat revised the 'Nebular Hypothesis', though differing in details.
- However, scientists in later period took up the problems of origin of universe rather than that of just the earth or the planets.
- The most popular argument regarding the origin of the universe is the **Big Bang Theory**. It is also called 'Expanding Universe Hypothesis'.
- The Big Bang Theory considers the following stages in the development of the universe:
  - In the beginning, all matter forming the universe existed in one place in the form of a "tiny ball" (singular atom) with an unimaginably small volume, infinite temperature and infinite density.
  - At the Big Bang the "tiny ball" exploded violently. This led to a huge expansion. It is now generally accepted that the event of Big Bang took place 13.7 billion years before the present. The expansion continues even to the present day. As it grew, some energy was converted into matter. There was particularly rapid expansion within fractions of a second after the bang. Thereafter, the expansion has slowed down. Within first three minutes from the Big Bang event, the first atom began to form.
  - Within 300,000 years from the Big Bang, temperature dropped to 4,500 K and gave rise to atomic matter. The universe became transparent. The expansion of the universe means increase in space between the galaxies.

- A galaxy contains a large number of stars. Galaxies spread over vast distances that are measured in thousands of light years.
- The diameters of individual galaxies range from 80,000-150,000 light years. A galaxy starts to form by accumulation of hydrogen gas in the form of a very large cloud called nebula.
- Eventually, growing nebula develops localised clumps of gas. These clumps continue to grow into even denser gaseous bodies, giving rise to formation of stars. The formation of stars is believed to have taken place some 5-6 billion years ago.
- The following are considered to be the stages in the development of planets :
  - The stars are localised lumps of gas within a nebula. The gravitational force within the lumps leads to the formation of a core to the gas cloud and a huge rotating disc of gas and dust develops around the gas core.
  - In the next stage, the gas cloud starts getting condensed and the matter around the core develops into small-rounded objects. These small-rounded objects by the process of cohesion develop into what is called planetesimals. Larger bodies start forming by collision, and gravitational attraction causes the material to stick together. Planetesimals are a large number of smaller bodies.
  - In the final stage, these large number of small planetesimals accrete to form a fewer large bodies in the form of planets.

Know the Terms

- **Nebular Hypothesis :** Nebular Hypothesis considered that the planets were formed out of a cloud of material associated with a youthful sun, which was slowly rotating.
- **Nebula :** A galaxy starts to form by accumulation of hydrogen gas in the form of a very large cloud. This slow circular moving gaseous clouds are called nebula.
- **Big Bang Theory :** This theory is the most universally accepted theory regarding the formation of the earth.

Multiple Choice Questions (1 mark each)

Q. 1. The Big Bang Theory is also called the : A

(a) Galaxy Theory
(b) Expanding Universe Hypothesis
(c) Nebular Hypothesis
(d) Galaxy Expansion Theory

Ans. (b) Expanding Universe Hypothesis 1

Q. 2. The expansion of the universe means increase in space between the: R

(a) universe (b) gases
(c) galaxies (d) bodies

Ans. (c) galaxies 1

Q. 3. The stars are localised lumps of gas within a: U

(a) nebula (b) core
(c) gas (d) hydrogen

Ans. (a) nebula 1

Very Short Answer Type Questions (1 mark each)

Q. 1. What do you know about 'Nebular Hypothesis'? A

Ans. Nebular Hypothesis considered that the planets were formed out of a cloud of material associated with a youthful sun, which was slowly rotating. 1

Q. 2. What is a nebula? A

Ans. A galaxy starts to form by accumulation of hydrogen gas in the form of a very large cloud. This slow circular moving gaseous clouds are called nebula. 1

Q. 3. Define the term Planetesimals? R

Ans. The gas cloud starts getting condensed and the matter around the core develops into small-rounded objects. These small-rounded objects by the process of cohesion develop into what is called planetesimals. 1

Q. 4. Define the term Galaxy. R

Ans. Galaxy is defined as a cluster of millions of stars and solar systems. 1

Q. 5. What does the light year measure? A

Ans. A light year is a measure of distance and not of time. 1

Commonly Made Error

- The concept of light year is not clear to the students.

Answering Tip

- A light year is the distance that light travels in empty space in one year.

AI Q.6. **Name the most popular argument regarding the origin of the universe?** U

Ans. The most popular argument regarding the origin of universe is the Big Bang Theory. 1

Q. 7. What is the other name for the Big Bang Theory? A

Ans. Expanding Universe Hypothesis. 1

Q. 8. Which hypothesis was given by Hoyle? U

Ans. The hypothesis given by Hoyle was that of Steady State. This hypothesis considered the universe to be roughly the same size at any given point of time. 1

Commonly Made Error

- The students are not aware of the fact that when the size of the universe is being referred in the Big Bang Theory, is it being referred as observable universe or entire universe.

Answering Tip

- When the size of the universe at Big Bang is described, it refers to the size of the observable universe, and not the entire universe.

Q. 9. Explain the formation of stars? U

Ans. A star is formed when atoms of light elements are squeezed under enough pressure for their nuclei to undergo fusion. 1

Q. 10. Which evidence was given by Edwin Hubble? R

Ans. Edwin Hubble provided the evidence that the universe is expanding. With time, the galaxies move further and further away. 1

Q. 11. Name a theory which is associated with the origin of the earth? A

Ans. Nebular Hypothesis is associated with the origin of earth. 1

Q. 12. Which theory is most widely accepted regarding origin of the universe at present? A

Ans. The Big Bang Theory is mostly accepted regarding the origin of universe. 1

Q. 13. Who was the propounder of the Nebular Hypothesis? R

Ans. The Nebular Hypothesis was propounded by Sir James and Harold Jeffery. 1

Short Answer Type Questions (3 marks each)

Q. 1. What do you mean by light year? U

Ans. A light year is equal to the number of kilometres travelled by light per second. It is a measure of distance and not of time. Light travels at a speed of 300,000 km/second. Considering this, the distances the light will travel in one year is taken to be one light year. This equals to 9.461×10^{12} km. The mean distance between the sun and the earth is 149,598,000 km. In terms of light years, it is 8.311 minutes of a year. Light travels at a speed of 300,000 km/second. Therefore, the distances that the light will travel in one year is taken to be one light year. 3

Q. 2. Name the various hypothesis associated with the formation of the earth. U

Ans. The various hypothesis associated with the formation of the earth are:

(i) **Nebular Hypothesis :** It was given by Laplace. The hypothesis considered that the planets were formed out of a cloud of material associated with a youthful sun which was slowly rotating.

(ii) **Collision Hypothesis :** It was given by Sir James and Harold Jeffrey. This theory suggests that the moon was formed out of the debris left over from a collision between the earth and an astronomical body the size of mars, approximately 4.5 billion years ago.

(iii) **Accretion Hypothesis :** It was given by Schmidt and Carl Weizascar. This hypothesis argues that about 4.6 million years ago our solar system formed from a cloud of gas and dust which slowly contracted under mutual gravity of all its particles.

(iv) **The Big Bang Theory :** It was given by Edwin Hubble. He argued that the universe was ever expanding. As time passes, galaxies move further and further apart. **(Any three) (1 × 3 = 3)**

Q. 3. Name the experts who modified Nebular Hypothesis. R

Ans. In 1950, Otto Schmidt in Russia and Carl Weizascar in Germany revised the 'Nebular Hypothesis', though they differed in details. They were of the opinion that the sun was surrounded by solar nebula containing mostly hydrogen and helium along with what may be termed as dust .

The friction and collision of particles led to formation of a disk -shaped cloud and the planets were formed through the process of accretion. However, scientists in later period took up the problems of origin of universe rather than that of just the earth or the planets. 3

Commonly Made Error

- The students fail to understand what does the Nebular Hypothesis explains.

Answering Tip

- The Nebular Hypothesis explains the formation and evolution of the Solar System .

Q. 4. What do you know about the formation of stars? R

Ans. The distribution of matter and energy was not even in the early universe. These initial density differences gave rise to differences in gravitational forces and it caused the matter to get drawn together. These formed the bases for development of galaxies which contains millions of stars. 3

Long Answer Type Questions

(5 marks each)

Q. 1. Explain the Big Bang Theory in detail. A

Ans. Refer to NCERT Corner Long Ans. (1) in (C) section.

Q. 2. Explain the earliest theory associated with the origin of the earth. U

Ans. **(i)** A large number of hypotheses were put forth by different philosophers and scientists regarding the origin of the earth. One of the earlier and popular arguments was by German philosopher Immanuel Kant. Mathematician Laplace revised it in 1796. It is known as Nebular Hypothesis.

(ii) The hypothesis considered that the planets were formed out of a cloud of material associated with a youthful sun, which was slowly rotating. Later in 1900, Chamberlain and Moulton considered that a wandering star approached the sun. As a result, a cigar-shaped extension of material was separated from the solar surface.

(iii) As the passing star moved away, the material separated from the solar surface continued to revolve around the sun and it slowly condensed into planets. Sir James Jeans and later Sir Harold Jeffrey supported this argument. At a later date, the arguments considered of a companion to the sun to have been coexisting.

(iv) These arguments are called the Binary Theories. In 1950, Otto Schmidt in Russia and Carl Weizascar in Germany somewhat revised the 'Nebular Hypothesis', though differing in details. They considered that the sun was surrounded by solar nebula containing mostly the hydrogen and helium along with what may be termed as dust.

(v) The friction and collision of particles led to formation of a disk-shaped cloud and the planets were formed through the process of accretion. **(1 × 5 = 5)**

AI **Q.3. Which modern theory is associated with the evolution of the earth?** R

Ans. **(i)** The most popular argument regarding the origin of the universe is the Big Bang Theory. It is also called the Expanding Universe Hypothesis. Edwin Hubble, in 1920, provided evidence that the universe is expanding. As time passes, galaxies move further and further apart. In the beginning, all matter forming the universe existed in one place in the form of a "tiny ball" (singular atom) with an unimaginably small volume, infinite temperature and infinite density.

(ii) At the Big Bang the "tiny ball" exploded violently. This led to a huge expansion. It is now generally accepted that the event of Big Bang took place 13.7 billion years before the present. The expansion continues even to the present day.

(iii) As it grew, some energy was converted into matter. There was particularly rapid expansion within fractions of a second after the bang. Thereafter, the expansion has slowed down. Within first three minutes from the Big Bang event, the first atom began to form.

(iv) Within 300,000 years from the Big Bang, temperature dropped to 4,500 K and gave rise to atomic matter. The universe became transparent. The expansion of universe means increase in space between the galaxies. An alternative to this was Hoyle's concept of steady state. It considered the universe to be roughly the same at any point of time.

(v) However, with greater evidence becoming available about the expanding universe, scientific community at present favours argument of expanding universe. **(1 × 5 = 5)**

Q. 4. Explain the various stages involved in the development of planets? R

Ans. The following are considered to be the stages in the development of planets :

(i) The stars are localised lumps of gas within a nebula. The gravitational force within the lumps leads to the formation of a core to the gas cloud and a huge rotating disc of gas and dust develops around the gas core.

(ii) In the next stage, the gas cloud starts getting condensed and the matter around the core develops into small-rounded objects.

(iii) These small-rounded objects by the process of cohesion develop into what is called planetesimals. Larger bodies start forming by collision, and gravitational attraction causes the material to stick together.

(iv) Planetesimals are a large number of smaller bodies.

(v) In the final stage, these large number of small planetesimals accrete to form a fewer large bodies in the form of planets. **(1 × 5 = 5)**

Commonly Made Error

- It is generally not clear as to why the planets are not perfectly spherical.

Answering Tip

- The planets are not perfectly spherical because they also spin.

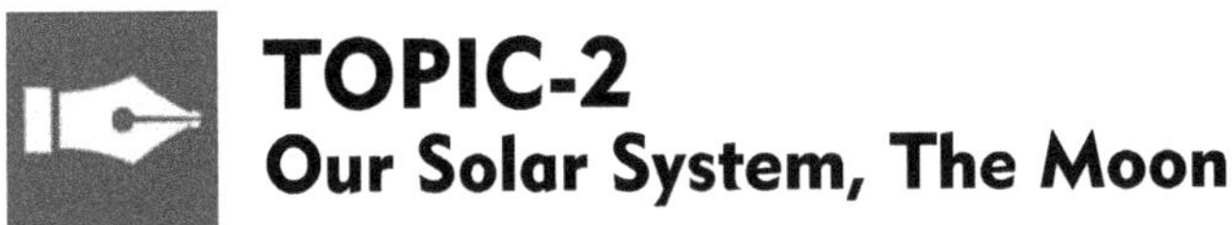

TOPIC-2
Our Solar System, The Moon

Revision Notes

- Our solar system consists of eight planets. A Pluto like dwarf planet 2003 UB_{313} has also been recently sighted.
- Our solar system consists of the sun (the star), 8 planets, 63 moons, millions of smaller bodies like asteroids and comets and huge quantity of dust-grains and gases.
- Out of the eight planets, mercury, venus, earth and mars are called as the inner planets as they lie between the Sun and the belt of asteroids the other four planets are called the outer planets.
- Alternatively, the first four are called Terrestrial, meaning earth-like as they are made up of rock and metals, and have relatively high densities. The rest five are called Jovian or Gas Giant planets. Jovian means jupiter-like.
- All the planets were formed in the same period sometime about 4.6 billion years ago.
- The moon is the only natural satellite of the earth. Like the origin of the earth, there have been attempts to explain how the moon was formed.
- In 1838, Sir George Darwin suggested that initially, the earth and the moon formed a single rapidly rotating body.
- However, the present scientists do not accept either of the explanations. It is now generally believed that the formation of moon, as a satellite of the earth, is an outcome of 'giant impact' or what is described as "the big splat".
- A body of the size of one to three times that of mars collided into the earth sometime shortly after the earth was formed. It blasted a large part of the earth into space. This portion of blasted material then continued to orbit the earth and eventually formed into the present moon about 4.44 billion years ago.

Know the Terms

- **Planetesimals :** The gas cloud that starts getting condensed and the matter around the core develops into small-rounded objects. These small-rounded objects by the process of cohesion develop into what is called planetesimals.
- **Big Splat :** The origin of the moon as a satellite of the earth is the result of big collision which is called the Big Splat.
- **Galaxy :** It is a cluster of millions of stars and solar systems.
- **Outer planets :** Jupiter, Saturn ,Uranus and Neptune are called outer planets.
- **Inner planets :** Mercury, Venus, Earth and Mars are called inner planets.
- **Jovian planets :** Jupiter, Saturn, Uranus and Neptune are called Jovian or Gas Giant planets. Jovian means Jupiter-like. Most of them are much larger than the terrestrial planets and have thick atmosphere, mostly of helium and hydrogen.

Multiple Choice Questions (1 mark each)

Q. 1. There are ___ inner planets. [A]

(a) four (b) five
(c) six (d) seven

Ans. (a) four 1

Q. 2. How many outer planets are there? [R]

(a) Two (b) Three
(c) Four (d) Five

Ans. (c) Four 1

[AI] **Q.3. The only natural satellite of the earth is :** [R]

(a) moon (b) sun
(c) planets (d) galaxy

Ans. (a) moon 1

Q. 4. All planets were formed around : [R]

(a) 4.6 billion years ago
(b) 3.6 billion years ago
(c) 2.6 billion years ago
(d) 1. 6 billion years ago

Ans. (a) 4.6 billion years ago 1

Q. 5. In ______, Chamberlain and Moulton considered that a wandering star approached the sun. [R]

(a) 1700
(b) 1800
(c) 1900
(d) 2000

Ans. (c) 1900 1

Very Short Answer Type Questions (1 mark each)

Q. 1. What are Jovian Planets? U

Ans. Jupiter, Saturn, Uranus and Neptune are called Jovian or Gas Giant planets. Jovian means Jupiter-like. Most of them are much larger than the terrestrial planets and have thick atmosphere, mostly of helium and hydrogen. 1

Commonly Made Error

- The students don't have a clear understanding as to why Jovian Planets are known as gas giant planets.

Answering Tip

- They are called the gas planets because they consist mainly of hydrogen, or the giant planets because of their size.

Q. 2. Define the term Big Splat. R

Ans. The origin of the moon as a satellite of the earth is the result of the big collision called the 'Big Spat'.1

Q. 3. Define solar system ? A

Ans. It consists of the sun, 8 planets , 63 moons, millions of smaller bodies like asteroids and comets and huge quantity of dust grains and gases. 1

Q. 4. What are terrestrial planets ? R

Ans. Terrestrial planets are those planets which are formed in the close vicinity of the parent star where it was too warm for gases to condense to solid particles. Mercury, Venus , Earth and Mars are known terrestrial planets . 1

Q. 5. How many planets are there in our solar system? U

Ans. There are eight planets in our solar system. 1

Q. 6. What is the distance between the sun and the earth ? R

Ans. The distance between the sun and the earth is 149.6 million kms. 1

Q. 7. Name any two inner planets ? R

Ans. Mercury, Venus, Earth and Mars. ½ + ½=1

Q. 8. Name any two outer planets. R

Ans. Jupiter, Saturn , Uranus and Neptune.

(Any two) ½ + ½ =1

Q. 9. Name one natural satellite of earth? A

Ans. Moon is the only natural satellite of earth. 1

Q. 10. What is the diameter of the Milky Way ?

Ans. The diameter is between 80,000 to 1,50,000 light years. 1

Q. 11. Why do we study the celestial bodies. U

Ans. We study the celestial bodies to know about the origin, evolution and function of each and every celestial bodies. 1

Short Answer Type Questions (3 marks each)

AI **Q.1. What do you understand by dwarf planets?** A

Ans. According to the International Astronomical Union (IAU) on August 24, 2006, a planet is a celestial body that :

(i) Orbits the sun.

(ii) Has sufficient mass so that it assumes a hydrostatic equilibrium (nearly round) shape.

(iii) The non-satellites bodies fulfilling these two rules are called dwarf planets. Pluto is now considered a dwarf planet. Ceres, Eris , Makemake, Haumea are some other dwarf planets. **(1 × 3 = 3)**

Q. 2. What are the differences between terrestrial planet and Jovian planets ? R

Ans. The difference between terrestrial and Jovian planets can be attributed to the following conditions :

(i) The terrestrial planets were formed in the close vicinity of the parent star where it was too warm for gases to condense to solid particles. Jovian planets were formed at quite a distant location.

(ii) The solar wind was most intense nearer the sun; so, it blew off lots of gas and dust from the terrestrial planets. The solar winds were not all that intense to cause similar removal of gases from the Jovian planets.

(iii) The terrestrial planets are smaller and their lower gravity could not hold the escaping gases. However, Jovian planets are bigger and have high gravity. **(1 × 3 = 3)**

Q. 3. What opinion do the present day scientists hold about the origin of the moon ? A

Ans. (i) In 1838, Sir George Darwin suggested that initially, the earth and the moon formed a single rapidly rotating body. The whole mass became a dumb-bell-shaped body and eventually it broke. It was also suggested that the material forming the moon was separated from what we have at present the depression occupied by the Pacific Ocean.

(ii) However, the present scientists do not accept either of the explanations. It is now generally believed that the formation of moon, as a satellite of the earth, is an outcome of 'giant impact' or what is described as "the big splat". A body of the size of one to three times that of mars collided into the earth sometime shortly after the earth was formed.

(ii) It blasted a large part of the earth into space. This portion of blasted material then continued to orbit the earth and eventually formed into the present moon about 4.44 billion years ago. **(1 × 3 = 3)**

Q. 4. How the inner planets are terrestrial while outer planets are Jovian? Explain. ? U

Ans. (i) Inner planets are terrestrial while the outer planets are Jovian because the terrestrial planets are much smaller and hold less gravity and are thus unable to hold the escaping gases.

(ii) Jovian planets being bigger in size have high gravity. The solar winds also are more intense near the sun, so it blows off lot of gas and dust from the terrestrial planets.

(iii) The solar winds are not that intense to cause similar removal of gases from the Jovian planets.

(1 × 3 = 3)

Commonly Made Error

- The students are unaware as to how the outer planets got the name of Jovian Planets.

Answering Tip

- The so called Jovian planets derived their name from Jupiter, the largest planet in the Solar System.

Q. 5. Write any three points of difference between inner planets and outer planets ? R

Ans.

S.No.	Inner Planets	Outer Planets
1.	Mercury, venus, mars and earth are the inner planets.	jupiter, saturn , uranus and neptune are called the outer planets.
2.	Inner planets are found between the belt of asteroids and the sun.	Outer planets are found after the belt of asteroids.
3.	Inner planets are also called terrestrial planets. These planets are smaller in size.	Outer planets are called Jovian planets. These planets are larger in size.

Commonly Made Error

- The students tend to stick to the common differences that have been discussed about the inner and outer planets.

Answering Tip

- The inner planets don't have rings whereas all outer planets have rings.

TOPIC-3
Evolution of the Earth, Evolution of Lithosphere, Evolution of Atmosphere and Hydrosphere, Origin of Life.

Revision Notes

- The earth has a layered structure. From the outermost end of the atmosphere to the centre of the earth, the material that exists is not uniform.
- The atmospheric matter has the least density. From the surface to deeper depths, the earth's interior has different zones and each of these contains materials with different characteristics.
- The earth was mostly in a volatile state during its primordial stage. Due to gradual increase in density the temperature inside has increased.
- As a result, the material inside started getting separated depending on their densities. This allowed heavier materials (like iron) to sink towards the centre of the earth and the lighter ones to move towards the surface.
- With passage of time it cooled further and solidified and condensed into a smaller size. This later led to the development of the outer surface in the form of a crust.
- During the formation of the moon, due to the giant impact, the earth was further heated up. It is through the process of differentiation that the earth forming material got separated into different layers. Starting from the surface to the central parts, we have layers like the crust, mantle, outer core and inner core. From the crust to the core, the density of the material increases.
- There are three stages in the evolution of the present atmosphere. The first stage is marked by the loss of primordial atmosphere. In the second stage, the hot interior of the earth contributed to the evolution of the atmosphere. Finally, the composition of the atmosphere was modified by the living world through the process of photosynthesis.
- Sometime around 3,800 million years ago, life began to evolve. However, around 2,500-3,000 million years before the present, the process of photosynthesis got evolved. Life was confined to the oceans for a long time.
- Oceans began to have the contribution of oxygen through the process of photosynthesis. Eventually, oceans were saturated with oxygen, and 2,000 million years ago, oxygen began to flood the atmosphere.
- Modern scientists refer to the origin of life as a kind of chemical reaction, which first generated complex organic molecules and assembled them.
- It can be assumed that life began to evolve sometime 3,800 million years ago. The record of life that existed on this planet in different periods is found in rocks in the form of fossils.

Know the Terms

- **Differentiation :** The process through which the earth forming material got separated into different layers is called differentiation.
- **Volatile state :** State of being liable to change rapidly and unpredictably at normal temperatures.
- **Primordial stage :** The beginning or the basic stage.
- **Photosynthesis :** The process by which green plants and some other organisms use sunlight to synthesize nutrients from carbon dioxide and water.

Multiple Choice Questions (1 mark each)

Q. 1. There are________ stages in the evolution of the present atmosphere. [A]

(a) two
(b) three
(c) four
(d) five

Ans. (b) three 1

Q. 2. The earth has a_________ structure. [R]

(a) layered
(b) non-layered
(c) piled on
(d) single

Ans. (a) layered 1

Very Short Answer Type Questions (1 mark each)

Q. 1. What you do you understand by the term 'Degassing'? [A]

Ans. The early atmosphere largely contained water vapour, nitrogen, carbon dioxide, methane, ammonia and very little of free oxygen. The process through which the gases are outpoured from the interior is called degassing. 1

Q. 2. Define the term 'Differentiation'. [U]

Ans. The process through which the earth forming material got separated into different layers is called differentiation. 1

Q. 3. The earth was in a volatile state in which phase? [U]

Ans. The earth was in a volatile state during the primordial stage. 1

Short Answer Type Questions (3 marks each)

Q. 1. Explain the three stages of the evolution of the present atmosphere. [U]

Ans. There are three stages in the evolution of the present atmosphere.

(i) The first stage is marked by the loss of primordial atmosphere.
(ii) In the second stage, the hot interior of the earth contributed to the evolution of the atmosphere.
(iii) Finally, the composition of the atmosphere was modified by the living world through the process of photosynthesis. (1 × 3 = 3)

Commonly Made Error

- The concept as to how did the atmosphere get oxygen is not very clear.

Answering Tip

- Scientists think that algae first evolved approximately 2.7 billion years ago; and soon after this, oxygen began to exist in the atmosphere. Photosynthesis by primitive plants and algae released oxygen, gradually built up in the atmosphere.

Q. 2. How did the atmosphere originate? [A]

Ans. (i) Gases were released from the earth's interior such as water vapour and other gases.
(ii) These were water vapour, nitrogen, carbon dioxide, methane, ammonia and little free oxygen.
(iii) The process of outpouring the gases from the interior of the earth is called degassing. The process of differentiation created the present atmosphere. (1 × 3 = 3)

[AI] **Q.3. How did the earth develop its different layers?** [R]

Ans. During the formation of the moon, due to the giant impact, the earth was further heated up. It is through the process of differentiation that the earth forming material got separated into different layers. Starting from the surface to the central parts, we have layers like the crust, mantle, outer core and inner core. The density of the material increases from the crust to the core. 3

Q. 4. What do you know about the evolution of life on the earth? [A]

Ans. The evolution of life on the earth traces the processes by which both living organisms and fossil organisms evolved since life emerged on the planets, until the present. Earth formed about 4.5 billion years ago and evidence suggest that life appeared as early as 4.1 to 4.28 billion years. This evidence remains controversial due to the non-biological mechanisms that may have formed these potential signatures of past life. The earliest evidences of life on earth are biogenic carbon signatures and stromatolites fossils discovered in 307 billion years old in Greenland. 3

Q. 5. Explain the role played by carbon dioxide in the formation of oceans?

Ans. The carbon dioxide in the atmosphere got dissolved in rainwater and the temperature further decreased causing more condensation and more rains. The rainwater falling onto the surface got collected in the depressions to give rise to oceans. The earth's oceans were formed within 500 million years from the formation of the earth. 3

Q. 6. How did the oceans come into being?

Ans. The earth's oceans were formed within 500 million years from the formation of the earth. This tells us years. Sometime around 3,800 million years ago, life began to evolve. However, around 2,500-3,000 million years before the present, the process of photosynthesis got evolved. Life was confined to the oceans for a long time. Oceans began to have the contribution of oxygen through the process of photosynthesis. Eventually, oceans were saturated with oxygen, and 2,000 million years ago, oxygen began to flood the atmosphere. 3

Long Answer Type Questions (5 marks each)

Q. 1. Explain how did the life originate on the earth. A

Ans. (i) The last phase in the evolution of the earth relates to the origin and evolution of life. It is undoubtedly clear that the initial or even the atmosphere of the earth was not conducive for the development of life.

(ii) Modern scientists refer to the origin of life as a kind of chemical reaction, which first generated complex organic molecules and assembled them.

(iii) This assemblage was such that they could duplicate themselves converting inanimate matter into living substance. The record of life that existed on this planet in different periods is found in rocks in the form of fossils.

(iv) The microscopic structures closely related to the present form of blue algae have been found in geological formations that are much older than these were some 3,000 million years ago.

(v) It can be assumed that life began to evolve sometime 3,800 million years ago. This is the summary of evolution of life from unicellular bacteria to the modern man. **($1 \times 5 = 5$)**

Q. 2. Explain in detail the collision and accretion hypothesis associated with the evolution of the earth. R

Ans. Collision Hypothesis was given by Sir James and Harold Jeffery. According to this theory , a large nebula wandering in the space came very close to a smaller nebula which is the sun, and its huge upsurge of matter in the surface of the smaller nebula. The matter was detected from the smaller nebula and on cooling condensed into planets.

Accretion Hypothesis was given by Schmidt and Carl Weizascar. According to them, the solar system started out as a cloud of gas and dust drifting in a space called nebula. The gaseous cloud exploded violently to form supernova. The exploitation left the vast spinning cloud and gases and thus to collapse under its own gravity and develop as denser core.

This denser core became larger and hotter and be got separated into different layers. 5

Q. 4. Explain the evolution of atmosphere. A

Ans. The present composition of earth's atmosphere is chiefly contributed by nitrogen and oxygen. There are three stages in the evolution of the present atmosphere :

The first stage is marked by the loss of primordial atmosphere. In the second stage, the hot interior of the earth contributed to the evolution of the atmosphere. Finally, the composition of the atmosphere was modified by the living world through the process of photosynthesis.

The early atmosphere, with hydrogen and helium, is supposed to have been stripped off as a result of the solar winds. This happened not only in case of the earth, but also in all the terrestrial planets, which were supposed to have lost their primordial atmosphere through the impact of solar winds.

During the cooling of the earth, gases and water vapour were released from the hot interior of solid earth. This started the evolution of the present atmosphere.

The early atmosphere largely contained water vapour, nitrogen, carbon dioxide, methane, ammonia and very little of free oxygen. The process through which the gases were outpoured from the interior is called degassing. Continuous volcanic eruptions contributed water vapour and gases to the atmosphere. As the earth cooled, the water vapour released started getting condensed. The carbon dioxide in the atmosphere got dissolved in rainwater and the temperature further decreased causing more condensation and more rains. The rainwater falling onto the surface got collected in the depressions to give rise to oceans. The earth's oceans were formed within 500 million years from the formation of the earth. This tells us that the oceans are as old as 4,000 million years. Sometime around 3,800 million years ago, life began to evolve. However, around 2,500-3,000 million years before the present, the process of photosynthesis got evolved. Life was confined to the oceans for a long time. Oceans began to have the contribution of oxygen through the process of photosynthesis. Eventually, oceans were saturated with oxygen, and 2,000 million years ago, oxygen began to flood the atmosphere. 5

NCERT CORNER

(A) Multiple choice questions :

Q. 1. Which one of the following figures represents the age of the earth : R

(a) 4.6 million years (b) 13.7 billion years
(c) 4.6 billion years (d) 13.7 trillion years

Ans. (c) 4.6 billion years.

Q. 2. Which one of the following has the longest duration : R

(a) Eons (b) Period
(c) Era (d) Epoch

Ans. (a) Eons.

Q. 3. Which one of the following is not related to the formation or modification of the present atmosphere : A

(a) Solar winds (b) Differentiation
(c) Degassing (d) Photosynthesis

Ans. (b) Differentiation.

Q. 4. Which one of the following represents the inner planets : A

(a) Planets between the sun and the earth
(b) Planets between the sun and the belt of asteroids
(c) Planets in gaseous state
(d) Planets without satellite(s)

Ans. (d) Planets without satellite(s).

Q. 5. Life on the earth appeared around how many years before the present : U

(a) 13.7 billion
(b) 3.8 million
(c) 4.6 billion
(d) 3.8 billion

Ans. (d) 3.8 billion.

(B) Answer the following questions in about 30 words :

Q. 1. Why are the terrestrial planets rocky? A

Ans. Terrestrial planets are rocky because :

(i) The terrestrial planets were formed in the close vicinity of the parent star where it was too warm for gases to condense to solid particles.

(ii) The solar wind was most intense nearer the sun, so , it blew off lots of gas and dust from the terrestrial planets.

(iii) The terrestrial planets are smaller and their lower gravity could not hold the escaping gases.

(1 × 3 = 3)

Q. 2. What is the basic difference in the arguments related to the origin of the earth given by :
(a) Kant and Laplace
(b) Chamberlain and Moulton R

Ans. Kant and Laplace Principle : The hypothesis considered that the planets were formed out of a cloud of material associated with a youthful sun, which was slowly rotating. According to the principle emerged in 1796, the interior of the earth must be gaseous because the earth has originated from gas form.

Chamberlain and Moulton : In 1900, Chamberlain and Moulton considered that a wandering star approached the sun. As a result, a cigar-shaped extension of the material was separated from the solar surface. As the passing star moved away, the material separated from the solar surface continued to revolve around the Sun and it slowly condensed into planets. Later on, the arguments considered of a companion to the sun to have been coexisting. These arguments are called Binary Theories.

Q. 3. What is meant by the process of differentiation? R

Ans. Starting from the surface to the central parts, we have layers like the crust, mantle, outer core and the inner core. As we move from the crust to the core we realise that the density of the material increases. This process of the earth forming material getting separated into different layers is called differentiation.

Q. 4. What was the nature of the earth surface initially? R

Ans. The planet earth initially was a barren, rocky and hot object with a thin atmosphere of hydrogen and helium. This is far from the present day picture of the earth.

It is concluded that in the initial stage the earth was in liquid form. A number of events that took place over millions of years has turned the earth into what it looks like today, i.e., beautiful planet with ample amount of water and conductive atmosphere favouring the existence of life.

Q. 5. What were the gases which initially formed the earth's atmosphere? A

Ans. The gases which initially formed the earth's atmosphere were namely hydrogen and helium. The early atmosphere, with hydrogen and helium, is supposed to have been stripped off as a result of the solar winds. This happened not only in case of the earth, but also in all the terrestrial planets, which were supposed to have lost their primordial atmosphere through the impact of solar winds.

During the cooling of the earth, gases and water vapour were released from the interior solid earth. This started the evolution of the present atmosphere. The early atmosphere largely contained water vapour, nitrogen, carbon dioxide, methane, ammonia and very little of free oxygen.

(C) Answer the following questions in about 150 words :

Q. 1. Write an explanatory note on the 'Big Bang Theory'. U

Ans. The most popular argument regarding the origin of the universe is the Big Bang Theory. It is also called the Expanding Universe Hypothesis. Edwin Hubble, in 1920, provided evidence that the universe is expanding. As time passes, galaxies move further and further apart. The universe appears to be growing larger.

The Big Bang Theory considers the following stages in the development of the universe.

(i) In the beginning, all matter forming the universe existed in one place in the form of a "tiny ball" (singular atom) with an unimaginably small volume, infinite temperature and infinite density.

(ii) At the Big Bang the "tiny ball" exploded violently. This led to a huge expansion. It is now generally accepted that the event of Big Bang took place 13.7 billion years before the present. The expansion continues even to the present day. As it grew, some energy was converted into matter. There was particularly rapid expansion within fractions of a second after the bang. Thereafter, the expansion has slowed down. Within first three minutes from the Big Bang event, the first atom began to form.

(iii) Within 300,000 years from the Big Bang, temperature dropped to 4,500 K and gave rise to atomic matter. The universe became transparent.

(iv) The expansion of universe means increase in space between the galaxies. An alternative to this was Hoyle's concept of steady state. It considered the universe to be roughly the same at any point of time.

(v) However, with greater evidence becoming available about the expanding universe, scientific community at present favours argument of expanding universe.

AI **Q.2. List the stages in the evolution of the earth and explain each stage in brief.** A

Ans. During the primordial stage the earth was mostly in the volatile state. Due to the gradual increase in density the temperature inside increased. As a result, the material inside started getting separated depending on their densities.

This allowed the heavy material to sink inside the centre of the earth and the lighter ones to move towards the surface. With the passage of time, it cooled further and solidified and condensed into smaller size.

This movement led to the development of the outer surface in the form of a crust. It is through the process of differentiation that the earth forming material got separated into different layers. Starting from the surface to the central parts, we have layers like the crust, mantle, outer core and the inner core.

During the cooling of the Earth, gases and water vapour were released from the interior solid earth. This started the evolution of the present atmosphere. The early atmosphere largely contained water vapour, nitrogen, carbon dioxide, methane, ammonia and very little of free oxygen. The process through which the gases were outpoured from the interior is called degassing.

The origin of life as a kind of chemical reaction , which first generated complex organic molecules and assembled them. This assemblage was such that they could duplicate themselves converting inanimate matter into living substances. It can be assumed that the life on earth began to evolve some 3,800 million years ago.

☐☐

CHAPTER

3 INTERIOR OF THE EARTH

Syllabus

> *Sources of Information About the Interior: Direct Sources, Indirect Sources; Earthquake, Earthquake waves, Types of Earthquakes, Effects of Earthquake.*
> *Structure of the Earth, Volcanoes and Volcanic Landforms.*

TOPIC-1
Sources of Information about the Interior, Earthquake and its Effects

Rivision Notes

- The configuration of the surface of the earth is largely a product of the processes operating in the interior of the earth.
- To understand why the earth shakes or how a tsunami wave is generated, it is necessary that we know certain details of the interior of the Earth.
- It is interesting to know how scientists have gathered information about these layers and what are the characteristics of each of these layers.
- The earth's radius is 6,370 km. No one can reach the centre of the earth.
- Most of our knowledge about the interior of the earth is largely based on estimates and inferences. Yet, a part of the information is obtained through direct observations and analysis of materials.
- The most easily available solid earth material is surface rock or the rocks we get from mining areas.
- Besides mining, scientists have taken up a number of projects to penetrate deeper depths to explore the conditions in the crustal portions.
- Scientists world over are working on two major projects such as "Deep Ocean Drilling Project" and "Integrated Ocean Drilling Project".
- Volcanic eruption forms another source of obtaining direct information. As and when the molten material (magma) is thrown onto the surface of the earth, during volcanic eruption it becomes available for laboratory analysis.
- Analysis of properties of matter indirectly provides information about the interior.
- Another source of information are the meteors that at times reach the earth. However, it may be noted that the material that becomes available for analysis from meteors, is not from the interior of the earth.
- The material and the structure observed in the meteors are similar to that of the earth. They are solid bodies developed out of materials same as, or similar to, our planet. Hence, this becomes yet another source of information about the interior of the earth.
- The other indirect sources include gravitation, magnetic field, and seismic activity.
- An earthquake in simple words is shaking of the earth. It is a natural event. It is caused due to release of energy, which generates waves that travel in all directions.
- The point where the energy is released is called the focus of an earthquake, alternatively, it is called the hypocentre.
- The energy waves travelling in different directions reach the surface. The point on the surface, nearest to the focus, is called epicentre.
- An instrument called 'seismograph' records the waves reaching the surface.

- Earthquake waves are basically of two types — body waves and surface waves. Body waves are generated due to the release of energy at the focus and move in all directions travelling through the body of the earth.
- The body waves interact with the surface rocks and generate new set of waves called surface waves.
- There are two types of body waves. They are called P and S-waves. P-waves move faster and are the first to arrive at the surface.
- The P-waves are similar to sound waves. They travel through gaseous, liquid and solid materials. S-waves arrive at the surface with some time lag. These are called secondary waves.
- Reflection causes waves to rebound whereas refraction makes waves move in different directions. The variations in the direction of waves are inferred with the help of their record on seismograph.
- Different types of earthquake waves travel in different manners. As they move or propagate, they cause vibration in the body of the rocks through which they pass.
- Earthquake waves get recorded in seismographs located at far off locations. However, there exist some specific areas where the waves are not reported. Such a zone is called the 'shadow zone'.
- The most common type of earthquakes are the tectonic earthquakes. These are generated due to sliding of rocks along a fault plane.
- A special class of tectonic earthquake is sometimes recognised as volcanic earthquake. However, these are confined to areas of active volcanoes.
- In the areas of intense mining activity, sometimes the roofs of underground mines collapse causing minor tremors. These are called collapse earthquakes.
- Ground shaking may also occur due to the explosion of chemical or nuclear devices. Such tremors are called explosion earthquakes.
- The earthquakes that occur in the areas of large reservoirs are referred to as reservoir induced earthquakes.
- The earthquake events are scaled either according to the magnitude or intensity of the shock. The magnitude scale is known as the Richter Scale.
- Tsunamis are waves generated by the tremors and not an earthquake in itself. Though the actual quake activity lasts for a few seconds, its effects are devastating provided the magnitude of the quake is more than 5 on the Richter Scale.

Know the Terms

- **Earthquake :** An earthquake is the shaking of the earth. It is a natural event. It is caused due to the release of energy.
- **Gravity Anomalies :** The differences in readings from the expected values is called gravity anomaly. Gravity anomalies give us information about the distribution of mass of the material in the crust of the earth.
- **Richter Scale :** The earthquake events are scaled either according to the magnitude or intensity of the shock. The magnitude scale is known as the Richter Scale.
- **P-waves :** They are known as primary waves. They move faster and are the first to arrive at the surface.
- **S-waves :** They are known as secondary waves. They arrive at the surface with some time lag.
- **Shadow Zone :** There exists some specific areas where the waves are not reported. Such a zone is called the shadow zone.

Multiple Choice Questions

(1 mark each)

Q. 1. The earth's radius is : [A]

(a) 6,370 km
(b) 7,370 km
(c) 8,370 km
(d) 9,370 km

Ans. (a) 6,370 km 1

Q. 2. P-waves are similar to : [R]

(a) sound waves
(b) heat waves
(c) earth waves
(d) plane waves

Ans. (a) sound waves 1

Q. 3. S-waves are also known as : [R]

(a) primary waves
(b) secondary waves
(c) major waves
(d) minor waves

Ans. (b) secondary waves 1

Q. 4. The earthquakes are measured on : [R]

(a) Victor Scale
(b) Richter Scale
(c) Shadow Scale
(d) Gravity Scale

Ans. (b) Richter Scale 1

Very Short Answer Type Questions (1 mark each)

AI **Q.1. Define the term 'Earthquake'.** A

Ans. An earthquake is the shaking of the earth. It is a natural event. It is caused due to the release of energy, which generates waves that travel in all directions. 1

Q. 2. Define the term Focus? R

Ans. When the earthquake occurs, the point where the energy is released is called the focus of an earthquake. 1

Q. 3. Define the term Epicentre? U

Ans. When the earthquake occurs, the point on the surface ,nearest to the focus is called epicentre. 1

Q. 4. Define the term Tsunami. U

Ans. Tsunami are waves generated by the tremors and not an earthquake in itself. 1

Commonly Made Error

- The students are not aware whether the tsunami can be predicted or not.

Answering Tip

- Scientists predict tsunamis by assessing data, so how and what data is acquired is crucial. Seismic readings are usually the first sign of an impending tsunami. Seismic waves travel much faster than water, meaning they can be recorded by seismograph stations some minutes before the tsunami hits.

Q. 5. The earthquake waves are of how many types? U

Ans. The earthquake waves are of two types :

(i) Body waves

(ii) Surface waves 1

Q. 6. What is the earth's radius? A

Ans. 6,371 km. 1

Q. 7. From where do we get the surface rock for the study of the interior of the earth? U

Ans. We get the surface rock from mining areas. 1

Q. 8. Name the two projects on which the scientists world over are working in order to study the interior of the earth. A

Ans. The two projects are :

(i) Deep Ocean Drilling Project

(ii) Integrated Ocean Drilling Project 1

Q. 9. Name any two direct sources of obtaining information about the interior of the earth. R

Ans. The two sources are :

(i) Volcanic eruptions

(ii) Drilling

(iii) Mining **(Any two)**

Q. 10. Name any two sources of indirect information about the interior of the earth's surface. A

Ans. The two sources are :

(i) Meteors

(ii) Gravitation

(iii) Magnetic field

(iv) Seismic activity **(Any two)**

Q. 11. How do we measure the magnitude of earthquake? R

Ans. We measure the magnitude of earthquake on the Richter Scale. 1

Commonly Made Error

- The students are not aware as to how the Richter Scale is measured.

Answering Tip

- The Richter Scale is calculated using information gathered by a seismograph. The Richter Scale is logarithmic, meaning that whole-number jumps indicate a tenfold increase. In this case, the increase is in wave amplitude.

Q. 12. How is the intensity of the earthquake measured? U

Ans. The intensity of the earthquake is measured on the Mercalli Scale. 1

Q. 13. What do we get to know about the interior of the earth through mining? A

Ans. We get to know through the mining activity that temperature and pressure increase with the increasing distance from the surface towards the interior in deeper depths. Moreover, it is also known that the density of the material also increases with depth. 1

Q. 14. When can an earthquake cause tsunami? U

Ans. An earthquake can take form of tsunami if its epicentre is below ocean and its magnitude is very high. An earthquake of magnitude more than 5 on the Richter Scale can prove to be very dangerous. 1

Q. 15. What is the interior part of the earth called? What is its depth? R

Ans. The interior part of the earth is called the core. Its depth is 2,900 km to 6,373 km . 1

Q. 16. `How are gravitational anomalies useful? A

Ans. Gravitational anomalies give us information about the distribution of mass of the material in the crust of the earth. 1

Short Answer Type Questions (3 marks each)

Q. 1. What are earthquakes? Discuss focus/hypocentre and epicentre. How do we measure its magnitude and intensity. [A]

Ans. An earthquake in simple words is shaking of the earth. It is a natural event. It is caused due to release of energy, which generates waves that travel in all directions.

(i) Focus/hypocentre : The point where the energy is released is called the focus of an earthquake, alternatively, it is called the hypocentre.

(ii) Epicentre : The energy waves travelling in different directions reach the surface. The point on the surface, nearest to the focus, is called epicentre. It is the first one to experience the waves. It is a point directly above the focus.

(iii) We measure earthquake's magnitude by Richter Scale.The intensity is measured by Mercalli Scale. **(1 × 3 = 3)**

Q. 2. Write any three points of difference between body waves and surface waves. [U]

Ans.

S.No.	Body Waves	Surface Waves
1.	Body waves are generated due to the release of energy at the focus.	The body waves interact with the surface rocks and generate new set of waves called the surface waves.
2.	These waves move in all directions travelling through the body of the earth.	These waves move along the surface.
3.	These waves are less destructive than the surface waves.	These waves are more destructive as compared to the body waves.

(1 × 3 = 3)

Commonly Made Error

- The students have limited knowledge about how the surface waves travel.

Answering Tip

- The surface waves are waves that travel across the surface of the earth and not through it.

Q. 3. Write any three points of difference between primary waves and secondary waves? [A]

Ans.

S.No.	Primary waves	Secondary waves
1.	They are also known as P-waves.	They are also known as S-waves.
2.	These waves move faster and are first to arrive at the surface.	These waves arrive after the P-waves.
3.	The shadow zone of P-waves is much smaller.	The shadow zone of S-waves is much larger .

(1 × 3 = 3)

Q. 4. How does the shadow zone emerge? [R]

Ans. Earthquake waves get recorded in Seismographs located at far off locations. However, there exist some specific areas where the waves are not reported. Such a zone is called the shadow zone. The study of different events reveals that for each earthquake, there exists an altogether different shadow zone. 3

Q. 5. What makes the earth shake ? [R]

Ans. The release of energy occurs along a fault. A fault is a sharp break in the crustal rocks. Rocks along a fault tend to move in opposite directions. As the overlying rock strata press them, the friction locks them together. However, their tendency to move apart at some point of time overcomes the friction. As a result, the blocks get deformed and eventually, they slide past one another abruptly. This causes a release of energy, and the energy waves travel in all directions. This energy movement causes the earth to shake. 3

Long Answer Type Questions (5 marks each)

Q. 1. Discuss the various sources of information related to the interior of the earth. [R]

Ans. Most of our knowledge about the interior of the earth is largely based on estimates and inferences. Yet, a part of the information is obtained through indirect and direct observations and analysis of materials . Various sources of information are :

(i) Mining : The most easily available solid earth material is surface rock or the rocks we get from mining areas. Gold mines in South Africa are as deep as 3 - 4 km. Going beyond this depth is not possible as it is very hot at this depth. Through mining precious stones, rocks and fuels are extracted which gives us valuable information.

(ii) Drilling : Scientists have taken up a number of projects to penetrate deeper depths to explore the conditions in the crustal portions. Scientists world over are working on two major projects such as "Deep Ocean Drilling Project" and "Integrated Ocean Drilling Project". The deepest drill at Kola, in Arctic Ocean, has so far reached a depth of 12 km. This and many deep drilling projects have provided large volume of information through the analysis of materials collected at different depths.

(iii) Volcanic eruptions : Volcanic eruption forms another source of obtaining direct information. As and when the molten material (magma) is thrown onto the surface of the earth, during volcanic eruption it becomes available for laboratory analysis. However, it is difficult to ascertain the depth of the source of such magma. To know about the thickness of the earth, scientists have estimated the values of temperature, pressure and density of materials at different depths.

(iv) Meteors that reach the Earth : Another source of information are the meteors that at times reach the earth. However, it may be noted that the material that becomes available for analysis from meteors, is not from the interior of the earth. The material and the structure observed in the meteors are similar to that of the earth. They are solid bodies developed out of materials same as, or similar to, our planet. Hence, this becomes yet another source of information about the interior of the earth.

(v) Gravitation : The gravitation force (g) is not the same at different latitudes on the surface. It is greater near the poles and less at the Equator. This is because of the distance from the centre at the equator being greater than that at the poles. The gravity values also differ according to the mass of material. The uneven distribution of mass of material within the earth influences this value. The reading of the gravity at different places is influenced by many other factors. These readings differ from the expected values. Such a difference is called gravity anomaly. Gravity anomalies give us information about the distribution of mass of the material in the crust of the earth.

(vi) Magnetic surveys : Magnetic surveys also provide information about the distribution of magnetic materials in the crustal portion, and thus, provide information about the distribution of materials in this part.

(vii) Seismic activity : It is one of the most important sources of information. The seismic waves provides a complete picture of the layered interior. **(Any five) (1 × 5 = 5)**

Q. 2. What do you know about the different types of earthquake waves. R

Ans. Earthquake waves are of two types :

(i) Body waves : Body waves are generated due to the release of energy at the focus and move in all directions travelling through the body of the earth. Hence, the name body waves.

Body waves are further divided into two types:

(a) P-waves : P-waves move faster and are the first to arrive at the surface. These are also called 'primary waves'. The P-waves are similar to sound waves. They travel through gaseous, liquid and solid materials.

(b) S-waves : S-waves arrive at the surface with some time lag. These are called secondary waves. An important fact about S-waves is that they can travel only through solid materials. This characteristic of the S-waves is quite important. It has helped scientists to understand the structure of the interior of the earth. Reflection causes waves to rebound whereas refraction makes waves move in different directions. The variations in the direction of waves are inferred with the help of their record on seismograph. The surface waves are the last to report on seismograph. These waves are more destructive. They cause displacement of rocks, and hence, the collapse of structures occurs.

Commonly Made Error

- Surface waves and body waves are considered to be similar.

Answering Tip

- Surface waves usually have larger amplitudes and longer wavelengths than body waves and they travel more slowly than body waves.

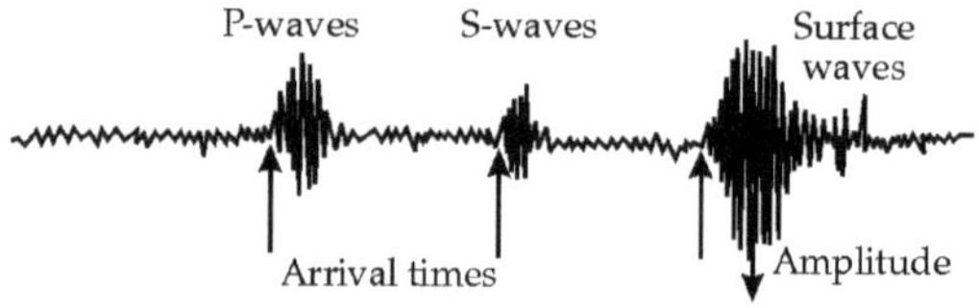

(ii) Surface waves : The body waves interact with the surface rocks and generate new set of waves called surface waves. These waves move along the surface. These waves are more destructive. They cause displacement of rocks and hence, the collapse of structures occurs. The velocity of waves changes as they travel through materials with different densities. The denser the material, the higher is the velocity. Their direction also changes as they reflect or refract when coming across materials with different densities.

(2½+2½=5)

Q. 3. Explain with the help of a diagram how does the shadow zone emerge? A

Ans. (i) Earthquake waves get recorded in seismographs located at far off locations. However, there exist some specific areas where the waves are not reported. Such a zone is called the 'shadow zone'. The study of different events reveals that for each earthquake, there exists an altogether different shadow zone.

(ii) Seismographs located at any distance within 105° from the epicentre, recorded the arrival of both P and S-waves. However, the seismographs located beyond 145° from epicentre, record the arrival of P-waves, but not that of S-waves. Thus, a zone between 105° and 145° from epicentre was identified as the shadow zone for both the types of waves.

(iii) The entire zone beyond 105° does not receive S-waves. The shadow zone of S-waves is much larger than that of the P-waves. The shadow zone of P-waves appears as a band around the earth between 105° and 145° away from the epicentre. The shadow zone of S-waves is not only larger in extent but it is also a little over 40 per cent of the earth's surface. 5

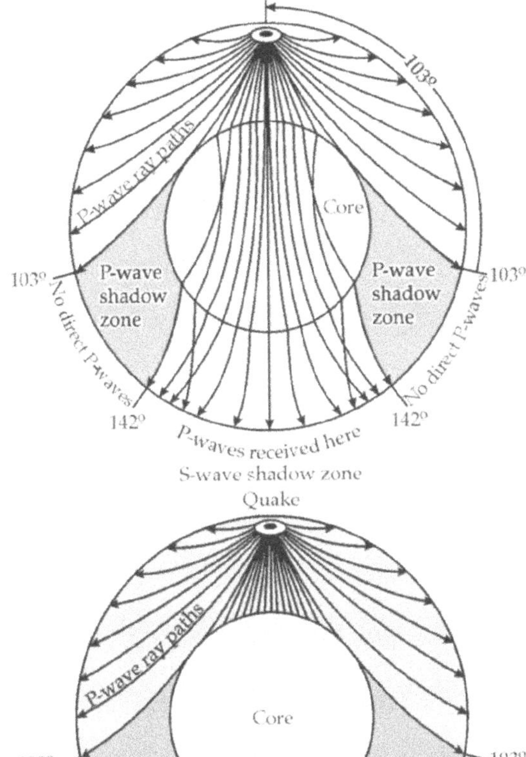

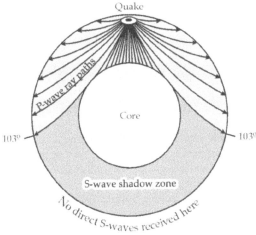

AI Q.4. Explain in detail different types of earthquakes. R

Ans. The different types of earthquakes are :

(i) Tectonic earthquake : The most common ones are the tectonic earthquakes. These are generated due to sliding of rocks along a fault plane.

(ii) Volcanic earthquake : A special class of tectonic earthquake is sometimes recognised as volcanic earthquake. However, these are confined to areas of active volcanoes.

(iii) Collapse earthquake : In the areas of intense mining activity, sometimes the roofs of underground mines collapse causing minor tremors. These are called collapse earthquakes.

(iv) Explosion earthquake : Ground shaking may also occur due to the explosion of chemical or nuclear devices. Such tremors are called explosion earthquakes.

(v) Reservoir induced earthquake : The earthquakes that occur in the areas of large reservoirs are referred to as reservoir induced earthquakes.

(1 × 5 = 5)

Q. 5. What are the effects of the earthquake. R

Ans. Earthquake is a natural hazard. The following are the immediate hazardous effects of earthquake :

(i) Ground shaking
(ii) Land and mud slides
(iii) Destruction of means of communication and transportation
(iv) Avalanches
(v) Ground displacement
(vi) Floods from dam and levee failures
(vii) Fire
(viii) Tsunami

Detailed Answer :

(i) Ground Shaking : Ground shaking is an hazard created by earthquakes and also triggers for other hazards such as liquefaction and landslides. The ground shaking is caused due to the seismic waves passing beneath buildings , roads and other structures.

(ii) Land and mud slides : When the earthquake occurs many times areas of steep slopes slip causing landslides. It also triggers mass movement of the soil.

(iii) Destruction of means of communication and transportation : It leads to the destruction of means of communication and transportation. It creates problems in sending help and relief to the victims.

(iv) Avalanches : Large earthquakes can trigger avalanches by suddenly cascading or dislodging the snow from the down side of the mountain which have catastrophic effects.

(v) Ground displacement : If a structure such as a building, road, etc., is built across a fault, the ground displacement during an earthquake could cause serious damage or rip apart that structure.

(vi) Floods from dam and levee failures : An earthquake can rupture or break dams or levees along a river. The water from the river or the reservoir would then flood the area, damaging buildings and maybe sweeping away or drowning people.

(vii) Fire : The fire can be started by broken gas lines and power lines or tipped over wood or coal stoves. There can be a serious problem, especially of the water lines that feed the hydrants are broken.

(viii) Tsunami : By and large the most destructive tsunamis are generated from large, shallow earthquakes with an epicentre or fault line near or on the ocean floor. These usually occur in regions of the earth characterized by tectonic subduction along tectonic plate boundaries.

(Any five) (1 × 5 = 5)

Commonly Made Error

- The students are not aware of what causes the earthquake

Answering Tip

- The most common cause of earthquake is the breaking of the underground rock along a fault.

Q. 6. How can we locate an epicentre of an earthquake? R

Ans. Steps involved in locating an epicentre of an earthquake are :

(i) Check the scale on the map. The scale should look like a piece of ruler.

(ii) Though all maps are different , 1 centimetre can be equal to 100 kilometres or something near to it.

(iii) Figure out the distance to the epicentre in your map. For instance, your map has a scale where one centimetre is equal to 100 kilometres. If the epicentre of the earthquake is 215 kilometres away, that equals 2.15 centimetres on the map.

(iv) Using your compass, draw a circle with a radius equal to the number you came up within the centre will be the location of your seismograph.

(v) The epicentre of the earthquake is somewhere on the edge of that circle. **(1 × 5 = 5)**

TOPIC-2
Structure of the Earth, Volcanoes and Volcanic Landforms

Revision Notes

- The crust is the outermost solid part of the earth. It is brittle in nature. The thickness of the crust varies under the oceanic and continental areas. Oceanic crust is thinner as compared to the continental crust.
- The mean thickness of oceanic crust is 5 km whereas that of the continental is around 30 km.
- The portion of the interior beyond the crust is called the mantle.
- The upper portion of the mantle is called asthenosphere. The word 'astheno' means weak. It is considered to be extending upto 400 km.
- The crust and the uppermost part of the mantle are called lithosphere. Its thickness ranges from 10-200 km. The lower mantle extends beyond the asthenosphere. It is in solid state.
- The core-mantle boundary is located at the depth of 2,900 km. The outer core is in liquid state while the inner core is in solid state. The density of material at the mantle core boundary is around 5g and at the centre of the earth at 6,300 km, the density value is around $13g/cm^3$.
- The core is made up of very heavy material mostly constituted by nickel and iron. It is sometimes referred to as the nife layer.
- A volcano is a place where gases, ashes and/or molten rock material – lava – escape to the ground.
- A volcano is called an active volcano if the materials mentioned are being released or have been released out in the recent past. The layer below the solid crust is mantle. It has higher density than that of the crust. The mantle contains a weaker zone called asthenosphere.
- The material in the upper mantle portion is called magma. Once it starts moving towards the crust or it reaches the surface, it is referred to as lava.
- Barring the basalt flows, the shield volcanoes are the largest of all the volcanoes on the earth. These volcanoes are mostly made up of basalt, a type of lava that is very fluid when erupted.
- Composite volcanoes are characterised by eruptions of cooler and more viscous lavas than basalt. These volcanoes often result in explosive eruptions.
- Caldera are the most explosive of the earth's volcanoes. They are usually so explosive that when they erupt, they tend to collapse on themselves rather than building any tall structure.
- Flood basalt provinces volcanoes outpour highly fluid lava that flows for long distances. Some parts of the world are covered by thousands of sq km of thick basalt lava flows.
- Mid-ocean ridge volcanoes occur in the oceanic areas. There is a system of mid-ocean ridges more than 70,000 km long that stretches through all the ocean basins.
- The lava that is released during volcanic eruptions on cooling develops into igneous rocks.
- Batholiths is a large body of magmatic material that cools in the deeper depth of the crust develops in the form of large domes. They appear on the surface only after the denudation processes remove the overlying materials.
- Lacoliths are large dome-shaped intrusive bodies with a level base and connected by a pipe-like conduit from below.

- The near horizontal bodies of the intrusive igneous rocks are called sill or sheet, depending on the thickness of the material.
- As and when the lava moves upwards, a portion of the same may tend to move in a horizontal direction wherever it finds a weak plane. It may get rested in different forms. In case it develops into a saucer shape, concave to the sky body, it is called lapolith.
- When the lava makes its way through cracks and the fissures developed in the land, it solidifies almost perpendicular to the ground. It gets cooled in the same position to develop a wall-like structure. Such structures are called dykes.

Know the Terms

- **Magma :** Magma is a mixture of molten or semi-molten rock, volatiles and solids that is found beneath the surface of the earth.
- **Volcano :** A volcano is a place where gases, ashes and molten rock materials lava escape to the ground.
- **Lava :** When magma reaches the crust of the earth, it is called lava.
- **Batholiths :** A large body of magmatic material that cools in the deeper depth of the crust develops in the form of large domes.
- **Lacoliths :** These are large dome-shaped intrusive bodies with a level base and connected by a pipe-like plane.
- **Phacolith :** A wavy mass of intrusive rocks, at times, is found at the base of synclines or at the top of anticline in folded igneous country. Such wavy materials have a definite conduit to source beneath in the form of magma chambers (subsequently developed as batholiths). These are called the phacoliths.
- **Asthenosphere :** The upper portion of the mantle is called asthenosphere.

Multiple Choice Questions (1 mark each)

Q. 1. The ______ is the outermost solid part of the earth. [A]

(a) crust (b) mantle
(c) magma (d) lava

Ans. (a) crust 1

Q. 2. The thickness of the continental crust is : [U]

(a) 10 km
(b) 20 km
(c) 30 km
(d) 40 km

Ans. (c) 30 km 1

Q. 3. The most explosive of the earth's volcanoes are called : [A]

(a) Caldera (b) Lapoliths
(c) Dykes (d) Asthenosphere

Ans. (a) Caldera 1

Q. 4. __________ Volcanoes are characterised by eruptions of cooler and more viscous lavas than basalt. [R]

(a) Intrinsic (b) Composite
(c) Caldera (d) Nife

Ans. (b) Composite 1

Very Short Answer Type Questions (1 mark each)

Q. 1. Define the term 'Volcano'? [A]

Ans. A volcano is a place where gases, ashes and molten rock materials–lava–escape to the ground. 1

Q. 2. Define the term 'Crust'. [A]

Ans. It is the outermost solid part of the earth. It is brittle in nature. The thickness of the crust varies under the oceanic and continental areas. Oceanic crust is thinner as compared to the continental crust. The mean thickness of oceanic crust is 5 km whereas that of the continental is around 30 km. 1

Q. 3. Define the term 'Mantle'. [A]

Ans. The portion of the interior beyond the crust is called the mantle. The mantle extends from Moho's discontinuity to a depth of 2,900 km. 1

Q. 4. What is 'Magma'? [R]

Ans. Magma is a mixture of molten or semi-molten rock, volatiles and solids that is found beneath the surface of the earth. 1

Q. 5. What is meant by mid-ocean ridge volcanoes ? [R]

Ans. These volcanoes occur in the oceanic areas. There is a system of mid-ocean ridges more than 70,000 km long that stretches through all the ocean basins. The central portion of this ridge experiences frequent eruptions. 1

Q. 6. What do you understand by the term 'Sill'? [U]

Ans. The near horizontal bodies of the intrusive igneous rocks are called sill or sheet, depending on the thickness of the material. The thinner ones are called sheets while the thick horizontal deposits are called sills. 1

Q. 7. What do you understand by the term 'Dykes'. [A]

Ans. When the lava makes its way through cracks and the fissures developed in the land, it solidifies almost perpendicular to the ground. It gets cooled in the same position to develop a wall-like structure. Such structures are called dykes. **1**

Q. 8. Define the term 'Lapoliths'? [A]

Ans. As and when the lava moves upwards, a portion of the same may tend to move in a horizontal direction wherever it finds a weak plane. It may get rested in different forms. In case it develops into a saucer shape, concave to the sky body, it is called lapolith. **1**

Q. 9. Define the term 'Lacoliths'? [A]

Ans. Lacoliths are large dome-shaped intrusive bodies with a level base and connected by a pipe-like conduit from below . It resembles the surface volcanic domes of composite volcano, only these are located at deeper depths. **1**

Answering Tip

- A lacolith is a sheet intrusion that has been injected between two layers of sedimentary rock.

Q. 10. Define the term 'Phacoliths'. [R]

Ans. A wavy mass of intrusive rocks, at times, is found at the base of synclines or at the top of anticline in folded igneous country. Such wavy materials have a definite conduit to source beneath in the form of magma chambers (subsequently developed as batholiths). These are called the phacoliths. **1**

Short Answer Type Questions

(3 marks each)

Q. 1. Explain the uppermost layer of the earth's crust? [U]

Ans. It is the outermost solid part of the earth. It is brittle in nature.

(i) The thickness of the crust varies under the oceanic and continental areas. Oceanic crust is thinner as compared to the continental crust. The mean thickness of oceanic crust is 5 km whereas that of the continental is around 30 km. The continental crust is thicker in the areas of major mountain systems. It is as much as 70 km thick in the Himalayan region.

(ii) It is made up of heavier rocks having density of 3 g/cm^3. This type of rock found in the oceanic crust is basalt.

(iii) The mean density of material in oceanic crust is 2.7 g/cm^3. **(1 × 3 = 3)**

Answering Tip

- The layers of the earth's crust are based on the chemical composition.

Q. 2. What do you know about the middle layer of the earth? [A]

Ans. The portion of the interior beyond the crust is called the mantle. The mantle extends from Moho's discontinuity to a depth of 2,900 km.

(i) The upper portion of the mantle is called asthenosphere. The word 'astheno' means weak. It is considered to be extending upto 400 km. It is the main source of magma that finds its way to the surface during volcanic eruptions.

(ii) It has a density higher than the crust's (3.4 g/cm^3). The crust and the uppermost part of the mantle are called lithosphere. Its thickness ranges from 10-200 km.

(iii) The lower mantle extends beyond the asthenosphere. It is in solid state. **(1 × 3 = 3)**

Answering Tip

- Rocks in earth's mantle experience temperatures of up to 4000 degrees Celsius (near the core), but stay solid due to enormous pressure.

[AI] **Q.3. What do you know about the innermost layer of the earth?** [R]

Ans. (i) The innermost layer of the earth is known as the core.

(ii) The earthquake wave velocities helped in understanding the existence of the core of the earth. The core-mantle boundary is located at the depth of 2,900 km.

(iii) The outer core is in liquid state while the inner core is in solid state. The density of material at the mantle-core boundary is around 5 g/cm^3 and at the centre of the earth at 6,300 km, the density value is around 13 g/cm^3.

(iv) The core is made up of very heavy material mostly constituted by nickel and iron. It is sometimes referred to as the nife layer. **(1 × 3 = 3)**

Q. 4. What do you know about the composite volcanoes? [R]

Ans. (i) These volcanoes are characterised by eruptions of cooler and more viscous lavas than basalt.

(ii) These volcanoes often result in explosive eruptions. Along with lava, large quantities of pyroclastic material and ashes find their way to the ground.

(iii) This material accumulates in the vicinity of the vent openings leading to formation of layers, and this makes the mounts appear as composite volcanoes. **(1 × 3 = 3)**

Q. 5. Write a note on shield volcanoes. [R]

Ans. A broad domed volcano with gently sloping sides, characteristic of the eruption of fluid basaltic lava is called shield volcano. The shield volcanoes are the largest of all the volcanoes on the earth.

The Hawaiian volcanoes are the most famous examples. These volcanoes are mostly made up of basalt, a type of lava that is very fluid when erupted. For this reason, these volcanoes are not steep.

They become explosive if somehow water gets into the vent; otherwise, they are characterised by low-explosivity. The upcoming lava moves in the form of a fountain and throws out the cone at the top of the vent and develops into cinder cone. **3**

Answering Tip

- The largest shield volcano is Mauna Loa on the Big Island of Hawaii; all the volcanoes in the Hawaiian Islands are shield volcanoes.
- There are also shield volcanoes, for example, in Washington, Oregon, and the Galapagos Islands.

Long Answer Type Questions

(5 marks each)

AI **Q.1. Explain with the help of a diagram the interior of the earth.** A

Ans. The structure of the earth can be divided into three parts :

(i) Crust

(ii) Mantle

(ii) Core

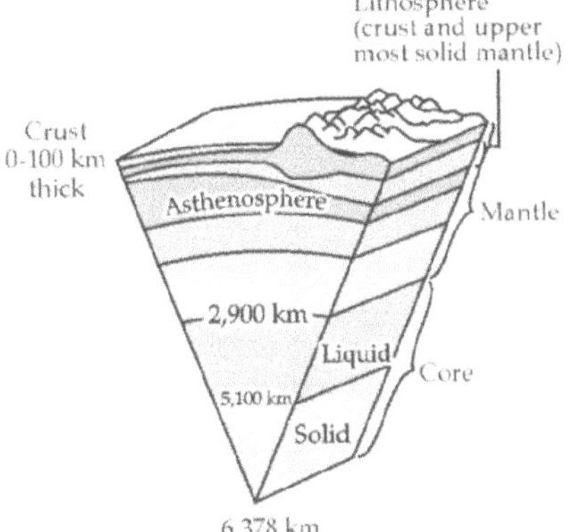

(i) Crust : It is the outermost solid part of the earth. It is brittle in nature. The thickness of the crust varies under the oceanic and continental areas. Oceanic crust is thinner as compared to the continental crust. The mean thickness of oceanic crust is 5 km whereas that of the continental is around 30 km.

The continental crust is thicker in the areas of major mountain systems. It is as much as 70 km thick in the Himalayan region. It is made up of heavier rocks having density of 3 g/cm^3.

This type of rock found in the oceanic crust is basalt. The mean density of material in oceanic crust is 2.7 g/cm^3.

(ii) Mantle : The portion of the interior beyond the crust is called the mantle. The mantle extends from Moho's discontinuity to a depth of 2,900 km. The upper portion of the mantle is called asthenosphere. The word 'astheno' means weak.

It is considered to be extending upto 400 km. It is the main source of magma that finds its way to the surface during volcanic eruptions. It has a density higher than the crust's (3.4 g/cm^3).

The crust and the uppermost part of the mantle are called lithosphere. Its thickness ranges from 10-200 km. The lower mantle extends beyond the asthenosphere. It is in solid state.

(iii) Core : The earthquake wave velocities helped in understanding the existence of the core of the earth. The core-mantle boundary is located at the depth of 2,900 km. The outer core is in liquid state while the inner core is in solid state.

The density of material at the mantle-core boundary is around 5 g/cm^3 and at the centre of the earth at 6,300 km, the density value is around 13 g/cm^3. The core is made up of very heavy material mostly constituted by nickel and iron. It is sometimes referred to as the nife layer.

(2+1+1+1=5)

Q. 2. Write a note on the various types of volcanoes classified on the basis of nature of eruption and the form developed at the surface. R

Ans. Volcanoes are classified on the basis of nature of eruption and the form developed at the surface. Major types of volcanoes are as follows :

(i) Shield Volcanoes : Barring the basalt flows, the shield volcanoes are the largest of all the volcanoes on the earth. The Hawaiian volcanoes are the most famous examples. These volcanoes are mostly made up of basalt, a type of lava that is very fluid when erupted. For this reason, these volcanoes are not steep. They become explosive if somehow water gets into the vent; otherwise, they are characterised by low-explosivity. The upcoming lava moves in the form of a fountain and throws out the cone at the top of the vent and develops into cinder cone.

(ii) Composite Volcanoes : These volcanoes are characterised by eruptions of cooler and more viscous lavas than basalt. These volcanoes often result in explosive eruptions. Along with lava, large quantities of pyroclastic material and ashes find their way to the ground. This material accumulates in the vicinity of the vent openings leading to formation of layers, and this makes the mounts appear as composite volcanoes.

(iii) Caldera : These are the most explosive of the earth's volcanoes. They are usually so explosive that when they erupt they tend to collapse on themselves rather than building any tall structure. The collapsed depressions are called calderas. Their explosiveness indicates that the magma chamber supplying the lava is not only huge but is also in close vicinity.

(iv) **Flood Basalt Provinces :** These volcanoes outpour highly fluid lava that flows for long distances. Some parts of the world are covered by thousands of sq km of thick basalt lava flows. There can be a series of flows with some flows attaining thickness of more than 50 m. Individual flows may extend for hundreds of km. The Deccan Traps from India, presently covering most of the Maharashtra Plateau, are a much larger flood basalt province. It is believed that initially the trap formations covered a much larger area than the present.

(v) **Mid-Ocean Ridge Volcanoes :** These volcanoes occur in the oceanic areas. There is a system of mid-ocean ridges more than 70,000 km long that stretches through all the ocean basins. The central portion of this ridge experiences frequent eruptions. **(1 × 5 = 5)**

Answering Tip

- Mid-ocean ridge volcanoes form where two plates are moving apart.

Q. 3. Write a note on the volcanic landforms. [A]

Ans. When Volcanic eruption takes place, it formed a structure called as volcanic landforms. These landforms are divided into extrusive and intrusive landforms which are based on weather magma cools within the crust or above the crust.

Extrusive Volcanic Landforms : They are formed from material thrown out during volcanic activity. The materials throughout during volcanic activity includes lava flows pyroclastic debris, volcanic bombs, ash and dust and gases such as nitrogen compounds, sulphur compounds and minor amounts of chlorine, hydrogen and argon. The extrusive volcano landforms includes; mid-ocean ridge, cinder cone, caldera lake, lava plateaus, shield landforms, etc.

Intrusive Volcanic Landforms : These are formed when magma cools within the crust. On the other words, the Lava that cools within the crustal portions assumes different forms. These forms are called intrusive volcanic landforms. They include; bathoiths, lacoliths, phacolithe, sills and dyke.

NCERT CORNER

(A) Multiple choice questions :

Q. 1. Which one of the following earthquake waves is more destructive : [R]

(a) P-waves **(b) S-waves**
(c) Surface waves **(d) None of the above**

Ans. (a) P-waves.

Q. 2. Which one of the following is a direct source of information about the interior of the earth : [R]

(a) Earthquake waves **(b) Volcanoes**
(c) Gravitational force **(d) Earth magnetism**

Ans. (a) Earthquake waves.

Q. 3. Which type of volcanic eruptions have caused Deccan Trap formations : [R]

(a) Shield **(b) Flood**
(c) Composite **(d) Caldera**

Ans. (b) Flood.

Q. 4. Which one of the following describes the lithosphere : [A]

(a) upper and lower mantle
(b) crust and upper mantle
(c) crust and core
(d) mantle and core

Ans. (b) crust and upper mantle.

(B) Answer the following questions in about 30 words :

Q. 1. What are body waves? [R]

Ans. Body waves are generated due to the release of energy at the focus and move in all directions travelling through the body of the earth. Hence, the name body waves. Body waves are of two types: P-waves and S-waves.

Q. 2. Name the direct sources of information about the interior of the earth. [R]

Ans. **Mining :** The most easily available solid earth material is surface rock or the rocks we get from mining areas.

Drilling : Scientist world over are working on two projects such as 'Deep Ocean Drilling Project' and 'Integrated Ocean Drilling Project'. The deepest drill at Kola, in Arctic Ocean , has so far reached a depth of 12 km.

Volcanic eruption : This forms another source of obtaining direct information. As and when the molten material (magma) is thrown onto the surface of the earth, during volcanic eruption it becomes available for laboratory analysis.

Q. 3. Why do earthquake waves develop shadow zone? [A]

Ans. Earthquake waves get recorded in seismographs located at far off locations. However, there exist some specific areas where the waves are not reported. Such a zone is called the 'shadow zone'. The study of different events reveals that for each earthquake, there exists an altogether different shadow zone.

Q. 4. Briefly explain the indirect sources of information of the interior of the earth other than those of seismic activity? [A]

Ans. An indirect source of information of the interior of the earth are the meteors that at times reach the earth. However, it may be noted that the material that becomes available for analysis from meteors, is not from the interior of the earth. The material and the structure observed in the meteors are similar to that of the earth. They are solid bodies developed out of materials same as, or similar to, our planet. Hence, this becomes yet another source of information about the interior of the earth.

The other indirect sources include gravitation, magnetic field and seismic activity.

(C) Answer the following questions in about 150 words :

Q. 1. What are the effects of propagation of earthquake waves on the rock mass through which they travel? R

Ans. Earthquake waves are basically of two types — body waves and surface waves. Body waves are generated due to the release of energy at the focus and move in all directions travelling through the body of the earth. Hence, the name body waves.

The body waves interact with the surface rocks and generate new set of waves called surface waves. These waves move along the surface. The velocity of waves changes as they travel through materials with different densities. The denser the material, the higher is the velocity. Their direction also changes as they reflect or refract when coming across materials with different densities.

The denser the material, the higher the velocity. The direction of vibrations of S-waves is perpendicular to the wave direction in the vertical plane. Hence, they create troughs and crests in the material through which they pass.

Surface waves are considered to be the most destructive waves. Seismographs located at any distance within 105° from the epicentre, recorded the arrival of both the P and S waves.

Thus, the zone between 105° and 145° from epicentre, record the arrival of P-waves, but not that of S-waves. Thus, a zone between 105° and 145° from epicentre was identified as the shadow zone for both the types of waves. The entire zone beyond 105° does not receive S-waves. The shadow zone of S-waves is much larger than that of the P-waves. The shadow zone of P-waves appears as a band around the earth between 105° and 145° away from the epicentre. The shadow zone of S-waves is not only larger in extent but it is also a little over 40 per cent of the earth's surface.

Q. 2. What do you understand by intrusive forms? Briefly describe various intrusive forms? R

Ans. The lava that cools within the crustal portions assumes different forms. These forms are called intrusive forms. Some of the intrusive forms are:

(i) Batholiths : A large body of magmatic material that cools in the deeper depth of the crust develops in the form of large domes. They appear on the surface only after the denudational processes remove the overlying materials. They cover large areas, and at times, assume depth that may be several km. These are granitic bodies. Batholiths are the cooled portion of magma chambers.

(ii) Lacoliths : These are large dome-shaped intrusive bodies with a level base and connected by a pipe-like conduit from below. It resembles the surface volcanic domes of composite volcano, only these are located at deeper depths. It can be regarded as the localised source of lava that finds its way to the surface. The Karnataka plateau is spotted with domal hills of granite rocks.

(iii) Phacoliths : A wavy mass of intrusive rocks, at times, is found at the base of synclines or at the top of anticline in folded igneous country. Such wavy materials have a definite conduit to source beneath in the form of magma chambers (subsequently developed as batholiths). These are called the phacoliths.

(iv) Sills : The near horizontal bodies of the intrusive igneous rocks are called sill or sheet, depending on the thickness of the material. The thinner ones are called sheets while the thick horizontal deposits are called sills.

(v) Dykes : When the lava makes its way through cracks and the fissures developed in the land, it solidifies almost perpendicular to the ground. It gets cooled in the same position to develop a wall-like structure. Such structures are called dykes. These are the most commonly found intrusive forms in the western Maharashtra area.

OSWAAL LEARNING TOOLS

For Suggested Online Videos

Visit : *https://qrgo.page.link/m25VZ* **Or Scan the Code**

To learn from NCERT Prescribed Videos

Visit : *https://qrgo.page.link/1czVM* **Or Scan the Code**

❑❑

CHAPTER

4 DISTRIBUTION OF OCEANS AND CONTINENTS

Syllabus

> *Continental Drift, Evidence in Support of the Continental Drift, Force for Drifting, Post-Drift Studies.*
> *Ocean Floor Configuration, Distribution of Earthquakes and Volcanoes, Concept of Sea Floor Spreading.*
> *Plate Tectonics, Divergent Boundaries, Convergent Boundaries, Rates of Plate Movement, Force for the Plate Movement, Movement of the Indian Plate .*

TOPIC-1
Continental Drift

Revision Notes

- The position of the continents and the ocean bodies, as we see them in the map, have not been the same in the past. Moreover, it is now a well-accepted fact that oceans and continents will not continue to enjoy their present positions in times to come.
- Observe the shape of the coastline of the Atlantic Ocean. You will be surprised by the symmetry of the coastlines on either side of the ocean.
- Many scientists thought of this similarity and considered the possibility of the two Americas, Europe and Africa, to be once joined together.
- From the known records of the history of science, it was Abraham Ortelius, a Dutch map maker, who first proposed such a possibility as early as 1596. Antonio Pellegrini drew a map showing the three continents together.
- However, it was Alfred Wegener, a German meteorologist, who put forth a comprehensive argument in the form of the "Continental Drift Theory " in 1912.
- According to Wegener, all the continents formed a single continental mass, a mega ocean surrounded by the same. The super continent was named PANGAEA, which meant all earth. The mega-ocean was called PANTHALASSA, meaning all water.
- He argued that, around 200 million years ago, the super continent, Pangaea, began to split. Pangaea first broke into two large continental masses as Laurasia and Gondwanaland forming the northern and southern components respectively.
- The shorelines of Africa and South America facing each other have a remarkable and unmistakable match.
- The radiometric dating methods developed in the recent period have facilitated correlating the rock formation from different continents across the vast ocean.
- It is the sedimentary rock formed out of deposits of glaciers. The Gondawana System of sediments from India is known to have its counter parts in six different landmasses of the Southern Hemisphere.
- The occurrence of rich placer deposits of gold in the Ghana coast and the absolute absence of source rock in the region is an amazing fact.
- The observations that Lemurs occur in India, Madagascar and Africa led some to consider a contiguous landmass "Lemuria" linking these three landmasses. Mesosaurus was a small reptile adapted to shallow brackish water. The skeletons of these are found only in two localities : The Southern Cape province of South Africa and Iraver formations of Brazil. The two localities presently are 4,800 km apart with an ocean in between them.
- Wegener suggested that the movement responsible for the drifting of the continents was caused by pole-fleeing force and tidal force.

- The polar-fleeing force relates to the rotation of the earth. The second force that was suggested by Wegener, the tidal force which is due to the attraction of the moon and the sun that develops tides in oceanic waters.
- It is interesting to note that for continental drift, most of the evidence was collected from the continental areas in the form of distribution of flora and fauna or deposits like tillite.
- Arthur Holmes in 1930s discussed the possibility of convection currents operating in the mantle portion.
- Detailed research of the ocean configuration revealed that the ocean floor is not just a vast plain but it is full of relief.

Know the Terms

- **Tillite :** Tillite is the sedimentary rock formed out of the deposits of glaciers.
- **Pangaea :** According to Wegener, all the continents formed a single continental mass, a mega ocean surrounded by the same. The super continent was named PANGAEA, which meant all earth.
- **Panthalassa :** The mega-ocean was known as Panthalassa, meaning all water.

Multiple Choice Questions (1 mark each)

Q. 1. The Continental Drift Theory was given in : A

(a) 1911 (b) 1921
(c) 1931 (d) 1941

Ans. (b) 1921 1

Q. 2. The mega-ocean meaning all water was called : A

(a) Panthalassa
(b) Lurasia
(c) Pangaea
(d) Tillite

Ans. (a) Panthalassa 1

Q. 3. Arthur Holmes discussed the possibility of convection currents operating in the mantle portion in : A

(a) 1920s (b) 1930s
(c) 1940s (d) 1950s

Ans. (b) 1930s 1

Q. 4. Pangaea began to split around : A

(a) 100 million years ago
(b) 200 million years ago
(c) 300 million years ago
(d) 400 million years ago

Ans. (b) 200 million years ago 1

Very Short Answer Type Questions (1 mark each)

Q. 1. Define the term 'Pangaea'. A

Ans. According to Wegener, all the continents formed a single continental mass, a mega ocean surrounded by the same. The super continent was named PANGAEA, which meant all earth. 1

Q. 2. What is Tillite? A

Ans. Tillite is the sedimentary rock formed out of the deposits of glaciers. It also provides the evidence of continental drift. For example, ancient tillites on opposite sides of the South Atlantic Ocean. 1

Q. 3. What is Panthalassa? U

Ans. According to Wegener, all the continents formed a single continental mass, a mega ocean surrounded by the same. The mega ocean was called PANTHALASSA, meaning all water. 1

AI **Q. 4. Which theory was propounded by Alfred Wegener?** U

OR

Who was the propounder of the Continental Drift Theory?

Ans. Alfred Wegener, a German meteorologist who put forth a comprehensive argument in the form of "the Continental Drift Theory" in 1912. 1

Answering Tip

- The most easy way to keep in mind the concept of the Continental Drift Theory is that the earth's continents have moved over geologic time relative to each other, thus appearing to have 'drifted' across the ocean bed.

Q. 5. Which is the smallest continent. R

Ans. Australia. 1

Q. 6. Who was the propounder of the Conventional Current Theory? U

Ans. Conventional current or simply current theory was propounded by Arthur Holmes. 1

Q. 7. What percent of the earth is covered with land and water respectively? A

Ans. The earth is covered with 29% land and 71% water. 1

Q. 8. What was the name given by Alfred Wegener to a large continent surrounded with water? U

Ans. Pangaea was the name given by Alfred Wegner to a large continent surrounded with water. 1

Q. 9. Pangaea was divided into how many land forms? A

Ans. Pangaea was divided into two landforms namely Lurasia and Gondwanaland. 1

Q. 10. What are the causes given by Wegener for the drifting of continents? R

Ans. The two causes given by Wegener are :

(i) Polar -fleeing force

(ii) Tidal force 1

Q. 11. Give any two examples of placer deposits? U

Ans. The occurrence of rich placer deposits of gold in the Ghana Coast and the gold bearing veins in Brazil. 1

Q. 12. What is the fleeing force related to? A

Ans. The fleeing force is related to the rotation of the earth. The earth is not a perfect sphere. It has a bulge at the equator. This bulge is caused due to the rotation of the earth. 1

Q. 13. What is tidal force related to? A

Ans. Tidal force is related to the to the attraction of the moon and the sun that develops tides in oceanic waters. 1

Q. 14. How is radiometric method helpful to the scientists? U

Ans. The radiometric dating methods developed in the recent period have facilitated correlating the rock formation from different continents across the vast ocean . 1

Short Answer Type Questions (3 marks each)

Q. 1. Explain in detail the Continental Drift Theory. A

Ans. The Continental Drift Theory can be understood through following points :

(i) Alfred Wegener, a German meteorologist who put forth a comprehensive argument in the form of "the Continental Drift Theory" in 1912. This was regarding the distribution of the oceans and the continents.

(ii) According to Wegener, all the continents formed a single continental mass, a mega ocean surrounded by the same. The super continent was named PANGAEA, which meant all earth. The mega-ocean was called PANTHALASSA, meaning all water. He argued that, around 200 million years ago, the super continent, Pangaea, began to split. Pangaea first broke into two large continental masses as Laurasia and Gondwanaland forming the northern and southern components respectively.

(iii) Subsequently, Laurasia and Gondwanaland continued to break into various smaller continents that exist today. A variety of evidence was offered in support of the continental drift. **(1 × 3 = 3)**

Q. 2. Why has the Continental Drift Theory been discarded? R

Ans. Arthur Holmes in 1930s discussed the possibility of convection currents operating in the mantle portion. These currents are generated due to radioactive elements causing thermal differences in the mantle portion. Holmes argued that there exists a system of such currents in the entire mantle portion.

This was an attempt to provide an explanation to the issue of force, on the basis of which contemporary scientists discarded the continental drift theory. **(1 × 3 = 3)**

Q. 3. Discuss the forces that are held responsible for the drifting of the continents? U

Ans. Forces that are held responsible for the drafting of the continents are as follows :

Wegener suggested that the movement responsible for the drifting of the continents was caused by pole-fleeing force and tidal force.

(i) The polar-fleeing force relates to the rotation of the earth. You are aware of the fact that the earth is not a perfect sphere; it has a bulge at the equator. This bulge is due to the rotation of the earth.

(ii) The second force that was suggested by Wegener is the tidal force which occurs due to the attraction of the moon and the sun that develops tides in oceanic waters.

(iii) Wegener believed that these forces would become effective when applied over many million years. However, most of scholars considered these forces to be totally inadequate. **(1 × 3 = 3)**

Answering Tip

- Apart from the main reasons , the students should remember that the movement of the tectonic plates is also considered one of the major reasons that has led to the drifting of the continents.

Long Answer Type Questions (5 marks each)

Q. 1. Discuss the evidences available in support of the Continental Drift Theory. R

Ans. Evidences in support of Continental Drift Theory are as follows :

(i) The Matching of Continents (Jig-Saw-Fit) : The shorelines of Africa and South America facing each other have a remarkable and unmistakable match. It may be noted that a map produced using a computer programme to find the best fit of the Atlantic margin was presented by Bullard in 1964. It proved to be quite perfect. The match was tried at 1,000 fathom line instead of the present shoreline.

(ii) Rocks of Same Age Across the Oceans : The radiometric dating methods developed in the recent period have facilitated correlating the rock formation from different continents across the vast ocean. The belt of ancient rocks of 2,000 million years from Brazil coast matches with those from western Africa. The earliest marine deposits along the coastline of South America and Africa are of the Jurassic Age. This suggests that the ocean did not exist prior to that time.

(iii) Tillite : It is the sedimentary rock formed out of deposits of glaciers. The Gondawana System of sediments from India is known to have its counter parts in six different landmasses of the Southern Hemisphere. At the base the system has thick tillite indicating extensive and prolonged glaciation. Counter parts of this succession are found in Africa, Falkland Island, Madagascar, Antarctica and Australia besides India. Overall resemblance of the Gondawana type sediments clearly demonstrates that these landmasses had remarkably similar histories.

(iv) Placer Deposits : The occurrence of rich placer deposits of gold in the Ghana coast and the absolute absence of source rock in the region is an amazing fact. The gold bearing veins are in Brazil and it is obvious that the gold deposits of Ghana are derived from the Brazil Plateau when the two continents lay side by side.

(v) Distribution of Fossils : When identical species of plants and animals adapted to living on land or in fresh water are found on either side of the marine barriers, a problem arises regarding accounting for such distribution. The observations that Lemurs occur in India, Madagascar and Africa led some to consider a contiguous landmass "Lemuria" linking these three landmasses.

(Any five) (1 × 5 = 5)

Answering Tip

- The look-alike animals, plant fossils and similar rock formations that are found on different continents act as evidences that support the Continental Drift Theory.

TOPIC-2
Ocean Floor Configuration

Revision Notes

- ➤ The ocean floor configuration help us in the understanding of the distribution of continents and oceans.
- ➤ The ocean floor may be segmented into three major divisions based on the depth as well as the forms of relief. These divisions are continental margins, deep-sea basins and mid-ocean ridges.
- ➤ Continental Margins form the transition between continental shores and deep-sea basins. They include continental shelf, continental slope, continental rise and deep-oceanic trenches.
- ➤ Abyssal Plains are extensive plains that lie between the continental margins and mid-oceanic ridges. The Abyssal Plains are the areas where the continental sediments that move beyond the margins get deposited.
- ➤ Mid-Oceanic Ridges form an interconnected chain of mountain system within the ocean. It is the longest mountain-chain on the surface of the earth though submerged under the oceanic waters.
- ➤ The mapping of the ocean floor and paleomagnetic studies of rocks from oceanic regions revealed the following facts about the sea floor spreading :
  - It was realised that all along the mid-oceanic ridges, volcanic eruptions are common and they bring huge amounts of lava to the surface in this area.
  - Rocks closer to the mid-oceanic ridges are normal polarity and are the youngest. The age of the rocks increases as one moves away from the crest.
  - The ocean crust rocks are much younger than the continental rocks.
  - The sediments on the ocean floor are unexpectedly very thin. However, nowhere was the sediment column found to be older than 200 million years.
  - The deep trenches have deep-seated earthquake occurrences while in the midoceanic ridge areas, the quake foci have shallow depths.
- ➤ Hess argued that constant eruptions at the crest of oceanic ridges cause the rupture of the oceanic crust and the new lava wedges into it, pushing the oceanic crust on either side. The ocean floor, thus spreads.

Know the Terms

- ➤ **Abyssal Plains :** The abyssal plains are the areas where the continental sediments that move beyond the margins get deposited.
- ➤ **Continental Margins :** These form the transition between continental shores and deep-sea basins.
- ➤ **Sea-floor spreading :** Hess argued that constant eruptions at the crest of oceanic ridges cause the rupture of the oceanic crust and the new lava wedges into it, pushing the oceanic crust on either side. The ocean floor, thus spreads.

Multiple Choice Questions (1 mark each)

Q. 1. The ocean crust rocks are much younger than the : [A]

(a) continental rocks

(b) continental bay

(c) continental shore

(d) continental sediments

Ans. (a) continental rocks 1

Q. 2. Rocks closer to the mid-oceanic ridges are : [A]

(a) oldest (b) youngest

(c) thinnest (d) heaviest

Ans. (b) youngest 1

Q. 3. The sediments on the ocean floor are unexpectedly very : [U]

(a) thick (b) polluted

(c) thin (d) fine

Ans. (c) thin 1

Very Short Answer Type Questions (1 mark each)

Q. 1. Define the term Abyssal Plains? [R]

Ans. Abyssal plains are extensive plains that lie between the continental margins and mid-oceanic ridges. The abyssal plains are the areas where the continental sediments that move beyond the margins get deposited. 1

Q. 2. Define the term Continental Margins. [R]

Ans. Continental margins form the transition between continental shores and deep-sea basins. They include continental shelf, continental slope, continental rise and deep-oceanic trenches. 1

Answering Tip

- Always remember that the Continental Margin is the shallow water area found in proximity to continent.

Q. 3. What are mid-oceanic ridges? [R]

Ans. Mid-oceanic ridges forms an interconnected chain of mountain system within the ocean. It is the longest mountain-chain on the surface of the earth though submerged under the oceanic waters. It is characterised by a central rift system at the crest, a fractionated plateau and flank zone all along its length. 1

Q. 4. Name the major divisions of the ocean floor based on the depth as well as the forms of relief. [A]

Ans. The ocean floor may be segmented into three major divisions based on the depth as well as the forms of relief. These divisions are continental margins, deep-sea basins and mid-ocean ridges. 1

Q. 5. Who gave the hypothesis of the 'sea floor spreading'? [U]

Ans. Harry Hess proposed the hypothesis of the 'sea floor spreading' in the early 1960s. 1

Q. 6. What is referred to as the 'Rim of Fire' and why? [A]

Ans. The Rim of the Pacific is considered as the 'Rim of Fire' due to the existence of active volcanoes in this area. 1

Short Answer Type Questions (3 marks each)

[AI] **Q. 1. Discuss the three major divisions of the ocean floor based on the depth as well as the forms of relief?** [R]

Ans. The ocean floor may be segmented into three major divisions based on the depth as well as the forms of relief. These divisions are continental margins, deep-sea basins and mid-ocean ridges.

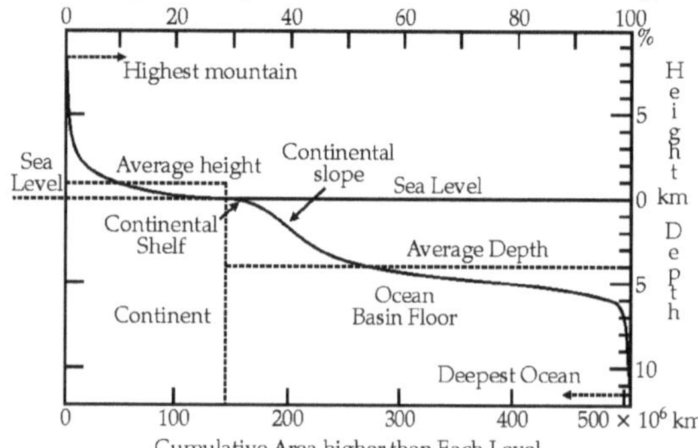

(i) Continental Margins : These form the transition between continental shores and deep-sea basins. They include continental shelf, continental slope, continental rise and deep-oceanic trenches. Of these, the deep-sea trenches are the areas which are of considerable interest in so far as the distribution of oceans and continents is concerned.

(ii) Abyssal Plains : These are extensive plains that lie between the continental margins and mid-oceanic ridges. The abyssal plains are the areas where the continental sediments that move beyond the margins get deposited.

(iii) Mid-Oceanic Ridges : This forms an interconnected chain of mountain system within the ocean. It is the longest mountain-chain on the surface of the earth though submerged under the oceanic waters. It is characterised by a central rift system at the crest, a fractionated plateau and flank zone all along its length. **(1 × 3 = 3)**

Commonly Made Error

- The students are not aware that the Continental Margins are further divided into two parts.

Answering Tip

- The Continental margins are divided into active and passive margins.

AI **Q. 2. Explain the 'hypothesis, known as the "sea floor spreading" given by Hess?** A

Ans.

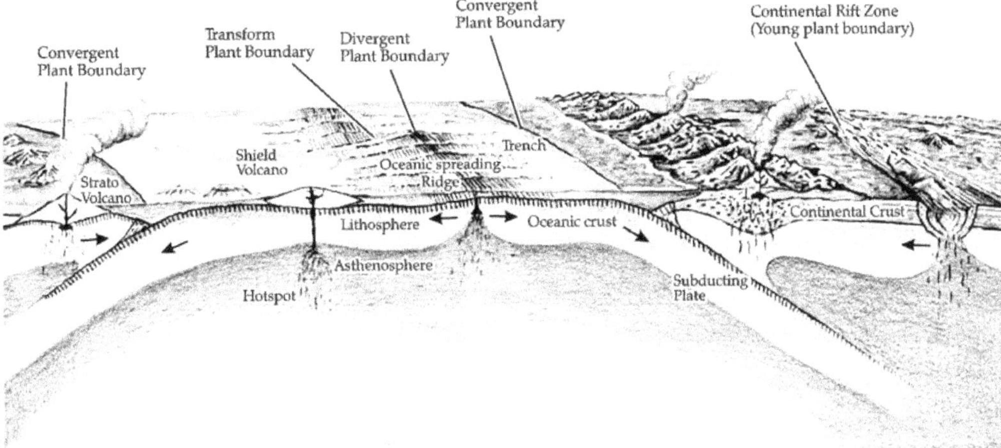

Harry Hess argued that constant eruptions at the crest of oceanic ridges cause the rupture of the oceanic crust and the new lava wedges into it, pushing the oceanic crust on either side. The ocean floor, thus spreads.

The younger age of the oceanic crust as well as the fact that the spreading of one ocean does not cause the shrinking of the other, made Hess think about the consumption of the oceanic crust. He further maintained that the ocean floor that gets pushed due to volcanic eruptions at the crest, sinks down at the oceanic trenches and gets consumed. **(1 × 3 = 3)**

Q. 3. On the basis of the depth as well as the forms of the relief, the ocean floor has been segmented into how many divisions? Explain. A

Ans. On the basis of the depth as well as the forms of the relief, the ocean floor has been segmented into :

(i) Continental margins :

(a) They form transitional zone between continental shore and deep sea basins .

(b) They include continental slope, shelf, continental rise and deep oceanic trenches.

(ii) Abyssal plains :

(a) They are extensive plains.

(b) They are found between continental margin and mid-oceanic ridge.

(c) Continental sediments get deposited.

(iii) Mid – Oceanic Ridges :

(a) This ridges has the distribution of volcanoes and earthquakes.

(b) All the volcanoes and earthquakes run parallel to the coast.

(c) The mid-oceanic ridges coincides with the Mid-Atlantic ridge and Alpine Himalayan System. **(1 × 3 = 3)**

Q. 4. Discuss the distribution of the earthquake and volcanic plates on the earth. U

Ans. Distribution of the earthquake and the volcanic plates on the earth.

(i) The plates moves from the Atlantic Ocean almost parallel to the coastlines. It further extends into the Indian Ocean. It bifurcates a little south of the Indian subcontinent with one branch moving into East Africa and the other meeting a similar line from Myanmar to New Guiana.

(ii) Another area of concentration coincides with the Alpine-Himalayan system and the rim of the Pacific Ocean.

(iii) In general, the foci of the earthquake in the areas of mid-oceanic ridges are at shallow depths whereas along the Alpine-Himalayan belt as well as the rim of the Pacific, the earthquakes are deep-seated ones. **(1 × 3 = 3)**

Long Answer Type Questions **(5 marks each)**

Q. 1. What information do we get from the mapping of the ocean floor and paleomegnetic studies of rocks from oceanic regions? A

Or

What facts have been revealed by the study of the mapping of the ocean floor and the paleo-magnetic studies of rocks from oceanic regions?

Ans. The mapping of the ocean floor and paleomagnetic studies of rocks from oceanic regions gave the following information :

(i) It was realised that all along the mid-oceanic ridges, volcanic eruptions are common and they bring huge amounts of lava to the surface in this area.

(ii) The rocks equidistant on either sides of the crest of mid-oceanic ridges show remarkable similarities in terms of period of formation, chemical compositions and magnetic properties. Rocks closer to the mid-oceanic ridges are normal polarity and are the youngest. The age of the rocks increases as one moves away from the crest.

(iii) The ocean crust rocks are much younger than the continental rocks. The age of rocks in the oceanic crust is nowhere more than 200 million years old. Some of the continental rock formations are as old as 3,200 million years.

(iv) The sediments on the ocean floor are unexpectedly very thin. Scientists were expecting, if the ocean floors were as old as the continent, to have a complete sequence of sediments for a period of much longer duration. However, nowhere was the sediment column found to be older than 200 million years.

(v) The deep trenches have deep-seated earthquake occurrences while in the mid-oceanic ridge areas, the quake foci have shallow depths. **(1 × 5 = 5)**

Answering Tip

- Mapping of ocean floor is important as it helps us explore our oceans and gather information.

TOPIC-3
Plate Tectonics

Revision Notes

- It was in 1967, McKenzie and Parker and also Morgan, independently collected the available ideas and came out with another concept termed Plate Tectonics.
- A tectonic plate (also called lithospheric plate) is a massive, irregularly-shaped slab of solid rock, generally composed of both continental and oceanic lithosphere.
- A plate may be referred to as the continental plate or oceanic plate depending on which of the two occupy a larger portion of the plate. Pacific plate is largely an oceanic plate whereas the Eurasian plate may be called a continental plate.
- The Theory of Plate Tectonics proposes that the earth's lithosphere is divided into seven major and some minor plates.
- The major plates are :
  - Antarctica and the surrounding oceanic plate
  - North American (with western Atlantic floor separated from the South American plate along the Caribbean islands) plate
  - South American (with western Atlantic floor separated from the North American plate along the Caribbean islands) plate
  - Pacific plate
  - India-Australia-New Zealand plate
  - Africa with the eastern Atlantic floor plate
  - Eurasia and the adjacent oceanic plate
- Some important minor plates are :
  - **Cocos plate :** Between Central America and Pacific plate
  - **Nazca plate :** Between South America and Pacific plate
  - **Arabian plate :** Mostly the Saudi Arabian landmass
  - **Philippine plate :** Between the Asiatic and Pacific plate
  - **Caroline plate :** Between the Philippine and Indian plate (North of New Guinea)
  - **Fuji plate :** North-east of Australia
- These plates have been constantly moving over the globe throughout the history of the earth. It is not the continent that moves as believed by Wegener. Continents are part of a plate and what moves is the plate.
- Wegener had thought of all the continents to have initially existed as a super continent in the form of Pangaea.
- Scientists using the paleomagnetic data have determined the positions held by each of the present continental landmass in different geological periods.
- Where new crust is generated as the plates pull away from each other. The sites where the plates move away from each other are called spreading sites.
- Where the crust is destroyed as one plate dived under another. The location where sinking of a plate occurs is called a **Subduction Zone.**
- Transform faults are the planes of separation generally perpendicular to the mid-oceanic ridges.

- The strips of normal and reverse magnetic field that parallel the mid-oceanic ridges help scientists determine the rates of plate movement.
- The Arctic Ridge has the slowest rate (less than 2.5 cm/yr), and the East Pacific Rise near Easter Island, in the South Pacific about 3,400 km west of Chile, has the fastest rate (more than 15 cm/yr).
- The fact that the plates move is now a well-accepted fact. The mobile rock beneath the rigid plates is believed to be moving in a circular manner. The heated material rises to the surface, spreads and begins to cool, and then sinks back into deeper depths. This cycle is repeated over and over to generate what scientists call a convection cell or convective flow.
- The Indian plate includes Peninsular India and the Australian continental portions.
- India was a large island situated off the Australian coast, in a vast ocean. The Tethys Sea separated it from the Asian continent till about 225 million years ago. India is supposed to have started her northward journey about 200 million years ago at the time when Pangaea broke.
- India collided with Asia about 40-50 million years ago causing rapid uplift of the Himalayas.
- The two major plates were separated by the Tethys Sea and the Tibetan block was closer to the Asiatic landmass. During the movement of the Indian plate towards the Asiatic plate, a major event that occurred was the outpouring of lava and formation of the Deccan Traps.
- This started somewhere around 60 million years ago and continued for a long period of time.
- Scientists believe that the process is still continuing and the height of the Himalayas is rising even to this date

Know the Terms

- **Paleomagnetic data :** It is the data used by scientist that has helped them determine the positions held by each of the present continental landmass in different geological periods.
- **Spreading sites :** Where new crust is generated as the plates pull away from each other. The sites where the plates move away from each other are called spreading sites.
- **Subduction zone :** It is the location where the sinking of the plates occurs.
- **Convergent Boundaries :** When the crust is neither produced nor destroyed as the plates slide horizontally past each other is known as convergent boundaries.
- **Transform faults :** They are the planes of separation generally perpendicular to the mid-oceanic ridges.
- **Divergent boundaries :** They are those where new crust is generated as the plates pull away from each other.
- **Tectonic plate :** A tectonic plate (also called lithospheric plate) is a massive, irregularly-shaped slab of solid rock, generally composed of both continental and oceanic lithosphere.

Multiple Choice Questions

(1 mark each)

Q. 1. India is supposed to have started her northward journey about : A

(a) 200 million years ago
(b) 400 million years ago
(c) 500 million years ago
(d) 600 million years ago

Ans. (a) 200 million years ago 1

Q. 2. The location where sinking of a plate occurs is called a : A

(a) Subduction Zone
(b) Reduction Zone
(c) Induction Zone
(d) Deduction Zone

Ans. (a) Subduction Zone 1

Very Short Answer Type Questions

(1 mark each)

Q. 1. Define the term 'Tectonic Plate'. R

Ans. A tectonic plate (also called lithospheric plate) is a massive, irregularly-shaped slab of solid rock, generally composed of both continental and oceanic lithosphere. Plates move horizontally over the asthenosphere as rigid units. 1

Q. 2. What does the term 'plate' refer to? R

Ans. A plate may be referred to as the continental plate or oceanic plate depending on which of the two occupy a larger portion of the plate. Pacific plate is largely an oceanic plate whereas the Eurasian plate may be called a continental plate. 1

Q. 3. What do you mean by 'Spreading Sites'? R

Ans. The sites where new crust is generated as the plates move away from each other are called spreading sites. 1

AI **Q.4. What do you understand by the term 'Convergent Boundaries'?** U

Ans. It is a region of active deformation where two or more tectonic plates or fragments of the lithosphere are near the end of their life cycle. It is also called as destructive plate boundary. 1

Answering Tip

- The most common feature of the convergent boundaries is that many earthquakes occur in this boundary.

Q. 5. What do you understand by the term 'Divergent Boundaries'? [U]

Ans. Divergent boundaries are those where new crust is generated as the plates pull away from each other. 1

Answering Tip

- The divergent boundaries exist between two tectonic plates that are moving away from each other.

Q. 6. Define the term 'Transform Boundaries'? [A]

Ans. Transform boundaries are those where the crust is neither produced nor destroyed as the plates slide horizontally past each other. 1

Q. 7. Define the term 'Subduction Zone'. [A]

Ans. Subduction zone is the location where the sinking of the plates occurs. 1

[AI] **Q.8. Define the term 'Convention Flow'.** [A]

Ans. The fact that the plates move is now a well-accepted fact. The mobile rock beneath the rigid plates is believed to be moving in a circular manner. The heated material rises to the surface, spreads and begins to cool, and then sinks back into deeper depths. This cycle is repeated over and over to generate what scientists call a convection cell or convective flow. 1

Q. 9. Which facts helped the scientists to understand plate movement? [R]

Ans. The rock equidistant on either sides of the crest of mid-oceanic ridges show remarkable similarities in terms of period of formation, chemical compositions and magnetic properties. Rocks closer to the mid-oceanic ridges have normal polarity and are younger. The age of the rocks tend to increase as one moves away from the crest. 1

Q. 10. The earth has been divided into how many plates? [U]

Ans. The earth has been divided into seven major plates and some minor plates. 1

Q. 11. Explain how the Himalayas were formed. [A]

Ans. About 200 million years ago, when the Pangaea broke, that is the time when India started its northward journey. India's collision with Asia caused a rapid uplift of the Himalayas. This uplift of Himalayas occurred 40-50 million years ago. 1

Q. 12. Describe the formation of the Deccan Traps. [R]

Ans. During the movement of the Indian Plate towards the Asian Plate, a major event that occurred was the outpouring of the lava. It led to the formation of the Deccan Traps. The formation of the Deccan Traps started around 60 million years ago and continued for a very long time. 1

Answering Tip

- The Deccan Trap is located on the Deccan Plateau of West-Central India.

Q. 13. Explain India's condition at the time the Pangaea broke. Before the breaking of the Pangaea what was India's status? [U]

Ans. Before the Pangaea broke up India was a large island which was situated in the vast ocean off the Australian Coast. The Tethys Sea separated it from the Asian continent till about 225 million years ago. It is estimated that India started its northward journey about 200 million years ago . This is the time when the Pangaea broke. India collided with Asia about 40 -50 million years ago which led to the rapid uplift of the Himalayas. 1

Q. 14. Name the three different ways in which the convergence can take place. [A]

Ans. There are three ways in which convergence can occur. These are: between an oceanic and continental plate , between two oceanic plates and between two continental plates. 1

Short Answer Type Questions (3 marks each)

Q. 1. What was the main emphasis of the sea floor spreading and the Plates Tectonic Theory? [U]

Ans. Sea floor spreading and the plate tectonic theory can be summarised in the following points :

(i) These theories emphasised that the earth is divided into plates and these plates have been constantly moving over the globe throughout the history of the earth.

(ii) It is not the continent that moves as believed by Wegener. Continents are part of a plate what moves is the plate.

(iii) All the plates, without the exception , have moved in the geological past and shall continue to move in the future as well. **(1 × 3 = 3)**

Q. 2. Name a few facts that helped the scientists to understand the plate movement. [A]

Ans. A few facts that have helped the scientists in understanding the plate movement are :

(i) The rocks equidistant on either sides of the crest of mid-oceanic ridges show remarkable similarities in terms of period of formation, chemical compositions and magnetic properties.

(ii) Rocks closer to the mid-oceanic ridges have normal polarity and are not considered as young rocks.

(iii) The age of the rocks increases as one moves away from the crest. **(1 × 3 = 3)**

Q. 3. Explain the Plate Tectonic Theory. U

Ans. The Plate Tectonic Theory was given by Mckenzie, Parker and Morgan in 1967. A tectonic plate (also called lithospheric plate) is a massive, irregularly-shaped slab of solid rock, generally composed of both continental and oceanic lithosphere.

Plates move horizontally over the asthenosphere as rigid units. The lithosphere includes the crust and top mantle with its thickness range varying between 5-100 km in oceanic parts and about 200 km in the continental areas. The plates are moving constantly throughout geological time not the continent. The Theory of Plate Tectonics proposes that the earth's lithosphere is divided into seven major and some minor plates. **(1 × 3 = 3)**

Q. 4. Name the major and minor plates into which the Earth has been divided. A

Ans. The major plates are as follows :

(i) Antarctica and the surrounding oceanic plate
(ii) North American (with western Atlantic floor separated from the South American plate along the Caribbean islands) plate
(iii) South American (with western Atlantic floor separated from the North American plate along the Caribbean islands) plate
(iv) Pacific plate
(v) India-Australia-New Zealand plate
(vi) Africa with the eastern Atlantic floor plate
(vii) Eurasia and the adjacent oceanic plate

Some of the minor plates are :

(i) **Cocos plate** : Between Central America and Pacific plate
(ii) **Nazca plate :** Between South America and Pacific plate
(iii) **Arabian plate :** Mostly the Saudi Arabian landmass
(vi) **Philippine plate :** Between the Asiatic and Pacific plate
(v) **Caroline plate** : Between the Philippine and Indian plate (North of New Guinea)
(vi) **Fuji plate :** North-east of Australia. **(1 × 3 = 3)**

AI **Q.5. Name the different boundaries that form as a result of tectonic plates. Explain each of the boundaries.** U

Ans. There are three types of plate boundaries :

(i) **Divergent Boundaries :** Where new crust is generated as the plates pull away from each other. The sites where the plates move away from each other are called spreading sites. The best-known example of divergent boundaries is the Mid-Atlantic Ridge. At this, the American Plate(s) is/are separated from the Eurasian and African Plates.

(ii) **Convergent Boundaries :** Where the crust is destroyed as one plate dived under another. The location where sinking of a plate occurs is called a subduction zone. There are three ways in which convergence can occur. These are :

(a) between an oceanic and continental plate;
(b) between two oceanic plates; and
(c) between two continental plates.

(iii) **Transform Boundaries :** Where the crust is neither produced nor destroyed as the plates slide horizontally past each other. Transform faults are the planes of separation generally perpendicular to the mid-oceanic ridges. As the eruptions do not take all along the entire crest at the same time, there is a differential movement of a portion of the plate away from the axis of the earth. Also, the rotation of the earth has its effect on the separated blocks of the plate portions. **(1 × 3 = 3)**

Q. 6. How do you think the rate of plate movement varies considerably ?

Ans. The rate of plate movement varies considerably as the strips of normal and reverse magnetic field that runs parallel to the mid-oceanic ridges help scientists in determining the rates of plate movement. The rates vary considerably. They can be divided into :

The Arctic Ridge has the slowest rate, less than 2.5 cm/yr.

The East Pacific Rise near the Eastern Island , in the South Pacific about 3,400 km West of Chile, has the fastest rate, more than 15 cm/yr. **3**

Answering Tip

- The plate movements take place because of the intense heat in the earth's core that causes molten rock in the mantle layer to move.

Long Answer Type Questions

(5 marks each)

Q. 1. Explain the movement of the Indian Plate? U

Ans. Movement of the Indian Plate :

(i) The Indian plate includes Peninsular India and the Australian continental portions. India was a large island situated off the Australian coast, in a vast ocean. The Tethys Sea separated it from the Asian continent till about 225 million years ago.

(ii) India is supposed to have started her northward journey about 200 million years ago at the time when Pangaea broke. India collided with Asia about 40-50 million years ago causing rapid uplift of the Himalayas.

(iii) About 140 million years before the present, the subcontinent was located as south as 50°S. latitude. The two major plates were separated by the Tethys Sea and the Tibetan block was closer to the Asiatic landmass. During the movement of the Indian plate towards the Asiatic plate, a major event that occurred was the outpouring of lava and formation of the Deccan Traps.

(iv) This started somewhere around 60 million years ago and continued for a long period of time. The subcontinent was still close to the equator.

(v) From 40 million years ago and thereafter, the event of formation of the Himalayas took place. Scientists believe that the process is still continuing and the height of the Himalayas is rising even to this date. **1×5**

Answering Tip

- The Indian Plate was originally a part of the ancient continent of Gondwana.

Q. 2. How many theories explain the movement of the continents? [A]

Ans. Many scientists thought of the similarity and considered the possibility of the two Americas, Europe and Africa, to be once joined together. The various theories that explain the movement of the continents are :

(i) Continental Drift Theory : Alfred Wegener, a German meteorologist who put forth a comprehensive argument in the form of "the Continental Drift Theory" in 1912. This was regarding the distribution of the oceans and the continents.

According to Wegener, all the continents formed a single continental mass, a mega ocean surrounded by the same. The super continent was named PANGAEA, which meant all earth. The mega-ocean was called PANTHALASSA, meaning all water. He argued that, around 200 million years ago, the super continent, Pangaea, began to split. Pangaea first broke into two large continental masses as Laurasia and Gondwanaland forming the northern and southern components respectively. Subsequently, Laurasia and Gondwanaland continued to break into various smaller continents that exist today.

There are various evidences in support of this theory. Some of the evidences are :

(a) The matching of the continents

(b) Rocks of same age across the oceans.

(c) The sedimentary rocks formed out of the deposits of the glaciers.

(d) The distribution of the fossils.

(e) The occurrence of the rich placer deposits of gold in various places.

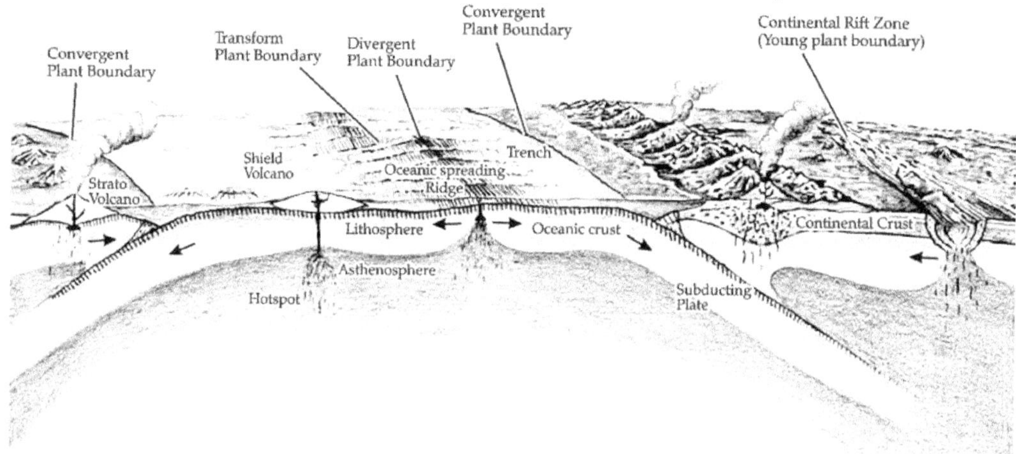

(ii) Sea-floor Spreading : A detailed analysis of magnetic properties of the rocks on either sides of the mid-oceanic ridge led Hess (1961) to propose his hypothesis, known as the "sea floor spreading". Hess argued that constant eruptions at the crest of oceanic ridges cause the rupture of the oceanic crust and the new lava wedges into it, pushing the oceanic crust on either side. The ocean floor, thus spreads. The younger age of the oceanic crust as well as the fact that the spreading of one ocean does not cause the shrinking of the other, made Hess think about the consumption of the oceanic crust. He further maintained that the ocean floor that gets pushed due to volcanic eruptions at the crest, sinks down at the oceanic trenches and gets consume.

(iii) Theory of Plate tectonics : It was in 1967, McKenzie and Parker and also Morgan, independently collected the available ideas and came out with another concept termed Plate Tectonics. A tectonic plate (also called lithospheric plate) is a massive, irregularly-shaped slab of solid rock, generally composed of both continental and oceanic lithosphere. plate may be referred to as the continental plate or oceanic plate depending on which of the two occupy a larger portion of the plate. Pacific plate is largely an oceanic plate whereas the Eurasian plate may be called a continental plate. The Theory of Plate Tectonics proposes that the earth's lithosphere is divided into seven major and some minor plates.

(iv) Movement of the Indian Plate : India was a large island situated off the Australian coast, in a vast ocean. The Tethys Sea separated it from the Asian continent till about 225 million years ago. India is supposed to have started her northward journey about 200 million years ago at the time when Pangaea broke. India collided with Asia about 40-50 million years ago causing rapid uplift of the Himalayas. About 140 million years before the present, the subcontinent was located as south as 50°S. latitude. The two major plates were separated by the Tethys Sea and the Tibetan block was closer to the Asiatic landmass. During the movement of the Indian plate towards the Asiatic plate, a major event that occurred was the outpouring of lava and formation of the Deccan Traps. This started somewhere around 60 million years ago and continued for a long period of time.

The subcontinent was still close to the equator. From 40 million years ago and thereafter, the event of formation of the Himalayas took place. Scientists believe that the process is still continuing and the height of the Himalayas is rising even to this date. **(1 × 5 = 5)**

Map Work

(5 marks each)

Q. 1. Study the outline map of the world given below and identify them with the help of the information given below and write the correct names.

(i) A tectonic plate between the Asiatic and Pacific plate.

(ii) A tectonic plate between Central America and Pacific plate.

(iii) A tectonic plate between South America and Pacific plate.

(iv) The tectonic plate in the Saudi Arabian landmass.

(v) A tectonic plate between the Philippine and Indian plate.

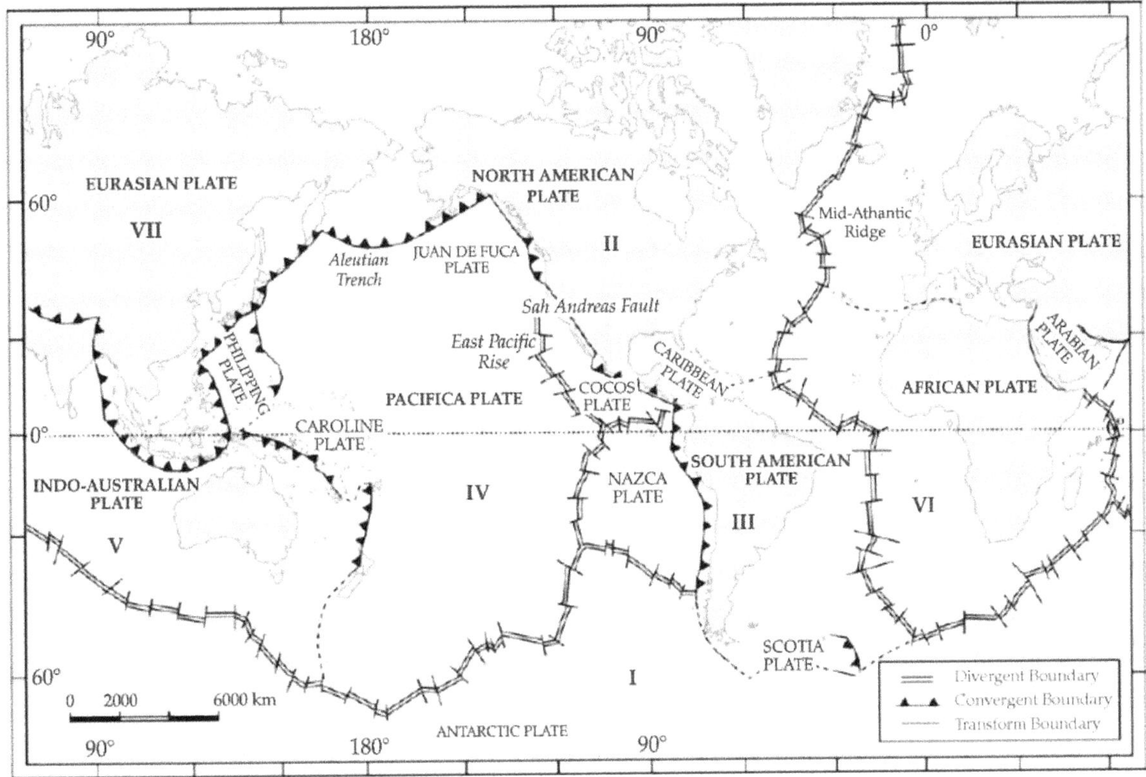

Ans. (i) Philippine plate
(ii) Cocos Plate
(iii) Nazca plate
(iv) Arabian plate
(v) Caroline plate

NCERT CORNER

(A) Multiple choice questions :

Q. 1. Who amongst the following was the first to consider the possibility of Europe, Africa and America having been located side by side : R

(a) Alfred Wegener (b) Antonio Pellegrini
(c) Abraham Ortelius (d) Edmond Hess

Ans. (c) Abraham Ortelius .

Q. 2. Polar-fleeing force relates to : A

(a) Revolution of the earth (b) Gravitation
(c) Rotation of the earth (d) Tides

Ans. (c) Rotation of the earth .

Q. 3. Which one of the following is not a minor plate : R

(a) Nazca (b) Arabia
(c) Philippines (d) Antarctica

Ans. (d) Antartica.

Q. 4. Which one of the following facts was not considered by those while discussing the concept of sea floor spreading : A

(a) Volcanic activity along the mid-oceanic ridges.
(b) Stripes of normal and reverse magnetic field observed in rocks of ocean floor.

(c) Distribution of fossils in different continents
(d) Age of rocks from the ocean floor

Ans. (c) Distribution of fossils in different continents.

Q. 5. Which one of the following is the type of plate boundary of the Indian plate along the Himalayan mountains : [A]

(a) Ocean-continent convergence
(b) Divergent boundary
(c) Transform boundary
(d) Continent-continent convergence

Ans. (d) Continent-continent convergence.

(B) Answer the following questions in about 30 words :

Q. 1. What were the forces suggested by Wegener for the movement of the continents? [A]

Ans. According to Wegener, all the continents formed a single continental mass, a mega ocean surrounded by the same. He suggested that the drifting of the continents was caused by two forces:

(i) Pole-fleeing force : This force is related to the rotation of the earth. The bulge in the earth is due to the rotation.

(ii) Tidal force : This force is due to the attraction of the moon and the sun that develops tides in the oceanic waters.

Q. 2. How are the convectional currents in the mantle initiated and maintained? [R]

Ans. Arthur Holmes in 1930s discussed the possibility of convection currents operating in the mantle portion. These currents are generated due to radioactive elements causing thermal differences in the mantle portion. Holmes argued that there exists a system of such currents in the entire mantle portion.

This was an attempt to provide an explanation to the issue of force, on the basis of which contemporary scientists discarded the continental drift theory.

[AI] **Q.3. What is the major difference between the transform boundary and the convergent or divergent boundaries of plates?** [R]

Ans. The major differences are :

(i) Transform Boundaries : Where the crust is neither produced nor destroyed as the plates slide horizontally past each other. Transform faults are the planes of separation generally perpendicular to the mid-oceanic ridges.

(ii) Convergent Boundaries : Where the crust is destroyed as one plate dived under another, it is called convergent boundaries.

(iii) Divergent Boundaries : Where new crust is generated as the plates pull away from each other, these are called divergent boundaries.

Q. 4. What was the location of the Indian landmass during the formation of the Deccan Traps? [R]

Ans. About 140 million years before the present, the subcontinent was located as south as 50°S. latitude. The two major plates were separated by the Tethys Sea and the Tibetan block was closer to the Asiatic landmass. During the movement of the Indian Plate towards the Asiatic plate, a major event that occurred was the outpouring of lava and formation of the Deccan Traps. This started somewhere around 60 million years ago and continued for a long period of time.

Note that the subcontinent was still close to the equator. From 40 million years ago and thereafter, the event of formation of the Himalayas took place. Scientists believe that the process is still continuing and the height of the Himalayas is rising even to this date

(C) Answer the following questions in about 150 words :

Q. 1. What are the evidences in support of the Continental Drift Theory? [U]

Ans. The various evidences in support of the Continental Drift Theory are :

(i) The Matching of Continents (Jig-Saw-Fit) : The shorelines of Africa and South America facing each other have a remarkable and unmistakable match. It may be noted that a map produced using a computer programme to find the best fit of the Atlantic margin was presented by Bullard in 1964 .

(ii) Rocks of Same Age Across the Oceans : The radiometric dating methods developed in the recent period have facilitated correlating the rock formation from different continents across the vast ocean. The belt of ancient rocks of 2,000 million years from Brazil coast matches with those from western Africa. The earliest marine deposits along the coastline of South America and Africa are of the Jurassic Age.

(iii) Tillite : It is the sedimentary rock formed out of deposits of glaciers. The Gondawana System of sediments from India is known to have its counter parts in six different landmasses of the Southern Hemisphere. At the base the system has thick tillite indicating extensive and prolonged glaciation. Counter parts of this succession are found in Africa, Falkland Island, Madagascar, Antarctica and Australia besides India. Overall resemblance of the Gondawana type sediments clearly demonstrates that these landmasses had remarkably similar histories.

(iv) Placer Deposits : The occurrence of rich placer deposits of gold in the Ghana coast and the absolute absence of source rock in the region is an amazing fact. The gold bearing veins are in Brazil and it is obvious that the gold deposits of the Ghana are derived from the Brazil plateau when the two continents lay side by side.

(v) Distribution of Fossils : When identical species of plants and animals adapted to living on land or in fresh water are found on either side of the marine barriers, a problem arises regarding accounting for such distribution. The observations that Lemurs occur in India, Madagascar and Africa led some to consider a contiguous landmass "Lemuria" linking these three landmasses. Mesosaurus was a small reptile adapted to shallow brackish water. The skeletons of these are found only in two localities : the Southern Cape province of South Africa and Iraver formations of Brazil. The two localities presently are 4,800 km apart with an ocean in between the them.

Q. 2. Bring about the basic difference between the Drift Theory and Plate tectonics. U

Ans.

S.No.	Drift Theory	Plate Tectonics
1.	This theory was put forth by a German meteorologist Alfred Wegener.	This theory was put forth by McKenzie and Parker.
2.	According to this theory , all continents formed a single continental mass called Pangaea.	According to this theory , the earth's lithosphere is divided into 7 major and some minor plates.
3.	Wegener argued that around 200 million years ago the super continent, Pangaea, began to split.	A tectonic plate is also called lithospheric plate.
4.	Pangaea first broke into two large continental masses as Laurasia and Gondawanaland forming Northern and Southern components respectively.	The plates moves horizontally over the asthenosphere as rigid units.
5.	Laurasia and Gondawanaland continue to break into various smaller continents that exist today.	Pacific plate is largely an oceanic plate whereas the Eurasian plate may be called a continental plate.

Q. 2. What were the major post-drift discoveries that rejuvenated the interest of scientists in the study of distribution of oceans and continents? A

Ans. A number of discoveries during the post-war period added new information to geological literature. Particularly, the information collected from the ocean floor mapping provided new dimensions for the study of distribution of oceans and continents.

(i) Currents are generated due to radioactive elements causing thermal differences in the mantle portion. Holmes argued that there exists a system of such currents in the entire mantle portion. This was an attempt to provide an explanation to the issue of force, on the basis of which contemporary scientists discarded the continental drift theory.

(ii) Detailed research of the ocean configuration revealed that the ocean floor is not just a vast plain but it is full of relief.

(iii) Expeditions to map the oceanic floor in the post-war period provided a detailed picture of the ocean relief and indicated the existence of submerged mountain ranges as well as deep trenches, mostly located closer to the continent margins.

(iv) The mid-oceanic ridges were found to be most active in terms of volcanic eruptions. The dating of the rocks from the oceanic crust revealed the fact that the latter is much younger than the continental areas.

(v) Rocks on either side of the crest of oceanic ridges and having equidistant locations from the crest were found to have remarkable similarities both in terms of their constituents and their age.

OSWAAL LEARNING TOOLS

For Suggested Online Videos

Visit : *https://qrgo.page.link/19H4K* **Or Scan the Code**

To learn from NCERT Prescribed Videos

Visit : *https://qrgo.page.link/2fcPn* **Or Scan the Code**

UNIT-III

Landforms

CHAPTER

5 MINERALS AND ROCKS

Syllabus

➢ *Physical Characteristics of the Some Major Minerals +, Characteristics of Metallic and Non-Metallic Minerals.*

➢ *Rocks: Igneous Rocks, Sedimentary Rocks, Metamorphic Rocks; Rock Cycle.*

TOPIC-1
Some Major Minerals and their Characteristics

Rivision Notes

➢ The earth is composed of various kinds of elements. These elements are in solid form in the outer layer of the Earth and in hot and molten form in the interior.

➢ The elements in the earth's crust are rarely found exclusively but are usually combined with other elements to make various substances.

➢ These substances are recognised as minerals. Thus, a mineral is a naturally occurring inorganic substance, having an orderly atomic structure and a definite chemical composition and physical properties.

➢ Though the number of elements making up the lithosphere are limited they are combined in many different ways to make up many varieties of minerals.

➢ Almost all the commonly occurring ones are related to six major mineral groups that are known as major rock forming minerals.

➢ The basic source of all minerals is the hot magma in the interior of the earth. When magma cools, crystals of minerals appear and a systematic series of minerals are formed in sequence to solidify so as to form rocks.

➢ Minerals such as coal, petroleum and natural gas are organic substances found in solid, liquid and gaseous forms respectively.

➢ Some important characteristics of the minerals are :

- **External crystal form :** Determined by internal arrangement of the molecules — cubes, octahedrons, hexagonal prisms, etc.
- **Cleavage :** Tendency to break in given directions producing relatively plane surfaces.
- **Fracture :** Internal molecular arrangement so complex the crystal will break in an irregular manner.
- **Lustre :** Appearance of a material without regard to colour; each mineral has a distinctive lustre like metallic, silky, glossy ,etc.
- **Colour :** Some minerals have characteristic colour determined by their molecular structure.
- **Streak :** Colour of the ground powder of any mineral. It may be of the same colour as the mineral or may differ.
- **Transparency :** Some minerals might be transparent, translucent or opaque.
- **Structure :** Particular arrangement of the individual crystals; fine, medium or coarse grained; fibrous — separable, divergent, radiating.
- **Hardness :** Some minerals are measured on the basis of their hardness.
- **Specific gravity :** The ratio between the weight of a given object and the weight of an equal volume of water.

➢ Some major minerals and their characteristics are as follows :
  - **Feldspar :** Half of the earth's crust is composed of feldspar. It has light cream to salmon pink colour. It is used in ceramics and glass making.
  - **Quartz :** It is one of the most important components of sand and granite. It is white or colourless and used in radio and radar.
  - **Pyroxene :** It forms 10 per cent of the earth's crust. It is commonly found in meteorites. It is in green or black colour.
  - **Amphibole :** They form 7 per cent of the earth's crust. It is in green or black colour and is used in asbestos industry.
  - **Mica :** It is commonly found in igneous and metamorphic rocks. It is used in electrical instruments.
  - **Olivine :** It is used in jewellery. It is usually a greenish crystal, often found in basaltic rocks.

➢ **Metallic Minerals :** These minerals contain metal content and can be sub-divided into three types:
  - **Precious metals :** Gold, silver, platinum, etc.
  - **Ferrous metals :** Iron and other metals often mixed with iron to form various kinds of steel.
  - **Non-ferrous metals :** Include metals like copper, lead, zinc, tin, aluminium, etc.

➢ **Non-Metallic Minerals :** These minerals do not contain metal content. Sulphur, phosphates and nitrates are examples of non-metallic minerals. Cement is a mixture of non-metallic minerals.

Know the Terms

➢ **Mineral :** A mineral is a naturally occurring inorganic substance, having an orderly atomic structure and a definite chemical composition and physical properties.

➢ **Cleavage :** The tendency to break the crystal in given directions producing relatively plane surfaces is known as cleavage.

➢ **Metallic minerals :** These are minerals which contain metal in the raw form.

➢ **Non-metallic minerals :** These are the minerals which do not contain metal content.

Multiple Choice Questions (1 mark each)

Q. 1. _____contains calcium, aluminium, magnesium, iron and silica. [A]
(a) Pyroxene
(b) Coal
(c) Sodium
(d) Graphite
Ans. (a) Pyroxene 1

Q. 2. ___________ is used in jewellery. It is usually a greenish crystal, often found in basaltic rocks. [U]
(a) Amphibole
(b) Olivine
(c) Quartz
(d) Feldspar
Ans. (b) Olivine 1

Very Short Answer Type Questions (1 mark each)

Q. 1. What is a mineral? [U]
Ans. A mineral is a naturally occurring inorganic substance, having an orderly atomic structure and a definite chemical composition and physical properties. 1

Answering Tip
- Minerals always occur naturally in pure form.

Q. 2. Define the term 'Cleavage'. [U]
Ans. The tendency to break the crystal in given directions producing relatively plane surfaces is known as cleavage. 1

Q. 3. What are metallic minerals? [R]
Ans. Metallic minerals contain metal in the raw form. 1

Q. 4. What are non-metallic minerals. [A]
Ans. Non-metallic minerals do not contain metal content. 1

Q. 5. Name any two elements that help in composing 98% of the total crust of the earth. [R]
Ans. About 98 per cent of the total crust of the earth is composed of elements like oxygen, silicon, aluminium, iron, calcium, sodium, potassium and magnesium. **(Any two) (½ + ½=1)**

Q. 6. What is the basic source of all minerals? [U]
Ans. The basic source of all minerals is the hot magma in the interior of the earth. 1

Commonly Made Error

- The students do not know how minerals are formed.

Answering Tip

- When liquid magma cools, it crystallizes to form an igneous rock composed of a variety of different minerals.

Q. 7. Give an example of the solid, liquid and gaseous form of minerals? [A]

Ans. Coal is an example of the solid form, petroleum is an example of the liquid form and natural gas is an example of the gaseous form. **1**

Answering Tip

- Always remember that the minerals are classified according to their chemical and crystal form.

Q. 8. Name any two types of metallic minerals? [R]

Ans. The types of metallic minerals are :

(i) Precious metals : Gold, silver, platinum, etc.

(ii) Ferrous metals : Iron and other metals often mixed with iron to form various kinds of steel.

(iii) Non-ferrous metals : Include metals like copper, lead, zinc, tin, aluminium ,etc.

(Any two) (½ + ½=1)

Q. 9. Give any two examples of non-metallic minerals? [A]

Ans. Sulphur, phosphates and nitrates are examples of non-metallic minerals. **1**

Q. 10. How does the systematic formation of minerals take place? [A]

Ans. The basic source of all minerals is the hot magma in the interior of the earth. When magma cools, crystals of minerals appear and a systematic series of minerals are formed in sequence to solidify so as to form rocks. **1**

Q. 11. What kind of quality do minerals have? [R]

Ans. A mineral is a naturally occurring organic and inorganic substance having an orderly atomic structure and a definite chemical composition and physical properties. **1**

[AI] **Q.12. Name any two minerals having single element?** [U]

Ans. Copper, sulphur, gold, silver, graphite.

(Any two) 1

Q. 13. Which is the hardest and the softest mineral? [A]

Ans. Hardest mineral is diamond and the softest mineral is talc. **1**

Q. 14. Name any two common elements found in all types of feldspar? [U]

Ans. Silicon and oxygen are found in all types of feldspar. **1**

Q. 15. What does pyroxene contain? [A]

Ans. Pyroxene contains calcium, aluminium, magnesium , iron and silica . **1**

Short Answer Type Questions **(3 marks each)**

Q. 1. Describe the major characteristics of feldspar and quartz . [A]

Ans. Feldspar :

(i) Silicon and oxygen are common elements in all types of feldspar and sodium, potassium, calcium, aluminium, etc., are found in specific feldspar variety.

(ii) Half of the earth's crust is composed of feldspar. It has light cream to salmon pink colour.

(iii) It is used in ceramics and glass making.

Quartz :

(i) It is one of the most important components of sand and granite. It consists of silica.

(ii) It is a hard mineral virtually insoluble in water.

(iii) It is white or colourless and used in radio and radar. It is one of the most important components of granite. **(1 × 3 = 3)**

Answering Tip

- Feldspar occurs in igneous, metamorphic and sedimentary rocks throughout the world.
- Quartz is one of the most common minerals in the earth's crust.

Q. 2. Describe the major characteristics of amphibole and mica? [R]

Ans. Amphibole :

(i) Aluminium, calcium, silica, iron, magnesium are the major elements of amphiboles.

(ii) They form 7 per cent of the earth's crust.

(iii) It is in green or black colour and is used in asbestos industry.

Mica :

(i) It comprises of potassium, aluminium, magnesium, iron, silica, etc. It forms 4 per cent of the earth's crust.

(ii) It is commonly found in igneous and metamorphic rocks.

(iii) It is used in electrical instruments. **(1 × 3 = 3)**

[AI] **Q. 3. Is it true that metallic minerals are more useful than the non-metallic minerals? Justify your answer?** [U]

Ans. No, it is not true that metallic minerals are more useful than the non-metallic minerals , as metallic minerals contain metal content and can be divided into: precious metals, ferrous metals and non-ferrous metals.

Whereas, non-metallic minerals do not have metal content. For example, cement is a mixture of non-metallic mineral. These minerals have there own utility .Therefore, both are very useful in the development of industries. **3**

 Long Answer Type Questions (5 marks each)

Q. 1. Explain any five physical characteristics of the minerals. [A]

Ans. The five physical characteristics of the minerals are :

(i) External crystal form : Determined by internal arrangement of the molecules — cubes, octahedrons, hexagonal prisms, etc.

(ii) Cleavage : Tendency to break in given directions producing relatively plane surfaces — result of internal arrangement of the molecules — may cleave in one or more directions and at any angle to each other.

(iii) Fracture : Internal molecular arrangement so complex there are no planes of molecules; the crystal will break in an irregular manner, not along planes of cleavage.

(iv) Lustre : Appearance of a material without regard to colour; each mineral has a distinctive lustre like metallic, silky, glossy, etc.

(v) Colour : Some minerals have characteristic colour determined by their molecular structure — malachite, azurite, chalcopyrite etc., and some minerals are coloured by impurities. For example, because of impurities quartz may be white, green, red, yellow ,etc.

(vi) Streak: Colour of the ground powder of any mineral. It may be of the same colour as the mineral or may differ — malachite is green and gives green streak, fluorite is purple or green but gives a white streak.

(vii) Transparency : Transparent: light rays pass through so that objects can be seen plainly; translucent — light rays pass through but will get diffused so that objects cannot be seen; opaque — light will not pass at all.

(viii) Structure : Particular — arrangement of the individual crystals; fine, medium or coarse grained; fibrous — separable, divergent, radiating.

(xi) Hardness : Relative resistance being scratched; ten minerals are selected to measure the degree of hardness from 1-10. They are: 1. talc; 2. gypsum; 3. calcite; 4. fluorite; 5. apatite; 6. feldspar; 7. quartz; 8. topaz; 9. corundum; 10. diamond. Compared to this for example, a fingernail is 2.5 and glass or knife blade is 5.5.

(x) Specific gravity : The ratio between the weight of a given object and the weight of an equal volume of water; object weighed in air and then weighed in water and divide weight in air by the difference of the two weights. **(Any five) (1 × 5=5)**

Commonly Made Error

- The students are unable to understand how are minerals characterized.

Answering Tip

- Most minerals can be characterized and classified by their unique physical properties: hardness, lustre, colour, streak,specific gravity, cleavage, fracture and tenacity.

Q. 2. Discuss any five important minerals along with their characteristics. [U]

Ans. Some of the important minerals and their characteristics are :

(i) Feldspar : Silicon and oxygen are common elements in all types of feldspar and sodium, potassium, calcium, aluminium, etc., are found in specific feldspar variety. Half of the earth's crust is composed of feldspar. It has light cream to salmon pink colour. It is used in ceramics and glass making.

(ii) Quartz : It is one of the most important components of sand and granite. It consists of silica. It is a hard mineral virtually insoluble in water. It is white or colourless and used in radio and radar. It is one of the most important components of granite.

(iii) Pyroxene : Pyroxene consists of calcium, aluminium, magnesium, iron and silica. Pyroxene forms 10 per cent of the earth's crust. It is commonly found in meteorites. It is in green or black colour.

(iv) Amphibole : Aluminium, calcium, silica, iron, magnesium are the major elements of amphiboles. They form 7 per cent of the earth's crust. It is in green or black colour and is used in asbestos industry. Hornblende is another form of amphiboles.

(v) Mica : It comprises of potassium, aluminium, magnesium, iron, silica, etc., It forms 4 per cent of the earth's crust. It is commonly found in igneous and metamorphic rocks. It is used in electrical instruments.

(vi) Olivine : Magnesium, iron and silica are major elements of olivine. It is used in jewellery. It is usually a greenish crystal, often found in basaltic rocks. Besides these main minerals, other minerals like chlorite, calcite, magnetite, haematite, bauxite and barite are also present in some quantities in the rocks. **(Any five) (1 × 5=5)**

TOPIC-2
Rocks and Rock Cycle

Revision Notes

- The earth's crust is composed of rocks. A rock is an aggregate of one or more minerals. Rocks may be hard or soft and in varied colours.
- Rocks do not have definite composition of mineral constituents. Feldspar and quartz are the most common minerals found in rocks.
- As there is a close relation between rocks and landforms, rocks and soils; a geographer requires basic knowledge of rocks.
- There are many different kinds of rocks which are grouped under three families on the basis of their mode of formation. They are :
  - **Igneous Rocks :** Solidified from magma and lava.
  - **Sedimentary Rocks :** The result of deposition of fragments of rocks by exogenous processes.
  - **Metamorphic Rocks :** Formed out of existing rocks undergoing recrystallisation.
- As igneous rocks form out of magma and lava from the interior of the earth, they are known as primary rocks.
- The igneous rocks are formed when magma cools and solidifies. When magma in its upward movement cools and turns into solid form it is called igneous rock.
- Granite, gabbro, pegmatite, basalt, volcanic breccia and tuff are some of the examples of igneous rocks.
- The word 'sedimentary' is derived from the Latin word sedimentum, which means settling.
- Rocks (igneous, sedimentary and metamorphic) of the earth's surface are exposed to denudation agents, and are broken up into various sizes of fragments. Such fragments are transported by different exogenous agencies and deposited. These deposits through compaction turn into rocks. This process is called **lithification**.
- Depending upon the mode of formation, sedimentary rocks are classified into three major groups:
  - **Mechanically formed :** Sandstone, conglomerate, limestone, shale, loess, etc., are examples.
  - **Organically formed :** Geyserite, chalk, limestone, coal, etc., are some examples.
  - **Chemically formed :** Chert, limestone, halite, potash, etc., are some examples.
- The word metamorphic means 'change of form'. These rocks form under the action of pressure, volume and temperature (PVT) changes.
- Metamorphism is a process by which already consolidated rocks undergo recrystallisation and reorganisation of materials within original rocks.
- Mechanical disruption and reorganisation of the original minerals within rocks due to breaking and crushing without any appreciable chemical changes is called **dynamic metamorphism.**
- The materials of rocks chemically alter and recrystallise due to thermal metamorphism.
- In regional metamorphism, rocks undergo recrystallisation due to deformation caused by tectonic shearing together with high temperature or pressure or both.
- In the process of metamorphism in some rocks grains or minerals get arranged in layers or lines. Such an arrangement of minerals or grains in metamorphic rocks is called **foliation or lineation.**
- Sometimes minerals or materials of different groups are arranged into alternating thin to thick layers appearing in light and dark shades. Such a structure in metamorphic rocks is called banding and rocks displaying banding are called banded rocks.
- Metamorphic rocks are classified into two major groups: foliated rocks and non-foliated rocks.
- Rocks do not remain in their original form for long but may undergo transformation. Rock cycle is a continuous process through which old rocks are transformed into new ones.
- Igneous rocks are primary rocks and other rocks (sedimentary and metamorphic) form from these primary rocks. Igneous rocks can be changed into metamorphic rocks. The fragments derived out of igneous and metamorphic rocks form into sedimentary rocks.
- Sedimentary rocks themselves can turn into fragments and the fragments can be a source for formation of sedimentary rocks.
- The crustal rocks (igneous, metamorphic and sedimentary) once formed may be carried down into the mantle (interior of the earth) through subduction process (parts or whole of crustal plates going down under another plate in zones of plate convergence) and the same melt down due to increase in temperature in the interior and turn into molten magma, the original source for igneous rocks.

Know the Terms

- **Rock :** A rock is the solid mineral material forming part of the surface of the earth.
- **Rock cycle :** Rock cycle is a continuous process through which old rocks are transformed into new ones.
- **Petrology :** Petrology is science of rocks.
- **Petrologist :** A petrologist studies rocks in all their aspects viz., mineral composition, texture, structure, origin, occurrence, alteration and relationship with other rocks.
- **Igneous rocks :** Igneous rocks are those rocks which are formed through the cooling and solidification of magma or lava.
- **Sedimentary rocks :** Sedimentary rocks are those rocks which are formed by the deposition and subsequent cementation of that material at the earth's surface and within the bodies of water.
- **Metamorphic rocks :** Metamorphic rocks are those rocks which are formed under the action of pressure.
- **Lithification :** It is a process in which unconsolidated sediments are converted into solid stone or rock.
- **Metamorphism :** It is the process by which the rocks are changed in composition, texture or structure by extreme heat and pressure.
- **Foliation :** It refers to repetitive layering in metamorphic rocks.
- **Dynamic metamorphism :** Mechanical disruption and reorganisation of the original minerals within rocks due to breaking and crushing without any appreciable chemical changes is called dynamic metamorphism.
- **Contact metamorphism :** In contact metamorphism the rocks come in contact with hot intruding magma and lava and the rock materials recrystallise under high temperatures.
- **Banding :** Sometimes minerals or materials of different groups are arranged into alternating thin to thick layers appearing in light and dark shades. Such a structure in metamorphic rocks is called banding.
- **Banding rocks :** Rocks displaying banding are called banded rocks.

Multiple Choice Questions (1 mark each)

Q. 1. The solid mineral material forming part of the surface of the earth is called : [A]
(a) rock
(b) magma
(c) sand
(d) silt

Ans. (a) rock 1

Q. 2. Foliated rocks and non-foliated rocks are classifications of : [U]
(a) Igneous rocks
(b) Metamorphic rocks
(c) Sedimentary rocks
(d) Crystal rocks

Ans. (b) Metamorphic rocks 1

Q. 3. Igneous, metamorphic and sedimentary rocks are known as : [R]
(a) crustal rocks
(b) banding rocks
(c) consolidated rocks
(d) broken rocks

Ans. (a) crustal rocks 1

Very Short Answer Type Questions (1 mark each)

Q. 1. Define the term 'Petrology'? [A]

Ans. Petrology is a branch of science which concerned with the origin, structure, and composition of rocks. 1

Q. 2. Define the term 'Rock'. [A]

Ans. A rock is the solid mineral material forming part of the surface of the earth . 1

Q. 3. Define the term 'Rock Cycle'. [U]

Ans. Rock cycle is a continuous process through which old rocks are transformed into new ones. 1

Q. 4. What does a petrologist do? [A]

Ans. A petrologist studies rocks in all their aspects viz., mineral composition, texture, structure, origin, occurrence, alteration and relationship with other rocks. 1

Q. 5. What are igneous rocks? [A]

Ans. Igneous rocks are those rocks which are formed through the cooling and solidification of magma or lava. 1

Answering Tip

- Igneous rocks are formed at the crust's surface as a result of the partial melting of rocks within the mantle and crust.

Q. 6. What are metamorphic rocks? [A]

Ans. Metamorphic rocks are those rocks which are formed under the action of pressure. 1

Q. 7. What are sedimentary rocks? [A]

Ans. Sedimentary rocks are those rocks which are formed by the deposition and subsequent cementation of that material at the earth's surface and within the bodies of water. 1

Q. 8. What is lithification? [U]

Ans. Rocks of the earth's surface are exposed to denudation agents, and are broken up into various sizes of fragments. Such fragments are transported by different exogenous agencies and deposited. These deposits through compaction turn into rocks. This process is called lithification. 1

Q. 9. What is metamorphism? R

Ans. Metamorphism is a process by which already consolidated rocks undergo recrystallisation and reorganisation of materials within original rocks. 1

Answering Tip

- In metamorphism, the structure of the rock is altered by heat, pressure or other natural agency.

Q. 10. What is foliation or lineation? R

Ans. In the process of metamorphism in some rocks grains or minerals get arranged in layers or lines. Such an arrangement of minerals or grains in metamorphic rocks is called foliation or lineation. 1

Q. 11. What is dynamic metamorphism? A

Ans. Mechanical disruption and reorganisation of the original minerals within rocks due to breaking and crushing without any appreciable chemical changes is called dynamic metamorphism. 1

Q. 12. What is banding? A

Ans. Sometimes minerals or materials of different groups are arranged into alternating thin to thick layers appearing in light and dark shades. Such a structure in metamorphic rocks is called banding. 1

Q. 13. What is contact metamorphism? R

Ans. In contact metamorphism, the rocks come in contact with hot intruding magma and lava and the rock materials recrystallise under high temperatures. 1

Q. 14. Metamorphic rocks can be classified into how many groups? U

Ans. Metamorphic rocks are classified into two groups: foliated group and non-foliated group. 1

Q. 15. What are the root sources of igneous rocks? A

Ans. Magma is the root source of igneous rocks. The igneous rocks are formed when the magma cools and solidifies. When the magma in its upward movement cools and turns into solid form , called igneous rocks. 1

Short Answer Type Questions (3 marks each)

Q. 1. Describe the characteristics of sedimentary rocks? A

Ans. Characteristics of sedimentary rocks :

(i) The word 'sedimentary' is derived from the Latin word sedimentum, which means settling. Rocks (igneous, sedimentary and metamorphic) of the earth's surface are exposed to denudation agents, and are broken up into various sizes of fragments. Such fragments are transported by different exogenous agencies and deposited.

(ii) These deposits through compaction turn into rocks. This process is called lithification. In many sedimentary rocks, the layers of deposits retain their characteristics even after lithification.

(iii) Hence, we see a number of layers of varying thickness in sedimentary rocks like sandstone, shale, etc. **(1 × 3 = 3)**

Commonly Made Error

- The students are not aware as to how the sediments are formed which ultimately lead to the formation of sedimentary rocks.

Answering Tip

- Sediments are often formed when weathering and erosion break down a rock into loose material in a source area.

Q. 2. Depending upon the mode of formation, sedimentary rocks can be classified into how many groups? A

Ans. Depending upon the mode of formation, sedimentary rocks are classified into three major groups :

(i) Mechanically formed : Sandstone, conglomerate, limestone, shale, loess, etc., are some of the examples.

(ii) Organically formed : Geyserite, chalk, limestone, coal, etc., are some of the examples.

(iii) Chemically formed : Chert, limestone, halite, potash etc., are some of the examples .**(1 × 3 = 3)**

AI **Q. 3. Explain the rock cycle.** A

OR

Rocks do not remain in their original form for long but may undergo transformation . Explain.

Ans. The Rock cycle is a group of changes. Igneous rock can change into sedimentary rock or into metamorphic rock. Sedimentary rock can change into metamorphic rock or into igneous rock. Metamorphic rock can change into igneous or sedimentary rock. **(1 × 3 = 3)**

IMAGE of ROCK CYCLE

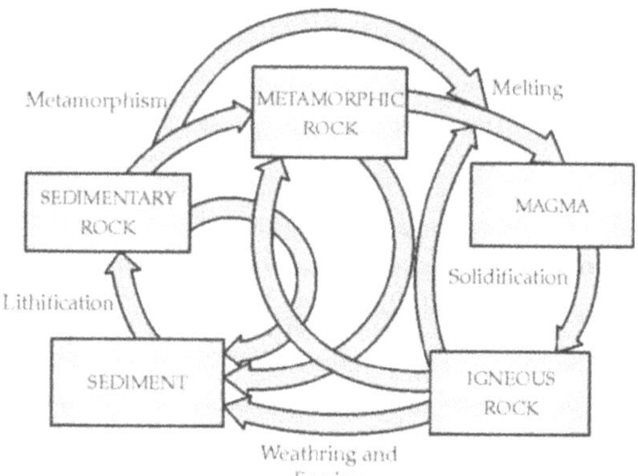

Q. 4. Differentiate between extrusive igneous and intrusive igneous. U

Ans.

S.No.	Extrusive Igneous	Intrusive Igneous
1.	Lava cools rapidly on the surface of the earth.	Cooling and solidification occurs inside the Earth's surface and is a slow process.
2.	Minerals crystals of extrusive igneous rocks change their structure and can become very small in size.	They are the coarse granule structure .
3.	Example of extrusive igneous is basalt.	Example of intrusive igneous is granite doloride.

(1 × 3 = 3)

Q. 5. Differentiate between minerals and rocks. A

Ans.

S.No.	Minerals	Rocks
1.	Minerals can be defined as naturally occurring substances with the definite chemical and physical composition.	Rocks are the solid mineral material forming part of the surface of the earth's crust.
2.	Minerals can be made up of two or more elements.	Rocks are of basically three types.
3.	There are more than 2000 minerals that exist.	Rocks can be classified into : igneous, sedimentary and metamorphic rocks.

(1 × 3 = 3)

Answering Tip

- The main point of difference between a rock and a mineral is that the former is not homogeneous and does not have a specific chemical composition. It can be a mix of one or more minerals and can also contain organic traces.

Long Answer Type Questions (5 marks each)

AI **Q. 1. Differentiate between sedimentary rocks and igneous rocks.** R

Ans.

S.No.	Sedimentary rocks	Igneous rocks
1.	These rocks are made up of sediments.	These rocks are made up of solidified lava.
2.	Sedimentary rocks form in layers.	Igneous rocks are compact.
3.	These rocks contain fossils.	These rocks do not contain fossils.
4.	These rocks are permeable and hence allow the water to seep.	These rocks are not permeable and do not allow water to seep.
5.	These rocks are also known as secondary rocks. Example: granite.	These rocks are also known as primary rocks. Example : sandstone.

(1×5=5)

Q. 2. Differentiate between igneous rocks and metamorphic rocks. A

Ans.

S.No.	Igneous rocks	Metamorphic rocks
1.	Igneous rocks are those rocks which are formed through the cooling and solidification of magma or lava.	Metamorphic rocks are those rocks which are formed under the action of pressure.
2.	These rocks are hard, impermeable in nature.	These rocks are also hard but have formed due to change in igneous and sedimentary rocks.
3.	In these types of rocks no bands can be seen.	In these types of rocks banding is visible.
4.	These rocks are of two types: intrusive and extrusive.	These rocks are of two types: contact metamorphism and regional metamorphism.
5.	As igneous rocks form out of magma and lava from the interior of the earth, they are known as primary rocks.	These rocks form under the action of pressure, volume and temperature (PVT) changes.

(1×5=5)

Q. 3. It is said that the igneous rocks act as a source of all other types of rocks. Do you agree? Justify the statement? [U]

Ans. It is true that the igneous rocks act as a source of all other types of rocks. This is the reason, igneous rocks are called primary rocks.

Igneous rocks are primary rocks and other rocks , *i.e.*, sedimentary and metamorphic rocks form from these primary rocks. Igneous rocks can be changed into metamorphic rocks.

The fragments derived out of igneous and metamorphic rocks form into sedimentary rocks. Sedimentary rocks themselves can turn into fragments and the fragments can be a source for formation of sedimentary rocks.

The crustal rocks (igneous, metamorphic and sedimentary) once formed may be carried down into the mantle (interior of the earth) through subduction process (parts or whole of crustal plates going down under another plate in zones of plate convergence) and the same melt down due to increase in temperature in the interior and turn into molten magma, the original source for igneous rocks. 5

NCERT CORNER

(A) Multiple choice questions :

Q. 1. Which one of the following are the two main constituents of granite :

(a) Iron and nickel
(b) Iron and silver
(c) Silica and aluminium
(d) Iron Oxide and potassium

Ans. (c) Silica and aluminium .

Q. 2. Which one of the following is the salient feature of metamorphic rocks :

(a) Changeable
(b) Quite
(c) Crystalline
(d) Foliation

Ans. (a) Changeable .

[AI] **Q. 3. Which one of the following is not a single element mineral :**

(a) Gold (b) Silver
(c) Mica (d) Graphite

Ans. (c) Mica.

Q. 4. Which one of the following is the hardest mineral :

(a) Topaz (b) Diamond
(c) Quartz (d) Feldspar

Ans. (b) Diamond

Q. 5. Which one of the following is not a sedimentary rock :

(a) Tillite (b) Borax
(c) Breccia (d) Marble

Ans. (d) Marble.

(B) Answer the following questions in about 30 words :

Q. 1. What do you mean by rocks? Name the three major classes of rocks.

Ans. A rock is an aggregate of one or more minerals. Rock may be hard or soft and in varied colours. Rocks do not have definite composition of mineral constituents. The earth's crust is composed of rocks.

The three major classes of rocks are :

(i) **Igneous Rocks :** Solidified from magma and lava.

(ii) **Sedimentary Rocks :** The result of deposition of fragments of rocks by exogenous processes.

(iii) **Metamorphic Rocks :** Formed out of existing rocks undergoing recrystallisation.

Q. 2. What is an igneous rock? Describe the method of formation and characteristics of igneous rock.

Ans. The igneous rocks are those rocks which are formed when magma cools and solidifies. As igneous rocks form out of magma and lava from the interior of the earth, they are known as primary rocks.

Formation of igneous rocks :

When magma in its upward movement cools and turns into solid form it is called igneous rock. The process of cooling and solidification can happen in the earth's crust or on the surface of the earth.

Features of igneous rocks :

Igneous rocks are made up of solidified lava. The liquid lava gets solidified by gradual cooling. Igneous rocks do not have fossils.

Q. 3. What is meant by sedimentary rock? Describe the mode of formation of sedimentary rock?

Ans. The word 'sedimentary' is derived from the Latin word sedimentum, which means settling. Sedimentary rocks are formed by the accumulation of the sediments.

Mode of formation of sedimentary rocks :

Rocks of the earth's surface are exposed to denudational agents, and are broken up into various sizes of fragments. Such fragments are transported by different exogenous agencies and deposited. These deposits through compaction turn into rocks. This process is called lithification. In many sedimentary rocks, the layers of deposits retain their characteristics even after lithification. Hence, we see a number of layers of varying thickness in sedimentary rocks like sandstone, shale ,etc.

Q. 4. What relationship explained by rock cycle between the major type of rock?

Ans. Rocks do not remain in their original form for long but may undergo transformation. Rock cycle is a continuous process through which old rocks are transformed into new ones.

Igneous rocks are primary rocks and other rocks (sedimentary and metamorphic) form from these primary rocks. Igneous rocks can be changed into metamorphic rocks. The fragments derived out of igneous and metamorphic rocks form into sedimentary rocks. Sedimentary rocks themselves can turn into fragments and the fragments can be a source for formation of sedimentary rocks.

The crustal rocks (igneous, metamorphic and sedimentary) once formed may be carried down into the mantle (interior of the earth) through subduction process (parts or whole of crustal plates going down under another plate in zones of plate convergence) and the same melt down due to increase in temperature in the interior and turn into molten magma, the original source for igneous rocks.

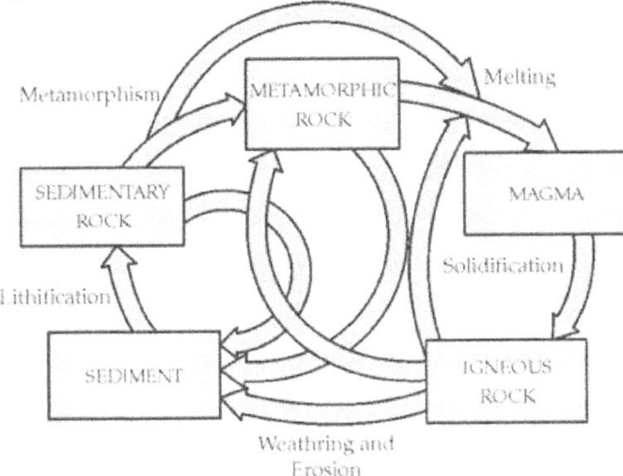

(C) Answer the following questions in about 150 words :

Q. 1. Define the term 'mineral' and name the major classes of minerals with their physical characteristics.

Ans. A mineral is a naturally occurring inorganic substance, having an orderly atomic structure and a definite chemical composition and physical properties. A mineral is composed of two or more elements. But, sometimes single element minerals like sulphur, copper, silver, gold, graphite etc., are found.

There are at least 2,000 minerals that have been named and identified in the earth's crust; but almost all the commonly occurring ones are related to six major mineral groups that are known as major rock forming minerals.

Some of the major classes of minerals with their physical characteristics are :

(i) Feldspar : Silicon and oxygen are common elements in all types of feldspar and sodium, potassium, calcium, aluminium, etc., are found in specific feldspar variety. Half of the earth's crust is composed of feldspar. It has light cream to salmon pink colour. It is used in ceramics and glass making.

(ii) Quartz : It is one of the most important components of sand and granite. It consists of silica. It is a hard mineral virtually insoluble in water. It is white or colourless and used in radio and radar.

(iii) Pyroxene : Pyroxene consists of calcium, aluminum, magnesium, iron and silica. It is in green or black colour.

(iv) Amphibole : Aluminium, calcium, silica, iron, magnesium are the major elements of amphiboles. They form 7 per cent of the earth's crust. It is in green or black colour and is used in asbestos industry.

(v) Mica : It comprises of potassium, aluminium, magnesium, iron, silica etc. It forms 4 per cent of the earth's crust. It is commonly found in igneous and metamorphic rocks.

(vi) Olivine : Magnesium, iron and silica are major elements of olivine. It is used in jewellery. It is usually a greenish crystal, often found in basaltic rocks.

Q. 2. Describe the nature and mode of origin of the chief types of rock at the earth's crust. How will you distinguish them?

Ans. The earth's crust is composed of rocks. A rock is an aggregate of one or more minerals. Rock may be hard or soft and in varied colours. For example, granite is hard, soapstone is soft.

There are many different kinds of rocks which are grouped under three families on the basis of their mode of formation. They are: Igneous rocks, sedimentary rocks and metamorphic rocks.

(i) Igneous rocks : The igneous rocks are formed when magma cools and solidifies. You already know what magma is. When magma in its upward movement cools and turns into solid form it is called igneous rock. The process of cooling and solidification can happen in the earth's crust or on the surface of the earth.

If molten material is cooled slowly at great depths, mineral grains may be very large. Sudden cooling (at the surface) results in small and smooth grains. Intermediate conditions of cooling would result in intermediate sizes of grains making up igneous rocks.

(ii) Sedimentary rocks : These rocks are the result of deposition of fragments of rocks by exogenous processes. In many sedimentary rocks, the layers of deposits retain their characteristics even after lithification. Hence, we see a number of layers of varying thickness in sedimentary rocks like sandstone, shale ,etc.

(iii) Metamorphic rocks : The word metamorphic means 'change of form'. These rocks form under the action of pressure, volume and temperature (PVT) changes. Metamorphism occurs when rocks are forced down to lower levels by tectonic processes or when molten magma rising through the crust comes in contact with the crustal rocks or the underlying rocks are subjected to great amounts of pressure by overlying rocks. Metamorphism is a process by which already consolidated rocks undergo recrystallisation and reorganisation of materials within original rocks.

Q. 3. What are metamorphic rocks? Describe the types of metamorphic rock and how are they formed?

Ans. The word metamorphic means 'change of form'. These rocks form under the action of pressure, volume and temperature (PVT) changes. Metamorphism occurs when rocks are forced down to lower levels by tectonic processes or when molten magma rising through the crust comes in contact with the crustal rocks or the underlying rocks are subjected to great amounts of pressure by overlying rocks. Metamorphism is a process by which already consolidated rocks undergo recrystallisation and reorganisation of materials within original rocks.

Mechanical disruption and reorganisation of the original minerals within rocks due to breaking and crushing without any appreciable chemical changes is called dynamic metamorphism. The materials of rocks chemically alter and recrystallise due to thermal metamorphism.

There are two types of thermal metamorphism namely contact metamorphism and regional metamorphism.

(i) Contact metamorphism : In contact metamorphism the rocks come in contact with hot intruding magma and lava and the rock materials recrystallise under high temperatures. Quite often new materials form out of magma or lava are added to the rocks.

(ii) Regional metamorphism : In regional metamorphism, rocks undergo recrystallisation due to deformation caused by tectonic shearing together with high temperature or pressure or both. In the process of metamorphism in some rocks grains or minerals get arranged in layers or lines. Such an arrangement of minerals or grains in metamorphic rocks is called foliation or lineation. Sometimes minerals or materials of different groups are arranged into alternating thin to thick layers appearing in light and dark shades. Such a structure in metamorphic rocks is called banding and rocks displaying banding are called banded rocks. Types of metamorphic rocks depend upon original rocks that were subjected to metamorphism.

Metamorphic rocks are classified into two major groups :

(a) Foliated rocks : These rocks have layered or banded appearance that is produced by exposure to heat and direct pressure.

(b) Non-foliated rocks : These rocks do not have a layered or banded appearance.

OSWAAL LEARNING TOOLS

For Suggested Online Videos

Visit : *https://qrgo.page.link/npjeV* **Or Scan the Code**

To learn from NCERT Prescribed Videos

Visit : *https://qrgo.page.link/AuBBK* **Or Scan the Code**

❑❑

CHAPTER

6 GEOMORPHIC PROCESSES

Syllabus

- *Geomorphic Processes, Endogenic Processes, Diastrophism, Volcanism, Exogenic Processes.*
- *Weathering, Chemical Weathering Processes, Physical Weathering Processes, Biological Activity and Weathering, Special Effects of Weathering, Significance of Weathering.*
- *Mass Movements, Slow Movements, Rapid Movements, Landslides, Erosion and deposition.*
- *Soil Formation, Process of Soil Formation, Soil-forming Factors.*

TOPIC-1
Geomorphic Processes : Endogenic Processes, Diastrophism and Volcanism

Revision Notes

- Now it is time to know in detail about the surface of the earth on which we live. The differences in the internal forces operating from within the earth which built up the crust have been responsible for the variations in the outer surface of the crust.
- The earth's surface is being continuously subjected to external forces induced basically by energy (sunlight). That means, the earth's surface is being continuously subjected to by external forces originating within the earth's atmosphere and by internal forces from within the earth.
- The external forces are known as exogenic forces and the internal forces are known as endogenic forces.
- The actions of exogenic forces result in wearing down (degradation) of relief/elevations and filling up (aggradation) of basins/depressions, on the earth's surface. The phenomenon of wearing down of relief variations of the surface of the earth through erosion is known as gradation.
- The endogenic forces continuously elevate or build up parts of the earth's surface and hence the exogenic processes fail to even out the relief variations of the surface of the earth.
- In general terms, the endogenic forces are mainly land building forces and the exogenic processes are mainly land wearing forces.
- Most of the surface of the earth had and has been shaped over very long periods of time (hundreds and thousands of years) and because of its use and misuse by humans its potential is being diminished at a fast rate.
- The endogenic and exogenic forces causing physical stresses and chemical actions on earth materials and bringing about changes in the configuration of the surface of the earth are known as geomorphic processes.
- Weathering, mass wasting, erosion and deposition are exogenic geomorphic processes.
- Any exogenic element of nature (like water, ice, wind, etc.) capable of acquiring and transporting earth materials can be called a geomorphic agent.
- Geomorphic processes and geomorphic agents especially exogenic, unless stated separately, are one and the same.
- Gravity besides being a directional force activating all downslope movements of matter also causes stresses on the earth's materials. Indirect gravitational stresses activate wave and tide induced currents and winds. Without gravity and gradients there would be no mobility and hence no erosion, transportation and deposition are possible.
- Gravity is the force that is keeping us in contact with the surface and it is the force that switches on the movement of all surface material on earth.
- The energy emanating from within the earth is the main force behind endogenic geomorphic processes. This energy is mostly generated by radioactivity, rotational and tidal friction and primordial heat from the origin of the earth.

- All processes that move, elevate or build up portions of the earth's crust come under diastrophism.
- They include :
  - Orogenic processes involving mountain building through severe folding and affecting long and narrow belts of the Earth's crust.
  - Epeirogenic processes involving uplift or warping of large parts of the earth's crust.
  - Earthquakes involving local relatively minor movements.
  - Plate tectonics involving horizontal movements of crustal plates.
- Volcanism includes the movement of molten rock (magma) onto or toward the earth's surface and also formation of many intrusive and extrusive volcanic forms.

Know the Terms

- **Gradation :** The phenomenon of wearing down of relief variations of the surface of the earth through erosion is known as gradation.
- **Exogenic forces :** The external forces are known as exogenic forces.
- **Geomorphic processes :** The endogenic and exogenic forces causing physical stresses and chemical actions on earth materials and bringing about changes in the configuration of the surface of the earth are known as geomorphic processes.
- **Geomorphic agents :** An agent is a mobile medium (like running water, moving ice masses, wind, waves and currents, etc.) which removes, transports and deposits earth materials. Running water, groundwater, glaciers, wind, waves and currents, etc., can be called geomorphic agents.
- **Diastrophism :** All processes that move, elevate or build up portions of the earth's crust come under diastrophism.
- **Volcanism :** It is the phenomenon of eruption of molten rock onto the surface of the earth where lava and volcanic gases erupt through a break in the surface called vent.

Multiple Choice Questions (1 mark each)

Q. 1. The earth's surface is being continuously subjected to external forces induced basically by : [A]

(a) sunlight
(b) wind
(c) water
(d) power

Ans. (a) sunlight 1

Q. 2. The land building forces are known as the : [R]

(a) endogenic forces
(b) exogenic forces
(c) geomorphic forces
(d) orogeny

Ans. (a) endogenic forces 1

Very Short Answer Type Questions (1 mark each)

Q. 1. Define the term 'Gradation'? [A]

Ans. The phenomenon of wearing down of relief variations of the surface of the earth through erosion is known as gradation. 1

Answering Tip
- Always remember that gradation involves three processes: weathering, transport and deposition.

Q. 2. Define the term 'Exogenic forces'. [A]

Ans. Exogenic forces refer to the external forces and the phenomena that occur on or above the surface of the earth. 1

Q. 3. Define the term 'Endogenic forces'? [A]

Ans. The endogenic forces refer to the forces that are coming from within the earth and causing horizontal and vertical movements. 1

[AI] **Q. 4. Define the term 'Geomorphic processes'.** [U]

Ans. The endogenic and exogenic forces causing physical stresses and chemical actions on earth materials and bringing about changes in the configuration of the surface of the earth are known as geomorphic processes. 1

Answering Tip
- Geomorphic processes help in generating sediments that circulate in the Rock Cycle.

Q. 5. What do you understand by 'geomorphic agents'? Give examples. [U]

Ans. An agent is a mobile medium which removes, transports and deposits earth materials. Running water, groundwater, glaciers, wind, waves and currents, etc., can be called geomorphic agents.

(Any two)(½ + ½ = 1)

Q. 6. What do you understand by the term 'diastrophism'?

Ans. All processes that move, elevate or build up portions of the earth's crust come under diastrophism. 1

Q. 7. Define the term 'volcanism'.

Ans. Volcanism includes the movement of molten rock (magma) onto or toward the earth's surface and also formation of many intrusive and extrusive volcanic form. 1

Q. 8. Cite one difference between epeirogeny and orogeny? [A]

Ans. Epeirogeny is strictly verticle movement of continent and it acts along the radius of the earth whereas orogeny is horizontal movement of plates act tangentially to the earth surface, as in plate tectonics. 1

Q. 9. Why is the surface of the earth uneven? [A]

Ans. The differences in the internal forces operating from within the earth which built up the crust have been responsible for the variations in the outer surface of the crust. Thus, the earth's surface is uneven. 1

Q. 10. What type of changes are brought by internal forces on the earth? [U]

Ans. Internal forces give rise to new landforms on the earth's surface. 1

Q. 11. What type of changes are brought by the external forces in the Earth? [A]

Ans. The external forces continuously keep on bringing changes in the earth's landform. Through the process of erosion and deposition they keep on bringing changes in the topography of the earth. 1

Q. 12. Are geomorphic processes and geomorphic agents same or different? [U]

Ans. Geomorphic processes and geomorphic agents especially exogenic, unless stated separately, are one and the same. 1

Q. 13. What does the indirect gravitational stresses do? [A]

Ans. Indirect gravitational stresses activate wave and tide induced currents and winds. 1

Q. 14. What would happen if gravity did not exist? [A]

Ans. Gravity is the force that is keeping us in contact with the surface and it is the force that switches on the movement of all surface material on earth. Without gravity and gradients there would be no mobility and hence no erosion, transportation and deposition are possible. 1

Q.15. What is the main force behind the endogenic processes? [U]

Ans. The energy emanating from within the earth is the main force behind endogenic geomorphic processes . 1

Q. 16. Give an example of the endogenic forces? [A]

Ans. Volcanism is one of the best example of endogenic forces. 1

Short Answer Type Questions (3 marks each)

[AI] **Q. 1. What makes the earth's surface uneven?** [A]

Ans. (i) The differences in the internal forces operating from within the earth which built up the crust have been responsible for the variations in the outer surface of the crust.

(ii) The earth's surface is being continuously subjected to by external forces originating within the earth's atmosphere and by internal forces from within the earth.

(iii) Due to the variations in the geothermal gradients and the strength, the actions of endogenic forces will not be uniform and hence the tectonically controlled original crystal surface is uneven.

(1 × 3 = 3)

Q. 2. How without gravity and gradient there will be no erosion? Explain? [A]

Ans. Gravity besides being a directional force activating all downslope movements of matter also causes stresses on the earth's materials.

(i) Without gravity and gradients there would be no mobility and hence no erosion, transportation and deposition are possible. So, gravitational stresses are as important as the other geomorphic processes.

(ii) Gravity is the force that is keeping us in contact with the surface and it is the force that switches on the movement of all surface material on earth.

(iii) All the movements either within the earth or on the surface of the earth occur due to gradients — from higher levels to lower levels, from high pressure to low pressure areas, etc. **(1 × 3 = 3)**

Q. 3. Differentiate between orogenic movements and epeirogenic movements? [U]

Ans.

S.No.	Orogenic Movements	Epeirogenic Movements
1.	In the process of orogenic the crust is severely deformed into folds.	Due to epeirogenic movements, there may be simple deformation.
2.	It is mountain building process.	It is a continental building process .
3.	It affects long and narrow belt of earth's crust.	It involves uplift or wrapping of large part of the earth's crust.

(1 × 3 = 3)

Answering Tip

- Orogenic movements are the primary mechanism by which mountains are built on continents,whereas epeirogenic movements are continent building movements.

Q. 4. Name the factors that cause diastrophism? [U]

Ans. All processes that move, elevate or build up portions of the earth's crust come under diastrophism.

They include :

(i) **Orogenic processes :** It involves mountain building through severe folding and affecting long and narrow belts of the earth's crust.

(ii) **Epeirogenic processes :** It involves uplift or warping of large parts of the earth's crust.

(iii) **Earthquakes :** It involves local relatively minor movements.

(iv) **Plate tectonics :** It involves horizontal movements of crustal plates. 3

AI **Q. 5. Differentiate between exogenic forces and endogenic forces?** A

Ans.

S.No.	Exogenic forces	Endogenic forces
1.	The external forces are known as exogenic forces.	The internal forces are known as endogenic forces.
2.	Solar energy is the sole driving force behind the exogenic forces.	Gravity is the sole driving force behind the endogenic forces.
3.	Example of exogenic forces are erosion, flood, mining, etc.	Example of endogenic forces are earthquake, volcanic eruptions, etc.

(1 × 3 = 3)

Commonly Made Error

- The students are not aware of the sources of where the exogenic and endogenic forces derive their energy.

Answering Tip

- Endogenic forces are forces which originate within the earth's crust;whereas exogenic forces derive their energy from solar radiation.

Q. 6. State how geomorphic agents are different from geomorphic processes? A

Ans. Geomorphic agents are different from geomorphic processes in the following ways :

Geomorphic agents : An agent is a mobile medium which removes, transports and deposits earth materials. Running water, groundwater, glaciers, wind, waves and currents, etc., can be called geomorphic agents.

Geomorphic processes : The endogenic and exogenic forces causing physical stresses and chemical actions on earth material and bringing about changes in the configuration of the surface of the earth is known as geomorphic processes. 3

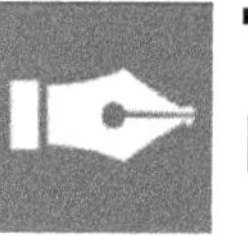

TOPIC-2
Exogenic Processes and Weathering

Revision Notes

- The exogenic processes derive their energy from atmosphere determined by the ultimate energy from the sun and also the gradients created by tectonic factors.
- Gravitational force acts upon all earth materials having a sloping surface and tend to produce movement of matter in downslope direction. Force applied per unit area is called stress.
- Stress is produced in a solid by pushing or pulling. Forces acting along the faces of earth materials are shear stresses (separating forces). The shear stresses result in angular displacement or slippage.
- As there are different climatic regions on the earth's surface, the exogenic geomorphic processes vary from region to region. Temperature and precipitation are the two important climatic elements that control various processes.
- All the exogenic geomorphic processes are covered under a general term, denudation. The word 'denude' means to strip off or to uncover. Weathering, mass wasting/movements, erosion and transportation are included in denudation.
- The effects of most of the exogenic geomorphic processes are small and slow and may be imperceptible in a short time span, but will in the long run affect the rocks severely due to continued fatigue.
- Weathering is defined as mechanical disintegration and chemical decomposition of rocks through the actions of various elements of weather and climate.
- There are three major groups of weathering processes :
  - Chemical
  - Physical or mechanical
  - Biological
- A group of weathering processes viz; solution, carbonation, hydration, oxidation and reduction acts on the rocks to decompose, dissolve or reduce them to a fine clastic state through chemical reactions by oxygen, surface and/ or soil water and other acids.

- When something is dissolved in water or acids, the water or acid with dissolved contents is called solution. This process involves removal of solids in solution and depends upon solubility of a mineral in water or weak acids.
- Carbonation is the reaction of carbonate and bicarbonate with minerals and is a common process helping the breaking down of feldspars and carbonate minerals.
- Hydration is the chemical addition of water. Minerals take up water and expand; this expansion causes an increase in the volume of the material itself or rock.
- In weathering, oxidation means a combination of a mineral with oxygen to form oxides or hydroxides. Oxidation occurs where there is ready access to the atmosphere and oxygenated waters.

➢ Physical or mechanical weathering processes depend on some applied forces. Most of the physical weathering processes are caused by thermal expansion and pressure release.

➢ Biological weathering is contribution to or removal of minerals and ions from the weathering environment and physical changes due to growth or movement of organisms. Burrowing and wedging by organisms like earthworms, termites, rodents etc., help in exposing the new surfaces to chemical attack and assists in the penetration of moisture and air.

➢ Decaying plant and animal matter help in the production of humic, carbonic and other acids which enhance decay and solubility of some elements. Algae utilise mineral nutrients for growth and help in concentration of iron and manganese oxides. Plant roots exert a tremendous pressure on the earth materials mechanically breaking them apart.

➢ Significance of weathering is that weathering of rocks and deposits helps in the enrichment and concentrations of certain valuable ores of iron, manganese, aluminium, copper, etc., which are of great importance for the national economy.

➢ Weathering is an important process in the formation of soils.

Know the Terms

➢ **Endogenic forces :** The internal forces are known as endogenic forces.

➢ **Stress :** Gravitational force acts upon all earth materials having a sloping surface and tend to produce movement of matter in downslope direction. Force applied per unit area is called stress.

➢ **Weathering :** Weathering is defined as mechanical disintegration and chemical decomposition of rocks through the actions of various elements of weather and climate.

➢ **Shear stress :** Forces acting along the faces of earth materials are shear stresses (separating forces).

➢ **Denudation :** All the exogenic geomorphic processes are covered under a general term, denudation. The word 'denude' means to strip off or to uncover. Weathering, mass wasting/movements, erosion and transportation are included in denudation.

➢ **Solution :** When something is dissolved in water or acids, the water or acid with dissolved contents is called solution.

➢ **Carbonation :** Carbonation is the reaction of carbonate and bicarbonate with minerals and is a common process helping the breaking down of feldspar and carbonate minerals.

➢ **Hydration :** Hydration is the chemical addition of water.

➢ **Oxidation :** Oxidation means combination of a mineral with oxygen to form oxides or hydroxides.

➢ **Enrichment :** When rocks undergo weathering, some materials are removed through chemical or physical leaching by groundwater and thereby the concentration of remaining (valuable) materials increases. Without such a weathering taking place, the concentration of the same valuable material may not be sufficient and economically viable to exploit, process and refine. This is what is called enrichment.

➢ **Reduction :** When oxidised minerals are placed in an environment where oxygen is absent, reduction takes place.

➢ **Tors :** In rocks like granites, smooth surfaced and rounded small to big boulders form due to exfoliation. It is called tors.

Multiple Choice Questions

(1 mark each)

Q. 1. Thermal expansion and pressure release lead to : [A]

(a) physical weathering
(b) hydration
(c) carbonation
(d) denudation

Ans. (a) physical weathering 1

Q. 2. The chemical addition of water is called as : [A]

(a) hydration
(b) dehydration
(c) reduction
(d) oxidation

Ans. (a) hydration 1

Very Short Answer Type Questions (1 mark each)

Q. 1. Define the term 'Stress'. A

Ans. Gravitational force acts upon all earth materials having a sloping surface and tend to produce movement of matter in downslope direction. Force applied per unit area is called stress. 1

Q. 2. Define the term 'Weathering'. A

Ans. Weathering is defined as mechanical disintegration and chemical decomposition of rocks through the actions of various elements of weather and climate. 1

Q. 3. What do you understand by the term 'shear stress'? A

Ans. Forces acting along the faces of earth materials are shear stresses (separating forces). 1

Q. 4. What do you understand by the term 'denudation'? U

Ans. All the exogenic geomorphic processes are covered under a general term, denudation. The word 'denude' means to strip off or to uncover. Weathering, mass wasting/movements, erosion and transportation are included in denudation. 1

Q. 5. Define the term 'Solution'. A

Ans. When something is dissolved in water or acids, the water or acid with dissolved contents is called solution. 1

Q. 6. Define the term 'Carbonation'. U

Ans. Carbonation is the reaction of carbonate and bicarbonate with minerals and is a common process helping the breaking down of feldspar and carbonate minerals. 1

Q. 7. What do you understand by the term 'Hydration'? A

Ans. Hydration is the chemical addition of water. 1

Q. 8. What do you understand by the term 'Oxidation'? A

Ans. Oxidation means combination of a mineral with oxygen to form oxides or hydroxides. 1

Q. 9. Where does oxidation occur?

Ans. Oxidation occurs where there is ready access to the atmosphere and oxygenated waters. 1

Q. 10. Define the term 'Reduction'. U

Ans. When oxidised minerals are placed in an environment where oxygen is absent, reduction takes place. 1

Q. 11. What do you understand by the term 'Enrichment'? A

Ans. When rocks undergo weathering, some materials are removed through chemical or physical leaching by groundwater and thereby the concentration of remaining (valuable) materials increases. Without such a weathering taking place, the concentration of the same valuable material may not be sufficient and economically viable to exploit, process and refine. This is what is called enrichment. 1

Q. 12. Name any two factors that condition the weathering process. A

Ans. Weathering processes are conditioned by many complex geological, climatic, topographic and vegetative factors, Climate is of particular importance. 1

Q. 13. Apart from the gravitational stress, the earth material becomes subjected to what kind of stress?

Ans. Besides the gravitational stress, earth materials become subjected to molecular stresses that may be caused by a number of factors amongst which temperature changes, crystallisation and melting are the most common. 1

Q. 14. How is stress produced in a solid? U

Ans. Stress is produced in a solid by pushing or pulling. 1

Q. 15. Weathering can take place in how many forms? A

Ans. Weathering can take place in physical, chemical and biological form. 1

Q. 16. Why do salts in rocks expand? U

Ans. Salts in rocks expand due to thermal action, hydration and crystallisation. 1

Q. 17. How does frost weathering occur? U

Ans. Frost weathering occurs due to the growth of ice within pores and cracks of rocks during repeated cycles of freezing and melting. 1

Commonly Made Error

- The students are not aware of the meaning of frost weathering.

Answering Tip

- Frost weathering is the collective name for several processes where ice is present. These processes include frost shattering, frost-wedging and freeze-thaw weathering.

Q. 18. How do weathering activities work? A

Ans. A group of weathering processes viz; solution, carbonation , hydration, oxidation and reduction acts on the rocks to decompose, dissolve or reduce them to a fine elastic state through chemical reactions by oxygen, surface and/or soil water and other acids. 1

Q. 19. Which is the most effective salt weathering processes?

Ans. Salt crystallisation is the most effective of all the salt weathering processes. 1

Commonly Made Error

- The students are not aware as to in which weather the salt weathering occurs.

Answering Tip

- Salt weathering is primarily a concern in marine areas where the presence of the ocean ensures a high level of salt in water vapor. Salt weathering also tends to happen in climates that are hot and dry.

Q. 20. Where does oxidation occur?

Ans. Oxidation occurs where there is ready access to the atmosphere and oxygenated waters. **1**

Q. 21. Name any two minerals which get affected by oxidation? [U]

Ans. Iron, manganese, sulphur, etc. **1**

Q. 22. Why is weathering of rocks important for the economy? [A]

Ans. Weathering of rocks is important for the economy because it helps in the enrichment and concentrations of certain valuable ores of iron, manganese, aluminium, copper, etc., which are of great importance for the national economy. **1**

Q. 23. What are tors? [U]

Ans. In rocks like granites, smooth surfaced and rounded small to big boulders form due to exfoliation. It is called tors. **1**

Q. 24. Name any two applied forces on which physical weathering depends? [A]

Ans. **(i)** Gravitational forces such as overburden pressure, load and shearing stress.

(ii) Expansion forces due to temperature changes, crystal growth or animal activity.

(iii) Water pressures controlled by wetting and drying cycles. **(Any two) (½ + ½ = 1)**

Short Answer Type Questions

(3 marks each)

Q. 1. Explain different types of physical weathering. [A]

Ans. Different types of physical weathering are :

(i) Exfoliation : Exfoliation can occur due to expansion and contraction induced by temperature changes. Exfoliation domes and tors result due to unloading and thermal expansion respectively. Due to differential heating and resulting expansion and contraction of surface layers and their subsequent exfoliation from the surfaces results in smooth rounded surfaces in rocks.

(ii) Frost : Frost is an active agent in cold climatic regions in high altitudes and the cracks are filled with water during the day time, this water is frozen at night when temperature falls below freezing point.

(iii) Pressure : Many igneous and metamorphic rocks crystallise deep in the interior under the combine influence of high pressure and temperature. The salt near surface pores cause splitting of the grains within the rocks which eventually falls off, this results into granules disintegration. **(1 × 3 = 3)**

Q. 2. Name the three applied forces on which the physical weathering depends? [U]

Ans. The applied forces could be :

(i) Gravitational forces such as overburden pressure, load and shearing stress.

(ii) Expansion forces due to temperature changes, crystal growth or animal activity.

(iii) Water pressures controlled by wetting and drying cycles. Many of these forces are applied both at the surface and within different earth materials leading to rock fracture. **(1 × 3 = 3)**

Q. 3. Explain the sole driving force behind all the exogenic processes. [A]

Ans. The energy derived from the sun i.e., the solar energy is the sole driving force behind all the exogenic processes.

(i) Various minerals in rocks possess their own limits of expansion and contraction.

(ii) With rise in temperature, every mineral expands and pushes against its neighbour and as temperature falls, a corresponding contraction takes place. Because of the diurnal changes in the cause splitting of individual grains within rocks, which eventually fall off. This process of falling off of individual grain may result in granular disintegration of granular foliation.

(iii) In areas with alternating wetting and frying conditions, salt crystal growth is favoured and the neighbouring grains are pushed aside. With salt crystal growth , chalk breaks down most readily, followed by limestone, sandstone, shale, gneiss and granite, etc. **(1 × 3 = 3)**

[AI] **Q. 4. What is the significance of weathering?** [U]

Ans. Significance of weathering :

(i) Weathering processes are responsible for breaking down the rocks into smaller fragments and preparing the way for formation of not only regolith and soils, but also erosion and mass movements.

(ii) Biomes and biodiversity is basically a result of forests (vegetation) and forests depend upon the depth of weathering mantles.

(iii) Weathering of rocks and deposits helps in the enrichment and concentrations of certain valuable ores of iron, manganese, aluminium, copper etc., which are of great importance for the national economy. Weathering is an important process in the formation of soils. **(1 × 3 = 3)**

Q. 5. Name the various types of physical weathering. [A]

Ans. The various types of physical weathering are :

(i) Unloading and Expansion : Removal of overlying rock load because of continued erosion causes vertical pressure release with the result that the upper layers of the rock expand producing disintegration of rock masses. Fractures will develop roughly parallel to the ground surface. In areas of curved ground surface, arched fractures tend to produce massive sheets or exfoliation slabs of rock. Exfoliation sheets resulting from expansion due to unloading and pressure release may measure hundreds or even thousands of metres in horizontal extent.

(ii) **Temperature Changes and Expansion :** Various minerals in rocks possess their own limits of expansion and contraction. With rise in temperature, every mineral expands and pushes against its neighbour and as temperature falls, a corresponding contraction takes place. Because of diurnal changes in the temperatures, this internal movement among the mineral grains of the superficial layers of rocks takes place regularly. This process is most effective in dry climates and high elevations where diurnal temperature changes are drastic.

(iii) **Freezing, Thawing and Frost Wedging :** Frost weathering occurs due to growth of ice within pores and cracks of rocks during repeated cycles of freezing and melting. This process is most effective at high elevations in mid-latitudes where freezing and melting is often repeated. Glacial areas are subject to frost wedging daily. In this process, the rate of freezing is important.

(iv) **Salt Weathering :** Salts in rocks expand due to thermal action, hydration and crystallisation. Many salts like calcium, sodium, magnesium, potassium and barium have a tendency to expand. Expansion of these salts depends on temperature and their thermal properties. High temperature ranges between 30 and 50°C of surface temperatures in deserts favour such salt expansion. **(Any three) 1 × 3 = 3**

Answering Tip

- Pressure, warm temperatures, water and ice cause physical weathering.

Q. 6. How does biological weathering take place? A

Ans. Biological weathering takes place in the following ways :

(i) **Animals :** Animals like rats, rabbits, etc., make burrows and holes in the rocks. They consume large quantity of soils and rocks for making their habitat and destruction of food. This loosens the rock strata and disintegration occurs.

(ii) **Vegetation :** Long roots of plants work down into cracks of rocks. The roots of shrubs and trees reach deep into them and this lodge large blocks.

(iii) **Human activities :** Mining, deforestation, indiscriminate cultivation of land and construction activities contribute to the biological weathering. **(1 × 3 = 3)**

Answering Tip

- Biological weathering is the weakening and subsequent disintegration of rock by plants, animals and microbes.

Long Answer Type Questions

(5 marks each)

AI **Q.1. Name the various types of chemical weathering processes.**

Ans. The various types of chemical weathering processes are :

(i) **Solution :** When something is dissolved in water or acids, the water or acid with dissolved contents is called solution. This process involves removal of solids in solution and depends upon solubility of a mineral in water or weak acids. On coming in contact with water many solids disintegrate and mix up as suspension in water. Soluble rock forming minerals like nitrates, sulphates, and potassium etc. are affected by this process.

(ii) **Carbonation :** Carbonation is the reaction of carbonate and bicarbonate with minerals and is a common process helping the breaking down of feldspars and carbonate minerals. Carbon dioxide from the atmosphere and soil air is absorbed by water, to form carbonic acid that acts as a weak acid.

(iii) **Hydration :** Hydration is the chemical addition of water. Minerals take up water and expand; this expansion causes an increase in the volume of the material itself or rock. Calcium sulphate takes in water and turns to gypsum, which is more unstable than calcium sulphate. This process is reversible and long, continued repetition of this process causes fatigue in the rocks and may lead to their disintegration.

(iv) **Oxidation :** In weathering, oxidation means a combination of a mineral with oxygen to form oxides or hydroxides. Oxidation occurs where there is ready access to the atmosphere and oxygenated waters. The minerals most commonly involved in this process are iron, manganese, sulphur, etc. In the process of oxidation rock breakdown occurs due to the disturbance caused by addition of oxygen. Red colour of iron upon oxidation turns to brown or yellow.

(v) **Reduction :** When oxidised minerals are placed in an environment where oxygen is absent, reduction takes place. Such conditions exist usually below the water table, in areas of stagnant water and waterlogged ground. Red colour of iron upon reduction turns to greenish or bluish grey. **(1 × 5 = 5)**

Q. 2. Differentiate between physical weathering and chemical weathering. [A]

Ans.

S.No.	Physical weathering	Chemical weathering
1.	Physical forces disintegrates the rocks.	Rocks are decomposed by chemical changes.
2.	In this kind of weathering no physical changes occur.	In this kind of weathering chemical changes occur due to air and water.
3.	This type of weathering is more effective in dry and cold areas.	This type of weathering is more effective in hot and humid areas.
4.	The various agents are : insulation, frost and pressure.	The various agents are: oxidation, reduction, carbonation, hydration and soil.
5.	In this type of weathering, the rocks are affected at the greater depth.	In this type of weathering, the rocks are affected at the surface only.

(1 × 5 = 5)

TOPIC-3
Mass Movements

Revision Notes

- Mass movements transfer the mass of rock debris down the slopes under the direct influence of gravity. That means, air, water or ice do not carry debris with them from place to place but on the other hand the debris may carry with it air, water or ice.
- The movements of mass may range from slow to rapid, affecting shallow to deep columns of materials and include creep, flow, slide and fall.
- Mass movements are aided by gravity and no geomorphic agent like running water, glaciers, wind, waves and currents participate in the process of mass movement.
- Weak unconsolidated materials, thinly bedded rocks, faults, steeply dipping beds, vertical cliffs or steep slopes, abundant precipitation and torrential rains and scarcity of vegetation etc., favour mass movements.
- Several activating causes precede mass movements. They are :
  - Removal of support from below to materials above through natural or artificial means
  - Increase in gradient and height of slopes
  - Overloading through addition of materials naturally or by artificial filling
  - Overloading due to heavy rainfall, saturation and lubrication of slope materials
  - Removal of material or load from over the original slope surfaces
  - Occurrence of earthquakes, explosions or machinery
  - Excessive natural seepage
  - Heavy drawdown of water from lakes, reservoirs and rivers leading to slow outflow of water from under the slopes or river banks
  - Indiscriminate removal of natural vegetation.
- Mass movements can be grouped under three major classes :
  - Slow movements
  - Rapid movements
  - Landslides
  - **Slow Movements :** Creep is one type under this category which can occur on moderately steep, soil covered slopes. Movement of materials is extremely slow and imperceptible except through extended observation. Materials involved also included in this group is solifluction which involves slow downslope flowing soil mass or fine grained rock debris saturated or lubricated with water. This process is quite common in moist temperate areas where surface melting of deeply frozen ground and long continued rain respectively, occur frequently can be soil or rock debris.
  - **Rapid Movements :** These movements are mostly prevalent in humid climatic regions and occur over gentle to steep slopes. Movement of water-saturated clayey or silty earth materials down low-angle terraces or hillsides is known as earthflow.

    Another type in this category is mudflow. In the absence of vegetation cover and with heavy rainfall, thick layers of weathered materials get saturated with water and either slowly or rapidly flow down along definite channels.

A third type is the debris avalanche, which is more characteristic of humid regions with or without vegetation cover and occurs in narrow tracks on steep slopes. This debris avalanche can be much faster than the mudflow. Debris avalanche is similar to snow avalanche.

- **Landslides :** These are known as relatively rapid and perceptible movements. Slump is slipping of one or several units of rock debris with a backward rotation with respect to the slope over which the movement takes place. Rapid rolling or sliding of earth debris without backward rotation of mass is known as debris slide. Sliding of individual rock masses down bedding, joint or fault surfaces is rockslide.

- Erosion involves acquisition and transportation of rock debris. When massive rocks break into smaller fragments through weathering and any other process, erosional geomorphic agents like running water, groundwater, glaciers, wind and waves remove and transport it to other places depending upon the dynamics of each of these agents.
- It is erosion that is largely responsible for continuous changes that the earth's surface is undergoing.
- The erosion and transportation of earth materials is brought about by wind, running water, glaciers, waves and groundwater.
- The erosion can be defined as "application of the kinetic energy associated with the agent to the surface of the land along which it moves".
- The work of the other two agents of erosion waves and groundwater is not controlled by climate.
- Deposition is a consequence of erosion. The erosional agents lose their velocity and hence energy on gentler slopes and the materials carried by them start to settle themselves.

Know the Terms

- **Solifluction :** Solifluction can defined as the gradual mass movement of wet soil or other material down a slope affected by alternate freezing and thawing.
- **Earthflow :** Movement of water-saturated clayey or silty earth materials down low-angle terraces or hillsides is known as earthflow.
- **Mudflow :** In the absence of vegetation cover and with heavy rainfall, thick layers of weathered materials get saturated with water and either slowly or rapidly flow down along definite channels.
- **Rockslide :** Sliding of individual rock masses down bedding, joint or fault surfaces is rockslide.
- **Slump :** Slump is slipping of one or several units of rock debris with a backward rotation with respect to the slope over which the movement takes place.

Multiple Choice Questions (1 mark each)

Q. 1. Mass movements are aided by: A

(a) gravity (b) water

(c) air (d) pressure

Ans. (a) gravity 1

Q. 2. The application of the kinetic energy associated with the agent to the surface of the land along which it moves is termed as: U

(a) deposition

(b) erosion

(c) solifluction

(d) slump

Ans. (b) erosion 1

AI **Q. 3. The consequence of erosion is :** U

(a) rockslide

(b) sliding

(c) deposition

(d) landslide

Ans. (c) deposition 1

Very Short Answer Type Questions (1 mark each)

Q. 1. Define the term 'Solifluction'. A

Ans. Solifluction can defined as the gradual mass movement of wet soil or other material down a slope affected by alternate freezing and thawing. 1

Answering Tip

- Solifluction is the name for the slow downhill flow of soil in arctic regions.

Q. 2. Define the term 'Earthflow'. U

Ans. Movement of water-saturated clayey or silty earth materials down low-angle terraces or hillsides is known as earthflow. 1

Q. 3. Define the term 'Mudflow'? A

Ans. In the absence of vegetation cover and with heavy rainfall, thick layers of weathered materials get saturated with water and either slowly or rapidly flow down along definite channels. It looks like a stream of mud within a valley. This is known as mudflow. 1

Q. 4. Define the term 'Rockslide'.

Ans. Sliding of individual rock masses down bedding, joint or fault surfaces is rockslide. 1

Answering Tip

- Erosion and earthquakes cause rockslide.

Q. 5. Define the term 'slump'?

Ans. Slump is slipping of one or several units of rock debris with a backward rotation with respect to the slope over which the movement takes place. 1

Q. 6. Define the term 'Debris slide'? [A]

Ans. Rapid rolling or sliding of earth debris without backward rotation of mass is known as debris slide. 1

Q. 7. Define the term 'Erosion'?

Ans. Erosion can be defined as application of the kinetic energy associated with the agent to the surface of the land along which it moves. 1

Q. 8. What is deposition? [A]

Ans. Deposition is a consequence of erosion. It is not actually the work of any agent . 1

Q. 9. Mass movement can be grouped into how many classes?

Ans. It can be grouped into three classes:

(i) Slow movement

(ii) Rapid movement

(iii) Landslides 1

Q. 10. Name any two factors that help in mass movement.

Ans. Weak unconsolidated materials, thinly bedded rocks, faults, steeply dipping beds, vertical cliffs or steep slopes, abundant precipitation and torrential rains and scarcity of vegetation, etc., help in mass movement. **(Any two) 1**

Short Answer Type Questions **(3 marks each)**

Q. 1. What are the different types of mass movements. [U]

Ans. The different types of mass movements are:

(i) Slow Movements : Creep is one type under this category which can occur on moderately steep soil covered slopes. Movement of materials is extremely slow and imperceptible except through extended observation. Materials involved can be soil or rock debris. Depending upon the type of material involved, several types of creep viz., soil creep, talus creep, rock creep, rock-glacier creep, etc., can be identified.

(ii) Rapid Movements : These movements are mostly prevalent in humid climatic regions and occur over gentle to steep slopes. Movement of water-saturated clayey or silty earth materials down low-angle terraces or hillsides is known as earthflow. Quite often the materials slump making steplike terraces and leaving arcuate scarps at their heads and an accumulation bulge at the toe. When slopes are steeper, even the bedrock especially of soft sedimentary rocks like shale or deeply weathered igneous rock may slide downslope.

(iii) Landslides : These are known as relatively rapid and perceptible movements. The materials involved are relatively dry. The size and shape of the detached mass depends on the nature of discontinuities in the rock, the degree of weathering and the steepness of the slope.

Landslides are of four types:

(i) Slumps : The slipping of one or several units of rock debris with a backward rotation with respect to the slope over which the movement takes place.

(ii) Debris slide : It is the rapid rolling or sliding of Earth debris without backward rotation of mass.

(iii) Rockslide : Sliding of individual rock masses down bedding, joint or fault surface is known as rockslide.

(iv) Rock fall : It is the free falling of rock blocks over any steep slope keeping itself away from the slope. **(1 × 3 = 3)**

Commonly Made Error

- The students do not know on what categories the mass movements are classified.

Answering Tip

- The mass movements classifications are based on how quickly the rock and sediment move and how much water there is.

Q. 1. "All corners of the earth do not have same slope." Justify. [A]

Ans. The differences in the internal forces operating from within the earth which built up the crust have been responsible for the variations in the outer surface of the crust.

The earth's surface is being continuously subjected to external forces induced basically by energy (sunlight). Of course, the internal forces are still active though with different intensities. Due to variations in the geothermal gradients and the strength, the actions of endogenic forces are not uniform and hence the tectonically controlled original crystal surface is uneven. 3

Q. 2. Is it true that slopes or gradients are created by tectonic forces? If yes then argue. [U]

Ans. Yes, it is true that slopes and gradients are created by tectonic forces. Those areas where there is excessive magma formation, have higher slopes and they have emerged as mountains. The strength of gradients also determine the types of landforms. 3

Long Answer Type Question

(5 marks)

Q. 1. Write a note on erosion and deposition. R

Ans. Erosion involves acquisition and transportation of rock debris. When massive rocks break into smaller fragments through weathering and any other process, erosional geomorphic agents like running water, groundwater, glaciers, wind and waves remove and transport it to other places depending upon the dynamics of each of these agents. Abrasion by rock debris carried by these geomorphic agents also aids greatly in erosion.

By erosion, relief degrades, i.e., the landscape is worn down. That means, though weathering aids erosion it is not a pre-condition for erosion to take place. Weathering, mass-wasting and erosion are degradational processes. It is erosion that is largely responsible for continuous changes that the earth's surface is undergoing.

The work of the other two agents of erosion-waves and groundwater is not controlled by climate. In case of waves it is the location along the interface of lithosphere and hydrosphere — coastal region — that will determine the work of waves, whereas the work of groundwater is determined more by the lithological character of the region. If the rocks are permeable and soluble and water is available only then karst topography develops.

Deposition is a consequence of erosion. The erosional agents loose their velocity and hence energy on gentler slopes and the materials carried by them start to settle themselves.

In other words, deposition is not actually the work of any agent. The coarser materials get deposited first and finer ones later. By deposition depressions get filled up. The same erosional agents viz., running water, glaciers, wind, waves and groundwater act as aggradational or depositional agents also. 5

TOPIC-4
Soil Formation

Revision Notes

- A pedologist who studies soils, defines soil as a collection of natural bodies on the earth's surface containing living matter and supporting or capable of supporting plants.
- Soil is a dynamic medium in which many chemical, physical and biological activities go on constantly. Soil is a result of decay, it is also the medium for growth.
- It is a changing and developing body. It has many characteristics that fluctuate with the seasons. It may be alternatively cold and warm or dry and moist.
- The soil chemistry, the amount of organic matter, the soil flora and fauna, the temperature and the moisture, all change with the seasons as well as with more extended periods of time.
- Soil formation or pedogenesis depends first on weathering. First, the weathered material or transported deposits are colonised by bacteria and other inferior plant bodies like mosses and lichens. Also, several minor organisms may take shelter within the mantle and deposits. The dead remains of organisms and plants help in humus accumulation.
- Five basic factors control the formation of soils :
  - **Parent material :** Parent material is a passive control factor in soil formation. Parent materials can be any insitu or on-site weathered rock debris (residual soils) or transported deposits (transported soils).

    Nature and rate of weathering and depth of weathering mantle are important consideration under parent materials. Also, in case of some limestone areas, where the weathering processes are specific and peculiar, soils will show clear relation with the parent rock.
  - **Topography :** Topography like parent materials is another passive control factor. The influence of topography is felt through the amount of exposure of a surface covered by parent materials to sunlight and the amount of surface and sub-surface drainage over and through the parent materials.
  - **Climate :** Climate is an important active factor in soil formation. The climatic elements involved in soil development are : **(i)** moisture in terms of its intensity, frequency and duration of precipitation — evaporation and humidity; **(ii)** temperature in terms of seasonal and diurnal variations. Precipitation gives soil its moisture content which makes the chemical and biological activities possible. Excess of water helps in the downward transportation of soil components through the soil (eluviation) and deposits the same down below (illuviation).

In climates like wet equatorial rainy areas with high rainfall, not only calcium, sodium, magnesium, potassium etc., but also a major part of silica is removed from the soil. Removal of silica from the soil is known as desilication.

- **Biological activity :** The vegetative cover and organisms that occupy the parent materials from the beginning and also at later stages help in adding organic matter, moisture retention, nitrogen, etc. Dead plants provide humus, the finely divided organic matter of the soil. Some organic acids which form during humification aid in decomposing the minerals of the soil parent materials. The influence of large animals like ants, termites, earthworms, rodents, etc., is mechanical, but, it is nevertheless important in soil formation as they rework the soil up and down.
- **Time :** Time is the third important controlling factor in soil formation. The length of time the soil forming processes operate, determines maturation of soils and profile development. A soil becomes mature when all soil-forming processes act for a sufficiently long time developing a profile.

Know the Terms

- **Soil :** Soil can be defined as a collection of natural bodies on the earth's surface containing living and non-living organisms.
- **Desilication:** Removal of silica from the soil is termed as desilication.
- **Hardpans :** In dry climates, because of high temperature, evaporation exceeds precipitation and hence ground-water is brought up to the surface by capillary action and in the process the water evaporates leaving behind salts in the soil. Such salts form into a crust in the soil known as hardpans.
- **Precipitation :** It can defined as ran, snow, sleet or hail—any kind of weather condition where something's falling from the sky.

Multiple Choice Question (1 mark)

Q. 1. Soil formation or pedogenesis depends first on: [A]

(a) weathering
(b) erosion
(c) deposition
(d) desilication

Ans. (a) weathering 1

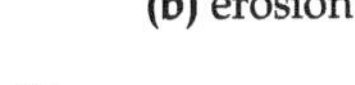

Very Short Answer Type Questions (1 mark each)

Q. 1. Define the term 'Soil'. [A]

Ans. Soil can be defined as a collection of natural bodies on the earth's surface containing living and non-living organisms. Soil is a dynamic medium in which many chemical, physical and biological activities go on constantly. Soil is a result of decay, it is also the medium for growth. It is a changing and developing body. 1

Q. 2. Define the term 'Pedology'. [U]

Ans. Pedology is the study of soil. It is a branch of science. 1

Q. 3. Who is a pedologist? [A]

Ans. A pedologist is a soil scientist. 1

Q. 4. What do you understand by the word pedogenesis. [U]

Ans. Pedogenesis is the process of soil formation. 1

Q. 5. What is desilication? [A]

Ans. Removal of silica from the soil is termed as desilication. 1

Commonly Made Error

- The students are not aware as to what leads to desilication.

Answering Tip

- Intense weathering and leaching leads to desilication.

Q. 6. What are hardpans? [U]

Ans. In dry climates, because of high temperature, evaporation exceeds precipitation and hence groundwater is brought up to the surface by capillary action and in the process the water evaporates leaving behind salts in the soil. Such salts form into a crust in the soil known as hardpans. 1

Q. 7. Name the climatic elements involved in soil formation. [R]

OR

Name any two climatic factors involved in the formation of soil.

Ans. The climatic elements involved in soil development are :

(i) Moisture in terms of its intensity, frequency and duration of precipitation—evaporation and humidity.

(ii) Temperature in terms of seasonal and diurnal variations. 1

Q. 8. In what type of topography soil formation is very favourable? [A]

Ans. Over gentle slopes where erosion is slow and percolation of water is good, soil formation is very favourable. 1

Q. 9. How is precipitation useful for soil? U

Ans. Precipitation gives soil its moisture content which makes the chemical and biological activities possible. 1

Q. 10. How is time a passive role player in the soil formation. U

Ans. Time is passive controlling factor in soil formation. The length of time the soil formatting processes operate determines maturation of soils and profile development. 1

Q. 11. How is parent material a passive factor in the soil formation? A

Ans. It is a passive factor as parent material can be moved or transported debris. Soil formation depends upon the texture, structure as well as mineral and chemical composition of the rock debris/deposits. 1

Q. 12. How does temperature help in soil formation? A

Ans. Temperature acts in two ways in soil formation — increasing or reducing chemical and biological activity. 1

Answering Tip

- Rock starts becoming soil the moment it is exposed to the environment.

Q. 13. When is the soil considered mature? R

Ans. A soil becomes mature when all soil-forming processes act for a sufficiently long time developing a profile. 1

Short Answer Type Questions (3 marks)

AI **Q. 1. Explain the process of soil formation.** A

Ans. Soil formation or pedogenesis depends first on weathering. It is the weathering mantle which is the basic input for soil to form.

(i) First, the weathered material or transported deposits are colonised by bacteria and other inferior plant bodies like mosses and lichens .

(ii) Also, several minor organisms may take shelter within the mantle and deposits. The dead remains of organisms and plants help in humus accumulation. Minor grasses and ferns may grow; later, bushes and trees will start growing through seeds brought in by birds and wind.

(iii) Plant roots penetrate down, burrowing animals bring up particles, mass of material becomes porous and spongelike with a capacity to retain water and to permit the passage of air and finally a mature soil, a complex mixture of mineral and organic products forms. **(1 × 3 = 3)**

Answering Tip

- Soils form from the interplay of five main factors namely: Parent material, time, climate, relief and organisms.

Long Answer Type Questions (5 marks)

Q. 1. Explain in detail the five basic factors that control the formation of soils. A

Ans. The five factors that control the formation of soils are :

(i) Parent Material : Parent material is a passive control factor in soil formation. Parent materials can be any in situ or on-site weathered rock debris (residual soils) or transported deposits (transported soils). Soil formation depends upon the texture (sizes of debris) and structure (disposition of individual grains/particles of debris) as well as the mineral and chemical composition of the rock debris/deposits . Nature and rate of weathering and depth of weathering mantle are important consideration under parent material.

(ii) Topography : Topography like parent materials is another passive control factor. The influence of topography is felt through the amount of exposure of a surface covered by parent materials to sunlight and the amount of surface and sub-surface drainage over and through the parent materials. Soils will be thin on steep slopes and thick over flat upland areas. Over gentle slopes where erosion is slow and percolation of water is good, soil formation is very favourable.

(iii) Climate : Climate is an important active factor in soil formation. The climatic elements involved in soil development are : **(i)** moisture in terms of its intensity, frequency and duration of precipitation—evaporation and humidity; **(ii)** temperature in terms of seasonal and diurnal variations. Precipitation gives soil its moisture content which makes the chemical and biological activities possible. Excess of water helps in the downward transportation of soil components through the soil (eluviation) and deposits the same down below (illuviation).

Temperature acts in two ways — increasing or reducing chemical and biological activity. Chemical activity is increased in higher temperatures, reduced in cooler temperatures (with an exception of carbonation) and stops in freezing conditions. That is why, tropical soils with higher temperatures show deeper profiles and in the frozen tundra regions soils contain largely mechanically broken materials.

(iv) Biological Activity : The vegetative cover and organisms that occupy the parent materials from the beginning and also at later stages help in adding organic matter, moisture retention, nitrogen, etc. Dead plants provide humus, the finely divided organic matter of the soil. Some organic acids which form during humification aid in decomposing the minerals of the soil parent materials.

In humid tropical and equatorial climates, bacterial growth and action is intense and dead vegetation is rapidly oxidised leaving very low humus content in the soil. Further, bacteria and other soil organisms take gaseous nitrogen from the air and convert it into a chemical form that can be used by plants. This process is known as nitrogen fixation.

(v) Time : Time is the third important controlling factor in soil formation. The length of time the soil forming processes operate, determines maturation of soils and profile development. A soil becomes mature when all soil-forming processes act for a sufficiently long time developing a profile. Soils developing from recently deposited alluvium or glacial till are considered young and they exhibit no horizons or only poorly developed horizons.

(1 × 5 = 5)

NCERT CORNER

(A) Multiple choice questions :

Q. 1. Which one of the following processes is a gradational process : [A]

(a) Deposition
(b) Diastrophism
(c) Volcanism
(d) Erosion

Ans. (d) Erosion .

Q. 2. Which one of the following materials is affected by hydration process : [A]

(a) Granite
(b) Clay
(c) Quartz
(d) Salts

Ans. (d) Salts.

Q. 3. Debris avalanche can be included in the category of : [U]

(a) Landslides
(b) Slow flow mass movements
(c) Rapid flow mass movements
(d) Subsidence

Ans. (c) Rapid flow mass movements.

(B) Answer the following questions in about 30 words :

Q. 1. It is weathering that is responsible for bio-diversity on the earth. How? [U]

Ans. Weathering is responsible for biodiversity on the earth as weathering processes are responsible for breaking down the rocks into smaller fragments and preparing the way for formation of not only regolith and soils, but also erosion and mass movements. Biomes and biodiversity is basically a result of forests (vegetation) and forests depend upon the depth of weathering mantles. Erosion cannot be significant if the rocks are not weathered. That means, weathering aids mass wasting, erosion and reduction of relief and changes in landforms are a consequence of erosion.

Q. 2. What are mass movements that are real rapid and perceptible? List. [R]

Ans. These movements transfer the mass of rock debris down the slopes under the direct influence of gravity. That means, air, water or ice do not carry debris with them from place to place but on the other hand the debris may carry with it air, water or ice. The movements of mass may range from slow to rapid, affecting shallow to deep columns of materials and include creep, flow, slide and fall.

Mass movements can be grouped under three major classes :

(i) Slow movements;
(ii) Rapid movements;
(iii) Landslides.

Q. 3. What are the various mobile and mighty exogenic geomorphic agents and what is the prime job they perform? [R]

Ans. All the exogenic geomorphic processes are covered under a general term, denudation. The word 'denude' means to strip off or to uncover. Weathering, mass wasting/movements, erosion and transportation are included in denudation. As there are different climatic regions on the earth's surface owing to thermal gradients created by latitudinal, seasonal and land and water spread variations, the exogenic geomorphic processes vary from region to region. The density, type and distribution of vegetation which largely depend upon precipitation and temperature exert influence indirectly on exogenic geomorphic processes.

Q. 4. Is weathering essential as a pre-requisite in the formation of soils? Why? [A]

Ans. Yes, weathering is an essential pre-requisite in the formation of soils as it is an action of elements of weather and climate over earth material. Weathering is the mechanical disintegration and chemical decomposition of rocks through the actions of various elements of weather and climate. Weathering processes are responsible for breaking down the rocks into smaller fragments and preparing the way for formation of regolith and soils.

Weathering is an important process in the formation of soils. It is when the rocks undergo weathering , rocks start to break up and take form of soil gradually.

(C) Answer the following questions in about 150 words :

Q. 1. "Our earth is a playfield for two opposing groups of geomorphic processes." Discuss. U

Ans. The statement holds correct as the earth is a playground of two forces : exogenic and endogenic forces. Exogenic forces are the external forces and the endogenic forces are the internal forces.

The differences in the internal forces operating from within the earth which built up the crust have been responsible for the variations in the outer surface of the crust. The Earth's surface is being continuously subjected to external forces induced basically by energy (sunlight). Of course, the internal forces are still active though with different intensities.

That means, the earth's surface is being continuously subjected to by external forces originating within the earth's atmosphere and by internal forces from within the earth.

The actions of exogenic forces result in wearing down (degradation) of relief/elevations and filling up (aggradation) of basins/depressions, on the earth's surface.

The endogenic forces continuously elevate or build up parts of the earth's surface and hence the exogenic processes fail to even out the relief variations of the surface of the earth. So, variations remain as long as the opposing actions of exogenic and endogenic forces continue. In general terms, the endogenic forces are mainly land building forces and the exogenic processes are mainly land wearing forces.

Q. 2. Exogenic geomorphic processes derive their ultimate energy from the sun's heat. Explain? U

Ans. The exogenic processes derive their energy from atmosphere determined by the ultimate energy from the sun and also the gradients created by tectonic factors.

Various minerals in rocks possess their own limits of expansion and contraction. With rise in temperature, every mineral expands and pushes against its neighbour and as temperature falls, a corresponding contraction takes place.

Because of diurnal changes in temperatures, this internal movement among the mineral grains of the superficial layers of rocks takes place regularly. This process is most effective in dry climates and high elevations where diurnal temperature changes are drastic.

High temperature ranges between 30 and 50°C of surface temperatures in deserts favour such salt expansion. Salt crystals in near-surface pores cause splitting of individual grains within rocks, which eventually fall off. This process of falling off of individual grains may result in granular disintegration or granular foliation.

Sodium chloride and gypsum crystals in desert areas heave up overlying layers of materials and with the result polygonal cracks develop all over the heaved surface. With salt crystal growth, chalk breaks down most readily, followed by limestone, sandstone, shale, gneiss and granite.

Q. 3. Are physical and chemical weathering processes independent of each other? If not, why? Explain with examples? A

Ans. No, physical and chemical weathering processes are not independent of each other. They are very much different but still interdependent in some way. The physical or mechanical weathering processes depend on some applied forces. The applied forces could be: **(i)** gravitational forces such as overburden pressure, load and shearing stress; **(ii)** expansion forces due to temperature changes, crystal growth or animal activity; **(iii)** water pressures controlled by wetting and drying cycles.

Chemical weathering depends on a groups of weathering processes viz; solution, carbonation, hydration, oxidation and reduction act on the rocks to decompose, dissolve or reduce them to a fine clastic state through chemical reactions by oxygen, surface and/or soil water and other acids. Water and air (oxygen and carbon dioxide) along with heat must be present to speed up all chemical reactions. Over and above the carbon dioxide present in the air, decomposition of plants and animals increases the quantity of carbon dioxide underground. These chemical reactions on various minerals are very much similar to the chemical reactions in a laboratory.

Q. 4. How do you distinguish between the process of soil formation and soil forming factors? What is the role of climate and biological activity as two important control factors in the formation of soils? U

Ans. The process of soil formation refers to the step by step procedure that explains the way in which soil comes into existence. Whereas, soil forming factors are those factors which cause the formation of the soil.

The process of soil formation is also known as pedogenesis. Soil formation or pedogenesis depends first on weathering. The weathered material or transported deposits are colonised by bacteria and other inferior plant bodies like mosses and lichens. Also, several minor organisms may take shelter within the mantle and deposits.

The dead remains of organisms and plants help in humus accumulation. Minor grasses and ferns may grow; later, bushes and trees will start growing through seeds brought in by birds and wind. Plant roots penetrate down, burrowing animals bring up particles, mass of material becomes porous and spongelike with a capacity to retain water and to permit the passage of air and finally a mature soil, a complex mixture of mineral and organic products forms.

The soil-forming factors are:

(i) Parent material : Parent material is a passive control factor in soil formation. Parent materials can be any in situ or on-site weathered rock debris (residual soils) or transported deposits (transported soils). Soil formation depends upon the texture (sizes of debris) and structure (disposition of individual grains/particles of debris) as well as the mineral and chemical composition of the rock debris/deposits.

(ii) Topography : Topography like parent materials is another passive control factor. The influence of topography is felt through the amount of exposure of a surface covered by parent materials to sunlight and the amount of surface and sub-surface drainage over and through the parent materials. Soils will be thin on steep slopes and thick over flat upland areas. Over gentle slopes where erosion is slow and percolation of water is good, soil formation is very favourable.

(iii) Climate : Climate is an important active factor in soil formation. The climatic elements involved in soil development are :

(a) Moisture in terms of its intensity, frequency and duration of precipitation — evaporation and humidity.

(b) Temperature in terms of seasonal and diurnal variations.

In climates like wet equatorial rainy areas with high rainfall, not only calcium, sodium, magnesium, potassium, etc., but also a major part of silica is removed from the soil.

In dry climates, because of high temperature, evaporation exceeds precipitation and hence groundwater is brought up to the surface by capillary action and in the process the water evaporates leaving behind salts in the soil.

(iv) Biological activity : The vegetative cover and organisms that occupy the parent materials from the beginning and also at later stages help in adding organic matter, moisture retention, nitrogen, etc. Dead plants provide humus, the finely divided organic matter of the soil. Some organic acids which form during humification aid in decomposing the minerals of the soil parent materials. In humid tropical and equatorial climates, bacterial growth and action is intense and dead vegetation is rapidly oxidised leaving very low humus content in the soil.

The influence of large animals like ants, termites, earthworms, rodents, etc., is mechanical, but, it is nevertheless important in soil formation as they rework the soil up and down. In case of earthworms, as they feed on soil, the texture and chemistry of the soil that comes out of their body changes.

(v) Time : The length of time the soil forming processes operate is also an important factor. A soil becomes mature when all soil-forming processes act for a sufficiently long time developing a profile. Soils developing from recently deposited alluvium or glacial till are considered young and they exhibit no horizons or only poorly developed horizons. No specific length of time in absolute terms can be fixed for soils to develop and mature.

OSWAAL LEARNING TOOLS

For Suggested Online Videos

Visit : *https://qrgo.page.link/f2LRR* **Or Scan the Code**

To learn from NCERT Prescribed Videos

Visit : *https://qrgo.page.link/1bKSV* **Or Scan the Code**

❑❑

CHAPTER 7

LANDFORMS AND THEIR EVOLUTION

Syllabus

> *Running Water, Erosional Landforms, Depositional Landforms*
> *Groundwater, Erosional Landforms, Depositional Landforms*
> *Glaciers, Erosional Landforms, Depositional Landforms, Waves and Currents, Erosional Landforms, Depositional Landforms*
> *Winds, Erosional Landforms, Depositional Landforms.*

TOPIC-1
Running Water, Erosional Landforms, Depositional Landforms

Revision Notes

- After weathering processes have had their actions on the earth materials making up the surface of the earth, the geomorphic agents like running water, groundwater, wind, glaciers, waves perform erosion.
- What is a landform? In simple words, small to medium tracts or parcels of the earth's surface are called landforms.
- Several related landforms together make up landscapes, (large tracts of earth's surface). Each landform has its own physical shape, size, materials and is a result of the action of certain geomorphic processes and agent(s).
- Actions of most of the geomorphic processes and agents are slow, and hence the results take a long time to take shape. Every landform has a beginning. Landforms once formed may change in their shape, size and nature slowly or fast due to continued action of geomorphic processes and agents. A landmass passes through stages of development somewhat comparable to the stages of life — youth, mature and old age.
- Geomorphology deals with the reconstruction of the history of the surface of the earth through a study of its forms, the materials of which it is made up of and the processes that shape it.
- In humid regions, which receive heavy rainfall running water is considered the most important of the geomorphic agents in bringing about the degradation of the land surface.
- There are two components of running water. One is overland flow on general land surface as a sheet. Another is linear flow as streams and rivers in the valleys.
- With time, stream channels over steep gradients turn gentler due to continued erosion, and as a consequence, lose their velocity, facilitating active deposition.
- When the stream beds turn gentler due to continued erosion, downward cutting becomes less dominant and lateral erosion of banks increases and as a consequence the hills and valleys are reduced to plains.
- Overland flow causes sheet erosion. Depending upon irregularities of the land surface, the overland flow may concentrate into narrow to wide paths.
- In the early stages, Streams are few during this stage with poor integration and flow over original slopes showing shallow V-shaped valleys with no floodplains or with very narrow floodplains along trunk streams. Waterfalls and rapids may exist where local hard rock bodies are exposed.

- During the middle stage streams are plenty with good integration. The valleys are still V-shaped but deep; trunk streams are broad enough to have wider floodplains within which streams may flow in meanders confined within the valley. Waterfalls and rapids disappear.
- Smaller tributaries during old age are few with gentle gradients. Streams meander freely over vast floodplains showing natural levees, ox-bow lakes, etc. Most of the landscape is at or slightly above sea level.
- **Erosional Landforms :**
  - **Valleys :** They start as small and narrow rills; the rills will gradually develop into long and wide gullies; the gullies will further deepen, widen and lengthen to give rise to valleys. Depending upon dimensions and shape, many types of valleys like V-shaped valley, gorge, canyon, etc., can be recognised. A gorge is almost equal in width at its top as well as its bottom. Valley types depend upon the type and structure of rocks in which they form.
  - **Potholes and Plunge Pools :** Over the rocky beds of hill-streams more or less circular depressions called potholes form because of stream erosion aided by the abrasion of rock fragments. Once a small and shallow depression forms, pebbles and boulders get collected in those depressions and get rotated by flowing water and consequently the depressions grow in dimensions. A series of such depressions eventually join and the stream valley gets deepened.
  - **Incised or Entrenched Meanders :** In streams that flow rapidly over steep gradients, normally erosion is concentrated on the bottom of the stream channel. Also, in the case of steep gradient streams, lateral erosion on the sides of the valleys is not much when compared to the streams flowing on low and gentle slopes. Because of active lateral erosion, streams flowing over gentle slopes, develop sinuous or meandering courses.
  - **River terraces :** They are surfaces marking old valley floor or floodplain levels. They may be bedrock surfaces without any alluvial cover or alluvial terraces consisting of stream deposits. River terraces are basically products of erosion as they result due to vertical erosion by the stream into its own depositional floodplain.
- **Depositional Landforms :**
  - **Alluvial fans :** They are formed when streams flowing from higher levels break into foot slope plains of low gradient. Normally very coarse load is carried by streams flowing over mountain slopes. This load becomes too heavy for the streams to be carried over gentler gradients and gets dumped and spread as a broad low to high cone shaped deposit called alluvial fan.
  - **Deltas :** Deltas are like alluvial fans but develop at a different location. The load carried by the rivers is dumped and spread into the sea. If this load is not carried away far into the sea or distributed along the coast, it spreads and accumulates as a low cone. Unlike in alluvial fans, the deposits making up deltas are very well sorted with clear stratification. As the delta grows, the river distributaries continue to increase in length and delta continues to build up into the sea.
  - **Floodplains, Natural Levees and Point Bars :** Deposition develops a floodplain just as erosion makes valleys. Floodplain is a major landform of river deposition. The floodplain above the bank is inactive floodplain. Inactive floodplain above the banks basically contain two types of deposits — flood deposits and channel deposits. Natural levees are found along the banks of large rivers . The levee deposits are coarser than the deposits spread by flood waters away from the river. When rivers shift laterally, a series of natural levees can form. Point bars are also known as meander bars.
  - **Meanders :** In large flood and delta plains, rivers rarely flow in straight courses. Loop-like channel patterns called meanders develop over flood and delta plains. Meander is not a landform but is only a type of channel pattern. Normally, in meanders of large rivers, there is active deposition along the convex bank and undercutting along the concave bank.
  - **Braided Channels :** When rivers carry coarse material, there can be selective deposition of coarser materials causing formation of a central bar which diverts the flow towards the banks; and this flow increases lateral erosion on the banks. Deposition and lateral erosion of banks are essential for the formation of braided pattern.

Know the Terms

- **Landforms :** A small to medium tracts or parcels of the earth's surface are called landforms.
- **Landscape :** Several related landforms together make up landscapes.
- **Evolution :** Evolution implies stages of transformation of either a part of the earth's surface from one landform into another or transformation of individual landforms after they are once formed
- **Geomorphology :** Geomorphology deals with the reconstruction of the history of the surface of the earth through a study of its forms, the materials of which it is made up of and the processes that shape it.

- **Monadnocks :** The divides between drainage basins are likewise lowered until they are almost completely flattened leaving finally, a lowland of faint relief with some low resistant remnants called monadnocks.
- **Peneplain :** The plain formed as a result of stream erosion is called a peneplain.
- **Gorge :** A gorge is a deep valley with very steep to straight sides.
- **Canyon :** A canyon is characterised by steep step-like side slopes and may be as deep as a gorge.
- **Plunge pools :** At the foot of waterfalls also, large potholes, quite deep and wide, form because of the sheer impact of water and rotation of boulders. Such large and deep holes at the base of waterfalls are called plunge pools.
- **Plunge tools :** A series of depressions eventually join and the stream valley gets deepened. At the foot of waterfalls also, large potholes, quite deep and wide, form because of the sheer impact of fwater and rotation of boulders. Such large and deep holes at the base of waterfalls are called potholes.
- **Incised or entrenched meanders :** They are very deep and wide meanders that can be found cut in hard rocks.
- **Paired terraces :** The river terraces may occur at the same elevation on either side of the rivers, these are called paired terraces.
- **Lunpaired terraces :** When a terrace is present only on one side of the stream and with none on the other side or one at quite a different elevation on the other side, the terraces are called lunpaired terraces.
- **Delta plains :** The floodplains in a delta are called delta plains.
- **Natural levees :** Natural levees are found along the banks of large rivers. They are low, linear and parallel ridges of coarse deposits along the banks of rivers, quite often cut into individual mounds.
- **Meanders :** In large flood and delta plains, rivers rarely flow in straight courses. Loop-like channel patterns are formed they are called meanders.
- **Ox-bow lakes :** As meanders grow into deep loops, the same may get cut-off due to erosion at the inflection points and are left as ox-bow lakes.

Multiple Choice Questions

(1 mark each)

Q. 1. The floodplains in a delta are called : [A]

(a) delta plains
(b) meanders
(c) ox-bow lakes
(d) levees

Ans. (a) delta plains 1

Q. 2. A deep valley with very steep to straight sides is called : [A]

(a) gorge
(b) delta
(c) canyon
(d) ox-bow lakes

Ans. (a) gorge 1

Q. 3. The plain formed as a result of stream erosion is called : [U]

(a) paired terraces
(b) meanders
(c) peneplain
(d) canyon

Ans. (c) peneplain 1

Very Short Answer Type Questions

(1 mark each)

Q. 1. Define the term landform. [A]

Ans. A small to medium tracts or parcels of the earth's surface are called landforms. 1

Answering Tip

- The world's oceans are the most common landform on earth.

Q. 2. Define the term geomorphology. [U]

Ans. Geomorphology deals with the reconstruction of the history of the surface of the earth through a study of its forms, the materials of which it is made up of and the processes that shape it. 1

Q. 3. What is monadnocks. [A]

Ans. The divides between drainage basins are likewise lowered until they are almost completely flattened, leaving finally, a lowland of faint relief with some low resistant remnants called monadnocks. 1

Q. 4. Define the term delta. [R]

Ans. On the mouth , the river flows not on one but many sides. It is called a delta. 1

Q. 5. What type of a landform is formed by the rivers in the youth stage. [U]

Ans. V-shaped valley is formed in the youth stage. 1

Q. 6. What are the loop-like channel pattern that develop in the river called? [A]

Ans. Meanders are the loop-like channel pattern that develop in the river. 1

Q. 7. Which type of landforms are formed by rivers in the youth stage? U

Ans. They form V-shaped valleys, waterfalls, canyons and meanders. 1

Q. 8. Which type of landforms are formed by rivers in their mature stage ? U

Ans. They form alluvial fans, mountainous plains, cirques, etc. 1

Q. 9. Which type of landforms are formed by rivers in their old stage? A

Ans. Rivers make floodplains, delta, lakes, volcanic plains. 1

Q. 10. Name any two factors that influence the evolution of landforms. A

Ans. Stability of sea level; tectonic stability of landmasses and climate, influence the evolution of landforms . 1

Q. 11. How are alluvial fans formed? U

Ans. Alluvial fans are formed when the streams flowing from the higher levels break into foot slope plains of low gradient. 1

Commonly Made Error

- The students are not aware of the shape formed by the alluvial fans.

Answering Tip

- An alluvial fan is a triangle-shaped deposit of gravel, sand, and even smaller pieces of sediment, such as silt.

Q. 12. Name any two types of valleys depending upon the dimensions and shapes? R

Ans. Depending upon dimensions and shape, many types of valleys like V-shaped valley, gorge, canyon, etc., can be recognised. 1

Q. 13. Why do geomorphic processes take a long time to shape. A

Ans. Actions of most of the geomorphic processes and agents are slow, and hence the results take a long time to take shape. 1

Short Answer Type Questions (3 marks each)

Q. 1. Differentiate between gorge and a canyon. A

Ans.

S.No.	Gorge	Canyon
1.	A gorge is a deep valley with very steep to straight sides.	A canyon is characterised by steep step-like side slopes and may be as deep as a gorge.
2.	A gorge is almost equal in width at its top as well as its bottom.	A canyon is wider at its top than at its bottom.
3.	Gorges form in hard rocks.	Canyons commonly form in horizontal bedded sedimentary rocks.

$(1 \times 3 = 3)$

Q. 2. How are river terrace formed? R

Ans. The terraces may result due to :

(i) Receding water after a peak flow;

(ii) Change in hydrological regime due to climatic changes;

(iii) Tectonic uplift of land;

(iv) Sea level changes in case of rivers closer to the sea. 3

Answering Tip

- Terraces can be formed in many ways and in several geologic and environmental settings.

AI **Q. 3. What are the causes behind the formation of river meander landform?** U

OR

How is meander not a landform but is only a type of channel pattern?

OR

Meander is not a landform but is only a type of channel pattern. Justify?

Ans. Meander is not a landform but is only a type of channel pattern. This is because of—

(i) Propensity of water flowing over very gentle gradients to work laterally on the banks.

(ii) Unconsolidated nature of alluvial deposits making up the banks with many irregularities which can be used by water exerting pressure laterally.

(iii) Coriolis force acting on the fluid water deflecting it like it deflects the wind. When the gradient of the channel becomes extremely low, water flows leisurely and starts working laterally. Slight irregularities along the banks slowly get transformed into a small curvature in the banks; the curvature deepens due to deposition on the inside of the curve and erosion along the bank on the outside. If there is no deposition and no erosion or undercutting, the tendency to meander is reduced. Normally, in meanders of large rivers, there is active deposition along the convex bank and undercutting along the concave bank. The concave bank is known as cut-off bank which shows up as a steep scarp and the convex bank presents a long, gentle profile and is known as slip-off bank. As meanders grow into deep loops, the same may get cut-off due to erosion at the inflection points and are left as ox-bow lakes. 3

Q. 4. What do you know about braided channels? [R]

Ans. When rivers carry coarse material, there can be selective deposition of coarser materials causing formation of a central bar which diverts the flow towards the banks; and this flow increases lateral erosion on the banks.

As the valley widens, the water column is reduced and more and more materials get deposited as islands and lateral bars developing a number of separate channels of water flow. Deposition and lateral erosion of banks are essential for the formation of braided pattern.

Or, alternatively, when discharge is less and load is more in the valley, channel bars and islands of sand, gravel and pebbles develop on the floor of the channel and the water flow is divided into multiple threads. These thread-like streams of water re-join and subdivide repeatedly to give a typical braided pattern. 3

Answering Tip

- The braided channel, also known as a braided river, refers to a network of small channels that are separated by minute and temporary islands known as braid bars, creating a unique appearance.

Q. 5. Write a note on the important landforms associated with floodplains? [A]

Ans. Natural levees and point bars are some of the important landforms found associated with floodplains. Natural levees are found along the banks of large rivers. They are low, linear and parallel ridges of coarse deposits along the banks of rivers, quite often cut into individual mounds. During flooding as the water spills over the bank, the velocity of the water comes down and large sized and high specific gravity materials get dumped in the immediate vicinity of the bank as ridges. They are high nearer the banks and slope gently away from the river. The levee deposits are coarser than the deposits spread by flood waters away from the river. When rivers shift laterally, a series of natural levees can form.

Point bars are also known as meander bars. They are found on the convex side of meanders of large rivers and are sediments deposited in a linear fashion by flowing waters along the bank. They are almost uniform in profile and in width and contain mixed sizes of sediments. If there more than one ridge, narrow and elongated depressions are found in between the point bars. Rivers build a series of them depending upon the water flow and supply of sediment. As the rivers build the point bars on the convex side, the bank on the concave side will erode actively. 3

Q. 6. What do you know about deltas? [U]

Ans. (i) Deltas are like alluvial fans but develop at a different location. The load carried by the rivers is dumped and spread into the sea. If this load is not carried away far into the sea or distributed along the coast, it spreads and accumulates as a low cone.

(ii) Unlike in alluvial fans, the deposits making up deltas are very well sorted with clear stratification. The coarsest materials settle out first and the finer fractions like silts and clays are carried out into the sea.

(iii) As the delta grows, the river distributaries continue to increase in length and delta continues to build up into the sea. 3

Answering Tip

- The sediment is dropped at the mouth of the river. Some rivers drop so much sediment that waves and tides can't carry it all away. It builds up in layers forming a delta.

[AI] **Q. 7. Write the characteristics of each of the stages that the running water or river undergoes.** [A]

OR

Explain the three stages of running water?

Ans. The characteristics of each of the stages of landscapes developing in running water regimes may be summarised as follows :

(i) Youth : Streams are few during this stage with poor integration and flow over original slopes showing shallow V-shaped valleys with no floodplains or with very narrow floodplains along trunk streams. Streams divides are broad and flat with marshes, swamp and lakes. Meanders if present develop over these broad upland surfaces. These meanders may eventually entrench themselves into the uplands. Waterfalls and rapids may exist where local hard rock bodies are exposed.

(ii) Mature : During this stage streams are plenty with good integration. The valleys are still V-shaped but deep; trunk streams are broad enough to have wider floodplains within which streams may flow in meanders confined within the valley. The flat and broad inter stream areas and swamps and marshes of youth disappear and the stream divides turn sharp. Waterfalls and rapids disappear.

(iii) Old : Smaller tributaries during old age are few with gentle gradients. Streams meander freely over vast floodplains showing natural levees, ox-bow lakes, etc. Divides are broad and flat with lakes, swamps and marshes. Most of the landscape is at or slightly above sea level. 3

Q. 8. How does weathering help in the formation of landforms?

Ans. After the weathering processes have had their actions on the earth materials making up the surface of the earth, the geomorphic agents like running water, groundwater, wind, glaciers, wave perform erosion. Due to changes in climatic conditions and vertical or horizontal movements of landmasses, either the intensity of processes or the processes themselves might change leading to new modifications in the landforms. By alluvium brought by rivers, plains are formed. In limestone regions, caves and sinkholes are formed. Many types of landforms are formed by weathering. **3**

Long Answer Type Questions

(5 marks each)

Q. 1. What kinds of landforms are seen in the upper part of the river. A

Ans. Some of the landforms that are seen in the upper part of the river are :

(i) V-shaped valleys : Valleys start as small and narrow rills; the rills will gradually develop into long and wide gullies; the gullies will further deepen , widen and lengthen to give rise to valleys. Depending upon dimensions and shape, many types of valleys like V-shaped valley, gorge, canyon , etc., can be recognised.

(ii) Gorge : It is deep valley with very steep to straight line. A gorge is almost equal in width at its top as well as its bottom. Gorges form in hard rocks.

(iii) Canyon : Canyon is characterised by steep step-like side slopes and may be as deep as a gorge. A canyon is wider at its top than at its bottom. In fact, a canyon is a variant of gorge. Canyons commonly form in horizontal bedded sedimentary rocks .

(iv) Waterfall : When the rivers start falling in pits in mountainous regions, it makes waterfall. Waterfalls also occur where meltwater drops over the edge of a tabular iceberg or ice shelf.

(v) Plunge Pools : At the foot of waterfalls also, large potholes, quite deep and wide, form because of the sheer impact of water and rotation of boulders. Such large and deep holes at the base of waterfalls are called plunge pools. These pools also help in the deepening of valleys. Waterfalls are also transitory like any other landform and will recede gradually and bring the floor of the valley above waterfalls to the level below.

(1 × 5 = 5)

Q. 2. Explain the depositional landforms made by the rivers? R

Ans. The depositional landforms made by the rivers are :

(i) Alluvial fans : They are formed when streams flowing from higher levels break into foot slope plains of low gradient. Normally very coarse load is carried by streams flowing over mountain slopes. This load becomes too heavy for the streams to be carried over gentler gradients and gets dumped and spread as a broad low to high cone shaped deposit called alluvial fan. Alluvial fans in humid areas show normally low cones with gentle slope from as a low cone.

(ii) Floodplains : Deposition develops a floodplain just as erosion makes valleys. Floodplain is a major landform of river deposition. Large sized materials are deposited first when stream channel breaks into a gentle slope. Thus, normally, fine sized materials like sand, silt and clay are carried by relatively slow moving waters in gentler channels usually found in the plains and deposited over the bed and when the waters spill over the banks during flooding above the bed.

(iii) Natural levees and point bars : Natural levees and point bars are some of the important landforms found associated with floodplains. Natural levees are found along the banks of large rivers. They are low, linear and parallel ridges of coarse deposits along the banks of rivers, quite often cut into individual mounds. During flooding as the water spills over the bank, the velocity of the water comes down and large sized and high specific gravity materials get dumped in the immediate vicinity of the bank as ridges. They are high nearer the banks and slope gently away from the river. The levee deposits are coarser than the deposits spread by flood waters away from the river. When rivers shift laterally, a series of natural levees can form. Point bars are also known as meander bars. They are found on the convex side of meanders of large rivers and are sediments deposited in a linear fashion by flowing waters along the bank. They are almost uniform in profile and in width and contain mixed sizes of sediments. If there more than one ridge, narrow and elongated depressions are found in between the point bars.

(iv) Meanders : In large flood and delta plains, rivers rarely flow in straight courses. Loop-like channel patterns called meanders develop over flood and delta plains. Meander is not a landform but is only a type of channel pattern. This is because of **(i)** propensity of water flowing over very gentle gradients to work laterally on the banks; **(ii)** unconsolidated nature of alluvial deposits making up the banks with many irregularities which can be used by water exerting pressure laterally; **(iii)** coriolis force acting on the fluid water deflecting it like it deflects the wind.

(v) Braided Channels : When rivers carry coarse material, there can be selective deposition of coarser materials causing formation of a central bar which diverts the flow towards the banks; and this flow increases lateral erosion on the banks. As the valley widens, the water column is reduced and more and more materials get deposited as islands and lateral bars developing a number of separate channels of water flow. Deposition and lateral erosion of banks are essential for the formation of braided pattern. 5

Commonly Made Error

- The students are not aware of the most common examples of depositional landform.

Answering Tip

- The most common examples include beaches, deltas, glacial moraines, sand dunes and salt domes.

Q. 3. Explain the erosional landforms made by the rivers. R

Ans. The various erosional landforms made by the rivers are :

(i) Valleys : They start as small and narrow rills; the rills will gradually develop into long and wide gullies; the gullies will further deepen, widen and lengthen to give rise to valleys. Depending upon dimensions and shape, many types of valleys like V-shaped valley, gorge, canyon, etc., can be recognised. A gorge is a deep valley with very steep to straight sides and a canyon is characterised by steep step-like side slopes and may be as deep as a gorge. A gorge is almost equal in width at its top as well as its bottom.

(ii) Potholes and plunge pools : Over the rocky beds of hill-streams more or less circular depressions called potholes form because of stream erosion aided by the abrasion of rock fragments. Once a small and shallow depression forms, pebbles and boulders get collected in those depressions and get rotated by flowing water and consequently the depressions grow in dimensions. A series of such depressions eventually join and the stream valley gets deepened. At the foot of waterfalls also, large potholes, quite deep and wide, form because of the sheer impact of water and rotation of boulders. Such large and deep holes at the base of waterfalls are called plunge pools. These pools also help in the deepening of valleys.

(iii) Incised or Entrenched Meanders : In streams that flow rapidly over steep gradients, normally erosion is concentrated on the bottom of the stream channel. Also, in the case of steep gradient streams, lateral erosion on the sides of the valleys is not much when compared to the streams flowing on low and gentle slopes. Because of active lateral erosion, streams flowing over gentle slopes, develop sinuous or meandering courses. It is common to find meandering courses over floodplains and delta plains where stream gradients are very gentle. But very deep and wide meanders can also be found cut in hard rocks. Such meanders are called incised or entrenched meanders.

(iv) River terraces : River terraces are surfaces marking old valley floor or floodplain levels. They may be bedrock surfaces without any alluvial cover or alluvial terraces consisting of stream deposits. River terraces are basically products of erosion as they result due to vertical erosion by the stream into its own depositional floodplain. There can be a number of such terraces at different heights indicating former river bed levels. The river terraces may occur at the same elevation on either side of the rivers in which case they are called paired terraces. When a terrace is present only on one side of the stream and with none on the other side or one at quite a different elevation on the other side, the terraces are called non-paired terraces. Unpaired terraces are typical in areas of slow uplift of land or where the water column changes are not uniform along both the banks.

Figure 7.3 : Paired and unpaired river terraces

5

Commonly Made Error

- The students are not aware what creates river landforms.

Answering Tip

- The processes of erosion and deposition create different river landforms.

TOPIC-2
Groundwater, Erosional Landforms, Depositional Landforms

Revision Notes

- The surface water percolates well when the rocks are permeable, thinly bedded and highly jointed and cracked. After vertically going down to some depth, the water under the ground flows horizontally through the bedding planes, joints or through the materials themselves.
- Physical or mechanical removal of materials by moving groundwater is insignificant in developing landforms. That is why, the results of the work of groundwater cannot be seen in all types of rocks.
- Any limestone or dolomitic region showing typical landforms produced by the action of groundwater through the processes of solution and deposition is called Karst topography after the typical topography developed in limestone rocks of Karst region in the Balkans adjacent to Adriatic Sea.
- **Erosional Landforms :**
  - **Pools, Sinkholes, Lapies and Limestone Pavements :** Small to medium sized round to sub-rounded shallow depressions called swallow holes form on the surface of limestones through solution. Sinkholes are very common in limestone/karst areas. A sinkhole is an opening more or less circular at the top and funnel-shapped towards the bottom with sizes varying in area from a few sq m to a hectare and with depth from a less than half a metre to thirty metres or more. Gradually, most of the surface of the limestone is eaten away by these pits and trenches, leaving it extremely irregular with a maze of points, grooves and ridges or lapies. Especially, these ridges or lapies form due to differential solution activity along parallel to sub-parallel joints. The lapie field may eventually turn into somewhat smooth limestone pavements.
  - **Caves :** In areas where there are alternating beds of rocks (shales, sandstones, quartzites) with limestones or dolomites in between or in areas where limestones are dense, massive and occurring as thick beds, cave formation is prominent. Caves normally have an opening through which cave streams are discharged. Caves having openings at both the ends are called tunnels.
- **Depositional Landforms :**
  - **Stalactites, Stalagmites and Pillars :** Stalactites hang as icicles of different diameters. Normally they are broad at their bases and taper towards the free ends showing up in a variety of forms. Stalagmites rise up from the floor of the caves. In fact, stalagmites form due to dripping water from the surface or through the thin pipe, of the stalactite, immediately below it. Stalagmites may take the shape of a column, a disc, with either a smooth, rounded bulging end or a miniature crater like depression. The stalagmites and stalactites eventually fuse to give rise to columns and pillars of different diameters.

Know the Terms

- **Karst topography :** Any limestone or dolomitic region showing typical landforms produced by the action of groundwater through the processes of solution and deposition is called Karst topography.
- **Sinkhole :** A sinkhole is an opening more or less circular at the top and funnel-shapped towards the bottom with sizes varying in area from a few sq m to a hectare and with depth from a less than half a metre to thirty metres or more.
- **Doline :** It is a shallow usually funnel-shaped depression of the ground surface formed by solution in limestone regions.
- **Valley sinks or Uvalas :** A closed karst depression, a terrain form usually of elongated or compound structure and of larger size than a sinkhole.
- **Ridges or lapies :** It is the grooved , fluted features in an open limestone field.
- **Stalactites :** A tapering structure hanging like an icicle from the roof of a cave, formed of calcium salts deposited by dripping water.
- **Stalagmites :** A mound or tapering column rising from the floor of a cave, formed of calcium salts deposited by dripping water and often uniting with a stalactite.

Multiple Choice Questions (1 mark each)

Q. 1. Stalagmites: A

(a) rise up from the floor of the caves
(b) rise from the roof of a cave
(c) rise from underground
(d) rise from the sinkhole

Ans. (a) rise up from the floor of the caves 1

Q. 2. The grooved , fluted features in an open limestone field is known as : U

(a) uvalas
(b) ridges
(c) doline
(d) valley sink

Ans. (b) ridges 1

Q. 3. Caves having openings at both the ends are called: A

(a) stalactites
(b) tunnels
(c) sinkholes
(d) cave holes

Ans. (b) tunnels 1

Very Short Answer Type Questions (1 mark each)

Q. 1. Define the term 'Karst Topography'. A

Ans. Any limestone or dolomitic region showing typical landforms produced by the action of groundwater through the processes of solution and deposition is called Karst topography. 1

Commonly Made Error

- The students are not aware as to where the Karst topography is formed.

Answering Tip

- Karst topography usually forms in regions of plentiful rainfall where bedrock consists of carbonate-rich rock, such as limestone, gypsum, or dolomite, that is easily dissolved.

Q. 2. Give any two features of stalactites. A

Ans. Stalactites hang as icicles of different diameters. Normally they are broad at their bases and taper towards the free ends showing up in a variety of forms. 1

Q. 3. Differentiate between stalactites and stalagmites. U

Ans.

S.No.	Stalactites	Stalagmites
1.	Stalactites hang as icicles of different diameters.	Stalagmites rise up from the floor of the caves.
2.	They are broad at the bases and taper towards the free ends showing up in a variety of forms.	It may take the shape of a disc, a column with either a smooth , rounded bulging end.

Q. 4. Differentiate between sinkholes and uvalas. R

Ans.

S.No.	Sinkholes	Uvalas
1.	A sinkhole is an opening more or less circular at the top and funnel-shaped towards the bottom.	When the sinkholes and dolines join together because of slumping of material along their margins the uvalas are formed.

Q. 5. Name the landforms made by groundwater? A

Ans. Pools, sinkholes, lapies and limestone pavements, caves, stalactites , stalagmites and pillars stalactites are formed by groundwater. 1

Commonly Made Error

- Caves are taken to be man-made.

Q. 6. What are caves? U

Ans. Some of the blow outs become deeper and wider. These are called caves. 1

Answering Tip

- A cave is a natural void in the ground, specifically a space large enough for a human to enter.

Short Answer Type Questions (3 marks each)

Q. 1. Explain the depositional landforms formed by groundwater. A

Ans. The various depositional landforms formed by groundwater are:

(i) **Stalactites :** They hang as icicles of different diameters. Normally they are broad at their bases and taper towards the free ends showing up in a variety of forms.

(ii) **Stalagmites :** Stalagmites rise up from the floor of the caves. In fact, stalagmites form due to dripping water from the surface or through the thin pipe, of the stalactite, immediately below it. Stalagmites may take the shape of a column, a disc, with either a smooth, rounded bulging end or a miniature crater like depression. The stalagmite and stalactites eventually fuse to give rise to columns and pillars of different diameters. 3

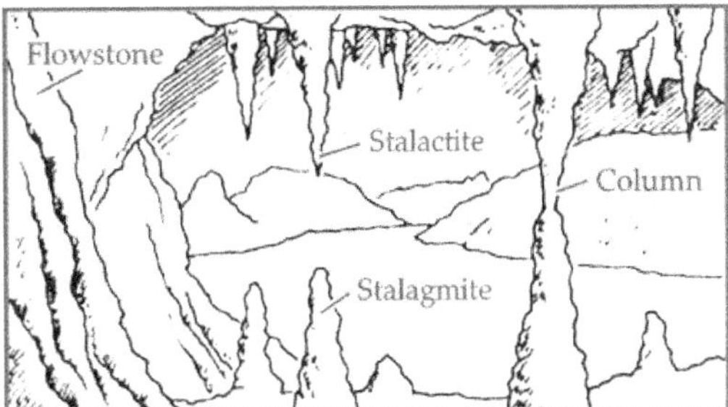

Long Answer Type Question (5 marks)

Q. 1. What are the erosional landforms made by the groundwater? [A]

Ans. The various erosional landforms made by the groundwater are :

(i) **Pools, Sinkholes, Lapies and Limestone Pavements :** Small to medium sized round to sub-rounded shallow depressions called swallow holes form on the surface of limestones through solution. Sinkholes are very common in limestone/karst areas. A sinkhole is an opening more or less circular at the top and funnel-shapped towards the bottom with sizes varying in area from a few sq m to a hectare and with depth from a less than half a metre to thirty metres or more. Some of these form solely through solution action (solution sinks) and others might start as solution forms first and if the bottom of a sinkhole forms the roof of a void or cave underground, it might collapse leaving a large hole opening into a cave or a void below (collapse sinks). Quite often, sinkholes are covered up with soil mantle and appear as shallow water pools. Anybody stepping over such pools would go down like it happens in quicksands in deserts. The term doline is sometimes used to refer the collapse sinks. Solution sinks are more common than collapse sinks. Quite often the surface run-off simply goes down swallow and sink holes and flow as underground streams and re-emerge at a distance downstream through a cave opening. When sinkholes and dolines join together because of slumping of materials along their margins or due to roof collapse of caves, long, narrow to wide trenches called valley sinks or Uvalas form. Gradually, most of the surface of the limestone is eaten away by these pits and trenches, leaving it extremely irregular with a maze of points, grooves and ridges or lapies. Especially, these ridges or lapies form due to differential solution activity along parallel to sub-parallel joints. The lapie field may eventually turn into somewhat smooth limestone pavements.

(ii) **Caves :** In areas where there are alternating beds of rocks (shales, sandstones, quartzites) with limestones or dolomites in between or in areas where limestones are dense, massive and occurring as thick beds, cave formation is prominent. Water percolates down either through the materials or through cracks and joints and moves horizontally along bedding planes. It is along these bedding planes that the limestone dissolves and long and narrow to wide gaps called caves result. There can be a maze of caves at different elevations depending upon the limestone beds and intervening rocks. Caves normally have an opening through which cave streams are discharged. Caves having openings at both the ends are called tunnels. 5

Answering Tip

- Groundwater deposits material in caves to create stalactites, stalagmites, and columns.

TOPIC-3

Glaciers, Erosional Landforms, Depositional Landforms, Waves and Currents, Erosional Landforms, Depositional Landforms

Revision Notes

➢ Masses of ice moving as sheets over the land (continental glacier or piedmont glacier if a vast sheet of ice is spread over the plains at the foot of mountains) or as linear flows down the slopes of mountains in broad trough-like valleys (mountain and valley glaciers) are called glaciers. Glaciers move basically because of the force of gravity.

➢ Erosion by glaciers is tremendous because of friction caused by sheer weight of the ice.

➢ Glaciers can cause significant damage to even un-weathered rocks and can reduce high mountains into low hills and plains.

➢ **Erosional Landforms :**

- **Cirques :** They are the most common of landforms in glaciated mountains. The cirques quite often are found at the heads of glacial valleys. The accumulated ice cuts these cirques while moving down the mountain tops. They are deep, long and wide troughs or basins with very steep concave to vertically dropping high walls at its head as well as sides.
- **Horns and Serrated Ridges :** Horns form through headward erosion of the cirque walls. If three or more radiating glaciers cut headward until their cirques meet, high, sharp pointed and steep-sided peaks called horns form.
- **Glacial Valleys/Troughs :** Glaciated valleys are trough-like and U-shaped with broad floors and relatively smooth, and steep sides. The valleys may contain littered debris or debris shaped as moraines with swampy appearance. Very deep glacial troughs filled with sea water and making up shorelines (in high latitudes) are called fjords/fiords.

➢ **Depositional Landforms :**

- **Moraines :** They are long ridges of deposits of glacial till. Terminal moraines are long ridges of debris deposited at the end (toe) of the glaciers. Lateral moraines form along the sides parallel to the glacial valleys. Many valley glaciers retreating rapidly leave an irregular sheet of till over their valley floors. Such deposits varying greatly in thickness and in surface topography are called ground moraines.
- **Eskers :** When glaciers melt in summer, the water flows on the surface of the ice or seeps down along the margins or even moves through holes in the ice. These waters accumulate beneath the glacier and flow like streams in a channel beneath the ice.
- **Outwash Plains :** The plains at the foot of the glacial mountains or beyond the limits of continental ice sheets are covered with glacio-fluvial deposits in the form of broad flat alluvial fans which may join to form outwash plains of gravel, silt, sand and clay.
- **Drumlins :** It are smooth oval shaped ridge-like features composed mainly of glacial till with some masses of gravel and sand. The long axes of drumlins are parallel to the direction of ice move.
- One end of the drumlins facing the glacier called the stoss end is blunter and steeper than the other end called tail. Drumlins give an indication of direction of glacier movement.

➢ Most of the changes along the coasts are accomplished by waves. When waves break, the water is thrown with great force onto the shore, and simultaneously, there is a great churning of sediments on the sea bottom.

➢ Constant impact of breaking waves drastically affects the coasts. As wave environment changes, the intensity of the force of breaking waves changes.

➢ Along the high rocky coasts, the rivers appear to have been drowned with highly irregular coastline. The coastline appears highly indented with extension of water into the land where glacial valleys (fjords) are present.

➢ Along high rocky coasts, waves break with great force against the land shaping the hill sides into cliffs. Waves gradually minimise the irregularities along the shore.

➢ When waves break over a gently sloping sedimentary coast, the bottom sediments get churned and move readily building bars, barrier bars, spits and lagoons. The maintenance of these depositional features depends upon the steady supply of materials.

➢ **Erosional Landforms :**

- **Cliffs, Terraces, Caves and Stacks :** Wave-cut cliffs and terraces are two forms usually found where erosion is the dominant shore process. Almost all sea cliffs are steep and may range from a few m to 30 m or even more. The lashing of waves against the base of the cliff and the rock debris that gets smashed against the cliff along with lashing waves create hollows and these hollows get widened and deepened to form sea caves. Retreat of the cliff may leave some remnants of rock standing isolated as small islands just off the shore. Such resistant masses of rock, originally parts of a cliff or hill are called sea stacks.

➢ **Depositional Landforms :**

- **Beaches and Dunes :** Beaches are characteristic of shorelines that are dominated by deposition, but may occur as patches along even the rugged shores. Most of the sediment making up the beaches comes from land carried by the streams and rivers or from wave erosion. Most of the beaches are made up of sand sized materials. Beaches called shingle beaches contain excessively small pebbles and even cobbles.
- **Bars, Barriers and Spits :** A ridge of sand and shingle formed in the sea in the off-shore zone (from the position of low tide waterline to seaward) lying approximately parallel to the coast is called an off-shore bar. An off-shore bar which is exposed due to further addition of sand is termed a barrier bar. Sometimes such barrier bars get keyed up to one end of the bay when they are called spits.

Know the Terms

- **Fjords :** Very deep glacial troughs filled with sea water and making up shorelines (in high latitudes) are called fjords/fiords.
- **Glacier :** Masses of ice moving as sheets over the land or as linear flows down the slopes of mountains in broad trough-like valleys are called glaciers.
- **Glacier till :** The unassorted coarse and fine debris dropped by the melting glaciers is called glacial till.
- **Outwash deposits :** Some amount of rock debris small enough to be carried by such melt-water streams is washed down and deposited. Such glacio-fluvial deposits are called outwash deposits.
- **Moraines :** They are long ridges of deposits of glacial till.
- **Tarn lakes :** A lake of water can be seen quite often within the cirques after the glacier disappears. Such lakes are called cirque or tarn lakes.
- **Drumlins :** They are smooth oval shaped ridge-like features composed mainly of glacial till with some masses of gravel and sand.
- **Wave cut terrace :** At the foot of such cliffs there may be a flat or gently sloping platform covered by rock debris derived from the sea cliff behind. Such platforms occurring at elevations above the average height of waves is called a wave-cut terrace.
- **Barrier bar :** Bars are submerged features and when bars show up above water, they are called barrier bars.
- **Wave cut terrace :** The gently sloping platform occurring at elevations above the average height of waves is called a wave-cut terrace.
- **Sea stacks :** The resistant masses of rock, originally parts of a cliff or hill are called sea stacks.
- **Spits :** Sometimes the barrier bars get keyed up to one end of the bay when they are called spits.

Multiple Choice Questions (1 mark each)

Q. 1. _______ can cause significant damage to even un-weathered rocks and can reduce high mountains into low hills and plains. [A]

(a) Cirques
(b) Glacier
(c) Fjords
(d) Drumlins

Ans. (b) Glacier 1

Q. 2. A ridge of sand and shingle formed in the sea in the off-shore zone lying approximately parallel to the coast is called an: [U]

(a) off-shore bar
(b) in-shore bar
(c) Outside shore bar
(d) Inside shore bar

Ans. (a) off-shore bar 1

Very Short Answer Type Questions (1 mark each)

Q. 1. Define the term 'Glacier'. [R]

Ans. Masses of ice moving as sheets over the land or as linear flows down the slopes of mountains in broad trough-like valleys are called glaciers. 1

Answering Tip

- Glaciers are often called "rivers of ice."

Q. 2. What are cirques? [U]

Ans. Cirques are deep, long and wide troughs or basins with very deep concave to vertically dropping high walls at its head as well as sides . 1

Q. 3. What is glacier till? [A]

Ans. The unassorted coarse and fine debris dropped by the melting glaciers is called glacial till. 1

Q. 4. What are outwash deposits. [U]

Ans. Some amount of rock debris small enough to be carried by melt-water streams is washed down and deposited. Such glacio-fluvial deposits are called outwash deposits. 1

Q. 5. What are fjords? [A]

Ans. Very deep glacial troughs filled with sea water and making up shorelines (in high latitudes) are called fjords/fiords. 1

Q. 6. What are ground moraines? [U]

Ans. The deposits varying greatly in thickness and in surface topography are called ground moraines. 1

Q. 7. What are drumlins? [R]

Ans. Drumlins are smooth oval shaped ridge-like features composed mainly of glacial till with some masses of gravel and sand. 1

Answering Tip

- Most drumlins are composed of till, but they may vary greatly in their composition.

Q. 8. What are barrier bars? [R]

Ans. Bars are submerged features and when bars show up above water, they are called barrier bars. 1

Q. 9. What are sea stacks? U

Ans. Retreat of the cliff may leave some remnants of rock standing isolated as small islands just off the shore. Such resistant masses of rock, originally parts of a cliff or hill are called sea stacks. 1

Q. 10. Name any two landforms made by the glaciers. R

Ans. Cirque, Eskers, moraines and drumlins. **(Any two) 1**

Q. 11. What happens when the waves break? R

Ans. When waves break, the water is thrown with great force onto the shore, and simultaneously, there is a great churning of sediments on the sea bottom. Constant impact of breaking waves drastically affects the coasts. 1

Q. 12. How are lagoons formed? U

Ans. When barrier bars and spits form at the mouth of a bay and block it, a lagoon forms. 1

Commonly Made Error

- How the lagoons are separated from the larger bodies is not known to most of the students.

Answering Tip

- Lagoons are separated from larger bodies of water by sandbars, barrier reefs, coral reefs, or other natural barriers.

Q. 13. How does ocean barriers prevent storm and tsunami? R

Ans. The coastal off-shore bars offer the first buffer or defence against storm or tsunami by absorbing most of their destructive force. 1

Short Answer Type Questions

(3 marks each)

Q. 1. Explain the erosion caused by glaciers. A

Ans. Erosion by glaciers is tremendous because of friction caused by sheer weight of the ice. The material plucked from the land by the glaciers get dragged along the floors or sides of the valleys and cause great damage through abrasion and plucking. Glaciers can cause significant damage to even un-weathered rocks and can reduce high mountains into lowhills and plains. Stalagmites may take the shape of a column, a disc, with either a smooth, rounded bulging end or a miniature crater like depression. The stalagmite and stalactites eventually fuse to give rise to columns and pillars of different diameters.

As glaciers continue to move, debris gets removed, divides get lowered and eventually the slope is reduced to such an extent that glaciers will stop moving leaving only a mass of low hills and vast outwash plains along with other depositional features. 3

Q. 2. Name the erosional landforms made by the glacier. U

Ans. Some of the erosional landforms are:

(i) Cirques : They are the most common of landforms in glaciated mountains. The cirques quite often are found at the heads of glacial valleys. The accumulated ice cuts these cirques while moving down the mountain tops. They are deep, long and wide troughs or basins with very steep concave to vertically dropping high walls at its head as well as sides . A lake of water can be seen quite often within the cirques after the glacier disappears. Such lakes are cirque or tarn lakes. There can be two or more cirques one leading into another down below in a stepped sequence.

(ii) Horns and Serrated Ridges : Horns form through headward erosion of the cirque walls. If three or more radiating glaciers cut headward until their cirques meet, high, sharp pointed and steep sided peaks called horns form. The divides between cirque side walls or head walls get narrow because of progressive erosion and turn into serrated or saw-toothed ridges sometimes referred to as arêtes with very sharp crest and a zig-zag outline.

(iii) Glacial Valleys/Troughs : Glaciated valleys are trough-like and U-shaped with broad floors and relatively smooth, and steep sides. The valleys may contain littered debris or debris shaped as moraines with swampy appearance. There may be lakes gouged out of rocky floor or formed by debris within the valleys. There can be hanging valleys at an elevation on one or both sides of the main glacial valley. 3

AI **Q. 3. What do you know about drumlin?** A

Ans. Drumlins are smooth oval shaped ridge-like features composed mainly of glacial till with some masses of gravel and sand. The long axes of drumlins are parallel to the direction of ice movement.

Measurement : They may measure up to 1 km in length and 30 m or so in height. One end of the drumlins facing the glacier called the stoss end is blunter and steeper than the other end called tail.

Formation : The drumlins form due to dumping of rock debris beneath heavily loaded ice through fissures in the glacier. The stoss end gets blunted due to pushing by moving ice. Drumlins give an indication of direction of glacier movement. 3

Answering Tip

- Drumlins rarely occur singly, however, and are found in groups or swarms, with the tapered end of each hill pointing in the direction of glacier flow.

Q. 4. Name the erosional landforms formed by the waves. U

Ans. Cliffs, Terraces, Caves and Stacks :

Wave-cut cliffs and terraces are two forms usually found where erosion is the dominant shore process. Almost all sea cliffs are steep and may range from a few m to 30 m or even more. At the foot of such cliffs there may be a flat or gently sloping platform covered by rock debris derived from the sea cliff behind. Such platforms occurring at elevations above the average height of waves is called a wave-cut terrace.

The lashing of waves against the base of the cliff and the rock debris that gets smashed against the cliff along with lashing waves create hollows and these hollows get widened and deepened to form sea caves. The roofs of caves collapse and the sea cliffs recede further inland. Retreat of the cliff may leave some remnants of rock standing isolated as small islands just off the shore. Such resistant masses of rock, originally parts of a cliff or hill are called sea stacks.

Like all other features, sea stacks are also temporary and eventually coastal hills and cliffs will disappear because of wave erosion giving rise to narrow coastal plains, and with onrush of deposits from over the land behind may get covered up by alluvium or may get covered up by shingle or sand to form a wide beach. **3**

Long Answer Type Questions **(5 marks each)**

Q. 1. Name the depositional landforms made by the glacier? [A]

Ans. The various depositional landforms are:

(i) Moraines : They are long ridges of deposits of glacial till. Terminal moraines are long ridges of debris deposited at the end (toe) of the glaciers. Lateral moraines form along the sides parallel to the glacial valleys. The lateral moraines may join a terminal moraine forming a horse-shoe shaped ridge. There can be many lateral moraines on either side in a glacial valley. These moraines partly or fully owe their origin to glacio-fluvial waters pushing up materials to the sides of glaciers.

(ii) Eskers : When glaciers melt in summer, the water flows on the surface of the ice or seeps down along the margins or even moves through holes in the ice. These waters accumulate beneath the glacier and flow like streams in a channel beneath the ice. Such streams flow over the ground (not in a valley cut in the ground) with ice forming its banks. Very coarse materials like boulders and blocks along with some minor fractions of rock debris carried into this stream settle in the valley of ice beneath the glacier and after the ice melts can be found as a sinuous ridge called esker.

(iii) Outwash Plains : The plains at the foot of the glacial mountains or beyond the limits of continental ice sheets are covered with glacio-fluvial deposits in the form of broad flat alluvial fans which may join to form outwash plains of gravel, silt, sand and clay.

(iv) Drumlins : They are smooth oval shaped ridge-like features composed mainly of glacial till with some masses of gravel and sand. The long axes of drumlins are parallel to the direction of ice movement. They may measure up to 1 km in length and 30 m or so in height. One end of the drumlins facing the glacier called the stoss end is blunter and steeper than the other end called tail. The drumlins form due to dumping of rock debris beneath heavily loaded ice through fissures in the glacier. The stoss end gets blunted due to pushing by moving ice. Drumlins give an indication of direction of glacier movement. **5**

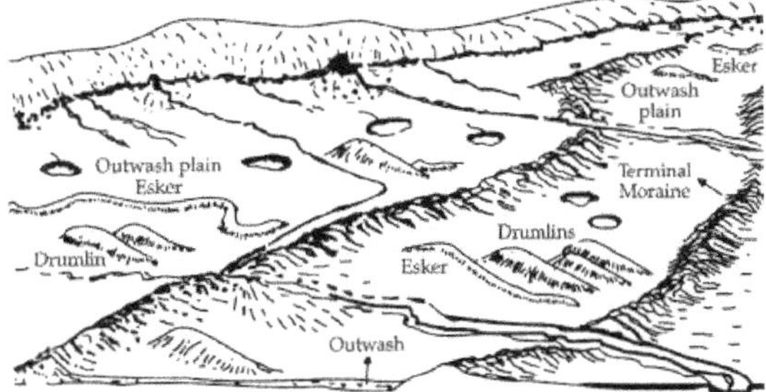

A panoramic diagram of glacial landscape with various depositional landforms (adapted and modified from Spancer, 1962)

Q. 2. Differentiate between high rocky coasts and low sedimentary coasts. [U]

Ans.

S.No.	High Rocky Coasts	Low Sedimentary Coasts
1.	Along the high rocky coasts, the rivers appear to have been drowned with highly irregular coastline.	Along low sedimentary coasts the rivers appear to extend their length by building coastal plains and deltas.
2.	The coastline appears highly indented with extension of water into the land where glacial valleys (fjords) are present.	The coastline appears smooth with occasional incursions of water in the form of lagoons and tidal creeks.
3.	The hill sides drop off sharply into the water.	The land slopes gently into the water.
4.	Shores do not show any depositional landforms initially.	Marshes and swamps may abound along the coasts.
5.	Erosion features dominate.	Depositional features dominate.

(1 × 5 = 5)

Commonly Made Error

- The students are not aware of the examples of high rocky coasts and low sedimentary coasts.

Answering Tip

- The example of high rocky coast is the West Coast of India and the example of low sedimentary coast is the East Coast of India.

TOPIC-4
Winds, Erosional Landforms, Depositional Landforms

Revision Notes

- Wind is one of the two dominant agents in hot deserts. The desert floors get heated up too much and too quickly because of being dry and barren.
- Winds also move along the desert floors with great speed and the obstructions in their path create turbulence.
- Winds cause deflation, abrasion and impact. Deflation includes lifting and removal of dust and smaller particles from the surface of rocks. In the transportation process sand and silt act as effective tools to abrade the land surface.
- The wind action creates a number of interesting erosional and depositional features in the deserts. The wind moves fine materials and general mass erosion is accomplished mainly through sheet floods or sheet wash.
- **Erosional Landforms :**
  - **Pediments and Pediplains :** Landscape evolution in deserts is primarily concerned with the formation and extension of pediments. Gently inclined rocky floors close to the mountains at their foot with or without a thin cover of debris, are called pediments. Erosion starts along the steep margins of the landmass or the steep sides of the tectonically controlled steep incision features over the landmass.
  - **Playas :** Plains are by far the most prominent landforms in the deserts. In times of sufficient water, these plains are covered up by a shallow water body. Such types of shallow lakes are called as playas where water is retained only for short duration due to evaporation and quite often the playas contain good deposition of salts.
  - **Deflation Hollows and Caves :** Weathered mantle from over the rocks or bare soil, gets blown out by persistent movement of wind currents in one direction. This process may create shallow depressions called deflation hollows. Deflation also creates numerous small pits or cavities over rock surfaces. The rock faces suffer impact and abrasion of wind-borne sand and first shallow depressures called blow outs are created, and some of the blow outs become deeper and wides fit to be called cares.
  - **Mushroom, Table and Pedestal Rocks :** Many rock-outcrops in the deserts easily susceptible to wind deflation and abrasion are worn out quickly leaving some remnants of resistant rocks polished beautifully in the shape of mushroom with a slender stalk and a broad and rounded pear shaped cap above. Sometimes, the top surface is broad like a table top and quite often, the remnants stand out like pedesta.
- **Depositional Landforms :**
  - **Sand Dunes :** Dry hot deserts are good places for sand dune formation. Obstacles to initiate dune formation are equally important. There can be a great variety of dune forms.
  - **Barchans :** Crescent shaped dunes called barchans with the points or wings directed away from wind direction *i.e.,* downwind, form where the wind direction is constant and moderate and where the original surface over which sand is moving is almost uniform. Parabolic dunes form when sandy surfaces are partially covered with vegetation. Seif is similar to barchan with a small difference. Seif has only one wing or point. This happens when there is shift in wind conditions. The lone wings of seifs can grow very long and high. When sand is plenty, quite often, the regular shaped dunes coalesce and lose their individual characteristics. Most of the dunes in the deserts shift and a few of them will get stabilised especially near human habitations.

Know the Terms

- **Wind :** The perceptible natural movement of the air, especially in the form of a current of air blowing from a particular direction.
- **Pediments :** Gently inclined rocky floors close to the mountains at their foot with or without a thin cover of debris, are called pediments.
- **Pediplain :** It is an extensive plain formed in a desert by the coalescence of neighbouring pediments.
- **Inselberg :** It is an isolated rock hill, knob, ridge or small mountain that rises abruptly from a gently sloping or virtually level surrounding plain.
- **Alkali Flats :** The playa plain covered up by salts is called alkali flats.
- **Deflation hollows :** Weathered mantle from over the rocks or bare soil, gets blown out by persistent movement of wind currents in one direction. This process may create shallow depressions called deflation hollows.

- **Barchans :** Crescent shaped dunes called barchans.
- **Parabolic Dunes :** Parabolic dunes form when sandy surfaces are partially covered with vegetation.
- **Seif :** Seif is similar to barchan with a small difference. Seif has only one wing or point. This happens when there is shift in wind conditions.
- **Longitudinal dunes :** They are formed when supply of sand is poor and wind direction is constant. They appear as long ridges of considerable length but low in height.
- **Transverse dunes :** They are aligned perpendicular to wind direction. These dunes form when the wind direction is constant and the source of sand is an elongated feature at right angles to the wind direction.

Multiple Choice Questions (1 mark each)

Q. 1. __________ is one of the two dominant agents in hot deserts. A

(a) Wind
(b) Water
(c) Pediplain
(d) Salt

Ans. (a) Wind 1

Q. 2. Dry hot deserts are good places for the formation of : U

(a) rain
(b) flats
(c) sand dune
(d) vegetation

Ans. (c) sand dune 1

Q. 3. A crescent-shaped shifting sand dune is known as: U

(a) barchan
(b) hollows
(c) inselberg
(d) seif

Ans. (a) barchan 1

Very Short Answer Type Questions (1 mark each)

Q. 1. Define the term 'Pediments'. A

Ans. Landscape evolution in deserts is primarily concerned with the formation and extension of pediments. Gently inclined rocky floors close to the mountains at their foot with or without a thin cover of debris, are called pediments. 1

Answering Tip

- The process through which pediplains are formed is called pediplanation.

Q. 2. Define the term 'Pediplains'. U

Ans. Through parallel retreat of slopes, the pediments extend backwards at the expense of mountain front, and gradually, the mountain gets reduced leaving an inselberg which is a remnant of the mountain. That's how the high relief in desert areas is reduced to low featureless plains called pediplains. 1

Q. 3. What are deflation hollows? A

Ans. Weathered mantle from over the rocks or bare soil, gets blown out by persistent movement of wind currents in one direction. This process may create shallow depressions called deflation hollows. 1

Q. 4. What are blow outs? R

Ans. Deflation creates numerous small pits or cavities over rock surfaces. The rock face suffers impact and abrasion of wind-borne sand and first shallow depressions called blow outs are created. 1

Q. 5. What are caves? A

Ans. Some of the blow outs become deeper and wider. These are called caves. 1

Q. 6. Define 'Saltation'. U

Ans. Depending upon the velocity of wind, different sizes of grains are moved along the floors by rolling and carried in suspension and in his process of transportation itself, the materials get sorted . These are called saltation. 1

Q. 7. How are pediments formed? A

Ans. Pediments are formed through the erosion of mountain front through a combination of lateral erosion by streams and sheet flooding. 1

Q. 8. How do inselberg get formed? R

Ans. Once, pediments are formed with a steep wash slope followed by cliff or free face above it, the steep wash slope and free face retreat backwards. This method of erosion is termed as parallel retreat of slopes through backwasting. So, through parallel retreat of slopes, the pediments extend backwards at the expense of mountain front, and gradually, the mountain gets reduced leaving an inselberg which is a remnant of the mountain. 1

Commonly Made Error

- The students are not aware of what is an inselberg.

Answering Tip

- An inselberg is an isolated rock hill, knob, ridge, or small mountain that rises abruptly from a gently sloping or virtually level surrounding plain.

Short Answer Type Questions (3 marks each)

Q. 1. What do you know about deflation hollows and caves? [A]

Ans. Weathered mantle from over the rocks or bare soil, gets blown out by persistent movement of wind currents in one direction. This process may create shallow depressions called deflation hollows. Deflation also creates numerous small pits or cavities over rock surfaces. The rock faces suffer impact and abrasion of wind-borne sand and first shallow depressions called blow outs are created, and some of the blow outs become deeper and wider fit to be called caves. 3

Q. 2. Name the depositional landforms made by the winds. [U]

Ans. The various depositional landforms made by the winds are :

(i) Sand dunes : Dry hot deserts are good places for sand dune formation. Obstacles to initiate dune formation are equally important. There can be a great variety of dune forms.

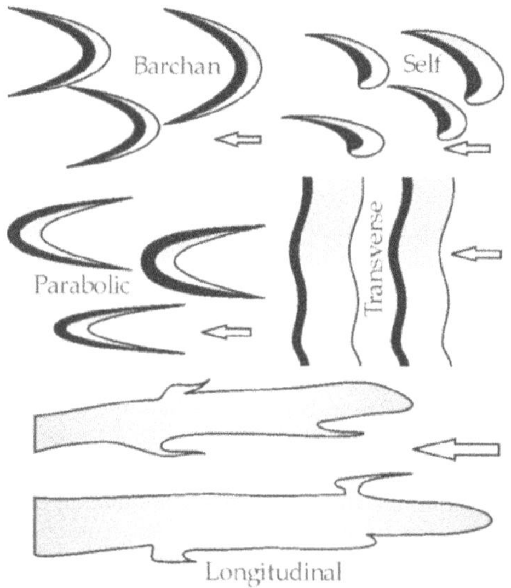

Fig. 7.16 : Various types of sand dunes Arrows indicate wind direction

(ii) Barchans : Crescent shaped dunes called barchans with the points or wings directed away from wind direction i.e., downwind, form where the wind direction is constant and moderate and where the original surface over which sand is moving is almost uniform. Parabolic dunes form when sandy surfaces are partially covered with vegetation. That means parabolic dunes are reversed barchans with wind direction being the same. 3

Q. 3. What are playas or alkali regions? Explain their formation? [U]

Ans. Plains are by far the most prominent landforms in the deserts. In basins with mountains and hills around and along, the drainage is towards the centre of the basin and due to gradual deposition of sediment from basin margins, a nearly level plain forms at the centre of the basin. In times of sufficient water, this plain is covered up by a shallow water body. Such types of shallow lakes are called as playas where water is retained only for short duration due to evaporation and quite often the playas contain good deposition of salts. The playa plain covered up by salts is called alkali flats. 3

[AI] **Q. 4. Explain the depositional landforms made by wind.** [A]

Ans. The various depositional landforms made by wind are :

(i) Barchans : Crescent shaped dunes called barchans with the points or wings directed away from wind direction i.e., downwind, form where the wind direction is constant and moderate and where the original surface over which sand is moving is almost uniform.

(ii) Parabolic dunes : Parabolic dunes form when sandy surfaces are partially covered with vegetation. That means parabolic dunes are reversed barchans with wind direction being the same.

(iii) Longitudinal dunes : Longitudinal dunes form when supply of sand is poor and wind direction is constant. They appear as long ridges of considerable length but low in height.

(iv) Transverse dunes : They are aligned perpendicular to wind direction. These dunes form when the wind direction is constant and the source of sand is an elongated feature at right angles to the wind direction. 3

Long Answer Type Questions (5 marks each)

Q. 1. Explain the process of formation of sand dunes. [A]

Ans. Sand dunes are of two types :

(i) Sand dunes in deserts : Dry hot deserts are good places for sand dunes formation. Obstacles to initiate dune formation are equally important. There can be a great variety of dune forms. Most of the dunes in the deserts shift and a few of them will get stabilised especially near human habitations:

(a) Barchans : Crescent shaped dunes called barchans with the points or wings directed away from wind direction i.e., downwind, form where the wind direction is constant and moderate and where the original surface over which sand is moving is almost uniform.

(b) **Parabolic dunes :** Parabolic dunes form when sandy surfaces are partially covered with vegetation. That means parabolic dunes are reversed barchans with wind direction being the same.

(c) **Longitudinal dunes :** Longitudinal dunes form when supply of sand is poor and wind direction is constant. They appear as long ridges of considerable length but low in height.

(d) **Transverse dunes :** They are aligned perpendicular to wind direction. These dunes form when the wind direction is constant and the source of sand is an elongated feature at right angles to the wind direction. They may be very long and low in height. When sand is plenty, quite often, the regular shaped dunes coalesce and lose their individual characteristics.

(ii) **Sand dunes formed by waves :** The sandy beach which appears so permanent may be reduced to a very narrow strip of coarse pebbles in some other season. Most of the beaches are made up of sand sized materials. Beaches called shingle beaches contain excessively small pebbles and even cobbles. Just behind the beach, the sands lifted and winnowed from over the beach surfaces will be deposited as sand dunes. Sand dunes forming long ridges parallel to the coastline are very common along low sedimentary coasts. 5

Answering Tip

- The sand that results in the formation of sand dunes is eroded from rocks by physical and chemical processes such as wind and water.

Q. 2. Explain the landforms created by erosion through wind. [A]

Ans. The various erosional landforms are :

(i) **Pediments :** Landscape evolution in deserts is primarily concerned with the formation and extension of pediments. Gently inclined rocky floors close to the mountains at their foot with or without a thin cover of debris, are called pediments. Such rocky floors form through the erosion of mountain front through a combination of lateral erosion by streams and sheet flooding.

Erosion starts along the steep margins of the landmass or the steep sides of the tectonically controlled steep incision features over the landmass.

(ii) **Pediplains :** Once, pediments are formed with a steep wash slope followed by cliff or free face above it, the steep wash slope and free face retreat backwards. This method of erosion is termed as parallel retreat of slopes through backwasting. So, through parallel retreat of slopes, the pediments extend backwards at the expense of mountain front, and gradually, the mountain gets reduced leaving an inselberg which is a remnant of the mountain. That's how the high relief in desert areas is reduced to low featureless plains called pediplains.

(iii) **Playas :** Plains are by far the most prominent landforms in the deserts. In basins with mountains and hills around and along, the drainage is towards the centre of the basin and due to gradual deposition of sediment from basin margins, a nearly level plain forms at the centre of the basin. In times of sufficient water, this plain is covered up by a shallow water body.

Such types of shallow lakes are called as playas where water is retained only for short duration due to evaporation and quite often the playas contain good deposition of salts. The playa plain covered up by salts is called alkali flats.

(iv) **Deflation Hollows and Caves :** Weathered mantle from over the rocks or bare soil, gets blown out by persistent movement of wind currents in one direction. This process may create shallow depressions called deflation hollows. Deflation also creates numerous small pits or cavities over rock surfaces. The rock faces suffer impact and abrasion of wind-borne sand and first shallow depressions called blow outs are created, and some of the blow outs become deeper and wider fit to be called caves.

(v) **Mushroom, Table and Pedestal Rocks :** Many rock-outcrops in the deserts easily susceptible to wind deflation and abrasion are worn out quickly leaving some remnants of resistant rocks polished beautifully in the shape of mushroom with a slender stalk and a broad and rounded pear shaped cap above. Sometimes, the top surface is broad like a table top and quite often, the remnants stand out like pedestals. 5

Q. 3. What is the role of wind in deserts? [R]

Ans. Wind is one of the two dominant agents in hot deserts. The desert floors get heated up too much and too quickly because of being dry and barren. The heated floors heat up the air directly above them and result in upward movements in the hot lighter air with turbulence, and any obstructions in its path sets up eddies, whirlwinds, updrafts and downdrafts. Winds also move along the desert floors with great speed and the obstructions in their path create turbulence.

Of course, there are storm winds which are very destructive. Winds cause deflation, abrasion and impact. Deflation includes lifting and removal of dust and smaller particles from the surface of rocks. In the transportation process sand and silt act as effective tools to abrade the land surface. The impact is simply sheer force of momentum which occurs when sand is blown into or against a rock surface. It is similar to sandblasting operation. The wind action creates a number of interesting erosional and depositional features in the deserts. In fact, many features of deserts owe their formation to mass wasting and running water as sheet floods. 5

Answering Tip

- Wind helps in the formation of rock pedestals, yardangs, desert pavements, deflation hollows, oasis and sand dunes in the deserts.

NCERT CORNER

(B) Multiple choice questions :

Q. 1. In which of the following stages of landform development, downward cutting is dominated : R

(a) Youth stage (b) Late mature stage
(c) Early mature stage (d) Old stage

Ans. (a) Youth stage.

Q. 2. A deep valley characterised by steep step-like side slopes is known as : A

(a) U-shaped valley (b) Gorge
(c) Blind valley (d) Canyon

Ans. (d) Canyon.

Q. 3. In which one of the following regions the chemical weathering process is more dominant than the mechanical process : A

(a) Humid region (b) Limestone region
(c) Arid region (d) Glacier region

Ans. (b) Limestone region.

Q. 4. Which one of the following sentences best defines the term 'Lapies' : R

(a) A small to medium sized shallow depression
(b) A landform whose opening is more or less circular at the top and funnel-shaped towards bottom
(c) A landform forms due to dripping water from surface
(d) An irregular surface with sharp pinnacles, grooves and ridges

Ans. (a) A small to medium sized shallow depression.

Q. 5. A deep, long and wide trough or basin with very steep concave high walls at its head as well as in sides is known as: A

(a) Cirque
(b) Glacial valley
(c) Lateral Moraine
(d) Esker

Ans. (a) Cirque.

(B) Answer the following questions in about 30 words :

Q. 1. What do incised meanders in rocks and meanders in plains of alluvium indicate? A

Ans. Incised meanders in rocks and meanders in plains of alluvium indicate on the status of original land surfaces over which streams have developed.

Q. 2. Explain the evolution of valley sinks or uvalas. U

Ans. When sinkholes and dolines join together because of slumping of materials along their margins of sue to roof collapse of caves, long , narrow to wide trenches called valley sinks or uvalas form.

Q. 3. Underground flow of water is more common than surface run-off in limestone areas. Why? A

Ans. The results of the work of groundwater cannot be seen in all types of rocks. But in rocks like limestones or dolomites rich in calcium carbonate, the surface water as well as groundwater through the chemical process of solution and precipitation deposition develop varieties of landforms. These two processes of solution and precipitation are active in limestones or dolomites occurring either exclusively or interbedded with other rocks. Therefore, underground flow of water is more common than surface run off in limestone areas.

Q. 4. Glacial valleys show up many linear depositional forms. Give their locations and names? A

Ans. Glacial valleys show up many linear depositional forms . their locations and names are as follows :

(i) **Moraines :** They are long ridges of deposits of glacial till. Terminal moraines are long ridges of debris deposited at the end (toe) of the glaciers.

(ii) **Eskers :** When glaciers melt in summer, the water flows on the surface of the ice or seeps down along the margins or even moves through holes in the ice. These waters accumulate beneath the glacier and flow like streams in a channel beneath the ice. Such streams flow over the ground (not in a valley cut in the ground) with ice forming its banks.

(iii) **Outwash Plains :** The plains at the foot of the glacial mountains or beyond the limits of continental ice sheets are covered with glacio-fluvial deposits in the form of broad flat alluvial fans which may join to form outwash plains of gravel, silt, sand and clay.

(iv) **Drumlins :** They are smooth oval shaped ridge-like features composed mainly of glacial till with some masses of gravel and sand.

Q. 5. How does wind perform its task in desert areas? Is it the only agent responsible for the erosional features in the deserts? U

Ans. The desert floors get heated up too much and too quickly because of being dry and barren. Winds also move along the desert floors with great speed and the obstructions in their path create turbulence. Of course, there are storm winds which are very destructive. The impact is simply sheer force of momentum which occurs when sand is blown into or against a rock surface. It is similar to sandblasting operation. The wind action creates a number of interesting erosional and depositional features in the deserts.

No, wind is not the only agent responsible for the erosional and depositional features in the deserts. The other factor is rain or sheet wash.

(C) Answer the following questions in about 150 words :

Q. 1. Running water is by far the most dominating geomorphic agent in shaping the earth's surface in humid as well as in arid climates. Explain? U

Ans. In humid regions, which receive heavy rainfall running water is considered the most important of the geomorphic agents in bringing about the degradation of the land surface. There are two components of running water. One is overland flow on general land surface as a sheet. Another is linear flow as streams and rivers in valleys. Most of the erosional landforms made by running water are associated with vigorous and youthful rivers flowing along gradients. With time, stream channels over steep gradients turn gentler due to continued erosion, and as a consequence, lose their velocity, facilitating active deposition. There may be depositional forms associated with streams flowing over steep slopes. But these phenomena will be on a small scale compared to those associated with rivers flowing over medium to gentle slopes. The gentler the river channels in gradient or slope, the greater is the deposition. When the stream beds turn gentler due to continued erosion, downward cutting becomes less dominant and lateral erosion of banks increases and as a consequence the hills and valleys are reduced to plains.

In dry regions, most of the landforms are formed by the erosion and deposition of flood sheet. Although , in deserts, rain is scarce, it comes down torrentially in a short period of time. The desert rocks devoid of vegetation , exposed to mechanical and chemical weathering processes due to drastic diurnal temperature changes, decay faster and the torrential rains help in removing the weathering material easily. This means that the weathered material is moved by not only wind but also by rain/sheet wash.

Q. 2. Limestones behave differently in humid and arid climates. Why? What is the dominant and almost exclusive geomorphic process in limestone areas and what are its results? [A]

Ans. Many depositional forms develop within the limestone caves. The chief chemical in limestone is calcium carbonate which is easily soluble in carbonated water (carbon dioxide absorbed rainwater). This calcium carbonate is deposited when the water carrying it in solution evaporates or loses its carbon dioxide as it trickles over rough rock surfaces.

Stalactites hang as icicles of different diameters. Normally they are broad at their bases and taper towards the free ends showing up in a variety of forms. Stalagmites rise up from the floor of the caves. In fact, stalagmites form due to dripping water from the surface or through the thin pipe, of the stalactite, immediately below it.

The results of the work of groundwater cannot be seen in all types of rocks. But in rocks like limestones or dolomites rich in calcium carbonate, the surface water as well as groundwater through the chemical process of solution and precipitation deposition develop varieties of landforms. These two processes of solution and precipitation are active in limestones or dolomite occurring either exclusively or interbedded with other rocks. Therefore, underground flow of water is more common than surface run off in limestone areas.

Q. 3. How do glaciers accomplish the work of reducing high mountains into low hills and plains? [U]

Ans. Masses of ice moving as sheets over the land (continental glacier or pidmont glacier if a vast sheet of ice is spread over the plains at the foot of mountains) or as linear flows down the slopes of mountains in broad trough-like valleys (mountain and valley glaciers) are called glaciers . The movement of glaciers is slow unlike water flow. The movement could be a few centimetres to a few metres a day or even less or more. Glaciers move basically because of the force of gravity.

Erosion by glaciers is tremendous because of friction caused by sheer weight of the ice. The material plucked from the land by glaciers (usually large-sized angular blocks and fragments) get dragged along the floors or sides of the valleys and cause great damage through abrasion and plucking. Glaciers can cause significant damage to even un-weathered rocks and can reduce high mountains into low hills and plains.

As glaciers continue to move, debris gets removed, divides get lowered and eventually the slope is reduced to such an extent that glaciers will stop moving leaving only a mass of low hills and vast outwash plains along with other depositional features.

OSWAAL LEARNING TOOLS

For Suggested Online Videos

Visit : *https://qrgo.page.link/tMtLD* **Or Scan the Code**

To learn from NCERT Prescribed Videos

Visit : *https://qrgo.page.link/YQCnV* **Or Scan the Code**

□□

UNIT-IV

Climate

CHAPTER 8

COMPOSITION AND STRUCTURE OF ATMOSPHERE

Syllabus

- *Atmosphere, composition of atmosphere.*
- *Structure of the atmosphere.*

TOPIC-1
Atmosphere, composition of Atmosphere

Revision Notes

- Air is essential to the survival of all organisms. Some organisms like humans may survive for some time without food and water but can't survive even a few minutes without breathing air.
- Atmosphere is a mixture of different gases and it envelopes the earth all round. It contains life-giving gases like oxygen for humans and animals and carbon dioxide for plants.
- The air is an integral part of the earth's mass and 99 per cent of the total mass of the atmosphere is confined to the height of 32 km from the earth's surface.
- The atmosphere is composed of gases, water vapour and dust particles.
- The proportion of gases changes in the higher layers of the atmosphere in such a way that oxygen will be almost in negligible quantity at the height of 120 km.
- Carbon dioxide is meteorologically a very important gas as it is transparent to the incoming solar radiation but opaque to the outgoing terrestrial radiation.
- It absorbs a part of terrestrial radiation and reflects back some part of it towards the earth's surface. It is largely responsible for the green house effect.
- Ozone is another important component of the atmosphere found between 10 and 50 km above the earth's surface and acts as a filter and absorbs the ultraviolet rays radiating from the sun and prevents them from reaching the surface of the earth.
- Water vapour is also a variable gas in the atmosphere, which decreases with altitude. It acts like a blanket allowing the earth neither to become too cold nor too hot. Water vapour also contributes to the stability and instability in the air.
- Atmosphere has a sufficient capacity to keep small solid particles, which may originate from different sources and include sea salts, fine soil, smoke-soot, ash, pollen, dust and disintegrated particles of meteors.
- Dust particles are generally concentrated in the lower layers of the atmosphere; yet, convectional air currents may transport them to great heights.
- Dust and salt particles act as hygroscopic nuclei around which water vapour condenses to produce clouds.

Know the Terms

- **Atmosphere :** An atmosphere is layer of gases surrounding a planet or other material body.
- **Ozone :** It is a region of earth's stratosphere that absorbs most of the sun's ultraviolet radiations.

Multiple Choice Questions (1 mark each)

Q. 1. ______ is essential to the survival of all organisms. [A]

(a) House (b) Clothes

(c) Air (d) Ozone

Ans. (c) Air 1

Q. 2. The gas that is transparent to the incoming solar radiation but opaque to the outgoing terrestrial radiation is known as : [U]

(a) carbon dioxide

(b) oxygen

(c) nitrogen

(d) helium

Ans. (a) carbon dioxide 1

Q. 3. __________ acts like a blanket allowing the earth neither to become too cold nor too hot. [U]

(a) Dust particles

(b) Water vapour

(c) Ozone layer

(d) Carbon dioxide

Ans. (b) Water vapour 1

Very Short Answer Type Questions (1 mark each)

Q. 1. Define the term atmosphere? [A]

Ans. An atmosphere is layer of gases surrounding a planet or other material body. 1

Q. 2. Define the term ozone. [U]

Ans. It is a region of earth's stratosphere that absorbs most of the sun's ultraviolet radiations. 1

Answering Tip

- Ozone is a special form of oxygen, made up of three oxygen atoms rather than the usual two oxygen atoms.

Q. 3. Name any two important components of atmosphere? [U]

Ans. The atmosphere is composed of gases, water vapour and dust particles. 1

Q. 4. Why is carbon dioxide meteorologically a very important gas? [A]

Ans. Carbon dioxide is meteorologically a very important gas as it is transparent to the incoming solar radiation but opaque to the outgoing terrestrial radiation. 1

Q. 5. Why has the volume of carbon dioxide rising in the past few decades? [U]

Ans. The volume of carbon dioxide has been rising in the past few decades mainly because of the burning of the fossil fuels. 1

Q. 6. To what height carbon dioxide and water vapour are found in the atmosphere?

Ans. Carbon dioxide and water vapour are found only up to 90 km from the surface of the earth. 1

Q. 7. The ozone layer is found till what height? [A]

Ans. The ozone layer is found till 10 to 50 km. 1

Q. 8. Where are the dust particles concentrated in the atmosphere? [U]

Ans. The dust particles are concentrated in the lower layers of the atmosphere. 1

Commonly Made Error

- The students are not aware of the significance of the dust particles found in the atmosphere.

Answering Tip

- Dust particles help in the formation of rain.

Q. 9. Where is the higher concentration of dust particles found? [A]

Ans. The higher concentration of dust particles is found in subtropical and temperate regions due to dry winds. 1

Q. 10. What per cent of the earth mass is constituted by air and to what height is it confined ?

Ans. 99% of the earth mass is constituted by air and it is confined to the height of 32 km the earth's surface. 1

[AI] **Q.11. Why is ozone an important constituent of atmosphere?** [A]

Ans. Ozone is an important constituent of the atmosphere as it acts as a filter and absorbs the ultraviolet rays radiating from the sun and prevents them from reaching the surface of the earth. 1

Q. 12. Explain the change in composition of air in the upper layers of the earth.? [A]

Ans. The proportion of gases changes in the higher layers of the atmosphere in such a way that oxygen will be almost in negligible quantity at the height of 120 km. Similarly, carbon dioxide and water vapour are found only up to 90 km from the surface of the earth. 1

Short Answer Type Questions (3 marks each)

Q. 1. What do you know about the presence of gases, water vapour and dust particles present in the atmosphere? [A]

Ans. Gases : The volume of other gases is constant but the volume of carbon dioxide has been rising in the past few decades mainly because of the burning of fossil fuels. This has also increased the temperature of the air.

Water vapour : Water vapour is also a variable gas in the atmosphere, which decreases with altitude. It also absorbs parts of the insolation from the sun and preserves the earth's radiated heat. It thus, acts like a blanket allowing the earth neither to become too cold nor too hot. Water vapour also contributes to the stability and instability in the air.

Dust particles : Dust particles are generally concentrated in the lower layers of the atmosphere; yet, convectional air currents may transport them to great heights. Dust and salt particles act as hygroscopic nuclei around which water vapour condenses to produce clouds. **(1 × 3 = 3)**

Q. 2. How is ozone layer an important constituent of atmosphere? U

Ans. Ozone is another important component of the atmosphere found between 10 and 50 km above the earth's surface and acts as a filter and absorbs the ultraviolet rays radiating from the sun and prevents them from reaching the surface of the earth. **(1 × 3 = 3)**

Q. 3. What do you know about the composition of atmosphere. A

Ans. The atmosphere is composed of gases, water vapour and dust particles. The proportion of gases changes in the higher layers of the atmosphere in such a way that oxygen will be almost in negligible quantity at the height 120 km. Similarly, carbon dioxide and water vapour are found only up to 90 km from the surface of the earth. **3**

Q. 4. Discuss the important gases present in the atmosphere. U

Ans. The important gases present in the atmosphere are :

(i) Oxygen : Oxygen is important for breathing. It is the most combustible and helps in the burning of the fuel. Oxygen is the main source of energy and provides solid base to industries. Oxygen extends upto 64 km but it is concentrated at 16 km.

(ii) Carbon dioxide : It is the heaviest gas and is confined to lower layers. Carbon dioxide can be found upto the height of 32 km. Though it present in negligible quantity , it is important for vegetation. Carbon dioxide is meteorologically a very important gas as it is transparent to the incoming solar radiation but opaque to the outgoing terrestrial radiation. It absorbs a part of terrestrial radiation and reflects back some part of it towards the earth's surface. It is largely responsible for the green house effect.

(iii) Nitrogen : Nitrogen has no colour , odour or taste. Nitrogen generates protein in plants which is the main source of food. Nitrogen extends upto 128 km. The atmosphere is composed of 78% nitrogen.

(iv) Hydrogen : Hydrogen is a light gas and extends upto 11 km over the heavier gases. It accounts for 0.01% of our atmosphere. **(Any three) (1 × 3 = 3)**

Answering Tip

- Nitrogen accounts for 78% of the atmosphere, oxygen 21% and argon 0.9%. Gases like carbon dioxide, nitrous oxide, methane, and ozone are trace gases that account for about a tenth of one per cent of the atmosphere.

Q. 5. Discuss the role of dust particles in atmosphere. A

Ans. Atmosphere has a sufficient capacity to keep small solid particles, which may originate from different sources and include sea salts, fine soil, smoke-soot, ash, pollen, dust and disintegrated particles of meteors. Dust particles are generally concentrated in the lower layers of the atmosphere; yet, convectional air currents may transport them to great heights. Dust and salt particles act as hygroscopic nuclei around which water vapour condenses to produce clouds. **3**

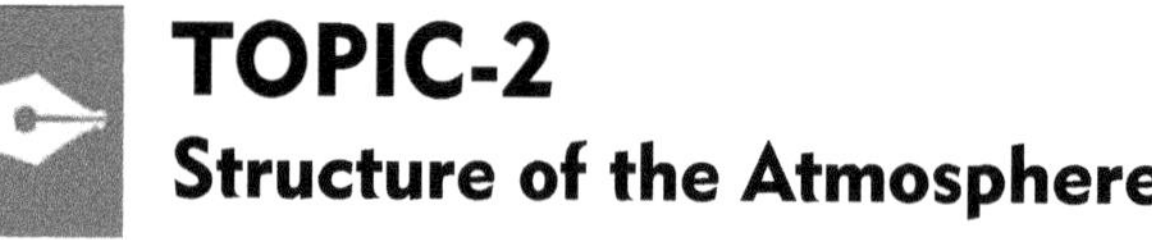

TOPIC-2
Structure of the Atmosphere

Revision Notes

- The atmosphere consists of different layers with varying density and temperature.
- Density is highest near the surface of the earth and decreases with increasing altitude.
- Atmosphere is divided into five different layers depending upon the temperature condition. They are: troposphere, stratosphere, mesosphere, ionosphere and exosphere.
- The troposphere is the lowermost layer of the atmosphere. Its average height is 13 km and extends roughly to a height of 8 km near the poles and about 18 km at the equator.
- Thickness of the troposphere is greatest at the equator because heat is transported to great heights by strong convectional currents.
- All changes in climate and weather take place in this layer. The temperature in this layer decreases at the rate of 1°C for every 165 m of height.

- This is the most important layer for all biological activity.
- The zone separating the troposphere from stratosphere is known as the tropopause.
- The air temperature at the tropopause is about minus 80°C over the equator and about minus 45°C over the poles.
- The stratosphere is found above the tropopause and extends up to a height of 50 km.
- One important feature of the stratosphere is that it contains the ozone layer. This layer absorbs ultraviolet radiation and shields life on the earth from intense, harmful form of energy.
- The mesosphere lies above the stratosphere, which extends up to a height of 80 km. In this layer, once again, temperature starts decreasing with the increase in altitude and reaches up to minus 100°C at the height of 80 km.
- The upper limit of mesosphere is known as the mesopause.
- The ionosphere is located between 80 and 400 km above the mesopause. It contains electrically charged particles known as ions, and hence, it is known as ionosphere.
- The uppermost layer of the atmosphere above the ionosphere is known as the exosphere. This is the highest layer but very little is known about it.
- Whatever contents are there, these are extremely rarefied in this layer, and it gradually merges with the outer space.

Know the Terms

- **Ion :** Ion are the electrically charged particles.
- **Tropopause :** The zone that separates the troposphere from stratosphere is known as the tropopause.
- **Mesopause :** The upper limit of mesosphere is known as mesopause.

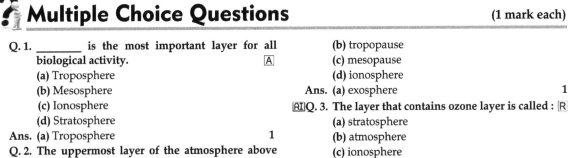

Multiple Choice Questions (1 mark each)

Q. 1. ________ is the most important layer for all biological activity. A

(a) Troposphere
(b) Mesosphere
(c) Ionosphere
(d) Stratosphere

Ans. (a) Troposphere 1

Q. 2. The uppermost layer of the atmosphere above the ionosphere is known as the : U

(a) exosphere
(b) tropopause
(c) mesopause
(d) ionosphere

Ans. (a) exosphere 1

AI **Q. 3. The layer that contains ozone layer is called :** R

(a) stratosphere
(b) atmosphere
(c) ionosphere
(d) mesosphere

Ans. (a) stratosphere 1

Very Short Answer Type Questions (1 mark each)

Q. 1. Define the term ion. A

Ans. Ions are the electrically charged particles. 1

Q. 2. What is tropopause?

Ans. The zone separating the troposphere from stratosphere is known as tropopause. 1

Commonly Made Error

- The students are not aware as to why tropopause is higher at the equator.

Answering Tip

- The troposphere is thicker over the equator than the poles because the equator is warmer. Heat differential on the planet's surface causes convection currents to flow from the equator to the poles. This implies that the warmer the weather, the thicker is the troposphere.

Q. 3. What is mesopause? U

Ans. The upper limit of mesosphere is known as mesopause. 1

AI **Q. 4. Which is the most important layer for human beings.** A

Ans. Troposphere is the most important layer for a biological activity, therefore, it is most important layer for human beings. 1

Q. 5. Name any two important elements of weather and climate?

Ans. Temperature, pressure, wind and humidity. (Any two) 1

Q. 6. Where is ionosphere located? A

Ans. Ionosphere is located between 80 to 400 km above the mesosphere. 1

Short Answer Type Questions (3 marks each)

Q. 1. What makes troposphere an important layer of the atmosphere? [U]

Ans. The troposphere is the lowermost layer of the atmosphere. Its average height is 13 km and extends roughly to a height of 8 km near the poles and about 18 km at the equator. It is an important layer of the atmosphere because :

(i) This layer contains dust particles and water vapour. Thickness of the troposphere is greatest at the equator because the heat is transported to great heights by strong conventional currents.

(ii) All climatic and weather changes take place in this layer. All biological activities also take place in this layer.

(iii) The temperature in this layer decreases at the rate of 1°C for every 165 m of height. **(1 × 3 = 3)**

Q. 2. Write important characteristics of stratosphere , mesosphere and ionosphere? [A]

Ans. Important characteristics of :

(i) Stratosphere :

(a) The stratosphere is found above the tropopause and extends up to a height of 50 km.

(b) One important feature of the stratosphere is that it contains the ozone layer.

(c) This layer absorbs ultraviolet radiation and shields life on the earth from intense, harmful form of energy.

(ii) Mesosphere :

(a) The mesosphere lies above the stratosphere, which extends up to a height of 80 km.

(b) In this layer, once again, temperature starts decreasing with the increase in altitude and reaches up to minus 100°C at the height of 80 km.

(c) The upper limit of mesosphere is known as the mesopause.

(iii) Ionosphere :

(a) The ionosphere is located between 80 and 400 km above the mesopause.

(b) It contains electrically charged particles known as ions, and hence, it is known as ionosphere.

(c) Radio waves transmitted from the earth are reflected back to the earth by this layer. Temperature here starts increasing with height.

(1 × 3 = 3)

Commonly Made Error

- The students are not aware as to what makes ionosphere so special.

Answering Tip

- Ionosphere is not a separate layer, but part of the thermosphere. Different regions of the ionosphere make long distance radio communication possible by reflecting the radio waves back to earth.

[AI] **Q. 3. What would be the consequences if there would be no ozone in the atmosphere?** [U]

Ans. The ozone acts as a filter and absorbs the ultraviolet rays radiating from the sun and prevents them from reaching the surface of the earth. If there would be no ozone, there would be no protection from the harmful UV rays and we would be exposed to these rays. In the absence of ozone, we would suffer from severe skin problems such as cancer and there is a probability that life would not have been possible on the earth. **3**

Long Answer Type Questions (5 marks each)

Q. 1. Explain the structure of the atmosphere with the help of a labelled diagram. [U]

Ans. Refer to NCERT Corner, Long Ans (2).

Answering Tip

- The atmosphere consists of 4 layers: the troposphere, stratosphere, mesosphere, and thermosphere. This is the layer where we live and where weather happens.

NCERT CORNER

(A) Multiple choice questions :

Q. 1. Which one of the following gases constitutes the major portion of the atmosphere : [R]

(a) Oxygen
(b) Nitrogen
(c) Argon
(d) Carbon dioxide

Ans. **(b)** Nitrogen .

Q. 2. Atmospheric layer important for human beings is : [A]

(a) Stratosphere
(b) Mesosphere
(c) Troposphere
(d) Ionosphere

Ans. **(c)** Troposphere.

Q. 3. Sea salt, pollen, ash, smoke-soot, fine soil — these are associated with : U

(a) Gases

(b) Dust particles

(c) Water vapour

(d) Meteors

Ans. (b) Dust particles.

Q. 4. Oxygen gas is in negligible quantity at the height of atmosphere : A

(a) 90 km

(b) 120 km

(c) 100 km

(d) 150 km

Ans. (b) 120 km.

Q. 5. Which one of the following gases is transparent to incoming solar radiation and opaque to outgoing terrestrial radiation : R

(a) Oxygen

(b) Nitrogen

(c) Helium

(d) Carbon dioxide

Ans. (d) Carbon dioxide .

(B) Answer the following questions in about 30 words :

Q. 1. What do you understand by atmosphere? A

Ans. Atmosphere is a mixture of different gases and it envelops the earth all round. It contains life-giving gases like oxygen for humans and animals and carbon dioxide for plants.

Q. 2. What are the elements of weather and climate. A

Ans. The important elements of weather and climate which are subject to change and which influence human life on earth are temperature, pressure, winds, humidity, clouds and precipitation.

AI **Q. 3. Describe the composition of atmosphere?** U

Ans. The atmosphere is composed of gases, water vapour and dust particles. The proportion of gases changes in the higher layers of the atmosphere in such a way that oxygen will be almost in negligible quantity at the height of 120 km. Similarly, carbon dioxide and water vapour are found only up to 90 km from the surface of the earth.

Other gases include helium, krypton, xenon, hydrogen , neon,etc.

Q. 4. Why is troposphere the most important of all the layers of the atmosphere? A

Ans. The troposphere is the lowermost layer of the atmosphere. This layer contains dust particles and water vapour. All changes in climate and weather take place in this layer. The temperature in this layer decreases at the rate of 1°C for every 165 m of height. This is the most important layer for all biological activity.

(C) Answer the following questions in about 150 words :

Q. 1. Describe the composition of the atmosphere. U

Ans. The atmosphere is composed of gases, water vapour and dust particles. The proportion of gases changes in the higher layers of the atmosphere in such a way that oxygen will be almost in negligible quantity at the height of 120 km.

Carbon dioxide is meteorologically a very important gas as it is transparent to the incoming solar radiation but opaque to the outgoing terrestrial radiation. The volume of other gases is constant but the volume of carbon dioxide has been rising in the past few decades mainly because of the burning of fossil fuels.

Ozone is another important component of the atmosphere found between 10 and 50 km above the earth's surface and acts as a filter and absorbs the ultra-violet rays radiating from the sun and prevents them from reaching the surface of the earth.

Water vapour is also a variable gas in the atmosphere, which decreases with altitude. It also absorbs parts of the insolation from the sun and preserves the earth's radiated heat. It thus, acts like a blanket allowing the earth neither to become too cold nor too hot. Water vapour also contributes to the stability and instability in the air.

Dust particles are generally concentrated in the lower layers of the atmosphere; yet, convectional air currents may transport them to great height. Dust and salt particles act as hygroscopic nuclei around which water vapour condenses to produce clouds.

Permanent Gases of the Atmosphere

Constituent	Formula	Percentage by Volume
Nitrogen	N_2	78.08
Oxygen	O_2	20.95
Argon	Ar	0.93
Carbon dioxide	CO_2	0.036
Neon	Ne	0.002
Helium	He	0.0005
Krypton	Kr	0.001
Xenon	Xe	0.00009
Hydrogen	H_2	0.00005

Q. 2. Draw a suitable diagram for the structure of the atmosphere and label it and describe it? U

Ans. The atmosphere consists of different layers with varying density and temperature. Density is highest near the surface of the earth and decreases with increasing altitude. The atmosphere is divided into five different layers depending upon the temperature condition.

They are: troposphere, stratosphere, mesosphere, ionosphere and exosphere.

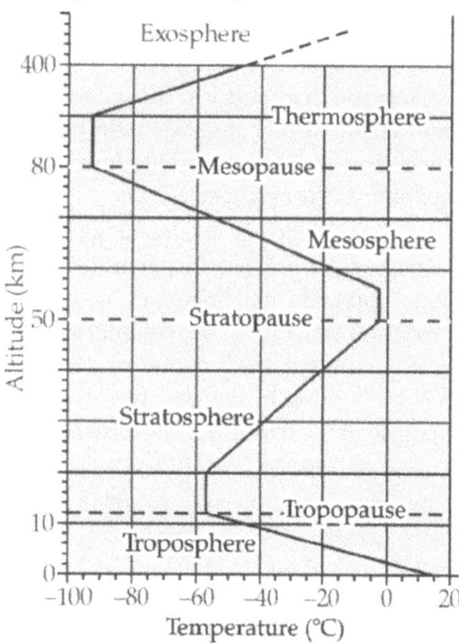

(i) **Troposphere:** The troposphere is the lowermost layer of the atmosphere. Its average height is 13 km and extends roughly to a height of 8 km near the poles and about 18 km at the equator. Thickness of the troposphere is greatest at the equator because heat is transported to great heights by strong convectional currents.
This layer contains dust particles and water vapour. All changes in climate and weather take place in this layer. The temperature in this layer decreases at the rate of 1°C for every 165 m of height. This is the most important layer for all biological activity.

(ii) **Stratosphere:** The stratosphere is found above the tropopause and extends up to a height of 50 km. One important feature of the stratosphere is that it contains the ozone layer. This layer absorbs ultraviolet radiation and shields life on the earth from intense, harmful form of energy.

(iii) **Mesosphere:** The mesosphere lies above the stratosphere, which extends up to a height of 80 km. In this layer, once again, temperature starts decreasing with the increase in altitude and reaches up to minus 100°C at the height of 80 km.

(iv) **Ionosphere :** The ionosphere is located between 80 and 400 km above the mesopause. It contains electrically charged particles known as ions, and hence, it is known as ionosphere. Radio waves transmitted from the earth are reflected back to the earth by this layer. Temperature here starts increasing with height.

(v) **Exosphere :** The uppermost layer of the atmosphere above the ionosphere is known as the exosphere. This is the highest layer but very little is known about it. Whatever contents are there, these are extremely rarefied in this layer, and it gradually merges with the outer space. Although all layers of the atmosphere must be exercising influence on us, geographers are concerned with the first two layers of the atmosphere.

OSWAAL LEARNING TOOLS

For Suggested Online Videos

Visit : *https://qrgo.page.link/WSWqy*

Or Scan the Code

Visit : *https://qrgo.page.link/5WDMV*

Or Scan the Code

To learn from NCERT Prescribed Videos

Visit : *https://qrgo.page.link/FX9Jk*   **Or Scan the Code**

❑❑

CHAPTER 9

SOLAR RADIATION, HEAT BALANCE AND TEMPERATURE

Syllabus

> *Solar Radiation, Variability of Insolation at the Surface of the Earth, Heating and Cooling of Atmosphere, Terrestrial Radiation.*
> *Heat Budget of the Planet Earth, Temperature, Factors Controlling Temperature Distribution, Inversion of Temperature.*

TOPIC-1
Solar Radiation, Variability of Insolation at the Surface of the Earth, Heating and Cooling of Atmosphere, Terrestrial Radiation

Revision Notes

- The earth receives almost all of its energy from the sun. The earth in turn radiates back to space the energy received from the sun. As a result, the earth neither warms up nor does it get cooled over a period of time.
- Thus, the amount of heat received by different parts of the earth is not the same. This variation causes pressure differences in the atmosphere. This leads to transfer of heat from one region to the other by winds.
- The earth's surface receives most of its energy in short wavelengths. The energy received by the earth is known as incoming solar radiation which in short is termed as insolation.
- As the earth is a geoid resembling a sphere, the sun's rays fall obliquely at the top of the atmosphere and the earth intercepts a very small portion of the sun's energy.
- The solar output received at the top of the atmosphere varies slightly in a year due to the variations in the distance between the earth and the sun.
- During its revolution around the sun, the earth is farthest from the sun (152 million km on 4th July). This position of the earth is called aphelion.
- On 3rd January, the earth is the nearest to the sun (147 million km). This position is called perihelion.
- The variation in the solar output does not have great effect on daily weather changes on the surface of the earth.
- The amount and the intensity of insolation vary during a day, in a season and in a year. The factors that cause these variations in insolation are :
  - the rotation of earth on its axis;
  - the angle of inclination of the sun's rays;
  - the length of the day;
  - the transparency of the atmosphere;
  - the configuration of land in terms of its aspect.

  The last two however, have less influence.
- The atmosphere is largely transparent to short wave solar radiation. The incoming solar radiation passes through the atmosphere before striking the earth's surface.
- The insolation received at the surface varies from about 320 Watt/m^2 in the tropics to about 70 Watt/m^2 in the poles. Maximum insolation is received over the subtropical deserts, where the cloudiness is the least.
- Equator receives comparatively less insolation than the tropics.

- The Earth after being heated by insolation transmits the heat to the atmospheric layers near to the earth in long wave form.
- The air in contact with the land gets heated slowly and the upper layers in contact with the lower layers also get heated. This process is called conduction.
- Conduction takes place when two bodies of unequal temperature are in contact with one another, there is a flow of energy from the warmer to cooler body.
- The air in contact with the earth rises vertically on heating in the form of currents and further transmits the heat of the atmosphere. This process of vertical heating of the atmosphere is known as convection.
- The transfer of heat through horizontal movement of air is called advection.
- In tropical regions particularly in northern India during summer season local winds called 'loo' is the outcome of advection process.
- The insolation received by the earth is in short waves forms and heats up its surface. The earth after being heated itself becomes a radiating body and it radiates energy to the atmosphere in long wave form. This energy heats up the atmosphere from below. This process is known as terrestrial radiation.
- The long wave radiation is absorbed by the atmospheric gases particularly by carbon dioxide and the other green house gases. Thus, the atmosphere is indirectly heated by the earth's radiation.

Know the Terms

- **Insolation :** The energy received by the earth is known as incoming solar radiation which in short is termed as insolation.
- **Aphelion :** During its revolution around the sun, the earth is farthest from the sun (152 million km on 4th July). This position of the earth is called aphelion.
- **Perihelion :** On 3rd January, the earth is the nearest to the sun (147 million km). This position is called perihelion.
- **Incoming Solar Radiation :** The earth's surface receives most of its energy in short wavelengths. The energy received by the earth is known as incoming solar radiation.
- **Conduction :** The air in contact with the land gets heated slowly and the upper layers in contact with the lower layers also get heated. This process is called conduction.
- **Convection :** The air in contact with the earth rises vertically on heating in the form of currents and further transmits the heat of the atmosphere. This process of vertical heating of the atmosphere is known as convection.
- **Advection :** The transfer of heat through horizontal movement of air is called advection.
- **Terrestrial Radiation :** The insolation received by the earth is in short waves forms and heats up its surface. The earth after being heated itself becomes a radiating body and it radiates energy to the atmosphere in long wave form. This energy heats up the atmosphere from below. This process is known as terrestrial radiation.

Multiple Choice Questions (1 mark each)

Q. 1. The atmosphere is indirectly heated by the earth's: R

(a) radiation
(b) insulation
(c) convection
(d) advection

Ans. (a) radiation 1

Q. 2. The insolation received by the Earth is in: U

(a) long waves forms
(b) short waves forms
(c) medium waves forms
(d) wide waves forms

Ans. (b) short waves forms 1

Q. 3. The earth after being heated by insolation transmits the heat to the atmospheric layers near to the earth in: R

(a) long wave form
(b) short wave form
(c) medium wave form
(d) average wave form

Ans. (a) long wave form 1

Very Short Answer Type Questions (1 mark each)

Q. 1. What is insolation? U

Ans. The earth's surface receives most of its energy in short wavelengths. The energy received by the earth is known as incoming solar radiation which in short is termed as insolation. 1

Q. 2. What is aphelion? U

Ans. During its revolution around the sun, the earth is farthest from the sun (152 million km on 4th July). This position of the earth is called aphelion. 1

Q. 3. What is perihelion? U

Ans. On 3rd January, the earth is the nearest to the sun (147 million km). This position is called perihelion. 1

Q. 4. Define the term 'Conduction'. R

Ans. The earth after being heated by insolation transmits the heat to the atmospheric layers near to the earth in long wave form. The air in contact with the land gets heated slowly and the upper layers in contact with the lower layers also get heated. This process is called conduction. 1

Q. 5. Define the term 'Convection'. R

Ans. The air in contact with the earth rises vertically on heating in the form of currents and further transmits the heat of the atmosphere. This process of vertical heating of the atmosphere is known as convection. 1

Q. 6. What is advection? A

Ans. The transfer of heat through horizontal movement of air is called advection. 1

Commonly Made Error

- The students are not aware of the examples of advection.

Answering Tip

- An example of advection is the transport of pollutants or silt in a river by bulk water flow downstream.

Q. 7. What is terrestrial radiation? U

Ans. The insolation received by the earth is in short waves forms and heats up its surface. The earth after being heated itself becomes a radiating body and it radiates energy to the atmosphere in long wave form. This energy heats up the atmosphere from below. This process is known as terrestrial radiation. 1

Q. 8. Why the annual insolation received by the earth on 3rd January is slightly more than the amount received on 4th July? A

Ans. On 3rd January, the earth is the nearest to the sun (147 million km). This position is called perihelion. Therefore, the annual insolation received by the earth on 3rd January is slightly more than the amount received on 4th July. 1

Q. 9. How much per cent of sun's rays are received by the upper layer of the atmosphere reach the earth? A

Ans. 51 per cent of sun's rays are received by the upper layer of the atmosphere reach the earth. 1

AI **Q.10. List any two factors that cause variations in insolation ?** U

Ans. The factors that cause these variations in insolation are :

(i) The rotation of earth on its axis;

(ii) The angle of inclination of the sun's rays;

(iii) The length of the day;

(iv) The transparency of the atmosphere;

(v) The configuration of land in terms of its aspect.

(Any two) 1

Q. 11. What causes the red colour of the rising and the setting Sun and the blue colour of the sky? A

Ans. Very small-suspended particles in the troposphere scatter visible spectrum both to the space and towards the earth surface. This process adds colour to the sky. The red colour of the rising and the setting sun and the blue colour of the sky are the result of scattering of light within the atmosphere. 1

Q. 12. What causes loo in the tropical regions?

Ans. Loo in the tropical regions especially north India is the outcome of advection process. 1

Q. 13. Write one point of differentiation between Perihelion and Aphelion.

Ans.

S.No.	Perihelion	Aphelion
1.	During its revolution around the sun, the earth is farthest from the sun (152 million km on 4th July). This position of the earth is called aphelion.	On 3rd January, the earth is the nearest to the sun (147 million km). This position is called perihelion.

1

Commonly Made Error

- It is believed that the difference of distance between the Perihelion and Aphelion cause changes in season.

Answering Tip

- The difference in distance is not the cause of our seasons. Instead, seasons are caused by the tilt of earth's axis.

Short Answer Type Questions (3 marks each)

Q. 1. Atmosphere gets heated up indirectly by terrestrial radiation and not directly by sun's rays. Explain? A

Ans. The atmosphere gets heated up indirectly by terrestrial radiation and not directly by sun's rays because :

(i) The long wave radiation is absorbed by the atmospheric gases particularly by carbon dioxide and the other green house gases.

(ii) Thus, the atmosphere is indirectly heated by the earth's radiation. The atmosphere in turn radiates and transmits heat to the space.

(iii) Finally the amount of heat received from the sun is returned to space, thereby maintaining constant temperature at the earth's surface and in the atmosphere. **(1 × 3 = 3)**

Q. 2. How does the energy received in upper layer of the atmosphere keep changing at different times of the year? U

Ans. The solar output received at the top of the atmosphere varies slightly in a year due to the variations in the distance between the earth and the sun. During the revolution of the earth around the sun, the Earth is farthest from the sun (152 million km on 4th July). This position of the earth is called aphelion. On 3rd January, the earth is the nearest to the sun (147 million km). This position is called perihelion. Therefore, the annual insolation received by the earth on 3rd January is slightly more than the amount received on 4th July. However, the effect of this variation in the solar output is masked by other factors like the distribution of land and sea and the atmospheric circulation. Hence, this variation in the solar output does not have great effect on daily weather changes on the surface of the earth. **(1 × 3 = 3)**

Q. 3. "The amount of insolation received depends on the angle of inclination of the rays". How? A

Ans. The amount of insolation received is the angle of inclination of the rays.

(i) This depends on the latitude of a place. The higher the latitude the less is the angle they make with the surface of the earth resulting in slant sun rays.

(ii) The area covered by vertical rays is always less than the slant rays. If more area is covered, the energy gets distributed and the net energy received per unit area decreases.

(iii) Moreover, the slant rays are required to pass through greater depth of the atmosphere resulting in more absorption, scattering and diffusion. **3**

Answering Tip

- Insolation affects temperature. The more the insolation, the higher the temperature.

Q. 4. What do you know about the spatial distribution of insolation on the earth's surface? A

Ans. The insolation received at the surface varies from about 320 Watt/m^2 in the tropics to about 70 Watt/m^2 in the poles. Maximum insolation is received over the subtropical deserts, where the cloudiness is the least. Equator receives comparatively less insolation than the tropics. Generally, at the same latitude the insolation is more over the continent than over the oceans. In winter, the middle and higher latitudes receive less radiation than in summer. **3**

Q. 5. Differentiate between conduction and convection.

Ans.

S.No.	Conduction	Convection
1.	The air in contact with the land gets heated slowly and the upper layers in contact with the lower layers also get heated. This process is called conduction.	The process of vertical heating of the atmosphere is known as convection.
2.	The Earth after being heated by insolation transmits the heat to the atmospheric layers near to the earth in long wave form.	The air in contact with the earth rises vertically on heating in the form of currents and further transmits the heat of the atmosphere.
3.	Conduction takes place when two bodies of unequal temperature are in contact with contact with each other , there is flow of energy from the warmer to cooler body.	The convection transfer of energy is confined only to the troposphere.

3

Answering Tip

- While conduction is the transfer of heat energy by direct contact, convection is the movement of heat by actual motion of matter; radiation is the transfer of energy with the help of electromagnetic waves.

Long Answer Type Questions **(5 marks each)**

Q. 1. Explain the factors that affect the insolation of the surface of the earth. A

Ans. The factors that affect the insolation of the surface of the earth are :

(i) The rotation of earth on its axis : The fact that the earth's axis makes an angle of 66½ with the plane of its orbit round the sun has a greater influence on the amount of insolation received at different latitudes.

(ii) The angle of inclination of the sun's rays : The higher the latitude the less is the angle they make with the surface of the earth resulting in slant sun's rays. The area covered by vertical rays is always less than the slant rays. If more area is covered, the energy gets distributed and the net energy received per unit area decreases. Moreover, the slant rays are required to pass through greater depth of the atmosphere resulting in more absorption, scattering and diffusion.

(iii) **The length of the day :** The duration of the day affects the amount of solar radiation received at the surface of the earth. The longer length of the day ensures larger supply of radiation which a particular area of the earth will receive. The latitude exercises the most dominant control over the length of the day.

(iv) **The transparency of the atmosphere :** The atmosphere is largely transparent to short wave solar radiation. The incoming solar radiation passes through the atmosphere before striking the earth's surface. Within the troposphere water vapour, ozone and other gases absorb much of the near infrared radiation.

(v) **The configuration of land in terms of its aspect :** The insolation received at the surface varies from about 320 Watt/m^2 in the tropics to about 70 Watt/m^2 in the poles. Maximum insolation is received over the subtropical deserts, where the cloudiness is the least. Equator receives comparatively less insolation than the tropics. Generally, at the same latitude the insolation is more over the continent than over the ocean. 3

Q. 2. Explain the heating and cooling mechanism of atmosphere. U

Ans. The heating and cooling mechanism of atmosphere includes :

(i) **Conduction :**

(a) The earth after being heated by insolation transmits the heat to the atmospheric layers near to the earth in long wave form. The air in contact with the land gets heated slowly and the upper layers in contact with the lower layers also get heated. This process is called conduction.

(b) Conduction takes place when two bodies of unequal temperature are in contact with one another, there is a flow of energy from the warmer to cooler body. The transfer of heat continues until both the bodies attain the same temperature or the contact is broken. Conduction is important in heating the lower layers of the atmosphere.

(ii) **Convection :**

(a) The air in contact with the earth rises vertically on heating in the form of currents and further transmits the heat of the atmosphere. This process of vertical heating of the atmosphere is known as convection.

(b) The convective transfer of energy is confined only to the troposphere.

(iii) **Advection :**

(a) The transfer of heat through horizontal movement of air is called advection. Horizontal movement of the air is relatively more important than the vertical movement. In middle latitudes, most of diurnal (day and night) variation in daily weather are caused by advection alone.

(b) In tropical regions particularly in northern India during summer season local winds called 'loo' is the outcome of advection process.

(Any three) (1 × 3 = 3)

Commonly Made Error

- The students have no idea what effect can the heating and cooling of the atmosphere have.

Answering Tip

- The heating or cooling of earth's surface and oceans can cause changes in the natural sources and sinks of these gases, and thus change greenhouse gas concentrations in the atmosphere.

TOPIC-2
Heat Budget of the Planet Earth, Temperature, Factors Controlling Temperature Distribution, Inversion of Temperature

Revision Notes

- The earth as a whole does not accumulate or loose heat. It maintains its temperature. This can happen only if the amount of heat received in the form of insolation equals the amount lost by the earth through **terrestrial radiation.**
- Consider that the insolation received at the top of the atmosphere is 100 per cent. While passing through the atmosphere some amount of energy is reflected, scattered and absorbed. Only the remaining part reaches the earth's surface.
- Roughly 35 units are reflected back to space even before reaching the earth's surface. Of these, 27 units are reflected back from the top of the clouds and 2 units from the snow and ice-covered areas of the earth. The reflected amount of radiation is called the albedo of the earth.
- Some part of the earth has surplus radiation balance while the other part has deficit.
- The surplus heat energy from the tropics is redistributed pole wards and as a result the tropics do not get progressively heated up due to the accumulation of excess heat or the high latitudes get permanently frozen due to excess deficit.

- The interaction of insolation with the atmosphere and the earth's surface creates heat which is measured in terms of temperature.
- While heat represents the molecular movement of particles comprising a substance, the temperature is the measurement in degrees of how hot (or cold) a thing (or a place) is.
- The various factors controlling temperature distribution are :
  - **The Latitude :** The temperature of a place depends on the insolation received. It has been explained earlier that the insolation varies according to the latitude hence the temperature also varies accordingly.
  - **The Altitude :** The temperature generally decreases with increasing height. The rate of decrease of temperature with height is termed as the normal lapse rate. It is 6.5°C per 1,000 m.
  - **Distance for the Sea :** As compared to land, the sea gets heated slowly and loses heat slowly. Land heats up and cools down quickly. Therefore, the variation in temperature over the sea is less compared to land.
  - **Air mass and Ocean Currents :** The places, which come under the influence of warm air masses experience higher temperature and the places that come under the influence of cold air masses experience low temperature. Similarly, the places located on the coast where the warm ocean currents flow record higher temperature than the places located on the coast where the cold currents flow.
  - **Distribution of Temperature :** The temperature distribution is generally shown on the map with the help of isotherms. The isotherms are lines joining places having equal temperature. The global distribution of temperature can well be understood by studying the temperature distribution in January and July.
- The temperature decreases with increase in elevation. It is called normal lapse rate. At times, the situations are reversed and the normal lapse rate is inverted. It is called inversion of temperature. Inversion is usually of short duration but quite common nonetheless.
- A long winter night with clear skies and still air is ideal situation for inversion. Over polar areas, temperature inversion is normal throughout the year.
- The inversion takes place in hills and mountains due to air drainage. Cold air at hills and mountains ,produced during night , flow under the influence of gravity . Being heavy and dense , the cold air acts almost like water and moves down the slopes to pile up deeply in pockets and valley bottoms with warm air above. This is called drainage. It protects plants from frost damages.

Know the Terms

- **Albedo of the earth :** While passing through the atmosphere some amount of energy is reflected , scattered and absorbed. Only the remaining part reached the earth surface. The reflected amount of radiation is called the albedo of the earth.
- **Heat budget :** The balance between incoming and outgoing solar radiation is termed as heat budget.
- **Normal lapse time :** The temperature generally decreases with increasing height. The rate of decrease of temperature with height is termed as the normal lapse time.
- **Loo :** It is the strong , gusty , hot and dry summer wind which blows in the summer season.
- **Isotherms :** They are lines joining places having equal temperature.
- **Inversion of temperature :** A reversal in the normal behaviour of temperature in the troposphere in which a layer of cool air at the surface is overlain by a layer of warmer air.
- **Planck's Law :** This law states that hotter a body, the more energy it radiates and shorter the wavelength of that radiation.
- **Air drainage :** The downslope flow of relatively cold air .
- **Specific heat :** It is the energy needed to raise the temperature of one gram of substance by one Celsius.

Multiple Choice Questions (1 mark each)

Q. 1. Earth as a whole maintains its: [A]
(a) heat
(b) coolness
(c) temperature
(d) height

Ans. (c) temperature 1

Q. 2. The temperature generally decreases with increasing: [U]
(a) height (b) pressure
(c) heat (d) time

Ans. (a) height 1

Q. 3. The temperature distribution is generally shown on the map with the help of: [R]
(a) heat budget
(b) isotherms
(c) mesotherms
(d) radiotherms

Ans. (b) isotherms 1

Very Short Answer Type Questions (1 mark each)

Q. 1. What do you mean by Albedo of the Earth? A

Ans. While passing through the atmosphere some amount of energy is reflected, scattered and absorbed. Only the remaining part reached the Earth surface. The reflected amount of radiation is called the albedo of the earth. 1

Answering Tip

- The range of albedo on the earth's surface can be as little as 3% (0.03) for water and as high as 95% (0.95) for fresh snow cover.

Q. 2. Define the term 'Heat Budget'. U

Ans. The balance between incoming and outgoing solar radiation is termed as heat budget. 1

Q. 3. What is normal lapse time? A

Ans. The temperature generally decreases with increasing height. The rate of decrease of temperature with height is termed as the normal lapse rate. 1

AI **Q. 4. Define Plank's Law.** U

Ans. Plank's law states that hotter a body, the more energy it will radiate and shorter the wavelength of that radiation. 1

Q. 5. What is specific heat?

Ans. Specific heat is the energy needed to raise the temperature of one gram of substance by one Celsius. 1

Commonly Made Error

- The students are not aware of the importance of specific heat.

Answering Tip

- Specific heat plays a very important role as it is able to absorb a lot of heat without a significant rise in the temperature.

Q. 6. How are temperature and heat interrelated? A

Ans. The earth as a whole does not accumulate or loose heat. It maintains its temperature. This can happen only if the amount of heat received in the form of insolation equals the amount lost by the earth through terrestrial radiation. 1

Short Answer Type Questions (3 marks each)

Q. 1. How do sun's rays while passing through atmosphere gets absorbed? U

Ans. Out of 100% sun's rays received by atmosphere, roughly 35 units are reflected back to the space.

The remaining 65 units are absorbed, 14 units within the atmosphere and 51 units by the earth's surface.

The earth radiates back 51 units in the form of terrestrial radiation. Of these, 17 units are radiated to space directly and the remaining 34 units are absorbed by the atmosphere (6 units absorbed directly by the atmosphere, 9 units through convection and turbulence and 19 units through latent heat of condensation. 48 units absorbed by the atmosphere, that are also radiation back into space. **(1 × 3 = 3)**

Q. 2. What is inversion of temperature? When and in what regions does it take place? A

Ans. At times, the situations are reversed and the normal lapse rate is inverted. It is called inversion of temperature. Inversion is usually of short duration but quite common nonetheless. A long winter night with clear skies and still air is ideal situation for inversion. The heat of the day is radiated off during the night, and by early morning hours, the earth is cooler than the air above. Over polar areas, temperature inversion is normal throughout the year. Surface inversion promotes stability in the lower layers of the atmosphere. Smoke and dust particles get collected beneath the inversion layer and spread horizontally to fill the lower strata of the atmosphere. Dense fogs in the mornings are common occurrences especially in winter season. This inversion commonly lasts for few hours until the sun comes up and begins to warm the earth. The inversion takes place in hills and mountains due to air drainage. **(1 × 3 = 3)**

Commonly Made Error

- What causes inversion of temperature is not clear to the students.

Answering Tip

- Temperature inversions occur most often when a warm, less dense air mass moves over a dense, cold air mass. This cold air then pushes under the warmer air rising from the valley, creating the inversion.

Q. 3. What do you know about the distribution of temperature in July? A

Ans. During this period, the sun shines vertically over head near the Tropic of Cancer. It is summer for the Northern Hemisphere and winter for the Southern Hemisphere. In the Northern Hemisphere the isotherm bends to the equator wards while crossing the oceans and polewards while crossing the landmass. In the Southern Hemisphere it is vice-versa.

In July, the isotherms generally run parallel to the latitude. The equatorial oceans record warmer temperature, more than 27°C. Over the land more than 30°C is noticed in the subtropical continental region of Asia, along the 30° N latitude. Along the 40° N runs the isotherm of 10° C and along the 40° S the temperature is 10° C. The lowest temperature below 0° C is recorded over Northern Hemisphere in the Central parts of Greenland. 3

Q. 4. What do you know about the temperature distribution in January? A

Ans. In January, the isotherms deviate to the north over the ocean and to the south over the continent. This can be seen on the North Atlantic Ocean. The presence of warm ocean currents, Gulf Stream and North Atlantic drift, make the Northern Atlantic Ocean warmer and the isotherms bend towards the north. Over the land the temperature decreases sharply and the isotherms bend towards south in Europe. It is much pronounced in the Siberian plain. The mean January temperature along 60° E longitude is – 20°C both at 80° N and 50° N latitudes. The mean monthly temperature for January is over 27°C, in equatorial oceans over 24°C in the tropics and 2°C – 0°C in the middle latitudes and – 18°C to – 48°C in the Eurasian continental interior. The effect of the ocean is well pronounced in the Southern Hemisphere. Here the isotherms are more or less parallel to the latitudes and the variation in temperature is more gradual than in the Northern Hemisphere. The isotherm of 20°C, 10° C, and 0°C runs parallel to 35° S, 45° S and 60° S latitudes respectively. 3

Q. 5. How does the distance from the sea affect the temperature of an area?

Ans. The temperature of an area varies with respect to the distance from the sea. Compared to land, the sea gets heated slowly and loses heat slowly. Land gets heated up and cools down fast. Therefore, the variation in temperature over the sea is less compared to land. Thus, the distance from the sea affects the temperature of an area. 3

Long Answer Type Questions

(5 marks each)

AI **Q. 1. Explain the factors that control the temperature distribution of any place.**

Ans. The temperature of air at any place is influenced by (i) the latitude of the place; (ii) the altitude of the place; (iii) distance from the sea, the airmass circulation; (iv) the presence of warm and cold ocean currents; (v) local aspects

(i) The latitude: The latitude can be explained as an angular distance of a place North or South of the earth's equator or of the equator of celestial object usually expressed in degrees and minutes. The temperature of a place depends on the insolation received. The insolation varies according to the latitude hence the temperature also varies accordingly.

(ii) The altitude : The atmosphere is indirectly heated by terrestrial radiation from below. Therefore, the places near the sea-level record higher temperature than the places situated at higher elevations. In other words, the temperature generally decreases with increasing height. The rate of decrease of temperature with height is termed as the normal lapse rate. It is 6.5°C per 1,000 m.

(iii) Distance from the sea : Another factor that influences the temperature is the location of a place with respect to the sea. Compared to land, the sea gets heated slowly and loses heat slowly. Land heats up and cools down quickly. Therefore, the variation in temperature over the sea is less compared to land. The places situated near the sea come under the moderating influence of the sea and land breezes which moderate the temperature.

(iv) Air mass : An air mass is a volume of air defined by its temperature and water vapour content. Air masses may cover many hundreds or thousands of square miles and adapt to the characteristics of the surface below them. Like the land and sea breezes, the passage of air masses also affects the temperature. The places, which come under the influence of warm air masses experience higher temperature and the places that come under the influence of cold air masses experience low temperature.

(v) Ocean currents: An ocean current is a seasonal directed movement of sea water generated by forces acting upon this mean flow, such as breaking waves, wind, the Coriolis effect, temperature and salinity differences, while tides are caused by the gravitational pull of the sun and moon. the places located on the coast where the warm ocean currents flow record higher temperature than the places located on the coast where the cold currents flow. 5

Q. 2. What do you know about the heat budget of the earth? A

Ans. The heat budget of the earth :

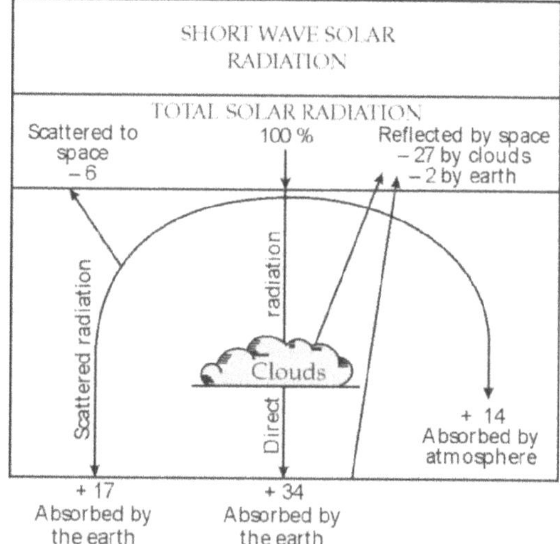

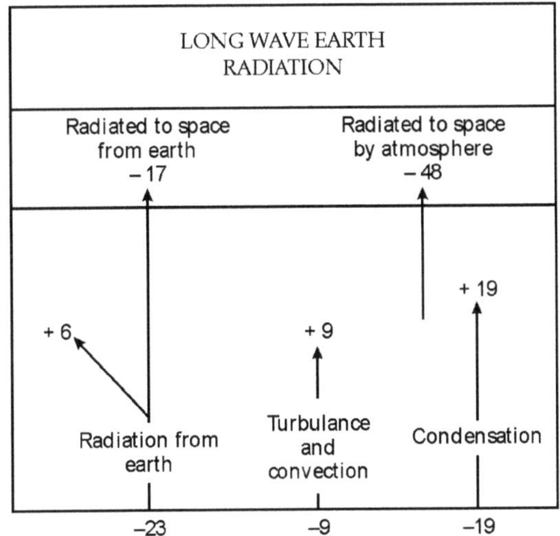

Heat budget of the earth

(i) The earth as a whole does not accumulate or loose heat. It maintains its temperature. This can happen only if the amount of heat received in the form of insolation equals the amount lost by the earth through terrestrial radiation. Consider that the insolation received at the top of the atmosphere is 100 per cent. While passing through the atmosphere some amount of energy is reflected, scattered and absorbed.

(ii) Only the remaining part reaches the earth's surface. Roughly 35 units are reflected back to space even before reaching the earth's surface. Of these, 27 units are reflected back from the top of the clouds and 2 units from the snow and ice-covered areas of the earth. The reflected amount of radiation is called the albedo of the earth.

(iii) The remaining 65 units are absorbed, 14 units within the atmosphere and 51 units by the earth's surface. The earth radiates back 51 units in the form of terrestrial radiation. Of these, 17 units are radiated to space directly and the remaining 34 units are absorbed by the atmosphere (6 units absorbed directly by the atmosphere, 9 units through convection and turbulence and 19 units through latent heat of condensation). 48 units absorbed by the atmosphere (14 units from insolation +34 units from terrestrial radiation) are also radiated back into space.

(iv) Thus, the total radiation returning from the earth and the atmosphere respectively is 17+48=65 units which balance the total of 65 units received from the sun. This is termed the heat budget or heat balance of the earth.

Answering Tip

- The atmosphere and the surface of the earth together absorb 71 per cent of incoming solar radiation, so together, they must radiate that much energy back to space for the planet's average temperature to remain stable.

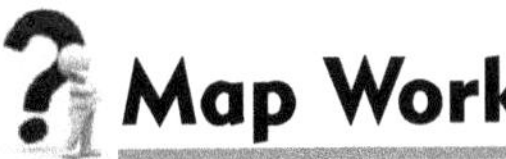

Map Work

(5 marks each)

Q.1. On an outline map of the world, locate the distribution of surface air temperature in the month of July.

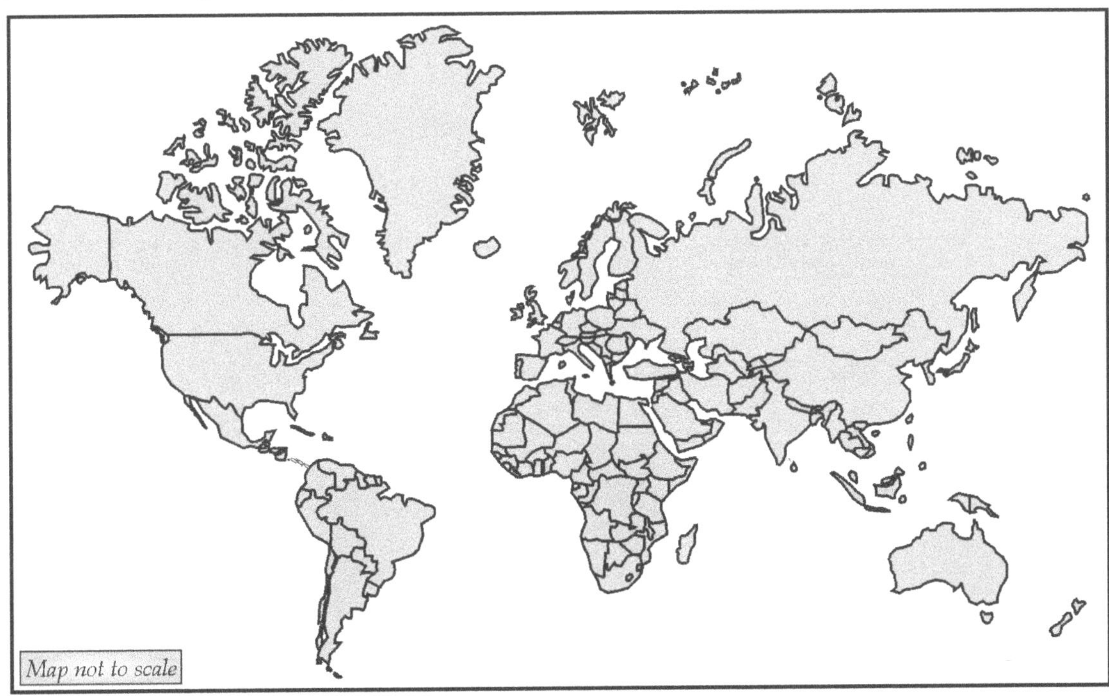

Ans.

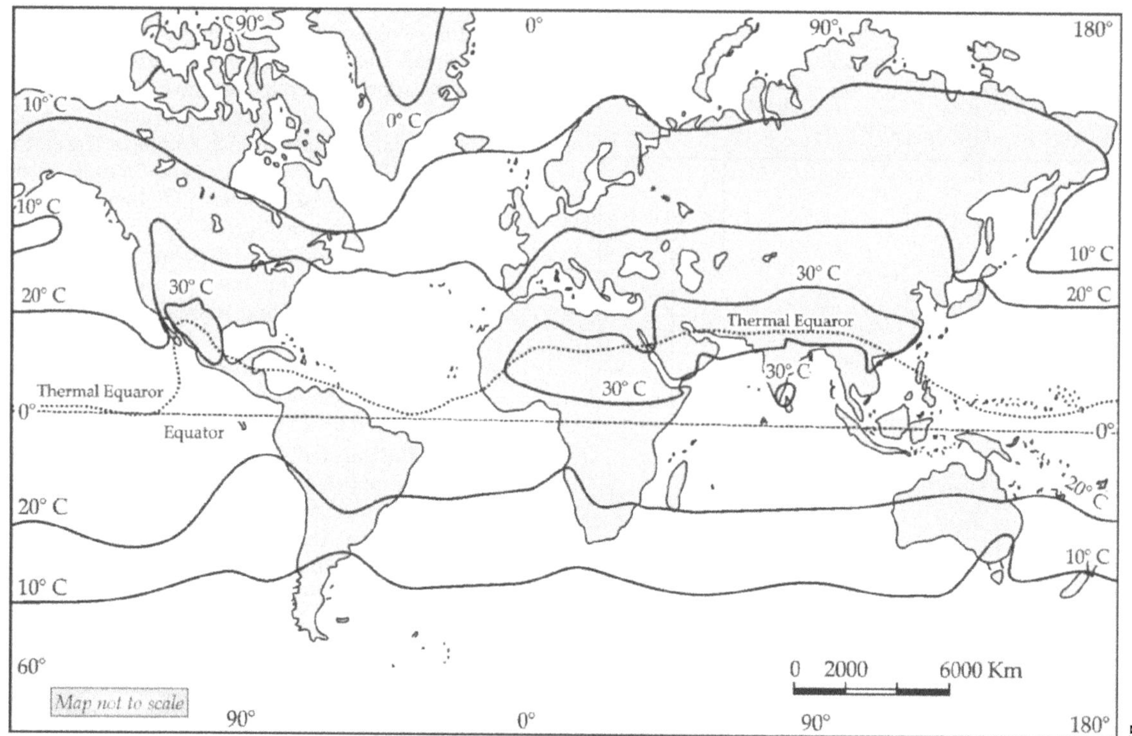

5

Figure 9.4 (b) : The distribution of surface air temperature in the month of July

Q. 2. On an outline map of the world , locate the distribution of surface air temperature in the month of January.

Ans.

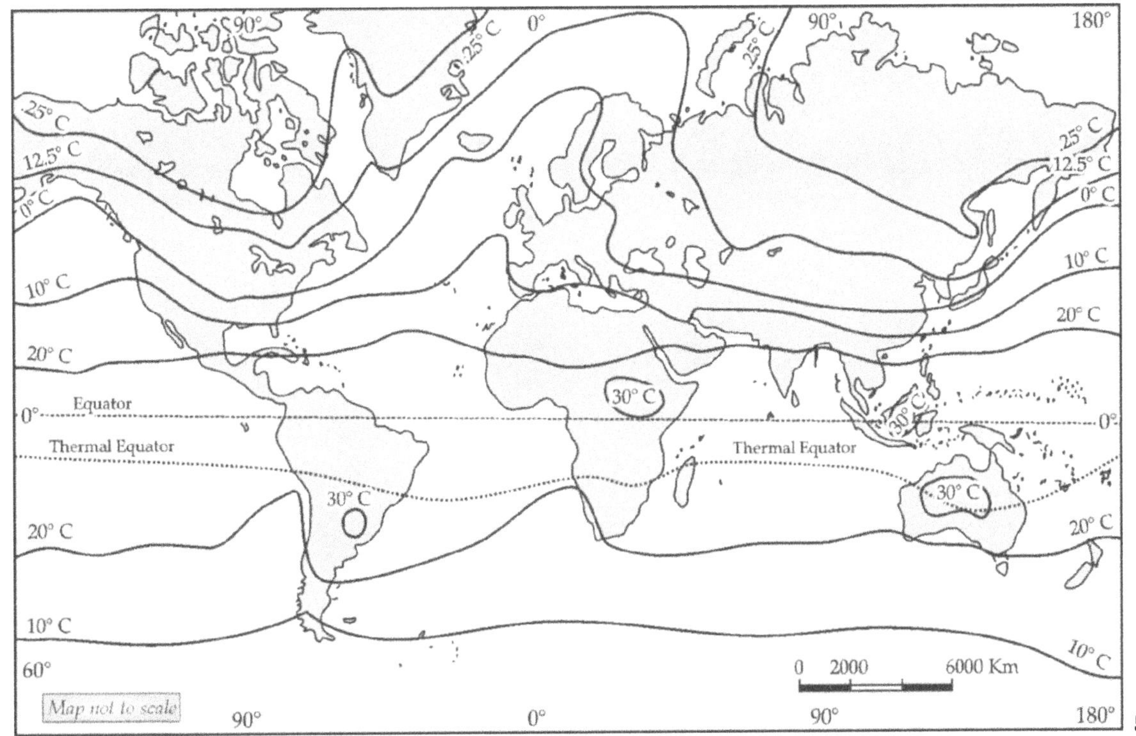

5

Q. 3. On an outline map of the world locate the range of temperature between January and July.

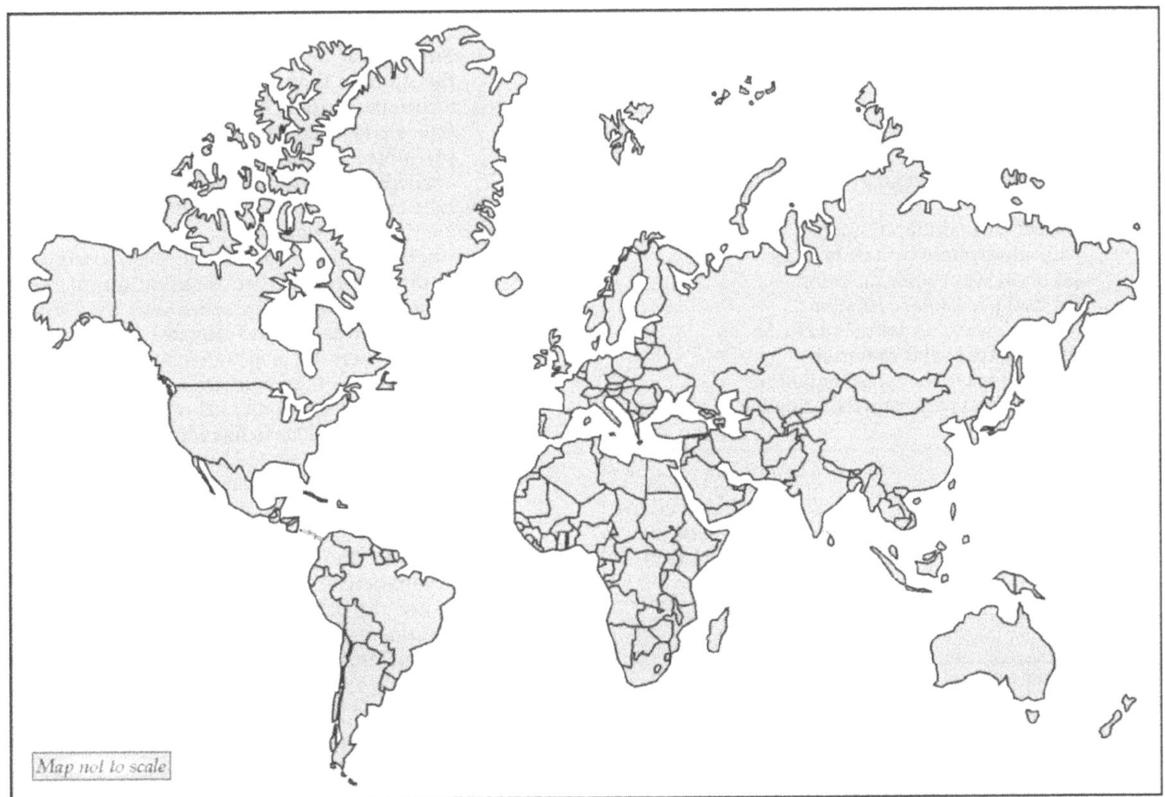

Ans.

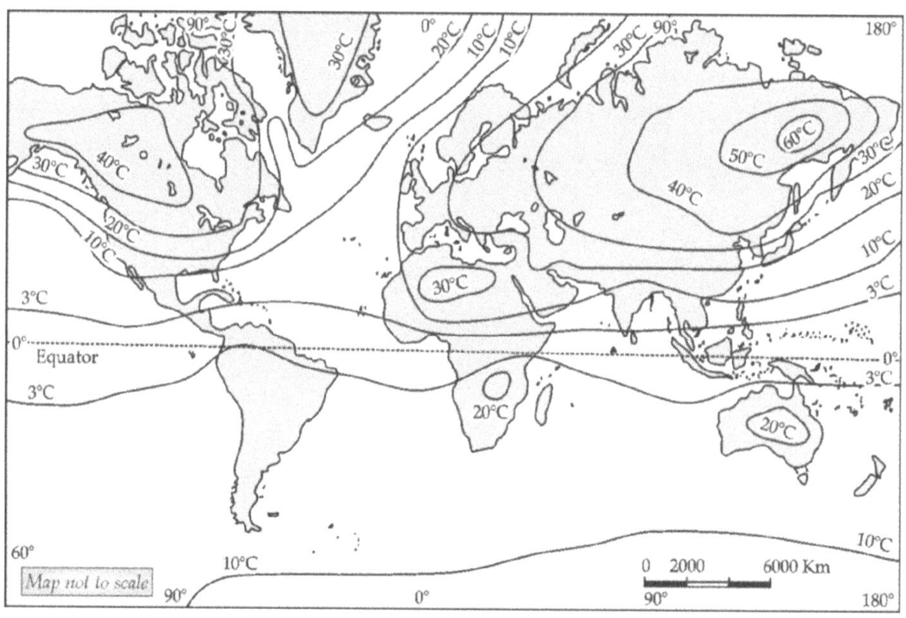

5

The range of temperature between January and July

NCERT CORNER

(A) Multiple choice questions :

Q. 1. The sun is directly overhead at noon on 21st June at : R

(a) The equator (b) 23.5° S
(c) 23.5° N (d) 66.5° N

Ans. (a) The equator .

Q. 2. In which one of the following cities, are the days the longest : R

(a) Thiruvananthapuram (b) Chandigarh
(c) Hyderabad (d) Nagpur

Ans. (a) Thiruvananthapuram.

Q. 3. The atmosphere is mainly heated by the : A

(a) Short wave solar radiation
(b) Reflected solar radiation
(c) Long wave terrestrial radiation
(d) Scattered solar radiation

Ans. (c) Long wave terrestrial radiation.

Q. 4. Make correct pairs from the following two columns : U

Column I	Column II
(i) Insolation	(a) The difference between the mean temperature of the warmest and the coldest months
(ii) Albedo	(b) The lines joining the places of equal temperature
(iii) Isotherm	(c) The incoming solar radiation
(iv) Annual range	(d) The percentage of visible light reflected by an object.

Ans. (i) (c); (ii) (d); (iii) (b); (iv) (a).

Q. 5. The main reason that the earth experiences highest temperatures in the subtropics in the Northern Hemisphere rather than at the equator is : U

(a) Subtropical areas tend to have less cloud cover than equatorial areas.
(b) Subtropical areas have longer day hours in the summer than the equatorial.
(c) Subtropical areas have an enhanced "green house effect" compared to equatorial areas.
(d) Subtropical areas are nearer to the oceanic areas than the equatorial locations.

Ans. (b) Subtropical areas have longer day hours in the summer than the equatorial.

(B) Answer the following questions in about 30 words :

Q. 1. How does the unequal distribution of heat over the planet earth in space and time cause variations in weather and climate? U

Ans. The areas where there is high temperature , wind blows from low temperature areas. Therefore, wind move upward from equatorial regions and blows towards two poles. Due to this wind, the pressure on both the poles increases. Unequal distribution of temperature is the main cause of blowing of wind. The unequal distribution of temperature, gives rise to rainfall and cyclone. Thus, unequal distribution of heat over the planet earth in space and time cause variations in weather and climate.

Q. 2. What are the factors that control temperature distribution on the surface of the earth? A

Ans. The temperature of air at any place is influenced by :

(i) The latitude of the place;
(ii) The altitude of the place;
(iii) Distance from the sea, the air mass circulation;
(iv) The presence of warm and cold ocean currents;
(v) Local aspects.

Q. 3. In India, why is the day temperature maximum in May and why not after the summer solstice? U

Ans. In India, the day temperature is maximum in May because at that time, the sun shines straight on the Tropic of Capricorn. It passes through the middle of India. The summer solstice stays till end of May. After this , the rains start on Malabar Coast at the end of May. It is because of this that the temperature does not increase in South India.

Q. 4. Why is the annual range of temperature high in the Siberian plains? [A]

Ans. Uneven climate is a characteristic of places located far off from the oceans and seas.

The mean monthly temperature for January is between – 18°C to – 48°C in the Siberian plains. In summers, it is upto 20° Celsius. This means that the annual range of temperature is – 68° which is extremely high. The presence of warm ocean currents, Gulf Stream and North Atlantic drift, make the Northern Atlantic Ocean warmer and the isotherms bend towards the north. Over the land the temperature decreases sharply and the isotherms bend towards south in Europe.

(C) Answer the following questions in about 150 words :

Q. 1. How do the latitude and the tilt in the axis of rotation of the earth affect the amount of radiation received at the earth's surface? [U]

Ans. Effect of Latitude: The amount of insolation received by a place on the surface of earth depnde upon the angle of inclination of the rays. The angle of inclination of the sun's rays depend upon the latitude of a place. The higher the latitude, the less is the angle the rays make with the surface of the earth resulting in slant rays. The area covered by the vertical rays is always less than the slant rays. If more area is covered, the energy gets distributed and the net energy received per unit area decreases. Moreover slant rays are required to pass through greater depth of the atmosphere resulting in more absorption, scattering and diffusion. Hence the high latitude areas get less net insolation as compared to the low latitudinal areas.

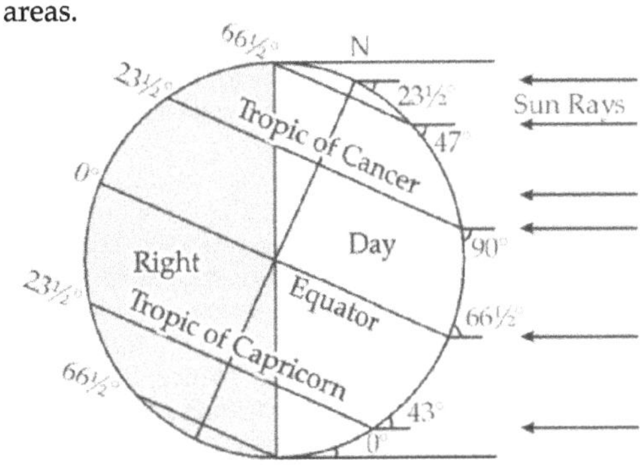

Figure 9.1 : Summer Solstice

Effect of the tilt in the axis of rotation of the earth: If all the other conditions are favourable to a place on the earth's surface then longer duration of sunshine or a day of the length and shorter duration of night enable the place to receive more amount of insolation.

The duration of sunshine or the day of length varies at all places except at the equator due to the tilt in the inclination in the axis of rotation of the earth (66 ½°)

The length of the day is almost 12 hours on the equator because the light circle always divides the equator in two equal halves. The length of day increases polewards with the northward march of the sun in the Northern Hemisphere while it decrease in the Southern Hemisphere at the time of summer solstice(21st June).

In contrast the length of day increases from the equator poleward in the Southern Hemisphere but it decreases in the Northern Hemisphere at the time of winter solstice. The following table describes this variation in the length of day on solstices due to the tilt in the axis of rotation of the earth.

Latitude	0°	20°	40°	60°	90°
December 22	12 h 00 m	10 h 48 m	9 h 8 m	5 h 33 m	0
June 21	12 h	13 h 12 m	14 h 52 m	18 h 27 m	6 months

Q. 2. Discuss the processes through which the earth-atmosphere system maintains heat balance. [U]

Ans. The earth receives most of its energy in the form of short wave radiation from the sun. All the solar energy entering the earth-atmosphere system is radiated back to the space maintaining the temperature of the earth-atmosphere system.

(i) A variety of processes—absorption, scattering, diffusion, reflection, terrestrial radiation, etc., make this possible.

(ii) Out of the total incoming solar radiation entering the earth's atmosphere, 35 per cent is sent back to space through scattering by dust particles, reflection from the clouds and from the ground surface. The 51 per cent solar energy received by the earth comprises 34 per cent as direct solar radiation and 17 per cent as diffuse day light. The earth after being heated by insolation transits the heat to the atmospheric layers near to the earth in long wave form. The air in contact with the land gets heated slowly and the upper layers in contact with the lower layers also get heated.

(iii) The earth after being heated itself becomes a radiating body and it radiates energy to the atmosphere in long wave forms. This energy heats up the atmosphere from below , a process called terrestrial radiation. The transfer of heat continues until both the bodies attain the same temperature or the contact is broken. Conduction is important in heating the lower layers of the atmosphere.

(iv) The long wave radiation is absorbed by the atmospheric gases particularly by carbon di-oxide and the other greenhouse gases. Thus, the atmosphere is indirectly heated by the earth's radiation. The air in contact with the earth rises vertically on heating in the form of currents and further transmits the heat of the atmosphere.

(v) The atmosphere in turn radiates and transits heat to the space. Finally the amount of heat received from the sun is returned to space, thereby maintaining the heat balance of the earth-atmosphere system.

Q. 3. Compare the global distribution of temperature in January over the Northern and the Southern Hemisphere of the earth. [U]

Ans. The global distribution of temperature can well be understood by studying the temperature distribution in January and July. The temperature distribution is generally shown on the map with the help of isotherms.

The isotherms are lines joining places having equal temperature. The deviation from this general trend is more pronounced in the month of January than in July, especially in the Northern Hemisphere. In the Northern Hemisphere the land surface area is much larger than in the Southern Hemisphere. Hence, the effects of land mass and the ocean currents are well pronounced. In January, the isotherms deviate to the north over the ocean and to the south over the continent. This can be seen on the North Atlantic Ocean. The presence of warm ocean currents, Gulf Stream and North Atlantic drift, make the Northern Atlantic Ocean warmer and the isotherms bend towards the north. Over the land the temperature decreases sharply and the isotherms bend towards south in Europe. The effect of the ocean is quite evident in the Southern Hemisphere. Here the isotherms are more or less parallel to the latitudes and the variation in temperature is ore gradual than in the Northern Hemisphere.

The mean January temperature along 60° E longitude is – 20°C both at 80° N and 50° N latitudes. The mean monthly temperature for January is over 27°C, in equatorial oceans over 24°C in the tropics and 2°C - 0°C in the middle latitudes and – 18°C to – 48°C in the Eurasian continental interior. The isotherms of 20 °C, 10°C and 0°C run parallel to 35 ° S , 45 ° S and 60 ° S latitudes, respectively.

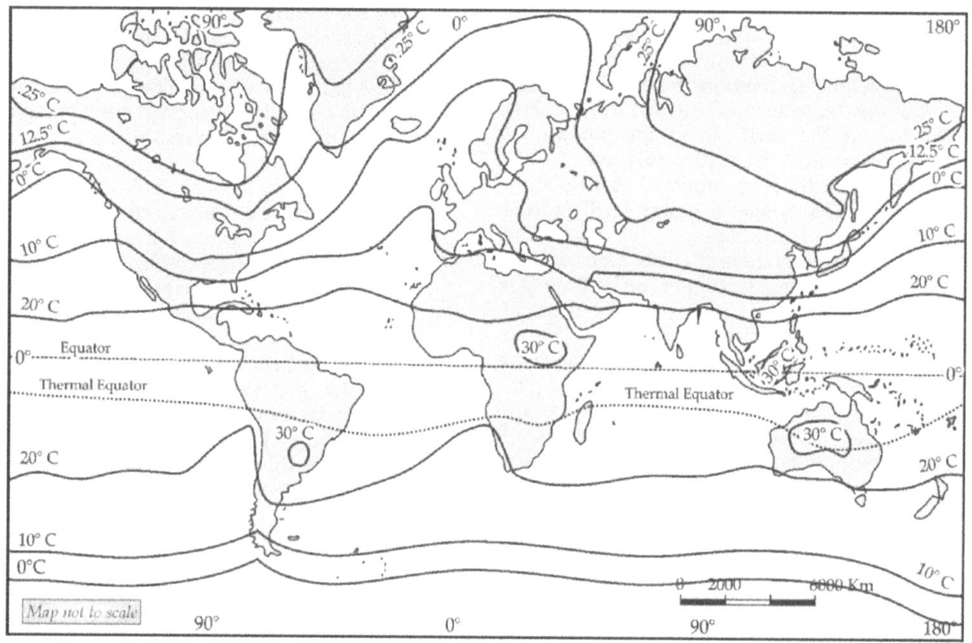

OSWAAL LEARNING TOOLS

For Suggested Online Videos

Visit : *https://qrgo.page.link/apYrA*

Or Scan the Code

Visit : *https://qrgo.page.link/3uzyU*

Or Scan the Code

To learn from NCERT Prescribed Videos

Visit : *https://qrgo.page.link/CTnjx*

Or Scan the Code

□□

CHAPTER

10 ATMOSPHERIC CIRCULATION AND WEATHER SYSTEMS

Syllabus

- *Atmospheric Pressure, Vertical Variation of Pressure, Horizontal Distribution of Pressure, World Distribution of Sea Level Pressure, Forces Affecting the Velocity and Direction of Wind.*
- *General Circulation of the Atmosphere.*

TOPIC-1

Atmospheric Pressure, Vertical Variation of Pressure, Horizontal Distribution of Pressure, World Distribution of Sea Level Pressure, Forces Affecting the Velocity and Direction of Wind.

Revision Notes

- Air expands when heated and gets compressed when cooled. This results in variations in the atmospheric pressure. The result is that it causes the movement of air from high pressure to low pressure, setting the air in motion.
- Atmospheric pressure also determines when the air will rise or sink. The wind redistributes the heat and moisture across the planet, thereby, maintaining a constant temperature for the planet as a whole. The vertical rising of moist air cools it down to form the clouds and bring precipitation.
- The weight of a column of air contained in a unit area from the mean sea level to the top of the atmosphere is called the atmospheric pressure.
- The atmospheric pressure is expressed in units of milibar (mb). Air pressure is measured with the help of a mercury barometer or the aneroid barometer.
- The pressure decreases with height. At any elevation it varies from place to place and its variation is the primary cause of air motion, i.e. wind which moves from high pressure areas to low pressure areas.
- The vertical pressure gradient force is much larger than that of the horizontal pressure gradient.
- Horizontal distribution of pressure is studied by drawing isobars at constant levels. Isobars are lines connecting places having equal pressure.
- Near the equator the sea level pressure is low and the area is known as **equatorial low**.
- Along 30° N and 30° S are found the high-pressure areas known as the subtropical highs.
- Further pole wards along 60 °N and 60° S, the low-pressure belts are termed as the sub polar lows.
- Near the poles the pressure is high and it is known as the polar high.
- These pressure belts are not permanent in nature. They oscillate with the apparent movement of the Sun. In the Northern Hemisphere in winter they move southwards and in the summer northwards.
- The air in motion is called wind. The wind blows from high pressure to low pressure.
- The wind at the surface experiences friction. In addition, rotation of the earth also affects the wind movement.
- The force exerted by the rotation of the earth is known as the Coriolis Force.

- Thus, the horizontal winds near the Earth surface respond to the combined effect of three forces – the pressure gradient force, the frictional force and the Coriolis Force.
  - **Pressure Gradient Force :** The differences in atmospheric pressure produces a force. The rate of change of pressure with respect to distance is the pressure gradient.
  - **Frictional Force :** It affects the speed of the wind. It is greatest at the surface and its influence generally extends upto an elevation of 1 - 3 km. Over the sea surface the friction is minimal.
  - **Coriolis Force :** The rotation of the earth about its axis affects the direction of the wind. This force is called the Coriolis Force. The Coriolis Force is directly proportional to the angle of latitude. It is maximum at the poles and is absent at the Equator.
  - **Pressure and Wind :** The velocity and direction of the wind are the net result of the wind generating forces. The winds in the upper atmosphere, 2 - 3 km above the surface, are free from frictional effect of the surface and are controlled by the pressure gradient and the Coriolis Force. Coriolis Force and the resultant wind blows parallel to the isobar. This wind is known as the geostrophic wind.
- The wind circulation around a low is called cyclonic circulation. Around a high it is called anti cyclonic circulation. The direction of winds around such systems changes according to their location in different hemispheres.

Know the Terms

- **Atmospheric Pressure :** The pressure exerted by the Earth's atmosphere at any given point of time, being the product of the mass of the atmospheric column of the unit area above the given point and of the gravitational acceleration at the given point.
- **Isobars :** They are lines connecting places having equal pressure.
- **Vertical pressure force:** The force that counteracts gravity and keeps the air up in the atmosphere is called the vertical pressure gradient force.
- **Horizontal pressure force :** The horizontal pressure forces are forces that are directed from higher towards lower pressure.
- **Equatorial low :** Near the Equator the sea level pressure is low and the area is known as equatorial low.
- **Polar high :** Near the poles the pressure is high and it is known as the polar high.
- **Sub-polar low :** The low-pressure belts are termed as the sub-polar lows.
- **Wind :** A natural movement of air of any velocity.
- **Pressure Gradient Force :** The differences in atmospheric pressure produces a force. The rate of change of pressure with respect to distance is the pressure gradient.
- **Frictional force :** It is the force resisting the relative motion of solid surfaces, fluid layers and material elements sliding against each other.
- **Coriolis force :** The rotation of the earth about its axis affects the direction of the wind. This force is called the Coriolis force.
- **Geostrophic wind :** These winds result from an exact balance between the Coriolis force and the pressure gradient force.
- **Cyclonic circulation :** The wind circulation around a low pressure condition is known as cyclonic circulation.
- **Anti-cyclonic circulation :** The wind circulation around the high pressure condition is known as anti-cyclonic circulation.

Multiple Choice Questions

(1 mark each)

Q. 1. Air pressure is measured with the help of a: R

(a) mercury barometer
(b) thermometer
(c) pressure force
(d) liquid barometer

Ans. (a) mercury barometer **1**

Q. 2. The wind circulation around a low is called : U

(a) frictional circulation
(b) cyclonic circulation
(c) atmospheric circulation
(d) anti-frictional circulation

Ans. (a) frictional circulation **1**

Q. 3. The Coriolis Force is the maximum at the: R

(a) Equator
(b) Poles
(c) Arctic Circle
(d) Antarctic Ocean

Ans. (b) Poles **1**

Q. 4. Coriolis Forces blow parallel to the : U

(a) hemispheres
(b) poles
(c) isobars
(d) poles

Ans. (c) isobars **1**

Very Short Answer Type Questions (1 mark each)

Q. 1. Define the term 'Atmospheric Pressure'? A

Ans. The weight of a column of air contained in a unit area from the mean sea level to the top of the atmosphere is called the atmospheric pressure. 1

Q. 2. What are isobars?

Ans. They are lines connecting places having equal pressure. 1

Q. 3. What is equatorial low? A

Ans. Near the Equator the sea level pressure is low and the area is known as equatorial low. 1

Q. 4. What is wind?

Ans. The air in motion is known as wind. 1

Q. 5. Define the term 'Corolis Force'. A

Ans. The force exerted by the rotation of the Earth is known as the Coriolis force. 1

Q. 6. Define the term Frictional Force?

Ans. It is the force resisting the relative motion of solid surfaces, fluid layers and material elements sliding against each other. 1

Q. 7. Define the term 'Pressure Gradient'. A

Ans. The differences in atmospheric pressure produces a force. The rate of change of pressure with respect to distance is the pressure gradient. 1

Answering Tip

- Winds are directed and driven by the pressure gradient force.

Q. 8. Define the term 'Vertical Pressure Gradient Force. U

Ans. The force that counteracts gravity and keeps the air up in the atmosphere is called the vertical pressure gradient force. 1

Q. 9. At what rate does pressure decrease with rise in height? U

Ans. In the lower atmosphere, the pressure decreases rapidly with height. The decrease amounts to about 1 mb for each 10m increase in elevation. It does not always decrease at the same rate. 1

Q. 10. How do the horizontal winds near the Earth's surface respond to the combined effect of forces? A

Ans. The horizontal winds near the Earth's surface respond to the combined effect of forces by—the pressure gradient force, the Coriolis force and the frictional force. 1

Q. 11. How is the atmospheric pressure expressed?

Ans. The atmospheric pressure is expressed in units of mb and Pascals. 1

AI **Q. 12. How is the air pressure measured?** A

Ans. Air pressure is measured with the help of a mercury barometer or the aneroid barometer. 1

Q. 13. How is the horizontal distribution of pressure studied? U

Ans. It is studied by drawing isobars at constant levels.

Q. 14. Differentiate between cyclonic circulation and anti-cyclonic circulation . A

Ans. The wind around low pressure is called cyclonic circulation, whereas; the wind circulation around a high pressure is called anti-cyclonic circulation. 1

Q. 15. Differentiate between low pressure and high-pressure system. U

Ans. Low pressure system is enclosed by one or more isobars with the lowest pressure in the centre. High-pressure system is also enclosed by one or more isobars with the highest pressure in the centre. 1

Answering Tip

- High pressure systems entail sinking air, while lows entail rising air.

Q. 16. Mention any one cause behind differences in atmospheric pressure . A

Ans. Air expands when heated and gets compressed when cooled. This results in variations in the atmospheric pressure. 1

Short Answer Type Questions (3 marks each)

Q. 1. Differentiate between vertical variation of pressure and horizontal distribution of pressure? A

Ans.

S.No.	Vertical variation of pressure	Horizontal distribution of pressure
1.	In the lower atmosphere the pressure decreases rapidly with height.	Small differences in pressure are highly significant in terms of wind direction and purposes of comparison.
2.	The decrease amounts to about 1 mb for each 10m increase in elevation.	Low pressure system is enclosed by one or more isobars with the lowest pressure in the centre.
3.	It does not always decrease at the same rate.	It is studied by drawing isobars at constant levels.

(1 × 3 = 3)

Long Answer Type Questions (5 marks each)

Q. 1. Discuss the factors that affect the direction and velocity of winds. U

Ans. The velocity and direction of the wind are the net result of the wind generating forces. The winds in the upper atmosphere, 2-3 km above the surface, are free from frictional effect of the surface, and are controlled mainly by the pressure gradient and the coriolis force.

When isobars are straight and when there is no friction, the pressure gradient force is balanced by the coriolis force and the resultant wind blows parallel to the isobar. This wind is known as the genostrophic wind . **3**

Q. 2. Write a note on Coriolis Force. A

Ans. The rotation of the earth about its axis affects the direction of the wind. This force is called the Coriolis Force after the French physicist who described it in 1844. It deflects the wind to the right direction in the Northern Hemisphere and to the left in the Southern Hemisphere.

The deflection is more when the wind velocity is high. The Coriolis force is directly proportional to the angle of latitude. It is maximum at the poles and is absent at the Equator. The Coriolis Force acts perpendicular to the pressure gradient force. The pressure gradient force is perpendicular to an isobar.

The higher the pressure gradient force, the more is the velocity of the wind and the larger is the deflection in the direction of wind.

As a result of these two forces operating perpendicular to each other, in the low-pressure areas the wind blows around it.

At the Equator, the Coriolis Force is zero and the wind blows perpendicular to the isobars. The low pressure gets filled instead of getting intensified. That is the reason why tropical cyclones are not formed near the Equator. **(Any Three) (1 × 3 = 3)**

Commonly Made Error

- The students are not aware what causes the Coriolis Force

Answering Tip

- Coriolis Force is the result of Earth's rotation on weather patterns and ocean currents.

TOPIC-2
General Circulation of the Atmosphere

Quick Review

➢ The pattern of planetary winds largely depends on :
- Latitudinal variation of atmospheric heating
- Emergence of pressure belts
- The migration of belts following apparent path of the sun
- The distribution of continents and oceans
- The rotation of Earth.

➢ The pattern of the movement of the planetary winds is called the **general circulation of the atmosphere.**

➢ The general circulation of the atmosphere also sets in motion the ocean water circulation which influences the Earth's climate.

➢ The air at the **Inter Tropical Convergence Zone** (ITCZ) rises because of convection caused by high insolation and a low pressure is created.

➢ The winds from the tropics converge at this low pressure zone. The converged air rises along with the convective cell. It reaches the top of the troposphere up to an altitude of 14 km. and moves towards the poles.

➢ This causes accumulation of air at about 30° N and S. Part of the accumulated air sinks to the ground and forms a subtropical high. Another reason for sinking is the cooling of air when it reaches 30° N and S latitudes.

➢ Down below near the land surface the air flows towards the Equator as the easterlies. The easterlies from either side of the Equator converge in the Inter Tropical Convergence Zone (ITCZ).

➢ Such circulations from the surface upwards and vice-versa are called cells. Such a cell in the tropics is called **Hadley Cell.**

➢ In the middle latitudes the circulation is that of sinking cold air that comes from the poles and the rising warm air that blows from the subtropical high. At the surface these winds are called westerlies and the cell is known as the **Ferrel Cell.**

➢ At polar latitudes the cold dense air subsides near the poles and blows towards middle latitudes as the polar easterlies. This cell is called the polar cell. These three cells set the pattern for the general circulation of the atmosphere.

➢ The local deviations from the general circulation system are as follows.

- **Seasonal Wind :** The pattern of wind circulation is modified in different seasons due to the shifting of regions of maximum heating, pressure and wind belts. The most pronounced effect of such a shift is noticed in the monsoons, especially over southeast Asia.
- **Local Winds :** Differences in the heating and cooling of Earth surfaces and the cycles those develop daily or annually can create several common, local or regional winds.
- **Land and Sea breeze :** The land and sea absorb and transfer heat differently. During the day the land heats up faster and becomes warmer than the sea. Therefore, over the land the air rises giving rise to a low pressure area, whereas the sea is relatively cool and the pressure over sea is relatively high. In the night the reversal of condition takes place. The land loses heat faster and is cooler than the sea. The pressure gradient is from the land to the sea and hence land breeze results.
- **Mountain and Valley Winds :** In mountainous regions, during the day the slopes get heated up and air moves upslope and to fill the resulting gap the air from the valley blows up the valley. This wind is known as the valley breeze. The cool air, of the high plateaus and ice fields draining into the valley is called katabatic wind.
- **Air Masses :** The air with distinctive characteristics in terms of temperature and humidity is called an airmass. It is defined as a large body of air having little horizontal variation in temperature and moisture.
- **Fronts :** When two different air masses meet, the boundary zone between them is called a front. The process of formation of the fronts is known as frontogenesis. When the front remains stationary, it is called a stationary front. When the cold air moves towards the warm air mass, its contact zone is called the cold front, whereas if the warm air mass moves towards the cold air mass, the contact zone is a warm front. If an air mass is fully lifted above the land surface, it is called the occluded front.
- **Extra Tropical Cyclones :** The systems developing in the mid and high latitude, beyond the tropics are called the middle latitude or extra tropical cyclones. The passage of front causes abrupt changes in the weather conditions over the area in the middle and high latitudes. Extra tropical cyclones form along the polar front. Initially, the front is stationary. In the Northern Hemisphere, warm air blows from the South and cold air from the North of the front.

  The extra tropical cyclone differs from the tropical cyclone in number of ways. The extra tropical cyclones have a clear frontal system which is not present in the tropical cyclones. They cover a larger area and can originate over the land and sea. Whereas the tropical cyclones originate only over the seas and on reaching the land they dissipate. The extra tropical cyclone affects a much larger area as compared to the tropical cyclone. The wind velocity in a tropical cyclone is much higher and it is more destructive. The extra tropical cyclones move from west to east but tropical cyclones, move from East to West.
- **Tropical Cyclones :** Tropical cyclones are violent storms that originate over oceans in tropical areas and move over to the coastal areas bringing about large scale destruction caused by violent winds, very heavy rainfall and storm surges. This is one of the most devastating natural calamities. Tropical cyclones originate and intensify over warm tropical oceans.
- The conditions favourable for the formation and intensification of tropical storms are : **(i)** Large sea surface with temperature higher than 27° C; **(ii)** Presence of the Coriolis force; **(iii)** Small variations in the vertical wind speed; **(iv)** A pre-existing weaklow-pressure area or low-level-cyclonic circulation; **(v)** Upper divergence above the sea level system.
- The place where a tropical cyclone crosses the coast is called the landfall of the cyclone. The cyclones, which cross 20° N latitude generally, recurve and they are more destructive.
- A mature tropical cyclone is characterised by the strong spirally circulating wind around the centre, called the eye. The diameter of the circulating system can vary between 150 and 250 km.
- **Thunderstorms and Tornadoes :** Other severe local storms are thunderstorms and tornadoes. They are of short duration, occurring over a small area but are violent. Thunderstorms are caused by intense convection on moist hot days. A thunderstorm is a well-grown cumulonimbus cloud producing thunder and lightening.
- A thunderstorm is characterised by intense updraft of rising warm air, which causes the clouds to grow bigger and rise to greater height. This causes precipitation. Later, downdraft brings down to earth the cool air and

the rain. From severe thunderstorms sometimes spiralling wind descends like a trunk of an elephant with great force, with very low pressure at the centre, causing massive destruction on its way. Such a phenomenon is called a tornado. Tornadoes generally occur in middle latitudes. The tornado over the sea is called water sprouts.

Know the Terms

- **General circulation of the atmosphere :** The pattern of the movement of the planetary winds is called the general circulation of the atmosphere.
- **Hadley cell :** A cell in the tropics is called the Hadley Cell.
- **Ferrel cell :** In the middle latitudes the circulation is that of sinking cold air that comes from the poles and the rising warm air that blows from the subtropical high. At the surface these winds are called westerlies and the cell is known as the Ferrel Cell.
- **Polar cell :** At polar latitudes the cold dense air subsides near the poles and blows towards middle latitudes as the polar easterlies. This cell is called the Polar Cell.
- **Cell :** The easterlies from either side of the Equator converge in the Inter Tropical Convergence Zone(ITCZ). Such circulations from the surface upwards and vice-versa are called cells.
- **El Nino :** The warm water of the central Pacific Ocean slowly drifts towards South American coast and replaces the cool Peruvian current. Such appearance of warm water off the coast of Peru is known as the El Nino.
- **Southern Oscillation :** The change in pressure condition over Pacific is known as the southern oscillation.
- **Westerlies :** They are the prevailing winds from the West towards the East in the middle latitudes between 30° and 60° degrees respectively.
- **Easterlies :** They are the winds which blow from the East towards the West .
- **Polar easterlies :** They are the dry, cold prevailing winds that blow from the high-pressure areas of polar highs at the North and South Poles towards low-pressure areas within the Westerlies at high latitudes. They blow from the pole to Equator.
- **ENSO :** The combined phenomenon of southern oscillation and El Nino is known as ENSO.
- **Katabatic winds :** The cool air, of the high plateaus and ice fields draining into the valley is called katabatic wind.
- **Adiabatic process :** It is the process which occurs without transfer of heat or matter between a thermodynamic system and its surroundings.
- **Airmass :** It is a volume of air defined by its temperature and water vapour content.
- **Source regions :** The homogenous surfaces, over which air masses form, are called the source regions.
- **Front :** When two different air masses meet, the boundary zone between them is called a front.
- **Frontogenesis :** The process of formation of the fronts is known as frontogenesis.
- **Stationary front :** When the front remains stationary, it is called a stationary front.
- **Cold front :** When the cold air moves towards the warm air mass, its contact zone is called the cold front.
- **Warm front :** If the warm air mass moves towards the cold air mass, the contact zone is a warm front.
- **Occluded front :** If an air mass is fully lifted above the land surface, it is called the occluded front.
- **Cyclone :** A cyclone is a large scale air mass that rotates around a strong centre of low atmospheric pressure.
- **Extra tropical cyclones :** The systems developing in the mid and high latitude, beyond the tropics are called the middle latitude or extra tropical cyclones.
- **Hurricane :** It is a large swirling storms which form over tropical or subtropical waters.
- **Landfall of the cyclone :** The place where a tropical cyclone crosses the coast is called the landfall of the cyclone.
- **Cumulous cloud :** They are the clouds which have flat bases and are often described as puffy , cotton-like or fluffy in appearance.
- **Cumulonimbus cloud :** They are dense, towering vertical cloud associated with thunderstorms and atmospheric instability , forming water vapour carried by powerful upward air currents.
- **Tornado :** They are rapidly rotating violent column of air that is in contact with both the surface of the Earth and the cumulonimbus cloud.
- **Water spouts :** The tornado over the sea is called water sprouts.
- **The eye :** It is a region of calm with subsiding air.
- **Eye Wall :** Around the eye is the eye wall, where there is a strong spiralling ascent of air to greater height reaching the tropopause.

Multiple Choice Questions (1 mark each)

Q. 1. The winds that blow from the west toward the east in the middle latitudes between 30 and 60 degrees latitude are known as : R

(a) easterlies wind (b) westerlies wind
(c) hurricane (d) cyclone

Ans. (b) westerlies wind 1

Q. 2. If the winds move from east to west, they are called: U

(a) easterlies (b) westerlies
(c) El Nino (d) hurricane

Ans. (a) easterlies 1

Q. 3. The puffy clouds that sometimes look like pieces of floating cotton: A

(a) cotton cloud (b) cumulus cloud
(c) front cloud (d) occulant cloud

Ans. (b) cumulus cloud 1

Q. 4. Tornadoes generally occur in: U

(a) upper latitudes
(b) down latitudes
(c) middle latitudes
(d) intermediate latitudes

Ans. (c) middle latitudes 1

Very Short Answer Type Questions (1 mark each)

Q. 1. What do you understand by the general circulation of the atmosphere? A

Ans. The pattern of the movement of the planetary winds is called the general circulation of the atmosphere. 1

Q. 2. Define the term 'El Nino'. U

Ans. The warm water of the central Pacific Ocean slowly drifts towards South American coast and replaces the cool Peruvian current. Such appearance of warm water off the coast of Peru is known as the El Nino. 1

Answering Tip

- The El Nino cycle begins when warm water in the western tropical Pacific Ocean shifts eastward along the equator toward the coast of South America.

Q. 3. What is airmass? A

Ans. It is a volume of air defined by its temperature and water vapour content. 1

Q. 4. What is front? U

Ans. When two different air masses meet, the boundary zone between them is called a front. 1

Q. 5. What sets the motion in the ocean water circulation?

Ans. The general circulation of the atmosphere sets in motion the ocean water circulation. 1

Q. 6. Differentiate between westerlies and easterlies. A

Ans. Westerlies are the prevailing winds from the West towards the East in the middle latitudes between 30° and 60° degrees respectively. Whereas, easterlies are the winds which blow from the East towards the West. 1

Q. 7. How many types of fronts are there? Mention any two?

Ans. There are four types of fronts: cold, warm, stationary and occluded. 1

Q. 8. How does front affect the weather? A

Ans. Front brings abrupt changes in the temperature and cause the air to rise to form clouds and cause precipitation. 1

Q. 9. Mention one important feature of front. U

Ans. Front occur in middle latitudes and are characterised by steep gradient in temperature and pressure. 1

Q.10. Mention any two different names by which the tropical cyclones are known. A

Ans. Tropical Cyclones are known as : cyclones in the Indian Ocean, hurricanes in the Atlantic, typhoons in the Western Pacific and South China Sea, and willy-willies in the Western Australia. 1

Q.11. Differentiate between Hadley Cell and Ferrell Cell. U

Ans. A cell in the tropics is called the Hadley Cell. Whereas, in the middle latitudes the circulation is that of sinking cold air that comes from the poles and the rising warm air that blows from the subtropical high. At the surface these winds are called westerlies and the Cell is known as the Ferrell Cell. 1

Q. 12. Differentiate between cold front and warm front. A

Ans. When the cold air moves towards the warm air mass, its contact zone is called the cold front. Whereas, if the warm air mass moves towards the cold air mass, the contact zone is a warm front. 1

Q. 13. Differentiate between stationary front and occluded front.

Ans. When the front remains stationary, it is called a stationary front. If an air mass is fully lifted above the land surface, it is called the occluded front. 1

Q. 14. Differentiate between cumulous cloud and cumulonimbus cloud.

Ans. Cumulous cloud are the clouds which have flat bases and are often described as puffy , cotton-like or fluffy in appearance.

Cumulonimbus cloud are dense, towering vertical cloud associated with thunderstorms and atmospheric instability , forming water vapour carried by powerful upward air currents. 1

Short Answer Type Questions (3 marks each)

Q. 1. Define the term 'Wind'. Explain different types of winds. [A]

Ans. The air in motion is known as wind. The different types of winds are :

(i) Seasonal Wind : The pattern of wind circulation is modified in different seasons due to the shifting of regions of maximum heating, pressure and wind belts. The most pronounced effect of such a shift is noticed in the monsoons, especially over southeast Asia.

(ii) Local Winds : Differences in the heating and cooling of earth surfaces and the cycles those develop daily or annually can create several common, local or regional winds.

(iii) Mountain and Valley Winds : In mountainous regions, during the day the slopes get heated up and air moves upslope and to fill the resulting gap the air from the valley blows up the valley. This wind is known as the valley breeze.

(1 × 3 = 3)

Answering Tip

- High winds can cause downed trees and power lines, flying debris and building collapses, which may lead to power outages, transportation disruptions, damage to buildings and vehicles, and injury or death.

Q. 2. Define the term 'Front'. How many types of front are there? Explain each of them. [A]

Ans. When two different air masses meet, the boundary zone between them is called a front. There are four different types of front.

(i) Stationary front : When the front remains stationary, it is called a stationary front.

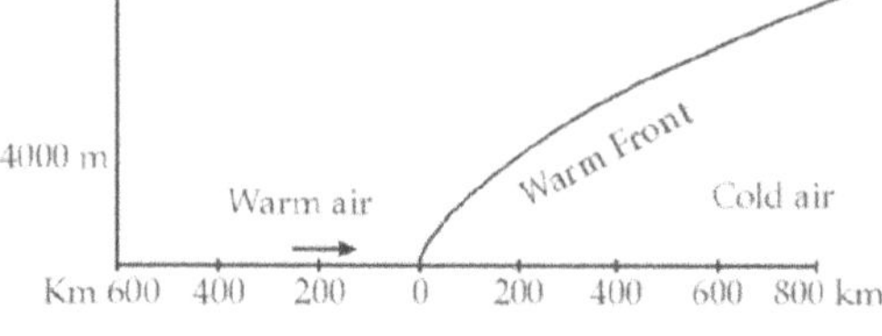

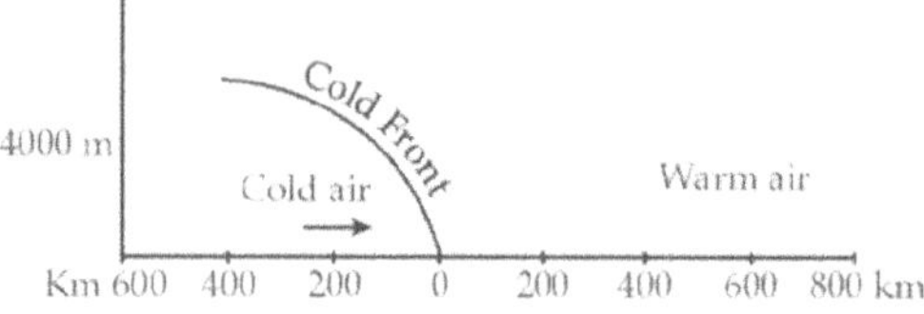

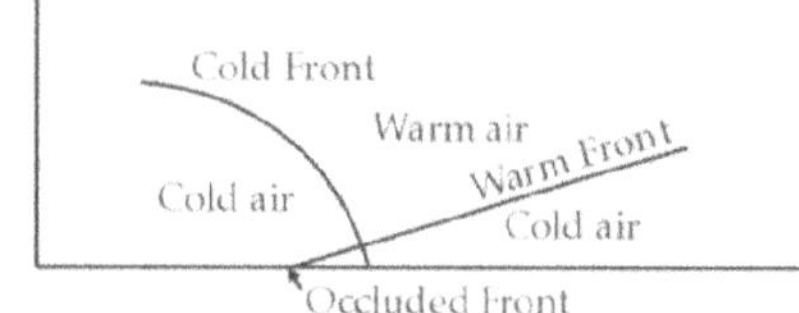

(ii) Cold front : When the cold air moves towards the warm air mass, its contact zone is called the cold front.

(iii) Warm front : The warm air mass moves towards the cold air mass, the contact zone is a warm front. **(1 × 3 = 3)**

Q. 3. What do you know about mountain and valley winds?

Ans. In mountainous regions, during the day the slopes get heated up and air moves upslope and to fill the resulting gap the air from the valley blows up the valley. This wind is known as the valley breeze. During the night the slopes get cooled and the dense air descends into the valley as the mountain wind. The cool air, of the high plateaus and ice fields draining into the valley is called katabatic wind. Another type of warm wind occurs on the leeward side of the mountain ranges. The moisture in these winds, while crossing the mountain ranges condense and precipitate. When it descends down the leeward side of the slope the dry air gets warmed up by adiabatic process. This dry air may melt the snow in a short time. **3**

Q. 4. What do you know about air mass? [U]

Ans. When the air remains over a homogenous area for a sufficiently longer time, it acquires the characteristics of the area. The homogenous regions can be the vast ocean surface or vast plains. The air with distinctive characteristics in terms of temperature and humidity is called an airmass. It is defined as a large body of air having little horizontal variation in temperature and moisture. The homogenous surfaces, over which air masses form, are called the source regions. The air masses are classified according to the source regions. **3**

Answering Tip

- The air of cold air masses is more dense than warmer air masses.

Q. 5. What do you know about thunderstorms? [A]

Ans. The severe local storms are thunderstorms and tornadoes. They are of short duration, occurring over a small area but are violent. Thunderstorms are caused by intense convection on moist hot days. A thunderstorm is a well-grown cumulonimbus cloud producing thunder and lightening. When the clouds extend to heights where sub-zero temperature prevails, hails are formed and they come down as hailstorm. If there is insufficient moisture, a thunderstorm can generate dust storms. A thunderstorm is characterised by intense updraft of rising warm air, which causes the clouds to grow bigger and rise to greater heights. This causes precipitation. **3**

Q. 6. What do you mean by ENSO?

Ans. The warm water of the central Pacific Ocean slowly drifts towards South American coast and replaces the cool Peruvian current. Such appearance of warm water off the coast of Peru is known as the El Nino. The El Nino event is closely associated with the pressure changes in the Central Pacific and Australia. This change in pressure condition over Pacific is known as the southern oscillation. The combined phenomenon of southern oscillation and El Nino is known as ENSO. **3**

Long Answer Type Questions

(5 marks each)

AI **Q. 1. Explain tropical cyclone.**

Ans. Tropical cyclones are violent storms that originate over oceans in tropical areas and move over to the coastal areas bringing about large scale destruction caused by violent winds, very heavy rainfall and storm surges

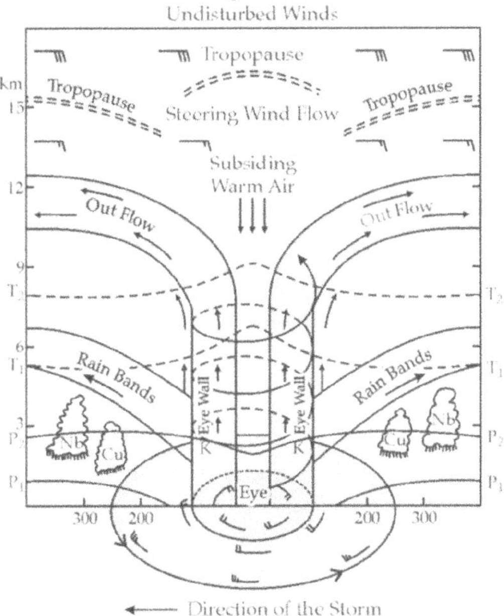

Vertical section of the tropical cyclone (after Rama Sastry)

This is one of the most devastating natural calamities. They are known as Cyclones in the Indian Ocean, Hurricanes in the Atlantic, Typhoons in the Western Pacific and South China Sea, and Willy-willies in the Western Australia.

Tropical cyclones originate and intensify over warm tropical oceans. The conditions favourable for the formation and intensification of tropical storms are: **(i)** Large sea surface with temperature higher than 27° C; **(ii)** Presence of the Coriolis Force; **(iii)** Small variations in the vertical wind speed; **(iv)** A pre-existing weaklow-pressure area or low-level-cyclonic circulation; **(v)** Upper divergence above the sea level system.

The energy that intensifies the storm, comes from the condensation process in the towering cumulonimbus clouds, surrounding the centre of the storm. With continuous supply of moisture from the sea, the storm is further strengthened. On reaching the land the moisture supply is cut off and the storm dissipates. The place where a tropical cyclone crosses the coast is called the landfall of the cyclone. The cyclones, which cross 20° N latitude generally, recurve and they are more destructive.

A mature tropical cyclone is characterised by the strong spirally circulating wind around the centre, called the eye. The diameter of the circulating system can vary between 150 and 250 km. The cyclone creates storm surges and they inundate the coastal low lands. The storm peters out on the land.

Answering Tip

- The tropical cyclone is characterized by a low-pressure centre, a closed low-level atmospheric circulation, strong winds, and a spiral arrangement of thunderstorms that produce heavy rain.

Q. 2. What do you know about the general atmospheric circulation and its effect on oceans? U

Ans. Warming and cooling of the Pacific Ocean is most important in terms of general atmospheric circulation. The warm water of the central Pacific Ocean slowly drifts towards The South American coast and replaces the cool Peruvian current.

Such appearance of warm water off the coast of Peru is known as the El Nino. The El Nino event is closely associated with the pressure changes in the Central Pacific and Australia. This change in pressure condition over Pacific is known as the southern oscillation.

The combined phenomenon of southern oscillation and El Nino is known as ENSO. In the years when the ENSO is strong, large-scale variations in weather occur over the world.

The arid west coast of South America receives heavy rainfall, drought occurs in Australia and sometimes in India and floods in China. This phenomenon is closely monitored and is used for long range forecasting in major parts of the world. **5**

Commonly Made Error

- The students are not aware as to how the general atmospheric circulation affects climate.

Answering Tip

- High and low pressure zones related to the atmospheric circulation cells are important in determining a region's climate. Prevailing winds influence the climate of a region because they bring in weather from the upwind area.

Q. 3. Explain how the general circulation of the atmosphere takes place.

Ans. The pattern of the movement of the planetary winds is called the general circulation of the atmosphere. The general circulation of the atmosphere also sets in motion the ocean water circulation which influences the Earth's climate.

The air at the Inter Tropical Convergence Zone (ITCZ) rises because of convection caused by high insolation and a low pressure is created. The winds from the tropics converge at this low pressure zone. The converged air rises along with the convective cell. It reaches the top of the troposphere up to an altitude of 14 km. and moves towards the poles.

This causes accumulation of air at about 30o N and S. Part of the accumulated air sinks to the ground and forms a subtropical high. Another reason for sinking is the cooling of air when it reaches 30° N and S latitudes. Down below near the land surface the air flows towards the Equator as the easterlies.

The easterlies from either side of the Equator converge in the Inter Tropical Convergence Zone (ITCZ). Such circulations from the surface upwards and vice-versa are called cells. Such a cell in the tropics is called Hadley Cell. In the middle latitudes the circulation is that of sinking cold air that comes from the poles and the rising warm air that blows from the subtropical high.

At the surface these winds are called westerlies and the cell is known as the Ferrel Cell. At polar latitudes the cold dense air subsides near the poles and blows towards middle latitudes as the polar easterlies. This cell is called the polar cell. These three cells set the pattern for the general circulation of the atmosphere. The transfer of heat energy from lower latitudes to higher latitudes maintains the general circulation. 5

NCERT CORNER

(A) Multiple choice questions :

Q. 1. If the surface air pressure is 1,000 mb, the air pressure at 1 km above the surface will be :

(a) 700 mb

(b) 1,100 mb

(c) 900 mb

(d) 1,300 mb

Ans. (c) 900 mb .

Q. 2. The Inter Tropical Convergence Zone normally occurs :

(a) Near the Equator

(b) Near the Tropic of Cancer

(c) Near the Tropic of Capricorn

(d) Near the Arctic Circle

Ans. (a) Near the Equator.

AI **Q. 3. The direction of wind around a low pressure in northern hemisphere is :**

(a) Clockwise

(b) Perpendicular to isobars

(c) Anti-clock wise

(d) Parallel to isobars

Ans. (c) Anti-clock wise.

Q. 4. Which one of the following is the source region for the formation of air masses :

(a) The Equatorial forest

(b) The Himalayas

(c) The Siberian Plain

(d) The Deccan Plateau

Ans. (c) The Siberian Plain

(B) Answer the following questions in about 30 words :

Q. 1. What is the unit used in measuring pressure? Why is the pressure measured at station level reduced to the sea level in preparation of weather maps? A

Ans. The unit used in measuring pressure is the milibar(mb) or Pascal. The pressure measured at station level reduced to the sea level in preparation of weather maps as the gravity of air at the surface is denser and hence has higher pressure.

Q. 2. While the pressure gradient force is from North to South, i.e. from the subtropical high pressure to the Equator in the Northern Hemisphere, why are the winds north easterlies in the tropics? U

Ans. The winds blow from high pressure to the low pressure, so this pressure gradient force is from North to South. Therefore, the North easterlies blow from North East to South West.

Q. 3. What are the geostrophic winds?

Ans. When isobars are straight and when there is no friction, the pressure gradient force is balanced by the Coriolis force and the resultant wind blows parallel to the isobar. This wind is known as the geostrophic wind.

Q. 4. Explain the land and sea breezes? U

Ans. During the day the land heats up faster and becomes warmer than the sea. Therefore, over the land the air rises giving rise to a low pressure area, whereas the sea is relatively cool and the pressure over sea is relatively high. Thus, pressure gradient from sea to land is created and the wind blows from the sea to the land as the sea breeze.

In the night the reversal of condition takes place. The land loses heat faster and is cooler than the sea. The pressure gradient is from the land to the sea and hence land breeze results..

(C) Answer the following questions in about 150 words :

Q. 1. Discuss the factors affecting the speed and direction of wind? U

Ans. The air in motion is called wind. The wind blows from high pressure to low pressure. The wind at the surface experiences friction. In addition, rotation of the earth also affects the wind movement. The force exerted by the rotation of the earth is known as the Coriolis force. Thus, the horizontal winds near the earth surface respond to the combined effect of three forces – the pressure gradient force, the frictional force and the Coriolis force. In addition, the gravitational force acts downward.

(i) Pressure Gradient Force : The differences in atmospheric pressure produces a force. The rate of change of pressure with respect to distance is the pressure gradient. The pressure gradient is strong where the isobars are close to each other and is weak where the isobars are apart.

(ii) Frictional Force : It affects the speed of the wind. It is greatest at the surface and its influence generally extends upto an elevation of 1 - 3 km. Over the sea surface the friction is minimal.

(iii) Coriolis Force : The rotation of the earth about its axis affects the direction of the wind. This force is called the Coriolis Force. It deflects the wind to the right direction in the Northern Hemisphere and to the left in the Southern Hemisphere. The deflection is more when the wind velocity is high. The Coriolis Force is directly proportional to the angle of latitude. It is maximum at the poles and is absent at the Equator. At the equator, the Coriolis Force is zero and the wind blows perpendicular to the isobars. The low pressure gets filled instead of getting intensified. That is the reason why tropical cyclones are not formed near the Equator.

(iv) Pressure and Wind : The velocity and direction of the wind are the net result of the wind generating forces. The winds in the upper atmosphere, 2 - 3 km above the surface, are free from frictional effect of the surface and are controlled by the pressure gradient and the Coriolis force. When isobars are straight and when there is no friction, the pressure gradient force is balanced by the Coriolis force and the resultant wind blows parallel to the isobar.

Q. 2. Draw a simplified diagram to show the general circulation of the atmosphere over the globe. What are the possible reasons for the formation of subtropical high pressure over 30° N and S latitudes. A

Ans.

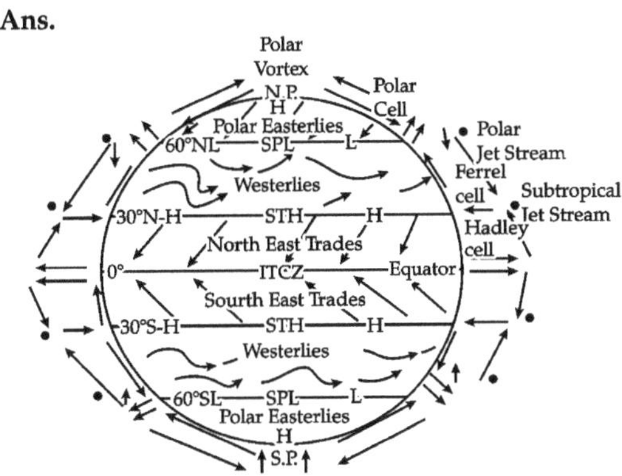

Simplified general circulation of the atmosphare

The air at the Inter Tropical Convergence Zone (ITCZ) rises because of convection caused by high insolation and a low pressure is created. The winds from the tropics converge at this low pressure zone. The converged air rises along with the convective cell. It reaches the top of the troposphere up to an altitude of 14 km. and moves towards the poles. This causes accumulation of air at about 30° N and S. Part of the accumulated air sinks to the ground and forms a subtropical high. The cooling of air when it reaches 30° N and S latitudes. Down below near the land surface the air flows towards the Equator as the easterlies. The easterlies from either side of the equator converge in the Inter Tropical Convergence Zone (ITCZ).

In the middle latitudes the circulation is that of sinking cold air that comes from the poles and the rising warm air that blows from the subtropical high. At polar latitudes the cold dense air subsides near the poles and blows towards middle latitudes as the polar easterlies.

The transfer of heat energy from lower latitudes to higher latitudes maintains the general circulation. Thus, this forms the subtropical high pressure over 30° N and S latitudes.

Q. 3. Why does tropical cyclone originate over the seas? In which part of the tropical cyclone do torrential rains and high velocity winds blow and why.

Ans. Tropical cyclones are violent storms that originate over oceans in tropical areas and move over to the coastal areas bringing about large scale destruction caused by violent winds, very heavy rainfall and storm surges. This is one of the most devastating natural calamities.

The tropical cyclones originate over the seas as the Coriolis Force is zero at the Equator and the wind blows perpendicular to the isobars. The low pressure gets filled instead of getting intensified. Thus, the tropical cyclones originate over the seas and not at the Equator.

Tropical cyclones originate and intensify over warm tropical oceans. Torrential rains occurs in the eye of the cyclone. The eye is a region of calm with subsiding air. Around the eye is the eye wall, where there is a strong spiralling ascent of air to greater height reaching the tropopause. The wind reaches maximum velocity in this region, reaching as high as 250 km per hour. Torrential rain occurs here. From the eye wall rain bands may radiate and trains of cumulus and cumulonimbus clouds may drift into the outer region.

The diameter of the storm over the Bay of Bengal, Arabian sea and Indian ocean is between 600 - 1200 km. The system moves slowly about 300 - 500 km per day. Due to the torrential rain, wind blowing from those regions are humid. It brings precipitation in oceanic regions. Due to torrential rains, heavy rain takes place on eastern coast of India and North East coast of China.

OSWAAL LEARNING TOOLS

For Suggested Online Videos

Visit : *https://qrgo.page.link/fvMWb* **Or Scan the Code**

To learn from NCERT Prescribed Videos

Visit : https://qrgo.page.link/f6sZb **Or Scan the Code**

CHAPTER

11 WATER IN THE ATMOSPHERE

Syllabus

- *Evaporation and Condensation, Clouds.*
- *Precipitation, Types of Rainfall, World Distribution of Rainfall.*

TOPIC-1
Evaporation and Condensation, Clouds

Revision Notes

- The air contains water vapour. It varies from zero to four per cent by volume of the atmosphere and plays an important role in the weather phenomena.
- Water is present in the atmosphere in three forms namely – gaseous, liquid and solid.
- Water vapour present in the air is known as humidity. It is expressed quantitatively in different ways. The actual amount of the water vapour present in the atmosphere is known as the absolute humidity.
- The absolute humidity differs from place to place on the surface of the earth. The percentage of moisture present in the atmosphere as compared to its full capacity at a given temperature is known as the relative humidity.
- It is the weight of water vapour per unit volume of air and is expressed in terms of grams per cubic metre.
- The air containing moisture to its full capacity at a given temperature is said to be saturated.
- The temperature at which saturation occurs in a given sample of air is known as dew point.
- Evaporation is a process by which water is transformed from liquid to gaseous state. Heat is the main cause for evaporation. The temperature at which the water starts evaporating is referred to as the latent heat of vapourisation.
- The transformation of water vapour into water is called condensation. Condensation is caused by the loss of heat. When moist air is cooled, it may reach a level when its capacity to hold water vapour ceases. Then, the excess water vapour condenses into liquid form. If it directly condenses into solid form, it is known as sublimation.
- Condensation also takes place when the moist air comes in contact with some colder object and it may also take place when the temperature is close to the dew point. Condensation, therefore, depends upon the amount of cooling and the relative humidity of the air.
- Condensation is influenced by the volume of air, temperature, pressure and humidity.
- Condensation takes place:
  - When the temperature of the air is reduced to dew point with its volume remaining constant;
  - When both the volume and the temperature are reduced;
  - When moisture is added to the air through evaporation. However, the most favourable condition for condensation is the decrease in air temperature.
- Condensation takes place when the dew point is lower than the freezing point as well as higher than the freezing point.
- After condensation the water vapour or the moisture in the atmosphere takes one of the following forms such as dew, frost, fog and clouds.
- When the moisture is deposited in the form of water droplets on cooler surfaces of solid objects (rather than nuclei in air above the surface) such as stones, grass blades and plant leaves, it is known as dew.

- Frost forms on cold surfaces when condensation takes place below freezing point (0^0C), i.e. the dew point is at or below the freezing point.
- The ideal conditions for the formation of white frost are the same as those for the formation of dew, except that the air temperature must be at or below the freezing point.
- When the temperature of an air mass containing a large quantity of water vapour falls all of a sudden, condensation takes place within itself on fine dust particles. So, the fog is a cloud with its base at or very near to the ground. Because of the fog and mist, the visibility becomes poor to zero.
- In urban and industrial centres smoke provides plenty of nuclei which help the formation of fog and mist. Such a condition when fog is mixed with smoke, is described as smog.
- In mist each nuclei contains a thicker layer of moisture. Mists are frequent over mountains as the rising warm air up the slopes meets a cold surface.
- Cloud is a mass of minute water droplets or tiny crystals of ice formed by the condensation of the water vapour in free air at considerable elevations.
- According to their height, expanse, density and transparency or opaqueness clouds are grouped under four types :
  - **Cirrus :** Cirrus clouds are formed at high altitudes (8,000 - 12,000m). They are thin and detached clouds having a feathery appearance. They are always white in colour.
  - **Cumulus :** Cumulus clouds look like cotton wool. They are generally formed at a height of 4,000 7,000 m. They exist in patches and can be seen scattered here and there. They have a flat base.
  - **Stratus :** As their name implies, these are layered clouds covering large portions of the sky. These clouds are generally formed either due to loss of heat or the mixing of air masses with different temperatures.
  - **Nimbus :** Nimbus clouds are black or dark grey. They form at middle levels or very near to the surface of the earth. These are extremely dense and opaque to the rays of the sun. Sometimes, the clouds are so low that they seem to touch the ground. Nimbus clouds are shapeless masses of thick vapour.

Know the Terms

- **Humidity :** Water vapour present in the air is known as humidity.
- **Absolute humidity :** The actual amount of the water vapour present in the atmosphere is known as the absolute humidity.
- **Relative humidity :** The percentage of moisture present in the atmosphere as compared to its full capacity at a given temperature is known as the relative humidity.
- **Dew point :** The temperature at which saturation occurs in a given sample of air is known as dew point.
- **Latent heat of Vaporisation :** The temperature at which the water starts evaporating is referred to as the latent heat of vapourisation.
- **Condensation :** The transformation of water vapour into water is called condensation.
- **Sublimation :** The change from solid to gas without passing through the liquid phase is known as sublimation.
- **Dew :** When the moisture is deposited in the form of water droplets on cooler surfaces of solid objects such as stones, grass blades and plant leaves, it is known as dew.
- **Frost :** It is the coating or deposit of ice that may form in humid air in cold conditions, usually overnight.
- **Fog :** A weather condition in which very small drops of water come together to form a thick cloud close to the land or sea , ocean making it difficult to see.
- **Mist :** A cloud of tiny water droplets suspended in the atmosphere at or near the Earth's surface limiting visibility.
- **Smog :** It is combination of smoke and fog.
- **Cloud :** Cloud is a mass of minute water droplets or tiny crystals of ice formed by the condensation of the water vapour in free air at considerable elevations.

Multiple Choice Questions (1 mark each)

Q. 1. The air contains: [A]
(a) water vapour
(b) wind
(c) cloud
(d) mist
Ans. (a) water vapour 1

Q. 2. The transformation of water vapour into water is called: [U]
(a) vaporisation
(b) condensation
(c) smog
(d) sublimation
Ans. (b) condensation 1

Very Short Answer Type Questions (1 mark each)

Q. 1. Define the term humidity. [A]

Ans. Water vapour present in the air is known as humidity. 1

[AI] **Q. 2. Define the term dew point.** [U]

Ans. The temperature at which saturation occurs in a given sample of air is known as dew point. 1

Q. 3. Define the term condensation.

Ans. The transformation of water vapour into water is called condensation. 1

Q. 4. Define the term dew. [A]

Ans. When the moisture is deposited in the form of water droplets on cooler surfaces of solid objects (rather than nuclei in air above the surface) such as stones, grass blades and plant leaves, it is known as dew. 1

Answering Tip

- Dew is the result of water changing from a vapor to a liquid.

Q. 5. What do you understand by the term latent heat of vapourisation?

Ans. The temperature at which the water starts evaporating is referred to as the latent heat of vapourisation. 1

Q. 6. What is the main cause of evaporation? [A]

Ans. Heat is the main cause of evaporation. 1

Q. 7. What causes condensation? [U]

Ans. Condensation is caused by the loss of heat. 1

Q. 8. Differentiate between absolute humidity and relative humidity. [A]

Ans.

S.No.	Absolute humidity	Relative humidity
1.	The actual amount of the water vapour present in the atmosphere is known as the absolute humidity.	The percentage of moisture present in the atmosphere as compared to its full capacity at a given temperature is known as the relative humidity.
2.	It is expressed in terms of grams per cubic metre.	It is measured in percentage and hence is unit free.

1

Q. 9. What are the ideal conditions for the formation of dew? [U]

Ans. The ideal conditions for its formation are clear sky, calm air, high relative humidity, and cold and long nights. For the formation of dew it is necessary that the dew point is above the freezing point. 1

Q. 10. How is smog formed? [A]

Ans. In urban and industrial centres smoke provides plenty of nuclei which help the formation of fog and mist. Such a condition when fog is mixed with smoke, is described as smog. 1

Commonly Made Error

- The students are not aware what is smog made of.

Answering Tip

- Smog is composed of nitrogen oxides, sulphur oxides, ozone, smoke and other particulates. Man-made smog is derived from coal combustion emissions, vehicular emissions, industrial emissions, forest and agricultural fires and photochemical reactions of these emissions.

Short Answer Type Questions (3 marks each)

Q. 1. When does condensation take place?

Ans. In free air, condensation results from cooling around very small particles termed as hygroscopic condensation nuclei. Particles of dust, smoke and salt from the ocean are particularly good nuclei because they absorb water. Condensation also takes place when the moist air comes in contact with some colder object and it may also take place when the temperature is close to the dew point. Condensation, therefore, depends upon the amount of cooling and the relative humidity of the air. 3

OR

Condensation takes place :

(i) When the temperature of the air is reduced to dew point with its volume remaining constant.

(ii) When both the volume and the temperature are reduced.

(iii) When moisture is added to the air through evaporation. However, the most favourable condition for condensation is the decrease in air temperature. 3

Answering Tip

- Condensation is the change of the physical state of matter from the gas phase into the liquid phase, and is the reverse of vaporisation.

AI **Q. 2. Differentiate between fog and mist.** A

Ans.

S.No.	**Fog**	**Mist**
1.	Fogs are drier than mist..	Mist has more moisture than fog.
2.	Fog is prevalent where warm currents of air come in contact with cold currents.	Mist is prevalent over mountains as the warm air rising up the slope meets a cold surface.
3.	Fogs are mini clouds in which condensation takes place around nuclei provided by dust, smoke and the salt particles.	In mist each nuclei contains a thicker layer of moisture.

(1 × 3 = 3)

Q. 3. Explain the process of evaporation. A

Ans. Evaporation is a process by which water is transformed from liquid to gaseous state. Heat is the main cause for evaporation. The temperature at which the water starts evaporating is referred to as the latent heat of vapourisation.

Increase in temperature increases water absorption and retention capacity of the given parcel of air. Similarly, if the moisture content is low, air has a potentiality of absorbing and retaining moisture. Movement of air replaces the saturated layer with the unsaturated layer. Hence, the greater the movement of air, the greater is the evaporation.**3**

Q. 4. How does continuous exchange of water take place? R

Ans. The air contains water vapour. It varies from zero to four per cent by volume of the atmosphere and plays an important role in the weather phenomena. Water is present in the atmosphere in three forms namely – gaseous, liquid and solid. The moisture in the atmosphere is derived from water bodies through evaporation and from plants through transpiration. Thus, there is a continuous exchange of water between the atmosphere, the oceans and the continents through the processes of evaporation, transpiration, condensation and precipitation. **3**

Long Answer Type Questions

(5 marks each)

Q. 1. What are clouds? Explain the various types of clouds. U

Ans. Cloud is a mass of minute water droplets or tiny crystals of ice formed by the condensation of the water vapour in free air at considerable elevations. As the clouds are formed at some height over the surface of the earth, they take various shapes. According to their height, expanse, density and transparency or opaqueness clouds are grouped under four types : **(i)** cirrus; **(ii)** cumulus; **(iii)** stratus; **(iv)** nimbus.

(i) Cirrus : Cirrus clouds are formed at high altitudes (8,000 - 12,000m). They are thin and detached clouds having a feathery appearance. They are always white in colour.

(ii) Cumulus : Cumulus clouds look like cotton wool. They are generally formed at a height of 4,000 7,000 m. They exist in patches and can be seen scattered here and there. They have a flat base.

(iii) Stratus : As their name implies, these are layered clouds covering large portions of the sky. These clouds are generally formed either due to loss of heat or the mixing of air masses with different temperatures.

(iv) Nimbus : Nimbus clouds are black or dark grey. They form at middle levels or very near to the surface of the Earth. These are extremely dense and opaque to the rays of the sun. Sometimes, the clouds are so low that they seem to touch the ground. Nimbus clouds are shapeless masses of thick vapour. **(1 × 5 = 5)**

Answering Tip

- The highest clouds in the atmosphere are cirrocumulus, cirrus, and cirrostratus. Cumulonimbus clouds can also grow to be very high. Mid-level clouds include altocumulus and altostratus. The lowest clouds in the atmosphere are stratus, cumulus, and stratocumulus.

Q. 2. Explain the process of condensation.

Ans. The transformation of water vapour into water is called condensation. Condensation is caused by the loss of heat. When moist air is cooled, it may reach a level when its capacity to hold water vapour ceases.

Then, the excess water vapour condenses into liquid form. If it directly condenses into solid form, it is known as sublimation. In free air, condensation results from cooling around very small particles termed as hygroscopic condensation nuclei. Particles of dust, smoke and salt from the ocean are particularly good nuclei because they absorb water.

Condensation also takes place when the moist air comes in contact with some colder object and it may also take place when the temperature is close to the dew point. Condensation, therefore, depends upon the amount of cooling and the relative humidity of the air.

Condensation is influenced by the volume of air, temperature, pressure and humidity. Condensation takes place: **(i)** when the temperature of the air is reduced to dew point with its volume remaining constant; **(ii)** when both the volume and the temperature are reduced; **(iii)** when moisture is added to the air through evaporation.

However, the most favourable condition for condensation is the decrease in air temperature. After condensation the water vapour or the moisture in the atmosphere takes one of the following forms — dew, frost, fog and clouds. 5

TOPIC-2
Precipitation, Types of Rainfall, World Distribution of Rainfall

Revision Notes

- The process of continuous condensation in free air helps the condensed particles to grow in size. When the resistance of the air fails to hold them against the force of gravity, they fall on to the earth's surface. So after the condensation of water vapour, the release of moisture is known as precipitation.
- The precipitation in the form of water is called rainfall, when the temperature is lower than the 00C, precipitation takes place in the form of fine flakes of snow and is called snowfall.
- Besides rain and snow, other forms of precipitation are sleet and hail.
- Sleet is frozen raindrops and refrozen melted snow-water. When a layer of air with the temperature above freezing point overlies a subfreezing layer near the ground, precipitation takes place in the form of sleet.
- Sometimes, drops of rain after being released by the clouds become solidified into small rounded solid pieces of ice and which reach the surface of the earth are called hailstones.
- On the basis of origin, rainfall may be classified into three main types – the convectional, orographic or relief and the cyclonic or frontal.
  - **Conventional Rain :** The, air on being heated, becomes light and rises up in convection currents. As it rises, it expands and loses heat and consequently, condensation takes place and cumulous clouds are formed. With thunder and lightening, heavy rainfall takes place but this does not last. It is very common in the equatorial regions and interior parts of the continents, particularly in the northern hemisphere.
  - **Orographic Rain :** When the saturated air mass comes across a mountain, it is forced to ascend and as it rises, it expands; the temperature falls, and the moisture is condensed. The chief characteristic of this sort of rain is that the windward slopes receive greater rainfall. The area situated on the leeward side, which gets less rainfall is known as the rain-shadow area. It is also known as the relief rain.
  - **Cyclonic Rain :** The rain caused by cyclonic activity is called cyclonic rain. It occurs along the fronts of the cyclone. It is formed when two masses of air of different temperature , humidity and density meets.
- Different places on the earth's surface receive different amounts of rainfall in a year and that too in different seasons.
- The coastal areas of the world receive greater amounts of rainfall than the interior of the continents. The rainfall is more over the oceans than on the landmasses of the world because of being great sources of water. Between the latitudes 35^0 and 40^0 N and S of the Equator, the rain is heavier on the eastern coasts and goes on decreasing towards the west. But, between 45^0 and 65^0 N and S of Equator, due to the westerlies, the rainfall is first received on the western margins of the continents and it goes on decreasing towards the east.
- Wherever mountains run parallel to the coast, the rain is greater on the coastal plain, on the windward side and it decreases towards the leeward side.
- The equatorial belt, the windward slopes of the mountains along the western coasts in the cool temperate zone and the coastal areas of the monsoon land receive heavy rainfall of over 200 cm per annum.
- Interior continental areas receive moderate rainfall varying from 100 - 200 cm per annum. The coastal areas of the continents receive moderate amount of rainfall. The central parts of the tropical land and the eastern and interior parts of the temperate lands receive rainfall varying between 50-100 cm per annum.
- Areas lying in the rain shadow zone of the interior of the continents and high latitudes receive very low rainfall-less than 50 cm per annum. Seasonal distribution of rainfall provides an important aspect to judge its effectiveness.
- In some regions rainfall is distributed evenly throughout the year such as in the equatorial belt and in the western parts of cool temperate regions.

Know the Terms

- **Precipitation :** After the condensation of water vapour, the release of moisture is known as precipitation.
- **Rainfall :** The precipitation in the form of water is called rainfall.
- **Snowfall :** When the temperature is lower than the 0°C, precipitation takes place in the form of fine flakes of snow and is called snowfall.

- **Orographic rain :** Orographic rainfall is caused when masses of air pushed by wind are forced up the side of elevated land formations, such as large mountains.
- **Cyclonic rain :** The rain caused by cyclonic activity is called cyclonic rain.
- **Hailstones :** The drops of rain after being released by the clouds become solidified into small rounded solid pieces of ice and which reach the surface of the earth are called hailstones.
- **Sleet :** Sleet is frozen raindrops and refrozen melted snow-water. When a layer of air with the temperature above freezing point overlies a subfreezing layer near the ground, precipitation takes place in the form of sleet.
- **Conventional rain :** Conventional rain occurs when the energy of the Sun heats the Earth's surface and causes water to evaporate changing to water vapour.
- **Rain shadow area :** The area situated on the leeward side, which gets less rainfall is known as the rain-shadow area.

Multiple Choice Questions (1 mark each)

Q. 1. Interior continental areas receive moderate rainfall varying from : [A]

(a) 90-100 cm per annum
(b) 100 - 200 cm per annum
(c) 200-300 cm per annum
(d) 400-500 cm per annum

Ans. (b) 100-200 cm per annum 1

Q. 2. The rain caused by cyclonic activity is known as : [U]

(a) cyclonic rain
(b) hydrolic rain
(c) conventional rain
(d) orographic rain

Ans. (a) cyclonic rain 1

Very Short Answer Type Questions (1 mark each)

Q. 1. Define the term precipitation. [A]

Ans. After the condensation of water vapour, the release of moisture is known as precipitation. 1

Q. 2. What is sleet? [U]

Ans. Sleet is frozen raindrops and refrozen melted snow-water. 1

Q. 3. What are hailstones?

Ans. Sometimes, drops of rain after being released by the clouds become solidified into small rounded solid pieces of ice and which reach the surface of the earth are called hailstones. 1

Q. 4. What is rain shadow area? [U]

Ans. Rain shadow area: The area situated on the leeward side, which gets less rainfall is known as the rain-shadow area. 1

Q. 5. How is orographic rain caused? [A]

Ans. Orographic rainfall is caused when masses of air pushed by wind are forced up the side of elevated land formations, such as large mountains. 1

Commonly Made Error

- The students are not aware as to where the orographic rain takes place in India.

Answering Tip

- Orographic rainfall occurs in the mountainous regions near the coastal lines in general. Conditions favoring orographic rainfall in India is seen only over the Western Ghats during monsoon period.

Q. 6. How does snowfall take place? [U]

Ans. When the temperature is lower than the 0°C, precipitation takes place in the form of fine flakes of snow and is called snowfall. 1

Short Answer Type Questions (3 marks each)

Q. 1. Explain the various types of rains. [A]

Ans. On the basis of origin, rainfall may be classified into three main types – the convectional, orographic or relief and the cyclonic or frontal.

(i) **Conventional Rain :** The, air on being heated, becomes light and rises up in convection currents. As it rises, it expands and loses heat and consequently, condensation takes place and cumulous clouds are formed. With thunder and lightening, heavy rainfall takes place but this does not last long. Such rain is common in the summer or in the hotter part of the day. It is very common in the equatorial regions and interior parts of the continents, particularly in the northern hemisphere.

(ii) **Orographic Rain :** When the saturated air mass comes across a mountain, it is forced to ascend and as it rises, it expands; the temperature falls, and the moisture is condensed. The chief characteristic of this sort of rain is that the windward slopes receive greater rainfall. After giving rain on the windward side, when these winds reach the other slope, they descend, and their temperature rises.

(iii) **Cyclonic rain :** The rain caused by cyclonic activity is called cyclonic rain. These rains take place in low pressure areas where air moves from low pressure area to high pressure area and this movement brings rainfall. **(1 × 3 = 3)**

Q. 2. Differentiate between precipitation and condensation. A

Ans.

S.No.	Precipitation	Condensation
1.	After the condensation of water vapour, the release of moisture is known as precipitation.	The transformation of water vapour into water is called condensation.
2.	Precipitation takes place after condensation.	Condensation takes place after precipitation .
3.	Precipitation takes form of rainfall, snowfall, hailstorms, sleet , etc.	Condensation takes form of dew, smog, clouds, fog and mist, etc.

(1 × 3 = 3)

Q. 3. Differentiate between convectional rain and orographic rain? U

Ans.

S.No.	Convectional rain	Orographic rain
1.	Conventional rain occurs when the energy of the Sun heats the Earth's surface and causes water to evaporate changing to water vapour.	Orographic rain is produced when moist air is lifted as it moves over a mountain range.
2.	As it rises, it expands and loses heat and consequently, condensation takes place and cumulous clouds are formed.	The chief characteristic of this sort of rain is that the windward slopes receive greater rainfall. After giving rain on the windward side, when these winds reach the other slope, they descend, and their temperature rises .
3.	It is very common in the equatorial regions and interior parts of the continents, particularly in the northern hemisphere.	Then their capacity to take in moisture increases and hence, these leeward slopes remain rainless and dry.

(1 × 3 = 3)

Long Answer Type Question (5 marks)

Q. 1. What do you know about the distribution of rainfall across the world?

Ans. Refer to NCERT Corner, Long Ans (1) .

NCERT CORNER

(A) Multiple choice questions :

Q. 1. Which one of the following is the most important constituent of the atmosphere for human beings :

(a) Water vapour
(b) Nitrogen
(c) Dust particle
(d) Oxygen

Ans. (a) Water vapour.

Q. 2. Which one of the following process is responsible for transforming liquid into vapour :

(a) Condensation
(b) Transpiration
(c) Evaporation
(d) Precipitation

Ans. (c) Evaporation.

Q. 3. The air that contains moisture to its full capacity :

(a) Relative humidity
(b) Specific humidity
(c) Absolute humidity
(d) Saturated air

Ans. (d) Saturated air.

Q. 4. Which one of the following is the highest cloud in the sky :

(a) Cirrus
(b) Stratus
(c) Nimbus
(d) Cumulus

Ans. (a) Cirrus

(B) Answer the following questions in about 30 words :

Q. 1. Name the three types of precipitation?

Ans. The three types of precipitation are :

(i) **Rainfall :** The precipitation in the form of water is called rainfall.

(ii) **Snowfall :** when the temperature is lower than the 0^0C, precipitation takes place in the form of fine flakes of snow and is called snowfall.

(iii) **Hailstones :** Sometimes, drops of rain after being released by the clouds become solidified into small rounded solid pieces of ice and which reach the surface of the earth are called hailstones.

Q. 2. Explain relative humidity. A

Ans. The percentage of moisture present in the atmosphere as compared to its full capacity at a given temperature is known as the relative humidity. With the change of air temperature, the capacity to retain moisture increases or decreases and the relative humidity is also affected. It is greater over the oceans and least over the continents.

Q. 3. Why does the amount of water vapour decreases rapidly with altitude? U

Ans. The quantity of water vapour existing in the air depends upon the rate of evaporation and the temperature of the air which determines its holding capacity of water vapour. Both temperature and evaporation decreases with altitude and as a result water vapour also decreases with the decrease in altitude.

Q. 4. How are clouds formed? Classify them? U

Ans. Cloud is a mass of minute water droplets or tiny crystals of ice formed by the condensation of the water vapour in free air at considerable elevations. As the clouds are formed at some height over the surface of the earth, they take various shapes. According to their height, expanse, density and transparency or opaqueness clouds are grouped under four types : **(i)** cirrus; **(ii)** cumulus; **(iii)** stratus; **(iv)** nimbus.

(C) Answer the following questions in about 150 words :

Q. 1. Discuss the salient features of the world distribution of precipitation?

Ans. After the condensation of water vapour, the release of moisture is known as precipitation. The salient features of the world distribution of precipitation are :

(i) Different places on the Earth's surface receive different amounts of rainfall in a year and that too in different seasons. In general, as we proceed from the equator towards the poles, rainfall goes on decreasing steadily. The coastal areas of the world receive greater amounts of rainfall than the interior of the continents.

(ii) The rainfall is more over the oceans than on the landmasses of the world because of being great sources of water. Between the latitudes 35^0 and 40^0 N and S of the Equator, the rain is heavier on the eastern coasts and goes on decreasing towards the west. But, between 45^0 and 65^0 N and S of equator, due to the westerlies, the rainfall is first received on the western margins of the continents and it goes on decreasing towards the east. Wherever mountains run parallel to the coast, the rain is greater on the coastal plain, on the windward side and it decreases towards the leeward side.

(iii) On the basis of the total amount of annual precipitation, major precipitation regimes of the world are identified as follows. The equatorial belt, the windward slopes of the mountains along the western coasts in the cool temperate zone and the coastal areas of the monsoon land receive heavy rainfall of over 200 cm per annum. Interior continental areas receive moderate rainfall varying from 100 - 200 cm per annum.

(iv) The coastal areas of the continents receive moderate amount of rainfall. The central parts of the tropical land and the eastern and interior parts of the temperate lands receive rainfall varying between 50-100 cm per annum. Areas lying in the rain shadow zone of the interior of the continents and high latitudes receive very low rainfall-less than 50 cm per annum.

(v) Seasonal distribution of rainfall provides an important aspect to judge its effectiveness. In some regions rainfall is distributed evenly throughout the year such as in the equatorial belt and in the western parts of cool temperate regions.

Q. 2. What are forms of condensation? Describe the process of dew and frost formation?

Ans. The transformation of water vapour into water is called condensation. Condensation is caused by the loss of heat. When moist air is cooled, it may reach a level when its capacity to hold water vapour ceases. Condensation also takes place when the moist air comes in contact with some colder object and it may also take place when the temperature is close to the dew point. The various forms of condensation are :

(i) Dew : When the moisture is deposited in the form of water droplets on cooler surfaces of solid objects (rather than nuclei in air above the surface) such as stones, grass blades and plant leaves, it is known as dew. The ideal conditions for its formation are clear sky, calm air, high relative humidity, and cold and long nights. For the formation of dew, it is necessary that the dew point is above the freezing point.

(ii) Frost : Frost forms on cold surfaces when condensation takes place below freezing point (0^0C), i.e. the dew point is at or below the freezing point. The excess moisture is deposited in the form of minute ice crystals instead of water droplets. The ideal conditions for the formation of white frost are the same as those for the formation of dew, except that the air temperature must be at or below the freezing point.

(iii) Fog and Mist : When the temperature of an air mass containing a large quantity of water vapour falls all of a sudden, condensation takes place within itself on fine dust particles. So, the fog is a cloud with its base at or very near to the ground. Because of the fog and mist, the visibility becomes poor to zero. In urban and industrial centres smoke provides plenty of nuclei which help the formation of fog and mist. Such a condition when fog is mixed with smoke, is described as smog. The only difference between the mist and fog is that mist contains more moisture than the fog. In mist each nuclei contains a thicker layer of moisture. Mists are frequent over mountains as the rising warm air up the slopes meets a cold surface. Fogs are drier than mist and they are prevalent where warm currents of air come in contact with cold currents. Fogs are mini clouds in which condensation takes place around nuclei provided by the dust, smoke, and the salt particles.

(iv) Clouds : Cloud is a mass of minute water droplets or tiny crystals of ice formed by the condensation of the water vapour in free air at considerable elevations. As the clouds are formed at some height over the surface of the earth, they take various shapes. According to their height, expanse, density and transparency or opaqueness clouds are grouped under four types : **(i)** cirrus; **(ii)** cumulus; **(iii)** stratus; **(iv)** nimbus.

OSWAAL LEARNING TOOLS

For Suggested Online Videos

Visit : *https://qrgo.page.link/ppG4k* **Or Scan the Code**

To learn from NCERT Prescribed Videos

Visit : *https://qrgo.page.link/FkG5g* **Or Scan the Code**

CHAPTER

12 WORLD CLIMATE AND CLIMATE CHANGE

Syllabus

> *Koeppen's Scheme of Classification of Climate, Tropical Humid Climates, Dry Climates, Cold Snow Forest Climates, Polar Climates, Highland Climates.*
> *Climate Change, Climate in the Past, Causes of Climate Change ,Global Warming.*

TOPIC-1
Koeppen's Scheme of Classification of Climate, Tropical Humid Climates, Dry Climates, Cold Snow Forest Climates, Polar Climates, Highland Climates.

Revision Notes

- The most widely used classification of climate is the empirical climate classification scheme developed by V. Koeppen.
- Koeppen identified a close relationship between the distribution of vegetation and climate.
- He selected certain values of temperature and precipitation and related them to the distribution of vegetation and used these values for classifying the climates.
- He introduced the use of capital and small letters to designate climatic groups and types. Although developed in 1918 and modified over a period of time, Koeppen's scheme is still popular and in use.
- Koeppen recognised five major climatic groups, four of them are based on temperature and one on precipitation.
- The climatic groups are subdivided into types, designated by small letters, based on seaonality of precipitation and temperature characteristics. The seasons of dryness are indicated by the small letters namely - f, m, w and s, where f corresponds to no dry season, m - monsoon climate, w - winter dry season and s - summer dry season. The small letters a, b, c and d refer to the degree of severity of temperature.
- The english capital letters such as A, B, C, D and E present the Koeppen climate groups in which A, C, D and E delineate humid climates and B dry climates. later he added new climate zone called H types.
- **Tropical Humid Climates A :** Tropical humid climates exist between Tropic of Cancer and Tropic of Capricorn. The Sun being overhead throughout the year and the presence of Inter Tropical Convergence Zone (ITCZ) make the climate hot and humid. The tropical group is divided into three types, namely:
  - **Af-Tropical wet climate :** Tropical wet climate is found near the Equator. The major areas are the Amazon Basin in South America, western equatorial Africa and the islands of East Indies. The maximum temperature on any day is around 30°C while the minimum temperature is around 20°C.
  - **Am-Tropical monsoon climate :** These type of climate are found over the Indian sub-continent, North Eastern part of South America and Northern Australia.
  - **Aw-Tropical wet and dry climate :** This type of climate occurs North and South of Af type climate regions. It borders with dry climate on the western part of the continent and Cf or Cw on the eastern part. The annual rainfall in this climate is considerably less than that in Af and Am climate types and is variable also. Temperature is high throughout the year and diurnal ranges of temperature are the greatest in the dry season. Deciduous forest and tree-shredded grasslands occur in this climate.
- **Dry Climates B :** Dry climates are characterised by very low rainfall that is not adequate for the growth of plants. These climates cover a very large area of the planet extending over large latitudes from 15° - 60° North and South

of the Equator. At low latitudes, from 15° - 30°, they occur in the area of subtropical high where subsidence and inversion of temperature do not produce rainfall. In middle latitudes, from 35° - 60° North and South of the Equator, they are confined to the interior of continents where maritime-humid winds do not reach and to areas often surrounded by mountains.

➢ Dry climates are divided into steppe or semi-arid climate (BS) and desert climate (BW).

- **Subtropical Steppe (BSh) and Subtropical Desert (BWh) Climates :** Subtropical steppe (BSh) and subtropical desert (BWh) have common precipitation and temperature characteristics. Located in the transition zone between humid and dry climates, subtropical steppe receives slightly more rainfall than the desert, adequate enough for the growth of sparse grasslands. Fog is common in coastal deserts bordering cold currents. Maximum temperature in the summer is very high. The annual and diurnal ranges of temperature are also high.

➢ **Warm Temperate (Mid-Latitude) Climates-C :** This type of climates extend from 30° - 50° of latitude mainly on the eastern and western margins of continents. They are grouped into four types:

(a) Humid Subtropical Climate (Cwa) : Humid subtropical climate occurs poleward of Tropic of Cancer and Capricorn, mainly in North Indian plains and South China interior plains. The climate is similar to Aw climate except that the temperature in winter is warm.

(b) Mediterranean Climate (Cs) : As the name suggests, Mediterranean climate occurs around the Mediterranean Sea, along the west coast of continents in subtropical latitudes between 30° - 40° latitudes *e.g.*, Central California, Central Chile, along the coast in south eastern and south western Australia. Monthly average temperature in summer is around 25° C and in winter below 10°C. The annual precipitation ranges between 35 - 90 cm.

(c) Humid Subtropical (Cfa) Climate : Humid subtropical climate lies on the eastern parts of the continent in subtropical latitudes. In this region the air masses are generally unstable and cause rainfall throughout the year. They occur in eastern United States of America, southern and eastern China, southern Japan, North-eastern Argentina, coastal south Africa and eastern coast of Australia. Thunderstorms in summer and frontal precipitation in winter are common.

(d) Marine West Coast Climate (Cfb) : Marine west coast climate is located poleward from the Mediterranean climate on the west coast of the continents. The main areas are: Northwestern Europe, west coast of North America, north of California, southern Chile, southeastern Australia and New Zealand. The annual and daily ranges of temperature are small. Precipitation occurs throughout the year. Precipitation varies greatly from 50-250cm.

➢ **Cold Snow Forest Climates (D) :** Cold snow forest climates occur in the large continental area in the northern hemisphere between 40°-70° north latitudes in Europe, Asia and North America. The severity of winter is more pronounced in higher latitudes. Cold snow forest climates are divided into two types:

(a) Cold Climate with Humid Winters (Df) : Cold climate with humid winter occurs poleward of marine west coast climate and mid latitude steppe. The frost free season is short. The annual ranges of temperature are large. The weather changes are abrupt and short. Poleward, the winters are more severe.

(b) Cold Climate with Dry Winters (Dw) : Cold climate with dry winter occurs mainly over Northeastern Asia. The development of pronounced winter anti- cyclone and its weakening in summer sets in monsoon like reversal of wind in this region. The annual precipitation is low from 12-15 cm.

➢ **Polar Climates (E) :** Polar climates exist poleward beyond 70° latitude. Polar climates consist of two types:

(a) Tundra Climate (ET) : The tundra climate (ET) is so called after the types of vegetation, like low growing mosses, lichens and flowering plants. This is the region of permafrost where the sub soil is permanently frozen. During summer, the tundra regions have very long duration of day light.

(b) Ice Cap Climate (EF) : The ice cap climate (EF) occurs over interior Greenland and Antartica. Even in summer, the temperature is below freezing point. This area receives very little precipitation. The snow and ice get accumulated and the mounting pressure causes the deformation of the ice sheets and they break.

➢ **Highland Climates (H) :** Highland climates are governed by topography. In high mountains, large changes in mean temperature occur over short distances. Precipitation types and intensity also vary spatially across high lands. There is vertical zonation of layering of climatic types with elevation in the mountain environment.

Know the Terms

➢ **Koeppen's scheme of classification of climate :** It is scheme developed by Koeppen. Koeppen identified a close relationship between the distribution of vegetation and climate.

➢ **Empirical Classification :** This classification is based on observed data, particularly on temperature and precipitation.

➢ **Genetic Classification :** This classification attempts to organise climates according to their causes.

➢ **Applied Classification :** This is used when classification is done for specific purpose.

➢ **Frontal precipitation :** It results when the leading edge of a warm, moist air mass meets a cool and dry air mass.

➢ **Annual rainfall :** It is the total accumulated rainfall in a year.

➢ **Diurnal ranges of temperature :** It is the difference between the daily maximum and minimum temperature.

➢ **Icebergs :** It is a large piece of freshwater ice that has broken off a glacier or an ice shelf and is floating freely in open water.

Multiple Choice Questions (1 mark each)

Q. 1. The english capital letters such as A, B, C, D and E present the: U

(a) Perennial climate groups
(b) Koeppen climate groups
(c) Ratzel climate groups
(d) Mackinder climate groups

Ans. (b) Koeppen climate groups 1

Q. 2. The small letters a, b, c and d refer to the degree of severity of: U

(a) temperature
(b) weather
(c) climate
(d) humidity

Ans. (a) temperature 1

Q. 3. Temperature is high throughout the year and diurnal ranges of temperature are the greatest in the dry season. This is a characteristic of : A

(a) Tropical wet and dry climate
(b) Tropical wet climate
(c) Tropical monsoon climate
(d) Tropical dry climate

Ans. (a) Tropical wet and dry climate 1

Q. 4. Precipitation varies greatly from 50-250 cm in the: U

(a) Tundra type of climate
(b) Marine west coast climate
(c) Polar climate
(d) Ice type climate

Ans. (b) Marine west coast climate. 1

Very Short Answer Type Questions (1 mark each)

Q. 1. Name the climate classification scheme developed by Koeppen. A

Ans. The most widely used classification of climate is the empirical climate classification scheme developed by V. Koeppen. 1

Q. 2. What is the empirical classification based on? U

Ans. An empirical classification is based on mean annual and mean monthly temperature and precipitation data. 1

Q. 3. Koeppen has recognised how many climatic groups? U

Ans. Koeppen has recognised five major climatic groups. 1

Answering Tip

- Koeppen Climate Classification Categories are based on the annual and monthly averages of temperature and precipitation.

Q. 4. What kind of climate is expressed by the letter code-BSh? A

Ans. BSh expresses the subtropical dry steppes. 1

Q. 5. What type of climate is expressed by the letter code- ET? U

Ans. Et expresses the Tundra type of climate. 1

Q. 6. What type of climate is expressed by the letter code-EF? A

Ans. EF expresses the Perennial Ice type of climate. 1

Q. 7. What is the average temperature of dry tropical climate? U

Ans. The average temperature of dry tropical climate is 18°C. 1

Q. 8. Where is the tropical monsoon climate found? R

Ans. Tropical monsoon climate (Am) is found over the Indian sub-continent, North Eastern part of South America and Northern Australia. 1

Q. 9. Where is the tropical wet and dry climate found? R

Ans. The tropical wet and dry climate is found in the Amazon Basin in South America, western equatorial Africa and the islands of East Indies.1

Q. 10. The dry climates can be divided into how many parts? R

Ans. Dry climates are divided into steppe or semi-arid climate (BS) and desert climate (BW). 1

Q. 11. Where was the highest shade temperature recorded? U

Ans. The highest shade temperature of 58° C was recorded at Al Aziziyah, Libya on 13 September 1922. 1

Q. 12. Which type of climate exist in Plateau Station, Antarctice, 79°S according to Koeppen? R

Ans. Ice cap climate exist in Plateau Station, Antarctice, 79°S. 1

Q. 13. Which part of the world experiences the humid subtropical climate? A

Ans. Humid subtropical climate occurs poleward of Tropic of Cancer and Capricorn, mainly in North Indian plains and South China interior plains. 1

AI **Q. 14. Write any two characteristics of dry climates?** U

Ans. (i) Dry climates are characterised by very low rainfall that is not adequate for the growth of plants.

(ii) These climates cover a very large area of the planet extending over large latitudes from 15° - 60° north and south of the Equator. 1

Q. 15. Where is the marine west coast climate found? U

Ans. Marine west coast climate is located poleward from the Mediterranean climate on the west coast of the continents. The main areas are:

North-western Europe, west coast of North America, north of California, southern Chile, South-eastern Australia and New Zealand. 1

Q. 16. Polar climates can be divided into how many types? [A]

Ans. Polar climates exist poleward beyond 70° latitude. Polar climates consist of two types: **(i)** Tundra (ET); **(ii)** Ice Cap (EF). 1

Commonly Made Error

- The students are not aware of the countries which experience polar climate.

Answering Tip

- Countries with claims to Arctic regions which experience Polar climate are the United States (Alaska), Canada (Yukon, the Northwest Territories and Nunavut), Denmark (Greenland), Norway, Finland, Sweden, Iceland, and Russia.

Q. 17. What type of climate did Rajasthan experience in 8000 BC? [R]

Ans. In 8000 BC Rajasthan experienced humid and cold climate. 1

Q. 18. Write any one climatic characteristic of Group A? [A]

Ans. The average temperature of the coldest month is 18°C or higher. 1

Q.19. Write any one climate characteristic of Group D? [U]

Ans. The average temperature of the coldest month is minus 3° C or below. 1

Q.20. What is the role of genetic classification? [A]

Ans. Genetic classification attempts to organise climates according to their causes. 1

Commonly Made Error

- The students don't know on what information is the genetic classification of climate based.

Answering Tip

- A genetic system relies on information about climate elements like solar radiation, air masses, pressure systems, etc.

Q. 21. Differentiate between genetic classification and applied classification. [A]

Ans. Genetic classification attempts to organise climates according to their causes. Applied classification is for specific purpose. 1

Q. 22. Write one feature of warm temperate climate? [U]

Ans. One feature of warm temperate climate are:

(i) Warm temperate (mid-latitude) climates extend from 30°-50° of latitude mainly on the eastern and western margins of continents. These climates generally have warm summers with mild winters. 1

Short Answer Type Questions (3 marks each)

Q. 1. According to Koeppen, into how many categories can we classify the type A-climate? [A]

Ans. The type A climate can be classified into three types :

(i) Af- Tropical wet climate : Tropical wet climate is found near the Equator. The major areas are the Amazon Basin in South America, western equatorial Africa and the islands of East Indies. Significant amount of rainfall occurs in every month of the year as thunder showers in the afternoon. The temperature is uniformly high and the annual range of temperature is negligible. The maximum temperature on any day is around 30°C while the minimum temperature is around 20°C.

(ii) Am-Tropical monsoon climate : Tropical monsoon climate (Am) is found over the Indian sub-continent, North Eastern part of South America and Northern Australia. Heavy rainfall occurs mostly in summer. Winter is dry.

(iii) Aw-Tropical wet and dry climate : Tropical wet and dry climate occurs north and south of Af type climate regions. It borders with dry climate on the western part of the continent and Cf or Cw on the eastern part. Extensive Aw climate is found to the north and south of the Amazon forest in Brazil and adjoining parts of Bolivia and Paraguay in South America, Sudan and south of Central Africa. The annual rainfall in this climate is considerably less than that in Af and Am climate types and is variable also. 3

Q. 2. Where is the tropical climate found? Mention its features?

Ans. Tropical humid climates exist between Tropic of Cancer and Tropic of Capricorn. The sun being overhead throughout the year and the presence of Inter Tropical Convergence Zone (ITCZ) make the climate hot and humid.

The main features are :

(i) Annual range of temperature is very low and annual rainfall is high. There is no dry season.

(ii) The temperature is uniformly high and the annual range of temperature is negligible. The maximum temperature on any day is around 30°C while the minimum temperature is around 20°C.

(iii) Winters are dry. Significant amount of rainfall occurs in every month of the year as thunder showers in the afternoon. 3

Answering Tip

- In tropical climates, there are often only two seasons: a wet season and a dry season.

Q. 3. Where is cold snow forest climate found? Mention its features? [A]

Ans. Cold snow forest climates occur in the large continental area in the Northern Hemisphere between 40°-70° north latitudes in Europe, Asia and North America.

The main features are :

(i) The severity of winter is more pronounced in higher latitudes. Precipitation occurs in summer. The annual precipitation is low from 12-15 cm.

(ii) The winters are cold and snowy. The frost free season is short. The annual ranges of temperature are large. The weather changes are abrupt and short. Poleward, the winters are more severe.

(iii) Poleward summer temperatures are lower and winter temperatures are extremely low with many locations experiencing below freezing point temperatures for up to seven months in a year. 3

[AI] **Q. 4. What do you know about the Mediterranean climate?** [A]

Ans. (i) As the name suggests, Mediterranean climate occurs around the Mediterranean Sea, along the west coast of continents in subtropical latitudes between 30° - 40° latitudes *e.g.,* — Central California, Central Chile, along the coast in south eastern and south western Australia.

(ii) These areas come under the influence of sub tropical high in summer and westerly wind in winter. Hence, the climate is characterised by hot, dry summer and mild, rainy winter.

(iii) Monthly average temperature in summer is around 25° C and in winter below 10°C. The annual precipitation ranges between 35 - 90 cm.3

Q. 5. What do you know about the tundra climate? [U]

Ans. (i) The tundra climate (ET) is so called after the types of vegetation, like low growing mosses, lichens and flowering plants.

(ii) This is the region of permafrost where the sub soil is permanently frozen.

(iii) The short growing season and water logging support only low growing plants. During summer, the tundra regions have very long duration of day light. 3

Q. 6. Write any three features of the highland climate? [R]

Ans. The three features of the highland climate are:

(i) Highland climates are governed by topography. In high mountains, large changes in mean temperature occur over short distances.

(ii) Precipitation types and intensity also vary spatially across high lands.

(ii) There is vertical zonation of layering of climatic types with elevation in the mountain environment. 3

Answering Tip

- Highland climate is the climate of 'high' 'land'. So, this climate is found in high mountain areas. It is found on single mountains such as Mount Kilimanjaro and also large areas of high elevation such as the Plateau of Tibet.

Q. 7. Discuss about the region where there is no permanent settlements for human beings. [A]

Ans. Polar climates exist poleward beyond 70° latitude. There are no permanent human settlements here. Polar climates consist of two types: **(i)** Tundra (ET); **(ii)** Ice Cap (EF).

Tundra Climate (ET) : The tundra climate (ET) is so called after the types of vegetation, like low growing mosses, lichens and flowering plants. This is the region of permafrost where the sub soil is permanently frozen. The short growing season and water logging support only low growing plants. During summer, the tundra regions have very long duration of day light.

Ice Cap Climate (EF) : The ice cap climate (EF) occurs over interior Greenland and Antartica. Even in summer, the temperature is below freezing point. This area receives very little precipitation. The snow and ice get accumulated and the mounting pressure causes the deformation of the ice sheets and they break. They move as icebergs that float in the Arctic and Antarctic waters. Plateau Station, Antarctica, 79°S, portray this climate. 3

Long Answer Type Questions

(5 marks each)

Q. 1. Discuss in detail the major climate categories given by Koeppen. [U]

Ans. The major climate categories given by Koeppen can be divided into six major climatic types designated by small letters, based on seasonality of precipitation and temperature characteristics.

(i) Group A- Tropical humid climate : Tropical humid climates exist between Tropic of Cancer and Tropic of Capricorn. The Sun being overhead throughout the year and the presence of Inter Tropical Convergence Zone (ITCZ) make the climate hot and humid. Annual range of temperature is very low and annual rainfall is high. The tropical group is divided into three types, namely **(i)** Af- Tropical wet climate; **(ii)** Am - Tropical monsoon climate; **(iii)** Aw- Tropical wet and dry climate.

(ii) Group B- Dry climate : Dry climates are characterised by very low rainfall that is not adequate for the growth of plants. These climates cover a very large area of the planet extending over large latitudes from 15° - 60° north and south of the equator. At low latitudes, from 15° - 30°, they occur in the area of subtropical high where subsidence and inversion of temperature do not produce rainfall. On the western margin of the continents, adjoining the cold current, particularly over the west coast of South America, they extend more Equator wards and occur on the coast land. Dry climates are divided into steppe or semi-arid climate (BS) and desert climate (BW). They are further subdivided as subtropical steppe (BSh) and subtropical desert (BWh) at latitudes from 15° - 35° and mid-latitude steppe (BSk) and mid-latitude desert (BWk) at latitudes between 35° - 60.

(iii) Group C- Warm Temperate Climate : Summer temperatures are warm to hot and winters are mild. The primary distinguishing characteristic of these climates is that the coldest month has an average temperature between 18° C and -3°C.

(iv) Group D- Cold Snow Forest Climates : Cold snow forest climates occur in the large continental area in the Northern Hemisphere between 40°-70° north latitudes in Europe, Asia and North America. Cold snow forest climates are divided into two types: **(i)** Df- cold climate with humid winter; **(ii)** Dw- cold climate with dry winter. The severity of winter is more pronounced in higher latitudes.

(v) Group E- Polar Climate : These climates have very cold winters and summers, with no real summer season. The primary distinguishing characteristic of these climates is the warmest month has an average temperature below 10 °C.

(vi) Group H- Highland Climates (H) : Highland climates are governed by topography. In high mountains, large changes in mean temperature occur over short distances. Precipitation types and intensity also vary spatially across high lands. There is vertical zonation of layering of climatic types with elevation in the mountain environment. **(1 × 5 = 5)**

Q. 2. What do you know about the dry climate? It can divided into how many types? U

Ans. Dry climates are characterised by very low rainfall that is not adequate for the growth of plants. These climates cover a very large area of the planet extending over large latitudes from 15° - 60° North and South of the Equator. At low latitudes, from 15° - 30°, they occur in the area of subtropical high where subsidence and inversion of temperature do not produce rainfall. On the western margin of the continents, adjoining the cold current, particularly over the west coast of South America, they extend more Equator wards and occur on the coast land.

It can be divided into the following types :

(i) Subtropical Steppe (BSh) and Subtropical Desert (BWh) Climates : Subtropical steppe (BSh) and subtropical desert (BWh) have common precipitation and temperature characteristics. Located in the transition zone between humid and dry climates, subtropical steppe receives slightly more rainfall than the desert, adequate enough for the growth of sparse grasslands. The rainfall in both the climates is highly variable.

(ii) Warm Temperate (Mid-Latitude) Climates-C : Warm temperate (mid-latitude) climates extend from 30° - 50° of latitude mainly on the eastern and western margins of continents. These climates generally have warm summers with mild winters.

(iii) Humid Subtropical Climate (Cwa) : Humid subtropical climate occurs poleward of Tropic of Cancer and Capricorn, mainly in North Indian plains and South China interior plains. The climate is similar to Aw climate except that the temperature in winter is warm.

(iv) Mediterranean Climate (Cs) : The Mediterranean climate occurs around the Mediterranean Sea, along the west coast of continents in subtropical latitudes between 30° - 40° latitudes *e.g.,* — Central California, Central Chile, along the coast in south eastern and south western Australia. These areas come under the influence of sub tropical high in summer and westerly wind in winter. Hence, the climate is characterised by hot, dry summer and mild, rainy winter. Monthly average temperature in summer is around 25° C and in winter below 10°C. The annual precipitation ranges between 35 - 90 cm.

(v) Humid Subtropical (Cfa) : Climate Humid subtropical climate lies on the eastern parts of the continent in subtropical latitudes. In this region the air masses are generally unstable and cause rainfall throughout the year. They occur in eastern United States of America, southern and eastern China, southern Japan, north-eastern Argentina, coastal south Africa and eastern coast of Australia.

(vi) Marine West Coast Climate (Cfb) : Marine west coast climate is located poleward from the Mediterranean climate on the west coast of the continents. The main areas are: Northwestern Europe, west coast of North America, north of California, southern Chile, southeastern Australia and New Zealand. Due to marine influence, the temperature is moderate and in winter, it is warmer than for its latitude. The mean temperature in summer months ranges from 15°-20°C and in winter 4°-10°C . 5

Answering Tip

- The places having Dry Climate experience very low precipitation, high evaporation rates that typically exceed precipitation and wide temperature swings both daily and seasonally.

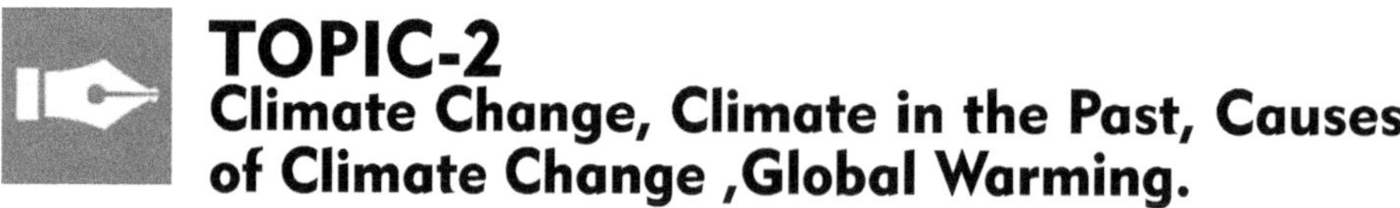

TOPIC-2
Climate Change, Climate in the Past, Causes of Climate Change ,Global Warming.

Revision Notes

- The type of climate we experience now might be prevailing over the last 10,000 years with minor and occasionally wide fluctuations.
- The planet earth has witnessed many variations in climate since the beginning. Geological records show alteration of glacial and inter-glacial periods.
- The geomorphological features, especially in high altitudes and high latitudes, exhibit traces of advances and retreats of glaciers.
- The sediment deposits in glacial lakes also reveal the occurrence of warm and cold periods.
- The rings in the trees provide clues about wet and dry periods. Historical records describe the vagaries in climate. All these evidences indicate that change in climate is a natural and continuous process.
- India also witnessed alternate wet and dry periods. Archaeological findings show that the Rajasthan desert experienced wet and cool climate around 8,000 B.C.
- The period 3,0001,700 B.C. had higher rainfall. From about 2,000-1,700 B.C., this region was the centre of the Harappan Civilization. Dry conditions accentuated since then.
- In the geological past, the earth was warm some 500-300 million years ago, through the Cambrian, Ordovician and Silurian periods.
- During the Pleistocene Epoch, glacial and inter-glacial periods occurred, the last major peak glacial period was about 18,000 years ago. The present inter-glacial period started 10,000 years ago.
- Variability in climate occurs all the time. The nineties decade of the last century witnessed extreme weather events.
- The 1990s recorded the warmest temperature of the century and some of the worst floods around the world.
- The worst devastating drought in the Sahel region, south of the Sahara Desert, from 1967-1977 is one such variability. During the 1930s, severe drought occurred in southwestern Great Plains of the United States, described as the dust bowl.
- A number of times Europe witnessed warm, wet, cold and dry periods, the significant episodes were the warm and dry conditions in the tenth and eleventh centuries, when the Vikings settled in Greenland.
- Europe witnessed "Little Ice Age" from 1550 to about 1850. From about 1885-1940 world temperature showed an upward trend. After 1940, the rate of increase in temperature slowed down.
- The causes for climate change are many. They can be grouped into astronomical and terrestrial causes.
- The astronomical causes are the changes in solar output associated with sunspot activities. Sunspots are dark and cooler patches on the sun which increase and decrease in a cyclical manner.
- According to some meteorologists, when the number of sunspots increase, cooler and wetter weather and greater storminess occur. A decrease in sunspot numbers is associated with warm and drier conditions. Yet, these findings are not statistically significant.
- An another astronomical theory is Millankovitch Oscillations, which infer cycles in the variations in the earth's orbital characteristics around the sun, the wobbling of the earth and the changes in the earth's axial tilt.
- All these alter the amount of insolation received from the sun, which in turn, might have a bearing on the climate.
- Volcanism is considered as another cause for climate change. Volcanic eruption throws up lots of aerosols into the atmosphere. These aerosols remain in the atmosphere for a considerable period of time reducing the sun's radiation reaching the Earth's surface.
- The most important anthropogenic effect on the climate is the increasing trend in the concentration of greenhouse gases in the atmosphere which is likely to cause global warming.
- Due to the presence of greenhouse gases, the atmosphere is behaving like a greenhouse. The atmosphere also transmits the incoming solar radiation but absorbs the vast majority of long wave radiation emitted upwards by the earth's surface.
- The gases that absorb long wave radiation are called greenhouse gases. The processes that warm the atmosphere are often collectively referred to as the greenhouse effect.
- The primary GHGs of concern today are carbon dioxide (CO_2), Chlorofluorocarbons (CFCs), methane (CH_4), nitrous oxide (N_2O) and ozone (O_3). Some other gases such as nitric oxide (NO) and carbon monoxide (CO) easily react with GHGs and affect their concentration in the atmosphere.
- The effectiveness of any given GHG molecule will depend on the magnitude of the increase in its concentration, its life time in the atmosphere and the wavelength of radiation that it absorbs.
- The chlorofluorocarbons (CFCs) are highly effective. Ozone which absorbs ultra violet radiation in the stratosphere is very effective in absorbing terrestrial radiation when it is present in the lower troposphere.

- Another important point to be noted is that the more time the GHG molecule remains in the atmosphere, the longer it take for Earth's atmospheric system to recover from any change brought about by the latter.
- The largest concentration of GHGs in the atmosphere is carbon dioxide. The emission of CO_2 comes mainly from fossil fuel combustion (oil, gas and coal). Forests and oceans are the sinks for the carbon dioxide.
- Doubling of concentration of CO_2 over pre-industrial level is used as an index for estimating the changes in climate in climatic models.
- Ozone occurs in the stratosphere where ultra-violet rays convert oxygen into ozone. Thus, ultra violet rays do not reach the earth's surface.
- The depletion of ozone concentration in the stratosphere is called the ozone hole. This allows the ultra violet rays to pass through the troposphere.
- International efforts have been initiated for reducing the emission of GHGs into the atmosphere. The most important one is the Kyoto protocol proclaimed in 1997.
- Kyoto protocol bounds the 35 industrialised countries to reduce their emissions by the year 2012 to 5 per cent less than the levels prevalent in the year 1990.
- The increasing trend in the concentration of GHGs in the atmosphere may, in the long run, warm up the earth. Once the global warming sets in, it will be difficult to reverse it.
- Rise in the sea level due to melting of glaciers and ice-caps and thermal expansion of the sea may inundate large parts of the coastal area and islands.
- One of the major concerns of the world today is global warming. An increasing trend in temperature was discernible in the 20th century. The greatest warming of the 20th century was during the two periods, 1901-44 and 1977-99.
- Over each of these two periods, global temperatures rose by about 0.4°C.
- The globally averaged annual mean temperature at the end of the 20th century was about 0.6°C above that recorded at the end of the 19th century. The seven warmest years during the 1856-2000 were recorded in the last decade.
- The year 1998 was the warmest year, probably not only for the 20th century but also for the whole millennium.

Know the Terms

- **Ozone hole :** A severe depletion of ozone in a region of the ozone layer, particularly over Antarctica and over the Arctic.
- **Sediment deposits :** It is the geological process in which sediments, soil and rocks are added to a landform or land mass.
- **Cambrian period :** It was the first geological period of the Paleozoic Era.
- **Ordovician periods :** It is a geologic period and system , the second of six periods of the Paleozoic Era.
- **Silurian periods :** It is a geologic period and system spanning 24.6 million years from the end of Ordovician Period.
- **Dust bowl :** During the 1930s, severe drought occurred in south western Great Plains of the United States. These are described as the 'Dust Bowl'.
- **Milllankovitch oscillations :** It infers cycles in the variations in the Earth's orbital characteristics around the Sun, the wobbling of the earth and the changes in the Earth's axial tilt. All these alter the amount of insolation received from the Sun, which in turn, might have a bearing on the climate.
- **Aerosols :** It is a colloidal system of solid or liquid particles in a gas.
- **Ozone :** It is a colourless unstable toxin gas with a pungent odour and powerful oxidizing properties, formed from oxygen by electrical discharges or ultraviolet light.
- **Ozone hole :** The depletion of ozone concentration in the stratosphere is called the ozone hole.
- **Kyoto protocol :** It is the name given to the protocol which was held for reducing the emission of GHGs into the atmosphere in 1997.
- **Global warming :** The increasing trend in the concentration of GHGs in the atmosphere may in the long run warm up the Earth. This is called global warming.
- **Greenhouse gases :** They are the gases in an atmosphere that absorbs and emits radiant energy within the thermal infrared range.
- **Greenhouse effect :** The processes that warm the atmosphere are often collectively referred to as the green house effect.
- **Greenhouse :** The term greenhouse is derived from the analogy to a greenhouse used in cold areas for preserving heat. A greenhouse is made up of glass. The glass which is transparent to incoming short wave solar radiation is opaque to outgoing long wave radiation.
- **Sunspots :** They are dark and cooler patches on the Sun which increase and decrease in a cyclic manner.
- **Daily range of temperature :** The differences between the highest and the lowest temperature of a place in a day is called daily range of temperature.

Multiple Choice Questions (1 mark each)

Q. 1. The warmest year, not only for the 20th century but also for the whole millennium was: [A]

(a) 1978

(b) 1988

(c) 1998

(d) 2008

Ans. (c) 1998 1

Q. 2. The greatest warming of the 20th century was during the period: [R]

(a) 1601-44

(b) 1701-44

(c) 1801-44

(d) 1901-44

Ans. (d) 1901-44 1

Q. 3. _______ protocol bounds the 35 industrialised countries to reduce their emissions by the year 2012 to 5 per cent less than the levels prevalent in the year 1990. [A]

(a) Nato

(b) Kyoto

(c) European

(d) UN

Ans. (b) Kyoto 1

Very Short Answer Type Questions (1 mark each)

Q. 1. Define the term 'Dust Bowl'. [A]

Ans. During the 1930s, severe drought occurred in south western Great Plains of the United States. These are described as the dust bowl. 1

Q. 2. Define the term 'Green House'. [A]

Ans. The term greenhouse is derived from the analogy to a greenhouse used in cold areas for preserving heat. A greenhouse is made up of glass. The glass which is transparent to incoming short wave solar radiation is opaque to outgoing long wave radiation. 1

[AI] **Q. 3. Define the term 'Ozone Hole'.** [U]

Ans. The depletion of ozone concentration in the stratosphere is called the ozone hole. 1

Q. 4. What is greenhouse effect? [A]

Ans. The processes that warm the atmosphere are often collectively referred to as the green house effect. 1

Commonly Made Error

- Maintaining suitable temperature for survival is possible without greenhouse effect.

Answering Tip

- Without the greenhouse effect, the Earth would have an average temperature of -18 °C and be covered in ice.

Q. 5. What are sunspots? [R]

Ans. They are dark and cooler patches on the Sun which increase and decrease in a cyclic manner. 1

Q. 6. What do you understand by the term 'Daily Range of Temperature'? [U]

Ans. The differences between the highest and the lowest temperature of a place in a day is called daily range of temperature. 1

Q. 7. What changes does the geological records show especially in the glaciers? [R]

Ans. The geomorphological features, especially in high altitudes and high latitudes, exhibit traces of advances and retreats of glaciers. 1

Q. 8. What type of climate did Rajasthan experience during 8000 BC? [R]

Ans. Rajasthan experienced humid and cold climate. 1

Q. 9. What kind of experiences did Europe witness from 1550 to about 1850? [A]

Ans. Europe experienced 'Little Ice Age'. 1

Q. 10. What kind of climate did the Earth experience during the Cambrian, Ordovician and Silurian periods? [U]

Ans. In the geological past, the earth was warm some 500-300 million years ago, through the Cambrian, Ordovician and Silurian periods. 1

Q. 11. How is volcanism considered as a cause for climatic change? [A]

Ans. Volcanism is considered as the a cause for climatic change because volcanic eruptions throws up lots of aerosols into the atmosphere. These aerosols remain in the atmosphere for a considerable period of time reducing the Sun's radiation reaching the Earth's surface. 1

Q. 12. Which protocol was held for reducing the emission of GHGs into the atmosphere in 1997? [R]

Ans. Kyoto Protocol, which as proclaimed in 1997, efforts have been initiated for reducing the emission of GHGs into the atmosphere . 1

Q. 13. What absorbs ultra-violet rays in the stratosphere? [R]

Ans. Ozone absorbs the ultra-violet rays in the stratosphere . 1

Q. 14. What can happen with the concentration of greenhouse gases in the atmosphere? [U]

Ans. It can cause global warming. 1

Q. 15. How is volcanism considered as a cause for climatic change? [A]

Ans. The largest concentration of GHGs in the atmosphere is the carbon dioxide. 1

Q. 16. Where does ozone occur in the atmosphere? [A]

Ans. Ozone occurs in the stratosphere where ultra-violet rays convert oxygen into ozone. 1

Q. 17. When was the Kyoto protocol come into effect? R

Ans. The Kyoto protocol was proclaimed in 1997. This protocol went into effect in 2005, satisfied by 41 nation. 1

Answering Tip

- The Nations that haven't signed 1997's Global Climate Treaty are Afghanistan, Sudan & the U.S.A. Even Somalia has ratified the Kyoto Protocol.

Q. 18. What is one of the major concerns of today's world? A

Ans. One of the major concerns of the world today is global warming. 1

Q. 19. When did the greatest warming of the 20th century take place? R

Ans. The greatest warming of the 20th century was during the two periods, 1901-44 and 1977-99. 1

Q. 20. Which year was the warmest in the whole millennium? A

Ans. The year 1998 was the warmest year, probably not only for the 20th century but also for the whole millennium. 1

Q. 21. What is the astronomical theory of Millankovitch oscillation? U

Ans. The astronomical theory is Millankovitch oscillations, infers cycles in the variations in the Earth's orbital characteristics around the sun, the wobbling of the earth and the changes in the Earth's axial tilt. All these alter the amount of insolation received from the Sun, which in turn, might have a bearing on the climate. 1

Short Answer Type Questions (3 marks each)

Q. 1. What is Kyoto Protocol? A

Ans. International efforts have been initiated for reducing the emission of GHGs into the atmosphere. The most important one is the Kyoto protocol proclaimed in 1997. This protocol went into effect in 2005, ratified by 141 nations. Kyoto protocol bounds the 35 industrialised countries to reduce their emissions by the year 2012 to 5 per cent less than the levels prevalent in the year 1990. 3

Q. 2. How does volcano affect the climate? U

Ans. Volcanic eruption throws up lots of aerosols into the atmosphere. These aerosols remain in the atmosphere for a considerable period of time reducing the sun's radiation reaching the Earth's surface. After the recent Pinatoba and El Cion volcanic eruptions, the average temperature of the earth fell to some extent for some years. 3

Answering Tip

- Most of the particles spewed from volcanoes cool the planet by shading incoming solar radiation. The cooling effect can last for months to years depending on the characteristics of the eruption.

AI **Q. 3. What do you know about the greenhouse effect?** A

Ans. The term 'greenhouse' is derived from the analogy to a greenhouse used in cold areas for preserving heat. A greenhouse is made up of glass. The glass which is transparent to incoming short wave solar radiation is opaque to outgoing long wave radiation. The glass, therefore, allows in more radiation and prevents the long wave radiation going outside the glass house, causing the temperature inside the glasshouse structure warmer than outside.

Due to the presence of greenhouse gases, the atmosphere is behaving like a greenhouse. The atmosphere also transmits the incoming solar radiation but absorbs the vast majority of long wave radiation emitted upwards by the earth's surface. The gases that absorb long wave radiation are called greenhouse gases. The processes that warm the atmosphere are often collectively referred to as the greenhouse effect. 3

Q. 4. What measures have been taken at international level to fight greenhouse effect? A

Ans. International efforts have been initiated for reducing the emission of GHGs into the atmosphere. The most important one is the Kyoto protocol proclaimed in 1997. This protocol went into effect in 2005, ratified by 141 nations. Kyoto protocol bounds the 35 industrialised countries to reduce their emissions by the year 2012 to 5 per cent less than the levels prevalent in the year 1990. 3

Q. 5. What are the repercussions of global warming? R

Ans. Once the global warming sets in, it will be difficult to reverse it. The effect of global warming may not be uniform everywhere. Nevertheless, the adverse effect due to global warming will adversely affect the life supporting system. Rise in the sea level due to melting of glaciers and ice-caps and thermal expansion of the sea may inundate large parts of the coastal area and islands, leading to social problems. 3

Answering Tip

- Global warming can lead to warming of the ocean surface, leading to increased temperature stratification.

Long Answer Type Questions

(5 marks each)

Q. 1. Write a note on the climatic changes that have taken place since the ancient times? [A]

Ans. The type of climate we experience now might be prevailing over the last 10,000 years with minor and occasionally wide fluctuations. The planet earth has witnessed many variations in climate since the beginning.

Geological records show alteration of glacial and inter-glacial periods. The geomorphological features, especially in high altitudes and high latitudes, exhibit traces of advances and retreats of glaciers.

The sediment deposits in glacial lakes also reveal the occurrence of warm and cold periods. The rings in the trees provide clues about wet and dry periods. Historical records describe the vagaries in climate. All these evidences indicate that change in climate is a natural and continuous process.

India also witnessed alternate wet and dry periods. Archaeological findings show that the Rajasthan desert experienced wet and cool climate around 8,000 B.C. The period 3,0001,700 B.C. had higher rainfall. From about 2,000-1,700 B.C., this region was the centre of the Harappan civilisation.

Dry conditions accentuated since then. In the geological past, the earth was warm some 500-300 million years ago, through the Cambrian, Ordovician and Silurian periods. During the Pleistocene epoch, glacial and inter-glacial periods occurred, the last major peak glacial period was about 18,000 years ago. The present inter-glacial period started 10,000 years ago. 5

Q. 2. Explain in detail the causes of climate changes? [A]

Ans. The causes for climate change are many. They can be grouped into astronomical and terrestrial causes.

The astronomical causes are the changes in solar output associated with sunspot activities. Sunspots are dark and cooler patches on the sun which increase and decrease in a cyclical manner. According to some meteorologists, when the number of sunspots increase, cooler and wetter weather and greater storminess occur. A decrease in sunspot numbers is associated with warm and drier conditions. Yet, these findings are not statistically significant.

An another astronomical theory is Millankovitch Oscillations, which infer cycles in the variations in the earth's orbital characteristics around the sun, the wobbling of the earth and the changes in the earth's axial tilt. All these alter the amount of insolation received from the Sun, which in turn, might have a bearing on the climate.

Volcanism is considered as another cause for climate change. Volcanic eruption throws up lots of aerosols into the atmosphere. These aerosols remain in the atmosphere for a considerable period of time reducing the sun's radiation reaching the Earth's surface. After the recent Pinatoba and El Cion volcanic eruptions, the average temperature of the earth fell to some extent for some years.

The most important anthropogenic effect on the climate is the increasing trend in the concentration of greenhouse gases in the atmosphere which is likely to cause global warming. 5

Commonly Made Error

- The students tend to ignore the effect that climate changes have on the environment.

Answering Tip

- As the climate warms, it changes the nature of global rainfall, evaporation, snow, stream flow and other factors that affect water supply and quality. Specific impacts include: Warmer water temperatures affect water quality and accelerate water pollution.

Q. 3. The planet has warmed up from the temperature records.' Explain? [A]

Ans. The planet has warmed up from the temperature records. Temperature data are available from the middle of the 19th century mostly for western Europe. The reference period for this study is 1961-90. The temperature anomalies for the earlier and later periods are estimated from the average temperature for the period 1961-90.

The annual average near-surface air temperature of the world is approximately 14°C. The time series show anomalies of annual near surface temperature over land from 1856-2000, relative to the period 1961-90 as normal for the globe. An increasing trend in temperature was discernible in the 20th century.

The greatest warming of the 20th century was during the two periods, 1901-44 and 1977-99. Over each of these two periods, global temperatures rose by about 0.4°C.

In between, there was a slight cooling, which was more marked in the Northern Hemisphere. The globally averaged annual mean temperature at the end of the 20th century was about 0.6°C above that recorded at the end of the 19th century.

The seven warmest years during the 1856-2000 were recorded in the last decade. The year 1998 was the warmest year, probably not only for the 20th century but also for the whole millennium.5

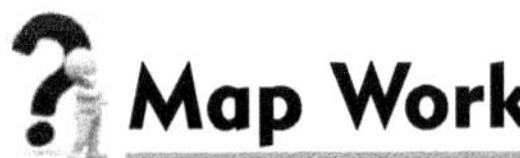

Map Work

(5 marks each)

Q.1. In the outline map of the world, mark the following:

(i) AF-Tropical Wet Climate
(ii) EF- Ice Cap Climate
(iii) Cfb-Marine West Coast Climate
(iv) Cwa -Humid Subtropical Climate
(v) Aw-Tropical Wet and Dry Climate

Ans. (i) AF-Tropical Wet Climate- Amazon Basin
(ii) EF- Ice Cap Climate- Antarctica
(iii) Cfb-Marine West Coast Climate- Australia
(iv) Cwa -Humid Subtropical Climate- South China
(v) Aw-Tropical Wet and Dry Climate-South of Central Africa.

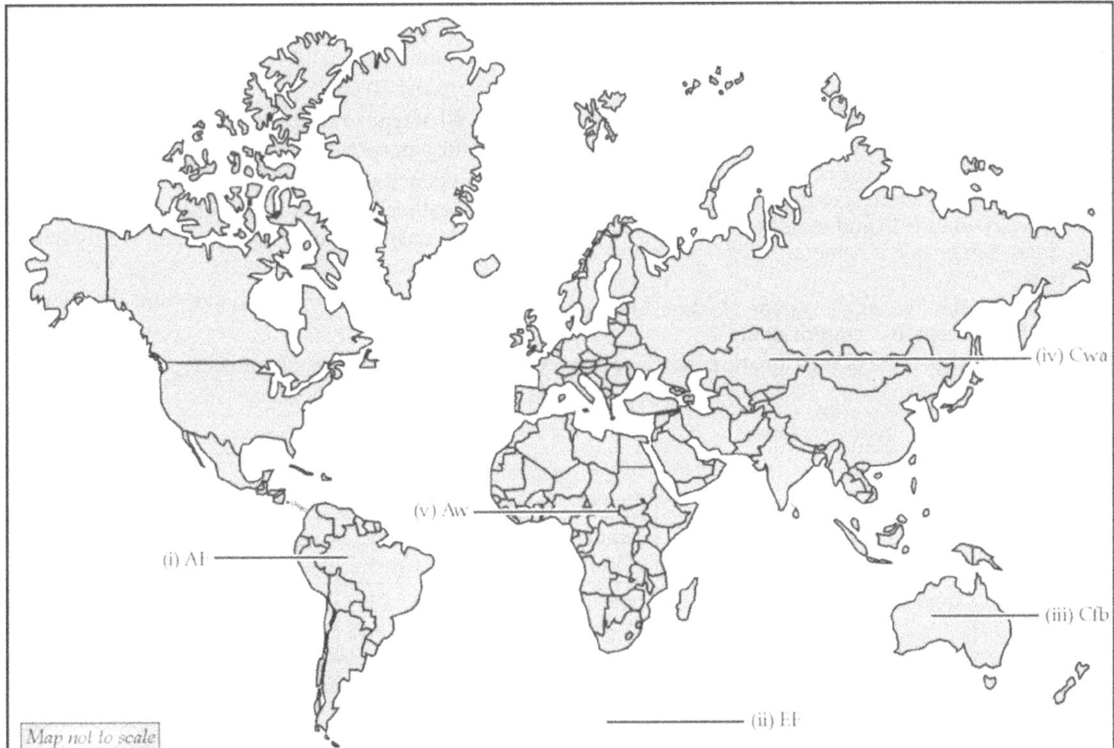

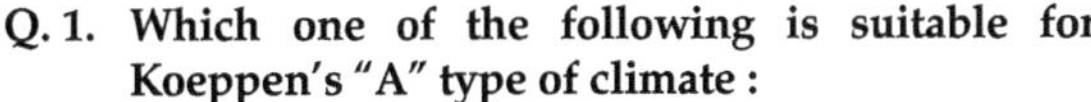

NCERT CORNER

Q. 1. Which one of the following is suitable for Koeppen's "A" type of climate :
(a) High rainfall in all the months
(b) Mean monthly temperature of the coldest month more than freezing point
(c) Mean monthly temperature of all the months more than 18°C
(d) Average temperature for all the months below 10°C

Ans. (a) High rainfall in all the months.

Q. 2. Koeppen's system of classification of climates can be termed as :
(a) Applied
(b) Systematic
(c) Genetic
(d) Empirical

Ans. (d) Empirical .

Q. 3. Most of the Indian Peninsula will be grouped according to Koeppen's system under :
(a) "Af"
(b) "BSh"
(c) "Cfb"
(d) "Am"

Ans. (d) "Am".

Q. 4. Which one of the following years is supposed to have recorded the warmest temperature the world over :
(a) 1990
(b) 1998
(c) 1885
(d) 1950

Ans. (b) 1998

Q. 5. Which one of the following groups of four climates represents humid conditions :

(a) A—B—C—E

(b) A—C—D—E

(c) B—C—D—E

(d) A—C—D—F

Ans. (b) A-C-D-E.

(B) Answer the following questions in about 30 words :

Q. 1. Which two climatic variables are used by Koeppen for classification of the climate? [A]

Ans. The most widely used classification of climate is the empirical climate classification scheme developed by V. Koeppen. Koeppen identified a close relationship between the distribution of vegetation and climate.

He introduced the use of capital and small letters to designate climatic groups and types. Although developed in 1918 and modified over a period of time, Koeppen's scheme is still popular and in use.

Q. 2. How is the "genetic" system of classification different from the "empirical one"?

Ans. The genetic system of classification attempts to organise climates according to their causes. Whereas, the empirical classification is based on observed data, particularly on temperature and precipitation.

Q. 3. Which types of climates have very low range of temperature?

Ans. Tropical wet climate found near the Equator has a very low range of temperature . The major areas covered are Amazon Basin in South America , western equatorial Africa and the islands of East Indies. The maximum temperature on nay day is around 30°C while the minimum temperature is around 20°C.

Q. 4. What type of climatic conditions would prevail if the sun spots increase?

Ans. When the sunspots increase, cooler and wetter weather and greater storminess occur. A decrease in sunspot numbers is associated with warm and drier conditions.

(C) Answer the following questions in about 150 words :

Q. 1. Make a comparison of the climatic conditions between the "A" and "B" types of climate?

Ans.

Groups	Types of climate	Comparison
Af	Tropical wet	Wet throughout the year. Rainfall evenly distributed all through the year. Average monthly temperature is greater than 18°C.
Am	Tropical Monsoon	Heavy rainfall occurs mostly in summer. Winter is dry. Average monthly temperature is greater than 18° C.
Aw	Tropical Wet and Dry Climate	The annual rainfall in this climate is considerably less than that in Af and Am climate types and is variable also. The wet season is shorter and the dry season is longer with the drought being more severe. Average temperature is greater than 18°C.
BSh	Subtropical Dry Semiarid (Steppe)	Located in the transition zone between humid and dry climates, subtropical steppe receives slightly more rainfall than the desert, adequate enough for the growth of sparse grasslands. The rainfall in both the climates is highly variable. Average temperature is more than 18°C.
BWh	Subtropical Dry Arid (Desert)	Evaporation exceeds precipitation on average but is less than potential evaporation . Average temperature is more than 18°C.
BSk	Mid-latitude Dry Semiarid	Mid-latitude is dry. Evaporation exceeds precipitation on average but is less than potential evaporation. Average temperature is less than 18°C.
BWk	Mid-latitude Dry Arid (Desert)	Mid-latitude desert. Winters are below freezing temperatures. Average temperature is less than 18°C.

Q. 2. What type of vegetation would you find in the "C" and "A" type(s) of climate?

Ans. Group A : Tropical humid climates exist between Tropic of Cancer and Tropic of Capricorn. The sun being overhead throughout the year and the presence of Inter Tropical Convergence Zone (ITCZ) make the climate hot and humid. Annual range of temperature is very low and annual rainfall is high.

The tropical group is divided into three types, namely :

(i) Af- Tropical wet climate;

(ii) Am - Tropical monsoon climate;

(iii) Aw- Tropical wet and dry climate

Group C : Warm temperate (mid-latitude) climates extend from 30° - 50° of latitude mainly on the eastern and western margins of continents. These climates generally have warm summers with mild winters.

They are grouped into four types:

(i) Humid subtropical, *i.e.*, dry in winter and hot in summer (Cwa);

(ii) Mediterranean (Cs);

(iii) Humid subtropical, i.e. no dry season and mild winter (Cfa);

(iv) Marine west coast climate (Cfb).

Q. 3. What do you understand by the term "Greenhouse Gases"? Make a list of greenhouse gases?

Ans. The term greenhouse is derived from the analogy to a greenhouse used in cold areas for preserving heat. A greenhouse is made up of glass. The glass which is transparent to incoming short wave solar radiation is opaque to outgoing long wave radiation. The glass, therefore, allows in more radiation and prevents the long wave radiation going outside the glass house, causing the temperature inside the glasshouse structure warmer than outside.

Due to the presence of greenhouse gases, the atmosphere is behaving like a greenhouse. The atmosphere also transmits the incoming solar radiation but absorbs the vast majority of long wave radiation emitted upwards by the earth's surface. The gases that absorb long wave radiation are called greenhouse gases. The processes that warm the atmosphere are often collectively referred to as the greenhouse effect.

Greenhouse gases are those gases which cause global warming and result in rise in atmospheric temperature. The greenhouse gases are :

The primary GHGs of concern today are carbon dioxide (CO_2), Chlorofluorocarbons (CFCs), methane (CH4), nitrous oxide (N_2O) and ozone (O_3). Some other gases such as nitric oxide (NO) and carbon monoxide (CO) easily react with GHGs and affect their concentration in the atmosphere. The effectiveness of any given GHG molecule will depend on the magnitude of the increase in its concentration, its life time in the atmosphere and the wavelength of radiation that it absorbs.

The largest concentration of GHGs in the atmosphere is carbon dioxide. The emission of CO_2 comes mainly from fossil fuel combustion (oil, gas and coal). Forests and oceans are the sinks for the carbon dioxide. Forests use CO_2 in their growth. So, deforestation due to changes in land use, also increases the concentration of CO_2.

Chlorofluorocarbons (CFCs) are products of human activity. Ozone occurs in the stratosphere where ultra-violet rays convert oxygen into ozone. Thus, ultra violet rays do not reach the earth's surface.

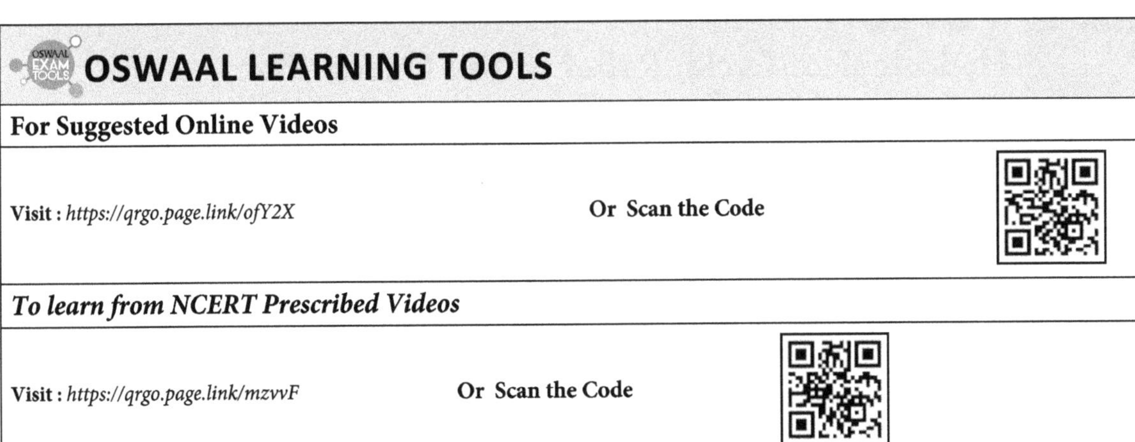
OSWAAL EXAM TOOLS
OSWAAL LEARNING TOOLS
For Suggested Online Videos
Visit : https://qrgo.page.link/ofY2X
Or Scan the Code
To learn from NCERT Prescribed Videos
Visit : https://qrgo.page.link/mzvvF
Or Scan the Code

❑❑

CHAPTER

13 WATER (OCEANS)

Syllabus

- *Hydrological Cycle, Relief of the Ocean Floor, Divisions of the Ocean Floor, Minor Relief Features.*
- *Temperature of Ocean Waters, Factors Affecting Temperature Distribution, Horizontal and Vertical Distribution of Temperature .*
- *Salinity of Ocean Waters, Horizontal Distribution of Salinity,Vertical Distribution of Salinity.*

TOPIC-1
Hydrological Cycle, Relief of the Ocean Floor, Divisions of the Ocean Floor, Minor Relief Features.

Revision Notes

- Water is a rare commodity in our solar system. There is no water on the sun or anywhere else in the solar system.
- The earth, fortunately has an abundant supply of water on its surface. Hence, our planet is called the **'Blue Planet'.**
- Water is a cyclic resource. It can be used and re-used. Water also undergoes a cycle from the ocean to land and land to ocean.
- The water cycle has been working for billions of years and all the life on earth depends on it.
- The distribution of water on earth is quite uneven. The hydrological cycle, is the circulation of water within the earth's hydrosphere in different forms i.e. the liquid, solid and the gaseous phases.
- Nearly 59 per cent of the water that falls on land returns to the atmosphere through evaporation from over the oceans as well as from other places.
- It is to be noted that the renewable water on the earth is constant while the demand is increasing tremendously.
- The oceans are confined to the great depressions of the earth's outer layer.
- The geographers have divided the oceanic part of the earth into four oceans, namely the Pacific, the Atlantic, the Indian and the Arctic. The various seas, bays, gulfs and other inlets are parts of these four large oceans.
- A major portion of the ocean floor is found between 3-6 km below the sea level.
- The floors of the oceans are rugged with the world's largest mountain ranges, deepest trenches and the largest plains.
- The ocean floors can be divided into four major divisions:
  - **The Continental Shelf :** The continental shelf is the extended margin of each continent occupied by relatively shallow seas and gulfs. It is the shallowest part of the ocean showing an average gradient of 1° or even less. The shelf typically ends at a very steep slope, called the shelf break.

    The continental shelves are covered with variable thicknesses of sediments brought down by rivers, glaciers, wind, from the land and distributed by waves and currents.
  - **The Continental Slope :** The continental slope connects the continental shelf and the ocean basins. It begins where the bottom of the continental shelf sharply drops off into a steep slope. The depth of the slope region varies between 200 and 3,000 m. The slope boundary indicates the end of the continents. Canyons and trenches are observed in this region.

- **The Deep Sea Plain :** Deep sea plains are gently sloping areas of the ocean basins. These are the flattest and smoothest regions of the world. These plains are covered with fine-grained sediments like clay and silt.
- **The Oceanic Deeps :** These areas are the deepest parts of the oceans. The trenches are relatively steep sided, narrow basins. They are some 3-5 km deeper than the surrounding ocean floor. As many as 57 deeps have been explored so far; of which 32 are in the Pacific Ocean; 19 in the Atlantic Ocean and 6 in the Indian Ocean.

➢ Some of the minor relief features are :

- **Mid-Oceanic Ridges :** A mid-oceanic ridge is composed of two chains of mountains separated by a large depression. The mountain ranges can have peaks as high as 2,500 m and some even reach above the ocean's surface.
- **Seamount :** It is a mountain with pointed summits, rising from the seafloor that does not reach the surface of the ocean. Seamounts are volcanic in origin. These can be 3,000-4,500 m tall.
- **Submarine Canyons :** These are deep valleys, some comparable to the Grand Canyon of the Colorado river. They are sometimes found cutting across the continental shelves and slopes, often extending from the mouths of large rivers.
- **Guyots :** It is a flat topped seamount. It is estimated that more than 10,000 seamounts and guyots exist in the Pacific Ocean alone.
- **Atoll :** These are low islands found in the tropical oceans consisting of coral reefs surrounding a central depression.

Know the Terms

➢ **Blue planet :** The earth, has an abundant supply of water on its surface. Hence, our planet is called the 'Blue Planet'.
➢ **Hydrological cycle :** It is the circulation of water within the earth's hydrosphere in different forms i.e. the liquid, solid and the gaseous phases.
➢ **Continental shelf :** The continental shelf is the extended margin of each continent occupied by relatively shallow seas and gulfs.
➢ **Continental slope :** The continental slope connects the continental shelf and the ocean basins.
➢ **Deep sea plains :** They are gently sloping areas of the ocean basins.
➢ **Oceanic Deeps or Trenches :** These areas are the deepest parts of the oceans .
➢ **Shelf break :** The shelf typically ends at a very steep slope, called the shelf break.
➢ **Seamount :** It is a mountain with pointed summits, rising from the seafloor that does not reach the surface of the ocean.
➢ **Submarine Canyons :** These are deep valleys, some comparable to the Grand Canyon of the Colorado river.
➢ **Guyots :** It is a flat topped seamount.

Multiple Choice Questions **(1 mark each)**

Q. 1. _____________ is a rare commodity in our solar system. A
(a) Oxygen
(b) Water
(c) Living beings
(d) Mountains
Ans. (b) Water 1

Q. 2. The distribution of water on earth is quite: R
(a) uneven
(b) even
(c) scattered
(d) abundant
Ans. (a) uneven 1

Very Short Answer Type Questions **(1 mark each)**

Q. 1. Define the term 'Blue Planet'. A
Ans. There is no water on the sun or anywhere else in the solar system. The earth, fortunately has an abundant supply of water on its surface. Hence, our planet is called the 'Blue Planet'. 1

Q. 2. Define the term 'Hydrological cycle'. U
Ans. The hydrological cycle, is the circulation of water within the earth's hydrosphere in different forms *i.e.*, the liquid, solid and the gaseous phases. 1

Commonly Made Error
- It is thought that the hydrological cycle ends after one cycle.

Answering Tip
- A fundamental characteristic of the hydrologic cycle is that it has no beginning and it has no end. It is a continuous ongoing process.

Q. 3. Define the term 'Shelf Break'. U

Ans. The continental shelf is the extended margin of each continent occupied by relatively shallow seas and gulfs. It is the shallowest part of the ocean showing an average gradient of 1° or even less. The shelf typically ends at a very steep slope, called the shelf break. 1

Answering Tip

- A shelf break is characterized by markedly increased slope gradients toward the deep ocean bottom.

Q. 4. What is deep sea plains? R

Ans. Deep sea plains are gently sloping areas of the ocean basins. These are the flattest and smoothest regions of the world. 1

Q. 5. Define the term 'seamount'. A

Ans. Seamount is a mountain with pointed summits, rising from the seafloor that does not reach the surface of the ocean. 1

Q. 6. What is guyots? U

Ans. Guyots It is a flat topped seamount. They show evidences of gradual subsidence through stages to become flat topped submerged mountains. 1

Q. 7. What is atoll? A

Ans. Atoll are low islands found in the tropical oceans consisting of coral reefs surrounding a central depression. 1

Q. 8. What are submarine canyons? A

Ans. They are sometimes found cutting across the continental shelves and slopes, often extending from the mouths of large rivers. 1

Answering Tip

- Submarine canyons are so called because they resemble canyons made by rivers on land.

Q. 9. Where is 71 per cent of the planetary water found? R

Ans. About 71 per cent of the planetary water is found in the oceans. 1

Q. 10. The oceanic part of the Earth has been divided into how many oceans? U

Ans. The geographers have divided the oceanic part of the earth into four oceans, namely the Pacific, the Atlantic, the Indian and the Arctic. 1

Q. 11. Name the deepest part of the oceans. A

Ans. Oceanic deeps or trenches. 1

Q. 12. Why are oceanic deeps significant in the study of plate movements? R

Ans. They occur at the bases of continental slopes and along island arcs and are associated with active volcanoes and strong earthquakes. That is why they are very significant in the study of plate movements. 1

Q. 13. Give one example of submarine canyon. A

Ans. The Hudson Canyon is the best-known canyon in the world. 1

Q. 14. Give an example of the mid-Atlantic Ridge? U

Ans. Iceland, a part of the mid-Atlantic Ridge, is an example. 1

Q.15. Give an example of the seamount. A

Ans. The Emperor Seamount, an extension of the Hawaiian Islands in the Pacific Ocean, is a good example. 1

Q. 16. What is the average depth of the continental shelf? U

Ans. The depth of the shelves also varies. It may be as shallow as 30 m in some areas while in some areas it is as deep as 600 m. 1

Q. 17. What is the depth of the continental slope? U

Ans. The depth of the continental slope region varies between 200 and 3,000 m. 1

Short Answer Type Questions

(3 marks each)

AI **Q. 1. 'Water is a cyclic resource.' Explain.** U

Ans. Water is a cyclic resource. It can be used and re-used. Water also undergoes a cycle from the ocean to land and land to ocean. The hydrological cycle describes the movement of water on, in, and above the earth. The water cycle has been working for billions of years and all the life on earth depends on it. 3

Q. 2. Explain the process of hydrological cycle? A

Ans. The hydrological cycle, is the circulation of water within the earth's hydrosphere in different forms i.e. the liquid, solid and the gaseous phases. It also refers to the continuous exchange of water between the oceans atmosphere, land surface and subsurface and the organisms. About 71 per cent of the planetary water is found in the oceans. The remaining is held as freshwater in glaciers and icecaps, groundwater sources, lakes, soil moisture, atmosphere, streams and within life. Nearly 59 per cent of the water that falls on land returns to the atmosphere through evaporation from over the oceans as well as from other places. The remainder runs-off on the surface, infiltrates into the ground or a part of it becomes glacier. 3

Answering Tip

- In the hydrologic cycle, water from oceans, lakes, swamps, rivers, plants, and even you, can turn into water vapor. Water vapor condenses into millions of tiny droplets that form clouds. ... Water that was absorbed into the ground is taken up by plants.

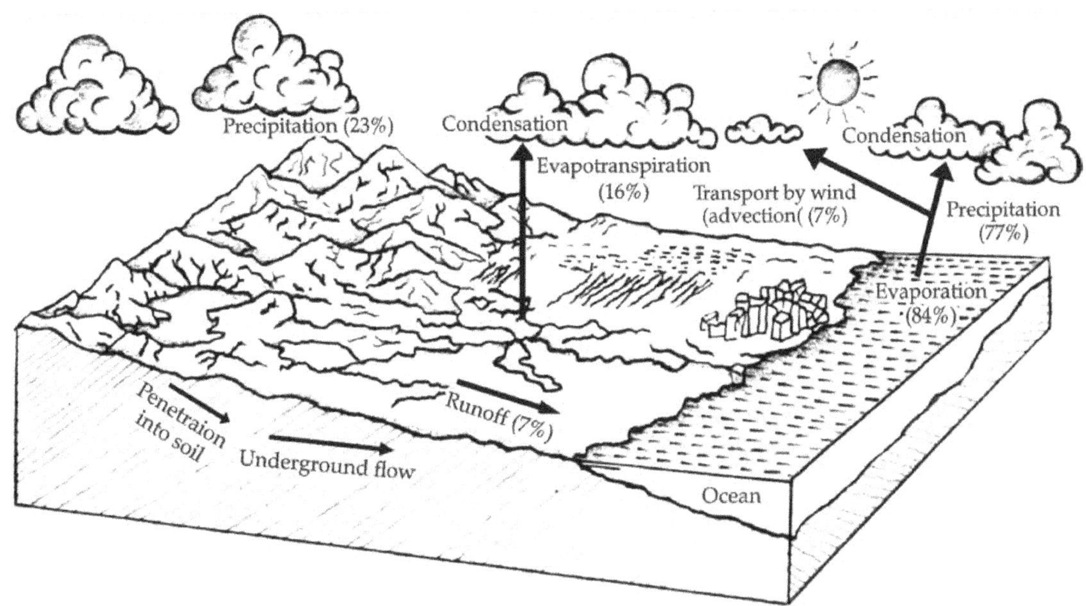

Hydrological Cycle

Q. 3. What do you know about the deepest trench of various oceans across the world? U

Ans. As many as 57 deeps have been explored so far; of which 32 are in the Pacific Ocean, 19 in the Atlantic Ocean and 6 in the Indian Ocean. Some important trenches of the world are as follows:

(i) **Mariana Trench :** It is the world's deepest trench. It lies in the Pacific Ocean. It is 11034 km below the ocean.

(ii) **Puritonko Trench :** It is the deepest trench in the Atlantic Ocean.

(iii) **Sunda Trench :** It is the deepest trench in the Indian Ocean. 3

Q. 4. What do you know about the relief features of the ocean floor?

Ans. The oceans are confined to the great depressions of the earth's outer layer. In this section, we shall see the nature of the ocean basins of the earth and their topography. The oceans, unlike the continents, merge so naturally into one another that it is hard to demarcate them.

The geographers have divided the oceanic part of the earth into four oceans, namely the Pacific, the Atlantic, the Indian and the Arctic. The various seas, bays, gulfs and other inlets are parts of these four large oceans. A major portion of the ocean floor is found between 3-6 km below the sea level.

The 'land' under the waters of the oceans, that is, the ocean floor exhibits complex and varied features as those observed over the land . The floors of the oceans are rugged with the world's largest mountain ranges, deepest trenches and the largest plains. These features are formed, like those of the continents, by the factors of tectonic, volcanic and depositional processes. 3

Answering Tip

- The relief features of the oceans are quite different from the continental features because the Oceanic crust is less than 60-70 million years old whereas continental features are of Proterozoic age (Over 1 billion years old).

Q. 5. How has the water been distributed on the Earth's surface? U

Ans. The distribution of water on earth is quite uneven. Many locations have plenty of water while others have very limited quantity. The hydrological cycle, is the circulation of water within the earth's hydrosphere in different forms i.e. the liquid, solid and the gaseous phases. It also refers to the continuous exchange of water between the oceans, atmosphere, landsurface and subsurface and the organisms.

About 71 per cent of the planetary water is found in the oceans. The remaining is held as freshwater in glaciers and icecaps, groundwater sources, lakes, soil moisture, atmosphere, streams and within life.

Nearly 59 per cent of the water that falls on land returns to the atmosphere through evaporation from over the oceans as well as from other places. The remainder runs-off on the surface, infiltrates into the ground or a part of it becomes glacier. 3

Long Answer Type Questions

(5 marks each)

Q. 1. Differentiate between continental shelf and continental slope. U

Ans.

S.No.	Continental Shelf	Continental Slope
1.	The continental shelf is the extended margin of each continent occupied by relatively shallow seas and gulfs.	The continental slope connects the continental shelf and the ocean basins.
2.	It is the shallowest part of the ocean showing an average gradient of 1° or even less.	The gradient of the slope region varies between 2-5°.
3.	The shelf typically ends at a very steep slope, called the shelf break.	It begins where the bottom of the continental shelf sharply drops off into a steep slope.
4.	The depth of the shelves also varies. It may be as shallow as 30 m in some areas while in some areas it is as deep as 600 m.	The depth of the slope region varies between 200 and 3,000 m.
5.	The continental shelves are covered with variable thicknesses of sediments brought down by rivers, glaciers, wind, from the land and distributed by waves and currents.	The slope boundary indicates the end of the continents. Canyons and trenches are observed in this region.

(1 × 5 = 5)

Answering Tip

- The Continental Shelf is the submerged edge of a continent which is gently sloping plain, whereas; the Continental slope is the the slope between the outer edge of the continental shelf and the deep ocean floor.

Q. 2. Explain the minor relief features of the ocean floor? A

Ans. The various relief features of the ocean floor are:

(i) Mid-Oceanic Ridges : A mid-oceanic ridge is composed of two chains of mountains separated by a large depression. The mountain ranges can have peaks as high as 2,500 m and some even reach above the ocean's surface. Iceland, a part of the midAtlantic Ridge, is an example.

(ii) Seamount : It is a mountain with pointed summits, rising from the seafloor that does not reach the surface of the ocean. Seamounts are volcanic in origin. These can be 3,000-4,500 m tall. The Emperor Seamount, an extension of the Hawaiian Islands in the Pacific Ocean, is a good example.

(iii) Submarine Canyons : These are deep valleys, some comparable to the Grand Canyon of the Colorado river. They are sometimes found cutting across the continental shelves and slopes, often extending from the mouths of large rivers. The Hudson Canyon is the best-known canyon in the world.

(iv) Guyots : It is a flat topped seamount. They show evidences of gradual subsidence through stages to become flat topped submerged mountains. It is estimated that more than 10,000 seamounts and guyots exist in the Pacific Ocean alone.

(v) Atoll : These are low islands found in the tropical oceans consisting of coral reefs surrounding a central depression. It may be a part of the sea (lagoon), or sometimes form enclosing a body of fresh, brackish, or highly saline water . 5

Q. 3. Explain in detail the division of the ocean floors? U

Ans. The ocean floors can be divided into four major divisions : **(i)** the Continental Shelf; **(ii)** the Continental Slope; **(iii)** the Deep Sea Plain; **(iv)** the Oceanic Deeps.

(i) Continental Shelf : The continental shelf is the extended margin of each continent occupied by relatively shallow seas and gulfs. It is the shallowest part of the ocean showing an average gradient of 1° or even less. The shelf typically ends at a very steep slope, called the shelf break.

The width of the continental shelves vary from one ocean to another. The average width of continental shelves is about 80 km. The shelves are almost absent or very narrow along some of the margins like the coasts of Chile, the west coast of Sumatra, etc. On the contrary, the Siberian shelf in the Arctic Ocean, the largest in the world, stretches to 1,500 km in width. The depth of the shelves also varies. It may be as shallow as 30 m in some areas while in some areas it is as deep as 600 m.

(ii) Continental Slope : The continental slope connects the continental shelf and the ocean basins. It begins where the bottom of the continental shelf sharply drops off into a steep slope. The gradient of the slope region varies between 2-5°. The depth of the slope region varies between 200 and 3,000 m. The slope boundary indicates the end of the continents. Canyons and trenches are observed in this region.

(iii) Deep Sea : Plain Deep sea plains are gently sloping areas of the ocean basins. These are the flattest and smoothest regions of the world. The depths vary between 3,000 and 6,000m. These plains are covered with fine-grained sediments like clay and silt.

(iv) Oceanic Deeps or Trenches : These areas are the deepest parts of the oceans. The trenches are relatively steep sided, narrow basins. They are some 3-5 km deeper than the surrounding ocean floor. They occur at the bases of continental slopes and along island arcs and are associated with active volcanoes and strong earthquakes.

Q. 4. 'Ocean seems to be water body but it has many types of landforms within it.' Justify the statements by giving some examples? [A]

Ans. The statement states true. Like the surface of the Earth ocean flow is neither level or flat, it is undulating and varying. It comprises of different types of landforms. Some of them are :

(i) Continental Shelf : The continental shelf is the extended margin of each continent occupied by relatively shallow seas and gulfs. It is the shallowest part of the ocean showing an average gradient of 1° or even less. The shelf typically ends at a very steep slope, called the shelf break.

(ii) Continental Slope : The continental slope connects the continental shelf and the ocean basins. It begins where the bottom of the continental shelf sharply drops off into a steep slope. The gradient of the slope region varies between 2-5°. The depth of the slope region varies between 200 and 3,000 m. The slope boundary indicates the end of the continents. Canyons and trenches are observed in this region .

(iii) Deep Sea : Plain Deep sea plains are gently sloping areas of the ocean basins. These are the flattest and smoothest regions of the world. The depths vary between 3,000 and 6,000m. These plains are covered with fine-grained sediments like clay and silt.

(iv) Sub Marine Ridges : Oceanic floors have submarine narrow and elongated ridges. They resemble mountain ridges on the Earth's surface. Peak of these ridges may rise above the sea-level to form islands. For example: Philippines Ice land is a mid-Atlantic ridge.

(v) Oceanic deeps of sub-marine trenches : Deep narrow steep sided depression found along the abyssal plain. The depth of these trenches may vary from 6,000 to 11,000m. **(1 x 5 = 5)**

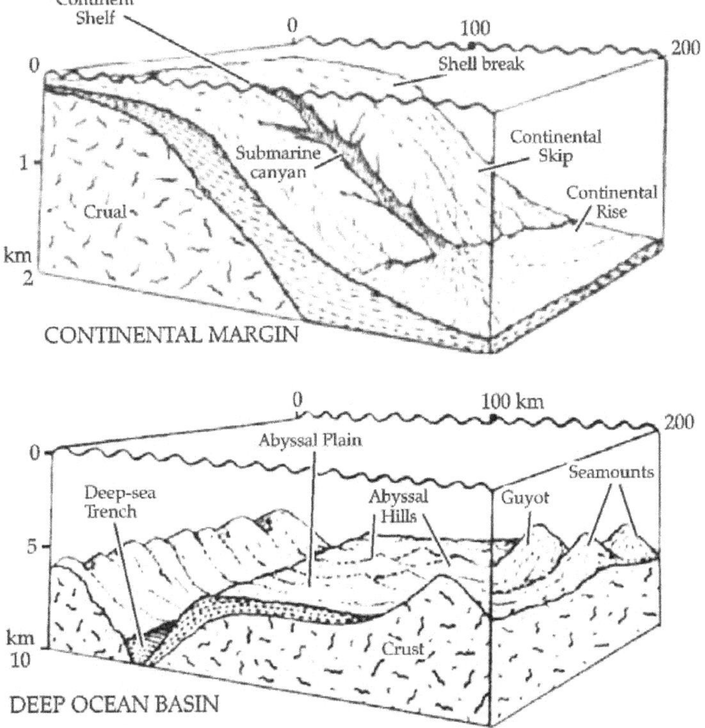

(1 × 5 = 5)

TOPIC-2
Temperature of Ocean Waters, Factors Affecting Temperature Distribution, Horizontal and Vertical Distribution of Temperature

Revision Notes

- Ocean waters get heated up by the solar energy just as land. The process of heating and cooling of the oceanic water is slower than land.
- The factors which affect the distribution of temperature of ocean water are :
  - **Latitude :** The temperature of surface water decreases from the Equator towards the poles because the amount of insolation decreases poleward.
  - **Unequal distribution of land and water :** The oceans in the Northern Hemisphere receive more heat due to their contact with larger extent of land than the oceans in the Southern Hemisphere.
  - **Prevailing wind :** The winds blowing from the land towards the oceans drive warm surface water away from the coast resulting in the upwelling of cold water from below.
  - **Ocean currents :** Warm ocean currents raise the temperature in cold areas while the cold currents decrease the temperature in warm ocean areas.
- The temperature-depth profile for the ocean water shows how the temperature decreases with the increasing depth.
- This boundary region, from where there is a rapid decrease of temperature, is called the thermocline.
- About 90 per cent of the total volume of water is found below the thermocline in the deep ocean. In this zone, temperatures approach 0° C.
- The temperature structure of oceans over middle and low latitudes can be described as a three-layer system from surface to the bottom.
- The first layer represents the top layer of warm oceanic water and it is about 500m thick with temperatures ranging between 20° and 25° C .
- The second layer called the thermocline layer lies below the first layer and is characterised by rapid decrease in temperature with increasing depth.
- The highest temperature is not recorded at the equator but slightly towards north of it. The average annual temperatures for the Northern and Southern Hemisphere are around 19° C and 16° C respectively.
- It is a well known fact that the maximum temperature of the oceans is always at their surfaces because they directly receive the heat from the sun and the heat is transmitted to the lower sections of the oceans through the process of conduction.
- The temperature falls very rapidly up to the depth of 200 m and thereafter, the rate of decrease of temperature is slowed down.

Know the Terms

- **Latitude :** It is the angular distance of a place north or south of the Earth's Equator.
- **Ocean currents :** It is the steady flow of surface ocean water in a prevailing direction.
- **Thermocline :** The boundary region, from where there is a rapid decrease of temperature, is called the thermocline.
- **The process of conduction :** It is the process in which the energy is transferred from the Earth's atmosphere to the air.

Multiple Choice Questions **(1 mark each)**

Q. 1. The process of heating and cooling of the oceanic water is : [A]

(a) slower than land
(b) faster than land
(c) equal to that of land
(d) moderate than land

Ans. (a) slower than land. 1

Q. 2. The average annual temperatures for the Northern Hemisphere are around : [U]

(a) 22° C
(b) 21° C
(c) 20° C
(d) 19° C

Ans. (d) 19° C 1

Very Short Answer Type Questions (1 mark each)

Q. 1. Define the term 'Thermocline'. [A]

Ans. The boundary region, from where there is a rapid decrease of temperature, is called the thermocline.

Commonly Made Error

- The students think that the thermocline remains constant in the ocean.

Answering Tip

- In the ocean, the depth and strength of the thermocline vary from season to season and year to year.

[AI] **Q. 2. How does latitude affect the temperature distribution of ocean water?** [A]

Ans. The temperature of surface water decreases from the Equator towards the poles because the amount of insolation decreases poleward. 1

Q. 3. How does ocean currents affect the temperature distribution of ocean water? [U]

Ans. The warm ocean currents raise the temperature in cold areas while the cold currents decrease the temperature in warm ocean areas. 1

Q. 4. Why is the temperature-depth profile important? [A]

Ans. The temperature-depth profile for the ocean water is important as it shows how the temperature decreases with the increasing depth. 1

Q. 5. What does the first layer of the temperature structure of oceans over middle and low latitudes represent? [R]

Ans. The first layer represents the top layer of warm oceanic water and it is about 500m thick with temperatures ranging between 20° and 25° C. This layer, within the tropical region, is present throughout the year but in mid latitudes it develops only during summer. 1

Q. 6. What does the second layer of the temperature structure of oceans over middle and low latitudes represent? [R]

Ans. The second layer called the thermocline layer lies below the first layer and is characterised by rapid decrease in temperature with increasing depth. The thermocline is 500 -1,000 m thick. 1

Q. 7. What is the average temperature of the surface water of the oceans? [R]

Ans. The average temperature of surface water of the oceans is about 27°C and it gradually decreases from the equator towards the poles. 1

Q. 8. What is the rate of decrease of temperature with increasing latitude? [U]

Ans. The rate of decrease of temperature with increasing latitude is generally 0.5°C per latitude.1

Q. 9. What is the average temperatures for the Northern and Southern Hemisphere? [R]

Ans. The average annual temperatures for the Northern and Southern hemisphere are around 19° C and 16° C respectively. 1

Q. 10. Why is the maximum temperature of the oceans always recorded at the surface? [A]

OR

Why do oceans have the highest temperature at the topmost layer?

Ans. The maximum temperature of the oceans is always at their surfaces because they directly receive the heat from the sun and the heat is transmitted to the lower sections of the oceans through the process of conduction. 1

Q. 11. Draw and label the diagram of thermocline. [A]

Ans.

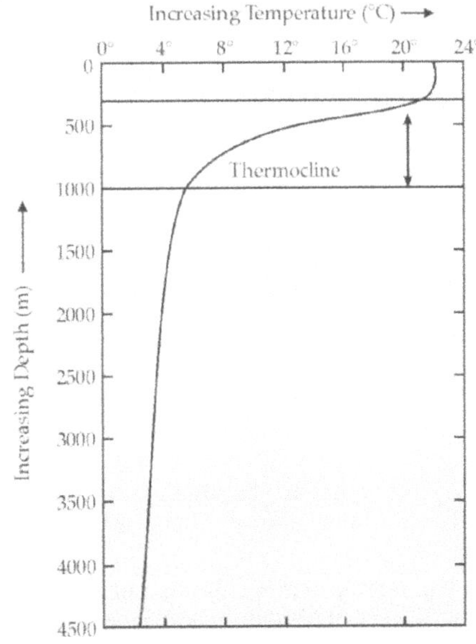

1

Q. 12. What is the rate of decrease of temperature with increasing latitude? [R]

Ans. The rate of decrease of temperature with increasing latitude is generally 0.5°C per latitude. 1

Short Answer Type Questions (3 marks each)

Q. 1. Describe the three-layer system of temperature structure of oceans. [A]

OR

Describe the vertical distribution of temperature.

OR

When you move into the ocean what thermal layers would you encounter ? Why does the temperature vary with depth?

Ans. The temperature structure of oceans over middle and low latitudes can be described as a three-layer system from surface to the bottom.

(i) The first layer represents the top layer of warm oceanic water and it is about 500m thick with temperatures ranging between 20° and 25° C. This layer, within the tropical region, is present throughout the year but in mid latitudes it develops only during summer.

(ii) The second layer called the thermocline layer lies below the first layer and is characterised by rapid decrease in temperature with increasing depth. The thermocline is 500 -1,000 m thick.

(iii) The third layer is very cold and extends upto the deep ocean floor. In the Arctic and Antarctic circles, the surface water temperatures are close to 0° C and so the temperature change with the depth is very slight. Here, only one layer of cold water exists, which extends from surface to deep ocean floor. **3**

Q. 2. Mention the factors that affect the distribution of temperature of ocean water?

Ans. The factors which affect the distribution of temperature of ocean water are :

(i) Latitude : The temperature of surface water decreases from the equator towards the poles because the amount of insolation decreases poleward.

(ii) Unequal distribution of land and water : The oceans in the northern hemisphere receive more heat due to their contact with larger extent of land than the oceans in the southern hemisphere.

(iii) Prevailing wind : The winds blowing from the land towards the oceans drive warm surface water away form the coast resulting in the upwelling of cold water from below. It results into the longitudinal variation in the temperature. Contrary to this, the onshore winds pile up warm water near the coast and this raises the temperature.

(iv) Ocean currents : Warm ocean currents raise the temperature in cold areas while the cold currents decrease the temperature in warm ocean areas. Gulf stream (warm current) raises the temperature near the eastern coast of North America and the West Coast of Europe while the Labrador current (cold current) lowers the temperature near the north-east coast of North America. **(Any Three)**

(1 × 3 = 3)

Long Answer Type Question **(5 marks)**

Q. 1. The average temperature of water on oceans floor keeps on falling from the Equator to poles systematically. Explain? [A]

Ans. The average temperature of surface water of the oceans is about 27°C and it gradually decreases from the equator towards the poles. The rate of decrease of temperature with increasing latitude is generally 0.5°C per latitude. The average temperature is around 22°C at 20° latitudes, 14° C at 40° latitudes and 0° C near poles. The oceans in the northern hemisphere record relatively higher temperature than in the southern hemisphere.

The highest temperature is not recorded at the equator but slightly towards north of it. The average annual temperatures for the northern and southern hemisphere are around 19° C and 16° C respectively. This variation is due to the unequal distribution of land and water in the northern and southern hemispheres. It is a well known fact that the maximum temperature of the oceans is always at their surfaces because they directly receive the heat from sun and the heat is transmitted to the lower sections of the oceans through the process of convection. It results into decrease of temperature with the increasing depth, but the rate of decrease is not uniform throughout the temperature falls very rapidly up to he depth of 200 m and thereafter, the rate of decrease of temperature is slowed down. **5**

TOPIC-3
Salinity of Ocean Waters, Horizontal Distribution of Salinity, Vertical Distribution of Salinity

Revision Notes

- All waters in nature, whether rain water or ocean water, contain dissolved mineral salts.
- Salinity is the term used to define the total content of dissolved salts in sea water.
- It is calculated as the amount of salt (in gm) dissolved in 1,000 gm (1 kg) of seawater.
- Salinity of 24.7 $\%_0$ has been considered as the upper limit to demarcate *'brackish water'*.
- Factors affecting ocean salinity are mentioned below :
  - The salinity of water in the surface layer of oceans depend mainly on evaporation and precipitation.

- Surface salinity is greatly influenced in coastal regions by the fresh water flow from rivers, and in polar regions by the processes of freezing and thawing of ice.
- Wind, also influences salinity of an area by transferring water to other areas.
- The ocean currents contribute to the salinity variations. Salinity, temperature and density of water are interrelated.

➢ The salinity for normal open ocean ranges between $33\%_0$ and $37\%_0$. In hot and dry regions, where evaporation is high, the salinity sometimes reaches to $70\%_0$.

➢ The average salinity of the Atlantic Ocean is around $36\%_0$. The highest salinity is recorded between 15° and 20° latitudes. Maximum salinity ($37\%_0$) is observed between 20° N and 30° N and 20° W – 60.

➢ The North Sea, in spite of its location in higher latitudes, records higher salinity due to more saline water brought by the North Atlantic Drift.

➢ The Baltic Sea records low salinity due to influx of river waters in large quantity.

➢ The average salinity of the Indian Ocean is $35\%_0$. The low salinity trend is observed in the Bay of Bengal due to influx of river water by the River Ganga.

➢ Salinity changes with depth, but the way it changes depends upon the location of the sea.

➢ Salinity at depth is very much fixed, because there is no way that water is 'lost', or the salt is 'added.'

➢ The lower salinity water rests above the higher salinity dense water.

➢ Salinity, generally, increases with depth and there is a distinct zone called the halocline, where salinity increases sharply.

➢ High salinity seawater, generally, sinks below the lower salinity water. This leads to stratification by salinity.

Know the Terms

➢ **Salinity :** Salinity is the term used to define the total content of dissolved salts in sea water.

➢ **Halocline :** Salinity, generally, increases with depth and there is a distinct zone called the halocline, where salinity increases sharply.

Multiple Choice Questions (1 mark each)

Q. 1. The salt water and fresh water mixed together to form the : [A]

(a) brackish water
(b) saline water
(c) dark water
(d) drinking water

Ans. (a) brackish water. 1

Q. 2. The average salinity of the Atlantic Ocean is around : [A]

(a) 34%
(b) 35%
(c) 36%
(d) 37%

Ans. (c) 36% 1

Q. 3. The salinity of water in the surface layer of oceans depend mainly on: [U]

(a) evaporation
(b) condensation
(c) temperature
(d) hydration

Ans. (a) evaporation 1

Very Short Answer Type Questions (1 mark each)

Q. 1. Define the term 'Salinity'.

Ans. Salinity is the term used to define the total content of dissolved salts in sea water. 1

Q. 2. Define the term 'Halocline'. [A]

Ans. Salinity, generally, increases with depth and there is a distinct zone called the halocline, where salinity increases sharply . 1

Q. 3. How is salinity calculated? [U]

Ans. It is calculated as the amount of salt (in gm) dissolved in 1,000 gm (1 kg) of seawater. 1

Q. 4. Name the areas of the world with highest salinity. [A]

Ans. Highest salinity in water bodies are Lake Van in Turkey, Dead Sea, Great Salt Lake. 1

Q. 5. What is the average salinity of the Indian Ocean? [U]

Ans. 35% is the average salinity of the Indian Ocean. 1

Short Answer Type Questions (3 marks each)

Q. 1. Describe the salinity of sea water? [A]

Ans. Salinity is the term used to define the total content of dissolved salts in sea water . It is calculated as the amount of salt (in gm) dissolved in 1,000 gm (1 kg) of seawater. It is usually expressed as parts per thousand ($\%_0$) or ppt. Salinity is an important property of sea water. Salinity of 24.7 $\%_0$ has been considered as the upper limit to demarcate 'brackish water'. Salinity changes with depth, but the way it changes depends upon the location of the sea. Salinity at the surface increases by the loss of water to ice or evaporation , or decreases by the input of fresh water, such as from the rivers. Salinity at depth is very much fixed because there is no way that water is lost or the salt is added. 3

Answering Tip

- Water in the world's oceans has a salinity of approximately 3.5%, or 35 parts per thousand.

Q. 2. Mention the factors that affect the ocean salinity? [A]

Ans. Factors affecting ocean salinity are mentioned below:

(i) The salinity of water in the surface layer of oceans depend mainly on evaporation and precipitation.

(ii) Surface salinity is greatly influenced in coastal regions by the fresh water flow from rivers, and in polar regions by the processes of freezing and thawing of ice.

(iii) Wind, also influences salinity of an area by transferring water to other areas.

(iv) The ocean currents contribute to the salinity variations. Salinity, temperature and density of water are interrelated. Hence, any change in the temperature or density influences the salinity of an area. 3

Commonly Made Error

- The students are not aware of what causes salinity in the sea water.

Answering Tip

- Salt in the ocean comes from rocks on land. The rain that falls on the land contains some dissolved carbon dioxide from the surrounding air. This causes the rainwater to be slightly acidic due to carbonic acid (which forms from carbon dioxide and water).

Long Answer Type Questions (5 marks each)

Q. 1. What do you know about the horizontal distribution of salinity? [A]

Ans. The salinity for normal open ocean ranges between 33$\%_0$ and 37 $\%_0$. In the land locked Red Sea, it is as high as 41$\%_0$, while in the estuaries and the Arctic, the salinity fluctuates from 0 - 35 $\%_0$, seasonally. In hot and dry regions, where evaporation is high, the salinity sometimes reaches to 70 $\%_0$.

The salinity variation in the Pacific Ocean is mainly due to its shape and larger areal extent. Salinity decreases from 35 $\%_0$ - 31 $\%_0$ on the western parts of the Northern Hemisphere because of the influx of melted water from the Arctic region. In the same way, after 15° - 20° south, it decreases to 33 $\%_0$.

The average salinity of the Atlantic Ocean is around 36 $\%_0$. The highest salinity is recorded between 15° and 20° latitudes. Maximum salinity (37 $\%_0$) is observed between 20° N and 30° N and 20° W - 60° W. It gradually decreases towards the north. The North Sea, in spite of its location in higher latitudes, records higher salinity due to more saline water brought by the North Atlantic Drift. Baltic Sea records low salinity due to influx of river waters in large quantity. The Mediterranean Sea records higher salinity due to high evaporation.

Salinity is, however, very low in Black Sea due to enormous fresh water influx by rivers. See the atlas to find out the rivers joining the Black Sea. The average salinity of the Indian Ocean is 35 $\%_0$. The low salinity trend is observed in the Bay of Bengal due to influx of river water by the river Ganga. On the contrary, the Arabian Sea shows higher salinity due to high evaporation and low influx of fresh water. 5

Answering Tip

- The surface salinity of oceans decreases on either side of the tropics.

Q. 2. Discuss the vertical distribution of salinity? [A]

Ans. Salinity changes with depth, but the way it changes depends upon the location of the sea. Salinity at the surface increases by the loss of water to ice or evaporation, or decreased by the input of fresh waters, such as from the rivers.

Salinity at depth is very much fixed, because there is no way that water is 'lost', or the salt is 'added.'

There is a marked difference in the salinity between the surface zones and the deep zones of the oceans. The lower salinity water rests above the higher salinity dense water.

Salinity, generally, increases with depth and there is a distinct zone called the halocline, where salinity increases sharply.

Other factors being constant, increasing salinity of seawater causes its density to increase. High salinity seawater, generally, sinks below the lower salinity water. This leads to stratification by salinity. 5

Map Work

(5 marks each)

Q. 1. On the given political outline map of the world, show the spatial distribution of surface temperature.

Ans.

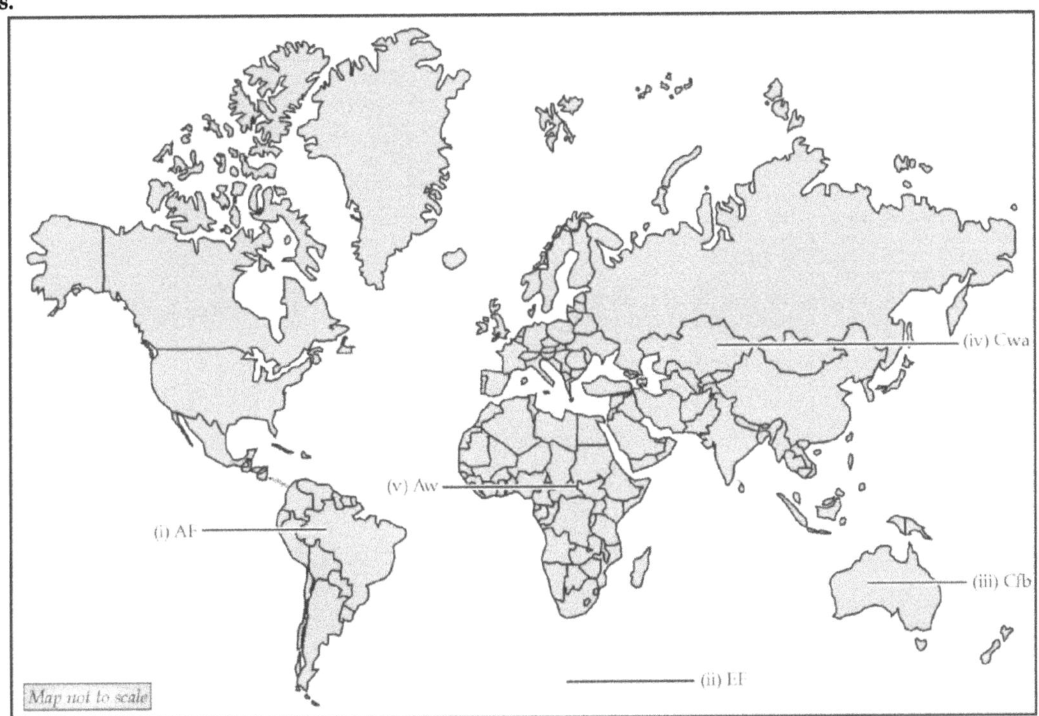

Q. 2. On the given political outline map of the world, show the surface salinity of the different oceans.

Ans.

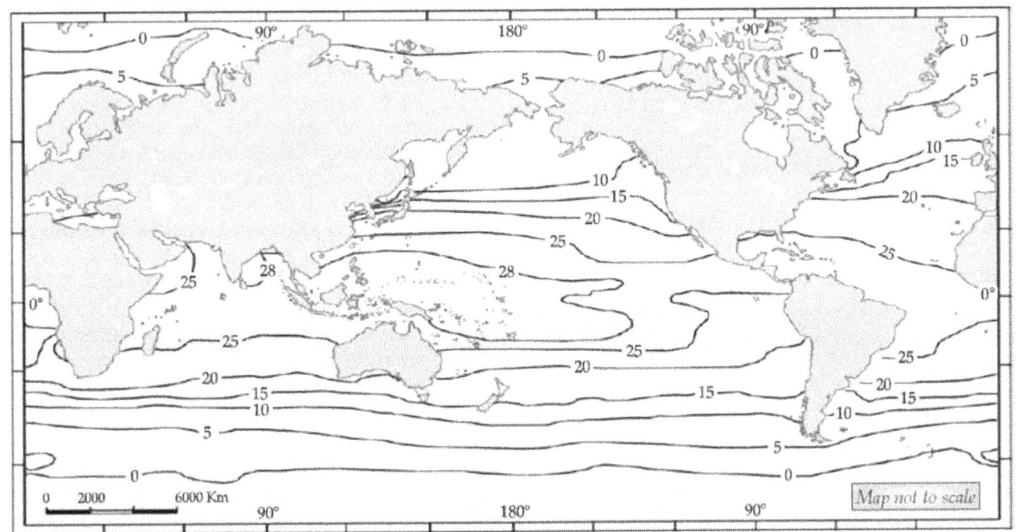

Figure 13.5 : Surface salinity of the World's Oceans

Q. 3. On the given political outline map of the world, locate the following trenches .
(i) Puerto Rico Trench
(ii) Peru-Chile Trench
(iii) Java Trench
(iv) Kurile and Japan Trench
(v) South Sandwich Trench

Ans.

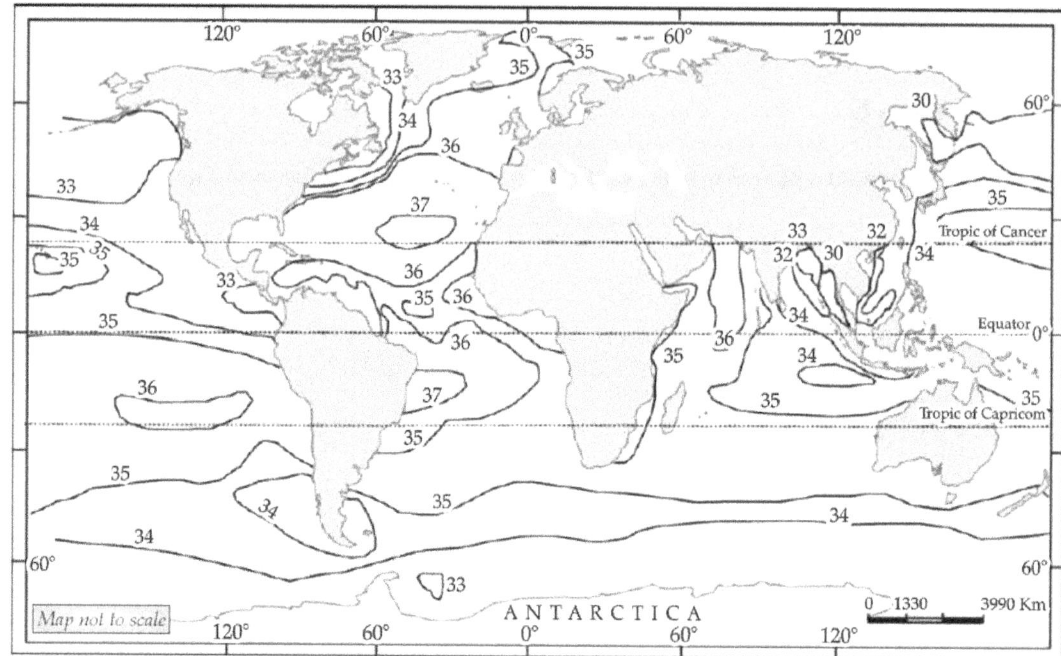

NCERT CORNER

(A) Multiple choice questions :

Q. 1. Identify the element which is not a part of the hydrological cycle :
(a) Evaporation (b) Hydration
(c) Precipitation (d) Condensation

Ans. (b) Hydration.

Q. 2. The average depth of continental slope varies between :
(a) 2-20m (b) 200-2,000m
(c) 20-200m (d) 2,000-20,000m

Ans. (b) 200-2000m.

Q. 3. Which one of the following is not a minor relief feature in the oceans :
(a) Seamount (b) Atoll
(c) Oceanic Deep (d) Guyot

Ans. (b) Atoll

Q. 4. Salinity is expressed as the amount of salt in grams dissolved in sea water per :
(a) 10 gm (b) 1,000 gm
(c) 100 gm (d) 10,000 gm

Ans. (b) 1,000gm.

Q. 5. Which one of the following is the smallest ocean :
(a) Indian Ocean (b) Arctic Ocean
(c) Atlantic Ocean (d) Pacific Ocean

Ans. (b) Arctic Ocean .

(B) Answer the following questions in about 30 words :

Q. 1. Why do we call the earth a Blue Planet? [A]

Ans. There is no water on the sun or anywhere else in the solar system. The earth, fortunately has an abundant supply of water on its surface. Hence, our planet is called the 'Blue Planet'.

Q. 2. What is a continental margin? [U]

Ans. The continental shelf is the extended margin of each continent occupied by relatively shallow seas and gulfs. It is the shallowest part of the ocean showing an average gradient of 1° or even less. The shelf typically ends at a very steep slope, called the shelf break .

Q. 3. List out the deepest trenches of various oceans.

Ans. (i) **Mariana Trench :** It is the world's deepest trench. It lies in the Pacific Ocean . It is 11034km below the ocean.

(ii) **Puritonko Trench :** It is the deepest trench in the Atlantic Ocean.

(iii) **Sunda Trench :** It is the deepest trench in the Indian Ocean.

Q. 4. What is a thermocline?

Ans. The temperature-depth profile for the ocean water shows how the temperature decreases with the increasing depth. The profile shows a boundary region between the surface waters of the ocean and the deeper layers. The boundary usually begins around 100 - 400 m below the sea surface and extends several hundred of m downward . This boundary region, from where there is a rapid decrease of temperature, is called the thermocline.

Q. 5. When you move into the ocean what thermal layers would you encounter? Why the temperature varies with depth?

Ans. The temperature structure of oceans over middle and low latitudes can be described as a three-layer system from surface to the bottom. The first layer represents the top layer of warm oceanic water and it is about 500m thick with temperatures ranging between 20° and 25° C. The second layer called the thermocline layer lies below the first layer and is characterised by rapid decrease in temperature with increasing depth. The third layer is very cold and extends upto the deep ocean floor.

Q. 6. What is salinity of sea water?

Ans. All waters in nature, whether rain water or ocean water, contain dissolved mineral salts. Salinity is the term used to define the total content of dissolved salts in sea water. Salinity is an important property of sea water.

(C) Answer the following questions in about 150 words :

Q. 1. How are various elements of the hydrological cycle interrelated? U

Ans. Water is a cyclic resource. It can be used and re-used. Water also undergoes a cycle from the ocean to land and land to ocean. hydrological cycle describes the movement of water on, in, and above the earth.

The water cycle has been working for billions of years and all the life on earth depends on it. Next to air, water is the most important element required for the existence of life on earth. The distribution of water on earth is quite uneven. Many locations have plenty of water while others have very limited quantity.

The hydrological cycle, is the circulation of water within the earth's hydrosphere in different forms i.e. the liquid, solid and the gaseous phases. It also refers to the continuous exchange of water between the oceans, atmosphere, land surface and subsurface and the organisms.

About 71 per cent of the planetary water is found in the oceans. The remaining is held as freshwater in glaciers and icecaps, groundwater sources, lakes, soil moisture, atmosphere, streams and within life. Nearly 59 per cent of the water that falls on land returns to the atmosphere through evaporation from over the oceans as well as from other places. The remainder runs-off on the surface, infiltrates into the ground or a part of it becomes glacier.

Q. 2. Examine the factors that influence the temperature distribution of the oceans?

Ans. The factors which affect the distribution of temperature of ocean water are:

(i) **Latitude :** The temperature of surface water decreases from the equator towards the poles because the amount of insolation decreases poleward.

(ii) **Unequal distribution of land and water :** The oceans in the northern hemisphere receive more heat due to their contact with larger extent of land than the oceans in the southern hemisphere.

(iii) **Prevailing wind :** The winds blowing from the land towards the oceans drive warm surface water away form the coast resulting in the upwelling of cold water from below. It results into the longitudinal variation in the temperature. Contrary to this, the onshore winds pile up warm water near the coast and this raises the temperature.

(iv) **Ocean currents :** Warm ocean currents raise the temperature in cold areas while the cold currents decrease the temperature in warm ocean areas. Gulf stream (warm current) raises the temperature near the eastern coast of North America and the West Coast of Europe while the Labrador Current (cold current) lowers the temperature near the north-east coast of North America.

(v) **Salinity :** Saline water absorbs more heat and its temperature rises much higher than fresh water.

OSWAAL LEARNING TOOLS

For Suggested Online Videos

Visit : *https://qrgo.page.link/q2xgB* **Or Scan the Code**

To learn from NCERT Prescribed Videos

Visit : *https://qrgo.page.link/4xgZT* **Or Scan the Code**

❑❑

CHAPTER

14 MOVEMENTS OF OCEAN WATER

Syllabus

> ➢ *Waves, Tides, Types of Tides, Importance of Tides.*
> ➢ *Ocean Currents, Types of Ocean Currents.*

TOPIC-1
Waves, Tides, Types of Tides, Importance of Tides

Revision Notes

- The ocean water is dynamic. Its physical characteristics like temperature, salinity, density and the external forces like of the sun, moon and the winds influence the movement of ocean water.
- The horizontal motion refers to the ocean currents and waves.
- The vertical motion refers to tides. The vertical motion refers to the rise and fall of water in the oceans and seas.
- Ocean currents are the continuous flow of huge amount of water in a definite direction while the waves are the horizontal motion of water.
- Water moves ahead from one place to another through ocean currents while the water in the waves does not move, but the wave trains move ahead.
- Due to attraction of the sun and the moon, the ocean water is raised up and falls down twice a day.
- Waves are actually the energy, not the water as such, which moves across the ocean surface.
- Wind provides energy to the waves. Wind causes waves to travel in the ocean and the energy is released on shorelines.
- As a wave approaches the beach, it slows down. This is due to the friction occurring between the dynamic water and the sea floor.
- Most of the waves are caused by the wind driving against water.
- Waves may travel thousands of km before rolling ashore, breaking and dissolving as surf.
- A wave's size and shape reveal its origin.
- Steep waves are fairly young ones and are probably formed by local wind. Slow and steady waves originate from far away places, possibly from another hemisphere.
- Waves travel because wind pushes the water body in its course while gravity pulls the crests of the waves downward.
- The periodical rise and fall of the sea level, once or twice a day, mainly due to the attraction of the sun and the moon, is called a tide.
- Movement of water caused by meteorological effects (winds and atmospheric pressure changes) are called surges.
- The study of tides is very complex, spatially and temporally, as it has great variations in frequency, magnitude and height.
- The moon's gravitational pull to a great extent and to a lesser extent the sun's gravitational pull, are the major causes for the occurrence of tides.

- Another factor is centrifugal force, which is the force that acts to counter the balance the gravity.
- On the side of the earth facing the moon, a tidal bulge occurs while on the opposite side though the gravitational attraction of the moon is less as it is farther away, the centrifugal force causes tidal bulge on the other side.
- The 'tide-generating' force is the difference between these two forces; *i.e.*, the gravitational attraction of the moon and the centrifugal force.
- On the surface of the earth, nearest the moon, pull or the attractive force of the moon is greater than the centrifugal force, and so there is a net force causing a bulge towards the moon.
- On the opposite side of the earth, the attractive force is less, as it is farther away from the moon, the centrifugal force is dominant. Hence, there is a net force away from the moon. It creates the second bulge away from the moon.
- When the tide is channelled between islands or into bays and estuaries they are called tidal currents.
- Tides may be grouped into various types based on their frequency of occurrence in one day or 24 hours or based on their height.
- **Tides based on Frequency :**
  - **Semi-diurnal tide :** The most common tidal pattern, featuring two high tides and two low tides each day. The successive high or low tides are approximately of the same height.
  - **Diurnal tide :** There is only one high tide and one low tide during each day. The successive high and low tides are approximately of the same height.
  - **Mixed tide :** Tides having variations in height are known as mixed tides. These tides generally occur along the west coast of North America and on many islands of the Pacific Ocean.
- **Tides based on the Sun, Moon and the Earth Positions:**
  - **Spring tides :** The position of both the sun and the moon in relation to the earth has direct bearing on tide height.
  - **Neap tides :** Normally, there is a seven day interval between the spring tides and neap tides. At this time the sun and moon are at right angles to each other and the forces of the sun and moon tend to counteract one another.
- Once in a month, when the moon's orbit is closest to the earth (perigee), unusually high and low tides occur. During this time the tidal range is greater than normal.
- Two weeks later, when the moon is farthest from earth (apogee), the moon's gravitational force is limited and the tidal ranges are less than their average heights.
- The time between the high tide and low tide, when the water level is falling, is called the ebb. The time between the low tide and high tide, when the tide is rising, is called the flow or flood.
- Since tides are caused by the earth-moon-sun positions which are known accurately, the tides can be predicted well in advance. This helps the navigators and fishermen plan their activities.
- Tidal flows are of great importance in navigation.
- Tidal heights are very important, especially harbours near rivers and within estuaries having shallow 'bars' at the entrance, which prevent ships and boats from entering into the harbour.
- Tides are also helpful in desilting the sediments and in removing polluted water from river estuaries.
- Tides are used to generate electrical power (in Canada, France, Russia, and China). A 3 MW tidal power project at Durgaduani in Sunderbans of West Bengal is under way.

Know the Terms

- **Waves :** Waves are actually the energy, not the water as such, which moves across the ocean surface.
- **Wave height :** It is the vertical distance from the bottom of a trough to the top of a crest of a wave.
- **Crest :** The highest point of a wave is called the crest.
- **Trough:** The lowest point of a wave is called trough.
- **Wave amplitude :** It is one-half of the wave height.
- **Wave period :** It is merely the time interval between two successive wave crests or troughs as they pass a fixed point.
- **Wavelength :** It is the horizontal distance between two successive crests.
- **Tides :** The periodical rise and fall of the sea level, once or twice a day, mainly due to the attraction of the sun and the moon, is called a tide.
- **Tidal currents :** When the tide is channelled between islands or into bays and estuaries they are called tidal currents.
- **Semi-diurnal tide :** The most common tidal pattern, featuring two high tides and two low tides each day.
- **Diurnal tide :** An area has diurnal tide if it experiences one high and one low tide every lunar day.
- **Mixed tide :** It is tidal cycle which consists of two unequal high tides and two unequal low tides in approximately a 24 hour period.

- **Spring tide :** When the sun, the moon and the earth are in a straight line, the height of the tide will be higher. These are called spring tides.
- **Neap tide :** A tide just after the first or third quarters of the moon when there is least difference between high and low water.
- **Perigee :** Once in a month, when the moon's orbit is closest to the earth , unusually high and low tides occur , it is called perigee.
- **Apogee :** When the moon is farthest from earth, the moon's gravitational force is limited and the tidal ranges are less than their average heights, it is called apogee.
- **Perihelion :** When the earth is closest to the sun.
- **Aphelion :** When the earth is farthest from the sun.
- **Flow :** The time between the low tide and high tide, when the tide is rising, is called the flow or flood.
- **Ebb :** The time between the high tide and low tide, when the water level is falling, is called the ebb.

Multiple Choice Questions (1 mark each)

Q. 1. The ocean water is: [A]

(a) dynamic
(b) static
(c) horizontal
(d) vertical

Ans. (a) dynamic 1

Q. 2. Tidal flows are of great importance in: [A]

(a) formation of day and night
(b) navigation
(c) fishing
(d) surges

Ans. (b) navigation 1

Q. 3. Mixed tides usually occur along the : [U]

(a) east coast of South America
(b) west coast of South America
(c) east coast of North America
(d) west coast of North America

Ans. (d) west coast of North America 1

Very Short Answer Type Questions (1 mark each)

Q. 1. Define the term 'Wave height'. [R]

Ans. It is the vertical distance from the bottom of a trough to the top of a crest of a wave. 1

Commonly Made Error

- The students do not know what causes wave height.

Answering Tip

- Waves located on the ocean's surface are commonly caused by wind transferring its energy to the water, and big waves, or swells, can travel over long distances.

Q. 2. Define the term 'wave period'. [R]

Ans. It is merely the time interval between two successive wave crests or troughs as they pass a fixed point. 1

Q. 3. What is wave frequency? [R]

Ans. It is the number of waves passing a given point during a one second time interval. 1

[AI] **Q. 4. What is wavelength?** [U]

Ans. It is the horizontal distance between two successive crests. 1

Q. 5. What is tide? [A]

Ans. The periodical rise and fall of the sea level, once or twice a day, mainly due to the attraction of the sun and the moon, is called a tide. 1

Q. 6. What are surges? [A]

Ans. Movement of water caused by meteorological effects (winds and atmospheric pressure changes) are called surges. 1

Q. 7. What are tidal currents? [U]

Ans. When the tide is channelled between islands or into bays and estuaries they are called tidal currents. 1

Commonly Made Error

- The students do not know when is the tidal current the strongest.

Answering Tip

- The tidal currents are the strongest before or near the time of the high and low tides.

Q. 8. Define the term 'Spring Tide'. [U]

Ans. The position of both the sun and the moon in relation to the earth has direct bearing on tide height. When the sun, the moon and the earth are in a straight line, the height of the tide will be higher. These are called spring tides. 1

Q. 9. How does a wave's size and shape reveal its origin? [U]

Ans. A wave's size and shape reveal its origin. Steep waves are fairly young ones and are probably formed by local wind. Slow and steady waves originate from far away places, possibly from another hemisphere . 1

Q. 10. How do winds provide energy to the waves? A

Ans. Wind provides energy to the waves. Wind causes waves to travel in the ocean and the energy is released on shorelines.. 1

Q. 11. Where does the highest tide occur in the world? R

Ans. The highest tides in the world occur in the Bay of Fundy in Nova Scotia, Canada. 1

Q. 12. What does the horizontal motion of the ocean water refer to ? A

Ans. The horizontal motion of the ocean water refers to the ocean currents and waves. 1

Q. 13. What does the vertical motion of the ocean water refer to? A

Ans. The vertical motion of the ocean water refers to tides. 1

Q. 14. Name any two forms of vertical motion of ocean water. R

Ans. Due to attraction of the sun and the moon, the ocean water is raised up and falls down twice a day. The upwelling of cold water from subsurface and the sinking of surface water are also forms of vertical motion of ocean water. 1

Q. 15. How are waves caused? U

Ans. Most of the waves are caused by the wind driving against water. When a breeze of two knots or less blows over calm water, small ripples form and grow as the wind speed increases until white caps appear in the breaking waves. 1

Q. 16. Why do waves travel? U

Ans. Most of the waves are caused by the wind driving against water. When a breeze of two knots or less blows over calm water, small ripples form and grow as the wind speed increases until white caps appear in the breaking waves. 1

Q. 17. Draw and label the diagram of motions of waves. A

Ans.

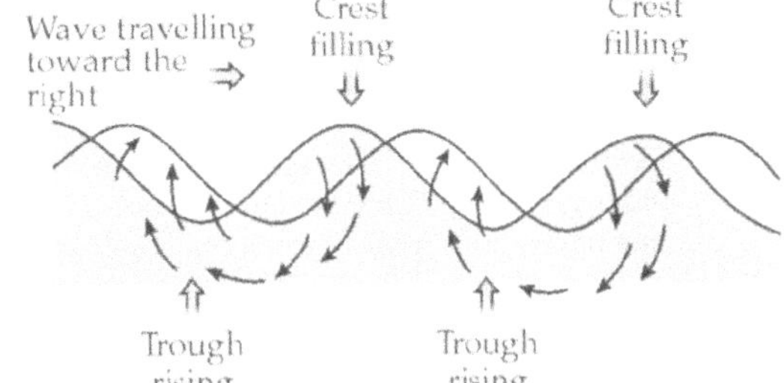

Motion of waves and water molecules 1

Q. 18. What cause the occurrence of tides? U

OR

What factors cause tides?

Ans. The moon's gravitational pull to a great extent and to a lesser extent the sun's gravitational pull, are the major causes for the occurrence of tides. The moon's gravitational pull to a great extent and to a lesser extent the sun's gravitational pull, are the major causes for the occurrence of tides. Another factor is centrifugal force, which is the force that acts to counter the balance the gravity. 1

Q. 19. Name any two tides based on frequency. R

Ans. The tides based on frequency are semi-diurnal tide, diurnal tide and mixed tide. 1

Short Answer Type Questions **(3 marks each)**

Q. 1. Differentiate between spring tides and neap tides. A

Ans.

S.No.	Spring tides	Neap tides
1.	It occurs twice each month -new moon day because the sun, moon and earth are in the straight line.	They occur at first and third quarter of the moon. Because during these days the sun, moon form a right angle with each other.
2.	When the rise and fall is more than the normal then it is called the spring tides.	The rise and fall is considerably low than the normal level.
3.	It is due to complimentary gravitational effect and cause sun, moon and earth are in the same.	The sun, moon are in the right angles and so the velocity of tidal currents slows down.

(1 × 3 = 3)

Q. 2. Describe any three characteristics of waves? A

Ans. The various characteristics of waves are :

(i) Wave crest and trough : The highest and lowest points of a wave are called the crest and trough respectively.

(ii) Wave height : It is the vertical distance from the bottom of a trough to the top of a crest of a wave.

(iii) Wave amplitude : It is one-half of the wave height.

(iv) Wave period : It is merely the time interval between two successive wave crests or troughs as they pass a fixed point.

(v) Wavelength : It is the horizontal distance between two successive crests.

(vi) Wave speed : It is the rate at which the wave moves through the water, and is measured in knots.

(vii) Wave frequency : It is the number of waves passing a given point during a one second time interval. **(Any three) (1 × 3 = 3)**

Answering Tip

- A wave's size depends on wind speed, wind duration, and the area over which the wind is blowing (the fetch).

Q. 3. Why are tides important? [U]

Ans. Meander is not a landform but is only a type of tides are important because :

(i) Since tides are caused by the earth-moon-sun positions which are known accurately, the tides can be predicted well in advance. This helps the navigators and fishermen plan their activities.

(ii) Tidal flows are of great importance in navigation. Tidal heights are very important, especially harbours near rivers and within estuaries having shallow 'bars' at the entrance, which prevent ships and boats from entering into the harbour.

(iii) Tides are also helpful in desilting the sediments and in removing polluted water from river estuaries. Tides are used to generate electrical power (in Canada, France, Russia, and China). A 3 MW tidal power project at Durgaduani in Sunderbans of West Bengal is under way. 3

Long Answer Type Questions

(5 marks each)

Q. 1. State the relationship between the gravitational forces and tides. [A]

Ans. The moon's gravitational pull to a great extent and to a lesser extent the sun's gravitational pull, are the major causes for the occurrence of tides. Another factor is centrifugal force, which is the force that acts to counter the balance the gravity. Together, the gravitational pull and the centrifugal force are responsible for creating the two major tidal bulges on the earth.

On the side of the earth facing the moon, a tidal bulge occurs while on the opposite side though the gravitational attraction of the moon is less as it is farther away, the centrifugal force causes tidal bulge on the other side.

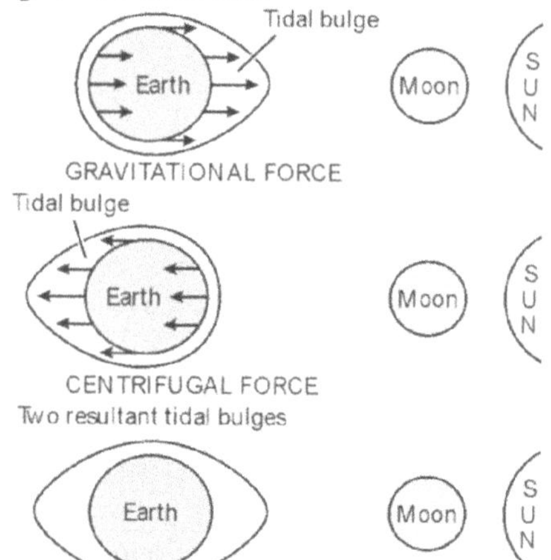

The 'tide-generating' force is the difference between these two forces; i.e. the gravitational attraction of the moon and the centrifugal force. On the surface of the earth, nearest the moon, pull or the attractive force of the moon is greater than the centrifugal force, and so there is a net force causing a bulge towards the moon. On the opposite side of the earth, the attractive force is less, as it is farther away from the moon, the centrifugal force is dominant. Hence, there is a net force away from the moon. It creates the second bulge away from the moon. On the surface of the earth, the horizontal tide generating forces are more important than the vertical forces in generating the tidal bulges.

The tidal bulges on wide continental shelves, have greater height. When tidal bulges hit the mid-oceanic islands they become low. The shape of bays and estuaries along a coastline can also magnify the intensity of tides. (1 × 5 = 5)

Q. 2. Into how many categories can tides be classified on the basis of their height and frequency? [A]

Ans. Tides may be grouped into various types based on their frequency of occurrence in one day or 24 hours or based on their height.

(a) Tides based on Frequency :

(i) Semi-diurnal tide : The most common tidal pattern, featuring two high tides and two low tides each day. The successive high or low tides are approximately of the same height.

(ii) Diurnal tide : There is only one high tide and one low tide during each day. The successive high and low tides are approximately of the same height.

(iii) Mixed tide : Tides having variations in height are known as mixed tides. These tides generally occur along the west coast of North America and on many islands of the Pacific Ocean.

(b) Tides based on the Sun, Moon and the Earth Positions : The height of rising water (high tide) varies appreciably depending upon the position of sun and moon with respect to the earth. Spring tides and neap tides come under this category.

(i) Spring tides : The position of both the sun and the moon in relation to the earth has direct bearing on tide height. When the sun, the moon and the earth are in a straight line, the height of the tide will be higher. These are called spring tides and they occur twice a month, one on full moon period and another during new moon period.

(ii) Neap tides : Normally, there is a seven day interval between the spring tides and neap tides. At this time the sun and moon are at right angles to each other and the forces of the sun and moon tend to counteract one another. The moon's attraction, though more than twice as strong as the sun's, is diminished by the counteracting force of the sun's gravitational pull . 5

TOPIC-2
Ocean Currents, Types of Ocean Currents

Revision Notes

➢ Ocean currents are like river flow in oceans. They represent a regular volume of water in a definite path and direction.

➢ **Ocean currents are influenced by two types of forces namely :**
- The primary forces that influence the currents are :
- **Heating by solar energy :** Heating by solar energy causes the water to expand. That is why, near the equator the ocean water is about 8 cm higher in level than in the middle latitudes.
- **Wind :** Wind blowing on the surface of the ocean pushes the water to move. Friction between the wind and the water surface affects the movement of the water body in its course.
- **Gravity :** Gravity tends to pull the water down to pile and create gradient variation.
- **Coriolis force :** The coriolis force intervenes and causes the water to move to the right in the Northern Hemisphere and to the left in the Southern Hemisphere.

➢ **The secondary forces that influence the currents to flow :**

➢ Water with high salinity is denser than water with low salinity and in the same way cold water is denser than warm water.

➢ Denser water tends to sink, while relatively lighter water tends to rise. Cold-water ocean currents occur when the cold water at the poles sinks and slowly moves towards the equator.

➢ **The ocean currents may be classified based on their depth as surface currents and deep water currents :**
- **Surface currents :** Constitute about 10 per cent of all the water in the ocean, these waters are the upper 400 m of the ocean.
- **Deep water currents :** Make up the other 90 per cent of the ocean water. These waters move around the ocean basins due to variations in the density and gravity.

➢ **Ocean currents can also be classified based on temperature : As cold currents and warm currents :**
- **Cold currents :** Bring cold water into warm water areas. These currents are usually found on the west coast of the continents in the low and middle latitudes (true in both hemispheres) and on the east coast in the higher latitudes in the Northern Hemisphere.
- **Warm currents :** Bring warm water into cold water areas and are usually observed on the east coast of continents in the low and middle latitudes (true in both hemispheres). In the Northern Hemisphere they are found on the west coasts of continents in high latitudes.

➢ Major ocean currents are greatly influenced by the stresses exerted by the prevailing winds and Coriolis Force.

➢ Due to the coriolis force, the warm currents from low latitudes tend to move to the right in the Northern Hemisphere and to their left in the Southern Hemisphere.

➢ The oceanic circulation transports heat from one latitude belt to another in a manner similar to the heat transported by the general circulation of the atmosphere.

➢ Ocean currents have a number of direct and indirect influences on human activities.

➢ Their average temperatures are relatively low with a narrow diurnal and annual ranges.

➢ Warm currents flow parallel to the east coasts of the continents in tropical and subtropical latitudes. This results in warm and rainy climates.

➢ The mixing of warm and cold currents helps to replenish the oxygen and favour the growth of planktons, the primary food for fish population. The best fishing grounds of the world exist mainly in these mixing zones.

Know the Terms

➢ **Ocean currents :** It is a seasonal directed movement of sea water generated by forces acting upon this mean flow.

➢ **Coriolis force :** It is an inertial force described by the 19th century French engineer-mathematician. Gaspart-Gustave de coridis, in connection with the theory of water wheels.

➢ **Gravity :** It is the natural phenomenon by which all things with mass are brought towards one another.

- **Drift :** At depths, currents are generally slow with speeds less than 0.5 knots. We refer to the speed of a current as its "drift.
- **Surface current :** The movement of the water at the surface of the ocean is known as surface currents.
- **Deep water current :** Deep water currents move very slowly, usually around 0.8-1.2 in per second.
- **Cold currents :** Cold currents bring cold water into warm water areas.
- **Warm currents :** Warm currents bring warm water into cold water areas.
- **Gyres :** It is any large system of circulating ocean currents, particularly those involved with large wind movements.

Multiple Choice Questions (1 mark each)

Q. 1. The __________ causes the water to move to the right in the Northern Hemisphere and to the left in the Southern Hemisphere. A

(a) coriolis force
(b) ocean currents
(c) warm currents
(d) cold currents

Ans. (a) coriolis force 1

Q. 2. Water with high salinity is : U

(a) thinner
(b) slummy
(c) denser
(d) cold

Ans. (c) denser 1

Q. 3. Heating by solar energy causes the water to: U

(a) expand
(b) contract
(c) darken
(d) circulate

Ans. (a) expand 1

Very Short Answer Type Questions (1 mark each)

Q. 1. Define the term 'Ocean Currents'. A

Ans. It is a seasonal directed movement of sea water generated by forces acting upon this mean flow. Ocean currents are the continuous flow of huge amount of water in a definite direction. 1

Answering Tip

- Currents are cohesive streams of sea water that circulate through the ocean.

Q. 2. Define the term 'Gyres'. U

Ans. The coriolis force intervenes and causes the water to move to the right in the Northern Hemisphere and to the left in the Southern Hemisphere. These large accumulations of water and the flow around them are called Gyres. 1

Q. 3. When do cold water currents occur? R

Ans. Cold-water ocean currents occur when the cold water at the poles sinks and slowly moves towards the equator. 1

Q. 4. How are ripples formed? U

Ans. When a breeze of two knots or less blows over calm water, small ripples form and grow as the wind speed increases until white caps appear in the breaking waves. 1

Q. 5. What are the two factors that influence the ocean currents? A

Ans. Ocean currents are influenced by two types of forces namely :

(i) Primary forces that initiate the movement of water;

(ii) Secondary forces that influence the currents to flow. 1

Q. 6. What is the percentage of spread of the surface current ? U

Ans. Surface currents constitute about 10 per cent of all the water in the ocean, these waters are the upper 400 m of the ocean. 1

AI **Q. 7. What influences the ocean currents?** R

Ans. Major ocean currents are greatly influenced by the stresses exerted by the prevailing winds and coriolis force. 1

Q. 8. How are fishing and oceanic currents related? U

Ans. The mixing of warm and cold currents helps to replenish the oxygen and favour the growth of planktons, the primary food for fish population. The best fishing grounds of the world exist mainly in these mixing zones. 1

Answering Tip

- Currents are important in marine ecosystems because they redistribute water, heat, nutrients, and oxygen about the ocean.

Short Answer Type Questions (3 marks each)

Q. 1. How does ocean currents affect the climate? Explain? A

Ans. Ocean currents affect the climate :

(i) Warm currents make the place warmer where as the cold currents makes the place colder. Example, warm currents of Kuroshio makes Southern Japan less cold in winter whereas the cold currents of Kuroshio makes the winter longer and severe in North Japan.

(ii) Winds passing over warm currents absorbs lot of moisture and cause heavy rainfall in coastal areas. On the other hand, winds passing over long currents do not get any warm currents as such they make the climate of coastal areas dry. This is the reason why hot deserts are located near the coastal areas from where the cold current passes.

(iii) The places where cold current and warm current near the coastal areas are found in abundance are rich fishing ground. For example, Newfoundland, the east coast of North America where Labrador Current and Gulf Stream meet. 3

Q. 2. Explain the different types of ocean currents. A

Ans. The ocean currents may be classified based on their depth as surface currents and deep water currents :

(i) Surface currents : It constitute about 10 per cent of all the water in the ocean, these waters are the upper 400 m of the ocean.

(ii) Deep water currents : It make up the other 90 per cent of the ocean water. These waters move around the ocean basins due to variations in the density and gravity. Deep waters sink into the deep ocean basins at high latitudes, where the temperatures are cold enough to cause the density to increase .

On the basis of temperature :

(i) Cold currents bring cold water into warm water areas. These currents are usually found on the west coast of the continents in the low and middle latitudes (true in both hemispheres) and on the east coast in the higher latitudes in the Northern Hemisphere.

(ii) Warm currents bring warm water into cold water areas and are usually observed on the east coast of continents in the low and middle latitudes (true in both hemispheres). In the Northern Hemisphere they are found on the west coasts of continents in high latitudes. 3

AI **Q. 3. What are the primary forces that influence the currents?** A

Ans. The primary forces that influence the currents are :

(i) Heating by solar energy : It causes the water to expand. That is why, near the equator the ocean water is about 8 cm higher in level than in the middle latitudes. This causes a very slight gradient and water tends to flow down the slope.

(ii) Wind : Wind blowing on the surface of the ocean pushes the water to move. Friction between the wind and the water surface affects the movement of the water body in its course.

(iii) Gravity : Gravity tends to pull the water down to pile and create gradient variation.

(iv) The coriolis force : It intervenes and causes the water to move to the right in the Northern Hemisphere and to the left in the Southern Hemisphere. 3

Q. 4. What are the characteristics of ocean currents? R

Ans. Currents are referred to by their "drift". Usually, the currents are strongest near the surface and may attain speeds over five knots. At depths, currents are generally slow with speeds less than 0.5 knots. We refer to the speed of a current as its "drift." Drift is measured in terms of knots. The strength of a current refers to the speed of the current. A fast current is considered strong. A current is usually strongest at the surface and decreases in strength (speed) with depth. Most currents have speeds less than or equal to 5 knots.

Answering Tip

- Ocean currents play an important role in determining the climates of coastal regions.

Long Answer Type Questions (5 marks each)

Q.1. Differentiate between warm currents and cold currents. A

Ans.

S.No.	Warm Currents	Cold Currents
1.	They flow from equatorial regions to high altitudes.	They flow from polar regions to low latitudes.
2.	Their temperature is higher than the surrounding water.	Their temperature is below than the surrounding water.

3.	They raise the temperature of coastal areas and are observed normally on the east coast of lower and middle latitude.	They reduce the temperature of the coastal area and are observed on the west of continent in lower and middle latitude.
4.	Warm currents are of great help to navigation because they melt icebergs.	Cold currents hinder navigation because they create icebergs.
5.	Warm currents keep the ports open in the polar regions free from ice.	Cold currents make the parts unoperational in lower latitudes as they are ice bound.

5

Answering Tip

- The actual difference in temperature of warm and cold currents is only a few degrees.

Q. 2. Why are some currents warm or cold? [A]

Ans. There are several warm ocean currents that move warm water away from the equator. These currents of water have warm air above the water. The warm air raises the temperature of the land it touches. These areas enjoy a much warmer climate than other places at the same latitude. Areas such as England would be much colder without the warm Gulf Stream. Warm ocean currents flow on the eastern side of the continent. They only reach the western side in high latitude areas. Another characteristic is that they flow away from the equator. Warm currents have higher temperatures, so they are less dense than cold water. Usually warm water has a higher salinity, but it remains less dense than the cold water, so cold water is heavier and flows under warm water. The water is warmed on the surface, so warm currents flow across the surface of the ocean. As a warm current cools down, it drops down and becomes a cold water current. **5**

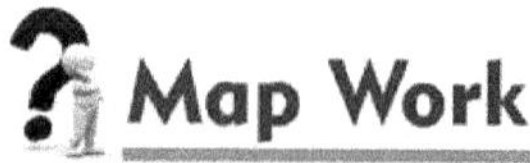

Map Work

(5 marks)

Q. 1. On the outline map of the world mark the following :

(i) West wind drift

(ii) North Atlantic drift

(iii) Brazilian current

(iv) Labrador current

(v) Equatorial counter current

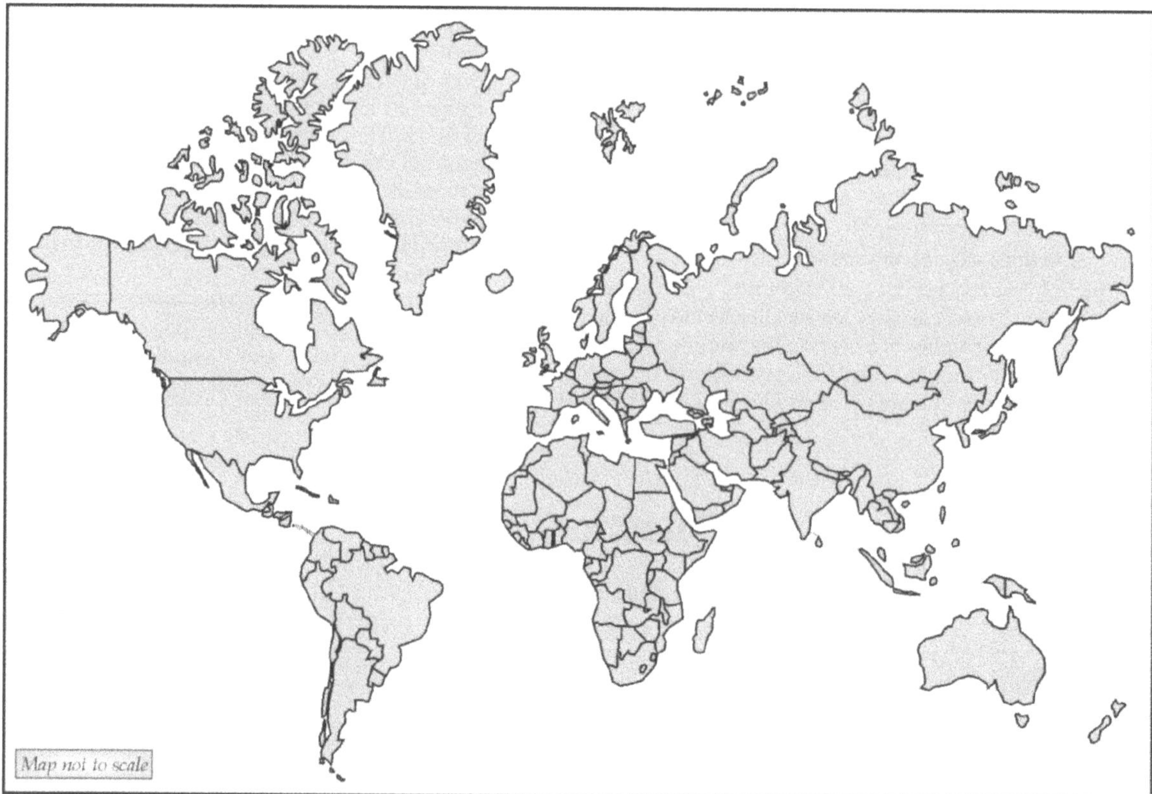

Ans.

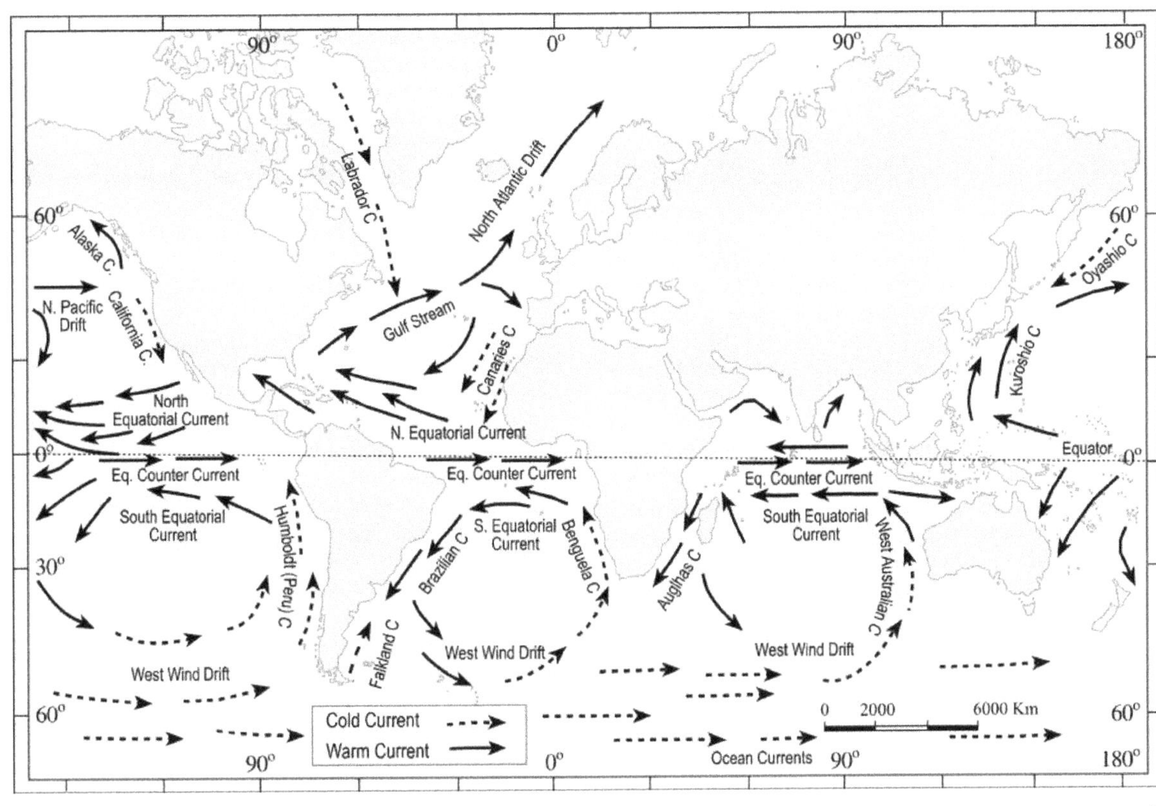

5

NCERT CORNER

(A) Multiple choice questions :

Q. 1. Upward and downward movement of ocean water is known as the : [A]

(a) tide **(b) current**

(c) wave **(d) None of the above**

Ans. (a) tide.

Q. 2. Spring tides are caused : [A]

(a) as result of the moon and the sun pulling the earth gravitationally in the same direction

(b) as result of the moon and the sun pulling the earth gravitationally in the opposite direction

(c) indention in the coast line

(d) None of the above

Ans. (a) as result of the moon and the sun pulling the earth gravitationally in the same direction.

Q. 3. The distance between the earth and the moon is minimum when the moon is in : [R]

(a) Aphelion **(b) Perigee**

(c) Perihelion **(d) Apogee**

Ans. (b) Perigee.

Q. 4. The earth reaches its perihelion in : [R]

(a) October **(b) September**

(c) July **(d) January**

Ans. (d) January .

(B) Answer the following questions in about 30 words :

Q. 1. What are waves? [A]

Ans. Waves are actually the energy, not the water as such, which moves across the ocean surface. Waves are oscillatory movements in water, manifested by an alternate rise and fall of the sea surface.

Q. 2. Where do waves in the ocean get their energy from? [U]

Ans. Wind provides energy to the waves. Wind causes waves to travel in the ocean and the energy is released on shorelines. The motion of the surface water seldom affects the stagnant deep bottom water of the oceans. As a wave approaches the beach, it slows down. This is due to the friction occurring between the dynamic water and the sea floor .

Q. 3. What are tides? [R]

Ans. The periodical rise and fall of the sea level, once or twice a day, mainly due to the attraction of the sun and the moon, is called a tide.

Q. 4. How are tides caused? [U]

Ans. The moon's gravitational pull to a great extent and to a lesser extent the sun's gravitational pull, are the major causes for the occurrence of tides. Another factor is centrifugal force, which is the force that acts to counter the balance the gravity.

Together, the gravitational pull and the centrifugal force are responsible for creating the two major tidal bulges on the earth.

Q. 5. How are tides related to navigation? [U]

Ans. Since tides are caused by the earth-moon-sun positions which are known accurately, the tides can be predicted well in advance. This helps the navigators and fishermen plan their activities. Tidal flows are of great importance in navigation. Tidal heights are very important, especially harbours near rivers and within estuaries having shallow 'bars' at the entrance, which prevent ships and boats from entering into the harbour.

(C) Answer the following questions in about 150 words :

Q. 1. How do currents affect the temperature? How does it affect the temperature of coastal areas in the N. W. Europe? [U]

Ans. Impact of currents on temperature varies depending on whether currents are warm or cold.

(i) **Cold currents :** Cold currents bring cold water into warm water areas. These currents are usually found on the west coast of the continents in the low and middle latitudes (true in both hemispheres) and on the east coast in the higher latitudes in the Northern Hemisphere.

(ii) **Warm currents :** Warm currents bring warm water into cold water areas and are usually observed on the east coast of continents in the low and middle latitudes (true in both hemispheres). In the Northern Hemisphere they are found on the west coasts of continents in high latitudes.

In North West Europe, warm currents exist. They increase the temperature in coastal areas of NW Europe.

Q. 2. What are the causes of currents? [A]

Ans. Ocean currents are like river flow in oceans. They represent a regular volume of water in a definite path and direction. Ocean currents are influenced by two types of forces namely :

(i) Primary forces that initiate the movement of water

(ii) Secondary forces that influence the currents to flow

Primary Forces : The primary forces that influence the currents are:

(i) **Heating by solar energy :** Heating by solar energy causes the water to expand. That is why, near the equator the ocean water is about 8 cm higher in level than in the middle latitudes. This causes a very slight gradient and water tends to flow down the slope.

(ii) **Wind :** Wind blowing on the surface of the ocean pushes the water to move. Friction between the wind and the water surface affects the movement of the water body in its course.

(iii) **Gravity :** Gravity tends to pull the water down to pile and create gradient variation.

(iv) **Coriolis force :** The coriolis force intervenes and causes the water to move to the right in the Northern Hemisphere and to the left in the Southern Hemisphere. These large accumulations of water and the flow around them are called Gyres. These produce large circular currents in all the ocean basins.

For Suggested Online Videos

Visit : *https://qrgo.page.link/fkTg5* **Or Scan the Code**

UNIT-VI

Life on the Earth

CHAPTER

15 LIFE ON THE EARTH

Syllabus

> *Ecology, Types of Ecosystems, Structure and Functions of Ecosystems.*
> *Types of Biomes, Biogeochemical Cycles, Ecological Balance.*

TOPIC-1
Ecology, Types of Ecosystems, Structure and Functions of Ecosystems.

Revision Notes

- There are three major realms of the environment, that is, the lithosphere, the atmosphere and the hydrosphere.
- The living organisms of the earth, constituting the biosphere, interact with other environmental realms.
- The biosphere includes all the living components of the earth. It consists of all plants and animals, including all the micro-organisms that live on the planet earth and their interactions with the surrounding environment.
- The biosphere and its components are very significant elements of the environment. These elements interact with other components of the natural landscape such as land, water and soil.
- The interactions of biosphere with land, air and water are important to the growth.
- The interactions of a particular group of organisms with abiotic factors within a particular habitat resulting in clearly defined energy flows and material cycles on land, water and air, are called ecological systems.
- The term ecology is derived from the Greek word 'oikos' meaning 'house', combined with the word 'logy' meaning the 'science of' or 'the study of'. Literally, ecology is the study of the earth as a 'household', of plants, human beings, animals and micro-organisms.
- A habitat in the ecological sense is the totality of the physical and chemical factors that constitute the general environment.
- A system consisting of biotic and abiotic components is known as ecosystem. All these components in ecosystem are inter related and interact with each other.
- Different types of ecosystems exist with varying ranges of environmental conditions where various plants and animal species have got adapted through evolution. This phenomenon is known as ecological adaptation.
- Ecosystems are of **two** major types : terrestrial and aquatic.
- Terrestrial ecosystem can be further be classified into 'biomes'. A biome is a plant and animal community that covers a large geographical area.
- A biome can be defined as the total assemblage of plant and animal species interacting within specific conditions. These include rainfall, temperature, humidity and soil conditions.
- Some of the major biomes of the world are: forest, grassland, desert and tundra biomes.
- Aquatic ecosystems can be classed as marine and freshwater ecosystems. Marine ecosystem includes the oceans, coastal estuaries and coral reefs. Freshwater ecosystem includes lakes, ponds, streams, marshes and bogs.
- From a structural point of view, all ecosystems consist of abiotic and biotic factors.

- Abiotic factors include rainfall, temperature, sunlight, atmospheric humidity, soil conditions, inorganic substances (carbon dioxide, water, nitrogen, calcium, phosphorus, potassium, etc.).
- Biotic factors include the producers, (primary, secondary, tertiary) the consumers and the decomposers. The producers include all the green plants, which manufacture their own food through photosynthesis.
- The primary consumers include herbivorous animals like deer, goats, mice and all plant-eating animals.
- The secondary consumers *i.e.,* carnivores include all the flesh-eating animals like snakes, tigers and lions.
- Decomposers are those that feed on dead organisms (for example, scavengers like vultures and crows), and further breaking down of the dead matter by other decomposing agents like bacteria and various microorganisms.
- Organisms of an ecosystem are linked together through a food chain.
- For example, a plant eating beetle feeding on a paddy stalk is eaten by a frog, which is, in turn, eaten by a snake, which is then consumed by a hawk. This sequence of eating and being eaten and the resultant transfer of energy from one level to another is known as the food-chain.
- Transfer of energy that occurs during the process of a foodchain from one level to another is known as flow of energy.
- The food- chains get interlocked with one another. This interconnecting network of species is known as food web. Generally, two types of food-chains are recognised : grazing food-chain and detritus food-chain.
- In a grazing food-chain, the first level starts with plants as producers and ends with carnivores as consumers as the last level, with the herbivores being at the intermediate level. There is a loss of energy at each level which may be through respiration, excretion or decomposition.
- A detritus food-chain is based on autotrophs energy capture initiated by grazing animals and involves the decomposition or breaking down of organic wastes and dead matter derived from the grazing food-chain.

Know the Terms

- **Biosphere :** The biosphere includes all the living components of the earth.
- **Ecological systems :** The interactions of a particular group of organisms with abiotic factors within a particular habitat resulting in clearly defined energy flows and material cycles on land, water and air, are called ecological systems.
- **Ecology :** Ecology can be defined as a scientific study of the interactions of organisms with their physical environment and with each other.
- **Science of ecology :** The study of interactions between life forms (biotic) and the physical environment (abiotic) is the science of ecology.
- **Habitat :** A habitat in the ecological sense is the totality of the physical and chemical factors that constitute the general environment.
- **Ecological adaptation :** Different types of ecosystems exist with varying ranges of environmental conditions where various plants and animal species have got adapted through evolution. This phenomenon is known as ecological adaptation.
- **Biomes :** A biome is a plant and animal community that covers a large geographical area.
- **Abiotic factors :** They are the non living condition or thing such as climate or habitat , that influences or affects an ecosystem and the organisms in it.
- **Biotic factors :** Biotic factors can be described as any living component that affects another organism, or shapes the ecosystem.
- **Marine ecosystem :** Marine ecosystems are among the largest of Earth's aquatic ecosystems.
- **Freshwater ecosystem :** Freshwater ecosystem: Freshwater ecosystems are a subset of Earth's aquatic ecosystems. They include lakes , rivers, ponds, streams, etc.
- **Primary consumers :** The primary consumers include herbivorous animals like deer, goats, mice and all plant-eating animals.
- **Carnivores :** The carnivores include all the flesh-eating animals like snakes, tigers and lions.
- **Decomposers :** They are those that feed on dead organisms.
- **Food chain :** The sequence of eating and being eaten and the resultant transfer of energy from one level to another is known as the food-chain.
- **Flow of energy :** Transfer of energy that occurs during the process of a food-chain from one level to another is known as flow of energy.
- **Food web :** The interconnecting network of species is known as food web.
- **Grazing food chain :** In a grazing food-chain, the first level starts with plants as producers and ends with carnivores as consumers as the last level, with the herbivores being at the intermediate level.
- **Detritus food-chain :** A detritus food-chain is based on autotrophs energy capture initiated by grazing animals and involves the decomposition or breaking down of organic wastes and dead matter derived from the grazing food-chain.

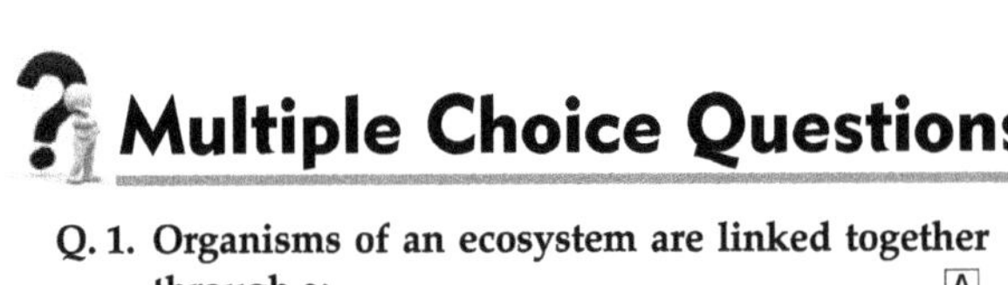

Multiple Choice Questions (1 mark each)

Q. 1. Organisms of an ecosystem are linked together through a: [A]
(a) food chain
(b) ecology
(c) biosphere
(d) habitat
Ans. (a) food chain 1

Q. 2. The total assemblage of plant and animal species interacting within specific conditions is known as : [A]
(a) ecosystem
(b) biomes
(c) flow of energy
(d) food chain
Ans. (b) biomes 1

Q. 3. The interactions of ________ with land, air and water are important to the growth. [U]
(a) hydrosphere
(b) biosphere
(c) ecology
(d) habitat
Ans. (b) biosphere 1

Q. 4. A connection of multiple food chains is known as: [R]
(a) ecosystem
(b) multiple food chains
(c) food web
(d) consumers
Ans. (c) food web 1

Very Short Answer Type Questions (1 mark each)

Q. 1. What is biosphere? [A]
Ans. The biosphere includes all the living components of the earth. It consists of all plants and animals, including all the micro- organisms that live on the planet earth and their interactions with the surrounding environment. 1

Q. 2. Define the term 'Ecology'. [U]
Ans. Ecology can be defined as a scientific study of the interactions of organisms with their physical environment and with each other. 1

Commonly Made Error
- The students tend to ignore the important role played by the ecology.

Answering Tip
- Ecology helps us understand how the world works. It provides useful evidence on the interdependence between people and the natural world and, as well the consequences of human activity on the environment.

Q. 3. What is the known as the science of ecology? [A]
Ans. The study of interactions between life forms (biotic) and the physical environment (abiotic) is the science of ecology. 1

Q. 4. Define the term 'Ecological Systems'. [A]
Ans. The interactions of a particular group of organisms with abiotic factors within a particular habitat resulting in clearly defined energy flows and material cycles on land, water and air, are called ecological systems. 1

Q. 5. What is a habitat? [A]
Ans. A habitat in the ecological sense is the totality of the physical and chemical factors that constitute the general environment. 1

Answering Tip
- The examples of terrestrial habitat are forest, steppe, grassland, semi-arid or desert.

Q. 6. Define the term 'Ecosystem'. [A]
Ans. A system consisting of biotic and abiotic components is known as ecosystem. 1

Q. 7. What is ecological adaptation? [R]
Ans. Different types of ecosystems exist with varying ranges of environmental conditions where various plants and animal species have got adapted through evolution. This phenomenon is known as ecological adaptation. 1

Q. 8. What is biome? [U]
Ans. Biome is a plant and animal community that covers a large geographical area. 1

Q. 9. Aquatic system can be classified into how many categories? [R]
Ans. Aquatic ecosystems can be classed as marine and freshwater ecosystems. 1

Q. 10. What does ecosystem consist of? [U]
Ans. From a structural point of view, all ecosystems consist of abiotic and biotic factors. 1

[AI] **Q.11. Differentiate between abiotic and biotic factors.** [A]
Ans. Abiotic factors include rainfall, temperature, sunlight, atmospheric humidity, soil conditions, inorganic substances (carbon dioxide, water, nitrogen, calcium, phosphorus, potassium, etc.). Biotic factors include the producers, (primary, secondary, tertiary) the consumers and the decomposers. 1

Q. 12. Who are the primary consumers? [A]
Ans. The primary consumers include herbivorous animals like deer, goats, mice and all plant-eating animals. 1

Q. 13. Who are the secondary consumers? A

Ans. The secondary consumers are all the flesh-eating animals like snakes, tigers and lions. 1

Q. 14. Who are decomposers? A

Ans. Decomposers are those that feed on dead organisms (for example, scavengers like vultures and crows), and further breaking down of the dead matter by other decomposing agents like bacteria and various microorganisms. 1

Q. 15. What do you know about food chain? U

Ans. The sequence of eating and being eaten and the resultant transfer of energy from one level to another is known as the food-chain. 1

Answering Tip

- From the food chain, we get to know how organisms are connected with each other.

Q. 16. Give an example of the food chain. U

Ans. Plants are eaten by the beetle. Beetle is eaten by the paddy-stalk. Paddy-stalk is eaten by the frog, frog is eaten by the snake and snake is eaten by the hawk. 1

Q. 17. Differentiate between grazing food chain and detritus food-chain. R

Ans. In a grazing food-chain, the first level starts with plants as producers and ends with carnivores as consumers as the last level, with the herbivores being at the intermediate level.

A detritus food-chain is based on autotrophs energy capture initiated by grazing animals and involves the decomposition or breaking down of organic wastes and dead matter derived from the grazing food-chain. 1

Q. 18. On whom do primary , secondary and tertiary producers depend? A

Ans. Primary consumers depend on producers who make the food themselves. Secondary consumers depend on primary consumers and tertiary consumers in turn depend on secondary consumers. 1

Q. 19. How many types of decomposers are there? R

Ans. There are two types of decomposers: scavengers and micro-organisms. Scavengers feed on dead organisms, like vultures and crows. Further breaking down of the dead matter is done by other decomposing agents like bacteria and various micro-organisms 1

Short Answer Type Questions

(3 marks each)

Q. 1. How does biosphere get formed? A

Ans. (i) The biosphere includes all the living components of the earth. It consists of all plants and animals, including all the micro- organisms that live on the planet earth and their interactions with the surrounding environment.

(ii) The biosphere and its components are very significant elements of the environment.

(iii) These elements interact with other components of the natural landscape such as land, water and soil.

The interactions of biosphere with land, air and water are important to the growth, development and evolution of the organism. 3

Answering Tip

- The biosphere is the global ecological system integrating all living beings and their relationships, including their interaction with the elements of the lithosphere, geosphere, hydrosphere, and atmosphere.

Q. 2. Differentiate between terrestrial ecosystem and aquatic ecosystem. U

Ans.

S.No.	Terrestrial ecosystem	Aquatic ecosystem
1.	It is an ecosystem that exists on land rather than water.	It is an ecosystem that exists on water rather than land.
2.	It can be classified into biomes.	It can be classified into marine and freshwater ecosystems.
3.	Rainfall, temperature, soil types, latitude, height, etc, determines the boundaries of terrestrial ecosystem.	Water bodies determine the boundaries of aquatic ecosystem.

3

Q. 3. Explain biome. R

Ans. A biome is a plant and animal community that covers a large geographical area. The boundaries of different biomes on land are determined mainly by climate.

(i) Therefore, a biome can be defined as the total assemblage of plant and animal species interacting within specific conditions. These include rainfall, temperature, humidity and soil conditions.

(ii) Some of the major biomes of the world are: forest, grassland, desert and tundra biomes. Aquatic ecosystems can be classed as marine and freshwater ecosystems.

(iii) Marine ecosystem includes the oceans, coastal estuaries and coral reefs. Freshwater ecosystem includes lakes, ponds, streams, marshes and bogs.3

Answering Tip

- A biome is a community of plants and animals that have common characteristics for the environment they exist in.

Q. 4. How does an ecosystem work? [A]

Ans. An ecosystem works with the help of producers and consumers. The producers includes all the green plants, which manufacture their own food through photosynthesis.

The primary consumers include herbivorous animals like deer, goats, mice and all plant-eating animals. The carnivores include all the flesh-eating animals like snakes, tigers and lions.

Certain carnivores that feed also on carnivore are known as top-carnivores like hawks and mongooses. Decomposers are those that feed on dead organisms and further breaking down of the dead matter by other decomposing agents like bacteria and various micro-organisms. 3

Q. 5. Differentiate between grazing food chain and detritus food chain.

Ans.

S.No.	Grazing Food Chain	Detritus Food Chain
1.	In a grazing food-chain, the first level starts with plants as producers and ends with carnivores as consumers as the last level, with the herbivores being at the intermediate level.	A detritus food-chain is based on autotrophs energy capture initiated by grazing animals and involves the decomposition or breaking down of organic wastes and dead matter derived from the grazing food-chain.
2.	The levels involved in a grazing food-chain ranges between three to five.	The levels involved in a detritus food chain ranges between three to seven.
3.	Plants-Cow-Lion.	Insects-Rat-Cat-Dog-Lion.

(1 × 3 = 3)

Q. 6. Give causes of ecological imbalance? [A]

Ans. Ecological balance may be disturbed due to the introduction of new species, natural hazards or human causes. Human interference has affected the balance of plant communities leading to disturbances in the ecosystems. Such disturbances bring about numerous secondary successions. Human pressure on the earth's resources has put a heavy toll on the ecosystem. This has destroyed its originality and has caused adverse effects to the general environment. Ecological imbalances have brought many natural calamities like floods, landslides, diseases, erratic climatic occurrences, etc. There is a very close relationship between the plant and animal communities within particular habitats. 3

Long Answer Type Questions

(5 marks each)

Q. 1. Explain about the working and structure of ecosystem. [A]

Ans. The structure of an ecosystem involves a description of the available plant and animal species. From a structural point of view, all ecosystems consist of abiotic and biotic factors. Abiotic factors include rainfall, temperature, sunlight, atmospheric humidity, soil conditions, inorganic substances (carbon dioxide, water, nitrogen, calcium, phosphorus, potassium, etc.).

Biotic factors include the producers, (primary, secondary, tertiary) the consumers and the decomposers. The producers include all the green plants, which manufacture their own food through photosynthesis.

The primary consumers include herbivorous animals like deer, goats, mice and all plant-eating animals. The carnivores include all the flesh-eating animals like snakes, tigers and lions. Certain carnivores that feed also on carnivores are known as top carnivores like hawks and mongooses.

Decomposers are those that feed on dead organisms (for example, scavengers like vultures and crows), and further breaking down of the dead matter by other decomposing agents like bacteria and various microorganisms. The producers are consumed by the primary consumers whereas the primary consumers are, in turn, being eaten by the secondary consumers. Further, the secondary consumers are consumed by the tertiary consumers.

The decomposers feed on the dead at each and every level. They change them into various substances such as nutrients, organic and inorganic salts essential for soil fertility. Organisms of an ecosystem are linked together through a foodchain. **1 x 5 = 5**

Commonly Made Error

- The students are not aware as to what does the structure of an ecosystem describes.

Answering Tip

- Ecosystem structure describes the physical features (abiotic) and organisms (biotic) of an environment including the distribution of nutrients and other prevailing climatic conditions, and the relationships between them.

Q. 2. Explain the food chain. U

Ans. The sequence of eating and being eaten and the resultant transfer of energy from one level to another is known as the food-chain. Transfer of energy that occurs during the process of a foodchain from one level to another is known as flow of energy. However, food-chains are not isolated from one another. For example, a mouse feeding on grain may be eaten by different secondary consumers (carnivores) and these carnivores may be eaten by other different tertiary consumers (top carnivores). In such situations, each of the carnivores may consume more than one type of prey. As a result, the food-chains get interlocked with one another. This interconnecting network of species is known as food web. For example: a plant eating beetle feeding on a paddy stalk is eaten by a frog, which is, in turn, eaten by a snake, which is then consumed by a hawk.

(i) Producers : The producers include all the green plants, which manufacture their own food through photosynthesis.

(ii) Primary consumers : The primary consumers include herbivorous animals like deer, goats, mice and all plant-eating animals.

(iii) Carnivores : The carnivores include all the flesh-eating animals like snakes, tigers and lions. Certain carnivores that feed also on carnivorous are known as top carnivores like hawks and mongooses.

(iv) Decomposers : Decomposers are those that feed on dead organisms (for example, scavengers like vultures and crows), and further breaking down of the dead matter by other decomposing agents like bacteria and various microorganisms.

There are two -types of food chains :

(i) Grazing food chain : In a grazing food-chain, the first level starts with plants as producers and ends with carnivores as consumers as the last level, with the herbivores being at the intermediate level. There is a loss of energy at each level which may be through respiration, excretion or decomposition. The levels involved in a food-chain range between three to five and energy is lost at each level.

(ii) Detritus food chain : A detritus food-chain is based on autotrophs energy capture initiated by grazing animals and involves the decomposition or breaking down of organic wastes and dead matter derived from the grazing food-chain . **5**

Q. 3. Differentiate between food chain and food web. R

Ans.

S.No.	Food chain	Food web
1.	Food chain follows a single path as animals eat each other.	Food webs show how plants and animals are inter connected by different paths.
2.	The Sun provides food for grass.	Trees produce acorns which act as food for many mice and insects.
3.	The grass is eaten by a grasshopper.	Because there are many mice, weasels and snakes have food.
4.	The grasshopper is eaten by a frog.	The insects and the acorns also attract birds, skunks and opossums.
5.	The frog is eaten by a snake.	With the skunks , opossums, weasels and mice around, hawks, foxes and owls can find food.
6.	The snake is eaten by a hawk.	They are all connected. Like a spiders web, if one part is removed, it can affect the whole web.

(Any five) (1 × 5 = 5)

Q. 4. How do human activities impact the ecological system? U

Ans. Ecological balance is a state of dynamic equilibrium within a community of organisms in a habitat or ecosystem. It can happen when the diversity of the living organisms remains relatively stable. Gradual changes do take place but that happens only through natural succession. Human interference has affected the balance of plant communities leading to disturbances in the ecosystems. Such disturbances bring about numerous secondary successions. Human pressure on the earth's resources has put a heavy toll on the ecosystem. This has destroyed its originality and has caused adverse effects to the general environment. Ecological imbalances have brought many natural calamities like floods, landslides, diseases, erratic climatic occurrences, etc. **5**

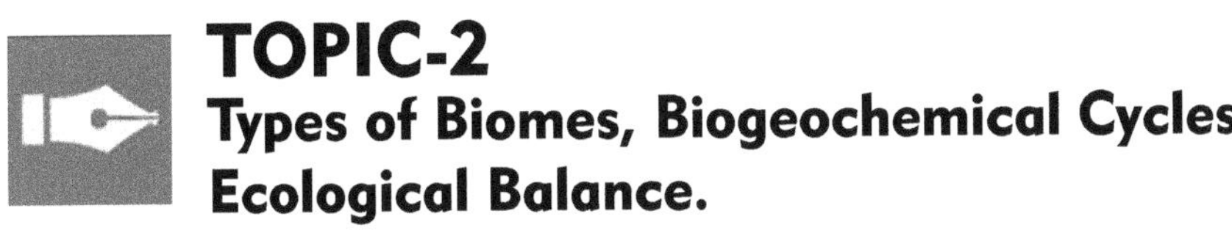

TOPIC-2
Types of Biomes, Biogeochemical Cycles, Ecological Balance.

Revision Notes

- There are five major biomes — forest, desert, grassland , aquatic and attitudinal biomes.
- The Sun is the basic source of energy on which all life depends.
- During photosynthesis, carbon dioxide is converted into organic compounds and oxygen. Out of the total solar insolation that reaches the earth's surface, only a very small fraction (0.1 per cent) is fixed in photosynthesis.
- More than half are used for plant respiration and the remaining part is temporarily stored or is shifted to other portions of the plant.
- Studies have shown that for the last one billion years, the atmosphere and hydrosphere have been composed of approximately the same balance of chemical components.
- This balance of the chemical elements is maintained by a cyclic passage through the tissues of plants and animals.
- These cyclic movements of chemical elements of the biosphere between the organism and the environment are referred to as biogeochemical cycles. 'Bio' refers to living organisms and 'geo' to rocks, soil, air and water of the earth.
- There are two types of biogeochemical cycles : the gaseous and the sedimentary cycle.
- In the gaseous cycle, the main reservoir of nutrients is the atmosphere and the ocean. In the sedimentary cycle, the main reservoir is the soil and the sedimentary and other rocks of the earth's crust.
- All living organisms, the atmosphere and the lithosphere maintain between them a circulation of water in solid, liquid or gaseous form referred to as the water or hydrologic cycle.
- The carbon cycle is mainly the conversion of carbon dioxide. This conversion is initiated by the fixation of carbon dioxide from the atmosphere through photosynthesis.
- During this process, more carbon dioxide is generated and is released through its leaves or roots during the day. The remaining carbohydrates not being utilised by the plant become part of the plant tissue.
- Oxygen is the main by-product of photosynthesis. It is involved in the oxidation of carbohydrates with the release of energy, carbon dioxide and water. The cycling of oxygen is a highly complex process. Oxygen occurs in a number of chemical forms and combination.
- Much of oxygen is produced from the decomposition of water molecules by sunlight during photosynthesis and is released in the atmosphere through transpiration and respiration processes of plants.
- Nitrogen is a major constituent of the atmosphere comprising about seventy-nine per cent of the atmospheric gases.
- Only a few types of organisms like certain species of soil bacteria and blue green algae are capable of utilising it directly in its gaseous form. Generally, nitrogen is usable only after it is fixed. Ninety per cent of fixed nitrogen is biological.
- Nitrogen can also be fixed in the atmosphere by lightning and cosmic radiation.
- Dead plants and animals, excretion of nitrogenous wastes are converted into nitrites by the action of bacteria present in the soil.
- There are still other types of bacteria capable of converting nitrates into free nitrogen, a process known as denitrification.
- Other than carbon, oxygen, nitrogen and hydrogen being the principal geochemical components of the biosphere, many other minerals also occur as critical nutrients for plant and animal life.
- All living organisms fulfil their mineral requirements from mineral solutions in their environments.
- Ecological balance is a state of dynamic equilibrium within a community of organisms in a habitat or ecosystem.
- It can happen when the diversity of the living organisms remains relatively stable.
- This occurs through competition and cooperation between different organisms where population remains stable.
- This balance is also attained by the fact that some species depend on others for their food and sustenance.
- In the plants, any disturbance in the native forests such as clearing the forest for shifting cultivation usually brings about a change in the species distribution.
- This change is due to competition where the secondary forest species such as grasses, bamboos or pines overtakes the native species changing the original forest structure. This is called succession.
- Ecological balance may be disturbed due to the introduction of new species, natural hazards or human causes.
- Human pressure on the earth's resources has put a heavy toll on the ecosystem.
- Ecological imbalances have brought many natural calamities like floods, landslides, diseases, erratic climatic occurrences, etc.

Know the Terms

- **Biogeochemical cycles :** The cyclic movements of chemical elements of the biosphere between the organism and the environment are referred to as biogeochemical cycles.
- **Gaseous cycle :** In the gaseous cycle, the main reservoir of nutrients is the atmosphere and the ocean.
- **Sedimentary cycle :** In the sedimentary cycle, the main reservoir is the soil and the sedimentary and other rocks of the earth's crust.
- **Photosynthesis :** The process by which green plants and some other organisms use sunlight to synthesize nutrients from carbon dioxide and water.
- **Water cycle :** All living organisms, the atmosphere and the lithosphere maintain between them a circulation of water in solid, liquid or gaseous form. This is known as the water or hydrologic cycle.
- **Oxygen cycle :** Oxygen is the main by-product of photosynthesis. It is involved in the oxidation of carbohydrates with the release of energy, carbon dioxide and water. The cycling of oxygen is a highly complex process.
- **Biogeochemical cycle :** The cyclic movements of chemical elements of the biosphere between the organism and the environment are referred to as biogeochemical cycles. Bio refers to living organisms and geo to rocks, soil, air and water of the earth.
- **Denitrification :** Some bacteria can even convert nitrites into nitrates that can be used again by green plants. There are still other types of bacteria capable of converting nitrates into free nitrogen, a process known as denitrification.

Multiple Choice Questions **(1 mark each)**

Q. 1. The basic source of energy on which all life depends is the : [A]

(a) Sun
(b) Moon
(c) Water
(d) Land

Ans. (a) Sun 1

Q. 2. Bio refers to the : [U]

(a) non-living beings
(b) living beings
(c) environment
(d) hydrosphere

Ans. (b) living beings 1

Q. 3. __________ can be fixed in the atmosphere by lightning and cosmic radiation. [A]

(a) Oxygen
(b) Nitrogen
(c) Carbon dioxide
(d) Sulphur

Ans. (b) Nitrogen 1

Very Short Answer Type Questions **(1 mark each)**

Q. 1. Define the term 'Biochemical Cycles'. [A]

Ans. The cyclic movements of chemical elements of the biosphere between the organism and the environment are referred to as biogeochemical cycles. 1

Q. 2. What is denitrification? [R]

Ans. Dead plants and animals, excretion of nitrogenous wastes are converted into nitrites by the action of bacteria present in the soil. Some bacteria can even convert nitrites into nitrates that can be used again by green plants. There are still other types of bacteria capable of converting nitrates into free nitrogen, a process known as denitrification. 1

Commonly Made Error

- The students are not aware of the effect denitrification has on the soil.

Answering Tip

- Denitrification depletes soil fertility and reducing agricultural productivity.

Q. 3. What is water cycle? [U]

Ans. All living organisms, the atmosphere and the lithosphere maintain between them a circulation of water in solid, liquid or gaseous form referred to as the water or hydrologic cycle. 1

Q. 4. What is succession? [A]

Ans. The change due to competition where the secondary forest species such as grasses, bamboos or pines overtakes the native species changing the original forest structure is called succession. 1

Q. 5. Differentiate between gaseous cycle and sedimentary cycle. [R]

Ans. In the gaseous cycle, the main reservoir of nutrients is the atmosphere and the ocean. In the sedimentary cycle, the main reservoir is the soil and the sedimentary and other rocks of the earth's crust. 1

Q. 6. How many types of biomes are there? [A]

Ans. There are five major biomes — forest, desert, grassland, aquatic and altitudinal biomes. 1

Q. 7. How is the ecological balance disturbed? R

Ans. Ecological balance may be disturbed due to the introduction of new species, natural hazards or human causes. 1

Q. 8. Forest biome can be sub divided into how many parts? U

Ans. Forest biome can be sub divided into tropical and temperate parts. 1

Q. 9. Desert biome can be subdivided into how many parts? A

Ans. It can be sub divided into : hot and dry desert, semi arid desert, coastal desert and cold desert. 1

Q. 10. Name the subtypes of grassland? A

Ans. The subtypes of grassland are: tropical savannah and temperate steppe. 1

Q. 11. Name the sub types of aquatic biomes. R

Ans. Freshwater and marine are the two sub types of aquatic biomes. 1

Short Answer Type Questions

(3 marks each)

Q. 1. What do you know about the oxygen cycle? R

Ans. Oxygen is the main by-product of photosynthesis. It is involved in the oxidation of carbohydrates with the release of energy, carbon dioxide and water. The cycling of oxygen is a highly complex process. Oxygen occurs in a number of chemical forms and combinations.

It combines with nitrogen to form nitrates and with many other minerals and elements to form various oxides such as the iron oxide, aluminium oxide and others.

Much of oxygen is produced from the decomposition of water molecules by sunlight during photosynthesis and is released in the atmosphere through transpiration and respiration processes of plants. 3

Commonly Made Error

- The students tend to ignore the major components of the oxygen cycle.

Answering Tip

- The major components of the oxygen cycle are the terrestrial biosphere , marine biosphere, lithosphere, and atmosphere.

Q. 2. How does nitrogen get fixed? A

Ans. Nitrogen is a major constituent of the atmosphere comprising about seventy-nine per cent of the atmospheric gases.

It is also an essential constituent of different organic compounds such as the amino acids, nucleic acids, proteins, vitamins and pigments. Only a few types of organisms like certain species of soil bacteria and blue green algae are capable of utilising it directly in its gaseous form. Generally, nitrogen is usable only after it is fixed. Ninety per cent of fixed nitrogen is biological.

The principal source of free nitrogen is the action of soil micro-organisms and associated plant roots on atmospheric nitrogen found in pore spaces of the soil. Nitrogen can also be fixed in the atmosphere by lightning and cosmic radiation. 3

AI **Q. 3. What type of changes take place during photosynthesis?** U

Ans. The carbon cycle is mainly the conversion of carbon dioxide. This conversion is initiated by the fixation of carbon dioxide from the atmosphere through photosynthesis. Such conversion results in the production of carbohydrate, glucose that may be converted to other organic compounds such as sucrose, starch, cellulose, etc.

Here, some of the carbohydrates are utilised directly by the plant itself. During this process, more carbon dioxide is generated and is released through its leaves or roots during the day. The remaining carbohydrates not being utilised by the plant become part of the plant tissue. Plant tissues are either being eaten by the herbivorous animals or get decomposed by the microorganisms.

The herbivores convert some of the consumed carbohydrates into carbon dioxide for release into the air through respiration. The micro-organisms decompose the remaining carbohydrates after the animal dies. 3

Answering Tip

- During photosynthesis light energy from the sun is being converted to chemical potential energy.

Long Answer Type Questions

(5 marks each)

Q. 1. Explain the bio-geochemical cycle. A

Ans. Life on earth consists of a great variety of living organisms. These living organisms exist and survive in a diversity of associations. Such survival involves the presence of systemic flows such as flows of energy, water and nutrients.

These flows show variations in different parts of the world, in different seasons of the year and under varying local circumstances. Studies have shown that for the last one billion years, the atmosphere and hydrosphere have been composed of approximately the same balance of chemical components.

This balance of the chemical elements is maintained by a cyclic passage through the tissues of plants and animals. The cycle starts by absorbing the chemical elements by the organism and is returned to the air, water and soil through decomposition.

These cycles are largely energised by solar insolation. These cyclic movements of chemical elements of the biosphere between the organism and the environment are referred to as biogeochemical.

There are two types of biogeochemical cycles :

(a) The gaseous and the sedimentary cycle. In the gaseous cycle, the main reservoir of nutrients is the atmosphere and the ocean.

(b) In the sedimentary cycle, the main reservoir is the soil and the sedimentary and other rocks of the earth's crust. 5

Q. 2. Explain in detail the carbon cycle. Draw and label the diagram. [R]

Ans. Carbon is one of the basic elements of all living organisms. It forms the basic constituent of all the organic compounds. The biosphere contains over half a million carbon compounds in them.

The carbon cycle is mainly the conversion of carbon dioxide. This conversion is initiated by the fixation of carbon dioxide from the atmosphere through photosynthesis. Such conversion results in the production of carbohydrate, glucose that may be converted to other organic compounds such as sucrose, starch, cellulose, etc.

Here, some of the carbohydrates are utilised directly by the plant itself. During this process, more carbon dioxide is generated and is released through its leaves or roots during the day. The remaining carbohydrates not being utilised by the plant become part of the plant tissue. Plant tissues are either being eaten by the herbivorous animals or get decomposed by the microorganisms.

The herbivores convert some of the consumed carbohydrates into carbon dioxide for release into the air through respiration. The micro-organisms decompose the remaining carbohydrates after the animal dies. The carbohydrates that are decomposed by the micro-organisms then get oxidised into carbon dioxide and are returned to the atmosphere. 5

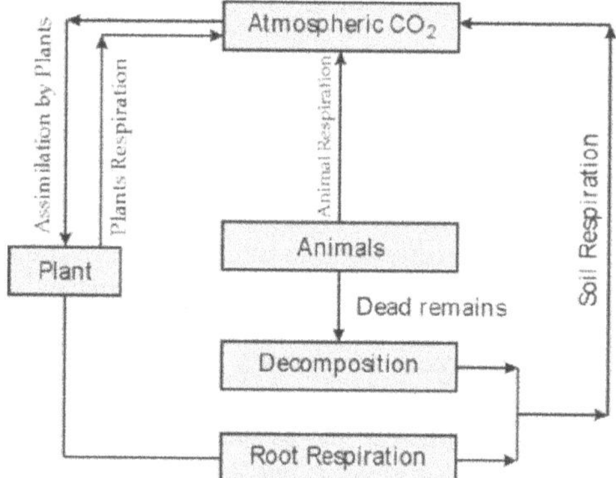

[AI]**Q. 3. Explain in detail about the nitrogen cycle. Draw and label the diagram.** [A]

Ans. Nitrogen is a major constituent of the atmosphere comprising about seventy-nine per cent of the atmospheric gases. It is also an essential constituent of different organic compounds such as the amino acids, nucleic acids, proteins, vitamins and pigments.

Only a few types of organisms like certain species of soil bacteria and blue green algae are capable of utilising it directly in its gaseous form. Generally, nitrogen is usable only after it is fixed. Ninety per cent of fixed nitrogen is biological. The principal source of free nitrogen is the action of soil micro-organisms and associated plant roots on atmospheric nitrogen found in pore spaces of the soil.

Nitrogen can also be fixed in the atmosphere lightning and cosmic radiation. In the oceans, some marine animals can fix it. After atmospheric nitrogen has been fixed into an available form, green plants can assimilate it. Herbivorous animals feeding on plants, in turn, consume some of it. Dead plants and animals, excretion of nitrogenous wastes is converted into nitrites by the action of bacteria present in the soil.

Some bacteria can even convert nitrites into nitrates that can be used again by green plants. There are still other types of bacteria capable of converting nitrates into free nitrogen, a process known as denitrification. 5

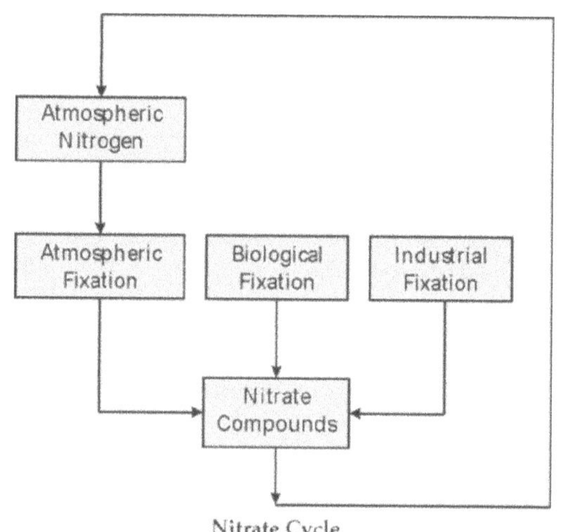

Nitrate Cycle

Answering Tip

- The nitrogen cycle is the biogeochemical cycle by which nitrogen is converted into multiple chemical forms as it circulates among atmosphere, terrestrial, and marine ecosystems.

(A) Multiple choice questions :

Q. 1. Which one of the following is included in biosphere :

(a) only plants
(b) all living and non-living organisms
(c) only animals
(d) all living organisms

Ans. (b) All living and non-living organisms.

Q. 2. Tropical grasslands are also known as :

(a) the prairies
(b) the savannas
(c) the steppes
(d) none of the above

Ans. (b) The savannas.

Q. 3. Oxygen combines with iron found in the rocks to form :

(a) iron carbonate
(b) iron nitrites
(c) iron oxides
(d) iron sulphate

Ans. (c) Iron oxides.

Q. 4. During photosynthesis, carbon dioxide combines with water in the presence of sunlight to form:

(a) proteins
(b) amino acids
(c) carbohydrates
(d) vitamins

Ans. (c) Carbohydrates .

(B) Answer the following questions in about 30 words :

Q. 1. What do you understand by the term 'ecology'? [A]

Ans. Ecology can be defined as a scientific study of the interactions of organisms with their physical environment and with each other.

Q. 2.What is an ecological system? Identify the major types of ecosystems in the world? [U]

Ans. The interactions of a particular group of organisms with abiotic factors within a particular habitat resulting in clearly defined energy flows and material cycles on land, water and air, are called ecological systems.

The major types od ecosystems in the world are, terrestrial and aquatic. Terrestrial ecosystem can further be classified into biomes. Aquatic ecosystem can be classified as marine and freshwater ecosystems.

Q. 3. What is a food-chain? Give one example of a grazing food-chain identifying the various levels?

Ans. The sequence of eating and being eaten and the resultant transfer of energy from one level to another is known as the food-chain.

In a grazing food-chain, the first level starts with plants as producers and ends with carnivores as consumers as the last level, with the herbivores being at the intermediate level. There is a loss of energy at each level which may be through respiration, excretion or decomposition. The levels involved in a food-chain range between three to five and energy is lost at each level.

Q. 4. What do you understand by the term 'food web'? Give examples?

Ans. The inter-connecting network of species is known as food-web. A mouse , feeding on grain may be eaten by different secondary consumers (carnivores) and these carnivores may be eaten by other different tertiary consumers (top carnivores). In such situations, each of the carnivores may consume more than one type of prey. As a result, the food- chains get interlocked with one another.

Q. 5. What is a biome?

Ans. A biome is a plant and animal community that covers a large geographical area. The boundaries of different biomes on land are determined mainly by climate.

(C) Answer the following questions in about 150 words :

Q. 1. What are bio-geochemical cycles? Explain how nitrogen is fixed in the atmosphere? [U]

Ans. The sun is the basic source of energy on which all life depends. This energy initiates life processes in the biosphere through photosynthesis, the main source of food and energy for green plants. During photosynthesis, carbon dioxide is converted into organic compounds and oxygen. Out of the total solar insolation that reaches the earth's surface, only a very small fraction (0.1 per cent) is fixed in photosynthesis. More than half is used for plant respiration and the remaining part is temporarily stored or is shifted to other portions of the plant.

The balance of the chemical elements is maintained by a cyclic passage through the tissues of plants and animals. The cycle starts by absorbing the chemical elements by the organism and is returned to the air, water and soil through decomposition. These cycles are largely energised by solar insolation. These cyclic movements of chemical elements of the biosphere between the organism and the environment are referred to as biogeochemical cycles.

Q. 2. What is an ecological balance? Discuss the important measures needed to prevent ecological imbalances?

Ans. Ecological balance is a state of dynamic equilibrium within a community of organisms in a habitat or ecosystem. It can happen when the diversity of the living organisms remains relatively stable. Gradual changes do take place but that happens only through natural succession. It can also be explained as a stable balance in the numbers of each species in an ecosystem. This occurs through competition and cooperation between different organisms where population remains stable. This balance is brought about by the fact that certain species compete with one another determined by the environment in which they grow. This balance is also attained by the fact that some species depend on others for their food and sustenance. Such accounts are encountered in vast grasslands where the herbivorous animals (deer, zebras, buffaloes, etc.) are found in plenty. On the other hand, the carnivorous animals (tigers, lions, etc.) that are not usually in large numbers, hunt and feed on the herbivores, thereby controlling their population.

In the plants, any disturbance in the native forests such as clearing the forest for shifting cultivation usually brings about a change in the species distribution. This change is due to competition where the secondary forest species such as grasses, bamboos or pines overtakes the native species changing the original forest structure. This is called succession.

Ecological balance may be disturbed due to the introduction of new species, natural hazards or human causes. Human interference has affected the balance of plant communities leading to disturbances in the ecosystems. Such disturbances bring about numerous secondary successions.

OSWAAL LEARNING TOOLS

For Suggested Online Videos

Visit : *https://qrgo.page.link/vLQs4* **Or Scan the Code**

❑❑

CHAPTER

16 BIODIVERSITY AND CONSERVATION

Syllabus

> *Genetic Diversity, Species Diversity, Ecosystem Diversity, Importance of Diversity, Ecological Role of Biodiversity, Economic Role of Biodiversity, Scientific Role of Biodiversity, Loss Of Biodiversity, Endangered Species, Vulnerable Species, Rare Species, Conservation of Biodiversity.*

Revision Notes

- Biodiversity as we have today is the result of 2.5-3.5 billion years of evolution. Before the advent of humans, our earth supported more biodiversity than in any other period.
- The number of species globally vary from 2 million to 100 million, with 10 million being the best estimate. New species are regularly discovered most of which are yet to be classified (an estimate states that about 40 per cent of fresh water fishes from South America are not classified yet). Tropical forests are very rich in bio-diversity.
- Biodiversity is a system in constant evolution, from a view point of species, as well as from view point of an individual organism.
- Biodiversity is not found evenly on the earth. It is consistently richer in the tropics. As one approaches the polar regions, one finds larger and larger populations of fewer and fewer species.
- Biodiversity is our living wealth. It is a result of hundreds of millions of years of evolutionary history.
- **Genetic biodiversity :** It refers to the variation of genes within species. Groups of individual organisms having certain similarities in their physical characteristics are called species. The genetic diversity is essential for a healthy breeding of population of species.
- **Species Diversity :** This refers to the variety of species. It relates to the number of species in a defined area. The diversity of species can be measured through its richness, abundance and types.
- **Ecosystem diversity :** The broad differences between ecosystem types and the diversity of habitats and ecological processes occurring within each ecosystem type constitute the ecosystem diversity.
- Biodiversity plays the following roles :
    - **Ecological role :** The more diverse an ecosystem, better are the chances for the species to survive through adversities and attacks, and consequently, is more productive. Hence, the loss of species would decrease the ability of the system to maintain itself. Just like a species with a high genetic diversity, an ecosystem with high biodiversity may have a greater chance of adapting to environmental change. In other words, the more the variety of species in an ecosystem, the more stable the ecosystem is likely to be.
    - **Economic role :** Some of the important economic commodities that biodiversity supplies to humankind are: food crops, livestock, forestry, fish, medicinal resources, etc.
    - **Scientific role :** Biodiversity also helps in understanding how life functions and the role of each species in sustaining ecosystems of which we are also a species. This fact must be drawn upon every one of us so that we live and let other species also live their lives.
- Since the last few decades, growth in human population has increased the rate of consumption of natural resources.
- It has accelerated the loss of species and habitation in different parts of the world. Tropical regions which occupy only about one-fourth of the total area of the world, contain about three fourth of the world human population.

- Overexploitation of resources and deforestation have become rampant to fulfil the needs of large population.
- Natural calamities such as earthquakes, floods, volcanic eruptions, forest fires, droughts, etc. cause damage to the flora and fauna of the earth, bringing change the biodiversity of respective affected regions.
- Pesticides and other pollutants such as hydrocarbons and toxic heavy metals destroy the weak and sensitive species.
- During the last few decades, some animals like tigers, elephants, rhinoceros, crocodiles, minks and birds were hunted mercilessly by poachers for their horn, tusks, hides, etc. It has resulted in the rendering of certain types of organisms as endangered category.
- The International Union of Conservation of Nature and Natural Resources (IUCN) has classified the threatened species of plants and animals into **three** categories for the purpose of their conservation.
  - **Endangered Species :** It includes those species which are in danger of extinction.
  - **Vulnerable Species :** This includes the species which are likely to be in danger of extinction in near future if the factors threatening to their extinction continue.
  - **Rare Species :** Population of these species is very small in the world; they are confined to limited areas or thinly scattered over a wider area.
- There is an urgent need to educate people to adopt environment-friendly practices and reorient their activities in such a way that our development is harmonious with other life forms and is sustainable.
- The critical problem is not merely the conservation of species nor the habitat but the continuation of process of conservation.
- The Government of India along with 155 other nations have signed the Convention of Biodiversity at the Earth Summit held at Rio-de Janeiro, Brazil in June 1992.
- The world conservation strategy has suggested the following steps for biodiversity conservation :
  - Efforts should be made to preserve the species that are endangered.
  - Prevention of extinction requires proper planning and management.
  - Varieties of food crops, forage plants, timber trees, livestock, animals and their wild relatives should be preserved.
  - Each country should identify habitats of wild relatives and ensure their protection.
  - Habitats where species feed, breed, rest and nurse their young should be safeguarded and protected.
  - International trade in wild plants and animals be regulated.
- There are some countries which are situated in the tropical region; they possess a large number of the world's species diversity.
- They are called mega diversity centres. There are 12 such countries, namely Mexico, Columbia, Ecuador, Peru, Brazil, Zaire, Madagascar, China, India, Malaysia, Indonesia and Australia in which these centres are located.
- In order to concentrate resources on those areas that are most vulnerable, the International Union for the Conservation of Nature and Natural Resources (IUCN) has identified certain areas as biodiversity hotspots.
- Hotspots are defined according to their vegetation. Plants are important because these determine the primary productivity of an ecosystem. Most, but not all, of the hotspots rely on species rich ecosystems for food, firewood, cropland, and income from timber.
- In Madagascar about 85 percent of the plants and animals are found nowhere else in the world. Other hotspots in wealthy countries are facing different types of pressure.
- The Islands of Hawaii have many unique plants and animals that are threatened by introduces species and land development.

Know the Terms

- **Biodiversity :** Biodiversity is the number and variety of organisms found within a specified geographic region. It refers to the varieties of plants, animals and micro-organisms, the genes they contain and the ecosystems they form.
- **Genetic biodiversity :** Genetic biodiversity refers to the variation of genes within Species
- **Species :** Groups of individual organisms having certain similarities in their physical characteristics are called species
- **Species diversity :** It refers to the variety of species. It relates to the number of species in a defined area.
- **Ecosystem diversity :** The broad differences between ecosystem types and the diversity of habitats and ecological processes occurring within each ecosystem type constitute the ecosystem diversity.
- **Hotspots :** Areas rich in species diversity are called hotspots of diversity.

- **Crop diversity/agro biodiversity :** It includes all components of biological diversity of relevance to food and agriculture.
- **Exotic species :** Species which are not the natural inhabitants of the local habitat but are introduced into the system, are called exotic species.
- **Sensitive species :** Pesticides and other pollutants such as hydrocarbons and toxic heavy metals destroy the weak species. These are called sensitive species.
- **Mega diversity centre :** There are some countries which are situated in the tropical region; they possess a large number of world's species diversity. They are called mega diversity centre.
- **IUCN :** The International Union of Conservation of Nature and Natural Resources.
- **Endangered species :** It includes the species which are likely to be in danger of extinction.
- **Rare species :** They are those species whose population is very small in the world and they are confined to limited areas or thinly scattered over a wider area.
- **Vulnerable species :** It includes those species which are likely to be in danger of extinction in near future if the factors threatening to their extinction continue.

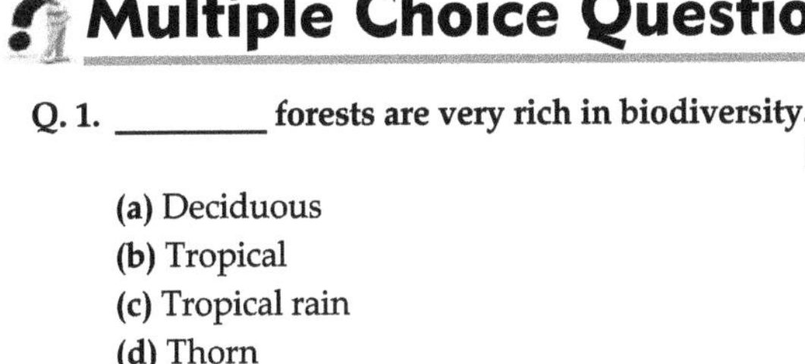

Multiple Choice Questions (1 mark each)

Q. 1. ________ forests are very rich in biodiversity. [A]

(a) Deciduous
(b) Tropical
(c) Tropical rain
(d) Thorn

Ans. (b) Tropical 1

Q. 2. Biodiversity as we have today is the result of__________ years of evolution. [U]

(a) 1.5-2.5 million
(b) 2.5-3.5 million
(c) 3.5-4.5 million
(d) 5.5-6.5 million

Ans. (b) 2.5-3.5 million 1

Q. 3. About 85 per cent of the plants and animals that are found nowhere else in the world are found in: [U]

(a) India
(b) Madagascar
(c) Russia
(d) Iceland

Ans. (b) Madagascar 1

Very Short Answer Type Questions (1 mark each)

[AI] **Q. 1. Define the term 'Biodiversity'.** [A]

Ans. Biodiversity refers to the varieties of plants, animals and micro-organisms, the genes they contain and the ecosystems they form. 1

Q. 2. Define the term 'Exotic Species'. [R]

Ans. They are the species which are not the natural inhabitants of the local habitat but are introduced into the system. 1

Q. 3. Define the term endangered species. [U]

Ans. Endangered species includes the species which are likely to be in danger of extinction.

Rare species : They are those species whose population is very small in the world and they are confined to limited areas or thinly scattered over a wider area. 1

Q. 5. What are mega diversity centres? [R]

Ans. There are some countries which are situated in the tropical region; they possess a large number of world's species diversity. They are called mega diversity centre. 1

Q. 6. What is agro diversity? [U]

Ans. It includes all components of biological diversity of relevance to food and agriculture. 1

Q. 7. What is genetic bio diversity? [A]

Ans. Genetic biodiversity refers to the variation of genes within species . 1

> **Answering Tip**
> - Genetic diversity serves as a way for populations to adapt to changing environments.

Q. 8. What does the word 'Bio' and 'Diversity' mean? [A]

Ans. Bio means life and diversity means variety. 1

Q. 9. When and where was the Conservation of Biodiversity at the Earth Summit held? [U]

Ans. It was held in 1992 at Rio de Janeiro, Brazil. 1

Q. 9. What are the causes behind biodiversity? [R]

Ans. Weathering mantle is the basis for the diversity of vegetation and thereby of the biodiversity. The basic cause for such weathering is the input of solar energy and water. 1

Q. 10. Why is bio diversity not evenly distributed over the Earth? [U]

Ans. Bio diversity is not evenly distributed over the Earth. It is consistently richer in the tropics. As one approached the polar regions, one finds larger and larger populations of fewer and fewer species. 1

Q. 11. Why is diversity required? U

Ans. Diversity is required for the development and prosperity of all living beings. 1

Q. 12. What is the average half-life of a species? A

Ans. The average half-life of a species is estimated at between one and four million years. 1

Q. 13. Name the countries which have highest bio diversity.

Ans. There are 12 such countries, namely Mexico, Columbia, Ecuador, Peru, Brazil, Zaire, Madagascar, China, India, Malaysia, Indonesia and Australia. 1

Q. 14. What provisions have been made under Wild Life Protection Act, 1972? U

Ans. The Wild Life Protection Act, 1972, provides for the protection of wild animals, birds and plants. This act governs wildlife conservation and protection of endangered species by establishing national parks, wildlife sanctuaries and biosphere reserves. 1

Short Answer Type Questions (3 marks each)

Q. 1. What do you know about genetic biodiversity? A

Ans. Genetic biodiversity refers to the variation of genes within species. Groups of individual organisms having certain similarities in their physical characteristics are called species. Human beings genetically belong to the homo sapiens group and also differ in their characteristics such as height, colour, physical appearance, etc., considerably. This is due to genetic diversity. This genetic diversity is essential for a healthy breeding of population of species. 3

Q. 2. What do you know about species diversity? U

Ans. This refers to the variety of species. It relates to the number of species in a defined area. The diversity of species can be measured through its richness, abundance and types. Some areas are more rich in species than others. Areas rich in species diversity are called hotspots of diversity.3

Q. 3. What is the economic role of biodiversity? A

Ans. (i) **Crop diversity :** For all humans, biodiversity is an important resource in their day-to-day life. One important part of biodiversity is 'crop diversity', which is also called agro-biodiversity.

(ii) **Manufacturing :** Biodiversity is seen as a reservoir of resources to be drawn upon for the manufacture of food, pharmaceutical, and cosmetic products. This concept of biological resources is responsible for the deterioration of biodiversity.

(iii) **Economic diversity :** At the same time, it is also the origin of new conflicts dealing with rules of division and appropriation of natural resources. Some of the important economic commodities that biodiversity supplies to humankind are: food crops, livestock, forestry, fish, medicinal resources, etc. 3

Q. 4. What do you know about bio diversity? U

Ans. Biodiversity is a system in constant evolution, from a view point of species, as well as from view point of an individual organism.

The average half-life of a species is estimated at between one and four million years, and 99 per cent of the species that have ever lived on the earth are today extinct. Biodiversity is not found evenly on the earth. It is consistently richer in the tropics. As one approaches the polar regions, one finds larger and larger populations of fewer and fewer species. Biodiversity is our living wealth. It is a result of hundreds of millions of years of evolutionary history. 3

Answering Tip

- Biodiversity boosts ecosystem productivity where each species, no matter how small, all have an important role to play.

AI **Q. 5. Mention the importance of biodiversity.** R

Ans. Biodiversity is important in the following ways :

(i) **Ecological :** Species of many kinds perform some function or the other in an ecosystem. every organism, besides extracting its needs, also contributes something of useful to other organisms. Can you think of the way we, humans contribute to the sustenance of ecosystems. Species capture and store energy, produce and decompose organic materials, help to cycle water and nutrients throughout the ecosystem, fix atmospheric gases and help regulate the climate.

(ii) **Economic :** Some of the important economic commodities that biodiversity supplies to humankind are: food crops, livestock, forestry, fish, medicinal resources, etc.

(iii) **Scientific :** Biodiversity is important because each species can give us some clue as to how life evolved and will continue to evolve. Biodiversity also helps in understanding how life functions and the role of each species in sustaining ecosystems of which we are also a species. 3

Q. 6. Into how many categories has the International Union of Conservation of Nature and Natural Resources (IUCN) classified the threatened species of plants and animals? A

Ans. The International Union of Conservation of Nature and Natural Resources (IUCN) has classified the threatened species of plants and animals into three categories for the purpose of their conservation :

(i) **Endangered Species :** It includes those species which are in danger of extinction. The IUCN publishes information about endangered species world-wide as the Red List of threatened species.

(ii) **Vulnerable Species :** This includes the species which are likely to be in danger of extinction in near future if the factors threatening to their extinction continue. Survival of these species is not assured as their population has reduced greatly.

(iii) **Rare Species :** Population of these species is very small in the world; they are confined to limited areas or thinly scattered over a wider area. 3

Q. 7. Tropical regions are most diverse regions of the world. Explain?

Ans. Tropical regions which occupy only about one-fourth of the total area of the world , contain about three-fourth of the world human population. Over-exploitation of resources and deforestation has become rampant to fulfil the needs of large population. As these tropical rain forests contain 50 percent of the species on the earth, destruction of natural habitats have proved disastrous for the entire biosphere. 3

Long Answer Type Questions

(5 marks each)

Q. 1. How do natural calamities and illegal hunting harm biodiversity. [A]

Ans. Natural calamities such as earthquakes, floods, volcanic eruptions, forest fires, droughts, etc. cause damage to the flora and fauna of the earth, bringing change the biodiversity of respective affected regions. Pesticides and other pollutants such as hydrocarbons and toxic heavy metals destroy the weak and sensitive species.

Species which are not the natural inhabitants of the local habitat but are introduced into the system, are called exotic species. There are many examples when a natural biotic community of the ecosystem suffered extensive damage because of the introduction of exotic species.

During the last few decades, some animals like tigers, elephants, rhinoceros, crocodiles, minks and birds were hunted mercilessly by poachers for their horn, tusks, hides, etc. It has resulted in the rendering of certain types of organisms as endangered category.

Illegal hunting and habitat destruction contributed to a second wave of extinctions after European settlement including:

(i) 16 land birds (nine species and seven subspecies)

(ii) One of three native bat species

(iii) Atleast 12 invertebrates, such as snails and insects. **(1 × 5 = 5)**

[AI]**Q.2. How can biodiversity be conserved?** [A]

Ans. If species of plants and animals become endangered, they cause degradation in the environment, which may threaten human being's own existence.

There is an urgent need to educate people to adopt environment-friendly practices and reorient their activities in such a way that our development is harmonious with other life forms and is sustainable.

There is an increasing consciousness of the fact that such conservation with sustainable use is possible only with the involvement and cooperation of local communities and individuals. For this, the development of institutional structures at local levels is necessary.

The critical problem is not merely the conservation of species nor the habitat but the continuation of process of conservation. The Government of India along with 155 other nations have signed the Convention of Biodiversity at the Earth Summit held at Riode Janeiro, Brazil in June 1992. The world conservation strategy has suggested the following steps for biodiversity conservation :

(i) Efforts should be made to preserve the species that are endangered.

(ii) Prevention of extinction requires proper planning and management

(iii) Varieties of food crops, forage plants, timber trees, livestock, animals and their wild relatives should be preserved;

(iv) Each country should identify habitats of wild relatives and ensure their protection.

(v) Habitats where species feed, breed, rest and nurse their young should be safeguarded and protected.

(vi) International trade in wild plants and animals be regulated . **(1 × 5 = 5)**

Answering Tip

- Biodiversity conservation is vital for economic growth and poverty reduction.

[AI]**Q. 3. How can it be said that biodiversity is important not for geographers but also for economists?** [U]

Ans. It is correct that biodiversity is not only important for geographers but also for economists. For all humans biodiversity is an important resource in their day to day life.

One important part of biodiversity is 'crop diversity', which is also called agro-biodiversity. Biodiversity is seen as a reservoir of resources to be drawn upon for the manufacture of food, pharmaceutical, and cosmetic product .

At the same time, it is also the origin of new conflicts dealing with rules of division and appropriation of natural resources. Some of the important economic commodities that biodiversity supplies to humankind are: food crops, livestock, forestry, fish, medicinal resources, etc.

Biodiversity is a reservoir of resources to be drawn upon for the manufacturing of food, pharmaceutical and cosmetic products. Biodiversity has given boost to tourism industry. 5

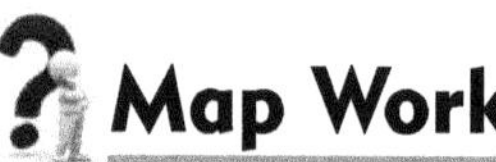

Map Work

(5 marks each)

Q. 1. On the outline map of the world, locate the label the following.

(i) Tropical Andes

(ii) Atlantic Forest

(iii) Eastern Madagascar

(iv) Western Ghats

(v) Central American Highlands Forests

Ans.

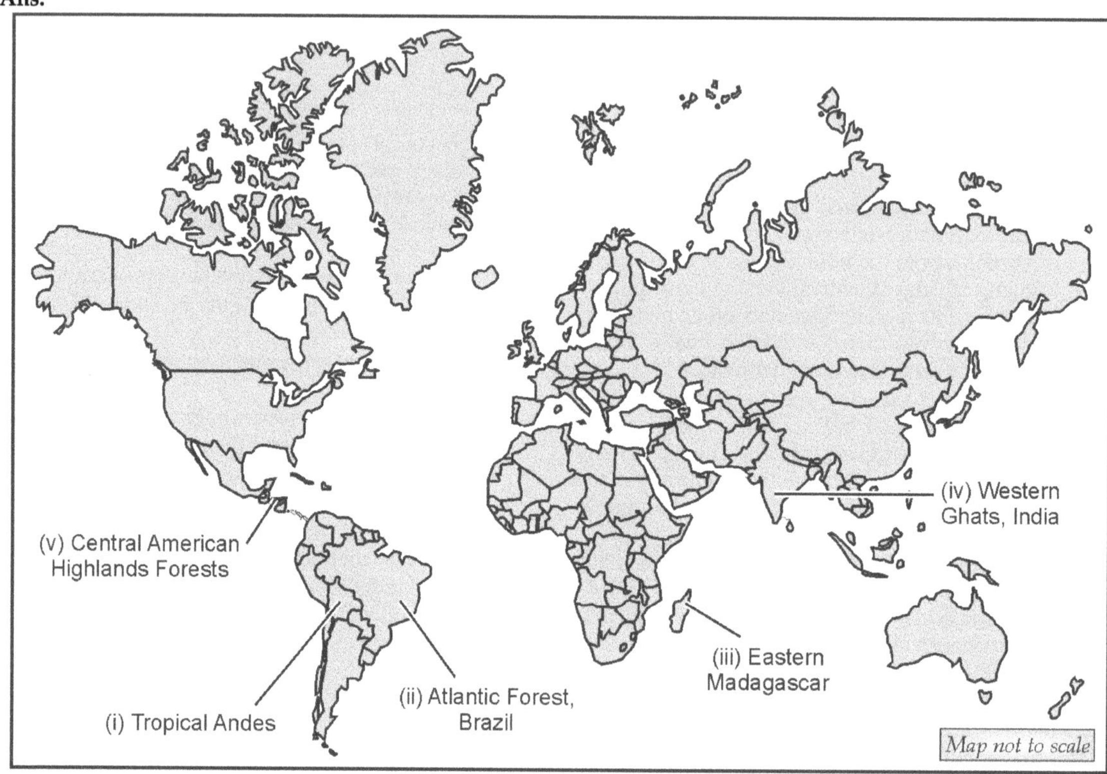

NCERT CORNER

(A) Multiple choice questions :

Q. 1. Conservation of biodiversity is important for :

(a) Animals

(b) Animals and plants

(c) Plants

(d) All organisms

Ans. (d) All organisms.

Q. 2. Threatened species are those which :

(a) threaten others

(b) Lion and tiger

(c) are abundant in number

(d) are suffering from the danger of extinction

Ans. (d) Are suffering from the danger of extinction.

Q. 3. National parks and sanctuaries are established for the purpose of :

(a) Recreation

(b) Hunting

(c) Pets

(d) Conservation

Ans. (d) Conservation.

Q. 4. Biodiversity is richer in :

(a) Tropical Regions

(b) Polar Regions

(c) Temperate Regions

(d) Oceans

Ans. (a) Tropical regions.

Q. 5. In which one of the following countries, the 'Earth Summit' was held?

(a) the UK

(b) Mexico

(c) Brazil
(d) China

Ans. (c) Brazil .

(B) Answer the following questions in about 30 words:

Q. 1. What is biodiversity?

Ans. In simple terms, biodiversity is the number and variety of organisms found within a specified geographic region. It refers to the varieties of plants, animals and micro-organisms, the genes they contain and the ecosystems they form.

Q. 2. What are the different levels of biodiversity?

Ans. Biodiversity can be discussed at three levels :

(i) **Genetic diversity :** Ity refers to the variation of genes within species.

(ii) **Species diversity :** This refers to the variety of species. It relates to the number of species in a defined area.

(iii) **Ecosystem diversity :** The broad differences between ecosystem types and the diversity of habitats and ecological processes occurring within each ecosystem type constitute the ecosystem diversity.

Q. 3. What do you understand by 'hotspots'?

Ans. The areas rich in species diversity are called hotspots of diversity. In order to concentrate resources on those areas that are most vulnerable, the International Union for the Conservation of Nature and Natural Resources (IUCN) has identified certain areas as biodiversity hotspots. Hotspots are defined according to their vegetation. Plants are important because these determine the primary productivity of an ecosystem. Most, but not all, of the hotspots rely on species rich ecosystems for food, firewood, cropland, and income from timber.

Q. 4. Discuss briefly the importance of animals to human kind?

Ans. The Earth and its ecosystem are all deeply connected. Thus, the existence of many species depends on the survival of the others. Many animals actually help people just by performing their natural roles in their environment. And we're benefiting from their services for free. Similarly there are many animals we rely on for our benefits and well being.

Q. 5. What do you understand by 'exotic species'?

Ans. Species which are not the natural inhabitants of the local habitat but are introduced into the system, are called exotic species.

(C) Answer the following questions in about 150 words :

Q. 1. What are the roles played by biodiversity in the shaping of nature? U

Ans. (i) Biodiversity has contributed in many ways to the development of human culture and in turn human communities have played a major role in shaping the diversity of nature at the genetic, species and ecological levels.

(ii) Species capture and store energy, produce and decompose organic materials, help to cycle water, gases and minerals . They fix atmospheric gases and help regulate the climate. These functions are important for eco-system.

(iii) The more diverse an ecosystem , better are the chances for the species to survive through adversities and attacks , and consequently , is more productive.

(iv) The more diverse an ecosystem, better are the chances for the species to survive through adversities and attacks and consequently is more productive .

(v) Hence, the loss of species would decrease the ability of the system to maintain itself. Just like a species with a high genetic diversity, an ecosystem with high biodiversity may have a greater chance of adapting to environmental change.

(vi) In other words, the more the variety of species in an ecosystem, the more stable the ecosystem is likely to be.

Q. 2. What are the major factors that are responsible for the loss of biodiversity? What steps are needed to prevent them?

Ans. (i) Since the last few decades, growth in human population has increased the rate of consumption of natural resources. It has accelerated the loss of species and habitation in different parts of the world. Tropical regions which occupy only about one-fourth of the total area of the world, contain about three fourth of the world human population.

(ii) Overexploitation of resources and deforestation have become rampant to fulfil the needs of large population. As these tropical rain forests contain 50 per cent of the species on the earth, destruction of natural habitats have proved disastrous for the entire biosphere.

(iii) Natural calamities such as earthquakes, floods, volcanic eruptions, forest fires, droughts, etc., cause damage to the flora and fauna of the earth, bringing change the biodiversity of respective affected regions.

(iv) Pesticides and other pollutants such as hydrocarbons and toxic heavy metals destroy the weak and sensitive species. Species which are not the natural inhabitants of the local habitat but are introduced into the system, are called exotic species.

(v) There are many examples when a natural biotic community of the ecosystem suffered extensive damage because of the introduction of exotic species. During the last few decades, some animals like tigers, elephants, rhinoceros, crocodiles, minks and birds were hunted mercilessly by poachers for their horn, tusks, hides, etc. It has resulted in the rendering of certain types of organisms as endangered category.

OSWAAL LEARNING TOOLS

For Suggested Online Videos

Visit : *https://qrgo.page.link/TTFjA* **Or Scan the Code**

To learn from NCERT Prescribed Videos

Visit : *https://qrgo.page.link/mzvvF* **Or Scan the Code**

PART B :
UNIT-VII
Introduction

CHAPTER

1 INDIA-LOCATION

Syllabus

➢ *Extent, Size, India and its Neighbours.*

Revision Notes

- The mainland of India, extends from Kashmir in the North to Kanyakumari in the South and Arunachal Pradesh in the East to Gujarat in the West.
- India's territorial limit further extends towards the sea upto 12 nautical miles (about 21.9 km) from the coast.
- Our southern boundary extends upto 6°45' N latitude in the Bay of Bengal.
- If you work out the latitudinal and longitudinal extent of India, they are roughly about 30 degrees, whereas the actual distance measured from North to South extremity is 3,214 km and that from east to west only 2,933 km.
- From the values of latitude, it is understood that the southern part of the country lies within the tropics and the northern part lies in the sub-tropical zone or the warm temperate zone.
- From the values of longitude, it is quite discernible that there is a variation of nearly 30 degrees, which causes a time difference of nearly two hours between the easternmost and the westernmost parts of our country.
- There is a general understanding among the countries of the world to select the standard meridian in multiples of 7°30' of longitude. That is why 82°30' E has been selected as the 'Standard Meridian' of India. Indian Standard Time is ahead of Greenwich Mean Time by 5 hours and 30 minutes.
- India with its area of 3.28 million sq. km accounts for 2.4 per cent of the world's land surface area and stands as the seventh largest country in the world.
- The size of India has endowed her with great physical diversity.
- India has the presence of lofty mountains in the North; large rivers such as Ganga, Brahmaputra, Mahanadi, Krishna, Godavari and Kaveri; green forested hills in North East and South India; and the vast sandy expanse of Marusthali.
- Bounded by the Himalayas in the North, Hindukush and Sulaiman ranges in the North West, Purvachal hills in the North-East and by the large expanse of the Indian ocean in the South, it forms a great geographic entity known as the Indian subcontinent. It includes the countries — Pakistan, Nepal, Bhutan, Bangladesh and India.
- The Himalayas, together with other ranges, have acted as a formidable physical barrier in the past.
- Except for a few mountain passes such as the Khyber, the Bolan, the Shipkila, the Nathula, the Bomdila, etc., it was difficult to cross it.
- Peninsular part of India extends towards the Indian Ocean. This has provided the country with a coastline of 6,100 km in the mainland and 7,517 km in the entire geographical coast of the mainland plus the island groups Andaman and Nicobar located in the Bay of Bengal and the Lakshadweep in the Arabian Sea.
- India is located in the south-central part of the continent of Asia, bordering the Indian ocean and its two arms extending in the form of Bay of Bengal and the Arabian Sea. This maritime location of Peninsular India has provided links to its neighbouring regions through the sea and air routes.
- Sri Lanka and Maldives are the two island countries located in the Indian Ocean, which are our neighbours. Sri Lanka is separated from India by the Gulf of Mannar and Palk Strait.

Know the Terms

- **Indira point :** It is the southernmost point of India.
- **Subcontinent :** A subcontinent is part of a larger continent , made up of a number of countries that form a large mass of land.

Multiple Choice Questions (1 mark each)

Q. 1. The length of international border between India and Pakistan is: [A]

(a) 3310 km (b) 2210 km

(c) 1110 km (d) 1010 km

Ans. (a) 3310 km 1

Q. 2. India is located in the ______ part of the continent of Asia: [U]

(a) south-eastern (b) south-central

(c) south-western (d) south-coastal

Ans. (b) south-central 1

Q. 3. India has an area of : [R]

(a) 1.28 million sq km

(b) 3.28 million sq km

(c) 4.28 million sq km

(d) 5.28 million sq km

Ans. (b) 3.28 million sq km 1

Q. 4. The southernmost part of India is : [U]

(a) Sonia Point (b) Indira Point

(c) Nehru Point (d) Gandhi Point

Ans. (b) Indira Point 1

Very Short Answer Type Questions (1 mark each)

Q. 1. Define the term 'Subcontinent'. [A]

Ans. A subcontinent is part of a larger continent , made up of a number of countries that form a large mass of land. 1

Answering Tip

- India is often called a subcontinent because it is a distinct landmass, not just a country.

Q. 2. Define the term 'Gulf'. [A]

Ans. A gulf can be described as a large body of water that is almost encircled by land except for a small mouth that is opened out to the ocean. 1

Q. 3. Define the term 'Strait'. [U]

Ans. A strait can be defined as a naturally formed narrow strip of water between two continents, islands or two larger bodies of water. It is used for navigational purposes and is sometimes referred to as a channel when it s found between two land masses. 1

Q. 4. Name any two countries which are included in the Indian subcontinent. [A]

Ans. Pakistan, Nepal , India and Bangladesh are jointly called as Indian Subcontinent. **(Any Two)** 1

Q. 5. What is India's position in the world from the point of view of area? [U]

Ans. The areas point of view India's position is 7th in the world. 1

Q. 6. How much area does India cover? [R]

Ans. 328.7 million sq.Km. 1

Q. 7. What is the latitudinal and longitudinal extent of India? [U]

Ans. The latitudinal and longitudinal extent of india are roughly about 30 degree. 1

Commonly Made Error

- The important role played by the latitudinal and longitudinal extend of a region is ignored.

Answering Tips

- Longitudinal extent influences the climate in the region.
- The latitudinal extent influences the duration of day and night as one moves from south to north.

Q. 8. What is India's length from West to East? [A]

Ans. 2933km is the length from West to East f India. 1

Q. 9. What is India's length from North to South? [U]

Ans. 3214 km is the length from North to South. 1

Q. 10. How does India get separated from Sri Lanka? [A]

Ans. India is separated from Sri Lanka by Palk Strait. 1

Q. 11. Name the northern most neighbour of India. [U]

Ans. China is the northern most neighbour of India. 1

Q. 12. Name the southernmost neighbours of India. [A]

Ans. Maldives and Sri Lanka is the southernmost neighbours of India. 1

Q. 13. Name the eastern most neighbour of India. [U]

Ans. Myanmar and Bangladesh.(Any One) 1

Q. 14. Name the countries with which India shares its boundaries in the North-East. [R]

Ans. Nepal and Bhutan. 1

Q. 15. Name the southernmost part of India. [A]

Ans. The Southernmost part of India is Indira Point. 1

Q. 16. What is the length of landmass of India? [U]

Ans. 15200 km is the length of landmass of India. 1

Short Answer Type Questions (3 marks each)

Q. 1. Why is there a time variation of 2 hours between the easternmost and westernmost part of the country? [A]

Ans. The time variation of 2 hours is due to the fact that the Sun rises two hours earlier in Arunachal Pradesh as compared to Gujarat. This is because the earth is tilted and also it rotates in the East to West direction. So , during rotation , the eastern parts of the world experiences the sun rays earlier as compared to the western parts of the world. **3**

Q. 2. What do you know about the size of India with reference to the world? Which countries are larger than India in terms of size? What do you know about India's location on the globe? [A]

Ans. India with its area of 3.28 million sq. km accounts for 2.4 per cent of the world's land surface area and stands as the seventh largest country in the world.

Russia, China, Canada, Brazil and Australia are larger than India in terms of size.

India lies in the Northern hemisphere. The mainland of India, extends from Kashmir in the north to Kanniyakumari in the south and Arunachal Pradesh in the East to Gujarat in the West. India's territorial limit further extends towards the sea upto 12 nautical miles (about 21.9 km) from the coast. It extends between latitudes 8°4'N(Kanniyakumari, Cape Caverian) and 37°6'N(Indira Point, J&K) and longitudes 68°7'E (Dwarka , Gujarat) and 97°25'E (Arunachal Pradesh).

Q. 3. What do you know about India's neighbours? [R]

Ans. Pakistan, Nepal, Bhutan , Bangladesh along with India form a part of the Indian subcontinent. India is located in the south-central part of the continent of Asia, bordering the Indian ocean and its two arms extending in the form of Bay of Bengal and the Arabian Sea. This maritime location of Peninsular India has provided links to its neighbouring regions through the sea and air routes. Sri Lanka and Maldives are the two island countries located in the Indian Ocean, which are our neighbours. Sri Lanka is separated from India by the Gulf of Mannar and Palk Strait. **3**

Answering Tip

- In total there are 7 countries that India shares its borders with.

Q. 4. What makes the North-South longer by 300 km as compared to East West extend? [R]

Ans. The actual distance measured from North South is 3,214 km and that from East West is 2,933 km. This difference is based on the fact that the distance between two longitudes decreases towards the poles whereas the distance between two latitudesremains the same everywhere. **3**

Long Answer Type Questions (5 marks each)

[AI] **Q. 1. 'The size of India has endowed her with great physical diversity'. Explain.** [A]

Ans. The size of India has endowed her with great physical diversity. Thus, you may appreciate the presence of lofty mountains in the north; large rivers such as Ganga, Brahmaputra, Mahanadi, Krishna, Godavari and Kaveri; green forested hills in the North East and South India; and the vast sandy expanse of Marusthali. Further appreciate that India is bounded by the Himalayas in the north, Hindukush and Sulaiman ranges in the northwest, Purvachal hills in the North-East and by the large expanse of the Indian ocean in the South, it forms a great geographic entity known as the Indian subcontinent. It includes the countries — Pakistan, Nepal, Bhutan, Bangladesh and India.

The Himalayas, together with other ranges, have acted as a formidable physical barrier in the past. Except for a few mountain passes such as the Khyber, the Bolan, the Shipkila, the Nathula, the Bomdila, etc. it was difficult to cross it. It has contributed towards the evolving of a unique regional identity of the Indian subcontinent. Peninsular part of India extends towards the Indian Ocean. This has provided the country with a coastline of 6,100 km in the mainland and 7,517 km in the entire geographical coast of the mainland plus the island groups Andaman and Nicobar located in the Bay of Bengal and the Lakshadweep in the Arabian Sea. Thus India, as a country, is a physically diverse land providing occurrence of varied resources. **5**

Commonly Made Error

- The students are not aware as to why India has different physical features.

Answering Tip

- India is a large landmass formed during different geological periods which has influenced her relief.

Q. 2. What do you know about the extension of our country? [R]

Ans. India lies entirely in the Northern Hemisphere. The mainland of India, extends from Kashmir in the North to Kanyakumari in the South and Arunachal Pradesh in the East to Gujarat in the West.

India's territorial limit further extends towards the sea upto 12 nautical miles (about 21.9 km) from the coast. Our southern boundary extends upto 6°45' N latitude in the Bay of Bengal. the latitudinal and longitudinal extent of India, they are roughly about 30 degrees, whereas the actual distance measured from North to South extremity is 3,214 km, and that from East to West is only 2,933 km.

India has a total area of 32, 87,263 sq.km. India's land length is 15, 200 km and it has a coastline of 6,100 km in the mainland and 7, 517 km in the entire geographical coast of the mainland plus the island groups of Andaman and Nicobar located in the Bay of Bengal and the Lakshadweep in the Arabian Sea. The mainland extends between latitudes 8°4'N(Kanniyakumari, Cape Caverian) and 37°6'N(Indira Point, J&K) and longitudes 68°7'E(Dwarka , Gujarat) and 97°25'E (Arunachal Pradesh).

Q. 3. How does India's size make it physically diverse? U

Ans. The size of India has endowed her with great physical diversity. Thus, you may appreciate the presence of lofty mountains in the north; large rivers such as Ganga, Brahmaputra, Mahanadi, Krishna, Godavari and Kaveri; green forested hills in the North East and South India; and the vast sandy expanse of Marusthali. You may further appreciate that bounded by the Himalayas in the north, Hindukush and Sulaiman ranges in the northwest, Purvachal hills in the North-East and by the large expanse of the Indian ocean in the south, it forms a great geographic entity known as the Indian subcontinent. It includes the countries — Pakistan, Nepal, Bhutan, Bangladesh and India.

The Himalayas, together with other ranges, have acted as a formidable physical barrier in the past. Except for a few mountain passes such as the Khyber, the Bolan, the Shipkila, the Nathula, the Bomdila, etc. it was difficult to cross it. It has contributed towards the evolving of a unique regional identity of the Indian subcontinent. Peninsular part of India extends towards the Indian Ocean. This has provided the country with a coastline of 6,100 km in the mainland and 7,517 km in the entire geographical coast of the mainland plus the island groups Andaman and Nicobar located in the Bay of Bengal and the Lakshadweep in the Arabian Sea. Thus India, as a country, is a physically diverse land providing occurrence of varied resources. 5

Map Work

(5 marks each)

Q. 1. Locate and label the following five features with appropriate symbols on the given political outline map of India:

(i) The Great Plains of North India.

(ii) The Himalayan Mountain.

(iii) The Coastal Plains

(iv) The Great Indian Desert

(v) The Island group

Ans.

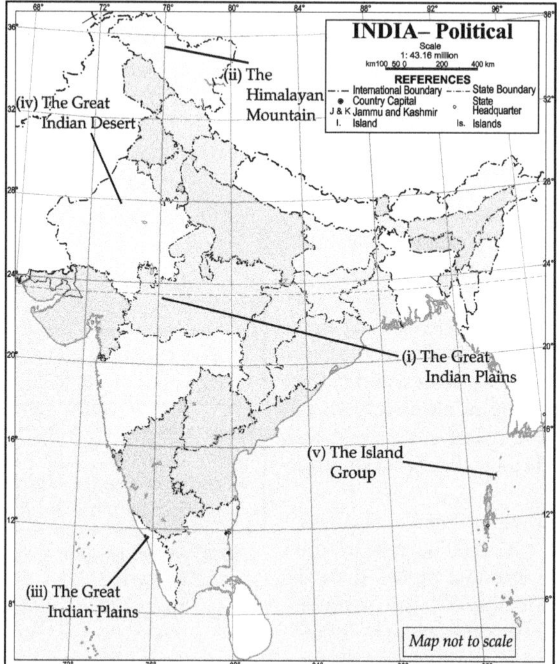

Q. 2. Locate and label the following five features with appropriate symbols on the given political outline map of India.

(i) Locate a state which shares its border with Pakistan.

(ii) Locate a state which shares its border with China.

(iii) Locate a state which shares its border with Bhutan.

(iv) Locate a state which shares its border with Nepal.

(v) Locate a state which shares its border with Bangladesh.

Ans.

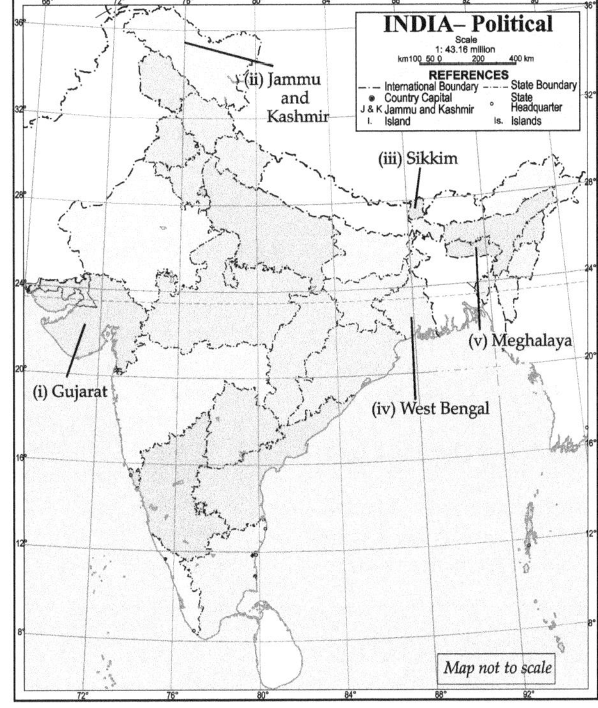

(i) Gujarat
(ii) Jammu and Kashmir
(iii) Sikkim
(iv) Bihar
(v) Meghalaya

(A) Multiple choice questions :

Q. 1. Which one of the following latitudinal extent is relevant for the extent of India's area :

(a) 8°41'N - 35°7'N
(b) 8°4'N - 37°6'N
(c) 8°4'N - 35°6'N
(d) 6°45'N - 37°6'N

Ans. (b) 8°4'N - 37°6'N.

Q. 2. Which one of the following countries shares the longest land frontier with India :

(a) Bangladesh
(b) China
(c) Pakistan
(d) Myanmar

Ans. (a) Bangladesh.

Q. 3. Which one of the following countries is larger in area than India :

(a) China
(b) Egypt
(c) France
(d) Iran

Ans. (a) China.

Q. 4. Which one of the following longitudes is the standard meridian for India :

(a) 69°30'E
(b) 82°30'E
(c) 75°30'E
(d) 90°30'E

Ans. (b) 82°30'E .

(B) Answer the following questions in about 30 words :

Q. 1. Does India need to have more than one standard time? If yes, why do you think so?

Ans. Yes, in my view India needs to have more than one standard time as India has a large longitudinal extent of about 30 °.

(i) When the Sun is still shining in western coast it is already night in northeast so we need two or more time zones to clearly reflect day to day changes.

(ii) Time variation of 2 hours between Easternmost and the westernmost parts of our country. The Sun rises two hours earlier in Arunachal Pradesh as compared to Gujarat because the earth is tilted and also it rotates in East to Wests direction during rotation the Eastern part of the world experiences that sun rays earlier as compared to the western parts of the world.

(iii) Other countries like USA, Canada and Russia have more than one standard time because their longitudinal extend is large. India's longitudinal extend is also 30 °. Therefore it is advisable to use more than one standard time.

Q. 2. What are the implications of India having a long coastline?

Ans. The implications of India having a long coastline is that it helps India establish close contacts with West Asia Africa and Europe from the western coast and with Southeast Asia and East Asia from the Eastern coast. The coastline also provides a strategic central location to India. It also ensures good trade relations with other countries.

Q. 3. How is the latitudinal spread of India advantageous to her?

Ans. The latitudinal spread of India is advantageous as:

(i) The Tropic of Cancer divides India into two parts. Southern part is in the tropical zone while northern part is in the temperate zone.

(ii) It brings climatic diversity in India which has many advantages.

(iii) As we move from Kanyakumari to J&K, the duration of day and night decreases by more than 4 ½ hours.

Q. 4. While the sun rises earlier in the east, say Nagaland and also sets earlier, how do the watches at Kohima and New Delhi show the same time?

Ans. This is because India follows one standard time all over the country. There is a general understanding among the countries of the world to select the standard meridian in multiples of 7°30' of longitude. That is why 82°30' E has been selected as the 'standard meridian' of India. Indian Standard Time is ahead of Greenwich Mean Time by 5 hours and 30 minutes.

❑❑

UNIT-VIII

Physiography

CHAPTER

2 STRUCTURE AND PHYSIOGRAPHY

Syllabus

> - *The Peninsular Block, The Northern and North-Eastern Mountains.*
> - *The Northern Plains*
> - *The Peninsular Plateau*
> - *The Indian Desert,The coastal Plains, The Islands.*

TOPIC-1
The Peninsular Block, The Northern and North-Eastern Mountains

Revision Notes

- Do you know that the Indian plate was to the South of the Equator millions of years ago?
- Over millions of years, this plate broke into many parts and the Australian plate moved towards the South Eastern direction and the Indian plate to the North.
- This northward movement of the Indian plate is still continuing and it has significant consequences on the physical environment of the Indian subcontinent.
- It is primarily through the interplay of these endogenic and exogenic forces and lateral movements of the plates that the present geological structure and geomorphologic processes active in the Indian subcontinent came into existence.
- The Peninsula is formed essentially by a great complex of very ancient gneisses and granites, which constitutes a major part of it.
- As a part of the Indo-Australian Plate, it has been subjected to various vertical movements and block faulting.
- **The Himalayas and Other Peninsular Mountains :** The Himalayas along with other Peninsular mountains are young, weak and flexible in their geological structure unlike the rigid and stable Peninsular Block.
- These mountains are tectonic in origin, dissected by fast-flowing rivers which are in their youthful stage. Various landforms like gorges, V-shaped valleys, rapids, waterfalls, etc., are indicative of this stage.
- **Indo-Ganga-Brahmaputra Plain :** The third geological division of India comprises the plains formed by the river Indus, the Ganga and the Brahmaputra. Originally, it was a geo-synclinal depression which attained its maximum development during the third phase of the Himalayan mountain formation approximately about 64 million years ago.
- **The North and North eastern Mountains :** The North and North eastern Mountains consist of the Himalayas and the North eastern hills . The Himalayas consist of a series of parallel mountain ranges. Some of the important ranges are the Greater Himalayan range, which includes the Great Himalayas and the Trans Himalayan range, the Middle Himalayas and the Shiwalik.
- The approximate length of the Great Himalayan range, also known as the central axial range, is 2,500 km from East to West, and their width varies between 160-400 km from North to South.
- Himalayas are not only the physical barrier, they are also a climatic, drainage and cultural divide. There are large-scale regional variations within the Himalayas. On the basis of relief, alignment of ranges and other geomorphological features, the Himalayas can be divided into the following sub-divisions :

- **Kashmir or Northwestern Himalayas :** It comprise a series of ranges such as the Karakoram, Ladakh, Zaskar and Pir Panjal. The northeastern part of the Kashmir Himalayas is a cold desert, which lies between the Greater Himalayas and the Karakoram ranges. Between the Great Himalayas and the Pir Panjal range, lies the world famous valley of Kashmir and the famous Dal Lake. The Kashmir Himalayas are also famous for Karewa formations, which are useful for the cultivation of Zafran, a local variety of saffron.

➢ Some of the important passes of the region are Zoji La on the Great Himalayas, Banihal on the Pir Panjal, Photu La on the Zaskar and Khardung La on the Ladakh range.

➢ Srinagar, capital city of the state of Jammu and Kashmir is located on the banks of Jhelum river.

➢ Jhelum in the valley of Kashmir is still in its youth stage and yet forms meanders – a typical feature associated with the mature stage in the evolution of fluvial land form.

- **The Himachal and Uttarakhand Himalayas :** This part lies approximately between the Ravi in the West and the Kali (a tributary of Ghaghara) in the East. It is drained by two major river systems of India, *i.e.*, the Indus and the Ganga. Tributaries of the Indus include the river Ravi, the Beas and the Satluj, and the tributaries of Ganga flowing through this region include the Yamuna and the Ghaghara.

➢ The three ranges of Himalayas are prominent in this section also. These are the Great Himalayan range, the Lesser Himalayas (which is locally known as Dhaoladhar in Himachal Pradesh and Nagtibha in Uttaranchal) and the Shiwalik range from the North to the South.

➢ The two distinguishing features of this region from the point of view of physiography are the 'Shiwalik' and 'Dun formations'.

➢ Dehra Dun is the largest of all the duns with an approximate length of 35-45 km and a width of 22-25 km.

- **The Darjiling and Sikkim Himalayas :** They are flanked by Nepal Himalayas in the west and Bhutan Himalayas in the East. It is relatively small but is a most significant part of the Himalayas.

➢ The higher reaches of this region are inhabited by Lepcha tribes while the southern part, particularly the Darjiling Himalayas, has a mixed population of Nepalis, Bengalis and tribals from Central India.

➢ As compared to the other sections of the Himalayas, these along with the Arunachal Himalayas are conspicuous by the absence of the Shiwalik formations.

- **The Arunachal Himalayas :** These extend from the east of the Bhutan Himalayas up to the Diphu pass in the East. The general direction of the mountain range is from South West to North East. Some of the important mountain peaks of the region are Kangtu and Namcha Barwa. Bhramaputra flows through a deep gorge after crossing Namcha Barwa.

➢ An important aspect of the Arunachal Himalayas is the numerous ethnic tribal community inhabiting in these areas. Some of the prominent ones from west to east are the Monpa, Daffla, Abor, Mishmi, Nishi and the Nagas.

➢ Most of these communities practise Jhumming. It is also known as shifting or slash and burn cultivation. Due to rugged terrain inter-valley transportation linkages are nominal. Hence, most of the interactions are carried through the duar region along the Arunachal-Assam border.

- **The Eastern Hills and Mountains :** These are part of the Himalayan mountain system having their general alignment from the north to the south direction. They are known by different local names. In the north, they are known as Patkai Bum, Naga hills, the Manipur hills and in the south as Mizo or Lushai hills.

➢ The Barak is an important river in Manipur and Mizoram. The physiography of Manipur is unique by the presence of a large lake known as 'Loktak' lake at the centre, surrounded by mountains from all sides.

➢ Mizoram which is also known as the 'Molassis basin' which is made up of soft unconsolidated deposits. Most of the rivers in Nagaland form the tributary of the Brahmaputra.

➢ While two rivers of Mizoram and Manipur are the tributaries of the Barak river, which in turn is the tributary of Meghna; the rivers in the eastern part of Manipur are the tributaries of Chindwin, which in turn is a tributary of the Irrawady of Myanmar.

Know the Terms

➢ **Physiography :** Physiography of an area is the outcome of structure, process and the stage of development.

➢ **Geomorphological processes :** The internal and external forces causing changes in the configuration of the surface of the earth are known as geomorphological processes.

➢ **Geo-synclinal depression :** It is a water depression characterized by sedimentation.

➢ **Karewas :** Karewas are the thick deposits of glacial clay and other materials embedded with moraines.

➢ **Central Axial Range :** The approximate length of the Great Himalayas range is known as the central axial range. It is 2,500 km from East to West.

➢ **Dhaoladhar :** The Lesser Himalayas is locally known as the Himachal Pradesh.

➢ **Nagtibha :** The Lesser Himalayas are known as the Nagtibha in Himachal Pradesh.

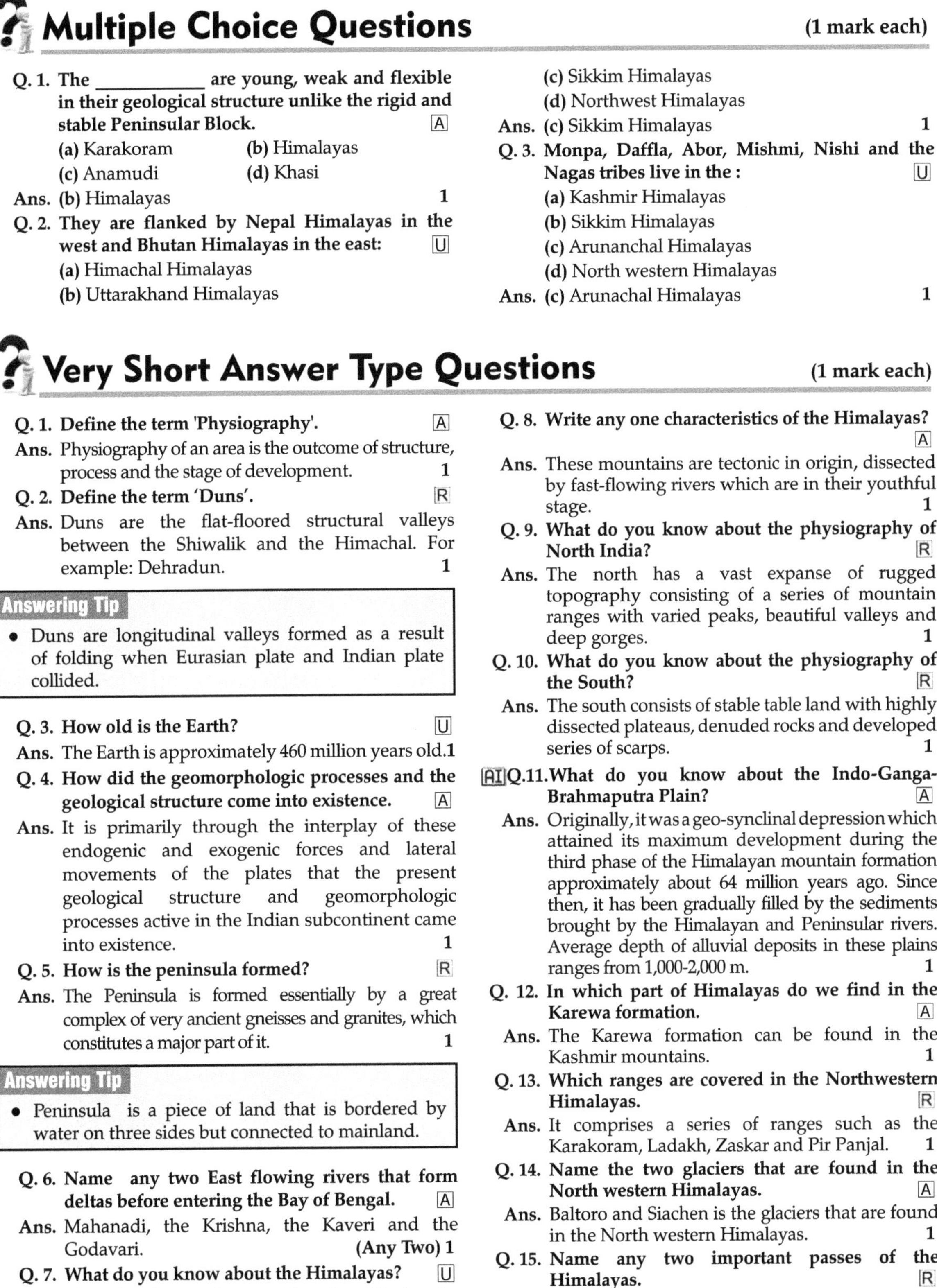

Multiple Choice Questions (1 mark each)

Q. 1. The __________ are young, weak and flexible in their geological structure unlike the rigid and stable Peninsular Block. [A]

(a) Karakoram (b) Himalayas

(c) Anamudi (d) Khasi

Ans. (b) Himalayas 1

Q. 2. They are flanked by Nepal Himalayas in the west and Bhutan Himalayas in the east: [U]

(a) Himachal Himalayas

(b) Uttarakhand Himalayas

(c) Sikkim Himalayas

(d) Northwest Himalayas

Ans. (c) Sikkim Himalayas 1

Q. 3. Monpa, Daffla, Abor, Mishmi, Nishi and the Nagas tribes live in the : [U]

(a) Kashmir Himalayas

(b) Sikkim Himalayas

(c) Arunanchal Himalayas

(d) North western Himalayas

Ans. (c) Arunachal Himalayas 1

Very Short Answer Type Questions (1 mark each)

Q. 1. Define the term 'Physiography'. [A]

Ans. Physiography of an area is the outcome of structure, process and the stage of development. 1

Q. 2. Define the term 'Duns'. [R]

Ans. Duns are the flat-floored structural valleys between the Shiwalik and the Himachal. For example: Dehradun. 1

Answering Tip

- Duns are longitudinal valleys formed as a result of folding when Eurasian plate and Indian plate collided.

Q. 3. How old is the Earth? [U]

Ans. The Earth is approximately 460 million years old.1

Q. 4. How did the geomorphologic processes and the geological structure come into existence. [A]

Ans. It is primarily through the interplay of these endogenic and exogenic forces and lateral movements of the plates that the present geological structure and geomorphologic processes active in the Indian subcontinent came into existence. 1

Q. 5. How is the peninsula formed? [R]

Ans. The Peninsula is formed essentially by a great complex of very ancient gneisses and granites, which constitutes a major part of it. 1

Answering Tip

- Peninsula is a piece of land that is bordered by water on three sides but connected to mainland.

Q. 6. Name any two East flowing rivers that form deltas before entering the Bay of Bengal. [A]

Ans. Mahanadi, the Krishna, the Kaveri and the Godavari. **(Any Two) 1**

Q. 7. What do you know about the Himalayas? [U]

Ans. The Himalayas along with other Peninsular mountains are young, weak and flexible in their geological structure unlike the rigid and stable Peninsular Block. 1

Q. 8. Write any one characteristics of the Himalayas? [A]

Ans. These mountains are tectonic in origin, dissected by fast-flowing rivers which are in their youthful stage. 1

Q. 9. What do you know about the physiography of North India? [R]

Ans. The north has a vast expanse of rugged topography consisting of a series of mountain ranges with varied peaks, beautiful valleys and deep gorges. 1

Q. 10. What do you know about the physiography of the South? [R]

Ans. The south consists of stable table land with highly dissected plateaus, denuded rocks and developed series of scarps. 1

[AI] **Q.11. What do you know about the Indo-Ganga-Brahmaputra Plain?** [A]

Ans. Originally, it was a geo-synclinal depression which attained its maximum development during the third phase of the Himalayan mountain formation approximately about 64 million years ago. Since then, it has been gradually filled by the sediments brought by the Himalayan and Peninsular rivers. Average depth of alluvial deposits in these plains ranges from 1,000-2,000 m. 1

Q. 12. In which part of Himalayas do we find in the Karewa formation. [A]

Ans. The Karewa formation can be found in the Kashmir mountains. 1

Q. 13. Which ranges are covered in the Northwestern Himalayas. [R]

Ans. It comprises a series of ranges such as the Karakoram, Ladakh, Zaskar and Pir Panjal. 1

Q. 14. Name the two glaciers that are found in the North western Himalayas. [A]

Ans. Baltoro and Siachen is the glaciers that are found in the North western Himalayas. 1

Q. 15. Name any two important passes of the Himalayas. [R]

Ans. Some of the important passes of the region are Zoji La on the Great Himalayas, Banihal on the Pir Panjal, Photu La on the Zaskar and Khardung La on the Ladakh range. **(Any Two) 1**

Q. 16. What do you know about the location of the Himachal and Uttaranchal Himalayas? U

Ans. This part lies approximately between the Ravi in the west and the Kali (a tributary of Ghaghara) in the east. 1

Q. 17. Name the two major drainage systems of the Himachal and Uttaranchal Himalayas. A

Ans. It is drained by two major river systems of India, *i.e.*, the Indus and the Ganga. 1

Q. 18. What are the two distinguishing features of the Himachal and Uttaranchal Himalayas? U

Ans. The two distinguishing features of this region from the point of view of physiography are the 'Shiwalik' and 'Dun formations'. 1

Q. 19. Name one important feature of the Darjiling and Sikkim Himalayas. R

Ans. The most important feature is the 'duar formations', which have also been used for the development of tea gardens. 1

Answering Tip

- Duar formations are also known for its wildlife sanctuaries where one can spot herds of deer, one-horned rhinos, elephants, guars and reptiles.

Q. 20. What do you know about the location of the Arunachal Himalayas? U

Ans. These extend from the East of the Bhutan Himalayas up to the Diphu pass in the East. 1

Q. 21. Name any two important peaks the Arunachal Himalayas. A

Ans. Some of the important mountain peaks of the region are Kangtu and Namcha Barwa. 1

Answering Tip

- The Arunachal Himalayas form the eastern frontier of the Eastern Himalayas.

Q. 22. The Eastern Hills and Mountains are known by which names. R

Ans. In the north, they are known as Patkai Bum, Naga hills, the Manipur hills and in the south as Mizo or Lushai hills. **(Any Two)** 1

Q. 23. The Lesser Himalayas are called by what name in Uttaranchal. R

Ans. Nagtia. 1

Q. 24. What is the East-West length of greater Himalayas. A

Ans. 2500km is the East-West length of greater Himalayas. 1

Short Answer Type Questions (3 marks each)

AI **Q. 1. Into how many geological divisions can India be divided?** A

Ans. India can be divided into three geological divisions :

(i) The Peninsular Block : The northern boundary of the Peninsular Block may be taken as an irregular line running from Kachchh along the western flank of the Aravali Range near Delhi and then roughly parallel to the Yamuna and the Ganga as far as the Rajmahal Hills and the Ganga delta. Apart from these, the Karbi Anglong and the Meghalaya Plateau in the North East and Rajasthan in the West are also extensions of this block.

(ii) The Himalayas and other Peninsular Mountains : The Himalayas along with other Peninsular mountains are young, weak and flexible in their geological structure unlike the rigid and stable Peninsular Block. Consequently, they are still subjected to the interplay of exogenic and endogenic forces, resulting in the development of faults, folds and thrust plains. These mountains are tectonic in origin, dissected by fast-flowing rivers which are in their youthful stage.

(iii) Indo-Ganga-Brahmaputra Plain : The third geological division of India comprises the plains formed by the river Indus, the Ganga and the Brahmaputra. Originally, it was a geo-synclinal depression which attained its maximum development during the third phase of the Himalayan mountain formation approximately about 64 million years ago. Since then, it has been gradually filled by the sediments brought by the Himalayan and Peninsular rivers. Average depth of alluvial deposits in these plains ranges from 1,000-2,000 m. 3

Q. 2. What do you know about the Sikkim and Darjeeling Himalayas? A

Ans. The Sikkim and Darjeeling Himalayas :

(i) They are flanked by Nepal Himalayas in the West and Bhutan Himalayas in the East. It is relatively small but is a most significant part of the Himalayas.

(ii) The higher reaches of this region are inhabited by Lepcha tribes while the southern part, particularly the Darjiling Himalayas, has a mixed population of Nepalis, Bengalis and tribals from Central India.

(iii) In place of the Shiwaliks here, the 'duar formations' are important, which have also been used for the development of tea gardens. Sikkim and Darjiling Himalayas are also known for their scenic beauty and rich flora and fauna, particularly various types of orchids. 3

Q. 3. Write a note on the Arunachal Himalayas? R

Ans. The Arunachal Himalayas:

(i) These extend from the East of the Bhutan Himalayas up to the Diphu pass in the East. The general direction of the mountain range is from Southwest to Northeast.

(ii) Some of the important mountain peaks of the region are Kangtu and Namcha Barwa.

(iii) An important aspect of the Arunachal Himalayas is the numerous ethnic tribal community inhabiting in these areas. Some of the prominent ones from West to East are the Monpa, Daffla, Abor, Mishmi, Nishi and the Nagas. 3

Answering Tip

- Arunachal Himalayas are endowed with wide topographical variations, vegetation and wild life.

Long Answer Type Questions

(5 marks each)

Q. 1. The Himalayas can be sub-divided into how many divisions? Explain each in detail? R

Ans. On the basis of relief, alignment of ranges and other geomorphological features, the Himalayas can be divided into the following sub-divisions :

(i) Kashmir or Northwestern Himalayas : It comprise a series of ranges such as the Karakoram, Ladakh, Zaskar and Pir Panjal. The northeastern part of the Kashmir Himalayas is a cold desert, which lies between the Greater Himalayas and the Karakoram ranges. Important glaciers of South Asia such as the Baltoro and Siachen are also found in this region. The Kashmir Himalayas are also famous for Karewa formations, which are useful for the cultivation of Zafran, a local variety of saffron.

Some of the important passes of the region are Zoji La on the Great Himalayas, Banihal on the Pir Panjal, Photu La on the Zaskar and Khardung La on the Ladakh range. Some of the important fresh lakes such as Dal and Wular and salt water lakes such as Pangong Tso and Tso Moriri are also in this region.

(ii) The Himachal and Uttarakhand Himalayas : This part lies approximately between the Ravi in the west and the Kali (a tributary of Ghaghara) in the east. It is drained by two major river systems of India, *i.e.*, the Indus and the Ganga. Tributaries of the Indus include the river Ravi, the Beas and the Satluj, and the tributaries of Ganga flowing through this region include the Yamuna and the Ghaghara.

The two distinguishing features of this region from the point of view of physiography are the 'Shiwalik' and 'Dun formations'. Some important duns located in this region are the Chandigarh-Kalka dun, Nalagarh dun, Dehra Dun, Harike dun and the Kota dun, etc. Dehra Dun is the largest of all the duns with an approximate length of 35-45 km and a width of 22-25 km.

(iii) The Darjiling and Sikkim Himalayas : They are flanked by Nepal Himalayas in the West and Bhutan Himalayas in the East. It is relatively small but is a most significant part of the Himalayas. The higher reaches of this region are inhabited by Lepcha tribes while the southern part, particularly the Darjiling Himalayas, has a mixed population of Nepalis, Bengalis and tribals from Central India.

In place of the Shiwaliks here, the 'duar formations' are important, which have also been used for the development of tea gardens. Sikkim and Darjiling Himalayas are also known for their scenic beauty and rich flora and fauna, particularly various types of orchids.

(iv) The Arunachal Himalayas : These extend from the East of the Bhutan Himalayas up to the Diphu pass in the East. The general direction of the mountain range is from the Southwest to Northeast. Some of the important mountain peaks of the region are Kangtu and Namcha Barwa. An important aspect of the Arunachal Himalayas is the numerous ethnic tribal community inhabiting in these areas. Some of the prominent ones from west to east are the Monpa, Daffla, Abor, Mishmi, Nishi and the Nagas.

Due to the rugged topography , the inter-valley transportation linkages are nominal. Hence, most of the interactions are carried through the duar region along the Arunachal-Assam border.

(v) The Eastern Hills and Mountains : These are part of the Himalayan mountain system having their general alignment from the north to the south direction. They are known by different local names. In the North, they are known as Patkai Bum, Naga hills, the Manipur hills and in the south as Mizo or Lushai hills. These are low hills, inhabited by numerous tribal groups practising Jhum cultivation.

The Barak is an important river in Manipur and Mizoram. The physiography of Manipur is unique by the presence of a large lake known as 'Loktak' lake at the centre, surrounded by mountains from all sides. Mizoram which is also known as the 'Molassis basin' which is made up of soft unconsolidated deposits. 5

Q. 2. Write a detailed note on Kashmir or North-Western Himalayas? A

Ans. Kashmir or the North-Western Himalayas:

(i) It comprises a series of ranges such as the Karakoram, Ladakh, Zaskar and Pir Panjal. The northeastern part of the Kashmir Himalayas is a cold desert, which lies between the Greater Himalayas and the Karakoram ranges.

(ii) Important glaciers of South Asia such as the Baltoro and Siachen are also found in this region. The Kashmir Himalayas are also famous for Karewa formations, which are useful for the cultivation of Zafran, a local variety of saffron.

(iii) Some of the important passes of the region are Zoji La on the Great Himalayas, Banihal on the Pir Panjal, Photu La on the Zaskar and Khardung La on the Ladakh range. Some of the important fresh lakes such as Dal and Wular and salt water lakes such as Pangong Tso and Tso Moriri are also in this region.

(iv) The Kashmir and north western Himalayas are well-known for their scenic beauty and picturesque landscape. The landscape of Himalayas is a major source of attraction for adventure tourists. Srinagar, capital city of the state of Jammu and Kashmir is located on the banks of Jhelum river. Dal Lake in Srinagar presents an interesting physical feature. Jhelum in the valley of Kashmir is still in its youth stage and yet forms meanders – a typical feature associated with the mature stage in the evolution of fluvial land form.

(v) The southernmost part of this region consists of longitudinal valleys known as 'duns'. Jammu dun and Pathankot dun are important examples.

(1 × 5 = 5)

Commonly Made Error

- The important role played by the Kashmir Himalayas is generally ignored.

Answering Tip

- The Kashmir Himalayas act as a barrier to cold winds, they give tropical touch and beauty to the land of India. They block the rain bearing monsoon winds from Arabian Sea and Bay of Bengal. They protect India from severe cold blowing from North Asia.

AI **Q. 3. How are Arunachal, Himachal , Purvachal and Uttaranchal Himalayas different from each other?** R

Ans. Arunachal Himalayas:

(i) These extend from the East of the Bhutan Himalayas up to the Diphu Pass in the East.

(ii) Some of the important mountain peaks of the region are Kangtu and Namcha Barwa.

(iii) These ranges are dissected by fast-flowing rivers from the North to the South, forming deep gorges.

(iv) Brahmaputra flows through a deep gorge after crossing Namcha Barwa.

(v) An important aspect of the Arunachal Himalayas is the numerous ethnic tribal community inhabiting in these areas. Some of the prominent ones from West to East are the Monpa, Daffla, Abor, Mishmi, Nishi and the Nagas.

Purvachal Himalayas :

(i) General alignment from the North to South direction.

(ii) They are known by different local names. In the north, they are known as Patkai Bum, Naga hills, the Manipur hills and in the south as Mizo or Lushai hills.

(iii) These are low hills, inhabited by numerous tribal groups practising Jhum cultivation.

(iv) The Barak is an important river in Manipur and Mizoram.

(v) Mizoram which is also known as the 'Molassis basin' which is made up of soft unconsolidated deposits.

The Himachal and Uttarakhand Himalayas :

(i) This part lies approximately between the Ravi in the west and the Kali (a tributary of Ghaghara) in the east.

(ii) It is drained by two major river systems of India, *i.e.*, the Indus and the Ganga. Tributaries of the Indus include the river Ravi, the Beas and the Satluj, and the tributaries of Ganga flowing through this region include the Yamuna and the Ghaghara.

(iii) The two distinguishing features of this region from the point of view of physiography are the 'Shiwalik' and 'Dun formations'.

(iv) In the Great Himalayan range, the valleys are mostly inhabited by the Bhotia's. These are nomadic groups who migrate to 'Bugyals' (the summer glasslands in the higher reaches) during summer months and return to the valleys during winters.

(v) The famous 'Valley of flowers' is also situated in this region. **5**

TOPIC-2
The Northern Plains

Revision Notes

- The Northern Plains are formed by the alluvial deposits brought by the rivers – the Indus, the Ganga and the Brahmaputra.
- These plains extend approximately 3,200 km from the East to the West. The average width of these plains varies between 150-300 km.
- The maximum depth of alluvium deposits varies between 1,000-2,000 m. From the North to the South, these can be divided into three major zones : the Bhabar, the Tarai and the alluvial plains. The alluvial plains can be further divided into the Khadar and the Bhangar.
- Bhabar is a narrow belt ranging between 8-10 km parallel to the Shiwalik foothills at the break-up of the slope.
- South of the Bhabar is the Tarai belt, with an approximate width of 10-20 km where most of the streams and rivers re-emerge without having any properly demarcated channel, thereby, creating marshy and swampy conditions known as the Tarai.

- The Brahmaputra plains are known for their riverine islands and sand bars. Most of these areas are subjected to periodic floods and shifting river courses forming braided streams.
- Otherwise, this is a featureless plain with a general elevation of 50-150 m above the mean sea level. The states of Haryana and Delhi form a water divide between the Indus and the Ganga river systems.
- The river valley plains have a fertile alluvial soil cover which supports a variety of crops like wheat, rice, sugarcane and jute, and hence, supports a large population.

Know the Terms

- **Indo-Ganga-Brahmaputra Plain :** It is a geological division of India that comprises the plains formed by the river Indus, the Ganga and the Brahmaputra.
- **Bhabar :** It is a narrow belt ranging between 8-10 km parallel to the Shiwalik foothills at the break-up of the slope.
- **Khadar :** The South of Tarai is a belt consisting of new alluvial deposits is known as khadar.
- **Tarai :** South of the Bhabar is the Tarai belt, with an approximate width of 10-20 km where most of the streams and rivers re-emerge without having any properly demarcated channel, thereby, creating marshy and swampy conditions known as the Tarai.

Multiple Choice Questions (1 mark each)

Q. 1. They are formed by the alluvial deposits brought by the rivers – the Indus, the Ganga and the Brahmaputra: A

(a) Brahmaputra Plains
(b) The Northern Plains
(c) Ganga Plains
(d) Indo Plains

Ans. (b) The Northern Plains 1

Q. 2. Khadar and the Bhangar are divisions of : U

(a) Alluvial plains
(b) Ganga plains
(c) Brahmaputra plains
(d) Northern plains

Ans. (a) Alluvial plains 1

Very Short Answer Type Questions (1 mark each)

Q. 1. What is Bangar? A

Ans. The old alluvial soil is called bangar. 1

Q. 2. What is khadar? U

Ans. The new alluvial soil is known as khadar. 1

Q. 3. What is Bhabar? A

Ans. Bhabar is a narrow belt ranging between 8-10 km parallel to the Shiwalik foothills at the break up of the slope. As a result of this, the streams and rivers coming from the mountains deposit heavy materials of rocks and boulders , and at times, disappear in this zone. 1

Q. 4. What is Tarai? R

Ans. South of the Bhabar is the Tarai belt, with an approximate width of 10-20 km where most of the streams and rivers re-emerge without having any properly demarcated channel, thereby, creating marshy and swampy conditions known as the Tarai. 1

Answering Tip

- Tarai is characterized by tall grasslands, scrub Savannah, sal forests and clay rich swamps.

Q. 5. When and how was the Indo-Ganga-Brahmaputra plain was formed? R

Ans. Indo-Ganga-Brahmaputra Plain is a geological division of India that comprises the plains formed by the river Indus, the Ganga and the Brahmaputra. Originally , it was a geo-synclinal depression which attained its maximum development during the third phase of the Himalayan mountain formation approximately about 64 million years ago. Since then, it has been gradually filled by the sediments brought by the Himalayan and Peninsular rivers. 1

Q. 6. The Northern Plains are formed by the alluvial deposits of which rivers? R

Ans. The Northern Plains are formed by the alluvial deposits brought by the rivers – the Indus, the Ganga and the Brahmaputra. 1

Q. 7. What types of crops are grown in the river valley plains? U

Ans. The river valley plains have a fertile alluvial soil cover which supports a variety of crops like wheat, rice, sugarcane and jute. 1

Q. 8. The alluvial plains can be divided into how many types? R

Ans. The alluvial plains can be further divided into the Khadar and the Bhangar. 1

Q. 9. What are the Brahmaputra plains famous for? A

Ans. The Brahmaputra plains are known for their riverine islands and sand bars. 1

Q. 10. What are North-western Himalayas? R

Ans. It comprises a series of ranges such as the Karakoram, Ladakh, Zaskar and Pir Panjal. The North- eastern part of the Kashmir Himalayas is a cold desert, which lies between the Greater Himalayas and the Karakoram ranges. 1

Short Answer Type Questions (3 marks each)

Q. 1. Dfferentiate between Bhabar and Tarai. R

Ans. Ref to Long Ans 1. 3

Q. 2. Differentiate between Bhangar and Khadar. R

Ans. Ref to Long Ans 2. 3

Q. 3. What is the relevance of the Northern Plains for our country? U

Ans. The Northern Plains are very relevant for our country because :

(i) It is made up of alluvial deposits brought by rivers due to which it is very fertile.

(ii) It is plain, therefore, it is easier to develop means of transport and communication in this region.

(iii) It is suitable for human habitation. 3

Long Answer Type Questions (5 marks each)

Q. 1. How is Bhabar different from Tarai? R

Ans.

S.No.	Bhabar	Tarai
1.	It lies along the foot of Shivalik from Indus to Tista.	It lies to the South of Bhabar and runs parallel to it.
2.	It is 8 to 16 km wide.	It is 20 to 30 km wide.
3.	It comprises of pebbles studded rocks in the shape of porous bed.	It is composed of finer alluvial particles and is covered by forests.
4.	Due to the porosity of rocks the stream disappear and flow underground.	The underground streams of Bhabar reappear here giving rise to a wet marshian.
5.	It is not suitable for agriculture.	It is reclaimed for agriculture purpose.

(1 × 5 = 5)

Q. 2. How is Bhangar different from Khadar? R

Ans.

S.No.	Bhangar	Khadar
1.	It is a highland composed of old alluvium.	It's a lowland composed of new alluvium.
2.	It is always above the level of flood plains.	It is flooded almost every year.
3.	It comprises of canvanious nodules.	It comprises of clay soil which is normally fertile.
4.	It is not much suited for agriculture.	It is suited for agriculture. Intensive agriculture is practiced.
5.	It is known as dhaya in Punjab.	It is known as bate in Punjab.

(1 × 5 = 5)

Answering Tip

- Bhangar soil is not as fertile as the khadar soil.

AI **Q. 3. Write a detailed note on the Northern Plains.** A

Ans. The Northern Plains are formed by the alluvial deposits brought by the rivers – the Indus, the Ganga and the Brahmaputra. These plains extend approximately 3,200 km from the East to the West. The average width of these plains varies between 150-300 km. The maximum depth of alluvium deposits varies between 1,000-2,000 m. From the North to the South, these can be divided into three major zones: the Bhabar, the Tarai and the alluvial plains.

Bhabar : Bhabar is a narrow belt ranging between 8-10 km parallel to the Shiwalik foothills at the break-up of the slope. As a result of this, the streams and rivers coming from the mountains deposit heavy materials of rocks and boulders, and at times, disappear in this zone.

Tarai : Its approximate width is 20-30km where most of the streams and river re-emerge without having any properly demarcated channel, thereby, creating marshy and swampy condition known as the Tarai. It has a luxurious growth of natural vegetation and houses a varied wild life.

Alluvial Plains : These plains have characteristic features of mature stage of fluvial erosional and depositional landforms such as sand bars, meanders, oxbow lakes and braided channels. The Brahmaputra plains are known for their riverine islands and sand bars. Most of these areas are subjected to periodic floods and shifting river courses forming braided streams. The mouths of these mighty rivers also form some of the largest deltas of the world, for example, the famous Sunderbans delta.

This is a featureless plain with a general elevation of 50-150 m above the mean sea level. The states of Haryana and Delhi form a water divide between the Indus and the Ganga river systems. As opposed to this, the Brahmaputra river flows from the northeast to the southwest direction before it takes an almost 90° southward turn at Dhubri before it enters into Bangladesh. 5

TOPIC-3
The Peninsular Plateau

Revision Notes

- Rising from the height of 150 m above the river plains up to an elevation of 600-900 m is the irregular triangle known as the Peninsular Plateau.
- The Peninsular India is made up of a series of patland plateaus such as the Hazaribagh plateau, the Palamu plateau, the Ranchi plateau, the Malwa plateau, the Coimbatore plateau and the Karnataka plateau, etc.
- This is one of the oldest and the most stable landmass of India. The general elevation of the plateau is from the West to the East, which is also proved by the pattern of the flow of rivers.
- Some of the important physiographic features of this region are tors, block mountains, rift valleys, spurs, bare rocky structures, series of hummocky hills and wall-like quartzite dykes offering natural sites for water storage. The western and northwestern part of the plateau has an emphatic presence of black soil.
- On the basis of the prominent relief features, the Peninsular Plateau can be divided into three broad groups :
  - **The Deccan Plateau :** This is bordered by the Western Ghats in the West, Eastern Ghats in the East and the Satpura, Maikal range and Mahadeo hills in the North. Western Ghats are locally known by different names such as Sahyadri in Maharashtra, Nilgiri hills in Karnataka and Tamil Nadu and Anaimalai hills and Cardamom hills in Kerala.
- Western Ghats are comparatively higher in elevation and more continuous than the Eastern Ghats.
- Their average elevation is about 1,500 m with the height increasing from North to South.
- Most of the Peninsular rivers have their origin in the Western Ghats. Eastern Ghats comprising the discontinuous and low hills are highly eroded by the rivers such as the Mahanadi, the Godavari, the Krishna, the Kaveri, etc.
- Some of the important ranges include the Javadi Hills, the Palconda Range, the Nallamala Hills, the Mahendragiri Hills, etc. The Eastern and the Western Ghats meet each other at the Nilgiri hills.
  - **The Central Highlands :** They are bounded to the west by the Aravali range. The Satpura range is formed by a series of scarped plateaus on the South, generally at an elevation varying between 600-900 m above the mean sea level.
- The extension of the Peninsular Plateau can be seen as far as Jaisalmer in the West, where it has been covered by the longitudinal sand ridges and crescent-shaped sand dunes called barchans.
- This region has undergone metamorphic processes in its geological history, which can be corroborated by the presence of metamorphic rocks such as marble, slate, gneiss, etc.
- The general elevation of the Central Highlands ranges between 700-1,000 m above the mean sea level and it slopes towards the North and northeastern directions.
- Banas is the only significant tributary of the river Chambal that originates from the Aravalli in the West. An eastern extension of the Central Highland is formed by the Rajmahal Hills, to the South of which lies a large reserve of mineral resources in the Chotanagpur Plateau.
  - **The Northeastern Plateau :** In fact it is an extension of the main Peninsular Plateau. It is believed that due to the force exerted by the northeastward movement of the Indian Plate at the time of the Himalayan origin, a huge fault was created between the Rajmahal Hills and the Meghalaya Plateau.
- Today, the Meghalaya and Karbi Anglong Plateau stand detached from the main Peninsular Block.
- The Meghalaya Plateau is further sub-divided into three : **(i)** The Garo Hills; **(ii)** The Khasi Hills; **(iii)** The Jaintia Hills, named after the tribal groups inhabiting this region.
- An extension of this is also seen in the Karbi Anglong Hills of Assam.
- The Meghalaya Plateau has a highly eroded surface. Cherrapunji displays a bare rocky surface devoid of any permanent vegetation cover.

Know the Terms

- **Peninsular Plateau :** Rising from the height of 150 m above the river plains up to an elevation of 600-900 m is the irregular triangle known as the Peninsular Plateau.
- **Central highlands :** They are bound to the West by the Aravali Range.
- **Satpura range :** They are formed by a series of scraped plateaus on the South , generally at an elevation varying between 600-900m above the mean sea level.

Multiple Choice Questions

(1 mark each)

Q. 1. The largest plateau in western and southern India is the: U

(a) Deccan Plateau **(b)** Sahyadri Plateau
(c) Nilgiri Plateau **(d)** Central Plateau

Ans. (a) Deccan Plateau 1

Q. 2. A bare rocky surface devoid of any permanent vegetation cover is displayed in : U

(a) Satpura range **(b)** Central Highlands
(c) Cherrapunji **(d)** Ghats

Ans. (c) Cherrapunji 1

Very Short Answer Type Questions

(1 mark each)

Q. 1. What is Peninsular Plateau? R

Ans. Rising from the height of 150 m above the river plains up to an elevation of 600-900 m is the irregular triangle known as the Peninsular Plateau. 1

AI **Q. 2. Name any two important physiographic features of the Peninsular Plateau.** A

Ans. Some of the important physiographic features of this region are tors, block mountains, rift valleys, spurs, bare rocky structures, series of hummocky hills and wall-like quartzite dykes offering natural sites for water storage. **(Any Two) 1**

Q. 3. On the basis of the relief features, the Peninsular Plateau can be divided into how many groups? R

Ans. On the basis of the prominent relief features, the Peninsular Plateau can be divided into three broad groups: **(i)** The Deccan Plateau **(ii)** The Central Highlands **(iii)** The Northeastern Plateau. 1

Q. 4. Give any two names of the Western Ghats. A

Ans. Western Ghats are locally known by different names such as Sahyadri in Maharashtra, Nilgiri hills in Karnataka and Tamil Nadu and Anaimalai hills and Cardamom hills in Kerala. 1

Q. 5. What is the height of the Western Ghats? R

Ans. Their average elevation is about 1,500 m with the height increasing from north to south. 1

Q. 6. Which is the highest peak of the Peninsular Plateau? U

Ans. Anaimudi, located on the Anaimalai hills of the Western Ghats followed by Dodabetta (2,637 m) on the Nilgiri hills is the highest peak of the Peninsular Plateau. 1

Q. 7. Name any two important ranges of the Deccan Plateau. A

Ans. Some of the important ranges include the Javadi hills, the Palconda range, the Nallamala hills, the Mahendragiri hills, etc. 1

Answering Tip

- The Deccan Plateau lies between three mountain ranges and extends over eight Indian states.

Q. 8. Where do the Eastern and the Western Ghats meet? U

Ans. They meet at the Nilgiri Hills. 1

Q. 9. What is the general elevation of the Central Highlands? A

Ans. The general elevation of the Central Highlands ranges between 700-1,000 m above the mean sea level and it slopes towards the north and northeastern directions. 1

Q. 10. The Meghalaya Plateau can be sub-divided into how many parts? R

Ans. The Meghalaya Plateau is further sub-divided into three: **(i)** The Garo Hills; **(ii)** The Khasi Hills; **(iii)** The Jaintia Hills, named after the tribal groups inhabiting this region . 1

Commonly Made Error

- The students are not aware of the highest peak in the Meghalaya Plateau.

Answering Tip

- The highest peak in the Meghalaya Plateau is the Shillong Peak.

Q. 11. Give sub-divisions of the Meghalaya Plateau. U

Ans. The sub-divisions of the Meghalaya Plateau are:

(i) The Garo Hills
(ii) The Khasi Hills
(iii) The Jaintia Hills 1

Q. 12. Give any two features of the Chotta Nagpur Plateau. A

Ans. (i) It is rich in mineral resources like coal, iron ore, limestone and uranium.

(ii) This area receives maximum rainfall from the south-west monsoon. 1

Short Answer Type Questions (3 marks each)

Q. 1. Write the features of Central Highlands. [A]

Ans. The features of the Central Highlands are :

(i) They are bounded to the west by the Aravali range. The Satpura range is formed by a series of scarped plateaus on the South, generally at an elevation varying between 600-900 m above the mean sea level. This forms the northernmost boundary of the Deccan plateau.

(ii) This region has undergone metamorphic processes in its geological history, which can be corroborated by the presence of metamorphic rocks such as marble, slate, gneiss, etc.

(iii) The general elevation of the Central Highlands ranges between 700-1,000 m above the mean sea level and it slopes towards the North and northeastern directions. 3

Answering Tips

- The Central Highlands of India are a biogeographic region in India formed by the disjunct ranges of the Satpura and Vindhya Hills.

Q. 2. Write a note on the features of the Peninsular Plateau. [R]

Ans. The various features of the Peninsular Plateau are:

(i) Rising from the height of 150 m above the river plains up to an elevation of 600-900 m is the irregular triangle known as the Peninsular plateau.

(ii) The Peninsular India is made up of a series of patland plateaus such as the Hazaribagh plateau, the Palamu plateau, the Ranchi plateau, the Malwa plateau, the Coimbatore plateau and the Karnataka plateau, etc. This is one of the oldest and the most stable landmass of India.

(iii) Some of the important physiographic features of this region are tors, block mountains, rift valleys, spurs, bare rocky structures, series of hummocky hills and wall-like quartzite dykes offering natural sites for water storage. The western and northwestern part of the plateau has an emphatic presence of black soil. 3

Q. 3. Write a note on the Deccan Plateau. [U]

Ans. The Deccan Plateau:

(i) This is bordered by the Western Ghats in the west, Eastern Ghats in the east and the Satpura, Maikal range and Mahadeo hills in the north.

(ii) Western Ghats are locally known by different names such as Sahyadri in Maharashtra, Nilgiri hills in Karnataka and Tamil Nadu and Anaimalai hills and Cardamom hills in Kerala.

(iii) Some of the important ranges include the Javadi hills, the Palconda range, the Nallamala hills, the Mahendragiri hills, etc. 3

Answering Tip

- The Peninsular plateau is a tableland. It is composed of the oldest rocks because it was formed from the drifted part of the Gondwana land. Broad and shallow valleys and rounded hills are the characteristic features of this plateau.

[AI] **Q. 4. On the basis of the prominent relief features, the Peninsular plateau can be divided into how many groups.** [A]

Ans. On the basis of the prominent relief features, the Peninsular plateau can be divided into three groups :

(i) The Deccan Plateau : This is bordered by the Western Ghats in the West, Eastern Ghats in the East and the Satpura, Maikal range and Mahadeo hills in the North. Western Ghats are locally known by different names such as Sahyadri in Maharashtra, Nilgiri hills in Karnataka and Tamil Nadu and Anaimalai hills and Cardamom hills in Kerala. Some of the important ranges include the Javadi hills, the Palconda range, the Nallamala hills, the Mahendragiri hills, etc. The Eastern and the Western Ghats meet each other at the Nilgiri hills.

(ii) The Central Highlands : They are bounded to the West by the Aravali range. The Satpura range is formed by a series of scarped plateaus on the South, generally at an elevation varying between 600-900 m above the mean sea level. This region has undergone metamorphic processes in its geological history, which can be corroborated by the presence of metamorphic rocks such as marble, slate, gneiss, etc.

(iii) The Northeastern Plateau : In fact it is an extension of the main Peninsular Plateau. It is believed that due to the force exerted by the northeastward movement of the Indian Plate at the time of the Himalayan origin, a huge fault was created between the Rajmahal Hills and the Meghalaya Plateau. The Meghalaya Plateau is further sub-divided into three : **(i)** The Garo Hills; **(ii)** The Khasi Hills; **(iii)** The Jaintia Hills, named after the tribal groups inhabiting this region. 3

Long Answer Type Questions (5 marks each)

Q. 1. Differentiate between the Western Ghats and the Eastern Ghats? [A]

Ans.

S.No.	Western Ghats	Eastern Ghats
1.	They are having an elevation of 900-1100m.	They are denuded peaks and have lesser elevation than 900km.
2.	They are divided as four regions or the four hills Sahyadri Hills in Maharasthra, Nilgiri in Karnataka and Tamil Nadu, Anaimalai Hills and Cardamom Hills in Kerala.	Some of the important ranges include the Javadi Hills, the Palconda range, the Nallamala Hills, the Mahendragiri Hills.
3.	The westward flowing rivers are Narmada and Tapi.	The eastward flowing rivers are Krishna, Kaveri and Mahanadi.
4.	The Western Ghats get southward monsoon.	The Eastern Ghats get rainfall from North-East monsoon.
5.	The height of the mountain increases from North to South.	The height increases from South to North.

(1 × 5 = 5)

Answering Tip

- Easter Ghats and Western Ghats meet at Nilgiri Hills.

TOPIC-4
The Indian Desert, The Coastal Plains, The Islands

Revision Notes

- To the Northwest of the Aravali Hills lies the Great Indian Desert.
- It is a land of undulating topography dotted with longitudinal dunes and barchans.
- This region receives low rainfall below 150 mm per year; hence, it has arid climate with low vegetation cover. It is because of these characteristic features that this is also known as Marusthali.
- Though the underlying rock structure of the desert is an extension of the Peninsular Plateau, yet, due to extreme arid conditions, its surface features have been carved by physical weathering and wind actions.
- On the basis of the orientation, the desert can be divided into two parts: the northern part is sloping towards Sindh and the southern towards the Rann of Kachchh.
- Most of the rivers in this region are ephemeral. The Luni river flowing in the southern part of the desert is of some significance.
- Low precipitation and high evaporation makes it a water deficit region.
- The lakes and the playas have brackish water which is the main source of obtaining salt.
- On the basis of the location and active geomorphological processes, the coastal plains can be broadly divided into two :
  - **The western coastal plains :** The western coastal plains are an example of submerged coastal plain. It is believed that the city of Dwarka which was once a part of the Indian mainland situated along the West coast is submerged under water.
- Because of this submergence it is a narrow belt and provides natural conditions for the development of ports and harbours.
- Kandla, Mazagaon, JLN port Navha Sheva, Marmagao, Mangalore, Cochin, etc., are some of the important natural ports located along the West coast.
- The the western Coast may be divided into following divisions – the Kachchh and Kathiawar coast in Gujarat, Konkan Coast in Maharashtra, Goan Coast and Malabar Coast in Karnataka and Kerala respectively.
  - **The eastern coastal plains :** As compared to the western coastal plain, the eastern coastal plain is broader and is an example of an emergent coast.
- There are well developed deltas here, formed by the rivers flowing eastward in to the Bay of Bengal.

- The continental shelf extends up to 500 km into the sea, which makes it difficult for the development of good ports and harbours. Name some ports on the eastern coast.
- There are **two** major island groups in India – one in the Bay of Bengal and the other in the Arabian Sea.
- The Bay of Bengal island groups consist of about 572 islands/islets. These are situated roughly between 6°N-14°N and 92°E -94°E.
- The two principal groups of islets include the Ritchie's Archipelago and the Labrynth Island.
- The entire group of island is divided into two broad categories – the Andaman in the North and the Nicobar in the South.
- They are separated by a water body which is called the Ten Degree Channel.
- It is believed that these islands are an elevated portion of submarine mountains. However, some smaller islands are volcanic in origin. The Barren Island, the only active volcano in India is also situated in the Nicobar Islands.
- The islands of the Arabian Sea include Lakshadweep and Minicoy. These are scattered between 8°N-12°N and 71°E -74°E longitude.
- The entire island group is built of coral deposits.
- There are approximately 36 islands of which 11 are inhabited. Minicoy is the largest island with an area of 453 sq. km.
- The islands of this archipelago have storm beaches consisting of unconsolidated pebbles, shingles, cobbles and boulders on the eastern seaboard.

Know the Terms

- **11° Channel :** It is the water body which separates the Andaman from the Nicobar.
- **Barren Island :** Barren island, the only active volcano in India is also situated in the Nicobar islands.

Very Short Answer Type Questions (1 mark each)

Q. 1. The only active volcano of India is the : [A]

(a) Narcondam Island (b) Barren Island

(c) Heaven Island (d) Halo Island

Ans. (b) Barren Island 1

Q. 2. The Bay of Bengal island groups consist of about: [U]

(a) 372 islands (b) 472 islands

(c) 572 islands (d) 672 islands

Ans. (c) 572 islands 1

Very Short Answer Type Questions (1 mark each)

Q. 1. Define the term 'Barchans'. [R]

Ans. They are crescent-shaped sand dunes produced by the action of wind predominately from one direction. 1

Q. 2. Where is the Great Indian Desert located? [A]

Ans. To the northwest of the Aravali hills lies the Great Indian desert. 1

Q. 3. Why is the Great Indian Desert referred to as Marusthali? [R]

Ans. This region receives low rainfall below 150 mm per year; hence, it has arid climate with low vegetation cover. It is because of these characteristic features that this is also known as Marusthali. 1

Answering Tip

- The Great Indian Desert is also known as the Thar Desert.

Q. 4. What makes Rajasthan water deficit region? [U]

Ans. Low precipitation and high evaporation makes it a water deficit region. 1

Q. 5. What is the main source of obtaining salt in the desert? [A]

Ans. The lakes and the playas have brackish water which is the main source of obtaining salt. 1

Q. 6. On the basis of the location and active geomorphological processes, the coastal plains can be divided into how many groups? [R]

Ans. On the basis of the location and active geomorphological processes, it can be broadly divided into two : **(i)** the western coastal plains; **(ii)** the eastern coastal plains. 1

Q. 7. Give on example of the submerged coastal plain. [U]

Ans. The western coastal plains are an example of submerged coastal plain. 1

Q. 8. Name any two natural ports located along the west coast. [A]

Ans. Kandla, Mazagaon, JLN port Navha Sheva, Marmagao, Mangalore, Cochin, etc., are some of the important natural ports located along the west coast. 1

Q. 9. Name one distinguishing feature of the Malabar Coast? [R]

Ans. The Malabar Coast has got certain distinguishing features in the form of 'Kayals' (backwaters), which are used for fishing, inland navigation and also due to its special attraction for tourists. 1

Q. 10. Where is the Nehru Trophy Vallamkali held? A

Ans. Every year the famous Nehru Trophy Vallamkali (boat race) is held in Punnamada Kayal in Kerala. 1

Q. 11. How is the eastern coastal plain different from the western coastal plain? U

Ans. As compared to the western coastal plain, the eastern coastal plain is broader and is an example of an emergent coast. 1

Q. 12. Name any deltas found at the eastern coast. A

Ans. These include the deltas of the Mahanadi, the Godavari, the Krishna and the Kaveri. 1

Q. 13. Name the two major island groups of India. R

Ans. The Andaman & Nicobar Islands and the Lakshadweep Islands. 1

Q. 14. Where are the two major island groups in India located? U

Ans. There are two major island groups in India – one in the Bay of Bengal and the other in the Arabian Sea. 1

Short Answer Type Questions (3 marks each)

AI **Q. 1. Write a note on Thar Desert.** A

Ans. To the northwest of the Aravali hills lies the Great Indian desert. It is a land of undulating topography dotted with longitudinal dunes and barchans. This region receives low rainfall below 150 mm per year; hence, it has arid climate with low vegetation cover. It is because of these characteristic features that this is also known as Marusthali.

The vegetaion commom in the region are Cacti, Kher, Kikar, Babool , Aclacia, Rhododendrons, etc. During the rainy season some streams appear which disappear in summer. Luni is an important river of the region.

Some of the well pronounced desert land features present here are mushroom rocks, shifting dunes and oasis. On the basis of the orientation, the desert can be divided into two parts: the northern part is sloping towards Sindh and the southern towards the Rann of Kachchh. Most of the rivers in this region are ephemeral. 3

Answering Tip

- Thar Desert is the world's 17th largest desert, and the world's 9th largest sub-tropical desert.

Q. 2. Write a short note on the island groups of India. R

Ans. There are two major island groups in India – one in the Bay of Bengal and the other in the Arabian Sea. The Bay of Bengal island groups consist of about 572 islands/islets. These are situated roughly between 6°N-14°N and 92°E -94°E. The two principal groups of islets include the Ritchie's Archipelago and the Labrynth Island. The entire group of island is divided into two broad categories – the Andaman in the north and the Nicobar in the south. They are separated by a water body which is called the Ten degree channel.

The islands of the Arabian Sea include Lakshadweep and Minicoy. These are scattered between 8°N-12°N and 71°E -74°E longitude. These islands are located at a distance of 280 km-480 km off the Kerala coast. The entire island group is built of coral deposits. There are approximately 36 islands of which 11 are inhabited. Minicoy is the largest island with an area of 453 sq. km. 3

Answering Tip

- While the Lakshadweep islands are located in the Arabian Sea, the Andaman and Nicobar islands lie in the Bay of Bengal

Q. 3. Why ports and harbours are less on the East Coast? R

Ans. Ports and harbours are less on the East Coast because :

(i) River flowing eastward into the Bay of Bengal include the deltas of Mahanadi, the Godavari, the Krishna and the Kaveri are well developed deltas.

(ii) Because of its emergent nature, it has less number of ports and harbours.

(iii) The continental shelf extends up to 500 km into the sea, which makes it difficult for the development of good ports and harbours. Name some ports on the eastern coast. 3

Q. 4. All physical divisions of India have their own importance. Which value does it reflect? How do we need to incorporate this value in our life? A

Ans. It is very much clear that all landforms are important in their own ways. Mountains provide scenic beauty, biodiversity, flora and fauna;plains provide arable land, living conditions for human habitation; plateau provides minerals and coastal plains sea products. It teaches us the value of respect for all. This value is very important to maintain peace and harmony in the society. The world could not be place of human survival without diversity. Therefore, each one of us need to learn to respect people who are not alike. Each human being is unique like landforms but has its own relevance. 3

Long Answer Type Questions (5 marks each)

Q. 1. Differentiate western coastal plain and eastern coastal plain? A

Ans.

S.No.	Western coastal plain	Eastern coastal plain
1.	They lie between the Western Ghats and Arabian Sea.	They lie between the Eastern Ghats and Bay of Bengal.
2.	They are narrow alluvial plain which are separated by hilly terrains.	They are wider plain (80-120km) with well developed deltas of the rivers.
3.	They are divided into : Konkan Coast and Malabar Coast.	They are divided into : Northern Circus and Coromandel Coast.
4.	They receive rainfall from south-west monsoons.	They receive rainfall by retreating or north-west monsoon.
5.	Narmada and Tapi are important rivers.	Krishna, Kaveri and Mahanadi are important rivers.

(1 × 5 = 5)

Q. 2. Differentiate between the Northern Plains and the Coastal Plains? A

Ans.

S.No.	Northern Plains	Coastal Plains
1.	They are located on foot hills of the Himalayas and above peninsular plateau.	They lie between the Arabian Sea, Western Ghats and Bay of Bengal.
2.	They spread between the area of 3200 sq.km and width is 240-320km.	They spread from Gujarat to Kanyakumari and Odisha to Kanyakumari.
3.	Due to fertile alluvial soil and water supply they are known for agriculture.	They are drained by perennial rivers and are important for fishing, lagoons and harbours.
4.	They are divided into Indus plains, Ganga plains and Brahmaputra plains.	They are divided into Konkan Coast and Malabar Coast, Northern Circar on eastern side and Coromandel Coast.
5.	Rivers orginiating from Himalayas and Peninsular Plateau has formed these plains by depositing sediments brought by rivers.	Most of the rivers originating from Pennisular Plateau like Krishna, Kaveri, Godavari , Mahanadi move eastward and form delta whereas Narmada and Tapi move westward from estuaries.

(1 × 5 = 5)

AI **Q. 3. Write a note on the physical features of the coastal plains?** R

Ans. On the basis of the location and active geomorphological processes, it can be broadly divided into two:

(i) The western coastal plains

(ii) The eastern coastal plains

The western coastal plains are an example of submerged coastal plain. It is believed that the city of Dwaraka which was once a part of the Indian mainland situated along the west coast is submerged under water. Because of this submergence it is a narrow belt and provides natural conditions for the development of ports and harbours. Kandla, Mazagaon, JLN port Navha Sheva, Marmagao, Mangalore, Cochin, etc. are some of the important natural ports located along the west coast. Extending from the Gujarat coast in the north to the Kerala coast in the south, the western coast may be divided into following divisions – the Kachchh and Kathiawar coast in Gujarat, Konkan coast in Maharashtra, Goa coast and Malabar coast in Karnataka and Kerala respectively. The western coastal plains are narrow in the middle and get broader towards north and south. The rivers flowing through this coastal plain do not form any delta. The Malabar coast has got certain distinguishing features in the form of 'Kayals' (backwaters), which are used for fishing, inland navigation and also due to its special attraction for tourists.

As compared to the western coastal plain, the eastern coastal plain is broader and is an example of an emergent coast. There are well developed deltas here, formed by the rivers flowing eastward in to the Bay of Bengal. These include the deltas of the Mahanadi, the Godavari, the Krishna and the Kaveri. Because of its emergent nature, it has less number of ports and harbours. The continental shelf extends up to 500 km into the sea, which makes it difficult for **5**

Answering

- A coastal plain is flat, low-lying land adjacent to a sea coast.

Q. 4. 'Physical divisions of India are alternative to each other.' Justify? [U]

Ans. The physical divisions of India are alternative to each other because :

(i) Himalayas are the storehouse of water as they rise to Perennial rivers which provide ample water for irrigation. Himalayas are also a source of forest produce and serve as a climatic divide.

(ii) The Northern Plains have fertile soil which is suitable for agriculture and also provides raw materials for industries. The Northern Plains are also known as the 'Food Bowl of India'.

(iii) The Peninsular India is the store house of minerals, which are of great use to industries and are exported across the world. The Ghats are responsible for generating hydroelectricity.

(iv) The coastal plains are important for ports, arrival of monsoons, international trade, fishing. Etc. the coastal plains are world famous for the spices which are exported world wide.

(v) The deserts are known for tourist attraction. The lakes and the playas have brackish water which is the main source of obtaining salt. The island group is known for the corals, volcanoes and are a major tourist destination.

Thus, no part of India can grow and develop in isolation .They all are interdependent and cannot grow without each other. One part needs the support and cooperation of other. **5**

Map Work

(5 marks each)

Q. 1. Locate and label the following five features with appropriate symbols on the given political outline map of India.

(i) Highest peak of India. **(ii) Palk Strait.**
(iii) Mahanadi Delta **(iv) Lowest point of India**
(v) Indira Point

Ans.

Q. 2. Locate and label the following five features with appropriate symbols on the given political outline map of India.

(i) Konkan coast **(ii) Malabar coast**
(iii) Central highlands **(iv) Coromandal coast**
(v) Deccan Plateau **(vi) The Great Indian Desert**

Ans.

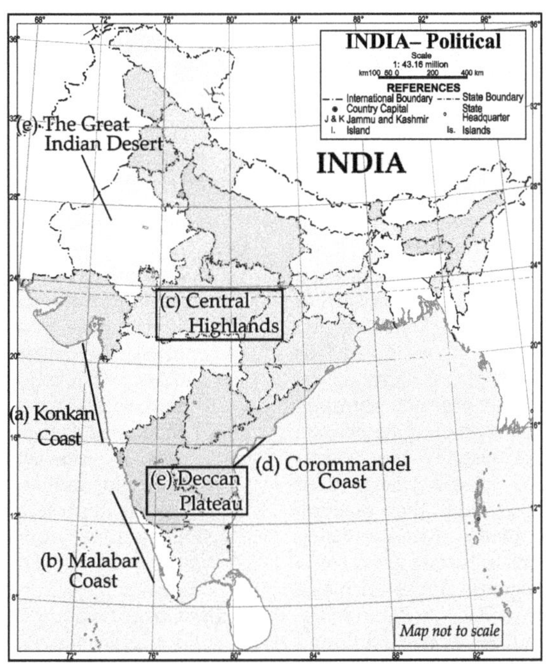

NCERT CORNER

(A) Multiple choice questions :

Q. 1. In which part of Himalayas do we find the Karewa formation :

(a) North-eastern Himalayas
(b) Himachal-Uttaranchal Himalayas
(c) Eastern Himalayas
(d) Kashmir Himalayas

Ans. (d) Kashmir Himalayas .

Q. 2. In which of the following states is Loktak lake situated :

(a) Kerala (b) Uttaranchal
(c) Manipur (d) Rajasthan

Ans. (c) Manipur .

Q. 3. Which one of the water bodies separates the Andaman from the Nicobar :

(a) 11°Channel (b) Gulf of Mannar
(c) 10° Channel (d) Andaman Sea

Ans. (a) 11° Channel .

Q. 4. On which of the following hill range is the 'Dodabeta' peak situated :

(a) Nilgiri hills (b) Anaimalai hills
(c) Cardamom hills (d) Nallamala hills

Ans. (a) Nilgiri Hills .

(B) Answer the following questions in about 30 words :

Q. 1. If a person is to travel to Lakshadweep, from which coastal plain does he prefer and why?

Ans. If a person is to travel to Lakshadweep, he will have to prefer the Malabar Coast ,as the islands are situated at a distance of 280km-480km off the Kerala Coast. It takes the least distance from the Malabar Coast to reach Lakshadweep.

Q. 2. Where in India will you find a cold desert? Name some important ranges of this region?

Ans. The cold desert is found in the North-eastern part of the Kashmir Himalayas. It lies between the Greater Himalayas and the Karakoram Ranges. Main ranges of this region are Ladakh, Karakoram , Zaskar and Pir Panjal.

Q. 3. Why is the western coastal plain being devoid of any delta?

Ans. The slope of the western coast is very steep. Therefore, these rivers flow not in different parts but in one part. And hence, they do not form any delta. As a result, we do not find any delta in the western coast.

(C) Answer the following questions in about 125 words :

Q. 1. Make a comparison of the island groups of the Arabian Sea and the Bay of Bengal.

Ans.

S.No.	Andaman and Nicobar Islands	Lakshadweep Islands
1.	It lies 1200 km away from the Indian mainland in the Bay of Bengal.	It lies opposite to the coast of Kerala in the Arabian Sea at a distance of 280-480km.
2.	Port Blair is the capital.	Kavarati is the capital.

3.	They are approx. 572 islands.	They are approx. 36 islands.
4.	They have two volcanic islands: Barren Island-active volcano and Norkandom Island -extinct Island.	Minicoy is the largest island and is a major tourist hub.
5.	The water body separating the Andaman and Nicobar Islands is called the 10 Degree Channel.	The water body separating the Lakshadweep Islands is called the eleventh degree channel.

Q. 2. What are the important geomorphological features found in the river valley plains?

Ans. Alluvial fans are formed when streams flowing from higher levels break into foot slope plains of low gradient. Normally very coarse load is carried by streams glowing over mountain slopes. This load becomes too heavy for the streams to be carried over gentler gradients and gets dumped and spread as a broad low to high cone shaped deposit called alluvial fan. Usually, the streams which flow over fans are not confined to their original channels for long and shift their position across the fan forming many channels called distributaries. Alluvial fans in humid areas show normally low cones with gentle slopes form as a low cone.

Delta is like alluvial fans but develop at a different location. The load carried by the rivers is dumped and spread into the sea. If this load is not carried far away into the sea or distributed along the coast, it spreads and accumulates. Such areas over flood plains build up by abandoned or cut off channels contain coarse deposits. The flood deposits of spilled waters carry relatively finer materials like silt and clay. The flood plains in a delta are called delta plains.

Floodplain is a major landform of river deposition. Large sized materials are deposited first when stream channel breaks into a gentle slope. Thus, normally, fine sized materials like sand, silt and clay are carried by relatively slow moving waters in gentler channels usually found in the plains and deposited over the bed and when the waters spill over the banks during flooding above the bed.

These river valley plains have a fertile alluvial soil cover which supports a variety of crops like wheat, rice, sugarcane and jute, and hence, supports a large population.

Q. 3. If you move from Badrinath to Sunderbans delta along the course of the river Ganga, what major geomorphological features will you come across?

Ans. If you move from Badrinath to Sunderbans delta along the course of the river Ganga, we come across the following major geomorphological features :

(i) V shaped valleys : Valleys start as small narrow rills, the rills will gradually develop into long and wide gullies, the gullies will further deepen, widen and lengthen to give rise to valleys. Depending upon dimensions and shape, many types of valleys like v-shaped valley, gorge, canyon , etc., can be recognised.

(ii) Gorge : A gorge is a deep valley with very steep to straight sides.

(iii) Canyon : A canyon is characterised by steep step-like slopes and may be as deep as a gorge. A gorge is almost equal in width at its top as well as at its bottom. In contrast, a canyon is wider at its top than at its bottom. In fact, a canyon is a variant of gorge.

(iv) Waterfall : When the rivers start falling in pits in mountainous regions, it makes waterfall.

(v) Plunge pools : Once a small and shallow depression forms, pebbles and boulders get collected in those depressions and get rotated by flowing water and consequently the depressions grow in dimensions. A series of such depressions eventually join and the stream valley gets deepened. At the foot of waterfalls also, large potholes, quite deep and wide , form because of the sheer impact of water and rotation of boulders. Such large and deep holes at the base of waterfalls are called plunge pools.

□□

CHAPTER

3 DRAINAGE SYSTEM

Syllabus

➢ *The Himalayan Drainage System : Evolution of the Himalayan Drainage System, The River Systems of the Himalayan Drainage System.*

➢ *The Peninsular Drainage System : The Evolution of the Peninsular Drainage System, River Systems of the Peninsular Drainage, River Regimes.*

TOPIC-1
The Himalayan Drainage System : Evolution of the Himalayan Drainage System, The River Systems of the Himalayan Drainage System

Revision Notes

➢ The flow of water through well-defined channels is known as 'drainage' and the network of such channels is called a 'drainage system'.

➢ The drainage pattern of an area is the outcome of the geological time period, nature and structure of rocks, topography, slope, amount of water flowing and the periodicity of the flow.

➢ A river drains the water collected from a specific area, which is called its 'catchment area'. An area drained by a river and its tributaries is called a drainage basin. The boundary line separating one drainage basin from the other is known as the watershed. The catchments of large rivers are called river basins while those of small rivulets and rills are often referred to as watersheds.

➢ Indian Drainage System may be divided on various bases. On the basis of discharge of water (orientations to the sea), it may be grouped into : **(i)** the Arabian Sea Drainage; and **(ii)** the Bay of Bengal Drainage.

➢ Nearly 77 per cent of the drainage area consisting of the Ganga, the Brahmaputra, the Mahanadi, the Krishna, etc., is oriented towards the Bay of Bengal while 23 per cent comprising the Indus, the Narmada, the Tapi, the Mahi and the Periyar systems discharge their waters in the Arabian Sea.

➢ On the basis of the size of the watershed, the drainage basins of India are grouped into three categories : **(i)** Major river basins with more than 20,000 sq. km of catchment area. **(ii)** Medium river basins with catchment area between 2,000-20,000 sq. km.

➢ On the basis of the mode of origin, nature and characteristics, the Indian drainage may also be classified into the Himalayan drainage and the Peninsular drainage.

➢ **The Himalayan Drainage :** The Himalayan drainage system has evolved through a long geological history. It mainly includes the Ganga, the Indus and the Brahmaputra river basins. Since these are fed both by melting of snow and precipitation, rivers of this system are perennial.

➢ These rivers pass through the giant gorges carved out by the erosional activity carried on simultaneously with the uplift of the Himalayas.

- In the Himalayan reaches, the course of these rivers is highly tortuous, but over the plains they display a strong meandering tendency and shift their courses frequently.
- River Kosi, also know as the 'sorrow of Bihar', has been notorious for frequently changing its course.
- There are difference of opinion about the evolution of the Himalayan rivers. However, geologists believe that a mighty river called Shiwalik or Indo-Brahma traversed the entire longitudinal extent of the Himalaya from Assam to Punjab and onwards to Sind, and finally discharged into the Gulf of Sind near lower Punjab during the Miocene period some 5-24 million years ago.
- It is opined that in due course of time Indo– Brahma river was dismembered into three main drainage systems : **(i)** the Indus and its five tributaries in the western part; **(ii)** the Ganga and its Himalayan tributaries in the central part; and **(iii)** the stretch of the Brahmaputra in Assam and its Himalayan tributaries in the eastern part.
- The Himalayan drainage consists of several river systems but the following are the major river systems:
- **The Indus System :** It is one of the largest river basins of the world, covering an area of 11,65,000 sq. km (in India it is 321, 289 sq. km and a total length of 2,880 km (in India 1,114 km). It originates from a glacier near Bokhar Chu (31°15' N latitude and 81°40' E longitude) in the Tibetan region at an altitude of 4,164 m in the Kailash Mountain range.
- The Indus receives a number of Himalayan tributaries such as the Shyok, the Gilgit, the Zaskar, the Hunza, the Nubra, the Shigar, the Gasting and the Dras.
- The other important tributaries joining the right bank of the Indus are the Khurram, the Tochi, the Gomal, the Viboa and the Sangar. They all originate in the Sulaiman ranges. The river flows southward and receives 'Panjnad' a little above Mithankot. The Panjnad is the name given to the five rivers of Punjab, namely the Satluj, the Beas, the Ravi, the Chenab and the Jhelum.
- The Indus flows in India only through the Leh district in Jammu and Kashmir.
- The Jhelum, an important tributary of the Indus, rises from a spring at Verinag situated at the foot of the Pir Panjal in the south-eastern part of the valley of Kashmir.
- The Chenab is the largest tributary of the Indus. It is formed by two streams, the Chandra and the Bhaga, which join at Tandi near Keylong in Himachal Pradesh.
- The Ravi is another important tributary of the Indus. It rises west of the Rohtang Pass in the Kullu hills of Himachal Pradesh and flows through the Chamba Valley of the state.
- The Beas is another important tributary of the Indus, originating from the Beas Kund near the Rohtang Pass at an elevation of 4,000 m above the mean sea level.
- The Satluj originates in the Rakas lake near Mansarovar at an altitude of 4,555 m in Tibet where it is known as Langchen Khambab.
- **The Ganga System :** The Ganga is the most important river of India both from the point of view of its basin and cultural significance . The Ganga basin covers about 8.6 lakh sq. km area in India alone. The Ganga river system is the largest in India having a number of perennial and non-perennial rivers originating in the Himalayas in the north and the Peninsula in the south, respectively.
- The Yamuna, the western most and the longest tributary of the Ganga, has its source in the Yamunotri Glacier on the western slopes of Banderpunch range (6,316 km).
- The Chambal rises near Mhow in the Malwa Plateau of Madhya Pradesh and flows northwards through a gorge up wards of Kota in Rajasthan, where the Gandhisagar Dam has been constructed.
- The Gandak comprises two streams, namely Kaligandak and Trishulganga. It rises in the Nepal Himalayas between the Dhaulagiri and Mount Everest and drains the central part of Nepal.
- The Ghaghara originates in the glaciers of Mapchachungo. After collecting the waters of its tributaries – Tila, Seti and Beri, it comes out of the mountain, cutting a deep gorge at Shishapani.
- The Kosi is an antecedent river with its source to the north of Mount Everest in Tibet, where its main stream Arun rises.
- The Ramganga is comparatively a small river rising in the Garhwal Hills near Gairsain.
- The Damodar occupies the eastern margins of the Chotanagpur Plateau where it flows through a rift valley and finally joins the Hugli. The Barakar is its main tributary.
- The Sarda or Saryu river rises in the Milan Glacier in the Nepal Himalayas where it is known as the Goriganga.
- The Mahananda is another important tributary of the Ganga rising in the Darjiling Hill.
- The Son is a large south bank tributary of the Ganga, originating in the Amarkantak Plateau.
- **The Brahmaputra System :** The Brahmaputra, one of the largest rivers of the world, has its origin in the Chemayungdung Glacier of the Kailash range near the Mansarovar Lake.
- The Brahmaputra receives numerous tributaries in its 750 km long journey through the Assam valley.
- The Brahmaputra enters into Bangladesh near Dhubri and flows southward. In Bangladesh, the Tista joins it on its right bank from where the river is known as the Yamuna.

Know the Terms

- **Drainage :** The flow of water through well-defined channels is known as 'drainage'.
- **Drainage system :** The network of drainage channels is called a 'drainage system'.
- **Dendritic drainage pattern :** The drainage pattern resembling the branches of a tree is known as "dendritic" the examples of which are the rivers of northern plain.
- **Radial drainage pattern :** When the rivers originate from a hill and flow in all directions, the drainage pattern is known as 'radial'.
- **Trellis drainage pattern :** When the primary tributaries of rivers flow parallel to each other and secondary tributaries join them at right angles, the pattern is known as 'trellis'.
- **Centripetal drainage pattern :** When the rivers discharge their waters from all directions in a lake or depression, the pattern is known as 'centripetal'.
- **Catchment area :** A river drains the water collected from a specific area, which is called its 'catchment area'.
- **Drainage basin :** An area drained by a river and its tributaries is called a drainage basin.
- **Watershed :** The boundary line separating one drainage basin from the other is known as the watershed.
- **River basins :** The catchments of large rivers are called river basins.
- **River system :** A river or a river system is a body of water flowing in a channel through the surface of the Earth. It consists of four important parts; river course, river source, tributaries and river mouth.

Multiple Choice Questions (1 mark each)

Q. 1. The Chenab is the largest tributary of the: A

(a) Beas (b) Brahmaputra
(c) Indus (d) Jhelum

Ans. (c) Indus 1

Q. 2. A river drains the water collected from a specific area, which is called its : U

(a) catchment area (b) attachment area
(c) drainage area (d) watershed area

Ans. (a) catchment area 1

Q. 3. Name the river which in Tibet is known as Langchen Khambab : U

(a) Ravi (b) Teesta
(c) Satluj (d) Beas

Ans. (c) Satluj 1

Very Short Answer Type Questions (1 mark each)

Q. 1. Define the term 'Drainage'. A

Ans. The flow of water through well-defined channels is known as 'drainage'. 1

Q. 2. Define the term 'Drainage System'. A

Ans. The network of drainage channels is called a 'drainage system'. 1

Q. 3. Define the term 'Drainage Basin'. U

Ans. An area drained by a river and its tributaries is called a drainage basin. 1

Commonly Made Error

- The students are not aware how the drainage basin is formed.

Answering Tip

- A drainage basin is formed by the action of water as it forms streams and rivers that flow downhill.

Q. 4. What is watershed? A

Ans. The boundary line separating one drainage basin from the other is known as the watershed. 1

Q. 5. What is river system? R

Ans. A river or a river system is a body of water flowing in a channel through the surface of the Earth. It consists of four important parts; river course, river source, tributaries and river mouth. 1

Q. 6. What is regime? U

Ans. The pattern of flow of water in a river channel over a year is known as regime. 1

Q. 7. What is Panjnad? A

Ans. The Panjnad is the name given to the five rivers of Punjab, namely Satluj, Beas, Ravi, Chenab and Jhelum. 1

Q. 8. On the basis of discharge of water , the Indian Drainage System can be divided into how many groups? R

Ans. Indian Drainage System may be divided on various bases. On the basis of discharge of water (orientations to the sea), it may be grouped into: **(i)** the Arabian Sea Drainage; and **(ii)** the Bay of Bengal Drainage. 1

Q. 9. On the basis of origin, form and features in how many groups can we classify river of India? A

Ans. On the basis of origin, form and features , we can classify the rivers of India into four parts:

(i) Himalayan rivers
(ii) Peninsular rivers

(iii) Coastal rivers
(iv) Internal basin river. 1

Q. 10. The Brahmaputra River is known by how many names? R

Ans. In Tibet, Brahmaputra is known as Tsango, in the Central Himalayas , it is known as Siang or Dihang. In India it is known as Brahmaputra. In Bangladesh it is known as Yamuna. 1

Q. 11. Name the river basins of the Himalayan Drainage System? U

Ans. It mainly includes the Ganga, the Indus and the Brahmaputra river basins. 1

Q. 12. Which river is known as the 'Sorrow of Bihar'? Why? A

Ans. River Kosi, is known as the 'Sorrow of Bihar', because it has been notorious for frequently changing its course. 1

Answering Tip

- The Kosi River is known as the "Sorrow of Bihar" as the annual floods affect about 21,000 km^2 of fertile agricultural land thereby disturbing the rural economy.

Q. 13. Name any two tributaries of the Brahmaputra River System. R

Ans. Burhi Dihing, Dhansari (South), Subansiri, Kameng,Manas and Sankosh. **(Any Two) 1**

Q. 14. Into how many parts is the Indo-Brahma Drainage System dismembered? Name any two? R

Ans. It is opined that in due course of time, Indo-Brahma river was dismembered into three main drainage systems:
(i) The Indus and its five tributaries in the western part.
(ii) The Ganga and its Himalayan tributaries in the central part
(iii) **The stretch of the Brahmaputra in Assam and its Himalayan tributaries in the eastern part.**

(Any two) 1

Q. 15. Name the factors on which the drainage pattern depends. R

Ans. The drainage pattern of an area is the outcome of the geological time period, nature and structure of the rocks, topography, slope , amount of water flowing and the periodicity of the flow. 1

Q. 16. Indus is known by how many different names? U

Ans. In India , Indus is also known as Sindhu and in Tibet, it is known as 'Singi Khamban; or Lion's mouth. **(Any two) 1**

Q. 17. Name the rivers falling into the Arabian Sea. R

Ans. Indus and its tributaries, Narmada, Tapti, Sabarmati rivers fall into the Arabian Sea. 1

Q. 18. Why are river basins and watersheds marked by unity? U

Ans. River basins and watersheds are marked by unity. What happens in one part of the basin or watershed directly affects the other parts and the unit as a whole. That is why, they are accepted as the most appropriate micro, meso or macro planning regions. 1

Q. 19. Differentiate between radial drainage pattern and centripetal drainage pattern. R

Ans.

S.No.	Radial Drainage Pattern	Centripetal Drainage Pattern
1.	When the rivers originate from a hill and flow in all directions, the drainage pattern is known as 'radial'.	When the rivers discharge their waters from all directions in a lake or depression, the pattern is known as 'centripetal'.
2.	The rivers originating from Amarkantak range present a good example of it.	Sambhar Lake of Rajasthan is a good example of it.

(Any One) (½ + ½ = 1)

Answering Tip

- Radial drainage : When the rivers radiate from a hill, the pattern is called radial drainage. Centripetal drainage : The rivers flowing into a depression or a lake, is called a centripetal drainage.

Short Answer Type Questions

(3 marks each)

Q. 1. On the basis of the size of the watershed, the drainage basins of India can be divided into how many groups? A

Ans. On the basis of the size of the watershed, the drainage basins of India are grouped into three categories:
(i) Major river basins with more than 20,000 sq. km of catchment area. It includes 14 drainage basins such as the Ganga, the Brahmaputra, the Krishna, the Tapi, the Narmada, the Mahi, the Pennar, the Sabarmati, the Barak, etc.
(ii) Medium river basins with catchment area between 2,000-20,000 sq. km incorporating 44 river basins such as the Kalindi, the Periyar, the Meghna, etc.
(iii) Minor river basins with catchment area of less than 2,000 sq. km include fairly good number of rivers flowing in the area of low rainfall. 3

Q. 2. Differentiate between the features of the River Ganga and Jhelum? R

Ans.

S.No.	Ganga	Jhelum
1.	It is an important river of India from the point of view of its basin and cultural significance	Jhelum is an important tributary of the Indus.
2.	It rises in the Gangotri Glacier near Gaumukh in the Uttarkashi district of Uttarakhand.	It rises from a spring at Verinag situated at the foot of the Pir Panjal in the South-eastern part of the valley of Kashmir.
3.	It discharges itself into the Bay of Bengal near the Sagar Island.	It flows into Pakistan through a deep narrow gorge.

(1 × 3 = 3)

Q. 3. Explain the important features of the Brahmaputra River System? A

Ans. The Brahmaputra River System:

(i) The Brahmaputra, one of the largest rivers of the world, has its origin in the Chemayungdung Glacier of the Kailash range near the Mansarovar lake. From here, it traverses eastward longitudinally for a distance of nearly 1,200 km in a dry and flat region of southern Tibet, where it is known as the Tsangpo, which means 'the purifier.'

(ii) The Brahmaputra receives numerous tributaries in its 750 km long journey through the Assam valley.

(iii) The Brahmaputra is well-known for floods, channel shifting and bank erosion. This is due to the fact that most of its tributaries are large, and bring large quantity of sediments owing to heavy rainfall in its catchment area. 3

Answering Tip

- The river Brahmaputra in Tibet/ China, is called Yarlung Tsangpo. In Assam and Arunachal Pradesh, it is called Lohit or Luit meaning blood.

Q. 4. Explain the important features of Yamuna? A

Ans. (i) The Yamuna, the western most and the longest tributary of the Ganga, has its source in the Yamunotri Glacier on the western slopes of Banderpunch range (6,316 km).

(ii) It joins the Ganga at Prayag (Allahabad). It is joined by the Chambal, the Sind, the Betwa and the Ken on its right bank which originates from the Peninsular Plateau while the Hindan, the Rind, the Sengar, the Varuna, etc., join it on its left bank.

(iii) Much of its water feeds the western and eastern Yamuna and the Agra canals for irrigation purposes. 3

AI **Q. 5. Why the flow of Ganga is not uniform throughout the year?** A

Ans. The Ganga has its minimum flow during the January -June period. The maximum flow is attained either in August or in September. After September, there is a steady fall in the flow. The river, thus, has a monsoon regime during the rainy season. There are striking differences in the river regimes in the eastern and the western parts of the Ganga Basin. The Ganga maintains a sizeable flow in the early parts of summer due to snow melt before the monsoon rains begin. The mean maximum discharge of the Ganga at Farakka is about 55,000 cusecs while the mean minimum is only 1,300 cusecs. 3

Q. 6. What do you know about the Indus River System? R

Ans. The Indus River System :

(i) It is one of the largest river basins of the world, covering an area of 11,65,000 sq. km (in India it is 321, 289 sq. km and a total length of 2,880 km (in India 1,114 km). The Indus also known as the Sindhu, is the westernmost of the Himalayan rivers in India. It originates from a glacier near Bokhar Chu (31°15' N latitude and 81°40' E longitude) in the Tibetan region at an altitude of 4,164 m in the Kailash Mountain range.

(ii) The Indus receives a number of Himalayan tributaries such as the Shyok, the Gilgit, the Zaskar, the Hunza, the Nubra, the Shigar, the Gasting and the Dras. It finally emerges out of the hills near Attock where it receives the Kabul river on its right bank.

(iii) The river flows southward and receives 'Panjnad' a little above Mithankot. The Panjnad is the name given to the five rivers of Punjab, namely the Satluj, the Beas, the Ravi, the Chenab and the Jhelum. It finally discharges into the Arabian Sea, east of Karachi. The Indus flows in India only through the Leh district in Jammu and Kashmir. 3

Q. 7. Explain the evolution of the Himalayan Drainage System? A

Ans. There are difference of opinion about the evolution of the Himalayan rivers. However, geologists believe that a mighty river called Shiwalik or Indo-Brahma traversed the entire longitudinal extent of the Himalaya from Assam to Punjab and onwards to Sind, and finally discharged into the Gulf of Sind near lower Punjab during the Miocene period some 5-24 million years ago . The remarkable continuity of the Shiwalik and its lacustrine origin and alluvial deposits consisting of sands, silt, clay, boulders and conglomerates support this viewpoint . 3

Commonly Made Error

- The students are not aware of the importance of the Indus River System.

Answering Tip

- The Indus is the most important supplier of water resources to the Punjab and Sindh plains - it forms the backbone of agriculture and food production in Pakistan. The river is especially critical as rainfall is meagre in the lower Indus valley.

Long Answer Type Questions

(5 marks each)

Q. 1. Write a note on the tributaries of the Indus River System. [A]

Ans. The tributaries of Indus:

(i) The Jhelum, an important tributary of the Indus, rises from a spring at Verinag situated at the foot of the Pir Panjal in the south-eastern part of the valley of Kashmir. It flows through Srinagar and the Wular lake before entering Pakistan through a deep narrow gorge. It joins the Chenab near Jhang in Pakistan.

(ii) The Chenab is the largest tributary of the Indus. It is formed by two streams, the Chandra and the Bhaga, which join at Tandi near Keylong in Himachal Pradesh. Hence, it is also known as Chandrabhaga. The river flows for 1,180 km before entering into Pakistan.

(iii) The Ravi is another important tributary of the Indus. It rises west of the Rohtang pass in the Kullu hills of Himachal Pradesh and flows through the Chamba valley of the state. Before entering Pakistan and joining the Chenab near Sarai Sidhu, it drains the area lying between the southeastern part of the Pir Panjal and the Dhauladhar ranges.

(iv) The Beas is another important tributary of the Indus, originating from the Beas Kund near the Rohtang Pass at an elevation of 4,000 m above the mean sea level. The river flows through the Kullu valley and forms gorges at Kati and Largi in the Dhaoladhar range. It enters the Punjab plains where it meets the Satluj near Harike.

(v) The Satluj originates in the Rakas lake near Mansarovar at an altitude of 4,555 m in Tibet where it is known as Langchen Khambab. It flows almost parallel to the Indus for about 400 km before entering India, and comes out of a gorge at Rupar. It passes through the Shipki La on the Himalayan ranges and enters the Punjab plains. It is an antecedent river. It is a very important tributary as it feeds the canal system of the Bhakra Nangal Project. 5

Q. 2. Write a note on the important tributaries of the Ganga System? [A]

Ans. The Ganga is the most important river of India both from the point of view of its basin and cultural significance. Important tributaries of the Ganga System are :

(i) The Yamuna, the western most and the longest tributary of the Ganga, has its source in the Yamunotri glacier on the western slopes of Banderpunch range (6,316 km). It joins the Ganga at Prayag (Allahabad). Much of its water feeds the western and eastern Yamuna and the Agra canals for irrigation purposes.

(ii) The Chambal rises near Mhow in the Malwa plateau of Madhya Pradesh and flows northwards through a gorge up wards of Kota. in Rajasthan, where the Gandhisagar dam has been constructed. From Kota, it traverses down to Bundi, Sawai Madhopur and Dholpur, and finally joins the Yamuna. The Chambal is famous for its badland topography called the Chambal ravines.

(iii) The Gandak comprises two streams, namely Kaligandak and Trishulganga. It rises in the Nepal Himalayas between the Dhaulagiri and Mount Everest and drains the central part of Nepal. It enters the Ganga plain in Champaran district of Bihar and joins the Ganga at Sonpur near Patna.

(iv) The Ghaghara originates in the glaciers of Mapchachungo. After collecting the waters of its tributaries – Tila, Seti and Beri, it comes out of the mountain, cutting a deep gorge at Shishapani. The river Sarda (Kali or Kali Ganga) joins it in the plain before it finally meets the Ganga at Chhapra.

(v) The Kosi is an antecedent river with its source to the north of Mount Everest in Tibet, where its main stream Arun rises. After crossing the Central Himalayas in Nepal, it is joined by the Son Kosi from the West and the Tamur Kosi from the east. It forms Sapt Kosi after uniting with the river Arun.

(vi) The Damodar occupies the eastern margins of the Chotanagpur Plateau where it flows through a rift valley and finally joins the Hugli. The Barakar is its main tributary. Once known as the 'sorrow of Bengal', the Damodar has been now tamed by the Damodar Valley corporation, a multipurpose project.

(vii) The Mahananda is another important tributary of the Ganga rising in the Darjiling hills. It joins the Ganga as its last left bank tributary in West Bengal.

(viii) The Son is a large south bank tributary of the Ganga, originating in the Amarkantak plateau. After forming a series of waterfalls at the edge of the plateau, it reaches Arrah, west of Patna, to join the Ganga. **(Any five) 5**

[AI] **Q. 3. Name the important drainage patterns?** [A]

Ans. The important drainage patterns are :

(i) Dendritic : The drainage pattern resembling the branches of a tree is known as "dendritic" the examples of which are the rivers of northern plain like Ganga, Yamuna, etc.

(ii) Radial : When the rivers originate from a hill and flow in all directions, the drainage pattern is known as 'radial'. The rivers originating from the Amarkantak range and the Central Highlands present a good example of it.

(iii) Trellis : When the primary tributaries of rivers flow parallel to each other and secondary tributaries join them at right angles, the pattern is known as 'trellis'. Peninsular rivers such as Godavari , Krishna, etc are good examples.

(iv) Centripetal : When the rivers discharge their waters from all directions in a lake or depression, the pattern is known as 'centripetal'. These rivers form cascades/rapids and waterfalls.

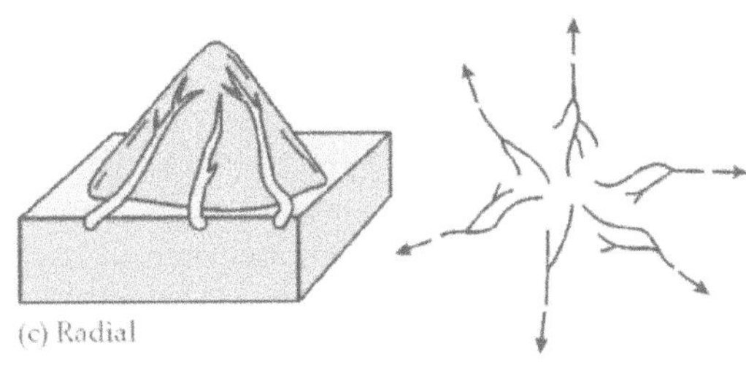

(c) Radial

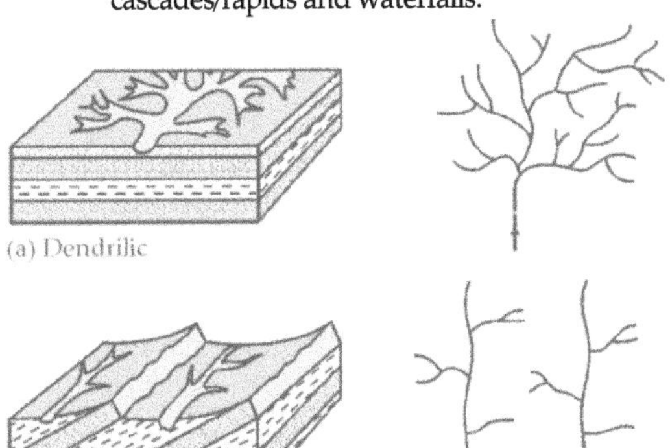

(a) Dendrilic

(b) Trellis

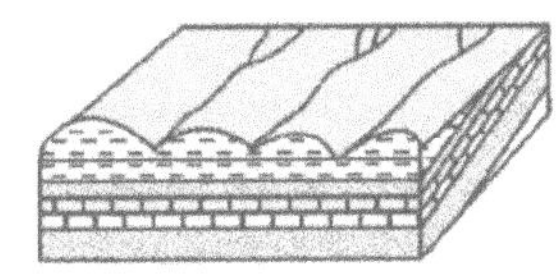

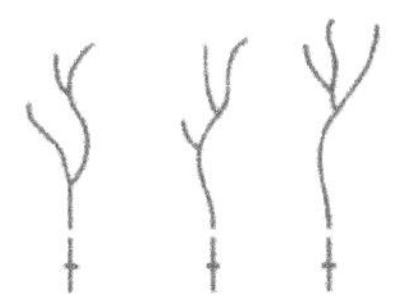

(d) Parallel

5

Answering Tip

- The drainage pattern are governed by the topography of the land, whether a particular region is dominated by hard or soft rocks, and the gradient of the land.

TOPIC-2

The Peninsular Drainage System : The Evolution of the Peninsular Drainage System, River Systems of the Peninsular Drainage, River Regimes.

Revision Notes

- The Peninsular Drainage System is older than the Himalayan one.
- The Western Ghats running close to the western coast act as the water divide between the major Peninsular rivers, discharging their water in the Bay of Bengal and as small rivulets joining the Arabian Sea.
- Most of the major Peninsular rivers except Narmada and Tapi flow from west to East.
- The other major river systems of the Peninsular drainage are – the Mahanadi the Godavari, the Krishna and the Kaveri. Peninsular rivers are characterised by fixed course, absence of meanders and non perennial flow of water.
- Three major geological events in the distant past have shaped the present drainage systems of Peninsular India :
  - Subsidence of the western flank of the Peninsula leading to its submergence below the sea during the early tertiary period.
  - Upheaval of the Himalayas when the northern flank of the Peninsular block was subjected to subsidence and the consequent trough faulting. Slight tilting of the Peninsular block from northwest to the southeastern direction gave orientation to the entire drainage system towards the Bay of Bengal during the same period.
- The Mahanadi rises near Sihawa in Raipur district of Chhattisgarh and runs through Odisha to discharge its water into the Bay of Bengal. It is 851 km long and its catchment area spreads over 1.42 lakh sq.km.
- The Godavari is the largest Peninsular river system. It is also called the Dakshin Ganga. It rises in the Nasik district of Maharashtra and discharges its water into the Bay of Bengal.
- The Krishna is the second largest eastflowing Peninsular river which rises near Mahabaleshwar in Sahyadri.
- The Kaveri rises in Brahmagiri hills (1,341m) of Kogadu district in Karnataka. Its length is 800 km and it drains an area of 81,155 sq. km.
- The Narmada originates on the western flank of the Amarkantak plateau at a height of about 1,057 m.
- The Tapi is the other important westward flowing river. It originates from Multai in the Betul district of Madhya Pradesh.
- Luni is the largest river system of Rajasthan, west of Aravali. It originates near Pushkar in two branches, i.e. the Saraswati and the Sabarmati, which join with each other at Govindgarh.

- Goa has two important rivers which are Mandovi and Jauri.
- Kerala has a narrow coastline. The longest river of Kerala, Bharathapuzha rises near Annamalai hills. It is also known as Ponnani.
- The Periyar is the second largest river of Kerala.
- The pattern of flow of water in a river channel over a year is known as its regime. The north Indian rivers originating from the Himalayas are perennial as they are fed by glaciers through snow melt and also receive rainfall water during rainy season.
- The discharge is the volume of water flowing in a river measured over time. It is measured either in cusecs (cubic feet per second) or cumecs (cubic metres per second).
- The two Peninsular rivers display interesting differences in their regimes compared to the Himalayan rivers.
- The rivers of India carry huge volumes of water per year but it is unevenly distributed both in time and space.
- There are perennial rivers carrying water throughout the year while the non-perennial rivers have very little water during the dry season.

Know the Terms

- **Meanders :** It is a series of regular sinuous curves, bends, loops , turns or windings in the channel of a river or a stream.
- **Cusecs :** It means cubic feet per second.
- **Cumecs :** It stands for cubic meters per second.

Multiple Choice Questions (1 mark each)

Q. 1. The largest Peninsular river system is the: A
(a) Narmada
(b) Tapi
(c) Godavari
(d) Periyar

Ans. (c) Godavari 1

Q. 2. Mandovi and Jauri are the important rivers of : U
(a) Goa
(b) Varanasi
(c) Madhya Pradesh
(d) Punjab

Ans. (a) Goa 1

Q. 3. The second largest river of Kerala is : U
(a) Vaigai
(b) Periyar
(c) Penner
(d) Subarnarekha

Ans. (b) Periyar 1

Very Short Answer Type Questions (1 mark each)

Q. 1. What is Cumecs ? U

Ans. Cubic metres per second is known as Cumecs. 1

Q. 2. Name any two small rivers flowing towards the East. A

Ans. The Shetruniji , the Bhadra , the Dhadhar, Sabarmati and Mahi. 1

Q. 3. What do you know about the Periyar River? A

Ans. The Periyar is the second largest river of Kerala. Its catchment area is 5,243 sq. km. 1

Answering Tip

- It is one of the few perennial rivers in the region and provides drinking water for several major towns.

AI **Q. 4. Name the important rivers flowing towards the West.** U

Ans. The Subarnrekha, the Baitarni, the Brahmani, the Vamsadhara, the Penner, the Palar and the Vaigai are important rivers. 1

Short Answer Type Questions (3 marks each)

Q. 1. What do you know about the flood prone areas of India. R

Ans. The states falling within the periphery of 'India Flood Prone Areas' are West Bengal, Odisha, Andhra Pradesh, Kerala, Assam, Bihar, Gujarat, Uttar Pradesh, Haryana and Punjab. The intense monsoons from the South-West causes the rivers like Brahmaputra, Ganga, Yamuna, etc., to swell their banks, which in turn floods the adjacent areas. Over the past decades, Central India has become familiar with the precipitation events like the torrential rains and flash floods. The major flood prone areas in India are the river banks and the deltas of Ravi, Yamuna-Sahibi, Gandak, Sutlej,

Ganga, Ghaggar, Kosi, Teesta, Brahmaputra, Mahanadi, Mahananda, Damodar, Godavari, Mayurakshi, Sabarmati and their tributaries.

During the rainy season, much of the water is wasted in floods and flows downs to the sea. Similarly, when there is a flood in one part of the country , the other area suffer from drought. The Godavari is subjected to heavy floods in its lower reaches to the south of Polavaram , where it forms a picturesque gorge. 3

Q. 2. What are the characteristics of the rivers of South? U

Ans. Characteristics of the rivers of South :

(i) These rivers originate in the Peninsular Plateau and central highlands. These are seasonal as it is dependent on monsoon rainfall.

(ii) **They reflect super imposed type of drainage pattern and rejuvenated resulting in trellis, radial and rectangular patterns.**

(iii) These rivers are smaller having fixed course with well-adjusted valleys. Their catchment area is relatively smaller basin. These rivers are old rivers with graded profile and have almost reached their base levels. . 3

Q. 3. The two peninsular rivers display interesting differences in their regimes compared to the Himalayan rivers. Explain? A

Ans. The two peninsular rivers display interesting differences in their regimes compared to the Himalayan rivers.

The Narmada has a very low volume of discharge from January to July but it suddenly rises in August when the maximum flow is attained. The fall in October is as spectacular as the rise in August. The flow of water in the Narmada, as recorded at Garudeshwar, shows that the maximum flow is of the order of 2,300 cusecs, while the minimum flow is only 15 cusecs.

The Godavari has the minimum discharge in May, and the maximum in July-August. After August, there is a sharp fall in water flow although the volume of flow in October and November is higher than that in any of the months from January to May. The mean maximum discharge of the Godavari at Polavaram is 3,200 cusecs while the mean minimum flow is only 50 cusecs. 3

Q. 4. Write a note on River Luni. A

Ans. (i) Luni is the largest river system of Rajasthan, west of Aravali. It originates near Pushkar in two branches, *i.e.*, the Saraswati and the Sabarmati, which join with each other at Govindgarh.

(ii) From here, the river comes out of Aravali and is known as Luni.

(iii) It flows towards the west till Telwara and then takes a southwest direction to join the Rann of Kuchchh. The entire river system is ephemeral. 3

Q. 5. What do you know about River Tapi? R

Ans. The Tapi is the other important westward flowing river. It originates from Multai in the Betul district of Madhya Pradesh. It is 724 km long and drains an area of 65,145 sq. km. Nearly 79 per cent of its basin lies in Maharashtra, 15 per cent in Madhya Pradesh and the remaining 6 per cent in Gujarat. 3

Answering Tip

- The Tapi River is a river in central India between the Godavari and Narmada rivers.

Q. 6. Explain important features of Kaveri Basin. R

Ans. Important features of Kaveri Basin are as follows :

(i) The Kaveri rises in Brahmagiri hills (1,341m) of Kogadu district in Karnataka. Its length is 800 km and it drains an area of 81,155 sq. km.

(ii) Since the upper catchment area receives rainfall during the southwest monsoon season (summer) and the lower part during the northeast monsoon season (winter), the river carries water throughout the year with comparatively less fluctuation than the other Peninsular rivers.

(iii) About 3 per cent of the Kaveri basin falls in Kerala, 41 per cent in Karnataka and 56 per cent in Tamil Nadu. 3

AI **Q. 7. How did the Peninsular Drainage System evolve?** A

Ans. Three major geological events in the distant past have shaped the present drainage systems of Peninsular India:

(i) Subsidence of the western flank of the Peninsula leading to its submergence below the sea during the early tertiary period. Generally, it has disturbed the symmetrical plan of the river on either side of the original watershed.

(ii) Upheaval of the Himalayas when the northern flank of the Peninsular block was subjected to subsidence and the consequent trough faulting. The Narmada and The Tapi flow in trough faults and fill the original cracks with their detritus materials. Hence, there is a lack of alluvial and deltaic deposits in these rivers.

(iii) Slight tilting of the Peninsular block from northwest to the southeastern direction gave orientation to the entire drainage system towards the Bay of Bengal during the same period. 3

Answering Tip

- Most of the major Peninsular Rivers except Narmada and Tapi flow from west to east.

Q. 8. Name any three factors that affect the speed of a river. U

Ans. Factors affecting the speed of a river :

(i) **Gradient :** If refer to the drop in the elevation of the river channel as the river flows down the hill. If the gradient is steep, the rivers flow quickly, whereas, if the gradient is gentle the river flows slowly. In the upper course, the river flows rapidly through a steep gradient. On the other hand, in the middle and the lower course , the river flows gently through a greater gradient.

(ii) Speed : around the perimeter of the river, at the sides and along the river bed friction is created as water flows against the edges . Water flowing through a wide, deep river channel encounters less resistance than water flowing in a narrow, shallow channel.

(iii) Volume of water : The volume of water that flows through a river within a given amount of time-known as the discharge-also affects its velocity. As the volume of water in a river increase, through smaller streams flowing into it, for example, the velocity of the river increases. An increase in water volume can also affect a river's velocity in the long term. **3**

Long Answer Type Questions (5 marks each)

Q. 1. Why are the rivers in India considered important? U

Ans. Importance of the rivers in India:

(i) Source of water : Rivers carry water and nutrients to areas all around the Earth. They play a very important part in the water cycle, acting as drainage channels for surface water. Rivers drain nearly 75% of the Earth's land surface.

(ii) Habitats : Rivers provide excellent habitat and food for many of the Earth's organisms. Many rare plants and trees grow by rivers. Ducks, voles, otters and beavers make their homes on the river banks. Reeds and other plants like bulrushes grow along the river banks. Other animals use the river for food and drink. Birds such as kingfishers eat small fish from the river.

(iii) Delta : River deltas have many different species of wildlife. Insects , mammals and birds use the delta for their homes and for food.

(iv) Transport : Rivers provide travel routes for exploration , commerce and recreation. Many heavy industries prefer water transport for the movement of bulky raw as well as finished goods.

(v) Farming : River valleys and plain provide fertile soils. Farmers in dry regions irrigate their cropland using water carried by irrigation ditched from nearby rivers.

(vi) Energy : Rivers are an important energy source. During the early industrial era, mills, shops and factories were built near fast-flowing rivers where water could be used to power machines. Today steep rivers are still used to power hydroelectric plants and their water turbines. **(Any five) 5**

AI **Q. 2. How are the Himalayan rivers different from the Peninsular rivers?** A

Ans. Followings are the important differences between Himalayan rivers and Peninsular rivers :

S.No.	Himalayan Rivers	Peninsular Rivers
1.	Himalayan mountain covered with glacier thus, they are perennial in nature.	Peninsular plateau and central highland thus, they are seasonal in nature.
2.	They are antecedent and consequent leading to dendritic pattern in plains.	Super imposed, rejuvenated resulting in trellis radial and rectangular patterns.
3.	They are relatively very large basins.	They are relatively very smaller basins.
4.	They are long course.	They are smaller and fixed course.
5.	They are young and youthful as well as active and make deepening in the valleys.	They are old river with graded profile, and have almost reached their based level.

Answering Tip

- For the Himalayan Rivers, glaciers act as a major sources of water, whereas the monsoon rain acts as a major source of water for the peninsular rivers.

Q. 3. Write a note on the river system of the peninsular drainage? R

Ans. There are a large number of river systems in the Peninsular drainage. A brief account of the major Peninsular river systems is given below:

(i) The Mahanadi : It rises near Sihawa in Raipur district of Chhattisgarh and runs through Odisha to discharge its water into the Bay of Bengal. It is 851 km long and its catchment area spreads over 1.42 lakh sq. km. Some navigation is carried on in the lower course of this river. Fifty three per cent of the drainage basin of this river lies in Madhya Pradesh and Chhattisgarh, while 47 per cent lies in Orissa.

(ii) The Godavari : It is the largest Peninsular river system. It is also called the Dakshin Ganga. It rises in the Nasik district of Maharashtra and discharges its water into the Bay of Bengal. Its tributaries run through the states of Maharashtra, Madhya Pradesh, Chhattisgarh, Odisha and Andhra Pradesh. It is 1,465 km long with a catchment area spreading over 3.13 lakh sq. km 49 per cent of this, lies in Maharashtra, 20 per cent in Madhya Pradesh and Chhattisgarh, and the rest in Andhra Pradesh.

(iii) The Krishna : It is the second largest eastflowing Peninsular river which rises near Mahabaleshwar in Sahyadri. Its total length is 1,401 km. The Koyna, the Tungbhadra and the Bhima are its major tributaries.

Of the total catchment area of the Krishna, 27 per cent lies in Maharashtra, 44 per cent in Karnataka and 29 per cent in Andhra Pradesh.

(iv) The Kaveri : It rises in Brahmagiri hills (1,341m) of Kogadu district in Karnataka. Its length is 800 km and it drains an area of 81,155 sq. km. Since the upper catchment area receives rainfall during the southwest monsoon season (summer) and the lower part during the northeast monsoon season (winter), the river carries water throughout the year with comparatively less fluctuation than the other Peninsular rivers.

(v) The Narmada : It originates on the western flank of the Amarkantak plateau at a height of about 1,057 m. Flowing in a rift valley between the Satpura in the south and the Vindhyan range in the north, it forms a picturesque gorge in marble rocks and Dhuandhar waterfall near Jabalpur. After flowing a distance of about 1,312 km, it meets the Arabian sea south of Bharuch, forming a broad 27 km long estuary. Its catchment area is about 98,796 sq. km.

(vi) The Tapi : It is the other important westward flowing river. It originates from Multai in the Betul district of Madhya Pradesh. It is 724 km long and drains an area of 65,145 sq. km. Nearly 79 per cent of its basin lies in Maharashtra, 15 per cent in Madhya Pradesh and the remaining 6 per cent in Gujarat.

(vii) Luni : It is the largest river system of Rajasthan, west of Aravali. It originates near Pushkar in two branches, *i.e.,* the Saraswati and the Sabarmati, which join with each other at Govindgarh. From here, the river comes out of Aravali and is known as Luni. It flows towards the west till Telwara and then takes a southwest direction to join the Rann of Kuchchh. **(Any Five) 5**

Q. 4. What factors determine the volume of water in a river? [A]

Ans. Factors that determine the volume of water in a river are :

(i) Size of the drainage basin : A drainage basin in an area drained by one main river and its tributaries determines the volume of water in a river. If the drainage basin is large, the volume of water in the river will be more. When the drainage is large the surface the surface run off flourished the river is more runoff in the amount of rainwater that flows in the ground and ultimately into the river or lake. On the other hand, if the drainage basin is small volume of water in the river will be less because there is less surface area for the rain to fall on.

(ii) Vegetation : Leaves of trees intercept rainwater and allow more water to sweep into the ground in groundwater . As a result, the amount of surface runoff reduces. Therefore , the volume of water in the river is less where vegetation is dense. Spare vegetation prevents rainwater from getting trapped in the leaves and branches, thereby allowing more water to flow through as surface runoff. So in areas with less vegetation volume of water is more.

(iii) Permeability of rocks : In areas with permeable or porous rocks, much of the rainwater sweeps through the pores in the rocks into the ground. In such areas, surface run off is less and water flowing into the river channel will also be less.

(iv) Climate : In areas with hot and wet climate such as equatorial area, volume of water in rivers will be high. However, the amount of water will be less in areas with dry climate receiving less rainfall. In areas with prominent wet or dry seasons, volume of water in the river will vary according to the amount of rainfall received.

(v) Riverbed gradient : The gradient of a river refers to how steep its slope is, this also has a significant effect on the velocity of a river. When a river flows down a steep slope, the gravitational force that pulls the water downward is stronger than it would be on water flowing down a gentle slope. **5**

Q. 5. What are the major causes of pollution of river water? [U]

Ans. The major causes of pollution of river water are:

(i) Sewage and waste water : Sewage , garbage and liquid waste of households , agricultural lands and factories are discharged into lakes and rivers. These wastes contain harmful chemicals and toxins which make the river water poisonous for aquatic animals and plants.

(ii) Dumping : Dumping of solid wastes and litters in water bodies causes huge problems. Litters include plastic, aluminium, Styrofoam, etc. Different things take different amount of time to degrade in water. They affect aquatic plants and animals.

(iii) Industrial waste : Industrial waste contains pollutants like asbestos, lead, mercury and petrochemicals which are extremely harmful to both people and environment. Industrial waste is discharged into rivers and forms a thick sludge polluting the water.

(iv) Global warming : Due to global warming, there is an increase in water temperature. This increase results in death of aquatic plants and animals. This also results in bleaching of coral reefs in water.

(v) Urbanisation : Many towns and cities which came up on the banks of rivers has given rise to problems such as disposal of wastewater in the rivers, sewage problems, etc which has led to pollution of river water. 5

Answering Tip

- Humans are the main cause of river pollution.

Q. 6. Can the problems of flood and drought be solved or minimised by transferring the surplus water from one basin to the water deficit basins? Do we have some schemes of inter-basin linkage? [A]

Ans. Yes ,the problems of flood and drought can be solved or minimised by transferring the surplus water from one basin to the water deficit basins. During the rainy season, much of the water is wasted in floods and flows down to the sea. When there is a flood in one part of the country , the other area suffers from drought. The government does have a number of schemes of inter-basin linkage:

(i) Periyar Diversion Scheme
(ii) Indira Gandhi Canal Scheme
(iii) Kurnool-Cuddapah Canal
(iv) Beas-Satluj Link Canal
(v) Ganga-Kaveri Link Canal 5

AI **Q.7. What problems will the world face if they misuse the river water?** R

Ans. If the world misuses the river water it will lead to a number of problems such as:

(i) No availability in sufficient quantity : The volume of river water will gradually start decreasing if we don't make sensible use of the available river water. There will be no substitute left for the deficit river water.

(ii) River water pollution : Dumping of solid wastes and litters in water bodies causes huge problems. Litters include plastic, aluminium, Styrofoam, etc. Different things take different amount of time to degrade in water. They affect aquatic plants and animals and also pollute the river water.

(iii) River water disputes between states : There will arise river water disputes between many states. One such dispute witnessed in India is the Cauvery dispute between Karnataka and Tamil Nadu.

(iv) Sediment pollution : Misuse of river water will lead to siltation or sediment pollution . It refers to the increased concentration of suspended sediments on bottoms where they are undesired.

(v) Uneven seasonal flow of water : Due to misuse of river water, the sufficient quantity required for maintaining the flow of water will also decrease hence leading to uneven season flow of water. 5

Map Work (5 marks)

Q. 1. Locate and label the following five rivers with appropriate symbols on the given political outline map of India.

(i) Kaveri **(ii) Narmada**
(iii) Luni **(iv) Tapi**
(v) Indus

Ans.

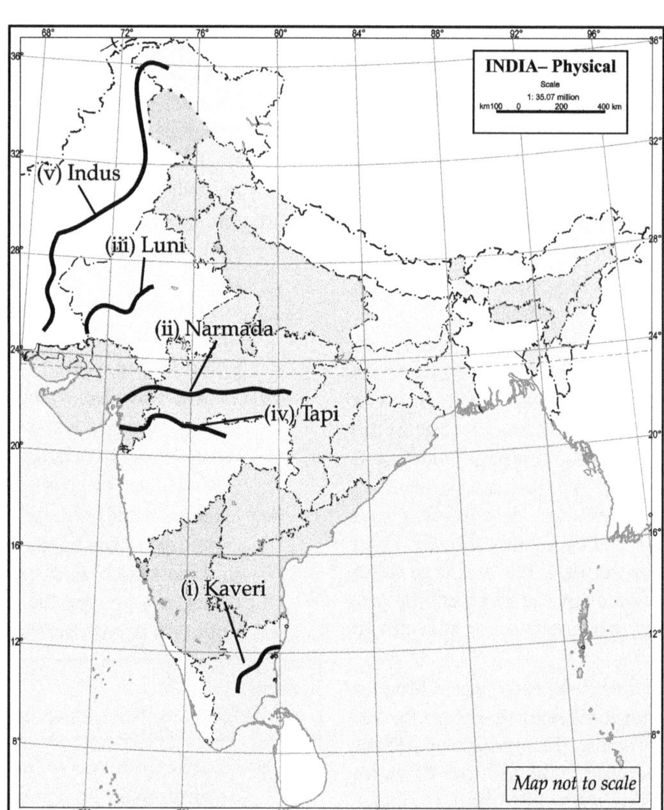

NCERT CORNER

(A) **Multiple choice questions :**

Q. 1. Which one of the following rivers was known as the 'Sorrow of Bengal' :

(a) The Gandak

(b) The Son

(c) The Kosi

(d) The Damodar

Ans. (d) The Damodar .

Q. 2. Which one of the following rivers has the largest river basin in India :

(a) The Indus

(b) The Brahmaputra

(c) The Ganga

(d) The Krishna

Ans. (c) The Ganga .

Q. 3. Which one of the following rivers is not included in 'Panchnad' :

(a) The Ravi

(b) The Chenab

(c) The Indus

(d) The Jhelum

Ans. (c) The Indus .

Q. 4. Which one of the following rivers flows in a rift valley :

(a) The Son

(b) The Narmada

(c) The Yamuna

(d) The Luni

Ans. (b) The Narmada .

Q. 5. Which one of the following is the place of confluence of the Alkananda and the Bhagirathi:

(a) Vishnu Prayag

(b) Rudra Prayag

(c) Karan Prayag

(d) Deva Prayag

Ans. (d) Deva Prayag .

(B) State the differences between the following.

Q. 1. River Basin and Watershed ?

Ans.

S.No.	River Basin	Watershed
1.	The catchments of large rivers are called river basins.	Catchment of small rivulets and rills are often referred to as watersheds.
2.	River basins collect water and moisture from different sources and drains them out into other bodies of water.	Watershed divides the river basins or collection points that contain the water that is collected.
3.	River basins are larger in area.	Watersheds are smaller in area.

Q. 2. Dendritic and Trellis drainage pattern.

Ans.

S.No.	Dendritic	Trellis
1.	The drainage pattern resembling the branches of a tree is known as dendritic.	When the primary tributaries of rivers flow parallel to each other and secondary tributaries join them at right angles, the pattern is known as trellis.
2.	Dendritic drainage develops in plains topography.	Trellis drainage develops in folded topography.
3.	Dendritic systems form in V-shaped valleys as a result, the rock types must be impervious and non-porous.	The rectangular drainage pattern is found in regions that have undergone faulting.

Q. 3. Radial and Centripetal drainage pattern?

Ans.

S.No.	Radial Drainage Pattern	Centripetal Drainage Pattern
1.	When the rivers originate from a hill and flow in all directions, the drainage pattern is known as 'radial'.	When the rivers discharge their waters from all directions in a lake or depression, the pattern is known as 'centripetal'.
2.	The rivers originating from the Amarkantak range present a good example of it.	Sambhar Lake of Rajasthan is the example of centripetal drainage system.

Q. 4. Delta and Estuary .

Ans.

S.No.	Delta	Estuary
1.	The triangular deposits made by the rivers at their mouth form delta.	The shard edged mouth of rivers, devoid of any deposits is known as estuary.
2.	Deltas are formed in the regions of low tides and coastal plains.	Regions of high tides and rift valleys witness estuaries.
3.	Deltas are fertile lands.	Estuary does not have fertile land.

(C) Answer the following questions in about 30 words:

Q. 1. What are the socio-economic advantages of inter-linking of rivers in India.

Ans. Rivers in India bear a large amount of water every year. Most of the water gets wasters in floods during rainy seasons, agriculture is also ruined. If the rivers are inter-linking to each other through canals, then the problems of floods and drought will get solved. It will also solve the problem of drinking water and millions of rupees will be saved. It will also lead to increase in productivity. It will also improve economic conditions of the farmers.

Q. 2. Write three characteristics of the Peninsular river?

Ans. The characteristics of the Peninsular river :

(i) The Peninsular drainage system is older than the Himalayan one. This is evident from the broad, largely-graded shallow valleys, and the maturity of the rivers.

(ii) The rivers originate in peninsular plateau and central highlands. These are seasonal as it dependents on monsoon rainfall.

(iii) They reflect super imposed type of drainage pattern and rejuvenated resulting in trellis , radial and rectangular patterns.

(D) Answer the following questions in about 125 words:

Q. 1. What are the important characteristic features of north Indian rivers? How are these different from Peninsular rivers?

Ans.

S.No.	North Indian Rivers	Peninsular rivers
1. Place of origin	They originate in Himalayan mountain covered with glaciers.	They originate in the Peninsular Plateau and the Central Highland
2. Nature of flow	They are perennial because they receive water from glacier and rainfall.	They are seasonal as it is dependent on monsoon rainfall.
3. Drainage pattern	These are antecedent and consequently lead to dendritic pattern in plains.	Super imposed, rejuvenated re-sulting in trellis, radial and rectan-gular patterns.
4. Nature of river	It has long course, flowing through the rugged mountains experiencing headward erosion and river capturing; in plains it exhibits meandering and shifting of course.	It is smaller, fixed course with well adjusted valleys.
5. Catchment area	Its catchment areas include very large basins.	Its catchment areas include rela-tively smaller basin.
6. Age of the river	These rivers are young and youthful. These are active and deepening in the valleys.	Old rivers with graded profile and have almost reached their base levels.

Q. 2. Suppose you are travelling from Hardwar to Siliguri along the foothills of the Himalayas. Name the important rivers you will come across. Describe the characteristics of any one of them?

Ans. While travelling from Hardwar to Siliguri along the foothills of the Himalayas, we shall come across the Tons, Gomti, Saryu, Ramganga, Sharda, Gandak, Old Gandak, Kamla, Bagmati, Kosi and Ganga.

The Ganga is the most important river of India both from the point of view of its basin and cultural significance. It rises in the Gangotri glacier near Gaumukh (3,900 m) in the Uttarkashi district of Uttaranchal. Here, it is known as the Bhagirathi. It cuts through the Central and the Lesser Himalayas in narrow gorges. At Devprayag, the Bhagirathi meets the Alaknanda; hereafter, it is known as the Ganga.

The Alaknanda has its source in the Satopanth glacier above Badrinath. The Alaknanda consists of the Dhauli and the Vishnu Ganga which meet at Joshimath or Vishnu Prayag. The other tributaries of Alaknanda such as the Pindar join it at Karna Prayag while Mandakini or Kali Ganga meets it at Rudra Prayag.

The Ganga enters the plains at Haridwar. From here, it flows first to the south, then to the south-east and east before splitting into two distributaries, namely the Bhagirathi and the Hugli. The river has a length of 2,525 km. It is shared by Uttarakhand (110 km) and Uttar Pradesh (1,450 km), Bihar (445 km) and West Bengal (520 km).

The Ganga basin covers about 8.6 lakh sq. km area in India alone. The Ganga river system is the largest in India having a number of perennial and non-perennial rivers originating in the Himalayas in the north and the Peninsula in the south, respectively. The Son is its major right bank tributary. The important left bank tributaries are the Ramganga, the Gomati, the Ghaghara, the Gandak, the Kosi and the Mahanada. The river finally discharges itself into the Bay of Bengal near the Sagar Island.

OSWAAL LEARNING TOOLS

For Suggested Online Videos

Visit : *https://qrgo.page.link/CZ6c4* **Or Scan the Code**

To learn from NCERT Prescribed Videos

Visit : *https://qrgo.page.link/d9Wxj* **Or Scan the Code**

UNIT-IX

Climate, Vegetation and Soil

CHAPTER

4 CLIMATE

Syllabus

➤ *Unity and Diversity in the Monsoon Climate, Factors Determining the Climate of India,*

➤ *The Nature of the Indian Monsoon, The Rhythm of Seasons, Distribution of Rainfall, Climatic Regions of India, Monsoon and the Economic Life in India.*

TOPIC-1
Unity and Diversity in the Monsoon Climate, Factors Determining the Climate of India

Revision Notes

➤ Weather is the momentary state of the atmosphere while climate refers to the average of the weather conditions over a longer period of time. ➤ There are variations in weather conditions during different seasons. These changes occur due to the changes in the elements of weather (temperature, pressure, wind direction and velocity, humidity and precipitation, etc.).

➤ Weather changes quickly, may be within a day or week but climate changes imperceptivity and may be noted after 50 years or even more.

➤ Monsoon connotes the climate associated with seasonal reversal in the direction of winds. India has hot monsoonal climate which is the prevalent climate in south and southeast Asia.

➤ The climate of India has many regional variations expressed in the pattern of winds, temperature and rainfall, rhythm of seasons and the degree of wetness or dryness.

➤ India's climate is controlled by a number of factors which can be broadly divided into two groups —

➤ **Factors related to location and relief :**

- **Latitude :** The Tropic of Cancer passes through the central part of India in east-west direction. Thus, northern part of the India lies in sub-tropical and temperate zone and the part lying south of the Tropic of Cancer falls in the tropical zone. The tropical zone being nearer to the equator, experiences high temperatures throughout the year with small daily and annual range.
- **The Himalayan Mountains :** The lofty Himalayas in the north along with its extensions act as an effective climatic divide. The towering mountain chain provides an invincible shield to protect the subcontinent from the cold northern winds . The Himalayas also trap the monsoon winds, forcing them to shed their moisture within the subcontinent.
- **Distribution of Land and Water :** India is flanked by the Indian Ocean on three sides in the south and girdled by a high and continuous mountain-wall in the north. As compared to the landmass, water heats up or cools down slowly. This differential heating of land and sea creates different air pressure zones in different seasons in and around the Indian subcontinent.

- **Distance from the Sea :** Areas in the interior of India are far away from the moderating influence of the sea. Such areas have extremes of climate. Whereas, the coastal areas hardly have any idea of extremes of temperature and the seasonal rhythm of weather.
- **Altitude :** Temperature decreases with height. Due to thin air, places in the mountains are cooler than places on the plains.
- **Relief :** The physiography or relief of India also affects the temperature, air pressure, direction and speed of wind and the amount and distribution of rainfall.

➢ **Factors related to air pressure and winds :**

- To understand the differences in local climates of India, we need to understand the mechanism of the following three factors :

➢ Distribution of air pressure and winds on the surface of the earth.

➢ Upper air circulation caused by factors controlling global weather and the inflow of different air masses and jet streams.

➢ Inflow of western cyclones generally known as disturbances during the winter season and tropical depressions during the south-west monsoon period into India, creating weather conditions favourable to rainfall. The mechanism of these three factors can be understood with reference to winter and summer seasons of the year separately.

➢ **Mechanism of weather in the winter season :**

- **Surface Pressure and Winds :** In winter months, the weather conditions over India are generally influenced by the distribution of pressure in Central and Western Asia.
- A high pressure centre in the region lying to the north of the Himalayas develops during winter. This centre of high pressure gives rise to the flow of air at the low level from the north towards the Indian subcontinent, south of the mountain range.
- The surface winds blowing out of the high pressure centre over Central Asia reach India in the form of a dry continental air mass. These continental winds come in contact with trade winds over northwestern India. The position of this contact zone is not, however, stable.
- **Jet Stream and Upper Air Circulation :** In the lower troposphere about 3 km above the surface of the earth, a different pattern of air circulation is observed. All of Western and Central Asia remains under the influence of westerly winds along the altitude of 9-13 km from West to East. These winds blow across the Asian continent at latitudes north of the Himalayas roughly parallel to the Tibetan highlands . These are known as jet streams.
- **Western Cyclonic Disturbance and Tropical Cyclones :** The western cyclonic disturbances originate over the Mediterranean Sea and are brought into India by the westerly jet stream. An increase in the prevailing night temperature generally indicates an advance in the arrival of these cyclones disturbances. Most of these cyclones are very destructive due to high wind velocity and torrential rain that accompanies.

➢ **Mechanism of Weather in the Summer Season :**

- **Surface Pressure and Winds :** By the middle of July, the low pressure belt nearer the surface [termed as Inter Tropical Convergence Zone (ITCZ) shifts northwards, roughly parallel to the Himalayas between 20° N and 25° N. By this time, the westerly jet stream withdraws from the Indian region. The maritime tropical airmass (mT) from the Southern Hemisphere, after crossing the Equator, rushes to the low pressure area in the general southwesterly direction. It is this moist air current which is popularly known as the southwest monsoon.
- **Jet Streams and Upper Air Circulation :** An easterly jet stream flows over the southern part of the Peninsula in June, and has a maximum speed of 90 km per hour . In August, it is confined to 15oN latitude, and in September up to 22o N latitudes. The easterlies normally do not extend to the north of 30o N latitude in the upper atmosphere.
- **Easterly Jet Stream and Tropical Cyclones :** The easterly jet stream steers the tropical depressions into India. These depressions play a significant role in the distribution of monsoon rainfall over the Indian subcontinent. The frequency at which these depressions visit India, their direction and intensity, all go a long way in determining the rainfall pattern during the southwest monsoon period.

Know the Terms

➢ **Weather :** Weather is the momentary state of the atmosphere.

➢ **Climate :** Climate refers to the average of the weather conditions over a longer period of time.

➢ **Monsoon :** It is traditionally defined as a seasonal reversing wind accompanied by corresponding changes in precipitation .

- **Break in the monsoon :** During the south-west monsoon period after having rains for a few days, if rain fails to occur for one or more weeks, it is known as break in the monsoon.
- **Jet Streams :** Winds blow across the Asian continent at latitudes north of the Himalayas roughly parallel to the Tibetan highlands are known as jet streams.
- **ITCZ :** The Inter Tropical Convergence Zone (ITCZ) is a low pressure zone located at the Equator where trade winds converge, and so, it is a zone where air tends to ascend.
- **Monsoon Trough :** In July, the ITCZ is located around 20° N-25°N latitudes over the Gangetic plain.

Multiple Choice Questions (1 mark each)

Q. 1. Weather changes : [A]
(a) quickly
(b) slowly
(c) gradually
(d) never

Ans. (a) quickly 1

Q. 2. A high pressure centre in the region lying to the north of the Himalayas develops during: [U]
(a) summer
(b) winter
(c) autumn
(d) monsoon

Ans. (b) winter 1

Q. 3. The western cyclonic disturbances originate over the: [U]
(a) Arabian Sea
(b) Mediterranean Sea
(c) Bay of Bengal
(d) Caspian Sea

Ans. (b) Mediterranean Sea 1

Very Short Answer Type Questions (1 mark each)

Q. 1. Define the term 'Weather'. [A]

Ans. Weather is the momentary state of the atmosphere. 1

Q. 2. Define the term 'Climate'. [A]

Ans. Climate refers to the average of the weather conditions over a longer period of time. 1

Q. 3. Define the term 'Monsoon'. [U]

Ans. It is traditionally defined as a seasonal reversing wind accompanied by corresponding changes in precipitation. 1

Answering Tip

- A monsoon is a seasonal shift in the prevailing wind direction, that usually brings with it a different kind of weather.

Q. 4. Define the term 'Jet stream'. [R]

Ans. Winds blow across the Asian continent at latitudes north of the Himalayas roughly parallel to the Tibetan highlands are known as jet streams. 1

Answering Tip

- The winds blow from west to east in jet streams but the flow often shifts to the north and south.

[AI] **Q. 5. What do you understand by the term ITCZ?** [A]

Ans. The Inter Tropical Convergence Zone (ITCZ) is a low pressure zone located at the Equator where trade winds converge, and so, it is a zone where air tends to ascend. 1

[AI] **Q. 6. Differentiate between weather and climate.** [A]

Ans. Refer to Short Ans 1.

Q. 7. Name any two regional variations experienced by the climate of India. [A]

Ans. The climate of India has many regional variations expressed in the pattern of winds, temperature and rainfall, rhythm of seasons and the degree of wetness or dryness. 1

Q. 8. Give one example of regional variation in precipitation? [U]

Ans. While snowfall occurs in the Himalayas, it only rains over the rest of the country is an apt example of regional variation in precipitation. 1

Q. 9. What is the amount of annual precipitation received in Meghalaya? [R]

Ans. The annual precipitation in Meghalaya exceeds 400 cm . 1

Q. 10. Name the two factors that control India's climate? [A]

Ans. India's climate is controlled by a number of factors which can be broadly divided into two groups — factors related to location and relief, and factors related to air pressure and winds. 1

Answering Tip

- Most of India is a sub-tropical country and that means very hot summers, humid rainy season and mild winters.

Q. 11. Why is the temperature range of Delhi more than Mumbai? [R]

Ans. Range of temperature is low in areas which are near to sea and high in areas which are far off from the sea. Delhi is far off from the sea and Mumbai is near to sea. Hence, the temperature range of Delhi is more than Mumbai. 1

Short Answer Type Questions (3 marks each)

Q. 1. Differentiate between weather and climate. A

Ans.

S.No.	Weather	Climate
1.	Weather is the momentary state of the atmosphere.	Climate refers to the average of the weather conditions over a longer period of time.
2.	Weather changes quickly, may be within a day or week.	Climate changes imperceptivity and may be noted after 50 years or even more.
3.	Frequency of weather change can be many times a day.	Frequency of climate change is very long process and can't be seen so easily.

(1 × 3 = 3)

Answering Tip

- Weather is the day-to-day state of the atmosphere, and its short-term variation in minutes to weeks. Climate is the weather of a place averaged over a period of time.

Q. 2. Explain with examples the regional variations in temperature, winds and rainfall. A

Ans. While in the summer the mercury occasionally touches 55°C in the western Rajasthan, it drops down to as low as minus 45°C in winter around Leh. Churu in Rajasthan may record a temperature of 50°C or more on a June day while the mercury hardly touches 19°C in Tawang (Arunachal Pradesh) on the same day. On a December night, temperature in Drass (Jammu and Kashmir) may drop down to minus 45°C while Thiruvananthapuram or Chennai on the same night records 20°C or 22°C. These examples confirm that there are seasonal variations in temperature from place to place and from region to region in India.

While snowfall occurs in the Himalayas, it only rains over the rest of the country. Similarly, variations are noticeable not only in the type of precipitation but also in its amount. While Cherrapunji and Mawsynram in the Khasi Hills of Meghalaya receive rainfall over 1,080 cm in a year, Jaisalmer in Rajasthan rarely gets more than 9 cm of rainfall during the same period.

The Ganga delta and the coastal plains of Orissa are hit by strong rain-bearing storms almost every third or fifth day in July and August while the Coromandal Coast, a thousand km to the south, goes generally dry during these months. Most parts of the country get rainfall during June-September, but on the coastal areas of Tamil Nadu, it rains in the beginning of the winter season. **3**

Q. 3. What is annual range of temperature? Explain it with the help of an example? R

Ans. The difference between the maximum average temperature and minimum average temperature of a place over twelve months is known as annual range of temperature.

Example :

The maximum average temperature at Jodhpur is 33.9°C and the minimum average temperature is 14.9°C. Hence the annual range of temperature at Jodhpur is 19°C (33.9°C -14.9°C). **3**

Long Answer Type Questions (5 marks each)

AI **Q. 1. Explain any five factors that determine the climate of India based on location and relief.** A

Ans. Factors related to Location and Relief:

(i) Latitude : The Tropic of Cancer passes through the central part of India in East-West direction. Thus, northern part of the India lies in sub-tropical and temperate zone and the part lying south of the Tropic of Cancer falls in the tropical zone. The tropical zone being nearer to the equator, experiences high temperatures throughout the year with small daily and annual range. Area north of the Tropic of Cancer being away from the Equator, experiences extreme climate with high daily and annual range of temperature.

(ii) The Himalayan Mountains : The lofty Himalayas in the north along with its extensions act as an effective climatic divide. The towering mountain chain provides an invincible shield to protect the subcontinent from the cold northern winds. The Himalayas also trap the monsoon winds, forcing them to shed their moisture within the subcontinent.

(iii) Distribution of Land and Water : India is flanked by the Indian Ocean on three sides in the south and girdled by a high and continuous mountain-wall in the north. As compared to the landmass, water heats up or cools down slowly. This differential heating of land and sea creates different air pressure zones in different seasons in and around the Indian subcontinent.

(iv) Distance from the Sea : With a long coastline, large coastal areas have an equable climate. Areas in the interior of India are far away from the moderating influence of the sea. Such areas have extremes of climate. That is why, the people of Mumbai and the Konkan Coast have hardly any idea of extremes of temperature and the seasonal rhythm of weather.

(v) Altitude : Temperature decreases with height. Due to thin air, places in the mountains are cooler than places on the plains. For example, Agra and Darjiling are located on the same latitude, but temperature of January in Agra is 16°C whereas it is only 4°C in Darjiling.

(vi) Relief : The physiography or relief of India also affects the temperature, air pressure, direction and speed of wind and the amount and distribution of rainfall. The windward sides of Western Ghats and Assam receive high rainfall during June-September whereas the southern plateau remains dry due to its leeward situation along the Western Ghats. **(Any Five) 5**

Q. 2. Explain the spatial variation in the rainfall throughout the country. [A]

Ans. There is great variation in rainfall throughout the country.

(i) While Cherrapunji and Mawsynram in the Khasi Hills of Meghalaya receive rainfall over 1,080cm in a year, Jaisalmer in Rajasthan rarely gets more than 9 cm of rainfall during the same period.

(ii) Tura situated in the Garo Hills of Meghalaya may receive an amount of rainfall in a single day which is equal to 10 years of rainfall at Jaisalmer. While the annual precipitation is less than 10 cm in the North-West Himalayas and the western deserts, it exceeds 400 cm in Meghalaya.

(iii) The highest rainfall occurs along the west coast, on the Western Ghats s well as in the sub-Himalayan areas in the North-West and the hills of Meghalaya, rainfall exceeding 200 cm. In some parts of the Khasi and Jaintia hills , the rainfall exceeds 1,000 cm. in the Brahmaputra valley and the adjoining hills, rainfall is less than 200 cm.

(iv) Rainfall between 100-200 cm is received in southern parts of Gujarat, east Tamil Nadu, North-eastern Peninsular covering Odisha, Jharkhand, Bihar, eastern Madhya Pradesh , Northern Ganga Plain along the sub-Himalayas and the Cachar Valley and Manipur.

(v) Western Uttar Pradesh, Delhi,Haryana, Punjab, Jammu and Kashmir, eastern Rajasthan, Gujarat and Deccan Plateau receive rainfall between 50-100 cm. 5

Answering Tip

- Spatial variability occurs when a quantity that is measured at different spatial locations exhibits values that differ across the locations.

TOPIC-2

The Nature of the Indian Monsoon, The Rhythm of Seasons, Distribution of Rainfall, Climatic Regions of India, Monsoon and the Economic Life in India

Revision Notes

➢ Systematic studies of the causes of rainfall in the South Asian region help to understand the causes and salient features of the monsoon, particularly some of its important aspects, such as :

- **The onset of the monsoon :** The differential heating of land and sea during the summer months is the mechanism which sets the stage for the monsoon winds to drift towards the subcontinent. During April and May when the sun shines vertically over the Tropic of Cancer, the large landmass in the north of Indian ocean gets intensely heated. This causes the formation of an intense low pressure in the northwestern part of the subcontinent.
  The southwest monsoon sets in over the Kerala coast by 1st June and moves swiftly to reach Mumbai and Kolkata between 10th and 13th June. By mid July, southwest monsoon engulfs the entire subcontinent.
- **Rain bearing Systems and Rainfall Distribution :** There seem to be two rain-bearing systems in India. First originate in the Bay of Bengal causing rainfall over the plains of north India. Second is the Arabian Sea current of the southwest monsoon which brings rain to the west coast of India. The intensity of rainfall over the west coast of India is, however, related to two factors:
- The offshore meteorological conditions
- The position of the equatorial jet stream along the eastern coast of Africa
  The rain which comes in spells, displays a declining trend from west to east over the west coast, and from the southeast towards the northwest over the North Indian Plain and the northern part of the Peninsula.
- **Break in the Monsoon :** During the south-west monsoon period after having rains for a few days, if rain fails to occur for one or more weeks, it is known as break in the monsoon. These dry spells are quite common during the rainy season. These breaks in the different regions are due to different reasons.
- In northern India rains are likely to fail if the rain-bearing storms are not very frequent along the monsoon trough or the ITCZ over this region.

- Over the west coast the dry spells are associated with days when winds blow parallel to the coast.
- The meteorologists recognise the following four seasons :
- **The Cold Weather Season :**
- **Temperature :** Usually, the cold weather season sets in by mid-November in northern India. December and January are the coldest months in the northern plain. The mean daily temperature remains below 21°C over most parts of northern India. There are three main reasons for the excessive cold in north India during this season :
- States like Punjab, Haryana and Rajasthan being far away from the moderating influence of sea experience continental climate.
- The snowfall in the nearby Himalayan ranges creates cold wave situation; and
- Around February, the cold winds coming from the Caspian Sea and Turkmenistan bring cold wave along with frost and fog over the north-western parts of India.
- There is hardly any seasonal change in the distribution pattern of the temperature in coastal areas because of moderating influence of the sea and the proximity to equator.
- **Pressure and Winds :** Due to low pressure gradient, the light winds with a low velocity of about 3-5 km per hour begin to blow outwards. By and large, the topography of the region influences the wind direction.
- During the winters, the weather in India is pleasant. The pleasant weather conditions, however, at intervals, get disturbed by shallow cyclonic depressions originating over the east Mediterranean Sea and travelling eastwards across West Asia, Iran, Afghanistan and Pakistan before they reach the north western parts of India.
- **Rainfall :** Winter monsoons do not cause rainfall as they move from land to the sea. It is because firstly, they have little humidity; and secondly, due to anti cyclonic circulation on land, the possibility of rainfall from them reduces. During October and November, northeast monsoon while crossing over the Bay of Bengal, picks up moisture and causes torrential rainfall over the Tamil Nadu coast, southern Andhra Pradesh, southeast Karnataka and southeast Kerala.
- **The Hot Weather Season :**
- **Temperature :** With the apparent northward movement of the sun towards the Tropic of Cancer in March, temperatures start rising in North India. April, May and June are the months of summer in north India. The hot weather season in South India is mild and not so intense as found in North India. Due to altitude, the temperatures in the hills of Western Ghats remain below 25°C. The mean daily minimum temperature during the summer months also remains quite high and rarely goes below 26°C.
- **Pressure and Winds :** The summer months are a period of excessive heat and falling air pressure in the northern half of the country. Because of the heating of the subcontinent, the ITCZ moves northwards occupying a position centred at 25°N in July. In the heart of the ITCZ in the northwest, the dry and hot winds known as 'Loo', blow in the afternoon, and very often, they continue to well into midnight. Dust storms in the evening are very common during May in Punjab, Haryana, Eastern Rajasthan and Uttar Pradesh.
- **The South West Monsoon Season** :
- The rain in the southwest monsoon season begins rather abruptly. One result of the first rain is that it brings down the temperature substantially.
- This sudden onset of the moisture-laden winds associated with violent thunder and lightening, is often termed as the "break" or "burst" of the monsoons. The monsoon may burst in the first week of June in the coastal areas of Kerala, Karnataka, Goa and Maharashtra while in the interior parts of the country, it may be delayed to the first week of July.
- **The monsoon approaches the landmass in two branches :**
- **The Arabian Sea branch :** The monsoon winds originating over the Arabian Sea further split into three branches:
- It's one branch is obstructed by the Western Ghats. These winds climb the slopes of the Western Ghats from 900-1200 m. Soon, they become cool, and as a result, the windward side of the Sahyadris and Western Coastal Plain receive very heavy rainfall ranging between 250 cm and 400 cm.
- Another branch of the Arabian sea monsoon strikes the coast north of Mumbai. Moving along the Narmada and Tapi river valleys, these winds cause rainfall in extensive areas of central India.
- A third branch of this monsoon wind strikes the Saurashtra Peninsula and the Kachchh. It then passes over west Rajasthan and along the Aravallis, causing only scanty rainfall.
- **The Bay of Bengal branch :** The Bay of Bengal branch strikes the coast of Myanmar and part of southeast Bangladesh. But the Arakan Hills along the coast of Myanmar deflect a big portion of this branch towards the Indian subcontinent. The other branch moves up the Brahmaputra Valley in the north and the northeast, causing widespread rains. Its sub-branch strikes the Garo and Khasi hills of Meghalaya. Mawsynram, located on the crest of Khasi hills, receives the highest average annual rainfall in the world.
- **Season of Retreating Monsoon :**
- The months of October and November are known for retreating monsoons.

- The monsoon retreats from the western Rajasthan by the first week of September. It withdraws from Rajasthan, Gujarat, Western Ganga plain and the Central Highlands by the end of the month. By the beginning of October, the low pressure covers northern parts of the Bay of Bengal and by early November, it moves over Karnataka and Tamil Nadu. By the middle of December, the centre of low pressure is completely removed from the Peninsula.
- The weather in the retreating monsoon is dry in north India but it is associated with rain in the eastern part of the Peninsula. Here, October and November are the rainiest months of the year.
- The widespread rain in this season is associated with the passage of cyclonic depressions which originate over the Andaman Sea and manage to cross the eastern coast of the southern Peninsula.
- A bulk of the rainfall of the Coromandal Coast is derived from these depressions and cyclones. Such cyclonic storms are less frequent in the Arabian Sea.
- The average annual rainfall in India is about 125 cm, but it has great spatial variations.
- The highest rainfall occurs along the west coast, on the Western Ghats, as well as in the sub-Himalayan areas is the northeast and the hills of Meghalaya. In some parts of Khasi and Jaintia hills, the rainfall exceeds 1,000 cm.
- Rainfall between 100-200 cm is received in the southern parts of Gujarat, east Tamil Nadu, north eastern Peninsula covering Odisha, Jharkhand, Bihar, eastern Madhya Pradesh, northern Ganga plain along the sub-Himalayas and the Cachar Valley and Manipur.
- Western Uttar Pradesh, Delhi, Haryana, Punjab, Jammu and Kashmir, eastern Rajasthan, Gujarat and Deccan Plateau receive rainfall between 50-100 cm.
- Parts of the Peninsula, especially in Andhra Pradesh, Karnataka and Maharashtra, Ladakh and most of western Rajasthan receive rainfall below 50 cm.
- A climatic region has a homogeneous climatic condition which is the result of a combination of factors.
- Temperature and rainfall are two important elements which are considered to be decisive in all the schemes of climatic classification.
- **Major climatic types of India based on Koeppen's scheme have been described below :**
  - Tropical climates, where mean monthly temperature throughout the year is over 18°C.
  - Dry climates, where precipitation is very low in comparison to temperature, and hence, dry.
  - Warm temperate climates, where mean temperature of the coldest month is between 18°C and minus 3°C.
  - Cool temperate climates, where mean temperature of the warmest month is over 10°C, and mean temperature of the coldest month is under minus 3°C.
  - Ice climates, where mean temperature of the warmest month is under 10°C.
- Regional variations in monsoon climate help in growing various types of crop.
- Sudden monsoon burst creates problem of soil erosion over large areas in India.
- Besides the natural causes, human activities such as large scale industrialisation and presence of polluting gas in the atmosphere are also important factors responsible for global warming.
- The mean annual surface temperature of the earth in the past 150 years has increased. It is projected that by the year 2,100, global temperature will warm about 2°C.
- According to the current prediction, on an average, the sea level will rise 48 cm by the end of twenty first century.

Know the Terms

- **Mango Shower :** Towards the end of summer, there are pre-monsoon showers which are a common phenomena in Kerala and coastal areas of Karnataka. Locally, they are known as mango showers since they help in the early ripening of mangoes.
- **Nor Westers :** These are dreaded evening thunderstorms in Bengal and Assam. Their notorious nature can be understood from the local nomenclature of 'Kalbaisakhi', a calamity of the month of Baisakh. These showers are useful for tea, jute and rice cultivation. In Assam, these storms are known as "Bardoli Chheerha".
- **Loo :** Hot, dry and oppressing winds blowing in the Northern plains from Punjab to Bihar with higher intensity between Delhi and Patna.
- **Dust storms :** A strong turbulent wind which carriers clouds of fine dust, soil and sand over a large area.
- **Northeast Monsoon :** In winters, the ITCZ moves southward, and so the reversal of winds from the northeast to south and southwest, takes place. They are called northeast monsoons.
- **Tropical Depression :** Inflow of western cyclones is generally known as tropical depressions.
- **Bardoli Chheerha :** In Assam, North Western storms are known as 'Bardoli Chheerha'.
- **Bursting of the monsoon :** High velocity winds with extreme thundering and lightening cause sudden rainfall, which is called bursting of the monsoon.

- **Western cyclone :** It is the extratropical storm originating in the Mediterranean region that brings sudden winter rain to India.
- **Tropical cyclone :** It is a rapidly rotating storm system characterised by a low-pressure centre, a closed low-level atmospheric circulation , strong winds and a spiral arrangement of thunderstorms that produce heavy rains.
- **October heat :** Owing to the condition of high temperature and humidity, the weather becomes rather oppressive and this is known as October heat.
- **Blossom showers :** With this shower, coffee flowers blossom in Kerala and nearby areas.

Multiple Choice Questions (1 mark each)

Q. 1. During April and May when the sun shines vertically over the: A

(a) Tropic of Cancer
(b) Tropic of Capricorn
(c) Equator
(d) Poles

Ans. (a) Tropic of Cancer 1

Q. 2. The mean monthly temperature throughout the year is over 18°C in: U

(a) Dry climate
(b) Tropical climate
(c) Rainy climate
(d) Temperate climate

Ans. (b) Tropical climate 1

Q. 3. The mean temperature of the warmest month is under 10°C in the: A

(a) temperate climate
(b) tropical climate
(c) ice climate
(d) monsoon climate

Ans. (c) ice climate 1

Very Short Answer Type Questions (1 mark each)

Q. 1. Define the term 'Mango Showers'. A

Ans. Towards the end of summer, there are pre-monsoon showers which are a common phenomena in Kerala and coastal areas of Karnataka. Locally, they are known as mango showers since they help in the early ripening of mangoes. 1

Answering Tip

- Sometimes Mango Showers are referred to generically as 'April rains' or 'Summer showers'.

Q. 2. What is 'Loo'? A

Ans. Hot, dry and oppressing winds blowing in the Northern Plains from Punjab to Bihar with higher intensity between Delhi and Patna. 1

Q. 3. What is 'October Heat'? U

Ans. Owing to the condition of high temperature and humidity, the weather becomes rather oppressive and this is known as October heat. 1

Q. 4. What is meant by 'bursting of monsoon'? R

Ans. High velocity winds with extreme thundering and lightening cause sudden rainfall, which is called bursting of the monsoon. 1

Q. 5. What is 'El-Nino'? A

Ans. El-Nino can be defined as the complex weather system that appears once every three to seven years bringing drought, floods and other weather extremes to different parts of the world. 1

Answering Tip

- El Nino is a climate cycle in the Pacific Ocean with a global impact on weather patterns.

Q. 6. Explain the two factors helpful in affecting Indian monsoon. R

Ans. The two factors helpful in affecting the Indian Monsoon are :

(i) Jet stream winds
(ii) Difference in atmospheric pressure. 1

Q. 7. Why does winter monsoon do not cause rainfall as they move from land to the sea? U

Ans. Winter monsoon do not cause rainfall as they move from land to the sea because

(i) They have little humidity
(ii) **Due to the anti-cyclonic circulation on land, the possibility of rainfall from them reduces.** 1

Q. 8. What directions do the winds follow in Kerala during the retreating monsoon? A

Ans. The winds blow from North to East and from East to West. 1

Q. 9. Differentiate between loo and chilled wave. U

Ans. Loo is the hot, dry and oppressing winds blowing in the Northern Plains from Punjab to Bihar with higher intensity between Delhi and Patna.

Chilled waves are the winds blowing in the Northern plains when the temperature falls too much. 1

AI **Q.10. What formula is used to measure variability in rainfall?** R

Ans. The formula used is :

$$\text{C.V.} = \frac{\text{Standard Deviation}}{\text{Mean}} \times 100$$ 1

Q. 11. Name one such place in India where polar climate is found. A

Ans. It is found in upper portions of the Himalayas located at 4000 mt above the sea level. **1**

Q. 12. Name one such place which experiences 31°C during January. U

Ans. Thiruvananthapuram **1**

Q. 13. Give two reasons stating the cause of Tamil Nadu remaining dry during South-West Monsoon. A

Ans. The two reasons are :

(i) The Tamil Nadu coast is situated parallel to the Bay of Bengal branch of the South west Monsoon.

(ii) It lies in the rain shadow area of the Arabian Sea branch of the South West Monsoon. **1**

Q. 14. Locate the origin of the tropical cyclones. R

Ans. The tropical cyclones originate over the Bay of Bengal and the Indian Ocean. These tropical cyclones have very high wind velocity and heavy rainfall. **1**

Commonly Made Error

- The students are not aware what causes the tropical cyclones to occur.

Answering Tip

- The tropical cyclones begin as a group of storms when the water gets as hot as 80 °F (27 °C) or hotter.

Q. 15. Name any two places which are affected by the tropical cyclones. R

Ans. Tamil Nadu, Andhra Pradesh , Odisha Coast. **(Any Two) (½ + ½ =1)**

Q. 16. Which places receive rainfall from South-West Monsoon? A

Ans. The coastal areas of Tamil Nadu. **1**

Q. 17. Mention any two important features of Kalbaisakhi. R

Ans. The two important features of Kalbaisakhi are :

(i) Kalbaisakhi are dreaded evening thunderstorms which occur in Bengal and Assam.

(ii) This calamity usually occurs at the month of Baisakhi. **(½ + ½ =1)**

Q. 18. Name any two climatic classification given by Koeppen. U

Ans. The two climate classification by Keoppen are :

(i) Tropical climates, where means monthly temperature throughout the year is over 18^0 C.

(ii) Ice climates, where mean temperature of the warmest month is under 100 C.

Answering Tip

- The Koppen climate classification system is a widely-utilized vegetation-based climate classification system.

Q. 19. Which place receives the heaviest rainfall in the world? R

Ans. Mawsynram, 1080cm annually receives the heaviest rainfall in the world. **1**

Q. 20. Name any features of monsoons in India. A

Ans. The two features of monsoons in India are:

(i) They are irregular and uneven.

(ii) They are uncertain and unreliable. **(½ + ½ =1)**

Answering Tip

- Monsoon rains in India mainly occur during four months June, July, August and September.
- It goes on decreasing from east to west.

Q. 21. What factors determine the intensity of rainfall over the west coast of India ? R

Ans. The intensity of rainfall over the west coast of India is, however, related to two factors :

(i) The offshore meteorological conditions.

(ii) The position of the equatorial jet stream along the eastern coast of Africa. **1**

Q. 22. Differentiate between advancing monsoon and retreating monsoon. A

Ans.

Advancing Monsoon	Retreating Monsoon
The season when rainy season begins in India, is called advancing monsoon.	The season of retreating monsoon is the period of transition.

(½ + ½ =1)

Q. 23. Why does North-West India receive rainfall even in winter season? U

Ans. The North-West India receives rainfall even in winter season because some of the occurrence of weak temperate cyclones from the Mediterranean Sea which cause rainfall in Punjab, Haryana, Delhi and Western Uttar Pradesh . Although the amount is meagre, it is highly beneficial for Rabi crops. **1**

Q. 24. Why does Tamil Nadu receive more rainfall in winter season as compared to summer season? A

Ans. Tamil Nadu receives more rainfall in winter season as compared to summer season because the North-west monsoon winds passing over the Bay of Bengal get moisture and when they reach Tamil Nadu coast they cause rainfall there. **1**

Q. 25. Why does highest rainfall occur in Mawsynram and Cherrapunji? R

Ans. Highest rainfall occurs in Mawsynram and Cherrapunji because it is covered by Garo , Khasi and Jantia hills on three sides. Being covered from hills from three sides, makes it difficult for the moisture laden winds which have entered this area to leave. They strike the mountains and cause rainfall. **1**

Short Answer Type Questions (3 marks each)

Q. 1. Differentiate between South-west monsoon and retreating monsoon. [A]

Ans.

S.No.	South-West Monsoon	Retreating Monsoon
1.	These winds blow from June to September.	These winds blow during October and November.
2.	The direction of these winds is from West to the North East.	These winds are calm. These flow from North to South.
3.	During June to September these winds cover whole of India and give heavy rainfall.	During retreating monsoon, Tamil Nadu receives the maximum rainfall .

1 × 3 = 3

Q. 2. Explain the climatic conditions as described by Koeppen? [R]

Ans. Koeppen based his scheme of Climatic classification on monthly values of temperature and precipitation. He identified five major climatic types, namely :

(i) Tropical climates, where mean monthly temperature throughout the year is over 18°C.

(ii) Dry climates, where precipitation is very low in comparison to temperature, and hence, dry. If dryness is less, it is semiarid (S); if it is more, the climate is arid(W).

(iii) Warm temperate climates, where mean temperature of the coldest month is between 18°C and minus 3°C.

(iv) Cool temperate climates, where mean temperature of the warmest month is over 10°C, and mean temperature of the coldest month is under minus 3°C.

(v) Ice climates, where mean temperature of the warmest month is under 10°C.

(Any Three) 1 × 3 = 3

[AI] **Q. 3. Mention the characteristics of monsoonal rainfall in India.** [U]

Ans. The characteristics of monsoonal rainfall in India are :

(i) Rainfall received from the South-West monsoons is seasonal in character , which occurs between June and September. The monsoon rainfall has a declining trend with increasing distance from the sea. For example, Kolkata receives 119cm of rain during south-west monsoon whereas, Allahabad receives 76 cm.

(ii) The summer rainfall comes in a heavy downpour leading to considerable runoff and soil erosion. Monsoon also plays a pivotal role in the agrarian economy of India because over three-fourth of the total rain in the country is received during the South-west monsoon season.

(iii) The spatial distribution of monsoon across the country is uneven. It ranges from 12cm to more than 250cm. The beginning of the rains sometimes is considerably delayed over the whole or a part of the country. 3

Answering Tip

- Monsoon rains that exceed 10% typically lead to major floods, while a 10% shortfall is a significant drought.

Q. 4. Explain the concept of 'Break in the Monsoon'. [R]

Ans. During the south-west monsoon period after having rains for a few days, if rain fails to occur for one or more weeks, it is known as break in the monsoon. These dry spells are quite common during the rainy season. These breaks in the different regions are due to different reasons:

(i) In northern India rains are likely to fail if the rain-bearing storms are not very frequent along the monsoon trough or the ITCZ over this region.

(ii) Over the west coast the dry spells are associated with days when winds blow parallel to the coast.3

Q. 5. Explain the features of El-Nino . [A]

Ans. El-Nino is a complex weather system that appears once every three to seven years, bringing drought, floods and other weather extremes to different parts of the world.

The various features of El-Nino are :

(i) The system involves oceanic and atmospheric phenomena with the appearance of warm currents off the coast of Peru in the Eastern Pacific and affects weather in many places including india.

(ii) El-Nino is merely an extension of the warm equatorial current which gets replaced temporarily by cold Peruvian current or Humbolt current.

(iii) This current increases the temperature of water on the Peruvian coast by 10 °C . 3

Q. 6. Why does India gets a monsoon named as South-West Monsoon? [R]

Ans. India gets a monsoon named as South-West Monsoon because :

(i) The low pressure conditions by early June are powerful enough to attract the trade winds of Southern Hemisphere coming from the Indian Ocean. These South-East trade winds cross the Equator and enter the Bay of Bengal and the Arabian Sea , only to be caught up in the air circulation over India.

(ii) Passing over the equatorial warm currents they bring with them moisture in abundance.

(iii) After crossing the Equator, they follow south westerly directions and they are known as south-west monsoon. 3

**Q.7. 'In spite of abundant rainfall , India is a water thirsty land.' Explain.** [A]

Ans. Inspite of abundant rainfall, India is a water thirsty land because :

(i) The occurrence of rainfall is restricted to a few months, i.e., June to September.

(ii) Even though monsoons occur, due to high temperature, there is a quick evaporation of rainwater and rapid run off.

(iii) Monsoons suffer from delay and long breaks. 3

Q. 8. Why does rainfall on the Western Ghats decrease from South to North? [A]

Ans. Rainfall on the Western Ghats decrease from South to North because the height of the Western Ghats in the south is maximum and it goes on decreasing northwards allowing progressively less condensation. It results in the decrease of rainfall from South to North. Moreover, the period of onset and withdrawal of monsoon in South is more than that in the North. It results in more rainfall in southern parts than in the northern parts of the Western Ghats. 3

Long Answer Type Questions (5 marks each)

Q. 1. Explain the features of hot weather season. [A]

Ans. The features of hot season are :

(i) April, May and June are the months of summer in north India. In most parts of India, temperatures recorded are between 30°-32°C. In March, the highest day temperature of about 38°C occurs in the Deccan Plateau while in April, temperature ranging between 38°C and 43°C are found in Gujarat and Madhya Pradesh.

(ii) The hot weather season in south India is mild and not so intense as found in north India. The Peninsular situation of south India with moderating effect of the oceans keeps the temperatures lower than that prevailing in north India. So, temperatures remain between 26°C and 32°C.

(iii) The mean daily minimum temperature during the summer months also remains quite high and rarely goes below 26°C.

(iv) The summer months are a period of excessive heat and falling air pressure in the northern half of the country. Because of the heating of the subcontinent, the ITCZ moves northwards occupying a position centred at 25°N in July. Roughly, this elongated low pressure monsoon trough extends over the Thar desert in the north-west to Patna and Chotanagpur plateau in the east-southeast.

(v) The location of the ITCZ attracts a surface circulation of the winds which are southwesterly on the west coast as well as along the coast of West Bengal and Bangladesh. They are easterly or southeasterly over north Bengal and Bihar. It has been discussed earlier that these currents of southwesterly monsoon are in reality 'displaced' equatorial westerlies. The influx of these winds by mid-June brings about a change in the weather towards the rainy season. 5

Answering Tip

- During the hot weather season in the Northern and North-Westem plain, there is occurrence of 'Loo'—strong, hot, dry wind.

Q. 2. Explain the important features of winter season of India. [R]

Ans. The important features of winter season of India are:

(i) Usually, the cold weather season sets in by mid-November in northern India. December and January are the coldest months in the northern plain. The mean daily temperature remains below 21°C over most parts of northern India.

(ii) The night temperature may be quite low, sometimes going below freezing point in Punjab and Rajasthan.

(iii) The Peninsular region of India, however, does not have any well-defined cold weather season. There is hardly any seasonal change in the distribution pattern of the temperature in coastal areas because of moderating influence of the sea and the proximity to equator.

(iv) The isobars of 1019 mb and 1013 mb pass through northwest India and far south, respectively. As a result, winds start blowing from northwestern high pressure zone to the low air pressure zone over the Indian Ocean in the south.

(v) During the winters, the weather in India is pleasant. The pleasant weather conditions, however, at intervals, get disturbed by shallow cyclonic depressions originating over the east Mediterranean Sea and travelling eastwards across West Asia, Iran, Afghanistan and Pakistan before they reach the northwestern parts of India. 5

Q. 3. Explain the important features of the South West Monsoon Season. [R]

Ans. Important features of the South West Monsoon Season :

(i) The southeast trade winds cross the equator and enter the Bay of Bengal and the Arabian Sea, only to be caught up in the air circulation over India. Passing over the equatorial warm currents, they bring with them moisture in abundance. After crossing the equator, they follow a southwesterly direction. That is why they are known as southwest monsoons.

(ii) The rain in the southwest monsoon season begins rather abruptly. One result of the first rain is that it brings down the temperature substantially.

(iii) This sudden onset of the moisture-laden winds associated with violent thunder and lightening, is often termed as the "break" or "burst" of the monsoon. The monsoon may burst in the first week of June in the coastal areas of Kerala, Karnataka, Goa and Maharashtra while in the interior parts of the country, it may be delayed to the first week of July. The day temperature registers a decline of 5°C to 8°C between mid-June and mid-July.

(iv) As these winds approach the land, their southwesterly direction is modified by the relief and thermal low pressure over the northwest India. The monsoon approaches the landmass in two branches : (i) The Arabian Sea branch (ii) The Bay of Bengal branch.

(v) The monsoon winds originating from the Arabian Sea is further divided into three branches : Its one branch is obstructed by the Western Ghats. Another branch of the Arabian sea monsoon strikes the coast north of Mumbai. A third branch of this monsoon wind strikes the Saurashtra Peninsula and the Kachchh. The Bay of Bengal branch strikes the coast of Myanmar and part of southeast Bangladesh. 5

Answering Tip

- The Southwest Monsoon typically begins around early June and finishes in late September.

Q. 4. How is the economic life in India affected by monsoon? U

Ans. **(i)** Monsoon is that axis around which revolves the entire agricultural cycle of India. It is because about 64 per cent people of India depend on agriculture for their livelihood and agriculture itself is based on southwest monsoon.

(ii) Except Himalayas all the parts of the country have temperature above the threshold level to grow the crops or plants throughout the year.

(iii) Regional variations in monsoon climate help in growing various types of crops.

(iv) Variability of rainfall brings droughts or floods every year in some parts of the country.

(v) Agricultural prosperity of India depends very much on timely and adequately distributed rainfall. If it fails, agriculture is adversely affected particularly in those regions where means of irrigation are not developed.

(vi) Sudden monsoon burst creates problem of soil erosion over large areas in India. 5

Q. 5. What is global warming? What are the effects of global warming? A

Ans. Global warming also referred to as climatic change , is the observed century-scale rise in the average temperature of the Earth's climate system and its related effects.

Effects of global warming :

(i) The temperature of the world is significantly increasing. Carbon dioxide produced by human activities is a major source of concern. This gas, released to the atmosphere in large quantities by burning of fossil fuel, is increasing gradually.

(ii) Other gases like methane, chlorofluorocarbons, and nitrous oxide which are present in much smaller concentrations in the atmosphere, together with carbon dioxide are known as green house gases. These gases are better absorbers of long wave radiations than carbon dioxide, and so, are more effective at enhancing the green house effect.

(iii) Global warming has led to the rise in the sea level and melting of glaciers and sea-ice due to warming. According to the current prediction, on an average, the sea level will rise 48 cm by the end of twenty first century. This would increase the incidence of annual flooding.

(iv) Climatic change would promote insect-borne diseases like malaria, and lead to shift in climatic boundaries, making some regions wetter and others drier.

(v) Agricultural pattern would shift and human population as well as the ecosystem would experience change. 5

Q. 6. What are the characteristics of monsoonal rainfall? A

Ans. Characteristics of monsoonal rainfall are :

(i) Rainfall received from the southwest monsoons is seasonal in character, which occurs between June and September.

(ii) Monsoonal rainfall is largely governed by relief or topography. For instance the windward side of the Western Ghats register a rainfall of over 250 cm. Again, the heavy rainfall in the north eastern states can be attributed to their hill ranges and the Eastern Himalayas .

(iii) The monsoon rainfall has a declining trend with increasing distance from the sea. Kolkata receives 119 cm during the southwest monsoon period, Patna 105 cm, Allahabad 76 cm and Delhi 56 cm.

(iv) The monsoon rains occur in wet spells of few days duration at a time. The wet spells are interspersed with rainless interval known as 'breaks'. These breaks in rainfall are related to the cyclonic depressions mainly formed at the head of the Bay of Bengal, and their crossing into the mainland. Besides the frequency and intensity of these depressions, the passage followed by them determines the spatial distribution of rainfall.

(v) The summer rainfall comes in a heavy downpour leading to considerable run off and soil erosion. Monsoons play a pivotal role in the agrarian economy of India because over three-fourths of the total rain in the country is received during the southwest monsoon season.

(vi) Its spatial distribution is also uneven which ranges from 12 cm to more than 250 cm. The beginning of the rains sometimes is considerably delayed over the whole or a part of the country.

(vii) The rains sometimes end considerably earlier than usual, causing great damage to standing crops and making the sowing of winter crops difficult. **(Any Five) (1 × 5 = 5)**

Answering

- Over half of India's population works in agriculture, and monsoon rains directly affect their incomes and livelihood.

Q. 7. 'Monsoon is a gambling for Indian farmers.' Explain. U

Ans. Agriculture in India is highly dependent on monsoons. It the monsoons fail to come on time, agriculture is adversely affected particularly in those regions where means of irrigation are not developed. Monsoon is considered to be an axis around which the entire agriculture cycle of our country revolves. Around 64% people of India depend on agriculture for livelihood . except Himalayas all other parts of the country have temperature above the threshold level to grow the crops throughout the year. Regional variations in monsoon climate help in growing various types of crops. Variability of rainfall brings droughts and floods every year in some parts of the country. Thus, monsoons play a pivotal role in the agrarian economy of India because over three-fourths of the total rain in the country is received during the southwest monsoon season. 5

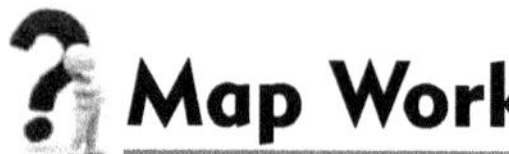

Map Work

(5 marks each)

Q.1. Locate and label on the outline map of India the amount of seasonal rainfall received in India.

(i) Place receiving more than 400 cm of rainfall.

(ii) Place receiving rainfall between 400-200 cm .

(iii) Place receiving rainfall between 200-100 cm.

(iv) Place receiving rainfall between 100 -60 cm.

(v) Place receiving rainfall between 60-40 cm.

Ans.

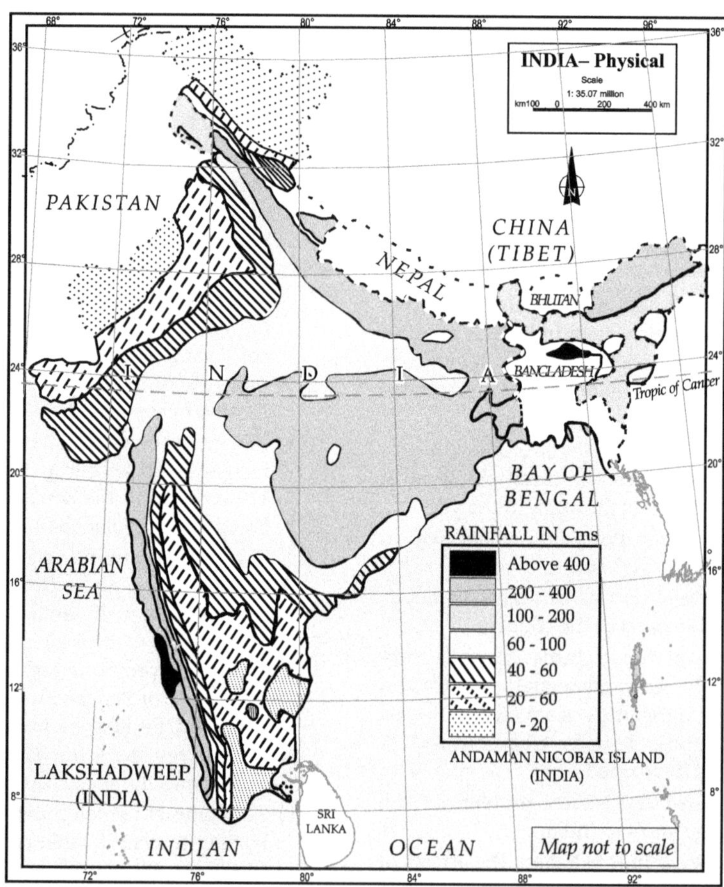

Q. 2. Locate and label on the outline map of India the annual rainfall received in different states of India.

(i) Place receiving annual rainfall of more than 400 cm.

(ii) Place receiving annual rainfall between 400-300 cm.

(iii) Place receiving annual rainfall between 300-200 cm.

(iv) Place receiving annual rainfall between 200-100 cm.

(v) Place receiving annual rainfall between 100-60 cm.

Ans.

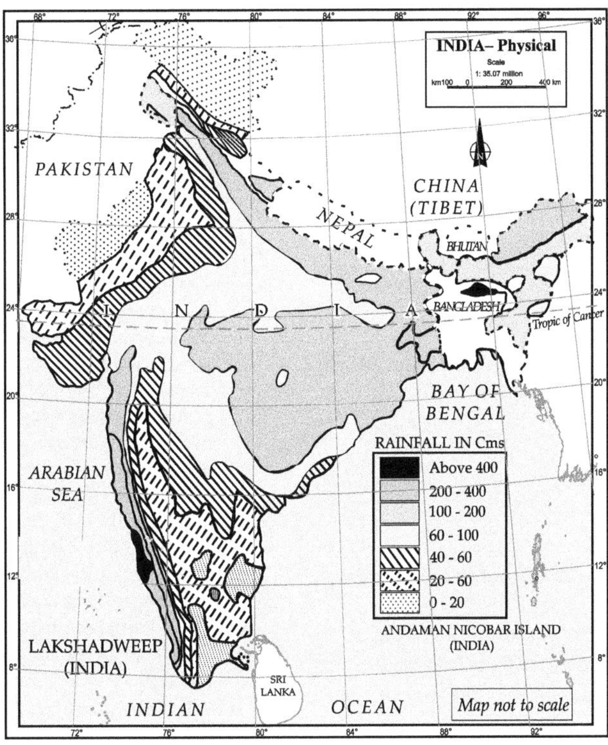

Q.3. Locate and label on the outline map of India , normal dates of onset of southwest monsoon in different states.

(i) Onset of monsoon in Chandigarh.
(ii) Onset of monsoon in Ahmadabad.
(iii) Onset of monsoon in Mumbai.
(iv) Onset of monsoon in Kolkata
(v) Onset of monsoon in Hyderabad.

Ans.

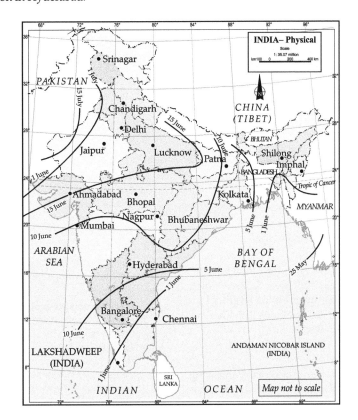

NCERT CORNER

(B) Multiple choice questions :

Q. 1. What causes rainfall on the coastal areas of Tamil Nadu in the beginning of winters :

(a) South-West monsoon
(b) Temperate cyclones
(c) North-Eastern monsoon
(d) Local air circulation

Ans. (c) North -Eastern monsoon .

Q. 2. What is the proportion of area of India which receives annual rainfall less than 75 cm :

(a) Half
(b) One-third
(c) Two-third
(d) Three-fourth

Ans. (d) Three-fourth .

Q. 3. Which one of the following is not a fact regarding South India :

(a) Diurnal range of temperature is less here.
(b) Annual range of temperature is less here.
(c) Temperatures here are high throughout the year.
(d) Extreme climatic conditions are found here.

Ans. (d) extreme climate conditions are found here.

Q. 4. Which one of the following phenomenon happens when the sun shines vertically over the Tropic of Capricorn in the southern hemisphere :

(a) High pressure develops over North-western India due to low temperatures.
(b) Low pressure develops over North-western India due to high temperatures.
(c) No changes in temperature and pressure occur in north-western India.
(d) 'Loo' blows in the North-western India.

Ans. (a) High pressure develops over North-eastern India due to low temperatures.

Q. 5. In which of the following states in India do we find 'As' type of climate as per Koeppen's classification :

(a) In Kerala and coastal Karnataka
(b) In Andaman and Nicobar Islands
(c) On Coromandal coast
(d) In Assam and Arunachal Pradesh

Ans. (c) On Coromandal Coast

(B) State the differences between the following.

Q. 1. What are the three important factors which influence the mechanism of Indian weather ?

Ans. The three important factors which influence the mechanism of Indian weather are :

(i) Distribution of air pressure and winds on the surface of the Earth.
(ii) Upper air circulation caused by factors controlling global weather and the inflow of different air masses and jet streams.
(iii) Inflow of western cyclones generally known as disturbances during the winter season and tropical depressions during the south-west monsoon period in India, creating weather conditions favourable for rainfall.

Q. 2. What is the Inter-Tropical Convergene Zone?

Ans. The Inter Tropical Convergence Zone (ITCZ) is a low pressure zone located at the equator where trade winds converge, and so, it is a zone where air tends to ascend. **In July, the ITCZ is** located around 20°N-25°N latitudes (over the Gangetic plain), sometimes called the monsoon trough. This monsoon trough encourages the development of thermal low over north and northwest India. Due to the shift of ITCZ, the trade winds of the southern hemisphere cross the equator between 40° and 60°E longitudes and start blowing from southwest to northeast due to the Coriolis force. It becomes southwest monsoon. In winter, the ITCZ moves southward, and so the reversal of winds from northeast to south and southwest, takes place. They are called northeast monsoons.

Q. 3. What is meant by 'bursting of monsoon'? Name the place of India which gets the highest rainfall.

Ans. High velocity winds with extreme thundering and lightening cause sudden rainfall. It is called bursting of the monsoon. The easterly jet stream sets in along 15°N latitude only after the western jet streams has withdrawn itself from the region. This easterly jet stream is held responsible for the burst of the monsoon in India.

The highest rainfall occurs along the west coast, on the Western Ghats, as well as in the sub-Himalayan areas is the North east and the hills of Meghalaya. Here the rainfall exceeds 1,000 cm.

Q. 4. Define 'climatic region'? What are the bases of Koeppen's classification?

Ans. A climatic region has a homogeneous climatic condition which is the result of a combination of factors. Temperature and rainfall are two important elements which are considered to be decisive in all the schemes of climatic classification. Koeppen recognised five major climatic groups, four of them are based in temperature and one on precipitation.

(a) Tropical climates
(b) Dry climates
(c) Warm temperature climates
(d) Cool temperature climates
(e) Ice climates

Q. 5. Which type(s) of cyclones cause rainfall in north-western India during winter? Where do they originate?

Ans. Western cyclonic disturbance cause rainfall in north western India during winter. The western cyclonic disturbances which enter the Indian subcontinent form the west and the north-west during the winter months originate over the

Mediterranean Sea and are brought into India by the westerly jet stream.

(C) Answer the following questions in about 125 words :

Q. 1. Notwithstanding the broad climatic unity, the climate of India has many regional variations. Elaborate this statement giving suitable examples.

Ans. The monsoon regime emphasises the unity of India with the rest of southeast Asian region. This view of broad unity of the monsoon type of climate should not, however, lead one to ignore its regional variations which differentiate the weather and climate of different regions of India. For example, the climate of Kerala and Tamil Nadu in the south are so different from that of Uttar Pradesh and Bihar in the north, and yet all of these have a monsoon type of climate.

While in the summer the mercury occasionally touches 55°C in the western Rajasthan, it drops down to as low as minus 45°C in winter around Leh. Churu in Rajasthan may record a temperature of 50°C or more on a June day while the mercury hardly touches 19°C in Tawang (Arunachal Pradesh) on the same day. On a December night, temperature in Drass (Jammu and Kashmir) may drop down to minus 45°C while Tiruvanantapuram or Chennai on the same night records 20°C or 22°C. These examples confirm that there are seasonal variations in temperature from place to place and from region to region in India.

Not only this, if we take only a single place and record the temperature for just one day, variations are no less striking. In Kerala and in the Andaman Islands, the difference between day and night temperatures may be hardly seven or eight degree Celsius. But in the Thar desert, if the day temperature is around 50°C, at night, it may drop down considerably upto 15°-20°C.

While snowfall occurs in the Himalayas, it only rains over the rest of the country. Similarly, variations are noticeable not only in the type of precipitation but also in its amount. While Cherrapunji and Mawsynram in the Khasi Hills of Meghalaya receive rainfall over 1,080 cm in a year, Jaisalmer in Rajasthan rarely gets more than 9 cm of rainfall during the same period.

Tura situated in the Garo Hills of Meghalaya may receive an amount of rainfall in a single day which is equal to 10 years of rainfall at Jaisalmer. While the annual precipitation is less than 10 cm in the northwest Himalayas and the western deserts, it exceeds 400 cm in Meghalaya.

The Ganga delta and the coastal plains of Orissa are hit by strong rain-bearing storms almost every third or fifth day in July and August while the Coromandal coast, a thousand km to the south, goes generally dry during these months. Most parts of the country get rainfall during June-September, but on the coastal areas of Tamil Nadu, it rains in the beginning of the winter season. In spite of these differences and variations, the climate of India is monsoonal in rhythm and character.

Q. 2. How many distinct seasons are found in India as per the Indian Meteorological Department? Discuss the weather conditions associated with any one season in detail.

Ans. The distinct seasons found in India as per the Indian Meteorological Department are :

(i) The cold weather : Usually, the cold weather season sets in by mid-November in northern India. December and January are the coldest months in the northern plain. The mean daily temperature remains below 21°C over most parts of northern India. The night temperature may be quite low, sometimes going below freezing point in Punjab and Rajasthan. The snowfall in the nearby Himalayan ranges creates cold wave situation. There is hardly any seasonal change in the distribution pattern of the temperature in coastal areas because of moderating influence of the sea and the proximity to equator.

(ii) The hot weather : With the apparent northward movement of the sun towards the Tropic of Cancer in March, temperatures start rising in north India. April, May and June are the months of summer in north India. In most parts of India, temperatures recorded are between 30°-32°C. In March, the highest day temperature of about 38°C occurs in the Deccan Plateau while in April, temperature ranging between 38°C and 43°C are found in Gujarat and Madhya Pradesh. The hot weather season in south India is mild and not so intense as found in north India.

(iii) The Southwest Monsoon : The rain in the southwest monsoon season begins rather abruptly. One result of the first rain is that it brings down the temperature substantially. This sudden onset of the moisture-laden winds associated with violent thunder and lightening, is often termed as the "break" or "burst" of the monsoons. The monsoon may burst in the first week of June in the coastal areas of Kerala, Karnataka, Goa and Maharashtra while in the interior parts of the country, it may be delayed to the first week of July.

(iv) Season of Retreating Monsoon : The monsoon retreats from the western Rajasthan by the first week of September. It withdraws from Rajasthan, Gujarat, Western Ganga plain and the Central Highlands by the end of the month. The retreating southwest monsoon season is marked by clear skies and rise in temperature. The land is still moist. Owing to the conditions of high temperature and humidity, the weather becomes rather oppressive. This is commonly known as the 'October heat'.

Project Work

Q. 1. On the outline map of India, show the following :

(i) **Areas of winter rain**

(ii) **Wind direction during the summer season**

(iii) **Areas having variability of rainfall over 50 per cent**

(iv) **Areas having less than 15°C temperature in January**

(v) **Isohyet of 100 cm.**

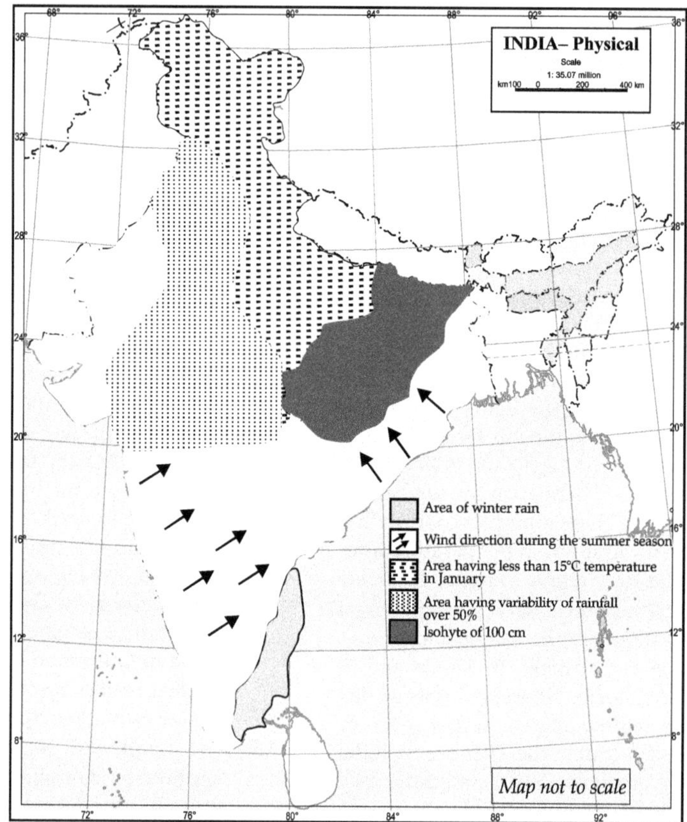

OSWAAL LEARNING TOOLS

For Suggested Online Videos

Visit : *https://qrgo.page.link/4a7W3* **Or Scan the Code**

To learn from NCERT Prescribed Videos

Visit : *https://qrgo.page.link/Tvsph* **Or Scan the Code**

❑❑

CHAPTER

5 NATURAL VEGETATION

Syllabus

➢ *Types of Forests, Forest Cover in India*
➢ *Forest Conservation, Social Forestry, Farm Forestry, Wildlife Conservation in India, Biosphere Reserves.*

TOPIC-1
Types of Forests, Forest Cover in India

Revision Notes

➢ Natural vegetation refers to a plant community that has been left undisturbed over a long time, so as to allow its individual species to adjust themselves to climate and soil conditions as fully as possible.

➢ India is a land of great variety of natural vegetation.

➢ Depending upon the variations in the climate and the soil, the vegetation of India changes from one region to another.

➢ Indian forests can be divided into the following groups :

- **Tropical Evergreen and Semi Evergreen Forests :** These forests are found in the western slope of the Western Ghats, hills of the north eastern region and the Andaman and Nicobar Islands. They are found in warm and humid areas with an annual precipitation of over 200 cm and mean annual temperature above 22°C.

➢ Tropical evergreen forests are well stratified, with layers closer to the ground and are covered with shrubs and creepers, with short structured trees followed by tall variety of trees.

➢ The trees reach great heights up to 60 m or above.

➢ There is no definite time for trees to shed their leaves, flowering and fruition.

➢ As such these forests appear green all the year round. Species found in these forests include rosewood, mahogony, aini, ebony, etc

➢ The semi evergreen forests are found in the less rainy parts of these regions.

➢ The undergrowing climbers provide an evergreen character to these forests. Main species are white cedar, hollock and kail.

- **Tropical Deciduous Forests :** These are the most widespread forests in India. They are also called the monsoon forests.

➢ They spread over regions which receive rainfall between 70-200 cm.

➢ **On the basis of the availability of water, these forests are further divided into :**

- **The Moist deciduous forests :** They are more pronounced in the regions which record rainfall between 100-200 cm. Teak, sal, shisham, hurra, mahua, amla, semul, kusum, and sandalwood etc. are the main species of these forests.

➢ **Dry deciduous forest :** It covers vast areas of the country, where rainfall ranges between 70 -100 cm. Tendu, palas, amaltas, bel, khair, axlewood, etc. are the common trees of these forests.

- **Tropical thorn forests :** It occur in the areas which receive rainfall less than 50 cm. These consist of a variety of grasses and shrubs. It includes semi-arid areas of south west Punjab, Haryana, Rajasthan, Gujarat, Madhya Pradesh and Uttar Pradesh.

- Important species found are babool, ber, and wild date palm, khair, neem, khejri, palas, etc.
  - **Montane Forests :** In mountainous areas, the decrease in temperature with increasing altitude leads to a corresponding change in natural vegetation. Mountain forests can be classified into two types :
- **The northern mountain forests :** Deciduous forests are found in the foothills of the Himalayas. Deodar, a highly valued endemic species grows mainly in the western part of the Himalayan range. The southern slopes of the Himalayas carry a thicker vegetation cover because of relatively higher precipitation than the drier north-facing slopes.
- **The southern mountain forests :** These forests are found in the Western Ghats, the Vindhyas and the Nilgiris. Some of the other trees of this forest of economic significance include, magnolia, laurel, cinchona and wattle. Such forests are also found in the Satpura and the Maikal ranges.
  - **Littoral and Swamp Forests :** India has a rich variety of wetland habitats. About 70 per cent of this comprises areas under paddy cultivation. The total area of wet land is 3.9 million hectares. Crisscrossed by creeks of stagnant water and tidal flows, these forests give shelter to a wide variety of birds. In India, the mangrove forests spread over 6,740 sq. km which is 7 per cent of the world's mangrove forests. They are highly developed in the Andaman and Nicobar Islands and the Sunderbans of West Bengal.
- According to state records, the forest area covers 23.28 per cent of the total land area of the country. The forest area is the area notified and recorded as the forest land irrespective of the existence of trees, while the actual forest cover is the area occupied by forests with canopy.
- In 2011, the actual forest cover was only 21.05 per cent. Of the forest cover, the share of dense and open forests was 12.29 per cent and 8.75 per cent respectively.
- Both forest area and forest cover vary from state to state. Lakshadweep has zero per cent. Andaman and Nicobar Icelands have 83.93 percent.
- Most of the states with less than 10 per cent of the forest area lie in the north and north western part of the country. These are Rajasthan, Gujarat, Punjab, Haryana and Delhi.
- States with 10-20 per cent forest area are Tamil Nadu and West Bengal. In Peninsular India, excluding Tamil Nadu, Dadra and Nagar Haveli and Goa, the area under forest cover is 20-30 per cent.
- There is a lot of variation in actual forest cover, which ranges from 9.56 per cent in Jammu and Kashmir to 84.01 per cent in Andaman and Nicobar Islands.

Know the Terms

- **Natural vegetation :** It refers to a plant community that has been left undisturbed over a long time, so as to allow its individual species to adjust themselves to climate and soil conditions as fully as possible.
- **Planted vegetation :** It refers to planting of trees under human supervision.
- **Tropical evergreen forests :** They occur in areas receiving more than 200 cm of rainfall and having a temperature of 15 to 30 degree Celsius.
- **Tropical Deciduous forests :** In these types of forests biome is dominated by deciduous trees which lose their leaves seasonally.
- **Tropical thorn forests :** They are found in semi-arid area with seasonal rainfall averaging 250 to 500 millimetres.
- **Montane forest :** These forests are found in the mountains.
- **Littoral and swamp forest :** They are forests which are inundated with freshwater, either permanently or seasonally.
- **Forest Area :** The forest area is the area notified and recorded as the forest land irrespective of the existence of trees.
- **Forest cover :** The forest cover is the area occupied by forests with canopy.

Multiple Choice Questions

(1 mark each)

Q. 1. The trees reach great heights up to 60 m or above in the: [A]

(a) Mountain forests
(b) Swamp forests
(c) Tropical evergreen forests
(d) Montane forests

Ans. (c) Tropical evergreen forests 1

Q. 2. Tamil Nadu and West Bengal's percentage of forest area is: [U]

(a) 10-20 per cent (b) 20-30 per cent
(c) 30-40 per cent (d) 40-50 per cent

Ans. (a) 10-20 per cent 1

Q. 3. In 2011, the actual forest cover was only: [U]

(a) 19.5% (b) 20.5%
(c) 21.5 % (d) 22.5%

Ans. (c) 21.5% 1

Q. 4. Lakshadweep has _______ per cent forest area and cover. [U]

(a) 0
(b) 2
(c) 4
(d) 6

Ans. (a) 0 1

Very Short Answer Type Questions (1 mark each)

Q. 1. Define the term 'Natural vegetation'. R

Ans. It refers to a plant community that has been left undisturbed over a long time, so as to allow its individual species to adjust themselves to climate and soil conditions as fully as possible. 1

Q. 2. What is planted vegetation? A

Ans. It refers to planting of trees under human supervision. 1

Q. 3. Define the term 'Forest Area'. U

Ans. The forest area is the area notified and recorded as the forest land irrespective of the existence of trees. 1

Answering Tip

- Russia has the largest forest area.

Q. 4. Define the term 'Forest Cover'. R

Ans. The forest cover is the area occupied by forests with canopy. 1

Q. 5. Where are tropical evergreen forests found? U

Ans. They are found in warm and humid areas with an annual precipitation of over 200cm and mean annual temperature above 22°C. 1

Answering Tip

- In India, tropical evergreen forests are found in the western slopes of the Western Ghats in States such as Kerala and Karnataka.

Q. 6. What types of trees are found in the tropical evergreen forests? A

Ans. Species found in these forests include rosewood, mahogony, aini, ebony, etc. 1

Q. 7. Where can you find natural vegetation? R

Ans. We can find natural vegetation in those areas where climate and soil are suitable for plant growth. Depending upon the variations in the climate and the soil, the vegetation of India changes from one region to another. 1

Q. 8. Where do you find semi-evergreen forests? U

Ans. The semi evergreen forests are found in the less rainy parts of the Western Ghats, hills of the northeastern region and the Andaman and Nicobar Islands. 1

Answering Tip

- In the semi-evergreen forests, the plants lose their foliage for a very short period, old leaves fall off and new foliage growth starts immediately.

Q. 9. What types of trees are found in the semi-evergreen forests? A

Ans. Main species are white cedar, hollock and kail. **(Any Two) (½ + ½ =1)**

Q. 10. Where do you find Tropical Deciduous Forests? R

Ans. They spread over regions which receive rainfall between 70-200 cm. 1

Q. 11. What is the other name of Tropical Deciduous Forests?? U

Ans. They are also called the monsoon forests. 1

Q. 12. On the basis of availability of water,Tropical Deciduous forests can be divided into how many parts? A

Ans. On the basis of the availability of water, these forests are further divided into moist and dry deciduous. 1

Q. 13. What types of trees are found in the moist deciduous forests? R

Ans. Teak, sal, shisham, hurra, mahua, amla, semul, kusum, and sandalwood etc. are the main species of these forests. **(Any two) (½ + ½ =1)**

Q. 14. What types of trees are found in the dry deciduous forests? A

Ans. Tendu, palas, amaltas, bel, khair, axlewood, etc. are the common trees of these forests. **(Any two) (½ + ½ =1)**

Q. 15. Where are Tropical Thorn Forests found? U

Ans. Tropical thorn forests occur in the areas which receive rainfall less than 50 cm. These consist of a variety of grasses and shrubs. It includes semi-arid areas of South West Punjab, Haryana, Rajasthan, Gujarat, Madhya Pradesh and Uttar Pradesh. 1

Q. 16. Montane forests can be classified into how many groups? R

Ans. Mountain forests can be classified into two types, the northern mountain forests and the southern mountain forests. 1

Q. 17. Name the tribes inhabiting in the montane forests. A

Ans. These pastures are used extensively by tribes like the Gujjars, the Bakarwals, the Bhotiyas and the Gaddis. 1

Q. 18. What do you know about the mangrove spread in India? U

Ans. In India, the mangrove forests spread over 6,740 sq. km which is 7 per cent of the world's mangrove forests. They are highly developed in the Andaman and Nicobar Islands and the Sunderbans of West Bengal. Other areas of significance are the Mahanadi, the Godavari and the Krishna deltas. 1

Answering Tip

- Sundarban is the largest mangrove forest in the world, consisting of various types of trees and shrubs that grow in saline waters and sediment habitats.

Q. 19. Which state has the highest and lowest percentage of forests? R

Ans. Mizoram has the highest percentage of forests and Haryana has the lowest percentage of forests. **1**

Q. 20. Which Union Territory has the highest and the lowest percentage of forests? A

Ans. Andaman and Nicobar Islands have got the highest percentage of forests, whereas, Chandigarh and Puducherry have got the lowest percentage of forests. **1**

Q. 21. Which island group has got the highest and lowest percentage of forest area? R

Ans. Lakshadweep has zero per cent forest area; Andaman and Nicobar Islands have 86.93 per cent. **1**

AI **Q.22. Why vegetation in thorn forests have sukleen stem and small leaves?** A

Ans. Vegetation in thorn forests have sukleen stem and small leaves because this forest lies in the areas which receives rainfall less than 50cm. **1**

Short Answer Type Questions

(3 marks each)

Q. 1. Differentiate between natural vegetation and forests. A

Ans.

S.No.	Natural Vegetation	Forests
1.	It refers to a plant community that has been left undisturbed over a long time, so as to allow its individual species to adjust themselves to climate and soil conditions as fully as possible.	Group and community of plants and trees which are found in a particular climatic conditions are called forests.
2.	It includes forests.	Forests are kind of natural vegetation.
3.	The collection of natural vegetation may not be similar.	Theses are generally similar.

(1 × 3 = 3)

Q. 2. Differentiate between dry deciduous forest and moist deciduous forest. U

Ans.

S.No.	Dry Deciduous Forest	Moist Deciduous Forest
1.	Its rainfall ranges between 70-100 cm.	Its rainfall ranges between 100-200 cm.
2.	These forests are found in the rain areas of the Peninsular and the plains of Uttar Pradesh and Bihar.	These forests are found in the northern-eastern states along the foothills of Himalayas , eastern slopes of the western Ghats and Odisha.
3.	Main species are Tendu, palas, khair , axlewood, etc.	Main species are Teak, sal, sheesham, kusum, sandalwood , etc.

(1 × 3 = 3)

Q. 3. Differentiate between forest cover and forest area. A

Ans.

S.No.	Forest Cover	Forest Area
1.	The forest cover is the area occupied by forests with canopy.	The forest area is the area notified and recorded as the forest land irrespective of the existence of land.
2.	It is based on aerial photography and satellite imageries.	It is based in the records of the State Revenue Department.
3.	The actual forest cover is only 20.55 %.	The forest cover area is 23.28% of the total area of the country. .

(1 × 3 = 3)

Q. 4. What do you know about montane forests? R

Ans. In mountainous areas, the decrease in temperature with increasing altitude leads to a corresponding change in natural vegetation. Mountain forests can be classified into two types, the northern mountain forests and the southern mountain forests.

The Himalayan ranges show a succession of vegetation from the tropical to the tundra, which change in with the altitude. Deciduous forests are found in the foothills of the Himalayas. It is succeeded by the wet temperate type of forests between an altitude of 1,000-2,000 m. Between 1,500-1,750 m, pine forests are also well-developed in this zone, with Chir Pine as a very useful commercial tree. Deodar, a highly valued endemic species grows mainly in the western part of the Himalayan range. Deodar is a durable wood mainly used in construction activity. Blue pine and spruce appear at altitudes of 2,225-3,048 m. But in the higher reaches there is a transition to Alpine forests and pastures. Silver firs, junipers, pines, birch and rhododendrons, etc. occur between 3,000-4,000 m.

The southern mountain forests include the forests found in three distinct areas of Peninsular India viz; the Western Ghats, the Vindhyas and the Nilgiris. As they are closer to the tropics, and only 1,500 m above the sea level, vegetation is temperate in the higher regions, and subtropical on the lower regions of the Western Ghats, especially in Kerala, Tamil Nadu and Karnataka. 3

Answering Tip

- The montane forests ecosystems are strongly affected by climate, which gets colder as elevation increases.

Q. 5. Into how many groups has wetland been divided in our country? [A]

Ans. The country's wetlands have been grouped into eight categories, They are :

(i) The reservoirs of the Deccan Plateau in the south together with the lagoons and other wetlands of the southern west coast;

(ii) The vast saline expanses of Rajasthan, Gujarat and the Gulf of Kachchh;

(iii) Freshwater lakes and reservoirs from Gujarat eastwards through Rajasthan (Keoladeo National Park) and Madhya Pradesh;

(iv) The delta wetlands and lagoons of India's east coast (Chilika Lake);

(v) The freshwater marshes of the Gangetic Plain;

(vi) The floodplains of the Brahmaputra; the marshes and swamps in the hills of northeast India and the Himalayan foothills;

(vii) The lakes and rivers of the montane region of Kashmir and Ladakh; and

(viii) The mangrove forest and other wetlands of the island arcs of the Andaman and Nicobar Islands. Mangroves grow along the coasts in the salt marshes, tidal creeks, mud flats and estuaries. 3

Long Answer Type Questions (5 marks each)

Q. 1. 'The percentage of forest cover varies state to state.' Explain. [R]

Ans. According to state records, the forest area covers 23.28 per cent of the total land area of the country. In 2011, the actual forest cover was only 21.05 per cent. Of the forest cover, the share of dense and open forests was 12.29 per cent and 8.75 per cent respectively. Both forest area and forest cover vary from state to state. Lakshadweep has zero per cent forest area; Andaman and Nicobar Islands have 86.93 per cent. Most of the states with less than 10 per cent of the forest area lie in the north and northwestern part of the country. These are Rajasthan, Gujarat, Punjab, Haryana and Delhi. Most of the forests in Punjab and Haryana have been cleared for cultivation.

States with 10-20 per cent forest area are Tamil Nadu and West Bengal. In Peninsular India, excluding Tamil Nadu, Dadra and Nagar Haveli and Goa, the area under forest cover is 20-30 per cent. The northeastern states have more than 30 per cent of the land under forest. Hilly topography and heavy rainfall are good for forest growth. There is a lot of variation in actual forest cover, which ranges from 9.56 per cent in Jammu and Kashmir to 84.01 per cent in Andaman and Nicobar Islands. 5

Q. 2. 'Natural vegetation is an outcome of climate.' Substantiate the statement by taking example of Indian vegetation. [A]

Ans. India is a land of great variety of natural vegetation. Himalayan heights are marked with temperate vegetation; the Western Ghats and the Andaman Nicobar Islands have tropical rain forests, the deltaic regions have tropical forests and mangroves; the desert and semi desert areas of Rajasthan are known for cactii, a wide variety of bushes and thorny vegetation. Depending upon the variations in the climate and the soil, the vegetation of India changes from one region to another.

(i) Tropical Evergreen and Semi Evergreen Forests: These forests are found in the western slope of the Western Ghats, hills of the northeastern region and the Andaman and Nicobar Islands. They are found in warm and humid areas with an annual precipitation of over 200 cm and mean annual temperature above 22°C. There is no definite time for trees to shed their leaves, flowering and fruition. As such these forests appear green all the year round. Species found in these forests include rosewood, mahogony, aini, ebony, etc.

The semi evergreen forests are found in the less rainy parts of these regions. Such forests have a mixture of evergreen and moist deciduous trees. The undergrowing climbers provide an evergreen character to these forests. Main species are white cedar, hollock and kail.

(ii) Tropical Deciduous Forests : These are the most widespread forests in India. They are also called the monsoon forests. They spread over regions which receive rainfall between 70-200 cm. On the basis of the availability of water, these forests are further divided into moist and dry deciduous. The Moist deciduous forests are more pronounced in the regions which record rainfall between 100-200 cm. Teak, sal, shisham, hurra, mahua, amla, semul, kusum, and sandalwood etc. are the main species of these forests.

Dry deciduous forest covers vast areas of the country, where rainfall ranges between 70 -100 cm. On the wetter margins, it has a transition to the moist deciduous, while on the drier margins to thorn forests. As the dry season begins, the trees shed their leaves completely and the forest appears like a vast grassland with naked trees all around. Tendu, palas, amaltas, bel, khair, axlewood, etc. are the common trees of these forests.

(iii) **Tropical thorn forests :** It occur in the areas which receive rainfall less than 50 cm. These consist of a variety of grasses and shrubs. It includes semi-arid areas of south west Punjab, Haryana, Rajasthan, Gujarat, Madhya Pradesh and Uttar Pradesh. Important species found are babool, ber, and wild date palm, khair, neem, khejri, palas, etc. Tussocky grass grows upto a height of 2 m as the under growth.

(iv) **Montane Forests :** In mountainous areas, the decrease in temperature with increasing altitude leads to a corresponding change in natural vegetation. Mountain forests can be classified into two types, the northern mountain forests and the southern mountain forests. The Himalayan ranges show a succession of vegetation from the tropical to the tundra, which change in with the altitude. Deciduous forests are found in the foothills of the Himalayas. It is succeeded by the wet temperate type of forests between an altitude of 1,000-2,000 m. The southern mountain forests include the forests found in three distinct areas of Peninsular India viz; the Western Ghats, the Vindhyas and the Nilgiris. As they are closer to the tropics, and only 1,500 m above the sea level, vegetation is temperate in the higher regions, and subtropical on the lower regions of the Western Ghats, especially in Kerala, Tamil Nadu and Karnataka.

(v) **Littoral and Swamp Forests :** India has a rich variety of wetland habitats. About 70 per cent of this comprises areas under paddy cultivation. The total area of wet land is 3.9 million hectares. Two sites — Chilika Lake (Orissa) and Keoladeo National Park (Bharatpur) are protected as water-fowl habitats under the Convention of Wetlands of International Importance (Ramsar Convention). **5**

Q. 3. On the basis of the percentage of the actual forest cover, in how many categories have Indian states been divided? R

Ans. On the basis of the percentage of the actual forest cover, the states have been grouped into four regions :

(i) **The region of high concentration > 40 :** It contains Andaman and Nicobar Islands, Mizoram, Nagaland, Arunachal Pradesh which have 80% of their total area under forests. Manipur, Tripura, Meghalaya, Sikkim and Dadar and Haveli have forest cover between 40-80%.

(ii) **The region of medium concentration 20-40 :** It includes Madhya Pradesh, Odisha, Goa, Kerala, Assam and Himachal Pradesh. In Goa, actual forest cover is 33.27% which is highest in this range. Thereafter, comes Assam and Odisha. In other states, 30 % of their area is covered with forests.

(iii) **The region of low concentration 10-20 :** It includes states of Maharashtra, Andhra Pradesh, Karnataka, Tamil Nadu, Bihar and Uttar Pradesh.

(iv) The region of very low concentration <10 : It includes states of Rajasthan, Punjab, Haryana and Gujarat. It also includes union territories of Delhi and Chandigarh. It also includes West Bengal.

S.No.	The Region	Percentage Cover of the Forest
1.	The region of high concentration.	>40
2.	The region of medium concentration	20-40
3.	The region of low concentration.	10-20
4.	The region of very low concentration	<10

(1 × 5 = 5)

Q. 4. 'Mangroves are unique in their own way.' Explain. A

Ans. In India, the mangrove forests spread over 6,740 sq. km which is 7 per cent of the world's mangrove forests. They are highly developed in the Andaman and Nicobar Islands and the Sunderbans of West Bengal. Other areas of significance are the Mahanadi, the Godavari and the Krishna deltas.

(i) Mangrove forests can survive both in fresh and salty water. The trees have stilt like breathing or support rots, sticking out of mud and water.

(ii) They are exposed at low tides and get submerged at high tides.

(iii) Hot and wet climate favours their dense growth. **5**

TOPIC-2

Forest Conservation, Social Forestry, Farm Forestry, Wildlife Conservation in India, Biosphere Reserves.

Revision Notes

- Forests have an intricate interrelationship with life and environment. These provide numerous direct and indirect advantages to our economy and society.
- Hence, conservation of forest is of vital importance to the survival and prosperity of humankind.
- Accordingly, the Government of India proposed to have a nation-wide forest conservation policy, and adopted a forest policy in 1952, which was further modified in 1988.
- The forest policy aimed at :
  - Bringing 33 per cent of the geographical areas under forest cover;
  - Maintaining environmental stability and to restore forests where ecological balance was disturbed;
  - Conserving the natural heritage of the country, its biological diversity and genetic pool;
  - Checks soil erosion, extension of the desert lands and reduction of floods and droughts;
  - Increasing the forest cover through social forestry and afforestation on degraded land;
  - Increasing the productivity of forests to make timber, fuel, fodder and food available to rural population dependant on forests, and encourage the substitution of wood;
  - Creating of a massive peoples movement involving women to encourage planting of trees, stop felling of trees and thus, reduce pressure on the existing forest .
- Forest and tribals are very closely related. The age-old knowledge of tribals regarding forestry can be used in the development of forests. Rather than treating tribals as minor forest produce collectors they should be made growers of minor forest produce and encouraged to participate in conservation.
- Social forestry means the management and protection of forests and afforestation on barren lands with the purpose of helping in the environmental, social and rural development.
- The National Commission on Agriculture (1976) has classified social forestry into three categories :
  - **Urban forestry :** It pertains to the raising and management of trees on public and privately owned lands in and around urban centres such as green belts, parks, roadside avenues, industrial and commercial green belts, etc.
  - **Rural forestry :** It lays emphasis on promotion of agro-forestry and community-forestry.
  - **Agro-forestry :** It is the raising of trees and agriculture crops on the same land inclusive of the waste patches. It combines forestry with agriculture, thus, altering the simultaneous production of food, fodder, fuel, timber and fruit.
- Community forestry involves the raising of trees on public or community land such as the village pasture and temple land, roadside, canal bank, strips along railway lines, and schools etc. Community forestry programme aims at providing benefits to the community as a whole.
- Forest departments of various states distribute seedlings of trees free of cost to small and medium farmers. Several lands such as the margins of agricultural fields, grasslands and pastures, land around homes and cow sheds may be used for raising trees under non-commercial farm forestry.
- Wildlife of India is a great natural heritage. It is estimated that about 4-5 per cent of all known plant and animal species on the earth are found in India.
- Over the years, their habitat has been disturbed by human activities and as a result, their numbers have dwindled significantly. There are certain species that are at the brink of extinction.
- Some of the important reasons of the declining of wildlife are as follows :
  - Industrial and technological advancement brought about a rapid increase in the exploitation of forest resources.
  - More and more lands were cleared for agriculture, human settlement, roads, mining, reservoirs, etc.
  - Pressure on forests mounted due to lopping for fodder and fuelwood and removal of small timber by the local people.
  - Grazing by domestic cattle caused an adverse effect on wildlife and its habitat.
  - Hunting was taken up as a sport by the elite and hundreds of wild animals were killed in a single hunt. Now commercial poaching is rampant.
  - Incidence of forest fire.
- In 1972, comprehensive Wildlife Act was enacted, which provides the main legal framework for conservation and protection of wildlife in India.

- The two main objectives of the Act are; to provide protection to the endangered species listed in the schedule of the Act and to provide legal support to the conservation areas of the country classified as National parks, sanctuaries and closed areas.
- There are 103 National parks and 535 wildlife sanctuaries covering an area of 15.67 million hectares in the country.
- For the purpose of effective conservation of flora and fauna, special steps have been initiated by the Government of India in collaboration with UNESCO's 'Man and Biosphere Programme'.
- Special schemes like Project Tiger (1973) and Project Elephant (1992) have been launched to conserve these species and their habitat in a sustainable manner.
- Initially, the Project Tiger was launched in nine tiger reserves, covering an area of 16,339 sq. km, which has now increased to 44 tiger reserves, encompassing 36,988.28sq. km of tiger habitats distributed in 17 states. The tiger population in the country has registered an increase from 1,411 in 2006 to 1,706 in 2010.
- Project Elephant was launched in 1992 to assist states having free ranging population of wild elephants.
- Apart from this, some other projects such as Crocodile Breeding Project, Project Hangul and conservation of Himalayan Musk deer have also been launched by the Government of India.
- A **Biosphere Reserve** is a unique and representative ecosystem of terrestrial and coastal areas which are internationally recognised within the framework of UNESCO's Man and Biosphere (MAB) Programme.
- There are 18 Biosphere Reserves, in India. Ten Biosphere Reserves have been recognized by UNESCO on World Network of Biosphere Reserves.
  - **Nilgiri Biosphere Reserve :** The Nilgiri Biosphere Reserve (NBR), the first of the fourteen biosphere reserves of India, was established in September 1986. The Nilgiri Biosphere Reserve possesses different habitat types, unspoilt areas of natural vegetation types with several dry scrubs, dry and moist deciduous, semievergreen and wet evergreen forests, evergreen sholas, grasslands and swamps. The largest south Indian population of elephant, tiger, gaur, sambar and chital as well as a good number of endemic and endangered plants are also found in this reserve.
  - **Nanda Devi Biosphere Reserve :** The Nanda Devi Biosphere Reserve situated in Uttaranchal includes parts of Chamoli, Almora, Pithoragarh and Bageshwar districts. The biosphere reserve has a rich fauna, for example the snow leopard, black bear, brown bear, musk deer, snowcock, golden eagle and black eagle.
  - **Sunderbans Biosphere Reserve :** It is located in the swampy delta of the river Ganga in West Bengal. It extends over a vast area of 9,630 sq. km and consists of mangrove forests, swamps and forested islands. Sunderbans is the home of nearly 200 Royal Bengal tigers. Adapting itself to the saline and fresh water environment, the tigers at the park are good swimmers, and they hunt scarce preys such as chital deer, barking deer, wild pig and even macaques.
  - **Gulf of Mannar Biosphere Reserve :** The Gulf of Mannar Biosphere Reserve covers an area of 105,000 hectares on the southeast coast of India. The biosphere reserve comprises 21 islands with estuaries, beaches, forests of the nearshore environment, sea grasses, coral reefs, salt marshes and mangroves.

Know the Terms

- **Social forestry :** It means the management and protection of forests and afforestation on barren lands with the purpose of helping in the environmental, social and rural development.
- **Urban forestry :** It pertains to the raising and management of trees on public and privately owned lands in and around urban centres such as green belts, parks, roadside avenues, industrial and commercial green belts, etc.
- **Rural forestry :** It lays emphasis on promotion of agro-forestry and community-forestry.
- **Agro-forestry :** It is the raising of trees and agriculture crops on the same land inclusive of the waste patches.
- **Community forestry :** It involves the raising of trees on public or community land such as the village pasture and temple land, roadside, canal bank, strips along railway lines, and schools etc.
- **Community forestry programme :** It aims at providing benefits to the community as a whole.
- **Farm forestry :** It is a term applied to the process under which farmers grow trees for commercial and non-commercial purposes on their farm lands.
- **Biosphere reserve :** It is a unique and representative ecosystem of terrestrial and coastal areas which are internationally recognised within the framework of UNESCO's Man and Biosphere(MAB) Programme.
- **National Park :** It is an area which is strictly reserved for the protection of the wildlife and where activities such as forestry, grazing or cultivation are not allowed.
- **Reserved forest :** An area notified under the provisions of Indian Forest Acts having full degree of protection. In protected forests, all activities are permitted unless prohibited.
- **Sanctuary :** It is an area which is reserved for the conservation of animals only and operations such as harvesting of timber, collection of minor forest products are allowed as long as that do not affect the animals adversely.

Multiple Choice Questions (1 mark each)

Q. 1. The project launched in 1992 to assist states having free ranging population of wild elephants was known as : A

(a) Project Pilot
(b) Project Elephant
(c) Project Park
(d) Project Animal

Ans. (b) Project Elephant 1

Q. 2. There are ________ National Parks in our country. U

(a) 105 (b) 104
(c) 103 (d) 102

Ans. (c) 103 1

Q. 3. The biosphere reserve situated in Uttarakhand includes parts of Chamoli, Almora, Pithoragarh and Bageshwar districts is known as : A

(a) Sunderbans Biosphere Reserve
(b) Nanda Devi Biosphere Reserve
(c) Gulf of Mannar Biosphere Reserve
(d) Kalka Devi Biosphere Reserve

Ans. (b) Nanda Devi Biosphere Reserve 1

Very Short Answer Type Questions (1 mark each)

Q. 1. Define the term 'Social Forestry'. A

Ans. It means the management and protection of forests and afforestation on barren lands with the purpose of helping in the environmental, social and rural development. 1

Q. 2. Define the term 'Urban Forestry'. A

Ans. It pertains to the raising and management of trees on public and privately owned lands in and around urban centres such as green belts, parks, roadside avenues, industrial and commercial green belts, etc. 1

Q. 3. Define the term 'Rural Forestry'. U

Ans. It lays emphasis on promotion of agro-forestry and community-forestry. 1

Q. 4. What are national parks? U

Ans. A national park is an area which is strictly reserved for the protection of the wildlife and where activities such as forestry, grazing or cultivation are not allowed. 1

Answering Tip

- National park : an area set aside by a national government for the preservation of the natural environment.

Q. 5. How many wildlife sanctuaries are there in India? R

Ans. There are 535 wildlife sanctuaries in the country. 1

AI **Q. 6. Name the first biosphere of India.** U

Ans. The Nilgiri Biosphere Reserve is the first biosphere of India. 1

Q. 7. When was the National Forest Policy adopted in India?

Ans. National Forest Policy was adopted in 1962 under which Forest Conservation Board was formed. This policy was modified in 1988. 1

Q. 8. When was the Project Tiger and Project Elephant launched? R

Ans. Project Tiger was launched in 1973 and Project Elephant was launched in 1992. 1

Q. 9. When was the new forest policy implemented? A

Ans. The new forest policy was adopted in 1952 and was further modified in 1988. 1

Q. 10. Where was the Sunderbans Biosphere Reserve located? U

Ans. It is located in the swampy delta of the river Ganga in West Bengal. 1

Q. 11. Where is the Nanda Devi Biosphere Reserve located? A

Ans. The Nanda Devi Biosphere Reserve situated in Uttaranchal includes parts of Chamoli, Almora, Pithoragarh and Bageshwar districts. 1

Q. 12. What is the objective of Project Elephant? R

Ans. Project Elephant was launched in 1992 to assist states having free ranging population of wild elephants. It was aimed at ensuring long-term survival of identified viable population of elephants in their natural habitat. The project is being implemented in 17 states. 1

Answering Tip

- Project Elephant (PE), a centrally sponsored scheme.

Short Answer Type Questions (3 marks each)

Q. 1. Differentiate between national park and sanctuary. A

Ans.

S.No.	National Park	Sanctuary
1.	A national park is an area which is strictly reserved for the protection of the wildlife and where activities such as forestry , grazing or cultivation are not allowed.	A sanctuary is an area which is reserved for the conservation of animals only and operations such as harvesting of timber, collection of minor forest products are allowed so long as they do not affect the animals adversely.
2.	There are 103 national parks in India..	There are 535 wildlife sanctuaries.
3.	National parks have properly marked boundaries.	Sanctuaries usually do not have properly marked boundaries.

(1 × 3 = 3)

Q. 2. Differentiate between national park and biosphere reserve. R

Ans.

S.No.	National Park	Biosphere Reserve
1.	National parks have reserved area of land ,owned by the government.	It has notified area which cover a larger area of land which may cover multiple National Parks, Sanctuaries and reserves as well.
2.	No cutting, grazing allowed. Outside species allowed.	Area are meant for conservation of biodiversity of a specific area.
3.	Conservation of wild nature for prosperity and as a symbol of national pride.	No outside species allowed .

(1 × 3 = 3)

Q. 3. When was the comprehensive Wildlife Act enacted and what are its objectives? A

Ans. The comprehensive Wildlife Act was enacted in 1972. The main objectives of this Act are :

(i) To protect the endangered species listed in the schedule of the Act.

(ii) To provide legal support to the conservation areas of the country classified as national parks, sanctuaries and closed areas.

(iii) Making punishments more stringent and has also made provisions for the protection of specified plant species and conservation of endangered species of wild animals. 3

Q. 4. What is a biosphere reserves? What are the objectives of biosphere reserves? U

Ans. A Biosphere Reserve is a unique and representative ecosystem of terrestrial and coastal areas which are internationally recognised within the framework of UNESCO's Man and Biosphere (MAB) Programme. The main objectives of biosphere reserves are :

(i) Conservation of the biodiversity and ecosystem.

(ii) Association of environment and development.

(iii) International network for research and monitoring. 3

Answering Tip

- Biosphere reserves help ensure the environmental, economic, and social sustainability of the region, by encouraging wise use of natural and human resources.

Q. 5. What are the objectives of Project Tiger? U

Ans. The main objective of the scheme is to ensure maintenance of viable population of tigers in India for scientific, aesthetic, cultural and ecological values, and to preserve areas of biological importance as natural heritage for the benefit, education and enjoyment of the people.

Initially, the Project Tiger was launched in nine tiger reserves, covering an area of 16,339 sq. km, which has now increased to 44 tiger reserves, encompassing 36,988.28sq. km of tiger habitats distributed in 17 states.

The tiger population in the country has registered an increase from 1,411 in 2006 to 1,706 in 2010. 3

Q. 6. Why do you think forests are important to us?

Ans. They are important to us because :

(i) They provide numerous direct and indirect advantages to our economy and society.

(ii) To a vast number of tribes, forest is a home, a livelihood , their very existence. They provide people with material which help them in building houses.

(iii) It provides us food, fodder, shelter, fruits, plants of medicinal value and helps in maintaining ecological balance by helping in oxygen cycle. 3

Answering Tip

- Forests offer watershed protection, prevent soil erosion and mitigate climate change.

Long Answer Type Questions (5 marks each)

Q. 1. Explain the three categories of social forestry. R

Ans. Social forestry can be classified into :

(i) **Urban forestry :** It pertains to the raising and management of trees on public and privately owned lands in and around urban centres such as green belts, parks, roadside avenues, industrial and commercial green belts, etc.

(ii) Rural forestry lays emphasis on promotion of agro-forestry and community-forestry.

(a) **Agro-forestry :** It is the raising of trees and agriculture crops on the same land inclusive of the waste patches. It combines forestry with agriculture, thus, altering the simultaneous production of food, fodder, fuel, timber and fruit.

(b) **Community forestry :** It involves the raising of trees on public or community land such as the village pasture and temple land, roadside, canal bank, strips along railway lines, and schools etc. Community forestry programme aims at providing benefits to the community as a whole. Community forestry provides a means under which the people of landless classes can associate themselves in treeraising and thus, get those benefits which otherwise are restricted for landowners.

(iii) **Farm forestry :** It is a term applied to the process under which farmers grow trees for commercial and non-commercial purposes on their farm lands. Forest departments of various states distribute seedlings of trees free of cost to small and medium farmers. Several lands such as the margins of agricultural fields, grasslands and pastures, land around homes and cow sheds may be used for raising trees under non-commercial farm forestry. 5

Q. 2. What objectives have been determined for the conservation of forests according to National Forest Policy? R

Ans. The forest policy aimed at :

(i) Bringing 33 per cent of the geographical areas under forest cover;

(ii) Maintaining environmental stability and to restore forests where ecological balance was disturbed;

(iii) Conserving the natural heritage of the country, its biological diversity and genetic pool;

(iv) Checks soil erosion, extension of the desert lands and reduction of floods and droughts;

(v) Increasing the forest cover through social forestry and afforestation on degraded land;

(vi) Increasing the productivity of forests to make timber, fuel, fodder and food available to rural population dependant on forests, and encourage the substitution of wood;

(vii) Creating of a massive peoples movement involving women to encourage planting of trees, stop felling of trees and thus, reduce pressure on the existing forest. **(Any five)(1 × 5 = 5)**

Answering Tip

- The National Forest Policy aims to maintain at least one-third of India's total land area under forest and tree cover.

Q. 3. What are the reasons for the decline of wildlife in India? U

Ans. Major reasons for the decline of wildlife in India are :

(i) **Industrial and technological advancement :** This brought about a rapid increase in the exploitation of forest resources by major industries in order to withstand the competition and market pressure .

(ii) **Commercial requirement :** More and more lands were cleared for agriculture, human settlement, roads, mining, reservoirs, etc. The wildlife was forced to move out of its habitat because to human greed.

(iii) **Demands of local population :** Pressure on forests mounted due to lopping for fodder and fuelwood and removal of small timber by the local people. Local population started exploiting the forests in order to meet their demands.

(iv) **Grazing :** Grazing by domestic cattle caused an adverse effect on wildlife and its habitat. The entire cycle got disturbed.

(v) **Hunting :** Hunting was taken up as a sport by the elite and hundreds of wild animals were killed in a single hunt. This led to wildlife disturbance. Now commercial poaching is rampant.

(vi) **Forest Fire :** Incidence of forest fire have also led to the decline of forest fire. Forest fires can be caused due to human negligence or sudden increase in temperature. **(Any Five) (1 × 5 = 5)**

AI **Q. 4. Write a note on the biospheres of India.** A

Ans. A Biosphere Reserve is a unique and representative ecosystem of terrestrial and coastal areas which are internationally recognised within the framework of UNESCO's Man and Biosphere (MAB) Programme. Ten Biosphere Reserves, have been recognised by the UNESCO on World Network of Biosphere Reserves. Some of the important Biosphere reserves are follows :

(i) **The Nilgiri Biosphere Reserve (NBR) :** The first of the fourteen biosphere reserves of India, was established in September 1986. It embraces the sanctuary complex of Wyanad, Nagarhole, Bandipur and Mudumalai, the entire forested hill slopes of Nilambur, the Upper Nilgiri plateau, Silent Valley and the Siruvani hills. The total area of the biosphere reserve is around 5,520 sq. km.

The Nilgiri Biosphere Reserve possesses different habitat types, unspoilt areas of natural vegetation types with several dry scrubs, dry and moist deciduous, semievergreen and wet evergreen forests, evergreen sholas, grasslands and swamps. It includes the largest known population of two endangered animal species, namely the Nilgiri Tahr and the Lion-tailed macaque. The largest south Indian population of elephant, tiger, gaur, sambar and chital as well as a good number of endemic and endangered plants are also found in this reserve. The habitat of a number of tribal groups remarkable for their traditional modes of harmonious use of the environment are also found here.

(ii) The Nanda Devi Biosphere Reserve : It is situated in Uttaranchal includes parts of Chamoli, Almora, Pithoragarh and Bageshwar districts. The major forest types of the reserve are temperate. A few important species are silver weed and orchids like latifolie and rhododendron. The biosphere reserve has a rich fauna, for example the snow leopard, black bear, brown bear, musk deer, snowcock, golden eagle and black eagle. Major threats to the ecosystem are the collection of endangered plants for medicinal use, forest fires and poaching.

(iii) Sunderbans Biosphere Reserve : It is located in the swampy delta of the river Ganga in West Bengal. It extends over a vast area of 9,630 sq. km and consists of mangrove forests, swamps and forested islands. Sunderbans is the home of nearly 200 Royal Bengal tigers. The tangled mass of roots of mangrove trees provide safe homes for a large number of species, from fish to shrimp. More than 170 birds species are known to inhabit these mangrove forests.

(iv) Gulf of Mannar Biosphere Reserve : The Gulf of Mannar Biosphere Reserve covers an area of 105,000 hectares on the southeast coast of India. It is one of the world's richest regions from a marine biodiversity perspective. The biosphere reserve comprises 21 islands with estuaries, beaches, forests of the nearshore environment, sea grasses, coral reefs, salt marshes and mangroves. Among the Gulf''s 3,600 plant and animal species are the globally endangered sea cow (Dugong dugon) and six mangrove species, endemic to Peninsular India. 5

Q. 5. 'It is important to conserve wildlife'. Mention the initiatives taken in this direction. [A]

Ans. The protection of wildlife has a long tradition in India. Many stories of Panchtantra and Jungle Books, etc. have stood the test of time relating to the love for wildlife. These have a profound impact on young minds.

In 1972, a comprehensive Wildlife Act was enacted, which provides the main legal framework for conservation and protection of wildlife in India.

The two main objectives of the Act are; to provide protection to the endangered species listed in the schedule of the Act and to provide legal support to the conservation areas of the country classified as National parks, sanctuaries and closed areas. This Act has been comprehensively amended in 1991, making punishments more stringent and has also made provisions for the protection of specified plant species and conservation of endangered species of wild animals.

There are 103 National parks and 535 wildlife sanctuaries covering an area of 15.67 million hectares in the country. Wildlife conservation has a very large ambit with unbounded potential for the wellbeing of humankind. However, this can be achieved only when every individual understands its significance and contributes his bit. For the purpose of effective conservation of flora and fauna, special steps have been initiated by the Government of India in collaboration with UNESCO's 'Man and Biosphere Programme'.

Special schemes like Project Tiger (1973) and Project Elephant (1992) have been launched to conserve these species and their habitat in a sustainable manner. Project Tiger has been implemented since 1973. The main objective of the scheme is to ensure maintenance of viable population of tigers in India for scientific, aesthetic, cultural and ecological values, and to preserve areas of biological importance as natural heritage for the benefit, education and enjoyment of the people.

Initially, the Project Tiger was launched in nine tiger reserves, covering an area of 16,339 sq. km, which has now increased to 44 tiger reserves, encompassing 36,988.28sq. km of tiger habitats distributed in 17 states. The tiger population in the country has registered an increase from 1,411 in 2006 to 1,706 in 2010. 5

Answering Tip

- In order to maintain a healthy ecological balance on this earth conservation of animals, plants and marine species is important.

Q. 6. 'Forest and tribals are very closely related.' Justify the statement. [U]

Ans. To a vast number of tribal people, the forest is a home, a livelihood, their very existence. It provides them food, fruits of all kinds, edible leaves, honey, nourishing roots and wild game. It provides them with material to build their houses and items for practising their arts. The importance of forests in tribal economy is well-known as they are the source of sustenance and livelihood for tribal communities. It is commonly believed that the tribal communities live in harmony with nature and protect forests. Out of a total of 593 districts 187 (2001) have been identified as tribal districts.

The tribal districts account for about 59.8 per cent of the total forest cover of the country whereas the geographical area of 187 tribal districts forms only 33.6 per cent of the total geographical area of the country. It demonstrates that tribal districts are generally rich in forest cover. Forest and tribals are very closely related. The age-old knowledge of tribals regarding forestry can be used in the development of forests. Rather than treating tribals as minor forest produce collectors they should be made growers of minor forest produce and encouraged to participate in conservation. 5

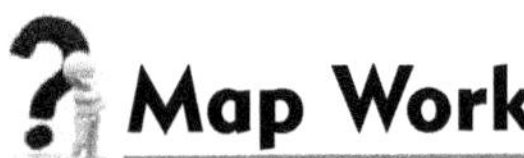

Map Work

(5 marks each)

Q.1. On the outline map of India, mark and label the following :

(i) Similipal **(ii) Sunderbans**

(iii) Panchmarhi **(iv) Manas**

(v) Great Andamans

Ans.

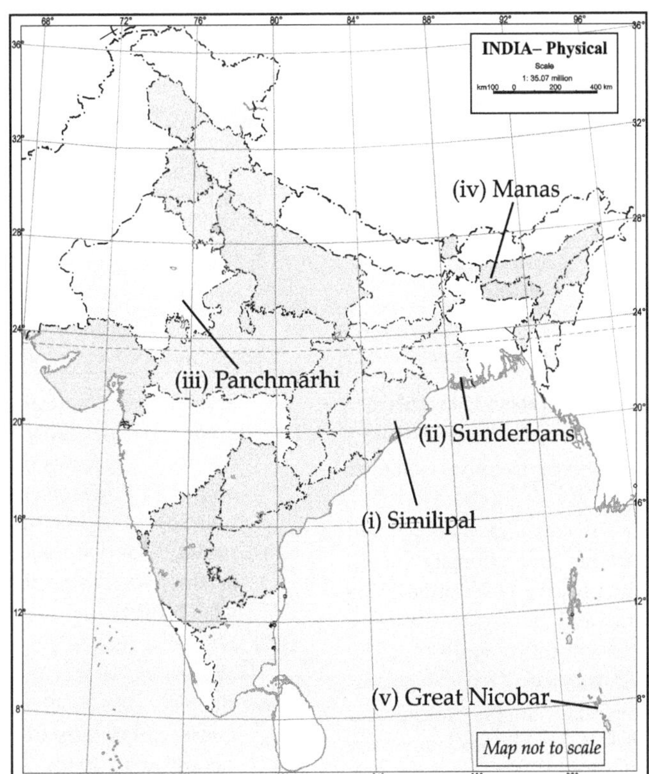

NCERT CORNER

(A) Multiple choice questions :

Q. 1. Sandalwood is an example of :

(a) Evergreen forest

(b) Deciduous forest

(c) Deltaic forest

(d) Thorny forest

Ans. (b) Deciduous forest.

Q. 2. Which one of the following was the purpose of Project Tiger :

(a) to kill tigers

(b) to put tigers in the Zoo

(c) to protect tigers from illegal hunting

(d) to make films on tigers

Ans. (c) To protect tigers from illegal hunting.

Q. 3. In which one of the following states is the Nandadevi Biosphere reserve situated :

(a) Bihar

(b) Uttar Pradesh

(c) Uttarakhand

(d) Odisha

Ans. (c) Uttarakhand.

Q. 4. How many of the following numbers of Biosphere reserves are recognised by the IUCN :

(a) One

(b) Two

(c) Ten

(d) Four

Ans. (c) Ten.

Q. 5. Which one of the following proportion of area of the country was targeted to be under forest in Forest Policy of India :

(a) 33 (b) 44

(c) 55 (d) 22

Ans. (a) 33

(B) Answer the following questions in about 30 words :.

Q. 1. What is natural vegetation? Under what climatic conditions are tropical evergreen forests develop?

Ans. Natural vegetation refers to a plant community that has been left undisturbed over a long time, so as to allow its individual species to adjust themselves to climate and soil conditions as fully as possible.

Tropical evergreen forests develop in warm and humid areas with an annual precipitation of over 200 cm and mean annual temperature above 22°C.

Q. 2. What do you understand by social forestry?

Ans. Social forestry means the management and protection of forests and afforestation on barren lands with the purpose of helping in the environmental, social and rural development.

Q. 3. Define Biosphere reserves.

Ans. A Biosphere Reserve is a unique and representative ecosystem of terrestrial and coastal areas which are internationally recognised within the framework of UNESCO's Man and Biosphere (MAB) Programme.

Q. 4. What is the difference between forest area and forest cover?

Ans.

S.No.	Forest Area	Forest Cover
1.	The forest area is the area notified and recorded as the forest land irrespective of the existence of trees.	The actual forest cover is the area occupied by forests with canopy.
2.	It is based on the records of the State Revenue Department.	It is based on the aerial photographs and satellite imageries.
3.	According to the state records, the forest area covers 23.28 percent of the total land area.	According to India State of Forest Report 2011, the actual forest cover in India is only 21.05 per cent.

(C) Answer the following questions in about 150 words :

Q. 1. What steps have been taken up to conserve forests?

Ans. Steps that have been taken up to conserve forests are:

(i) Social forestry : It means the management and protection of forests and afforestation on barren lands with the purpose of helping in the environmental, social and rural development. The National Commission on Agriculture (1976) has classified social forestry into three categories:

(a) Urban forestry : It pertains to the raising and management of trees on public and privately owned lands in and around urban centres such as green belts, parks, roadside avenues, industrial and commercial green belts, etc.

(b) Rural forestry : It lays emphasis on promotion of agro-forestry and community-forestry.

(c) Agro-forestry : It is the raising of trees and agriculture crops on the same land inclusive of the waste patches. It combines forestry with agriculture, thus, altering the simultaneous production of food, fodder, fuel, timber and fruit.

(ii) Community forestry : It involves the raising of trees on public or community land such as the village pasture and temple land, roadside, canal bank, strips along railway lines, and schools etc. Community forestry programme aims at providing benefits to the community as a whole. Community forestry provides a means under which the people of landless classes can associate themselves in tree raising and thus, get those benefits which otherwise are restricted for landowners.

(iii) Farm forestry : It is a term applied to the process under which farmers grow trees for commercial and non-commercial purposes on their farm lands. Forest departments of various states distribute seedlings of trees free of cost to small and medium farmers. Several lands such as the margins of agricultural fields, grasslands and pastures, land around homes and cow sheds may be used for raising trees under non-commercial farm forestry.

Q. 2. How can people's participation be effective in conserving forests and wildlife?

Ans. People's participation can be very effective in conserving forests and wildlife. It is the common people who harm and destroy the forests as well as the wildlife. They cut trees for shifting cultivation. They kill animals for entertainment. Therefore in 1972, Government of India passes the Wildlife Protection Act, whereby it is illegal to do hunting. Since then the hunting and poaching cases have reduced to a great extent. The two main objectives of the Act are; to provide protection to the endangered species listed in the schedule of the Act and to provide legal support to the conservation areas of the country classified as National parks, sanctuaries and closed areas. This Act has been comprehensively amended in 1991, making punishments more stringent and has also made provisions for the protection of specified plant species and conservation of endangered species of wild animals.

There are about 103 national parks and 535 wildlife sanctuaries covering an area of 15.67 million hectares in the country. These actions are taken by the government but their implementation and maintenance depend on the participation and cooperation of the people

Project Work

Q. 1. On the outline map of India, mark and label the following :

(i) Areas having Mangrove forests.

(ii) Biosphere reserves of Nanda Devi, Sunderbans, Gulf of Mannar and Nilgiri.

(iii) Mark the location of Forest Survey of India Head Quarter.

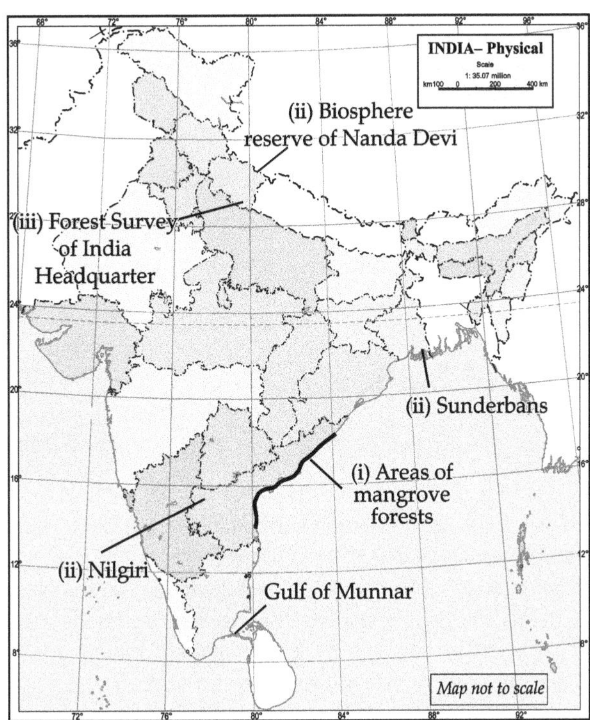

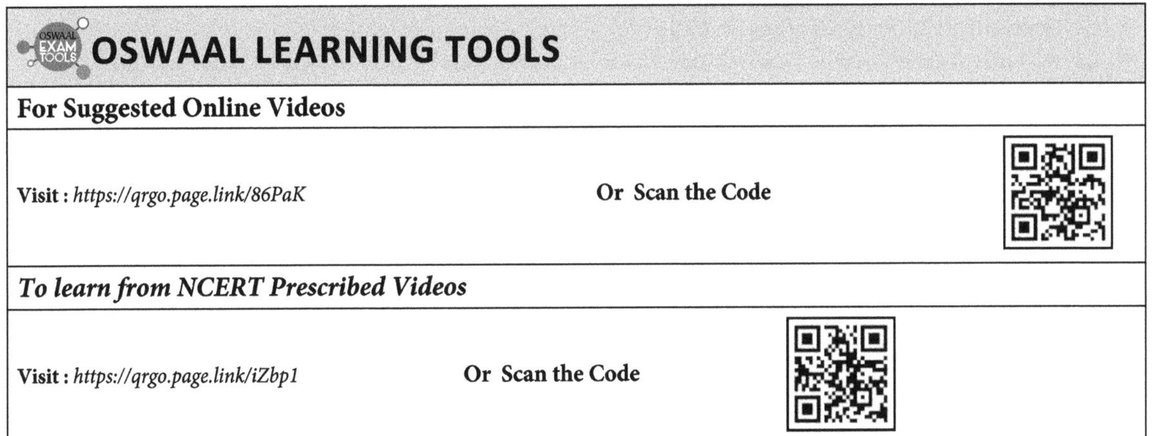

CHAPTER

6 SOILS

Syllabus

> *Classification of Soils*
> *Soil Degradation, Soil Erosion, Soil Conservation.*

TOPIC-1 Classification of Soils

Revision Notes

- Soil is the most important layer of the earth's crust. It is a valuable resource. The bulk of our food and much of our clothing is derived from land-based crops that grow in the soil.
- The soil on which we depend so much for our day-to-day needs has evolved over thousands of years.
- Soil is the mixture of rock debris and organic materials which develop on the earth's surface. The major factors affecting the formation of soil are relief, parent material, climate, vegetation and other life-forms and time.
- Components of the soil are mineral particles, humus, water and air.
- Some soils are deficient in one or more of these, while there are some others that have varied combinations.
- India has varied relief features, landforms, climatic realms and vegetation types. These have contributed in the development of various types of soils in India.
- **On the basis of genesis, colour, composition and location, the soils of India have been classified into :**
  - **Alluvial Soils :** Alluvial soils are widespread in the Northern Plains and the river valleys. Through a narrow corridor in Rajasthan, they extend into the plains of Gujarat. In the Peninsular region, they are found in deltas of the east coast and in the river valleys.
- The colour of the alluvial soils varies from the light grey to ash grey. Its shades depend on the depth of the deposition, the texture of the materials, and the time taken for attaining maturity. Alluvial soils are intensively cultivated.
  - **Black Soil :** Black soil covers most of the Deccan Plateau which includes parts of Maharashtra, Madhya Pradesh, Gujarat, Andhra Pradesh and some parts of Tamil Nadu.
- These soils are also known as the 'Regur Soil' or the 'Black Cotton Soil'.
- The black soils are generally clayey, deep and impermeable. They swell and become sticky when wet and shrink when dried.
- Chemically, the black soils are rich in lime, iron, magnesia and alumina. They also contain potash. But they lack in phosphorous, nitrogen and organic matter.
- The colour of the soil ranges from deep black to grey.
  - **Red and Yellow soil :** It develops on crystalline igneous rocks in areas of low rainfall in the eastern and southern part of the Deccan Plateau.
- Yellow and red soils are also found in parts of Odisha and Chhattisgarh and in the southern parts of the middle Ganga plain.
- The fine-grained red and yellow soils are normally fertile, whereas coarse-grained soils found in dry upland areas are poor in fertility.

- They are generally poor in nitrogen, phosphorous and humus.
  - **Laterite soil :** The word 'Laterite' has been derived from the Latin word 'Later' which means brick. The laterite soils develop in areas with high temperature and high rainfall.
- These soils are poor in organic matter, nitrogen, phosphate and calcium, while iron oxide and potash are in excess.
- Red laterite soils in Tamil Nadu, Andhra Pradesh and Kerala are more suitable for tree crops like cashewnut.
- Laterite soils are widely cut as bricks for use in house construction.
- The laterite soils are commonly found in Karnataka, Kerala, Tamil Nadu, Madhya Pradesh and the hilly areas of Odisha and Assam.
  - **Arid soils :** It ranges from red to brown in colour. In some areas, the salt content is so high that common salt is obtained by evaporating the saline water.
- Lower horizons of the soil are occupied by 'kankar' layers because of the increasing calcium content downwards.
- Arid soils are characteristically developed in western Rajasthan, which exhibit characteristic arid topography. These soils are poor and contain little humus and organic matter.
  - **Saline Soils :** They are also known as Usara soils. Saline soils contain a larger proportion of sodium, potassium and magnesium, and thus, they are infertile, and do not support any vegetative growth.
- They have more salts, largely because of dry climate and poor drainage.
- Excessive irrigation with dry climatic conditions promotes capillary action, which results in the deposition of salt on the top layer of the soil.
- They are more widespread in western Gujarat, deltas of the eastern coat and in suderban areas of West Bengal.
  - **Peaty Soils :** They are found in the areas of heavy rainfall and high humidity, where there is a good growth of vegetation.
- Organic matter in these soils may go even up to 40-50 per cent.
- This soil is black in colour.
- At many places, they are alkaline also. It occurs widely in the northern part of Bihar, southern part of Uttarakhand and the coastal areas of West Bengal, Odisha and Tamil.
  - **Forest soil :** forest soils are formed in the forest areas where sufficient rainfall is available. The soils vary in structure and texture depending on the mountain environment where they are formed.
- They are loamy and silty on valley sides and coarse-grained in the upper slopes.
- The soils found in the lower valleys are fertile.

Know the Terms

- **Soil :** Soil is the mixture of rock debris and organic materials which develop on the earth's surface.
- **Horizons :** If we dig a pit on land and look at the soil, we find that it consists of three layers which are called horizons.
- **Horizon A' :** It is the topmost zone, where organic materials have got incorporated with the mineral matter, nutrients and water, which are necessary for the growth of plants.
- **Horizon B' :** It is a transition zone between the 'horizon A' and 'horizon C', and contains matter derived from below as well as from above. It has some organic matter in it, although the mineral matter is noticeably weathered.
- **Horizon C' :** It is composed of the loose parent material. This layer is the first stage in the soil formation process and eventually forms the above two layers.
- **Soil profile :** The arrangement of layers in the three horizons is known as the soil profile.
- **Parent rock :** Underneath the three horizons there is the rock which is known as the parent rock or the bedrock.
- **Khadar :** Khadar is the new alluvium and is deposited by floods annually, which enriches the soil by depositing fine silt.
- **Bhangar :** It represents a system of older alluvium, deposited away from the flood plains.
- **Alluvial soil :** They are depositional soils, transported and deposited by the rivers and streams.
- **Laterite soil :** This soil develops in areas with high temperature and high rainfall.
- **Black soil :** These soils are made out of volcanic eruption.

Multiple Choice Questions (1 mark each)

Q. 1. The soil which is formed by the occurrence of volcanoes is known as : A
(a) black soil
(b) red soil
(c) yellow soil
(d) grey soil
Ans. (a) black soil 1

AI **Q.2. The soil which is formed by the deposition of rivers is known as :** U
(a) clay soil
(b) alluvial soil
(c) silt
(b) loamy soil
Ans. (b) alluvial soil 1

Q. 3. The colour of arid soil is: R
(a) red and green
(b) red and yellow
(c) red and brown
(d) red and grey
Ans. (b) red and brown 1

Q. 4. The total area covered with alluvial soil in India is: U
(a) 60%
(b) 50%
(c) 40%
(d) 30%
Ans. (c) 40% 1

Very Short Answer Type Questions (1 mark each)

Q. 1. Define the term 'Soil'. A
Ans. Soil is the mixture of rock debris and organic materials which develop on the earth's surface. 1

Q. 2. Define the term 'Khadar'. A
Ans. Khadar is the new alluvium and is deposited by floods annually, which enriches the soil by depositing fine silt. 1

Q. 3. Define the term 'Bhangar'. U
Ans. Bhangar represents a system of older alluvium, deposited away from the flood plains. 1

Q. 4. Where are alluvial soils found in India? R
Ans. Through a narrow corridor in Rajasthan, they extend into the plains of Gujarat. In the Peninsular region, they are found in deltas of the east coast and in the river valleys. 1

Commonly Made Error
- The students are not aware how the alluvial soil is formed.

Answering Tip
- Alluvial soils are formed mainly due to silt deposited by Indo-Gangetic-Brahmaputra rivers.

Q. 5. Where are black soils found in India? R
Ans. Black soil covers most of the Deccan Plateau which includes parts of Maharashtra, Madhya Pradesh, Gujarat, Andhra Pradesh and some parts of Tamil Nadu. 1

Q. 6. Where are red and yellow soils found in India? R
Ans. Yellow and red soils are found in parts of Orissa and Chhattisgarh and in the southern parts of the middle Ganga plain. It is also found in eastern and southern part of the Deccan Plateau and along the piedmont zone of the Western Ghats.1

Q. 7. Why are laterite soils not suitable for agriculture? U
Ans. These soils are poor in organic matter, nitrogen, phosphate and calcium, while iron oxide and potash are in excess. Hence, laterites are not suitable for cultivation. 1

Q. 8. Why do arid soils lack moisture and humus? A
Ans. Due to the dry climate, high temperature and accelerated evaporation, they lack moisture and humus. 1

Answering Tip
- Arid soils are mineral rich soils but the main limitation is the lack of water.

AI **Q.9. What are the physical features of soil?** U
Ans. Colour, texture, composition, capacity to absorb moisture ,erosion , depth, structure ,slope of land and density are included in the physical features of soil. **(Any Two) (½ + ½ =1)**

Q. 10. Mention the physical factors on which the fertility of soil depends? A
Ans. Size of the particles, nature and composition, result of its holes, form and depth of soil , flow and storage of water are some of the physical factors on which the fertility of soil depends. **(Any Two) (½ + ½ =1)**

Answering Tip
- Soil fertility can be improved by incorporating cover crops that add organic matter to the soil.

Q. 11. What does ICAR stand for? U
Ans. Indian Council of Agricultural Research. 1

Q. 12. What factors determine the various shades of the alluvial soil? A

Ans. Its shades depend on the depth of the deposition, the texture of the materials, and the time taken for attaining maturity. 1

Q. 13. Differentiate between Khadar and Bhangar. U

Ans.

S.No.	Khadar	Bhangar
1.	Khadar is the new alluvium and is deposited by floods annually, which enriches the soil by depositing fine silts.	Bhangar represents a system of older alluvium, deposited away from the flood plains.

1

Q. 14. What is the common feature of Khadar and Bhangar? R

Ans. Both the Khadar and Bhangar soils contain calcareous concretions (Kankars). These soils are more loamy and clayey in the lower and middle Ganga plain and the Brahamaputra valley. 1

Q. 15. What role does climate play in the formation of soil? U

Ans. Climate especially rainfall plays an important role in soil formation. It determines the nature of weathering, amount of water absorption , particles of humus and types of micro-organisms. 1

Q. 16. How does the topography affect the process of soil formation? R

Ans. Slope determines the flow of water and soil erosion. Therefore, places of gentle slope have better soil development. It is so because steepness of slope reduces the rate of soil erosion. 1

Q. 17. What determines the colour of the red and yellow soil? U

Ans. The soil develops a reddish colour due to a wide diffusion of iron in crystalline and metamorphic rocks. It looks yellow when it occurs in a hydrated form. 1

Answering Tip

- Yellow and red soil indicates the presence of oxidized ferric iron oxides.

Q. 18. How is soil useful to us? R

Ans. Soil is useful to us as it helps us to nurture plants and animals. It is an important resource without which we cannot get our food. 1

Answering Tip

- Soil acts as a drainage system when it rains to absorb water therefore preventing floods.

Q. 19. The Indian Agriculture Research Institute has classified the Indian soils on what basis? U

Ans. The Indian Agriculture Research Institute has classified the Indian soils on the basis of genesis, colour, composition and location. 1

Q. 20. Where is forest soil found? A

Ans. As the name suggests, forest soils are formed in the forest areas where sufficient rainfall is available. 1

Short Answer Type Questions (3 marks each)

Q. 1. What are the features of black soil? A

Ans. Features of black soil :

(i) These soils are also known as the 'Regur Soil' or the 'Black Cotton Soil'. The black soils are generally clayey, deep and impermeable.

(ii) They swell and become sticky when wet and shrink when dried. So, during the dry season, these soil develop wide cracks. Thus, there occurs a kind of 'self ploughing'.

(iii) Because of this character of slow absorption and loss of moisture, the black soil retains the moisture for a very long time, which helps the crops, especially, the rain fed ones, to sustain even during the dry season. **(1 × 3 = 3)**

Answering Tip

- Black soil is rich in calcium, potassium and magnesium but has poor nitrogen content.

Q. 2. How were soils classified in ancient times? U

Ans. In ancient times, soils used to be classified into two main groups – Urvara and Usara, which were fertile and sterile, respectively. In the 16th century A.D., soils were classified on the basis of their inherent characteristics and external features such as texture, colour, slope of land and moisture content in the soil. Based on texture, main soil types were identified as sandy, clayey, silty and loam, etc. On the basis of colour, they were red, yellow, black, etc. 3

AI **Q.3. What is soil made up of?** R

Ans. Soil is made up of the following things :

(i) **Clay :** It is the smallest particles of broken rock in soil , less than .0002 mm in diameter, so it is a fine dust. When wet, the individual particles stick together to form a solid mass. When they dry , they can bake to a hard crust. Clay holds water which does not drain away.

(ii) **Silt :** It is slightly larger pieces of rock than clay. It is also soft and smooth, with individual pieces close together. It too holds a lot of water,but the slightly larger particles make it a little better at draining then clay.

(iii) **Sand :** It is small piece of rock (2mm to .05mm diameter) such as quartz or sandstone. Sand particles are large enough to allow water to drain easily, but they do not hold water and are easily blown around when dry.

(iv) **Stones , rocks and boulders :** They are larger pieces of rock which are too big to form part of the soil but are found in many gardens. Under the surface layer of soil, they can help drainage.

(Any three) (1 × 3 = 3)

Q. 4. What do you know about saline soils? [A]

Ans. (i) They are also known as Usara soils. Saline soils contain a larger proportion of sodium, potassium and magnesium, and thus, they are infertile, and do not support any vegetative growth. They have more salts, largely because of dry climate and poor drainage.

(ii) They occur in arid and semi-arid regions, and in waterlogged and swampy areas. Their structure ranges from sandy to loamy.

(iii) They lack in nitrogen and calcium. Saline soils are more widespread in western Gujarat, deltas of the eastern coast and in Sunderban areas of West Bengal. In the Rann of Kuchchh, the Southwest Monsoon brings salt particles and deposits there as a crust. **(1 × 3 = 3)**

Commonly Made Error

- The students are not aware as to how the saline soils are formed.

Answering Tip

- The saline soils are formed due to evapotranspiration and lack of rainfall.

Q. 5. Differentiate between light soil and heavy soil? [R]

Ans.

S.No.	Light Soil	Heavy Soil
1.	It contains a vey high proportion of sand, which contains few plant nutrients. They easily dry out, when the surface layer is easily blown out.	They are those with a large component of clay in them , because the clay particles bind together to form a heavy ,sticky lump which is difficult to dig.
2.	It holds a lot of water and easily becomes waterlogged.	They are often acidic. It cannot hold water.
3.	Its quality can be improved by adding plenty of organic matter in the form of garden compost .	Its quality can be improved by adding humus or other organic matter and sharp sand for better drainage.

(1 × 3 = 3)

Long Answer Type Questions

(5 marks each)

Q. 1. Explain the features of the alluvial soil. [A]

Ans. Features of the alluvium soil :

(i) They are depositional soils, transported and deposited by rivers and streams. Through a narrow corridor in Rajasthan, they extend into the plains of Gujarat. In the Peninsular region, they are found in deltas of the east coast and in the river valleys.

(ii) Alluvial soils are widespread in the northern plains and the river valleys. These soils cover about 40 percent of the total area of the country.

(iii) The alluvial soils vary in nature from sandy loam to clay. They are generally rich in potash but poor in phosphorous. In the Upper and Middle Ganga plain, two different types of alluvial soils have developed, viz. Khadar and Bhangar.

(iv) Khadar is the new alluvium and is deposited by floods annually, which enriches the soil by depositing fine silts. Bhangar represents a system of older alluvium, deposited away from the flood plains. Both the Khadar and Bhangar soils contain calcareous concretions (Kankars).

(v) The colour of the alluvial soils varies from the light grey to ash grey. Its shades depend on the depth of the deposition, the texture of the materials, and the time taken for attaining maturity. Alluvial soils are intensively cultivated.

(Any Five) (1 × 5 = 5)

Answering Tip

- The alluvial soil is acidic, sandy, rich in total potash and phosphorus.

Q. 2. Explain the features of the black soil. [R]

Ans. Features of black soil :

(i) Black soil covers most of the Deccan Plateau which includes parts of Maharashtra, Madhya Pradesh, Gujarat, Andhra Pradesh and some parts of Tamil Nadu.

(ii) These soils are also known as the 'Regur Soil' or the 'Black Cotton Soil'. The black soils are generally clayey, deep and impermeable.

(iii) They swell and become sticky when wet and shrink when dried. So, during the dry season, these soil develop wide cracks. Thus, there occurs a kind of 'self ploughing'.

(iv) Because of this character of slow absorption and loss of moisture, the black soil retains the moisture for a very long time, which helps the crops, especially, the rain fed ones, to sustain even during the dry season.

(v) Chemically, the black soils are rich in lime, iron, magnesia and alumina. They also contain potash. But they lack in phosphorous, nitrogen and organic matter. The colour of the soil ranges from deep black to grey. **(1 × 5 = 5)**

Q. 3. Explain the features of the laterite soil. [R]

Ans. (i) Laterite has been derived from the Latin word 'Later' which means brick. The laterite soils develop in areas with high temperature and high rainfall.

(ii) These are the result of intense leaching due to tropical rains. With rain, lime and silica are leached away, and soils rich in iron oxide and aluminium compound are left behind.

(iii) Humus content of the soil is removed fast by bacteria that thrives well in high temperature. These soils are poor in organic matter, nitrogen, phosphate and calcium, while iron oxide and potash are in excess. Hence, laterites are not suitable for cultivation; however, application of manures and fertilisers are required for making the soils fertile for cultivation.

(iv) Red laterite soils in Tamil Nadu, Andhra Pradesh and Kerala are more suitable for tree crops like cashewnut.

(v) Laterite soils are widely cut as bricks for use in house construction. These soils have mainly developed in the higher areas of the Peninsular plateau. The laterite soils are commonly found in Karnataka, Kerala, Tamil Nadu, Madhya Pradesh and the hilly areas of Odisha and Assam. **(1 × 5 = 5)**

Answering Tip

- In some areas, laterite soils support grazing grounds and scrub forests.

Q. 4. Explain the features of saline soils. U

Ans. Important features of saline soils:

(i) They are also known as Usara soils. Saline soils contain a larger proportion of sodium, potassium and magnesium, and thus, they are infertile, and do not support any vegetative growth. They have more salts, largely because of dry climate and poor drainage.

(ii) They occur in arid and semi-arid regions, and in waterlogged and swampy areas. Their structure ranges from sandy to loamy.

(iii) Seawater intrusions in the deltas promote the occurrence of saline soils. In the areas of intensive cultivation with excessive use of irrigation, especially in areas of green revolution, the fertile alluvial soils are becoming saline.

(iv) Excessive irrigation with dry climatic conditions promotes capillary action, which results in the deposition of salt on the top layer of the soil.

(v) In such areas, especially in Punjab and Haryana, farmers are advised to add gypsum to solve the problem of salinity in the soil. **(1 × 5 = 5)**

TOPIC-2
Soil Degradation, Soil Erosion, Soil Conservation

Revision Notes

- Like any other organism, they too develop and decay, get degraded, respond to proper treatment if administered in time.
- **Soil degradation** can be defined as the decline in soil fertility, when the nutritional status declines and depth of the soil goes down due to erosion and misuse.
- The degree of soil degradation varies from place to place according to the topography, wind velocity and amount of the rainfall.
- The destruction of the soil cover is described as soil erosion. The soil forming processes and the erosional processes of running water and wind go on simultaneously.
- Human activities too are responsible for soil erosion to a great extent.
- Forest and other natural vegetation is removed for human settlement, for cultivation, for grazing animals and for various other needs.
- Wind and water are powerful agents of soil erosion because of their ability to remove soil and transport it. Wind erosion is significant in arid and semi-arid regions. In regions with heavy rainfall and steep slopes, erosion by running water is more significant.
- Sheet erosion takes place on level lands after a heavy shower and the soil removal is not easily noticeable.
- Gully erosion is common on steep slopes. Gullies deepen with rainfall, cut the agricultural lands into small fragments and make them unfit for cultivation.
- A region with a large number of deep gullies or ravines is called a badland topography.
- Besides this, they are also found in Tamil Nadu and West Bengal. The country is losing about 8,000 hectares of land to ravines every year.
- Soil erosion is a serious problem for Indian agriculture and its negative effects are seen in other spheres also.
- Eroded materials are carried down to rivers and they lower down their carrying capacity, and cause frequent floods and damage to agricultural lands.
- Deforestation is one of the major causes of soil erosion. Plants keep soils bound in locks of roots, and thus, prevent erosion.
- Chemical fertilisers in the absence of organic manures are also harmful to the soil. Unless the soil gets enough humus, chemicals harden it and reduce its fertility in the long run.
- According to estimates, about half of the total land of India is under some degree of degradation.
- If soil erosion and exhaustion are caused by humans; by corollary, they can also be prevented by humans.

- Soil conservation is a methodology to maintain soil fertility, prevent soil erosion and exhaustion, and improve the degraded condition of the soil.
- The first step in any rational solution is to check open cultivable lands on slopes from farming.
- Lands with a slope gradient of 15 - 25 per cent should not be used for cultivation.
- Over-grazing and shifting cultivation in many parts of India have affected the natural cover of land and given rise to extensive erosion.
- Contour terracing, regulated forestry, controlled grazing, cover cropping, mixed farming and crop rotation are some of the remedial measures which are often adopted to reduce soil erosion.
- Efforts should be made to prevent gully erosion and control their formation. Finger gullies can be eliminated by terracing.
- Special attention should be made to control headward extension of gullies. This can be done by gully plugging, terracing or by planting cover vegetation.
- Lands not suitable for cultivation should be converted into pastures for grazing. Experiments have been made to stabilise sand dunes in western Rajasthan by the Central Arid Zone Research Institute (CAZRI).
- The Central Soil Conservation Board, set up by the Government of India, has prepared a number of plans for soil conservation in different parts of the country.
- Integrated land use planning, therefore, seems to be the best technique for proper soil conservation.
- The final responsibility for achieving the conservation of land will rest on the people who operate on it and receive the benefits.

Know the Terms

- **Bad land topography :** A region with a large number of deep gullies or ravines is called a bad land topography.
- **Gully erosion :** It is the erosion of the soil and rock by the concentration of runoff into gullies.
- **Sheet erosion :** It is the uniform removal of soil in thin layers by the forces of raindrops and overland flow.
- **Soil erosion :** The destruction of the soil cover is described as soil erosion.
- **Soil degradation :** It is the decline in soil fertility when the nutritional status declines and depth of the soil goes down due to erosion and misuse.
- **Soil conservation :** It is a methodology to maintain soil fertility , prevent soil erosion and exhaustion and improve the degraded condition of the soil.

Multiple Choice Questions (1 mark each)

Q. 1. The decline in soil fertility when the nutritional status declines and depth of the soil goes down due to erosion and misuse is known as : A

(a) soil conservation **(b)** soil erosion

(c) soil degradation **(d)** soil utilization

Ans. (c) soil degradation 1

Q. 2. Lands with a slope gradient of _______ per cent should not be used for cultivation. U

(a) 5-10 **(b)** 10-15

(c) 15-25 **(d)** 25-35

Ans. (c) 15-25 1

AI **Q. 4. A region with a large number of deep gullies or ravines is called a:** A

(a) good land topography

(b) bad land topography

(c) arid land topography

(d) sandy land topography

Ans. (b) bad land topography 1

Very Short Answer Type Questions (1 mark each)

Q. 1. Define the term 'Soil Erosion'. A

Ans. The destruction of the soil cover is described as soil erosion. 1

Q. 2. Define the term 'Soil Conservation'. A

Ans. Soil conservation is a methodology to maintain soil fertility, prevent soil erosion and exhaustion, and improve the degraded condition of the soil. **1**

Q. 3. Define the term 'Ravine'. U

Ans. Gullies deepen with rainfall , cut the agricultural lands into small fragments and make them unfit for cultivation. These are called ravines. 1

Answering Tip

- Ravines are an example of soil erosion.

Q. 4. Name any two factors responsible for soil erosion and degradation? R

Ans. Running water, wind, snow, animals and human activities are responsible for soil erosion and degradation. **(Any Two) (½ + ½=1)**

Q. 5. Why is soil erosion harmful? U

Ans. Soil erosion is harmful as if removes the fertile layer of the soil, it also leads to sudden overflow of destructive floods, it makes the agricultural land unfit as it cuts the land into small fragments thus reducing the moisture of the soil. 1

Q. 6. How can we reduce soil erosion? U

Ans. Contour bunding, Contour terracing, regulated forestry, controlled grazing, cover cropping, mixed farming and crop rotation are some of the remedial measures which are often adopted to reduce soil erosion. 1

Q. 7. How does gully erosion make the soil unfit for agriculture? R

Ans. Gully erosion is common on steep slopes. Gullies deepen with rainfall, cut the agricultural lands into small fragments and make them unfit for cultivation. 1

Q. 8. How can soil be conserved in the arid and semi-arid areas? R

Ans. In arid and semi-arid areas, efforts should be made to protect cultivable lands from encroachment by sand dunes through developing shelter belts of trees and agro-forestry. 1

Short Answer Type Questions (3 marks each)

Q. 1. Differentiate between gentle slope and steep slope. A

Ans.

S.No.	Gentle Slope	Steep Slope
1.	Slope of 5 % of the land is called gentle slope.	Slope of 10% of the land is called steep slope.
2.	The steep slopes in the headwaters of drainage basins tend to generate more run off than do lowland areas.	On gentle slopes, water may temporarily pond and later soak in.
3.	On gentle slopes water tends to move slowly. Soils tend to be thicker, more infiltration can occur.	On steep mountainsides, water tends to move downward more rapidly.

(1 × 3 = 3)

Answering Tip

- When contour lines are closer to each other, then slope is called steep slope. When contour lines are further apart from each other, then slope is called gentle slope

Q. 2. Differentiate between soil erosion and soil degradation. A

Ans.

S.No.	Soil Erosion	Soil Degradation
1.	Destruction of soil cover is called as soil erosion.	Soil degradation is decline in soil fertility when the nutritional status declines and depth of the soil goes down.
2.	It happens due to action of running water, wind , deforestation, etc.	It happens as a result of soil erosion and misuse of land.
3.	Forestation, check open cultivation lands on slopes from farming, preventing overgrazing, etc., can help solve the problem of soil erosion.	Controlled use of fertilizers, land use planning, terrace farming, etc., can help solve the problem of soil degradation.

(1 × 3 = 3)

AI **Q.3. Mention the regions affected by soil erosion.** R

OR

Different regions exhibit different types of erosion. Substantiate.

Ans. The destruction of the soil cover is described as soil erosion. A fairly large area of arable land in the irrigated zones of India is becoming saline because of overirrigation. West Bengal, Uttar Pradesh, Maharashtra, Karnataka, Delhi, Rajasthan and many other parts of India are facing the problem of soil erosion.

The mountain regions of our country face a serious problem of over grazing. In Meghalaya and Nilgiri Hills face the problem due to excessive potato cultivation. In the Himalayas, the soil erosion has occurred due to over-grazing and deforestation.

Gully erosion is common on steep slopes. Gullies deepen with rainfall, cut the agricultural lands into small fragments and make them unfit for cultivation. A region with a large number of deep gullies or ravines is called a badland topography. Ravines are widespread, in the Chambal basin. Besides this, they are also found in Tamil Nadu and West Bengal. The country is losing about 8,000 hectares of land to ravines every year. 3

Long Answer Type Questions (5 marks each)

Q. 1. Mention the causes responsible for soil erosion. [A]

Ans. The causes responsible for soil erosion are :

(i) Human activities : The soil forming processes and the erosional processes of running water and wind go on simultaneously. But generally, there is a balance between these two processes. Sometimes, such a balance is disturbed by natural or human factors, leading to a greater rate of removal of soil. Human activities too are responsible for soil erosion to a great extent. As the human population increases, the demand on the land also increases. Forest and other natural vegetation is removed for human settlement, for cultivation, for grazing animals and for various other needs.

(i) Slope Gradient and Length : The steeper and longer the slope of a field, the higher the risk for erosion. Soil erosion by water increases as the slope length increases due to the greater accumulation of runoff. Consolidation of small fields into larger ones often results in longer slope lengths with increased erosion potential, due to increased velocity of water, which permits a greater degree of scouring (carrying capacity for sediment).

(iii) Cropping and Vegetation : The potential for soil erosion increases if the soil has no or very little vegetative cover of plants and/or crop residues. Plant and residue cover protects the soil from raindrop impact and splash, tends to slow down the movement of runoff water and allows excess surface water to infiltrate.

(iv) Wind and water : Wind and water are powerful agents of soil erosion because of their ability to remove soil and transport it. Wind erosion is significant in arid and semi-arid regions. In regions with heavy rainfall and steep slopes, erosion by running water is more significant. Water erosion which is more serious and occurs extensively in different parts of India, takes place mainly in the form of sheet and gully erosion. Sheet erosion takes place on level lands after a heavy shower and the soil removal is not easily noticeable. But it is harmful since it removes the finer and more fertile top soil.

(v) Deforestation : Deforestation is one of the major causes of soil erosion. Plants keep soils bound in locks of roots, and thus, prevent erosion. They also add humus to the soil by shedding leaves and twigs. Forests have been denuded practically in most parts of India but their effect on soil erosion are more in hilly parts of the country. 5

[AI] **Q. 2. Explain the different types of soil erosion.** [R]

Ans. The different types of soil erosion are :

(i) Surface erosion : When rain, wind or frost detaches soil particles form the surface, the particles are washed or blown off the paddock.

(a) Sheet erosion : Sheet erosion takes place on level lands after a heavy shower and the soil removal is not easily noticeable. But it is harmful since it removes the finer and more fertile top soil. It lowers the fertility of the soil.

(b) Wind erosion : Wind erosion has the ability to remove soil and transport it. Wind erosion is significant in arid and semi-arid regions. In regions with heavy rainfall and steep slopes, erosion by running water is more significant.

(c) Water erosion : Water erosion which is more serious and occurs extensively in different parts of India, takes place mainly in the form of sheet and gully erosion. Sheet erosion takes place on level lands after a heavy shower and the soil removal is not easily noticeable. But it is harmful since it removes the finer and more fertile top soil.

(ii) Fluvial erosion : This occurs when running water gouges shallow channels or deep gullies into the soil.

(a) Rill erosion : On sloping land, particularly if cultivated , water run-off may gather in small V-shaped channels or rills. These are particularly evident in pumice soils or those formed from loess , but can occur on all hillsides.

(b) Gully erosion : Gully erosion is common on steep slopes. It occurs on unconsolidated subsoils. Gullies deepen with rainfall, cut the agricultural lands into small fragments and make them unfit for cultivation. A region with a large number of deep gullies or ravines is called a badland topography. Ravines are widespread, in the Chambal basin. Besides this, they are also found in Tamil Nadu and West Bengal. 5

Q. 3. Mention the steps taken to conserve the soil. [U]

Ans. If soil erosion and exhaustion are caused by humans; by corollary, they can also be prevented by humans. Soil conservation is a methodology to maintain soil fertility, prevent soil erosion and exhaustion, and improve the degraded condition of the soil. Soil erosion is essentially aggravated by faulty practices.

The first step in any rational solution is to check open cultivable lands on slopes from farming.

Lands with a slope gradient of 15 - 25 per cent should not be used for cultivation. If at all the land is to be used for agriculture, terraces should carefully be made.

Over-grazing and shifting cultivation in many parts of India have affected the natural cover of land and given rise to extensive erosion. It should be regulated and controlled by educating villagers about the consequences. Contour bunding, Contour terracing, regulated forestry, controlled grazing, cover cropping, mixed farming and crop rotation are some of the remedial measures which are often adopted to reduce soil erosion.

Efforts should be made to prevent gully erosion and control their formation. Finger gullies can be eliminated by terracing. In bigger gullies, the erosive velocity of water may be reduced by constructing a series of check dams.

Special attention should be made to control headward extension of gullies. This can be done by gully plugging, terracing or by planting cover vegetation. In arid and semi-arid areas, efforts should be made to protect cultivable lands from encroachment by sand dunes through developing shelter belts of trees and agro-forestry. Lands not suitable for cultivation should be converted into pastures for grazing. Experiments have been made to stabilise sand dunes in western Rajasthan by the Central Arid Zone Research Institute (CAZRI). **5**

Answering Tip

- Soil Conservation is the name given to a handful of techniques aimed at preserving the soil.

Q. 4. In India, fertility of soil is also destroyed by over irrigation. Explain. [A]

Ans. A fairly large area of arable land in the irrigated zones of India is becoming saline because of overirrigation. The salt lodged in the lower profiles of the soil comes up to the surface and destroys its fertility. Chemical fertilisers in the absence of organic manures are also harmful to the soil. Unless the soil gets enough humus, chemicals harden it and reduce its fertility in the long run. This problem is common in all the command areas of the river valley projects, which were the first beneficiaries of the Green Revolution. According to estimates, about half of the total land of India is under some degree of degradation. Every year, India loses millions of tonnes of soil and its nutrients to the agents of its degradation, which adversely affects our national productivity. So, it is imperative to initiate immediate steps to reclaim and conserve soils. **5**

Q. 5. What kinds of steps have been taken by Central Soil Conservation Board, set up by the Government of India? [A]

Ans. The Central Soil Conservation Board, set up by the Government of India, has prepared a number of plans for soil conservation in different parts of the country. These plans are based on the climatic conditions, configuration of land and the social behaviour of people. Even these plans are fragmental in nature. Integrated land use planning, therefore, seems to be the best technique for proper soil conservation. Lands should be classified according to their capability; land use maps should be prepared and lands should be put to right uses. The final responsibility for achieving the conservation of land will rest on the people who operate on it and receive the benefits. **5**

Q. 6. Wind and water are two important agents of soil erosion. Explain. [A]

Ans. Wind and water are powerful agents of soil erosion because of their ability to remove soil and transport it. Wind erosion is significant in arid and semi-arid regions. In regions with heavy rainfall and steep slopes, erosion by running water is more significant. Water erosion which is more serious and occurs extensively in different parts of India, takes place mainly in the form of sheet and gully erosion. Sheet erosion takes place on level lands after a heavy shower and the soil removal is not easily noticeable. But it is harmful since it removes the finer and more fertile top soil. Gully erosion is common on steep slopes. Gullies deepen with rainfall, cut the agricultural lands into small fragments and make them unfit for cultivation. A region with a large number of deep gullies or ravines is called a badland topography. Ravines are widespread, in the Chambal basin. Besides this, they are also found in Tamil Nadu and West Bengal. The country is losing about 8,000 hectares of land to ravines every year. **5**

Map Work

(5 marks each)

Q.1. Label and locate the regions where the following soils are found on the outline map of India :

(i) Alluvial soil **(ii) Black soil**

(iii) Arid soil **(iv) Red and Yellow soil**

(v) Forest soil

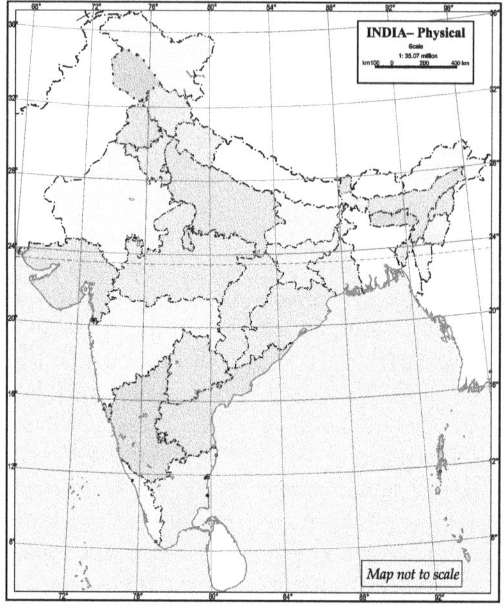

Ans.

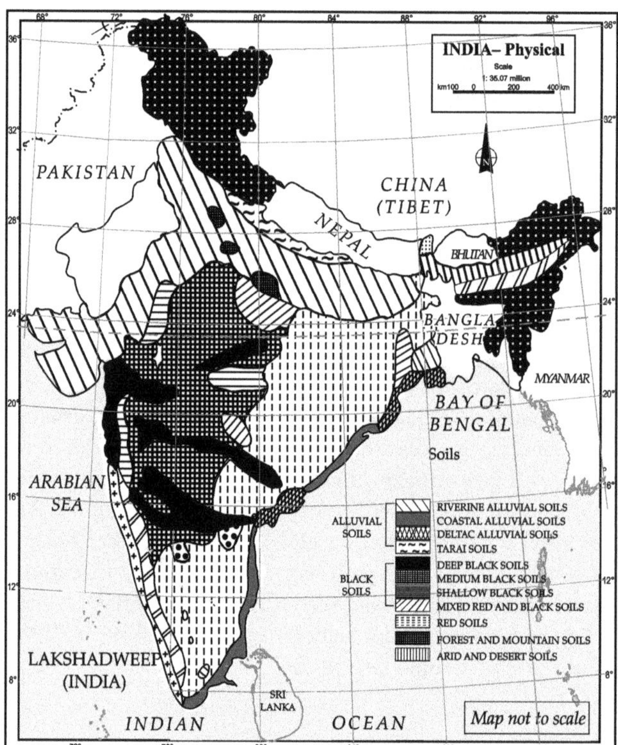

Fig. 7.1. Major Soil Groups of India

NCERT CORNER

(A) Multiple choice questions :

Q. 1. Which one of the following is the most widespread and most productive category of soil?

(a) Alluvial Soil (b) Laterite Soil
(c) Black Soil (d) Forest Soil

Ans. (a) Alluvial Soil.

Q. 2. 'Regur Soil' is another name for the :

(a) Saline Soil
(b) Arid Soil
(c) Black Soil
(d) Laterite Soil

Ans. (c) Black Soil.

Q. 3. Which one of the following is the main reason for the loss of the top soil in India?

(a) Wind erosion
(b) Water erosion
(c) Excessive leaching
(d) None of these

Ans. (a) Wind erosion.

Q. 4. Arable land in the irrigated zones of India is turning saline due to which of the following reasons?

(a) Addition of gypsum
(b) Over grazing
(c) Over irrigation
(d) Use of fertilisers

Ans. (c) Over irrigation.

Q. 5. What is the difference between Khadar and Bhangar?

Ans.

S.No.	Khadar	Bhangar
1.	It is a highland composed of old alluvium.	It is a lowland composed of new alluvium.
2.	It is always above the level of flood plains.	It comprises of clay soil which is normally fertile.
3.	It is not much suited for agriculture.	It is suited for agriculture.

(B) Answer the following questions in about 30 words :

Q. 1. What is soil?

Ans. Soil is the mixture of rock debris and organic materials which develop on the earth's surface.

Q. 2. What are the main factors responsible for the formation of soil?

Ans. The major factors affecting the formation of soil are relief, parent material, climate, vegetation and other life-forms and time. Besides these, human activities also influence it to a large extent. Components of the soil are mineral particles, humus, water and air. The actual amount of each of these depend upon the type of soil.

Q. 3. Mention the three horizons of a soil profile.

Ans. The three horizons of a soil profile are :

(i) **Horizon A :** It is the topmost zone, where organic materials have got incorporated with the mineral matter.

(ii) **Horizon B :** It is a transition zone between the 'horizon A' and 'horizon C' and contains matter derived from below as well as from above.

(iii) **Horizon C :** It is composed of the loose parent material. This layer is the first stage in the soil formation process and eventually forms the above two layers.

Q. 4. What is soil degradation?

Ans. Soil degradation can be defined as the decline in soil fertility, when the nutritional status declines and depth of the soil goes down due to erosion and misuse. Soil degradation is the main factor leading to the depleting soil resource base in India.

(C) Answer the following questions in about 125 words :

Q. 1. What are black soils? Describe their formation and characteristics?

Ans. The black soils are generally clayey, deep and impermeable. They swell and become sticky when wet and shrink when dried. So, during the dry season, these soil develop wide cracks. Thus, there occurs a kind of 'self ploughing'.They are formed by volcanoes. They are also known as 'Regur Soil' or the 'Black Cotton Soil'.

Features :

Black soil covers most of the Deccan Plateau which includes parts of Maharashtra, Madhya Pradesh, Gujarat, Andhra Pradesh and some parts of Tamil Nadu. In the upper reaches of the Godavari and the Krishna, and the north western part of the Deccan Plateau, the black soil is very deep.

Because of this character of slow absorption and loss of moisture, the black soil retains the moisture for a very long time, which helps the crops, especially, the rain fed ones, to sustain even during the dry season.

Chemically, the black soils are rich in lime, iron, magnesia and alumina. They also contain potash. But they lack in phosphorous, nitrogen and organic matter. The colour of the soil ranges from deep black to grey. The black soil is highly retentive of moisture. It swells greatly on accumulating moisture. Strenuous effort is required to work on such soil in rainy season as it gets very sticky.

Q. 2. What is soil conservation? Suggest some measures to conserve soil?

Ans. Soil conservation is a methodology to maintain soil fertility, prevent soil erosion and exhaustion, and improve the degraded condition of the soil.

Measures taken to conserve soil are :

(i) The first step in any rational solution is to check open cultivable lands on slopes from farming.

(ii) Lands with a slope gradient of 15 - 25 per cent should not be used. for cultivation. If at all the land is to be used for agriculture, terraces should carefully be made.

(iii) Over-grazing and shifting cultivation in many parts of India have affected the natural cover of land and given rise to extensive erosion. It should be regulated and controlled by educating villagers about the consequences.

(iv) Contour bunding g, Contour terracing, regulated forestry, controlled grazing, cover cropping, mixed farming and crop rotation should be encouraged.

(v) In arid and semi-arid areas, efforts should be made to protect cultivable lands from encroachment by sand dunes through developing shelter belts of trees and agro-forestry.

Q. 3. How do you know that a particular type of soil is fertile or not? Differentiate between naturally determined fertility and culturally induced fertility.

Ans. The fine-grained red and yellow soils are normally fertile, whereas, coarse-grained soils found in dry upland areas are poor in fertility. They are generally poor in nitrogen , phosphorous and humus.

Some soils have phosphorus , potassium , humus, nitrogen and calcium naturally. It increases the fertility of these soils. Such fertility is called naturally determined fertility. On the other hand, if soil is deficient in these substances, such substances are added in the form of fertilizers and manures. If fertility of soil is increased through human efforts, such fertility is called culturally induced fertility.

Naturally determined fertility makes human dependent on nature. culturally induced fertility indicates that man has become a master of the nature. it is an indicator of development of human race. Soils are living systems. Like any other organism, they too develop and decay, get degraded , respond to proper treatment if administered in time.

A human being amy be intelligent by birth or may be made intelligent by efforts. Similarly, soil may be fertile naturally or made fertile by human efforts. Former is called naturally determined fertility and the latter is called culturally induced fertility.

Project Work

Q. 1. On an outline map of India, mark the areas covered by the following soil categories :

(i) **Red soil** (ii) **Laterite soil** (iii) **Alluvial soil**

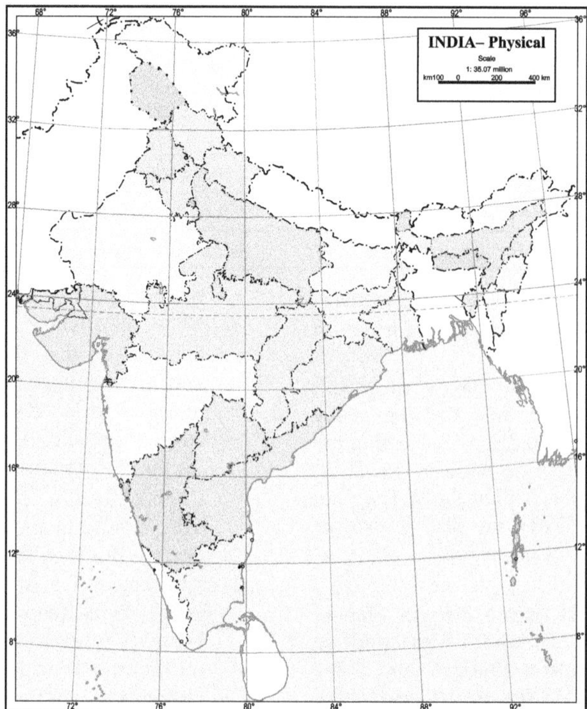

Ans.

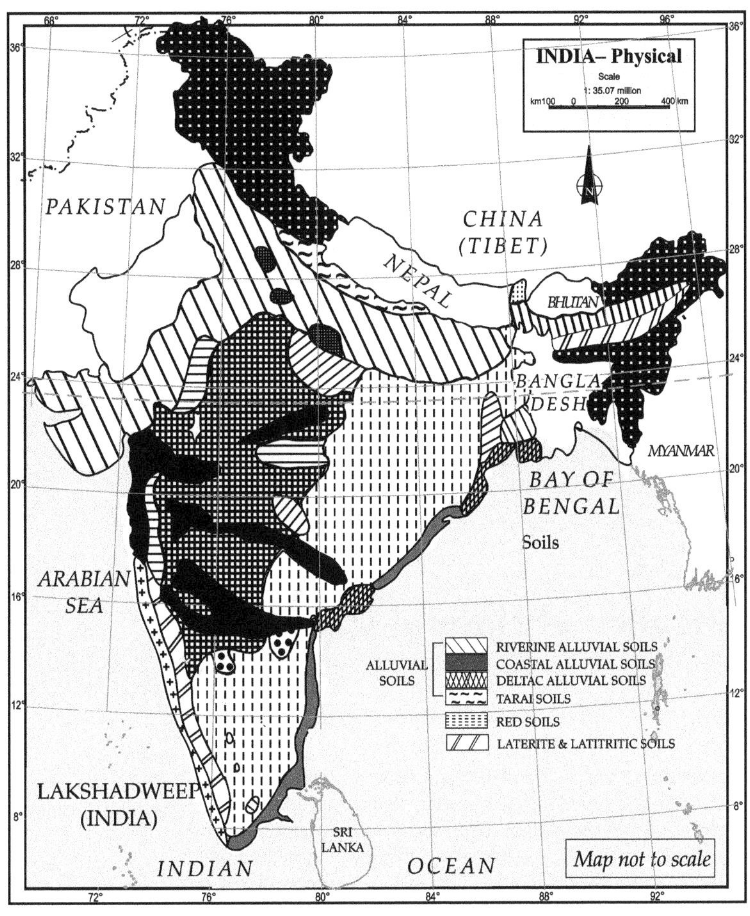

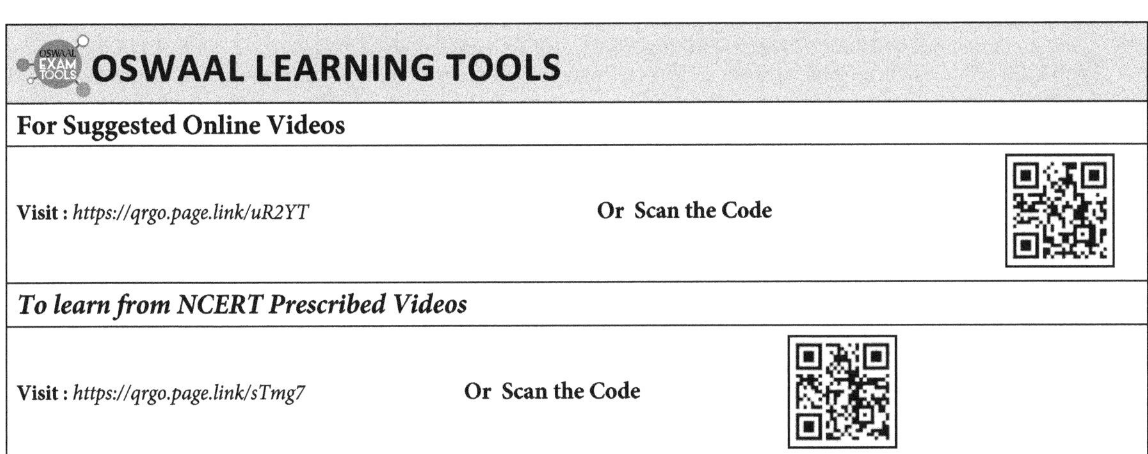

OSWAAL LEARNING TOOLS

For Suggested Online Videos

Visit : *https://qrgo.page.link/uR2YT* **Or Scan the Code**

To learn from NCERT Prescribed Videos

Visit : *https://qrgo.page.link/sTmg7* **Or Scan the Code**

❑❑

UNIT-X

Natural Hazards and Disasters: Causes, Consequences and Management

CHAPTER

7 NATURAL HAZARDS AND DISASTERS

Syllabus

> *Classification of Natural Disasters.*
> *Natural Disasters and Hazards in India, Disaster Management.*

TOPIC-1

Classification of Natural Disasters

Revision Notes

- Change is the law of nature. It is a continuous process that goes on uninterruptedly involving phenomena, big and small, material and nonmaterial that make our physical and sociocultural environment.
- Change can be a gradual or slow process like the evolution of landforms and organisms and it can be as sudden and swift as volcanic eruptions, tsunamis, earthquakes and lightening, etc.
- Disasters in general and natural disasters in particular, are some such changes that are always disliked and feared by humankind.
- "Disaster is an undesirable occurrence resulting from forces that are largely outside human control, strikes quickly with little or no warning, which causes or threatens serious disruption of life and property including death and injury to a large number of people, and requires therefore, mobilisation of efforts in excess of that which are normally provided by statutory emergency services."
- For a long time, geographical literature viewed disasters as a consequence of natural forces; and human beings were treated as innocent and helpless victims in front of the mighty forces of nature.
- Disasters are also caused by some human activities. There are some activities carried by human beings that are directly responsible for disasters.
- Bhopal Gas tragedy, Chernobyl Nuclear Disaster, wars, release of CFCs (Chlorofluorocarbons) and increase of green house gases, environmental pollutions like noise, air, water and soil are some of the disasters which are caused directly by human actions.
- Landslides and floods due to deforestation, unscientific land use and construction activities in fragile areas are some of the disasters that are the results of indirect human actions.
- Natural Hazards are elements of circumstances in the Natural environment that have the potential to cause harm to people or property or both.
- These may be swift or permanent aspects of the respective environmental settings like currents in the oceans, steep slope and unstable structural features in the Himalayas or extreme climatic conditions in deserts or glaciated areas.
- As compared to natural hazards, natural disasters are relatively sudden and cause large scale, widespread death, loss of property and disturbance to social systems and life over which people have a little or no control.
- Every disaster is unique in terms of the local socio-environmental factors that control it, the social response it generates, and the way each social group negotiates with it.
- Natural disasters have caused widespread loss of life and property. Concerted efforts are on at various levels to take appropriate measures to deal with the situation. It is also being felt that the damages caused by natural disasters have global repercussions that are beyond the means and capabilities of individual nation-states to cope up with.
- Identification and classification of disasters is being considered as an effective and scientific step to deal promptly and efficiently with the disasters.
- India is one of those countries which has experienced most of the natural disasters.
- Every year it loses thousands of lives and property worth millions of rupees due to these natural calamities.

Know the Terms

- **Disaster :** Disasters in general and natural disasters in particular, are some such changes that are always disliked and feared by humankind.
- **Natural Hazards :** They are elements of circumstances in the natural environment that have the potential to cause harm to people or property or both.

Multiple Choice Questions (1 mark each)

Q. 1. India is one of those countries which has experienced most of the : A

(a) natural disasters
(b) immigration
(c) migration
(d) trade

Ans. (a) natural disasters 1

Q. 2. ________ can be a gradual or slow process. U

(a) Birth
(b) Change
(c) Hurricanes
(d) Tornadoes

Ans. (b) Change 1

Very Short Answer Type Questions (1 mark each)

Q. 1. What is disaster? A

Ans. Disaster is an undesirable occurrence resulting from forces that are largely outside human control, strikes quickly with little or no warning, which causes or threatens serious disruption of life and property including death and injury to a large number of people, and requires therefore, mobilisation of efforts in excess of that which are normally provided by statutory emergency services. 1

Q. 2. Define the term 'Natural Hazards'. A

Ans. They are elements of circumstances in the natural environment that have the potential to cause harm to people or property or both. 1

Answering Tip

- Some natural hazards occur because of forces outside our control. For example, the movement of earth's crustal plates triggers earthquakes and tsunamis.

Q. 3. What are natural calamities? A

Ans. Natural calamities are elements of circumstances in the natural environment that have the potential to cause harm to people or property or both. 1

Q. 4. What effects can change have? U

Ans. Change can be a gradual or slow process like the evolution of landforms and organisms and it can be as sudden and swift as volcanic eruptions, tsunamis, earthquakes and lightening, etc. It may remain confined to a smaller area occurring within a few seconds like hailstorms, tornadoes and dust storms, and it can also have global dimensions such as global warming and depletion of the ozone layer. 1

Q. 5. Name some natural calamities. R

Ans. Earthquake, floods, tsunamis, drought, landslides, cyclones, volcanoes, tornado, hailstorms, dust storms, hurricanes, etc., are some of the natural calamities. 1

AI **Q. 6. On the basis of origin, in how many groups are calamities categorised.** A

Ans. On the basis of origin, calamities can be categorised into four groups :

(i) **Atmospheric :** Thunderstorms, Tornedoes, Drought and Hailstorm.
(ii) **Terrestrial :** Earthquakes, Volcanic eruptions, Avalanches , Soil erosion.
(iii) **Aquatic :** Floods, Tidal waves, Storm surge and Tsunami.
(iv) **Biological :** Viral Diseases, Plants and Animals as colonisers. 1

Q. 7. What does IDNDR stand for? R

Ans. International Decade for Natural Disaster Reduction. 1

Short Answer Type Questions (3 marks each)

Q. 1. Differentiate between man-made disaster and natural disaster. A

Ans.

S.No.	Man-made disaster	Natural disaster
1.	Natural hazards are those elements of the physical environment, harmful to man.	They are caused by natural forces.

2.	Can be avoided with promoting scientific and technical knowledge to reduce human and material losses.	Steps can be taken to minimise the effects.
3.	Example: avalanches and floods,extreme temperatures, drought and wildfires etc.	Examples: Floods, droughts, volcanic eruptions, avalanches, soil erosion, etc.

(1 × 3 = 3)

Q. 2. Differentiate between natural hazards and natural disasters. A

Ans.

S.No.	Natural hazards	Natural disasters
1.	They are caused by the activities of human beings.	They are caused by natural forces.
2.	Can be avoided with careful planning and prevention methods.	Steps can be taken to minimise the effects.
3.	Example: Hazardous material spills, explosions, chemical or biological attacks, etc.	Examples: Floods, droughts, volcanic eruptions, avalanches, soil erosion, etc.

(1 × 3 = 3)

Long Answer Type Question **(5 marks)**

Q. 1. How does disaster limit economic development? A

Ans. Disasters limit economic development as they wipe out the gains of economic development.

For example : Hurrican Isaac (1982) -destroyed 22% of Tonga's housing stock. Mozambique's flood (2000) resulted in over $165 million in costs to reconstruct and repair damage to water, sanitation, energy, telecommunication, roads and railway infrastructure.

Vietnam flooding each year results into destruction of 300,000 tons of food. Catastrophic disasters result in the destruction of nation's assets, and interrupts production, trade, investment and other economic engines. Larger countries with a greater geographical spread of economic assets relative to spatial impact of disasters are more able to avoid direct loss and minimise downstream, indirect or secondary losses. 5

Answering Tip

- Natural disasters destroy tangible assets such as buildings and equipment – as well as human capital – and thereby deteriorate their production capacity.

TOPIC-2
Natural Disasters and Hazards in India, Disaster Management

Revision Notes

➢ Let us focus on the major natural disasters in India.

- **Earthquakes :** Earthquakes are by far the most unpredictable and highly destructive of all the natural disasters. Earthquakes that are of tectonic origin have proved to be the most devastating and their area of influence is also quite large.

➢ These earthquakes result from a series of earth movements brought about by a sudden release of energy during the tectonic activities in the earth's crust.

➢ Some of the most vulnerable states are Jammu and Kashmir, Himachal Pradesh, Uttarakhand, Sikkim, and the Darjeeling and subdivision of West Bengal and all the seven states of the northeast.

➢ Earth scientists have found it difficult to explain the occurrence of earthquakes in one of the oldest, most stable and mature landmass of Peninsular block for a long time.

➢ National Institute of Disaster Management, have made an intensive analysis of more than 1,200 earthquakes that have occurred in India in different years in the past, and based on these, they divided India into the following five earthquake zones :

- Very high damage risk
- High damage risk zone

- Moderate damage risk zone
- Low damage risk zone
- Very low damage risk zone

➢ Out of these, the first two zones had experienced some of the most devastating earthquakes in India.

➢ **Socio-Environmental Consequences of Earthquakes :**

➢ It becomes a calamity when it strikes the areas of high density of population. It not only damages and destroys the settlements, infrastructure, transport and communication network, industries and other developmental activities but also robs the population of their material and socio-cultural gains that they have preserved over generations.

➢ It renders them homeless, which puts an extra-pressure and stress, particularly on the weak economy of the developing countries.

➢ **Effects of Earthquakes :**

➢ Surface seismic waves produce fissures on the upper layers of the earth's crust through which water and other volatile materials gush out, inundating the neighbouring areas.

➢ Earthquakes are also responsible for landslides and often these cause obstructions in the flow of rivers and channels resulting in the formation of reservoirs.

➢ Sometimes, rivers also change their course causing floods and other calamities in the affected areas.

➢ **Earthquake Hazard Mitigation :**

➢ The next best option is to emphasis on disaster preparedness and mitigation rather than curative measures such as :

- Establishing earthquake monitoring centres (seismological centres) for regular monitoring and fast dissemination of information among the people in the vulnerable areas.
- Use of Geographical Positioning System (GPS) can be of great help in monitoring the movement of tectonic plates.
- Preparing a vulnerability map of the country and dissemination of vulnerability risk information among the people and educating them about the ways and means minimising the adverse impacts of disasters.
- Modifying the house types and building designs in the vulnerable areas.
- Finally, making it mandatory to adopt earthquake-resistant designs and use light materials in major construction activities in the vulnerable areas.
- **Tsunami :** Earthquakes and volcanic eruptions that cause the sea-floor to move abruptly resulting in sudden displacement of ocean water in the form of high vertical waves are called tsunamis (harbour waves) or seismic sea waves.

➢ As a result of this, the impact of tsunami is less over the ocean and more near the coast where they cause large-scale devastations.

➢ Therefore, a ship at sea is not much affected by tsunami and it is difficult to detect a tsunami in the deeper parts of sea.

➢ Tsunamis are frequently observed along the Pacific ring of fire, particularly along the coast of Alaska, Japan, Philippines, and other islands of Southeast Asia, Indonesia, Malaysia, Myanmar, Sri Lanka, and India etc.

➢ After reaching the coast, the tsunami waves release enormous energy stored in them and water flows turbulently onto the land destroying port-cities and towns, structures, buildings and other settlements.

➢ Unlike other natural hazards, the mitigation of hazards created by tsunami is difficult, mainly because of the fact that losses are on a much larger scale.

- **Tropical cyclones :** These are intense low-pressure areas confined to the area lying between 30° N and 30° S latitudes, in the atmosphere around which high velocity winds blow.

➢ Horizontally, it extends up to 500-1,000 km and vertically from surface to 12-14 km.

➢ A tropical cyclone or hurricane is like a heat engine that is energised by the release of latent heat on account of the condensation of moisture that the wind gathers after moving over the oceans and seas.

➢ Some initial conditions for the emergence of a tropical cyclone are :

- Large and continuous supply of warm and moist air that can release enormous latent heat.
- Strong Coriolis force that can prevent filling of low pressure at the centre (absence of Coriolis force near the equator prohibits the formation of tropical cyclone between 0°-5° latitude).

- Unstable condition through the troposphere that creates local disturbances around which a cyclone develops.
- Finally, absence of strong vertical wind wedge, which disturbs the vertical transport of latent heat.

➢ **Structure of Tropical Cyclone :**

➢ The centre of the cyclone is mostly a warm and low-pressure, cloudless core known as eye of the storm.

➢ Normally, it varies between 14-17mb/100 km, but sometimes it can be as high as 60mb/100km. Expansion of the wind belt is about 10-150 km from the centre.

➢ **Spatio-temporal Distribution of Tropical Cyclone in India :**

➢ Though most of the cyclones originate between 10°-15° north latitudes during the monsoon season, yet in case of the Bay of Bengal, cyclones mostly develop during the months of October and November. Here, They originate between 16^0 - 2^0 N Latitudes and to the west of 92^0 E.

➢ **Consequences of Tropical Cyclones :**

➢ With the increase in distance from the sea, the force of the cyclone decreases.

➢ In India, the force of the cyclone decreases with increase in distance from the Bay of Bengal and the Arabian Sea.

➢ So, the coastal areas are often struck by severe cyclonic storms with an average velocity of 180 km/h. Often, this results in abnormal rise in the sea level known as Storm Surge.

- **Floods :** Floods are relatively slow in occurrences and often, occur in well-identified regions and within expected time in a year.

➢ Floods occur commonly when water in the form of surface run-off exceeds the carrying capacity of the river channels and streams and flows into the neighbouring low-lying flood plains.

➢ Floods can also be caused due to a storm surge (in the coastal areas), high intensity rainfall for a considerably longer time period, melting of ice and snow, reduction in the infiltration rate and presence of eroded material in the water due to higher rate of soil erosion.

➢ Floods in the South, Southeast and East Asian countries, particularly in China, India and Bangladesh, are frequent and equally disastrous.

➢ It has been noticed that states like Rajasthan, Gujarat, Haryana and Punjab are also getting inundated in recent decades due to flash floods.

➢ Sometimes, Tamil Nadu experiences flooding during November -January due to the retreating monsoon.

➢ **Consequence and Control of Floods :**

➢ Floods do not only destroy valuable crops every year but these also damage physical infrastructure such as roads, rails, bridges and human settlements.

➢ Millions of people are rendered homeless and are also washed down along with their cattle in the floods.

➢ Spread of diseases like cholera, gastro-enteritis, hepatitis and other water-borne diseases spread in the flood-affected areas.

➢ However, floods also make a few positive contributions. Every year, floods deposit fertile silt over agricultural fields which is good for the crops.

- **Droughts :** The term 'drought' is applied to an extended period when there is a shortage of water availability due to inadequate precipitation, excessive rate of evaporation and over-utilisation of water from the reservoirs and other storages, including the ground water.

➢ Drought is a complex phenomenon as it involves elements of meteorology like precipitation, evaporation, evapotranspiration, ground water, soil moisture, storage and surface run-off, agricultural practices, particularly the types of crops grown, socio-economic practices and ecological conditions.

➢ **Types of Droughts :**

➢ **Meteorological Drought :** It is a situation when there is a prolonged period of inadequate rainfall marked with mal-distribution of the same over time and space.

➢ **Agricultural Drought :** It is also known as soil moisture drought, characterised by low soil moisture that is necessary to support the crops, thereby resulting in crop failures.

➢ **Hydrological Drought :** It results when the availability of water in different storages and reservoirs like aquifers, lakes, reservoirs, etc.

➢ **Ecological Drought :** When the productivity of a natural ecosystem fails due to shortage of water and as a consequence of ecological distress, damages are induced in the ecosystem.

- **Drought Prone Areas in India :**
- Droughts and floods are the two accompanying features of Indian climate.
- About 30 per cent of the country's total area is identified as drought prone affecting around 50 million people.
- Drought is mainly because of the large-scale variations and unpredictability in the behaviour of the monsoon in India.
- Thus, droughts are widespread and common phenomena in most parts of the country, but these are most recurrent and severe in some and not so in others.
- **Consequences of Drought :**
- Crop failure leading to scarcity of food grains (akal), fodder (trikal), inadequate rainfall, resulting in shortage of water (jalkal), and often shortage in all the three (trikal) is most devastating.
- Large-scale death of cattle and other animals, migration of humans and livestock are the most common sight to be seen in the drought-affected areas.
- Scarcity of water compels people to consume contaminated water resulting in spread of many waterborne diseases like gastro-enteritis, cholera, hepatitis, etc.
- Droughts have both immediate as well as long-term disastrous consequences on the social and physical environments.
  - **Landslides :** Disasters due to landslides, are in general, far less dramatic than due to earthquakes, volcanic eruptions, tsunamis and cyclones but their impact on the natural environment and national economy is in no way less severe.
- Landslides are largely controlled by highly localised factors.
- Frequency and certain causal relationships with the controlling factors like geology, geomorphic agents, slope, land-use, vegetation cover and human activities are the major reasons for the landslides to occur.
- **Landslide Vulnerability Zones :**
  - **Very High Vulnerability Zone :** Highly unstable, relatively young mountainous areas in the Himalayas and Andaman and Nicobar, high rainfall regions with steep slopes in the Western Ghats and Nilgiris, the north-eastern regions.
  - **High Vulnerability Zone :** All the Himalayan states and the states from the north-eastern regions except the plains of Assam are included in the high vulnerability zones.
  - **Moderate to Low Vulnerability Zone :** Areas that receive less precipitation such as Trans-Himalayan areas of Ladakh and Spiti (Himachal Pradesh), rain shadow areas in the Western and Eastern Ghats and Deccan plateau also experience occasional landslides.
  - **Other Areas :** The remaining parts of India, particularly states like Rajasthan, Haryana, Uttar Pradesh, Bihar, West Bengal (except district Darjiling), Assam (except district Karbi Anglong) and Coastal regions of the southern States are safe as far as landslides are concerned.
- **Consequences of Landslides :**
- Landslides have relatively small and localised area of direct influence, but roadblock, destruction of railway lines and channel blocking due to rock-falls have far-reaching consequences.
- Diversion of river courses due to landslides can also lead to flood and loss of life and property.
- **Mitigation :**
- Restriction on the construction and other developmental activities such as roads and dams, limiting agriculture to valleys and areas with moderate slopes, and control on the development of large settlements in the high vulnerability zones, should be enforced.
- Terrace farming should be encouraged in the north-eastern hill states where Jhumming (Slash and Burn/Shifting Cultivation) is still prevalent.
- Construction of cyclone shelters , embankments, dykes, reservoirs and afforestation to reduce the speed of the winds are some of the steps that can help in minimising the damages .
- **There are three stages involved in disaster mitigation and management :**
  - Pre-disaster management involves generating data and information about the disasters, preparing vulnerability zoning maps and spreading awareness among the people about these.
  - During disasters, rescue and relief operations such as evacuation, construction of shelters and relief camps, supplying of water, food, clothing and medical aids etc. should be done on an emergency basis.
  - Post-disaster operations should involve rehabilitation and recovery of victims.
- Introduction of the Disaster Management Bill, 2005 and establishment of National Institute of Disaster Management are some examples of the positive steps taken by the Government of India.

Know the Terms

- **Drought :** It can be defined as the extended period when there is a shortage of water availability due to inadequate precipitation, excessive rate of evaporation and over-utilisation of water from the reservoirs and other shortages, including ground water.
- **Landslide :** It is a form of mass movement on which rock and debris moves rapidly downslope under the influence of gravity as a result of failure along a sheer plane.
- **Tsunamis :** Earthquakes and volcanic eruptions that cause the sea-floor to move abruptly resulting in sudden displacement of ocean water in the form of high vertical waves are called tsunamis.
- **Flood :** When a river bursts its banks and water spills out onto the floodplain , it is called floods.
- **Meteorological drought :** It is a situation when there is a prolonged period of inadequate rainfall marked with mal-distribution of the same over time and space.
- **Agricultural drought :** When there is low soil moisture that is necessary to support the crops, thereby resulting in crop failures it is termed as agricultural drought.
- **A tropical cyclone :** It is like a heat engine that is energised by the release of latent heat on account of the condensation of moisture that the wind gathers after moving over the oceans and seas.
- **Hydrological drought :** It results when the availability of water in different storages and reservoirs like aquifers, lakes, reservoirs, etc.
- **Ecological drought :** When the productivity of a natural ecosystem fails due to shortage of water and as a consequence of ecological distress, it is termed as ecological drought.
- **Eye of the storm :** The centre of the cyclone is mostly a warm and low-pressure, cloudless core. It is known as eye of the storm.
- **Storm surge :** Abnormal rise in the sea level is known as storm surge.
- **Famine :** Extreme scarcity of food as a result of drought is called famine.
- **Earthquake :** Earthquakes result from a series of earth movements brought about by a sudden release of energy during the tectonic activities in the earth's crust.
- **Seismicity :** It refers to the frequency , type and size of earthquake experienced over a period of time. It is also called as seismism or seismic activity.

Multiple Choice Questions (1 mark each)

Q. 1. The large-scale variations and unpredictability in the behaviour of the monsoon in India cause: [A]

(a) droughts
(b) earthquakes
(c) tsunami
(d) volcanoes

Ans. (a) droughts 1

Q. 2. Sometimes, rivers also change their course causing: [U]

(a) landslides
(b) floods
(c) cyclones
(d) tornadoes

Ans. (b) floods 1

Q. 3. The heat engine that is energised by the release of latent heat on account of the condensation of moisture that the wind gathers after moving over the oceans and seas is termed as : [A]

(a) drought
(b) landslide
(c) hurricane
(d) tsunami

Ans. (c) hurricane 1

Very Short Answer Type Questions (1 mark each)

Q. 1. Define the term 'Landslides'. [R]

Ans. Rapid sliding of large mass of bedrocks is called landslides. 1

Q. 2. What is disaster management? [R]

Ans. Disaster management is inclusive of all those processes and preparations which are undertaken to mitigate the losses from disasters. It includes steps that should be taken before disaster, during disaster and after disaster. 1

[AI] **Q.3. Define the term 'Earthquakes'.** [A]

Ans. An earthquake is the result of a sudden release of energy in the earth's crust that creates seismic waves. 1

Answering Tip

- An earthquake is a shaking of the ground caused by movement of the earth's crust.

Q. 4. Define the term 'Drought'. U

Ans. It can be defined as the extended period when there is a shortage of water availability due to inadequate precipitation, excessive rate of evaporation and over-utilization of water from the reservoirs and other shortages, including ground water. 1

Q. 5. Define the term 'Tsunamis'. A

Ans. Earthquakes and volcanic eruptions that cause the sea-floor to move abruptly resulting in sudden displacement of ocean water in the form of high vertical waves are called tsunamis. 1

Q. 6. What do you understand by the term 'Flood'? U

Ans. When a river bursts its banks and water spills out onto the floodplain , it is called floods. 1

Answering Tip

- Flooding is a temporary overflow of water onto land that is normally dry.

Q. 7. What is the eye of the storm? R

Ans. The centre of the cyclone is mostly a warm and low-pressure, cloudless core. It is known as eye of the storm. 1

Q. 8. What is 'Meteorological Drought'? U

Ans. It is a situation when there is a prolonged period of inadequate rainfall marked with mal-distribution of the same over time and space. 1

Q. 9. What is 'Natural Hazard'? A

Ans. Natural changes which have side effects on human life are called natural hazards. 1

Q.10. Name the region which has the highest number of landslides in India. U

Ans. Mountainous regions have the highest number of landslides. 1

Q. 11. What is the unit of measuring earthquake? A

Ans. Earthquakes are measured in Richter scale. 1

Q. 12. Which states have high risk of earthquake? U

Ans. The areas to the north of Darbhanga and Araria along the Indo-Nepal border in Bihar, Uttaranchal, Western Himachal Pradesh (around Dharamshala) and Kashmir Valley in the Himalayan region and the Kuchchh (Gujarat). These are included in the Very High Damage Risk Zone. 1

Q. 13. Mention the speed of cyclones. R

Ans. Cyclones move at a speed of 20km per hour. As it moves further, its energy keeps on reducing. Its duration is 5 to 7 days. 1

Q. 14. Mention the flood prone areas of India. U

Ans. Assam, West Bengal and Bihar are among the high flood-prone states of India. Apart from these, most of the rivers in the northern states like Punjab and Uttar Pradesh, are also vulnerable to occasional floods. 1

Q. 15. Name any two causes due to which the frequency of floods has increased in India. A

Ans. Deforestation, barrier in flow of water by means of transport and buildings and construction of dams have increased the frequency of floods in India. 1

Q. 16. Name landslide prone areas of India. U

Ans. Himalayas and Andaman and Nicobar, high rainfall regions with steep slopes in the Western Ghats and Nilgiris, the north-eastern regions, experiences frequent ground-shaking due to earthquakes, etc. 1

Q. 17. How can landslides be avoided? A

Ans. Restriction on the construction and other developmental activities such as roads and dams, limiting agriculture to valleys and areas with moderate slopes, and control on the development of large settlements in the high vulnerability zones, should be enforced. This should be supplemented by some positive actions like promoting large-scale afforestation programmes and construction of bunds to reduce the flow of water. 1

Q. 18. What are the consequences of drought? A

Ans. Scarcity of food crop, shortage of water, Large-scale death of cattle and other animals, migration of humans and livestock, Scarcity of water compels people to consume contaminated water resulting in spread of many waterborne diseases. 1

Answering Tip

- Long-term droughts can lead to war, famine, disease, or mass migrations.

Q. 19. How can we control droughts? R

Ans. Identification of ground water potential in the form of aquifers, transfer of river water from the surplus to the deficit areas, and particularly planning for inter-linking of rivers and construction of reservoirs and dams, etc., should be given a serious thought. Remote sensing and satellite imageries can be useful in identifying the possible river-basins that can be inter-linked and in identifying the ground water potential.

(Any Two) (½ +½=1)

AI **Q.20. How can we control floods?** A

Ans. Construction of flood protection embankments in the flood-prone areas, construction of dams, afforestation and discouraging major construction activities in the upper reaches of most of the flood-creating rivers, etc., are some steps that need to be taken up on urgent basis. Removal of human encroachment from the river channels and depopulating the flood plains can be the other steps.

(Any Two) (½+½=1)

Short Answer Type Questions

(3 marks each)

Q. 1. How can we do disaster management against earthquakes? U

Ans. It is not possible to prevent the occurrence of an earthquake; hence, the next best option is to emphasis on disaster preparedness and mitigation rather than curative measures such as :

(i) Establishing earthquake monitoring centres (seismological centres) for regular monitoring and fast dissemination of information among the people in the vulnerable areas. Use of Geographical Positioning System (GPS) can be of great help in monitoring the movement of tectonic plates.

(ii) Preparing a vulnerability map of the country and dissemination of vulnerability risk information among the people and educating them about the ways and means minimising the adverse impacts of disasters.

(iii) Modifying the house types and building designs in the vulnerable areas and discouraging construction of high-rise buildings, large industrial establishments and big urban centres in such areas.

(iv) Finally, making it mandatory to adopt earthquake-resistant designs and use light materials in major construction activities in the vulnerable areas.

(Any Three) (1 × 3 = 3)

Q. 2. What are the catastrophic effects of landslides? R

Ans. Landslides have relatively small and localised area of direct influence, but roadblock, destruction of railway lines and channelblocking due to rock-falls have far-reaching consequences. Diversion of river courses due to landslides can also lead to flood and loss of life and property. It also makes spatial interaction difficult, risky as well as a costly affair, which, in turn, adversely affects the developmental activities in these areas. 3

Answering Tip

- The negative economic effects of landslides include the cost to repair structures, loss of property value, disruption of transportation routes, medical costs in the event of injury, and indirect costs, such as lost timber and fish stocks. Water availability, quantity, and quality can be affected by landslides.

Q. 3. Explain the three stages involved in disaster mitigation and management. A

Ans. There are three stages involved in disaster mitigation and management :

(i) Pre-disaster management involves generating data and information about the disasters, preparing vulnerability zoning maps and spreading awareness among the people about these. Apart from these, disaster planning, preparedness and preventive measures are other steps that need to be taken in the vulnerable areas.

(ii) During disasters, rescue and relief operations such as evacuation, construction of shelters and relief camps, supplying of water, food, clothing and medical aids etc., should be done on an emergency basis.

(iii) Post-disaster operations should involve rehabilitation and recovery of victims. It should also concentrate on capacity building in order to cope up with future disasters, if any. 3

Q. 4. What are the effects of landslide on human life? U

Ans. Effects of landslide on human life :

(i) It also leads to loss of life and property .It can lead to diversion of river courses due to land slide which can lead to floods.

(ii) It leads to failure of transport and communication system. It can lead to road blocks, destruction of railway lines and channel-blocking due to rock-falls having far-reaching consequences.

(iii) It leads to hurdles in economic activities and destruction of natural beauty. It makes spatial interaction difficult, risky as well as a costly affair, which in turn, adversely affects the developmental activities in these areas.**(1× 3 = 3)**

Q. 5. What are the conditions for the occurrence of cyclones? A

Ans. Some initial conditions for the emergence of a tropical cyclone are :

(i) Large and continuous supply of warm and moist air that can release enormous latent heat.

(ii) Strong Coriolis force that can prevent filling of low pressure at the centre (absence of Coriolis force near the equator prohibits the formation of tropical cyclone between 0°-5° latitude).

(iii) Unstable condition through the troposphere that creates local disturbances around which a cyclone develops.

(iv) Finally, absence of strong vertical wind wedge, which disturbs the vertical transport of latent heat. 3

Q. 6. How can we mitigate instances of landslides? U

Ans. It is always advisable to adopt area-specific measures to deal with landslides.

(i) Restriction on the construction and other developmental activities such as roads and dams, limiting agriculture to valleys and areas with moderate slopes, and control on the development of large settlements in the high vulnerability zones, should be enforced.

(ii) Some positive actions like promoting large-scale afforestation programmes and construction of bunds to reduce the flow of water should be taken.

(iii) Terrace farming should be encouraged in the north-eastern hill areas. **(1 × 3 = 3)**

Q. 7. Explain the spatio-temporal distribution of tropical cyclones in India. [A]

Ans. (i) Owing to its Peninsular shape surrounded by the Bay of Bengal in the east and the Arabian Sea in the west, the tropical cyclones in India also originate in these two important locations.

(ii) Though most of the cyclones originate between 10°-15° north latitudes during the monsoon season, yet in case of the Bay of Bengal, cyclones mostly develop during the months of October and November. Here, they originate between 16°-2° N latitudes and to the west of 92° E.

(iii) By July the place of origin of these storms shifts to around 18° N latitude and west of 90°E near the Sundarbans Delta. **(1×3=3)**

Q. 8. What do you know about the drought prone areas in India? [R]

Ans. On the basis of severity of droughts, India can be divided into the following regions :

(i) Extreme Drought Affected Areas : It is evident from the Figure 7.8 that most parts of Rajasthan, particularly areas to the west of the Aravali hills, i.e. Marusthali and Kachchh regions of Gujarat fall in this category. Included here are also the districts like Jaisalmer and Barmer from the Indian desert that receive less that 90 mm average annual rainfall.

(i) Severe Drought Prone Area : Parts of eastern Rajasthan, most parts of Madhya Pradesh, eastern parts of Maharashtra, interior parts of Andhra Pradesh and Karnataka Plateau, northern parts of interior Tamil Nadu and southern parts of Jharkhand and interior Odisha are included in this category.

(i) Moderate Drought Affected Area : Northern parts of Rajasthan, Haryana, southern districts of Uttar Pradesh, the remaining parts of Gujarat, Maharashtra except Konkan, Jharkhand and Coimbatore plateau of Tamil Nadu and interior Karnataka are included in this category. The remaining parts of India can be considered either free or less prone to the drought. **(1 × 3 = 3)**

Answering Tip

- A drought prone area is defined as one in which the probability of a drought year is greater than 20%.

Q. 9. What do you know about the 'Disaster Management Bill'? [A]

Ans. The Disaster Management Bill, 2005, defines disaster as a catastrophe, mishap, calamity or grave occurrence affecting any area, arising from natural or man-made causes, or by accident or negligence which results in substantial loss of life or human suffering or damage to, and destruction of, environment, and is of such nature or magnitude as to be beyond the coping capacity of the community of the affected area. **3**

Answering Tip

- The Disaster Management Bill is considered a major step in streamlining appropriate mitigation measures and better preparedness for disaster.

Q. 10. How can we survive earthquakes?

Ans. A fairly large area of arable land in the irrigated Man can survive earthquakes by taking a few precautionary steps.

(i) When the earthquake occurs we should leave the building go and stand out at a safe distances. If it is not possible to move out of the building, stand in four corners of the house or take shelter under beds or table.

(ii) All the electrical connections in the house should be switched off.

(iii) Put off all types of fire like gas stove ,etc., do not drive any vehicle during earthquake. **3**

Long Answer Type Questions (5 marks each)

[AI] **Q.1. What are earthquakes? What are the socio-environmental consequences of earthquakes ?** [A]

Ans. These earthquakes result from a series of earth movements brought about by a sudden release of energy during the tectonic activities in the earth's crust.

Socio-environmental consequences of earthquake :

(i) The idea of an earthquake is often associated with fear and horror due to the scale, magnitude and suddenness at which it spreads disasters on the surface of the earth without discrimination. It becomes a calamity when it strikes the areas of high density of population. It not only damages and destroys the settlements, infrastructure, transport and communication network, industries and other developmental activities but also robs the population of their material and socio-cultural gains that they have preserved over generations.

(ii) It renders them homeless, which puts an extra-pressure and stress, particularly on the weak economy of the developing countries.

(iii) Earthquakes also have some serious and far-reaching environmental consequences. Surface seismic waves produce fissures on the upper layers of the earth's crust through which water and other volatile materials gush out, inundating the neighbouring areas.

(iv) Earthquakes are also responsible for landslides and often these cause obstructions in the flow of rivers and channels resulting in the formation of reservoirs. Sometimes, rivers also change their course causing floods and other calamities in the affected areas. **(1 × 5 = 5)**

Q. 2. What is drought? Explain the different types of droughts that occur in India. A

Ans. The term 'drought' is applied to an extended period when there is a shortage of water availability due to inadequate precipitation, excessive rate of evaporation and over-utilisation of water from the reservoirs and other storages, including the ground water.

Different types of droughts that occur in India are :

(i) Meteorological Drought : It is a situation when there is a prolonged period of inadequate rainfall marked with mal-distribution of the same over time and space.

(ii) Agricultural Drought : It is also known as soil moisture drought, characterised by low soil moisture that is necessary to support the crops, thereby resulting in crop failures. Moreover, if an area has more than 30 per cent of its gross cropped area under irrigation, the area is excluded from the drought-prone category.

(iii) Hydrological Drought : It results when the availability of water in different storages and reservoirs like aquifers, lakes, reservoirs, etc. falls below what the precipitation can replenish.

(iv) Ecological Drought : When the productivity of a natural ecosystem fails due to shortage of water and as a consequence of ecological distress, damages are induced in the ecosystem.

(1 × 5 = 5)

Answering Tip

- A drought can last for months or years, or may be declared after as few as 15 days.

Q. 3. Define landslides. India can be divided into how many landslide prone zones. R

Ans. Landslides can be defined as a form of mass movement in which rock and debris moves rapidly down the slope under the influence of gravity as a result of failure along a shear plane/

India has been divided into a number of landslide prone zones :

(i) Very High Vulnerability Zone : Highly unstable, relatively young mountainous areas in the Himalayas and Andaman and Nicobar, high rainfall regions with steep slopes in the Western Ghats and Nilgiris, the north-eastern regions, along with areas that experience frequent ground-shaking due to earthquakes, etc., and areas of intense human activities, particularly those related to construction of roads, dams, etc. are included in this zone.

(ii) High Vulnerability Zone : Areas that have almost similar conditions to those included in the very high vulnerability zone are also included in this category. The only difference between these two is the combination, intensity and frequency of the controlling factors. All the Himalayan states and the states from the north-eastern regions except the plains of Assam are included in the high vulnerability zones.

(iii) Moderate to Low Vulnerability Zone : Areas that receive less precipitation such as Trans-Himalayan areas of Ladakh and Spiti (Himachal Pradesh), undulated yet stable relief and low precipitation areas in the Aravali, rain shadow areas in the Western and Eastern Ghats and Deccan plateau also experience occasional landslides. Landslides due to mining and subsidence are most common in states like Jharkhand, Odisha, Chhattisgarh, Madhya Pradesh, Maharashtra, Andhra Pradesh, Karnataka, Tamil Nadu, Goa and Kerala.

(iv) Other Areas : The remaining parts of India, particularly states like Rajasthan, Haryana, Uttar Pradesh, Bihar, West Bengal (except district Darjiling), Assam (except district Karbi Anglong) and Coastal regions of the southern States are safe as far as landslides are concerned. **5**

Q. 4. Development can help in disaster management as well as cause management. Justify. U

Ans. Efforts with the help of development of techniques to monitor the behaviour of cyclones, their intensity, direction and magnitude, it has become possible to manage the cyclonic hazard to some extent.

Construction of cyclone shelters, embankments, dykes, reservoirs and afforestation to reduce the speed of the winds are some of the steps that can help in minimising the damages.

Unwise, uncoordinated or unsafe development can quickly and dramatically increase the disaster risk faced by the people of a country.

Practices that incorporate risk reduction methodologies, such as stringent building codes, resistant materials, proper land use planning and other important mitigation measures and practices often reduce the likelihood of disaster events or the consequences that result when events do occur.

Mass urbanisation and coastal migration which occur with little regard to wise building practices- as is often seen in the megacities of the developing world – is a primary contributor to increased risk of development. **5**

Map Work

(5 marks each)

Q. 1. Locate and label the following :

(i) Any one flood prone area

(ii) Any one drought prone area

(iii) Any one earthquake prone area

(iv) Any one landslide prone area

(v) Any one cyclone prone area

(vi) Forest soil

Ans.

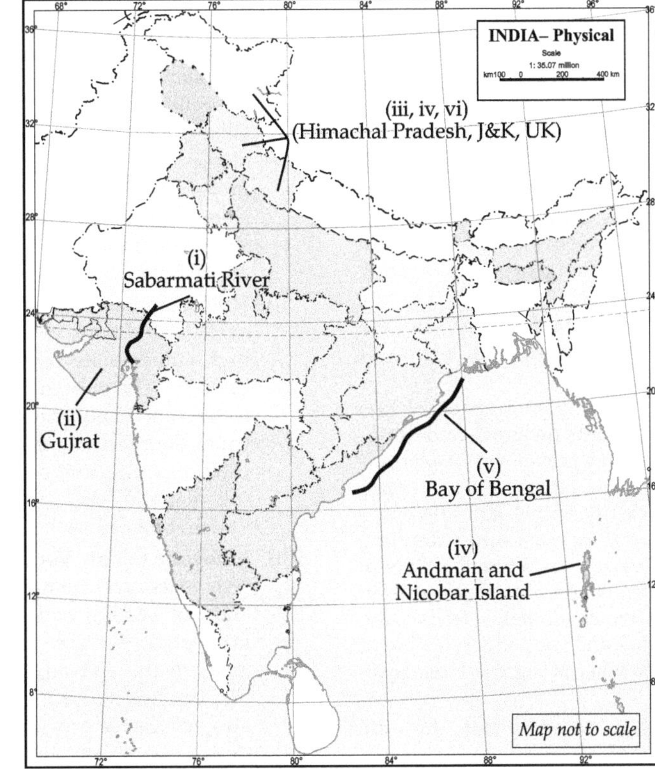

(i) Sabarmati

(ii) Gujarat

(iii) Himachal Pradesh

(iv) Andaman & Nicobar Islands

(v) Bay of Bengal

NCERT CORNER

(B) Multiple choice questions :

Q. 1. Which one of the following states of India experiences floods frequently?

(a) Bihar

(b) West Bengal

(c) Assam

(d) Uttar Pradesh

Ans. (c) Assam.

Q. 2. In which one of the following districts of Uttaranchal did Malpa Landslide disaster take place :

(a) Bageshwar

(b) Champawat

(c) Almora

(d) Pithoragarh

Ans. (d) Pithoragarh.

Q. 3. Which one of the following states receives floods in the winter months?

(a) Assam

(b) West Bengal

(c) Kerala

(d) Tamil Nadu

Ans. (d) Tamil Nadu.

Q. 4. In which of the following rivers is the Majuli River Island situated?

(a) Ganga
(b) Brahmaputra
(c) Godavari
(d) Indus

Ans. (b) Brahmaputra.

Q. 5. Under which type of natural hazards do blizzards come?

(a) Atmospheric
(b) Aquatic
(c) Terrestrial
(d) Biological

Ans. (a) Atmospheric.

(B) Answer the following questions in about 30 words :

Q. 1. When can a hazard become a disaster?

Ans. A hazard can becomes a disaster when either there are no mitigating circumstances to prevent the disaster from happening or the mitigating circumstances fail.

Q. 2. Why are there more earthquakes in the Himalayas and in the north-eastern region of India?

Ans. The Indian plate is moving at a speed of one centimetre per year towards the north and north-eastern direction and this movement of plates is being constantly obstructed by the Eurasian plate from the north. As a result of this, both the plates are said to be locked with each other resulting in accumulation of energy at different points of time. Excessive accumulation of energy results in building up of stress, which ultimately leads to the breaking up of the lock and the sudden release of energy causes earthquakes along the Himalayan arch.

Q. 3. What are the basic requirements for the formation of a cyclone?

Ans. Some initial conditions for the emergence of a tropical cyclone are :

(i) Large and continuous supply of warm and moist air that can release enormous latent heat.

(ii) Strong Coriolis force that can prevent filling of low pressure at the centre (absence of Coriolis force near the equator prohibits the formation of tropical cyclone between 0°-5° latitude).

(iii) Unstable condition through the troposphere that creates local disturbances around which a cyclone develops.

(iv) Finally, absence of strong vertical wind wedge, which disturbs the vertical transport of latent heat.

Q. 4. How are the floods in Eastern India different from the ones in Western India?

Ans. Floods in Eastern India are different from the ones in Western India because more rainfall takes place in eastern India as compared to western India. Moreover, floods of eastern India are more severe in comparison to western India.

Q. 5. Why are there more droughts in Central and Western India?

Ans. **Less rainfall, excessive evaporation, scarcity in** ground water and water bodies result in more droughts in central and western India. Western India consists of deserts and central India has plateaus and, in both regions, ground water level is less. It creates drought conditions.

(C) Answer the following questions in about 125 words :

Q. 1. Identify the Landslide-prone regions of India and suggest some measures to mitigate the disasters caused by these.

Ans. India has been divided into number of zones :

(i) **Very High Vulnerability Zone :** Highly unstable, relatively young mountainous areas in the Himalayas and Andaman and Nicobar, high rainfall regions with steep slopes in the Western Ghats and Nilgiris, the north-eastern regions, along with areas that experience frequent ground-shaking due to earthquakes, etc. and areas of intense human activities, particularly those related to construction of roads, dams, etc. are included in this zone.

(ii) **High Vulnerability Zone :** Areas that have almost similar conditions to those included in the very high vulnerability zone are also included in this category. The only difference between these two is the combination, intensity and frequency of the controlling factors. All the Himalayan states and the states from the north-eastern regions except the plains of Assam are included in the high vulnerability zones.

(iii) **Moderate to Low Vulnerability Zone :** Areas that receive less precipitation such as TransHimalayan areas of Ladakh and Spiti (Himachal Pradesh), undulated yet stable relief and low precipitation areas in the Aravali, rain shadow areas in the Western and Eastern Ghats and Deccan plateau also experience occasional landslides. Landslides due to mining and subsidence are most common in states like Jharkhand, Odisha, Chhattisgarh, Madhya Pradesh, Maharashtra, Andhra Pradesh, Karnataka, Tamil Nadu, Goa and Kerala.

(iv) **Other Areas :** The remaining parts of India, particularly states like Rajasthan, Haryana, Uttar Pradesh, Bihar, West Bengal (except district Darjiling), Assam (except district Karbi Anglong) and Coastal regions of the southern States are safe as far as landslides are concerned.

Measures to mitigate the disaster caused by the landslide :

(i) Restriction on the construction and other developmental activities such as roads and dams, limiting agriculture to valleys and areas with moderate slopes, and control on the development of large settlements in the high vulnerability zones, should be enforced.

(ii) This should be supplemented by some positive actions like promoting large-scale afforestation programmes.

(iii) Construction of bunds to reduce the flow of water.

(iv) Terrace farming should be encouraged in the northeastern hill states where Jhumming (Slash and Burn/Shifting Cultivation) is still prevalent.

Q. 2. What is vulnerability? Divide India into natural disaster vulnerability zones based on droughts and suggest some mitigation measures?

Ans. Vulnerability refers to the risk of becoming a victim to a disaster. Those areas which are more prone to natural calamities are more vulnerable :

India can be divided into the following regions :

(i) **Extreme drought affected areas :** It is evident from the Figure 7.8 that most parts of Rajasthan, particularly areas to the west of the Aravali hills, i.e. Marusthali and Kachchh regions of Gujarat fall in this category. Included here are also the districts like Jaisalmer and Barmer from the Indian desert that receive less that 90 mm average annual rainfall.

(ii) **Severe Drought Prone Area :** Parts of eastern Rajasthan, most parts of Madhya Pradesh, eastern parts of Maharashtra, interior parts of Andhra Pradesh and Karnataka Plateau, northern parts of interior Tamil Nadu and southern parts of Jharkhand and interior Odisha are included in this category.

(iii) **Moderate Drought Affected Area :** Northern parts of Rajasthan, Haryana, southern districts of Uttar Pradesh, the remaining parts of Gujarat, Maharashtra except Konkan, Jharkhand and Coimbatore plateau of Tamil Nadu and interior Karnataka are included in this category. The remaining parts of India can be considered either free or less prone to the drought.

Remedial measures :

Provision for the distribution of safe drinking water, medicines for the victims and availability of fodder and water for the cattle and shifting of the people and their livestock to safer places, etc. are some steps that need to be taken immediately.

Identification of ground water potential in the form of aquifers, transfer of river water from the surplus to the deficit areas, and particularly planning for inter-linking of rivers and construction of reservoirs and dams, etc. should be given a serious thought.

Remote sensing and satellite imageries can be useful in identifying the possible river-basins that can be inter-linked and in identifying the ground water potential. Dissemination of knowledge about drought-resistant crops and proper training to practise the same can be some of the long-term measures that will be helpful in drought-mitigation. Rainwater harvesting can also be an effective method in minimising the effects of drought.

Q. 3. When can developmental activities become the cause of disasters?

Ans. There are many times when developmental activities carried by human beings have become the cause of disasters.

Bhopal Gas tragedy, Chernobyl nuclear disaster, wars, release of CFCs (Chlorofluorocarbons) and increase of green house gases, environmental pollutions like noise, air, water and soil are some of the disasters which are caused directly by human actions. There are some other activities of human beings that accelerate or intensify disasters indirectly. Landslides and floods due to deforestation, unscientific land use and construction activities in fragile areas are some of the disasters that are the results of indirect human actions.

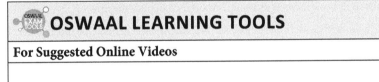

□□

PART C :
UNIT-I

Fundamentals of Maps

CHAPTER 1 INTRODUCTION TO MAPS

Syllabus

> *Essentials of Map Making, History of Map Making, Types of Maps , Uses of Maps..*

Revision Notes

- A map is a simplified depiction of whole or part of the earth on a piece of paper. In other words, it is a two-dimensional form of the three-dimensional earth.
- A map is, therefore, defined as selective, symbolised and generalised representation of whole or apart of the earth's surface on a plane surface at a reduced scale.
- Cartography, being an art and science of map-making, does include a series of processes that are common to all the maps.
- The certain essential features of map are:
  - **Scale :** The first decision that a map-maker has to take is about the scale of the map. The choice of scale is of utmost importance. The scale of a map sets limits of information contents and the degree of reality with which it can be delineated on the map.
  - **Projection :** The transformation of all-side-curved-geoidal surface into a plane surface is another important aspect of the cartographic process. We should know that such a radical transformation introduces some unavoidable changes in directions, distances, areas and shapes from the way they appear on a geoid. Hence, the choice, utilisation and construction of projections is of prime importance in map-making.
  - **Generalisation :** Every map is drawn with a definite objective. For example, a general purpose map is drawn to show information of a general nature such as relief, drainage, vegetation, settlements, means of transportation, etc. Similarly, a special purpose map exhibits information pertaining to one or more selected themes like population density, soil types or location of industries. It is, therefore, necessary to carefully plan the map contents while the purpose of the map must be kept in the forefront.
  - **Map Design :** The fourth important task of a cartographer is the map design. It involves the planning of graphic characteristics of maps including the selection of appropriate symbols, their size and form, style of lettering, specifying the width of lines, selection of colours and shades, arrangement of various elements of map design within a map and design for map legend.
  - **Map Construction and Production :** The drawing of maps and their reproduction is the fifth major task in the cartographic process. However, the map construction and reproduction has been revolutionalised with the addition of computer assisted mapping and photo-printing techniques in the recent past.
- The history of map making is as old as the history of mankind itself. The oldest map was found in Mesopotamia drawn on a clay tablet that belongs to 2,500 B.C.
- The measurement of the circumference of the Earth and the use of the system of geographical coordinates in map-making are some of the significant contributions of the Greeks and the Arabs.
- The foundation of map-making in India was laid during the Vedic period when the expressions of astronomical truths and cosmological revelations were made.

- Ancient Indian scholars divided the known world into seven 'dwipas'. Mahabharata conceived a round world surrounded by water surveying and map-making as an integral part of the revenue collection procedure. Besides, Sher Shah Suri's revenue maps further enriched the mapping techniques during the medieval period.
- The Survey of India was set up in 1767. Today, the Survey of India produces maps at different scales for the entire country.
- On the basis of scale, maps may be classified into large-scale and small-scale.
  - **Large scale maps :** Large scale maps are drawn to show small areas at a relatively large-scale. For example, the topographical maps drawn at a scale of 1: 250,000, 1:50,000 or 1:25,000 and the village maps, the zonal plans of the cities and house plans prepared on a scale of 1:4,000, 1:2,000 and 1:500 are large scale maps. Large-scale maps are further divided into the following types :

  (a) **Cadastral Maps :** These maps are drawn to show the ownership of landed property by demarcating field boundaries of agricultural land and the plan of individual houses in urban areas. The cadastral maps are prepared by the government agencies to realise revenue and taxes, along with keeping a record of ownership.

  (b) **Topographic Maps :** The topographical maps are based on precise surveys and are prepared in the form of series of maps made by the national mapping agencies of almost all countries of the world .These maps follow uniform colours and symbols to show topographic details such as relief, drainage, agricultural land, forest, settlements, means of communication, location of schools, post offices and other services and facilities.

  - **Small scale maps :** The small-scale maps are drawn to show large areas. For example, atlas maps, wall maps, etc. Small-scale maps are further divided into the following types:

  (a) **Wall Maps :** These maps are generally drawn on large size paper or on plastic base for use in classrooms or lecture halls.

  (b) **Atlas Maps :** Atlas maps are very small-scale maps. These maps represent fairly large areas and present highly generalised picture of the physical or cultural features. Even so, an atlas map serves as a graphic encyclopaedia of the geographical information about the world, continents, countries or regions.

- The maps may also be classified on the basis of their functions :
  - **Physical Maps :** Physical maps show natural features such as relief, geology, soils, drainage, elements of weather, climate and vegetation, etc.

  (a) **Relief Maps :** Relief maps show general topography of an area like mountains and valleys, plains, plateaus and drainage.

  (b) **Geological Maps :** These maps are drawn to show geological structures, rock types, etc.

  (c) **Climatic Maps :** These maps depict climatic regions of an area. Besides, maps are also drawn to show the distribution of temperature,rainfall, cloudiness, relative humidity, direction and velocity of winds and other elements of weather.

  (d) **Soil Maps :** Maps are also drawn to show the distribution of different types of soil(s) and their properties.

  - **Cultural Maps :** Cultural maps show man-made features. These include a variety of maps showing population distribution and growth, sex and age, social and religious composition, literacy, levels of educational attainment, occupational structure, location of settlements, facilities and services, transportation lines and production, distribution and flow of different commodities.

  (a) **Political Maps :** These maps show the administrative divisions of an area such as country, state or district.

  (b) **Population Maps :** The population maps are drawn to show the distribution, density and growth of population, age and sex composition,distribution of religious, linguistic and social groups, occupational structure of the population, etc.

  (c) **Economic Maps :** Economic maps depict production and distribution of different types of crops and minerals, location of industries and markets, routes for trade and flow of commodities.

  (d) **Transportation Maps :** These maps show roads, railway lines and the location of railway stations and airports.

- The maps are very useful for various purposes :
  - **Measurement of Distance :** The linear features shown on the maps fall into two broad categories, i.e. straight lines and erratic or zigzag lines. The measurement of straight line features like roads, railway lines and canals is simple.However, distances are required, more often, along erratic paths, i.e. the coastlines, rivers and streams.

The distances along all such features can be measured by placing a thread at the starting point and carrying it along the line up to the end point.

- **Measurement of direction :** Direction is defined as an imaginary straight line on the map showing the angular position to a common base direction. A map always shows the north direction. All other directions are determined in to this relation. The north direction enables the map user to locate different features with respect to each other. The four commonly known directions are North, South, East and West. These are also called the cardinal points. In between the cardinal points, one may have several intermediate directions.
- **Measurement of Area :** There are different methods in which areas can be determined. One of the simplest but not very accurate method to determine the area is by means of regular pattern of squares. In this method, the area to be measured is covered by squares by placing a sheet of graph paper beneath the map on an illuminated tracing table or by tracing the area onto the square sheet.

Know the Terms

- **Maps :** A map, is a simplified depiction of whole or part of the earth on a piece of paper.
- **Geoid :** An oblate spheroid whose shape resembles the actual shape of the Earth.
- **Cadastral map :** It is a large scale map drawn at a scale of 1:500 to 1:4000 to show property boundaries, designating each parcel of land with a number.
- **Cardinal Points :** North (N), South (S), East (E) and West (W).
- **Cartography :** Art, science and technology of making maps, charts, plans and other modes of graphical expression as well as their study and use.
- **Generalisation-Map :** A simplified representation of the features on the map, appropriate to its scale or purpose, without affecting their visual form.
- **Map series :** A group of maps produced at same scale, style and specifications for a country or a region.
- **Projection-Map :** The system of the transformation of the spherical surface onto a plane surface. Scale : The ratio between the distances of two points on the map, plan or photograph and the actual distance between the same two points on the ground.
- **Sketch Map :** A simplified map drawn freehand which fails to preserve the true scale or orientation.
- **Scale :** The ratio between the distances of two points on the map, plan or photograph and the actual distance between the same two points on the ground is called scale.
- **Zero direction :** The line pointing to the north is zero direction .
- **Ratometer :** It is an instrument which is used to measure distance on a map.
- **Large scale map :** Large scale maps are drawn to show small areas at a relatively large-scale.
- **Small scale map :** Small-scale maps are drawn to show large areas. For example, atlas maps, wall maps, etc.
- **Planimeter :** It is an instrument used to measure area on a map.

Multiple Choice Questions

(1 mark each)

Q. 1. Indian ancient scholars divided the world into: A

(a) seven dwipas

(b) eight dwipas

(c) nine dwipas

(d) four dwipas

Ans. (a) seven dwipas 1

Q. 2. The maps that are drawn on large size paper or on plastic base for use in classrooms or lecture halls are known as : U

(a) home maps

(b) wall maps

(c) ground maps

(d) distance maps

Ans. (b) wall maps 1

Q. 3. A/An_________ map serves as a graphic encyclopaedia of the geographical information about the world, continents, countries or regions. R

(a) small scale

(b) sketch

(c) atlas

(d) projection

Ans. (c) atlas 1

Q. 4. The maps that show the administrative divisions of an area such as country, state or district are known as : U

(a) Sketch maps

(b) cadastral maps

(c) political maps

(d) physical maps

Ans. (c) political maps 1

Very Short Answer Type Questions (1 mark each)

Q. 1. Define the term 'Map'. [A]

Ans. A map, is a simplified depiction of whole or part of the earth on a piece of paper. 1

Q. 2. What is map series? [U]

Ans. A group of maps produced at same scale, style and specifications for a country or a region. 1

Q. 3. What is cartography? [R]

Ans. Art, science and technology of making maps, charts, plans and other modes of graphical expression as well as their study and use is called as cartography. 1

> **Answering Tip**
> - Modern cartography also helps to quickly disseminate crucial information.

Q. 4. What are cardinal points? [A]

Ans. North (N), South (S), East (E) and West (W) are the cardinal points. 1

Q. 5. What is a scale? [U]

Ans. The ratio between the distances of two points on the map, plan or photograph and the actual distance between the same two points on the ground is called scale. 1

Q. 6. What is planimeter? [A]

Ans. It is an instrument used to measure area on a map. 1

> **Answering Tip**
> - The planimeter is a mechanical device for measuring areas in the plane. It has the shape of a ruler with two legs.

Q. 7. What is a ratometer? [R]

Ans. It is an instrument which is used to measure distance on a map. 1

Q. 8. How is a scale expressed on a map? [U]

Ans. Scale is expressed in three ways on a map: by a statement, by graphical or bar scale and by representative fraction method. (Any Two) (½ + ½ =1)

Q. 9. Name the two components of a map. [A]

Ans. The two components of a map are distance and direction. 1

Q. 10. Name any two important relationships that we search in maps. [U]

Ans. The important relationships that we search in maps are :

(i) Shapes of land forms, oceans and political units

(ii) Their areas

(iii) Distances between the places

(iv) Direction of each place in context to other places

(v) Location of different places in context of entire earth. (Any Two)(½ +½ = 1)

Q. 11. When was the oldest map drawn? [A]

Ans. The oldest map was found in Mesopotamia drawn on a clay tablet that belongs to 2,500 B.C. 1

Q. 12. When was the foundation of map-making laid in India? [R]

Ans. The foundation of map-making in India was laid during the Vedic period when the expressions of astronomical truths and cosmological revelations were made. 1

Q. 13. What is the purpose of large scale maps? [A]

Ans. Large scale maps are drawn to show small areas at a relatively large-scale. For example, the topographical maps drawn at a scale of 1: 250,000, 1:50,000 or 1:25,000 and the village maps, the zonal plans of the cities and house plans prepared on a scale of 1:4,000, 1:2,000 and 1:500 are large scale maps. 1

> **Answering Tip**
> - The geographic extent shown on a large scale map is small.

Q. 14. What is the purpose of small scale maps ? [A]

Ans. Small-scale maps are drawn to show large areas. For example, atlas maps, wall maps, etc. 1

Q.15. When was the Survey of India established? [R]

Ans. Survey of India was established in 1767. 1

Q. 16. When was the first map made by Survey of India? [U]

Ans. The first map was made by the Survey of India in 1785. 1

Q. 17. What do we call a system of transformation of the spherical surface to the plane surface? [A]

Ans. A system of transformation of the spherical surface to the plane surface is called Map Projection. 1

Q. 18. Give the formula for measuring distance used by geographers. [U]

Ans. $\text{Some of whole squares} + \dfrac{\text{Some of whole squares}}{2} \times \text{Map Scale}$ 1

Short Answer Type Questions (3 marks each)

Q. 1. Differentiate between a globe and map. A

Ans.

S.No.	Globe	Map
1.	Globe is such a model of the earth which gives us the right form of the Earth	Map is a simplified depiction of whole or part of earth on a piece of paper.
2.	It is more accurate but it is difficult to use it.	It is relatively less accurate but it is easy to be handled.
3.	It is three dimensional .	It is two dimensional

(1 × 3 = 3)

Answering Tip

- A map is easy to use and portable, whereas a globe is not.

Q.2. Write any three basic limitations of maps. A

Ans. The basic limitation of maps are:

(i) Maps are two dimensional representations. We cannot show the entire earth on a map without distributing its shape.

(ii) It is impossible to present the accurate shape of the earth with the help of map. When looking at maps we tend to forget that it is just an representation of something that may be approximated for better understanding of topic.

(iii) It can't be accurate in terms of area, volume and distance. It shows distorted shape and size of the landforms. 3

Q. 3. What makes maps an important tool for geographers? U

Ans. The following factors make the map an important tool for geographers :

(i) To get information about resources, their development and planning for their utilization. It is also important to study changes that are taking place on the Earth.

(ii) It is important to understand various physical factors ;between physical and human resources. Maps also enable human geographers to give visual evidence to support claims which can be manipulated into presentation techniques such as choropleth maps.

(iii) It is important to make a comparative analysis and to present facts in a way that has a memorizing effects. **(1 × 3 = 3)**

Q. 4. How is area of map measured using a planimeter? R

Ans. The area calculation is also carried out using Polar Planimeter. In this instrument, a measure is made of the movement of a rod whose locus is a radial arc . The area to be measured is traced along its perimeter in a clockwise direction with an index mark, starting from one convenient point to which the index of the tracing arm must exactly return.

Reading on the dial, before and after the tracing of area's perimeter, will give a value in instrumental units. These readings are multiplied by the same constant for the particular instrument to convert into areas in square inches or centimeters. 3

Q. 5. How are the directions measured on a map? A

Ans. Direction is defined as an imaginary straight line on the map showing the angular position to a common base direction. The line pointing to the north is zero direction or the base direction line. A map always shows the north direction. All other directions are determined in to this relation. The north direction enables the mapuser to locate different features with respect to each other. The four commonly known directions are North, South, East and West. These are also called the cardinal points. In between the cardinal points, one may have several intermediate directions. 3

Q. 6. How is the distance between maps measured by geographer, planner and other resource researchers? U

Ans. The linear features shown on the maps fall into two broad categories, i.e. straight lines and erratic or zigzag lines. The measurement of straight line features like roads, railway lines and canals is simple. It can be taken directly with a pair of dividers or a scale placed on the map surface. However, distances are required, more often, along erratic paths, i.e. the coastlines, rivers and streams. The distances along all such features can be measured by placing a thread at the starting point and carrying it along the line up to the end point. The thread is then stretched and measured to determine the distance. It can also be measured by using a simple instrument called Rotameter. The wheel of the 'rotameter' is moved along the route to measure the distance. 3

Q. 7. What do you know about the physical maps? R

Ans. **(i) Physical Maps :** Physical maps show natural features such as relief, geology, soils, drainage, elements of weather, climate and vegetation, etc. They can be further divided into:

(a) Relief Maps : Relief maps show general topography of an area like mountains and valleys, plains, plateaus and drainage.

(b) Geological Maps : These maps are drawn to show geological structures, rock types, etc.

(c) Climatic Maps : These maps depict climatic regions of an area. Besides, maps are also drawn to show the distribution of temperature,rainfall, cloudiness, relative humidity, direction and velocity of winds and other elements of weather.

(d) Soil Maps : Maps are also drawn to show the distribution of different types of soil(s) and their properties. **(Any Three) (1 × 3 = 3)**

Answering Tip

- The physical map of the world displays all the continents and various geographical features across the world. Water bodies such as oceans, seas, lakes, rivers, and river basins .

Long Answer Type Questions

(5 marks each)

Q. 1. Explain the essentials of map making? A

Ans. The essentials of map making include :

(i) Scale : We know that all maps are reductions. The first decision that a map-maker has to take is about the scale of the map. The choice of scale is of utmost importance. The scale of a map sets limits of information contents and the degree of reality with which it can be delineated on the map.

(ii) Projection : We also know that maps are a simplified representation of the three-dimensional surface of the earth on a plane sheet of paper. The transformation of all-side-curved-geoidal surface into a plane surface is another important aspect of the cartographic process. We should know that such a radical transformation introduces some unavoidable changes in directions, distances, areas and shapes from the way they appear on a geoid. A system of transformation of the spherical surface to the plane surface is called a map projection. Hence, the choice, utilisation and construction of projections is of prime importance in map-making .

(iii) Generalisation : Every map is drawn with a definite objective. For example, a general purpose map is drawn to show information of a general nature such as relief, drainage, vegetation, settlements, means of transportation, etc. Similarly, a special purpose map exhibits information pertaining to one or more selected themes like population density, soil types or location of industries. It is, therefore, necessary to carefully plan the map contents while the purpose of the map must be kept in the forefront. As maps are drawn at a reduced scale to serve a definite purpose, the third task of a cartographer is to generalise the map contents. In doing so, a cartographer must select the information (data) relevant to the selected theme and simplify it as per the needs.

(iv) Map Design : The fourth important task of a cartographer is the map design. It involves the planning of graphic characteristics of maps including the selection of appropriate symbols, their size and form, style of lettering, specifying the width of lines, selection of colours and shades, arrangement of various elements of map design within a map and design for map legend. The map design is, therefore, a complex aspect of mapmaking and requires thorough understanding of the principles that govern the effectiveness of graphic communication.

(v) Map Construction and Production : The drawing of maps and their reproduction is the fifth major task in the cartographic process. In earlier times, much of the map construction and reproduction work used to be carried out manually. Maps were drawn with pen and ink and printed mechanically. However, the map construction and reproduction has been revolutionalised with the addition of computer assisted mapping and photo-printing techniques in the recent past. **(1×5=5)**

Answering Tip

- The most important part of the map making is to put the symbols.

Q. 2. What do you know about the cultural maps? R

Ans. **Cultural Maps :** Cultural maps show man-made features. These include a variety of maps showing population distribution and growth, sex and age, social and religious composition, literacy, levels of educational attainment, occupational structure, location of settlements, facilities and services, transportation lines and production, distribution and flow of different commodities.

(i) **Political Maps :** These maps show the administrative divisions of an area such as country, state or district. These maps facilitate the administrative machinery in planning and management of the concerned administrative unit.

(ii) **Population Maps :** The population maps are drawn to show the distribution, density and growth of population, age and sex composition distribution of religious, linguistic and social groups, occupational structure of the population, etc. Population maps serve the most significant role in the planning and development of an area.

(iii) **Economic Maps :** Economic maps depict production and distribution of different types of crops and minerals, location of industries and markets, routes for trade and flow of commodities.

(iv) **Transportation Maps :** These maps show roads, railway lines and the location of railway stations and airports. **(1 × 5 = 5)**

NCERT CORNER

(A) Multiple choice questions :

Q. 1. Which one of the following is essential for the network of lines and polygons to be called a map :

(a) Map Legend

(b) Symbols

(c) North Direction

(d) Map Scale

Ans. (d) Map Scale .

Q. 2. A map bearing a scale of 1 : 4000 and larger is called :

(a) Cadastral map

(b) Topographical map

(c) Wall map

(d) Atlas map

Ans. (a) Cadastral Map

Q. 3. Which one of the following is NOT an essential element of maps :

(a) Map Projection

(b) Map Generalisation

(c) Map Design

(d) History of Maps

Ans. (d) History of Maps

(B) Answer the following questions in about 30 words :

Q. 1. What is map generalisation?

Ans. Every map is drawn with a definite objective. For example, a general purpose map is drawn to show information of a general nature such as relief, drainage, vegetation, settlements, means of transportation, etc. Similarly, a special purpose map exhibits information pertaining to one or more selected themes like population density, soil types or location of industries. It is, therefore, necessary to carefully plan the map contents while the purpose of the map must be kept in the forefront. As maps are drawn at a reduced scale to serve a definite purpose, the third task of a cartographer is to generalise the map contents.

Q. 2. Why is map design important ?

Ans. The map design is, therefore, a complex aspect of mapmaking and requires thorough understanding of the principles that govern the effectiveness of graphic communication. It involves the planning of graphic characteristics of maps including the selection of appropriate symbols, their size and form, style of lettering, specifying the width of lines, selection of colours and shades, arrangement of various elements of map design within a map and design for map legend.

Q. 3. What are different types of small-scale maps ?

Ans. Small-scale maps are further divided into the following types :

(i) **Wall Maps :** These maps are generally drawn on large size paper or on plastic base for use in classrooms or lecture halls.

(ii) **Atlas Maps :** Atlas maps are very small-scale maps. These maps represent fairly large areas and present highly generalised picture of the physical or cultural features.

Q. 4. List out two major types of large-scale maps.

Ans. The major types of large-scale maps are:

(i) **Cadastral Maps :** The term 'cadastral' is derived from the French word 'cadastre' meaning 'register of territorial property'. These maps are drawn to show the ownership of landed property by demarcating field boundaries of agricultural land and the plan of individual houses in urban areas.

(ii) **Topographical Maps :** These maps are also prepared on a fairly large scale. The topographical maps are based on precise surveys and are prepared in the form of series of maps made by the national mapping agencies of almost all countries of the world.

Q. 5. How is a map different from a sketch ?

Ans.

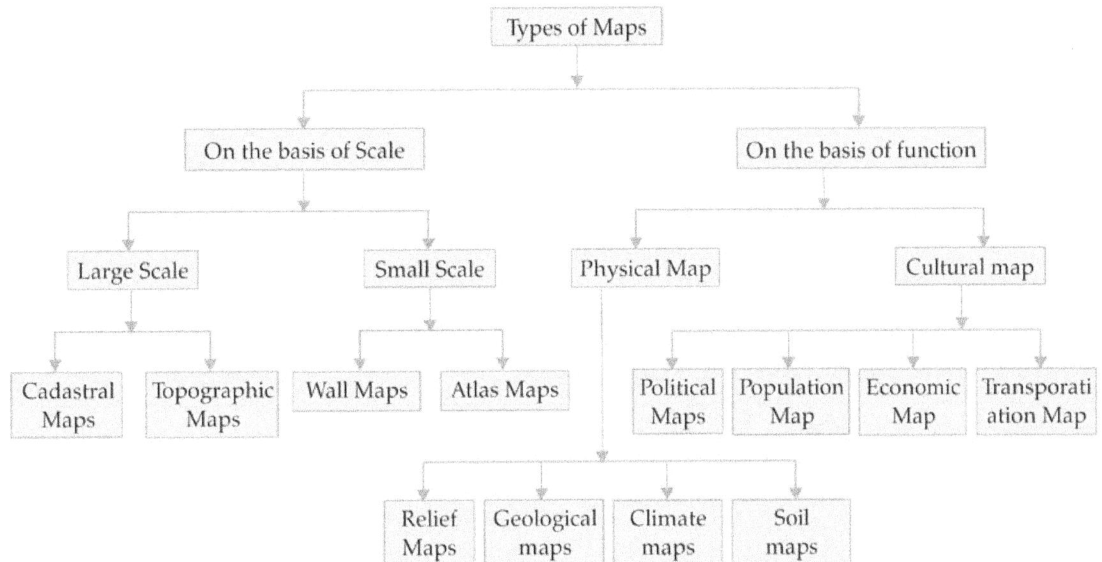

A map is a part of the Earth's surface on a plane surface at a reduced scale. A map is drawn scientifically whereas, the sketch is drawn roughly . A map has a specific scale and sketch does not.

(i) Large scale maps : Large scale maps are drawn to show small areas at a relatively large-scale. For example, the topographical maps drawn at a scale of 1: 250,000, 1:50,000 or 1:25,000 and the village maps, the zonal plans of the cities and house plans prepared on a scale of 1:4,000, 1:2,000 and 1:500 are large scale maps.

Large scale maps can be further divided into :

(a) Cadastral Maps : The term 'cadastral' is derived from the French word 'cadastre' meaning 'register of territorial property'. These maps are drawn to show the ownership of landed property by demarcating field boundaries of agricultural land and the plan of individual houses in urban areas. The cadastral maps are prepared by the government agencies to realise revenue and taxes, along with keeping a record of ownership.

(b) Topographical Maps : These maps are also prepared on a fairly large scale. The topographical maps are based on precise surveys and are prepared in the form of series of maps made by the national mapping agencies of almost all countries of the world . For example, the Survey of India undertakes the topographical mapping of the entire country at 1 : 250,000, 1 : 50,000 and 1 : 25,000 scale.

(ii) Small-scale maps : small-scale maps are drawn to show large areas. They are further divided into:

(a) Wall Maps : These maps are generally drawn on large size paper or on plastic base for use in classrooms or lecture halls. The scale of wall maps is generally smaller than the scale of topographical maps but larger than atlas maps.

(b) Atlas Maps : Atlas maps are very small-scale maps. These maps represent fairly large areas and present highly generalised picture of the physical or cultural features. Even so, an atlas map serves as a graphic encyclopaedia of the geographical information about the world, continents, countries or regions.

The maps may also be classified on the basis of their functions. Broadly, maps based on their functions may be classified into physical maps and cultural maps.

(i) Physical Maps : Physical maps show natural features such as relief, geology, soils, drainage, elements of weather, climate and vegetation, etc.

(a) Relief Maps : Relief maps show general topography of an area like mountains and valleys, plains, plateaus and drainage.

(b) Geological Maps : These maps are drawn to show geological structures, rock types, etc.

(c) Climatic Maps : These maps depict climatic regions of an area. Besides, maps are also drawn to show the distribution of temperature,rainfall, cloudiness, relative humidity, direction and velocity of winds and other elements of weather .

(d) Soil Maps : Maps are also drawn to show the distribution of different types of soil(s) and their properties

(ii) Cultural Maps : Cultural maps show man-made features. These include a variety of maps showing population distribution and growth, sex and age, social and religious composition, literacy, levels of educational attainment, occupational structure, location of settlements, facilities and services, transportation lines and production, distribution and flow of different commodities.

(a) Political Maps : These maps show the administrative divisions of an area such as country, state or district. These maps facilitate the administrative machinery in planning and management of the concerned administrative unit.

(b) Population Maps : The population maps are drawn to show the distribution, density and growth of population, age and sex composition,distribution of religious, linguistic and social groups, occupational structure of the population, etc.

(c) Economic Maps : Economic maps depict production and distribution of different types of crops and minerals, location of industries and markets, routes for trade and flow of commodities.

OSWAAL LEARNING TOOLS

For Suggested Online Videos

Visit : *https://qrgo.page.link/ZnFE3* **Or Scan the Code**

To learn from NCERT Prescribed Videos

Visit : *https://qrgo.page.link/4xY37* **Or Scan the Code**

CHAPTER

2 MAP SCALE

Syllabus

➢ *Methods of Scale, Conversion of Scale..*

Revision Notes

➢ A map scale provides the relationship between the map and the whole or a part of the earth's surface shown on it. We can also express this relationship as a ratio of distances between two points on the map and the corresponding distance between the same two points on the ground.

➢ There are at least three ways in which this relationship can be expressed. These are: 1. Statement of Scale 2. Representative Fraction (R. F.) 3. Graphical Scale.

➢ There are two different systems of measurement of the distances used in different countries of the world. Whereas the former system is referred to as the Metric System of Measurement and presently used in India and many other countries of the world, the latter system is known as the English System of Measurement and is prevalent in both the United States and the United Kingdom. India also used this system for measuring/showing linear distances before 1957.

➢ The scale of the map may be expressed using one or a combination of more than one **methods of scale**. Let us see how these methods are used and what are their advantages and limitations.

- **Statement of Scale :** The scale of a map may be indicated in the form of a written statement. For example, if on a map a written statement appears stating 1 cm represents 10 km, it means that on that map a distance of 1 cm is representing 10 km of the corresponding ground distance. It may also be expressed in any other system of measurement, i.e. 1 inch represents 10 miles.

➢ It is the simplest of the three methods. However, it may be noted that the people who are familiar with one system may not understand the statement of scale given in another system of measurement. Another limitation of this method is that if the map is reduced or enlarged, the scale will become redundant and a new scale is to be worked out.

- **Graphical or Bar Scale :** The second type of scale shows map distances and the corresponding ground distances using a line bar with primary and secondary divisions marked on it. This is referred to as the graphical scale or bar scale. n yet another bar scale the readings may be shown in miles and furlongs. Hence, like the statement of scale method, this method also finds restricted use for only those who can understand it.

- **Representative Fraction (R. F.) :** The third type of scale is R. F. It shows the relationship between the map distance and the corresponding ground distance in units of length. The use of units to express the scale makes it the most versatile method.

Know the Terms

➢ **Map scale :** A map scale provides the relationship between the map and the whole or a part of the earth's surface shown on.

➢ **Scale :** The ratio between the distances of two points on the map, plan or photograph and the actual distance between the same two points on the ground is called scale.

- **Denominator :** The number below the line in a fraction. For example, in a fraction of 1 : 50,000, 50,000 is the denominator.
- **Numerator :** The number above the line in a fraction. For example, in a fraction of 1 : 50,000, 1 is the numerator.
- **Representative Fraction :** A method of scale of a map or plan expressed as a fraction showing the ratio between a unit distance on the map or plan, and the distance measured in the same units on the ground.
- **Statement of scale :** The scale of a map may be indicated in the form of a written statement. For example, if on a map a written statement appears stating 1 cm represents 10 km, it means that on that map a distance of 1 cm is representing 10 km of the corresponding ground distance.
- **Graphical or Bar Scale :** The type of scale showing map distances and the corresponding ground distances using a line bar with primary and secondary divisions marked on it is known as the graphical scale or bar scale.
- **Representative Fraction (R. F.) :** It shows the relationship between the map distance and the corresponding ground distance in units of length. The use of units to express the scale makes it the most versatile method.

Multiple Choice Questions (1 mark each)

Q. 1. The number below the line in a fraction is known as : A

(a) denominator

(b) scale

(c) RF

(d) bar scale

Ans. (a) denominator 1

Q. 2. The system of measuring based on the metre, kilogram and second is known as : U

(a) syndicate system of measurement

(b) metric system of measurement

(c) graphic system of measurement

(d) statement system of measurement

Ans. (b) metric system of measurement 1

Very Short Answer Type Questions (1 mark each)

Q. 1. Define the term 'Map Scale'. A

Ans. A map scale provides the relationship between the map and the whole or a part of the earth's surface shown on. 1

Q. 2. Define the term 'Scale'. U

Ans. The ratio between the distances of two points on the map, plan or photograph and the actual distance between the same two points on the ground is called scale. 1

Q. 3. What is meant by 'Representative Fraction'? U

Ans. It shows the relationship between the map distance and the corresponding ground distance in units of length. The use of units to express the scale makes it the most versatile method. 1

Q. 4. What do you understand by the term 'Bar Scale'? R

Ans. The type of scale showing map distances and the corresponding ground distances using a line bar with primary and secondary divisions marked on it is known as the graphical scale or bar scale. 1

Q. 5. What is statement of scale? A

Ans. When the scale of a map is expressed in a written statement, it is called statement of scale. 1

Q. 6. What is the formula for representative fraction? A

Ans. $\frac{\text{Distance of Map}}{\text{Distance of Ground}}$ 1

Q. 7. Name the different methods of showing scale on a map. A

Ans. The different methods of showing scale on a map are :

(a) By scale statement ;

(b) By graphical or bar scale and

(c) By representative fraction. 1

Q. 8. State one advantage of representative fraction. U

Ans. The advantage of representative fraction is that this method can be used in all countries whether we are acquainted with their unit system or not. 1

Q. 9. What is the importance of map scale? A

Ans. The advantage of a map scale is that it provides the relationship between the map and the whole or part of the Earth's surface shown on it. 1

Answering Tip

- The scale on a map is important in order to give the map reader a sense of size.

Q. 10. What factors are kept in mind while selecting a scale? U

Ans. The following factors are kept in mind while selecting a scale :

(i) Purpose of map : If the map is drawn to study minor details than we should make use of large scale map and if the map is drawn physical features or large area we must make use of small scale map.

(ii) Space availability : Scale is also affected by availability of space for drawing maps. 1

Q. 11. Why do arid soils lack moisture and humus? A

Ans. Due to the dry climate, high temperature and accelerated evaporation, they lack moisture and humus. 1

Short Answer Type Questions (3 marks each)

Q. 1. Differentiate between Representative fraction and graphical scale. R

Ans.

S.No.	Representative Fraction	Graphical Scale
1.	It shows the relationship between the map distance and the corresponding ground distance in units of length. The use of units to express the scale makes it the most versatile method.	The type of scale showing map distances and the corresponding ground distances using a line bar with primary and secondary divisions marked on it is known as the graphical scale.
2.	It gets affected by changing the size of maps.	It is not affected by changing the size of maps proportionally.
3.	It has no unit.	It has a unit.

(1 × 3 = 3)

Q. 2. Discuss the utility of scale in a map. A

Ans. The utility of scale in a map is :

(i) A map scale provides the relationship between the map and the whole or a part of the earth's surface shown on it. We can also express this relationship as a ratio of distances between two points on the map and the corresponding distance between the same two points on the ground.

(ii) Scale of map determines whether it can reflect minor details on it . For example , to locate it on world map , it will be of no use. It is better to use a map of Punjab to locate Chandigarh on it.

(ii) On the basis of scale, maps can be classified into small scale maps and large scale maps. **(1 × 3 = 3)**

Answering Tip

- The scale helps to find a map of an area you want to use.

Q. 3. Write any three limitations of representative fraction? U

Ans. The limitations of representative fraction are :

(i) R.F method is only a fraction. It does not make use of any measurement system. Hence, it cannot be used to measure the direct distance between two places.

(ii) Whenever maps are changed using computers, theses fractions get changed.

(iii) It is not easy for a layman to understand this method. **(1 × 3 = 3)**

Long Answer Type Questions (5 marks each)

Q. 1. Construct a graphical scale for scale 1 inch= 1 mile and which can be read in furlongs and miles. A

Ans. For graphical scale , to know the length of the line we need to make the following calculations :

1 inch= 1 mile

Since , 1 inch = 1 mile

Therefore, 6 inches = 6 miles

The graphical scale can be drawn in the following way :

First of all draw a 6 inches line and divide it in 6 parts. Except one part from the left , give all parts a distance of 1 inch . now divide the first part into 4 equal parts and each part will be equal to 0.25 inch.

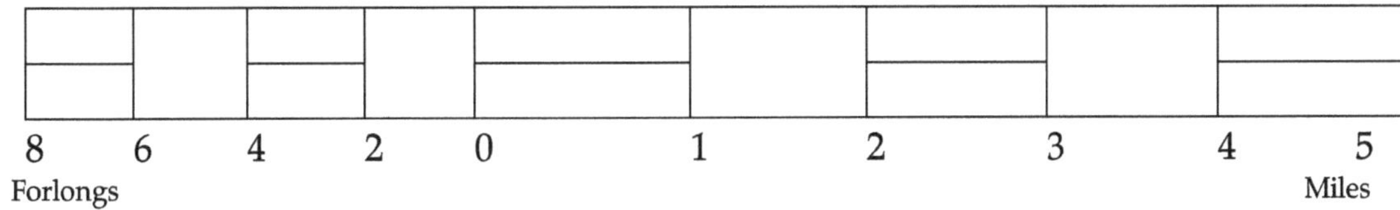

RF 1: 63360

NCERT CORNER

(A) Multiple choice questions :

Q. 1. Which one of the following methods of scale is a universal method?

(a) Simple Statement
(b) Representative Fraction
(c) Graphical Scale
(d) None of the above

Ans. (b) Representative Fraction.

Q. 2. (ii) Map distance in a scale is also known as :

(a) Numerator
(b) Denominator
(c) Statement of Scale
(d) Representative Fraction

Ans. (c) Representative Fraction.

Q. 3. 'Numerator' in scale represents :

(a) Ground distance
(b) Map distance
(c) Both the distances
(d) None of the above

Ans. (a) Ground distance.

(B) Answer the following questions in about 30 words :

Q. 1. What are the two different systems of measurement?

Ans. The two different systems of measurement are : Kilometre, metre , centimetre, etc. They are used to measure the linear distances between the two points on the ground. It is referred to as the Metric System of Measurement .

The other units are miles, furlongs, yards, feet, etc. It is known as the English System of Measurement.

Q. 2. Give one example each of statement of scale in Metric and English system.

Ans. Metric System of Measurement

1 km = 1000 Metres
1 Metre = 100 Centimetres
1 Centimetre = 10 Millimetres

English System of Measurement

1 Mile = 8 Furlongs
1 Furlong = 220 Yards
1 Yard = 3 feet
1 Foot = 12 Inches.

Q. 3. Why is the Representative Fraction Method called a Universal method?

Ans. Representative Fraction Method is called a Universal method because it shows the relationship between the map distance and the corresponding ground distance in units of length. While converting the fraction of units into Metric or English systems, units in centimetre or inch are normally used by convention. This quality of expressing scale in units in R.F makes it a universally acceptable and usable method.

Q. 4. What are the major advantages of the graphical method?

Ans. The major advantages of the graphical method are :

(i) It can express scale not only in kilometres and metres but the readings may also be shown in miles and furlongs.

(ii) This method unlike the statement of the scale method, stands valid even when the map is reduced or enlarged.

(C) Convert the given Statement of Scale into Representative Fraction (R. F.) :

Q. 1. 5 cm represents 10 km.

Ans. $\text{R. F.} = \dfrac{\text{Distance of Map}}{\text{Distance of Ground}}$

Distance on Map = 5 cm
Distance on Ground = 10 km

$\text{R.F.} = \dfrac{5}{10} = \dfrac{1\text{Km}}{2}$ or 2,00,000 cm

Therefore representative fraction = 1 : 2,00,000 cm

Q. 2. 2 inches represents 4 miles

Ans.

$\text{R.F.} = \dfrac{\text{Distance of map}}{\text{Distance on Ground}}$

Distance on Map = 2 inch
Distance on Ground = 4 miles
Therefore, 1 inch = 2 miles (63,360x2)
1 inch on map = 1,26,720 inch on ground
Therefore, representative fraction = 1 : 1,26,720

Q. 3. 1 inch represents 1 yard

Ans.

$\text{R.F.} = \dfrac{\text{Distance of map}}{\text{Distance on Ground}}$

Distance on Map = 1 inch
Distance on Ground = 1 yard
1 yard = 36 inches

$\text{R.F.} = \dfrac{1}{36}$

Therefore, RF= 1 : 36

Q. 4. 1 cm represents 100 metres

Ans.

$\text{R.F.} = \dfrac{\text{Distance of map}}{\text{Distance on Ground}}$

Distance on Map= 1 cm
Distance on Ground= 100 meters
1 cm= 100 meters

$\text{R.F.} = \dfrac{1}{10{,}000}$

Therefore, RF= 1 : 10,000

(D) Convert the given Representative Fraction (R. F.) into Statement of Scale in the System of Measurement shown in parentheses :

Q. 1. 1 : 100,000 (into km)

Ans. This means that 1,00,000 cm on map represents 1 km on ground

So, 1,00,000 cm on map represents 1,00,000 cm on ground

Thus, 1 cm represents 1 km.

Q. 2. 1 : 31680 (into furlongs)

Ans. 1 mile = 8 furlongs

1 furlong = 220 yards

Therefore, 31680 inches =31680

Divided by 12 × 3 × 220 furlongs = 4 furlongs

Therefore, 31680 inches = 4 furlongs

Q. 3. 1 : 126,720 (into miles)

Ans. 1 inch represents 1,26,720 inches

1 mile = 63,360 inches.

Therefore 1,26,720 inches = 2 miles

Hence, 1 inch represents 2 miles

Q. 4. 1 : 50,000 (into meters)

Ans. 1 cm represents = 50,000 cm

1 meter = 100 cm

Therefore, 1 cm represents 500 meters

Q. 5. Construct a graphical scale when the given RF is 1: 50,000 and read the distances in kilometre and metre.

Ans. According to a standard, generally a length of 15 cm is taken to draw a graphical scale. 1 : 50,000 means that 1 cm on map shows 50,000 cm on ground. In other words, 1 cm shows 50,000 cm.

15 cm shows 50,000 × 15/1,00,000

15cm = 7.5 km

Since 7.5 km is not an integer, so we can round it off to 5 or 10. Let us round it off to 5 km in this question.

Therefore, we need to make following calculations to express the scale on a length of 5 km.

7.5 km is shown by 15 cm line.

Therefore, for a 5 km we can express it as 15 × 5/7.5

0.5 km will be shown by 1 cm on line.

We can make the graph by flowing steps:

First of all draw a 10 cm line and divide it in 5 important parts. Except one part from the left, give all parts a distance of one km. now divide the first part in 10 equal parts and each part will be equal to 100 metres. We can divide it in five parts as well and taking one part as 200 meter and so on.

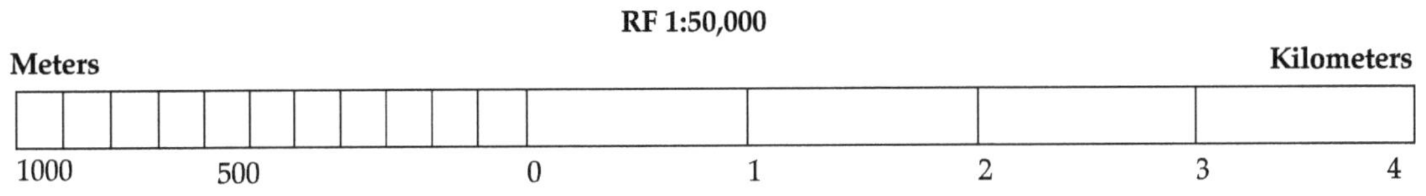

RF 1:50,000

Meters **Kilometers**

1000 500 0 1 2 3 4

OSWAAL LEARNING TOOLS

For Suggested Online Videos

Visit : *https://qrgo.page.link/LBEpB* Or Scan the Code	**Visit :** *https://qrgo.page.link/T7Ymb* Or Scan the Code

CHAPTER

3 LATITUDE, LONGITUDE AND TIME

Syllabus

➤ *Parallels of Latitude, Drawing the Parallels of Latitudes, Meridians of Longitude, Longitude and Time, International Date Line.*

Revision Notes

➤ The Earth is nearly a sphere. It is because of the fact that the equatorial radius and the polar radius of the earth is not the same.

➤ The shape of the earth presents some difficulties in positioning its surface features, as there is no point of reference from which to measure the relative positions of other points. Hence, a network of imaginary lines is drawn on a globe or a map to locate various places.

➤ The spinning of the earth on its axis from west to east provides two natural points of reference, i.e. North and South Poles. They form the basis for the geographical grid.

➤ A network of intersecting lines is drawn for the purpose of fixing the locations of different features. The grid consists of two sets of horizontal and vertical lines, which are called parallels of latitudes and the meridians of longitudes.

➤ Horizontal lines are drawn parallel to each other in East-West direction. The line drawn midway between the North Pole and the South Pole is called the Equator.

➤ It is the largest circle and divides the globe into two equal halves. It is also called a great circle. All the other parallels get smaller in size, in proportion to their distance from the Equator towards the poles and divide the earth into two unequal halves, also referred to as the small circles.

➤ These imaginary lines running East-West are commonly known as the parallels of latitude.

➤ The vertical lines running North-South, join the two poles. They are called the meridians of longitude.

➤ The latitudes and longitudes are commonly referred to as geographical coordinates as they provide systematic network of lines upon which the position of various surface features of the earth, can be represented.

➤ Although an infinite number of parallels and meridians may be drawn on a globe, only a selected number of them are usually drawn on a map.

➤ Latitudes and longitudes are measured in degrees (°) because they represent angular distances. Each degree is further divided into 60 minutes (′) and each minute into 60 seconds (″).

➤ The latitude of a place on the earth's surface is its distance north or south of the equator, measured along the meridian of that place as an angle from the centre of the earth.

➤ Lines joining places with the same latitudes are called parallels.

➤ If parallels of latitude are drawn at an interval of one degree, there will be 89 parallels in the Northern and the Southern Hemispheres each. The total number of parallels thus drawn, including the Equator, will be 179.

➤ Unlike the parallels of latitude which are circles, the meridians of longitude are semi-circles that converge at the poles.

➤ The meridians intersect the Equator at right angles. Unlike the parallels of latitude, they are all equal in length.

➤ For convenience of numbering, the meridian of longitude passing through the Greenwich observatory (near London) has been adopted as the Prime Meridian by an international agreement and has been given the value of 0°.

- The longitude of a place is its angular distance east or west of the Prime Meridian. It is also measured in degrees.
- The part of the earth east of the Prime Meridian is called the Eastern Hemisphere and in its west referred to as the Western Hemisphere.
- The Sun traverses 15^0 of longitudes per hour or one degree of longitude in every four minutes of time. It may further be noted that the time decreases when we move from west to east and increases with our westward movement.
- The rate of the time at which the sun traverses over certain degrees of longitudes is used to determine the local time of an area with respect to the time at the Prime Meridian (0°Longitude).
- In order to maintain uniformity of time as far as possible within the territorial limits of a country, the time at the central meridian of the country is taken as the Standard Meridian and its local time is taken as the standard time for the whole country.
- The Indian Standard Time is calculated from 82°30′E meridian passing through Mirzapur. Therefore, IST is plus 5.30 hours from the GMT ((82°30′ × 4) (60 minutes = 5 hours 30 minutes).
- Similarly, all countries of the world choose the standard meridian within their territory to determine the time within their administrative boundaries.
- The countries with large east west span may choose more than one standard meridian to get more than one time zone such as Russia, Canada and the United States of America. The world is divided into 24 major time zones.
- While the world is divided into 24 time zones, the 180° line of longitude is approximately where the International Date Line passes. The time at this longitude is exactly 12 hours from the 0° longitude, irrespective of one travels westward or eastward from the Prime Meridian.

Know the Terms

- **Parallels of Latitude :** The parallels of latitude refer to the angular distance, in degrees, minutes and seconds of a point North or South of the Equator. Lines of latitude are often referred to as parallels.
- **Meridians of Longitude :** The meridians of longitude refer to the angular distance, in degrees, minutes, and seconds, of a point East or West of the Prime (Greenwich) Meridian. Lines of longitude are often referred to as meridians.
- **Equator :** Imaginary line drawn midway between the North Pole and the South Pole is called the Equator.
- **International Date Line :** The 180° line of longitude is taken as international date line.
- **Prime Meridian :** It is a meridian in a geographic coordinate system at which longitude is defined to be 0°.
- **Great circle :** Equator is also known as Great Circle.
- **Eastern Hemisphere :** It refers to the part of the Earth East of the Prime Meridian .
- **Western Hemisphere :** It refers to the part of the Earth West of the Prime Meridian.
- **Parallel :** It refers to the lines joining places with the same latitudes.
- **Geographical grid :** The spinning of the earth on its axis from west to east provides two natural points of reference, *i.e.,* North and South Poles. They form the basis for the geographical grid.

Multiple Choice Questions (1 mark each)

Q. 1. The other name of Great Circle is the: [A]

(a) Poles
(b) Equator
(c) Parallel
(d) Meridians

Ans. (b) Equator 1

Q. 2. The latitudes are useful in determining the: [A]

(a) local time
(b) local dates
(c) local areas
(d) local places

Ans. (a) local time 1

Q. 3. The longitude of a place is its angular distance east or west of the: [U]

(a) Equator
(b) Arctic Circle
(c) Poles
(d) Prime Meridian

Ans. (d) Prime Meridian 1

Q. 4. The Indian Standard Time is calculated from 82°30′E meridian passing through : [A]

(a) Mirzapur
(b) Birzapur
(c) Hirzapur
(d) Chirzapur

Ans. (a) Mirzapur 1

Very Short Answer Type Questions (1 mark each)

Q. 1. Define the term 'Parallels of Latitude'. U

Ans. The parallels of latitude refer to the angular distance, in degrees, minutes and seconds of a point north or south of the Equator. Lines of latitude are often referred to as parallels. 1

Commonly Made Error

- The students are not aware as to what lead to the name 'Parallels of Latitude'.

Answering Tip

- Circles of latitude are often called parallels because they are parallel to each other.

Q. 2. Define the term 'Meridians of Longitude'. U

Ans. The meridians of longitude refer to the angular distance, in degrees, minutes, and seconds, of a point east or west of the Prime (Greenwich) Meridian. Lines of longitude are often referred to as meridians. 1

Q. 3. Name the longitude on which the International Date Line is fixed. A

Ans. 180° Longitude is fixed as the international Date Line. 1

Q. 4. Where is Greenwich located? R

Ans. Greenwich is located at 0° Longitude. 1

Q. 5. Indian Standard Time has been determined at which latitude? R

Ans. Indian Standard Time has been determined at 82 ½ Eastern Longitude. 1

Q. 6. The world has been divided into how many time zones? U

Ans. The world has been divided into 24 time zones. 1

Q. 7. State the relationship between longitude and time. R

Ans. When we move from West to East longitude, 4 minutes get added on and when we move from East to West, 4 minutes get subtracted. This states the relationship between longitude and time. 1

Answering Tip

- Relationship of Time and Longitude : Local time is the time at one particular meridian. ... The difference in time between two meridians is the time of the sun's passage from one meridian to the other.

Q. 8. What do you know about the longitudinal extent of the Earth? R

Ans. There are 180 Eastern longitudes and 180 Western Longitudes. The longitudes vary from 0° to 180 ° eastward and westward of the Prime Meridian. The part of the earth East of the Prime Meridian is called the Eastern Hemisphere and in its West is called Western Hemisphere. 1

Q. 9. What do you know about the latitudinal extent of the earth? U

Ans. There are 90 southern latitudes and 90 northern latitudes. 0° latitude is called Equator. The latitude to the South of Equator makes up Southern Hemisphere and latitudes to the north of the Equator makes up the Northern Hemisphere. 1

Q. 10. How can you prove that the earth is not a circle but sphere? A

Ans. The earth is not a circle but sphere, this can be proved because of the fact that the equatorial radius and the polar radius of the Earth is not the same. 1

Q.11. State one reason as to why latitudes and longitudes are measured in degrees. U

Ans. Latitudes and longitudes are measured in degrees because they represent angular distances. 1

Q. 12. What do you know about IST? R

Ans. IST refers to Indian Standard Time. IST is calculated from 82° 30′E meridian passing through Mirzapur. IST is plus 5.30 hours from the GMT. 1

Q. 13. Name any two countries which have more than one time zone. A

Ans. Canada, Russia and USA have more than one time zone. **(Any Two) (½ + ½ =1)**

Q. 14. How many latitudes are there? U

Ans. There are 180 latitudes, 90 in the South and 90 in the North. 1

Q. 15. How many longitudes are there? A

Ans. There are 360 ° of longitude , 180 ° each in the east and west of the Prime Meridian. 1

Short Answer Type Questions (3 marks each)

Q. 1. If it is 12 noon in Greenwich then what will be the time at the capital of Bhutan, Thimbu; which is located at 90° East? A

Ans. We must remember that at 1 degree time changes by 4 minutes.

Therefore the difference between Greenwich and Thimbu is equal to 90°. Thus, the time difference is 90 × 4 = 360 minutes or 6 hours.

Local time of Thimpu is 6 hours more than that at Greenwich, *i.e.*, 6.00 p.m. 3

Q. 2. What will be the time at New Orleans which is located at 90° west, when it is 12 noon at Greenwich? A

Ans. We must remember that at 1 degree time changes by 4 minutes.

Therefore, the difference between Greenwich and New Orleans is equal to 90°. Thus, the time difference is 90 × 4 = 360 minutes or 6 hours.

Local time of New Orleans is 6 hours less than that at Greenwich, *i.e.,* 6.00 a. m. 3

Long Answer Type Questions (5 marks each)

Q. 1. What do you know about International Date Line? State its importance? U

Ans. While the world is divided into 24 time zones, there has to be a place where there is a difference in days, somewhere the day truly "starts" on the planet. The 180° line of longitude is approximately where the International Date Line passes. The time at this longitude is exactly 12 hours from the 0^0 longitude, irrespective of one travels westward or eastward from the Prime Meridian. We know that time decreases east of the Prime Meridian and increases to its west. Hence, for a person moving east of the Prime Meridian, the time would be 12 hours less than the time at 0° longitude. For another person moving westward, the time would be 12 hours more than the Prime Meridian. For example, a person moving eastward on Tuesday will count the day as Wednesday once the International Date Line is crossed. Similarly, another person starting his journey on the same day, but moving westward will count the day as Monday after crossing the line. 5

Answering Tip

- International Date Line is located halfway round the world from the Prime Meridian.

Q. 2. How are longitude and time interrelated? A

Ans. The earth rotates from West to East over its axis. It makes the sun rise in the East and set in the West. The rotation of the earth over its axis takes 24 hours to complete one circle or 360° of longitudes. As 180° of longitudes fall both East and West of the Prime Meridian, the sun, thus takes 12 hours' time to traverse the eastern and western hemispheres. In other words, the sun traverses 15^0 of longitudes per hour or one degree of longitude in every four minutes of time. It may further be noted that the time decreases when we move from west to east and increases with our westward movement. The rate of the time at which the sun traverses over certain degrees of longitudes is used to determine the local time of an area with respect to the time at the Prime Meridian (0°Longitude). For example: when it is 2 p.m. in Greenwich, it will be 3 p.m. in 15° east. 5

Q. 3. Explain the process of drawing latitudes. U

Ans. The process of drawing latitudes includes the following steps :

(i) Draw a circle and divide it into two equal halves by drawing a horizontal line in the centre.

(ii) This represents the equator.

(iii) Place a protractor on this circle in a way that 0° and 180° line on the protractor coincide with the equator on the paper.

(iv) Now to draw 20°S, mark two points at an angle of 20° from the equator, east and west in the lower half of the circle.

(v) The arms of the angle cut the circle at two points. Join these two points by a line parallel to the equator. It will be 20°S. **(1 × 5 = 5)**

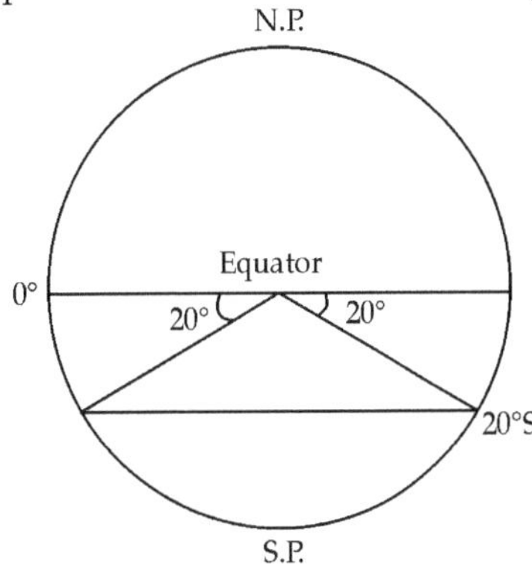

Q. 4. Explain the process of drawing longitudes. A

Ans. The process of drawing longitudes:

(i) Draw a circle whose centre represents the North Pole. The circumference will represent the equator. Draw a vertical line through the centre of the circle, i.e. crossing the North Pole.

(ii) This represents the 0° and 180° meridians, which meet at the North Pole. to draw a longitude, imagine that you are on the North Pole, i.e. at the centre of the circle.

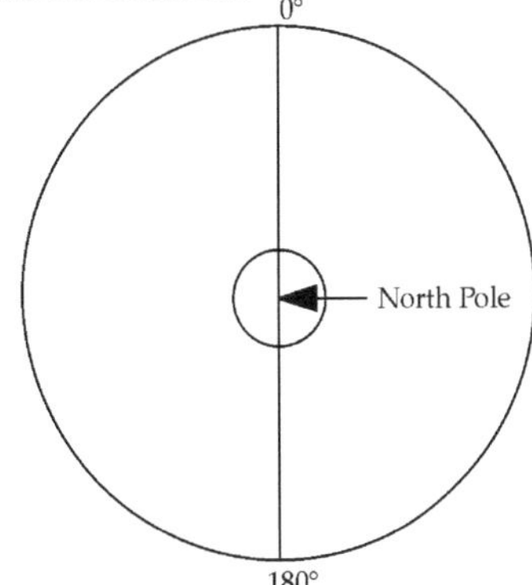

(iii) Observe now that the relative directions of east and west would reverse in this case and east would be towards your left while west would be towards your right. Now, draw 45° E and W.

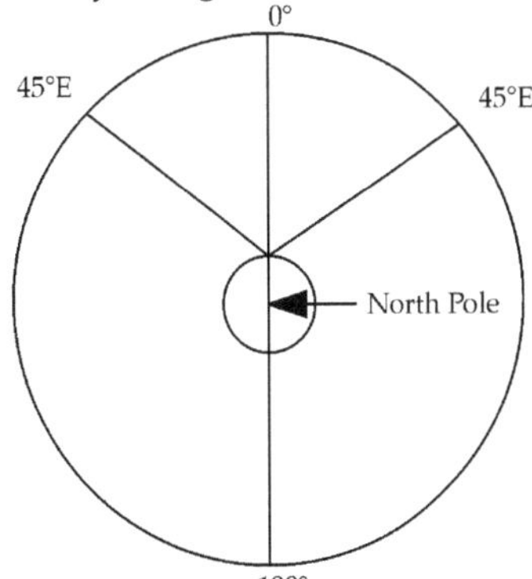

(iv) For this, place your protractor along the vertical line, coinciding with the 0° and 180° meridians and then measure 45° on both the sides, which will denote 45° E meridian and 45° W meridian on your left and right, respectively. The diagram will represent the appearance of the earth if we look at it from directly above the North Pole.

(1 × 5 = 5)

Answering Tip

- The distance per degree of longitude at the Equator is about 111.32 km (69.18 miles) and at the polesis 0.

NCERT CORNER

(A) Answer the following questions in about 30 words :

Q. 1. Which are the two natural points of references on the earth?

Ans. The two natural points of reference on the earth are the North Pole and the South Pole.

Q. 2. What is a great circle?

Ans. The Equator is referred to as the great circle. All the other parallels get smaller in size, in proportion to their distance from the equator towards the poles and divide the earth into two unequal halves.

Q. 3. What are coordinates?

Ans. The latitudes and longitudes are commonly referred to as geographical coordinates as they provide systematic network of lines upon which the position of various surface features of the earth, can be represented.

Q. 4. Why does the sun appear to be moving from east to west?

Ans. The earth rotates from West to East and thus, the sun appears to be moving from East to West.

Q. 5. What is meant by local time?

Ans. Local time can be defined as the rate of the time at which the sun traverses over certain degrees of longitudes is used to determine the local time of an area with respect to the time at the Prime Meridian.

Q. 6. Distinguish between latitudes and longitudes?

Ans.

S.No.	Latitudes	Longitudes
1.	Latitude is the angular distance of a point north or south of the equator as measured in degrees.	Longitude is the angular distance along the equator measured in degrees. It is measured east or west of Greenwich (0°), from 0° to 180°.
2.	All latitudes are parallel to the equator.	All meridians of longitude converge at the poles.
3.	The distance between approximately two longitudes is 111 km.	The distance between two longitudes is maximum at the equator (111.3 km) and minimum at the poles (0 km). Midway, at 45^0 of latitude, it is 79 km.
4.	The 0° latitude is referred to as the equator and the 90° as the poles.	There are 360° of as the equator and the 90° longitude, 180° each in as the poles. the east and west of the Prime Meridian.
5.	It divides the earth into northern hemisphere and southern hemisphere.	It divides the earth into eastern hemisphere and western hemisphere.

Project Work

Q. 1. Find out the locations of the following places with the help of your atlas and write their latitudes and longitudes.

Place	Latitudes	Longitudes
1. Mumbai	19°Northern Latitude	73°Eastern Longitude
2. Vladivostok	34°Northern Latitude	132° Eastern Latitude
3. Cairo	30 °Northern Latitude	30 ° Eastern Latitude
4. New York	41°Northern Latitude	74°Western Latitude
5. Ottawa	45°Northern Latitude	76°Western Latitude
6. Geneva	47°Northern Latitude	7° Western Latitude
7. Johannesburg	27°Southern Latitude	27° Western Latitude
8. Sydney	34°Southern Latitude	152°Eastern Latitude

Q. 2. What would be the time of the following cities if the time at Prime Meridian is 10 a.m.

(i) Delhi

(ii) London

(iii) Tokyo

(iv) Paris

(v) Cairo

(vi) Moscow

Ans. The time of the following cities if the time at Prime Meridian is 10 a.m. would be :

(i) Delhi 3 : 30 p.m.

(ii) London 10 a.m.

(iii) Tokyo 7: 18 p.m.

(iv) Paris 10: 8 a.m.

(v) Cairo 12 noon

(vi) Moscow 12:32 p.m.

❑❑

CHAPTER

4 MAP PROJECTIONS

Syllabus

> *Map Projection, Need for Map Projection, Elements of Map Projection.*
> *Classification of Map Projections, Construction of some Selected Projections.*

TOPIC-1
Map Projection, Need for Map Projection, Elements of Map Projection

Quick Review

- Map projection is the method of transferring the graticule of latitude and longitude on a plane surface. It can also be defined as the transformation of spherical network of parallels and meridians on a plane surface.
- The globe is divided into various segments by the lines of latitude and longitude. The horizontal lines represent the parallels of latitude and the vertical lines represent the meridians of the longitude. The network of parallels and meridians is called graticule. This network facilitates drawing of maps. Drawing of the graticule on a flat surface is called projection.
- The need for a map projection mainly arises to have a detailed study of a region, which is not possible to do from a globe.
- In map projection we try to represent a good model of any part of the earth in its true shape and dimension.
- But distortion in some form or the other is inevitable. To avoid this distortion, various methods have been devised and many types of projections are drawn.
- Due to this reason, map projection is also defined as the study of different methods which have been tried for transferring the lines of graticule from the globe to a flat sheet of paper.
- The various elements of map projection are:
  - **Reduced Earth :** A model of the earth is represented by the help of a reduced scale on a flat sheet of paper. This model is called the "reduced earth".
  - **Parallels of Latitude :** These are the circles running round the globe parallel to the equator and maintaining uniform distance from the poles. Each parallel lies wholly in its plane which is at right angle to the axis of the earth. They are not of equal length.
  - **Meridians of Longitude :** These are semi-circles drawn in north-south direction from one pole to the other, and the two opposite meridians make a complete circle, i.e. circumference of the globe. Each meridian lies wholly in its plane, but all intersect at right angle along the axis of the globe.
  - **Global Property :** In preparing a map projection the following basic properties of the global surface are to be preserved by using one or the other methods:

(a) Distance between any given points of a region;
(b) Shape of the region;
(c) Size or area of the region in accuracy;
(d) Direction of any one point of the region bearing to another point.

Know the Terms

- **Map projection :** It is the system of transformation of the spherical surface onto a plane surface. It is carried out by an orderly and systematic representation of the parallels of latitude and the meridians of longitude of the spherical earth or part of it on a plane surface on a conveniently chosen scale.
- **The Great Circle :** It represents the shortest route between two points, which is often used both in air and ocean navigation.
- **Graticule :** The horizontal lines represent the parallels of latitude and the vertical lines represent the meridians of the longitude. The network of parallels and meridians is called graticule.

Multiple Choice Questions (1 mark each)

Q. 1. Drawing of the graticule on a flat surface is called: U

(a) projection
(b) induction
(c) deduction
(d) reduction

Ans. (a) projection 1

Q. 2. The network of parallels and meridians is called: A

(a) gratitude
(b) graticule
(c) projection
(d) Great Circle

Ans. (b) graticule 1

Very Short Answer Type Questions (1 mark each)

Q. 1. What is map projection? A

Ans. Map projection is the system of transformation of the spherical surface onto a plane surface. It is carried out by an orderly and systematic representation of the parallels of latitude and the meridians of longitude of the spherical earth or part of it on a plane surface on a conveniently chosen scale. 1

Q. 2. Why does the need for map projection arise? R

Ans. The need for a map projection mainly arises to have a detailed study of a region, which is not possible to do from a globe. 1

Answering Tip

- Maps cannot be created without map projections.

Q. 3. What is reduced earth? U

Ans. A model of the earth is represented by the help of a reduced scale on a flat sheet of paper. This model is called the "reduced earth". 1

Q. 4. What do you know about the meridians of longitude? R

Ans. These are semi-circles drawn in North South direction from one pole to the other, and the two opposite meridians make a complete circle, i.e. circumference of the globe. 1

Answering Tip

- Meridians of longitude are drawn from the North Pole to the South Pole and are at right angles to the Equator.

Q. 5. Name any two basic properties of the global surface that are used in preparing a map projection. A

Ans. In preparing a map projection the following basic properties of the global surface are to be preserved by using one or the other methods :

(i) Distance between any given points of a region;
(ii) Shape of the region;
(iii) Size or area of the region in accuracy;
(iv) Direction of any one point of the region bearing to another point. 1

Short Answer Type Questions (3 marks each)

Q. 1. What are the advantages and limitations of a globe? A

Ans. The advantages of a globe are :

(i) A globe is the best model of the earth. Due to this property of the globe, the shape and sizes of the continents and oceans are accurately depicted on it.
(ii) The directions and distances are very accurately shown in it.
(iii) The lines of latitudes and lonngitudes helps in dividing the globe into various segments.

The limitations of a globe are :

(i) Globe is expensive.
(ii) It is very difficult to carry it every where. Besides, on the globe the meridians are semi-circles and the parallels are circles. When they are transferred on a plane surface, they become intersecting straight lines or curved lines.
(iii) Minors detailed cannot be shown on the globe.

(½ × 6 = 3)

Long Answer Type Question (5 marks)

Q. 1. What is the need of map projection? U

Ans. The need for a map projection mainly arises to have a detailed study of a region, which is not possible to do from a globe. Similarly, it is not easy to compare two natural regions on a globe. Therefore, drawing accurate large-scale maps on a flat paper is required.

Now, the problem is how to transfer these lines of latitude and longitude on a flat sheet. If we stick a flat paper over the globe, it will not coincide with it over a large surface without being distorted. If we throw light from the centre of the globe, we get a distorted picture of the globe in those parts of paper away from the line or point over which it touches the globe.

The distortion increases with increase in distance from the tangential point. So, tracing all the properties like shape, size and directions, etc. from a globe is nearly impossible because the globe is not a developable surface.

In map projection we try to represent a good model of any part of the earth in its true shape and dimension. But distortion in some form or the other is inevitable.

To avoid this distortion, various methods have been devised and many types of projections are drawn. Due to this reason, map projection is also defined as the study of different methods which have been tried for transferring the lines of graticule from the globe to a flat sheet of paper. **5**

TOPIC-2

Classification of Map Projections, Construction of some Selected Projections.

Revision Notes

- Map projections may be classified on the following bases :
  - **Drawing Techniques :** On the basis of method of construction, projections are generally classified into perspective, non-perspective and conventional or mathematical.

  (a) Perspective projections can be drawn taking the help of a source of light by projecting the image of a network of parallels and meridians of a globe on developable surface.

  (b) Non–perspective projections are developed without the help of a source of light or casting shadow on surfaces, which can be flattened.

  (c) Mathematical or conventional projections are those, which are derived by mathematical computation, and formulae and have little relations with the projected image.

  - **Developable Surface :** A developable surface is one, which can be flattened, and on which, a network of latitude and longitude can be projected. A non-developable surface is one, which cannot be flattened without shrinking, breaking or creasing.
  - **Global Properties :** As mentioned above, the correctness of area, shape, direction and distances are the four major global properties to be preserved in a map. But none of the projections can maintain all these properties simultaneously. Therefore, according to specific need, a projection can be drawn so that the desired quality may be retained. Thus, on the basis of global properties, projections are classified into equal area, orthomorphic, azimuthal and equi-distant projections.

  (a) **Equal Area Projection :** It is also called homolographic projection. It is that projection in which areas of various parts of the earth are represented correctly.

  (b) **Orthomorphic or True-Shape projection :** It is one in which shapes of various areas are portrayed correctly. The shape is generally maintained at the cost of the correctness of area.

  (c) **Azimuthal or True-Bearing projection :** It is one on which the direction of all points from the centre is correctly represented.

  (d) **Equi-distant or True Scale projection :** It is that where the distance or scale is correctly maintained. However, there is no such projection, which maintains the scale correctly throughout.

  - **Source of Light :** On the basis of location of source of light, projections may be classified as gnomonic, stereographic and orthographic.

  (a) **Gnomonic projection :** It is obtained by putting the light at the centre of the globe.

  (b) **Stereographic projection :** It is drawn when the source of light is placed at the periphery of the globe at a point diametrically opposite to the point at which the plane surface touches the globe.

  (c) **Orthographic projection :** It is drawn when the source of light is placed at infinity from the globe, opposite to the point at which the plane surface touches the globe.

- A conical projection is one, which is drawn by projecting the image of the graticule of a globe on a developable cone, which touches the globe along a parallel of latitude called the standard parallel. As the cone touches the globe located along AB, the position of this parallel on the globe coinciding with that on the cone is taken as the standard parallel. The length of other parallels on either side of this parallel are distorted.

➢ **The properties of the conical projection are :**
- All the parallels are arcs of concentric circle and are equally spaced.
- All meridians are straight lines merging at the pole. The meridians intersect the parallels at right angles.
- The scale along all meridians is true, i.e. distances along the meridians are accurate.
- An arc of a circle represents the pole.
- The scale is true along the standard parallel but exaggerated away from the standard parallel.
- Meridians become closer to each other towards the pole.
- This projection is neither equal area nor orthomorphic.

➢ **The limitations of conical projection are :**
- It is not suitable for a world map due to extreme distortions in the hemisphere opposite the one in which the standard parallel is selected.
- Even within the hemisphere, it is not suitable for representing larger areas as the distortion along the pole and near the equator is larger.

➢ **The uses of conical projection are :**
- This projection is commonly used for showing areas of mid-latitudes with limited latitudinal and larger longitudinal extent.
- A long narrow strip of land running parallel to the standard parallel and having east-west stretch is correctly shown on this projection.
- Direction along standard parallel is used to show railways, roads, narrow river valleys and international boundaries.
- This projection is suitable for showing the Canadian Pacific Railways, Trans-Siberian Railways, international boundaries between USA and Canada and the Narmada Valley.

➢ The cylindrical equal area projection, also known as the Lambert's projection, has been derived by projecting the surface of the globe with parallel rays on a cylinder touching it at the equator.

➢ Both the parallels and meridians are projected as straight lines intersecting one another at right angles. The pole is shown with a parallel equal to the equator; hence, the shape of the area gets highly distorted at the higher latitude.

➢ **The properties of cylindrical equal area projection are :**
- All parallels and meridians are straight lines intersecting each other at right angle.
- Polar parallel is also equal to the equator.
- Scale is true only along the equator.

➢ **The limitations of cylindrical equal area projection are :**
- Distortion increases as we move towards the pole.
- The projection is non-orthomorphic.
- Equality of area is maintained at the cost of distortion in shape.

➢ **The uses of the cylindrical equal area projection are :**
- The projection is most suitable for the area lying between 45º N and S latitudes.
- It is suitable to show the distribution of tropical crops like rice, tea, coffee, rubber and sugarcane.

➢ A Dutch cartographer Mercator Gerardus Karmer developed the Mercator projection in 1569. The projection is based on mathematical formulae. So, it is an orthomorphic projection in which the correct shape is maintained. The distance between parallels increases towards the pole.

➢ Like cylindrical projection, the parallels and meridians intersect each other at right angle. It has the characteristics of showing correct directions. A straight line joining any two points on this projection gives a constant bearing, which is called a Laxodrome or Rhumb line.

➢ **The properties of the Mercator projection are :**
- All parallels and meridians are straight lines and they intersect each other at right angles.
- All parallels have the same length which is equal to the length of equator.
- All meridians have the same length and equal spacing. But they are longer than the corresponding meridian on the globe.
- Spacing between parallels increases towards the pole.
- Scale along the equator is correct as it is equal to the length of the equator on the globe; but other parallels are longer than the corresponding parallel on the globe; hence the scale is not correct along them. For example, the 30º parallel is 1.154 times longer than the corresponding parallel on the globe.
- Shape of the area is maintained, but at the higher latitudes distortion takes place.

➢ **The limitations of this projection are :**
- There is greater exaggeration of scale along the parallels and meridians in high latitudes. As a result, size of the countries near the pole is highly exaggerated. For example, the size of Greenland equals to the size of USA, whereas it is 1/10th of USA.
- Poles in this projection cannot be shown as 90º parallel and meridian touching them are infinite.

➢ **The uses of this projection are :**
- More suitable for a world map and widely used in preparing atlas maps.
- Very useful for navigation purposes showing sea routes and air routes.
- Drainage pattern, ocean currents, temperature, winds and their directions, distribution of worldwide rainfall and other weather elements are appropriately shown on this map.

Know the Terms

➢ **Lexodrome or Rhumb Line :** It is a straight line drawn on Mercator's Projection joining any two points having a constant bearing. It is very useful in determining the directions during navigation.

➢ **Homolograhic Projection :** A projection in which the network of latitudes and longitudes is developed in such a way that every graticule on the map is equal in area to the corresponding graticule on the globe. It is also known as the equal-area projection.

➢ **Orthomorphic Projection :** A projection in which the correct shape of a given area of the earth's surface is preserved.

➢ **Perspective projections :** They can be drawn taking the help of a source of light by projecting the image of a network of parallels and meridians of a globe on developable surface.

➢ **Non–perspective projections :** They are developed without the help of a source of light or casting shadow on surfaces, which can be flattened.

➢ **Mathematical or conventional projections :** They are those, which are derived by mathematical computation, and formulae and have little relations with the projected image.

➢ **Cylindrical projections :** They are made through the use of cylindrical developable surface. A paper-made cylinder covers the globe, and the parallels and meridians are projected on it.

➢ **Normal projections :** If the developmental surface touches the globe at the Equator, it is called the equatorial or normal projections.

➢ **A Conical projection :** It is drawn by wrapping a cone round the globe and the shadow of graticule network is projected on it. When the cone is cut open, a projection is obtained on a flat sheet.

➢ **Zenithal projection :** It is directly obtained on a plane surface when plane touches the globe at a point and the graticule is projected on it.

Multiple Choice Questions (1 mark each)

Q. 1. A cylinder, a cone and a plane are: U

(a) undeveloped surface
(b) developed surface
(c) limited surface
(d) unlimited surface

Ans. (b) developed surface 1

Q. 2. Mercator's Projection is very useful for: A

(a) fishing purpose
(b) mining purpose
(c) navigation purpose
(d) irrigation purpose

Ans. (c) navigation purpose 1

Q. 3. The other name of cylindrical equal area projection is: U

(a) Lambert's projection
(b) Rhumb Line
(c) Lexodrome projection
(d) Conventional projection

Ans. (a) Lambert's projection 1

Very Short Answer Type Questions (1 mark each)

Q. 1. What do you understand by the term 'Lexodrome or Rhumb Line'? R

Ans. It is a straight line drawn on Mercator's Projection joining any two points having a constant bearing. It is very useful in determining the directions during navigation. 1

Q. 2. What is mathematical or conventional projection? R

Ans. They are those, which are derived by mathematical computation, and formulae and have little relations with the projected image. 1

Answering Tip
- Conventional projections are pure-mathematical constructions designed to map the entire sphere with minimal distortion.

Q. 3. What is conical projection? A

Ans. A conical projection is the one that is drawn by wrapping a cone round the globe and the shadow of graticule network is projected on it. When the cone is cut open, a projection is obtained on a flat sheet. 1

Q. 4. What is developable surface? U

Ans. A developable surface is the one which can be flattened and on which , a network of latitude and longitude can be projected. A cylinder, a cone and a plane have the property of developable surface. 1

Q. 5. How is the zenithal projection obtained? A

Ans. It is directly obtained on a plane surface when plane touches the globe at a point and the graticule is projected on it. 1

Q. 6. What do you know about the shapes of meridians and parallels in Mercator projection? U

Ans. The meridians and parallels in Mercator's projection are straight lines and they intersect each other at right angles. The length of all the parallels is the same and is equal to the length of the Equator. The length of all the meridians is the same with equal spacing . but they are longer than the corresponding meridian on the globe. Spacing between parallels increases towards the pole. 1

Q. 7. Describe how perspective and non-perspective projections be drawn. R

Ans. Perspective projections can be drawn taking the help of a source of light by projecting the image of a network of parallels and meridians of a globe on developable surface. Non- perspective projections are developed without the help of a source of light or casting shadow on surfaces, which can be flattened. 1

Q. 8. How can projection be obtained on a plane surface? A

Ans. A conical projection is drawn by wrapping a cone round the globe and the shadow of graticule network is projected on it. When the cone is cut open, a projection is obtained on a flat sheet. **1**

Q. 9. Mention any two limitations of Mercator Projection. A

Ans. The limitations of Mercator Projection are :

(i) There is greater exaggeration of scale along the parallels and meridians in high latitudes. As a result, size of the countries near the pole is highly exaggerated. For example, the size of Greenland equals to the size of USA, whereas it is 1/10th of USA.

(ii) Poles in this projection cannot be shown as 90º parallel and meridian touching them are infinite.

(Any Two) (½ + ½ =1)

Q. 10. Mention any two uses of Cylindrical Equal Area Projection. U

Ans. The uses of cylindrical equal area projection are :

(i) The projection is most suitable for the area lying between 45º N and S latitudes.

(ii) It is suitable to show the distribution of tropical crops like rice, tea, coffee, rubber and sugarcane.

(Any Two) (½ + ½=1)

Q. 11. Name any two global properties to be preserved in a map. R

Ans. The correctness of area, shape, direction and distances are the four major global properties to be preserved in a map. **(Any Two) (½ +½ =1)**

Short Answer Type Questions (3 marks each)

Q. 1. Classify the projections on the basis of the method of construction. A

Ans. On the basis of method of construction, projections are generally classified into perspective, non-perspective and conventional or mathematical.

(i) Perspective projections : It can be drawn taking the help of a source of light by projecting the image of a network of parallels and meridians of a globe on developable surface.

(ii) Non–perspective projections : These are developed without the help of a source of light or casting shadow on surfaces, which can be flattened.

(iii) Mathematical or conventional projections are those, which are derived by mathematical computation, and formulae and have little relations with the projected image. **(1 x 3=3)**

Q. 2. How are conical projections drawn? R

Ans. The conical projections are drawn by projecting the image of the graticule of a globe on a developable cone, which touches the globe along a parallel of latitude called the standard parallel. As the cone touches the globe located along AB, the position of this parallel on the globe coinciding with that on the cone is taken as the standard parallel. The length of other parallels on either side of this parallel are distorted. 3

Answering Tip

- The most famous example of a cylindrical projection is the mercator.

Q. 3. How can the projection be classified on the basis of global properties? U

Ans. On the basis of global properties, projections are classified into equal area, orthomorphic, azimuthal and equi-distant projections:

(i) Equal Area Projection : It is also called homolographic projection. It is that projection in which areas of various parts of the earth are represented correctly.

(ii) Orthomorphic or True-Shape projection : It is one in which shapes of various areas are portrayed correctly. The shape is generally maintained at the cost of the correctness of area.

(iii) Azimuthal or True-Bearing projection : It is one on which the direction of all points from the centre is correctly represented.

(iv) Equi-distant or True Scale projection : It is that where the distance or scale is correctly maintained.

Long Answer Type Questions

(5 marks each)

Q. 1. Explain the properties, uses and limitations of the cylindrical equal area projection. R

Ans. The cylindrical equal area projection, also known as the Lambert's projection, has been derived by projecting the surface of the globe with parallel rays on a cylinder touching it at the equator.

The properties are :

(i) All parallels and meridians are straight lines intersecting each other at right angle.

(ii) Polar parallel is also equal to the equator.

(iii) Scale is true only along the equator.

Limitations :

(i) Distortion increases as we move towards the pole.

(ii) The projection is non-orthomorphic.

(iii) Equality of area is maintained at the cost of distortion in shape.

Uses :

(i) The projection is most suitable for the area lying between 45º N and S latitudes.

(ii) It is suitable to show the distribution of tropical crops like rice, tea, coffee, rubber and sugarcane.

(1 + 2+ 2 = 5)

Q. 2. What do you know about the developable surface? A

Ans. A developable surface is one, which can be flattened, and on which, a network of latitude and longitude can be projected. On the basis of nature of developable surface, the projections are classified as cylindrical, conical and zenithal projections.

(i) Cylindrical projections : They are made through the use of cylindrical developable surface. A paper-made cylinder covers the globe, and the parallels and meridians are projected on it. When the cylinder is cut open, it provides a cylindrical projection on the plane sheet.

(ii) A Conical projection : It is drawn by wrapping a cone round the globe and the shadow of graticule network is projected on it. When the cone is cut open, a projection is obtained on a flat sheet.

(iii) Zenithal projection : It is directly obtained on a plane surface when plane touches the globe at a point and the graticule is projected on it. Generally, the plane is so placed on the globe that it touches the globe at one of the poles.

These projections are further subdivided into normal, oblique or polar as per the position of the plane touching the globe :

(i) If the developable surface touches the globe at the equator, it is called the equatorial or normal projection.

(ii) If it is tangential to a point between the pole and the equator, it is called the oblique projection.

(iii) If it is tangential to the pole, it is called the polar projection. 5

Answering Tip

- Developable surface is a surface that can be flattened onto a plane without distortion.

Q. 3. Explain the properties of the Mercator Projection. R

Ans. The properties of the Mercator Projection are:

(i) All parallels and meridians are straight lines and they intersect each other at right angles.

(ii) All parallels have the same length which is equal to the length of equator.

(iii) All meridians have the same length and equal spacing. But they are longer than the corresponding meridian on the globe.

(iv) Spacing between parallels increases towards the pole.

(v) Scale along the equator is correct as it is equal to the length of the equator on the globe; but other parallels are longer than the corresponding parallel on the globe; hence the scale is not correct along them. For example, the 30º parallel is 1.154 times longer than the corresponding parallel on the globe.

(vi) Shape of the area is maintained, but at the higher latitudes distortion takes place.

(vii) The shape of small countries near the equator is truly preserved while it increases towards poles.

(viii) It is an azimuthal projection.

(ix) This is an orthomorphic projection as scale along the meridian is equal to the scale along the parallel. **(Any Five) (1 × 5 = 5)**

Q. 4. Explain the limitations and uses of conical projection with one standard parallel. U

Ans. The cylindrical equal area projection, also known as the Lambert's projection, has been derived by projecting the surface of the globe with parallel rays on a cylinder touching it at the equator.

The limitations are :

(i) Distortion increases as we move towards the pole.

(ii) The projection is non-orthomorphic.

(iii) Equality of area is maintained at the cost of distortion in shape.

Uses :

(iv) The projection is most suitable for the area lying between 45º N and S latitudes.

(v) It is suitable to show the distribution of tropical crops like rice, tea, coffee, rubber and sugarcane.

(1 × 5 = 5)

Q. 5. Construct a cylindrical equal area projection for the world when the R.F. of the map is 1:300,000,000 taking latitudinal and longitudinal interval as 15º. [A]

Ans. Radius of the reduced earth

$$R = \frac{640,000,000}{300,000,000} = 2.1 \text{ cm}$$

Length of the equator 2ðR or

$$= \frac{2 \times 22 \times 2.1}{7} = 13.2 \text{ cm}$$

Interval along the equator

$$= \frac{13.2 \times 15^0}{360^0} = 0.55 \text{ cm}$$

Construction :

- Draw a circle of 2.1 cm radius;
- Mark the angles of 15º, 30º, 45º, 60º, 75º and 90º for both, northern and southern hemispheres;
- Draw a line of 13.2 cm and divide it into 24 equal parts at a distance of 0.55cm apart.
- This line represents the equator;
- Draw a line perpendicular to the equator at the point where 0° is meeting the circumference of the circle;
- Extend all the parallels equal to the length of the equator from the perpendicular line; and
- Complete the projection as shown below.

R.F. 1 : 300,000,000

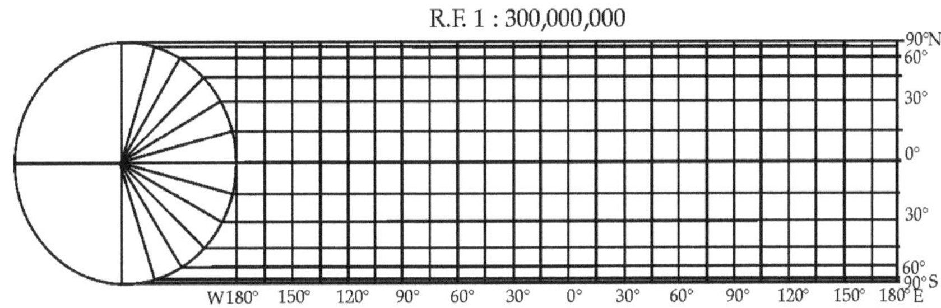

Q. 6. Draw a Mercator's Projection for the world map on the scale of 1:250,000,000 at 15º interval. [A]

Ans. Calculation :

Radius of the reduced earth is

$$R = \frac{250,000,000}{250,000,000} = 1" \text{ cm}$$

Length of the equator 2ðR or

$$R = \frac{1 \times 22 \times 2}{7} = 6.28" \text{ inch}$$

Interval along the equator

$$= \frac{6.28 \times 15^0}{360^0} = 0.26" \text{ inch}$$

Construction :

(i) Draw a line of 6.28" inches representing the equator as EQ :

(ii) Divide it into 24 equal parts. Determine the length of each division using the following.

$$\text{Formula} = \frac{\text{Length of Equator} \times \text{Interval}}{360}$$

(iv) Calculate the distance for latitude with the help of the table given below:
Latitude Distance 15° 0.25 x 1= 0.25″ inch 30° and so on.

Projection shown below :

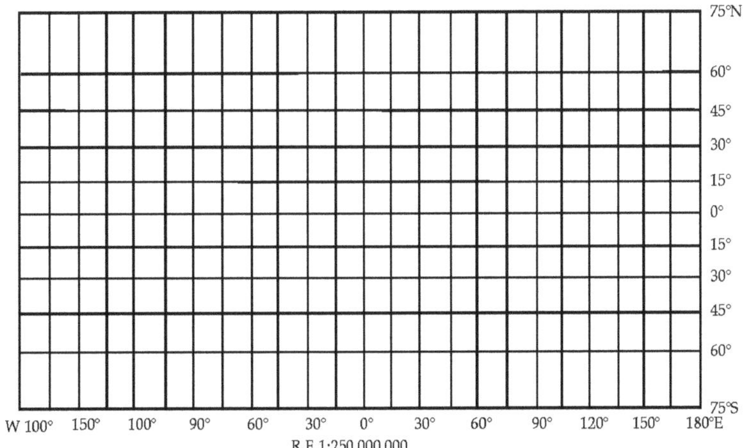

R.F. 1:250,000,000

NCERT CORNER

(A) Multiple choice questions :

Q. 1. A map projection least suitable for the world map :

(a) Mercator
(b) Simple Cylindrical
(c) Conical
(d) All the above

Ans. (c) Conical .

Q. 2. A map projection that is neither the equal area nor the correct shape and even the directions are also incorrect :

(a) Simple Conical
(b) Polar zenithal
(c) Mercator
(d) Cylindrical

Ans. (a) Simple Conical .

Q. 3. A map projection having correct direction and correct shape but area greatly exaggerated polewards is :

(a) Cylindrical Equal Area
(b) Mercator
(c) Conical
(d) All the above

Ans. (b) Mercator.

Q. 4. When the source of light is placed at the centre of the globe, the resultant projection is called :

(a) Orthographic
(b) Stereographic
(c) Gnomonic
(d) All the above

Ans. (c) Gnomonic.

(B) Answer the following questions in about 30 words :

Q. 1. Describe the elements of map projection.

Ans. The elements of map projection are :

(i) Reduced Earth : A model of the earth is represented by the help of a reduced scale on a flat sheet of paper. This model is called the "reduced earth".

(ii) Parallels of Latitude : These are the circles running round the globe parallel to the equator and maintaining uniform distance from the poles. Each parallel lies wholly in its plane which is at right angle to the axis of the earth. They are not of equal length.

(iii) Meridians of Longitude : These are semi-circles drawn in north-south direction from one pole to the other, and the two opposite meridians make a complete circle, *i.e.* circumference of the globe. Each meridian lies wholly in its plane, but all intersect at right angle along the axis of the globe.

(iv) Global Property : In preparing a map projection the following basic properties of the global surface are to be preserved by using one or the other methods.

Q. 2. What do you mean by global property?

Ans. Global Property: In preparing a map projection the following basic properties of the global surface are to be preserved by using one or the other methods :

(i) Distance between any given points of a region;
(ii) Shape of the region;
(iii) Size or area of the region in accuracy;
(iv) Direction of any one point of the region bearing to another point.

Q. 3. Not a single map projection represents the globe truly. Why?

Ans. Not a single map projection represents the globe truly because distortion in some form or the other is inevitable. To avoid this distortion, various methods have been devised and many types of projections are drawn. When the shape of the globe changes, certain inaccuracy comes in. thus, it can be rightly said that not a single map projection represents the globe truly.

Q. 4. How is the area kept equal in cylindrical equal area projection?

Ans. The area is kept equal in cylindrical area projection as both the parallels and meridians are projected as straight lines intersecting one another at right angles.

Q. 5. Differentiate between Developable and non-developable surfaces.

Ans.

S.No.	Developable Surfaces	Non-Developable Surfaces
1.	A developable surface is one, which can be flattened, and on which, a network of latitude and longitude can be projected.	A non-developable surface is one, which cannot be flattened without shrinking, breaking or creasing.
2.	A cylinder, a cone and a plane have the property of developable surface.	A globe or spherical surface has the property of non-developable surface.

Q. 6. Differentiate between Homolographic and orthographic projections.

Ans.

S.No.	Homolographic Projections	Orthographic Projections
1.	A projection in which the network of latitudes and longitudes is developed in such a way that every graticule on the map is equal in area to the corresponding graticule on the globe.	A projection in which the correct shape of a given area of the earth's surface is preserved.
2.	It is also known as the equal-area projection.	The shape is generally maintained at the cost of the correctness of area.

Q. 7. Differentiate between Normal and oblique projections .

Ans.

S.No.	Normal Projection	Oblique Projection
1.	If the developable surface touches the globe at the Equator, it is called the normal projection.	If the projection is tangential to a point between the pole and the equator, it is called the oblique projection.

Q. 8. Differentiate between Parallels of latitude and meridians of longitude.

Ans.

S.No.	Parallels of Latitude	Meridians of Longitude
1.	Lines of latitude are often referred to as parallels.	Lines of longitudes are often referred to as meridians.
2.	It divides the earth into northern hemisphere and southern hemisphere.	It divides the earth into eastern hemisphere and western hemisphere.
3.	0° latitude is called Equator.	0° longitude is called Prime Meridian.

(C) Answer the following questions in about 125 words :

Q. 1. Discuss the criteria used for classifying map projection and state the major characteristics of each type of projection.

Ans. Map Projections may be classified on the following bases :

(i) Drawing Techniques : On the basis of method of construction, projections are generally classified into perspective, non-perspective and conventional or mathematical. Perspective projections can be drawn taking the help of a source of light by projecting the image of a network of parallels and meridians of a globe on developable surface. Non–perspective projections are developed without the help of a source of light or casting shadow on surfaces, which can be flattened. Mathematical or conventional projections are those, which are derived by mathematical computation, and formulae and have little relations with the projected image.

(ii) Developable Surface : A developable surface is one, which can be flattened, and on which, a network of latitude and longitude can be projected. A non-developable surface is one, which cannot be flattened without shrinking, breaking or creasing. A globe or spherical surface has the property of non-developable surface whereas a cylinder, a cone and a plane have the property of developable surface. On the basis of nature of developable surface, the projections are classified as cylindrical, conical and zenithal projections.

(iii) Global Properties : The correctness of area, shape, direction and distances are the four major global properties to be preserved in a map. But none of the projections can maintain all these properties simultaneously. Therefore, according to specific need, a projection can be drawn so that the desired quality may be retained. Thus, on the basis of global properties, projections are classified into equal area, orthomorphic, azimuthal and equi-distant projections.

(iv) Source of Light : On the basis of location of source of light, projections may be classified as gnomonic, stereographic and orthographic. Gnomonic projection is obtained by putting the light at the centre of the globe. Stereographic projection is drawn when the source of light is placed at the periphery of the globe at a point diametrically opposite to the point at which the plane surface touches the globe. Orthographic projection is drawn when the source of light is placed at infinity from the globe, opposite to the point at which the plane surface touches the globe.

Q. 2. Which map projection is very useful for navigational purposes? Explain the properties and limitations of this projection?

Ans. Mercator's Projection is very useful for navigational purposes. A Dutch cartographer Mercator Gerardus Karmer developed this projection in 1569. The projection is based on mathematical formulae. So, it is an orthomorphic projection in which the correct shape is maintained.

Properties of Mercator's projections are :

(i) All parallels and meridians are straight lines and they intersect each other at right angles.

(ii) All parallels have the same length which is equal to the length of equator.

(iii) All meridians have the same length and equal spacing. But they are longer than the corresponding meridian on the globe.

(iv) Spacing between parallels increases towards the pole.

(v) Scale along the equator is correct as it is equal to the length of the equator on the globe; but other parallels are longer than the corresponding parallel on the globe; hence the scale is not correct along them. For example, the 30º parallel is 1.154 times longer than the corresponding parallel on the globe.

(vi) Shape of the area is maintained, but at the higher latitudes distortion takes place.

(vii) The shape of small countries near the equator is truly preserved while it increases towards poles.

(viii) It is an azimuthal projection.

(ix) This is an orthomorphic projection as scale along the meridian is equal to the scale along the parallel.

Limitations of Mercator's projections are :

(i) There is greater exaggeration of scale along the parallels and meridians in high latitudes. As a result, size of the countries near the pole is highly exaggerated. For example, the size of Greenland equals to the size of USA, whereas it is 1/10th of USA.

(ii) Poles in this projection cannot be shown as 90º parallel and meridian touching them are infinite.

Q. 3. Discuss the main properties of conical projection with one standard parallel and describe its major limitations.

Ans. A conical projection is one, which is drawn by projecting the image of the graticule of a globe on a developable cone, which touches the globe along a parallel of latitude called the standard parallel. As the cone touches the globe located along AB, the position of this parallel on the globe coinciding with that on the cone is taken as the standard parallel. The length of other parallels on either side of this parallel are distorted.

Properties of Conical Projection :

(i) All the parallels are arcs of concentric circle and are equally spaced.

(ii) All meridians are straight lines merging at the pole. The meridians intersect the parallels at right angles.

(iii) The scale along all meridians is true, i.e. distances along the meridians are accurate.

(iv) An arc of a circle represents the pole.

(v) The scale is true along the standard parallel but exaggerated away from the standard parallel.

(vi) Meridians become closer to each other towards the pole.

(vii) This projection is neither equal area nor orthomorphic.

Limitations of conical projection :

(i) It is not suitable for a world map due to extreme distortions in the hemisphere opposite the one in which the standard parallel is selected.

(ii) Even within the hemisphere, it is not suitable for representing larger areas as the distortion along the pole and near the equator is larger.

Project Work

Q. 1. Prepare graticule for a Cylindrical Equal Area Projection for the world when R.F. is1: 150,000,000 and the interval is 15º apart.

Ans. Construction :

Radius of reduced Earth :

$$= \frac{6,40,000,000}{150,000,000} = 4.26 \text{ cm}$$

(round off to 4.3 cm)

Draw a circle of 4.3 cm radius :

Mark the angles of 15°, 30 °, 45°, 60 °, 75° and 90° for both, northern and southern hemispheres.

Length of the Equator = $2\pi r$

$$= 2 \times \frac{22}{7} \times 4.3 = 27.03 \text{ cm}$$

Draw a line of 27.03 cm.

Divide it into 24 equal parts at a distance of 1.262 cm apart. This line represents the Equator.

Draw a perpendicular to the Equator at the point where 0° is meeting the circumference of the circle.

Extend all the parallels equal to the length of the Equator from the perpendicular line, and complete the projection.

R.F. 1 : 300,000,000

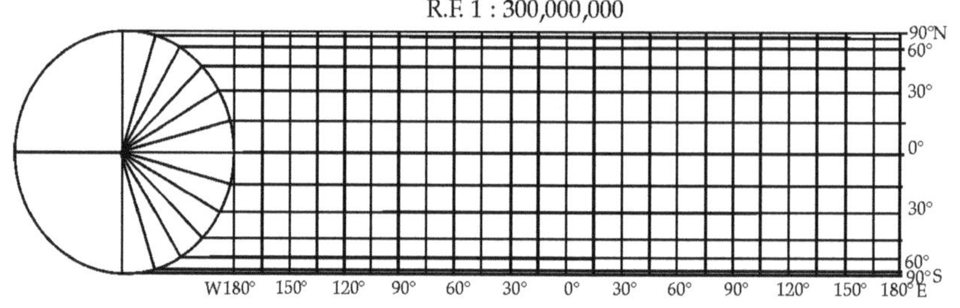

Q. 2. Draw a Mercator Projection for the world map when the R.F. is 1:400,000,000 and the interval between the latitude and longitude is 20º.

Ans. Calculation :

$$\frac{250,000,000}{400,000,000} = 0.625''$$

Radius of the reduced earth R is 0.625″ is 1 : 400,000,000

Length of the equator $2\pi r$ or

$$2 \times \frac{22}{7} \times 0.625$$

= 3.93″ inches

Interval along the equator

$$\frac{3.93 \times 20}{360^{\circ}} = 0.218''$$

Construction :

- Draw a line of 3.93″ inches representing the equator as EQ.
- Divide it into 24 equal parts. Determine the length of each division using the following formula. Length of the equator multiplied by interval divided by 360°.
- Calculate the distance for latitude with the help of the table given below :

Latitude	**distance**
20 °	218″x 0.625=0.136 inch
40°	0.437″x 0.625=0.273 inch

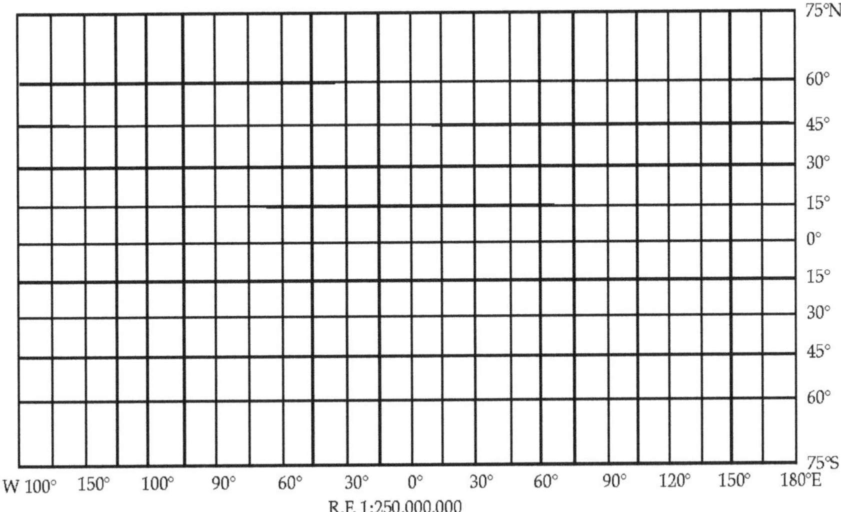

R.F. 1:250,000,000

UNIT-II

Topographic and Weather Maps

CHAPTER

5 TOPOGRAPHICAL MAPS

Syllabus

> *Topographical Maps, Methods of Relief Representation, Contours, Basic Features of Contour Lines. Types of Slope.*
> *Identification of Cultural Features from Topographical Sheets, Interpretation of Topographical Maps, Map Interpretation Procedure.*

TOPIC-1

Topographical Maps, Methods of Relief Representation, Contours, Basic Features of Contour Lines, Types of Slope.

Revision Notes

- The topographical maps are of utmost importance to geographers. They serve the purpose of base maps and are used to draw all the other maps.
- Topographical maps, also known as general purpose maps, are drawn at relatively large scales. These maps show important natural and cultural features such as relief, vegetation, water bodies, cultivated land, settlements, and transportation networks, etc. These maps are prepared and published by the National Mapping Organisation of each country.
- For example, the Survey of India prepares the topographical maps in India for the entire country.
- The topographical maps in India are prepared in two series, i.e. India and Adjacent Countries Series and The International Map Series of the World.
  - **India and Adjacent Countries Series :** The topographical maps of India are prepared on 1 : 10,00,000, 1 : 250,000, 1 : 1,25,000, 1 : 50,000 and 1: 25,000 scale providing a latitudinal and longitudinal coverage of 4° x 4°, 1° x 1°, 30' x 30', 15' x 15' and 5' x 7' 30", respectively.
  - **International Map Series of the World :** Topographical Maps under International Map Series of the World are designed to produce standardised maps for the entire World on a scale of 1: 10,00,000 and 1:250,000.
  - **Reading of Topographical Maps :** The study of topographical maps is simple. It requires the reader to get acquainted with the legend, conventional sign and the colours shown on the sheets.
  - **Methods of Relief Representation :**
- The elevation and depressions of the earth's surface are known as physical features or relief features of the earth. The map showing these features is called a relief map.
- A number of methods have been used to show the relief features of the Earth's surface on maps, over the years. These methods include hachure, hill shading, layer tints, benchmarks and spot heights and contours.
- Contours are imaginary lines joining places having the same elevation above mean sea level. A map showing the landform of an area by contours is called a contour map.
- The contour lines on a map provide a useful insight into the topography of an area.
- Contours are drawn at different vertical intervals (VI), like 20, 50, 100 metres above the mean sea level. It is known as contour interval.
- **Some of the basic features of contour lines are :**
  - A contour line is drawn to show places of equal heights.
  - Contour lines and their shapes represent the height and slope or gradient of the landform.

- Closely spaced contours represent steep slopes while widely spaced contours represent gentle slope.
- When two or more contour lines merge with each other, they represent features of vertical slopes such as cliffs or waterfalls.
- Two contours of different elevation usually do not cross each other.

➢ The slopes can broadly be classified into gentle, steep, concave, convex and irregular or undulating.

- **Gentle Slope :** When the degree or angle of slope of a feature is very low, the slope will be gentle. The contours representing this type of slope are far apart.
- **Steep Slope :** When the degree or angle of slope of a feature is high and the contours are closely spaced, they indicate steep slope.
- **Concave Slope :** A slope with a gentle gradient in the lower parts of a relief feature and steep in its upper parts is called the concave slope. Contours in this type of slope are widely spaced in the lower parts and are closely spaced in the upper parts.
- **Convex Slope :** Unlike concave slope, the convex slope is fairly gentle in the upper part and steep in the lower part. As a result, the contours are widely spaced in the upper parts and are closely spaced in the lower parts.

➢ **The various types of landforms are :**

- **Conical Hill :** It rises almost uniformly from the surrounding land. A conical hill with uniform slope and narrow top is represented by concentric contours spaced almost at regular intervals.
- **Plateau :** A widely stretched flat–topped high land, with relatively steeper slopes, rising above the adjoining plain or sea is called a plateau.

➢ A geomorphic feature lying between two hills or ridges and formed as a result of the lateral erosion by a river or a glacier is called a valley. The various types of valleys are:

- **'V'-shaped Valley :** It resembles the letter V. A V-shaped valley occurs in mountainous areas .The lowermost part of the V–shaped valley is shown by the innermost contour line with very small gap between its two sides and the lowest value of the contour is assigned to it. The contour value increases with uniform intervals for all other contour lines outward.
- **'U' – shaped Valley :** A U–shaped valley is formed by strong lateral erosion of glaciers at high altitudes. The flat wide bottom and steep sides makes it resemble the letter 'U'. The contour value increases with uniform intervals for all other contour lines outward.
- **Gorges :** In high altitudes, gorges form in the areas where the vertical erosion by river is more prominent than the lateral erosion. A gorge is represented by very closely-spaced contour lines on a map with the innermost contour showing small gap between its two sides.
- **Spur :** A tongue of land, projecting from higher ground into the lower is called a spur. It is also represented by Vshaped contours but in the reverse manner.
- **Cliff :** It is a very steep or almost perpendicular face of landform. On a map, a cliff may be identified by the way the contours run very close to one another, ultimately merging into one.
- **Waterfalls and Rapids :** A sudden and more or less perpendicular descent of water from a considerable height in the bed of a river is called a waterfall. Sometimes, a waterfall succeeds or precedes with a cascading stream forming rapids upstream or downstream of a waterfall. The contours representing a waterfall merge into one another while crossing a river stream and the rapids are shown by relatively distant contour lines on a map.

Know the Terms

➢ **Contours :** Imaginary lines joining all the points of equal elevation or altitude above mean sea level. They are also called "level lines".

➢ **Contour Interval :** Interval between two successive contours. It is also known as vertical interval, usually written as V. I. Generally, it is constant for a given map.

➢ **Cross-section :** A side view of the ground cut vertically along a straight line. It is also known as a section or profile.

➢ **Hachures :** Small straight lines drawn on the map along the direction of maximum slope, running across the contours. They give an idea about the differences in the slope of the ground.

➢ **Topographic Map :** A map of a small area drawn on a large scale depicting detailed surface features both natural and man made. Relief in this map is shown by contours.

➢ **Relief map :** The elevation and depressions of the earth's surface are known as physical features or relief features of the earth. The map showing these features is called a relief map.

➢ **Contour map :** A map showing the landform of an area by contours is called a contour map.

➢ **Concave slope :** A slope with a gentle gradient in the lower parts of a relief feature and steep in its upper parts is called concave slope.

➢ **Convex slope :** It is fairly gentle in the upper part and steep in the lower part. As a result, the contours are widely spaced in the upper parts and are closely spaced in the lower parts.

➢ **Conical hills :** It rises almost uniformly from the surrounding land. A conical hill with uniform slope and narrow top is represented by concentric contours spaced almost at regular.

Multiple Choice Questions (1 mark each)

Q. 1. Source of water, provision of food, nature of relief, nature and character of occupation and defence are the factors that determine the site of : [A]

(a) settlements
(b) dwellings
(c) developments
(d) organisations

Ans. (a) settlements 1

Q. 2. The elevation and depressions of the earth's surface are known as ___________features of the earth. [U]

(a) political
(b) physical
(c) chemical
(d) interval

Ans. (b) physical 1

Q. 3. The topographical maps in India for the entire country is prepared by the : [U]

(a) Survey of India
(b) Survey in India
(c) Survey by India
(d) Survey through India

Ans. (a) Survey of India 1

Very Short Answer Type Questions (1 mark each)

Q. 1. What do you know about topographical maps? [A]

Ans. Topographical maps, also known as general purpose maps, are drawn at relatively large scales. These maps show important natural and cultural features such as relief, vegetation, water bodies, cultivated land, settlements, and transportation networks, etc. These maps are prepared and published by the National Mapping Organisation of each country. 1

Answering Tip

- The topographic map is a two-dimensional representation of the earth's three-dimensional landscape.

Q. 2. Define the term 'Contour'. [A]

Ans. Imaginary lines joining all the points of equal elevation or altitude above mean sea level. They are also called "level lines". 1

Q. 3. What are contour intervals? [R]

Ans. Interval between two successive contours. It is also known as vertical interval, usually written as V. I. Generally, it is constant for a given map. 1

Q. 4. Define the term 'Contour Lines'. [R]

Ans. Contour lines are the imaginary lines joining all the points of equal elevation or altitude above the sea level. They are also known as 'level lines'. 1

Q. 5. What are Hachure? [A]

Ans. Small straight lines drawn on the map along the direction of maximum slope, running across the contours. They give an idea about the differences in the slope of the ground. 1

Answering Tip

- They show orientation of slope, and by their thickness and overall density; they provide a general sense of steepness.

Q. 6. Which organisation in India prepares the topographical maps? [U]

Ans. The Survey of India prepares the topographical maps. 1

Q. 7. Why are the international map series of the world designed? [A]

Ans. Topographical Maps under International Map Series of the World are designed to produce standardised maps for the entire World on a scale of 1 : 10,00,000 and 1 : 250,000. 1

Q. 8. Differentiate between gentle slope and steep slope. [R]

Ans. When the degree or angle of slope of a feature is very low, the slope will be gentle. The contours representing this type of slope are far apart.

Whereas, when the degree or angle of slope of a feature is high and the contours are closely spaced, they indicate steep slope. **(½ + ½ = 1)**

Q. 9. What do you know about the contours of concave slope? [U]

Ans. Contours in this type of slope are widely spaced in the lower parts and are closely spaced in the upper parts. 1

Q. 10. What do you know about the contours of convex slope? [U]

Ans. In the convex slope the contours are widely spaced in the upper parts and are closely spaced in the lower parts. 1

Answering Tip

- Convex slope is a geographical feature with inconstant slopes.

Q. 11. What do you know about the contour lines of waterfall and rapids? [A]

Ans. A sudden and more or less perpendicular descent of water from a considerable height in the bed of a river is called a waterfall. Sometimes, a waterfall succeeds or precedes with a cascading stream forming rapids upstream or downstream of a waterfall. The contours representing a waterfall merge into one another while crossing a river stream and the rapids are shown by relatively distant contour lines on a map. 1

Q. 12. How are the contour lines of the plateau placed? U

Ans. The contour lines representing a plateau are normally close spaced at the margins with the innermost contour showing wide gap between its two sides. 1

Short Answer Type Questions

(3 marks each)

Q. 1. Differentiate between topographical maps and relief maps. A

Ans.

S.No.	Topographical maps	Relief maps
1.	Topographical maps, also known as general purpose maps, are drawn at relatively large scales. These maps show important natural and cultural features such as relief, vegetation, water bodies, cultivated land, settlements, and transportation networks, etc. These maps are prepared and published by the National Mapping Organisation of each country.	The elevation and depressions of the earth's surface are known as physical features or relief features of the earth. The map showing these features is called a relief map.
2.	They are also called general purpose map.	They are also known as specific purpose map.
3.	These are drawn on relatively larger scale.	These are drawn on relatively smaller scale.

(1 × 3 = 3)

Q. 2. Differentiae between vertical interval and horizontal distance. A

Ans.

S.No.	Vertical Interval	Horizontal Distance
1.	Interval between two successive contours is called vertical interval.	The distance between two contours horizontally is known as horizontal distance.
2.	The vertical interval between the two successive contour lines remains constant.	The distance varies from place to place.
3.	It is expressed as VI (Vertical Interval).	It is also known as horizontal equivalent(HE).

(1 × 3 = 3)

Answering Tip

- Vertical Interval is the vertical distance between two contour lines. Horizontal distance is the actual distance between two points on two contour lines.

Q. 3. Mention any three features of contours. R

Ans. Some basic features of contour lines are :

(i) A contour line is drawn to show places of equal heights.

(ii) Contour lines and their shapes represent the height and slope or gradient of the landform.

(iii) Closely spaced contours represent steep slopes while widely spaced contours represent gentle slope.

(iv) When two or more contour lines merge with each other, they represent features of vertical slopes such as cliffs or waterfalls.

(v) Two contours of different elevation usually do not cross each other. **(Any Three)(1×3=3)**

Answering Tip

- Always remember, no two lines of the contour meet on intersect each other in any case.

Long Answer Type Questions

(5 marks each)

Q. 1. What are the steps involved in drawing a cross-section from their contours in different topographical landforms? R

Ans. The flowing steps are involved in drawing a cross-section from their contours in different topographical landforms :

(i) Draw a straight line cutting across the contours on the map and mark it as AB.

(ii) Take a strip of white paper or graph and place its edge along the AB line.

(iii) Mark the position and value of every contour that cuts the line AB.

(iv) Choose a suitable vertical scale, eg ½ cm =100 metres, to draw horizontal lines parallel to each other and equal to the length of AB. The number of such lines should be equal or more than the total contour lines.

(v) Mark the appropriate values corresponding to the contour values along the vertical of the cross-section. The numbering may be started with the lowest value represented by the contours.

(vi) Now place the edge of the marked paper along the horizontal line at the bottom line of the cross-section in such a way that AB of the paper corresponds to the AB of the map and mark the contour points.

(vii) Draw perpendiculars from AB line, intersecting contour lines, to the corresponding line at the cross-section base.

(viii) Smoothly join all the points marked on different lines at the cross section base. **5**

TOPIC-2

Identification of Cultural Features from Topographical Sheets, Interpretation of Topographical Maps, Map Interpretation Procedure

Revision Notes

➢ Settlements, buildings, roads and railways are important cultural features shown on topographical sheets through conventional signs, symbols and colours.
- Distribution of settlements:

➢ Four types of rural settlements may be identified on the map
- Compact
- Scattered
- Linear
- Circular

➢ Similarly, urban centres may also be distinguished as
- Cross-road town
- Nodal point
- Market centre
- Hill station
- Coastal resort centre
- Port
- Manufacturing centre with suburban villages or satellite towns
- Capital town
- Religious centre

➢ Various factors determine the site of settlements like
- Source of water
- Provision of food
- Nature of relief
- Nature and character of occupation
- Defence

➢ Density of settlement is directly related to food supply. Sometimes, village settlements form alignments, *i.e.*, they are spread along a river valley, road, embankment, coastline – these are called linear settlements.
- **Transport and Communication Pattern:** Relief, population, size and resource development pattern of an area directly influence the means of transport and communication and their density. Means of transport and communication provide useful information about the area shown on the map.

➢ Knowledge of map language and sense of direction are essential in reading and interpreting topo-sheets.

➢ You must first look for the north line and the scale of the map and orient yourself accordingly.

➢ You must have a thorough knowledge of the legends / key given in the map depicting various features. All topo-sheets contain a table showing conventional signs and symbols used in the map.

- Conventional signs and symbols are internationally accepted; so, anyone can read any map anywhere in the world without knowing the language of that particular country.
- A topographic sheet is usually interpreted under the following heads :
  - **Marginal Information :** It includes the topographical sheet number, its location, grid references, its extent in degrees and minutes, scale, the districts covered, etc.
  - **Relief of the Area :** The general topography of the area is studied to identify the plains, plateaus, hills or mountains along with peaks, ridges, spur and the general direction of the slope.
  - **Drainage of the Area :** The important rivers and their tributaries and the type and extent of valleys formed by them, the types of drainage pattern, i.e. dendritic, radial, ring, trellis, internal, etc.
  - **Land use :** It includes the use of land under different categories like natural vegetation and forest, agricultural, orchard, wasteland, industrial, etc. Facilities and services such as schools, colleges, hospitals, parks, airports, electric substations, etc.
  - **Transport and Communication :** The means of transportation include national or state highways, district roads, cart tracks, camel tracks, footpaths, railways, waterways, major communication lines, post offices, etc.
  - **Settlement :** Settlements are studied are rural settlement and urban settlement.
  - **Occupation :** The general occupation of the people of the area may be identified with the help of land use and the type of settlement. For example, in rural areas the main occupation of majority of the people is agriculture; in tribal regions, lumbering and primitive agriculture dominates and in coastal areas, fishing is practised. Similarly, in cities and towns, services and business appear to be the major occupations of the people.
- Map interpretation involves the study of factors that explain the causal relationship among several features shown on the map.
- **The following steps will help in map interpretation :**
  - Find out from the index number of the topographical sheet, the location of the area in India. Note the scale of the map and the contour interval, which will give the extent and general landform of the area.
  - Trace out the following features on tracing sheets: major landforms, drainage and water features, land use, settlement and transport pattern.
- Describe the distributional pattern of each of the features separately drawing attention to the most important aspect.
- Superimpose pairs of these maps and note down the relationship, if any, between the two patterns. For example, if a contour map is superimposed over a land use map, it provides the relationship between the degree of slope and the type of the land used.

Know the Terms

- **Linear settlements :** Sometimes, village settlements form alignments, i.e. they are spread along a river valley, road, embankment, coastline – these are called linear settlements.

Multiple Choice Question (1 mark)

Q. 1. The density of settlement is directly related to: A

(a) water supply
(b) food supply
(c) air supply
(d) fuel supply

Ans. (b) food supply 1

Very Short Answer Type Questions (1 mark each)

Q. 1. Define the term 'Linear Settlement'. R

Ans. Sometimes, village settlements form alignments, i.e. they are spread along a river valley, road, embankment, coastline – these are called linear settlements. 1

Q. 2. Name any two different settlements shown on a topographic sheet. A

Ans. The different settlements shown on a topographic sheet are: compact , scattered, linear, circular. Urban settlements are distinguished as : cross-road town, nodal point , market centre, hill station, coastal resort centre, port , manufacturing centre with suburban villages or satellite towns, capital town and religious centre.

(Any Two) (½+ ½ =1)

Short Answer Type Questions (3 marks each)

Q. 1. How can the topographical sheets be interpreted? [A]

Ans. Knowledge of map language and sense of direction are essential in reading and interpreting topo-sheets .You must first look for the northline and the scale of the map and orient yourself accordingly. You must have a thorough knowledge of the legends / key given in the map depicting various features. Thorough knowledge of the legends /key given in the map depicting various features is a must. All topo-sheets contain a table showing conventional signs and symbols used in the map. It is important to be acquainted with conventional symbols, signs and colours. 3

Long Answer Type Questions (5 marks each)

Q. 1. Explain the heads under which the topographical sheet is interpreted. [A]

OR

Under which heads are topographical maps explained?

Ans. A topographic sheet is usually interpreted under the following heads:

(i) Marginal Information : It includes the topographical sheet number, its location, grid references, its extent in degrees and minutes, scale, the districts covered, etc.

(ii) Relief of the Area : The general topography of the area is studied to identify the plains, plateaus, hills or mountains along with peaks, ridges, spur and the general direction of the slope. These features are studied under the following heads :

(a) Hill : With concave, convex, steep or gentle slope and shape.

(b) Plateau : Whether it is broad , narrow, flat, undulating or dissected.

(c) Plain : Its types, *i.e.,* alluvial, glacial, karst, coastal, marshy, etc.

(d) Mountain : General elevation, peak, passes, etc.

(e) Drainage of the Area : The important rivers and their tributaries and the type and extent of valleys formed by them, the types of drainage pattern, i.e. dendritic, radial, ring, trellis, internal, etc.

(iii) Land Use: It includes the use of land under different categories like : Natural vegetation and forest (which part of the area is forested, whether it is dense forest or thin, and the categories of forest found there like Reserved, Protected, Classified / Unclassified).

(iv) Agricultural, orchard, wasteland, industrial, etc. Facilities and Services such as schools, colleges, hospitals, parks, airports, electric substations, etc.

(v) Transport and Communication : The means of transportation include national or state highways, district roads, cart tracks, camel tracks, footpaths, railways, waterways, major communication lines, post offices, etc.

(vi) Settlement : Settlements are studied under the following heads :

(a) Rural Settlements : The types and patterns of rural settlements, *i.e.,* compact, semi-compact, dispersed, linear, etc.

(b) Urban Settlements : Type of urban settlements and their functions, *i.e.,* capital cities, administrative towns, religious towns, port towns, hill stations, etc.

(vii) Occupation : The general occupation of the people of the area may be identified with the help of land use and the type of settlement. For example, in rural areas the main occupation of majority of the people is agriculture; in tribal regions, lumbering and primitive agriculture dominates and in coastal areas, fishing is practised. Similarly, in cities and towns, services and business appear to be the major occupations of the people. 5

Q. 2. What is map interpretation? Explain the steps that help in map interpretation? [U]

Ans. Map interpretation involves the study of factors that explain the causal relationship among several features shown on the map. The following steps will help in map interpretation:

(i) Find out from the index number of the topographical sheet, the location of the area in India. This would give an idea of the general characteristics of the major and minor physiographic divisions of the area. Note the scale of the map and the contour interval, which will give the extent and general landform of the area.

(ii) Trace out the following features on tracing sheets.

(a) Major landforms – as shown by contours and other graphical features.

(b) Drainage and water features – the main river and its important tributaries.

(c) Land use – *i.e.,* forest, agricultural land, wastes, sanctuary, park, school, etc.

(d) Settlement and Transport pattern.

(iii) Describe the distributional pattern of each of the features separately drawing attention to the most important aspect.

(iv) Superimpose pairs of these maps and note down the relationship, if any, between the two patterns. For example, if a contour map is superimposed over a land use map, it provides the relationship between the degree of slope and the type of the land used.

(v) Aerial photographs and satellite imageries of the same area and of the same scale can also be compared with the topographical map to update the information. 5

Answering Tip

- Map interpretation is the process of looking at a map and figuring out what the symbols represent.

NCERT CORNER

(A) Answer the following questions in about 30 words :

Q. 1. What are topographical maps?

Ans. Topographical maps, also known as general purpose maps, are drawn at relatively large scales. These maps show important natural and cultural features such as relief, vegetation, water bodies, cultivated land, settlements, and transportation networks, etc. These maps are prepared and published by the National Mapping Organisation of each country.

Q. 2. Name the organisation which prepares the topographical maps of India.

Ans. Tropographical maps show important natural and cultural features such as relief, vegetation, water bodies, cultivated land, settlements and transportation networks, etc. These maps are prepared and published by the National Mapping Organisation of each country. The Survey of India prepares the topographical maps in India for the entire country.

Q. 3. Which are the commonly used scales for mapping our country used by the Survey of India?

Ans. The commonly used scales for mapping our country used by the Survey of India are:

(i) **India and Adjacent Countries Series :** The topographical maps of India are prepared on 1 : 10,00,000, 1 : 250,000, 1 : 1,25,000, 1 : 50,000 and 1 : 25,000 scale providing a latitudinal and longitudinal coverage of 4° × 4°, 1° × 1°, 30' × 30', 15' × 15' and 5' × 7' 30", respectively.

(ii) **International Map Series of the World :** Topographical Maps under International Map Series of the World are designed to produce standardised maps for the entire World on a scale of 1 : 10,00,000 and 1 : 250,000.

Q. 4. What are contours?

Ans. *Contours* are imaginary lines joining places having the same elevation above mean sea level. In other words, these are imaginary lines joining all the points of equal elevation or altitude above the mean sea level. They are also called 'level lines'.

Q. 5. What does the spacing of contours indicate?

Ans. The spacing of contours represents slope. Closely spaced contours represent slope and widely spaced contours represent steep slopes.

Q. 6. What are conventional signs?

Ans. Conventional signs are internally determined standard symbols, signs and colours which are used to depict settlements , buildings , roads and railways , etc. conventional signs are internally accepted so that anyone can read any map anywhere in the world without knowing the language of that particular country.

(C) Write short notes on :

Q. 1. Contours .

Ans. Contours are imaginary lines joining places having the same elevation above mean sea level. A map showing the landform of an area by contours is called a contour map. The method of showing relief features through contour is very useful and versatile. The contour lines on a map provide a useful insight into the topography of an area. A contour line is drawn to show places of equal heights. Contour lines and their shapes represent the height and slope or gradient of the landform.

Q. 2. 'Marginal Information' in Topographical sheets.

Ans. Marginal Information includes the topographical sheet number, its location, grid references, its extent in degrees and minutes, scale, the districts covered, etc. It provides information related to what exactly a topographical sheet is showing. Both marginal information and marginal sheet are interrelated.

Q. 3. The Survey of India.

Ans. The Survey of India prepares the topographical maps in India for the entire country. Topographical maps under India and Adjacent Countries Series were prepared by the Survey of India till the coming into existence of Delhi Survey Conference in 1937. Henceforth, the preparation of maps for the adjoining countries was abandoned and the Survey of India confined itself to prepare and publish the topographical maps for India as per the specifications laid down for the International Map Series of the World. However, the Survey of India for the topographical maps under the new series retained the numbering system and the layout plan of the abandoned India and Adjacent Countries Series.

Q. 4. Explain what is meant by 'map interpretation' and what procedure is followed for its interpretation.

Ans. Knowledge of map language and sense of direction are essential in reading and interpreting topo-sheets. Map interpretation involves the study of factors that explain the causal relationship among several features shown on the map. For example, the distribution of natural vegetation and cultivated land can be better understood against the background of landform and drainage. Likewise, the distribution of settlements can be examined in association with the levels of transport network system and the nature of topography.

The following steps will help in map interpretation :

(i) Find out from the index number of the topographical sheet, the location of the area in India. This would give an idea of the general characteristics of the major and minor physiographic divisions of the area. Note the scale of the map and the contour interval, which will give the extent and general landform of the area.

(ii) Find the scale on the map and the contour interval , which will give the extent and general landform of the area.

(iii) Trace out the following features on tracing sheets.

(a) Major landforms – as shown by contours and other graphical features.

(b) Drainage and water features – the main river and its important tributaries.

(c) Land use – *i.e.*, forest, agricultural land, wastes, sanctuary, park, school, etc.

(d) Settlement and Transport pattern.

(iv) Describe the distributional pattern of each of the features separately drawing attention to the most important aspect.

(v) Superimpose pairs of these maps and note down the relationship, if any, between the two patterns. For example, if a contour map is superimposed over a land use map, it provides the relationship between the degree of slope and the type of the land used.

Q. 5. If you are interpreting the cultural features from a topographical sheet, what information would you like to seek and how would you derive this information? Discuss with the help of suitable examples.

Ans. Settlements, buildings, roads and railways are important cultural features shown on topographical sheets through conventional signs, symbols and colours. The location and pattern of distribution of different features help in understanding the area shown on the map.

(i) Distribution Of Settlements : It can be seen in the map through its site, location pattern, alignment and density. The nature and causes of various settlement patterns may be clearly understood by comparing the settlement map with the contour map. Various factors determine the site of settlements like source of water , provision of food ,nature of relief ,nature and character of occupation and defence. In the case of an urban settlement, a cross-road town assumes a fan-shaped pattern, the houses being arranged along the roadside and the crossing being at the heart of the town and the main market place. In a nodal town, the roads radiate in all directions.

Transport and Communication Pattern : Relief, population, size and resource development pattern of an area directly influence the means of transport and communication and their density. These are depicted through conventional signs and symbols. Means of transport and communication provide useful information about the area shown on the map.

Settlements, occupation, means of communication, transportation , land use pattern are some of the cultural features which are shown on topographical sheet using conventional signs, colours and symbols. The general occupation of the people of the area may be identified with the help of land use and the type of settlement. For example , in urban areas the main occupation of majority of the people is agriculture, in tribal regions, lumbering and primitive agriculture dominates and in coastal areas , fishing is practised. Similarly, in cities and towns, services and business appear to be the major occupation of the people.

Q. 6. Draw the conventional signs and symbols for the following features :

(i) International Boundary

(ii) Bench Mark

(iii) Villages

(iv) Metalled Road

(v) Footpath with bridges

(vi) Places of Worship

(vii) Railway line.

Ans.

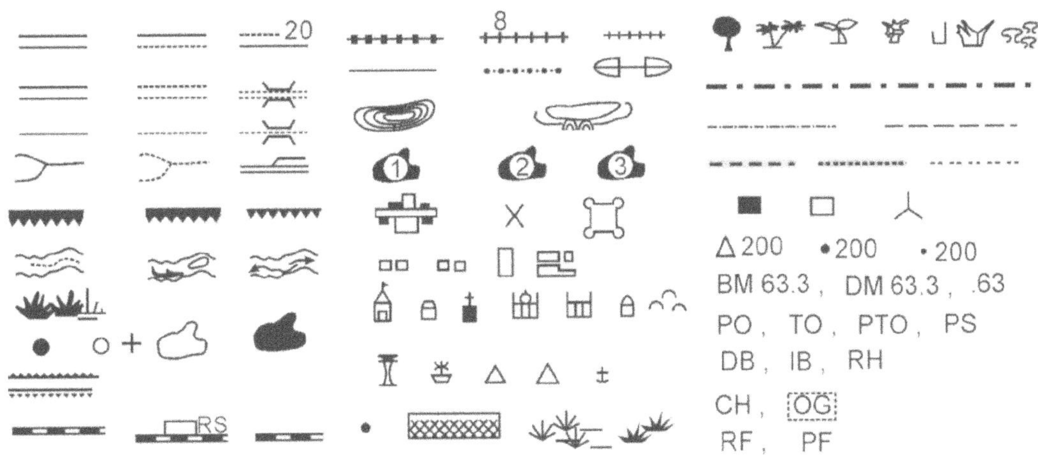

Project Work

Exercise A :

Q. 1. Study the contour pattern and answer the following questions :

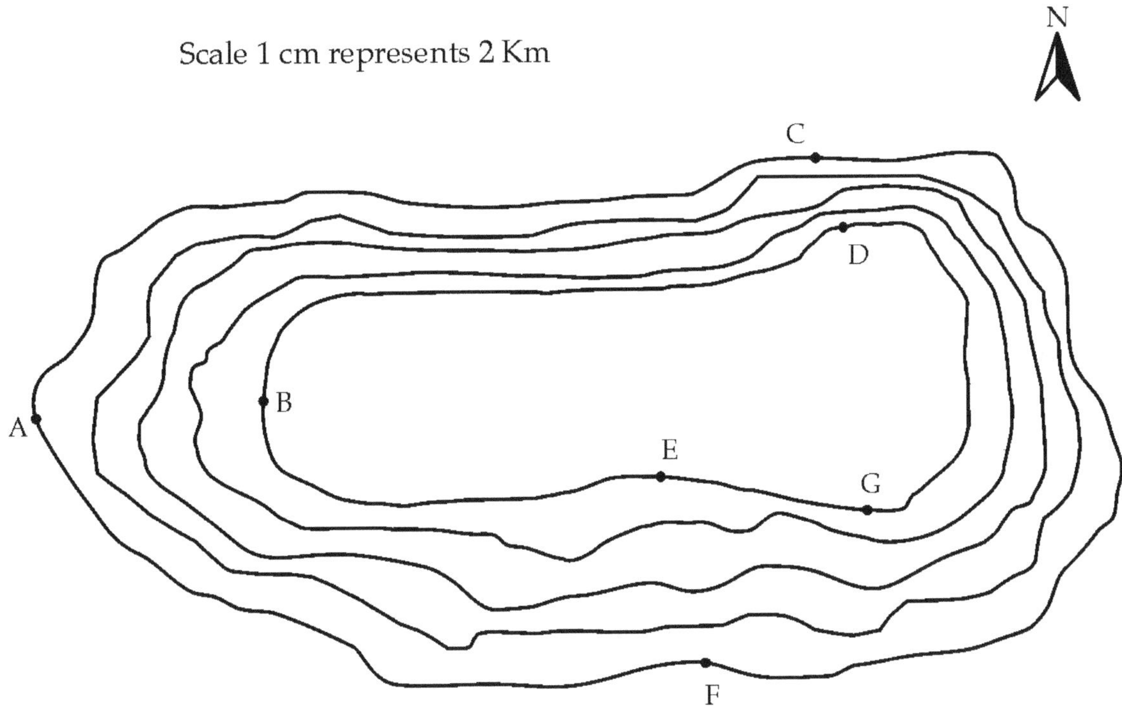

(i) Name the geographical feature formed by contours.

Ans. Plateau

Q. 2. Find out the contour interval in the map.

Ans. 100 metre.

Q. 3. Find out the map distance between E and F and convert it into ground distance.

Ans. 2 cm = 4 km on the ground.

Q. 4. Name the type of slope between A and B; C and D and E and F.

Ans. A and B Gentle Slope
C and D Steep Slope
E and F Gentle Slope .

Q. 5. Find out the direction of E, D and F from G.

Ans. From G, E is in West, D is in North and F is in South directions.

Exercise B :

Study the extract from the topographical sheet No. 63K/12, as shown in the figure below and answer the following questions :

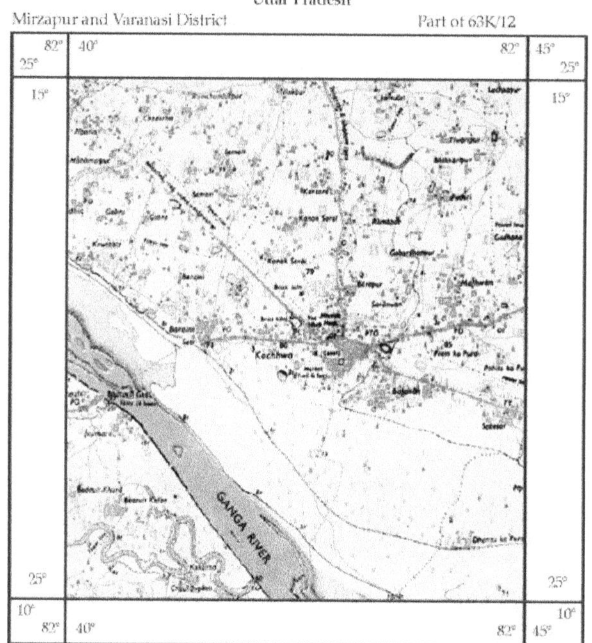

Q. 1. Convert 1:50,000 into a statement of scale.

Ans. 1 cm on the map is showing 50,000 cm on ground.

Q. 2. Name the major settlements of the area.

Ans. Kachhwa, Prem ka Pura, Bhatauli and Bahraini.

Q. 3. What is the direction of flow of the river Ganga.

Ans. North west to South east.

Q. 4. At which one of the banks of river Ganga, Bhatauli is located .

Ans. It is located in the middle of the River Ganga.

Q. 5. What is the pattern of rural settlements along the right bank of river Ganga?

Ans. The pattern of rural settlements is compact pattern.

Q. 6. Name the villages/settlements where Post Office/Post and Telegraph Office are located?

Ans. Villages indicating PO, and PTO have post office or post and telegraph office.

Q. 7. What does the yellow colour in the area refer to?

Ans. The yellow colour in the area refers to plains.

Q. 8. What means of transportation is used to cross the river by the people of Bhatauli village?

Ans. Boats are used by the people of Bhatauli village.

Exercise C :

Study the extract for topographical sheet 63K/12 shown in the figure given above and answer the following questions :

Q. 1. Give the height of the highest point on the map.

Ans. 208 mtrs.

Q. 2. River Jamtihwa Nadi is flowing through which quarter of the map?

Ans. It is flowing through the south east quarter of the map.

Q. 3. Which is the major settlement located in the east of the Kuardari Nala?

Ans. Bandhwa settlement.

Q. 4. What type of settlement does this area have?

Ans. Linear settlement .

Q. 5. Name the geographical feature represented by white patches in the middle of Sipu Nadi.

Ans. It is showing plains.

Q. 6. Name the two types of vegetation shown on part of the topographical sheet.

Ans. Tropical Deciduous vegetation.

Q. 7. What is the direction of the flow of the Kuardari?

Ans. South to North.

Q. 8. In which part of the sheet area is Lower Khajuri Dam located?

Ans. Khajuri Dam is located at the southern part.

CHAPTER

6 INTRODUCTION TO AERIAL PHOTOGRAPHS

Syllabus

> *Uses of Aerial Photographs, Advantages of Aerial Photographs, Types of Aerial Photographs.*
> *Geometry of an Aerial Photography, Difference between a Map and an Aerial Photography.*

TOPIC-1
Uses of Aerial Photographs, Advantages of Aerial Photographs, Types of Aerial Photographs

Quick Review

- The photographs taken from an aircraft or helicopter using a precision camera are termed aerial photographs.
- The photographs so obtained have been found to be indispensable tools in the topographical mapping and interpretation of the images of the objects.
- Aerial photographs are used in topographical mapping and interpretation. These two different uses have led to the development of photogrammetry and photo/image interpretation as two independent but related sciences.
  - **Photogrammetry :** It refers to the science and technology of making reliable measurements from aerial photographs. The principles used in photogrammetry facilitate precise measurements related to the length, breadth and height from such photographs. Hence, they are used as the data source for creating and updating topographic maps.
  - **Image Interpretation :** It is an art of identifying images of objects and judging their relative significance. The principles of image interpretation are applied to obtain qualitative information from the aerial photographs such as land use/land cover, topographical forms, soil types, etc.
- The basic advantages that aerial photographs offer over ground based observation are:
  - **Improved vantage point :** Aerial photography provides a bird's eye view of large areas, enabling us to see features of the earth surface in their spatial context.
  - **Time freezing ability :** An aerial photograph is a record of the surface features at an instance of exposure.
  - **Broadened Sensitivity :** Our eyes perceive only in the visible region of the electromagnetic spectrum, i.e. 0.4 to 0.7 μm whereas the sensitivity of the film ranges from 0.3 to 0.9 μm.
  - **Three Dimensional Perspective :** Aerial photographs are normally taken with uniform exposure interval that enables us in obtaining stereo pair of photographs.
- The types of the aerial photographs based on the position of optical axis and the scale are given below :
  - **Types of Aerial Photographs Based on the Position of the Camera Axis :** On the basis of the position of the camera axis, aerial photographs are classified into the following types :

  (a) **Vertical Photographs :** While taking aerial photographs, two distinct axes are formed from the camera lens centre, one towards the ground plane and the other towards the photo plane. When the photo plane is kept parallel to the ground plane, the two axes also coincide with each other. The photograph so obtained is known as vertical aerial photograph.

  (b) **Low Oblique :** An aerial photograph taken with an intentional deviation of 15° to 30° in the camera axis from the vertical axis is referred to as the low oblique photograph.

  (c) **High Oblique :** The high oblique are photographs obtained when the camera axis is intentionally inclined about 60° from the vertical axis.

- **Types of Aerial Photographs Based on Scale :** The aerial photographs may also be classified on the basis of the scale of photograph into three types :

(a) Large Scale Photographs : When the scale of an aerial photograph is 1 : 15,000 and larger, the photography is classified as large-scale photograph.

(b) Medium Scale Photographs : The aerial photographs with a scale ranging between 1 : 15,000 and 1 : 30,000 are usually treated as medium scale photographs.

(c) Small Scale Photographs : The photographs with the scale being smaller than 1 : 30,000, are referred to as small scale photographs.

Know the Terms

- **Aerial photographs :** The photographs taken from an aircraft or helicopter using a precision camera are termed aerial photographs.
- **Aerial perspective :** The bird's eye view which we get in aerial photographs, is termed as aerial perspective.
- **Aerial camera :** A precision camera specifically designed for use in aircrafts.
- **Aerial Film :** A roll film with high sensitivity, high intrinsic resolution power and dimensionally stable emulsion support.
- **Aerial photography :** Art, science and technology of taking aerial photographs from an air-borne platform.
- **Vertical aerial photography :** When the photo plane is kept parallel to the ground plane, the two axes also coincide with each other. The photograph so obtained is known as vertical aerial photograph.
- **Tilted photography :** Any photography with an unintentional deviation of more than 3o in the optical axis from the vertical axis is known as a tilted photograph.

Multiple Choice Questions (1 mark each)

Q. 1. The photographs with the scale being smaller than 1 : 30,000 are referred to as: [A]

(a) small scale photographs
(b) large scale photographs
(c) middle scale photographs
(d) intermittent scale photographs

Ans. (a) small scale photographs **1**

Q. 2. When the scale of an aerial photograph is 1 : 15,000 and larger, the photograph is classified as: [U]

(a) small-scale photograph
(b) large-scale photograph
(c) aerial -scale photograph
(d) medium-scale photograph

Ans. (b) large-scale photograph **1**

Q. 3. The photographs taken from the camera kept in the helicopter or aeroplane are known as : [U]

(a) bird-view photographs
(b) aerial photographs
(c) small-scale photographs
(d) serial photographs

Ans. (b) aerial photographs **1**

Q. 4. The images are taken from man made satellites launched in the space is known as : [U]

(a) satellite images
(b) aerial photographs
(c) photogrammetry
(d) image interpretation

Ans. (a) satellite images **1**

Very Short Answer Type Questions (1 mark each)

Q. 1. Define the term aerial photographs. [A]

Ans. The photographs taken from an aircraft or helicopter using a precision camera are termed aerial photographs. **1**

Q. 2. What is aerial photography? [A]

Ans. Art, science and technology of taking aerial photographs from an air-borne platform. **1**

Q. 3. What is aerial perspective? [U]

Ans. The bird's eye view which we get in aerial photographs, is termed as aerial perspective. **1**

Q. 4. What is photogrammetry? [A]

Ans. It refers to the science and technology of making reliable measurements from aerial photographs.**1**

Q. 5. How are aerial photographs useful? [R]

Ans. The photographs so obtained have been found to be indispensable tools in the topographical mapping and interpretation of the images of the objects. **1**

Q. 6. How is photogrammetry useful? [U]

Ans. Photogrammetry is useful as the principles used in photogrammetry facilitate precise measurements related to the length , breadth and height from such photographs. Hence, they are used as the data source for creating and updating topographic maps. 1

Q. 7. Where are the principles of image interpretation applied? [A]

Ans. The principles of image interpretation are applied to obtain qualitative information from the aerial photographs such as land use/land cover, topographical forms, soil types, etc. 1

Q. 8. How can an aerial photograph be used for historic records? [R]

Ans. An aerial photograph is a record of the surface features at an instance of exposure. It can, therefore, be used as a historical record. 1

Q. 9. How is the bird's eye view useful? [U]

Ans. Aerial photography provides a bird's eye view of large areas, enabling us to see features of the earth surface in their spatial context. 1

Q. 10. When and which city of India was the first aerial photography taken? [A]

Ans. The first aerial photography was taken in Agra in 1920. 1

Q. 11. Name the first country of the world where aerial photography was taken and when. [U]

Ans. The country where first aerial photography was taken was France in 1909. 1

Short Answer Type Questions

(3 marks each)

Q. 1. Write a short note on the development of aerial photography in India. [A]

Ans. Aerial photography in India goes back to 1920 when large-scale aerial photographs of Agra city were obtained. Subsequently, Air Survey Party of the Survey of India took up aerial survey of Irrawaddy Delta forests, which was completed during 1923–24. Subsequently, several similar surveys were carried out and advanced methods of mapping from aerial photographs were used. Today, aerial photography in India is carried out for the entire country under the overall supervision of the Directorate of Air Survey (Survey of India) New Delhi. Three flying agencies, i.e. Indian Air Force, Air Survey Company, Kolkata and National Remote Sensing Agency, Hyderabad have been officially authorised to take aerial photographs in India. 3

Commonly Made Error

- The students are not aware of the use of aerial photography.

Answering Tip

- Aerial photography is used in cartography, land-use planning, archaeology, movie production, environmental studies, espionage, commercial advertising, conveyancing, and other fields.

Q. 2. State the advantages of aerial photography. [U]

Ans. The advantages of aerial photography are:

(i) Improved vantage point : Aerial photography provides a bird's eye view of large areas, enabling us to see features of the earth surface in their spatial context.

(ii) Time freezing ability : An aerial photograph is a record of the surface features at an instance of exposure. It can, therefore, be used as a historical record.

(iii) Broadened Sensitivity : The sensitivity of the film used in taking aerial photographs is relatively more than the sensitivity of the human eyes. Our eyes perceive only in the visible region of the electromagnetic spectrum, i.e. 0.4 to 0.7 μm whereas the sensitivity of the film ranges from 0.3 to 0.9 μm.

(iv) Three-Dimensional Perspective : Aerial photographs are normally taken with uniform exposure interval that enables us in obtaining stereo pair of photographs. Such a pair of photographs helps us in getting a three-dimensional view of the surface photographed.

(Any Three) (1 x 3 =3)

Q. 3. Differentiate between vertical photograph and low oblique photograph. [A]

Ans.

S.No.	Attributes	Vertical Photographs	Low Oblique Photographs
1.	Optical axis	Tilt < 3° exactly or nearly coincides with the vertical axis.	Deviation is > 30° from the vertical axis.
2.	Coverage	Small area .	Relatively larger area.
3.	Appearance	Horizon does not appear.	Horizon does appear.
4.	Advantage	Useful in topographical and thematic mapping.	Reconnaissance Survey.

(Any Three)(1×3=3)

Q. 4. Differentiate between high oblique photograph and low oblique photograph. R

Ans.

S.No.	High Oblique Photograph	Low Oblique Photograph
1.	Deviation is more than 30^0 degrees from the vertical axis.	Deviation is more than 3^0 degrees from the vertical axis.
2.	It covers largest area.	It is greater with low oblique photographs.
3.	It is useful in illustrative comparison.	It is useful in reconnaissance survey

5

Q. 5. Differentiate between vertical and low oblique photograph. A

Ans.

S.No.	Vertical Photograph	High Oblique Photograph
1.	It covers small area.	It covers largest area.
2.	It is useful in topographical and thematic mapping.	It is useful in illustrative comparison.
3.	Horizon does not appear.	Horizon does appear

5

Answering Tip

- A vertical photograph is one which has been taken with the camera axis directed toward the ground as vertically as possible, while an oblique photograph is one which has been taken with the camera axis directed at an inclination to the ground.

Long Answer Type Questions (5 marks each)

Q. 1. On the basis of the position of the camera axis explain the different types of aerial photographs. R

Ans. On the basis of the position of the camera axis, the different types of aerial photographs are :

(i) Vertical Photographs : While taking aerial photographs, two distinct axes are formed from the camera lens centre, one towards the ground plane and the other towards the photo plane. The perpendicular dropped from the camera lens centre to the ground plane is termed as the vertical axis, whereas the plumb line drawn from the lens centre to the photo plane is known as the photographic/optical axis. When the photo plane is kept parallel to the ground plane, the two axes also coincide with each other. The photograph so obtained is known as vertical aerial photograph.

However, it is normally very difficult to achieve perfect parallelism between the two planes due to the fact that the aircraft flies over the curved surface of the earth. The photographic axis, therefore, deviates from the vertical axis. If such a deviation is within the range of plus or minus 3o, the near-vertical aerial photographs are obtained. Any photography with an unintentional deviation of more than 3o in the optical axis from the vertical axis is known as a tilted photograph.

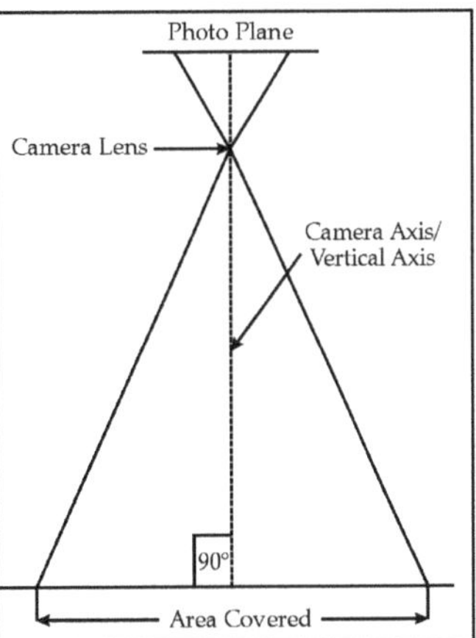

(ii) Low Oblique : An aerial photograph taken with an intentional deviation of 15° to 30° in the camera axis from the vertical axis is referred to as the low oblique photograph .This kind of photograph is often used in reconnaissance surveys.

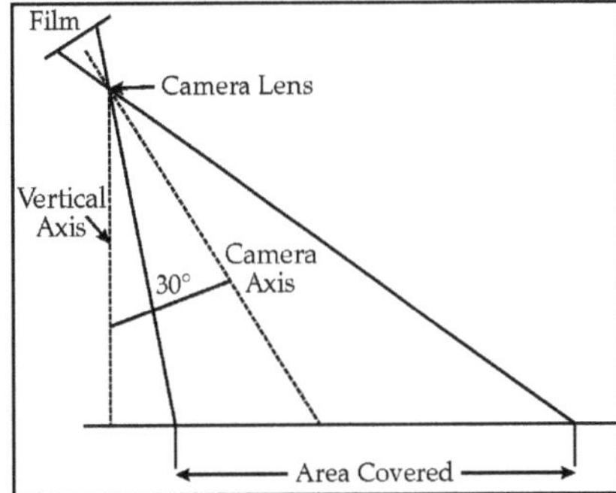

(iii) High Oblique : The high oblique are photographs obtained when the camera axis is intentionally inclined about 60° from the vertical axis. Such photography is useful in reconnaissance surveys.5

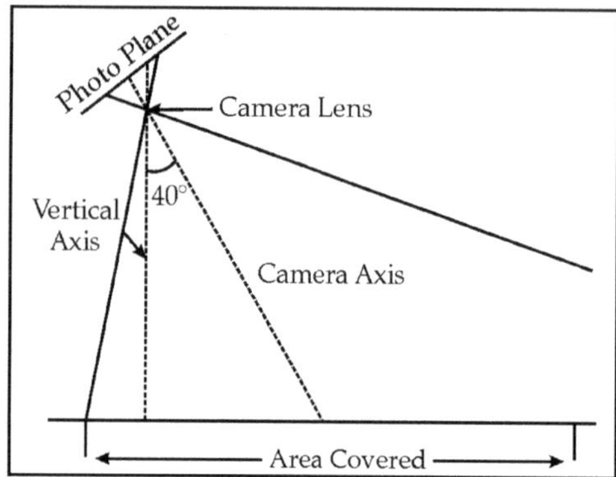

Q. 2. On the basis of scale, classify the aerial photography. [A]

Ans. The aerial photographs may also be classified on the basis of the scale of photograph into three types :

(i) Large Scale Photographs : When the scale of an aerial photograph is 1 : 15,000 and larger, the photography is classified as large-scale photograph.

(ii) Medium Scale Photographs : The aerial photographs with a scale ranging between 1 : 15,000 and 1 : 30,000 are usually treated as medium scale photographs.

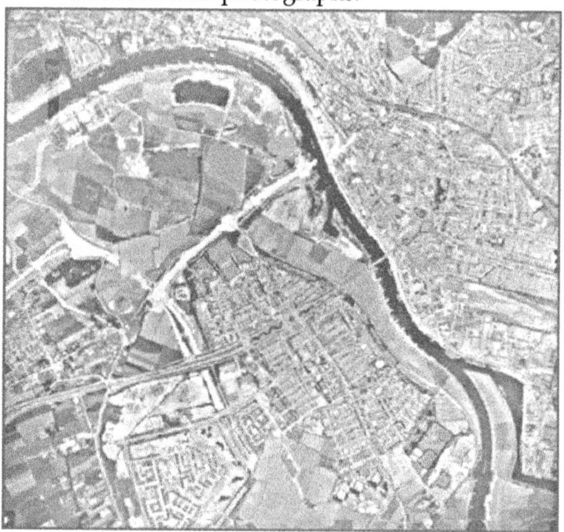

(iii) Small Scale Photographs : The photographs with the scale being smaller than 1 : 30,000, are referred to as small scale photographs.

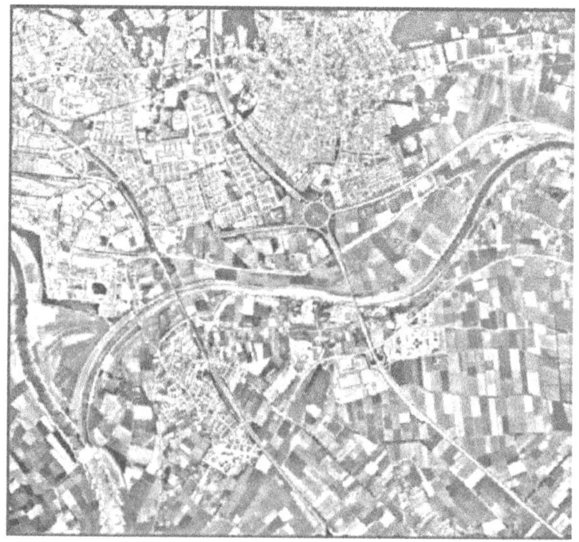

5

TOPIC-2
Geometry of an Aerial Photography, Difference between a Map and an Aerial Photography

Revision Notes

➢ To understand the geometry of an aerial photograph, it is important to appreciate the orientation of the photograph with respect to the ground, *i.e.*, the way the rays connect or 'project' onto the ground in relation to the ground representation. The following three examples of such projection would be useful in understanding the problem :

- **Parallel Projection :** In this projection, the projecting rays are parallel but not necessarily perpendicular.

- **Orthogonal Projection :** This is a special case of parallel projections. The advantage of this projection is that the distances, angles or areas on the plane are independent of the elevation differences of the objects.
- **Central Projection :** This is a case in which a projection of one plane onto a second plane such that a point on the first plane and its image on the second plane lie on a straight line through a fixed point not on either plane. the central projection is characterised by the fact that all straight lines joining corresponding points, *i.e.,* straight lines joining object points to their corresponding image points pass through one point.

➢ **The main differences between aerial photograph and map are as follows :**

- An aerial photograph is geometrically incorrect. The distortion in the geometry is minimum at the centre and increase towards the edges of the photographs. Whereas, a map is a geometrically correct representation of the part of the Earth projected.
- In aerial photography, the scale of photograph is not uniform. Whereas, in the map the scale of map is uniform throughout the map extent.
- Aerial photograph is a central projection, whereas, map is an orthogonal projection.
- Aerial photograph holds good for inaccessible and inhospitable areas. Whereas, the mapping of inaccessible and inhospitable area is very difficult and sometimes it becomes impossible.

➢ The concept of scale for aerial photographs is much the same as that of a map. Scale is the ratio of a distance on an aerial photograph the distance between the same two places on the ground in the real world.

➢ **There are three methods to compute the scale of an aerial photograph using different sets of information :**

- By Establishing Relationship Between Photo Distance and Ground Distance: If additional information like ground distances of two identifiable points in an aerial photograph is available, it is fairly simple to work out the scale of a vertical photograph. Provided that the corresponding ground distances (Dg) are known for which the distances on an aerial photograph (Dp) are measured. In such cases, the scale of an aerial photograph will be measured as a ratio of the two, *i.e.,* Dp/ Dg.
- By Establishing Relationship Between Photo Distance and Map Distance: In other words, the distances between two points identifiable both on a map and the aerial photograph enable us to compute the scale of the aerial photograph (Sp).
- By Establishing Relationship Between Focal Length (f) and Flying Height (H) of the Aircraft : If no additional information is available about the relative distances on photograph and ground/map, we can determine the photo-scale provided the information about the focal length of the camera (f) and the flying height of the aircraft (H) are known.

Know the Terms

➢ **Orthogonal projection :** This is a special case of parallel projections. Map are orthogonal projections of the ground.

➢ **Principal point :** It is the foot of the perpendicular drawn from the camera lens centre on the photo plane.

➢ **Principal distance :** It is the perpendicular distance from the perspective centre to the plane of the photograph.

➢ **Focal length :** The perpendicular distance between the camera lens and the negative plane is known as the focal length.

➢ **Flying height :** The perpendicular distance between the camera lens and the ground photographed is known as the flying height.

➢ **Perspective centre :** The point of origin(perspective point) of the bundle of light rays.

➢ **Nadir points :** The foot of the perpendicular drawn from the camera lens centre on the ground plane.

➢ **Orthophotos :** Aerial photographs need to be transformed from perspective view to the planimetric view before they can be used as map substitute. Such transformed photographs are known as orthophotos.

Multiple Choice Questions

(1 mark each)

Q. 1. The projecting rays are parallel but not necessarily perpendicular in: [A]

(a) parallel projection
(b) flying projection
(c) focal length
(d) principle projection

Ans. (a) parallel projection 1

Q. 2. In aerial photography, the scale of photograph is not: [U]

(a) parallel
(b) uniform
(c) collective
(d) central

Ans. (b) uniform 1

Very Short Answer Type Questions (1 mark each)

Q. 1. What is focal length? A

Ans. The perpendicular distance between the camera lens and the negative plane is known as the focal length. 1

Q. 2. What is flying height? R

Ans. The perpendicular distance between the camera lens and the ground photographed is known as the flying height. 1

Q. 3. What is orthophotos? A

Ans. Aerial photographs need to be transformed from perspective view to the planimetric view before they can be used as map substitute. Such transformed photographs are known as orthophotos. 1

Answering Tip

- An ortho-photograph can be used to measure true distances of features within the photograph.

Q. 4. What are nadir points? U

Ans. The foot of the perpendicular drawn from the camera lens centre on the ground plane. 1

Q. 5. What is a scale? R

Ans. Scale is the ratio of a distance on an aerial photograph the distance between the same two places on the ground in the real world. It can be expressed in unit equivalents like 1 cm = 1,000 km(or 12,000 inches) or as a representative fraction (1 : 100,000). 1

Q. 6. Why a map cannot be directly traced out of an aerial photograph? A

Ans. A map cannot be directly traced out of an aerial photograph. The reason is that there is a basic difference in the planimetry (projection) and perspective of a map and an aerial photograph. 1

Q. 7. What changes does the aerial photographs need to go before they can be used as map substitute? U

Ans. Aerial photographs need to be transformed from perspective view to the planimetric view before they can be used as map substitute. 1

Q. 8. The distance between two points on an aerial photograph is measured as 2 centimetres. The known distance between the same two points on the ground is 1 km. Compute the scale of the aerial photograph (Sp). R

Ans.

Sp = Dp : Dg

= 2cm : 1 km

= 2cm : 1 × 100,000 cm

= 1 : 100,000/2 =50,000 cm

= 1 unit represents 50,000 units

Therefore, Sp = 1: 50,000. 1

Q. 9. The distance measured between two points on a map is 2 cm. the corresponding distance on an aerial photograph is 10 cm. Calculate the scale of the photograph when the scale of the map is 1:50,000. U

Ans. Photo scale (Sp) = Photo distance (Dp) : Map distance (Dm) × Map scale factor (msf)

= 10 cm : 2cm × 50,000

=10 cm : 100,000 cm

= 1 : 100,000/10 = 10,000 units

= 1 unit represents 10,000 units

Therefore, Sp =1 : 10,000 1

Short Answer Type Questions (3 marks each)

Q. 1. Differentiate between aerial photography and map. R

Ans.

S.No.	Aerial photography	Map
1.	The photographs taken from an aircraft or helicopter using a precision camera are termed aerial photographs.	A map is geometrically correct representation of the part of the earth projection
2.	It is central projection.	It is an orthogonal projection.
3.	The scale of the photograph is not uniform.	The scale of the map is uniform throughout the map extent.

(1 × 3 = 3)

NCERT CORNER

(A) Multiple choice questions :

Q. 1. In which of the following aerial photographs the horizon appears :

(a) Vertical

(b) Near-vertical

(c) Low-oblique

(d) High-oblique

Ans. (c) Low-oblique.

Q. 2. In which of the following aerial photographs the Nadir and the principle points coincide :

(a) Vertical

(b) Near-vertical

(c) Low-oblique

(d) High-oblique

Ans. (d) High-oblique .

Q. 3. Which type of the following projections is used in aerial photographs :

(a) Parallel

(b) Orthogonal

(c) **Central**

(d) None of the above

Ans. (c) Central.

(B) Answer the following questions in about 60 words :

Q. 1. State any three advantages that an aerial photograph offers over ground-based observations.

Ans. The three advantages that an aerial photograph offers over ground-based observations are:

(i) **Broadened sensitivity :** The sensitivity of the film used in taking aerial photographs is relatively more than the sensitivity of the human eyes. Our eyes perceive only in the visible region of the electromagnetic spectrum, i.e. 0.4 to 0.7 μm whereas the sensitivity of the film ranges from 0.3 to 0.9 μm.

(ii) **Three Dimensional Perspective :** Aerial photographs are normally taken with uniform exposure interval that enables us in obtaining stereo pair of photographs. Such a pair of photographs helps us in getting a three-dimensional view of the surface photographed.

(iii) **Improved vantage point :** Aerial photography provides a bird's eye view of large areas, enabling us to see features of the earth surface in their spatial context.

(iv) **Time freezing ability :** An aerial photograph is a record of the surface features at an instance of exposure. It can, therefore, be used as a historical record.

Q. 2. How is an aerial photograph taken?

Ans. Aerial photographs are taken from the camera kept in aeroplane or helicopter. The photographs are taken from aerial camera which is a precision camera specifically designed for use in aircraft.

Q. 3. Present a concise account of aerial photography in India?

Ans. Aerial photography in India goes back to 1920 when large-scale aerial photographs of Agra city were obtained. Subsequently, Air Survey Party of the Survey of India took up aerial survey of Irrawaddy Delta forests, which was completed during 1923–24. Subsequently, several similar surveys were carried out and advanced methods of mapping from aerial photographs were used. Today, aerial photography in India is carried out for the entire country under the overall supervision of the Directorate of Air Survey (Survey of India) New Delhi. Three flying agencies, i.e. Indian Air Force, Air Survey Company, Kolkata and National Remote Sensing Agency, Hyderabad have been officially authorised to take aerial photographs in India.

(C) Answer the following questions in about 125 words :

Q. 1. What are the two major uses of an aerial photograph? Elaborate?

Ans. Aerial photographs are used in topographical mapping and interpretation. These two different uses have led to the development of photogrammetry and photo/image interpretation as two independent but related sciences.

Photogrammetry : It refers to the science and technology of making reliable measurements from aerial photographs. The principles used in photogrammetry facilitate precise measurements related to the length, breadth and height from such photographs. Hence, they are used as the data source for creating and updating topographic maps.

Image Interpretation : It is an art of identifying images of objects and judging their relative significance. The principles of image interpretation are applied to obtain qualitative information from the aerial photographs such as land use/land cover, topographical forms, soil types, etc. A trained interpreter can thus utilise aerial photographs to analyse the land-use changes.

Q. 2. What are the different methods of scale determination?

Ans. There are three methods to compute the scale of an aerial photograph using different sets of information.

(i) **By Establishing Relationship Between Photo Distance and Ground Distance :** If additional information like ground distances of two identifiable points in an aerial photograph is available, it is fairly simple to work out the scale of a vertical photograph. Provided that the corresponding ground distances (Dg) are known for which the distances on an aerial photograph (Dp) are measured. In such cases, the scale of an aerial photograph will be measured as a ratio of the two, *i.e.*, Dp/ Dg.

(ii) By Establishing Relationship Between Photo Distance and Map Distance : As we know, the distances between different points on the ground are not always known. However, if a reliable map is available for the area shown on an aerial photograph, it can be used to determine the photo scale. In other words, the distances between two points identifiable both on a map and the aerial photograph enable us to compute the scale of the aerial photograph (Sp). The relationship between the two distances may be expressed as under :

(Photo scale : Map scale) = (Photo distance : Map distance)

We can derive

Photo scale (Sp) = Photo distance (Dp) : Map distance (Dm) x Map scale factor (msf)

(iii) By Establishing Relationship Between Focal Length (f) and Flying Height (H) of the Aircraft : If no additional information is available about the relative distances on photograph and ground/map, we can determine the photo-scale provided the information about the focal length of the camera (f) and the flying height of the aircraft (H) are known. The photo scale so determined could be more reliable if the given aerial photograph is truly vertical or near vertical and the terrain photographed is flat. The focal length of the camera (f) and the flying height of the aircraft (H) are provided as marginal information on most of the vertical photographs.

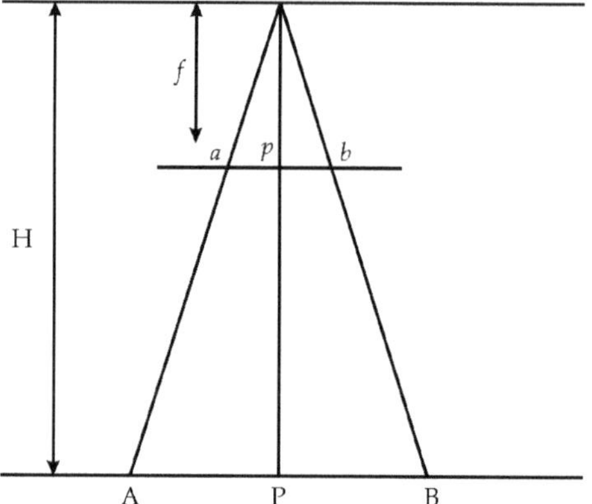

❑❑

CHAPTER

7 INTRODUCTION TO REMOTE SENSING

Syllabus

➢ *Stages in Remote Sensing, Sensors, Resolving Powers of the Satellites, Sensor Resolutions.*
➢ *Data Products, Interpretation of Satellite Imageries, Elements of Visual Interpretation.*

TOPIC-1
Stages in Remote Sensing, Sensors, Resolving Powers of the Satellites, Sensor Resolutions

Revision Notes

➢ The term remote sensing was first used in the early 1960s. Later, it was defined as the total processes used to acquire and measure the information of some property of objects and phenomena by a recording device (sensor) that is not in physical contact with the objects and phenomena in study.

➢ The stages in remote sensing involve the following steps :

- **Source of Energy :** Sun is the most important source of energy used in remote sensing.
- **Transmission of Energy from the Source to the Surface of the Earth :** The energy that emanates from a source propagates between the source and the object surface in the form of the waves of energy at a speed of light (300,000 km per second). Such energy propagation is called the Electromagnetic Radiation (EMR).
- **Interaction of Energy with the Earth's Surface :** The propagating energy finally interacts with the objects of the surface of the earth. This leads to absorption, transmission, reflection or emission of energy from the objects. The objects' responses to the energy they receive are also not uniform. Besides, one particular object also responds differently to the energy it receives in different regions of the spectrum.
- **Propagation of Reflected/Emitted Energy through Atmosphere :** When energy is reflected from objects of the earth's surface, it re–enters into the atmosphere. The energy reflected from the objects comes in contact with the atmospheric constituents and the properties of the original energy get modified.
- **Detection of Reflected/Emitted Energy by the Sensor :** The sensors recording the energy that they receive are placed in a near– polar sun synchronous orbit at an altitude of 700 – 900 km. These satellites are known as remote sensing satellites. Remote sensing satellites are deployed with sensors which are capable of collecting the EMR reflected by the objects. The sensors used in remote sensing satellites possess a mechanism that is different from photographic camera in collecting and recording the information.
- **Conversion of Energy Received into Photographic/ Digital Form of Data :** The radiations received by the sensor are electronically converted into a digital image. It comprises digital numbers that are arranged in rows and columns. These numbers may also be converted into an analogue (picture) form of data product.
- **Extraction of Information Contents from Data Products :** After the image data is received at the earth station, it is processed for elimination of errors caused during image data collection. Once the image is corrected, information extraction is carried out from digital images using digital image processing techniques and from analogue form of data products by applying visual interpretation methods.
- **Conversion of Information into Map/Tabular Forms :** The interpreted information is finally delineated and converted into different layers of thematic maps. Besides, quantitative measures are also taken to generate a tabular data.

➢ A sensor is a device that gathers electromagnetic radiations, converts it into a signal and presents it in a form suitable for obtaining information about the objects under investigation.

- Based upon the form of the data output, the sensors are classified into photographic (analogue) and non–photographic (digital) sensors.
- A photographic sensor (camera) records the images of the objects at an instance of exposure. On the other hand, a non–photographic sensor obtains the images of the objects in bit-by-bit form.
- In satellite remote sensing, the Multi-Spectral Scanners (MSS) are used as sensors. These sensors are designed to obtain images of the objects while sweeping across the field of view.
- A scanning sensor constructs the scene by recording a series of scan lines. The oscillation of the scanning mirror across the scene directs the received energy to the detectors, where it is converted into electrical signals. These signals are further converted into numerical values called Digital Number (DN Values) for recording on a magnetic tape. The Multi-Spectral Scanners are divided into the following types :
  - **Whiskbroom Scanners :** The whiskbroom scanners are made up of a rotating mirror and a single detector. The mirror is so oriented that when it completes a rotation, the detector sweeps across the field of view between 90° and 120° to obtain images in a large number of narrow spectral bands ranging from visible to middle infrared regions of the spectrum.
  - **Push broom Scanners :** The push broom scanners consist of a number of detectors which are equivalent to the number obtained by dividing the swath of the sensor by the size of the spatial resolution. In push broom scanner, all detectors are linearly arrayed and each detector collects the energy reflected by the ground cell (pixel) dimensions of 20 metres at a nadir's view.

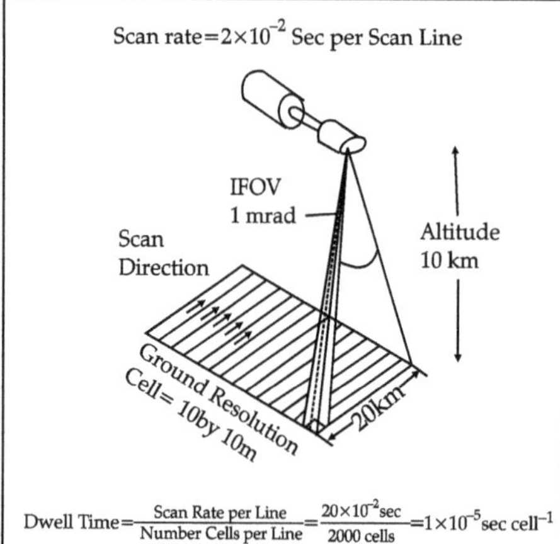

7.1 Whiskbroom Scanners

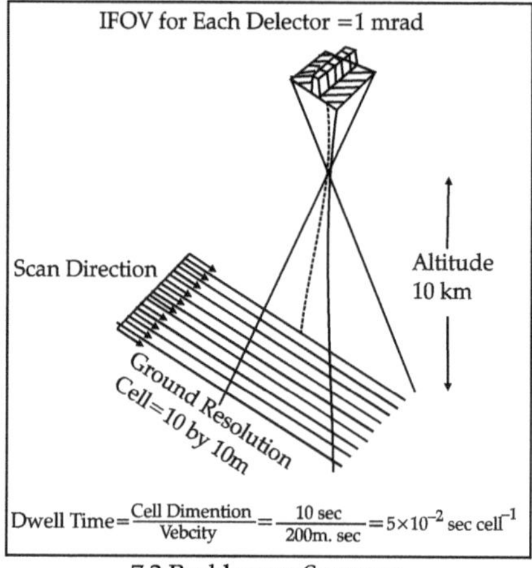

7.2 Pushbroom Scanners

- In satellite remote sensing, the sun-synchronous polar orbit enables the collection of images after a pre-determined periodical interval referred to as the temporal resolution or the revisit time of the satellite over the same area of the earth surface.
- Remote sensors are characterised by spatial, spectral and radiometric resolutions that enable the extraction of useful information pertaining to different terrain conditions:
  - **Spatial Resolution :** In remote sensing, the spatial resolution of the sensors refers to the same phenomena. It is the capability of the sensor to distinguish two closed spaced object surfaces as two different object surfaces. As a rule, with an increasing resolution the identification of even smaller object surfaces become possible.
  - **Spectral Resolution :** It refers to the sensing and recording power of the sensor in different bands of EMR (Electromagnetic radiation). Multi-spectral images are acquired by using a device that disperses the radiation received by the sensor and recording it by deploying detectors sensitive to specific spectral ranges.
  - **Radiometric Resolution :** It is the capability of the sensor to discriminate between two targets. Higher the radiometric resolution, smaller the radiance differences that can be detected between two targets.

Know the Terms

- **Sensor :** Any imaging or non–imaging device that receives EMR and converts it into a signal that can be recorded and displayed as photographic or digital image.
- **Remote sensing :** It can be defined as the total processes used to acquire and measure the information of some property of objects and phenomena by a recording device (sensor) that is not in physical contact with the objects and phenomena in study.
- **Electromagnetic Radiation (EMR) :** The energy propagated through a space or a medium at a speed of light.
- **Electromagnetic Spectrum :** The continuum of EMR that ranges from short wave high frequency cosmic radiations to long wavelength low frequency radio waves.
- **Sensor :** A sensor is a device that gathers electromagnetic radiations, converts it into a signal and presents it in a form suitable for obtaining information about the objects under investigation.
- **Digital image :** An array of digital numbers (DN) arranged in rows and columns, having the property of an intensity value and their locations.
- **Band :** The specific wavelength interval in the electromagnetic spectrum.
- **Swath :** The motor device which oscillates the scanning mirror through the angular field of view of the sensor, which determines the length of scan lines and is called swath.

Multiple Choice Questions (1 mark each)

Q. 1. The most important source of remote sensing is the : [A]

(a) Sun (b) Water
(c) Waves (d) Moon

Ans. (a) Sun 1

Q. 2. In satellite remote sensing, the Multi Spectral Scanners (MSS) are used as : [U]

(a) image (b) spectrum
(c) sensors (d) analogue

Ans. (b) spectrum 1

Very Short Answer Type Questions (1 mark each)

Q. 1. What is remote sensing? [R]

Ans. It can be defined as the total processes used to acquire and measure the information of some property of objects and phenomena by a recording device (sensor) that is not in physical contact with the objects and phenomena in study. 1

Q. 2. What is a sensor? [A]

Ans. A sensor is a device that gathers electromagnetic radiations, converts it into a signal and presents it in a form suitable for obtaining information about the objects under investigation. 1

Q. 3. Define the term 'Digital image'. [U]

Ans. An array of digital numbers (DN) arranged in rows and columns, having the property of an intensity value and their locations. 1

Answering Tip

- By itself, the term "digital image" usually refers to raster images or bitmapped images.

Q. 4. Define the term 'electromagnetic spectrum'. [U]

Ans. The continuum of EMR that ranges from short wave high frequency cosmic radiations to long wavelength low frequency radio waves. 1

Q. 5. Define the term 'electromagnetic radiation'. [U]

Ans. The energy propagated through a space or a medium at a speed of light. 1

Commonly Made Error

- The students are not aware of the examples of electromagnetic waves.

Answering Tip

- Radio waves, microwaves, visible light, and x-rays are all examples of electromagnetic waves that differ from each other in wavelength.

Q. 6. When was the term remote sensing first used? [A]

Ans. The term remote sensing was first used in early 1950s. 1

Q. 7. Based upon the form of the data output the sensors can be classified into how many group? [U]

Ans. Based upon the form of the data output, the sensors are classified into photographic (analogue) and non– photographic (digital) sensors. 1

Short Answer Type Questions (3 marks each)

Q. 1. What do you know about sensors? [A]

Ans. A sensor is a device that gathers electromagnetic radiations, converts it into a signal and presents it in a form suitable for obtaining information about the objects under investigation. Based upon the form of the data output, the sensors are classified into photographic (analogue) and non–photographic (digital) sensors. A photographic sensor (camera) records the images of the objects at an instance of exposure. On the other hand, a non–photographic sensor obtains the images of the objects in bit-by-bit form. These sensors are known as scanners. 3

Answering Tip

- A sensor is always used with other electronics.

Q. 2. Differentiate between photographic sensors and non-photographic sensors. [R]

Ans.

S.No.	Photographic sensors	Non- photographic sensors
1.	A photographic sensor (camera) records the images of the objects at an instance of exposure.	A non–photographic sensor obtains the images of the objects in bit-by-bit form.
2.	It is done through camera.	It is done through scanners.
3.	It is also called Analogue sensors.	It is also called digital sensors

(1 × 3 = 3)

Q. 3. What is a scanner? How does it work? R

Ans. A scanner is usually made up of a reception system consisting of a mirror and detectors. A scanning sensor constructs the scene by recording a series of scan lines. While doing so, the motor device oscillates the scanning mirror through the angular field of view of the sensor, which determines the length of scan lines and is called swath. It is because of such reasons that the mode of collection of images by scanners is referred bit–by–bit. Each scene is composed of cells that determine the spatial resolution of an image. The oscillation of the scanning mirror across the scene directs the received energy to the detectors, where it is converted into electrical signals. These signals are further converted into numerical values called Digital Number (DN Values) for recording on a magnetic tape. 3

Q. 4. Discuss about the different types of multi spectral scanners. A

Ans. In satellite remote sensing, the Multi Spectral Scanners (MSS) are used as sensors. These sensors are designed to obtain images of the objects while sweeping across the field of view. The different types of multi-spectral scanners are:

(i) Whiskbroom Scanners : The whiskbroom scanners are made up of a rotating mirror and a single detector. The mirror is so oriented that when it completes a rotation, the detector sweeps across the field of view between 90° and 120° to obtain images in a large number of narrow spectral bands ranging from visible to middle infrared regions of the spectrum. The total extent of the oscillating sensor is known as the Total Field of View (TFOV) of the scanner. While scanning the entire field, the sensor's optical head is always placed at a particular dimension called the Instantaneous Field of View (IFOV).

(ii) Pushbroom Scanners : The pushbroom scanners consist of a number of detectors which are equivalent to the number obtained by dividing the swath of the sensor by the size of the spatial resolution (Fig. 7.8). For example, the swath of High Resolution Visible Radiometer – 1 (HRVR – 1) of the French remote sensing satellite SPOT is 60 km and the spatial resolution is 20 metres. If we divide 60 km x 1000 metres/20 metres, we get a number of 3000 detectors that are deployed in SPOT HRV – 1 sensor. In pushbroom scanner, all detectors are linearly arrayed and each detector collects the energy reflected by the ground cell (pixel) dimensions of 20 metres at a nadir's view.3

Answering Tip

- A scanning system used to collect data over a variety of different wavelength ranges is called a multi-spectral scanner (MSS).

Q. 5. Explain the different types of sensor resolutions. A

Ans. Remote sensors are characterised by spatial, spectral and radiometric resolutions that enable the extraction of useful information pertaining to different terrain conditions.

(i) Spatial Resolution : You must have seen some people using spectacles while reading a book or newspaper. Have you ever thought as to why they do so. It is simply because of the fact that resolving power of their eyes to differentiate two closed spaced letters in a word is unable to identify them as two different letters. By using positive spectacles they try to improve their vision as well as the resolving power. In remote sensing, the spatial resolution of the sensors refers to the same phenomena. It is the capability of the sensor to distinguish two closed spaced object surfaces as two different object surfaces. As a rule, with an increasing resolution the identification of even smaller object surfaces become possible.

(ii) Spectral Resolution : It refers to the sensing and recording power of the sensor in different bands of EMR (Electromagnetic radiation). Multi-spectral images are acquired by using a device that disperses the radiation received by the sensor and recording it by deploying detectors sensitive to specific spectral ranges. The principles in obtaining such images is the extension of the dispersion of light in nature resulting in the appearance of the 'rainbow".

(iii) Radiometric Resolution : It is the capability of the sensor to discriminate between two targets. Higher the radiometric resolution, smaller the radiance differences that can be detected between two targets. **(1 × 3 = 3)**

Q. 6. Differentiate between whiskbroom scanners and push broom scanners. R

Ans.

S.No.	Whisk broom Scanners	Push broom Scanners
1.	The whiskbroom scanners are made up of a rotating mirror and a single detector.	The pushbroom scanners consist of a number of detectors which are equivalent to the number obtained by dividing the swath of the sensor by the size of the spatial resolution.
2.	While scanning the entire field, the sensor's optical head is always placed at a particular dimension called the Instantaneous Field of View.	In pushbroom scanner, all detectors are linearly arrayed and each detector collects the energy reflected by the ground cell (pixel) dimensions of 20 metres at a nadir's view.
3.	Refer by 7.1 'Revision Notes'	Refer by 7.2 'Revision Notes'

(1 × 3 = 3)

Long Answer Type Question (5 marks)

Q. 1. Name the basic processes of remote sensing that help in collecting information about the properties of the objects and phenomena of the earth surface. [A]

Ans. The basic processes that help in the collection of information about the properties of the objects and phenomena of the earth surface are as follows :

(i) Source of Energy : Sun is the most important source of energy used in remote sensing. The energy may also be artificially generated and used to collect information about the objects and phenomena such as flashguns or energy beams used in radar (radio detection and ranging).

(ii) Transmission of Energy from the Source to the Surface of the Earth : The energy that emanates from a source propagates between the source and the object surface in the form of the waves of energy at a speed of light (300,000 km per second). Such energy propagation is called the Electromagnetic Radiation (EMR). The energy waves vary in size and frequency. The plotting of such variations is known as the Electromagnetic Spectrum.

(iii) Interaction of Energy with the Earth's Surface: The propagating energy finally interacts with the objects of the surface of the earth. This leads to absorption, transmission, reflection or emission of energy from the objects. We all know that all objects vary in their composition, appearance forms and other properties. Hence, the objects' responses to the energy they receive are also not uniform. Besides, one particular object also responds differently to the energy it receives in different regions of the spectrum.

(iv) Propagation of Reflected/Emitted Energy through Atmosphere : When energy is reflected from objects of the earth's surface, it re–enters into the atmosphere. Hence, the energy that is either absorbed or scattered by the atmospheric constituents never reaches to sensor placed onboard a satellite and the properties of the objects carried by such energy waves are left unrecorded.

(v) Detection of Reflected/Emitted Energy by the Sensor : The sensors recording the energy that they receive are placed in a near– polar sun synchronous orbit at an altitude of 700 – 900 km. These satellites are known as remote sensing satellites (e.g. Indian Remote Sensing Series). As against these satellites, the weather monitoring and telecommunication satellites are placed in a Geostationary position (the satellite is always positioned over its orbit that synchronises with the direction of the rotation of the earth) and revolves around the earth (coinciding with the direction of the movement of the earth over its axis) at an altitude of nearly 36,000 km.

(vi) Conversion of Energy Received into Photographic/ Digital Form of Data : The radiations received by the sensor are electronically converted into a digital image. It comprises digital numbers that are arranged in rows and columns. These numbers may also be converted into an analogue (picture) form of data product.

(vii) Extraction of Information Contents from Data Products : After the image data is received at the earth station, it is processed for elimination of errors caused during image data collection. Once the image is corrected, information extraction is carried out from digital images using digital image processing techniques and from analogue form of data products by applying visual interpretation methods.

(viii) Conversion of Information into Map/Tabular Forms : The interpreted information is finally delineated and converted into different layers of thematic maps. Besides, quantitative measures are also taken to generate a tabular data. 5

TOPIC-2
Data Products, Interpretation of Satellite Imageries, Elements of Visual Interpretation.

Revision Notes

- We have seen that the electromagnetic energy may be detected either photographically or electronically.
- An image refers to pictorial representation, regardless of what regions of energy have been used to detect and record it. A photograph refers specifically to images that have been recorded on photographic film. Hence, it can be said that all photographs are images, but all images are not photographs.
- Based upon the mechanism used in detecting and recording, the remotely sensed data products may be broadly classified into two types :

- **Photographic Images :** Photographs are acquired in the optical regions of electromagnetic spectrum, *i.e.*, 0.3 – 0.9 μm. Four different types of light sensitive film emulsion bases are used to obtain photographs. These are black and white, colour, black and white infrared and colour infrared. Photographs may be enlarged to any extent without loosing information contents or the contrast.
- **Digital Images :** A digital image consists of discrete picture elements called pixels. Each one of the pixels in an image has an intensity value and an address in two-dimensional image space. In a digital image, the reproduction of the details pertaining to the images of the objects is affected by the size of the pixel. A smaller size pixel is generally useful in the preservation of the scene details and digital representation.

➢ The data obtained from the sensors is used for information extraction related to the forms, and patterns of the objects and phenomena of the earth's surface.

➢ The visual interpretation is a manual exercise. It involves reading of the images of objects for the purpose of their identification.

➢ Whether we are conscious of it or not we use the form, size, location of the objects and their relationships with the surrounding objects to identify them in our day-to-day life. These characteristics of objects are termed as elements of visual interpretation.

➢ We can further group the characteristics of the objects into two broad categories, i.e. image characteristics and terrain characteristics. The image characteristics include:

- **Tone or Colour :** We know that all objects receive energy in all regions of spectrum. The interaction of EMR with the object surface leads to the absorption, transmittance and reflection of energy. The variations in the tone or the colour depend upon the orientation of incoming radiations, surface properties and the composition of the objects. In other words, smooth and dry object surfaces reflect more energy in comparison to the rough and moist surfaces.
- **Texture :** The texture refers to the minor variations in tones of grey or hues of colour. These variations are primarily caused by an aggregation of smaller unit features that fail to be discerned individually such as high density and low density residential areas; slums and squatter settlements; garbage and other forms of solid waste; and different types of crops and plants. The textural differences in the images of certain objects vary from smooth to coarse textures.
- **Size :** The size of an object as discerned from the resolution or scale of an image is another important characteristic of individual objects.
- **Shape :** The general form and configuration or an outline of an individual object provides important clues in the interpretation of remote sensing images. The shape of some of the objects is so distinctive that make them easy to identify.
- **Shadow :** The shape of some of the objects is so typical that they could not be identified without finding out the length of the shadow they cast. For example, the Qutub Minar located in Delhi. It may , however, be noted that the shadow as an element of image interpretation is of less use in satellite images. However, it serves a useful purpose in large-scale aerial photography.
- **Pattern :** The spatial arrangements of many natural and man–made features show repetitive appearance of forms and relationships.
- **Association :** The association refers to the relationship between the objects and their surroundings along with their geographical location. For example, an educational institution always finds its association with its location in or near a residential area as well as the location of a playground within the same premises.

Know the Terms

➢ **Absorbance :** The ratio of the radiant energy absorbed by a substance to the energy it receives is called absorbance.

➢ **Digital number :** An intensity value of a pixel in a digital image.

➢ **Grey scale :** A medium to calibrate the variations in the brightness of an image that ranges from black to white with intermediate grey values is called grey scale.

➢ **Image :** It is the permanent record of a scene comprising of natural and man-made features and activities, produced by photographic and non-photographic means.

➢ **False Colour Composite (FCC) : An artificially generated colour image in which blue, green and red colours are assigned to the wavelength regions to which they do not belong in nature.**

Multiple Choice Questions **(1 mark each)**

Q. 1. The__________ refers to the relationship between the objects and their surroundings along with their geographical location. [A]

(a) association
(b) absorbance
(c) pattern
(d) shadow

Ans. (a) association 1

Q. 2. The minor variations in tones of grey or hues of colour is known as : [U]

(a) tone
(b) shadow
(c) colour
(d) texture

Ans. (d) texture 1

Very Short Answer Type Questions (1 mark each)

Q. 1. What is absorbance? A

Ans. The ratio of the radiant energy absorbed by a substance to the energy it receives is called absorbance. 1

Q. 2. What is false colour composite? R

Ans. False colour composite refers to an artificially generated colour image in which blue, green and red colours are assigned to the wavelength regions to which they do not belong in nature. 1

Answering Tip

- False colour composites allow us to visualize the wavelengths that the human eye does not see.

Q. 3. What is temporal resolution? U

Ans. In satellite remote sensing, the sun-synchronous polar orbit enables the collection of images after a pre-determined periodical interval. This interval is referred to as the temporal resolution or the revisit time of the satellite over the same area of the earth surface. 1

Q. 4. Differentiate between photographic process and a scanning device. U

Ans. The photographic process uses light sensitive film to detect and record energy variations . On the other hand, a scanning device obtains images in digital mode. 1

Q. 5. How can the arrangements be easily identified from the images? R

Ans. The arrangements can easily be identified from the images through the utilisation of the pattern they form. 1

Q. 6. What do you know about the shadow of an object? A

Ans. Shadow of an object is a function of the sun's illumination angle and the height of the object itself. The shape of some of the objects is so typical that they could not be identified without finding out the length of the shadow they cast. 1

Q. 7. How is the shape as an element of visual interpretation important? U

Ans. The general form and configuration or an outline of an individual object provides important clues in the interpretation of remote sensing images. 1

Short Answer Type Questions (3 marks each)

Q. 1. Differentiate between photographic image and digital image. R

Ans.

S.No.	Photographic image	Digital image
1.	Photographs are acquired in the optical regions of electromagnetic spectrum, i.e. 0.3 – 0.9 μm.	A digital image consists of discrete picture elements called pixels.
2.	Four different types of light sensitive film emulsion bases are used to obtain photographs.	Each one of the pixels in an image has an intensity value and an address in two-dimensional image space. In a digital image, the reproduction of the details pertaining to the images of the objects is affected by the size of the pixel.
3.	Photographs may be enlarged to any extent without loosing information contents or the contrast.	A smaller size pixel is generally useful in the preservation of the scene details and digital representation.

(1 × 3 = 3)

Q. 1. Differentiate between photograph and image. R

Ans.

S.No.	Photograph	Images
1.	A photograph refers specifically to images that have been recorded in photographic film.	An image refers to pictorial representation , regardless of what regions of energy have been used to detect and record it.
2.	All photographs are images.	All images are not photographs.
3.	Photographs are inclusive in images and its scope is narrow	Images can be digital images and photographic images. Therefore, its scope is wider.

(1 × 3 = 3)

Long Answer Type Questions

(5 marks each)

Q. 1. Which are the various elements of visual interpretation? R

Ans. The various elements of visual interpretation are :

(i) Tone or Colour : We know that all objects receive energy in all regions of spectrum. The interaction of EMR with the object surface leads to the absorption, transmittance and reflection of energy. It is the reflected amount of the energy that is received and recorded by the sensor in tones of grey, or hues of colour in black and white, and colour images respectively. The variations in the tone or the colour depend upon the orientation of incoming radiations, surface properties and the composition of the objects.

(ii) Texture : The texture refers to the minor variations in tones of grey or hues of colour. These variations are primarily caused by an aggregation of smaller unit features that fail to be discerned individually such as high density and low density residential areas; slums and squatter settlements; garbage and other forms of solid waste; and different types of crops and plants. The textural differences in the images of certain objects vary from smooth to coarse textures.

(iii) Size : The size of an object as discerned from the resolution or scale of an image is another important characteristic of individual objects. It helps in distinctively identifying the industrial and industrial complexes with residential dwellings, etc.

(iv) Shape : The general form and configuration or an outline of an individual object provides important clues in the interpretation of remote sensing images. The shape of some of the objects is so distinctive that make them easy to identify.

(v) Shadow : Shadow of an object is a function of the sun's illumination angle and the height of the object itself. The shape of some of the objects is so typical that they could not be identified without finding out the length of the shadow they cast. It may , however, be noted that the shadow as an element of image interpretation is of less use in satellite images. However, it serves a useful purpose in large-scale aerial photography.

(vi) Pattern : The spatial arrangements of many natural and man–made features show repetitive appearance of forms and relationships. The arrangements can easily be identified from the images through the utilisation of the pattern they form.

(vii) Association : The association refers to the relationship between the objects and their surroundings along with their geographical location. **(Any Five) (1 × 5 = 5)**

NCERT CORNER

(A) Multiple choice questions :

Q. 1. Remote sensing of objects can be done through various means such as A. remote sensors, B. human eyes and C. photographic system. Which of the following represents the true order of their evolution :

(a) ABC

(b) BCA

(c) CAB

(d) None of the above

Ans. (b) BCA

Q. 2. Which of the following regions of Electromagnetic spectrum is not used in satellite remote sensing :

(a) Microwave region

(b) Infrared region

(c) X - rays

(d) Visible region

Ans. (c) X-rays.

Q. 3. Which of the following is not used in visual interpretation technique :

(a) Spatial arrangements of objects

(b) Frequency of tonal change on the image

(c) Location of objects with respect to other objects

(d) Digital image processing

Ans. (a) Spatial Arrangement of Objects.

(B) Answer the following questions in about 30 words :

Q. 1. Why is remote sensing a better technique than other traditional methods.

Ans. Remote sensing is a better technique than other traditional methods because :

(i) It presents the exact picture of a large area.

(ii) It provides real or nearly real pictures on time base line.

(iii) It is not affected by bad weather and inaccessible land.

(iv) It is less expensive as compared to land survey and we can easily collect information by using it.

Q. 2. Differentiate between IRS and INSAT series of satellites.

Ans.

S.No.	IRS	INSAT
1.	It stands for Indian Remote Sensing.	It stands for Indian Satellite System .
2.	It is the largest civilian remote sensing satellite constellation in the world.	It initiated a major revolution in India's communication sector .
3.	The sensors recording the energy that they receive are placed in a near– polar sun synchronous orbit at an altitude of 700 – 900 km. These satellites are known as remote sensing satellites.	The weather monitoring and telecommunication satellites are placed in a Geostationary position (the satellite is always positioned over its orbit that synchronises with the direction of the rotation of the earth) and revolves around the earth (coinciding with the direction of the movement of the earth over its axis) at an altitude of nearly 36,000 km. (*e.g.*, INSAT series of satellites)

Q. 3. Describe in brief the functioning of push broom scanner?

Ans. The pushbroom scanners consist of a number of detectors which are equivalent to the number obtained by dividing the swath of the sensor by the size of the spatial resolution (Fig. 7.8). For example, the swath of High Resolution Visible Radiometer – 1 (HRVR – 1) of the French remote sensing satellite SPOT is 60 km and the spatial resolution is 20 metres. If we divide 60 km x 1000 metres/20 metres, we get a number of 3000 detectors that are deployed in SPOT HRV – 1 sensor. In pushbroom scanner, all detectors are linearly arrayed and each detector collects the energy reflected by the ground cell (pixel) dimensions of 20 metres at a nadir's view.

(C) Answer the following questions in about 125 words :

Q. 1. Describe the operation of a whiskbroom scanner with the help of a diagram. Explain how it is different from push broom scanner.

Ans. The whiskbroom scanners are made up of a rotating mirror and a single detector. The mirror is so oriented that when it completes a rotation, the detector sweeps across the field of view between 90° and 120° to obtain images in a large number of narrow spectral bands ranging from visible to middle infrared regions of the spectrum. The total extent of the oscillating sensor is known as the Total Field of View (TFOV) of the scanner. While scanning the entire field, the sensor's optical head is always placed at a particular dimension called the Instantaneous Field of View (IFOV).

Q. 2. Identify and list the changes that can be observed in the vegetation of Himalayas.

Ans. The Himalayas show a succession of vegetation from the tropical to the tundra with changes in the altitude. Deciduous forests are found in the foothills of the Himalayas. It is succeeded by the wet temperate types of forests between the altitude of 1,000-2,000 mtrs.

After 3000 metres altitude, conical forests are found which have sharp leaves. Some of the important trees found in this region are Chid, Fur, Pine, Sprus, etc.

The red patches in May image refer to Coniferous vegetation. In November image, the additional red patches refer to Deciduous plants and the light red colour is related to the crops.

❑❑

CHAPTER

8 WEATHER INSTRUMENTS, MAPS AND CHARTS

Syllabus

➢ *Weather Observations, Weather Instruments. Weather Maps and Charts, Weather Symbols, Mapping the Climatic Data, Weather Map Interpretation*

Revision Notes

➢ Weather denotes the atmospheric conditions of weather elements at a particular place and time. The weather elements include temperature, pressure, wind, humidity and cloudiness.

➢ In India, weather-related information is collected and published under the auspices of the Indian Meteorological Department, New Delhi, which is also responsible for weather forecasting.

➢ Weather forecasts help in taking safety measures in advance in case of the likelihood of bad weather. Predicting weather a few days in advance may prove very useful to farmers and to the crew of ships, pilots, fishermen, defence personnel, etc.

➢ Globally, meteorological observations are recorded at three levels:

- **Surface Observatories :** A typical surface observatory has instruments for measuring and recording weather elements like temperature (maximum and minimum), air pressure, humidity, clouds, wind and rainfall. Specialised observatories also record elements like radiation, ozone atmospheric trace gases, pollution and atmospheric electricity.

➢ These observations are taken all over the globe at fixed times of the day as decided by the WMO and the use of instruments are made conforming to international standards, thus making observations globally compatible.

➢ In India, meteorological observations are normally classified into five categories depending upon their instruments and the number of daily observations taken.

➢ Typical instrumental facility available in a Class-I observatory consists of the following :

(a) Maximum and minimum thermometers

(b) Anemometer and wind vane

(c) Dry and Wet bulb thermometer

(d) Rain gauge

(e) Barometer

- **Space Based Observations :** Weather satellites make comprehensive and large-scale observations of different meteorological elements at the ground level as well in the upper layers of the atmosphere.

➢ The geo-stationary satellites provide space-based observations about weather conditions.

➢ The Indian National Satellite (INSAT) provides valuable observations of temperature, cloud cover, wind and associated weather phenomena.

➢ Various instruments are used for measuring different weather phenomena :

- **Thermometer :** Thermometer is used to measure air temperature. Most thermometers are in the form of a narrow-closed glass tube with an expanded bulb at one end.

➢ The bulb of the thermometer in contact with the air gets heated or cooled, as the case may be, as a result of which the mercury in the bulb rises or falls.

➢ A scale is marked on the glass tube and readings are taken from there.

- The two most common scales used in thermometers are Centigrade and the Fahrenheit.
- The maximum thermometer is designed to record the highest temperature during a day. As the temperature increases, the mercury moves up into the tube; however, as the mercury cools, it cannot move downwards because of a constriction in the tube.
- The minimum thermometer records the lowest reading in a day. In this thermometer, alcohol is used in place of mercury. When the temperature decreases, the metal pin in the tube goes down and strikes at the minimum temperature.
- The dry bulb and wet bulb thermometers are used for measuring humidity in the air. The dry bulb and wet bulb thermometers are two identical thermometers fixed to a wooden frame. The bulb of the dry thermometer is kept uncovered and is exposed to the air while the bulb of the wet bulb thermometer is wrapped up with a piece of wet muslin, which is kept continuously moist by dipping a strand of it into a small vessel of distilled water.
- The difference of the readings of the dry bulb and the wet bulb thermometers determines the state of the atmosphere with regard to its humidity. The larger the difference, the more arid is the air.
  - **Barometer :** The instrument used to measure atmospheric pressure is called a barometer.
- The most commonly used barometers are the mercury barometer, aneroid barometer and barographs.
- The unit of measurement is in the millibar. Mercury barometer is an accurate instrument and is used as a standard.
- Aneroid barometer gets its name from the Greek work, aneros (a- 'not', neros – 'moisture', meaning without liquid). It is a compact and portable instrument. It consists of a corrugated metal box made up of a thin alloy, sealed completely and made airtight after partial exhaustion of air. It has a thin flexible lid, which is sensitive to changes of pressure.
- Barograph works on the principle of aneroid barometer. There are a number of vacuum boxes placed one above the other so that the displacement is large.
  - **Wind Vane :** Wind vane is a device used to measure the direction of the wind. The wind vane is a lightweight revolving plate with an arrowhead on one end and two metal plates attached to the other end at the same angle.
- This revolving plate is mounted on a rod in such a manner that it is free to rotate on a horizontal plane.
- The arrow always points towards the direction from which the wind blows.
  - **Rain Gauge :** The amount of rainfall is measured with the help of a rain gauge. The rain gauge consists of a metal cylinder on which a circular funnel is fitted. The diameter of the funnel's rim is normally 20 cm.
- The rain drops are collected and measured in a measuring glass. Normally, rainfall is measured in the units of millimetres or centimetres.
- A weather map is the representation of weather phenomena of the earth or a part of it on a flat surface. It depicts conditions associated with different weather elements such as temperature, rainfall, sunshine and cloudiness, direction and velocity of winds, etc. on a particular day.
- The central office keeps a record of the observations, which forms the basis for making a weather map.
- Since the inception of the Indian Meteorological Department, the weather maps and charts are prepared regularly. Meteorological observatories transmit the data to the Central Observatory at Pune twice a day.
- A good progress has been made in the field of weather forecasting and observation with the establishment of weather observatories in Antarctica, the International Indian Ocean Expedition, and the launching of rockets and weather satellites.
- Weather charts provide the primary tools for weather forecasting. They help in locating and identifying different air masses, pressure systems, fronts and areas of precipitation.
- The messages received from all the observatories are plotted on the map using weather symbols standardised by the World Meteorological Organisation and the National Weather Bureaus.
- Much of the climatic data is represented by line symbols. The most common of these are the isometric lines. These lines are depicted on the map as isopleths.
- The Isopleth can be interpolated for places having the same mean values of temperature, rainfall, pressure, sunshine, clouds, etc.

Know the Terms

- **Weather :** The condition of the atmosphere at a given place and time with respect to atmospheric pressure, temperature, humidity, precipitation, cloudiness and wind. These factors are known as weather elements.

- **Weather Forecast :** Prediction with a reasonable amount of certainty about the conditions of weather that would prevail in the coming 12 to 48 hours in a certain area.
- **Weather elements :** Pressure, temperature, humidity , precipitation, cloudiness and wind are known as weather elements.
- **Weather forecast :** It is the weather prediction with a reasonable amount of certainty about the conditions of weather that would prevail in the coming 12 to 48 hours in a certain area.
- **Weather satellites :** These satellites make comprehensive and large-scale observations of different meteorological elements at the ground level as well in the upper layers of the atmosphere.
- **The geo-stationary satellites :** These satellites provide space-based observations about weather conditions.
- **Thermometer :** It is an instrument used to measure air temperature.
- **Wind vane :** It is a device used to measure the direction of the wind.
- **Rain gauge :** The amount of rainfall is measured with the help of a rain gauge.
- **Weather map :** A weather map is the representation of weather phenomena of the earth or a part of it on a flat surface. It depicts conditions associated with different weather elements such as temperature, rainfall, sunshine and cloudiness, direction and velocity of winds, etc. on a particular day.
- **Isobars :** Lines connecting places of equal air pressure.
- **Isotherms :** Lines connecting places of equal temperature.
- **Isohyets :** Lines connecting places of equal amount of rainfall over a given period of time.
- **Isohels :** Lines connecting places of same mean daily duration of sunshine.
- **Isonephs :** Lines connecting places of same mean value of cloud cover.

Multiple Choice Questions (1 mark each)

Q. 1. The amount of rainfall is measured with the help of a : [A]

(a) rain gauge
(b) rain metre
(c) rain thermometer
(d) rain scale

Ans. (a) rain gauge 1

Q. 2. The highest pressure isobar of 1018 mb passes through: [U]

(a) Maharasthra
(b) Rajasthan
(c) Goa
(d) Gujarat

Ans. (b) Rajasthan 1

Q. 2. The lines connecting places of equal temperature are known as : [U]

(a) barometer
(b) isobars
(c) isotherms
(d) gauge

Ans. (c) isotherms 1

Q. 4. The lines connecting places of equal air pressure are known as : [A]

(a) aneroid
(b) isobars
(c) isotherms
(d) charts

Ans. (b) isobars 1

Very Short Answer Type Questions (1 mark each)

Q. 1. What is weather? [A]

Ans. The condition of the atmosphere at a given place and time with respect to atmospheric pressure, temperature, humidity, precipitation, cloudiness and wind. These factors are known as weather elements. 1

Q. 2. Define the term weather forecast. [U]

Ans. It is the weather prediction with a reasonable amount of certainty about the conditions of weather that would prevail in the coming 12 to 48 hours in a certain area. 1

Q. 3. What is a barometer? [A]

Ans. The instrument used to measure atmospheric pressure is called a barometer. 1

Answering Tip

- Forecasters use changes in air pressure measured with barometers to predict short-term changes in the weather.

Q. 4. Name a few basic elements of weather. [A]

Ans. Pressure, temperature, humidity , precipitation, cloudiness and wind are known as weather elements. **(Any Two) (½ + ½ = 1)**

Q. 5. How can relative humidity be calculated? [R]

Ans. Relative humidity can be calculated by using the following formula :

$$\textbf{Relative humidity} = \frac{\textbf{Amount of moisture in air a given temperature}}{\textbf{Total moisture absorbing capacity of atmosphere on same temperature}} \times 100$$

1

Q. 6. What is the full form of IMD? [U]

Ans. IMD stands for the Indian Meteorological Department. **1**

Q. 7. When and where was the IMD established? [A]

Ans. The Indian Meteorological Department (IMD) was established in 1875, with its headquarters at Calcutta. The IMD headquarters are presently located at New Delhi. **1**

Q. 8. Predicting weather a few days in advance can prove helpful to whom? [R]

Ans. Predicting weather a few days in advance may prove very useful to farmers and to the crew of ships, pilots, fishermen, defence personnel, etc. **1**

Q. 9. How are weather charts helpful? [A]

Ans. Weather charts are helpful as they provide the primary tools for weather forecasting. They help in locating and identifying different air masses, pressure systems , fronts and areas of precipitation. **1**

Answering Tip

- Weather charts are the fundamental basis for weather analysis and forecasts.

Q. 10. How is INSAT helpful to us? [R]

Ans. The INSAT is helpful to us as it provides valuable observations of temperature, cloud cover, wind and associated weather phenomena. **1**

Q. 11. What is the unit of measurement for measuring the atmospheric pressure? [U]

Ans. The unit of measurement is in the millibar. **1**

Q. 12. What is an aneroid barometer? [R]

Ans. Aneroid barometer gets its name from the Greek work, aneros (a- 'not', neros – 'moisture', meaning without liquid). It is a compact and portable instrument. It consists of a corrugated metal box made up of a thin alloy, sealed completely and made airtight after partial exhaustion of air. It has a thin flexible lid, which is sensitive to changes of pressure. **1**

Short Answer Type Questions (3 marks each)

Q. 1. Write any three uses of weather forecasting. [A]

Ans. Weather forecasting is useful for :

(i) Weather forecasts help in taking safety measures in advance in case of the likelihood of bad weather.

(ii) It reduces the likely loss from natural calamities.

(iii) Predicting weather a few days in advance may prove very useful to farmers and to the crew of ships, fishermen, defence personnel, etc. **(1 × 3 = 3)**

Q. 2. Write a note on wind vane. [U]

Ans. Wind vane is a device used to measure the direction of the wind. The wind vane is a lightweight revolving plate with an arrowhead on one end and two metal plates attached to the other end at the same angle. This revolving plate is mounted on a rod in such a manner that it is free to rotate on a horizontal plane.

It responds even to a slight blow of wind. The arrow always points towards the direction from which the wind blows. **(1 × 3 = 3)**

Q. 3. Write a note on the working of the weather observatories in India. [A]

Ans. Every day weather maps are prepared for that day by the Meteorological Department from the data obtained from observations made at various weather stations across the world. In India, weather -related information is collected and published under the auspices of the Indian Meteorological Department, New Delhi, which is also responsible for weather forecasting. **3**

Q. 4. What do you know about rain gauge? [A]

Ans. Rain gauge :

(i) The amount of rainfall is measured with the help of a rain gauge. The rain gauge consists of a metal cylinder on which a circular funnel is fitted.

(ii) The diameter of the funnel's rim is normally 20 cm. The rain drops are collected and measured in a measuring glass.

(iii) Normally, rainfall is measured in the units of millimetres or centimetres. Snow is also measured in a similar manner by turning it into liquid form. **(1 × 3 = 3)**

Answering Tip

- The standard rain gauge instrument generally consists of a funnel connecting to a graduated cylinder which is marked in millimeters.

Q. 5. Write a short note on Anemometer. U

Ans. Aneroid barometer gets its name from the Greek work, aneros (a- 'not', neros – 'moisture', meaning without liquid). It is a compact and portable instrument. It consists of a corrugated metal box made up of a thin alloy, sealed completely and made airtight after partial exhaustion of air. It has a thin flexible lid, which is sensitive to changes of pressure.

As the pressure increases, the lid is pressed inward, and this, in turn, moves a system of levers connected to a pointer, which moves clockwise over the graduated dial and gives higher reading. When the pressure decreases, the lid is pushed outward and the pointer moves counter clockwise, indicating lower pressure.

Barograph works on the principle of aneroid barometer. There are a number of vacuum boxes placed one above the other so that the displacement is large. A system of levers magnifies this movement which is recorded by a pen on a paper attached to a rotating drum. The readings of a barograph are not always accurate, and therefore, they are standardised by comparing them with a mercury barometer reading.

(1 × 3 = 3)

Answering Tip

- Anemometers are important tools for meteorologists, who study weather patterns.

Q. 6. What do you know about Stevenson Screen? R

Ans. The Stevenson screen is designed to protect thermometers from precipitation and direct sunlight while allowing air to circulate freely around them. It is made from wood with louvered sides to allow free and even flow of air. It is painted white to reflect radiation. It stands on four legs and is about 3 feet 6 inches above the level of the ground.

The legs must be sufficiently rigid and be buried sufficiently in the ground to prevent shaking. The front panel is hinged at the bottom to form a door, which allows for maintenance and reading of the thermometers.

The door of Stevenson screen is always towards the north in the northern hemisphere and towards the south in the southern hemisphere because direct sunrays also affect mercury. The purpose of the Stevenson screen is to create a uniform temperature enclosure that closely represents the same temperature as the air outside.

Q. 7. Differentiate between dry bulb and wet bulb. A

Ans.

S.No.	Dry Bulb	Wet Bulb
1.	It is used to measure lowest humidity	It is used to measure highest humidity.
2.	The bulb is kept uncovered and is exposed to the air..	The bulb is kept wrapped up with a piece of wet muslin, which is kept continuously moist by dipping a strand of it into a small vessel of distilled water.
3.	Its temperature remains high.	The evaporation from the wet bulb lowers its temperature.

(1 × 3 = 3)

Q. 8. Differentiate between aneroid barometer and mercury barometer. A

Ans.

S.No.	Aneroid Barometer	Mercury Barometer
1.	It is a compact and portable instrument.	In this barometer, the atmospheric pressure of any place is balanced against the weight of a column of mercury in an inverted glass tube.
2.	It is filled with alcohol.	It is filled with mercury.
3.	It is used to measure lowest temperature.	It is used to measure highest temperature.

(1 × 3 = 3)

Q. 9. Differentiate between Centigrade and Fahrenheit. A

Ans. On the Centigrade thermometer, the temperature of melting ice is marked 0°C and that of boiling water as 100°C, and the interval between the two is divided into 100 equal parts. On the Fahrenheit thermometer, the freezing and boiling points of water are graduated as 32°F and 212°F respectively. **3**

Long Answer Type Questions

(5 marks each)

Q. 1. What do you know about thermometer? R

Ans. Thermometer is used to measure air temperature. Most thermometers are in the form of a narrow closed glass tube with an expanded bulb at one end. The bulb and the lower part of the tube are filled with liquid such as mercury or alcohol. Before the other end is sealed off, the air in the tube is released by heating it. The bulb of the thermometer in contact with the air gets heated or cooled, as the case may be, as a result of which the mercury in the bulb rises or falls. A scale is marked on the glass tube and readings are taken from there.

The two most common scales used in thermometers are Centigrade and the Fahrenheit. On the Centigrade thermometer, the temperature of melting ice is marked 00C and that of boiling water as 1000C, and the interval between the two is divided into 100 equal parts. On the Fahrenheit thermometer, the freezing and boiling points of water are graduated as 32°F and 212°F respectively.

While the maximum thermometer and minimum thermometer are used to measure the air temperature, the dry bulb and the wet bulb thermometers are used to determine the humidity in the air. A set of these thermometers is kept in the Stevenson Screen. The maximum thermometer is designed to record the highest temperature during a day. As the temperature increases, the mercury moves up into the tube; however, as the mercury cools, it cannot move downwards because of a constriction in the tube. It must be reset again to bring it down. The minimum thermometer records the lowest reading in a day. In this thermometer, alcohol is used in place of mercury. When the temperature decreases, the metal pin in the tube goes down and strikes at the minimum temperature. 5

Answering Tip

- A thermometer has two important elements: a temperature sensor in which some change occurs with a change in temperature; and some means of converting this change into a numerical value.

Q. 2. Name the instruments used to measure the atmospheric pressure. [A]

Ans. The instrument used to measure atmospheric pressure is called a barometer. The most commonly used barometers are the mercury barometer, aneroid barometer and barographs. The unit of measurement is in the millibar.

(i) Mercury barometer : It is an accurate instrument and is used as a standard. In it the atmospheric pressure of any place is balanced against the weight of a column of mercury in an inverted glass tube. The principle of a mercurial barometer can be explained by a simple experiment.

(ii) Aneroid barometer : It gets its name from the Greek work, aneros (a- 'not', neros – 'moisture', meaning without liquid). It is a compact and portable instrument. It consists of a corrugated metal box made up of a thin alloy, sealed completely and made airtight after partial exhaustion of air. It has a thin flexible lid, which is sensitive to changes of pressure.

(iii) Barograph : It works on the principle of aneroid barometer. There are a number of vacuum boxes placed one above the other so that the displacement is large. A system of levers magnifies this movement which is recorded by a pen on a paper attached to a rotating drum. The readings of a barograph are not always accurate, and therefore, they are standardised by comparing them with a mercury barometer reading. 5

Q. 3. How are thermometers designed to be protected from precipitation and direct sunlight while allowing air to circulate freely around them? [R]

Ans. The Stevenson screen is designed to protect thermometers from precipitation and direct sunlight while allowing air to circulate freely around them. It is made from wood with louvered sides to allow free and even flow of air. It is painted white to reflect radiation. It stands on four legs and is about 3 feet 6 inches above the level of the ground. The legs must be sufficiently rigid and be buried sufficiently in the ground to prevent shaking. The front panel is hinged at the bottom to form a door, which allows for maintenance and reading of the thermometers. The door of Stevenson screen is always towards the north in the northern hemisphere and towards the south in the southern hemisphere because direct sunrays also affect mercury. The purpose of the Stevenson screen is to create a uniform temperature enclosure that closely represents the same temperature as the air outside. 5

Q. 4. How is the information about weather and related facts collected organised and dispensed in India?

Ans. In India , weather related information is collected and published under the auspices of the Indian Meteorological Department, New Delhi, which is also responsible for weather forecasting.

A typical surface observatory has instruments for measuring and recording weather elements like temperature (maximum and minimum), air pressure, humidity, clouds, wind and rainfall. Specialised observatories also record elements like radiation, ozone atmospheric trace gases, pollution and atmospheric electricity. These observations are taken all over the globe at fixed times of the day as decided by the WMO and the use of instruments are made conforming to international standards, thus making observations globally compatible.

In India, meteorological observations are normally classified into five categories depending upon their instruments and the number of daily observations taken. The highest category is Class-I. Typical instrumental facility available in a Class-I observatory consists of the following:

(a) Maximum and minimum thermometers

(b) Anemometer and wind vane

(c) Dry and Wet bulb thermometer

(d) Rain gauge

(e) Barometer

Observations are taken in these observatories normally at 00,03,06,09,12,15,18,21 hours (Greenwich Mean Time) around the globe. However, for logistic reasons, some of the observatories take limited number of daily observations upper air observation during daytime only.

Weather satellites make comprehensive and large-scale observations of different meteorological elements at the ground level as well in the upper layers of the atmosphere. The geo-stationary satellites provide space-based observations about weather conditions. For example, The Indian National Satellite (INSAT) provides valuable observations of temperature, cloud cover, wind and associated weather phenomena. **5**

Map Work

(5 marks each)

Q. 1. Study the map given below and answer the following questions?

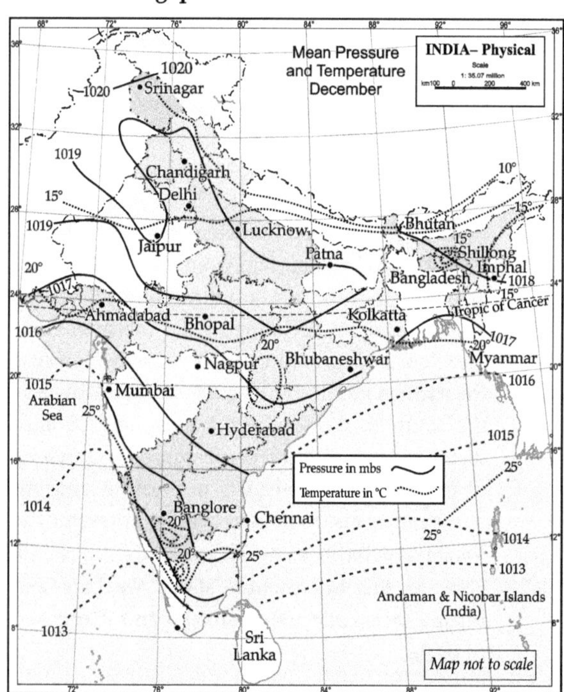

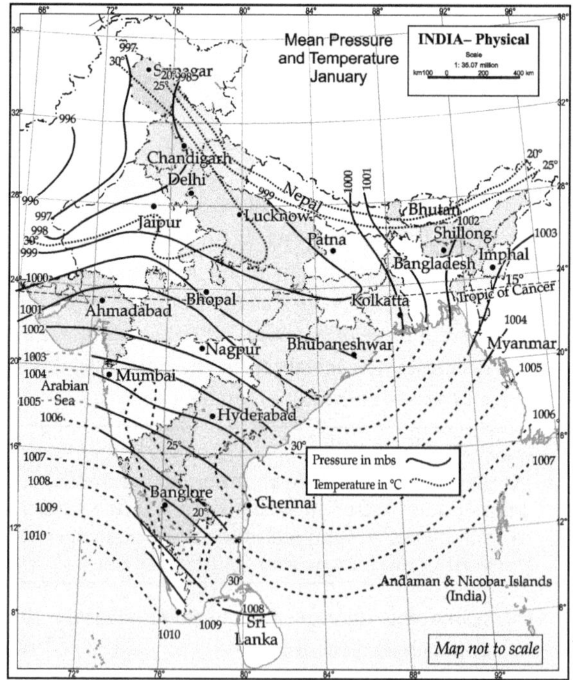

(i) Which seasons are shown in the maps given above?

(ii) What is the value of the highest isobars in the map showing mean pressure and temperature in July and through which part of the country does it pass?

(iii) What is the value of the highest and the lowest isobars in the map showing mean pressure and temperature in January and where are they located?

(iv) What is the patterns of temperature distribution in both the maps?

(v) What relationship do you see between the distribution of temperature and pressure in both the maps?

Ans. (i) The maps are showing winter and monsoon seasons.

(ii) The value of the highest isobar is 1010 millibar and it is passing through south-west part of the country.

(iii) The value of highest isobar is 1020 millibar, located in Lakshadweep and lowest isobar is 1013 millibar is located in Pakistan .

(iv) In the first map , the temperature of July in South India is 20 ° and the temperature of North India is between 20° to 30°. In the second map the temperature of January in North India is between 10° to 15° and temperature of South India is between 20° to 25°.

(v) As temperature increases, pressure decreases and vice versa. **(1 × 5 = 5)**

NCERT CORNER

(A) Multiple choice questions :

Q. 1. Which department prepares the weather map of India for each day :

(a) The World Meteorological Organisation

(b) The Indian Meteorological Department

(c) The Survey of India

(d) None of the above

Ans. (b) The Indian Meteorological Department

Q. 2. Which two liquids are used in maximum and minimum thermometers :

(a) Mercury and water

(b) Water and alcohol

(c) Mercury and alcohol

(d) None of the above

Ans. (b) Mercury and alcohol.

Q. 3. Lines connecting the places of equal pressure are called :

(a) Isobars

(b) Isohyets

(c) Isotherms

(d) Isohels

Ans. (a) Isobars.

Q. 4. The primary tool for weather forecasting is :

(a) Thermometer

(b) Barometer

(c) Maps

(d) Weather charts

Ans. (d) Weather charts

Q. 5. If there is more humidity in the air, the difference between the readings of a dry bulb and a wet bulb will be :

(a) Less

(b) More

(c) Equal

(d) None of the above

Ans. (a) Less

(B) Answer the following questions in about 30 words :

Q. 1. What are the basic elements of weather?

Ans. Pressure, temperature, humidity , precipitation, cloudiness and wind are known as weather elements.

Q. 2. What is a weather chart?

Ans. A date received from various weather observatories are in plenty and detailed. Therefore, they cannot be incorporated in one single chart unless the coding designed to give the economy of expression is used. These are called synoptic weather charts.

Q. 3. Which instruments are normally available in Class-I observatory to measure the weather phenomena?

Ans. The following instruments are available in Clasas -I observatory to measure the weather phenomena :

(a) Maximum and minimum thermometers

(b) Anemometer and wind vane

(c) Dry and wet bulb thermometer

(d) Rain gauge

(e) Barometer

Q. 4. What are Isotherms?

Ans. Isotherms are lines connecting places of equal temperature.

Q. 5. Which meteorological symbols are used to mark the following on a weather map?

(a) Rain

(b) Mist

(c) Sunshine

(d) Lightning

(e) Overcast Sky

Ans. (a) Rain •

(b) Mist =

(c) Sunshine ☉

(d) Lighting ϟ

(e) Overcast Sky •

(C) Answer the following questions in about 125 words :

Q. 1. Discuss how weather maps and charts are prepared and how they are useful to us.

Ans. Weather maps : A weather map is the representation of weather phenomena of the earth or a part of it on a flat surface. It depicts conditions associated with different weather elements such as temperature, rainfall, sunshine and cloudiness, direction and velocity of winds, etc. on a particular day. Such observations being taken at fixed hours are transmitted by code to the forecasting stations. The central office keeps a record of the observations, which forms the basis for making a weather map. The upper air observations which are procured from hill stations, aeroplanes, pilot balloons, etc. are plotted separately. Since the inception of the Indian Meteorological Department, the weather maps and charts are prepared regularly. Meteorological observatories transmit the data to the Central Observatory at Pune twice a day. Data is also collected on ships plying on the Indian seas. A good progress has been made in the field of weather forecasting and observation with the establishment of weather observatories in Antarctica, the International Indian Ocean Expedition, and the launching of rockets and weather satellites.

Usefulness :

(i) Weather maps help us to predict weather.

(ii) Weather forecasting helps farmers, fishermen, soldiers, navigators and pilots in many ways.

(iii) Disaster management is not possible without weather maps and charts.

Weather charts : The data received from various weather observatories are in plenty and detailed. As such, they cannot be incorporated in one single chart unless the coding designed to give the economy of expression is used. These are called synoptic weather charts and the codes used are called meteorological symbols. Weather charts provide the primary tools for weather forecasting. They help in locating and identifying different air masses, pressure systems, fronts and areas of precipitation.

Usefulness :

(i) Weather charts provide the primary tools for weather forecasting.

(ii) They help in locating and identifying different air masses, pressure systems , fronts and areas of precipitation.

MAP WORK

Part A : Fundamentals of Physical Geography

1. Map of all Continents of the World.

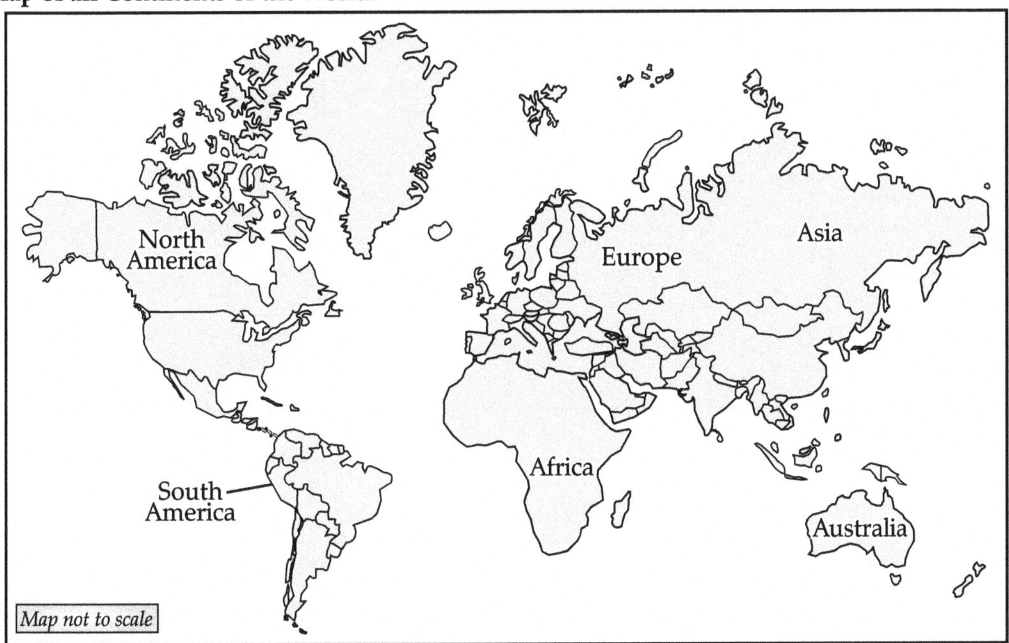

2. Major Oceans of the World

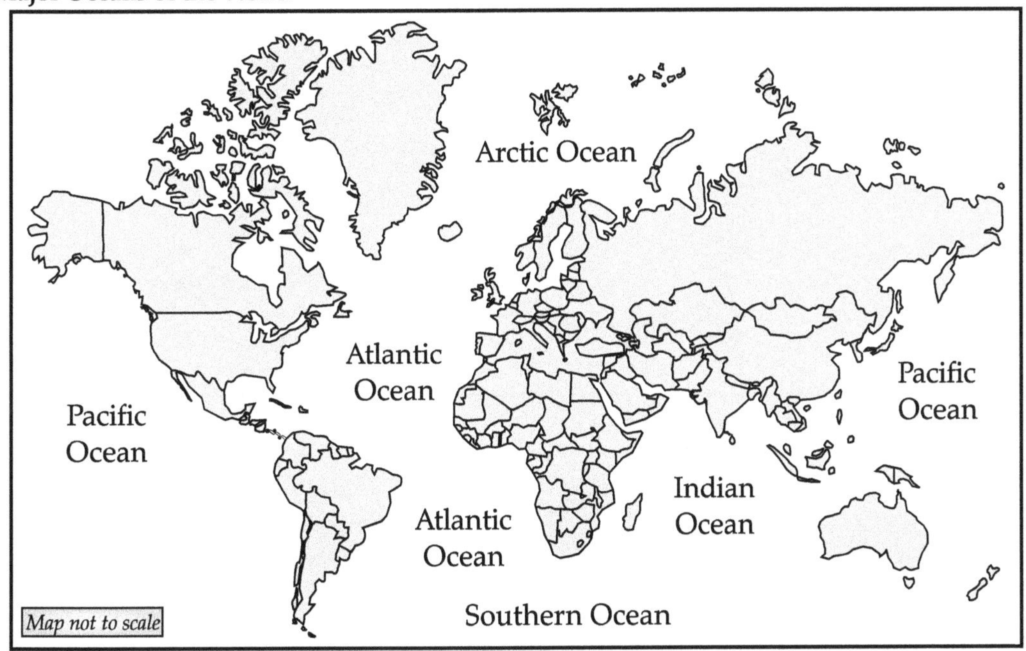

3. Major & Minor Lithospheric Plates

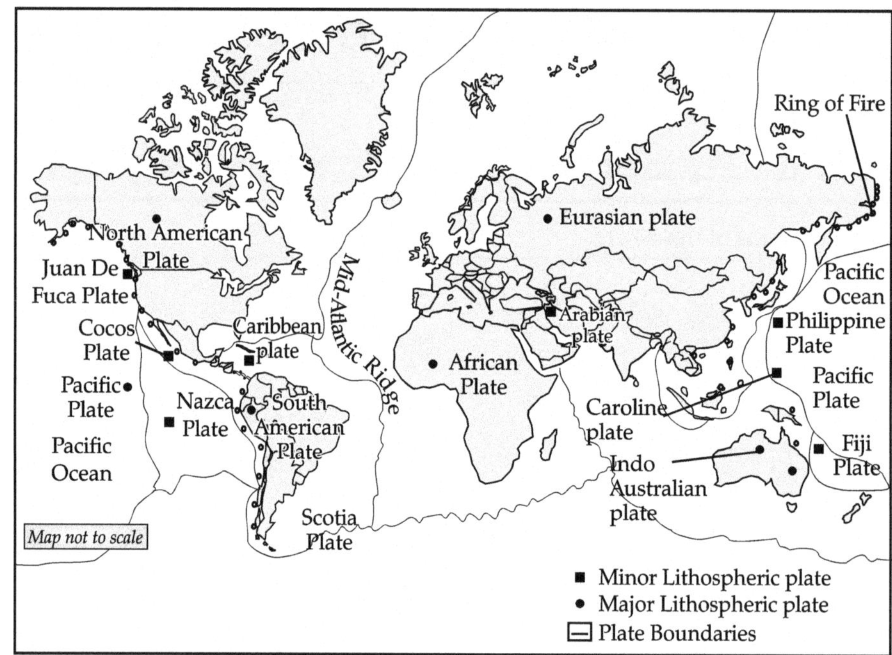

4. Major Hot Deserts of the World

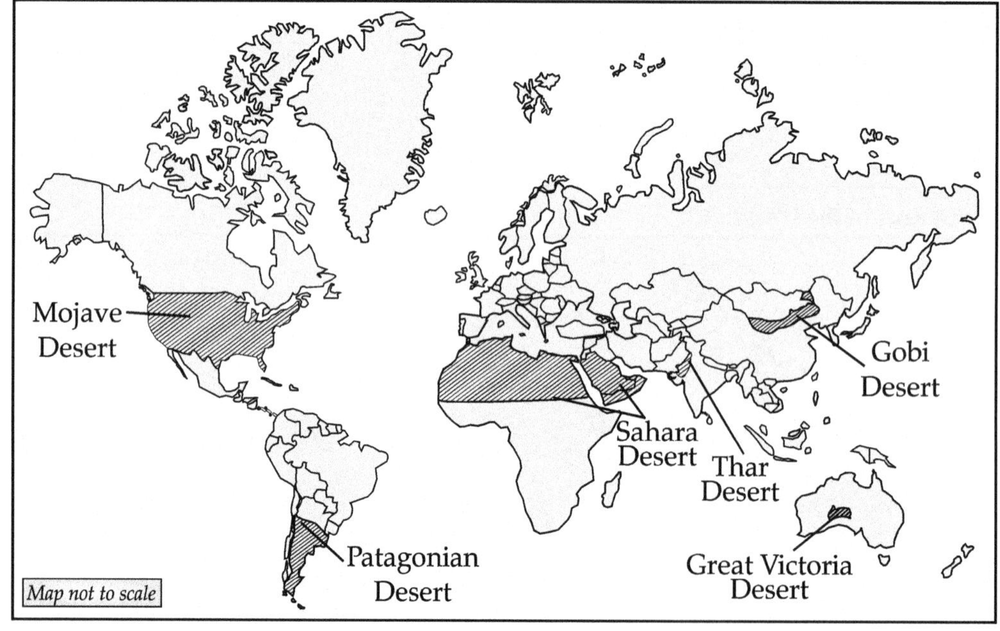

5. **Major Seas**

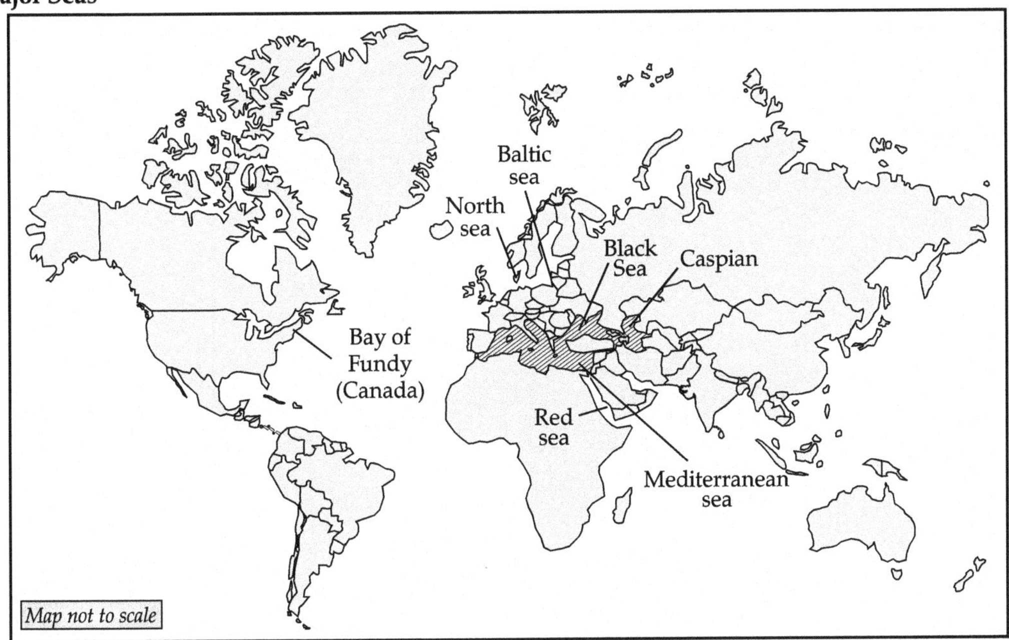

6. **Ecological Hotspots**

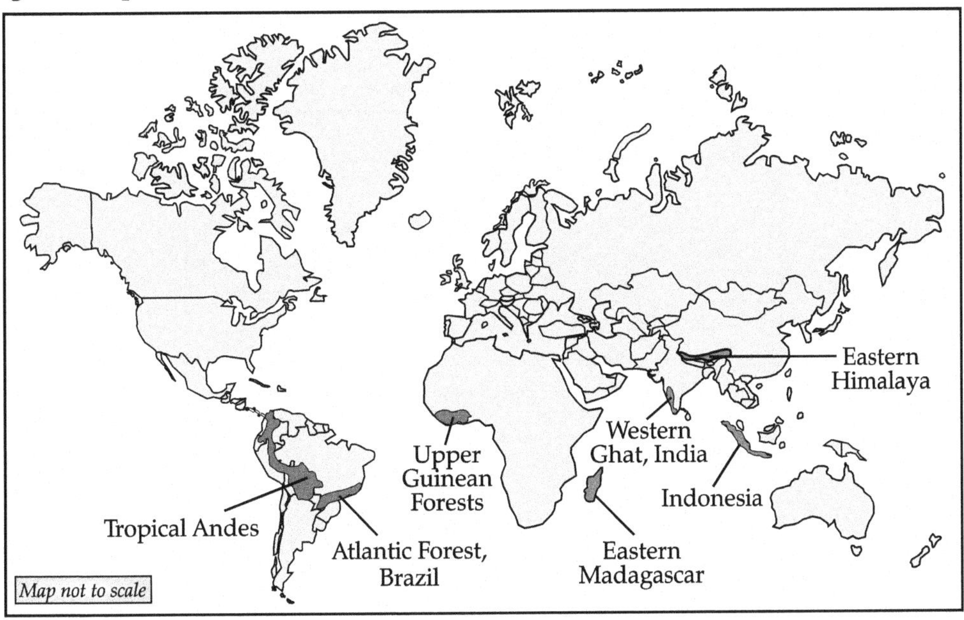

Part B : India Physical Environment

1. India-Location

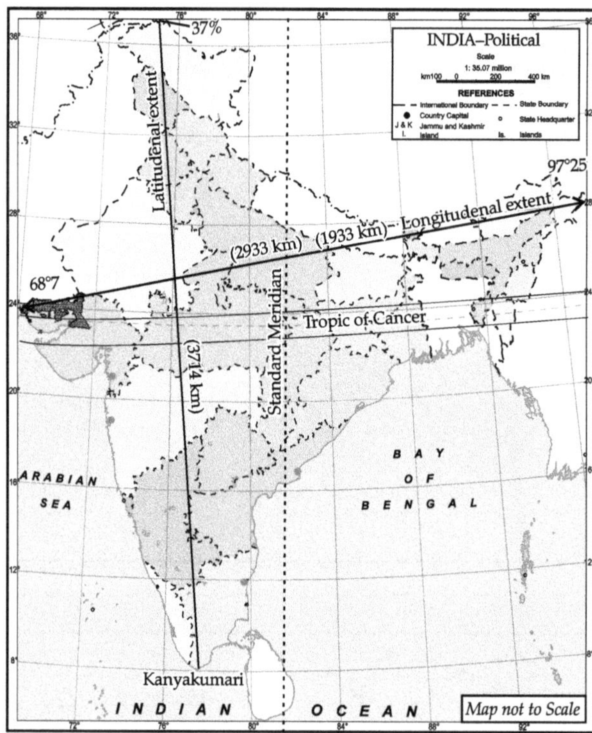

2. Mountains

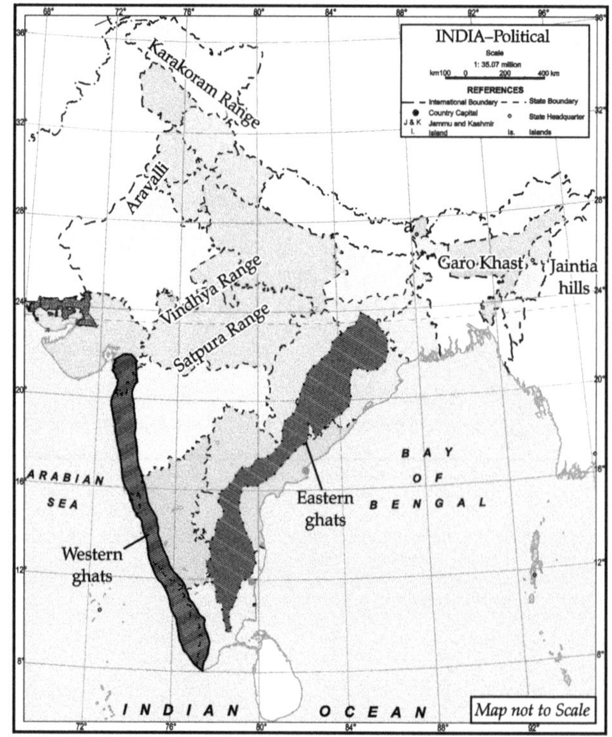

3. **Pleateaus**

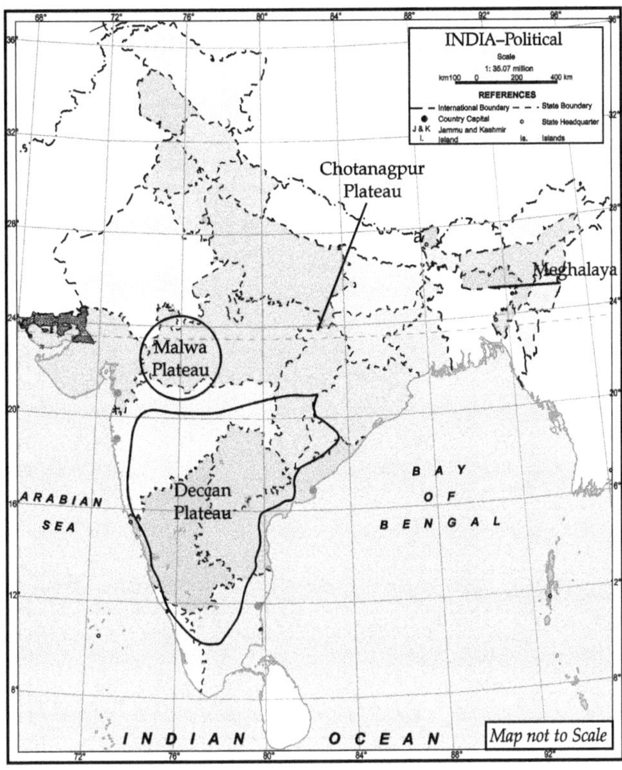

4. **Passes**

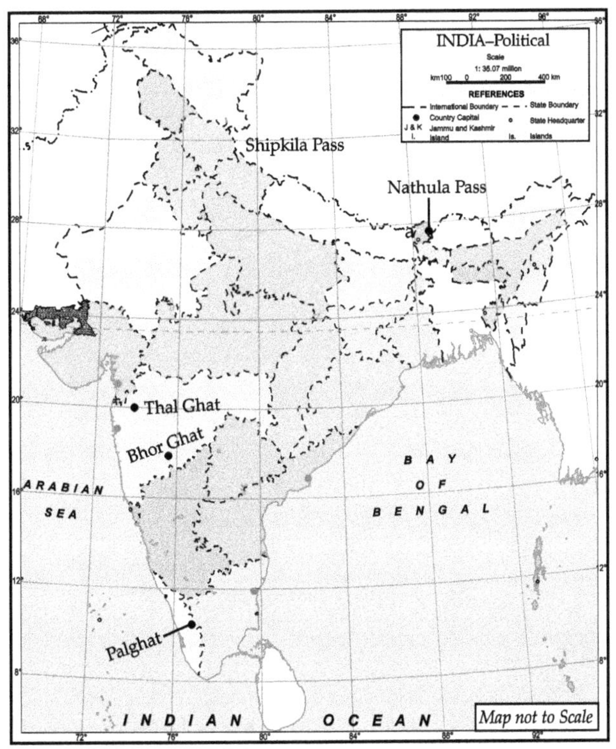

5. Peaks & Islands

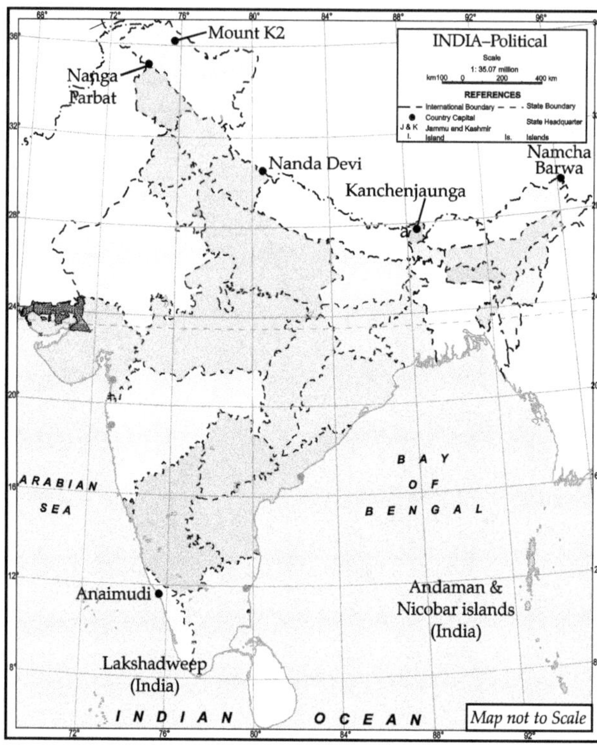

Peaks

6. Coastal Plains

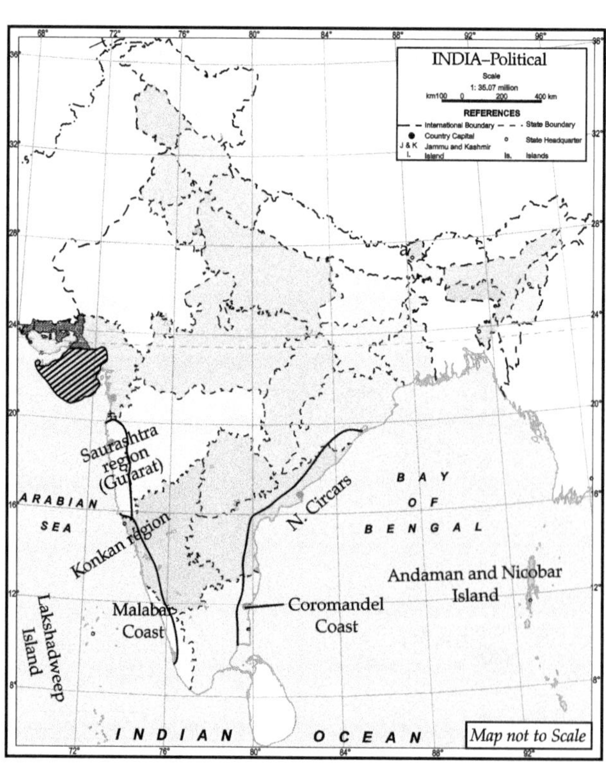

7. **Drainage System : Rivers, Lakes, Straits, Bays and Gulfs**

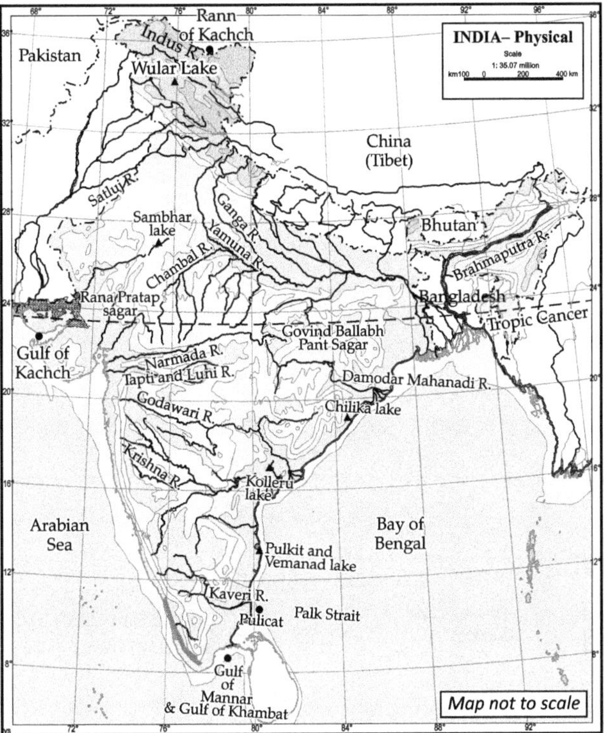

8. **Climate : Area with Highest & Lowest Temperature**

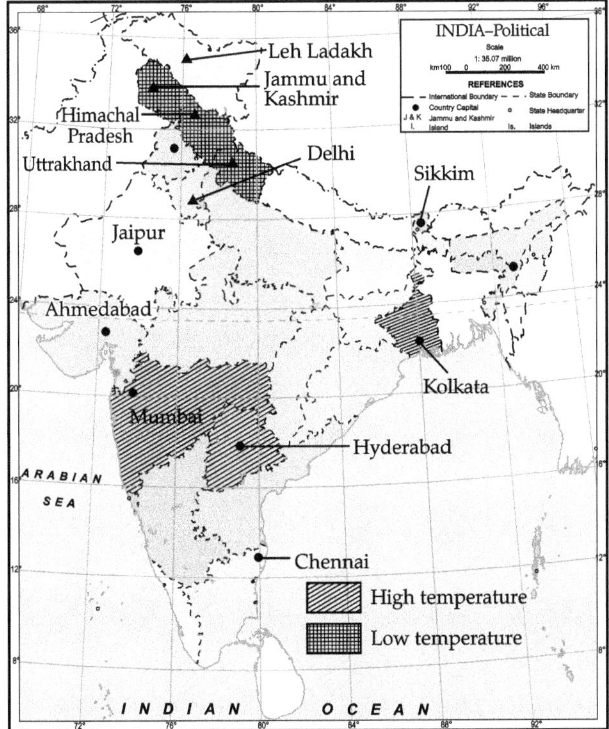

9. Natural Vegetation

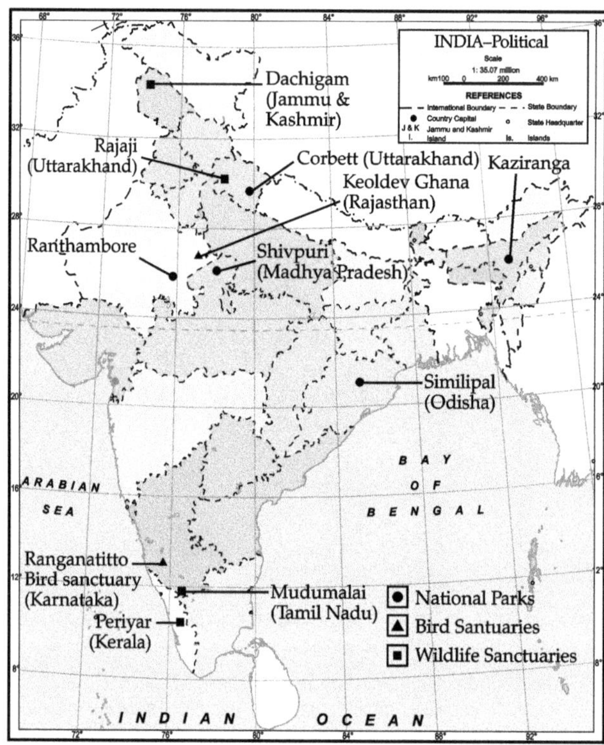

Milton Keynes UK
Ingram Content Group UK Ltd.
UKHW050953310723
426074UK00007B/685